69.50
C/
5/83

BIOGRAPHICAL DICTIONARY OF AMERICAN MAYORS, 1820–1980

Baltimore
Boston
Buffalo
Chicago
Cincinnati
Cleveland
Detroit
Los Angeles
Milwaukee
New Orleans
New York
Philadelphia
Pittsburgh
San Francisco
St. Louis

BIOGRAPHICAL DICTIONARY OF AMERICAN MAYORS, 1820–1980
Big City Mayors

Edited by MELVIN G. HOLLI
and PETER d'A. JONES

GREENWOOD PRESS WESTPORT, CONNECTICUT · LONDON, ENGLAND

Library of Congress Cataloging in Publication Data

Main entry under title:

Biographical dictionary of American mayors, 1820-1980.

   Bibliography: p. iv
   Includes index.
   1. Mayors—United States—Biography. I. Holli,
Melvin G. II. Jones, Peter d'Alroy.
E176.B5725   352′.008′0922 [B]   80-1796
ISBN 0-313-21134-5 (lib. bdg.)

Library of Congress Catalog Card Number: 80-1796
ISBN: 0-313-21134-5

First published in 1981

Greenwood Press
A division of Congressional Information Service, Inc.
88 Post Road West, Westport, Connecticut 06881

Printed in the United States of America

10 9 8 7 6 5 4 3 2 1

For
Susan and Steven Holli
as their own biographies
unfold

Barbara and Kathryn Jones
as they face entirely new
adventures

CONTENTS

Achenbaum, W. Andrew, *Canisius College*

Allswang, John M., *California State University* (Los Angeles)

Argersinger, Jo Ann Eady, *Dickinson College*

Arnold, Joseph L., *University of Maryland* (Baltimore)

Baker, Jean H., *Goucher College*

Barrett, Paul, *Illinois Institute of Technology* (Chicago)

Bauman, John F., *California State College* (California, Pennsylvania)

Baur, John E., *Los Angeles*

Biles, W. Roger, *University of Illinois* (Chicago Circle)

Blassingame, Lurton W., *University of Wisconsin* (Oshkosh)

Blouin, Francis X., Jr., *Bentley Historical Library* (Ann Arbor, Michigan)

Bolt, Robert, *Calvin College*

Browne, Gary L., *University of Maryland* (Baltimore)

Buenker, John D., *University of Wisconsin* (Parkside)

Bukowski, Douglas, *University of Illinois* (Chicago Circle)

Bulger, William T., *Central Michigan University*

Bullard, Thomas R., Oak Park, Illinois

Burns, Constance, *Boston College*

Campbell, Thomas, *Cleveland State University*

Carleton, Mark T., *Louisiana State University* (Baton Rouge)

Cocoltchos, Christopher, *Clark University*

Cornescu, Daniela, Chicago, Illinois

Crooks, James B., *University of North Florida*

Cumming, John, *Clarke Historical Library* (Mt. Pleasant, Michigan)

Densmore, Christopher, *State University of New York* (Buffalo)

Disbrow, Donald W., *Eastern Michigan University*

Duis, Perry R. *University of Illinois* (Chicago Circle)

Duncan, Richard H., *Georgetown University*

Durr, W. T., *University of Baltimore*

Dykes, De Witt S., Jr., *Oakland University*

Eberle, Scott, *State University of New York* (Buffalo)

Ebner, Michael H., *Lake Forest College*

Elenbaas, Jack D., *California State University* (Fullerton)

Engberg, George B., *University of Cincinnati*

Fairbanks, Robert B., *University of Cincinnati*

Findlay, John M., *University of California* (Berkeley)

Fine, Sidney, *University of Michigan* (Ann Arbor)

Gentile, Richard H., *Massachusetts Historical Society*

Gillette, Howard, Jr., *George Washington University*

Greene, Susan Ellery, *Morgan State University*

Griffith, Michael, Berkeley, California

Haas, Edward F., *Louisiana State Museum* (New Orleans)

Hammack, David C., *Princeton University*

CONTRIBUTORS

Hershkowitz, Leo, *Queens College*
Holli, Betsy B., *Rosary College*
Holli, Melvin G., *University of Illinois* (Chicago Circle)
Homel, Michael W., *Eastern Michigan University*
Jackson, Joy J., *Southeastern State University* (Louisiana)
Jacobs, Donald M., *Northeastern University* (Boston)
Jenkins, William D., *Youngstown State University*
Jones, Beau Fly, *Chicago Board of Education*
Jones, Peter d'A., *University of Illinois* (Chicago Circle)
Judd, Jacob, *City University of New York, Lehman College*
Karin, Donald B., *State University of New York* (Buffalo)
Kocolowski, Gary P., *Dyke College* (Cleveland)
Lapomarda, Vincent A., *Holy Cross College*
Lauer, Jeanette C., *St. Louis Community College at Florissant Valley*
Lewandowski, Eric C., *Ohio State University*
Lewis, Gene D., *University of Cincinnati*
Logsdon, Joseph, *University of New Orleans*
McGuire, Jack B., New Orleans, Louisiana
Magda, Matthew, Harrisburg, Pennsylvania
Maurer, David J., *Eastern Illinois State University*
Mazur, Edward H., *Chicago City Colleges*
Melvin, Patricia Mooney, Ohio Historical Society
Milligan, John D., *State University of New York* (Buffalo)
Mlemchukwu, Finny Ike, *Western Michigan University*
Mushkat, Jerome, *University of Akron*
O'Connor, Thomas H., *Boston College*
O'Malley, Peter J., *Lewis University*
Parkerson, D. H., *Newberry Library* (Chicago)
Posadas, Barbara M., *Northern Illinois University*
Prinz, Andrew K., *Elmhurst College*
Rakove, Milton, *University of Illinois* (Chicago Circle)
Richardson, James F., *University of Akron*
Ridgway, Whitman H., *University of Maryland* (College Park)
Rishel, Joseph F., *University of Pittsburgh*
Rosen, Christine M., *University of California* (Berkeley)

Schiesl, Martin J., *California State University*, Los Angeles
Shaw, Douglas V., *University of Akron*
Shaw, Ronald E., *Miami University*
Shumsky, Neil L., *Virginia Polytechnic Institute and State University*
Smith, Helene, Greensburg, Pennsylvania
Smith, Dwight L., *Miami University*
Sparks, Robert V., Massachusetts Historical Society
Spraul-Schmidt, Judith, *University of Cincinnati*
Strauss, W. Patrick, *Oakland University*
Sutherland, John F., *Manchester Community College* (Connecticut)
Swetnam, George (Pittsburgh, Pennsylvania)
Teaford, Jon C., *Purdue University*
Tingley, Donald F., *Eastern Illinois University*
Tischauser, Leslie V., *University of Illinois* (Chicago Circle)
Tompkins, C. David, *Northeastern Illinois University*
Touchstone, D. Blake, *Tulane University*
Tregle, Joseph G., Jr., *University of New Orleans*
Varbero, Richard A., *State University of New York* (New Paltz)
Viehe, Fred W., Santa Barbara, California
Vinyard, JoEllen, *Marygrove College* (Detroit)
Weber, R. David, *Los Angeles Harbor College*
Weiner, Howard R., *College of Staten Island, State University of New York*
Wilson, Ben C., *Western Michigan University*

CONSULTANTS

Barth, Gunther, *University of California* (Berkeley)
Clark, Terry N., *University of Chicago*
Frisch, Michael H., *State University of New York* (Buffalo)
Gerber, Richard, *City University of New York, Lehman College*
Miller, Zane, *University of Cincinnati*
Valone, James, *Canisius College*

The last executive office in America to remain in genuine, close, daily human contact with the voters is that of big-city mayors. Other executives have become increasingly remote from the people over the course of the twentieth century. U.S. senators are safely installed in six-year terms and are carefully insulated by layers of office staff in their somewhat remote Washington, D.C., offices. U.S. presidents, with their huge staffs, security men, cabinet officers, special assistants, and public relations experts are sadly isolated from the day-to-day life of the people, with effects only too apparent in such cases as Lyndon Johnson or Richard Nixon. Even the state governors are removed, ensconced in their executive mansions in state capitals that are only sometimes true cities. But the mayor has no such protective padding and cannot enjoy such artificial comforts. The mayor is not remote. Seven days a week the real world of the city streets is free to invade city hall and complain, cajole, demand. No important elective office in the nation has been so frequently buffeted, torn, shaped, and reshaped by popular demands and pressure group politics. The office of mayor is unique: a grass-roots, popular, elected executive office of considerable power and authority, often filled by men (and nowadays, women) of humble economic and social backgrounds and very diverse ethnic and religious origins.

The *Biographical Dictionary of American Mayors, 1820–1980* is the first and only definitive treatment of *all* the mayors of the fifteen leading American cities, from the very beginnings, when the office assumed a recognizably modern shape, to the present. The volume amasses a remarkably rich data base, the raw materials for a collective biography of 679 American mayors. It offers a slice through American society for a 160-year period of national history.

During the course of U.S. history, thousands of mayors have served in hundreds of cities and towns, often for single one-year terms (or less), many of whom made little impact on the office or on their community, and are forgotten by historians. Currently, the country has over 4,300 communities led by mayors, whether officially defined as "municipalities" or as "townships." In some communities, though not in many, the mayor is a figurehead or minor character on a purely nominal salary (for example, Dallas, Texas, $50 per council meeting), while a professional city manager runs the city on a day-to-day basis (Dallas salary, 1973: $43,888). Other cities have experimented with the commission system. But the historical trend in the evolution of the office of mayor in the United States has been towards increased executive power and responsibility, with diminishing authority of city councils. From time to time, state legislatures have tried to interfere with cities, bringing city demands for

PREFACE

greater "home rule." This has been a perennial struggle since the 1850s. Generally, however, the power of American mayors has grown, along with the problems of cities themselves. As early as 1918, Chicago was already paying its mayor as much as $18,000 a year, New York $15,000, and Philadelphia $12,000. In those cities, the mayor was a true "chief executive" and owed his political life to the voters.

In view of these and other difficulties, we decided from the outset to cover only the fifteen major cities, including every holder of that office. In most cases, we also included several mayors who held office *before* popular election became the norm in their city—taking an individual judgment on each city. For San Francisco, for example, we did include some early Spanish and American *alcaldes*. Complete, cross-indexed lists at the end of the volume make clear who is included for which city.

With the expert help of 100 scholars trained in urban history and working mainly with original sources in local city archives, it has been discovered that the official compilations put out by various mayoral offices listed some mayors incorrectly or not at all. This on-the-spot archival work has in many cases been checked and re-checked by the editors, and we believe our present listing to be the most accurate now available. We decided to cover biographically all the mayors of the top fifteen cities, however brief or ephemeral their tenure, in order to give a complete run of the history of the office in those selected cities. For many of these mayors, the *Dictionary* offers the only historical, biographical treatment they have ever received. This volume offers historians, social scientists, and humanists alike the most complete possible historical coverage for their potential use.

The choice of the top fifteen cities was made with great care, though no doubt the selection is open to differing judgments by scholars. Our final choice was of those cities that have maintained *consistent* leadership in population and historical importance since the 1820s. Naturally, as the nation evolved, the list of the top fifteen cities changed: the leading fifteen of 1820 were not those of 1850, 1890, or 1920. We excluded Washington D.C., on the grounds that its mayor was appointed, not elected; that the mayoralty was subject to the wishes of a small group of U.S. congressmen; and that the city had an artificial quality as a captive, federal capital. However, we will include the nation's capital in a future volume. The example of Washington is used here to illustrate the problems of inclusion and exclusion. Ideally, in a subsequent volume, which will be the third research product of the *Project for the Study of American Mayors*, fifty leading cities will be treated in the way the present *Dictionary* treats fifteen.

The fifteen cities selected included seven coastal cities (Boston, New York, Philadelphia, Baltimore, New Orleans, Los Angeles, and San Francisco); five inland lake cities (Chicago foremost, with Milwaukee, Detroit, Cleveland, and Buffalo); and three great river cities (Pittsburgh, St. Louis, and Cincinnati). The fifteen cities represent internal and external trade, finance, older and newer industries, varied ethnic mixes, and regional balance—the Heartland, the Pacific and Atlantic coasts, South, East, West, and North. Their ranking by population size, according to the 1970 Census, is New York, Chicago, Los Angeles, Philadelphia, Detroit, Baltimore, Cleveland, Milwaukee, San Francisco, Boston, St. Louis, New Orleans, Pittsburgh, Buffalo, and Cincinnati. The population ranges from just under 8 million (New York) to under half a million (Cincinnati).

The power of cities and of their mayors is seen in relative population ratios. New York City (according to the 1970 Census, which now includes the District of Columbia as a state) is still greater in size than forty-four out of fifty-one "states" of the Union. Chicago is still bigger than twenty-nine states. Even Cincinnati, the smallest of our fifteen cities and one that suffered a population loss of over 10 percent in the 1960s, remained by 1970 bigger than three states and close in size to two others. As long ago as 1918, with much urban growth still to come (Los Angeles was still only half a million strong), a study pointed out that three U.S. cities were larger than twenty-five of the then forty-eight states; twenty-five cities had populations greater than two states; nine cities exceeded the half million mark, but eleven states fell below that population level. Clearly, many mayors had more citizens under their care than did state governors. Moreover, state population figures *include* the cities—with which governors are rarely concerned on a day-to-day basis, given the powers of the executive office of mayor and the home rule principle. Jimmy Carter, who became president of the United States in 1976, had far less executive and administrative experience as governor of Georgia than he would have had as mayor of New York or Chicago.

We thus feel strongly that the office of mayor is a major American institution, worthy of much more study and attention than it has received in the past. We, along with our many contributors, hope that the *Biographical Dictionary* will not only become a useful tool and resource for future scholars, but will also encourage newer generations of students, who are beginning to look afresh at American social and political processes.

Melvin G. Holli and Peter d'A. Jones
Co-Directors
Project for the Study of American Mayors
Chicago, Illinois
May 1980

BIG CITY
MAYORS

A

ADAM, JAMES NOBLE (1842–1912), Mayor of Buffalo (1906–09). Scottish-born businessman-mayor, Adams was born in Peebles, Scotland, on 1 March 1842, the son of Thomas Adam, a preacher, and Isabella (Borthwick) Adam. The second of five children, he attended local schools until 1854 when he became an apprentice in the firm of Thomas Cooper and Son, a dry goods company in Edinburgh, the capital city. In 1865, he left that firm and started his own dry goods company. On 9 January 1872, Adam married Margaret L. Paterson of Edinburgh, and they emigrated to the United States that same year. Following the advice of an older brother, Adam settled in New Haven in 1874 where he ran a dry goods firm until 1881. In 1881, he moved to Buffalo and opened a full-scale department store (J. N. Adam and Company). He retired from this company twenty-four years later in 1905, to pursue the dream of a political career. Adam was a Presbyterian, a member of the Chamber of Commerce, and a supporter of the Buffalo Historical Society and Fine Arts Academy.

A Democrat, Adam had served a single term as an alderman (1895–96), but he intended to follow a full-time political career after 1905. He was elected mayor in November of that year, defeating Republican Charles L. Feldman 36,498 to 26,592. Buffalo had a population of 352,387 in 1900 and a mayor-council form of government. Mayor Adam supported reform of the police department and carried out a complete overhaul of city departments putting all of them on what he considered to be a good business basis. He intended to adopt further businesslike measures in a second term, but Democratic party leaders refused to support his candidacy again in 1909, and he was forced to retire from all political activity. He maintained personal ties to the administration which followed, but his dream was dashed. He died on 9 February 1912, following a stroke.

SOURCES: J. N. Larned, *A History of Buffalo*, 2 vols. (New York, 1916); New York *Times*, 10 February 1912; *Who's Who in New York, City and State* (New York, 1905 ed.).   *Thomas R. Bullard*

ADAMS, GABRIEL (1788?–1864), Mayor of Pittsburgh (1847–48). According to U.S. Census records, Adams was born around 1788 in Ireland. During the first

quarter of the nineteenth century, he migrated to America. Little is known of his early life and background. He and his wife, Margaret Jane, also born in Ireland, had one son, William. Adams was a wealthy grocer in Pittsburgh by the early 1830s. In 1833, he was a founding member of the Pittsburgh Savings Fund Company and was later president of that firm when it became the Farmers Deposit Bank in the early 1840s. Adams was a Presbyterian and a member of the Reformed Presbyterian Society, a temperance organization. In 1836, he attended an Allegheny County convention of temperance societies.

In 1840, Pittsburgh, located in Allegheny County, had a population of 21,115 (which more than doubled by the end of the decade) and a mayor-council form of government. Exercising both legislative and executive powers, the select and common councils held most municipal authority. The mayor served primarily as a magistrate and police chief. A well-known businessman, Adams received the Whig and Anti-Masonic nomination for mayor in December 1846. On 12 January 1847, he easily won the election with 1,719 votes to 1,089 for Andrew McIlwaine (Democrat), 263 for J. W. Cook (Independent), and 100 for Alexander Jaynes (Native American and Citizens' candidate). Adams was reelected on 11 January 1848 in a close vote, with 1,642 to 1,556 for Dr. William Kerr (Democrat) and 312 for Samuel Stackhouse (Native American). Whether by his own choice or because of the wishes of his party, Adams did not run for a third one-year term.

Adams' initial election victory stemmed mainly from popular resentment against the Democratic party over the Mexican-American War. His triumph signaled a return to the Whigs' usual domination of municipal affairs. Mayor Adams conducted a stable, although not distinguished, administration. During his first term, he helped provide relief for victims of a flood which inundated many city homes along the Ohio River. The mayor somewhat alienated the *Gazette*, the strongest Whig daily in the city, by ignoring that paper and bestowing municipal patronage to other, weaker, Whig newspapers. He favored the wealthy and native-born, especially manufacturers. Adams' administration helped check strikes by the journeyman tailors in 1847 and the women cotton-mill workers in the following year. His second term closed amid legal difficulties when he and a police officer were sued for false arrest. Adams was acquitted in January 1849.

After his mayoralty, Adams made an unsuccessful attempt to win his party's nomination for county commissioner. He was appointed an associate lay judge of the court of common pleas in 1852. Five years later, he was reappointed to another five-year term. Adams received high praise from his fellow judges and the press for the impartiality and soundness of his judicial decisions. On 4 June 1864, he died at his home in Lower St. Clair Township, Allegheny County.

SOURCES: Isaac Harris, *General Business Directory of the Cities of Pittsburgh and Allegheny* (Pittsburgh, 1841); Michael Fitzgibbon Holt, *Forging a Majority: The Formation of the Republican Party in Pittsburgh, 1848–1860* (New Haven, Conn., 1969); Allen Humphreys Kerr, "The Mayors and Recorders of Pittsburgh, 1816–1951" (unpublished manuscript, Historical Society of Western Pennsylvania, Pittsburgh, 1952); Pittsburgh *Gazette*, 11 and 21 January 1847, 28 and 30 December 1846, 9 and 10 January 1849); Pittsburgh *Post*, 9 January 1849; Catherine Elizabeth Reiser, *Pittsburgh's Commercial Development 1800–1850* (Harrisburg, Pa., 1951); Erasmus Wilson, ed., *Standard History of Pittsburgh* (Chicago, 1898).   *Matthew S. Magda*

AGUILAR, CRISTOBAL (1825?–86), Mayor of Los Angeles (1866–68, 1870–72). Mexican-American mayor of Los Angeles during years of important growth, Aguilar came from a well-established *Californio* family. His father, Don José Maria Aguilar, born in Spanish Mexico around 1790, was a man of means in the Los Angeles *pueblo*, though not a wealthy *ranchero*. (He lived into his nineties, dying in Los Angeles in 1883.) Cristobal worked on the family farm and at one time taught at the *pueblo* school (1833–34), resigning after being refused a raise. His mother, Doña Maria, was California-born, like her son; his wife, Dolores y Orba, was also born in the state, in about 1834. They were married when she was sixteen and Cristobal twenty-five (1850). The Aguilar family home, a well-known *adobe* south of the Plaza, lasted long into the U.S. period, serving as a jail and then as the town's first hospital (from 1858).

Aguilar served many times on the city council, from 1 July 1850, being successful in the very first American election at that time, when the Mexican *ayuniamento* system of town government was replaced by the U.S. mayor and council. He was mayor of Los Angeles from 10 May 1866 to 7 December 1868 and again from 9 December 1870 to 5 December 1872. Later, he served as county supervisor and in other public offices. Aguilar was a Democrat and a Roman Catholic. The first census

of the *pueblo* of Los Angeles, taken in 1850 when Aguilar joined the first elected council, numbered 1,610 people (excluding Indians).

During Aguilar's administrations, the park site was created which later became Pershing Square (1866 ordinance); the first agricultural fair was held at Exposition Park; the first city directory was printed (1872); the first steam fire engine was commissioned by the fire department; the Spanish-language newspaper *La Cronica* began; a woolen mill opened in the city, as well as the first town bank, capitalized at $100,000; an ice factory began selling ice at 4 cents a pound; the Merced Theatre opened (1871); and a race riot broke out in October 1871 in which at least twenty-two Chinese were lynched and no one arrested for the crimes. A council ordinance banned the carrying of firearms, knives, and swords, but nobody obeyed it.

One problem that Aguilar (and subsequent mayors) could not readily solve was that of the growing town's water supply—a recurring problem of drought or flood. Mayor Aguilar vetoed a scheme for city purchase of a private water works. He died suddenly, of a heart attack, on 11 April 1886, after a full life of service to Los Angeles.

SOURCES: California Biography File, Los Angeles Public Library; J. M. Guin, *History of California and Extended History of Its Southern Coast Counties* (Los Angeles, 1907), vol. 1.; Los Angeles Times, 13 April 1886 (obituary); John Waugh, "Los Angeles Mayors, The Great, Near-Great and Un-Great," Los Angeles *Times West* Magazine, 25 May 1969.
          Peter d'A. Jones

ALBERGER, FRANKLIN A. (1825–77), Mayor of Buffalo (1860–61). The first Republican mayor of Buffalo and a German-American butcher, Alberger was the eldest of six children of Job Alberger (1800–63) and Louisa (Frederick) Alberger (1804–92), both German Protestants, and was born on 14 January 1825 in Baltimore, Maryland. His parents took him at age eleven to Buffalo where his father continued his trade as butcher. Leaving school to be his father's apprentice, young Alberger henceforth educated himself. In time, he became the proprietor of stalls in the Terrace Square Market and then joined his brothers in a porkpacking business. He met and married Katherine Rice (1828–77) by whom he had three daughters and a son.

Originally a Whig devotee of Henry Clay, Alberger became, from its genesis, an active member of the new Republican party. If "his political rise was rapid," noted one newspaper, his "political ambition kept full pace with his opportunities." In 1854 and again in 1859, he was elected to Buffalo's common council. Supporting the concept of an international bridge to Canada, Alderman Alberger was appointed chairman of the bridge committee during his latter term. Holding promise of winning the German vote and supported by ex-Mayor F. P. Stevens (*q.v.*), now a Republican, Alberger was nominated as Republican candidate for mayor and in the fall of 1859 received 4,445 votes to Democrat Henry K. Viele's 4,100. The city of 81,129 had its first Republican mayor, bringing with him into office the entire Republican slate. Under his guidance the city council looked to the improvement of Buffalo's harbor, parks, schools, including "a wise liberality" in teachers' salaries, police department, and, with the purchase of new steam fire engines and conversion from a volunteer to a professional organization, the fire department. Alberger also fostered the Association for the Encouragement of Manufacturers to advertise the advantages of Buffalo as a business site. The city was in a cycle of prosperity when he left office. As another newspaper put it: "His capabilities were bounded by a narrower horizon than he would acknowledge; and, although in no sense a great man, within his limitations he was singularly apt and efficient."

Always a staunch unionist, Mayor Alberger used his influence to support Lincoln's policies. As a member of the Buffalo Committee on Defense of the Union, he helped raise the Forty-ninth New York Volunteer Regiment. While war usually brings criticism to public figures, Alberger had an honesty of purpose backed by a straightforwardness, candor and intelligence that people recognized and accepted.

In 1861, Alberger was elected for the first of two terms as Erie Canal commissioner (1862–67). Later, he was three times elected to the state assembly (1871–74). He was defeated, however, in his run for the state Senate and, afterwards, in his bid for renomination as candidate for the assembly. He died in 1877 of *cholera morbus*. A Mason since 1850, he was buried according to the rites of that order.

SOURCES: Buffalo *Commercial Advertiser*, 24 August 1877, and Buffalo *Daily Courier*, 25 August 1877; Sister Mary Jane and Sister Mercedes, "Mayors of Buffalo, 1832 to 1961" (B.A. thesis, Rosary Hill College, Buffalo, 1961.); Grace C. Sheldon, "Franklin A. Alberger," Buffalo *Times*, 31 August 1919; Truman C. White, *History of Erie County*, 2 vols. (Boston, 1898).   *John D. Milligan*

ALEXANDER, GEORGE (1839–1923), Mayor of Los Angeles (1909–13). Scottish-born reform mayor, born on 21 September 1839 in Glasgow, Alexander was the son of William Alexander, a farmer, and Mary (Cleland) Alexander. The family migrated to America in 1850 and settled in Chicago. With limited opportunities for edu-

cation, George Alexander left school at age twelve and sold newspapers. He went with his parents to Iowa in 1856 and worked on his father's farm. In 1862, he enlisted in the Twenty-fourth Iowa Volunteers and served under Generals Ulysses S. Grant and Philip H. Sheridan. Upon discharge in 1865, Alexander went to work in a grain warehouse in Belle Plain, Iowa, and in 1874 entered that business himself. He operated grain warehouses and a shipping business in Toledo and Dysart, Iowa. Moving to Los Angeles in 1886, aged forty-seven, he built a feed mill and later abandoned the business for public office.

Alexander married Anna Yeiser in 1862, and they had three children, two of whom, Lydia and Frank, survived to adulthood. Alexander was a Mason and a member of the Los Angeles Chamber of Commerce, the Municipal League, and the Los Angeles Grand Army of the Republic.

The 1890s saw the launching of Alexander's public service career. He served as Los Angeles street inspector, and in 1893 he was appointed chief deputy in the street department. Two years later, he entered the Los Angeles County recorder's office as a clerk and became chief deputy recorder. Elected county supervisor in 1901, he identified with the reform wing of the Republican party and made a record for honest service and protection against improper concessions to private interests. Alexander accepted the recall nomination of the Good Government Organization for mayor in March 1909 which he won by 14,043 votes to his Socialist opponent Fred C. Wheeler's 12,341. Nine months later, he was reelected with 20,291 votes to Republican candidate George A. Smith's 16,964. In the 1911 primary, Job Harriman, Socialist party candidate, polled a plurality and Alexander secured the second spot. Shortly before the runoff election, two labor militants confessed to the crime of dynamiting the Los Angeles *Times* building on 1 October 1910 in which twenty-one people died. Alexander soundly won by 85,739 to Harriman's 51,796. He retired at the end of his third term.

The population of Los Angeles jumped from 293,300 in 1909 to 430,000 by 1913. Mayor Alexander reorganized city departments along the lines of authority and responsibility, considerably expanded public facilities, and won approval for a municipal power system. He also suppressed vice operations, promoted tenement regulation, and forcefully advocated the municipalization of privately owned utilities.

After retiring from public office, Alexander led a quiet life with his family. He died on 2 August 1923 following a lingering illness and was buried in Los Angeles.

SOURCES: "George Alexander," *California Biography File*, Los Angeles Public Library; Los Angeles *Times*, 3 August 1923; Charles F. Lummis, *Out West*.

Los Angeles and Her Makers: A Record (Los Angeles, 1909); Press Reference Library, *Notables of the Southwest* (Los Angeles, 1912); Martin J. Schiesl, "Progressive Reform in Los Angeles under Mayor Alexander, 1909–1913," *California Historical Quarterly* 54 (Spring 1975).
                                                                    Martin J. Schiesl

ALIOTO, JOSEPH LAWRENCE (1916–   ), Mayor of San Francisco (1968–76). Reform mayor of San Francisco, Alioto was a native son, born in that city on 12 February 1916 of immigrant Sicilian parents, Giuseppe Alioto and Domenica Lazio Alioto. His father had founded a successful firm, the International Fish Company. Joseph had a Roman Catholic education, attaining a B.A., St. Mary's College (1937), and a J.D., Catholic University (1940), and he went straight from law school to work in the Justice Department. He married Angelina Genaro on 2 June 1941, and they had six children, five boys and one girl. During World War II, Alioto was special assistant in the Antitrust Division, 1942–44, under Judges Thurman Arnold and Tom Clark, and later worked for the Board of Economic Warfare. He was always an active Democrat and a liberal.

Returning home to San Francisco after the war, Alioto opened what became one of the nation's largest business law firms (antitrust specialties), numbering among his clients movie moguls Walt Disney and Sam Goldwyn. In the 1950s and early 1960s, he was president of the board of education, director of the city's urban renewal efforts, developer of the federal Food for Peace program, and adviser to the governments of Hawaii and Puerto Rico. A success in business, Alioto became president and general manager of the Rice Growers Association in 1959, expanding annual sales from $25 million to $70 million, with pioneering use of ships as seagoing silos to transport edible bulk rice.

In 1967, when the Democratic favorite to replace incumbent Mayor J. F. Shelley (*q.v.*) (State Senator E. McAteer) suddenly died, Shelley persuaded Alioto to run. On 7 November 1967, Alioto defeated Harold Dobbs, a perpetual candidate, in a landslide victory with an excess of 15,000 votes over the closest contender. Alioto ran well with minority voters, with waterfront labor and Harry Bridges (who had also supported Mayor Shelley earlier), and even with downtown business. Alioto's platform—that of a moderate, liberal Democrat—was a winner. He supported President Lyndon Johnson's Vietnam policy, stood for strict law enforcement, but also demanded new social and ethnic programs.

Mayor Alioto was immediately swept into an ongoing city press strike, which he mediated by February 1968. He walked through the ghetto areas of San Francisco, winning minority support for his efforts to improve conditions with expanded summer job programs, increased employment of blacks and Hispanics in city jobs, and city pressure on labor unions and employers to hire minority workers. Alioto rapidly became a major national spokesman for cities, mediating with the Democratic powers in Washington for greater devolution of authority to local governments. He threatened to tax suburbanites who worked in the central city and paid their taxes elsewhere, and to reduce taxes for inner-city dwellers. At the riotous Democratic national convention in Chicago in August 1968, it was Mayor Alioto who nominated Hubert H. Humphrey for president. Alioto even emerged from the conflict with student radicals on the San Francisco State University campus in the fall of 1968 with modest honor.

In 1969, at the peak of his career, as a potential U.S. vice-presidential candidate and possible gubernatorial nominee, Mayor Alioto suffered a severe setback—beginning with a *Look* magazine exposé claiming he had Mafia links. Withdrawing from the governorship battle in January 1970, he still managed to gain reelection as mayor (by 30,000 votes) in 1971. Although the charges against him did not stick, Alioto could not get the nomination for state governor in 1974, and he retired from the mayor's office in January 1976 after serving two full terms.

In addition to his success with the rice industry, Alioto became chairman of the board of the First San Francisco Bank, 1965–68, and he was general counsel of the Charles Krug Winery. He held various honors, including decorations from the French and Italian governments.

SOURCES: C. P. Larrowe, *Harry Bridges, the Rise and Fall of Radical Labor in the United States* (New York, 1972); F. W. Wirt, *Power in the City* (Berkeley, Calif., 1974).
                                                                    Peter d'A. Jones

ALLEN, JOHN W. (1802–87), Mayor of Cleveland (1841). Fourth mayor of Cleveland, and a transplanted Yankee, Allen had the most significant city, state, and national career among Cleveland's early mayors. He was born in 1802 in Litchfield, Connecticut, son of John Allen (congressman, lawyer, and poet, d. 1812) and Ursula McCurdy (d. 1819). His marriage to Anna Maria Perkins of Warren, Ohio, in 1828 ended with her death after three months, and in 1830 he married Harriet C. Mather in Lyme, Connecticut. They had three children: James, William, and Louisa. He was Episcopalian. Allen studied law at Oxford in Chenango County, New York, and then he moved to Cleveland in 1825 to study law with Judge Samuel Cowles. In 1826, he was third in Cleveland to be admitted to the bar and two years later was a village trustee.

From 1831 to 1835, Allen was elected annually to serve as president of the village board of trustees and then served a term in the Ohio Senate (1835–37). Elected to Congress as a Whig in 1836 (defeating Mayor John W. Willey—*q.v.*), he was reelected in 1838, becoming a close political friend of Henry Clay. In these years, Cleveland grew from a village of 500 (while Brooklyn on the west side of the Cuyahoga River had 200) in 1825 to a city of 6,071 in 1840, booming as the Lake Erie terminus of the Ohio and Erie Canal, which was begun the year Allen arrived. Allen was a lawyer, banker, land speculator, and railroad promoter. He served as a director of the Commercial Bank of Lake Erie, 1832–42; was the first editor of the (Whig) Cleveland *Advertiser* in 1831; established the board of health during the cholera epidemic of 1832; helped to establish the Cleveland Lyceum in 1833; was president of the Cleveland Insurance Company in 1836 and helped to organize the Society for Savings in 1849; was a leader in the Cuyahoga Colonization Society in 1839; was a founder of the Episcopal Trinity Church in 1828; helped to inaugurate medical education in Cleveland; and became president of the New England Society in 1846. He speculated in thousands of acres of land and operated a land sale office. He helped to organize the local Cleveland and Newburg Railroad in 1834, and the Ohio Railroad Company in 1836 which had banking powers and started a "stilt" line toward Elyria and the Maumee River. He was chief promoter of the Cleveland, Columbus, and Cincinnati Railroad in 1836, of which he became president in 1845, and he headed the Cleveland, Warren and Pittsburgh Railroad in 1846.

Allen was elected mayor of Cleveland as a Whig in 1841, five years after Cleveland had been chartered as a city, 421 votes, against 407 for ex-Mayor Joshua Mills (*q.v.*) (Locofoco). Nelson Hayward (*q.v.*) was elected alderman, later to be mayor. When the State Bank of Ohio was chartered in 1846, Allen was a commissioner to oversee its branches. He was commissioned as agent for Ohio for the settlement of land claims against the federal government remaining from land grants given for the Ohio canals, recovering some 120,000 acres for the state. In 1853, he was a promoter of the Cleveland Iron Mining Company. He died on 5 October 1887 and was buried in Cleveland.

SOURCES: Elroy McKendree Avery, *Cleveland and Its Environs: The Heart of New Connecticut*, (Chicago, 1918); E. Decker, *Cleveland Past and Present; Its Representative Men* (Cleveland, 1869); S. A. Fuller, "Biographical Sketch of John W. Allen, with Some Notes on His Lineage" (typescript, Western Reserve Historical Society, n.d.); Harlan Hatcher, *The Western Reserve: The Story of New Connecticut in Ohio*, rev. ed. (Cleve-

land, 1966); Gertrude Van Rensselaer Wickham, *The Pioneer Families of Cleveland 1796–1940* (Cleveland, 1914).

Ronald E. Shaw

ALLEN, ORLANDO (1803–74), Mayor of Buffalo (1848–49). Businessman-mayor, born in New Hartford, New York, on 10 February 1803, Allen was the son of Eli and Sarah (Lee) Allen, both old-stock New Englanders. He attended local schools until 1819 when he went to Buffalo and began working for the mercantile firm of M. Cyrenius Chapin. He became a leading salesman for Chapin and Pratt in 1821, and the following year the firm sent him to Detroit as its local representative. He remained there until 1824 and returned to Buffalo, working then for Pratt, who had started his own firm. In 1826, they formed Pratt, Allen and Company, and this partnership lasted until 1840. In 1826, Allen married Marilla Pratt (1807–92), and they had six children, four of whom died before 1874. The Allens were active in social affairs and supported the Buffalo Historic Society and the Fine Arts Academy. They attended the First Presbyterian Church.

A Whig, Allen served on the city council, 1836–37 and 1846–47. He was elected mayor in 1848, defeating Democrat Israel T. Hatch and Workingmen's party candidate C. Coburn by 1,970 to 1,855 and 756, respectively. Buffalo had 29,773 people in 1845 (according to a state census) and a mayor-council form of government. As mayor, Allen was most interested in civic improvements and the city's business success. He was especially concerned with the construction of the city's first major sewer system. He did not seek a second term in 1849.

Allen's political career did not end in 1849, for he was to spend a total of three terms in the New York legislature (1850–52 and 1861). In this phase of his career, Allen strongly supported internal improvements for the entire state, especially canals and the Buffalo and Pittsburgh Railroad. In 1856–57, Allen served on the board of supervisors in Buffalo. By this time he had become a Republican. He died at his home on 4 September 1874.

SOURCES: H. Perry Smith, ed., *History of the City of Buffalo and Erie County* 2 vols. (Syracuse, N.Y., 1884); U.S. Census returns for Buffalo, 1850.

Thomas R. Bullard

ALVORD, WILLIAM (1833–1904), Mayor of San Francisco (1871–73). Businessman, philanthropist, patron of the arts, leading citizen, and mayor, Alvord was born in Albany, New York, on 3 January 1833. His father was descended from an early colonial, English family. Alvord graduated in the class of 1850 from Albany Academy after winning medals in philosophy and mathematics. Three years later, he migrated to San Francisco, where he soon prospered as proprietor of a hardware store, partner in an import firm, and president of an ironworks.

By 1871, approximately 185,000 people lived in San Francisco. The coalition of Republican and Taxpayers parties supported Alvord as their mayoral candidate that year. He polled 13,402 votes in the election on 16 September, compared to the 11,053 of Tyler Curtis, his Democratic rival. On 4 December, Alvord embarked on a somewhat unsuccessful term as mayor. Despite his fiscal conservatism, a trait shared by many mayors in this depression decade, Alvord attempted to expand city services. He sought to enlarge the municipal police force in order to cope with increasing unrest from labor and the unemployed, but these efforts failed. So did his attempts to enhance fire safety. When Alvord opposed anti-Chinese ordinances passed by the board of supervisors, his vetoes were overridden. Alvord was most successful in his efforts to improve the local environment. He pressed hard for the development of the city's massive Golden Gate Park, a cause that consumed much of his life. He supported the arts and municipal efforts to beautify the city, reflecting the need of San Franciscans to develop cultural amenities in their crude metropolis. Finally, Alvord became the first mayor to ride on the city's cable cars.

Alvord declined to stand for reelection and endorsed his successor, James Otis (q.v.), in 1873. The ex-mayor then embarked on an even busier schedule. He served as city park commissioner (1873–82), police commissioner (1878–99), member of the board of health, president of the American Forestry Association (1890–91), president of the San Francisco Art Association (1871–75), trustee of the College of California (which later became the University of California), president of the California Academy of Sciences (1903–1904), and director, president, or board member for a number of businesses. In June 1884, Alvord married his first wife, Mary E. Keeney. He outlived both this wife and a second one. Neither of his marriages produced any children. He died as a result of heart failure on 21 December 1904.

SOURCES: Gunther Barth, *Instant Cities: Urbanization and the Rise of San Francisco and Denver* (New York, 1975); Biographical notes on William Alvord, n.d. (MS, Bancroft Library, University of California, Berkeley); William J. Heintz, *San Francisco's Mayors 1850–1880* (Woodside, Calif., 1975); Theodore H. Hittell, *William Alvord; Born January 3, 1833, Died December 21, 1904* (San Francisco, 1905).

John M. Findlay

ANDREWS, ANDRE M. (1792–1834), Mayor of Buffalo (1833–34). The second mayor of Buffalo,

Major Andre Andrews, named after the British officer hanged as a spy during the American Revolution, was born in Cornwall, Connecticut, on 8 July 1792, the son of Andrew and Mary (Morse) Andrews, an old-stock Yankee Protestant family. He married Sarah Mehitable Hosmer (d. 1834), granddaughter of General Samuel Holden Parsons (1737–89), in Middletown, Connecticut. Their first child, William Richard (1818–58), was born in Middletown; the remaining seven, Elizabeth Hosmer (1820-96), Harriet Hinsdale (1822-34), Edward C. (1825-65), John Ellsworth (1826-?), Lucia Hosmer (1829-1915), Henry (1831-86), and Harriet (1834–1918), were all born in Buffalo.

Andrews practiced law in Middletown, Connecticut, before moving to Buffalo in about 1820. Although he joined the Erie County Bar Association in 1821, his main interest was the management of his real estate in and around Buffalo. He was a trustee of the village of Buffalo in 1826 and 1827, and an unsuccessful candidate for the New York Assembly in 1829. Joseph Ellicott, agent of the Holland Land Company in western New York, told company officials that Andrews was the "Agrarius" who wrote articles against the company in the Buffalo *Republican* in 1829. Andrews was also a member of the 1832 Electoral College which named Andrew Jackson as president.

Between 1832, the year Buffalo received its city charter, and by 1835, the city had grown from 10,119 to 15,661 inhabitants. Government was by a common council, consisting of two aldermen from each of five wards, elected for one-year terms. The common council appointed the mayor and other city officials. Andrews was elected to the common council from the Fourth Ward in the first city election of 1832. During his term as alderman, he resisted efforts of the pro-temperance members of the council to raise the rates of liquor licenses for taverns and grocery stores. The second common council, elected in March 1833, reappointed Buffalo's first mayor, Dr. Ebenezer Johnson, but when Johnson refused a second term, the council unanimously appointed Andrews as mayor. The Buffalo *Patriot* reported that the aldermen elected in the Second and Third Wards were National Republicans, that the aldermen from the Fifth Ward was an Anti-Mason, and that the election in the First and Fifth Wards was conducted without reference to parties. The common council offered Andrews a second term in 1834, but he declined to serve.

Soon after leaving office, Andrews, along with his wife and his daughter Harriet, died in an epidemic of Asiatic cholera.

SOURCES: Grace Carew Sheldon, "Major Andrews Occupied the Chair at City Hall as Buffalo's Second Mayor," Buffalo *Times*, 26 January 1919; H. Perry

Smith, *History of the City of Buffalo and Erie County*, 2 vols. (Syracuse, N.Y., 1884); Truman C. White, *Our Country and Its People: A Descriptive Work on Erie County*, 2 vols., (Boston, 1898).

Christopher Densmore

ARMSTRONG, JOSEPH GRAY (1867–1931), Mayor of Pittsburgh (1914–18). Armstrong was born in old Allegheny, now Pittsburgh's North Side, on 2 February 1867. His father, William A. Armstrong, an Irish immigrant, was a graduate of Trinity College, Dublin, but the son was an elementary school dropout, worked as a department store cash-boy, and then was apprenticed as a glass blower. He became a leader in the Knights of Labor, and on 17 October 1892 married Clara B. Smith, who bore him five children. The family was Protestant, probably Presbyterian.

Armstrong was a member of the common council from 1896 to 1902 and was twice elected to the select council. He resigned to run for coroner, was elected twice but left this post in 1909 to become public works director under Mayor William A. Magee (*q.v.*).

In 1913, a short-lived nonpartisan ballot law was in force, and Mayor Magee was pushing Congressman Stephen G. Porter as his successor. Learning that Armstrong planned to run, he fired him as public works director, but Armstrong teamed up with the old political boss, William Flinn, and came within 304 votes of Porter in a three-man primary. In the runoff, Armstrong won 39,912 to 37,472. Pittsburgh at this time had about 550,000 people and a strong mayor, small council form of government.

Although four of the five councilmen elected were Porter men, Armstrong achieved a great deal. He issued all bonds within the city's borrowing power, built tunnels, roads, and a new city-county building and was elected county treasurer, and then in 1923 county commissioner, being chairman of the board for two terms.

Armstrong's wife had died in 1926, and in 1930 he married a widow, Mrs. Ethel Wilson. He missed renomination in 1931. He had become diabetic, and died on 19 November 1931 of that malady and pneumonia. He was buried with Masonic honors in South Side Cemetery.

SOURCES: Frank Harper, *Pittsburgh of Today* (New York, 1931); Kermit McFarland "Campaigns of Other Days," Pittsburgh *Press*, 2 November 1938; Pittsburgh *Post-Gazette* and *Press*, both 20 November 1931; *Western Pennsylvanians*, (Pittsburgh, 1912).

George Swetnam

ARMSTRONG, SAMUEL TURELL (1784–1850), Mayor of Boston (1836). Sixth mayor of Boston, Armstrong was born in Dorchester, Massachusetts, on 29

April 1784 the son of John (d. 1794) and Elizabeth Armstrong (d. 1797). He attended public school in Dorchester until the death of his father when he was eleven, and his mother sent him off to work in his uncle's paint shop. The death of his mother three years later freed him to look for something better. The ambitious fourteen-year old moved to the printing firm of Manning and Loring, becoming the youngest printer's apprentice. He finished his apprenticeship in April 1805, and after five months as a journeyman, left to start his own business with a friend, as a pamphlet jobber and publisher of literary and religious magazines. Although the company floundered and finally was dissolved in 1808, Armstrong went on to make an impressive career in printing and bookselling. In fact, in 1848, near the end of his life, a survey of the richest men in Boston estimated his wealth to be $200,000, most of which he had made selling *Scott's Family Bibles* across the United States. In 1812, while still struggling to make his fortune, Armstrong married Abigail Walker of Charlestown, Massachusetts; they had no children. He also took time out to serve as the captain of the "Warren Phalanx" in Charlestown in the War of 1812.

Armstrong entered politics in his thirties, serving in the Massachusetts House of Representatives in 1822–23 and 1828–29. As a Whig, he was elected lieutenant governor in 1833 and 1835. In 1835, he assumed the position of acting governor, after Governor John Davis was appointed to the Senate. He ran for governor in his own right later that year but failed to gain the support of Whig party leader Edward Everett, and so he had to run as an Independent, losing miserably to Everett, himself. Undeterred, he ran for mayor of Boston a month later on the Whig ticket and won.

In 1836, Boston had a population of approximately 81,500 and a mayor/bicameral council form of government. The city was suffering the pains of rapid economic and population growth. Unable to meet the challenges this posed, the Armstrong administration's only achievements were the construction of a fence around the Common and the extension of a mall through the burial ground on Boylston Street. The most important projects Armstrong considered were a plan to build a new county jail in South Boston to replace the antiquated Leverett Street jail and a plan to introduce fresh water into Boston to supplement and replace its inadequate and increasingly unsanitary well water. But both projects failed. The people of South Boston and local judicial leaders opposed the relocation of the jail to a still remote and undeveloped area, while the city council insisted that the water system be developed by a private company. Perhaps disillusioned, Armstrong chose not to run for a second term. He was elected to the state Senate in 1839 and died on

26 March 1850.

SOURCES: S. T. Armstrong Papers, Massachusetts Historical Society; Boston City Documents, (Boston, 1836); James M. Bugbee, "Boston Under the Mayors," in Justin Winsor (ed.), *The Memorial History of Boston* (Boston, 1881), vol. 3; *Inaugural Addresses of the Mayors of Boston 1822–1851* (Boston, 1894); *Our First Men: A Calendar of Wealth, Fashion, and Gentlemen Containing a List of Those Persons Taxed in the City of Boston Credibly Reported to Be Worth 100 Thousand Dollars* (Boston, 1846); Rollo G. Silver, "Belcher C. Armstrong Set Up Shop," *Studies in Bibliography: Papers of the Bibliographical Society of the University of Virginia* (1951–1952), vol. 4.   Christine M. Rosen

ASHBRIDGE, SAMUEL H. (1849–1906), Mayor of Philadelphia (1899–1903). The notorious "boodle mayor" was born in Philadelphia on 5 December 1849. Ashbridge attended the public schools, began clerking in a coal company office, and later entered the same business himself. He was chief clerk of the coroner's office (1880–86) and coroner (1899). Known as "Stars and Stripes Sam," Ashbridge went to lodges, Sunday schools, and prayer meetings, making patriotic speeches and civic promises to win favor and support of voters. When he was coerced by the "machine" to enter the election for sheriff as a Republican (which he lost), he exacted from Israel Durham, city boss for the Matthew S. Quay organization, the promise of nomination for mayor. He won the election in 1899.

As mayor, Ashbridge stunned even "corrupt and contented" Philadelphia (as Lincoln Steffens labeled the Ashbridge era) by his open, brazen, and wholesale boodle and graft. The mayor told another officeholder: "I mean to get out of this office everything there is in it for Samuel H. Ashbridge." When he was nominated for mayor, Ashbridge had a personal debt of $40,000; the debt was liquidated in the few intervening weeks before he was elected. When he left the office, he became president of a bank and reportedly was rich. The administration inflated a $3.7 million water purification plant loan into a $12 million bonanza for graft on payrolls, contracting, supplies, and excavating. Favored contractors charged 83 cents per yard for grading when the established rate was 30 cents. Feed contracts for the city's horses were awarded, not as required by law to the lowest bidders, but to the highest. Sidewalks, curbs, sewers, bridges, and buildings were all sources of lucrative profit for machine faithfuls, but even those paled next to the "great franchise sensation." The administration gave away free to a favored syndicate the rights to construct transit systems on streets not serviced by streetcars. John Wanamaker, the reformist millionaire retailer, offered to pay $2.5 million for those rights, but his offer was spurned by Mayor Ashbridge who signed the giveaway franchise. Lincoln Steffens, who immortalized Ashbridge in his exposé of urban graft, paid tribute to the mayor for having "broken through all the principles of moderate grafting" and for having established a new benchmark for wholesale plunder, reminiscent of New York's Tweed Ring of the mid-nineteenth century. Philadelphia's outstanding scoundrel died in March 1906.

SOURCES: *City of Firsts: Complete History of Philadelphia* (Philadelphia, 1926); Lincoln Steffens, "Philadelphia: Corrupt and Contended," *McClure's Magazine* 21 (July 1903).   Melvin G. Holli

B

BABCOCK, BRENTON D. (1830–1906), Mayor of Cleveland (1887–88). Businessman-mayor and advocate of the "federal plan," Babcock was born on 2 October 1830 on a farm in Adams, New York. He attended Adams Seminary and eventually graduated from Watertown College. His first job as a clerk in a general store culminated in a managerial position with another general store. Still a bachelor, he moved to Cleveland in 1865 as a bookkeeper for Cross, Payne and Company, local coal dealers. Having learned the coal business, he formed the Card and Babcock Coal Company in 1869, and in 1875 he sold out his share to his partner, becoming a traveling salesman for Tod, Morris and Company, another coal firm. By 1878, he had decided to reenter the business, and he founded a new coal mining company, Babcock, Morris Coal Company, with mines in Hocking Valley. Meanwhile, Babcock married Elizabeth C. Smith (1837–1926) from Buffalo, daughter of a doctor, on 6 November 1867, a union that produced no children. She was a prominent voluntary charity worker and a member of the Northern Ohio Woman's Press Association. Having joined the Freemasons in 1859, Babcock became a very prominent 33 degree Mason, holding several state offices and membership on the Supreme Council for the Northern Masonic Jurisdiction of the USA. Crediting him for starting the Scottish Rite Masonry in Cleveland, the Freemasons erected a $2,500 monument to his memory in 1908.

Cleveland had approximately 239,000 people in 1887 and a city government with power spread among the mayor, board of aldermen, and various elected commissioners. The board of trade had begun agitation for a federal plan such as was employed in Philadelphia with a strong mayor and city council. Babcock attended public meetings on the subject and became the head of a study committee. In 1887, the local Democrats were looking for a Mugwump type and selected Babcock to run against William M. Bayne, the Republican nominee. Bayne, a professional politician, proprietor of a job-printing firm, and a Sunday School superintendent, ousted George W. Gardner (*q.v.*), Republican mayor of Cleveland and a prominent businessman, in the party's convention. The *Plain Dealer*, a local Democratic organ, called on the board of trade to support Babcock, a businessman, who advocated careful management and municipal reform, while the *Leader*, the Republican newspaper, accused Babcock and the Democrats of favoring open saloons on Sunday. Babcock won easily with 14,166 votes to 10,845 for Bayne.

As mayor, Babcock continued to support the federal plan, but complications at the state legislature level held up matters. The only item of note was completion of the Central Viaduct connecting the South Side with the central city. During his term, the city treasurer, Thomas Axworthy, defalcated with $440,000, an amount eventually recovered, but the issue carried over into the next election. Babcock himself became disenchanted with politics, in his first few weeks throwing out officeseekers and deciding never to run for office again. In 1902, Babcock suffered a stroke that rendered him partially paralyzed. He died on 10 January 1906 from what was described as apoplexy.

SOURCES: Ceremonies of the Unveiling of the Brenton D. Babcock Monument in Lakeview Cemetery (1908), available in the Western Reserve Historical Society; William R. Coates, *A History of Cuyahoga County and the City of Cleveland* (New York, 1924); Charles Kennedy, *Fifty Years of Cleveland, 1875 to 1925* (Cleveland, 1925); James H. Kennedy, *A History of the City of Cleveland, 1796–1896* (Cleveland, 1896); The *Plain Dealer* and the *Leader*, 11 January 1906; W. Scott Robinson, *History of the City of Cleveland* (Cleveland, 1887).

William D. Jenkins

BABCOCK, EDWARD VOSE (1864–1948), Mayor of Pittsburgh (1918–22). Pittsburgh's World War I mayor, Babcock was born in 1864 on a small farm outside of Fulton in Oswego County, New York. His parents, Leman B. and Harriet (Vose) Babcock, had New England roots and raised a family of five: Edward (b. 1864); Fred (b. 1865); Oscar (b. 1870); Clarence (b. 1871); and Lena (b. 1873). Babcock attended district schools during the winter term and worked on the family farm during the summers. Hired as a teacher at age sixteen, Edward taught three terms before continuing his education at a Poughkeepsie business college. At age twenty-one, he migrated to Michigan where he worked as a "lumber hustler," and five years later, with his brother Fred, founded a lumber company headquartered in Pittsburgh. The Babcock Lumber Company, and the Babcock Coal and Coke Company founded in 1912, made Babcock a millionaire.

On 2 June 1903, Babcock married Mary Dundore Arnold of Reading, Pennsylvania, the daughter of a prominent local financier; the couple honeymooned in Europe. Active in reform politics, Babcock was appointed as one of the nine initial councilmen under a new mayor/small council city charter that took effect in 1911. Elected in his own right the following November, Babcock resigned halfway through his term to pursue what he claimed were neglected business interests. He remained active in Republican party affairs, however, and in 1917 entered the mayoral race with support among both Republicans and Democrats.

In the general election, Babcock received 40,604 votes, defeating former Mayor William A. Magee (*q.v.*) who drew 36,174. In 1920, Pittsburgh had a population of 588,343. Although promising a "business" administration in his campaign, Babcock offered a remarkably expansive program. He sponsored a $22 million bond issue for major road reconstruction and pushed the improvement of the water system and the construction of parks and playgrounds. As Pittsburgh's war mayor, Babcock and his wife led the drives to sell bonds and to encourage support for the war. During his term, the city annexed several adjacent townships.

Although eligible for reelection, Babcock chose not to run in 1921. He returned to his business and did not hold office again until 1925 when the judges of the county court of common pleas chose him to fill the unexpired term of a deceased county commissioner. Elected to a full term two years later, Babcock again supported bond issues for road, bridge, and airport improvements. What he considered his personal triumph, however, was the creation of North and South parks, the county's two largest recreation areas. Babcock personally optioned much of the land and turned it over to the county at cost.

Babcock returned to business after his commissioner's term expired in 1931 and worked until the morning of his death. He died at home on 2 September 1948, of a heart attack, aged seventy-four. Services were held at Shadyside Presbyterian Church, and he was buried in Homewood Cemetery.

SOURCES: Clipping file Pennsylvania Division, Carnegie Public Library, Pittsburgh; Allen Humphreys Kerr, "The Mayors and Recorders of Pittsburgh, 1816–1951." (unpublished manuscript Historical Society of Western Pennsylvania, Pittsburgh, 1952); Pittsburgh *Post-Gazette*, 3 September 1948.

Douglas V. Shaw

BACHRACH, WALTON H. (1904–   ), Mayor of Cincinnati (1960–67). Bachrach was born in Cincinnati on 22 December 1904, the son of Fisher Bachrach (1882–1938), a restaurant owner, and Rose (Silverglade) Bachrach (1883–   ), both of East European Jewish ancestry. Fisher Bachrach was born in Poland and his wife in Cincinnati. An only child, Walton Bachrach attended local schools, Culver Military Academy, Washington and Lee University (in Lexington, Virginia) and the University of Cincinnati Law School, graduating from the law school in 1929. On 4 February 1930, he married Ida May Henly, a student at Smith College, and they had two daughters. Bachrach practiced law and served two years as assistant county attorney, followed by two years as court clerk. In 1937, he joined his father in running the successful Wheel Cafe (founded in 1902) and continued in this profession until 1965.

A Republican, Bachrach was elected to the city council in 1953 and served for fourteen years. When Mayor Donald Clancy (*q.v.*) resigned to enter Congress in late 1960, the council chose Bachrach as his successor. He was chosen again for three consecutive two-year terms, serving until 1967. Cincinnati had 502,550 people in 1960 and a city manager-mayor-council form of government. Bachrach strongly supported the city manager system, considering it the best type for a "small" city like Cincinnati. He worked hard to increase river traffic and to make the city more attractive to industry. Bachrach supported sound and efficient municipal government and revival of the downtown area, including support for a new stadium. He belonged to the Citizens' Development Committee which helped meet the problems of the 1960s. After the second longest mayoral career in Cincinnati, Bachrach retired from both politics and business in 1967 and moved to Tucson, Arizona.

SOURCES: Cincinnati *Enquirer*, 1 and 3 December 1961; Interview, 28 July 1979; *Who's Who in American Politics* (New York, 1967).   *Thomas R. Bullard*

BADING, GERHARD A. (1870–1946), Mayor of Milwaukee (1912–16). First official nonpartisan mayor of Milwaukee, Dr. Bading was born in that city on 31 August 1870, the son of Dr. John Bading (1824–1913), a minister and long-time president of the Lutheran Synodical Conference of North America. He was educated at Northwestern College in Watertown, Wisconsin, and at Rush Medical College in Chicago, receiving his M.D. degree in 1896. On 15 December 1895, he married Carol Royal Clemmer, a Chicago German, a union that lasted until his death half a century later but that produced no children. Bading practiced medicine and taught surgery at the Milwaukee Medical College and the Wisconsin College of Physicians and Surgeons until his appointment as city health commissioner in 1906. He served in that capacity until 1910, introducing tuberculin tests for milk cows, licensing of food establishments, medical inspection in parochial schools, and vaccination programs.

Although a life-long Republican, Bading was first elected mayor in 1912 as a fusion candidate, endorsed by both major parties against the incumbent Social Democrats. Bading defeated Socialist Mayor Emil Seidel (*q.v.*) 43,176 to 30,272 in an election marked by class-conscious rhetoric. Partly in response to Socialist strength in the city of over 400,000, the Wisconsin legislature made municipal elections nonpartisan later that same year. In 1914, Bading became the first official nonpartisan mayor of the city by defeating Seidel again, 37,673 to 29,122. As mayor, Bading directed the initiation of municipal harbor facilities by acquiring riparian rights to the lakefront and Jones Island, and created the sewerage commission. He stirred up controversy by opposing an eight-hour day for city workers, by delaying public works projects, and by being charged with collusion in his dealings with the electric company and asphalt contractors. As a result, Bading lost his bid for reelection in 1916 to Socialist Daniel Hoan (*q.v.*) by a vote of 32,493 to 30,623.

Bading enlisted in the Army during World War I, rising to the rank of major and serving in the Philippines, Tientsin China, and Manchuria. In 1922, President Warren G. Harding appointed him an envoy to Ecuador, and he continued in the Foreign Service until 1930. After 1930, Bading resumed his medical practice in Milwaukee and was active in the American Legion, the American Medical Association, and the English-Speaking Union. He died in Milwaukee on 11 April 1946, after a long illness.

SOURCES: Milwaukee *Journal*, 5 March 1922, 12 April 1946; Bayrd Still, *Milwaukee: The History of a City*, (Madison, Wis., 1965); E. B. Usher, *History of Wisconsin* (Chicago, 1914).   *John D. Buenker*

BAEHR, HERMAN C. (1866–1942), Mayor of Cleveland (1910–11). German-American brewer and mayor of Cleveland, born on 16 March 1866 in Keokuk, Iowa, Baehr was the son of Jacob Baehr (1824–73), a cooper, and Magdalena (Zipf) Baehr (1833–1909), both German-born Mennonites. The second of nine children, Herman moved to Cleveland with his family at the age of six months; there the elder Baehr established a thriving brewery. Quitting school at fourteen, young Herman joined his father's firm and was sent to Lehmann's Scientific Academy in Worms, Germany, receiving a degree in medicine in 1883. Upon his return to the United States,

Baehr assumed control of the family brewery and merged it with the Cleveland and Sandusky Brewery Company. On 27 April 1898, he married Rose Schulte of Rochester, New York. Baehr was a Mason, a member of the Chamber of Commerce and the Cleveland Auto Club, a director of the Cleveland Trust Company, and president of the Forest City Savings and Trust Company.

Baehr was an ally of Senator Mark Hanna and entered politics by winning election as the county recorder in 1903. A Republican, Baehr was reelected for two more terms. In 1909, he was elected mayor, with 41,405 votes to 37,711 for Tom Johnson (*q.v.*) (Democrat) and 1,266 for John G. Willert (Socialist). Cleveland had 560,663 people in 1910 and a mayor-council form of government. Baehr had not expected to win the election, since Johnson, the incumbent, was a popular and well-known political leader in Cleveland.

Baehr was not an active mayor and is best remembered for the uproar caused by his decision to remove Fred Kohler as chief of police. Baehr was personally a popular man, but he had no further political ambitions. He returned to his brewery in 1912, and eventually retired. While on a vacation trip to Los Angeles, he suffered a fatal stroke on 4 February 1942.

SOURCES: Elroy M. Avery, *A History of Cleveland and Its Environs*, 4 vols. (Chicago, 1918); Cleveland *Plain Dealer*, 5 February 1942; W. R. Coates, *A History of Cuyahoga County and the City of Cleveland*, 3 vols., (Chicago, 1924).   *Thomas R. Bullard*

BAKER, CHARLES J. (–1937), Mayor *ex officio* of Baltimore (1862). Mayor *ex officio*, Baker was never elected and only briefly served as acting mayor, replacing Mayor *ex officio* John C. Blackburn (*q.v.*). The mayoral confusion evident in late 1861 and early 1862 resulted from the arrest of the popularly elected mayor, George William Brown (*q.v.*), who was imprisoned following his 12 September 1861 arrest by federal authorities.

Baker, a reformer, was elected to the Second Branch of the city council from the Thirteenth Ward on 10 October 1860. Never officially recognized as a Baltimore mayor, Baker nevertheless delivered the Mayor's Message as required by law on 6 January 1862. It was Baker, not Blackburn, who was acting mayor in January 1862 when John Lee Chapman (*q.v.*) was unanimously selected to become mayor *ex officio*, thereby ending the period of mayoral uncertainty.

SOURCES: Baltimore *Morning Sun*, 11 October 1860; 7 January 1862.   *Jo Ann Eady Argersinger*

BAKER, NEWTON DIEHL (1871–1937), Mayor of Cleveland (1912–15). Progressive mayor, reform Democrat, and later secretary of war, born on 5 December

1871 in Martinsburg, West Virginia, Baker was the son of Newton D. Baker, a cultured country doctor of English-Irish stock, and Mary Ann Dukehart of German-Irish background. While the father was Lutheran, the mother was high church Episcopalian, a denomination which Newton preferred. After education at an Episcopal high school, Baker entered Johns Hopkins University (1889–93) where he studied under Woodrow Wilson. After a postgraduate year studying Roman law and jurisprudence, Baker entered Washington and Lee University where he earned a bachelor of law degree in nine months. He began a law practice in 1894 but two years later was made assistant to the postmaster-general, 1896–97. Baker moved to Cleveland in 1899 at the suggestion of reformer Frederick C. Howe. On 5 July 1902, he married Elizabeth Leopold (1873–1951), a Presbyterian of Dutch ancestry, who came from Pottstown, Pennsylvania, and had been a faculty member of Wilson College in Chambersburg, Pennsylvania. The Bakers had three children: Elizabeth (b. 1905), Newton D. III (b. 1907), and Margaret (b. 1912).

In 1901, Baker became legal adviser and key aide to reform Mayor Tom L. Johnson (*q.v.*) (1901–1909) and was the reformer's closest confidant during the administration's battle for a 3-cent street fare and other attacks against "the forces of privilege." In 1902, Baker was elected to the new position of city solicitor, a position he retained until he ran for mayor in 1911 on a campaign platform to expand the municipal light plant with a 3-cent rate for electricity. He defeated the Republican, Frank G. Hogan, by a vote of 46,214 to 28,376; C. E. Ruthenberg got 8,147 and John Goerke 583. Baker governed a city of over 560,663 population (74.6 percent of whom were of foreign stock) that grew to 796,841 by 1920.

Baker continued Johnson's social reforms. Baker was a Progressive who added his own stamp with structural reforms, such as a successful drive for a home rule amendment to the state constitution in 1912 and Cleveland's first home rule charter which provided for a strong mayor-council form of government, eliminated party primaries, and introduced recall, initiative, and referendum.

Advocating 3-cent rates for electricity, streetcar fares, dances, and even fish, Baker became known as the "3-cent mayor," Baker was a strong advocate of women's suffrage and pioneered in placing women in leading city hall positions. Political and economic reforms were later joined by his efforts in cultural and recreational activities such as a municipal orchestra, city parks, and dance halls. He was reelected in 1913, winning his second election against Republican Harry L. Davis (*q.v.*) by a vote of 41,286 to 36,126, with 5,737 for J. E. Robb. Mayor Baker continued with the endeavors of his first

term and drew criticism for going into debt rather than increasing taxes. He did not seek reelection but joined the cabinet of President Wilson as secretary of war (1916–21), and earned a reputation as a brilliant administrator.

Baker returned to Cleveland in 1921 to rejoin the law firm of Baker, Hofstedter, and Sidlo, which he had organized when he left the mayor's office. Over the years, he acquired a large number of corporate clients and never again entered the public arena. Although he was critical of the TVA and other governmental centralization under President Franklin Roosevelt, he remained committed to the Democratic party until his death of a heart attack on 25 December 1937.

SOURCES: Newton D. Baker Papers at the Library of Congress total 106 linear feet and additional material in mayoral archives, Cleveland City Hall; Thomas F. Campbell, *Daniel E. Morgan: The Good Citizen in Politics: 1877–1949* (Cleveland 1966); C. H. Cramer, *Newton D. Baker: A Biography* (Cleveland and New York, 1931); Tom L. Johnson, *My Story* (Seattle, 1970; introduction by Melvin G. Holli); Hoyt Landon Warner, *Progressivism in Ohio* (Columbus, 1964).

Thomas F. Campbell and Thomas R. Bullard

BANKS, ROBERT TUNSTALL (1822–1901), Mayor of Baltimore (1867–71). Reconstruction Mayor Banks, born in Williamsburg, Virginia, on 2 April 1822, was the son of Major George W. Banks, a prominent member of the Virginia bar, and Charlotte (Martin) Banks of Snow Hill, Maryland. Banks received a common school education. When his father died, he was taken as a youngster into the office of Thomas Ritchie, founder of the Richmond *Enquirer*. At fifteen, Banks moved with his family to Baltimore, settling in the eastern part of the city in the old Fourth Ward. There he worked as a postal clerk for several years. In 1845 he married Mary B. Loane of Baltimore. They were members of the Christ Protestant Episcopal Church. She died in 1899, survived by three children—two sons and one daughter.

Banks entered politics as the Democratic-Conservative mayoral candidate in 1867. The 23 October municipal elections were the first held under the new state constitution that represented "self-reconstruction" and increased the mayoral term to four years. The term was changed back to two years in 1870. Banks easily defeated his Radical Republican opponent, General Andrew W. Denison, by 18,420 to 4,896 votes.

Baltimore in 1870 was overwhelmingly Democratic, had 267,354 people, and a mayor-council form of government. Banks began his administration on 4 November 1867, serving until 6 November 1871—the first and last four-year term until the adoption of the 1898 city charter. As mayor, he remained the traditionalist, attempting to soothe the city's sectional animosities. Ironically, it was during his term that blacks went to the polls in 1870 for the first time since 1802. Much to his satisfaction, the elections proceeded without violence, and the newly enfranchised black Republicans did little to disturb Democratic hegemony. Banks did approve numerous railroad and street improvements, including the first recorded asphalt paving in Baltimore. He consolidated earlier city hall construction efforts, urged modifications of Jones Falls in order to preclude another flood disaster such as the one in 1868, and authorized a million dollar loan to the Western Maryland Railroad—a company he also served as president in 1871.

In 1879, Banks was elected register of wills, serving two terms until 1892. During that time, he established a profitable wholesale crockery business. A gentleman who belonged to the old order of things, Banks died on 8 August 1901.

SOURCES: Wilbur F. Coyle, *The Mayors of Baltimore* (Baltimore, 1919); Enoch Pratt Free Library, Baltimore: Vertical File (newspaper clippings), Maryland Room; J. Thomas Scharf, *History of Baltimore City and County* (Philadelphia, 1891).   Jo Ann Eady Argersinger

BARKER, JOSEPH (1806?–62), Mayor of Pittsburgh (1850). Bigoted, nativist, anti-Catholic, rabble-rouser and the only mayor in Pittsburgh's history to be elected while serving out a prison term, the controversial and eccentric Barker was born, according to U.S. Census records, sometime around 1806 in the Pittsburgh area. Not much is known about his origins and background. His wife, Jane Barker, was born in Ireland. The Barkers had four children: William H., Augustine, Eliza, and David. Surviving information indicates that by the 1840s Joseph Barker resided in the Bayardstown section of Pittsburgh. He held petty city offices under the Whigs for short periods. He was elected street commissioner for Second Street in January 1839, and in 1841 he was appointed collector of tolls at the Allegheny River bridge.

Barker first came into prominence around 1840 as a street preacher. A good speaker, he had a large following, especially among working-class Protestants. Capitalizing on nativist fears and reform sentiments, Barker directed his harangues against Masons, foreigners, Roman Catholics, the economic elite, slavery, intemperance, and politicians. Because of his violent rhetoric and his constant violation of city ordinances, he was frequently in trouble with the law. In November 1849, after delivering a harsh anti-Catholic speech, he was arrested and convicted for using obscene language, obstructing the streets, and causing a riot. He was fined $250 and sentenced to a year's imprisonment.

Pittsburgh, located in Allegheny County, had a population of 46,601 in 1850 and was governed by a mayor-council system. Exercising both legislative and executive powers, the councils (select and common) held most municipal authority. The mayor served primarily as a magistrate and police chief. Barker's trial and incarceration made him a hero and martyr for many. His followers offered Barker as the People's and anti-Catholic candidate for mayor. While still in jail, Barker won the 8 January 1850 election with 1,787 votes to 1,584 for John B. Guthrie (q.v.) (Democratic, Citizens' candidate), and 1,034 for Robert McCutcheon (Whig and Anti-Mason). Soon after the election, Barker was pardoned by Governor William F. Johnston. On 11 January 1851, Barker ran for reelection as a reform candidate and lost, running third with 924 votes to 1,911 for John B. Guthrie (Democrat), and 1,206 for John J. Roggen (Whig and Anti-Mason). A year later, Barker ran as an Independent and lost. The vote on 13 January 1852 was 1,429 for incumbent Mayor Guthrie, 1,382 for B. C. Sawyer (Whig and Anti-Mason), and 785 for Barker. In a final attempt to win public office in October 1852, Barker ran for sheriff and lost.

Barker's term as mayor was characterized by constant conflict and municipal disorder. Catholics were harassed. Bishop Michael O'Connor was arrested twice on charges of maintaining a public nuisance. Barker personally arrested hucksters and merchants who obstructed sidewalks and used faulty weights and measures. He continued his street preaching, frequently attacking Catholics and the city councils. He fought a furious battle over control of the police forces with the police committee of the councils. This dispute resulted in the creation of two rival police forces which fought one another while patrolling the city. Barker also often interfered with arrests and defied the court. A man of reckless action, in October 1850, he was arrested twice for assault and battery, and a short time later for riot. In early 1851, he was tried on this latter charge and convicted. He remained incarcerated until June 1851.

By running for mayor three times (1850–1852), Barker upset the Whig party's traditional political dominance of Pittsburgh. By appealing to nativist, anti-Catholic, and reform sentiments, he drew the votes of poor Protestants who usually voted Whig. In many ways, he presaged the later political appeal of the Know-Nothing party.

Barker continued his street preaching after his mayoralty. He was thrown out of the Pennsylvania Senate chamber when he tried to address that body. During the late 1850s, he was arrested several times on a variety of charges, including assault with intent to kill. He slowly sank into obscurity and drunkenness.

With the advent of the Civil War, Barker helped arouse public opinion in support of the war. On 2 August 1862, while returning home from a war meeting in Ross Township, he was struck and killed by a passenger train.

SOURCES: Christine Altenburger, "The Pittsburgh Bureau of Police: Some Historical Highlights," *Western Pennsylvania Historical Magazine* 49 (January 1966); Leland D. Baldwin, *Pittsburgh: The Story of a City* (Pittsburgh, 1937); Michael Fitzgibbon Holt, *Forging a Majority: The Formation of the Republican Party in Pittsburgh, 1848–1860* (New Haven, Conn., 1969); Allen Humphreys Kerr, "The Mayors and Recorders of Pittsburgh, 1816–1951" (unpublished manuscript, Historical Society of Western Pennsylvania, Pittsburgh, 1952); Sarah H. Killkelly, *The History of Pittsburgh: Its Rise and Progress* (Pittsburgh, 1906).

Matthew S. Magda

BARKER, KIRKLAND C. (1819–75), Mayor of Detroit (1864, 1865). Transplanted Yankee and Republican mayor during the Civil War, Barker was born in East Schuyler, Herkimer County, New York, on 8 September 1819, the second son of Mason Barker, a contractor and builder of canals and railroads. Kirkland Barker attended public schools in East Schuyler and continued his training at the manual labor school in nearby Whitesboro. His first employment was as a clerk in a store at Frankfort, New York. From there he moved to Utica, New York, where he found similar employment. His next move was to Cleveland, Ohio, where he worked in a warehouse. In 1844, he moved to Detroit, where he became sales representative for a tobacco firm located in Logansport, Indiana. A few years later, he started his own tobacco business which eventually became the American Eagle Tobacco Company.

Barker was elected alderman in 1863 and was elected mayor in November of the same year. His administration was marked by Civil War problems, principally raising money through bond issues for bounties to be paid to enlisting soldiers. In October 1864, word was received from the U.S. consul in Toronto that a plot was under way to burn Detroit. Mayor Barker called for military aid and organized volunteer patrol groups to guard the city at night. Nothing developed, but according to Barker, a number of strangers were seen leaving the city as the protective measures were taken. As relations between Britain and the United States became strained, Secretary of State William H. Seward placed certain restrictions upon communication between the United States and Canada, one of which was the requirement of passports by Canadians who wished to cross the border. Because of the hardship such a requirement exerted upon the people of Detroit, Mayor Barker requested that the council pass resolutions in opposition to Secretary Seward's action.

Because of the alarm over the possibility of invasion or sabotage by the enemy and because more vagabonds and wanderers seemed to be visiting Detroit, Mayor Barker instituted plans for the establishment of Detroit's first permanent paid night police force.

Not long after his term as mayor, Barker moved to Grosse Isle, where he had built a fine home. He was recognized as a sportsman, participating in yachting races and following the turf. He was also an active supporter of the Audubon Club.

Barker was drowned in the Detroit River on 20 May 1875, when the sailboat in which he was transporting ballast-lead to his yacht *Cora* suddenly sank near Bois Blanc Island. He was survived by his wife (married in 1847), a daughter, and two sons.

SOURCES: Detroit *Free Press*, 21 May 1875; *Journal of the Proceedings of the Common Council of the City of Detroit*, 1864, 1865; Silas Farmer, *The History of Detroit and Michigan* (Detroit, 1889); Scrapbooks, Burton Historical Collection, Detroit Public Library.

John Cumming

BARKER, PIERRE AUGUSTUS (1790–1870), Mayor of Buffalo (1837–38). Early Buffalo mayor and an old-stock Yankee, Barker, born 17 April 1790 in LaGrange, New York, was the third child of Samuel Still Augustus Barker (1756–1819) and his first wife, Mary (Dalvin) Barker (1771–98). Samuel Barker, originally from Connecticut, had served in the Revolution as an aide to General Lafayette and later represented Dutchess County in the New York Assembly nine times between 1788 and 1811. In 1812, Pierre Barker married Annache G. Livingston (1790–1865), and eight of his nine children lived past infancy: Catherine (1812–35), William (1814–?), E. Marie (1816–83), (wife of another Buffalo mayor Philander Hodge), Louise (1818–46), Robert Rose S. (1821–46), Elizabeth King (1823–1905), James Stuart (1825–1909), and Pierre Augustus (1827–   ).

Barker owned property in and around Buffalo. He was a founder of the Bank of Buffalo in 1831, president of the Commercial Bank (c. 1835 to 1836), and president of the United States Bank at Buffalo (c. 1838 to 1840). From 1830 to 1838, he was collector of customs for the port of Buffalo, a major federal appointment.

Between 1835 and 1840, Buffalo grew from 15,661 to 18,231 inhabitants. The city, originally chartered in 1832, was governed by a common council, consisting of ten aldermen elected from the five wards, who appointed the mayor and other city officials. Barker was elected to the common council for a one-year term in March 1837. In December of that year, many radical refugees, including William Lyon Mackenzie, came to Buffalo from Canada as a result of the Rebellion of 1837. Support, including arms and men, was offered to the Canadian rebels. Barker, as a representative of U.S. government authority, and the mayor of Buffalo, Dr. Josiah

Trowbridge (*q.v.*) were in contact with federal officials and attempted to prevent any action that would bring the United States and Canada into conflict. Trowbridge, feeling that he was unable to keep order in the city, resigned on 22 December; Barker was appointed acting mayor immediately and full mayor in January 1838. In spite of the occupation of Navy Island in the Niagara River below Buffalo by the Canadian rebel Patriots, and the burning of the ship *Caroline*, conflict between the two countries was averted.

In 1838, Barker was replaced as collector of customs by George W. Clinton. Sometime after 1841, Barker left Buffalo. He died at the home of his son in Natchez, Mississippi, in 1870.

SOURCES: Elizabeth Frye Barker, *The Barker Genealogy* (New York, 1927); House Documents No. 74, 25th Congress, 2d Session; Grace Carew Sheldon, "Pierre A. Barker, Sixth Mayor of Buffalo, in Chair at Beginning of Patriot War," Buffalo *Times*, 9 March 1919; Orrin Edward Tiffany, "Relations of the United States to the Canadian Rebellion of 1837-1838," *Publications of the Buffalo Historical Society*, 8 (1905).

Christopher Densmore

BARR, JOSEPH MORAN (1906–   ), Mayor of Pittsburgh (1959–70). Barr was born in Pittsburgh on 28 May 1906, the sixth of seven children of James P. Barr, a Roman Catholic Irish-American general contractor. His great-grandfather had founded the Pittsburgh *Post* in about 1840. Barr attended the University of Pittsburgh where he was active in student affairs. He worked for an auto manufacturer and later as a salesman for a canning firm.

Barr helped organize Pittsburgh's first Young Democrat group. In 1936, he began an eighteen-year tenure as secretary of his party's county committee. He was president of the state Young Democrat group and vice-president of the national group. In 1940, Barr was elected to the state Senate, holding the post for twenty years. From 1954 to 1959, he was Democratic state chairman. On the departure of Mayor David L. Lawrence (*q.v.*) to become governor, Barr won a special election to fill out the unexpired term. He was twice reelected to four-year terms (in 1961 and 1965) (1961: Barr, 123,648; W. J. Crehan, 60,672; and R. A. Reis, 1,428; 1965: Barr, 109,799 and V. S. Rovitro, 65,944).

During his tenure as mayor, Pittsburgh completed a civic arena, finished most of the work on a sports stadium, and initiated a "land reserve bank" of space for industrial growth. It also acquired a new public safety building. The city at that time had a falling population of about 550,000, with a strong mayor-small council form of government. When a party split developed near the end of his second elective term, Barr declined to run again.

On 4 January 1949, Barr married Alice White of Glencoe, Illinois, a home economist and also an Irish Catholic. They had a daughter and a son. In 1966, Barr became a member of the Democratic National Committee and was named vice-president of the U.S. Conference of Mayors.

SOURCES: "The Mayoralty Candidates," Pittsburgh *Post-Gazette*, 20 October 1959; "One Mayor's Story," *U.S. News and World Report*, 21 April 1969; Lawrence Walsh "The Barr Years," Pittsburgh *Press Roto*, 28 December 1969.

George Swetnam

BARRET, ARTHUR B. (1835–75), Mayor of St. Louis (1875). Well-to-do farmer and politician, born in Springfield, Illinois, on 21 August 1835, Barret was the second son of Richard F. Barret (1804–60), a wealthy doctor, banker, farmer, and railroad promoter; and Maria Lewis (Buckner) Barret (1815–75), both Kentuckians. The second of five children, Barret went to private schools in Springfield and was then sent to Phillips Academy in Andover, Massachusetts. He finally graduated from St. Louis University and promptly went to Louisiana, to consider the idea of doing business in the South. In 1855, he made a lengthy trip on horseback through the rough country from Louisiana to St. Louis and became a successful farmer. He actively supported methods to modernize agriculture, and he organized various agricultural societies and exhibitions. On 16 June 1859, he married Anna Farrar Swearingen of St. Louis, and they had three children.

Barret, strongly desiring political office, sought the Democratic nomination for mayor of St. Louis in 1869 and 1871. In each case, he was narrowly defeated, but he refused to contest the results. In 1872, he was a presidential elector from Missouri, and in 1875 he finally won the mayoralty nomination. In the ensuing election, he was elected by 12,749 votes to 12,175 for Henry Overstolz (*q.v.*) (Independent Republican) and 4,445 for Maguire (the regular Republican). St. Louis had 310,864 people in 1870 and a mayor-council form of government.

Barret's campaign for the mayoralty was based on a platform of reform, and his inaugural speech suggested an emphasis on economic reform and measures for the public welfare. His plans came to nothing, for he died quite suddenly from an ulcerated appendix on 24 April 1875.

SOURCES: Charles H. Cornwell, *St. Louis Mayors: Brief Biographies* (St. Louis, 1965); William A. Crozier, *The Buckners of Virginia* (New York, 1907); William Hyde and Howard L. Conrad, eds., *Encyclopedia of the History of Saint Louis*, 4 vols. (New York, 1899); T. J.

Scharf, *History of Saint Louis City and County*, 5 vols. (Philadelphia, 1883). *Thomas R. Bullard*

BARRY, JAMES G. (1800–80), Mayor of St. Louis (1849–50). Mayor of St. Louis during the great fire and cholera outbreak of 1849, Barry was born in Ireland in 1800 and moved to the United States at some time prior to the late 1830's. He had little opportunity for any formal education in Ireland and does not seem to have attended any schools in the United States. His political career began with several terms on the St. Louis council (1839–41, 1842–43, and 1845–47). He also served as city auditor, 1848–49. On 26 September 1848, he married Elizabeth Scheuer of St. Louis, and they had one daughter.

Barry, a Democrat, was elected mayor in 1848, defeating Whig candidate Joseph Foster 3,181 to 3,038. St. Louis had 77,860 people and a mayor-council form of government. Mayor Barry had little chance to develop any specific programs, for the city was visited by two terrible calamities during his single term. The first was the great fire which struck St. Louis on 17 May 1849. Starting at the docks, the blaze destroyed twenty-three steamboats and most of the business district of the city, destroying $5 million worth of property. Barry had to spend much time raising funds to rebuild the city and to aid the homeless. That summer, while the fire damage was still visible, St. Louis was hit by a cholera epidemic that killed many people. Barry claimed the city council had not acted quickly enough in previous years to prepare for this catastrophe, while the city press blamed him. Perhaps the most positive accomplishment of Barry's short tenure in office was the establishment of a special news bureau that arranged to have all the ordinances passed by the council translated into German for the growing German-language press and citizenry.

After leaving office, Barry abandoned his political career, and he sold real estate for some years. He also was a prominent member of the Missouri Historical Society and helped raise funds for this organization in his later years. He died on 9 May 1880, virtually forgotten by the city he had once served.

SOURCES: Charles H. Cornwell, *St. Louis Mayors: Brief Biographies* (St. Louis, 1965); J. T. Scharf, *History of Saint Louis City and County*, 5 vols. (Philadelphia, 1883). *Thomas R. Bullard*

BARTLETT, WASHINGTON (1824–87), Mayor of San Francisco (1883–87). Democratic Mayor Washington Bartlett was born in Savannah, Georgia, on 29 February 1824 to Sarah E. (Melhado) Bartlett and Cosam Emir Bartlett (d. 1850). His father was a transplanted old-stock Yankee who gave up law practice to become a newspaper editor. One of at least five children, Washington grew up in the Southeast and learned printing from his father. In 1849, he decided to seek his fortune in California, sailing from Charleston, South Carolina, to San Francisco, where he arrived on 19 November. Using printing supplies shipped in advance, he quickly produced the first English-language book printed in California, Felix Wierzbicki's *California As It Is, and As It May Be* (1849). During the early 1850s, Bartlett expanded his businesses, publishing the *Daily Journal of Commerce* from 1850 to 1851 and, beginning in 1852, operating a job printing office with his brother Columbus. He founded the *Daily Evening News* (later the *True Californian*) in 1853, publishing it with his brother Cosam Julian and others until 1857. Of his ventures, real estate speculations were the most successful, and he eventually made around $100,000 from his investments. Bartlett also served as director and vice-president of the San Francisco Savings Union for fifteen years and joined several civic, fraternal, and business organizations, including the Mechanics Institute, the Odd Fellows, and the Chamber of Commerce, for which he acted as secretary for two years. In 1860, he helped organize the San Francisco Homestead Association which he served as president for several years, and he also founded the California Home for Feeble Minded Children near San Jose, which later became a state institution. He never married and never professed any religion; his mother was Jewish, and at his own death he called for a Congregational minister.

In 1856, Bartlett actively supported the Vigilance Committee, and in 1857, he received his first public office from county clerk William Duer who appointed him a deputy. In 1859, Bartlett was elected county clerk, being reelected in 1861 and 1867; in the interim, he practiced law with his brother Columbus and lost an 1866 campaign for city auditor on the ticket of the People's party, an outgrowth of the 1856 Vigilance Committee. In 1873, he won election to the state Senate on an Independent ticket, serving until 1877. He also was appointed a harbor commissioner for San Francisco in 1870 by Democratic Governor Henry Haight, and in 1879, he worked on the San Francisco Board of Freeholders which prepared the city charter rejected in the election of 8 September 1880.

In 1880, 233,959 people lived in San Francisco, and the city, consolidated with San Francisco County, was governed by a mayor and a board of supervisors. Bartlett accepted the 1882 Democratic nomination for mayor and won the 7 November election, with 20,612 votes to Republican Maurice C. Blake's (*q.v.*) 18,286. Bartlett was reelected on 4 November 1884, winning 25,010 votes to Republican William L. Merry's 22,176. Although limited in influence by the city charter, which dispersed power widely, Bartlett achieved some success. As mayor he interested himself chiefly in collecting due taxes and in preventing extravagance and illegality in spending for ongoing city activities rather than in instituting new projects. During his first term, he helped curtail water company tax evasion, vetoed gas price rises, enforced regulations requiring total city expenditures to be made in uniform amounts each month, and helped pass a limit on city taxes of $1 per $100 of assessed property. Some of Bartlett's activities coincided with the program of Democratic boss Christopher Buckley who sought victory through a platform of tax restriction and opposition to bond issues. During Bartlett's first term, when the Democrats controlled the board of supervisors, Buckley enriched and sustained his political organization within his self-imposed limits on taxation. During Bartlett's second term, the Republicans dominated the supervisors, and the mayor and board repeatedly clashed. In 1886, while serving his second term, Bartlett was nominated and won election as governor on the Democratic ticket. However, he died in Oakland of strain and overwork on 12 September 1887 and was buried in San Francisco.

SOURCES: Alexander Callow, Jr., "San Francisco's Blind Boss," *Pacific Historical Review* 25 (August 1956); [San Francisco Board of Supervisors], *San Francisco Municipal Reports, 1882/83* (San Francisco, 1883) and *San Francisco Municipal Reports, 1884/85* (San Francisco, 1885); San Francisco *Call*, 13 September 1887; San Francisco *Chronicle*, 13 September 1887; San Francisco *Examiner*, 13 September 1887; San Francisco *Wasp*, 18 September 1866; Oscar T. Shuck, *Historical Abstract of San Francisco* (San Francisco, 1897); [Society of California Pioneers], *Memorial of the Life and Services of Washington Bartlett . . .* (San Francisco, 1888); Norton B. Stern, "California's Jewish Governor," *Western States Jewish Historical Quarterly* 5 (July 1973); John Phillip Young, *San Francisco: A History of the Pacific Coast Metropolis*, 2 vols. (San Francisco, 1912). *Michael Griffith*

BARTLETT, WASHINGTON ALLON* (c. 1820–71), *Alcalde* of San Francisco (1846–47). First American *alcalde* of San Francisco (the *alcalde* was a Mexican executive and judicial office that preceded the American mayoralty), Washington Allon Bartlett was born in Maine in about 1820. Midshipman in the U.S. Navy (1833), he was promoted to past-midshipman (1839), acting lieutenant (1842), and, finally, lieutenant (1844). Serving on the U.S. sloop-of-war *Portsmouth* under Captain J. B. Montgomery during the American occupation of California, Lieutenant Bartlett was appointed *alcalde*

*Washington Allon Bartlett is not to be confused with a later mayor of San Francisco in the 1880s, of the same name, Washington Bartlett; a curious coincidence (no known relation).

of Yerba Buena by Montgomery on 26 August 1846, mainly because of his knowledge of Spanish. On 15 September 1846, his appointment was ratified by a local election, in which he defeated Robert T. Ridley and one other candidate.

Bartlett's term of office was notable for his ordinance of 30 January 1847, which changed the name of the town from the Mexican, Yerba Buena, to the American, San Francisco. As *alcalde*, Bartlett also named several major streets and retrieved (from a saloon wall!) the original survey of the bay area made by Jean Jacques Vioget in 1839. His position as first American *alcalde* was difficult; he faced a revolt of native *Californios* and was seized and held in the Montara hills by irregulars for some time (February 1847). He was blamed for not promoting the growth of San Francisco sufficiently and for not extending the survey. As an *alcalde*, he was supposed to pay attention to Mexican laws and customs, where these could be ascertained. Early American officials, however, tended to resort to English common law, if they knew it, and common sense. Bartlett had read Kent and Wheaton, and administered a civil court of common pleas, a court of records and probate, a customs house, a public safe, and a jail. Bartlett was chief magistrate, U.S. collector, and judge. He empaneled the first regular jury for the trial of any cause in California.

On his release by the rebels, Bartlett was ordered back to his ship, and General S. W. Kearny appointed a new *alcalde* (22 February 1847). Controversy surrounds this recall and Bartlett's later life. He commanded the *Argo* in 1847 and, in 1848–52, the schooner *Ewing*, an ex-revenue cutter which he sailed from New York to San Francisco, quelling a mutiny on the way and then proceeding to an important survey voyage of the Columbia River in order to open that region to world commerce. As special agent of the U.S. Treasury in Paris, 1852–54, his mission was to introduce the advanced Fresnel lenses from France for use in U.S. lighthouses on the East and West coasts. In 1855, while serving on the flagship of the U.S. African Squadron, Bartlett was dropped from the service by the navy board, an *ad hoc* body making economies in the Navy.

Bartlett's appeal of this decision uncovered a host of charges against him, chiefly involving finances. He had allegedly been ostracized by fellow officers on the *Portsmouth* in 1847, "placed in Coventry" for speculation and huckstering, for example, selling "indescribables," which turned out to be a shawl, "to a lady at Monterey" at high prices. In addition, his expense accounts in Paris were questioned. Friends defended him strenuously, especially Anna Ella Carroll, and a naval court of enquiry was held in May 1857.

Bartlett retired to live in New York, but not quietly. When his daughter, Frances Aurelia, married a "rich

Cuban,'' Señor Orviedo, in 1859, the huge ceremony, called ''The Diamond Wedding,'' was satirized in verse by Edmund C. Stedman. The bride's father, true to form, nearly involved himself in a duel with the unlucky poet. When her husband died, Frances married a certain Count Von Glumer (well-known in Mexican military circles). Washington Allon Bartlett, the man who named San Francisco, died in 1871.

SOURCES: Anna Ella Carroll, *The Star of the West, or National Men and National Measures*, 3d ed. (New York, 1857); *Defence of Washington A. Bartlett, Ex-Lt., U.S. Navy . . .* Washington, D.C., May 1857, in review of the Proceedings of the Navy Board of 1855 (New York, 1857); Z. S. Eldredge, *The Beginnings of San Francisco*, 2 vols. (San Francisco, 1912); Z. S. Eldredge, *History of California* (New York, n.d.), vol. 3; *Memorial of W. A. Bartlett*, U.S. Senate, 34th Congress, 1st Session, Rep. Comm. No. 237 (Washington, D.C., 1856).   *Peter d'A. Jones*

BARTON, HIRAM K. (1810–80), Mayor of Buffalo (1849–50 and 1852–53). Last Whig mayor of Buffalo, born on 20 May 1810 in Hebron, New York, Barton attended Caldwell School and Middlebury College in Vermont studying law. He moved to Buffalo in 1835 and quickly became a partner of Daniel Lockwood. Barton established a successful legal practice, earning a reputation as a first-rate lawyer whose knowledge of the law was considered superior to his courtroom style. In 1840, he married Lucy Ann Clark (1815–81) of Buffalo, and they had two daughters.

Barton served on the city council, 1841–45 and 1847–48, as a Whig. He first ran for mayor in 1843, losing to Democrat Joseph Masten (*q.v.*) 550 to 106. Barton was elected in 1849, defeating Elijah Ford (Hunker faction-Democrat) and M. Hersee (Barnburner faction-Democrat) 2,511 to 1,855 and 481, respectively. He did not run in 1850, but he was elected to another term in 1852, defeating William Williams (Democrat) 2,879 to 2,711. He was the last Whig to be elected to the office of mayor in Buffalo. Buffalo had 29,773 people in 1845 and 42,261 in 1850, and a mayor-council form of government.

Like so many mayors of his generation, Barton strongly supported a miserly administration, with limited expenditures. He especially hoped to see taxes reduced, or at least not increased. The only area of the budget which Barton felt merited more spending was education, since he strongly supported a good school system. He also wanted the city's health system reorganized to combat a threatened epidemic of cholera during his first term in office. After leaving office, Barton returned to his law practice. He retired in 1875 and died on 10 February 1880.

SOURCES: Buffalo *Courier-Express*, 8 February 1942; Buffalo *Daily Courier*, 11 February 1880; Buffalo *Express*, 11 February 1880; Buffalo *Sunday Times*, 29 June 1919, 20 July 1950.   *Thomas R. Bullard*

BEAME, ABRAHAM DAVID (1906–   ), Mayor of New York (1974–77). Beame, the first Jewish mayor of New York City, was born in London, England, on 19 March 1906 to Philip Birnbaum (1877–1961) and Esther (Goldfarb) Birnbaum (1879–1913), who had fled to Britain from their native Poland, where Beame's father had run a restaurant. Before Abraham was a year old, the Birnbaum family moved again, this time to America where the name Birnbaum was changed to Beame. Abe Beame grew up in a Lower East Side Manhattan coldwater tenement with his sister and two brothers. His mother died when he was young.

Beame attended the local New York City public elementary school and the High School of Commerce. Although he worked an eight-hour factory shift, he completed high school in three and a half years and graduated at the top of his class. Working his way through the City College of New York, he graduated cum laude, with a B.B.A. and accounting major in 1928. On 18 February 1928, he married Mary Ingerman (26 December 1906–   ). The couple had two sons: Edmond M. Beame and Bernard W. Beame.

After graduation, Beame and Bernard Greidinger founded a small accounting firm, and during the Depression Beame also taught in high schools and at Rutgers University.

Always active in politics, Beame in 1930 was one of the founders of the Haddingway Democratic Club. Mayor William O'Dwyer (*q.v.*) in 1946 appointed Beame assistant director of the budget, and within two years he had put into practice reforms that reportedly saved the city $40,000. In 1952, Mayor Vincent Impellitteri (*q.v.*) appointed Beame budget director, the most important appointive position in city government. In 1962, he joined Robert Wagner's (*q.v.*) third-term mayoralty bid, successfully running for the post of city comptroller. In that position, Beame headed the Department of Finance and controlled the capital and expense budgets.

In November 1965, Beame ran as the Democratic candidate for mayor, losing to the Republican-Liberal fusion candidate, John Lindsay (*q.v.*), 1,149,106 to 1,046,669. In the following four years, Beame founded his own financial consulting firm, was chairman of the finance committee of the American Bank and Trust Company, and was board chairman of the Arrow Lock Corporation.

In 1969, Beame ran successfully as the Democratic candidate for comptroller, thus becoming the city's ranking elected Democrat. In 1973, he won the mayoralty election, receiving 955,388 votes to 275,362 for Republican State Senator John J. Marchi; 263,604 for the Liberal party candidate, Albert Blumenthal; and 189,185 for the Conservative party candidate, Mario Biaggi.

During the mayoralty of Abe Beame, New York City experienced desperate fiscal problems, and efforts to keep the city from bankruptcy increasingly involved both the state and federal government. The city government was reorganized. Two new departments—Aging , and Cultural Affairs—and new top-level city management positions were created in a reorganization that eliminated the so-called superagencies and modernized the city's accounting procedures.

After losing to Edward Koch (*q.v.*) in the 1977 Democratic primary, Beame retired to private life as a consultant and continued to be active in numerous charitable and civic organizations.

SOURCES: Abraham Beame, Collected Papers, Municipal Archives, New York City; Robert Daley, ''The Realism of Abe Beame,'' New York *Times Magazine* (18 November 1973); ''The Quiet Safari of Abe Beame,'' New York *Times Magazine* (6 October 1974).

Lurton W. Blassingame

BEAUDRY, PRUDENT (1819–93), Mayor of Los Angeles (1874–76). Second French-Canadian mayor of Los Angeles and an eager land developer, Beaudry was born of a large Roman Catholic family at Ste. Anne des Plaines, Quebec, in 1819. His brothers were leading businessmen, one of them being mayor of Montreal several times. Beaudry was educated in Canada and New York, and worked as a merchant in New Orleans for two years. Returning to Canada in 1842, he worked with the family in Montreal until 1850, and then joined the rush to San Francisco where one brother, Victor, had made a small fortune supplying miners. In 1852, Beaudry moved his mercantile operation to Los Angeles; he made over $40,000 in the 1860s and after 1867 innovated in real estate, offering installment land and property purchases to less wealthy buyers. He became the main subdivider in Los Angeles. Some regarded him as a ''land-grabber,'' especially in the local land boom of 1868–74. It was rumored that in California Beaudry made five fortunes and lost four. He also donated several tracts for civic betterment and charity.

Beaudry was one of the organizers of the Los Angeles City Water Company. His speculations in land beyond the city limits helped to develop Pasadena and Alhambra. He built the Temple Street cable railway. Since city fathers failed to open and grade certain key streets, Beaudry did so himself. Appropriately, Beaudry Street was named for him. Meanwhile, he was one of the incorporators of Los Angeles's original Chamber of Commerce in 1873.

Beaudry was naturalized on 30 April 1863 and soon entered local politics. He served on the city council dur-

ing 1871–74. In November 1874, he ran for mayor against three candidates, getting 816 votes, or 90 more than his trio of opponents combined. One of his functions as mayor was to try minor offenses as judge on the mayor's court. Beaudry disposed of a large docket daily, besides presiding over council meetings and reporting municipal needs. He advocated that a special judge be elected to hear these 800 cases yearly, which took up so much of the mayor's time. Meanwhile, Beaudry continued his private business and was criticized for moving his official headquarters to his realty office. As mayor of 13,000 people, he advocated and got the paving of more streets and a modicum of city beautification *via* tree planting. On 6 September 1876, in his capacity as city chief executive, he witnessed the arrival of the railroad from northern California when the Southern Pacific's tracks finally reached Los Angeles.

Beaudry was an active mayor who used his veto when necessary. In his last official message, in December 1876, he mentioned the local and national hard times, yet he could boast of a substantial balance in the city treasury, fourteen more miles of streets, and better gas lighting. Even though he was one of southern California's largest taxpayers, Beaudry favored the expensive moving of city offices from the old ''miserable adobes'' of an earlier era, and the creation of the office of city auditor.

After his single term, Beaudry remained active in business affairs. He was a life-long bachelor. After suffering a paralytic stroke, he died in Los Angeles, on 29 May 1893. His funeral took place in the Catholic cathedral on 2 June, and his body was sent to Montreal for interment. One admirer summarized Beaudry's career aptly: ''His philanthropy was one of that best kind—he furnished work whereby a man could earn his livelihood.''

SOURCES: Files of the Los Angeles *Herald, Star*, and *Times*, 1872–1893 *passim; An Illustrated History of Los Angeles County, California* (Chicago, 1889); Remi A. Nadeau, *City Makers* (Garden City, N.Y., 1948); Harris Newmark, *Sixty Years in Southern California, 1853–1913* (New York, 1916); L. J. Rose, Jr., *L. J. Rose of Sunny Slope* (San Marino, Calif., 1959); William A. Spalding, *History of Los Angeles City and County, California*; Boyle Workman, *The City That Grew* (Los Angeles, 1935).

John E. Baur

BECKER, PHILIP (1830–98), Mayor of Buffalo (1876–77, 1886–90). A wealthy immigrant entrepreneur who twice served terms as Buffalo's mayor, Becker was born in Germany on 30 April 1830 at Ober-Rottenbach, Bavaria. He was the son of Frederick Becker, a prosperous farmer, and Catharina (Seibel) Becker, neither of whom left Germany. The second child and second son in a Roman Catholic family of four boys and a girl, Becker attended local German schools in Bavaria during

1836–42, went to a "French College" in 1843–44, and a German collegiate institute in 1845. He emigrated alone to Buffalo, directly from Bavaria, in 1847 at the age of seventeen. Starting modestly as a small grocer in 1848, Becker built his business into a huge wholesale food brokerage within a decade. By the 1870s and 1880s, he had diversified his business interests, which included the largest wholesale food brokerage/supply house and the largest glassworks in New York State outside of Manhattan. He also founded the Buffalo German Insurance Company in 1868.

Becker married Sarah Goetz, daughter of Jacob and Sarah (Philips) Goetz, on 14 May 1858. Born on 11 May 1832, Sarah and her family arrived in Buffalo from Brumath, Alsace-Lorraine, in 1840. Sarah Goetz was educated in Buffalo public schools, graduating in 1850. The couple was childless. A Roman Catholic, Becker was prominent among the Roman Catholic Germans and served twice as alderman before his first mayoral term.

Buffalo had a mayor-council form of government and, at the time of Becker's first term in 1876, a population of 142,000, increasing, by his last two terms, 1886–90, to 255,664 (1890 Census). Becker was elected mayor by a narrow margin in 1875 on the Republican ticket, 12,585 votes to 9,376 for Democrat A. P. Lansing. Becker's first term was unremarkable. Erie County was experiencing a political upheaval between the Democratic and Republican parties, which contributed to Becker's defeat by Democrat Solomon Scheu in 1877: 8,756 to 8,159, with 6,216 for Edward Bennett. Becker remained active in Buffalo politics as an alderman until his election to a second mayoral term, when he defeated William P. Taylor, Democrat, 18,311 to 15,633, in 1885. He was reelected again in 1887, defeating Solomon Scheu (q.v.) 17,925 to 17,451.

Becker's last two terms were highlighted by his streamlining and reorganization of city government. A dynamic businessman, he now became in turn a dynamic mayor. Becker altered the structure of the council of aldermen and changed the ward composition of Buffalo. He believed in nonpartisan city administration and lowest bidder contracts. He was firmly committed to attracting and promoting business, as well as improving public education, organizing public libraries, and trying to foster cultural growth. At the end of his third term, Becker announced that he no longer desired to hold political office: the council had often overridden his veto.

In the years following his political retirement, the wealthy Becker dedicated his time to philanthropic, social, and cultural pursuits. Continuing in his directorship of the Buffalo German Insurance Company, he also founded or was active in many organizations, including the Odd Fellows, German Old Folk's Society, German Young Men's Association, Buffalo Historical Society,

and the *Turner Verein*. Prominent in Buffalo society, the Beckers were noted for their lavish social and musical parties and for their financial support of various social and church groups. Becker died on 4 July 1898.

SOURCES: J. F. Barry, ed., *The Buffalo Text Book* (Buffalo, 1924); Buffalo *Commercial Advertiser*, 5 July, 7 June, 7 August, 7 December 1898; Buffalo *Times*, 21 December 1919; William H. Dolan and Mark S. Hubbard, eds., *Our Police and Our City . . . and a History of the City of Buffalo* (Buffalo, 1893); *The Men of New York*, 2 vols. (Buffalo, 1898); Truman C. White, ed., *A Descriptive Work on Erie County, New York* (Boston, 1898), vol. 2.

W. Andrew Achenbaum and Thomas R. Bullard

BECKER, SHERBURN M. (1876-1949), Mayor of Milwaukee (1906-1908). Erstwhile "boy-mayor" of Milwaukee, Becker, a Dutch-American, was born in that city on 13 November 1876. He was the only son of Washington Becker (1847–1929), a prominent Milwaukee financier, descended from an old-line colonial Dutch family of South Worcester, New York, and Sarah Worthing. Becker graduated from Harvard in 1897 and returned to Milwaukee to work for his father. He married Irene Booth Smith, an Anglo-American Episcopalian like his mother, on 12 December 1898, and they had three children. Seeking a fresh new candidate to oppose four-term Democratic Mayor David ("All the time Rosy") Rose (q.v.), the Republicans nominated the twenty-nine-year-old Becker in 1906. The campaign was one of the most colorful in the city's history. Becker hired a public relations agent, organized Young Men's clubs with a membership of 5,000, and offered a barrel of flour to the woman who could provide the best answer to the question of why he should be elected. The two candidates traded insults and quips, dealing with Becker's youth and corporation connections and Rose's questionable financial and moral machinations. Becker also promised a "thoroughly business administration" which would give Milwaukee voters "a full dollar's value for every dollar of their money expended." Becker upset the complacent Rose by a vote of 22,850 to 21,332; Socialist candidate William A. Arnold received 16,784 votes.

Becker's term as mayor was characterized largely by his colorful antics and lack of substantive actions. He toured the eastern half of the nation in a carmine-colored Pope-Toledo automobile called the "Red Devil," advertising the city and calling upon President Theodore Roosevelt at Oyster Bay, Long Island. Because he felt that the jewelers' signs and clocks on Wisconsin Avenue interfered with free passage, Becker and his associates dismantled them during a nocturnal raid. The mayor's antics prompted a series of suits and injunctions against the city and attracted newspaper coverage throughout the nation. Put off by such activities, the Republicans declined to nominate Becker for reelection in 1908.

Becker moved to New York City in 1911, but he maintained his Milwaukee ties as a director of the Marine National Exchange Bank and as president of the Hansen-Schmidt Tobacco Company. As a member of the New York Stock Exchange, Becker divided his time between New York City and the family estate in South Worcester, reportedly driving a tractor until he was seventy years old. He died in New York on 5 February 1949 but was buried in Milwaukee.

SOURCES: *Milwaukee Journal*, 10 December 1929, 6 February 1949; Bayrd Still, *Milwaukee: The History of a City* (Madison, Wis., 1965); Robert W. Wells, *This Is Milwaukee* (Garden City, N.Y., 1970).

John D. Buenker

BECKER, WILLIAM D. (1876–1943), Mayor of St. Louis (1941–43). One of a series of German-American mayors of St. Louis, Becker was born in East St. Louis, Illinois, on 23 October 1876, the son of John Philip Becker, a dry goods merchant, and Anna A. (Cammann) Becker, both born in Germany. The Beckers came to St. Louis in 1879, and young William attended public schools. He then went to Smith Academy in St. Louis, Harvard University (graduating in 1899) and Washington University Law School in St. Louis, graduating in 1901 with an LL.B. He began practicing law in 1901 as partner of Henry Troll. In 1905, Becker began an eight-year partnership with W. W. Henderson. Becker was a judge of the St. Louis Court of Appeals from 1916 until 1940. In 1902, he married Margaret Louise McIntosh, and they had two children, both reaching adulthood. The Beckers were Presbyterians and were members of the Scottish Rites Cathedral. Becker was a member of city, county, state, and national bar groups, as well as the St. Louis Chamber of Commerce.

In 1941, the Republican party leaders selected Becker to run against incumbent Mayor Bernard F. Dickmann (q.v.), emphasizing their candidate's integrity and political innocence versus Dickmann's personal machine. Much to his surprise, Becker won the election 183,112 to 147,428. St. Louis had 816,048 people in 1940 and a mayor-council form of government. The press regarded this as one of the few genuine upset victories in local political history.

As might be expected, Mayor Becker strongly supported the merit system and stated that he would retain qualified department heads from the previous administration rather than replace them with Republicans. He worked to improve the city's overall business output. With the outbreak of World War II, Becker supported various fund-raising drives. On 1 August 1943, he agreed to be a passenger in a new Army glider, as a stunt for

the war effort. The glider crashed, killing all ten people aboard, a tragic ending of Becker's career.

SOURCES: Charles H. Cornwell, *St. Louis Mayors: Brief Biographies* (St. Louis, 1965); St. Louis *Post-Dispatch*, 2 August 1939; Floyd C. Shoemaker, *Missouri and Missourians*, 5 vols. (Chicago, 1943).

Thomas R. Bullard

BEHAN, WILLIAM J. (1840–1928), Mayor of New Orleans (1882–84). Conservative (Democratic) mayor, Behan was born on 5 September 1840, in New Orleans, the son of John Holland and Katherine Behan, both natives of Ireland. William was educated locally and at Western Military Institute in Nashville, Tennessee. As an officer in the crack Washington Artillery of New Orleans, Behan fought in almost every battle waged in the eastern theater, including Appomattox. Back in New Orleans after the Civil War, Behan became successively a sugar planter, a manufacturer, and a merchant. He participated as a White Leaguer in 1874 in the "battle of Liberty Place" (a riot against federally imposed carpetbagger rule) and in 1877 was made commander of the state militia with the rank of major general. He married Katie Walker on 7 June 1866.

Behan was one of the ablest, wealthiest, and most respected citizens of New Orleans when he was chosen in 1882 to succeed reform Mayor Joseph Shakspeare (q.v.). Election returns gave Behan 14,897 votes to only 5,346 for his opponent, Abel W. Bosworth of the Citizens' Independent Movement. At the same time, Behan was the nominee of what had become the Democratic "Ring" in New Orleans, a tightly structured and "bossed" political machine controlled by three powerful magnates—James Houston, State Treasurer E. A. Burke, and future Mayor John Fitzpatrick. A year after taking office, Behan alienated these men by refusing to appoint their favorite, a political hack, chief of police. (Instead, Behan appointed a qualified professional policeman.)

Behan displayed similar courage and determination in successfully attacking the prevailing system of paying city employees—by depreciable certificates at irregular intervals rather than in cash on a monthly basis. Brokers purchased the certificates at a discount when funds in the city treasury were low, held on to them, and redeemed them at face value when city assets rose. Under pressure from the brokers, the practice was revived by Behan's successor. Mayor Behan also made notable progress in reducing the city's bonded and floating indebtedness, although in order to do so, property taxes had to be raised and strict economies enforced.

During Behan's term, a new city charter took effect, extending the mayor's tenure from two years to four. Many believed that Behan's demonstrated competence and integrity should be rewarded by a four-year term.

But the mayor's "Ring" associates thought otherwise, and in the election of 1884 they supported J. Valsin Guillotte (*q.v.*), Behan's comptroller and a reliable "Ring" politician. In an election marred by large-scale vote-buying and ballot-tinkering, Guillotte defeated Behan (who ran as an Independent) 18,278 votes to 6,612.

Behan became a Republican in 1894 after the Democratic Wilson-Gorman Tariff Act drastically reduced the protection given to Louisiana sugar. While serving as chairman of the Republican state executive committee, Behan was an unsuccessful candidate in 1904 for the governorship of Louisiana. On 4 May 1928, Behan died in New Orleans, aged eighty-eight. He was survived by two daughters.

SOURCES: Joy J. Jackson, *New Orleans in the Gilded Age: Politics and Urban Progress, 1880–1896* (Baton Rouge, La., 1969); John S. Kendall, *History of New Orleans* (Chicago, 1922), vol. 1; Works Progress Administration typescripts, "Administrations of the Mayors of New Orleans, 1803–1936," and "Biographies of the Mayors of New Orleans, 1803–1936" (New Orleans, 1940).
                                        Mark T. Carleton

BEHRMAN, MARTIN (1864–1926), Mayor of New Orleans (1904–20, 1925–26). Behrman was born on 14 October 1864 in New York City to German-Jewish parents, Henry Behrman, a cigar-maker, and Frederica, who moved to the French Quarter in New Orleans in 1865. His father died when Martin was twelve years old, and his mother, a woman of determination, opened a bazaar to support herself and her only child, though she also died shortly thereafter. Martin studied at the German-American School and at St. Philip's public school where he learned to speak both French and German. He withdrew from school when his mother died and went to work in a grocery store, becoming a traveling salesman for a wholesale grocery firm at age nineteen. He would later credit his success in politics to his success in selling merchandise.

Behrman began his long political career in 1888, at the bottom, as a minor Democratic ward politician and deputy city assessor. By 1892, he was recognized as the leader of his ward and was rewarded with a share of party patronage. During the same year, he began a four-year stint as clerk of the New Orleans City Council, and from 1892 to 1906 he was also a member of the board of education. To supplement his income he worked as a solicitor for the Edison Electric Company until 1896. He was elected state auditor in 1904 but resigned to run for the mayor's seat. Behrman married Julia Collins of Cincinnati, Ohio, in 1887, and she bore him eleven children, only two of whom survived childhood. Although born a Jew, Behrman became a Roman Catholic. He was known to New Orleans voters as a family man with never any scandal in his personal life.

New Orleans at the time of Behrman's first election had a population of 287,000 and a mayor-council form of government. With the support of the political machine, called the Choctaw Club, Behrman was easily elected mayor in 1904, garnering 13,962 votes to his Home Rule party opponent Charles F. Buck's 10,047, Republican John A. Wogan's 496, and Socialist W. Covington Hall's 179. As the Choctaw Club's power grew so did the size of Behrman's reelection victories. He was reelected in 1908 over token opposition and in 1912 beat the Good Government candidate, Judge Charles Claiborne, 23,371 to 13,917 to become New Orleans' first mayor under a new city commission charter. Although not a high school graduate, Behrman was credited by contemporaries as being of high intelligence, a keen student of the human condition, and a shrewd judge of public opinion. His easy reelection in 1916 and his last victory for mayor in 1925 attest to that assessment. Yet, by 1920, Behrman was clearly out of step with public sentiments in his open toleration of the vice district, his unsatisfactory explanation for poor city services, his opposition to pro-labor legislation, and the city's mounting debt. The voters turned him out of office, electing businessman-reformer Andrew McShane (*q.v.*) by 22,986 votes to the incumbent's 21,563. Chastened by defeat, Behrman spent the intervening time before the next election rebuilding his and the Choctaw Club's political influence. As a result, he won election as mayor in 1925 for a final term that was cut short by his death in 1926.

Behrman fit the mold of the classical boss in many ways: he had an ability to lead and select subordinates, he knew how to compromise, and he had personal charm, although he was not an effective public speaker. His personal character was a cut above that of his cronies; he was said to be "better than his crowd." His machine nullified the civil service and overcame such reforms as city-wide elections, direct primaries, and commission government. Although the Behrman administration was responsible for some public improvements, including new schools and roads, it seldom took the initiative in matters of progressive social legislation. Behrman's foot-dragging on the efforts of reformers and the U.S. Navy to close down the segregated vice district (Storyville) in 1917 helped defeat him in 1920. His views on black disfranchisement were expressed in his memoir: "I had a hand in putting the negroes out of politics, which was the best thing done for Louisiana in my time." Behrman's lack of enlightened social policies appeared to reflect not only his own limitations but also the attitudes of a majority of the city's voters. When he died on 26 January 1926, New York's gayblade Mayor Jimmie

Walker (*q.v.*) asserted Behrman "was a constant source of inspiration to me. . . . The Democratic Party has lost a class A soldier in Martin Behrman."

SOURCES: J. R. Kemp, ed., *Martin Behrman of New Orleans: Memoirs of a City Boss* (Baton Rouge, La., 1977); John S. Kendall, *History of New Orleans* (Chicago, 1922), vol. 2; George M. Reynolds, *Machine Politics in New Orleans 1897–1926* (New York, 1936).   *Betsy B. Holli* and *Melvin G. Holli*

BERRY, THEODORE M. (1905–   ), Mayor of Cincinnati (1972–75). Cincinnati's first black mayor, Berry was born in Maysville, Kentucky on 8 November 1905, moving to Cincinnati in childhood, attending Woodward High School, and becoming that institution's first black valedictorian (1924). He then attended the University of Cincinnati, receiving an A.B. in 1928 and a J.D. in 1931. He began practicing law the following year and was admitted to practice before the Supreme Court in 1937. On 23 June 1938, he married Johnnie Mae Newton, a librarian at Cincinnati's Technical College, and they had three children. Berry served with the Office of War Information in World War II. A Methodist, he became a member of city, state, national, and Washington, D.C., bar associations. He also served on the board of directors of the local NAACP, 1946 to 1968.

Berry was chairman of the Ohio Commission on Civil Rights Legislation, 1949–65. In 1950, he was a member of the city council, serving until his defeat in 1957. Initially a Republican, Berry became a leading member of the Charterite faction within the council and was the chief sponsor of fair employment measures considered by that body. He was again an alderman, 1963–65, and then resigned to serve as the director of community action programs in the Office of Economic Opportunity, 1965–69. Convinced that Congress was not willing to provide adequate funding, he resigned from that federal post. He practiced law in Washington, 1969–72, and then returned to Cincinnati and again served in the city council, 1972–75.

Berry became Cincinnati's first black mayor in 1972, completing the normal two-year term begun by Thomas Luken (*q.v.*). He was chosen mayor again in 1973 and 1974. As mayor, Berry strongly supported all measures to reduce unemployment among the city's youth, especially among minorities, claiming that this was the best way to lower the crime rate. He also backed efforts to improve the city's transit system. Berry sought ways to cooperate with suburban governments that shared common problems with the city. A man of principle, Berry often said that "power was persuasion" and thus avoided dramatic action while in office. He chose not to seek another term in 1975 and retired from public office in

December of that year. He currently practices law in Cincinnati.

SOURCES: Cincinnati *Enquirer*, 2 December 1972, 2 December 1973; *Profiles of Black Mayors in America* (Chicago, 1977); *Who's Who Among Black Americans* (Northbrook, Ill., 1978); *Who's Who in Government* (Chicago, 1977).   *Thomas R. Bullard*

BERTUS, PAUL (Not available), Acting Mayor of New Orleans, 10 April–12 May, 1938.

BIDDLE, JOHN (1792–1859), Mayor of Detroit (1827, 1828). Biddle, Detroit's fourth mayor, was born in Philadelphia in March 1792, the son of Charles Biddle, vice-president of Pennsylvania during the Revolutionary War and nephew of Commodore Nicholas Biddle of the Revolutionary Navy. He graduated from Princeton College and served in the U.S. Army for most of the War of 1812. Like his predecessor, Mayor Jonathan Kearsley (*q.v.*), he was a soldier—a captain in the artillery, promoted to major, who served on the Niagara frontier under Winfield Scott. Biddle remained in the Army for some time after the war. In 1817, he arrived in Detroit to assume command of Fort Shelby, but he resigned from the Army in 1819. Biddle went east and married Eliza F. Bradish of New York and returned to Detroit where he became active in local affairs. From 1823 to 1837, Biddle served as register of the land office, responsible for claims in the areas of Mackinaw, Sault Sainte Marie, Green Bay, and Prairie du Chien. In 1827, he was elected mayor, polling 137 votes to J. Kearsley's 40 and John R. Williams' (*q.v.*) 26. Biddle was reelected in 1828 with 129 votes to a scattering of 5 votes to his five opponents.

At the time of Biddle's mayoralty, the small city had a population of 2,000. In 1829, he gained election to the U.S. Congress from the territory and served there until 1831. In May 1835, he became president of the first Michigan Constitutional Convention. That same year he helped organize the corporation that built the Michigan Central Railroad, and subsequently he became its first president. Biddle ran unsuccessfully for mayor in 1836 losing to the incumbent, Levi Cook.

During those years, Biddle may have had interests in the western part of the state because 1835 saw him as president of the St. Joseph branch of the Farmer's and Merchant's Bank. In 1838, however, he became president of the Farmer's and Merchant's Bank in Detroit. In his later years, Biddle was a regent of the University of Michigan and a vestryman and patron of St. Paul's Episcopal Church in Detroit. These later activities reflected a life-long interest in education and church affairs. Some of his writings were published in 1834, entitled

Historical Sketches of Michigan. Toward the end of his life, he inherited a large estate near St. Louis, which occupied much of his time. He died on 25 August 1859 in White Sulfur Springs, Virginia, after taking a cold bath. He and Eliza had four children: William, James, Edward, and a fourth named in the records only as the "widow of Gen. Andrew Porter."

SOURCES: John Biddle, *Historical Sketches of Michigan* (Detroit, 1834); Stephen Bingham, *Early History of Michigan* (Lansing, Mich., 1898); Fred Carlisle, *Chronography of Notable Events in the history of the Northwest Territory and Wayne County* (Detroit, 1890); Silas Farmer, *The History of Detroit and Michigan* (Detroit, 1889); T. H. Hinchman, *Banks and Banking in Michigan* (Detroit, 1887).   *Francis X. Blouin, Jr.*

BIGELOW, JOHN PRESCOTT (1797–1872), Mayor of Boston (1849–51). Whig Mayor, born on 25 August 1797, in Groton, Massachusetts, Bigelow was the grandson of Colonel Timothy Bigelow of Revolutionary War fame and the son of Timothy Bigelow, Jr. (1767–1821), former Massachusetts speaker of the House, and of Lucy (Prescott) Bigelow (1771–1852) of New England stock. The third of seven children, John studied at Groton Academy (Lawrence Academy) and graduated from Harvard (1815). He married Luisa Anne Brown (1800–47), a native of Liverpool, England, who was the organist at Trinity Church, Boston, on 9 March 1824, and they had one son. Bigelow belonged to the First Unitarian Church of Boston.

A lawyer by profession, Bigelow served on the common council from the Ninth Ward (1827–1834) and was president for two years (1832–33). Around those years (1828–36), save for 1834, he was a state representative. Later, he became Massachusetts secretary of state (1836–43) and a member of the governor's council (1845–48).

Boston, with a mayor-alderman-council form of government, had a population of 136,000 when Bigelow became mayor. He was first elected in 1848, drawing 5,150 votes to J. W. James' 1,143, B. Sumner's 929, and J. V. C. Smith's (*q.v.*) 417. In 1849, Bigelow attracted 4,543 votes to J. Hall's 705 and B. Sumner's 349. In his last election, in 1850, Bigelow polled his largest vote of 5,394 defeating C. Amory's 1,146, C. B. Goodrich's 1,126, and B. B. Mussey's 771. Bigelow was popular with Bostonians because of his conservative fiscal policies, his realism in permitting the licensing of the sale of intoxicating liquors, his improvement of fire protection, his supplying of the city with a system of fresh water, and his celebration of the completion of the railroad linking the Great Lakes and Canada with Boston. Because some major property-owners moved out of Boston to escape taxation, the city itself had to bear a dis-

proportionate share of the state's financial burden. Although Bigelow's mayoralty saw the development of necessary projects like the water system, such progress offset the reduction in expenditures achieved—for example, in cutting down on the improvement of the city's streets. Since he was associated with the decision that prevented Daniel Webster from using Faneuil Hall due to fear of protests, Bigelow was turned out of office in the election of 1851.

Bigelow was particularly attentive to the victims and their families during the summer of 1849 when cholera claimed the lives of at least 5,000 people in Boston. On 23 October 1849, a group of Bostonians presented him with a purse for a silver vase which he later gave to the city for a library. This $1,000 was the first gift to the Boston Public Library, which continues to honor his memory. He died in Boston on 4 July 1872 and was buried in Mount Auburn Cemetery in Cambridge. He left $1,000 to the American Antiquarian Society and $10,000 to Groton Academy.

SOURCES: John P. Bigelow, *Statistical Tables* (Boston, 1838); John P. Bigelow Letters, Massachusetts Historical Society; John Prescott Bigelow Papers, Houghton Library, Harvard University; Boston *Journal*, 5 July 1872 (obituary); State Street Trust Company, *Mayors of Boston* (Boston, 1914); Annie Louisa (Bigelow) Vickery, "Bigelow Genealogy and History in Massachusetts" (typed manuscript, American Antiquarian Society, 1925); William H. Whitmore, ed., *The Inaugural Addresses of the Mayors of Boston*, 2 vols. (Boston, 1894–1896).   *Vincent A. Lapomarda*

BILANDIC, MICHAEL ANTHONY (1923–   ), Mayor of Chicago (1976–79). Chosen successor to Richard J. Daley (*q.v.*) as mayor of Chicago, quiet-spoken attorney Bilandic was born on 13 February 1923 in Chicago's Bridgeport neighborhood, the "Back of the Yards" training-ground for many ethnic mayors and politicians, and the Irish, Democratic power base of the influential Eleventh Ward. The son of Croatian-born immigrant parents, Matthew and Domenica (Lebedina) Bilandic, a Roman Catholic couple, he attended De La Salle High School (from which came several generations of ethnics) and finished his B.S. degree at Notre Dame (1947) and law degree (J.D., 1948) at De Paul University of Chicago. His education had been interrupted by four years of war service in the Pacific in World War II as a lieutenant in the Marines. Admitted to the Illinois bar in 1949, Bilandic worked for twenty-eight years as a corporate lawyer in the same Chicago firm, which eventually became Anixter, Delaney, Bilandic and Piggott. He was assistant to Cook County Circuit Court, 1964–67, and special assistant to the state attorney general, 1965–68.

A Democrat, Bilandic was a close friend of his Bridgeport neighbor, Richard J. Daley, canvassing on his behalf as early as 1955 and working politically in the neighborhood in a quiet way. Mayor Daley persuaded him to run for Eleventh Ward alderman in 1969, a shoo-in in view of his unbeatable backing. By 1970, Bilandic was a member of the crucial city council finance committee and was already asserting his leadership as marshal of Mayor Daley's legislative program. When Daley was excluded from the 1972 Democratic national convention by the ephemeral anti-Daley alliance of that unusual "radical" year, it was Bilandic who stood in his place and denounced the takeover of the convention. He rapidly became Mayor Daley's chief spokesman and right-hand man.

Bilandic became chairman of the finance committee in 1974, after the former chairman, Thomas E. Keane, was indicted for fraud. As Daley slowed down, following an early heart attack in 1974, Bilandic grew in power. A final heart attack removed the mayor on 20 December 1976, and after a complex week of political infighting (and some confusion as to what council rules actually meant with regard to mayoral succession), Bilandic emerged the victor. He was an available, compromise man who filled in as mayor of Chicago, until a special election could be held to complete the remaining two years of Daley's unexpired term. Bilandic promised not to run in that special election, and on 28 December 1976 he was elected nearly unanimously by the council as acting mayor. Just a month later, however, the Democratic Central Committee chose none other than Bilandic as its candidate, and he accepted, winning the across-the-board support of business, labor, and many minority and ethnic groups. His strength was firm knowledge of the budget and the promise of continuity and stability. In the primary campaign, much was made of Bilandic's closeness to the late mayor, and he even began to sound more and more like Daley. The primary of 19 April 1977 gave Bilandic 50.4 percent of total votes cast—an organization victory that proved the Daley machine was still alive—though Alderman (and former Congressman) Roman Pucinski did very well with 32 percent (a heavily ethnic vote). Bilandic received much black support, winning almost twice as many votes as a black candidate, State Senator Harold Washington. The special election that followed on 7 June 1977 was a rubber-stamp affair, Bilandic defeating the sole Republican city councillor, Dennis H. Block, 475,169 to 130,945. It was the lowest voter turnout for sixty-six years, a sign of what might happen to Bilandic, if his style remained so low-key, in the regular mayoral election of 1979.

Mayor Bilandic's 1977 June victory came only a day after he negotiated with Chicago Puerto Rican leaders, following two days of bitter fighting, looting, and burning in the northwest ethnic neighborhood, Humboldt Park, in which three people were killed and about one hundred injured. Bilandic had also successfully weathered, as acting mayor, a variety of strikes by gravediggers, butchers, and even the Chicago Lyric Opera's musicians. In addition, he had skillfully negotiated a major transportation agreement with Republican Governor James Thompson over a controversial crosstown expressway and downtown subway system plan—releasing $1.5 billion in federal funds to the city.

Mayor Bilandic married an attractive and talented Smith College graduate, Heather Morgan, who was executive director of the Chicago Arts Council, on 15 July 1977, and they had a son, Michael Morgan Bilandic. Mrs. Bilandic played an important role in the city's cultural life.

Bilandic's years as full mayor proved to be less spectacular than his early achievements seemed to promise as acting mayor. He survived a federally mandated school desegregation/busing plan in the fall of 1977; responded firmly and promptly to a press *exposé* of the lucrative concession contract at O'Hare International Airport by canceling the existing contract (the books had mysteriously vanished) and requiring new, open bids; failed to attract Ford to build a new plant in the city; and sacked Jane Byrne (*q.v.*), the Chicago commissioner for consumer sales (a Daley appointee), who failed to prove any impropriety on Bilandic's part with regard to a city taxi fare increase. What he could not overcome was the massive snowstorm of the winter of 1979, which crippled the city and exposed the inadequacy of its basic services. Daley's "City That Works" did *not* work in that winter, and on 27 February 1979 the insurgent Jane Byrne defeated Bilandic in the Democratic primary—a surprise victory that seemed, mistakenly, to indicate the final "death" of the machine in Chicago.

SOURCES: Chicago *Tribune*, numerous issues of the period; *Current Biography*, 1979; local sources.   *Daniela Cornescu* and *Peter d'A. Jones*

BINGHAM, FLAVEL WHITE (1803–67), Mayor of Cleveland (1849–50). One of a long series of Yankee mayors of Cleveland, Bingham was born in Utica, New York on 8 November 1803, the son of Flavel Bingham (1781–1804), a farmer, and Fanny (White) Bingham (1781–1804), both originally from Connecticut. An only child, Bingham was orphaned in the summer of 1804 when his parents were killed in a cholera epidemic. He was raised by his grandfather, Deacon David White of Utica. Bingham attended public schools and Union College (graduating in 1829). He studied law with General Joseph Kirkland and practiced in Utica until 1835 when he moved to Cleveland. There he developed a successful legal practice lasting until 1863. On 27 May 1835, he married Emmaline (or Eveline) Day of Connecticut, and they had three children. The Binghams were members of the "Old Stone Church," then switched to the First Presbyterian Church, of which Bingham became president of the board of trustees.

Bingham served on the city council, 1845–46 and 1847–49, being chosen president for all three terms. In 1848, he was city clerk. In 1849, he was elected mayor as a Democrat, defeating J. A. Root (Whig) and W. A. Otis (Free-Soil) 973 to 541 to 237, respectively. Cleveland had 17,034 people by 1850 and a mayor-council form of government. As mayor, Bingham supported civic improvements but did not leave any lasting impression on this office. Returning to his legal practice, he served as the county's first probate judge (1852–55). In 1863, during the Civil War, he joined the Sanitary Commission, being sent to Nashville, Tennessee, for a short period. In 1866, Bingham was a member of the Infirmary Board of Education. He then went to Memphis as an agent for the Freedmen's Bureau. This was followed by a trip to New Orleans, where he died on about 15 May 1867.

SOURCES: Theodore A. Bingham, *The Bingham Family in the United States*, 3 vols., (Easton, Pa., 1927); Cleveland *Leader*, 21 May 1867; Gertrude Wickham, *The Pioneer Families of Cleveland, 1796–1840*, 2 vols. (Chicago, 1914).   *Thomas R. Bullard*

BINGHAM, WILLIAM (1808–73), Mayor of Pittsburgh (1856–57). Know-Nothing Mayor Bingham came to Pittsburgh in 1837. Little is known of his youth. He was born in March 1808 and came to the city as an agent, forwarding canal and river freight. Later, he and his brother, George, engaged in this trade together and separately, by turns, and dealt in grain, flour, and feeds, sometimes as partners, again as rivals.

The election of 1856 was quiet but confusing. Mayor Ferdinand E. Volz (*q.v.*) was running on a fusion ticket, Bingham as a Native American, and John M. Irwin as a Democrat, with two minor candidates. Bingham's vote was 1,500 to 1,115 for Irwin and 1,036 to Volz. Escorted to council chambers by Volz, Bingham spoke briefly and frankly. He said he had no idea he might win, was completely surprised, and knew nothing of the duties of the post. The city of 48,000 had two councils, select and common. Thomas M. Marshall, the new head of the common council, responded, promising cooperation. Not much happened during Bingham's term, except for the first Republican national convention which opened on 22 February.

Bingham did not seek reelection but resumed his commission business. He was an active Methodist, a founder of Christ Methodist Church, and a trustee of Pittsburgh Female College, now Beaver College. He died at his home in East Liberty on 15 September 1873.

SOURCES: Allen H. Kerr, "The Mayors and Recorders of Pittsburgh. 1816–1951" (unpublished manuscript, Historical Society of Western Pennsylvania, Pittsburgh, 1952); Pittsburgh *Gazette*, 16 and 17 September 1873; Pittsburgh *Post*, 17 September 1873.   *George Swetnam*

BISHOP, CHARLES F. (1844–1913), Mayor of Buffalo (1890–94). Prosperous grocer and first Buffalo mayor to serve a three-year term, Bishop was born in Williamsville, New York on 4 October 1844. The Bishops moved to Buffalo when Charles was still a child, and he attended public schools until age thirteen. He then started work in a retail grocery store and in 1869 organized his own wholesale tea, coffee, and spice store, which soon became the largest of its kind in Buffalo. He also was president of the People's Bank and a trustee of the Western Savings Bank. On 6 August 1865, he married Kate Moran. Bishop was a Mason and served as deputy grand master of New York's Twenty-fifth District for four years. He was a member of the Orpheus Club, a Buffalo musical organization.

A Democrat, Bishop ran for county treasurer in 1887 and narrowly lost the election. It was suggested that he contest the result, but he preferred to return to his business. In 1889, he was elected mayor, defeating James H. Carmichael (Republican) 24,155 to 18,206. In 1891, he was reelected, defeating Peter A. Vogt, 23,596 to 18,955, and becoming the first mayor to serve a three-year term. At that time, Buffalo had 255,664 people and a mayor-council form of government.

Bishop was a popular mayor, noted for his sense of humor and easy-going nature. He once told President Grover Cleveland (*q.v.*) that the mayor should be no more than a "handy man" and a detective seeking out crooked politicians. Bishop strongly supported economy in city expenditures and insisted that city contracts go to the lowest bidder. He settled a longstanding conflict between the city and the local street railways, and he generally took the view that the mayor's office was a public trust and required a sense of civic duty. A believer in the merit system, he largely disregarded traditional party uses of patronage. In 1895, he returned to his business pursuits. He died on 14 September 1913.

SOURCES: William H. Dolan and Mark S. Hubbell, *Our Police and Our City . . . and a History of the City of Buffalo* (Buffalo, 1893); *The Men of New York*, 3 vols. (Buffalo, 1898); *Who's Who in New York, City and State* (New York, 1907).   *Thomas R. Bullard*

BISHOP, RICHARD MOORE (1812–93), Mayor of Cincinnati (1859–61). Mayor at the outbreak of the Civil War, and later governor of Ohio, "Papa Richard," as he was affectionately called when he was mayor, was born on 4 November 1812 in Fleming County, Kentucky, the son of a German father and an English mother, both Baptists, who had moved from Virginia in 1800. He received a common school education and began to work as a clerk in a country dry goods store where he became a partner in four years. From 1838 to 1841, he and a brother carried on a pork business until collapsed prices and bank closures forced them to quit. After other business ventures in Mount Sterling, Kentucky, Bishop moved to Cincinnati in 1848 and built a prosperous wholesale grocery firm in partnership with his three sons under the name of R. M. Bishop and Company. Bishop amassed a large estate, and his charities increased in ratio to the growth of his fortune. He was a member of the Central Christian Church and held several responsible positions there and at higher levels in the denomination. He served on boards of educational and charitable institutions, as well as banks, insurance companies, and railroads.

Cincinnati in 1860 had 161,044 people and a mayor-council form of government. In 1857, without his knowledge, Moore was nominated for city council on a Citizens' ticket and was elected by an overwhelming majority. His quiet, unobtrusive diligence won the respect of the council which chose him as its president the following year. Nominated for city mayor in 1859, again by a Citizens' convention, Moore was a reluctant candidate who did not campaign but won by 10,717 votes to his opponent William J. Flagg's 8,787. He refused renomination by both major political parties in 1861 and retired to his business.

Bishop persistently declined all suggestions to run for state and federal office. In 1873, he was elected as a Democratic delegate to the Ohio Constitutional Convention. He was elected Democratic governor of Ohio in 1878 by a huge plurality. At the end of his term in 1880, his name was among those mentioned for vice-president of the United States.

Bishop worked assiduously and courageously as mayor to enhance the material and social prosperity of Cincinnati. In 1860, he was host to a joint meeting of the legislatures of Kentucky, Tennessee, Indiana, and Ohio to encourage them to remain in the Union. He introduced police and prison reform. He insisted on enforcement and respect for municipal laws. One of the mayor's most lasting achievements was securing a right-of-way for the Cincinnati Southern Railroad through Kentucky and Tennessee.

Bishop was a relatively conservative governor under whom state penal and welfare institutions were reorganized. His administration was characterized as efficient, honest, and satisfactory. At the end of his term, he returned to private life in Cincinnati. He died in Jacksonville, Florida, on 2 March 1893 but was buried in Cincinnati.

SOURCES: Virginius C. Hall, "Richard M. Bishop," *The Governors of Ohio* (Columbus, 1954); [Robert Herron], *Cincinnati's Mayors* (Cincinnati, 1957); James Lundy, *Cincinnati Past and Present* (Cincinnati, 1872).
                                              Dwight L. Smith

BLACK, JOHN (1827–99), Mayor of Milwaukee (1878–80). French-born Catholic mayor of Milwaukee, Black was born in Biche, France on 12 August 1827, the son of Peter Black and his wife Magdalena, French farmers. One of five children, Black attended common schools and spent a few years in a college in Metz. In 1845, he emigrated to Lockport, New York, where he met the Ringueberg brothers, immigrant French liquor merchants. Black was their clerk until 1848, when he left to work for a rival firm. In 1854, he returned to the Ringuebergs and became their partner. They bought him out in 1857, and he arrived in Milwaukee, forming his own liquor business, one of the most successful in the city. On 17 September 1855, he married Elizabeth Schoeffel (d. 1891), of Rochester, New York, and they had two daughters, one of whom died in childhood. The Blacks attended St. Joseph's (Roman Catholic) Cathedral in Milwaukee. Black was a prominent member of Milwaukee's Old Settlers' Club and supported various artistic and social organizations.

Black entered politics in 1859, when he was elected the city's railroad commissioner, serving until 1864. A Democrat, he served on the city council in 1870, the Wisconsin Assembly (1872), and state Senate (1874–75), where he sponsored legislation to punish anyone who bribed a politician. He was elected mayor in 1878, defeating Republican Caspar Sanger 7,983 to 7,620 in a bitterly fought election. Milwaukee had 115,587 people in 1880 and a mayor-council form of government. Critics claimed that Black, as a liquor merchant, was a tool of gamblers and saloon-keepers. It was claimed that his occupation alone earned him more hostility from newspapers than anything seen before. Despite this dislike, Black was a popular mayor with the general public. While in office, he actively backed better schools and reform of the police department.

Black did not seek another term and returned to his liquor business in 1880. In 1886, he was an unsuccessful candidate for Congress. He retired from the liquor interests in 1889 and became a director of the Merchants' Exchange Bank. He was also a director of the Milwaukee Manufacturing Company and an active railroad promoter. Black remained active in these pursuits until his death on 25 October 1899.

SOURCES: *The Biographical Dictionary and Portrait Gallery of Eminent and Self-Made Men, Wisconsin Volume* (Chicago, 1877); *The Biographical Dictionary and Portrait Gallery of Representative Men of Chicago, Wisconsin and the World's Columbian Exposition* (Chicago, 1895); Herbert W. Rice, "John Black, Milwaukee's Twentieth Mayor," *Historical Messenger* (Milwaukee County Historical Society Journal) 14:3 (June 1958).

Thomas R. Bullard

BLACKBURN, JOHN C. Mayor *ex officio* of Baltimore (1861). Mayor *ex officio* Blackburn was never elected but temporarily replaced George William Brown (*q.v.*), who was arrested by federal authorities on 21 September 1861. A little-known figure, Blackburn emerged slightly from obscurity in 1919 when he was finally officially recognized as a one-time Baltimore mayor.

In 1861, Baltimore had a population of 212,418 and a mayor-council form of government. Elected to the city council from the Thirteenth Ward on 10 October 1860, as a reformer, Blackburn was chosen president of the council's First Branch. From that position he automatically succeeded Brown, serving in an era of municipal confusion and political unrest. Preoccupied with Brown's imprisonment, the press barely acknowledged Blackburn's new role, which lasted only a few months until he was succeeded by still another temporary mayor, Charles J. Baker (*q.v.*).

SOURCES: Baltimore *Sun*, 12 October 1919; Wilbur F. Coyle, *The Mayors of Baltimore* (Baltimore, 1919); Enoch Pratt Free Library, Baltimore: Vertical File (newspaper clippings), Maryland Room.

Jo Ann Eady Argersinger

BLACKMORE, JAMES (1821–75), Mayor of Pittsburgh (1868–69, 1872–75). Blackmore was born in Washington County, Pennsylvania, on 2 February 1821. His father, Thomas Blackmore, was a farmer and road contractor until he came to Pittsburgh in 1838, and entered the lumber business. Shortly, he set his son up in the same business. The family was Protestant, probably Methodist.

James had little education, though he later took a short course at what is now the University of Pittsburgh. When his father became county treasurer in 1855, he made James his clerk. From 1858 to 1873, father and son were coal dealers and shippers. In 1844, Blackmore married Sarah Jane Ewart, who bore him four sons and a daughter.

Blackmore ran for mayor as a Democrat in 1866 and was defeated by a faked charge of Civil War treason, put out on the morning of election day. Two years later, he was nominated by the Workingmen's party and defeated Republican J. W. Riddle 5,684 to 2,770. Pittsburgh at this time had a population of about 80,000, with government by a mayor and two councils. Both councils had solid Republican majorities, and in April 1868 the state legislature cut off half Blackmore's term with a "ripper bill," changing the term from two to three years but allowing the incumbent to run for a three-year term. There were many marching clubs and fights, and a mob once beat up the mayor. He lost the election to Republican Jared M. Brush (*q.v.*) 7,287 to 5,738.

In 1871, Blackmore defeated A. H. Gross, a prominent physician, for the Democratic nomination, and on 5 December beat Benjamin W. Morgan, Republican, 6,184 to 4,801. By this time Pittsburgh's population was about 90,000. Under the new law, Blackmore's term should have begun on 1 February; but on 8 January he took over the office, with no opposition from Brush, whose term still had three weeks to run.

Blackmore's election as a Democrat did him little good, as both councils were heavily Republican. But he did get them to approve a bill to purchase and free the city's toll bridges. Financially crushed and forced into bankruptcy by the Panic of 1873, Blackmore appointed a deputy and withdrew from active participation in the city's affairs. He died on 6 February 1875, five days after his term ended.

SOURCES: *Biographical Encyclopedia of Pennsylvania* (Philadelphia, 1874); J. Traintor King, "Hon. James Blackmore," *Leisure Hours* (October 1868); *People's Monthly* (February 1875); Pittsburgh *Bulletin*, NS 40:20, 10 March 1900; Pittsburgh *Post and Gazette*, 8 February 1875.

George Swetnam

BLACKWELL, JOHN KENNETH (1948–   ), Mayor of Cincinnati (1979–   ). Educator and Cincinnati's second black mayor, Blackwell was born 26 February 1948 in Cincinnati, the son of George L. Blackwell (1924–   ) an inspector for the Ohio Department of Agriculture, and Dana Jean (Hubbard) Blackwell (1928–   ), both Protestants. The elder of two children, Blackwell grew up in Cincinnati's West End, attending Hughes High School and Xavier University, receiving a B.S. in 1970, an M.A. in 1971 (both in psychology), and continuing postgraduate study in business administration while being mayor. A football player in college, Blackwell was drafted by the Dallas Cowboys, before deciding to pursue a career in education. He taught at Merry Junior High School and, from 1971, at Xavier University, also holding the position of director of community relations. On 10 August 1968, he married Rosa E. Smith (1948–   ), an education graduate of Xavier University, and they have two children. Blackwell joined various organizations, including the Better Housing league, Coalition of Neighborhoods, Cincinnati Opera Board, Queen City

Association, Charter Committee, and the Association of Black Psychologists.

A Charterite, Blackwell was elected alderman in 1977 and immediately served a one-year term as Cincinnati's vice-mayor. In 1979, following reelection to the city council, he was selected to serve one year as mayor, becoming Cincinnati's second black mayor and the youngest chief executive under the charter system. Cincinnati had 451,455 people in 1970 and a city manager-mayor-council form of government.

As mayor, Blackwell realizes that Cincinnati faces major problems and has made efforts to solve them. He has actively supported the existing plan for relieving unemployment and has helped create a program to improve relations between the police force and minority neighborhoods. His inaugural address stressed the need to stay within fiscal limits to combat inflation, thus avoiding the common fault of attempting to accomplish too much with too little funding. To provide better services for Cincinnati (transit, police and fire departments, garbage collection, health care, and schools), Blackwell has urged greater cooperation between the city and the surrounding county authorities. He also has stressed the desire to maintain open communications with the public. This was shown only three days after he took office when a riot at a local rock concert caused a stampede of fans, killing eleven people. Blackwell immediately called for a full investigation and continued to push for laws to prevent further tragedies at overcrowded public events.

SOURCES: Cincinnati *Enquirer*, 1979–80, especially 27 November 1979 and 2 December 1979; letter from Mayor J. K. Blackwell to author, 12 April 1980; *Who's Who Among Black Americans* (Northbrook, Ill., 1978).   *Thomas R. Bullard*

BLAKE, MAURICE CAREY (1815–97), Mayor of San Francisco (1881–83). Republican Mayor Blake was born on 20 October 1815 in Otisfield, Maine, to the Yankee Congregationalist family of Simon Blake (1785–1851), a doctor, and Sophia (Cary) Blake (b. 1785), both of New England ancestry. The third of six children, Blake grew up in Otisfield, attended Bowdoin College, graduating in 1838, and then studied law with General Samuel Fessenden in Portland. Admitted to the bar in 1841, he began practice in Camden, Maine. In 1846, he won a seat in the Maine legislature as a Whig and in 1849 was appointed collector of customs for the Belfast, Maine, district, a position he kept until removed in 1853. That year he left Maine for California, where he arrived in San Francisco on Thanksgiving Day, 1853, after a steamer voyage around Cape Horn. After examining opportunities and also visiting the Sandwich Islands in 1854, he began a law practice in the city in May 1854. He remained a bachelor all his life.

Blake began his political career by actively supporting the Vigilance Committee in 1856. Later in that year, he was elected on the ticket of the committee-backed People's party to the California legislature where he served as a Republican and chaired the San Francisco delegation. During 1857, Blake was elected a county judge, and he served through 1863. Elected as a probate judge in 1864, Blake strengthened English common law practice at the expense of civil law which had been introduced by early Spanish and Mexican settlers. In 1879, he served on the municipal criminal court.

In 1880, 233,959 people lived in San Francisco, and the city and the county of the same name were governed together by a mayor and board of supervisors. In 1881, Blake received the Republican nomination for mayor, and he won the 9 September election, with 17,770 votes to his Democratic opponent Robert Howe's 15,231. Like most San Francisco mayors during the 1880s, Blake recorded few achievements. The city charter, which dispersed power widely, limited a mayor's ability to provide leadership, and Blake's suspicions of the city's government reinforced these limitations, for he sought primarily to reduce waste and corruption rather than to undertake large projects. In addition, Blake had only a one-year term in which to work because the legislature required that city and state elections be held together, starting in 1882. Renominated in 1882, Blake lost the 7 November election to Democrat Washington Bartlett (*q.v.*) 18,286 votes to 20,612. Blake remained involved in Republican politics for some years, losing a bid for the 1886 gubernatorial nomination in convention. He also practiced law with his nephew Maurice Blake until the latter's death in 1885 and subsequently in partnership with George N. Williams and Edward C. Harrison. Weakened by age, Blake died of a stroke in San Francisco on 27 September 1897 and was buried in Marin County.

SOURCES: [Anon.], *The Bay of San Francisco*, 2 vols. (Chicago, 1892); Alexander Callow, Jr., "San Francisco's Blind Boss," *Pacific Historical Review* 25 (August 1956); Alphonso Moulton, Howard L. Sampson, and Granville Fernald, *Centennial History of Harrison, Maine* (Portland, Me., 1909); [San Francisco Bar Association], *Memorial to M. C. Blake Adopted . . . 1897* (n.p., n.d.); [San Francisco Board of Supervisors], *San Francisco Municipal Reports, 1881/82* (San Francisco, 1882), and *San Francisco Municipal Reports, 1882/83* (San Francisco, 1883); San Francisco *Call*, 28 September 1897; San Francisco *Chronicle*, 28 September 1897; Oscar T. Shuck, *Historical Abstract of San Francisco* (San Francisco, 1897); Oscar T. Shuck, ed., *History of the Bench and Bar of California* (Los Angeles, 1901); John Phillip Young, *San Francisco: A History of the Pacific Coast Metropolis*, 2 vols. (San Francisco, 1912).   *Michael Griffith*

BLANKENBURG, RUDOLPH (1843–1918), Mayor of Philadelphia (1912–16). Reform mayor, born in a small village in Germany on 16 February 1843, Blankenburg was the son of a German Reformed minister, Louis Blankenburg, and Sophie (Goede) Blankenburg. Educated at home by a tutor, Rudolph showed a facility for languages, studying Latin, Greek, French, English, and his native German. At age fourteen, he left home to attend the *Gymnasium* at Lippstadt, Germany, and although his parents had wanted him to follow his father's career as a clergyman, he began to work for a merchant uncle in Lippstadt. In 1865, Blankenburg followed his tutor to America, first settling in New Jersey and then in Philadelphia, where he became a traveling salesman and later a European buyer. In 1875, he began his own business and in 1909, retired from its active management. Blankenburg had been active in Philadelphia municipal reform circles, including the Committee of 100, the Committee of 70, and the Business Men's Good Government League. Although many of these groups were bipartisan or fusionist, in national politics he was a Republican. Blankenburg married Lucretia Longshore in a Quaker ceremony in 1867 and fathered three daughters, none of whom lived to adulthood. Lucretia, a Militant Quakeress, was also active in public affairs and was elected president of the Pennsylvania Women's Suffrage Association, a post she held for sixteen years.

Philadelphia in 1910 had a population of 1,549,000 and a mayor-council form of government. Blankenburg, who was nominated for mayor by the reformist Keystone party and supported by the Democrats, beat the Republican machine candidate, George H. Earle, Jr., 134,680 to 130,185.

Reform Mayor Blankenburg promised "honesty" and "efficiency" and brought into his administration young Progressives such as Morris L. Cooke to direct the city's scandal-ridden Department of Public Works. Cooke ended corrupt contracts, pared away padded payrolls, and revived the merit system, which had lain moribund under machine control, and reportedly saved the city $5 million. Blankenburg also brought in other experts, and improvements were effected in garbage collection, city streets, and purchasing supplies and in forcing lower electrical rates from a large utility. In addition, the city's oceanic municipal wharf space was doubled; dangerous grade crossings were eliminated; construction on a subway began; and open vice operations and bawdy houses were closed. Many of Blankenburg's reforms met stiff opposition from the Republican city council, as in that body's refusal to appropriate funds to enforce the new housing inspection law. Blankenburg also refused to distribute patronage "plums" to his own Keystone party, and its members began to desert him. With support for

his programs waning, the aging reformer decided not to seek reelection. He died on 12 April 1918. After a service in the Methodist Episcopal Church, he was buried in Philadelphia.

SOURCES: Lucretia Blankenburg, *The Blankenburgs of Philadelphia* (Philadelphia, 1928); *The City of Firsts: Complete History of Philadelphia* (Philadelphia, 1926); Donald W. Disbrow, "Reform in Philadelphia Under Mayor Blankenburg, 1912–1916, *Pennsylvania History* 27 (October 1960).   *Melvin G. Holli*

BLEE, ROBERT E. (1839–98), Mayor of Cleveland (1893–94). Irish-American Democrat and second mayor of Cleveland under the "federal plan," Blee was born in Glenville (later annexed to Cleveland) on 31 January 1839 to Hugh Blee, originally from Londonderry, Ireland, and Mary B. Porter, also of Irish descent. Blee grew up on a farm, one of eight Blee children, but remained a bachelor the rest of his life. At his graduation from Shaw Academy, Blee was inspired by the speaker to become a railroad brakeman in 1853 for the Cleveland, Columbus, and Cincinnati line. He rose to the position of manager and by 1869 was general superintendent of the Bee Line, later consolidated into the Big Four in 1888. Blee also organized the Bee Line Insurance Company, serving as its president for twenty-two years, and the Ohio National Building and Loan Company. Claiming that "every penny I possess I earned honestly," Blee kept a fifty cent piece, his only money in 1853, for over forty years.

Blee's first entry into politics came as police commissioner from 1875 to 1879; he was credited with ending the "star-chamber" proceedings that had characterized police arrests in the past. In 1893, the Democrats selected Blee over John H. Farley (*q.v.*), former mayor, as Cleveland's population reached 322,900. Blee promised an honest, businesslike administration. A split in the Republican party enabled Blee (16,288) to defeat William J. Akers (14,773), the Republican nominee, and General Edwin S. Meyer (6,189), who bolted and ran as an Independent. Meyer wanted municipal ownership of the gas utility and street railways, and accused Blee of being too close to the railroads with whom the city was having a dispute over some lakefront property. As mayor, Blee advocated the building of docks on the lake front and construction of a better harbor in order to promote trade. The day after his election, the city council passed the Park Act, which eventually led to the establishment of the Emerald Necklace, a chain of parks around the perimeter of Cleveland. Under Blee, the police department pursued a policy of registration for local prostitutes, but public uproar led to its abandonment. Blee's appointment of former Mayor Farley as director of public works created further problems for Blee because Farley did not appoint the party faithful. In spite of a lack of willingness to run again, Blee was drafted in 1895, but the Republicans had reunited, with Robert E. McKisson (*q.v.*) as their candidate. McKisson won easily by a vote of 25,058 to 17,850.

Blee's contributions to charity were well-known—turkeys to St. Alexis Hospital at Christmas, and to George A. Myers, local barber and prominent black politician at Thanksgiving. He particularly liked to help poor and struggling churches, and one year claimed to have given away over $11,000. Blee never ran again for office. He died on 26 February 1898 after a bout with pneumonia.

SOURCES: Annals of the Early Settlers' Association of Cuyahoga County, Ohio (Cleveland, 1898), vol. 4; Charles Kennedy, *Fifty Years of Cleveland, 1875 to 1925* (Cleveland, 1925); Samuel P. Orth, *A History of Cleveland, Ohio* (Cleveland, 1910); the *Plain Dealer* and the *Leader*, especially the obituary in each.

William D. Jenkins

BLYTHIN, EDWARD (1884–1958), Mayor of Cleveland (1940–41). Fourth Welshman to govern Cleveland, but the first Welsh-*born* Mayor, Blythin was born in Newmarket, Wales, on 10 October 1884, the son of Peter and Elizabeth (Roberts) Blythin. He attended the Newmarket Elementary School and Rhyl Intermediate School. He was bookkeeper for a British coal company 1904–1906, and in 1906 he emigrated to the United States, becoming a citizen in 1911. Between 1906 and 1916, he sold real estate as a means of financing his advanced education, and he attended both Cleveland Law School and Baldwin-Wallace College in Berea, Ohio, graduating from the latter with an LL.D. in 1916. He began a successful Cleveland legal practice in 1916, which lasted without interruption to 1940. On 5 April 1913, he married Jane Rankin and they had five children, four of whom outlived him. Blythin was a Mason and a member of the City Club.

Blythin was assistant director of law for the city, 1935–40, and director in 1940. Since this position is equivalent to deputy mayor, Blythin automatically became mayor in November 1940 when Mayor Harold Burton (*q.v.*) resigned to run for the U. S. Senate. Cleveland had 878,336 people and a mayor-council form of government. As mayor, Blythin basically continued Burton's policies, which had attempted to revive the city's business, following the impact of the Depression. In 1941, Blythin was the Republican candidate for a full term as mayor but was defeated by Democrat Frank Lausche (*q.v.*) 145,324 to 94,534.

Blythin resumed his law practice in 1942 but again entered public life in 1943 when he was appointed to the Cleveland Transit Board, holding this post until 1948.

He was also financial vice-president of Case Western Reserve University, 1943–48. In 1949, he became judge of the court of common pleas and gained considerable attention for presiding over the notorious Sam Sheppard murder trial in 1954. Blythin continued on the bench until his death on 14 February 1958.

SOURCES: Cleveland Plain Dealer, 15 February 1958; *New York Times*, 15 February 1958.

Thomas R. Bullard

BOHN, JOHN L. (1867–1955), Mayor of Milwaukee (1942–44, 1944–48). Seventy-six years old when elected mayor in his own right, Bohn was born on 2 August 1867 at Two Rivers, Wisconsin, one of thirteen children of German Lutheran immigrants, John C. Bohn, a hotel operator, and his wife, Regina. Educated in the Two Rivers public schools, Bohn moved with his family to Milwaukee following the death of his father. As a youth he worked as a newsboy, bellboy, and waiter, and as a messenger in the state Senate for three terms prior to running a hotel in Ishpeming, Michigan, and a saloon in Hurley. Bohn and his wife, Anna (1868–1950), were married in 1888. Upon his return to Milwaukee, he operated the Bohn Hotel, and after enactment of Prohibition, spent nine years as a partner in the real estate firm of Mikkelson and Bohn.

Bohn's service in local government began with one term on the Milwaukee County Board of Supervisors (1898–1902). In 1916, he was elected alderman of the city's Twenty-third Ward, the post in Milwaukee's mayor-council government which he would hold for the next twenty-eight years. As chairman of the common council's Legislative Committee for twenty years, he directed the city's lobbying efforts in the state legislature. In 1940, after a bitter contest with Harry J. Divine, Bohn was elected president of the common council, thus becoming acting mayor automatically in 1942 when his predecessor, Carl F. Zeidler (*q.v.*), was called to active service in the Navy during World War II and was subsequently declared missing in action. During this period, Bohn continued to serve as alderman and president of the council.

In the 1940s, Milwaukee's population grew from 587,472 to 637,392. On 4 April 1944, running for mayor in his own right as a nonpartisan, Bohn defeated John A. Seramur, a former policeman and Zeidler bodyguard, 79,516 to 67,531. Bohn's campaign pointed to the success of his service as acting mayor and emphasized that experience was needed to guide Milwaukee in the postwar years.

As mayor, Bohn continued Milwaukee's ''pay as you

go'' method of financing improvements and the building of a permanent improvement fund for postwar construction. He supported a city income tax which was rejected by the legislature. While advocating fair wages for municipal employees, Bohn opposed strikes by government workers. Defining housing as the major problem, resulting from the wartime black migration to Milwaukee, Bohn sought funds for slum clearance and began a program of public housing with construction of the low-rent Hillside Terrace project.

In 1947, the eighty-year-old Bohn announced that he would retire at the end of his term on the half-salary pension recently provided by law. He died of heart failure at his Milwaukee home on 20 April 1955.

SOURCES: John L. Bohn Mayor's Papers, 54 boxes, Milwaukee Public Library; John L. Bohn Papers, 3 boxes, Milwaukee County Historical Society; Milwaukee *Journal*, 21 April 1955; New York *Times*, 6 June 1947, 25 August 1947.   *Barbara M. Posadas*

BOND, LESTER LEGRANT (1829–1903), Acting Mayor of Chicago (August-November, 1873). Ten-week acting mayor of Chicago, Bond was born 27 October 1829 in Ravenna, Ohio, attended the local schools, read the law, and began a law practice as a specialist in the patent business in Chicago in 1854. Bond was alderman from 1863–66 and state legislator from 1867 to 1871. He married on 12 October 1856 to Amie Scott Aspinwall and was prominent and active in the Masons.

Chicago at the time Bond became mayor had a population of more than 300,000 and a mayor-council government. Bond was appointed by the city council as acting mayor in August 1873 when Mayor Joseph E. Medill resigned the office in the face of widespread public protest over his attempt to enforce the Sunday saloon closing law. Bond's term as a ten-week caretaker was uneventful. He ran unsuccessfully as Citizens' party candidate for mayor against Harvey D. Colvin (*q.v.*) who handily defeated him. Bond died in Chicago 15 April 1903.

Sources: A. T. Andreas, *History of Chicago,* 3 vols. (Chicago 1884-86); Fremont C. Bennett, *Politics and Politicians of Chicago, Cook County and Illinois* (Chicago, 1886).   *Besty B. Holli*

BONSALL, WILLIAM HARTSHORN (1846–1905), Acting Mayor of Los Angeles (1892). A member of the Los Angeles City Council, 1889–92, and its first full-time president under the new charter of 1889, Bonsall was born in Cincinnati on 10 February 1846, one of six children of Samuel Bonsall and Mary Mills Bonsall, both old-stock Yankees. Receiving only an elementary school education, he entered the First Ohio Heavy Artillery in 1862, rising from private to major by 1865. His father

died that year, and so Bonsall retired. On 2 October 1871, he married Ellen Doddridge McFarland, daughter of the treasurer of the Times-Mirror Company of Los Angeles, in Portsmouth, Ohio. He was in insurance and then was editor-publisher of the Portsmouth, Ohio *Tribune*, until moving to Elizabeth, New Jersey. In 1886, the Bonsalls moved to Los Angeles, where Bonsall worked in insurance and real estate until his death. They had five children.

An active Republican, Bonsall won the nomination for councilman for the Third Ward in a special election on 22 February 1889 to elect new officers under the city charter of 1889. He garnered 1,117 votes to his Democratic (Cassen) and Prohibitionist (Fuller) opponents' 535 and 31 votes. He was reelected on 1 December 1880, with 728 votes to Cassen's 402 and Bryant's (Municipal Reform) 135. The council elected him its president on 5 December 1890, and he served until 12 December 1892, declining to run for reelection at that time. Apparently, as president, Bonsall also served as acting mayor of Los Angeles for one week (5 to 12 December 1892). Los Angeles was at the time a small city of 57,000 with a mayor-council form of government.

Bonsall was neither a reformer nor an innovator. His political convictions strictly reflected the party-line Republicanism of the late nineteenth century. Bonsall's quick rise to power and his equally rapid retreat from the political arena testified to the opportunities available to a well-connected newcomer with the right ethnic background in Los Angeles and to the lack of an established party machinery. Like many other Los Angeles political leaders of this period, politics and real estate speculation enjoyed a symbiotic relationship during his career.

After leaving office, Bonsall became a traveling adjuster for a local insurance company. By this time, he had accumulated enough wealth to be listed in the local Blue Book of Wealth. In 1897, President McKinley appointed Bonsall to the board of organizers for the National Homes for Disabled Volunteer Soldiers. He managed the Sawtelle Veterans' facility in Los Angeles for six years until he resigned in 1903. On 20 July 1905, Bonsall died of endocarditis at his home in the then fashionable West Adams section of Los Angeles. He was a Christian Scientist.

SOURCES: California Biography File, Los Angeles Public Library; *The Los Angeles Blue Book 1894–1895* (Los Angeles, 1894); Los Angeles Churches Collection, Special Collections, UCLA Library; Los Angeles *Times*, 1890–92, 21 July 1905.

Christopher Cocoltchos and *John M. Allswang*

BOONE, LEVI DAY (1809–82), Mayor of Chicago (1855). Know-Nothing mayor, responsible for inciting Chicago's first fatal street riot, Boone, the grandnephew of the legendary Daniel Boone, was born on 8 December 1808 near Lexington, Kentucky, during an Indian attack. He was the seventh and last child born to Squire Boone (d. 1818) and Anna (Grubbs) Boone, both Virginians in origin. His father, a Baptist minister, was killed during an Indian fight at Horseshoe Bend when Levi was ten. As a teenager, his mother sent the precocious boy to Transylvania University to become a doctor. He completed his medical training in 1829 at the age of twenty. Boone set up his first practice in Edwardsville, Illinois and later moved to Hillsboro. With the outbreak of the Blackhawk War, Levi was commissioned a captain and appointed surgeon of the Second Illinois Regiment. Following the war, Levi married Louise M. Smith in March 1833, and the young couple, with their son Daniel, moved to Chicago in 1836, where Boone was selected that same year as the first secretary of the newly formed Cook County Medical Association. The Boones had eleven children, but only six lived to maturity: Daniel (b. 1834), Samuel (b. 1837), Clara (b. 1840), and 3 younger children. In Chicago, the Boone family lived in a substantial home at 106 State Street and employed one male and two young female servants.

During the next decade, Boone established himself as one of Chicago's most prominent doctors and in 1849 was appointed city physician. Elected alderman (First Ward, 1846, Second Ward, 1847 and 1854), Boone was drafted for mayor by the Native American or Know-Nothing party in 1855, primarily because of the great respect he commanded in Chicago. The party's bigoted slogan was: "Put None But Americans On Guard." No candidates were announced for the mayoral race until five days before the election, and in a very close contest, on 8 March 1855, Boone narrowly defeated the incumbent, Isaac Milliken (q.v.) by 346 votes. At that time the population of Chicago was about 80,000, one-half being foreign-born. Although associated with the anti-Catholic, anti-immigrant Know-Nothing party, Dr. Boone continued some of Milliken's liberal educational reforms. He was responsible for the establishment of Chicago's first high school at Halsted and Monroe Streets, an impressive three-story building costing $50,000, and the city's first reform school. He also increased the size of the police department to fifty men, appointing Chicago's first police chief, Cyrus P. Bradley. The first wooden pavement was installed on Wells Street, and E. S. Chesbrough's plan of draining sewage into the Chicago River, was begun.

Despite Boone's positive actions as mayor, he will probably be best remembered for the Lager Beer Riots of 1855. Shortly after his election, Boone, an anti-liquor man as well as a virulent xenophobe, enforced Chicago's first Sunday closing ordinance and drastically increased the saloon licensing fees from $50 to $300 per year. This action especially affected the large German community on the North Side of the city, and what began as a peaceful demonstration at Randolph Street ended in tragedy when the police fired on a crowd that had gathered in protest. One rioter was killed, and several rioters and policemen were seriously injured. With this stain on his political record, Boone never again ran for public office, but he nevertheless continued his active life. He made himself rich in local real estate and was the first owner to sell lots on State Street to Potter Palmer for a store, with the aim of relocating retail trade from Lake Street to State Street. A trustee of Chicago University, he also continued his support of the Michigan Avenue Baptist Church, to which he donated $200,000.

In 1862 Dr. Boone was again in the news. This time he was arrested and tried for conspiring to help a Confederate prisoner escape. Actually, he had treated a young rebel at Chicago's Camp Douglass prisoner-of-war facility. The youth's mother had sent Boone a letter and some money asking that the doctor help arrange for her son's release. When the young rebel escaped, Boone was immediately arrested. Since Boone was a Southerner, he was suspected of being a sympathizer and narrowly escaped imprisonment. Boone spent the rest of his colorful life dabbling in real estate and insurance. He died on 24 January 1882 at the age of seventy-three.

SOURCES: Biographical Sketches of the Leading Men of Chicago (Chicago, 1876); Weston A. Goodspeed and Daniel D. Healy, eds., *History of Cook County Illinois* (Chicago, 1909), vol. 1; Henry Justin Smith, *Chicago's Great Century: 1833 to 1933* (Chicago, 1933); Charles S. Winslow, *Historical Events of Chicago* (Chicago, 1937).   *D. H. Parkerson*

BOWLES, CHARLES A. (1884–1957), Mayor of Detroit (1930). Recalled from the mayoralty after only seven months in office (14 January–22 September 1930), Charles Bowles was born on 24 March 1884 in Yale, Michigan, where he attended the public schools. The son of Alfred and Mary (Lutz) Bowles, he studied at Ferris Institute in Big Rapids, Michigan, and then transferred to the University of Michigan, graduating with a law degree in 1909. He practiced law in Detroit, 1909–57. Bowles married Ruth Davis in June 1915 and was the father of one daughter. After his first wife died in 1935, Bowles remarried in 1937, but was divorced three years later.

Detroit in 1930 had a population of 1,568,000 and a mayor-council form of government elected by nonpartisan elections. Bowles, who had already served three terms as recorder court judge (1927–29), won the mayoralty election in 1929 for a term that began on 14 January 1930, but ended in his unusual recall by the voters the following September. A series of gangster killings in a gang war, soaring Prohibition era crime, and mounting corruption resulted in this dramatic recall of the mayor and in the assassination, by three unidentified gunmen, of the mayor's chief radio critic and reform crusader, Gerald E. Buckley. Although Bowles probably was not party to the crime, the gangland slaying of his chief critic finished Bowles' political career. He ran three times for public office thereafter but was defeated each time. Bowles was defeated in the mayoralty race of September 1930 by Frank Murphy (q.v.). He resumed law practice in Detroit until his death in 1957.

SOURCES: Biographical file, Detroit Public Library; Detroit *News*, 30 July 1957; *Literary Digest* 106 (9 August 1930).

Ben C. Wilson

BOWRON, FLETCHER (1887–1968), Mayor of Los Angeles (1938–53). Reform mayor, born on 13 August 1887 in Poway, California, Bowron was the son of two Mennonites of English descent, Samuel Bowron (1846–1915), a farmer, and Martha B. (Hershey) Bowron (1848–1924), a teacher. The youngest of five children, Fletcher Bowron moved with his family to Pasadena when he was fifteen and graduated from Los Angeles High School in 1905. Two years later, he entered the University of California at Berkeley and in 1909 transferred to the law school at the University of Southern California. Financial difficulties forced him to discontinue formal education in 1911, but he continued to study law while working as a reporter for the Los Angeles *Examiner* and the San Francisco *Sun*, and in 1917 passed the state bar. During World War I, Bowron was a first lieutenant with the 144th Field Artillery and General Staff Intelligence. In 1919, the thirty-one-year-old Bowron returned to Los Angeles and resumed his law practice with Z. B. West and Willis I. Morrison. On 16 September 1922, Bowron married Irene Martin, a registered nurse, and they adopted one son, Barrett. He joined many associations, including the American Legion, United Veterans, Native Sons of the Golden West, Masons, Elks, and Kiwanis.

Bowron's Republican political career began when Mike Daugherty, a newspaper colleague, persuaded him to become a deputy state corporation commissioner in 1923. Two years later, Bowron became the executive secretary to Governor F. W. Richardson, and on his last day in office, the governor appointed him to the Los Angeles Superior Court bench. Bowron was elected to this position in his own right in 1928 and was reelected in 1934. On 16 September 1938, he was elected mayor (232,686 to 128,895: a handy victory) in a successful recall election.

Prior to Bowron's election, Los Angeles was regarded as the most corrupt city in the nation, but under his stewardship it was considered the best governed city in the United States. Bowron restored faith in Los Angeles by proving that, with a professional civil service, government could achieve both honesty and efficiency. During Bowron's more than fourteen years in office, Los Angeles built the finest municipal facilities in the world, including an international airport, a modern harbor, and the nation's largest sewage treatment plant. Prior to 1938, Los Angeles was considered culturally backward, but Mayor Bowron made it a cultural center, bringing the city into the modern age. In 1952, however, championing the unpopular idea of public housing, he was denied a fifth term. On 6 May 1941, in his first reelection bid, he had won 174,237 to 142,546; on 3 April 1945, 146,323 to 125,004; and on 31 May 1949, his final success, 238,190 to 207,211. By 1952, this proven vote-winner had run out of steam.

Mayor Bowron left office but kept an interest in city affairs. In 1953, he was named to the air pollution hearing board. In 1956, he was reelected to the superior court, but he finally retired in 1962, devoting himself to urban history and founding the Los Angeles Metropolitan History Project. In one of his last civic acts, in 1967, he chaired a citizens committee on zoning.

Bowron's wife died in January 1961, and on the following 18 November he married Mrs. Albine P. Norton, a widow, who had served as his executive secretary throughout his career. Bowron died of a heart attack on 11 September 1968.

SOURCES: Carl W. Blume, "Los Angeles High-Activity Airport," *Aero Digest* (July 1949); California Ephemera Collection, Bowron, Fletcher file, Special Collections, *UCLA* Research Library; Francis M. Carney, "The Decentralized Politics of Los Angeles," *The Annals* (May 1964); Interview with Mrs. Fletcher Bowron and the author, September 1979; Robert G. Lane, "The Administration of Fletcher Bowron as Mayor of the City of Los Angeles" (M.A. thesis, USC, 1954); "Largest Sewage-Treatment Plant," *American City* (February 1949); Donald B. Robison, "A Study of Civil Service Administration in the City of Los Angeles from 1938 to 1952" (M.S. thesis, USC, 1952); William R. Warden, "The History and Development of the Artificial Harbor of Los Angeles" (M.A. thesis, USC, 1957).

Fred W. Viehe

BOXTON, CHARLES (1860–1927), Mayor of San Francisco (1907). Mayor of San Francisco for one week only, 9–16 July 1907, Boxton was a successful dentist by profession. Born in Shasta County, California, on 24 April 1860, he practiced dentistry until joining the California Volunteers to fight in the Philippines. He returned from that war with political ambitions which were soon encouraged by political boss Abe Ruef. He was elected to the board of supervisors in 1899, and the board selected him to fill in the remaining portion of Mayor Eugene Schmitz' (*q.v.*) term, when that incumbent was arrested and convicted of extortion of a city business. Boxton, a confessed, lesser criminal who had turned state's evidence to put Mayor Schmitz into jail, was reluctant to take the office. Public outrage over the prospect of another tainted chief executive forced Boxton to resign after one stormy week in the office. "But what a mayor!" declared *The Wasp*, ". . . His confession that he had been told that he must be Mayor until an honest man could be chosen . . . was cabled all over the world."

Boxton returned to dentistry and rose to dean of dentistry at the College of Physicians and Surgeons. He died in San Mateo on 29 August 1927.

SOURCES: Walton Bean, *Boss Ruef's San Francisco* (Berkeley, 1952); San Francisco *Municipal Reports*, 1907–1908; Lately Thomas, *A Debonair Scoundrel* (New York, 1962); *The Wasp*, 10 August 1907.

Peter d'A. Jones

BRADLEY, TOM (1917–   ), Mayor of Los Angeles (1973–   ). First black mayor of a major, predominantly white, American city, Bradley was born of a sharecropping family on an east central Texas cotton plantation at Calvert (population 500) on 29 December 1917. One of seven children, he was the son of Crenner (Hawkins) and Lee Thomas Bradley. The family moved to Los Angeles when Tom was seven, his mother working as a domestic servant and his father in various jobs, including waiter and Pullman porter. Tom had his own paper route at age nine. An athlete, he became an all-city football tackle and a state champion in the 440-yard dash. He also studied hard at Polytechnic High School in Los Angeles and went to UCLA on an athletic scholarship as a track star. In 1940, he dropped out of college to enter the police department as a juvenile officer. He married a girl he had met in the African Methodist Episcopal Church, Ethel Mae Arnold, on 4 May 1941, and they had two daughters. Bradley later became a trustee of this church. The temporary police job turned out to become a twenty-one-year career (1940–61), during which Bradley became a detective, rose to lieutenant, and began the first community relations program. Meanwhile, in the 1950s, he also studied law at night and was granted the LL.B. degree at Southwestern University in 1956, with admission to the California bar following.

This already remarkable career was soon to be capped by politics. A Democrat, Bradley was elected to the Los Angeles City Council in 1963—the first black ever to sit on that body. He was reelected, unopposed, in 1967 and again in 1971, representing a racially mixed (one-third white) district. As councillor, Bradley suggested the first

minibus scheme and opposed poorly planned coastal oil drilling. He was the first nonmayor to be made vice-president of the National League of Cities, and he gained a reputation as an expert on urban transit needs, conservation, and energy.

A candidate for mayor in 1969 against Sam Yorty (*q.v.*), Bradley was defeated in a bitter runoff election in which Yorty painted him as a black radical. The violence of the late 1960s helped Yorty's campaign. For his 1973 campaign, Bradley therefore prepared the way with great care, hiring a media expert from New York, David Garth, and spending $200,000 on television advertisements. The false radical image was dispelled, the times were now different, and Yorty could be attacked as an absent, do-nothing mayor. Bradley won a stunning victory—56 percent of the votes in a city with a black electorate of only 15 percent. Mayor Bradley took over the city on 1 July 1973 and began a vigorous program, based mainly on attracting millions of dollars in outside aid and grants: he increased federal grants to Los Angeles from $80 million to $800 million. Budgets were balanced, and no new taxes were introduced for six years in a row. A beginning was made on an ambitious rail rapid transit scheme (projected cost $4 billion); a moratorium was declared on freeway building to reduce pollution; further offshore oil drilling was prohibited; zoning changes were planned to limit the city's maximum population growth to 4 million; further efforts were made to revitalize the city core and the neighborhoods; and Bradley tried to draw the scattered city together by holding open house days around the region to meet people off the street, and by creating branch mayoral offices in San Fernando Valley and San Pedro. As the fuel crisis of the 1970s deepened, Mayor Bradley emerged as a national figure in the struggle for a solar energy policy; he planned to make Los Angeles the "Solar City" of the future and gained strong support from the Democratic president, Jimmy Carter. In 1977, Bradley was reelected by a sweeping 60 percent of the vote total, in the nation's third largest city (population 3 million). Bradley endorsed Carter for reelection in 1980, and Carter placed him in various national advisory jobs.

SOURCES: City of Los Angeles, *Mayor Tom Bradley: A Biography* (pamphlet, November 1979); *Ebony* 24:126 (June 1969), 28:113 (July 1973); *Newsday*, 31 May 1973; New York *Times*, 31 May 1973.   *Peter d'A. Jones*

BRADY, SAMUEL (1789–1871), Mayor of Baltimore (1840–42). Born in Delaware in 1789, Samuel Brady served as mayor of Baltimore from 1840 until his resignation in March 1842. Little is known of his background, and he is frequently confused with another Samuel Brady who lived in Baltimore County. He was the son of Benjamin Brady (1759–1839), a member of the Methodist Episcopal Church. He moved to Baltimore at an early age, entered the retail dry goods business on North Gay Street, and was active in Democratic politics as a printer and patronage holder. He married in 1831. Nominated for the House of Delegates in the 1830s, he was defeated but twice ran successfully for city council and was chosen president of the First Branch. Mayor Samuel Smith (*q.v.*) appointed him city collector in 1836, and he was always associated with the Jacksonian Democrats in politics.

Brady won election over the incumbent Whig mayor, Sheppard C. Leakin (*q.v.*), 7,119 votes to 6,887 in 1840. His tenure as mayor of a city that numbered over 100,000 was marked by significant administrative changes. In 1840, the city was redistricted from twelve to fourteen wards, necessitating new procedures for selecting school commissioners. Unlike some members of his party, Brady favored municipal support of internal improvements, and his annual messages to the city council were filled with statistics on the city's progress in shipping and commerce. Disagreement over the city's purchase of Baltimore and Ohio Railroad stock (which Brady supported but the council opposed) led to his resignation in 1842. Brady ran for Congress after his resignation but was defeated. Later, he was elected county commissioner, a position he held for many years. He died in 1871 at the age of eighty-two.

SOURCES: Baltimore *Sun*, 11 December 1871 (obituary); Wilbur Coyle, *Mayors of Baltimore* (Baltimore, 1919); Dielman-Hayward File, Maryland Historical Society; Whitman Ridgway, "A Social Analysis of Maryland Community Leaders, 1827–1836" (Ph.D. dissertation, University of Pennsylvania, 1973).

Jean H. Baker

BRADY, WILLIAM V. (1801–70), Mayor of New York (1847–48). A New York silversmith, Brady was elected mayor of the city on 13 April 1847. His administration was conservative and cost-cutting, and he advocated abandoning the new pioneer urban police force created for New York under Mayor James Harper (*q.v.*) (1844) on the grounds that the police system had "failed the just expectation of the community" and cost too much. The council did not carry out his suggestion. At this time the City College of New York was first established, as the "Free Academy," at Lexington and 22nd.

Mayor Brady's message of 11 May 1847 established the city's debt as almost $12 million. Almshouse costs had increased in the 1840s, from $238,000 in 1842 to $343,000 in 1846, and Brady suggested cutting staff and salaries, which he claimed had risen disproportionately to the number of inmates. Like several mayors before

him, he demanded a new workhouse as well as a wooden building on Randall's Island for child laborers, moved from former farm camps on Long Island. Other issues of his administration were typical of the period—street-cleaning costs, treatment of lunatics, and the rising costs of urban government.

SOURCES: Message of His Honor the Mayor, William V. Brady, Document No. I, Board of Alderman, 11 May 1847 (New York, 1847), New York Public Library; *The Renascence of City Hall: Mayors of New York* (New York 1956).

Peter d'A. Jones

BREITMEYER, PHILIP (1864–1941), Mayor of Detroit (1909–10). Famous horticulturist and one-term Republican mayor, Breitmeyer was born 3 May 1864 in Detroit of German-born, probably Lutheran, immigrant parents, John Breitmeyer (1834–1900) and Fredericka (Schneider) Breitmeyer (1837–1920). The second of seven children, Philip Breitmeyer ended his formal education in Detroit's public schools at age eleven when he went to work in his father's florist shop. He became a nationally known horticulturist, president of John Breitmeyer and Sons, founder of the Floral Telegraph Delivery service, and president of both Breitmeyer's Nursery and the Broadway Market Company. He married Katherine Grass of Philadelphia, a Christian Scientist, on 9 March 1886, and she bore him two children, Harry G. and Katherine. Breitmeyer attended the Christian Science Church of Detroit and was a member of the prestigious Detroit Athletic Club and the Detroit Golf Club.

In 1909, Detroit had a population of over 465,000 and a mayor-council form of government. Breitmeyer, a relative newcomer to local politics, served as commissioner of parks and boulevards (1907–1908) before becoming mayor in 1909. Breitmeyer won over the Democratic incumbent largely on the streetcar franchise issue. The Democrat William B. Thompson (*q.v.*) had won in 1906 on the promise of achieving municipal ownership of the street railway system by 1908, but he failed, and in his campaign Breitmeyer capitalized on this failure, promising to solve the streetcar issue. The wide coat-tails of Republican presidential candidate William Howard Taft also helped Breitmeyer win the mayoralty. Taft carried Detroit by 20,000 votes, giving Breitmeyer the needed margin. Breitmeyer defeated Thompson 32,240 to 32,608.

Breitmeyer's single term in office was dominated by the difficult streetcar franchise issue. He appointed a committee of 50 that came up with the Webster Plan which (depending upon the Detroit United Railway's acceptance) allowed for a ticket price of eight for a quarter, a five-man policy commission, a board of arbitration that would settle all labor disputes with the Detroit United Railway, and finally municipal ownership, scheduled to take effect in 1924. The Detroit United Railway Company rejected the Webster Plan, and Mayor Breitmeyer had nothing else to offer, thus sealing his political fate.

Breitmeyer's inability to solve the nagging problem of urban transportation coupled with the 1910 split in the Republican party between Roosevelt and Taft cost Breitmeyer the nomination, which went to a Roosevelt "insurgent."

After his defeat, Breitmeyer returned to his successful floral business. In 1933, he made another unsuccessful bit for the mayoral nomination, but in 1937 he won a seat on the Detroit Common Council. He died on 9 November 1941 and was buried in Detroit.

SOURCES: Philip Breitmeyer Papers, Correspondence, September–November 1910, scrapbooks, Burton Historical Collection, Detroit Public Library; Burton Historical Collection Biographical Index, Drawer no. 25; Clarence M. Burton, *The City of Detroit, Michigan, 1701–1922* (Detroit-Chicago, 1922); Jack D. Elenbaas, "Detroit and the Progressive Era: A Study of Urban Reform 1900–1914" (Ph.D. dissertation, Wayne State University, 1968); A. N. Marquis, *The Book of Detroiters* (Chicago, 1900).   *Jack D. Elenbaas*

BRENHAM, CHARLES JAMES (1817–75), Mayor of San Francisco (1851, 1852–3). Second and fourth mayor of San Francisco, Brenham was born in Frankfort, Kentucky, on 6 November 1817. He left home as a boy to work the rivers and by age twenty, had his own boat at Natchez. He became a well-known Mississippi steamboat captain, a success at a very tough and hazardous life. Gold fever took him to San Francisco (18 August 1849), but he took command of a steamer plying between that city and Sacramento. For eight months he hauled miners, supplies, and foodstuffs up the Sacramento River, helping people reach the Sierra foothills.

In 1850, the Whig party asked Brenham to run for mayor, but he was reluctant and refused to leave his steamer, the *McKim*. John Geary (*q.v.*) won the nomination and the election. The following year, however, Brenham changed his mind and campaigned well. His first administration as mayor of San Francisco ran from 5 May to 30 December 1851 and was dominated by the vigilante crisis. City crime, gang violence by the "Sydney Ducks" and "Hounds" (who controlled the foot of Telegraph Hill), and serious arson brought sharp citizen reaction with the formation of a vigilante group. Brenham, tough river captain that he was, took a courageous stand against the vigilantes, but they held midnight courts, arrested a total of ninety-one men, and executed four in 1851. Two massive city fires (one of which destroyed the city hall) scared the populace and gave power

to the Committee of Vigilance. When they threatened to lynch a certain Captain Waterman, Mayor Brenham faced down the mob, pulling out his watch and giving them ten minutes to disperse. The audacious bluff worked. However, the vigilantes did reduce crime in San Francisco.

More serious in the long run was the issue of city financing. Through corruption and mismanagement the city was heavily overspent and in debt. By March 1851, its liabilities were over $1 million, and it had spent nearly $2 million since August 1849—high figures for a still-simple town of about 30,000 or less. Broke, the city began to issue scrip—paper certificates that could be exchanged for gold dollars and that rapidly depreciated. Fortunately for Brenham, a new state charter to the city, granted on 15 April 1851, helped him move towards a solution. The charter set a debt ceiling for the city and controlled city salaries. Later, the public debt was properly funded.

The new charter also called for fresh elections in September to coincide with general state elections. The Whigs felt that no election was necessary until September 1852 and offered no candidates. The Democrats ran unopposed, and Dr. S. R. Harris (*q.v.*) was elected mayor in September 1851. Brenham refused to relinquish his office until the state supreme court confirmed Harris's election (27 December 1851). For nine months Brenham was out of politics, working at a local bank he helped found, Sanders and Brenham. He ran hard for reelection in late summer and regained power in September 1852.

Brenham's second term saw many improvements and changes in the city. He claimed to have reduced the budget to one-third or less. As failed miners turned increasingly to farming and industry, the city grew: brickyards, tanneries, flour mills, and iron forges flourished, together with over 500 saloons. The first public library, the Mercantile Library, was opened in January 1853 with Brenham's support. The mayor stood firm against Governor Bigler's state plans to fill in more of the Bay in order to sell lots to build up state revenues. He tackled the perennial water supply problem, without much success. Sand hills vanished from the city as the Bay was filled in and as ballast was needed for ships. Telegraph Hill itself was said to be reduced in size by one-third.

Despite all this activity, Brenham was replaced by C. K. Garrison (*q.v.*) in September 1853. Brenham did not vanish totally from public life thereafter. For a while he was agent of the California, Oregon, and Mexico Steamship Company. In 1852, he had declined President Fillmore's appointment as treasurer of the U.S. Mint. He did badly in the race for state controller on 6 July 1853, coming out sixth out of seven on the fourth ballot at the Whig nominating convention in Sacramento. He became an active Democrat, attending state party conventions in 1860 and as late as 1867. His death in San Francisco on 10 May 1875 attracted little notice.

SOURCES: Academy of Pacific Coast History, *Papers of the San Francisco Committee of Vigilance·of 1851* (Berkeley, 1919); W. J. Davis, *History of Political Conventions in California, 1849–92* (Sacramento, 1893); W. F. Heintz, *San Francisco's Mayors* (Woodside, Calif., 1975); W. F. White, *A Picture of Pioneer Times in California* (San Francisco, 1881); Mary F. Williams, *History of the San Francisco Committee of Vigilance, 1851* (Berkeley, 1921).   *Peter d'A. Jones*

BRIMMER, MARTIN (1793–1847), Mayor of Boston (1843–44). Ninth mayor of Boston, Brimmer was born on 8 June 1793 in Roxbury, Massachusetts, one of Martin (1742–1804) and Sarah (Watson) (d. 1832) Brimmer's four children. His father was of German-French and his mother of British descent. He studied with the Reverend H. H. Jenks, D.D., and entered Harvard as a divinity student. Graduating in 1814, he joined the military and then took up a career in business, entering the store of Theodore Lyman, Sr. He went on to become a successful merchant with Isaac Winslow and Company on Long Wharf. In addition to his commercial success, Brimmer was widely noted for his interest in public education. He became something of a local *cause célèbre* when he printed and distributed copies of *The School and The Schoolmaster*, by Alonzo Potter and George B. Emerson, to every school in Massachusetts at his own expense. He was active in the state militia, in which he held several commissions. Brimmer married Harriet E. Wadsworth of Genesco, New York, on 15 January 1829. They had one son, Martin (b. 9 December 1829).

Brimmer, a Whig, became mayor of Boston in 1843, following his victory over Bradford Sumner, the candidate of the Loco-Foco party. He served two one-year terms, leaving office at the end of 1844, having chosen not to run again. At that time, Boston had grown to about 110,000 inhabitants with an influx of Irish immigrants. Municipal services were strained. Brimmer's primary concern, however, like that of his predecessor, was to reduce the city debt. He pressed on with Chapman's retrenchment policies and also stepped up the selling off of city-owned property. Mayor Brimmer managed to bring the city's net funded debt down to roughly $1,121,000. Despite retrenchment, however, he supported the construction of several new schools, and he worked hard, but unsuccessfully, for the long-needed county jail in South Boston. His administration made the first significant headway on the question of the public water system, when, at the December 1844 election, a majority of the voters approved a ballot proposal to have

the city procure a public water supply from Long Pond. Brimmer's last major act as mayor was to apply to the state legislature for authority to begin this vital improvement. He died two and a half years later, on 25 April 1847.

SOURCES: *Boston City Documents* (Boston, 1843, 1844); James M. Bugbee, "Boston Under the Mayors," in Justin Winsor, ed., *The Memorial History of Boston* (Boston, 1881), vol. 3; Charles Philips Huse, *The Financial History of Boston from May 1, 1822 to January 31, 1909* (Cambridge, Mass., 1916); *Inaugural Addresses of the Mayors of Boston 1822–1851* (Boston, 1894); *Our First Men: A Calendar of Wealth, Fashion, and Gentlemen Containing a List of Those Persons Taxed in the City of Boston Credibly Reported to be Worth 100 Thousand Dollars* (Boston, 1846).

Christine M. Rosen

BRITTON, JAMES H. (1817–1900), Mayor of St. Louis (1875–76). Welsh-American mayor of St. Louis, Britton was born in Shenandoah County, Virginia, on 11 July 1817, the son of immigrants from Wales. Britton had little formal education. He was a clerk in Sparryville, Virginia, 1832–38, and then a partner of a Thompsonville (Virginia) merchant, 1838–40. He continued his general mercantile career in Virginia until 1857 when he moved to St. Louis, working as a cashier of the Southern Bank. By 1864, he had become president of that institution. Subsequently, he served as head of the National Bank of the State of Missouri. No information about his immediate family has come to light.

Britton, a Democrat, was the Missouri Senate's secretary during the 1848 session and served in the Missouri House of Representatives, 1852–56. He was chief clerk of that body, 1856–57. Britton was elected treasurer of Lincoln County, Missouri, and served a short while as postmaster of Troy. He secured the Democratic nomination for mayor of St. Louis for the special election following the sudden death of Mayor Arthur B. Barret (q.v.), one week after taking office in 1875. His opponent was Henry Overstolz (q.v.), and the election was a virtual tie. The official returns were not released, and a bitter court battle ensued. The election judges declared Britton the winner, and he took office late in May. St. Louis had a population of 310,864 in 1875 and a mayor-council form of government.

As mayor, Britton sponsored the typical civic improvements of the period, notably a new sewer system and an improved method of granting building permits (mainly to limit the number of wooden buildings, reducing the risk of fire). In February 1876, an official recount of the vote took place, and Britton discovered that he had actually been defeated by Overstolz 14,725 to 14,648. After leaving office, Britton retired from politics and moved to Ardsley, New York, where he died on 27 January 1900.

SOURCES: Howard L. Conrad, ed., *Encyclopedia of the History of Missouri*, 6 vols. (New York, 1901); Charles H. Cornwell, *St. Louis Mayors: Brief Biographies* (St. Louis, 1965); J. T. Scharf, *History of Saint Louis City and County*, 2 vols. (Philadelphia, 1883); Walter B. Stevens, *St. Louis History of the Fourth City, 1764–1909* (Chicago, 1909).   *Thomas R. Bullard*

BROENING, WILLIAM FREDERICK (1870–1953), Mayor of Baltimore (1919–23, 1927–31). Republican mayor, born on 2 June 1870, in Baltimore, Broening was the son of a Bavarian immigrant tailor, Henry Jacob Broening, and Catherine (Petri) Broening, born in Frankfort, Germany. The second of three sons, William Broening attended the Baltimore public schools and graduated from the University of Maryland Law School in 1897. He entered politics immediately, serving a two-year term (1897–99) on the Baltimore City Council and then working as secretary to Republican Congressman Frank Wachter (1899–1907) whose support boosted Broening's political career. In 1902, he was elected to a two-year term in the House of Delegates (Maryland's lower house.) From 1909 to 1911, he worked as secretary to Republican Congressman John Kronmiller. Broening was elected to a four-year term as states' attorney of Baltimore in 1911 and again in 1915. On 6 September 1905, he married Josephine Marie Gravel (1875–1954), a public school teacher from Baltimore. Both were Lutherans. They had three children: William Frederick, Jr., K. Ethel (Mrs. Fred Fulenwider), and E. Calvin. Broening was a member of the Masons, Oddfellows, Moose, Elks, and Knights of Pythias, and a director of the Gettysburg Theological Seminary.

During Broening's mayoralty, Baltimore was an expanding city (733,826 in 1920; 804,874 in 1930) and had a mayor-council form of government. The Democrats generally dominated city politics, but Republicans occasionally benefited from divisions within the Democratic party and won city-wide elections. In 1919, Broening, unopposed for the Republican nomination, defeated a weak Democratic candidate for mayor, George Weems Williams, by a vote of 60,298 to 51,060. In 1923, Broening was renominated but lost to a very popular Democrat, Howard Jackson (*q.v.*), by a vote of 74,124 to 49,919, despite the presence on the ballot of a Democratic primary loser, James Preston, who garnered 39,042 votes. In 1927, with the unusual support of Democratic boss Sonny Mahon, Broening won re-election as mayor over William Curran by a vote of 85,695 to 68,299.

Broening's popularity stemmed largely from his devotion to Baltimore, and his reputation as a representative of ordinary people and their neighborhoods, of the small businessmen rather than the wealthy. He was known as a humanitarian, interested in the health and welfare of all. During his term, he established the Bureau of Child Welfare in the Health Department, he sponsored safety regulations in various public utilities, and he built a new sports stadium.

After his retirement in 1931, Broening worked as a city tax collector and as chairman of the State Industrial Accident Commission. He died on 12 October 1953 and is buried in Baltimore.

SOURCES: Wilbur F. Coyle, *The Mayors of Baltimore* (Baltimore, 1919); Files of the Maryland Historical Society, the Enoch Pratt Free Library, and the Baltimore *Sun*.   *Suzanne Ellery Greene*

BROWN, ADAM M. (1829–1910), Recorder of Pittsburgh (1901). Brown was seventy-one when the governor appointed him recorder, a post which temporarily replaced the office of mayor for Pittsburgh. (A "Ripper Act," passed during a Republican factional fight for control of Pittsburgh, abolished the office of mayor in 1901, but was repealed in 1903). Brown was born on 3 August 1829 in Brownsdale, Butler County, Pennsylvania, a town named for his father, Joseph Brown, a merchant of British extraction. While "reading" medicine in 1849, he became interested in the California Gold Rush and led a party from Pittsburgh overland. Returning to Pittsburgh, he studied law with his uncle, Thomas Marshall, Sr., was admitted to the bar in 1853, and remained in partnership with him until 1865. Brown later practiced law with two of his sons, John D. and Thomas M. Brown.

As an organizer of the local Republican party, Brown was a delegate to the convention which nominated Lincoln. During the Civil War, he was chairman of the Republican County Committee. Brown did not fight, but he aided local civilian activities for the war effort.

In 1873, Major Brown (a title he got from militia duty prior to the war) was an organizer and first president of the Anchor Savings Bank while continuing his law practice. In addition, he was a member of the Pittsburgh City Council and a director of and counsel for the Pittsburgh *Dispatch*, and was engaged in the insurance business.

Brown's involvement in politics was not extensive until Governor William A. Stone suddenly appointed him recorder on 6 April 1901. He did not decide to accept the position until 27 May, a delay that was, in part, his political downfall. Brown had supported the Matthew Quay forces in their battle with the Magee-Flinn machine which, until Brown's appointment, had controlled the city. After he became recorder, Brown dismissed many corrupt Magee-Flinn men, but before this they had made peace with Governor Stone. Recorder Brown then allied himself with Senator Quay but vacillated in cleaning out city hall of the rest of the Magee-Flinn officeholders until 29 August 1901. Meanwhile, the governor failed to oblige the Magee-Flinn machine in removing Brown because the new "reform" recorder had the support of Pittsburgh's upper class.

All of this wrangling absorbed so much energy and interest that the only other events of importance during Brown's administration were the passage of McKinley's funeral train attended by numerous local speeches and the planning of a water filtration plant. Meanwhile, the irate Magee-Flinn forces promised Governor Stone a U.S. Senate seat after his term of office if he would remove Recorder Brown. On 21 November 1901, the governor removed Brown, accusing him of trying to build a political machine. He was replaced by J. O. Brown (no relation), an old Magee-Flinn supporter, whom he had previously fired. Brown returned to his law practice before retiring at age seventy-four.

Brown was married to Lucetta Turney of Greensburg, Pennsylvania, and was the father of six children. In addition to the two sons mentioned above, he was the father of William J. Brown who moved to Florida; Marshall, who became a judge; and two daughters, Sarah and Caroline, who respectively married Dr. Francis Herron and his cousin, John H. Herron, a wealthy coal merchant. Adam Brown was an elder and trustee of the First United Presbyterian Church. He published *Recollections of Bench and Bar* in 1878. He died on 17 August 1910 and was buried in Allegheny Cemetery, Pittsburgh.

SOURCES: L. H. Everts, *History of Allegheny County, Pennsylvania* (Philadelphia, 1876); Pittsburgh *Dispatch*, Editorial, "Death of a Great Citizen," 18 August 1910.   *Joseph F. Rishel*

BROWN, GEORGE WILLIAM (1812–90), Mayor of Baltimore (1860–61). Jailed Civil War mayor, Brown, born in Baltimore on 13 October 1812, was the son of George John Brown and Esther (Allison) Brown. His father, a wealthy merchant, was the son of a prominent physician born in Ireland, educated at the University of Edinburgh, Scotland, and an early Presbyterian settler of Baltimore. Brown's mother was a daughter of Reverend Patrick Allison, the first pastor of Baltimore's First Presbyterian Church. Brown attended a Quaker school and Baltimore City College. He entered Dartmouth at sixteen but left when his father died. Brown graduated from Rutgers with honors in 1831. That same year, he returned to Baltimore to study law and was admitted to the bar. In 1839, he formed a law partnership with Frederick Brune. Brown married Brune's sister, Clara Maria, daughter of Frederick William Brune of Bremen, Mary-

land, on 29 October 1839. They had seven children, four of whom survived. His eldest son, Arthur George, joined his law firm.

Throughout the 1850s, ardent Democrat Brown opposed Know-Nothing ruffianism. Denouncing municipal violence, he delivered speeches like "Lawlessness, the Evil of the Day." Dismayed by the politically successful Know-Nothings, Brown urged municipal reform, particularly the reorganization of the city police. He championed the 1859 law that shifted control of the police from the mayor to a board of commissioners, and he helped form the City Reform Association—a political organization that sought fair elections and Democratic control of Baltimore's mayor-council government.

On the reform ticket, Brown defeated Samuel Hindes, the Union party candidate, on 10 October 1860, by a vote of 17,779 to 9,675. Brown's administration began on 12 November 1860, but ended on 12 September 1861, when he was arrested by federal authorities as a result of the 19 April 1861 Baltimore riot against federal troops marching through Maryland. Although Brown had urged peaceful passage of the troops and had professed loyalty to the Union, he opposed Lincoln's policies. Following his arrest, he was confined at Fort Monroe until the expiration of his mayoral term (27 November 1862).

A city of 212,418 people, Baltimore in 1860 was disrupted by sectional conflict that overwhelmed Brown during his brief mayoral term. Although he consolidated earlier efforts at water and sewage improvements, he contributed most to the city in the years after the Civil War. He participated in the 1867 state constitutional convention, helped establish the Maryland Historical Society, worked as a Baltimore supreme court judge from 1872 to 1888, served as a trustee of numerous colleges, and founded the Baltimore Bar Library. Before his death, Brown published his own account of the infamous riot, *Baltimore and the 19th of April, 1861: A Study of War.* He died on 8 September 1890.

SOURCES: Jean H. Baker, *The Politics of Continuity: Maryland Political Parties from 1858 to 1870* (Baltimore, 1973); *The Biographical Cyclopedia of Representative Men in Maryland and District of Columbia* (Baltimore, 1879); George William Brown, *Baltimore and the 19th of April, 1861: A Study of War* (Baltimore, 1887); Wilbur F. Coyle, *The Mayors of Baltimore* (Baltimore, 1919); Clayton Colman Hall, ed., *Baltimore: Its History and Its People* (New York, 1921); Enoch Pratt Free Library, Baltimore: Vertical File (newspaper clippings), Maryland Room; J. Thomas Scharf, *History of Baltimore City and County* (Philadelphia, 1891).

Jo Ann Eady Argersinger

BROWN, JAMES S. (1824–78), Mayor of Milwaukee (1861–62). Born in Hampden, Maine, on 1 February

1824, of British descent, Brown attended public schools in Penobscot County. He read law in Cincinnati, Ohio, and was admitted to the bar in 1843. The following year he began his legal practice in Milwaukee. He married twice: his first wife was Elizabeth Shepard, and his second, a Miss Stetson of Bangor, Maine.

Brown was elected prosecuting attorney for Milwaukee County in 1846 and Wisconsin attorney general in 1848 and 1849. In 1861, he received the Democratic nomination for mayor and was easily elected when local Republicans also announced their support. He was elected to the Thirty-eighth Congress in 1862 but was unsuccessful in his bid for reelection two years later.

By 1860, Brown had acquired major real estate holdings in Milwaukee. He was dedicated to his community, as illustrated by his sponsorship of the city's first steam fire engine. His contemporaries noted that the community had lost a good German scholar when he succumbed to lengthy ill health on 15 April 1878.

SOURCES: H. Russell Austin, *The Milwaukee Story: The Making of an American City* (Milwaukee, 1946); John G. Gregory, *History of Milwaukee, Wisconsin* (Chicago, 1931), vol. 2; [Wisconsin] *State Journal*, 17 April 1878 (obituary).   *David J. Maurer*

BROWN, JOSEPH (1823–99), Mayor of St. Louis (1871–75). Scottish-born businessman mayor of St. Louis, born in Jedburg in 1823, Brown emigrated to the United States in 1831 when his family settled in St. Louis. They soon moved across the river to Alton, Illinois, where Brown attended public schools and started college. He quit school in 1845 and began work in the milling business. In 1854–55, he was mayor of Alton (the second mayor of Alton to have become mayor of St. Louis), actively promoting the Chicago and Alton Railroad. In 1854, he married Virginia Keach, and they had two daughters. Becoming interested in the steamboat business, Brown concluded that this line of work would be more successful if based in a large city, and he moved his family to St. Louis before the Civil War. During the war, his steamboat yards built gunboats for the U.S. Navy. In 1869, he served a brief term in the state Senate as a Democrat.

Brown was elected mayor in 1871, defeating Republican E. D. Stannard by a vote of 10,914 to 8,910. Two years later, he was reelected, defeating George Bain 15,348 to 10,991. St. Louis had 310,864 people in 1870 and a mayor-council form of government. During his first term, Mayor Brown supported various civic improvements, notably the great Eads Bridge. To finance these improvements he issued special city bonds nicknamed "Brownbacks." During his second term, he was forced to support a program of fiscal retrenchment as a response to the depression that began in 1873.

During his term in office, Brown was elected president of the Missouri Pacific Railroad. After leaving the mayoralty, he virtually retired from all business activities and lived quietly until his death on 3 December 1899.

SOURCES: Charles H. Cornwell, *St. Louis Mayors: Brief Biographies* (St. Louis, 1965); William Hyde and Howard L. Conrad, eds. *Encyclopedia of the History of St. Louis*, 4 vols. (New York, 1899); J. T. Schraf, *History of St. Louis City and County*, 2 vols. (Philadelphia, 1883); Walter B. Stevens, *St. Louis: History of the Fourth City, 1764–1909* (Chicago, 1909).   *Thomas R. Bullard*

BROWN, JOSEPH OWEN (1846–1903), Recorder of Pittsburgh (1901–1903). Brown was born in West Deer Township, Allegheny County, Pennsylvania, on 8 January 1846, the son of Jesse B. and Hannah Brown. After college, he taught school in Cincinnati, Ohio, eventually becoming principal. In 1873, he resigned, returned to Pittsburgh, and became chief clerk in the prothonotary's office. At this time, he studied law and in 1876 was admitted to the bar. When the Republican organization fell under the control of the Christopher Magee (and later William Flinn) faction in 1878, Brown joined it. The following year, he was rewarded with the party's endorsement for prothonotary. He was elected and served two terms. Brown then turned to his law practice until he was elected chief of the Department of Public Safety by the city council in 1887. He continued in this post until he was removed by Recorder Adam M. Brown (*q.v.*) in 1901.

Brown made a considerable number of improvements in his department, including efficient police and fire bureaus, reduced crime, and restrictions in gambling and prostitution to certain areas. This last-named policy was to cause feuding with Mayor Henry Gourley (*q.v.*) in 1891. In addition, through court action, the number of saloons was reduced in the city from more than a thousand to several hundred, but speakeasies emerged as a result. Brown was an avid builder, and some charges of corruption in construction contracts led to his trial by the city council. The affair was mainly windowdressing, however, and Brown was exonerated.

Upon firing Recorder Adam M. Brown, Governor William A. Stone appointed Joseph O. Brown to replace him on 21 November 1901. (A Republican factional fight for control of Pittsburgh politics resulted in the passage of a "Ripper Act" in 1901 that abolished the office of mayor replacing it with a recorder appointed by the governor. The Ripper Act was repealed in 1903.) Brown promptly reinstated the old Magee-Flinn machine officials. As recorder, Brown continued his old policy of regulating vice rather than attempting to eliminate it. He supported the first pension bill for Pittsburgh police and firemen. But Brown was absent from his office much of the time, often mysteriously. During his tenure as recorder, a business venture in oil begun ten years earlier in West Virginia became immensely successful. At this same time, his health also began to decline.

A new recorder was to be elected rather than appointed in 1903, but the Republicans nominated John C. Haymaker instead of Brown. After Haymaker's defeat, Brown resigned his office on 13 March. His resignation was to take effect on 16 March, just two weeks before the end of his term, but Brown died the day before.

Brown was married to Jane Walter in 1871. They had a daughter, Josephine Edna, and a boy who died in infancy. Mrs. Brown died in Philadelphia in 1896. The following year, Brown married a Pittsburgh school teacher, Ella Martin, but they separated after six months. Brown had built a new home and was attempting a reconciliation when he died. He was a Sunday School teacher and a member of the Fifth Avenue Methodist Episcopal Church.

SOURCES: Pittsburgh *Dispatch*, 16 March 1903; Pittsburgh *Post*, 16 March 1903; and Pittsburgh *Press*, 16 March 1903.   *Joseph F. Rishel*

BROWN, THOMAS H. (1839-1908), Mayor of Milwaukee (1880-82, 1888-90). The first Milwaukee-born, native son to become mayor, Brown was born on 3 April 1839, the second of four children of Samuel Brown (1804–74), a contractor and railroad promoter, and a Presbyterian, originally from Belchertown, Massachusetts, and Clarissa Brown (1813–87), a Methodist from New Hampshire. Both were pioneer settlers of the Milwaukee region, Clarissa being the first white woman to settle there. Their son attended local schools and Beloit College, until his father's business troubles forced him to abandon college before the junior year. After attempting schoolteaching and law, he spent some years wildcatting in the Pennsylvania oilfields (1861–67), returning to Milwaukee to invest his profits. Brown's investments turned sour, and he was again forced to work, becoming a partner in a wholesale hat business (Salomon, Brown and Fowler) and in 1870 forming a carriage manufacturing company, Wechselberg and Brown, later reorganized as T. H. Brown and Company. On 26 December 1866, he married Emma J. Fowler, but was soon widowed (1868); on 12 November 1872, he married Alice L. Davis, and they had two daughters, Fanny (b. 1874) and Edith (b. 1877).

A Republican, Brown was elected to the city council as an alderman from the Fourth Ward (1877–80). He acted as temporary mayor when Mayor John Black (*q.v.*) was out of town. A strong Republican partisan, he often opposed the mayor's policies, and in 1880, he was elected mayor in his own right. He defeated Joshua Stark

(Independent) 8,988 to 5,610. Milwaukee was a growing city, having 116,000 people by 1880 and 205,000 by 1890, with a mayor-bicameral council form of government. As mayor, Brown was pro-business and supported the merit system, refusing the dictates of local party stalwarts to make patronage appointments. He even retained many Democrats in their city jobs, showing an independence of spirit that cost him his own party's renomination in 1882.

Brown ran unsuccessfully for Congress in 1886, but two years later he recaptured the nomination for mayor on a fusion ticket of Republicans and Democrats. In a bitter three-way battle against heavy labor opposition, Brown was elected as a Citizens' party candidate, with 15,978 votes to 15,033 for Herman Kroeger (Union Laborite) and 904 for Colin Campbell (Socialist-Labor). The Milwaukee *Sentinel* termed Brown's barely successful coalition an alliance for the protection "of the sacred rights of property, in defense of the homes of thousands of workingmen as well as capitalists and against the building of a class party." Milwaukee was rapidly becoming one of the strongest Socialist cities in the United States.

In 1890, Brown sought a third term on the regular Republican ticket, only to lose to Democrat George W. Peck (*q.v.*), a popular humorist, 16,216 to 9,501. German voters defected in large members from the GOP, and Peck capitalized on widespread ethnic disaffection with the Republicans for their support in 1889 of the Bennett Law, a state measure requiring that school instruction be in English. The act was clearly intended to weaken parochial and German-language schools and was an "Americanizing" attempt.

A businessman-politician, Mayor Brown concentrated on efficient administration and the extension of municipal services. He presided over reforms in the police department, modernization of the sewage system, and creation of an adequate public park system. After his final defeat in 1890, Brown served nine years as city tax commissioner (1893–1902) before retiring again to his carriage firm. He died on 19 June 1908.

SOURCES: *History of Milwaukee, Wisconsin* (Chicago, 1881); Milwaukee *Sentinel*, 20 June 1908; Bayrd Still, *Milwaukee: The History of a City* (Madison, Wis., 1948); *U.S. Biographical Dictionary and Portrait Gallery of Eminent and Self-Made Men* Wisconsin Volume (Chicago, 1877); *Wisconsin Necrology* (prominent obituaries, compiled at State Historical Society on microfilm).

Thomas R. Bullard and *Douglas Bukowski*

BROWNELL, ABNER C. (1813–57), Mayor of Cleveland (1852–55). Politician and banker, Brownell was born in Massachusetts in 1813, and moved to Cleveland in the mid-1840s. He had spent some time in New York, where he was married around 1840. He and his wife Eliza had four children, two of whom died very young. The family was Protestant. Brownell was a dealer in iron and glass for W. A. Otis and Company in Cleveland, 1846–49. He then joined the banking firm of Wick, Otis and Brownell (1849–53). He was president of the New England Society, 1853–54.

A Democrat, Brownell served on the city council, 1849–52. He was elected mayor in 1852 with 1,694 votes; there was no opposition to him. In 1853, he became the first Cleveland mayor elected to a two-year term, defeating Buckley Stedman (Citizen's party) 1,754 to 1,078. Cleveland was growing fast, with over 20,000 people and a mayor-council form of government. Brownell supported the city departments, new schools, new sewers and loans to area railroads. After leaving office, he became a commission merchant and kept the position until his death in 1857.

SOURCES: Wilfred and Miriam R. Alburn, *This Cleveland of Ours*, 4 vols. (Chicago, 1933); William G. Rose, *Cleveland: The Making of a City* (Cleveland, 1950); U.S. Census, 1850, Cleveland.

Thomas R. Bullard

BRUSH, ALEXANDER (1824–92), Mayor of Buffalo (1870–73; 1879–81). An honest, Whiggish politician in the heyday of dirty Republican politics, Brush was born on 8 February 1824 in "Brushland," Delaware County, New York, the fifth child and third son of Jacob Brush (d. 1835) and Phoebe (Cushing) Brush, well-to-do Methodist farmers and millers. Shortly after the birth of his tenth child, Jacob died, leaving his young widow to manage a 600-acre farm. Even though Alexander's education was limited to a few weeks in a country school and one term in a public school, he acquired those traits that would ensure him security and respect in adulthood. When the Brush family moved to Buffalo in 1843, Alexander and two of his brothers established a brickmaking business. By the 1880s, the firm was producing over 20 million bricks a year.

In the 1860s, Brush applied his business acumen to civic affairs. Although his father and grandfather had been Democrats, Alexander aligned himself with Whigs and helped to establish the Republican party in western New York. Between 1860 and 1866, he served as an alderman on the Buffalo Common Council. In 1867, he was elected street commissioner, one of only two Republicans elected during that Democratic year. His effectiveness and popularity ensured his nomination and election to the mayoralty in 1870. In 1872, Brush carried his entire ticket into office. Buffalo's population in 1870 was 129,576, and in 1880, 155,134; they city had a mayor-council form of government. Brush peremptorily

declined renomination in order to direct his full attention to the affairs of his business. But in 1879, in the midst of a party scandal, the Republicans entreated Brush to clean up the local political arena (and his party's image) by running again for mayor. Brush reluctantly agreed, was elected, and served until 1881. He introduced no major changes in city operations during his six years as mayor; his administration was not "noted for any aggressive or radical efforts at reform." His integrity, however, was impeccable, and that was enough to ensure his election.

Brush spent the last decade of his life in political retirement. He contributed to various philanthropic groups and lived contentedly with his second wife until his death on 1 June 1892.

SOURCES: H. Perry Smith, ed., *History of the City of Buffalo and Erie County* (Syracuse, N.Y., 1884); Truman C. White, ed., *A Descriptive Work on Erie County, New York* (Boston, 1898).

W. Andrew Achenbaum

BRUSH, JARED M. (1814–95), Mayor of Pittsburgh (1869–72). Brush, born on 10 October 1814 in Pittsburgh, was left an orphan at the age of four and was bound out. He was apprenticed to a carpenter and worked at that trade, and became a contractor. He married Sarah Ward Dithridge, who bore him nine children, only two of whom lived past childhood. The family was Protestant.

Brush got into politics early and in 1842–45 was overseer of the poor in Pitt Township. He then became a deputy sheriff and agent for the Guardians of the Poor and in 1851 became clerk of courts. Three years later, he got into the business of ironmaking and was elected a councilman. He was active in helping organize the Republican party and was the last survivor of the committee on arrangements for the 1856 national convention in Pittsburgh.

During the Civil War, Brush was active in war work and served on the Sanitary Commission in order to provide rest, food and medical care for troops passing through the city. In the general election of 1868, he defeated the incumbent mayor, James Blackmore, Independent (q.v.), 7,287 to 5,738.

With a Republican majority in both councils, Brush launched a program of street construction and other improvements and built a new city hall. He proposed a system of city parks totaling 600 acres. The plan passed but was quickly repealed because of its cost. In October 1871, he sent Pittsburgh firemen by special train to fight the great Chicago fire.

Unable to succeed himself, Brush served successively as school director, poor farm superintendent, and clerk in the treasurer's and assessor's offices. He was appointed police magistrate in 1888. Brush died on 3 November 1895.

SOURCES: Allen H. Kerr, "The Mayors and Recorders of Pittsburgh, 1816–1951" (unpublished manuscript, Historical Society of Western Pennsylvania, Pittsburgh, 1952); Pittsburgh *Press, Gazette*, both 5 November 1895.   *George Swetnam*

BRYANT, ANDREW JACKSON (1832–82), Mayor of San Francisco (1875–79). Bryant, San Francisco mayor during a period of violent nativist and vigilante agitation in the late 1870s, was born the son of a farmer in Carroll County, New Hampshire, on 30 October 1832. Bryant's father, descended from British colonist ancestry, died when Bryant was four. With little education, Bryant traveled to the goldfields of California in 1850. After a brief, luckless period of prospecting, he became city marshal of Benecia, California, from 1851 to 1853. Afterwards, a short attempt at retailing in Sacramento was followed by success in the insurance and express businesses in San Francisco. Bryant's prosperity ushered him into politics. Always a Democrat, he nevertheless remained loyal to the Union during the Civil War. In 1865, he chaired a committee to appoint a new state supreme court justice. The next year, President Andrew Johnson commissioned him a naval officer until 1870, although Bryant never left port.

Bryant served two terms as mayor, drawing support from Democrats and workingmen's political groups. In 1875, his 9,792 votes topped the 9,486 of Republican candidate Charles Clayton and the 4,106 of People's Independent party nominee A. S. Hallidie. In 1877, Bryant tallied 17,517 votes against Republicans and Taxpayers candidate Monroe Ashbury's 15,856. As candidate, Bryant spoke out for an eight-hour day and for relocation of the city's Chinese population.

Bryant's support for labor demands secured his election to office, but those demands soon were pushed to extremes. The depression of the 1870s, which was especially acute in California as a result of drought and mining busts, had already stirred up some labor agitation, and in the summer of 1877 matters got out of hand. Thirty thousand unemployed men had flocked to the city of around 220,000 residents, and demonstrations against the Chinese and other targets had become frequent. Unable to control the lower class crowds, Bryant tacitly permitted a vigilante committee composed of more affluent citizens to restore order. Bryant's tactic reflected his increasing "moderation" on workers' issues and demonstrated his inability to control either the rioters or the vigilantes. The mayor's moderation became more apparent during his second term when he persuaded the state legislature to impose a "gag order" which curbed

public gatherings. Although workingmen had already begun to temper their protests, this action by Bryant undercut his basis of support. Moreover, frequent rumors of scandal had always tainted his reputation. These factors helped to explain his disappearance from politics after 1879.

After his mayoral term expired, Bryant returned to preside over his insurance business. On 11 May 1882, he drowned in San Francisco Bay after falling from a ferry.

SOURCES: Hubert Howe Bancroft, "Andrew Jackson Bryant," n.d. (MS, Bancroft Library, University of California, Berkeley); Gunther Barth, *Instant Cities: Urbanization and the Rise of San Francisco and Denver* (New York, 1975); William J. Heintz, *San Francisco's Mayors 1850–1880* (Woodside, Calif., 1975); Alonzo Phelps, *Contemporary Biography of California's Representative Men* (San Francisco, 1881), vol. 2.

John M. Findlay

BRYANT, EDWIN (1805–69), *Alcalde* of San Francisco (1847). Second American *alcalde* of San Francisco in the prestatehood pre-1850 period (the *alcalde* was a Mexican judicial and executive office that preceded and would become the American mayoralty), Bryant was born in Massachusetts in 1805, worked as a journalist in Kentucky, and then led a large overland expedition from Independence, Missouri, to California in 1846. The American conquest of California was taking place while his group was on the way, and Bryant joined up with Fremont's volunteers.

The American military governor General Stephen Kearny appointed Bryant *alcalde* to replace Lieutenant Washington Bartlett (*q.v.*) on 22 February 1847. Bryant made full use of the broad powers of an American *alcalde*, which stretched even to the granting of building lots in the town. He extended the town survey to include beach and water property, which the governor, General Kearny, renounced in favor of the town. Bryant had a clear vision of future greatness for San Francisco and for the Pacific Coast—a vision not always shared by other Anglo-Americans at the time. He saw San Francisco as a future commercial city and worked on harbor improvements. However, he left California to return east on 2 June 1847, and serve as witness at Fremont's court-martial.

Bryant is best remembered for his important chronicle of the period, *What I Saw in California* (1848), which remains a chief historical source on the tumultuous "events of 1846–47," the migrant route via South Pass (he had left letters for the Donner Party which might have saved them), and political, social and economic details of early California history in the Americanization period—the Bear Flag revolt, military operations, the missions, and the growth of the San Francisco and Los Angeles regions, even before the Gold Rush began.

Bryant returned during the Gold Rush of 1849 and stayed for about five years, becoming a prominent citizen, politician, and property owner. He served as one of the two first wardens of Grace Church (Protestant Episcopal). Returning finally to Kentucky, Bryant resumed journalism. He served in the Civil War in a California battalion and died in Louisville in 1869 at the age of sixty-four.

SOURCES: E. Bryant, *What I Saw in California . . .* (New York, 1848) (also published under the title, *Rocky Mountain Adventures*); F. Soule, J. H. Gihon, and J. Nisbet, *The Annals of San Francisco* (New York, 1855).

Peter d'A. Jones

BRYSON, JOHN, SR. (1819–1907), Mayor of Los Angeles (1888–89). One of the shortest-term mayors of Los Angeles, Bryson was born on 20 June 1819 in Mount Joy, Pennsylvania. One of thirteen children, he received no formal education but was apprenticed at age ten to a cabinetmaker. Bryson followed this trade until age thirty. In 1843, he married Emeline Sentman of Pennsylvania, and they had six sons and two daughters.

In 1847, Bryson and his family moved to Ohio where he opened his own lumberyard. In 1851, Bryson moved to Muscatine, Iowa, and then to Washington, Iowa, in 1856. Within a few years, his business prospered. He owned twelve lumberyards in Iowa and Kansas and a supply yard in Chicago. Bryson and his family moved to Los Angeles in 1879 and quickly became involved in construction and real estate speculation.

In 1888, Los Angeles had approximately 50,000 people and a mayor-council form of government. Bryson was not an active politician, but he was persuaded to accept the Democratic nomination for mayor. He won on 3 December 1888 by getting 5,351 votes to his Republican opponent's (D. E. Miles) 4,491. Bryson's victory marked a rare back-to-back capture of the mayoralty by the Democrats in a predominantly Republican city. His achievement was more noteworthy considering the collapse of the land boom by late 1888. Bryson's victory was short-lived. Voters had just approved a city charter giving Los Angeles home rule. A new city election was required and was held on 22 February 1889. Bryson was defeated by Republican Henry T. Hazard (*q.v.*) who won 5,322 votes to Bryson's 2,991 and the Prohibitionist Toberman's (*q.v.*) 1,268. Bryson's defeat stemmed from voter dissatisfaction with alleged graft in his administration, the town's inability to revitalize the real estate boom, and the reassertion of the town's Republican majority.

Bryson ran for office on a platform of fiscal conservatism and vice control—especially of the saloons and the liquor traffic. However, voter dissatisfaction quickly spread in a time of economic downturn when his fellow Democrats were unwilling to fulfill campaign pledges. Like other Angelenos, Bryson used business success as a catapult to political success and then employed his political notoriety to achieve greater financial returns after he left office.

After his defeat, Bryson continued his lumberyard and construction activities and branched out into banking, organizing one local institution and becoming an officer of two more. Bryson died of arterial sclerosis on 11 October 1907, leaving behind an estate valued at over $300,000. He was buried in Los Angeles.

SOURCES: James Miller Gwinn, *Historical and Biographical Record of Los Angeles and Vicinity* (Chicago, 1902); Los Angeles *Times*, 1888–89; William A. Spalding, *History of Los Angeles City and County, California* (Los Angeles, 1931), vols. 1–3; J. G. Warner, *An Illustrated History of Los Angeles County, California* (Chicago, 1889).

Christopher Cocoltchos

BUCK, GEORGE STURGES (1875–1931), Mayor of Buffalo (1918–21). A conservative lawyer and the first mayor of Buffalo under the new city commission plan of 1916, Buck was born in Chicago on 10 February 1875, the son of Roswell R. Buck (1826–1904), a grain elevator owner, and Maria Catherine (Barnes) Buck (d. 1905), both old-stock Americans. The youngest of three children, Buck was a sickly child and did not attend school until the age of nine, but completed grade school in four years, attended high school, and graduated from Yale in 1896. He then moved to Buffalo and attended the Buffalo Law School, graduating in 1898, and immediately began a law practice. Buck married Louise Hussey on 6 October 1903, and they had four children. The Bucks attended the First Presbyterian Church, and Buck was one of its deacons. He also was Sunday School superintendent at the Welfare Hall Settlement and a member of various legal fraternities.

Buck's political career began in 1899 with his election to the Erie County Republican Committee (serving until 1903). He was a member of the board of supervisors, 1903–11, and was county auditor, 1912–17. He was also a lecturer at the law school, specializing in contract law. He was elected mayor in 1917 as a Republican, defeating the popular Democrat, incumbent Louis Fuhrmann (*q.v.*), 38,144 to 27,391. In 1921, he lost his bid for a second term, being defeated by Frank X. Schwab (*q.v.*), 62,531 to 59,974. Although Schwab was a Democrat, the election was officially nonpartisan. Buffalo had

506,775 people in 1920 and a new mayor-commission form of government.

As mayor, Buck supported war bond drives and other wartime efforts. After 1918, he backed measures to help the returning soldiers. He reduced streetcar fares and favored Prohibition. He strongly believed the commission system was the best for the city, although some party leaders disagreed. On the one hand, he used the police to suppress Socialist rallies and on the other he prevented the police themselves from joining the American Federation of Labor. His own poor health and public hostility to Prohibition caused his defeat in 1921. He continued to practice law until his death on 5 July 1931.

SOURCES: Buffalo *Sunday Times*, 20 July 1924; William R. Cutler, *Genealogical and Family History of Central New York*, 3 vols. (New York, 1912).

Thomas R. Bullard

BUHL, CHRISTIAN H. (1812–94), Mayor of Detroit (1860–61). The son of a German farmer and merchant, and brother of an earlier mayor of Detroit, Buhl was born in Zelienople, Butler County, Pennsylvania, on 9 May 1812, one of five sons and two daughters of an immigrant German farmer and merchant from Saxony. At an early age, he learned the trade of hatter and at the age of twenty-one headed west. Arriving in Detroit in 1833, he found a hat shop whose owner had recently died. He enlisted the aid of his older brother Frederick Buhl (*q.v.*) to purchase the shop.

The hat business expanded to include the fur trade, and the Buhl brothers traded in furs throughout the Great Lakes area. In 1855, Christian withdrew from the fur and hat business to enter the wholesale hardware trade in partnership with Charles Ducharme. This business prospered and grew into the largest wholesale establishment in its field in the Midwest. In 1871, Buhl and associates purchased the Westerman Iron Works at Sharon, Pennsylvania, and renamed it the Sharon Iron Works. They produced bar, sheet iron, pigs, and nails. In subsequent years, Christian Buhl was one of the principal founders of the Detroit Copper and Brass Rolling Mills, Peninsula Car Works, Michigan Stove Company, Michigan Malleable Iron Company, Buhl Stamping Company, and Second National Bank of Detroit. He was also an active investor in railroads and real estate.

In 1843 Buhl was married to Caroline DeLong of Utica, New York, and they had five children. Two sons, Frank H. and Theodore, became associated with their father in business.

Buhl was elected an alderman in 1851, and in 1859 he was elected mayor with 3,613 votes over John H. Harmon's 2,815. At the time, Detroit's population had reached 45,327. It was still a period of expansion with new street openings, sewer line extensions, paving, and licensing problems dominating the council business, although a serious financial recession slowed development considerably. Buhl's administration continued to move from the volunteer fire department toward the paid professional system. During his term of office, Buhl entertained Prince Albert on a visit to Detroit. An ardent protectionist and a Republican from the beginning of that party, Buhl declined to continue in public office after the conclusion of his term. Buhl was the second member of his family to serve as mayor of Detroit, his brother Frederick (1806–90), having filled that post in 1848.

Buhl was active in civic affairs and was recognized as a philanthropist. He presented a large and valuable law library to the University of Michigan and was one of the original promoters of an art museum for the city. He died at his home in Detroit on 23 January 1894.

SOURCES: Detroit *Free Press*, 23 January 1894; Silas Farmer, *The History of Detroit and Michigan . . .* (Detroit, 1889); *Journal of the Proceedings of the Common Council of the City of Detroit*, 1860 and 1861; Scrapbooks, Burton Historical Collection, Detroit Public Library.

John Cumming

BUHL, FREDERICK (1806–90), Mayor of Detroit (1848). Buhl was another of the one-term businessmen-mayors who, along with prominent lawyers and doctors, characterized much of Detroit's early leadership. Unlike many of the mayors, however, Buhl's parents were of German rather than Yankee-English origin. The second son of seven children, Buhl was born on 27 November 1806, in Zelienople, Butler County, Pennsylvania to parents who had emigrated from Saxony. His father was a farmer as well as a leading businessman in their section of western Pennsylvania. It was a rural area, and the Buhl children had little opportunity for education. At the age of sixteen, Frederick left for Pittsburgh to learn the jeweler's trade.

In 1833, with his brother Christian (*q.v.*), he moved to Detroit. They established a wholesale and retail house for the sale of furs, hats, and caps. Arriving at a time when the city was experiencing a population explosion and economic boom, F. and C. H. Buhl Company prospered quickly. After his brother's retirement, Buhl joined in partnership with Henry Newland, another merchant. Frederick had meanwhile married Matilda Beatty (d. 1884), from his home county in Pennsylvania, and the couple had four sons and two daughters. When Newland withdrew from their business to form his own company, Buhl entered into partnership with his sons. Their company became one of the largest shippers of furs in the country.

The Buhl family belonged to the elite Fort Street Presbyterian Church, and Frederick long held a prominent place among local capitalist entrepreneurs. Buhl was a director of the State Bank of Michigan, of the Second National Bank of Detroit, and president of the Michigan Department of the American Life Association. He joined in an association with other wealthy businessmen in 1840s to build roads west to Lansing and east to Mount Clemens and Utica, where new population growth expanded trade possibilities. He was also president of the Fort Wayne and Elmwood Street Railroad Company. Civic service was common among the community leaders, and Buhl, with James Van Dyke and others, helped form the first fire department; he also served as trustee and president of the board of Harper Hospital, organized primarily by prominent Presbyterians.

In 1845 and 1846, Buhl was an alderman, representing the First Ward. In 1848, he agreed to accept the Whig party's nomination for mayor. He ran against Democrat Daniel Goodwin and won by a majority of 80 votes; the Democrats elected only one alderman that year. The political boundaries had just been revised to include a Seventh Ward, and Buhl sat with and presided over the fourteen-member common council. The city charter also charged him with presiding over the mayor's court.

By 1848, Detroit had about 20,000 people and was growing. Major concerns before the mayor and council were expansion of city services, keeping the public order, fiscal management, and economy in government. Buhl did not run for reelection, but his brother Christian served in the mayor's office in 1860–61.

Buhl saw his sons and nephews prosper and take important roles in the city. He continued an active interest in business affairs almost until his death on 12 May 1890.

SOURCES: Clarence M. Burton, *The City of Detroit, Michigan, 1701–1922* (Detroit, 1922), vol. 5; Frederick Carlisle, comp., *Wayne County Historical and Pioneer Society Chronography* (Detroit, 1890); Silas Farmer, *The History of Detroit and Michigan* (Detroit, 1889), vol. 2.
JoEllen Vinyard

BUHRER, STEPHEN (1825–1907), Mayor of Cleveland (1867–71). German-American mayor and liquor merchant, born in Lawrence, Ohio on 26 December 1825, Buhrer was the son of Johann Caspar and Anna Maria (Miller) Buhrer, German-born Quaker immigrants. The youngest of two children, Buhrer was raised in the community of Zoar, where the family had moved in 1827. The Quaker life-style (Stephen could only attend school at night) was restrictive, and he later claimed that this period of his life taught him the value of tolerance. He came to Cleveland in 1844 but left later that year for Detroit, where he opened a saloon. Losing money within the year, he toured the Midwest with a menagerie during

1845. He returned to Cleveland in 1847 and opened a ships' supply store. He operated a cooperage firm 1852–53 and in 1853 started a highly successful liquor business. His next-door neighbor was the young John D. Rockefeller. In 1848, Buhrer married Eva Maria Schneider (1828–89), and they had three children. Buhrer himself was a Mason and a religious liberal.

A strong Democrat, Buhrer served on the city council, 1855–57, supporting civic improvements. He served again in 1863–67, strongly supporting the Civil War. In 1867, he was elected mayor, defeating Peter Thatcher (Republican) 4,833 to 4,377. In 1869, he was reelected, with 6,530 votes to 3,872 for Clark (Republican) and 1,041 for Abbey (Temperance party). In 1871, he was defeated by Frederick Pelton (Republican) 7,085 to 5,939. Cleveland had 92,829 people by 1870 and a mayor-council form of government.

Buhrer believed in government for all the people and thus opposed organized political machines. He supported new jails, parks, improved police and fire departments, and other civic improvements. Oddly enough, despite his opposition to machines, critics charged that he had managed to gain personal control over the police force, and this issue probably led to his defeat in 1871. His only later political career was as director of the House of Corrections Board (1883–86). A year after his first wife died, Buhrer married Marguerite Paterson (1890). He spent his later years with his liquor business until his death from a sudden heart attack on 8 December 1907.

SOURCES: J. F. Brennan, ed., *A Biographical Cyclopedia and Portrait Gallery of Distinguished Men With an Historical Sketch of the State of Ohio* (Cincinnati, 1879); *Cleveland, Past and Present* (Cleveland, 1869); Cleveland *Plain Dealer*, 9 December 1907; *Memorial Record of the County of Cuyahoga and City of Cleveland, Ohio* (Chicago, 1894); W. Scott Robinson, ed., *History of the City of Cleveland* (Cleveland, 1887).
Thomas R. Bullard

BURKE, GLENDY (1805–79), Acting Mayor of New Orleans (8–28 June 1865). Prominent merchant who served as mayor of New Orleans for three weeks in June 1865, Burke was born in Baltimore, Maryland, on 31 December 1805. His grandfather, James Burke, of Irish Presbyterian gentry stock, had migrated to Maryland in about 1760. Glendy's father, David Burke, was engaged in the Baltimore shipping industry.

Glendy, whose first name was taken from his mother's Scottish family name, moved to New Orleans in 1826 seeking employment. He worked for commission merchant Abijah Fisk, and within five years Burke bought him out. Burke's business expanded rapidly, but in the Panic of 1837 he was faced with $3 million in debts which he paid off in ten years. By the 1850s, Burke had become a millionaire for the second time, owned sugar and cotton plantations and 1,000 slaves, was involved in banking as well as his business, and had been elected to the council of the city's Second Municipality and served two terms in the state legislature. Devoted to philanthropy and education, Burke helped to get the first public school system written into Louisiana law in the 1840s and served on the Charity Hospital Board of Administrators. He was a Whig and later a Know-Nothing. He was married three times—to Czarina Eliza Rogers of Baltimore (d. 1842); to Annie Hooke of Havana, Cuba (d. 1854); and to Victoria Catherine deBolle of Philadelphia (d. 1904). Three children survived him: Corneal, George B., and Mojesta Burke Carradine. Reared a Presbyterian and later becoming an Episcopalian, he became a lay minister in the Church of the New Jerusalem (the Swedenborgian faith).

After Louisiana was organized under Lincoln's Reconstruction Plan in 1865, Governor James Madison Wells appointed Dr. Hugh Kennedy (q.v.) as mayor. Dr. Kennedy named Glendy Burke chairman of the bureau of finance. But military commander Nathaniel P. Banks, in a power struggle with Governor Wells, replaced Kennedy with Colonel Samuel Miller Quincy (q.v.) on 5 May 1865. A change in command brought General Edward R. S. Canby to New Orleans, who reinstated Kennedy. Glendy Burke was asked to serve as mayor temporarily until Kennedy, who was in Washington, D.C., seeking presidential support, returned. Burke was mayor from 8 June until 28 June 1865. At that time, New Orleans (contiguous with Orleans Parish) had a population of approximately 170,000 and an aldermanic form of government. His three weeks in office were memorable for his orders to remove from their offices by force the state auditor and registrar of voters who had formerly been protected by General Banks against the governor's dismissal order.

The Civil War ruined Burke financially. He had only a modest income in his last years. He died on 21 June 1879 and was buried in the Girod Street Cemetery. Later, his remains were moved to Hope Mausoleum in New Orleans.

SOURCES: ''Gallery of Industry and Enterprise: Glendy Burke of New Orleans, Merchant,'' *DeBow's Southern and Western Review*, XI O.S. (August 1851); John S. Kendall, *History of New Orleans* (Chicago, 1922), vol. 1; New Orleans *Daily Picayune*, 22 June 1879; Works Program Administration, ''Administrations of the Mayors of New Orleans, 1803 to 1936'' (New Orleans, 1940). This manuscript is located in the main branch of the New Orleans Public Library.

Joy J. Jackson

BURKE, THOMAS A. (1898–1971), Mayor of Cleveland (1945–53). Mayor of Cleveland and U.S. senator, Burke was an Irish-American Catholic, born in Cleveland 30 October 1898, the son of physician Thomas A. Burke and Lillian (McNeil) Burke, both Catholics of Irish descent. Burke attended St. Agnes Parochial School, Loyola High School, Holy Cross College (Worcester, Massachusetts) and Western Reserve University Law School, graduating from Western Reserve in 1923. His college studies were interrupted by service in the U.S. Army in 1917–18. On 25 June 1924, he married a Catholic, Josephine Lyon, and they had two children.

Burke was assistant prosecuting attorney for Cuyahoga County, 1930–36, and special counsel to the State's Attorney's Office (Vote Fraud Division), 1937–41. He also belonged to the law firm of McConnell, Blackmore, Cory and Burke, 1937–41. He was named the city's law director in 1941 and was still serving in that post in 1944 when Mayor Frank Lausche (q.v.) was elected to the U.S. Senate. Since this position is the equivalent of vice-mayor, Burke automatically became mayor. He was elected to a full term in his own right as a Democrat in 1945, defeating Ray Miller (Republican) 125,596 to 59,707. In 1947, he was successfully reelected, defeating Eliot Ness 168,566 to 86,042. Two years later he won again, 158,115 votes to Republican Franklin A. Polk's 77,921, and in 1951 he was returned to city hall, defeating William J. McDermott 114,198 to 92,520. Cleveland had 914,808 people by 1950 and a mayor-council form of government.

As mayor, Burke worked to reorganize the transit system, beautify the lake front, and improve the downtown region. He won approval of a new charter giving him more control over the police and fire departments. Burke usually supported organized labor without antagonizing business leaders. In 1953, he resigned to serve in the U.S. Senate, where he supported measures to aid cities. He was defeated in the 1954 election and returned to his legal practice in Cleveland. His wife died on 26 October 1964 and on 15 December 1965 he married a widow, Mrs. Evelyn Sedgwick. He died on 5 December 1971.

SOURCES: Cleveland *Plain Dealer*, 6 December 1971; *Current Biography* (New York, 1954).

Thomas R. Bullard

BURNET, ISAAC G. (1784–1856), Mayor of Cincinnati (1819–31). First popularly-elected mayor after Cincinnati's incorporation as a city in 1819, Burnet was born in Newark, New Jersey, on 7 July 1784, the son of Continental Congress member Dr. William Burnet (1730–91), a New Jersey native of Scottish parents, and Gertrude Governeur Burnet. The family was Protestant. The fourth of five sons, Isaac received an excellent tutored education as a youth. In about 1804, he moved to Cincinnati to study law with his older brother Jacob and within two years became a member of the Hamilton County bar. In 1807, he married Catherine Gordon, whose family had moved to Cincinnati shortly after her birth in Fayette County, Kentucky, in 1791. Soon after his marriage, Burnet moved to Dayton, Ohio, north of Cincinnati. Over the next nine years, he became one of Dayton's leading citizens, serving in turn as county prosecuting attorney, member of the town council, and president of that body. Burnet also published the weekly newspaper, the *Ohio Sentinel*, 1810–13, and joined in a partnership to publish the *Ohio Republican*, 1814–15. In 1816, he returned to Cincinnati, where Jacob, his third and last child, was born in the following year, joining another son, D. S. (1808) and a daughter, Mary T. (c. 1812). Burnet set up a private law practice in Cincinnati, became a partner publishing the newspaper *Liberty Hall*, and was named in 1817 as a director of the branch office of the Bank of the United States.

In 1819, with its population approaching 9,000, Cincinnati held its first election as a chartered city. The popularly elected council chose Burnet as mayor, a post he would hold until 1831. With the first popular, direct election of mayor in 1827, Burnet was again victorious and defeated Elisha Hotchkiss, 1,004 to 984 votes. In his next and last mayoral race in 1829, Burnet, with 1,042 votes, defeated Andrew Mack (*q.v.*) (784 votes) and ex-*town* mayor William Corry (*q.v.*) (263 votes).

A physical disability forced Burnet to use crutches most of his life. His great firmness of character, however, compensated for this bodily deficiency, and he personally averted several public riots while mayor of Cincinnati. Burnet's administrations have been characterized as without the slightest hint of corruption. As mayor, he presided over numerous innovations in urban government, including the creation of a hook and ladder company, a public hospital, an underground sewer system, and public schools. As a politician, Burnet became known for his anti-Jacksonian views. In 1831, he retired from the mayor's office, although he probably could have been reelected.

In 1833, Burnet was appointed clerk of the supreme court of Hamilton County and held this office until 1851. He died in 1856.

SOURCES: Charles Cist, *Cincinnati in 1841: Its Early Annals and Future Prospects* (Cincinnati, 1841); James A. Green, *The Burnet Family* (Cincinnati, 1938); Charles T. Greve, *Centennial History of Cincinnati and Representative Citizens*, 2 vols. (Chicago, 1904); Isabella Burnet Neff, *Dr. William Burnet and His Sons, Jacob, Isaac and David* (Charlottesville, Va., 1938); Harry R. Stevens, "Cincinnati's Founding Fathers: Isaac Burnet,"

Bulletin of the Historical and Philosophical Society of Ohio 10 (July 1952).   *Gary Kocolowski*

BURR, EPHRAIM WILLARD (1809–94), Mayor of San Francisco (1856–59). Three-term, reform mayor of San Francisco, and last mayor of the Gold Rush decade, Burr was a New Englander, like his two predecessors, born in Rhode Island on 7 March 1809, the son of Nathan Miller Burr and Lucy Burr. Burr worked for a New England whaling company which sent him west in 1849 to recruit crews. The task was impossible: whaling was in decline, and ports of call like San Francisco or Honolulu proved too attractive to sailors, who often jumped ship. Burr became a merchant instead: he bought an empty ship and turned it into a store in San Francisco—Burr, Mattoon and Company (October 1850). His family arrived in 1852. Later, he established the first savings bank on the Pacific Coast, the San Francisco Accumulating Fund (evolving into a savings and loan society), known in town simply as the Clay Street Bank. Burr was a genius in making money. He was also a master of cheeseparing economy; probity and thrift were his hallmark.

Elected to the mayoralty an unprecedented three times in a row by the Vigilantes' People's party, 1856–59, Burr seems to have first been politicized by the death of his nineteen-year-old son—one of three victims of cholera in 1855. On 26 October 1855, Burr petitioned the common council to regulate the pollution of open streams in San Francisco by slaughterhouses.

Burr's election on 4 November 1856 was clean—and as many as 10,000 armed men at the polling booths made it so. He was the candidate of a crusading mass party, the first mayor to be elected under the new Consolidation Act which combined county and city government. That act had been written by two Know-Nothing men, William Hawkes and Horace Hawes. Its aims had been to economize as well as to clean up local administration. The city was divided into twelve wards, each with a supervisor. A board of supervisors, unpaid, and a president (replacing the former mayor's office, but with much less power) were to administer the city-county area. All officers had to post bonds of varying amounts ($2,000 for the president of the board of supervisors). Certainly, Burr managed to economize under the new charter. Combined county-city expenditures for 1854–55 had been $2,646,190; Burr's expenditures totaled only $353,292 for 1856–57. He was reelected with a big majority on 3 September 1857 (despite a shift towards the Democrats in the state) and again (not so strongly) on 1 September 1858.

Clearly, city services were cut to achieve Burr's economies. For instance, street lighting was reduced in order to cut monthly bills from the San Francisco Gas Company. Burr doubled up on jobs, making the supervisors act *ex-officio* as commissioners for the city's funded debt and giving more work to the city attorney to avoid outside fees. In addition, the city treasurer was now to be paid a regular, fixed salary. (Previously, he had extracted a percentage of all city financial transactions.) Burr tried to improve the water supply but like Mayor Charles Brenham (*q.v.*) before him had little success.

On the eve of the Civil War and as news of the rich Comstock Lode (Nevada silver) was about to engulf San Francisco with yet another rush of growth, Burr was replaced by an Englishman, a member also of the (Know-Nothing) People's party, Henry Teschemaker (*q.v.*). Burr devoted himself to the savings and loan business he had founded, ran a fire insurance company for five years, doubling its investment, and loaned money to Andrew S. Hallidie's cable car company (which began operation in San Francisco, 1873), saving it from failure. He finally retired in 1879. He was forced out after charges that he skimmed off 5 percent commissions when handling navy paymaster's certificates. This was the only blotch on his reputation.

Burr emerged at the sprightly age of eighty-two to protest the city extending Van Ness Avenue through his property in 1891. He died in San Francisco on 20 July 1894, leaving a carefully amassed fortune of $6 million.

SOURCES: Hubert Howe Bancroft, *Works, History of California* (San Francisco, 1886), vols. 18–24; W. F. Heintz, *San Francisco's Mayors* (Woodside, Calif., 1975); J. S. Hittell, *History of the City of San Francisco* (San Francisco, 1878); "Resignation of E. W. Burr of the Clay Street Bank," *San Francisco Real Estate Circular* (December 1878); San Francisco *Examiner,* 22 July 1894; San Francisco *Chronicle,* 22 July 1894; "Savings Bank Burr and His Crooked Commissions," *Coast Review* (November 1877); Benjamin C. Wright, *Banking in California* (San Francisco, 1910).

Peter d'A. Jones

BURTON, HAROLD H. (1888–1964), Mayor of Cleveland (1931–32, 1935–40). Republican mayor, U.S. senator, and Supreme Court justice, born on 22 June 1888, in Jamaica Plains, Massachusetts, Burton was the son of Alfred E. Burton (1857–1935), an old-stock Yankee engineer, professor, and dean at MIT, and Gertrude (Hitz) Burton (d. 1895), of Swiss ancestry. The younger of two sons, Harold Burton received his B.A. degree from Bowdoin College in 1909 and his LL.B. from Harvard in 1912. After graduation, he moved to Cleveland to practice law. He entered the Army in 1917 and served in France, rising to the rank of captain and being decorated. On his return to Cleveland he taught and practiced law and was active in veterans and civic organizations

and the Unitarian Church (though his father was a Swedenborgian). Burton married Wellesley graduate Selma Smith (1888–1970), on 15 June 1912, and they had four children: Barbara, William, Deborah, and Robert. In 1928, he was elected to the Ohio General Assembly, and in 1929 he was appointed law director of the city of Cleveland. When the voters by referendum overturned the city manager charter to return to a mayor-council form in 1931, Burton served as acting mayor until elections could be held (November 1931–February 1932).

In 1930, Cleveland had 900,429 residents and from 1931 on, a mayor-council form of government. After a few years in private practice, Burton won the mayoralty in 1935 (after defeating Republican incumbent Harry L. Davis [*q.v.*] in the party primary) by 154,199 votes to Democrat Ray T. Miller's (*q.v.*) 115,114. In 1937, Burton won reelection by 144,558 votes to John O. McWilliams' 110,026; in 1939 he was successful again, defeating Democrat John E. O'Donnell by 141,858 to 104,551. An Independent, conservative Republican, Burton centered his first campaign on issues of law and order at a time when the city experienced widespread racketeering. He appointed Eliot Ness as safety director and took a less pro-union position than his predecessor, Harry L. Davis. In subsequent years, Burton's most pressing problem was meeting relief needs in the face of the massive unemployment of the 1930s and the unwillingness of state officials to act. Burton had to struggle against both Democratic Governor Martin Davey and his fellow Republican John W. Bricker. The controversy with Bricker, who did not want to release federal funds for relief purposes, made headlines around the world. Burton won.

Burton resigned as mayor in 1940, upon his election as U.S. senator from Ohio. He remained in the Senate until 1945 when President Truman appointed him an associate justice of the Supreme Court. He retired from the court in 1958 because of Parkinson's disease and died on 28 October 1964.

SOURCES: Mary Frances Berry, *Stability, Security, and Continuity: Mr. Justice Burton and Decision-Making in the Supreme Court, 1945–1958* (Westport, Conn., 1978); Biographical Clipping File, Cleveland Public Library; Harold H. Burton Papers, Library of Congress; Philip W. Porter, *Cleveland: Confused City on a Seesaw* (Columbus, 1976).

James F. Richardson

BUSSE, FRED A. (1866–1914), Mayor of Chicago (1907–11). First Republican mayor of twentieth-century Chicago, born on 3 March 1866 in Chicago, Busse was one of three children of Gustave Busse, a Prussian immigrant, and Caroline (Gross) Busse. His father came to Chicago in 1855 and soon developed a successful hardware business. Fred Busse attended the Ogden and Sheldon schools on the north side of Chicago. After completing his basic education, he first worked for his father and then for the Northwestern Coal Company. A member of the Busse-Reynolds Company, he finally owned the successful Busse Coal and Ice Company. On 6 June 1908, he secretly married Josephine Lee (1878–1961) originally from Toledo, Ohio. Their marriage was childless.

Busse became interested in party politics early and spent most of his adult life in elected office. He held a variety of public posts, serving as town clerk for two years, 1890–92, bailiff of the city court, 1892–94, then Republican representative in Springfield, 1894–97. Next he advanced to the Illinois Senate, 1898–1902. He was selected by the Republican party to run for state treasurer and held that post 1902–1906. President Theodore Roosevelt appointed him postmaster general of Chicago, 1906–1907.

In 1907, Chicago had a growing population of over 2 million, with a weak mayor-strong council form of government. The council consisted of thirty-five wards, with two partisan aldermen per ward, one elected every year. The Republicans felt that Busse would be a strong candidate who would appeal to the many Germans in Chicago and thus defeat the incumbent mayor. This strategy proved correct when on 2 April 1907 Busse won 164,702, or 48.6 percent, to incumbent Democrat Edward F. Dunne's (q.v.) 151,779, or 45.7 percent; Socialist George Koop's 13,429, or 3.9 percent; and Progressive W. A. Brubaker's 6,020, or 1.8 percent.

Busse was the first Chicago mayor to serve a four-year term. A large and kindhearted person, he proved to be a pleasant surprise to many. He completely reorganized the board of education, revamped the traction system, and was the guiding influence behind the development of the Municipal Tuberculosis Sanitarium. While he was mayor, the famous Burnham Plan of 1909 was presented to the city, and to start implementation, Busse established the Chicago Plan Commission. A new city hall was constructed, and Busse made a number of improvements in virtually all city departments. Although he ran a "wide-open" city, he yielded to pressure and set up the Chicago Vice Commission in 1910.

Busse left office in 1911 and suffered from a lingering illness. He died on 9 July 1914 in Chicago. He left an unwelcome surprise for his wife; this wealthy man had spent or given away all of his money. She received only 15 cents and had to become a charwoman.

SOURCES: Donald S. Bradley, "The Historical Trends of the Political Elites in a Metropolitan Central City: The Chicago Mayor," Center for Social Organization Studies Working Paper no. 10 University of Chicago, Department of Sociology, May 1963; Paul Michael Green, "The Chicago Democratic Party 1840–1920: From Factionalism to Political Organization" (Ph.D. dissertation, University of Chicago, 1975); Ralph R. Tingley, "From Carter Harrison II to Fred Busse: A Study of Chicago Political Parties and Personages From 1896–1907" (Ph.D. dissertation, University of Chicago, 1950).
Andrew K. Prinz

BUTLER, AMMI A. R. (1821–1901), Mayor of Milwaukee (1876–78). Butler was born in Fairfield, Vermont, on 4 September 1821, the son of Ammi A. R. Butler, physician, and his wife. The family moved to Alexander, New York, in 1822, and Butler attended public schools and the local "Academy." He studied law in the office of Hiram Barton (in Buffalo) and moved to Milwaukee in 1846. He was one of the city's first lawyers. He was elected county district attorney in 1848, and was reelected in 1850 and 1852. The Whigs offered him the nomination for sheriff in 1850, but he declined, as his loyalties were with the Democrats. In 1853, Butler was one of the promoters of the Milwaukee and LaCrosse Railroad. He served as Milwaukee's superintendent of schools in 1855. Butler was also a member of the general assembly in 1866. His law practice grew to the point where he was forced to take on partners: Frederick C. Winkler in 1867 and Davis Flanders in 1875. In 1846, he had married Orvilla L. Tanner of New York, and they had one son.

Butler had run for mayor in 1858, losing to Republican William Prentiss (q.v.) 4,022 to 2,908. He showed no interest in the post until 1876 when he was nominated by the Democrats and was elected without opposition. Milwaukee had 71,440 people in 1870 and a mayor-bicameral council form of government. Butler believed in civic efficiency and economy, and opposed efforts by party leaders to control patronage. Newspapers of the period constantly printed criticisms by local politicians who complained that Butler was not a forceful or partisan mayor. He did not seek reelection in 1878 and never held a political position in later years. He was considered for the post of state supreme court justice, but he refused to be nominated. Butler retired from his legal practice around the time he became mayor, and he lived quietly in his home until his death on 4 April 1901.

SOURCES: The Biographical Dictionary and Portrait Gallery of Chicago, Wisconsin and the World's Columbian Exposition (Chicago, 1895); The Biographical Dictionary and Portrait Gallery of Eminent and Self-Made Men, Wisconsin Volume (Chicago, 1877); History of Milwaukee, Wisconsin (Chicago, 1881).
Thomas R. Bullard

BYRNE, JANE M. (1934–   ), Mayor of Chicago (1979–   ). First woman mayor, born on 24 May 1934 in Chicago, Byrne is the daughter of Edward Burke, vice president of Inland Steel Corporation, and Katherine Burke. The third oldest of six children of an Irish Catholic family, Jane is a graduate of Queen of All Saints Elementary School and Saint Scholastica High School. She received her B.A. from Barat College (Lake Forest, Illinois) and did graduate work in education at the University of Illinois at Chicago Circle. She was married in 1957 to William P. Byrne, a Marine Corps lieutenant. Fifteen months after the birth of their only child, Kathy, Lieutenant Byrne was killed in a plane crash. In 1978, Byrne married Chicago *Sun-Times* reporter Jay Mc-Mullen.

Byrne's first involvement in Democratic politics came in the 1960 presidential election when she served as secretary-treasurer in John F. Kennedy's Chicago headquarters, becoming acquainted with Mayor Richard J. Daley (*q.v.*). Daley gave her a position with the city's Head Start Program, later naming her a recruiter for the Chicago Committee on Urban Opportunity. In 1968, he appointed Byrne as the first commissioner of the city's Department of Consumer Sales, Weights, and Measures. In 1971, Byrne became a member of the Democratic National Committee. In 1975, Daley made her co-chairman with him of the Cook County Democratic Central Committee, a post she relinquished the year after Daley's death.

In November 1977, Byrne publicly called on Mayor Michael A. Bilandic (*q.v.*), Daley's successor, to roll back taxicab rate increases. Later, she leaked a scathing memo to the press on the rate increase negotiations, charging that Bilandic had improperly "greased" the way for rate hikes. Removed from her office by the mayor, Byrne announced her intention to challenge Bilandic in the approaching Democratic mayoral primary.

By the end of 1978, Byrne's chief issue—a federal grand jury investigation of Bilandic's role in the cabfare increase—had fizzled. But then at 8:00 P.M. on 13 January 1979 the snow began falling and thirty hours later when it stopped, more than twenty inches of new snow had piled up. The city was paralyzed, the rapid transit system was a "rolling disaster," and stranded cars prevented snow plows and salt trucks from doing their work. Bilandic, after the fact, announced an ineffectual snow-removal plan and presented to the public a business-as-usual-face, insisting all was well. Meanwhile, a freeze occurred and the city's side streets, many of which went unplowed for the winter, froze into single-lane, two-rutted ice roads. Garbage went uncollected, and the rat population soared. Vehicles buried in mounds of snow gave some parts of the city the appearance of Napoleon's retreat from Moscow. Bilandic continued to deflect quizzical reporters and angry voters by denying the seriousness of the problem. Immobilized Chicagoans were outraged by what they saw as the mayor's incompetence. The fiery and feisty challenger Jane Byrne charged that under Bilandic Chicago was no longer the "city that works." In her media presentations, she ran as the "rightful heir" to Daley, using sound transcriptions of the late mayor's voice praising her. While the city stumbled along with inadequate services, Byrne revealed instances of political favoritism and graft in city hall. The most damaging concerned a former top Bilandic aide who had been awarded a $90,000 no-bid consulting contract to produce a snow-removal plan, which in fact removed no snow and cut even less ice with the voters. In the February mayoral primary, an extraordinarily large number of annoyed, winter-weary voters slogged through the snow drifts to vote against the incumbent with a stunning result. The Democratic organization's hand-picked favorite and incumbent was repudiated by a groundswell of resentment, and the beneficiary was a political outsider, a relative novice, and a female. A political-machine Goliath had been felled by a short, scrappy blonde and a snowstorm.

The general election that followed in April was anticlimactic: Byrne buried Wallace Johnson, the Republican challenger with 671,189 votes to his 131,262 and captured 82 percent of the popular vote. Elected mayor by the largest majority in the city's history, surpassing Daley's 79.57 percent majority in 1975, Byrne promised the city a "clean machine." She sought a rapprochement with the regular Democratic organization, emphasizing her willingness to allow patronage to remain in the hands of the party. At the same time, however, she presided over a thorough reshuffling of personnel in city hall. Her dismissal of many department heads and clashes with powerful city agencies like the park board suggested a strong desire for independence, as did her rejection of the proposed Crosstown Expressway and Franklin Street Subway, pet projects of both Mayors Daley and Bilandic.

The mayor would face serious problems during the remainder of her four-year term, including public employees who demanded unions and higher wages; some deterioration in the city's bond rating; and the tax loss and the human loss occasioned by Chicago's expected population drop from 3,366,000 in 1970.

SOURCES: "Biography of Mayor Jane M. Byrne," Chicago Municipal Reference Library; Chicago *Sun-Times* 4, 5 April 1980; Chicago Tribune, 5 April 1980; Interview with Robert M. Saigh, assistant press secretary to Mayor Byrne, 5 July 1979.

W. Roger Biles

C

CALDWELL, JOHN ALEXANDER (1852–1927),
Mayor of Cincinnati (1894–97). Scots-Irish, Presbyterian
mayor and lieutenant governor of Ohio, Caldwell, was
born on 21 April 1852 in Fairhaven, Ohio, the son of
Alexander P. Caldwell, Scottish-born and Sarah (Pink-
erton) from Caldwell, North Ireland. Caldwell was educated in the Fairhaven common school system in which
he later taught for two years. He moved to Cincinnati
to read law with Colonel C. W. Moulton, entered the
Cincinnati Law School, and graduated in 1876. Caldwell
married a fellow Presbyterian, Anna Eversull of Cincinnati that same year, and they had three children, John
Alexander Jr., Bessie, and Robert.

Caldwell joined the law firm of Moulton, Johnson and
Levy in 1876. In 1881, with his election as city prosecutor on the Republican ticket, he began a distinguished
career in public service. He was reelected in 1883 and
in 1886 became a police court judge. In 1888, Caldwell
was elected to Congress from the Second District of
Cincinnati. He was reelected in 1890 and in 1892. While
in Washington, Caldwell supported the eight-hour day,
introduced a lottery bill, worked on the reclassification
of postal employees, and served as chairman of the Republican congressional committee. He resigned from his
third term in Congress in 1894 following his election as
mayor of Cincinnati.

Cincinnati in 1894 had over 325,000 people and a
mayor-council form of government. Caldwell ran against
Democrat Isaac J. Miller (11,855), Citizens' party's candidate Theodore C. Horstman (19,912), Populist John
H. Grover (255), and Populist Charles E. Ileff (79).
Caldwell received 26,672 votes, and his plurality of
6,755 was the largest secured by any of Cincinnati's
mayors since 1880. His election was one of the most
decisive city elections in the last quarter of the nineteenth
century and marked the emergence of George B. Cox as
Cincinnati's undisputed political boss. During Mayor
Caldwell's term, the city finally secured the annexation
of several wealthy suburbs.

Caldwell did not serve a second term. In 1899, he was
elected lieutenant governor of Ohio and then became a
judge on the Cincinnati Court of Common Pleas. There
he was instrumental in creating the Cincinnati Juvenile
Court and was the first judge of the Hamilton County

Juvenile Court. He was a Scottish Rite Mason and a
member of the Knights of Pythias, the National Union,
and the Independent Order of Oddfellows. He died in
Cincinnati on 24 May 1927.

*SOURCES: Biographical Cyclopedia and Portrait
Gallery* (Cincinnati, 1981); *Cincinnati's Mayors* (Cin-
cinnati, 1957); Charles T. Greve, *Centennial History of
Cincinnati and Representative Citizens* (Chicago, 1904);
History of Cincinnati and Hamilton County, Ohio (Cin-
cinnati, 1894); Zane L. Miller, *Boss Cox's Cincinnati:
Urban Politics in the Progressive Era* (New York, 1968);
William A. Taylor, *Ohio in Congress, 1803–1901* (Co-
lumbus, 1900).   *Patricia Mooney Melvin*

CALIGUIRI, RICHARD SYLVESTER (1931–   ),
Mayor of Pittsburgh (1977–   ). Caliguiri was born in
Pittsburgh on 20 October 1931, the son of Chris and
Virginia Curto Caliguiri, both second-generation Italian
Catholics (and she half-Hungarian). His father, a former
boxer, worked as a milkman and food distributor. As a
youth, Richard worked with his maternal grandfather,
a landscaping contractor.

After graduation from high school, Caliguiri enlisted
in the Air Force for four years. He then attended Pittsburgh Technical Institute, getting an industrial engineering certificate. His first public job was in the city
Parks Department, where he soon became a works supervisor. Later, he held supervisory posts in the Department of Public Works and became director of the
Department of Parks, and assistant secretary to Mayor
Joseph M. Barr (*q.v.*).

In 1970, he was appointed to fill a vacancy on the city
council, but he showed too much independence and so
was not slated by the party for election the following
year. He entered the primary, led the ticket by 3,000
votes, and then won in the general election. Two years
later he challenged Mayor Pete F. Flaherty (*q.v.*) in the
primary, losing, but only by a respectable 5 percent.

Caliguiri was president *pro tem* of the city council
from January 1976 until March 1977. After it became
known that Mayor Flaherty planned to resign, the council
elected Caliguiri its president only after he agreed not
to enter the primary against a party faithful. He agreed
and assumed the post on 14 March, becoming mayor on

11 April. Following the primary, Caliguiri announced he would run in the general election of 1977 as an Independent. He won and began a four-year term on 3 January 1978. The election results of 1977 were: Caliguiri, 67,848; T. Foerster, 62,911; and Joe Cosetti, 12,494.

Caliguiri proved a popular mayor, active in city improvements, and announced a "Renaissance II," similar to that of Mayor David L. Lawrence (*q.v.*) except that in addition to the alliance with business for large-scale renewal, he gave much attention to neighborhood renewal in rundown areas—improvement with a minimum of destruction.

SOURCES: Eileen Colianni, "Dick Caliguiri: The Mayor Nobody Hates," *Pittsburgh*, June 1979; Pittsburgh *Post-Gazette*, 14 February 1973 and 3 January 1977; Pittsburgh *Press Roto Magazine*, 23 April 1978; David Warner "Likable Caliguiri Ready for Test," 10 April 1977.   *George Swetnam*

CAMDEN, PETER G. (1801–73), Mayor of St. Louis (1846). American party (Know-Nothing) mayor, Camden was born on 23 May 1801 in Amherst County, Virginia. Orphaned as an infant, he was adopted and raised by his aunt and uncle. When Camden was twenty, he began attending Washington College in Virginia and then studied law under the instruction of Chancellor Taylor, a respected jurist of Cumberland County, Virginia. When his legal studies were completed, he moved west and eventually set up a successful law practice in Lincoln County, Kentucky. On 16 February 1830, he married his cousin, Anna B. Camden. In 1837, Camden decided to change both his work and residence; he moved to St. Louis and established a dry goods business, later becoming a commissions merchant.

St. Louis had a population of 51,000 and a mayor-council type of government in 1846 when Camden, as the nominee of the nativist American party, was elected mayor of the city. Under his leadership a regular police department was set up. Until then, there had only been night watchmen and some daytime patrols to safeguard the city. Moreover, at the mayor's strong urging, the city issued $25,000 in bonds to secure the eastern shore of the Mississippi River, a repair that was essential to the continued prosperity of St. Louis commerce. There was also additional improvement of the harbor and further installation of gas streetlights—a task that had been initiated by Camden's predecessor.

Camden remained active in St. Louis affairs after his term as mayor. In addition to his merchandising and commissions businesses, he served as a director of the Marine Insurance Company. Camden died on 23 July 1873 at Jennings, Missouri, a town on the outskirts of St. Louis.

SOURCES: Charles H. Cornwell, *St. Louis Mayors: Brief Biographies* (St. Louis, 1965); Richard Edwards and M. Hopewell, *Edwards' Great West* (St. Louis, 1860); William Hyde and Howard L. Conrad, eds., *Encyclopedia of St. Louis* (New York, 1899); J. T. Scharf, *History of Saint Louis City and County* (Philadelphia, 1883); Walter B. Stevens, *St. Louis: History of the Fourth City 1764–1909* (St. Louis, 1909).

Jeanette C. Lauer

CAPDEVILLE, PAUL (1845–1922), Mayor of New Orleans (1900–1904). Born in New Orleans, on 15 January 1845, Capdeville was the won of Augustin Capdeville, a prominent New Orleans merchant who had left his native France in 1825 for the Crescent City. Paul graduated from the city's Jesuits' College in 1861. At the outbreak of the Civil War, Capdeville enlisted in an infantry regiment called the New Orleans Guard, was taken prisoner by the Union forces in 1863, and was subsequently exchanged and returned to the South. He served the duration of the war in another Confederate unit which surrendered at Greensboro, North Carolina, in 1865. Returning to New Orleans, Capdeville enrolled at Tulane University where he completed his study of law in 1868 and from then to 1892 practiced his profession in his home city. He became president of the Merchants' Insurance Company in 1892, serving until 1905. He married Emma Larue and fathered three sons and two daughters.

New Orleans in 1900 had a population of 287,000 and a mayor-council form of government. Capdeville, who had served in some minor political offices including the state school board and the New Orleans levee board, accepted the nomination for mayor from the regular Democrats to oppose incumbent reform Mayor Walter C. Flower (*q.v.*), whom he defeated by a vote of 19,366 to 13,099. Although the loser, Flower had conducted a successful reform administration; he was rained out by extraordinarily bad weather which inundated parts of town and kept reform voters at home. The flood was so bad that in some instances voters were "carried on the backs of men" or conveyed by roughly made rafts to the polls.

Reformers feared the worst when Capdeville took office in 1900 and with some reason. The new mayor, through state legislation, emasculated the civil service and restored patronage to the regular Democratic organization. Yet, Capdeville also made some positive accomplishments in public building construction, in asserting city control over the public markets, and by continuing efforts set in motion by the reformers for better drainage, sewers, and water in New Orleans. During his administration, the city's privately owned street railways were consolidated into a single system, the New Orleans Railways Company. The Capdeville administration is best remembered for the Charles Riots and the Streetcar Strike of 1901. The riots were triggered in July 1900 when a Negro, Robert Charles, wounded one police officer and killed two others, causing white mobs to rampage indiscriminately after Negroes. A four-day mêlée ensued in which several Negroes and whites were wounded and killed, halted only by an armed force of 1,500 volunteers. The mayor's efforts to prosecute incendiaries of both races met with mixed success. The Streetcar Strike, which began in September 1901, stopped all public transportation for fifteen days and was broken when the state militia was mobilized. The governor intervened to force a settlement which was less than the strikers had demanded.

Capdeville was proud of his French ancestry and sought to establish ties between New Orleans and his father's homeland by work with French-American charities and sailors' relief. This effort won him the Legion of Honor from the French government in 1902. He died in New Orleans on 13 August 1922.

SOURCES: J. R. Kemp, ed., *Martin Behrman of New Orleans, Memoirs of a City Boss* (Baton Rouge, La., 1977); John S. Kendall, *History of New Orleans* (Chicago, 1922), vol. 2; George M. Reynolds, *Machine Politics in New Orleans, 1897–1926* (New York, 1936). *Betsy B. Holli* and *Melvin G. Holli*

CARREL, GEORGE P. (1865–1949), Mayor of Cincinnati (1922–25). Republican mayor, born on 4 September (or December) 1865 in Chillicothe, Ohio, Carrel was the son of nationally known riverboat captain and steamboat-builder Hercules Carrel (1801–90) of British descent and Eleanora K. (Prescott) Carrel. Probably the third of four children, George Carrel was brought to Cincinnati by his family in 1867 and grew up with a consuming interest in baseball. He had many contacts in the sport, which he later used to good advantage in his political career. He also attended Denison University in Granville, Ohio, completed a self-taught law course, and worked in his father's shipyard and as a mate on riverboats. On 31 December 1896, Carrel married Olive Sargent of Cincinnati; there were no children, or at least none who survived. He was an Episcopalian, as she was, and a Mason. Through his baseball connections, Carrel became chief deputy in the county probate office and served there from 1890 to 1917.

Cincinnati in the early 1920s had about 420,000 people with a mayor-council form of government run by the remnants of the George B. Cox Republican machine. In 1917, the machine under the new leadership of Rudolph K. Hynicka, chose Carrel to run for city auditor. He was reelected in 1919, carrying every ward and receiving the largest majority accorded to any candidate in a city election up to that time. When Mayor John Galvin (*q.v.*)

withdrew as a candidate for reelection in 1921 because of ill health, Carrel was the machine choice, in part because the poor state of municipal finances suggested that a candidate with experience as city auditor might be able to find a way to avoid municipal bankruptcy.

Carrel defeated Dr. Charles L. Bonifield, his Democratic opponent, 69,547 to 41,061, and two minor candidates so that he had an absolute majority of the vote cast. The elected council was also overwhelmingly Republican. State statutes limited total tax levies, the taxpayers refused additional bond issues, and Carrel was also opposed to increased indebtedness which would bring more interest charges. The council passed an ordinance to increase gas rates, and when it became known that Hynicka from his New York office had told the council what to do, there was a public outcry. Carrel vetoed the increase, but the council passed it over his veto. As political dissension mounted and city services deteriorated, the reform element again was aroused. This time the organization of the Charter Committee under the leadership of Murray Seasongood (*q.v.*) and others secured the adoption of a city manager type of government by a large majority. Thus began one of the longest municipal reform movements in American history.

After leaving the mayoralty, Carrel retired and spent much of his time traveling and hunting throughout the United States. He died in Cincinnati on 3 May 1949 and was buried there.

SOURCES: Cincinnati *Enquirer*, 4 May 1949; Cincinnati *Post*, 3 May 1949; Cincinnati *Times-Star*, 3 May 1949; Lewis A. Leonard, ed., *Greater Cincinnati and Its People, A History* (Cincinnati, 1927). *George B. Engberg*

CASE, WILLIAM (1818–62), Mayor of Cleveland (1850–52). First Cleveland-born mayor, Case was born in that city on 10 August 1818, the son of Leonard Case, Sr. (1786–1864), broker, real estate executive, lawyer, and philanthropist of German parentage, and Elizabeth (Gaylord) Case from Connecticut. The elder of two children, Case attended public schools and two years of college. The family was Protestant. Poor health led to his leaving school but convinced him of the need to follow outdoor activities (walking, hunting, and fishing) to preserve his physical well-being. He entered his father's varied businesses, earning enough money to have retired at an early age, yet preferring to work. He organized the Cleveland, Painesville and Ashtabula Railroad, and was one of its executives, 1853–58. He also was vice-president of the Lake Shore Railroad. Case never married; he spent his spare time supporting social and artistic organizations. He organized the famed "Ark," a literary club that met in his office. He was a director of Cleveland University.

Case served as an alderman, 1846–50 (president of the council, 1849–50). A Whig, he was elected mayor in 1850, defeating Democrat W. Harrington 1,655 to 743. He was reelected in 1851, this time on the "People's" ticket, with 1,152 votes to 787 for Democrat Robert Parks, and one each for J. Stoddard and Charles Lloyd. Cleveland had 17,034 people in 1850 and a mayor-council form of government. As mayor, Case actively supported a full-scale street-paving plan, using planks. He also backed more schools and a better system of sewers. After leaving office in 1852, he unsuccessfully sought a seat in Congress. He continued supporting various social and cultural institutions until his death from tuberculosis on 19 April 1862.

SOURCES: J. F. Brennan, ed., *A Biographical Cyclopedia and Portrait Gallery of Distinguished Men with an Historical Sketch of the State of Ohio* (Cincinnati, 1879); *Cleveland, Past and Present* (Cleveland, 1869); Henry Hall, ed., *America's Successful Men of Affairs*, 2 vols. (New York, 1896); Gertrude Wickham, *The Pioneer Families of Cleveland, 1796–1840*, 2 vols. (Chicago, 1914). The Case Family Papers, in the Western Reserve Historical Society in Cleveland, comprise some two feet of material, including William Case's letters and notebooks.   *Thomas R. Bullard*

CASH, ALBERT D. (1897–1952), Mayor of Cincinnati (1948–51). Lawyer and politician, born in Cincinnati, on 21 August 1897, Cash was the son of Denis F. Cash, local politician, and Margaret (Heister) Cash, both Roman Catholics. Cash received an A.B. from Xavier University in 1916 and spent the World War I era as an agent for the FBI. He attended the University of Cincinnati, graduating in 1920 with an LL.B. He began practicing law that same year on his own and was a member of the firm of Dolle, O'Donnell and Cash (1926–52). In 1926, he married Esther Boehnlein (d. 1940) a Catholic like himself, and they had four children. Cash belonged to the city, state, and national bar associations, and was president of the Xavier University Society.

Cash, like his father, was an ardent Democrat and managed the Hamilton County campaigns for Franklin Roosevelt in 1932, 1936, and 1940. He was elected to the city council in 1937, serving until 1952. One of the members of the council during this period was Elizabeth Cassatt Reid, a widow whom Cash married in 1947. He was selected as mayor in 1948, after several votes were taken by the council. Cincinnati had 503,998 people in 1950 and a city manager-mayor-council form of government.

Cash was unpopular with many local politicians because of his belief that the mayor should be a strong leader. Many felt that the charter system of government

had reduced the mayor to a mere figurehead, but Cash disagreed, calling the office a "pulpit" to reach the public. He used his office to back all measures to improve the city, especially smoke abatement which became something of a crusade with him. He also pushed a master plan which he saw as the only way for Cincinnati to prepare for the future. It called for large-scale rebuilding and drastic reduction in the city's traffic. After his second term ended in late 1951, Cash continued to support this plan as an alderman until 2 August 1952 when he drowned in a freak storm while fishing on a lake in Michigan.

SOURCES: Cincinnati Mayors (Cincinnati, c. 1957); New York *Times*, 16 November 1947 and 4 August 1952; Ralph A. Straetz, *PR: Politics in Cincinnati* (Washington Square, 1958).   *Thomas R. Bullard*

CASTLE, WILLIAM B. (1814–72), Mayor of Cleveland (1855–57). Businessman and a transplanted Yankee, born in Essex, Vermont, on 30 November 1814, Castle was the son of Jonathan Castle (1782–1834), an architect, and Frances P. Castle. The family moved to Ontario, Canada, in 1815, where Jonathan Castle established a successful architectural career. In 1827, they settled on a farm near Cleveland. The senior Castle opened a lumberyard, and William attended local schools. In 1834, when his father died, Castle moved to Vienna, Canada, running his own lumberyard. In 1836, he married Mary Derby, but she died the following year. In 1839, Castle returned to Ohio City, Ohio, forming the hardware company of Castle and Field in 1840. In 1843, he left this firm and joined the Cuyahoga Steam Furnace Company, a small ironmaking operation. He rose through the company's ranks, achieving the presidency in the late 1860s and making this company one of the most important in the area. On 13 May 1840, he had married Mary Newell (1819–1907), a Vermont farmer's daughter, and they had four children. The Castles belonged to St. John's Church.

Castle was mayor of Ohio City, 1853–55, and was a member of the special commission that produced the merger of Ohio City with Cleveland in 1854. He was considered the leader of the new west side of the city and was selected as the Whig candidate for mayor in 1855, defeating H. Wood (Democrat) 2,553 to 2,147. In 1857, he was himself defeated by former mayor Samuel Starkweather (*q.v.*) by 419 votes. Cleveland had about 35,000 people by then and a mayor-council form of government.

As mayor, Castle supported reduction of the city debt and tax levels. At the same time, he believed in more railroads, schools, and a greater development of the city's property. After leaving office, he returned to the Cuyahoga Steam Furnace Company and increased its business by adding a locomotive-construction foundry. He also was a trustee of the Savings Bank and the Citizens' Savings and Loan Association. In 1870, he took his family on a lengthy vacation in Germany. In late 1871, he developed sciatica, and the following year was discovered to be suffering from Bright's disease, which claimed his life on 28 February 1872.

SOURCES: Richard N. Campen, "The Story of Ohio City" (unpub. typescript, 1968); Cleveland *Leader*, 29 February 1872; Cleveland *Plain Dealer*, 19 February 1872, 2 March 1872; *Cleveland, Past and Present* (Cleveland, 1869). *Thomas R. Bullard*

CAVANAGH, JEROME PATRICK (1928–79), Mayor of Detroit (1962–70). Liberal reform Democratic mayor, born on 16 June 1928 in Detroit, Michigan, Cavanagh was the son of Sylvester J. Cavanagh (1892–1968), a steamfitter, and Mary Irene (Timmins) Cavanagh. Both parents were of Irish Catholic descent and lived on a 150-acre farm near Toronto, Canada, before emigrating to the United States by 1920. The middle son of three sons and three daughters, Jerome attended St. Cecilia High School and received two degrees from the University of Detroit: Ph.B. in 1950 and LL.B in 1954. Cavanagh was chairman of the Wayne County Young Democrats (1949–50), worked as a deputy sheriff and as a sales representative for the IBM Corporation, was appointed an administrative assistant with the Michigan State Fair Authority, and was appointed to two terms as a member of the Metropolitan Airport Board of Zoning Appeals. He also was a delegate to county and state conventions of the Democratic party. From 1955 to 1961, Cavanagh practiced law as a member of the firm of Sullivan, Romanoff, Cavanagh and Nelson.

On 22 November 1952, Cavanagh married a Catholic, Mary Helen Martin (1930–), a secretary born in Kokomo, Indiana, and they had eight children. Cavanagh was divorced from Mary Helen on 30 July 1968. In 1972, he married Kathleen Marie Disser (1943–), and they adopted a daughter, Katie.

Detroit in 1960 had 1,670,144 people, a strong mayor-council form of government, and nonpartisan elections. In 1961, on his first try for elective office, Cavanagh won the Detroit mayorship in an upset victory by 200,773 to the incumbent Mayor Louis C. Miriani's (q.v.) 158,679, becoming at age thirty-three Detroit's second youngest mayor in history. He was reelected mayor in 1965 by 295,991 votes to his opponent Walter C. Shamie's 144,866. Cavanagh declined to run for reelection in 1969.

As mayor, Cavanagh helped to solve Detroit's fiscal problems, erasing an inherited ($34.5 million) debt, in-

stituting a municipal income tax on both residents and nonresidents working in the city, reducing property taxes and a tax on industry, and achieving a prime rating for Detroit's municipal bonds. Only during his last year in office did the budget deficit return. Personally concerned about racial problems, Cavanagh pioneered by appointing several blacks to positions of high-level responsibility and instituting policies to gain fairer police treatment. He was imaginative and aggressive in securing federal financing for programs in Detroit to train high school dropouts, for housing, for water and sewer programs, for a new wing of the Detroit Art Institute, and for other redevelopment programs. In 1966, Detroit won the "All-America City" award from *Look* magazine and the National Municipal League.

Considered a rising political star, Cavanagh was named outstanding young man of the year in 1962 by the Michigan Junior Chamber of Commerce and again in 1963 by the National Junior Chamber of Commerce. In 1966 he was president of both the National League of Cities and the U.S. Conference of Mayors. He was also a member of national advisory committees on manpower problems, area redevelopment, and community relations.

In spite of programs to improve conditions for poor people, in July 1967, Detroit exploded into one of the worst civil disorders of a turbulent decade. In six days of violence, over forty people were killed, hundreds were injured, and extensive property damage was committed. Only bayonet-wielding federal troops could restore peace. "That riot, it was a crusher!" he lamented. It finished his political career. Cavanagh's image as a racial problem solver was damaged beyond repair. Nonetheless, his policies laid the basis for Detroit's Renaissance programs of the 1970s.

Cavanagh lost primary campaigns for the U.S. Senate in 1966 and for the Michigan governorship in 1974. He practiced law in Detroit, 1970–79, lectured part-time at universities (Michigan and Massachusetts Institute of Technology), and was president of the Incorporated Society of Irish-American Lawyers. On 27 November 1979, while in Lexington, Kentucky, to consult with a law client, Cavanagh died of a heart attack. He was buried in Detroit.

SOURCES: Jerome P. Cavanagh, biography file and miscellaneous material file, Burton Historical Collection, Detroit Public Library; Jerome P. Cavanagh Papers, Reuther Library, Wayne State University, Detroit; Robert Conot, *American Odyssey* (New York, 1974); "Jerry Cavanagh" and "He Presided During City's Revival, Riot," Detroit *Free Press*, 28 November 1979; Arthur M. Woodford, *Detroit: American Urban Renaissance* (Tulsa, Okla., 1979). *DeWitt S. Dykes, Jr.*

CAVE, JESSE S. Acting Mayor of New Orleans (15 July–17 August 1936).

CELEBREZZE, ANTHONY J. (1910–   ), Mayor of Cleveland (1953–62). Mayor of Cleveland and cabinet secretary (HEW.), Celebrezze was an immigrant Italian Catholic, born in Anzi, Italy, on 4 September 1910, the son of Rocco Celebrezze, a railroad track worker, and Dorothy (Marcoguiseppe) Celebrezze, two Italian immigrants who had temporarily gone back to Italy. The ninth of thirteen children, Celebrezze reached the United States two years after his birth. He attended public schools and Central High School in Cleveland. Starting in 1916, he, along with his brothers, sold newspapers. He attended John Carrol University, paying his way by boxing and working for the New York Central Railroad. He graduated from Ohio Northern University in 1936 and began practicing law. He was employed by the Ohio Bureau of Unemployment Compensation, 1936–39, but after 1939 he had his own office. In 1938, he married Anne Marco, a fellow ethnic and a Cleveland school teacher, and they had three children. A single term in the Ohio Senate (1951–53) earned Celebrezze attention as a popular Democratic vote-getter.

When Mayor Thomas A. Burke (*q.v.*) went to the U.S. Senate in 1953, the Democratic leader selected Celebrezze as his successor. He defeated William J. McDermott (Republican) 140,590 to 94,040. In 1955 and again in 1957, he was returned unopposed. In 1959, Celebrezze won 138,980 votes to 60,815 for T. Ireland (Republican) and 8,492 for A. G. Netrakos (Independent). In 1961, he overwhelmed Republican Albina Cermak 145,672 to 53,302. Cleveland had 914,808 people in 1950, a figure that declined to 876,050 in 1960, with a mayor-council form of government.

A highly successful campaigner, Celebrezze was often considered a maverick by party regulars. He supported massive bond issues for urban renewal and the Cleveland waterfront rebuilding. Celebrezze backed new housing, welfare payments, civil rights, and a reduced city work force. He was president of the American Municipal Association in 1958–59 and president of the U.S. Conference of Mayors in 1962. President John F. Kennedy selected him to be secretary of Health, Education and Welfare, a post Celebrezze held until 1965. Since 1965, he has been the judge for the Sixth Circuit Court of Appeals in Cleveland.

SOURCES: Current Biography (New York, 1963 ed.); *Who's Who in American Politics* (New York, 1977).

Thomas R. Bullard

CERMAK, ANTON J. (1873–1933), Mayor of Chicago (1931–33). Bohemian mayor and leader of Chicago's Democratic machine, Cermak was born on 9 May 1873 in Kladno, Bohemia, and was brought to America as an infant by his immigrant parents, Anton and Catherine (Frank) Cermak. His coal miner father, a Hussite Protestant, worked in Braidwood, Illinois, where Anton, the oldest of six children, received a few years of primary school education. He left for Chicago at age sixteen, finding employment as a seller of kindling wood in the Bohemian immigrant neighborhood of Lawndale. Cermak's financial interests eventually grew to include ownership of a coal and wood business, the presidency of a building and loan association, director of the Lawndale National Bank, and a real estate partnership. In 1894, he married Mary Horejs, a Bohemian-born Roman Catholic; they had three daughters: Lillian, Ella, and Helen. Cermak lacked any formal religious affiliation but was active in the Masons, the Knights of Pythias, Foresters, and Zoldaks.

Associating himself with Democratic ward politics, Cermak rose steadily through party ranks, serving as state representative (1902–1909), Chicago alderman (1909–12), and municipal court bailiff (1912–18). During this period, Cermak provided vigorous leadership for the United Societies for Local Self-Government, a federation of ethnic groups opposed to stringent state liquor control legislation. Defeated for Cook County sheriff in 1918, he returned to the Chicago City Council until 1922, when he was elected president of the Cook County Board of Commissioners. During the next decade Cermak organized the modern Democratic machine in Chicago, using patronage jobs and public works contracts to cement the loyalty of Chicago's "new immigrant" population to the party. Cermak capped his rise to political leadership in 1928 by becoming chairman of the Cook County Democratic party.

By 1931, Chicagoans had tired of a corrupt Republican administration and the criminal, gangster activity that flourished during Prohibition. The nation's second largest city, with a population of 3,378,000, also suffered severely from the mass unemployment brought on by the Great Depression. Backed by Chicago's reform groups and his own Democratic machine, Cermak defeated the incumbent William Hale Thompson (*q.v.*) 671,189 votes to 476,922 in the 1931 mayoral election.

Cermak's most pressing problem as mayor proved to be the relief costs of providing for Chicago's unemployed, further complicated by falling tax revenues that almost led to municipal bankruptcy. Unable to obtain necessary state aid, Cermak appealed to the federal government as the only source capable of providing the financial support cities needed. He effectively used his state-wide political power to assure a sweeping victory for Democrats in the 1932 Illinois election. On a trip to confer with Franklin D. Roosevelt in Miami, Florida, Cermak was mortally wounded during an assassination attempt against the president-elect on 15 February 1933. He died on 6 March 1933 and was buried in Chicago's Bohemian National Cemetery.

SOURCES: John Allswang, *Bosses, Machines and Urban Voters: An American Symbiosis* (Port Washington, N.Y., 1977); John Allswang, *A House for All People: Ethnic Politics in Chicago, 1890–1936* (Lexington, Ky., 1971); Alex Gottfried, *Boss Cermak of Chicago: A Study of Political Leadership* (Seattle, 1962).

Peter J. O'Malley

CERVANTES, ALFONSO J. (1920–   ), Mayor of St. Louis (1965–73). Spanish-American, Catholic mayor, and urban reformer, Cervantes was born on 27 August 1920 in St. Louis, the son of Augustine A. Cervantes, an insurance salesman of Spanish ancestry, and Victoria (Kussenberger) Cervantes, of Alsatian-German descent. Mrs. Cervantes was active in local Catholic charity work. The youngest of five children, Cervantes graduated from a local parochial school, but dropped out of high school and headed west during the 1930s. He was a paperhanger ar d dance contest promoter in Los Angeles until 1942 when he joined the Merchant Marine. In 1945, he returned to St. Louis and started selling insurance for trucks and taxis. This led to Cervantes assuming control of the Laclede Cab Company. In 1947, he married Carmen Davis, and they had six children.

A Democrat, Cervantes was elected to the city council in 1949 and served until 1965. He was president of the board of alderman, 1959–63. He soon realized the growing problems faced by the city and began to develop a reputation as a reformer. In 1965, Cervantes was elected mayor, defeating M. R. Zumwalt (Republican) 102,961 to 47,510. In 1969, he was reelected over G. Fischer (Republican) 64,813 to 41,825. Cervantes was defeated in the Democratic primary elections in 1973 and 1977. St. Louis had 750,026 people in 1960 and 622,236 by 1970, and a mayor-council form of government.

Cervantes considered public housing the number one problem in the city and the nation, and worked to secure more federal grants and construction of new low-income housing units. Recognizing crime as the second major issue, Cervantes supported the creation of the Commission for Crime and Law Enforcement. He constantly sought ways to attract more tourists to St. Louis (he called tourism the city's "smokeless industry") and felt that his most important achievement was the new sense of pride instilled in the public during his term in office. Cervantes urged construction of a new airport across the Mississippi River in Illinois and a broader tax base (through a merger of the city with St. Louis County),

thus looking to the future. He was constantly in touch with all groups within the city, keeping up with public opinion. Cervantes was an extremely popular politician, although his popularity suffered in 1970 after *Life* magazine claimed that some of his political aides were allied with organized crime. This article may well have caused his defeat in the 1973 primary. Since leaving office, he has returned to his insurance business, now known as Cervantes and Associates.

SOURCES: A. J. Cervantes, *Mr. Mayor* (Los Angeles, 1974); Charles H. Cornwell, *St. Louis Mayors: Brief Biographies* (St. Louis, 1965); *Who's Who in American Politics* (New York, 1977).   Thomas R. Bullard

CHAMBERLAIN, MARVIN H. (1842–1923), Mayor of Detroit (1886–87). Democratic mayor of Detroit, Chamberlain was born in Woodstock (Lenawee County), Michigan, on 5 November 1842. His father, Philonzo C. Chamberlain (1804–94), moved from a farm in western New York in 1835 to Lenawee County. Marvin, the youngest of eight children (six boys, two girls) in a Protestant farming family, taught district school locally before attending Hillsdale College. Moving to Detroit to enter business school in 1865, he began work as a bookkeeper and then as a traveling salesman for a firm he and a brother eventually took over. Renamed Marvin H. Chamberlain and Company, it became the leading wholesale liquor firm in Detroit. For some time he and his brother also ran the Fearless Tobacco Company. Chamberlain was married to Ellen Wilson (1857–1939) of Niagara County, New York (where his parents had lived earlier), in 1876. A good debater and speaker, Chamberlain was elected to the Detroit City Council in 1882.

Detroit in 1880 had 116,340 people and a mayor-council form of government. In 1883, the Democrats first nominated Chamberlain for mayor to oppose the Republican candidate, Stephen B. Grummond (*q.v.*), who won 9,770 to 9,304 votes. The Republicans continued to control the councils. In 1885, during his second term on the councils, Chamberlain was chosen president. The Democrats nominated him again the same year to contest Grummond, the incumbent mayor. Temperance became a heated political question and Chamberlain was vulnerable as a liquor dealer because of excitement over the "Beer-on-Belle-Isle" issue; he straddled the issue, agreeing to support the Sunday sale of beer on Belle Isle while promising to have the operation carefully supervised to keep good public order. This stand pulled him through, and he won with 11,972 votes to Grummond's 10,104. Carleton H. Mills of the Prohibition party trailed with 129 votes. Mayor Chamberlain was as business-minded as any Republican and escaped press censure despite the usual grumblings about alleged political malfeasance among the aldermen and city department heads. Not on particularly good terms with the William C. Maybury (*q.v.*) faction of the party (Don Dickinson captained another faction), Chamberlain was not renominated in 1887. He had to make room for John Pridgeon, Jr. (*q.v.*), a young business leader who won the election.

Chamberlain returned to his liquor business and died on 15 February 1923.

SOURCES: Richard Edwards, comp., *Industries of Michigan, City of Detroit: Historical and Descriptive Review* (Detroit, 1880); Silas Farmer, *The History of Detroit and Wayne County and Early Michigan* (Detroit, 1890), vol. 2; Paul Leake, *History of Detroit* (Chicago and New York, 1912), vol. 2.   *Donald W. Disbrow*

CHANDLER, ZACHARIAH (1813–79), Mayor of Detroit (1851–52). Whig mayor of Detroit, but later a founder of the Republican party, a radical abolitionist, and a U.S. senator, Chandler was born on 10 December 1813 at Bedford, New Hampshire, the son of Samuel Chandler (1774–1870), a farmer whose family came to Massachusetts from England in 1637, and Margaret (Orr) Chandler (1774–1855), who was of Scotch-Irish, Presbyterian ancestry. Zachariah Chandler was the sixth of seven children. Zachariah received his schooling in Bedford to age fifteen and then attended academies in Derry and Pembroke. He taught for one semester in a rural schoolhouse and worked several months as a store clerk in nearby Nashua. In 1833, Chandler moved to Detroit and opened a retail general store in partnership with his brother-in-law, Franklin Moore. Chandler enjoyed rapid business success. He terminated the Moore and Chandler partnership in 1836 and assumed sole control. His was the first Detroit firm to sell $50,000 worth of goods in one year. In the 1840s, Chandler discontinued retail trade and concentrated on wholesale transactions. As his wealth accumulated, he invested in downtown real estate, road building companies, banks, railroads, and timber land, thereby amassing a $2 million estate by the time he died. Meanwhile, Chandler had married Letitia Grace Douglass of New York, on 10 December 1844. The couple had one child, Mary Douglass Chandler, born in 1848.

Chandler came from a politically active family. Two uncles, Thomas Chandler and Benjamin Orr, served in Congress, and his father was elected to several positions in local government. Beginning in the late 1830s, Zachariah Chandler contributed his money, time, and talents to Whig campaigns in Detroit. In 1850, he was a delegate to the Whig state convention, and the following year he was the Whig nominee for mayor. Chandler was also an active Presbyterian and treasurer of the Young Men's Benevolent Society (1848), and belonged to a volunteer fire company.

In 1851, Detroit's population numbered about 25,000, and the Wayne County (Michigan) city had a mayor-council form of government. Mayors were elected annually by popular vote and served without pay, presiding over a sixteen-member city council (two from each of eight wards). After a strenuous personal campaign in which Chandler successfully appealed for Irish and German support, he won every ward and beat his Democratic opponent, former Mayor John R. Williams (*q.v.*), 1,909 to 1,558 (3 March 1851). Chandler's triumph was personal rather than partisan, as the Democrats won most city-wide posts and took six of the ten council seats at stake. As mayor, Chandler concentrated on physical improvements and budgetary matters. A major controversy ensued after the council awarded the city printing contract to a Whig at a meeting at which most Democrats were absent. As Chandler directed his ambitions toward state-wide office, he did not run for reelection when his term ended.

Chandler is best known for his political career after leaving the Detroit mayoralty. In 1852, he was the unsuccessful Whig candidate for governor of Michigan. Two years later, Chandler helped establish the Republican party. In 1857, the legislature chose him to succeed Lewis Cass in the U.S. Senate, where Chandler served three full terms and part of a fourth (1857–75, 1879). As a senator and an abolitionist, Chandler served on the Committee on the Conduct of the War, and supported the Wade-Davis bill (1863), black suffrage, and the impeachment and conviction of President Andrew Johnson (1867–68). After his defeat in 1875, he served briefly as secretary of the interior (1875–76) and Republican National Committee chairman (1876).

While campaigning for the Republican party, Chandler suffered a cerebral hemorrhage and died in his Chicago hotel room on 1 November 1879. He was buried in Elmwood Cemetery, Detroit.

SOURCES: Detroit *Post and Tribune, Zachariah Chandler: An Outline Sketch of His Life and Public Services* (Detroit, 1880); Mary Karl George, *Zachariah Chandler* (East Lansing, Mich., 1969); Wilmer C. Harris, *Public Life of Zachariah Chandler, 1851–1875* (Lansing, Mich., 1917); the Zachariah Chandler Papers are in the Library of Congress.   *Michael W. Homel*

CHAPIN, HERMAN MERRILL (1823–79), Mayor of Cleveland (1865–67). Meatpacker and businessman-mayor, born in Walpole, New Hampshire, on 29 July 1823, Chapin was the son of Nathaniel Chapin (1792–1876), merchant, and Fanny Booth (Brown) Chapin (1791–1852), both New Englanders of English descent. The fifth of ten children, young Herman attended common schools after the family moved to Chelsea, Massachusetts, around 1830. He quit school in 1838 and went to Boston, working as a clerk in a dry goods store. In 1848, he moved west to Cleveland and was employed as a clerk for Charles Bradburn and Company (wholesale grocers) until 1852. He then started a successful porkpacking operation, adding a cooperage company in 1862–67. In 1849, he married Sarah Matilda Fenno (1829–98) of Boston, and they had six children. They were members of the First Unitarian church in Cleveland, and Chapin was one of the founders of the Cleveland Public Library.

In 1865, while on a business trip, Chapin was nominated as the Republican candidate for mayor. He expected to lose the election and was astonished by his 3,304 to 2,323 victory over Democrat D. B. Sexton. Cleveland had over 65,000 people and a mayor-council form of government. Chapin tried to refuse the "prize" of election but reluctantly agreed to serve for patriotic reasons. He actively supported the Civil War, sponsoring the Twenty-ninth Regiment. He also backed the fire department and other civic agencies. He had no desire to continue in politics and would not seek a second term in 1867, completely ending his political career.

After leaving office, Chapin was busy with two insurance companies. (He was vice-president of the Sun Fire Insurance Company and organized the Huhnemman Company in 1865.) He moved his packing plant to Chicago, 1867–68, but returned to Cleveland after a single year. In May 1878, he caught a chill while in the plant's cooling room, and despite efforts by doctors, his health rapidly declined and he died on 24 May 1879.

SOURCES: Gilbert W. Chapin, comp., *The Chapin Book of Genealogical Data*, 2 vols. (Hartford, 1924); *Cleveland, Past and Present* (Cleveland, 1869); Cleveland *Plain Dealer*, 24 May 1879.   *Thomas R. Bullard*

CHAPIN, JOHN P. (1810–64), Mayor of Chicago (1846–47). One-term mayor of Chicago, Chapin was born in Rutland, Vermont on 21 April 1810 and moved to Chicago in 1833. He was descended from Revolutionary War General Israel Putnam. He worked as a commissioning and forewarding agent and opened up a meat packing plant which shipped the first beef ever put up in Chicago for a foreign market. Chapin built and operated the first line of canal boats on the Illinois and Michigan Canal. In March 1848, he helped organize the Chicago Board of Trade; and with W. B. Ogden (Chicago's first mayor), he organized the Chicago and Northwestern Railroad.

Chicago in 1846 had over 14,000 citizens and a mayor-council form of government with a one-year term for mayor. Chapin was a Whig and served one term as alderman in 1844 (First Ward) before he defeated Charles Follansbee, the Democratic candidate for mayor, 1,104 to 667 on 3 March 1846. The Liberty party (abolitionist)

candidate, Philo Carpenter, received 229 votes. During Chapin's term of office, Chicago's earlier designation as a port of entry by the federal government was opposed by many merchants in the city. They feared that British ships plying the Great Lakes would now be able to flood the Chicago area with cheap foreign-made products and thus have a commercial advantage over locally produced manufacturers. Railroad development made those fears groundless.

The United States went to war against Mexico in 1846, and Chapin, despite his political affiliation, joined the state militia and served as a captain. After the war, he returned to the board of trade where he worked until his death in Chicago on 27 June 1864 at the age of fifty-four.

SOURCES: A. T. Andreas, *History of Chicago* (Chicago, 1884); Don Fehrenbacher, *Chicago Giant: A Biography of "Long John" Wentworth* (Madison, Wis., 1957); Bessie L. Pierce, *History of Chicago* (New York, 1937–57).   *Leslie V. Tischauser*

CHAPIN, MARSHALL (1798–1838), Mayor of Detroit (1831, 1833). Detroit's fifth mayor was a transplanted New England doctor, whose father's family had lived in and around the Connecticut River Valley and Springfield (Massachusetts) for over a century. Marshall was born in Bernardstown, Massachusetts, of Caleb Chapin, a local physician, and Mary Wright Chapin (1765–1827), on 27 February 1798, and was one of nine children. When Chapin was a child, the family moved to Caledonia, New York, where he received his basic education at local schools. He then took a medical course at Geneva, New York, with his uncle, Dr. Cyrenius Chapin. He graduated in 1819 and immediately moved to Detroit where he established, with the help of his uncle, the first drugstore in the town located on Jefferson Avenue.

Soon after his arrival Dr. Chapin met Governor Lewis Cass, who appointed him surgeon of the garrison. In 1826 and 1827, he became alderman at large. In 1831 and again in 1833, he was elected mayor, as a Whig. In the meantime, in 1832, he was also appointed chief engineer of the fire department. According to most sources, Chapin's major contribution to the city was his extraordinary medical service during the cholera epidemics of 1832 and 1834. At the time, Detroit had a growing population of about 4,000. Chapin held the title "City Physician" in 1832. He failed to be reelected mayor on 3 April 1837, losing to the Democrat, Henry Howard (*q.v.*) 682 to 411. He died on 25 August 1838, at only forty years of age. He had married Mary Crosby (1796–1841) of New York in 1823 and had four children, Louisa, Helen, Charles, and Marshall.

SOURCES: C. B. Burr, *Medical History of Michigan* (Minneapolis, 1930); Fred Carlisle, *A Chronography of Notable Events in the History of the Northwest Territory and Wayne County* (Detroit, 1890); Silas Farmer, *A History of Detroit* (Detroit, 1889).   *Francis X. Blouin, Jr.*

CHAPMAN, JOHN LEE (1812–80), Mayor of Baltimore (1862–67). Very little is known about Chapman's early life. He was reportedly born in Harford County on 18 February 1812, but another source states that he was born in the Fells Point district of Baltimore City. His father was George Chapman (1789–1845), who was of Scottish descent but came from Derbyshire, England. He married his cousin, Elizabeth Chapman, around 1835, and by 1850 they had six children. John Lee first established himself in the city as a druggist, but in 1850 he went into the glass manufacturing business with his brother George. He affiliated with the Whig party and later with a reform party. He was elected to the city council in 1860 and was reelected in 1861. The 1861 council organized on 6 January 1862 and selected Chapman as council president. The mayor, George William Brown (*q.v.*), was suspected of secessionist activities by the federal military authorities in Maryland and had been imprisoned in September 1861. Therefore, Chapman, as president of the city council, became mayor *ex officio*. Since the arrival of federal troops in 1861, Baltimore was in fact governed by the military commander at Fort McHenry. A large number of other officeholders and political leaders had been arrested along with Mayor Brown, and in the city council election of 1861 only those loyal to the federal Union were permitted to run for office. Chapman and many other old Whigs, Know-Nothings, and pro-union Democrats slowly affiliated with the Union party and eventually with the Republicans.

With many of the leading political figures of the city out of politics, the Unionists and Republicans took the opportunity to pass a variety of city ordinances supporting the war and pursued other goals of interest to this political faction. Chapman, for example, was helpful in aiding the Western Maryland Railroad and served for two years as its president. He was affiliated with the moderate wing of the Republican party in Baltimore and the former Know-Nothing Mayor Thomas Swann (*q.v.*). In 1864, Chapman defeated the more radical Republican candidate, Archibald Stirling, for mayor by a vote of 11,237 to 3,290. However, when Chapman ran again in 1866 against a "Conservative" (Democrat) candidate, the police actively intervened on the Republican side and most Democratic voters either did not have their vote counted or stayed home. The Democrats finally managed to gain control of the state government and to write a new state constitution which required a new election for mayor in the city. In an effort to present a candidate who was not associated with the long period of Republican-military rule in the city, the party passed over Chapman and never again nominated him for a public office.

During these extremely turbulent years, Chapman had devoted all his time and energy to public office, and his glass business apparently failed or passed into other hands by 1867. His brief tenure as president of the Western Maryland Railroad did not enrich him either. That he left public office much poorer than he entered was thereafter alluded to as a measure of his personal integrity and honesty. The last years of his life were spent quietly in Baltimore in minor federal offices given him by Presidents Grant and Hayes. Chapman was Episcopalian. He died on 18 November 1880 at his home at 79 Harlem Avenue. The Baltimore *Morning Herald* summarized his life as that of a "quiet unobtrusive man . . . unaccustomed to the duties that were thrust upon him." He nevertheless "bore himself bravely" and displayed "the highest moral courage and strong common sense."

SOURCES: Wilbur F. Coyle, *The Mayors of Baltimore* (Baltimore: 1919); Dielman-Hayward File, Maryland Historical Society; E. M. Killough, *A History of the Western Maryland Railroad Including Biographies of the Presidents* (Baltimore, 1938).   *Joseph L. Arnold*

CHAPMAN, JONATHAN (1807–48), Mayor of Boston (1840–42). Eighth mayor of Boston, Chapman was born there on 23 January 1807, the son of Margaret Rogers of Stowe, Massachusetts, and Jonathan Chapman, a sea captain and former selectman of Boston. He studied at Phillips Academy and Harvard (graduating in 1825) and then studied law with Judge Lemuel Shaw. Chapman became a lawyer. Widely recognized for his wit and eloquence, he had the honor of being appointed city orator in 1837. He lectured widely and wrote for popular journals like the *North American Review*, in addition to professional publications such as *Proceedings at Law in Massachusetts*. Active in the Whig party and in the state militia, in which he held several commissions, he married Lucinda Dwight of Springfield, Massachusetts, on 25 April 1832. They had four daughters and a son.

Chapman's term as mayor of Boston was an economic turning-point for the city. When it began in 1840, the city's population had reached 93,383 people and its municipal debt had increased to over $1.5 million. When it ended three years later, the population was still growing rapidly. The economy, however, had begun to turn around, as had the city's financial situation.

The improvement in Boston's economic health resulted from natural factors, including the weakening of the national depression and enlargement of the city's foreign and domestic markets with the coming of a local Cunard steamship line and the opening of the Western Railroad in 1840 and 1841. Chapman himself managed to improve the city's fiscal condition by an almost draconian policy of retrenchment. This involved raising taxes in the face of calls for lower taxes, earmarking regular city revenues for debt retirement, tightening municipal accounting procedures, and postponing expenditures for permanent improvements like street-widenings and the much needed public water system and new county jail. It also included remodeling the old county courthouse into a city hall, instead of building an entirely new building for the purpose. While popular, such retrenchment was, of course, an essentially negative policy. The Chapman administration, however, made two positive contributions to the city in areas that did not require massive outlays of municipal funds: submitting a new revision of the city charter to the state legislature and pursuing a controversial, tougher enforcement of state liquor laws.

Chapman returned to private life in 1842 and died six years later on 25 May 1848. He was buried at Kings Chapel in Boston.

SOURCES: *Boston City Documents* (Boston, 1840, 1841, 1842); James M. Bugbee, "Boston Under the Mayors," in Justin Winsor, ed., *The Memorial History of Boston* (Boston, 1881), vol. 3; Charles Philips Huse, *The Financial History of Boston from May 1, 1822 to January 31, 1909* (Cambridge, Mass., 1916); *Inaugural Addresses of the Mayors of Boston 1822–1851* (Boston, 1894); James Spear Loring, *The Hundred Boston Orators Appointed by the Authorities and Other Public Bodies from 1770–1852* (Boston, 1855); *Our First Men: A Calendar of Wealth, Fashion and Gentlemen Containing a List of Those Persons Taxed in the City of Boston Credibly Reported to Be Worth 100 Thousand Dollars* (Boston, 1846).

Christine M. Rosen

CHASE, HORACE (1810–86), Mayor of Milwaukee (1862–63). Born on his father's farm near Derby, Vermont, on 25 December 1810 to Jacob and Hannah (Colby), both of British descent, Chase worked on the farm and in the family grist mill until he was apprenticed as a clerk in 1830 to a wholesale and retail grocery firm in Boston. In 1834, with several other pioneer settlers, he established himself in what was then the small village of Milwaukee. The following year he formed a partnership in a grocery store and organized the first Methodist service in the community. In 1836, he developed a commission business that brought him wealth and political success. He married Sarah Ann Grey of Hadley, Illinois, in October 1837 and served in the Wisconsin Constitu-

tional Convention as a delegate from Milwaukee County. In 1848, he was elected to the state legislature. His wife passed away in 1852, but he remarried in 1858, to Mary H. Davis of Mount Holly, Vermont.

In 1861, Chase was elected city alderman, and in the following year, running as a Democrat, he defeated William B. Hibbard for the mayoral office. Milwaukee was then over 46,000 in size, with a mayor-council form of government. Prior to his death on 1 September 1886, Chase was noted for his successful real estate and railroad promotions.

SOURCES: H. Russell Austin, *The Milwaukee Story: The Making of an American City* (Milwaukee, 1946); Frank Flower, *History of Milwaukee, Wisconsin* (Chicago, 1881); Charles R. Tuttle, *The State of Wisconsin* (Madison, Wis., 1875).

David J. Maurer

CHRISTOPHER, GEORGE (1907–), Mayor of San Francisco (1956–64). Greek-born mayor of San Francisco, Christopher was born in St. Peter's, Arcadia, Greece, on 8 December 1907. His father, James Christopheles, emigrated to Sacramento, California, in 1895, worked to earn money and gain U.S. citizenship, returned home to Greece to marry (Mary Koines), and subsequently returned to California in 1910, when little George was aged two. George grew up in the toughest section of San Francisco, south of Market Street; his father ran a "seven stool" restaurant at the corner of Third and Minna. After Lincoln Elementary School, George entered Galileo High School but had to drop out when his father died (1921). He worked full-time as an office-boy at the San Francisco *Examiner*, rising to head the payroll section. Meanwhile, George went to Humboldt Evening High School and later to Golden Gate College where he studied accounting. After eight long years of night study and full-time work, he graduated with a B.A. degree and then opened his own accounting office—characteristically, specializing in giving counsel to small businesses. From time to time, he invested in his clients' firms, including the Excelsior Dairy (1937) and the Meadow Glen Dairy, which eventually became the larger and successful Christopher Dairy. In 1930, he had already changed his name from Christopheles and had taken out U.S. citizenship. By the late 1930s, he was a successful businessman, as well as a pioneer of low milk prices. In 1936, he married a Greek girl, Tula Sarantitis.

Christopher entered local politics as a Republican and was elected to the city's board of supervisors in 1945, when San Francisco's population numbered about 700,000. The city was still growing at that time. Christopher was reelected in 1949, serving until 1955, twice as president of the board (1949, 1953). His reelection vote of 1949 was the largest single vote total ever won by a single candidate (170,756). Christopher had genuine leadership qualities, a keenness for the job, coupled with a personal humility that many found attractive. After being acting mayor on occasions, he was elected mayor of San Francisco on 8 November 1955 with a 2 to 1 victory over his Democratic opponent, George Reilly, who fought a partisan election. The totals were 158,244 to 75,824, which the Republicans claimed as the largest majority in the city's history.

As a supervisor, Christopher had stood for economy in government, encouragement of private business, and specific issues, such as a special clinic for alcoholics. He had failed to be elected mayor in 1951, being defeated by Elmer Robinson (q.v.) by 2,700 votes. He refused to be nominated for lieutenant governor of the state, preferring to try again for mayor in 1955.

As mayor Christopher reorganized the police department, fought against book banning, raised school taxes, and pushed a 1957 plan for a system of elevated streetcar tracks. He signed a bill banning job discrimination in city employment, and he began a series of weekly radio talks in July 1956 called ''Report to the People.'' He insisted on the city gaining revenues from offshore oil as a means of helping the port, and as supervisor he had already demanded structural improvements in labor-management relations on the waterfront.

Christopher's regime is best remembered for bringing the New York Giants baseball team to San Francisco, promising their president, among other things, a $10 million stadium.

Fortune magazine named San Francisco one of the best administered cities in the nation under Christopher. The mayor ran without success for William F. Knowland's U.S. Senate seat in the Republican primary in 1957. He also ran unsuccessfully against Ronald Reagan for the gubernatorial nomination in the 1966 primaries. Among his philanthropic and volunteer activities was his work with young people—an estimated 30,000 San Francisco children attended free sports activities because of Mayor Christopher.

SOURCES: Bill Boyarsky, *Rise of Ronald Reagan* (New York, 1968); G. Dorsey, *Christopher of San Francisco* (San Francisco, 1968); R. G. Minott, *The Sinking of the Lollipop* (San Francisco, 1968); *Nation*, 7 December 1957; ''The California Rebel,'' *Newsweek*, 25 November 1957.   *Peter d'A. Jones*

CLANCEY, DONALD D. (1921–   ), Mayor of Cincinnati (1957–60). Republican mayor and later U.S. congressman, Clancey was born in Cincinnati on 24 July 1921, the son of James Clancey, a livestock broker from Joplin, Missouri, and Margaret (Headley) Clancey, from

Henderson, Kentucky, both Irish-American Catholics. The first of two children, Clancy attended Elden High School and Xavier University, prior to serving with the Finance Department of the U.S. Army, 1943–44. He attended the University of Cincinnati, graduating in 1948 with an LL.B., and immediately began practicing law in Cincinnati. In 1949, he married Betty Jane Mangeot, also a Catholic, of Cincinnati, and they had three children. Clancy had belonged to the American Legion, Knights of Columbus, and the Hamilton County Republican Club (serving as its president in 1955–56).

Clancy was elected to the city council as a Republican in 1951, and he served for nearly ten years, becoming the Republican floor leader by the end of the 1950s. In 1957, the council selected him to be mayor, and he served until his resignation in December 1960. Cincinnati had 502,558 people in 1960 and a city manager-mayor-council form of government. Unlike some city Republicans who urged a return to traditional politics, Clancy supported the city manager concept. He favored preserving the high standards of city services but within reasonable financial limits. Clancy also backed such improvements as a new superhighway and off-street parking. In 1960, he was elected congressman from Ohio's Second District, forcing him to resign from city politics. He served eight terms in Congress, being defeated for reelection in 1976. After 1977, he continued to practice law in Cincinnati.

SOURCES: *Congressional Directory, 94th Congress, 2d Session* (Washington, D.C., 1976); Personal Interview of July 17, 1979; *Who's Who in American Politics* (New York, 1977).   *Thomas R. Bullard*

CLARK, AARON (1784?–1861), Mayor of New York (1837–39). Mayor of a dynamic city with a population of some 295,000, Clark was an extremely wealthy individual whose background remains shrouded by time. He was born in 1784 or 1788 at Northampton, Massachusetts, or Clinton, New York. His parents moved to Middlebury, Vermont, about the time he left Hamilton Oneida Academy for further studies at Union College, Schenectady, in 1808. After tutoring there, he may have become the private secretary to Governor Daniel D. Tompkins of New York for a time. Clark did serve as clerk of the state assembly from 1814 to 1820. Within those years, he read law with the esteemed legal talent, Erastus Root, married, and subsequently moved to New York City and engaged in law.

Clark entered local politics in 1835 as the aldermanic representative of the First Ward in the common council. In the mayoral election of 1837, he ran as the Whig, pro-Bank candidate opposing the Democrat, John J. Morgan, and an Equal Rights candidate, Moses Jaques. Clark received 17,044 votes to Morgan's 13,762 and Jaques'

4,239, and so became the city's second popularly elected mayor, replacing Van Wyck Lawrence. In addition to Whig support, Clark had acquired the political backing of the city's volunteer firemen, feuding with the local Democratic organization, already known as Tammany. Mayor Clark retained such support when he ran for re-election the following year. His opponents then became Isaac Leggett Varian (*q.v.*), Democrat, and a reconstituted local Democratic element under the banner of Conservatives who named Richard Riker as their candidate. Clark regained his seat with 19,723 votes to Varian's 19,204 and Riker's 395. He tried for a third term in 1839 but lost to Varian.

Retiring from politics in 1839, Clark devoted some time to the Hamilton College Alumni Association, and he received an honorary Master's degree in 1856. He died in New York City on 3 August 1861, having amassed a substantial fortune as an exchange broker, director of the Merchants' Insurance Company, and property owner.

SOURCES: Melvin G. Dodge and Daniel W. Burke, *The Clark Prize Book Containing an Account of the Foundation and History of the Prize . . .* (Clinton, N.Y., 1894); Stephen G. Ginsberg, "Above the Law: Volunteer Firemen in New York City, 1836–1837," *New York History* 50, no. 22 (April 1969); New-York *Herald*, 4 August 1861. *Jacob Judd*

CLARK, GEORGE, Acting Mayor of New Orleans, 19 March-11 May 1866. Clark, councilman and president *pro tem*, was acting mayor while federal authorities delayed the inauguration of Mayor-elect John T. Monroe (*q.v.*) 1866–67.

SOURCES: John S. Kendall, *History of New Orleans* (Chicago, 1922), vol. 1. *Melvin G. Holli*

CLARK, JOSEPH S., JR. (1901–   ), Mayor of Philadelphia, 1952–56. First post-World War II reform mayor, Clark was born 21 October 1901 in the posh Chestnut Hill section of Philadelphia. He was the only son of the prominent Philadelphia lawyer, Joseph S. Clark, Sr., and his wife, Kate Avery, of Avery Island, Louisiana. The Clarks belonged to the Philadelphia aristocracy, headed the investment firm of E. W. Clark, and owned extensive coal holdings in West Virginia. In 1946, oil was discovered on Avery Island.

Following his education in private schools, Harvard, and the University of Pennsylvania Law School, between 1926 and 1950 Clark pursued a traditional upper class law career in Philadelphia. He attended the Germantown Unitarian Church. In 1934, with his friend from summers at Southhampton, Long Island, Richardson Dilworth (*q.v.*), Clark dabbled unsuccessfully in Philadelphia

Democratic politics. During World War II, Clark served as deputy chief of staff in the Army Air Force in the China-Burma-India theatre.

Clark's first marriage in 1927 to Elizabeth Story Jenks ended in divorce in 1934. His second marriage to Noel C. Miller in 1935 lasted thirty-one years but ended in a politically disastrous divorce on the eve of Clark's third race for the Senate in 1967. His third marriage in 1967 was to Iris Cole Ritchy, a campaign worker. Clark has one child, Joseph S. Clark, III, from his first marriage, and another child, Noel, from his second.

During the 1930s, both Clark and Richardson Dilworth belonged to an organization of young Turk lawyers called the Democratic Warriors Club. After World War II, Clark and Dilworth seized power in the Democratic party and undertook to dethrone the scandal-ridden Republican machine. By 1949, the disclosures of the Committee of 15 and the reform spirit generated by the charter reform campaign made the time auspicious for reform. That year Clark ran for city controller and Dilworth for city treasurer. Their victory in 1949 set the stage for Clark's mayoral victory in 1951 in which he defeated Daniel A. Poling to a vote of 448,983 to 324,283.

Philadelphia's population in 1950 was 2,071,605. Under the new city charter of 1951, the city had a strong mayor-council form of government. As mayor, Clark concerned himself primarily with reform affecting the physical and economic development of the city. To foster progress, Clark staffed his government with skilled professionals and strove to involve business and civic organizations such as the Greater Philadelphia Movement in physical and social planning.

Clark's administration emphasized slum clearance and better housing for the poor. He also reformed the civil service and made city jobs available to the city's black population. After one term in office, Clark announced in 1956 that he would run for the U.S. Senate and designated Dilworth to be his successor.

As a senator, 1957–68, Clark campaigned to end the dominance of the so-called Senate Establishment. He also fought to reduce America's involvement in Vietnam. He wrote two books, *The Senate Establishment* (New York, 1963) and *Congress: The Sapless Branch* (New York, 1964). Clark's dovish stance on Vietnam, his marital problems, and an ill-fated series of debates within his 1968 opponent, Richard Schweiker, lost him his Senate seat.

After 1968, Clark taught at Temple University and from his home in Chestnut Hill spoke out on city issues. He was a vocal critic of Mayor Frank Rizzo (*q.v.*), 1971–79.

SOURCES: Steve Neal, "Joseph Clark: Our Last Angry Man," *Today Magazine, Philadelphia Inquirer*, 3

August 1975; Kirk R. Petshek, *The Challenge of Urban Reform: Politics and Progress in Philadelphia* (Philadelphia, 1973); Anthony Roth, ed., "Mayors of Philadelphia, 1691–1977: Collection of the Genealogical Society of Pennsylvania" (unpublished collection found at the Historical Society of Pennsylvania, Philadelphia).   *John F. Bauman*

CLEVELAND, STEPHEN GROVER (1837–1908), Mayor of Buffalo (1822). American statesman, mayor of Buffalo, governor of New York, and twice president of the United States, Cleveland was born on 18 March 1837 in Caldwell, New Jersey, the son of Richard F. Cleveland (1804–53) a Presbyterian preacher of old-stock ancestry, and Ann (Neal) Cleveland (1806–82), of Irish and French ancestry. The fifth of nine children, Grover (the Stephen was dropped by 1880) attended local schools and the Academy at Fayetteville, New York, where the family had moved in 1841. He spent one year (1850–51) at an academy at Clinton, followed by two years as a clerk in Fayetteville. He taught at the New York Institute for the Blind, (1853–54) and moved to Buffalo in 1855. Beginning as a clerk for Rogers, Bowen and Rogers, Cleveland embarked upon a successful legal career. He was a member of the Buffalo and Erie County Bar Associations and the City Club. He was technically a Presbyterian, although he did not attend church with any regularity.

Cleveland began working for local Democratic leaders in 1858 and was a ward supervisor by 1862. He served as assistant district attorney, 1862–65, and Erie County sheriff, 1870–73. During these years, his private legal career continued with various partners, but it became obvious that he would be a leading political figure. Seeking an honest candidate to capture the mayoralty in 1881, the Democrats selected Cleveland, who readily defeated George Beebe (Republican) 15,120 to 11,528. Buffalo had 182,511 people in 1882 (city census), and a mayor-council form of government.

As mayor, Cleveland actively opposed machine leaders, whom he felt to be corrupt. Claiming "public officials are the trustees of the people," Cleveland backed civil service reform and used vetoes to control the city council. The publicity created by his battle with the "bosses" won him the gubernatorial election in 1882 and the presidential election in 1884. Hence, he did not serve a full mayoral term, resigning on 20 November 1882. He continued his anti-boss course as governor (1883–85) and president (1885–89 and 1893–97), fighting Tammany Hall and frequently resisting other party leaders on various issues. During his first White House term, on 2 June 1886, Cleveland married Frances Folsom (1864–1947), the young daughter of a former law part-

ner. They had five children, one of whom died at age fourteen. Cleveland retired from politics in 1897, spending his last decade as a trustee of Princeton University, often clashing with that institution's president, Woodrow Wilson. He died on 24 June 1908.

SOURCES: Robert McElroy, *Grover Cleveland: The Man and the Statesman*, 2 vols. (New York, 1923); Horace S. Merrill, *Bourbon Leader: Grover Cleveland and the Democratic Party* (Boston, 1957); Allan Nevins, *Grover Cleveland: A Study in Courage* (New York, 1933); the Grover Cleveland Papers at the Library of Congress comprise roughly 100,000 letters; the Buffalo and Erie County Historical Society also possesses some thirty volumes of letters from his local political career.   *Thomas R. Bullard*

CLINTON, GEORGE W. (1807–85), Mayor of Buffalo (1842–43). Early mayor of Buffalo (and the first Democrat), Clinton was born in New Town, now Brooklyn, on 24 April 1807. He came from a distinguished political family, long prominent in New York. He was the grandson of James Clinton, a brigadier general in the Revolutionary War, and a grandnephew of George Clinton (1739–1812), first governor of New York and vice-president of the United States under Thomas Jefferson. De Witt Clinton (1769–1828), his father (and the son of James), was a state senator, a U.S. senator, a successful mayor of New York (1803–15), and a nominee for president, defeated in 1812 by James Madison. A reformer, De Witt Clinton was the motive force behind the construction of the Erie Canal, and like his uncle he served as governor of New York (1817–21, 1825–28). De Witt Clinton married Maria Franklin, daughter of Walter Franklin of New York City and of Mary Browne, a direct descendant of Adam Winthrop, founder of the famous Winthrop family. Their son, George W., attended the Pickett's School and graduated from Hamilton College in 1834. For two years, George was a student at the Fairfield Medical School, but after the death of his father in 1828 he read law with John Canfield Spencer, secretary of war under President Tyler and son of Chief Justice Ambrose Spencer. Clinton was admitted to the bar in 1831, and on 15 May 1832, he married Spencer's daughter, Laura Catherine (1810–91). They had nine children.

Clinton organized the local Democratic party shortly after his arrival in Buffalo in 1836, and on 1 March 1840 he became the first Democratic mayor by defeating the incumbent, Isaac R. Harrington (*q.v.*). Mayor Clinton accepted a salary of $100 a year. As mayor, he advocated better salaries for public servants and teachers, harbor improvements, and the licensing of liquor sales. Clinton is perhaps better known for the positions he held in addition to his mayoral duties, especially those related to law. He was appointed collector of customs by President Martin Van Buren; was elected president of the Young Man's Temperance Society in 1841; became district attorney under President James Polk; was elected to the New York Superior Court in 1854; and became chief judge in 1870, his term lasting until his retirement seven years later. Clinton also served as a regent of the University of Buffalo and became its vice-chancellor in 1881. During his tenure, he edited the papers of his great uncle, George.

Clinton brought the energy and talents of his legal career to his avocation, naturalism, and discovered and classified several plant and animal species. In 1866, he founded the Buffalo Society of Natural Sciences; an effective speaker, he lectured in botany and geology. As a practicing Episcopalian, strong religious feeling led Clinton to oppose Darwin's theory of natural selection on the grounds that it left no room for an intervening God. On a more scientific basis, and where Darwin (who had no knowledge of genetics) proved vulnerable, Clinton argued that the trope "the survival of the fittest" was founded on the "shadowy doctrine of transmutation." This shortcoming of Darwin's theory convinced Clinton that species were especially created and were immutable. Clinton collapsed and died while gathering flowers in Forest Lawn Cemetery on 7 September 1885. He was buried there four days later.

SOURCES: David F. Day, "An Address in Commemoration of George W. Clinton," 24 March 1890, Buffalo Historical Society Publications, vol. 17; John T. Horton, *Old Erie: The Growth of an American Community, History of Northwestern New York* (New York, 1947), vol. 1; Samuel M. Welch, *Home History: Recollections of Buffalo During the Decade, 1830–1840, or Fifty Years Since* (Buffalo, 1891).

Scott Eberle

COBB, SAMUEL CROCKER (1826–91), Mayor of Boston (1874–76). Nonpartisan reform mayor of Boston, Cobb was born in Taunton, Massachusetts, on 22 May 1826, the son of David George Washington Cobb and Abby (Crocker) Cobb, an established local family. He attended Bristol Academy in Taunton, a private school founded by his grandfather, and expected to go to Harvard in 1842 but had to give up his studies and take a job instead.

Cobb's work as a clerk in a shipping firm housed on Rowe's Wharf led in 1847 to his entry into business for himself with a friend, J. Henry Cunningham. They founded Cunningham and Cobb, a profitable mercantile firm that specialized in trade with Europe and South America. Cobb married Aurelia L. Beattie on 21 November 1848. At first affiliated with the Whig party,

after its dissolution in 1854 Cobb generally sided with the Democrats on most national issues. In local affairs, however, he followed an independent political course. He began his political career as a member of the Roxbury Board of Aldermen in 1860, and, after Roxbury's annexation by Boston in 1868, he became a member of the Boston Board of Aldermen.

Viewed positively by Republicans and Democrats alike, Cobb won easy election to the mayoralty in November 1873 by over 19,000 votes. His subsequent election victories in 1874 and 1875 demonstrated a strong positive feeling for him throughout much of the city. He won reelection in 1875, although he was opposed by candidates put up by both the Republican and Democratic parties.

After several unsuccessful efforts prior to his mayoralty, Cobb was able to secure legislative approval for an act permitting the designing of a system of public parks for the city. This set the stage for the later laying out of Boston's "Emerald Necklace" by Frederick Law Olmstead. Under Cobb, the Boston Water Board was created, as were a licensing board to control the sale of liquor and a board of registrars to prepare the city's voting lists in order to insure the honest election of candidates for municipal office. A champion of fiscal responsibility, Cobb also worked successfully to gain approval of legislation that would limit municipal indebtedness.

A public-spirited citizen, Cobb remained actively involved in a whole array of public and private institutions. He remained president of the Massachusetts Society of Cincinnati until his death on 18 February 1891.

SOURCES: Albert P. Langtry, ed., *Metropolitan Boston: A Modern History* (New York, 1929), vol. 2; New England Historic and Genealogical Society, *Memorial Biographies*, 1890–97, vol. 9; State Street Trust Company, *Mayors of Boston* (Boston, 1914); Justin Winsor, ed., *The Memorial History of Boston* (Boston, 1880–83), vol. 3.

Donald M. Jacobs

COBO, ALBERT EUGENE (1893–1957), Mayor of Detroit (1950–57). Credited with significantly altering the face of Detroit, Cobo was born on 2 October 1893 in Detroit, the son of a marine engineer, August Cobo, whose French-born father and Pennsylvania Dutch (German) mother had come to Michigan from Pennsylvania, and Elizabeth (Byrn) Cobo. Young Cobo attended the Craft, McKinstry, and Amos elementary schools and was a graduate of Detroit's Western High School. He studied at night for a year at the Detroit Business Institute and then received a diploma from the Alexander Hamilton Institute after completing a correspondence course. In 1910, he became an office-boy in the Detroit Copper and Brass Rolling Mills. The following year, he formed a partnership with his brother Edward, and the pair entered the candy and ice cream manufacturing business. In 1918, he joined the Burroughs Adding Machine Company as a junior salesman and within a year was promoted to senior salesman. In 1928, after working for the Sunstrand Adding Machine Company as a manager for three years, he returned to Burroughs as a salesman. In 1929, he was placed in charge of all governmental and utility accounts in Detroit. Cobo married Ethel Ruby Christie on 3 June 1914; the couple had two children, Elaine Elizabeth and Jean. Cobo was a member of the Masons, the Elks, the Optimists, the Detroit Economic Club, and the Mount Hope Congregational Church. He was president of the American Municipal Association, a director of the Great Lakes-St. Lawrence Association, and a member of the President's Civil Defense Advisory Council.

In 1933, Cobo entered public life as special adviser to Detroit's city government. In July of that year, he became deputy treasurer, and when the city treasurer, Charles L. Williams died, Cobo, in April 1935, became city treasurer, a post he held until he became mayor. As treasurer, he worked out a seven-year tax payment plan that made it possible for thousands of Detroiters to retain homes they would otherwise have lost for nonpayment of taxes.

In 1949 Detroit, a city of 1,825,000 with a mayor-council form of government, elected Cobo mayor over George Edwards, by a margin of 313,136 to 206,134. He was reelected to a two-year term in 1951 after he defeated Edgar M. Branigin 168,453 to 113,284, and to a further four-year term in 1953 after Cobo overcame James H. Lincoln 237,357 to 159,330.

As mayor, Cobo played an important role in the development of Detroit's $112 million Civic Center overlooking the Detroit River. Cobo Hall is named after him. He also deserves much credit for the construction of Detroit's expressway system. One of his most significant achievements was the development of the revenue-bond financing system which made it possible to complete twenty miles of expressway in seven years instead of the fifteen years it would have taken under a pay-as-you-go plan. In 1956, Cobo was the Republican candidate for governor, but incumbent G. Mennen Williams defeated him in the November election.

On 12 September 1957, Cobo suffered a fatal heart attack as his four-year term was coming to an end. He was buried in Detroit's Woodlawn Cemetery.

SOURCES: Albert E. Cobo Papers, 9 vols., scrapbooks, Burton Historical Collection, Detroit Public Library; Robert I. Vexler, *Detroit: A Chronological and Documentary History, 1701–1976* (Dobbs Ferry, N.Y., 1977).
                                              Robert Bolt

CODD, GEORGE P. (1869–1927), Mayor of Detroit (1905–1906). Republican Mayor Codd was born on 7 December 1869 in Detroit to George Calvin Codd, an Irish-born immigrant, and Eunice (Lawrence) Codd (1831–1903), a native of Vermont, both Presbyterians. George C. Codd (1829–1904), the father, was an important local politician, sheriff of Wayne County (1871–75), and then postmaster of Detroit (1877–84). Young George was educated in the Detroit public schools and in 1887 entered the University of Michigan, graduating in 1891 with an A.B. degree and a reputation as an outstanding baseball player. In 1892, he entered Michigan's law school, received a law degree, and was admitted to the bar. He began his law practice with the Detroit firm of Griffin, Warner and Codd. In 1894, he married Kathleen Warner (1874–1967), of Detroit and they had three children, John Warner, George Calvin, and Kathleen. Codd was active in a number of fraternal and social clubs, including the Masons, the Nobles of the Mystic Shrine of Moslem Temple, Delta Kappa Epsilon, the Detroit Athletic Club, and the Bloomfield Hills Country Club. He served as a member of the board of regents of the University of Michigan (1909–10). Codd and his family were members of the prestigious First Woodward Presbyterian Church.

Codd began his political career in 1893 as the assistant city attorney of Detroit (1893–96) after which he returned to his law practice with the new firm of Warner, Codd and Warner. He reentered local politics in 1902 as an alderman from Detroit's Fifteenth Ward, and was elected mayor in 1904.

Detroit in 1904 had over 290,000 people and a mayor-council form of government, and was growing rapidly. The streetcar franchise issue continued to be a vital issue, and the idea of municipal ownership of the city's streetcar system was growing in popularity. Codd campaigned on improving the transportation system and hinted at municipal ownership as his ultimate solution. That along with Theodore Roosevelt's presidential coattails gave Detroit Republicans an almost complete sweep of the city's political offices in 1904 and helped carry Codd to victory with 30,942 votes over Democrat William C. Maybury's (q.v.) 23,576.

As mayor, Codd was tormented by the streetcar franchise issue. As the 1906 election approached, he still had not produced a solution. Finally, with the cooperation of the Detroit United Railway's president, Jeremiah Hutchins, Mayor Codd unveiled the Codd-Hutchins Plan that called for a new eighteen-year franchise for Detroit United Railway and a "workingman's ticket" of ten tickets for a quarter. This plan proved to be very unpopular both with Democrats and Republicans, and in a city-wide referendum it was defeated 28,823 to 13,134.

Mayor Codd had staked his political career on the plan and as a result was defeated in his bid for a second term. Codd had the distinction of being the only Republican candidate of importance to be defeated in the 1906 city election, demonstrating the dangers the streetcar franchise issue held for Detroit mayors who failed to produce an acceptable solution.

Following his defeat, Codd returned to his local law practice and in 1911 was elected a circuit court judge for Wayne County, a position he held until 1921 when he was elected to Congress from Michigan's First District. Codd served one term in Washington, and in 1923 he returned to the Wayne County Circuit Court, serving until his death, on 16 February 1927.

SOURCES: Bench and Bar of Michigan, 1918 (Detroit, 1918); *Bench and Bar of Michigan, 1924* (Detroit, 1924); Clarence M. Burton, *The City of Detroit, Michigan, 1701–1922* (Detroit-Chicago, 1922), vol. 4; George P. Codd Papers, scrapbooks, Second Annual Message to the Common Council, 1906, Reading Room File and Biographical Index, Drawer No. 40, Burton Historical Collection, Detroit Public Library; Jack D. Elenbass, "Detroit and the Progressive Era: A Study of Urban Reform 1900–1914" (Ph.D. dissertation, Wayne State University, 1968).   *Jack D. Elenbaas*

COHN, BERNARD (1835–89), Mayor of Los Angeles (1878). First Jewish mayor of Los Angeles, Cohn was born on 7 November 1835 in Polish Prussia of local parents. He migrated to the United States in 1852, moving to Los Angeles in 1854 and clerking in a store before opening his own mercantile business in 1857. He was naturalized on 18 March 1858. In the early 1860s, Cohn was at the gold mines of La Paz, Arizona, on the Colorado River. He ran a forwarding and trading firm, and the later famous Goldwater brothers ran his store until they moved to Prescott. Cohn accumulated real estate in Los Angeles and elsewhere, and had a keen, legalistic mind. In the 1870s he was one of the founders of Hellman, Haas and Company, local grocers.

Cohn knew Los Angeles politics and law well and was famous for his fierce and fearless attacks on those who served the public badly. He thereby became highly controversial. Among Cohn's civic crusades were the removal of a police chief and opposition to a street railway franchise. He served on the Los Angeles City Council, 1876–77, was its president, 1877–78, acting mayor briefly in 1878, and again councilman, 1880–82 and 1887–89. While a councilman he served as chairman of the Finance Committee and was on the public works, water supply, and special committees. Remarkably well read, he was called probably the best and most effective councilman who ever served the city. Cohn was a framer

of a new city charter, worked for a responsible water system, and, like others, tried to solve the problems of effective sewage systems as a member of the sewer commission.

When Mayor MacDougall (*q.v.*) died suddenly on 16 November 1878, the council unanimously elected its colleague, Cohn, mayor *pro tem*. His term would last but two weeks, during which he presided over the council and a hearing, and reported the collection of fees. This was a unique period because, for the first time, Los Angeles had both a Jewish mayor and a Jewish chief of police. In 1877, Councilman Cohn had moved that the newly created post of police chief be filled by Emil Harris, who eventually got the job.

During his brief interim term, Cohn ran for a full term of two years as mayor. On 19 November, the People's convention nominated him. Opponents reacted by accusing him of being the candidate of the bank of which he was associated. Another journal exclaimed: "He may B. Cohn, but he'll never be Mayor." In the election of 2 December, he received 562 votes, about 300 less than his successful opponent, James R. Toberman (*q.v.*).

Cohn returned to the city council and in 1882 ran again for mayor, but he came in third, doing much less well than in 1878, since now he ran as an Independent against the Republican and Democratic candidates. Once more a Democrat, he was reelected to the council in 1887.

As his life drew to its close, Cohn planned to reorganize the Democratic organization locally. Socially, he was active as an Oddfellow, a founder of the Jewish Congregation Beth El, and president of the Congregation B'nai B'rith, and belonged to Los Angeles's pioneer Social Club.

Bernard Cohn died suddenly in Los Angeles of heart disease, on 1 November 1889. Three Los Angeles mayors, Hazard (*q.v.*), Spence (*q.v.*), and Workman (*q.v.*), were pallbearers at his mile-long funeral procession on 3 November to the Jewish Cemetery. His wife, Esther Norton Cohn, had died of apoplexy on 2 June 1885. Cohn left three children by her and four by his Mexican-Californian common-law wife, Delfina Verelas de Cohn, whose children were raised as Roman Catholics.

SOURCES: Chronological Record of Los Angeles City Officials, 1850–1938 (Los Angeles, 1966); files of Los Angeles *Express Herald*, and *Star*, 1876–89; *Great Register of Los Angeles County* (Los Angeles, 1873); Harris Newmark, *Sixty Years in Southern California, 1853–1913* (New York, 1916); Robert V. Hine, ed., *William Andrew Spalding: Los Angeles Newspaperman* (San Marino, 1961); Interview at Los Angeles with Dr. Norton B. Stern, O.D., expert on Bernard Cohn's early career and his 1878 campaign; Los Angeles County Hall of Records, Death Certificates; *United States 10th Census*, 1880:

''California, Los Angeles County''; Max Vorspan and Lloyd F. Gartner, *History of the Jews of Los Angeles* (Huntington Library, 1970).   *John E. Baur*

COLE, NATHAN (1825–1904), Mayor of St. Louis (1869–71). Successful merchant and reform mayor, Cole was born in St. Louis on 26 July 1825, the son of Nathan (d. 1840) and Sarah (Scott) Cole, originally from Ovid, New York. Nathan was the youngest of seven children. He attended school in Chester, Illinois, where the family had moved in 1837. He then went to Shurtleff College in Alton, Illinois, 1843–45. Cole returned to St. Louis as clerk for a local merchant. In 1851, he became a partner of W. L. Ewing, head of a large wholesale grocery. In 1864, he left that company and organized Cole Brothers, commission merchants, attaining equal success. On 30 January 1851, he married Rebecca Lane Fagin of St. Louis, and they had many children. Cole was an active Baptist and constantly stressed the need for religious teachings in daily life.

Cole was elected mayor in 1869, defeating incumbent James Thomas (*q.v.*) 8,961 to 6,033. Cole had defeated Thomas for the Republican nomination, and the latter ran as a Democrat. St. Louis had 310,864 people in 1870 and a mayor-council form of government. Cole was a reform mayor, supporting a new charter and efforts to restore public confidence in their elected officials. He also secured city purchase of the local gas company and improvements to the harbor. He did not particularly enjoy public office and refused to run for a second term, although party leaders thought he would win easily.

Cole returned to his grocery company and was elected president of the St. Louis Merchants' Exchange in 1876. That same year, much against his will, he was elected to Congress for a single term. He actively supported all legislation to improve the city's business opportunities, especially increased U.S. trade with Latin America. In 1879, he completely retired from politics and spent much of his time with the Bank of Commerce, serving as its vice-president until his death on 4 March 1904.

SOURCES: Charles H. Cornwell, *St. Louis Mayors: Brief Biographies* (St. Louis, 1965); William Hyde and Howard L. Conrad, eds., *Encyclopedia of the History of St. Louis*, 4 vols. (New York, 1889); J. T. Scharf, *History of Saint Louis City and County*, 2 vols. (Philadelphia, 1883).   *Thomas R. Bullard*

COLLINS, JOHN F. (1919–   ), Mayor of Boston (1960–68). Strong mayor and shaper of the ''New Boston,'' Collins was born on 20 July 1919 in the Roxbury section of the city. The first-born of three sons of Frederick B. Collins (1888–1959), a mechanic for the Boston Elevated Railway, and Margaret (Mellyn) Collins (1891–1969), both Irish-American Catholics, John Collins attended Roxbury schools and graduated first in his class at Suffolk University Law School in 1941. He also passed the bar in 1941. Collins enlisted in the U.S. Army during World War II and rose from private to the rank of captain in counter-intelligence. After his discharge in 1946, Collins ran successfully for a seat in the Massachusetts House of Representatives from Roxbury and was reelected in 1948. He married Mary Patricia Cunniff, an Irish-American secretary from the Jamaica Plain area of Boston, on 6 September 1947, and they had four children. In 1949, Collins gained a reputation as something of a maverick in Boston politics by supporting the insurgent mayoral candidacy of John B. Hynes (*q.v.*) against Roxbury's own ward boss, James Michael Curley (*q.v.*). Hynes won the election and, a year later, Collins was elected to the state Senate where he served two terms. As a senator, he sponsored tough anti-Communist and narcotics legislation. In 1954, he captured the Democratic nomination for state attorney general but lost the election to Republican incumbent George Fingold. During a campaign for the Boston City Council in 1955, Collins and three of his children were stricken with bulbar poliomyelitis. The children recovered, but their father was thereafter forced to move about by means of a wheelchair and crutches. Despite his condition, Collins remained in the 1955 council race and was victorious. Governor Foster Furcolo appointed him Suffolk County register of probate to fill a vacancy in 1957, and Collins won a full term as register in the election of 1958.

In 1959, Register Collins decided to take on a seemingly impossible race for the Boston mayoralty. He ran second to John E. Powers, the powerful Massachusetts Senate president, in the September preliminary election and thus won the right to compete again in November. Campaigning against ''power politics'' and for substantial urban redevelopment, Collins managed to upset Powers, who was backed by U.S. Senator John F. Kennedy and most of Boston's business and opinion leadership, by a vote of 114,210 to 90,142. He was elected to a second term in 1963 with 108,624 votes to Gabriel F. Piemonte's 73,067. In 1966, Collins lost a contest for Democratic U.S. Senate nomination to Endicott Peabody, who was then defeated by Republican Edward W. Brooke.

Boston had a population of 697,197 in 1960, down 104,000 since 1950. The city had a higher real estate tax than New York and Chicago. In addition, the old-fashioned urban center was losing trade and investment to the suburbs and other parts of the country, and its neighborhoods were deteriorating. As mayor, Collins instituted an economy program which resulted in property tax reductions for four straight years, and he pushed successfully for state assumption of Boston's welfare costs. Collins also brought in urban renewal expert Edward J. Logue from New Haven to head a reorganized Boston Redevelopment Authority. Collins and Logue were able to convince the federal government to fund ten areas of Boston for renewal and won state approval for substantial private development. The Prudential and Government Center projects, on paper during the previous administration, were actually begun and completed in Collins' term, and there were changes made in many areas of the city, including the Boston waterfront and the South End. In the Roxbury and Charlestown sections, hundreds of low- and moderate-income housing units were built. In 1963, Boston was a finalist in the "All-America City" competition, and Collins was president of the National League of Cities. Still, the mayor's support of a limited state sales tax, city personnel cuts, and the razing of parts of old neighborhoods for urban renewal won Collins angry opposition during his second term. In September 1966, he failed to carry Boston in the Democratic primary for the U.S. Senate nomination. The mayor did not seek reelection in 1967. The principal shaper of a "New Boston," Collins was a strong executive who changed the face of the old city fiscally and physically, and became a national spokesman for urban concerns.

In 1968, Collins, the first Boston mayor awarded an honorary doctorate of law by Harvard, was made visiting professor of urban affairs at the Alfred P. Sloan School of Management of MIT, and he has remained consulting professor at the school. He also has practiced law and was chosen president of the Greater Boston Chamber of Commerce in 1971. A member of the Elks, the Knights of Columbus, and the Disabled American Veterans, Collins served as vice-chairman of Democrats for Nixon in the presidential campaign of 1972.

SOURCES: City Record, 1960–1968, Government Documents Department, Boston Public Library; John F. Collins, Boston's Second Revolution (New York, 1962); John F. Collins, "Rebuilding an Old City," Journal of the Boston Society of Civil Engineers 48 (1961); John F. Collins clippings, Newspaper Morgue, School of Public Communication, Boston University; John F. Collins Papers, Boston Public Library; Documents of the City of Boston, 1960–1968, Microtext Department, Boston Public Library; Arnold M. Howitt, "Strategies of Governing: Electoral Constraints on Mayoral Behavior in Philadelphia and Boston" (Ph.D. dissertation, Harvard, 1976); Murray B. Levin, The Alienated Voter: Politics in Boston (New York, 1960); Edward J. Logue, "Boston, 1960–1967—Seven Years of Plenty," Proceedings of the Massachusetts Historical Society 84 (1972); Walter McQuade, "Urban Renewal in Boston," in James Q.

Wilson, ed., Urban Renewal: The Record and the Controversy (Cambridge, Mass., 1966); Daniel S. Pool, "Politics in the New Boston, 1960–1970: A Study of Mayoral Policy-Making" (Ph.D. dissertation, Brandeis, 1974); Proceedings of the City Council of Boston, (Government Documents, Boston Public Library) 1956–57, 1960–68; Stephan Thernstrom, Poverty, Planning and Politics in the New Boston: The Origins of ABCD (New York, 1969).
Richard H. Gentile

COLLINS, PATRICK ANDREW (1844–1905), Mayor of Boston (1902–1905). Called "one of Boston's greatest Irishmen," Collins was a "famine Irish" immigrant, born in Ballinfauna, near Fermoy, County Cork, Ireland, on 12 March 1844. He was the son of a substantial tenant farmer (who rented 200 acres until the potato blight), Bartholomew Collins, and his second wife, Mary Leahy. Bartholomew died in 1847, leaving some published poetry and a family without means, and Mary took her son to Chelsea, Massachusetts, arriving in March 1848. Patrick was aged four. A good Catholic, he went to local public schools, was an altar boy, and taught Sunday School. But his Yankee school peers, infected by the Know-Nothing movement of the day, persecuted him as Irish and Catholic; he was often beaten and had his arm broken. These experiences he did not forget, for, as he developed into a firmly Irish Nationalist politician, he never espoused violence. A poor boy, he did many jobs, including fishmarket work. In 1857, his mother took him to Ohio for two years—a temporary experiment. There he worked in the fields and coal mines at hard manual labor. In 1859, at age fifteen they returned to Boston, and he became an apprentice upholsterer at F. M. Holmes Company, rising to foreman by 1863. A founder-member of the upholsterers' union and a good worker, he earned high wages and much respect. Collins was honest, forthright, and a capable public speaker with a fine memory.

While working, Collins studied at night at the Boston Public Library, walking all the way to work from South Boston in the day, then returning at night to study. He began studying law in 1863 at age twenty-three in the law office of Boston Democrat James M. Keith, enrolling at Harvard Law School (LL.B. and admission to bar, 1871). Meanwhile, he became a leading Fenian from 1864. He gave up once he realized the futility of violence as a means to Irish liberation. He became the first American president of C. S. Parnell's Land League (his portrait hung with Parnell's in Dublin), but he took a conservative, nonradical stance. A strong Democrat, he was a state delegate to the conventions of 1876, 1880, 1888, and 1892, and at age twenty-nine he was chairman of the City Committee, 1874–75. While still a law student, this able and hardworking immigrant youngster was elected to the Massachusetts House (1868–69, age twenty four) and subsequently to the Senate (1870–71—the youngest state senator ever). In the Senate, he fought to abolish anti-Catholic prejudices, including the special "Catholic oath," and demanded Roman Catholic chaplains in hospitals and jails. He opened a successful business law practice in 1871, later forming a law partnership with Judge J. W. Corcoran (1893). Meanwhile, on 1 July 1873, he married Mary E. Carey of Boston, and they had two daughters and a son.

In 1874, for political services to Governor William Garton, Collins was made judge advocate-general (though he never liked the title "general"). In the 1876 election, he worked for the "proper Bostonian" C. F. Adams, arguing, in a famous ethnic speech, that the Irish should vote as Americans—the problem being that most Irish did not like Adams, believing him to be unsympathetic to the Irish cause. In this Marlboro address, Collins said:

I kneel at the altar of my fathers, and I love the land of my birth, but in American politics I know neither color, race nor creed. Let me say here and now that there are no Irish voters among us. There are Irish-born citizens, like myself, and there will be many more of us, but . . . Americans we are, Americans we will remain. . . .

Collins was elected to the U.S. House in 1882 and served until 1889, never liking Congress. Repeating his assimilationist arguments of 1876, Collins became and remained a Cleveland supporter, despite Irish suspicions of that president. He helped elect Cleveland in 1884, presided at the Democratic convention which chose him again in 1888 (when Cleveland lost), and spoke up for him in 1892. Despite all this support, Collins received surprisingly little federal preferment from Cleveland, though his own interests centered increasingly on local Boston politics. He did accept Cleveland's offer and became U.S. consul-general in London, for four years, 1893–97.

During the imperialist years, 1898–1900, Collins strongly supported the liberation of Cuba but bitterly opposed U.S. acquisition of the Philippines and Puerto Rico. He tried to become mayor of Boston in 1899 but lost, the Democrats being badly divided after the death of party boss Pat Maguire in 1896. "I came back (from London) to find the Democratic Party torn into shreds," said Collins. However, he was elected mayor in 1901 and again in 1903. He died in office during 1905, the remainder of his term being filled by Daniel A. Whelton (*q.v.*), chairman of the board of aldermen. As mayor, Collins was no radical: he stood for probity, high ethics, economy, and home rule for the city (as opposed to the authority of the state). He resisted corruption, although even Collins could not help being supported by people like Jimmy Walsh, who in 1903 boasted that he had voted twenty-eight times. Collins felt that Boston had

gone too far with "benevolent Socialism." He rigidly opposed city borrowing, reduced debt levels, and vetoed many spending ideas. However, he believed in the commercial and industrial growth of his city—"I may be counted as an expansionist of the most extreme type," he claimed—and he demanded more business centers to take the pressure off the downtown central business district. "The chief trouble with Boston," he said, "is that it seeks to do all its best business in one square mile of land."

Collins was not a great mayor, but he was easily the most distinguished Irishman of his day, and with his courtly bearing and high political standards he did much to improve the image of Irish Americans in city politics. He died suddenly, on 14 September 1905, in Hot Springs, Virginia, and was buried in Holyhood Cemetery, Boston. A crowd of 100,000 attended his funeral.

SOURCES: Boston *Globe*, 15 September 1905; J. H. Cutler, *"Honey Fitz": Three Steps to the White House* (Indianapolis and New York, 1962); John Koren, *Boston, 1822–1922: The Story of Its Government* (Boston, 1923); *A Memorial to Patrick A. Collins* (Boston 1909).

Peter d'A. Jones

COLVIN, HARVEY DOOLITTLE (1815–92), Mayor of Chicago (1873–76). Populist mayor of Chicago, and a transplanted Yankee, Colvin was born on 18 December 1815 in rural Herkimer County, New York, the son of Presbyterian parents, apparently of British origin. Colvin's father may have been a farmer, but almost nothing is known of the future mayor's early life except that he was educated in the local district schools.

Some time before 1854, Colvin married Nancy Churchill of Little Falls, Herkimer County, New York. He operated a boot factory in that town and held a number of local offices, including that of town supervisor. Colvin and his wife had five known children: John (a Chicago alderman, 1879–87), George P. (an auditor for the American Express Company), Horatio, Libby, and Helen (De-Long).

Colvin came to Chicago in 1854 as resident agent of the U.S. Express Company (later known as American Express)—a position which he held, except for the years of his mayoral term, until 1885. A "Douglas" Democrat, Colvin supported the North in the Civil War and became a Republican in 1864; by 1873, he had returned to the Democratic fold.

Chicago in 1873 had a mayor-council form of government and a population of approximately 380,000. The city's political life was much disturbed during that year by the attempts of the Joseph E. Medill (*q.v.*) administration to close saloons on Sundays, and by charges of misuse of the police power and opposition to the introduction of civil service. Unrest, fueled by the national depression, was centered in the city's immigrant community, especially among German Americans.

The Democratic party seized the opportunity and, in 1873, joined forces with the People's party to support Colvin (who had publicly opposed Sunday closing). This alliance included allegedly corrupt politicians and was compared with New York City's Tweed Ring. Such varied support helped Colvin defeat Republican Lester L. Bond (interim mayor from the time of the resignation of Joseph Medill) by a vote of 28,791 to 18,540 on 4 November 1873.

Colvin's term was beset with controversy. The mayor ended attempts to enforce Sunday closing, but five weeks after his election, the city treasurer—a carryover from the two previous administrations—defaulted and threw Chicago's finances into chaos. Colvin opposed a new city charter, presented for referendum in 1875, which centralized the police and fire departments and removed them further from public control, but the charter narrowly passed. When the state passed a law altering the terms of local officials, Colvin claimed, on a technicality, that his term should run through April 1877. A public furor followed, and conservative elements called a special election, without council authorization, for 18 April 1876. Thomas Hoyne, a prominent real estate man, ran without organized opposition and received 33,064 of 33,814 votes cast. Colvin denied Hoyne's right to office and for nearly two months the city had two mayors and two sets of officials. After the courts declared Hoyne's election illegal, Colvin resumed the mayoral office on 5 June 1876 and retained it until a legal special election on 7 July 1876, in which he did not run.

Colvin retired from political life after the election of 1876, but he did serve as a Democratic elector in 1884. He died on 16 April 1892 in Jacksonville, Florida.

SOURCES: Fremont O. Bennett, *Politics and Politicians of Chicago, Cook County, and Illinois* (Chicago, 1886); Chicago *Daily News*, 18 April 1892; Chicago *Tribune*, 19 April 1892; Francis A. Eastman, *Chicago City Manual* (Chicago, 1911); Frederick Rex, *The Mayors of the City of Chicago from March 4, 1837 to April 13, 1933* (typescript dated 1933 held by the Municipal Reference Library of Chicago).   *Paul Barrett*

COMAN, THOMAS (1836–1909), Acting Mayor of New York (1868). Born in 1836 in Ireland, Coman emigrated to New York with his parents and eventually served briefly as acting mayor. As a young man, he worked for James Gordon Bennett on the New York *Herald*, but at the age of twenty-five, he found employment with the Post Office. He left after facing charges of embezzlement. In 1864, he was appointed inspector

of incumberances. He married his wife, Martha, in that year; their first child Ada, a daughter, was born in 1865. Four other children followed—Thomas W. (b. 1874), Marjam J. (b. 1876), John H. (b. 1878), and Theresa D. (b. 1880). In 1866, Coman was nominated to run as alderman in the Second District on the Democratic ticket. This district consisted of two lower wards of the city, the Fourth and the notorious "Bloody Ould" Sixth Ward where elections were often violent affairs. Coman defeated his opponent, Michael C. Donahoe, 1,798 to 1,471. Coman's occupation at the time was given as a printer. He was elected to his office as alderman each year through 1872. He appears to have served as temporary mayor in 1868, between Mayor J. T. Hoffman (*q.v.*) and Mayor A. O. Hall (*q.v.*). From 1868 to 1870, Coman was president of the board of aldermen, and in 1870 he was also a county courthouse commissioner. The city had a population of over 800,000 and a mayor-council form of government, with weak executive power.

Coman's political world tumbled, along with that of many others, after the denunciation of Boss William M. Tweed by the New York *Times* beginning in July 1871. In June 1872, the *Times* involved Coman on unprosecuted charges of having, as acting mayor, fraudulently signed several warrants. Coman insisted that such bills had been approved by others and had only needed his official signature; moreover, Mayor John T. Hoffman was never away from his office longer than six days, and under the law Coman never really was acting mayor. He issued a statement of disgust with the new "Tammany Hall Management" in June 1872 and lost a fight to become president of the aldermen again. Coman promised to vote for U. S. Grant, as the Republican party was the only one that could effect "Reform."

In June 1873, writs were issued for the arrest of Coman and all former members of the County Courthouse Commission. The courthouse was already famed as the center of the "Ring Frauds," when Coman was indicted on six counts of bribery. He fled to Canada but returned in October 1874, and by June 1875 the state instituted suits to recover some $400,000 from the defendants. The ex-officials were found guilty, but on appeal the suit against Coman was dismissed. He retired from politics, and was involved in insurance. He died of pneumonia on 22 October 1909 at his home at 35 West 76th Street.

SOURCES: New York *Times*, various dates during the period 1871–78; David T. Valentine, *Minutes of the Common Council* (New York, 1860–70).

Leo Hershkowitz

CONNELL, GEORGE (1871–1955), Acting Mayor of Philadelphia (1939). Long-time politician, born in Philadelphia on 3 November 1871, Connell was the third son of Horatio P. Connell (1840–1927), politician, and his wife Anne (Laycock) Connell, both old-stock Americans of Scottish Protestant descent. The fifth of eight children, young George attended Newton Grammar School and Pierce Brown High School. He then started work as a stockboy for Boyd, White and Company, a major carpet firm. He spent a few years in West Philadelphia, selling real estate. In 1894, he entered local politics and was elected Republican ward committeeman in 1896, retaining this party post for forty-two years until defeated in 1938. He also married Caroline Fairman (1874–1933), the daughter of a prominent Philadelphia merchant, and they had two children. They soon bought a summer home in Maryland where Connell relaxed by hunting and fishing. He also served as director of the Mount Moriah Cemetery, founded by his grandfather in the nineteenth century.

Connell served on the common council, 1913–15, the select council, 1915–19, and the city council, 1919–39 (president, 1936–39). He was also a member of the Republican Central Committee of Philadelphia County, 1906–39. As presiding officer of the council, Connell became acting mayor on 11 August 1939, when Mayor Samuel Wilson (q.v.) resigned because of poor health. At that time, Philadelphia had a population of 1,935,086 and a mayor-council form of government.

As acting mayor, Connell strongly supported a city-wide tax to ease the financial crisis stemming from his predecessor's long illness. He also streamlined the police and fire departments, sending 210 desk officers out to the city streets. He secured a new budget, sold $4 million in city bonds, and settled a longstanding fight with the city's gas company. In 1940, Connell was appointed director of public welfare by Mayor Robert Lamberton (q.v.) and served until 1943 when he was paralyzed by a stroke. Connell spent the next twelve years in a nursing home until his death on 22 October 1955.

SOURCES: Herman L. Collins and Wilfred Jordan, *Philadelphia: A Story of Progress*, 4 vols. (New York, 1941), vol. 4; Philadelphia *Bulletin*, 4 December 1939, 23 October 1955; Philadelphia *Enquirer*, 23 October 1955; Philadelphia *Record*, 20 August 1939.

Thomas R. Bullard

CONRAD, ROBERT (1810–58), Mayor of Philadelphia (1854–56). Anti-immigrant, prohibitionist, Protestant mayor, born in Philadelphia in 1810, Conrad was educated for a career in law. But shortly after his admission to the bar in 1832, he, like his father before him, entered publishing, serving as editor of the Philadelphia *Daily Gazette*. Because of bad health he resigned his position in 1834 to return to law, quickly establishing a reputation as a brilliant orator. In 1835, he was elected

city recorder and in 1838 judge of the court of criminal sessions. When that court was dissolved shortly thereafter, Conrad returned to writing as a dramatist, as editor of *Graham's* literary magazine, and as political editor of the protectionist Whig paper, the *North American*. He also assumed the presidency of the Hempfield Railroad, which secured valuable city investments in the effort to open markets to the West.

Conrad's political ascendancy coincided with a turbulent period in Philadelphia politics, distinguished by the growth of a virulent anti-Catholic, "American Republican" party after the devastating riots of 1844 and subsequent decline of the Whig party. When the city and county of Philadelphia consolidated in 1854 (combining a population of 493,000), in part to assure law and order, Conrad sought the nomination for mayor from the American and prohibitionist parties by pledging to sustain the dominant Protestant morality through observance of the Sabbath, retention of Protestant Bible readings in public schools, and appointment of only native-born police. Arguing that a separate nomination would insure a Democratic victory, he used his endorsement by the American Republicans as a weapon in diverting support in the Whig convention away from the presiding mayor of Philadelphia, Charles Gilpin, to his own candidacy. With this support in hand, he defeated his Democratic opponent, Richard Vaux, 28,883 to 21,020.

Conrad quickly redeemed his pledges to his more moralistic supporters by dismissing all foreign-born members of the police force and by enforcing a long-dormant law prohibiting taverns from opening on Sundays. His political hold on office rapidly declined, however, as divisions between old-line Whigs and Americans sharpened and reports of extravagant expenditures plagued his administration. When the Americans offered their support for reelection in 1856, Conrad declined to run. Shortly after leaving office he was named judge of the court of quarter sessions to replace William Kelley, who had resigned upon becoming a Republican candidate for Congress. A year later Conrad retired to private law practice, which he pursued until his death, after a brief illness, at his home in West Philadelphia, on 28 June 1858.

SOURCES: Michael Feldberg, *The Philadelphia Riots of 1844: A Study of Ethnic Conflict* (Westport, Conn., 1975); Howard Gillette, Jr., "The Emergence of the Modern Metropolis: Philadelphia in the Age of its Consolidation," in William W. Cutler III and Howard Gillette, Jr., eds., *The Divided Metropolis: Social and Spatial Dimensions of Philadelphia, 1800–1975* (Westport, Conn., 1980); Sam Bass Warner, Jr., *The Private City: Philadelphia in Three Periods of Its Growth* (Philadelphia, 1968).

Howard Gillette, Jr.

CONWAY, JAMES F. (1933–   ), Mayor of St. Louis (1977–   ). Born on 27 June 1933 in St. Louis, Conway, the son of Charles F. Conway and Amelia (Buchholtz) Conway, both Roman Catholic natives of that city, attended local parochial schools and graduated from General Motors Institute in 1955 (with a B.S., receiving a M.B.A. in 1964). Conway served with the Thirteenth Infantry, rising in rank from private to Specialist, 1955–57. During the early 1960s, he was product manager for the Missouri Tank and Boilers Division of the Nooter Corporation. In 1967, he became president of ACI Plastics. On 4 June 1955, he married Joan Carol Newman, and they had five children. The Conways are members of St. Margaret of Scotland (Catholic) Church. Conway is a member of the Ancient Order of Hibernians, Express Club, St. Louis Chamber of Commerce, and the St. Vincent De Paul Society.

A Democrat, Conway served in the Missouri House of Representatives from 1967 to 1975, followed by a single term (1975–77) in the state Senate. In 1977, he was elected mayor of St. Louis, with 69,697 votes to 16,869 for J. A. Stemmler (Republican) and 16,861 write-in votes for W. L. Clay (Independent). St. Louis had 622,236 people in 1970 (a declining population) and a mayor-council form of government.

Mayor Conway's administration coincided with the ongoing effort to preserve St. Louis's historic buildings. He was able to negotiate a successful agreement with the Missouri Pacific Railroad, regarding trackage along the city's waterfront. Perhaps his most important accomplishment concerns the city's annual budget. Traditionally, the budgetary process was the responsibility of the comptroller and his staff, with final approval coming from the city council. Conway, in an effort to streamline the process, created a special mayoral budget staff which now does most of the work. His goal has been to reduce waste and to preserve necessary jobs and services, since the city has been hard hit by rising costs and inflation. Critics have charged that he is assuming more power than allowed by the city charter, but it would appear that his plan has public approval.

SOURCES: *Official Manual, State of Missouri, 1971–1972* (Jefferson City, 1971); St. Louis *Post-Dispatch*, various issues for January-April 1980; *Who's Who in American Politics* (New York, 1979).

Thomas R. Bullard

CONWAY, JOHN R. (1825–96), Mayor of New Orleans (1868–70). Born on 25 August 1825 in Alexandria, Virginia, to parents of Welsh extraction, Conway moved to New Orleans in 1843 and was employed in the cotton commission business until federal troops occupied the city in 1862. In 1865, he reentered business as a wholesale grocer and commission merchant. He married Eliza G. Waggaman in 1857 and was the father of two daughters.

New Orleans in 1868 had a population of about 180,000 and a mayor-council form of government under the control of a Radical Reconstruction legislature and military authorities. Having served as first chairman of the Orleans Parish Democratic Committee after the war, Conway accepted the Democratic nomination for mayor and beat his Republican opponent, Seth W. Lewis, by a close vote of 13,895 to 13,244. Conway's inauguration was delayed for several weeks until the occupying military authority had again canvassed the vote, and on 10 June 1868 the mayor-elect was installed.

Conway's mayoralty is not considered a brilliant chapter in the annals of New Orleans, but it was memorable because, as a result of Louisiana's readmission to the Union, military control over the municipal government ended. Yet, one outside force was merely replaced by another. The Radical Reconstruction government in the statehouse took control of the New Orleans police department with a state-controlled metropolitan police force, as well as of the city's schools with a state-appointed board, and invalidated the election of several Democratic city councilmen. In 1870, the state legislature abolished New Orleans' mayor-council government and in its place put in a weak mayor and seven administrators who were to be elected at large. The new charter also authorized the governor to appoint the first set of administrators and the new mayor, who was a Republican. The Democratic incumbent Conway, according to a local historian, lacked the vigor, both physical and mental, to deal with these problems. In the dying days of his administration, he clung desperately to his office, trying to resist change but to no avail. He died on 11 March 1896.

SOURCES: L. V. Howard and R. S. Friedman, *Government in Metropolitan New Orleans* (New Orleans, 1959); John S. Kendall, *History of New Orleans* (Chicago, 1922), vol. 1.

Betsy B. Holli and *Melvin G. Holli*

COOK, ELI, JR. (1814–65), Mayor of Buffalo (1853–55). Conservative lawyer and first mayor under the new two-year term charter of 1853, Cook was born in Palatine Bridge, New York, on 23 January 1814, the son of Joseph and Fanny Cook. The Cook family moved to Manlius, New York, in 1824, and young Eli attended local schools and then studied for the ministry, as his father had wished. He became dissatisfied with the life of a divinity student and switched to law in 1830. Cook moved to Utica and studied in the office of John Fleming. He subsequently became a clerk for Whittemore and

Denio, and then entered a private law partnership. This partnership was dissolved in 1837 when Cook went to the South. He traveled through Tennessee and Mississippi, as a partner of Simon B. Buckner, the future Confederate general. In 1838, this partnership was also dissolved, and Cook moved back to Buffalo. He married, but his first wife died soon after, and in 1843 he married for a second time. He and his second wife, Sarah (d. 1883), had no children. Cook was one of Buffalo's most popular courtroom lawyers, noted for his brilliant oratory.

A Democrat, Cook had served as Buffalo's city attorney in 1845–46. He was elected mayor in 1853, defeating Whig Leroy Farnham 3,138 to 2,389. A new charter went into effect during this term, and Cook was reelected to the first two-year mayoral term in November 1853 (the term beginning 1 January 1854). He defeated Whig James C. Harrison 3,093 to 3,021, with three other minor candidates receiving a total of 586 votes. Buffalo had 42,261 people and a mayor-council form of government.

As mayor, Cook supported fiscal conservatism and warned against allowing the city budget to grow beyond safe limits. He did believe that schools were worth extra expenses but only because they shaped future citizens. He constantly urged the city council to keep taxes low and to reduce them whenever possible. After three years in office, Cook showed no interest in another term and returned to his law practice. His health declined, and he died on 25 February 1865.

SOURCES: Buffalo *Daily Courier*, 27 February 1865; Buffalo *Express*, 27 February 1865; Buffalo *Sunday Times*, 27 July 1919.   *Thomas R. Bullard*

COOK, LEVI (1792–1866), Mayor of Detroit (1832, 1835, 1836). Three times mayor of Detroit and a transplanted New Englander, Cook was born in Bellingham, Massachusetts, on 16 December 1792, the son of a farmer. He was one of four children. As a young man, Cook taught school in Massachusetts and then moved to Buffalo, New York, where he entered the fur trade. In 1815, he moved to Detroit and taught school for a year. He then operated a grocery store but was not successful. In 1821, he opened a dry goods store with his brother, Orville.

Cook held numerous offices in the city of Detroit and the Territory of Michigan. He was a trustee of Detroit, 1821–22; treasurer of Detroit, 1822; a Wayne County commissioner, 1824–26; superintendent of the city poor, 1827–28; alderman-at-large, 1828; treasurer of the Territory of Michigan, 1830–36; chief engineer of Detroit's fire department, 1830, 1833–35; and township supervisor for Detroit, 1834. He married Eliza Stevens (d. 1866)

of Boston, a Presbyterian as he was. They had no children but adopted one daughter, Eliza Sanderson. He was active in the Masonic Lodge and served as a colonel in the state militia. Cook was a Whig, who in the 1850s joined the new Republican party.

Detroit had a population of about 4,000 when Cook was first elected mayor. On 2 April 1832, running as a National Republican with no opposition, he received 148 votes to win. The city had a mayor-council form of government. Under Cook's direction, the common council drew up rules of order for its meetings and established standing committees on claims and accounts, ways and means, streets, health, and fires. During the summer of 1832, Cook had to deal with a serious outbreak of cholera, brought to the city by troops on their way to the Blackhawk War. The mayor issued a proclamation requiring the medical inspection of all ships arriving at the city, and he set up a committee of physicians to assist the board of health in dealing with the epidemic. The disease caused the death of several hundred Detroit citizens.

As a Whig, Cook ran for reelection on 6 April 1835 defeating Andrew Mack (*q.v.*) by a vote of 234 to 188. Cook began his second term as mayor on 11 April 1835. The mayor and the council planned a new sewer system for the city. In October, they authorized a loan of $100,000 to pay for the sewers. The "Toledo War," a bloodless fight over the location of the border between Ohio and Michigan, took place at this time, and Cook led his city in supporting Michigan's claims. In July, the common council voted to permit the publication of their proceedings in the newspapers. A new city hall with a public market on the first floor was occupied on 18 November. A fresh outbreak of cholera during the summer slowed the large migration movement that passed through Detroit.

Cook was elected to his third and final term on 4 April 1836, defeating John Biddle (*q.v.*) 249 to 153. The city's population had grown to 6,927. The mayor and council revoked the charter of the Hydraulic Company that had provided Detroit with its water for many years. They bought out the company for $20,500 and made plans for a city-owned water plant to be constructed up the river. The first underground sewer was built. The city ordered street names at all street corners for the first time. In September 1836, the council drew up new bylaws and ordinances for the government of the city. Cook opposed the council's proposal to have the city subscribe $50,000 for the construction of the Michigan Central Railroad, but the council prevailed. On 9 February 1837, the mayor led the city's celebration to honor Michigan's admission to the Union on 26 January 1837.

In 1838, Cook was elected to the state legislature. He

served on the Detroit Board of Review, 1840–41, and was assessor for the Second Ward, 1840–41. He was connected with several banking organizations, serving as a director of the Farmers and Mechanics Bank in 1829 and as president, 1838–45. In 1835, he was secretary of the Detroit and St. Joseph Railroad, and in 1845, he became president of the Bank of St. Clair. He held large real estate holdings in the city. He died on 2 December 1866.

SOURCES: Clarence M. Burton, *History of Detroit, 1780–1850* (Detroit, 1917); Frederick Carlisle, comp., *Chronology of Notable Events in the History of the Northwest Territory and Wayne County* (Detroit, 1895); Detroit Common Council, *Journal of the Proceedings of the Common Council of the City of Detroit, 1824–1843* (n.p., n.d.); Detroit *Post*, 3 December 1866; Silas Farmer, *History of Detroit and Wayne County and Early Michigan*, 3d ed. (1890; reprint, Detroit, 1969); scattered papers in the Burton Historical Collection, Detroit Public Library.   *William T. Bulger*

COON, HENRY PERRIN (1822–84), Mayor of San Francisco (1863–67). Talented eleventh mayor of San Francisco and the last to represent the Vigilante-People's party, Coon was born of Dutch stock in Columbia County, New York, on 20 September 1822. One of thirteen children, he taught school before graduating from the Philadelphia School of Medicine in 1848. He practiced medicine in Syracuse, New York, then moved to San Francisco in 1853, where he opened a drug store and began the San Francisco Chemical Company to import drugs (February 1854). He also had strong real estate interests.

Coon favored the Vigilance Committee of 1856 and was easily elected police judge on 15 November 1856, serving until 1861. He was firm but fair, although he gained some notoriety by refusing to intervene in a famous duel in September 1859, when a California Supreme Court justice, David S. Terry, shot and killed a senator, David C. Broderick. Coon reluctantly allowed himself to be run as the People's party nominee for mayor and was elected on 19 May 1863, defeating an unlucky Democrat, Nathaniel Holland, who was burdened with owning rich waterfront property at a time when the Vigilantes were angry over land speculation and were out to impose regulations.

During Coon's first term, the city grew rapidly, helped by the silver boom, now at its peak, and Civil War prosperity. Hundreds of banks opened, five from Great Britain alone, all on Montgomery Street, and also one of the five largest in the United States, W. C. Ralston's Bank of California, which opened in July 1864 with $22 million capital. The city had three stock exchanges and up to forty manufacturing concerns, placing it ninth in the nation in manufacturing investment and net worth of goods manufactured ($2 million and $20 million, respectively) by 1865. Its population, always growing, was over 100,000. Mayor Coon was suited to an era of commercial growth: he was calm, quiet, an able administrator, with enormous faith in the future of San Francisco. He took very few actions, although he did have installed an advanced system of local fire alarm, crank-action magnetic boxes in contact with fire headquarters; and the magnetic telegraph reached the city, one day ahead of Lincoln's murder in April 1865 and in time to communicate that news. Perhaps Coon's leadership, such as it was, took the form of example. He certainly invested in his city: he was president of the King Morse Canning Company and director of the San Francisco Fire Insurance Company, Coon helped found the Calvary Presbyterian Church and served as the church's elder and trustee.

Coon was reelected on 16 May 1865. His victory was much narrower this time, however, a sign of the declining power of the People's party. His final term (extended to December 1867 by yet another change of city election schedules of the interfering state legislature) was less calm, although the city continued its growth. The mayor and the board lost a legal action against the Central Pacific Railroad over Coon's refusal to deliver $650,000 of city bonds in exchange for railroad bonds. The mayor opposed one of the city's leading capitalists, William C. Ralston, by vetoing an extension of Montgomery Street that would have enriched Ralston's property (though Coon spent his final seventeen years of retirement and died, in Ralston's famous Palace Hotel). Coon failed to solve many legal problems over *pueblo* titles dating back to the 1840s, but he did have one success, the Clement Ordinance of 1867, which set aside land for public use, including the future Golden Gate Park, which Coon had surveyed—pushing the visionary plans of Mayor James Van Ness (*q.v.*) one step further.

After 1867, Coon returned briefly to his practice, but he soon became totally involved in business and real estate. Very wealthy, he bought two large ranches, one of which became part of Stanford University in later years. He died in San Francisco on 4 December 1884.

SOURCES: Hubert Howe Bancroft, *Retrospection, Political and Personal* (New York, 1912); Stuart Daggett, *Chapters on the History of the Southern Pacific* (New York, 1922); W. F. Heintz, *San Francisco's Mayors* (Woodside, Calif., 1975); San Francisco *Evening Bulletin*, 4 October 1864; Oscar T. Shuck, *Historical Abstract of San Francisco* (San Francisco, 1897).

Peter d'A. Jones

COOPER, EDWARD (1824–1905), Mayor of New York (1879–80). Third mayor of the post-Tweed, limited reform era, Cooper was born in New York City on 26 October 1824. His father, Peter Cooper (1791–1883), a famous inventor, industrialist, and philanthropist, built the first successful American locomotive, worked to develop the nation's telegraph system, helped to create New York's school system, founded Cooper Union, and was a Greenback party presidential candidate in 1876. Edward was educated in public schools and at Columbia University (he did not graduate). After a tour abroad with Abram S. Hewitt (*q.v.*), another future New York mayor and manufacturer, he returned to Columbia in 1845 where he was awarded an honorary A.M. degree. With Hewitt, he organized Cooper, Hewitt and Company, manufacturers of iron and steel products. Cooper gained prominence in metallurgical engineering with his invention of the regenerative hot blast stove. Cooper, Hewitt expanded and absorbed the Peter Cooper, Trenton, Ringwood, Pequest and Durham Iron Works. Cooper served as director of the U.S. Trust Company, the American Sulphur Company, the New Jersey Steel and Iron Company, the New York and Greenwood Lake Railway, the American Elevator Company, the Chrysolite Silver Mining Company, and the Metropolitan Opera House. A late marriage (1886) to Mrs. James Redman of Utica, New York, resulted in the birth of a daughter Edith.

Cooper's political career began in 1860 as a delegate to the national Democratic convention. In 1871, he suggested to Governor Samuel J. Tilden, with whom he was identified in Democratic party battles, that Boss Tweed be investigated. As a member of the Committee of 70 Cooper was prominent in the prosecutions and reforms that followed. Cooper became known as the man who had investigated Tweed's bank accounts, favored sanitation reform, and opposed property qualifications for voting.

According to the 1880 Census, New York had 1,164,673 people and a mayor-aldermanic system. In the 1878 election, Cooper was the fusion candidate of the anti-Tammany Democrats and the Republicans. With his victory, the anti-Tammany party members supplanted Tammany as the regular Democrats. Cooper proclaimed an end to the niggardly policies of his immediate predecessors, but it was understood that levels of spending would not reach previous heights. He was unable to build a stable coalition to support his programs, as his efforts were seen in the context of Tilden's battles with Tammany's John Kelly. Cooper refused to reappoint Kelly as comptroller after the expiration of his term in 1880. Mayor Cooper was viewed as an earnest but heavyhanded reformer who continued the battle for cleaner streets and a more responsive police board. Under his administra-

tion, there was more a sense of marking time than of making clear-cut changes in the questionable conduct of the aldermen and the city departments. Cooper helped to enact the Tenement House Law of 1879 which prohibited building on more than 65 percent of a lot.

After his term, Cooper turned his attention to the Cooper Union (an educational institute in New York City) and his various corporation trusteeships. He suffered a stroke shortly before his eighty-first birthday at his home at 12 North Washington Square, where he lived with the family of his son-in-law, ex-Congressman Lloyd S. Bryce. He died on 25 February 1905 and was buried in Greenwood Cemetery.

SOURCES: Gordon Atkins, *Health, Housing and Poverty in New York City 1865–1898* (Ann Arbor, Mich., 1947); William T. Bonner, *New York: The World's Metropolis* (New York, 1924); William Herman, *Factbook: Mayors and Burgomasters* (New York, n.d.); New York *Herald*, 12 January 1879, Speech of John Kelly to Lotus Club (in Tammany Scrapbooks, Special Collections, Columbia University).   *Howard R. Weiner*

CORONEL, ANTONIO F. (1817–94), Mayor of Los Angeles, (1853–54). First Hispanic mayor of American Los Angeles, Coronel, born on 21 October 1817 in Mexico City, came to California in 1834. He was the third oldest of eleven children of Roman Catholic parents, Ygnacio Coronel (c. 1796–1862) and Francisca Romero de Coronel (c. 1800–71). Ygnacio Coronel struggled for several years to make a living but finally settled in 1837 in Los Angeles where he became a schoolteacher and minor civic official. His oldest surviving son, Antonio, also held local offices and, when U.S. troops invaded California in 1846, he attempted to reach Mexican Army officers in Sonora to seek assistance for the *Californios*, only to turn back when he encountered American troops. In 1848, he went north as a successful gold miner, but in the following years threats of violence against non-Americans soured him on gold mining. He then returned to Los Angeles where he owned substantial orchards and vineyards.

Antonio Coronel easily moved back into local politics when an American government was organized. He won office as assessor in the first Los Angeles County election in April 1850 and three months later was elected city assessor. After three terms as assessor, he was elected mayor of the city's approximately 2,400 residents in 1853. His major achievement was council suspension of payments to private schools and establishment of a board of education to provide for the construction of a public schoolhouse and to obtain money from the state school fund.

After his one year as mayor, Coronel ran for the common council and served nine terms between 1854 and 1867. During those years, he was also twice appointed to the board of education and once elected to the county board of supervisors. He became a leading member of the Democratic County Central Committee, and in 1860 he appeared as a presidential elector for the slate of John Breckenridge which carried Los Angeles but not California. By 1867, he had become one of the leading Hispanics in the Democratic party and was nominated for state treasurer. Although he won that office, his unfamiliarity with English limited his political future in the increasingly Anglo-dominated South. He served briefly on the Water Commission in 1870 but mostly confined himself to managing his property in Los Angeles, with several intensive agricultural operations near downtown. In 1873, he married Mariana Williamson (1851–?), daughter of a Yankee father and Mexican mother who had moved to Los Angeles from San Antonio when Mariana was a child. Until his death on 17 April 1894, Coronel and his wife, thirty-four years his junior and childless, remained socially prominent, a member of the State Horticultural Society, president of the Spanish-American Benevolent Society of Los Angeles, and founding member of the Historical Society of Southern California. For the thoroughly Americanized city of the late nineteenth century, the Coronels symbolized the romantic aspects of southern California in the years of the Mexican *dons*.

SOURCES: Hubert Howe Bancroft, *The Works of Hubert Howe Bancroft*, 39 vols., *History of California* (San Francisco, 1884–90), vols. 18–24; H. D. Barrows, "Antonio F. Coronel," *Historical Society of Southern California* 5 (1900); Antonio F. Coronel, "Cosas de California," unpublished mss., Bancroft Library, Berkeley, California; Richard Morefield, "The Mexican Adaptation in American California, 1846–1875" (M.A. Thesis, University of California, Berkeley, 1955).

R. David Weber

CORR, FRANK J. (1877–1934), Acting Mayor of Chicago (1933). The unknown mayor, who never wanted the job but instead a judgeship, was born in 1877 in Brooklyn, New York and brought to Chicago at age 12 by his father, a chewing-gum manufacturer. One of eight children, Corr attended the public schools, went to Kent College of Law, and then into private practice with a politically-connected friend. He held several minor political posts including assistant corporation counsel and was elected to the city council in 1931 and reelected in 1933.

When an assassin's bullet missed President-elect Franklin D. Roosevelt on 15 February 1933 and hit Chicago Mayor Anton Cermak—a train of events began that elevated the reluctant Corr into the mayorship. The ailing Cermak died on 6 March, and Cook County and Chicago political boss, Patrick J. Nash led the city council to choose Frank J. Corr, as temporary mayor. Chicago politicians, as startled as the newspapers, asked, "Who is Frank J. Corr?" Corr himself gasped: "I hadn't any idea that I was to be mayor at this time yesterday." Corr was simply a convenient, unknown caretaker who was temporarily to hold the mayorship until the Democratic political machine could agree upon a more permanent choice. When the organization decided upon Edward J. Kelly, Corr's twenty-eight day reign ended on April 17. One of the pleasant duties that Corr had enjoyed was presiding over what Chicagoan's called "New Beer's Eve," when prohibition ended and the foamy amber fluid flowed legally again in Chicago. Corr never achieved his goal of a judgeship. Although he was slated by the party to run in 1934, he took sick three weeks before the election and died on 3 June 1934, nineteen hours before the polls opened. Ironically he held a job that thousands wanted but which he did not desire; and death cheated him out of the judgeship he did want.

SOURCES: Files Municipal Reference Library; Chicago *Tribune*, March and April 1933; Chicago *Magazine*, 29 (October 1980).

Perry R. Duis

CORRY, WILLIAM (1779–1833), Mayor of Cincinnati (1815–19). Corry, the first mayor of the *town* of Cincinnati was born in 1779 in rural Virginia of immigrant parents born in Ireland. His patriot-soldier father was killed at the battle of King's Mountain in 1781. William worked on his mother's farm until he was nineteen, receiving an elementary education at a local schoolhouse. In 1798, he accepted the invitation of a relative, attorney William McMillan, to go to Cincinnati to study law. Corry was admitted to the Cincinnati bar in 1803, and, after McMillan's death in 1804, he was a law partner of John Reily in Dayton, Ohio. After Reily became clerk of courts in Dayton, Corry practiced law alone. Marrying in 1810, Corry returned to Cincinnati in 1811 to administer a large agricultural estate for which he had become an executor under McMillan's will. Corry set up a law practice in Cincinnati at the same time and also became librarian of the downtown library. He was elected in 1814 to the post of town clerk by the council. In 1815, the state legislature repealed the old town incorporation act of 1802, increasing Cincinnati's council membership to twelve—three elected from each of four newly created Wards—and changing the title of council president to mayor.

Corry was the first town mayor elected by the council under the new municipal system in 1815. The population of Cincinnati was then 6,200. During his four-year term,

Corry and the town marshal, James Chambers, successfully met a serious challenge to public order from lawless elements in this raw and wild river community. Attempts to mediate local disputes in the mayor's office often ended in brawls and knife duels. But the Corry administration ruled with an iron hand and punished lawbreakers severely, bringing law and order to Cincinnati. Corry was a capable administrator. During his term, a private water company was given rights to serve the town, a wharf was built on the Ohio River, and methods of preventing and fighting fires were improved.

After an exhausting four years, Corry chose to return to the private practice of law and to cultural pursuits. In 1829, however, he did run again in a public election for mayor, but he finished third with 263 votes to Isaac G. Burnet's (q.v.) 1,042 and Andrew Mack's (q.v.) 784. Corry's health deteriorated during the last years of his life, and he died in 1833 at the age of fifty-four.

SOURCES: Cincinnati Municipal Reference Bureau, *Origins of Municipal Activities in the City of Cincinnati* (Cincinnati, 1935); Charles Cist, *Cincinnati in 1841: Its Early Annals and Future Prospects* (Cincinnati, 1841); Charles T. Greve, *Centennial History of Cincinnati and Representative Citizens*, 2 vols. (Chicago, 1904).

Gary Kocolowski

COUZENS, FRANK (1902–50), Mayor of Detroit (1933–38). Detroit's youngest mayor, who became known nationally because he so ably handled fiscal problems during the Great Depression, Couzens was born on 28 February 1902 in Detroit, the son of a former mayor and U.S. senator, James Couzens (q.v.) (1872–1936), and Margaret Ann (Manning) Couzens. Couzens attended the Newman Preparatory School in Hackensack, New Jersey, and the Detroit public schools. He left school at age eighteen and joined an architectural firm where after three years he became assistant superintendent. He later joined with John Frazer to form a building firm of which he was vice-president until 1941 when the company was dissolved. Couzens married a Canadian, Margaret Lang, the daughter of a Kitchener, Ontario, manufacturer, on 19 October 1922; they had seven children. He was a member of the Roman Catholic Church. He served as chairman of the board of the Children's Fund of Michigan, as a board member of the Boys Club of Detroit, and on the Crippled Children's Commission of Michigan. He belonged to the Round Table of Catholics, Jews, and Protestants. Yachting, riding, golf, and bowling were his favorite pastimes, and so he belonged to several recreational organizations within the Detroit community.

Couzens entered public life at the age of twenty-one when he was appointed to the Detroit City Plan Commission. In 1929, he joined the city's Department of Street Railways. Two years later, he ran for the common council, led the ticket, and was elected president. He became acting mayor on 10 May 1933 at the age of thirty-one after Frank Murphy (q.v.) resigned to become governor-general of the Philippine Islands. Couzens was out of office briefly when he resigned to run for mayor, but when his fellow citizens elected him in November 1933, he served two terms, from 2 January 1934, to 3 January 1938. In the November 1933 election he defeated Philip Breitmeyer (q.v.) 141,811 to 76,450, and two years later he easily overcame Joseph Schemansky 130,339 to 30,503. Couzens always refused to spend large sums in his campaign saying, "I'm not going to have it said that I set too heavy a price for some candidates with less money to follow."

In 1933 Detroit, a city of 1,483,274 with a mayor-council form of government, had defaulted on bond payments and was paying city employees with scrip. Mayor Couzens restored the city's fiscal creditability by slashing the debt by $45 million and by balancing the budget. Couzens so improved the city's finances that Detroit's bonds were selling at a premium by the time he left office. He demonstrated leadership in establishing a better street-lighting program, encouraging the construction of a $20 million sewage disposal system, and improving traffic regulations.

Couzens chose not to run for a third term in 1937 and entered private business as a banker. He founded the Wabeek State Bank of Detroit, which later merged with the Wabeek State Bank of Birmingham, an institution founded by his father. In 1937, he also became president of the Wabeek Corporation, a company involved in real estate operations. During World War II, he was an officer in the U.S. Army serving as chief of the production service branch of the Detroit Ordnance District. Couzens died of cancer on 31 October 1950 at the young age of forty-eight.

SOURCES: Frank Couzens Papers, Miscellaneous material, Burton Historical Collection, Detroit Public Library; Detroit *Free Press*, 1 November 1950; Detroit *News*, 1 November 1950; New York *Times*, 1 November 1950; Robert I. Vexler, *Detroit: A Chronological and Documentary History*, 1701–1976 (Dobbs Ferry, N.Y., 1977).

Robert Bolt

COUZENS, JAMES (1872–1936), Mayor of Detroit (1919–22). Canadian-born Republican mayor and Ford automobile executive, Couzens was born on 26 August 1872 in Chatham, Ontario, to English immigrant parents, James Joseph and Emma (Clift) Couzens, and was the first of five children. Couzens' father had emigrated to Chatham, Ontario, in 1870 from London, and worked

CREGIER, DeWITT C.   83

as a grocery clerk, day laborer, and soapmaker. Later, he opened his own soap manufacturing establishment and achieved some status as a successful businessman. Raised in a strict Presbyterian household, young James attended Chatham grammar school, spent two years in the local high school and another two at the local business college. At age sixteen, he took a job as a newsbutcher for the Erie and Huron Railroad. In 1890, encouraged by a friend to come to Detroit, Couzens secured a position as a car checker in the Michigan Central railroad yard. In 1895, Alex Malcomson, owner of the Malcomson Fuel Company, hired him as an assistant bookkeeper.

In the next few years, Malcomson's company and James Couzens prospered, and he became a trusted manager. In 1903, when Malcomson decided to become Henry Ford's partner in the creation of the Ford Motor Company, Couzens was brought along as the business manager and secretary for the new company. Couzens also invested a borrowed $1,500 plus $1,000 of his own and his sister's money in the company and became one of the original Ford stockholders. In 1919, that original investment was sold for $30 million. By 1906, Couzens was the general manager and a director of the successful Ford Motor Company, the director of several Detroit banks, the president of the Highland Park Bank, and the founder of the Highland Park Land Company. Couzens was on his way to becoming one of Detroit's automobile millionaires. In 1915, he resigned as vice-president and general manager of Ford Motor Company in a dispute with Henry Ford over company policy and Ford's political opinions.

Couzens married a Roman Catholic, Margaret Manning of Detroit, on 31 August 1898, and they had five children, two boys and three girls. Couzens was a member of the Detroit Club, the Detroit Athletic Club, the Detroit Board of Commerce, and Bloomfield Hills Country Club. While his wife and children were members of the Roman Catholic Church, Couzens, as his biographer, Harry Barnard, described it, "kept religion at arms length."

Couzens' political life began in 1913 as chairman of the Detroit Street Railway Commission where he unsuccessfully attempted to get a municipal ownership referendum passed. In 1916, he was appointed police commissioner, a position he held until his election as mayor in 1918. Elected by a vote of 38,516 to 30,618 over William F. Connolly, Couzens was the first mayor under the new "strong mayor" charter of 1918. Strong-willed and temperamental Couzens fought a number of battles with the city council and with various companies that did business with the city. By 1920, Detroit had a population of over 990,000 and had doubled in area. The streetcar franchise was still a major political issue, and Couzens fought for and finally achieved municipal own-

ership of Detroit's streetcar lines. In 1922, the Detroit United Railway sold its property to the city for $19,850,000. Thus, an issue that had begun with Hazen Pingree (q.v.) in 1895 was finally resolved in 1922 by the feisty James Couzens.

Couzens was reelected mayor in 1921 by 70,719 votes over Daniel Smith's 38,905. In 1922, he was appointed by Governor Alex Groesbeck to fill the unexpired term of the retiring U.S. Senator Truman Newberry. Couzens served in the Senate until his death in Detroit on 22 October 1936. He was buried in Woodlawn Cemetery.

SOURCES: Harry Barnard, *Independent Man: The Life of Senator James Couzens* (New York, 1958); James Couzens Papers, general letters, notebooks, 1903-36, Library of Congress; James Couzens Papers, scrapbooks—see Reading Room File and Biographical Index, Drawer no. 44, Mayor's Message to the Common Council, 1919, 1920, Burton Historical Collection, Detroit Public Library; A. N. Marguis, *The Book of Detroiters* (Chicago, 1914).

Jack D. Elenbaas

CREGIER, DeWITT CLINTON (1829-98), Mayor of Chicago (1889-91). Civil engineer and Democratic mayor, born on 1 June 1829 in New York City, Cregier was the son of John L. Cregier (d. 1842), and Anne E. (LeFort) Cregier (d. 1842) of Franco-American ancestry. Orphaned in 1842, he lived with relatives and received less than a grade school education in New York City. Cregier was a self-made man, employed as a subengineer on a Long Island Sound steamboat until 1847 when he joined the Morgan Iron Works of New York City. He received on-the-job training in mechanical engineering and worked on U.S. mail steamers that plied between New York City, Havanna, Cuba, and New Orleans.

Cregier went to Chicago in 1853 to install and supervise the city's pumping machinery, serving as chief engineer of the North Side pumping station until 1880, when he was appointed city engineer. In 1882, Mayor Carter Harrison I (q.v.) appointed Cregier commissioner of public works. Cregier also served as superintendent of the West Chicago Street Railway Company, 1886-89. He married Mary S. Foggin (1832-1921), in 1853, and they had ten children, eight of whom survived to adulthood. Cregier was a Mason and an active member of the Western Society of Engineers.

Chicago in 1889 had 935,000 people and a mayor-council form of government. Cregier was elected Democratic mayor in 1889 by 57,340 votes to his Republican opponent, incumbent Mayor John A. Roche's (q.v.) 45,328. He sought reelection in 1891 but was defeated when former Mayor Carter Harrison successfully divided the Democratic vote, thereby permitting the election of a Republican, Hempstead Washburne (*q.v.*), who received 46,957 votes to Cregier's 46,588 and Harrison's 42,931.

During Cregier's term, plans were drawn up to bring the World's Fair of 1893 to Chicago. Mayor Cregier was president of the citizens' organizing committee, a director of the Columbian Exposition Corporation, and chairman of the committee on buildings and grounds. More important, in 1889, Chicago annexed a large area of territory, adding 120 square miles and more than 220,000 people to the city. The annexation increased the original municipal limits to an area of 160.4 square miles and placed Chicago over the one million mark in population (1,099,850). The consolidation, agreed to by both the citizenry of Chicago and the surrounding country towns, brought the city to Lake View, the towns of Hyde Park, Lake, and Jefferson, and part of the town of Cicero into the municipality of Chicago. The annexation made Chicago the second largest city in the United States.

Cregier resumed his civil engineering career after he left the mayoral office in 1891. In 1894, President Cleveland (*q.v.*) appointed him superintendent of the U.S. Indian warehouse in Chicago and special disbursing agent of public funds. After a two-year illness, Cregier died from kidney failure on 9 November 1898, and was buried in Rosehill Cemetery, Chicago.

SOURCES: Paul M. Green, *The Chicago Democratic Party 1840–1920: From Factionalism to Political Organization* (Ph.D. dissertation, University of Chicago, 1975); Claudius O. Johnson, *Carter Henry Harrison I: Political Leader* (Chicago, 1928); Bessie L. Pierce, *A History of Chicago* (New York, 1957), vol. 3; Frederick Rex, *The Mayors of the City of Chicago from March 4, 1837 to April 13, 1933* (Chicago, 1947).

Edward H. Mazur

CROCKER, HANS (1815–89), Mayor of Milwaukee (1852–53). Milwaukee's first Irish-born mayor, Crocker was born 11 June 1815 in Dublin, of Protestant parents and moved with them to the United States, settling in Utica, New York. After attending public school for a few years, he moved west to Chicago, studying law in the office of Butterfield and Collins. Crocker emigrated to Milwaukee in 1836, serving as editor of the Milwaukee *Advertiser* for a few months. That same year, he was appointed private secretary to Governor Henry Dodge, with the rank of colonel. Crocker was admitted to the bar in 1837 and opened an office with Horatio N. Wells and Asahel Finch. In 1839, he left this partnership and spent two years in private practice. Crocker then became the partner of John H. Tweedy in 1841. Finding the practice of law too distasteful, the two men retired from legal practice in 1847.

Crocker pursued a business career, serving as a director of the Marine Fire Insurance Company in 1839. He was a director of both the Milwaukee and Rock River Canal (1839) and the Watertown and Madison Plank Road (1850). In 1850, he was elected president of Milwaukee's board of trade and two years later was chosen president of the Lake Hydraulic Company. These business ventures earned Crocker enough money to allow him to retire in 1850. On 21 March 1844, he married Augusta Potter, daughter of a prominent Milwaukee business leader of old New York stock, and they had three children. Crocker was first president of the Milwaukee Lyceum and a founder of St. Paul's Episcopal Church. Despite his Irish birth, Crocker was essentially a "WASP" in outlook and background.

Crocker entered politics by serving as an East Side trustee (1841–42) and as a member of the territorial council (1842–44). Though a Democrat, he was elected mayor of Milwaukee on the People's party ticket in 1852, defeating regular Democrat James Kneeland 2,083 to 1,388. Milwaukee had 20,061 people in 1850 and a mayor-council form of government. As mayor, Crocker supported civic improvements, fiscal reform, honesty, and nonpartisanship in city government. His single term coincided with service as Third Ward school commissioner (1852–55).

After leaving office, Crocker showed little interest in politics, although he switched parties as the Civil War approached, and he was a delegate to the state Republican conventions of 1858 and 1860. Crocker was president of the Milwaukee Gas Company in 1853. He spent many years as a railroad promoter, mainly as an associate of Alexander Mitchell. Crocker was a director of the Milwaukee and Mississippi Railroad, 1860–63 (vice-president 1858–60) and receiver for the LaCrosse and Milwaukee Railroad, 1860–65. During 1872–74, he was a director of the Chicago, Milwaukee and St. Paul Railroad. In the 1880s, his health declined. He spent his last years as an invalid dying at his home on 15 March 1889.

SOURCES: Howard L. Conrad, *History of Milwaukee*, 2 vols. (Chicago, 1895), vol. 1: John G. Gregory, *History of Milwaukee, Wisconsin*, 4 vols. (Chicago, 1931), vol. 2; *History of Milwaukee, Wisconsin* (Chicago, 1881); Herbert N. Rice, "Milwaukee's Sixth Mayor," *Historical Messenger* (Milwaukee County Historical Society Publication, September 1955).

Thomas R. Bullard

CROSS, JAMES B. (1819–76), Mayor of Milwaukee (1855–58). Milwaukee's first three-term mayor, born on 17 December 1819 of old-stock Protestant parents in Phelps, New York, Cross worked on a farm until age sixteen, attending school in the winter months. After graduating from the Geneva Lyceum in 1840, he began the practice of law in Lyons, New York, with the firm of Sherwood and Smith, Cross moved to Milwaukee in 1841, joining the firm of Wells and Finch, and passing the Wisconsin bar the following year.

Cross belonged to the local Democratic machine and was a justice of the peace in 1846–48. He was elected Milwaukee County's first probate judge (1848–50) but declined a second term. Cross also served as a state assemblyman (1849–50), especially noted for his handsome appearance. During 1850–51, he served as city attorney. After winning a bitter election in 1854, he served one more term in the assembly (early 1855).

Cross was elected mayor in 1855, defeating Independent Democrat J. B. Martin 2,746 to 1,367. Milwaukee had 30,118 people (state census, 1855), and a mayor-council form of government. Cross was reelected in 1856 and 1857, without opposition. He opposed graft, supported civic improvements (especially new schools), and urged city support for local railroads. During his third term, he realized that city loans to the Milwaukee and Mississippi Railroad were out of control but was unable to halt the process. Embezzlement by the city comptroller created an additional financial scandal, and Cross was held responsible. During his second term, he had constructed a building and rented one floor to the city council for a large fee, again at the cost of his reputation. On 29 May 1856, he married Catherine L. Fuller (1823–57), and they spent their honeymoon in Cincinnati where Cross attended sessions of the national Democratic convention. Mrs. Cross died within a year. Cross ran for governor in 1857 and was narrowly defeated amidst widespread charges of corruption, mismanagement, and excessive use of his office to aid other Democratic candidates.

Cross was president of the Juneau Bank after leaving office (1857–61). In 1859, he married Eunice G. Osborn (b. 1838), of Edgartown, Massachusetts, and they had two children. Both of his wives were old-stock Protestants. In 1860, his large city block burned down—a severe blow to his personal finances. Cross sold real estate for a year or two, and was vice-president of the Milwaukee and Port Washington Railroad in 1867. During 1866–73, he owned a liquor store, while his second wife pursued a career as a choral singer to raise extra money. Cross was a probate court clerk in 1873–74 until suffering a stroke. In his last years, he was reduced to working as a postal clerk until his death from a second stroke on 3 February 1876.

SOURCES: Lawrence M. Carson, *A Financial and Administrative History of Milwaukee* (Madison, Wis., 1908); John Gregory, *A New and Vastly Improved Edition of the Industrial Resources of Wisconsin* (Milwau-

kee, 1870); *History of Milwaukee, Wisconsin* (Chicago, 1881); *Wisconsin Historical Collection* (1879), vol. 8.

Thomas R. Bullard

CROSSMAN, ABDIEL DAILY (1804–59), Mayor of New Orleans (1846–54). Born in 1804 in Green, Maine, of old Puritan stock, Crossman, who had very little formal education, was taught reading, writing, and arithmetic by his parents, and the skill of hatmaking by his father, a hatter. The apprentice hatter sought his fortune first in Philadelphia and then, in 1829, in New Orleans where he arrived with only $5 in his pockets. Opening a small shop, Crossman soon prospered, becoming a director of several banks and an important person in New Orleans' financial circles. He served on the municipal council of the First District, assisted that body in putting its finances in order, and was elected to the state legislature in 1844.

New Orleans in 1846 had a population in excess of 105,000 and a mayor, multicouncil form of government (three municipal councils drawn from three city districts and one general council).

Crossman accepted the Whig nomination for mayor and won with 2,989 votes because the opposition Democrats split their votes between two candidates: the incumbent Edgar Montegut (*q.v.*), 1,614, and A. J. Guirot, 2,743. In 1848, Crossman beat Democrat M. Reynolds 5,090 to 2,986, and in 1850 Crossman campaigned to abolish the three-municipality system in his bid for reelection, and won on both issues, defeating Democrat J. M. Bell 4,984 to 4,452. In 1852, he won his fourth and last term as mayor, defeating Democratic challenger John L. Lewis 4,993 to 4,877.

During the Mexican War, New Orleans became a central supply depot, and the city's streets were filled with military activity, which added to the city's commerce but also contributed to problems of maintaining public order. The "Spanish Riot" of 1851, although deriving from a different cause, was a source of embarrassment for the city and necessitated an indemnity payment by the U.S. government to Spain. An unsuccessful invasion by General Narciso López, who planned to liberate Cuba from Spain, resulted in the deaths and capture of a large contingent of Americans and others who had been recruited in New Orleans. The execution in Cuba of the remaining captives raised tempers in New Orleans, and when the Spanish consul's secretary refused to release the correspondence of the doomed captives, mobs began rioting in New Orleans, attacking Spanish businesses and the Spanish consulate. Although much property was destroyed, no deaths occurred. The Spanish flag was torn from the consulate and was destroyed in a ritual burning in Lafayette Square, which caused an international incident.

The riot also demonstrated the weakness of the three-municipality system in quelling disorders and strengthened the positions of Mayor Crossman and those who wanted a unitary city government. Accordingly, the state legislature passed an enabling act that became effective in 1852, creating a single city corporation with a bicameral council and a strong mayor. The new charter was greeted as an important step in ''Americanizing'' the city, since it ended the three municipalities which had represented the Creole, American, and foreign-born sections. Crossman's last term witnessed one of the worst yellow fever epidemics in the city's history; the epidemic caused 7,434 deaths in 1853. Partly as a result, New Orleans passed its first drainage tax. In 1854, the city ended public executions, moving them to the privacy of the parish prison. Crossman died on 13 June 1859, the year the state capital was moved from New Orleans to Baton Rouge.

SOURCES: L. V. Howard and R. S. Freidman, *Government of New Orleans* (New Orleans, 1959); John S. Kendall, *History of New Orleans* (Chicago, 1922), vol. 1; Leon C. Soule, *The Know Nothing Party in New Orleans* (Baton Rouge, La., 1961).   *C. David Tompkins*

CRYER, GEORGE E. (1875–1961), Mayor of Los Angeles (1921–29). Reform mayor, born on 13 May 1875 in Douglas County, Nebraska, to John B. Cryer and Elizabeth (Grange) Cryer, and an only child, George Cryer moved to California with his parents and attended Los Angeles High School. During the Spanish-American War, Cryer volunteered and quickly rose to the rank of first sergeant. He saw duty with Company G, Seventh California Infantry, United States Volunteers. Following his discharge on 1 January 1899, Cryer took a law degree at the University of Michigan in 1903 and opened his own practice in Los Angeles. On 5 September 1906, he married the former Isabel Gay and they had two children, Edward Gay and Catherine Christine. Cryer was a founding member of the Wilshire Presbyterian Church, a Mason, and an Elk.

Cryer, a staunch Republican but a reformer, began his political career in 1910 when he was appointed first assistant U.S. attorney in the Southern District. Over the next decade, he received similar appointments, and in 1912 became the first assistant city attorney for Los Angeles. In 1915, he was made chief deputy district attorney for Los Angeles County, holding the job until 1919. After a two-year respite from public office, Cryer was elected mayor on 7 June 1921 (37,510 to 33,411). He was reelected on 1 May 1923 with a massive majority (61,688 to 29,136) and under a new city charter, he was reelected to a four-year term, on 7 May 1925 (82,186 to 78,213). In 1929, he refused to seek a fourth term.

During Cryer's tenure, Los Angeles more than doubled its population (550,000 to 1,200,000) as it grew from a sunny resort town to the nation's fifth largest industrial metropolis. To provide its expanding industrial base with low-cost energy, Cryer established the Department of Water and Power, the nation's largest city-owned utility. The city purchased Southern California Edison's facilities, thereby forcing the remaining private power company, Los Angeles Gas and Electric, to lower its rates. Cryer also maintained amicable relations with organized labor and racial minorities by making appointments favorable to the Central Labor Council and by integrating the police and fire departments—a national first.

These achievements were militantly opposed by the ''Power Trust,'' a political conglomerate composed of the Los Angeles *Times*, Southern California Edison, and old guard Republicans. Initially, in 1921, Cryer had been elected with the Power Trust's support, but within a year, he switched allegiances and became a progressive Republican. As Cryer ran up one impressive victory after another, the *Times* charged that he ran a political machine and that he accepted contributions from the underworld. In 1927, he was threatened with recall by the Reverend Robert P. ''Bob'' Shuler, a fiery Southern Methodist, but Shuler failed to get public support. The following year, the grand jury indicted district attorney Asa Keys, a Cryer colleague, and in 1929, Keys was convicted of bribery. Public sentiment was against Cryer and the machine, and he did not seek reelection.

Cryer attempted to revive his political fortunes when he ran for city attorney in 1937 and, again, for mayor in 1941 but was defeated in both attempts. His wife died on 12 September 1945, and Cryer remarried on 24 September 1947. For the remainder of his life, Cryer practiced law and was active in church and fraternal affairs. He died after falling from a ladder on 24 May 1961.

SOURCES: Richard N. Baisden, ''Labor Unions in Los Angeles Politics'' (Ph.D. dissertation, Chicago, 1958); Lawrence B. DeGraag, ''The City of Black Angels,'' *Pacific Historical Review* (August 1970); Los Angeles *Times*, 25 May 1961; John R. Haynes Collection, Government Documents, *UCLA* Research Library; Vincent A. Ostrom, ''Government and Water'' (Ph.D. dissertation, UCLA, 1950).   *Fred W. Viehe*

CURLEY, JAMES MICHAEL (1874–1958), Mayor of Boston (1914–17, 1922–25, 1930–33, 1946–49). ''Last Hurrah'' mayor of Boston, a classic Irish city boss, but one who failed to build a permanent, effective machine, Curley was a personal political force for over half a century. Born in Boston on 20 November 1874, this future "mayor of the poor" was the son of immigrant parents, brought up in a fetid, rotting three-decker in Irish shantytown, where it was said that the children were born with clenched fists. Curley early learned an abiding hatred of upper class, Yankee, Protestant Boston which he never relinquished. His father, Michael Curley (1850–84) came from Galway at age fourteen and got a patronage job from the Seventeenth Ward boss P. J. ("Peajacket") Maguire as hod-carrier, at 10 cents an hour—until he was killed showing off by lifting a 400-pound stone onto a dray. He left two sons (the eldest, John, b. 1872), and his wife, Sarah Clancy (b. 1852), a "meagre-boned Connemara girl" who, to keep her little family alive, labored as a Beacon Hill maid and as a night scrubwoman in Boston offices.

As a schoolboy, Curley worked long part-time hours in a drugstore. After graduating in 1889, he worked as a grocer's assistant for eight years for the C. S. Johnson Company and used his horse-cart delivery route for political canvassing on the side. About a third of Boston's registered voters were Irish Catholics—at least 50,000 souls out of a city population of over 300,000. Curley learned ethnic politics at local centers like Curran's livery stable and "One-Arm" Peter Whalen's cigar store. He came of voting age in 1895 and the next year campaigned unsuccessfully *against* the ward boss choice for mayor: an early indication of his contrariness and independence, and the difficulty Curley had in personal relations with other Irish and Democratic leaders. He feuded with "Honey Fitz" (*q.v.*) and the Kennedys, with FDR, and others.

On 27 June 1906, Curley married a solid Irish girl, Mary E. Herlihy of Boston, who bore him nine children, seven of whom did not survive. Tragedy and frustration haunted his personal life. In 1950, for instance, his son Leo and his daughter Mary both died of cerebral hemorrhage on the same day. His first wife died in 1930, and Curley grew increasingly unrestrained and coarsened after her loss. In 1936, he married Gertrude Casey Dennis, a quiet Irish widow, who gave him some stability.

Curley lived for politics. When out, he only dreamed of getting back in. He ran unsuccessfully for the Boston Common Council in 1898 against a "Peajacket" candidate, and was counted out by the machine. The next year he ran again, using his own hired toughs, and won—at age twenty-six. Subsequently elected to the Massachusetts House (1902–1903), Curley spent sixty days in the Charles Street jail for impersonating one of his wardheelers in a civil service exam, an event he turned to good politics: "I did it for a friend!" From jail, Curley was elected to the board of aldermen (1904–1909), and later he moved onto the new Boston City Council (1910–11). In 1910, he was elected to the U.S. Congress

for the Twelfth District, was reelected in 1912, but served without distinction in Washington. He took etiquette lessons; elected mayor of Boston in November 1913, he quickly resigned from Congress.

In Curley's first mayoral election, a tidal wave from the slums, he defeated his rival, Thomas J. Kenny, by a majority of 5,700 votes and set back the "Honey Fitz" machine. Rewarding his friends and punishing his enemies in classic fashion, Curley immediately threw out many officeholders and opened up city hall to his followers. From the start, Mayor Curley was a big builder, a big spender, and a big employer. He spent money on parks, auditoriums, hospitals, and such developments as the Strandway (a recreational shore drive) and the South End Municipal Building. Creating jobs and increasing tax assessments, he alienated the business elite but reshaped the face of the city. He kept open house at city hall and spoke directly to as many as 200 people on any one day. But Curley failed to be reelected in 1917: the machine he had built was personal and limited. Although he was one of the first mayors to push industrial growth for Boston and was a strong advocate of home rule for the city, he was defeated in 1917 by a combination of business and politics. One of the few surviving ward bosses not eliminated by Curley, Martin Lomasney, ran two bogus candidates with Irish names, split the vote, and defeated the mayor.

Reelected in 1921 in a spectacular campaign, Curley defeated three opponents, J. R. Murphy, C. S. O'Connor, and C. S. Baxter, with a plurality of 2,470. His second mayoralty began in 1922, the year of the one hundredth anniversary of the city charter of 1822. Curley took immediate steps to create jobs, reducing city unemployment from 75,000 to 45,000 within the first two months and placing war veterans. He continued his building and industrial growth programs and served until 1925. Elected for the third time in 1929, Curley served as mayor, 1930–33. Defeating Democratic lawyer F. W. Mansfield by over 20,000 votes, Curley followed his habitual spending policies and demanded New Deal aid for Boston. He had a fist fight with the state party chairman, split with FDR, and was charged with theft from the city. The charge lasted three years, through thirty-four continuances, until Curley was ordered to pay back $42,629 to Boston. As for Roosevelt, Curley had supported him strongly in 1932, switching from Al Smith at risk to himself among the Boston Irish. He expected his due reward, a cabinet post (the Navy). When offered the ambassadorship to Poland, Curley snapped at FDR: "If it's such a goddam interesting place, why don't you resign the Presidency and take it yourself?" It was said that if he had accepted it, Curley would have paved the Polish Corridor.

In 1934, Curley was elected governor, serving until 1937. He failed to get into the Senate in 1936, to be reelected mayor in 1937, governor in 1938, and mayor in 1941: a string of defeats. As Massachusetts governor he played a New Deal role, as usual, building roads, bridges, and hospitals across the state and creating work. The city hall gang simply moved up Beacon Hill to occupy the statehouse. Curley was perhaps too extravagant a governor: the inaugural ball had 14,000 guests, and as chief executive Curley zoomed around the state with blue-and-gold-braided police escorts, much like Huey Long of Louisiana.

By 1941, at age sixty-seven, the old warhorse seemed finished. But he ran successfully for the U.S. Congress in 1942, was reelected in 1944, and was elected mayor of Boston in 1945 and again in 1947, retiring fully only after a final defeat in 1949, aged seventy-five.

A charge of influence-peddling in Congress struck home in 1947, and Curley served five months of an eighteen-month jail sentence—remaining mayor all along and beating off Republican attempts to force him out. An able political manager and orator, and a warm-hearted and spirited mayor of great courage and stamina, Curley nonetheless lacked overall political vision or philosophy. His impact, though enormous, was purely personal. He died on 12 November 1958, by then a revered elder statesman, and was buried in Calvary Cemetery, Dorchester, after an unusual two-day-long wake in the Hall of Flags at the statehouse.

SOURCES: J. M. Curley, *I'd Do It Again* (Boston, 1957); J. H. Cutler, *"Honey Fitz": Three Steps to the White House* (Indianapolis, 1962); J. F. Dinneen, *The Purple Shamrock: The Hon. James M. Curley of Boston* (New York, 1949); Edwin O'Connor, *The Last Hurrah* (New York, 1956), a popular novel based on Curley's life.   *Peter d'A. Jones*

CURTIS, EDWIN UPTON (1861–1922), Mayor of Boston (1895). A conservative Republican lawyer, Curtis is most remembered for his role as police commissioner during the famous Boston police strike of 1919 which threw Calvin Coolidge into national prominence. As a mayor of Boston twenty-four years earlier, Curtis was relatively undistinguished.

Born on 26 March 1861 in Roxbury, Massachusetts, Curtis was the son of Martha Ann (Upton) and George Curtis—an ex-alderman and picturesque Boston character known for his habitual blue coat and brass buttons. George Curtis was a sixth generation New England Curtis and a prosperous lumber merchant. Edwin, his seventh child, was sent to private schools and Bowdoin College (A.B. 1882, A.M. 1885, LL.D. 1914), where he was an athlete and oarsman. Edwin was admitted to the bar in 1885 after studying law privately and at Boston University. He practiced law in Boston, was an ardent Republican, and was secretary of the city committee in 1888. Edwin married Margaret Waterman, the daughter of Charles Waterman, of Thomaston, Maine, on 27 October 1897.

Curtis entered public service by being elected Boston city clerk in 1889, but he resigned after two years, taking a leadership role in the civic reform movement. In 1894, he was elected mayor as a Republican in a sweeping victory of over 2,500 votes. He began an instant structural reform of the city administration: he created a new board of electoral commissioners; placed each department under a single commissioner; and revised school finances. His whole aim was economy and tax-paring, although he also believed single commissioners governed better than committees. The confident Republicans pushed a law through the legislature to extend the mayor's term from one to two years, feeling certain Curtis would be reelected, but in 1895 the Democratic bosses, led by Martin Lomasney, brought in Josiah Quincy (*q.v.*), who defeated Curtis.

Curtis served on the city Park Commission (1896–1916) and later was assistant U.S. treasurer at Boston (1906) and collector of customs (1909–13). Governor McCall appointed him Boston police commissioner in December 1918, a post Curtis held to his death, and the police strike brought him public notice. When the mayor refused a pay increase and the police joined an AF of L affiliate union, Commissioner Curtis immediately suspended all police who joined the local. Three-quarters of the force thereupon went out on strike, on 9 September 1919. The strike was broken by blackleg volunteers and the Massachusetts State Guard, with strong support from the governor. Calvin Coolidge, the future U.S. president, had been lieutenant governor (1916–19) and now became governor (1919–21). As a result of the strike publicity and Coolidge's tough "law and order" stance with the police, he was elected Republican vice-president of the United States in November 1920. Curtis died on 28 March 1922.

SOURCES: *Annual Report, Police Commissioner for the City of Boston* (1920); J. H. Cutler, *"Honey Fitz": Three Steps to the White House* (Indianapolic, 1962); John Koren, *Boston, 1822–1922: The Story of Its Government* (Boston, 1923); W. A. White, *Puritan in Babylon* (New York, 1938).   *Peter d'A. Jones*

CURTISS, JAMES (1803–59), Mayor of Chicago (1847, 1850). An energetic reformer and two-term Democratic mayor, and a professional politician devoted to holding office, Curtiss was born on 7 April 1803 in Weathersford, Vermont, to a devout Presbyterian, native

New England family. Little is known of his early life until he was married at age twenty-seven in 1830 to Mary Curtiss, who was also a New England Presbyterian. But he did receive an academic and legal education and had been admitted to the bar before he moved west. Curtiss spent four years in New York, then migrated to Chicago in 1834, opened a law practice and bought a large home on Randolph Street between May and Ann streets. He had five children (Mary K., b. 1833; Sarah, b. 1836; Lucy, b. 1838; Elizabeth, b. 1840; and a son, C. C., b. 1847), and he adopted two orphans, a boy and a girl.

Curtiss tried other things before he settled down to politics. He became disenchanted with law and dropped it; then he tried a newspaper career and became editor of the *Daily Democrat*. But his career became public office, and he held a string of appointments before becoming mayor in 1847. He was clerk of the county court, states' attorney, alderman (elected from the Second Ward, 1838; from the Third Ward, 1846), and city clerk (elected 1842). In 1835, he sat on the first city board of health during the cholera epidemic—an ineffective body that failed to raise $2,000 to combat the disease. Curtiss attempted to become mayor of Chicago six times: 5 March 1839 (defeated by B. W. Raymond—*q.v.*), 2 March 1847 (elected), 7 March 1848 (defeated by J. H. Woodworth—*q.v.*), 5 March 1850 (elected), and 4 March 1851 and 2 March 1852 (defeated both times by W. S. Gurnee—*q.v.*).

Chicago had been incorporated in 1834, with a mayor-council form of government and a mayoral term of only one year, although a candidate could succeed himself and run as many times as he wished. Since the Democrats were the principal power, it was not unusual for several kinds of Democrats to be competing against each other. Chicago's population grew rapidly, from under 17,000 (1847) to 30,000 (1850) during Curtiss's terms of office as mayor. The city was then divided into nine wards.

Curtiss was twice elected mayor on the Democratic ticket. At the age of forty-four in 1847, he was elected over Whig John H. Kinzie 1,281 votes to 1,220—a close vote, with Abolitionist Philo Carpenter winning 238 votes. After an interval of two years, Curtiss was again elected mayor in March 1850, receiving 1,700 votes against 1,224 for Dr. Levi D. Boone (*q.v.*) and 805 for Lewis C. Kerchival. Curtiss was an active mayor, interested in education, city sanitation, and developing Chicago physically and culturally. In July 1847, a huge convention was held to boost Chicago's image and to encourage use of its superb geographical location and water facilities—a "people's" convention, under the official title "River and Harbor Convention"—to which 20,000 visitors came, including Abraham Lincoln (his first trip to the city). Out of the twenty-nine states, eighteen were represented. The meeting did much to promote Chicago's growth, and many people began buying real estate on the spot. In more mundane city matters, the state passed a new law giving Chicago complete ownership and control of all city sewers; the police force was increased (from six to nine constables).

Curtiss's second administration brought the first gas street-lighting to Chicago, in the central business district only (4 September 1850). Thirty-six gas burners lit up city hall, and Lake Street (at that time the chief shopping center) was brilliant at night. The Illinois Central Railroad—to become one of the keys to Chicago's rise as a major city—acquired lakefront land, part of the old Fort Dearborn reservation, for $45,000. Cultural life was brightened by the addition of Rice's Theater (owned and operated by a future mayor), though many citizens opposed its opening on moral grounds. Mayor Curtiss strongly supported the theater, wrote a letter on its behalf to the *Democrat*, and when it burned down after the first performance of the opera "Sonnambula," he helped to raise funds to rebuild it.

Mayor Curtiss's family was active socially. His wife, Mary, was one of the original thirty-five members of the Third Presbyterian Church, built on the west side of the river. After his second term, Curtiss retired to a farm in Champaign. He died on 2 November 1859 at Joliet, Illinois, at age fifty-six.

SOURCES: A. F. Andreas, *History of Chicago* (Chicago, 1884), vol. 1; *City of Chicago Census—1850*, Newberry Library, Chicago, microfilm; *The Press Tribune*, 4 November 1859, Chicago; Frederick Rex, comp., *Mayors of the City of Chicago* (Chicago, 1933); Charles S. Winslow, *Historical Events of Chicago* (Chicago, 1937).   *D. H. Parkerson*

CUTTER, LEONARD R. (1825–94), Mayor of Boston (1873–74). Interim mayor of the city of Boston for two months, December 1873–January 1874, Cutter was chairman of the board of aldermen when Mayor Henry Pierce (*q.v.*) successfully ran for election to Congress to fill an unexpired term and resigned the mayoralty early in December 1873. Cutter served as mayor only through the 1873 mayoralty campaign and was replaced by the victor in the contest, Samuel C. Cobb (*q.v.*) in 1874. Cutter was born on 1 July 1825 and died on 13 July 1894.

SOURCES: Boston *Transcript*, 14 July 1894; *Municipal Register*; Justin Winsor, ed., *The Memorial History of Boston* (Boston, 1880–83), vol. 3.

Donald M. Jacobs

CUTTING, HARMON S. (1830–84), Mayor of Buffalo (1882–83). Mayor for only two days, Cutting was born in England in 1830 and emigrated to the United States with his family in 1836. He began studying law in 1845 and started a practice in Buffalo in 1853. A Democrat, Cutting served as Buffalo's city attorney, 1862–63, then spent a single term in the New York legislature in 1865. He served on the board of police commissioners, 1870–72. Cutting was elected city clerk in 1881, and when Mayor Marcus Drake resigned on 29 December 1882, Cutting was appointed mayor by the council. Cutting thoroughly disliked party politics and preferred a legal career. He readily gave up the mayor's office on 9 January 1883 to J. B. Manning, who had won the special election. Cutting served as city clerk until his death at age fifty-four on 25 April 1884, as a result of pneumonia. Cutting was never married—one of the few bachelor mayors in Buffalo's history.

SOURCES: Buffalo *Evening News*, 25 April 1884; New York *Herald*, 26 April 1884; New York *Times*, 26 April 1884; New York *Tribune*, 26 April 1884.

Thomas R. Bullard

D

DAGGETT, JOHN D. (1793–1874), Mayor of St. Louis (1841). The fifth mayor of St. Louis was a transplanted New Englander, born at Attleborough, Massachusetts, on 4 October 1793, the son of Benjamin Daggett, a respected merchant of English ancestry. One of four children, Daggett began his formal education in the public schools of Attleborough. His schooling was cut short by the death of his father in 1807 which necessitated that he help his mother maintain the family business. At age sixteen he began an apprenticeship as a machinist, and, during the War of 1812, he worked at this trade, manufacturing musket-locks for the Army. After the war, Daggett decided to seek his fortune in the West. In 1817, he settled in St. Louis where he established himself in the retail merchandising business. He worked first for his benefactor and friend, Reuben Neal, and then opened his own business in 1822. Daggett added to the fortune he obtained in merchandising by successfully expanding into other ventures. He operated a steamboat which traveled from St. Louis to New Orleans and was superintendent of the Sectional Floating Dock Company. He was also a founder and eventually president of the Floating Dock Insurance Company as well as a director of the Citizens' Insurance Company. In addition, Daggett was active in civic affairs, serving on the board of aldermen, 1827–28, and as street commissioner in 1838. In February 1821, Daggett married Sarah Sparks of Maine. Their marriage produced twelve children, nine of whom lived to maturity.

In 1841, Daggett reluctantly accepted the nomination of the Whig party and was elected to a one-year term as mayor of St. Louis, with 1,263 votes against 881 for Hugh O'Neil (Locofoco) and 101 for B. Cleland (Independent). This was a time of rapid growth for the city which had a population of 21,800 and a mayor-council form of government when he assumed office. The accomplishments of his administration reflected the needs of the growing city and included the creation of an Engineering Department, composed of the city engineer, street commissioner, and superintendent of the waterworks; the establishment of the Office of City Counselor, responsible for drafting city contracts and representing the city in legal matters; and the continuation of harbor improvements, begun in the previous administration.

Although Daggett would not consider a second term as mayor, he continued to be active in St. Louis affairs. He held numerous Masonic offices and served as secretary of the public school board. In 1842, he became the president of the St. Louis Gas Light Company, and in 1849 he was named manager of the Sectional Dock Company, a position he held until his death on 10 May 1874.

SOURCES: Charles Cornwell, *St. Louis Mayors: Brief Biographies* (St. Louis, 1965); Richard Edwards and M. Hopewell, *Edwards' Great West and Her Commercial Metropolis* (St. Louis 1860); William Hyde and Howard L. Conrad, *Encyclopedia of the History of St. Louis* (New York, 1899); J. T. Scharf, *History of St. Louis City and County* (Philadelphia, 1883); Walter B. Stevens, *St. Louis: History of the Fourth City, 1764–1909* (St. Louis, 1909).

Jeanette C. Lauer

D'ALESANDRO, THOMAS J., III (1929–), Mayor of Baltimore (1967–71). D'Alesandro was born in Baltimore on 24 July 1929, the son of Thomas J. D'Alesandro, Jr. (*q.v.*) (born in Baltimore in 1903) and Annunciata Lombardi (born in Naples, Italy, in 1909). The father of Thomas J. D'Alesandro III was a congressman before becoming a three-term mayor of Baltimore (1947–59). Young Thomas was the first-born child of seven, in this Roman Catholic family. Thomas III attended Loyola High School and College and the University of Maryland School of Law. Following a brief career in the Army, 1952–55, he entered politics in Baltimore, and under Mayor J. Harold Grady (*q.v.*) became the administrative floor leader. In 1963, Thomas III was elected city council president.

Elected mayor in 1967, Thomas J. D'Alesandro III was inaugurated on 5 December. While feted by friends and family, D'Alesandro knew the city's grim situation: the school system and urban renewal program lacked leadership; public housing and the city's housing law enforcement capacity had deteriorated, and the budding model cities program was chaotic. The white middle class was retreating to the suburbs, and real estate exploitation was rampant. Crime was on the increase, and financial resources were badly strained. The only bright spots were a newly completed Charles Center business, hotel, and cultural complex, along with an awareness that Baltimore, unlike most large cities, had not suffered from urban riots. At that time, Baltimore's population was 970,000, and it had a strong mayor/charter form of government.

Prior to assuming office, D'Alesandro agreed on major goals. Aided by confidante and city council president William Donald Schaefer, work toward these goals was well under way at the end of his first year. Civil rights laws were enacted; close liaison with key agency, bureau, and finance heads was established; neighborhood multipurpose centers and mayor's stations were opened to improve delivery of city services; and a Department of Housing and Community Development was established to coordinate code enforcement, urban renewal, and related housing matters.

D'Alesandro was especially sensitive to the needs of the poor and to the aspirations of the city's black population. During his first four months in office, he appointed more Negroes to posts than any predecessor over an entire term. He would go out to meet black citizens at their offices. Yet, with the assassination of Martin Luther King, Jr., civil disorder broke out all over Baltimore. D'Alesandro, whose life had been threatened earlier because of his pro-civil rights activity, was extremely disheartened. Furthermore, a Republican governor, Spiro Agnew, seemed less and less interested in the city's plight.

A pall hung over many city leaders when several of them, including housing commissioner Robert Embry, suggested a city fair at its new Charles Center to celebrate its neighborhoods, ethnic customs, talents, and institutional strength. On the eve of the first fair, fearing that it would set up a riot-prone situation and under pressure from conservatives, D'Alesandro almost canceled it. However, the fair was held and became an annual event, drawing over a million visitors. The D'Alesandro years were filled with high energy and the inception of programs that would flower under the next mayor. Thomas D'Alesandro, a strong family man (married 8 June 1952) who by then had four children, decided to withdraw from politics and practice law as a private citizen.

SOURCES: Biographical files of Maryland Historical Society, the Enoch Pratt Free Library.   *W. T. Durr*

D'ALESANDRO, THOMAS LUDWIG JOHN, JR. (1903–), Mayor of Baltimore (1947–59). First Catholic and first Italian mayor of Baltimore, born on 1 August 1903, D'Alesandro was the second youngest son of thirteen children of Thomas (Tomaso) (1867–1952) and Mary Antoinette (Foppiano) D'Alesandro (1861–1938). Thomas, Sr., born in Montenero Domini, Italy, worked as a laborer in a rock quarry, in a grocery store, and

finally as a city employee after he emigrated to Baltimore. His wife was born in Baltimore of an Italian-American family. Staunch Catholics, the D'Alesandros raised their family in Little Italy, where the future mayor attended St. Leo's Parochial School. He later studied at the Calvert Business College. D'Alesandro, Jr., married an Italian-born neighbor, Annunciata M. Lombardi, on 30 September 1928. She attended high school at Notre Dame of Aisquith Street. They had six children, one of whom, Thomas III (*q.v.*), also became mayor of Baltimore (1967–71). At an early age, D'Alesandro worked in a box factory, as a pickle packer and tomato skinner, and as an office-boy in an insurance firm. He later owned his own insurance business. D'Alesandro did precinct work in Little Italy. His childhood work as a *Sabbath Goy* in a nearby Jewish neighborhood marked the beginning of his contact with other ethnic groups, contact which he later put to good political use. D'Alesandro won election to the House of Delegates, Maryland's lower house, 1926–1933. From 1933 to 1934, he served as general deputy collector of internal revenue, and from 1935 to 1938 as a city council member. In 1938, he was elected to the U.S. Congress, defeating his former benefactor, Vincent Palmisano, and he still held that seat in 1947 when he was elected mayor. D'Alesandro was a member of St. Leo's Catholic Church, the Knights of Columbus, Holy Name Society, Order of Alhambra, Shrine, Elks, Moose, Eagles, and Rotary Club.

Baltimore in 1950 had 949,708 people, and its population declined slightly to 939,024 by 1960. It had a mayor-council form of government. D'Alesandro defeated three different Republicans in his mayoral victories: in 1947, Deeley K. Nice (96,161 to 71,889); in 1951, Joseph L. Carter (112,924 to 61,801); and in 1955, Samuel Hopkins (119,413 to 95,349). D'Alesandro lost a race for the U.S. Senate in 1958 as well as the primary bid for a fourth term as mayor in 1959.

D'Alesandro's administration saw the completion of Friendship Airport and the building of Memorial Stadium, which resulted in bringing big league baseball to Baltimore. His mayoralty was heralded by Italian-Americans and other ethnic groups as a sign of their political coming-of-age.

After 1959, D'Alesandro retired from politics and worked in his insurance business, continuing always to reside in Little Italy.

SOURCES: Biographical files of the Maryland Historical Society, the Enoch Pratt Free Library, and the Baltimore *Sun*; Gilbert Sandler, *The Neighborhood* (Baltimore, 1974).   *Suzanne Ellery Greene*

DALEY, RICHARD J. (1902–76), Mayor of Chicago (1955–76). The most powerful mayor in Chicago's history, Daley was born in the Bridgeport neighborhood on 15 May 1902, the only son of Michael Daley, a sheet-metal worker and union organizer, and Lillian (Dunne) Daley. Both parents were Irish Catholics and sent Richard to a parochial elementary school, required of him a stint as altar boy, and then sent him to a Christian Brothers school, De La Salle High School. Finally, after several long terms of night courses, Daley won the coveted degree common to Chicago politicians, a law diploma from De Paul Law School in 1933. While studying, Daley clerked in the Cook County controller's office and made his first successful run for public office as a state representative in 1936. Two years later, Daley moved to the state Senate and remained there until 1946, when he suffered his only election defeat in a bid to become Cook County sheriff. Defeated but not without friends, Daley was picked by Governor Adlai Stevenson in 1949 to become director of the Illinois Department of Finance. There Daley honed and polished those budgeting skills that would serve him well as mayor. A year later, Daley returned to Chicago when elected clerk of Cook County, a post he held through 1955. He married Eleanor Guilfoyle on 23 June 1936, and fathered a family of four sons and three daughters. A devout Catholic, Daley attended Mass every morning.

Chicago in the mid-1950s had a population of 3,690,000 and a mayor-council form of government, with councilmen elected from the wards. Daley became chairman of the Cook County Democratic committee in 1953—the key that opened the mayor's office to him. In a primary fight, Daley defeated incumbent Mayor Martin H. Kennelly (q.v.) in 1955 and in the April election beat Republican challenger Robert E. Merriam by 708,660 votes to 581,461. During the next two decades, Daley was reelected mayor over a series of nominally nonpartisan but generally Republican contenders including Timothy Sheehan, 778,612 to 311,940 in 1959; Benjamin Adamowski, 678,347 to 540,816 in 1963; John Waner, 792,238 to 272,542 in 1967; Richard Friedman, 735,787 to 318,059 in 1971, and John Hoellen, 536,413 to 136,874 in 1975. The source of Daley's power was his dual role as mayor and party chairman. He combined a tightly organized party structure with control over 35,000 city workers and patronage employees and paid close attention to the delivery of municipal services in "the city that works." Daley first attracted national recognition as a political strategist for his key role in helping John F. Kennedy win the presidential nomination and election in 1960.

Committed to the physical development of Chicago, Daley encouraged the construction of downtown skyscrapers (including the world's "tallest" building, the Sears Tower); stimulated expressway expansion and mass transit facilities; and enlarged the world's busiest airport, O'Hare. His administrations also set a rapid pace for urban renewal, the demolition of blighted areas, and the building of public housing. As with all of his enterprises, he mixed politics and business—and for the scoffers Daley would repeat again and again "Good politics makes for good government." When reporters taunted Daley about the evils of the "machine," he generally snapped back: "Organization, not machine. Get that, organization, not machine." Although evidence of venality occasionally tainted Daley's cronies, the mayor himself appeared to have remained as "clean as a hound's tooth." Numerous clandestine investigations by federal, state, city, agencies, and the newspapers never dug up a single solid charge of boodle against the mayor personally.

In the wake of Martin Luther King's death in April 1968, a firestorm of arson, looting, and rioting swept through Chicago's black West Side, and an enraged mayor issued an order that was broadcast across the newspaper headlines and television screens of the nation: "shoot to kill any arsonist . . . with a Molotov cocktail in his hand." Daley's remarks provoked the wrath of the liberal news media. But that was only a foretaste of the bitter draught yet to come. Daley's attempt to host the 1968 Democratic presidential convention in Chicago in August turned into a week of antiwar turmoil, street violence by demonstrators, a "police riot," and a shambles that lessened Daley's reputation. Media liberals predicted that Daley was finished, and the lockout of the Daley delegation from the 1972 Democratic national convention by the McGovernites seemed to support that view. Yet, the prognosticators were wrong. Daley went on to win his largest political victory ever, in 1975, winning an unprecedented sixth four-year term. Early into his term on 20 December 1976 Daley died; he is buried in suburban Worth, Illinois.

A four-day symposium, held in 1977, including scholars, veteran city-watchers, journalists, and practicing politicians, examined Daley's twenty-one years in office. They concluded that Daley had won membership in a rare class of a dozen or so of the best and most effective big-city mayors in the twentieth century; he had played a key role in using the mayor's office to rescue the downtown Loop from impending blight; he used his superior ability as a money manager and expert on public finance to steer Chicago free of the rocky shoals that bankrupted New York City; and as a political broker and organizer had few peers in the nation. The mayor earned lower marks from the experts for his unwillingness to reach out to the suburbs; for the Democratic organization's slow accommodation of newcomer blacks and Latinos, and for his often stormy relationships with the press and the media. The city's bankers and real estate interests were pleased with Chicago's solid financial base and its high bond rating.

SOURCES: Melvin G. Holli and Peter d'A. Jones, ''Richard J. Daley's Chicago: A Conference'' (11–14 October 1977, Chicago); Eugene Kennedy, *Himself: The Life and Times of Mayor Richard J. Daley* (New York, 1978); Len O'Connor, *Clout: Mayor Daley and His City* (Chicago, 1975); Len O'Connor, *Requiem: The Decline and Demise of Mayor Daley and His Era* (Chicago, 1977); Milton Rakove, *Don't Make No Waves—Don't Back No Losers: An Insider's Analysis of the Daley Machine* (Bloomington, Ind., 1975); Mike Royko, *Boss: Richard J. Daley of Chicago* (New York, 1971).

Peter J. O'Malley

DARBY, JOHN FLETCHER (1803–82), Mayor of St. Louis (1835–37, 1840). Fourth mayor of St. Louis, Darby was born in the South on 10 December 1803 in Person County, North Carolina, the son of planter John Darby, a native of Lancaster County, Pennsylvania. In 1818, the Darby family moved to a farm in the western part of St. Louis County where young John continued his education, teaching himself Latin and mathematics. Following the death of both his parents in 1823, Darby returned to North Carolina and studied Latin and Greek under a learned clergyman for a year and a half. He then moved to Kentucky where he studied law in the office of a Frankfort attorney. In 1827, he began a law practice in St. Louis, and flourished in a practice that involved primarily debt collection and the management of business interests.

In 1834, Darby was elected to the board of aldermen; the following year, he won the office of mayor. During Darby's four one-year terms as mayor, the population of St. Louis approximately doubled from 8,000 to 16,000. The young chief executive responded to this growth by supporting a wide range of civic improvements. He urged the creation of public squares as parks, organized a convention to discuss the construction of railroads into St. Louis, and petitioned Congress for the extension of the National Road westward through the city. Moreover, he refinanced the city debt at a considerable savings to the taxpayers. While advancing his local political career, Darby found time in 1836 to wed Mary M. Wilkinson (1818–75), daughter of an Army captain of English ancestry and granddaughter on her mother's side of Francis Vallé, a descendant of one of the early French families in the Mississippi Valley and a grantee of property during the period of Spanish rule in Missouri. She was a staunch Catholic, and they had at least five children, all reared in that faith, though Darby himself was a Presbyterian. On his wife's death he converted to Catholicism.

Darby was reelected mayor in 1836 with 614 votes against 156 for Jabez Warner; in 1837, he was elected again with 630 votes against 151 for Beriah Cleveland. In 1838–39, between his two periods of service as mayor, Darby was a member of the Missouri State Senate where he was a proponent of railroad enterprises. Reelected to a final term as mayor in 1840 (Darby 502, James J. Purdy 328, and A. Wetmore 25), Darby continued his practice of law, expanded his business interests, and remained active in Whig politics. He failed to be reelected mayor in 1843. He founded the banking firm of Darby and Poulterer and served as treasurer of the Liberty's Fire Company. In 1850, he capped his political career by winning election to the U.S. House of Representatives where he served one term as a loyal Whig and a dedicated spokesman for St. Louis interests. He secured federal land grants for Missouri railroads and an appropriation of $115,000 for the St. Louis customshouse and post office. During his term as congressman, he suffered a severe contusion that resulted in a partial paralysis from which he never recovered. Consequently, he retired from public life, although he remained influential as an elder statesman and grand old man of the St. Louis bar. On 11 May 1882, he died near Pendleton Station, Warren County, Missouri. He is buried in Calvary (Catholic) Cemetery in St. Louis.

SOURCES: John Fletcher Darby, *Personal Recollections of Many Prominent People Whom I Have Known, and of Events . . .* (St. Louis, 1880); John Fletcher Darby Papers, Missouri Historical Society, St. Louis, Missouri; Richard Edwards and M. Hopewell, *Edwards' Great West and Her Commercial Metropolis* (St. Louis, 1860); *Missouri Republican*, 7 April 1836, 4 April 1837, 7 April 1840; L. U. Reavis, *St. Louis, The Future Great City of the World* (Biographical Edition) (St. Louis, 1875); J. T. Scharf, *History of Saint Louis City and County* (Philadelphia, 1883); Walter B. Stevens, *St. Louis: History of the Fourth City 1764–1909* (St. Louis, 1909).

Jon C. Teaford

DARRAGH, JOHN (1772–1828), Mayor of Pittsburgh (1817–25). Irish-born second mayor of Pittsburgh, Darragh (named for his father), served fourth longest of any Pittsburgh mayor. The younger of two sons, Darragh was born in Ireland in 1772, the son of a Presbyterian farmer.

Darragh came to America in 1774 with his family and settled south of Pittsburgh, but he moved into the city as a young man and established a store. He and his wife, Peggy Calhoun, had two sons and two daughters. One son, Cornelius, served in the state legislature and the federal House of Representatives. One of the daughters married the grandson of Darragh's business associate, the powerful William Wilkins. With several associates, they requested a bank charter and offered to contribute

$100,000 to the state for public improvements, but the offer was refused. When money became scarce in 1822, these men formed a partnership, the Pittsburgh Manufacturing Company, which functioned as a bank, purchasing products and paying in certificates that were payable when they were sold. They were chartered as the Bank of Pittsburgh in 1814. Darragh was a director and was president from 1819 until his death.

Darragh also helped secure for the young town a branch of the Bank of the United States. He was a trustee of the Western University of Pennsylvania, now the University of Pittsburgh.

A Federalist, Darragh was the last burgess of Pittsburgh in 1815 and became one of the original aldermen when it became a city. When Ebenezer Denny (*q.v.*) refused to serve a second term, Darragh was chosen mayor on 31 July 1817 and was unanimously reelected each year until 28 June 1825 when he resigned because of a new law prohibiting a bank director from holding any executive office in the state. At that time, Pittsburgh had a population of about 7,250.

Darragh was elected more times than any other Pittsburgh mayor. The two principal events of his eight years as mayor were the visits of President James Monroe in 1817 and of Lafayette in 1825. On each occasion, he and a civic committee planned impressive ceremonies. Two major civic improvements also occurred—the building of the first bridge over the Monongahela River in 1818 and that over the Allegheny River the following year. Sidewalks and sewers were constructed and streets opened. And the first issue of city bills ($5,000) was floated. The operation of the Monongahela wharf was placed under city control, and the first inventory of Pittsburgh's industry was taken.

Darragh died of consumption on 13 May 1828 and was buried in the Presbyterian churchyard.

SOURCES: History of Allegheny County, Pennsylvania (Chicago, 1889), vol. 1; Allen H. Kerr, "The Mayors and Recorders of Pittsburgh, 1816–1951" (Typescript, 1952, Carnegie Library of Pittsburgh); The Pittsburgh *Press*, "The Mayors' Notebook, No. 2," by George Swetnam, 17 September 1973.   *Helene Smith*

DARST, JOSEPH M. (1889–1953), Mayor of St. Louis (1949–53). One of a series of German-American mayors of St. Louis, Darst was born in St. Louis on 18 March 1889, the son of Joseph C. Darst, a realtor, and Annie (Miltenberger) Darst, both Roman Catholics of German ancestry. He attended various local schools, Christian Brothers College, and St. Louis University (graduating in 1913). In 1910, he joined his father's real estate company. Darst served with the Thirty-fifth Division in 1917–18. Upon his return to St. Louis, he became vice-president of his father's firm and president in 1930. The

company became J. M. Darst and Associates in 1941. On 12 February 1930, Darst married Lucille Rose. He belonged to the Key Club, Missouri Athletic Club, St. Louis Real Estate Board, and the Co-operative Club.

Darst became active in local Democratic politics around 1925. He was St. Louis's director of public welfare, 1933–41, acting as a major assistant to Mayor Bernard Dickman (*q.v.*). Darst ran for the presidency of the board of aldermen in 1943 but was defeated. In 1947, he began a two-year term as director of the Federal Housing Authority for the Eastern District of Missouri. In 1949, he was elected mayor, defeating J. E. Gragg (Republican) 110,507 to 92,761. St. Louis had 856,796 people by 1950 and a mayor-council form of government.

Darst considered public housing a major issue, and during his term of office 704 units were completed, with another 13,000 planned. Mayor Darst also supported projects to clear land for this major redevelopment program. He backed a special city earnings tax to finance these projects. Unfortunately, his health could not stand the strain of public office, and he was forced to resign the mayoralty in early 1953, a few weeks before his term was to expire. He died on 8 June of the same year.

SOURCES: Charles H. Cornwell, *St. Louis Mayors: Brief Biographies* (St. Louis, 1965); New York *Times*, 9 June 1953.   *Thomas R. Bullard*

DAVIDSON, ROBERT C. (1850–?), Mayor of Baltimore (1889–91). Democratic party mayor, Davidson was born in Lunenburg, Virginia, on 25 December 1850. His family moved to Richmond in 1860 and to Baltimore in 1865. Davidson eventually became a merchant and manufacturer in partnership with Daniel Miller and was president of the Baltimore Trust Company.

In 1890, Baltimore had a population of 434,439 and a mayor-council form of government. Davidson was the regular Democratic party candidate pitted against Major Alexander Shaw, the fusion (Republican and Independent Democrat) candidate, and Edward Eichelberger, the Prohibition candidate. On 5 November 1889, Davidson received 40,703 votes, Shaw 37,651, and Eichelberger 672. There were 92,567 registered voters in the city and 101,731 male citizens of voting age.

The achievements of Davidson's administration were considerable. Overhead-cable streetcars began operation; three bridges and twelve public schoolhouses were constructed; a new fireboat and water tower were authorized for the fire department; a municipal building code was adopted; the city expanded and paved its streets; storm-water facilities were expanded; the harbor was deepened; and the municipality tightened up its regulations of the sale of perishable foods.

Following his tenure as mayor, Davidson moved to Hastings-on-Hudson, established himself as a broker and financier in New York City, and married Laura Noyes (1877–?). The circumstances of their separation and divorce occasioned a certain notoriety, many years later, in 1923.

SOURCES: Wilbur F. Coyle, *The Mayors of Baltimore* (Baltimore, 1919); ''Robert C. Davidson,'' Dielman File, Maryland Historical Society, Baltimore; New York *Times*, 18 May, 28 June 1923.   *Gary L. Browne*

DAVIES, JACOB G. (1796–1857), Mayor of Baltimore (1844–48). Prominent Baltimore merchant and president of an insurance company, Davies was born in that city on 29 May 1796. In his early youth, Davies was very active in military affairs. In response to the War of 1812, he eagerly volunteered his services and participated in the battle of Bladensburg. Shortly thereafter, he received a commission as a lieutenant in the cavalry of the U.S. Army. After the war, he briefly toured Europe and on his return to Baltimore entered the mercantile business. He married Sarah Glen and they had four children.

Davies' interest in military affairs continued in private life. He joined the militia, became a brigade major, and was ultimately promoted to a colonelcy in the Second Regiment of cavalry. He retired from the militia but was called back into service in 1835 in response to a mob threat in Baltimore, was placed in command of the cavalry attached to the City Guards, and was made a colonel in the Fifty-third Regiment of volunteer militia, a post he held until 1851.

Politically, Davies became a Democrat and in 1844 was his party's candidate in the mayoralty, challenging his younger cousin, James O. Law (*q.v.*), a Whig and the incumbent. Davies carried the election by a margin of 498 votes, 8,468 to 7,970. Two years later, he ran for reelection and again won, but this time with a reduced margin of 106 in a heavier turnout of voters. During his administrations, two significant events took place. Politically, the state legislature divided the city into twenty wards, each being represented in the First Branch of the city council. The Second Branch, the upper, smaller, and more powerful house, was now composed of a representative from every two contiguous wards. However, the mayor's office remained fairly powerless. Economically, the basis of Baltimore's coal trade was laid, with the construction of roads from various coal mines in western Maryland to Cumberland and to Baltimore's important railroad link with that city. As a result, the Baltimore and Ohio Railroad expanded its Locust Point facilities.

Davies retired from office at the end of his term. Later, with the return of the Democratic party to national power after its defeat in 1848, he was appointed postmaster for Baltimore by President Franklin Pierce. Poor health ul-

timately forced his retirement from politics. He died on 7 December 1857 in Baltimore and was buried in St. Paul's Cemetery.

SOURCES: Baltimore *Sun*, 8 December 1857; Wilbur F. Coyle, *The Mayors of Baltimore* (Baltimore, 1919); Dielman File, Maryland Historical Society; Clayton Colman Hall, ed., *Baltimore: Its History and Its People* (New York, 1912).   *Richard R. Duncan*

DAVIES, SAMUEL W. (1776–1843), Mayor of Cincinnati (1833–43). Third elected mayor of Cincinnati, Davies was born in London, England, in 1776, the son of Jacob Davies, born in Wales, and Mary (Watts) Davies, of English birth. Along with two brothers and sisters, Samuel spent his youth in London, and in about 1799 the family emigrated to the United States. During the next two years, Samuel Davies became a grocer and then a merchant in New York City and, in 1800, married Mary Stall Thomas, of the wealthy Stall family of Philadelphia, a widow with three children. Davies had two sons, Edward (b. 1802) and Samuel, Jr., and two daughters, Agnes and Mary. In 1802, Davies moved with his family to Williamsburg, a small village in southwestern Ohio, where he quickly became immersed in politics. Although twice defeated as a candidate for the state legislature, Davies remained popular locally, running a general store and serving in the state militia, eventually reaching the rank of colonel. He moved again with his family, around 1809, to Cincinnati, where he continued his interest in politics. In 1811, he was made secretary of a county meeting of local Democratic-Republicans, in 1813 he was elected town recorder, in 1814 he was elected president of the Cincinnati Town Council for a year, and until 1819 he served as a member of the council. Davies became especially well known in Cincinnati for supporting a 1817 council ordinance to build a public water system and also gained fame as a leading banker and textile manufacturer.

Davies first ran for mayor of Cincinnati in 1831 but lost to Elisha Hotchkiss (*q.v.*) 1,697 to 931 votes. In the next mayoral contest, that of 1833, Davies proved victorious over Hotchkiss by a margin of 1,882 to 1,479 and went on to win the next four elections in a row—giving him ten years in office. In 1835, Davies defeated John C. Avery 1,560 to 1,168, with Hotchkiss coming in third with 364; in 1837, Davies won over Hotchkiss 1,754 to 1,521; in 1839, Davies garnered 2,048 votes to John A. Wiseman's 1,173 and Hotchkiss's 1,084; and in 1841, Davies tallied 3,658 votes to R. W. Lawrence's 417.

At the start of Davies' terms as mayor in 1833, the population of Cincinnati stood at 27,645; a decade later it had doubled. Davies was a popular and successful mayor during his early terms, presiding over local improvements such as examinations for teachers, creating a city budgetary procedure, developing a public waterworks, and granting a gas franchise. But Davies' strongly pro-Whig politics as well as his anti-abolitionist activities created hostilities in the Queen City, and, after a race riot in 1841 and a bank riot in 1842, he was tried and found guilty by the city council for negligence in the bank violence. Because of his poor health, Davies received no sentence, and he died shortly after the trial, on 21 December 1843.

SOURCES: Cincinnati Municipal Reference Bureau, *Origins of Municipal Activities in the City of Cincinnati* (Cincinnati, 1935); Charles Cist, *Cincinnati in 1841: Its Early Annals and Future Prospects* (Cincinnati, 1841); Charles T. Greve, *Centennial History of Cincinnati and Representative Citizens*, 2 vols. (Chicago, 1904); Harry R. Stevens, ''Samuel Watts Davies and the Industrial Revolution in Cincinnati,'' *Ohio Historical Quarterly* (April 1961).

Gary Kocolowski

DAVIS, HARRY LYMAN (1878–1950), Mayor of Cleveland (1915–20 and 1933–35). Welsh Baptist mayor, governor of Ohio, and a popular politician, born in Cleveland on 25 January 1878, Davis was the son of Evan Hicks (1841–1906) and Barbara (Jones) Davis, two Welsh immigrants. One of six children, Harry Davis attended public schools and started working in the Newburgh steel mills at thirteen. He took night classes at the Euclid Avenue Business School and served as a page in the Ohio House of Representatives, 1898–99, while his father, a former laborer, was a state legislator. He began working for the Bell Telephone Company in 1899 and started the Davis Rate Adjustment Company a few years later. He began the Davis and Farley Insurance Company in 1913, continuing until 1915. On 16 July 1902, he married Lucy V. Fagin (1880–1969) and had one son, Harry L., Jr. Davis was a Baptist, Mason, and Elk, an organizer of the Cleveland Chapter of the Loyal Order of Moose, and president of the Welsh Society of Cleveland.

Davis entered politics in 1910, serving as city treasurer, 1910–11, and as a member of the city's Republican Central Committee. In 1913, he ran for mayor but was defeated by Newton D. Baker (*q.v.*) 42,296 to 36,119, with Socialist Joseph Robb winning 5,737 votes. In 1915, he was successfully elected over Peter Witt, 47,697 to 45,912, with 59,689 for four other candidates. Davis was reelected mayor in 1917, defeating William Stinchcomb (Democrat) and three others 48,827 to 32,837 and 26,244. In 1919, Davis was again reelected, defeating R. H. Bishop (Democrat) and two others 63,001 to 32,053 and 13,304. During that period, Cleve-

land had 560,663 people and a mayor-council form of government.

As mayor, Davis supported the war effort and civic improvements. In 1920, he resigned to campaign successfully for governor, serving a single term, 1921–23, marked by support for tax reform, Prohibition enforcement, good roads, and economic retrenchment. He did not seek reelection in 1922 and was defeated in the 1924 election. He organized the Harry Davis Insurance Company in 1923. In 1933, he again ran for mayor and was elected, defeating Democrat Ray Miller (*q.v.*) 147,673 to 133,227. Now he had to struggle to overcome the Great Depression and revive the city. He fought an unsuccessful battle against crime and was defeated for the 1935 nomination. He returned to his insurance business, working until his death on 21 May 1950.

SOURCES: Elroy M. Avery, *A History of Cleveland and Its Environs*, 3 vols. (Chicago, 1918); James K. Mercer, *Ohio Legislative History*, 6 vols. (Columbus, 1916–26); The Harry Davis Papers in the Ohio Historical Society, Columbus, comprise some 3 feet of clippings, letters, and scrapbooks from his gubernatorial years only (1921–23).

Thomas R. Bullard

DAVIS, SIMON STEVENS (1817–97), Mayor of Cincinnati (1871–73). Businessman-mayor, S. S. Davis, as his contemporaries called him, was born in Rockingham, Vermont, on 17 December 1817 to Hiram Davis, a Yankee physician turned farmer, and Melinda (Stevens) Davis, daughter of a New York judge. Davis's early education was restricted by the demands of farm life, but he spent a few winter months each year as a student and then, later as a teacher, in the common schools. He left the farm in 1840 and traveled to Howell Works, New Jersey, to teach at an academy while pursuing studies in Latin, French, and higher mathematics, but he returned home the next year when his father fell ill. Davis journeyed to Cincinnati in 1843 and lived there, and in St. Louis and New Orleans for the next four years while following a mercantile career. In 1847, he moved to New York City, married Elizabeth Sayer, a farmer's daughter from Goshen, New York, on 12 February 1850, and remained in New York until August 1853 when he moved back to Cincinnati and founded the banking house of S. S. Davis. Later, in a partnership with a younger brother, he established the First National Bank of Memphis, Tennessee, which became that southern city's largest bank.

Davis, a Republican who had earlier been a Whig, held his first elected office in 1859 when he served a two-year term on the city council. During the Civil War, he organized a local committee system to care for the soldiers' families needing support.

Cincinnati by 1870 had 216,239 people and a mayor-council form of government. Davis received the Republican nomination for mayor in 1871 and defeated his Democratic opponent, Leonard A. Harris (q.v.), by 1,727 votes (16,599 to 14,872). He failed in a bid for reelection two years later when George W. C. Johnston (q.v.) amassed 16,509 votes to Davis's 14,872. Crucial in his defeat for reelection was his failure to fulfill a pledge of police reform as well as his indecisiveness over traction issues. His apparent shortcomings convinced the liberal Republicans to support his Democratic opponent in 1873.

After his defeat, Davis turned most of his attention to his Cincinnati banking house. He also remained active in philanthropic and social service, being a trustee of the Protestant Home for the Friendless and the Female Guardian Society, the public high schools, and the Cincinnati Relief Union. Davis died in Newton Highlands, Massachusetts, on 11 May 1896.

SOURCES: *The Biographical Cyclopedia and Portrait Gallery with an Historical Sketch of the State of Ohio* (Cincinnati, 1884), vol. 2; *The Biographical Encyclopedia of Ohio of the Nineteenth Century* (Cincinnati and Philadelphia, 1876); Cincinnati *Daily Gazette*, 26 March 1879; Cincinnati *Post*, 28 February 1913.

Robert B. Fairbanks

DAVIS, THOMAS ASPINWALL (1798–1845), Mayor of Boston (1845). Boston's first Native American party mayor and its first mayor to die in office, Davis was born on 11 December 1798, in Brookline, Massachusetts, into an old-line family. His parents were Ebenezer Davis (1759–1806) and Lucy (Aspinwall) Davis (1767–91) Ebenezer's second wife. He was the seventh of Ebenezer's nine children, the fifth of Lucy's seven. Davis attended public schools and, at age nineteen, went into business as a jeweler. On 11 November 1825, he married Sarah Jackson of Newton, Massachusetts; they had no children. A leader of local cultural affairs, Davis served as president of the Boston Temperance Society and the Boston Lyceum. He was an active member of the Central and the Bowdoin Street (Congregational) churches. A Whig, he held several minor offices in city government and was elected to the state House of Representatives in 1839, 1840, and 1842.

Davis became mayor of Boston in 1845, the year the city's population reached 114,366 (state census) and the Irish potato famine began. His election dramatized the social and political dislocations that Irish immigration was already causing. The election was a three-way race between Whig candidate Josiah Quincy, Jr. (q.v.), Democratic candidate Adam W. Thaxter, Jr., and Davis, the candidate of the Native American party, a new, anti-immigrant group that had emerged out of a split in the

Whig party over how to deal with the massive influx. On the first ballot, Davis came in second, with 3,907 votes to Quincy's 4,464 and Thaxter's 2,173. Because there was no majority, another election had to be held. Thomas Wetmore took Quincy's place, while Colonel Charles G. Greene replaced Thaxter. This time Davis won, but Greene prevented him from getting a majority. The indecisive balloting continued, with the Whig and Democratic parties repeatedly substituting new candidates, until 21 February 1845, when Davis finally received a bare majority on the eighth ballot. William Parker, chairman of the board of aldermen, served as acting mayor until Davis was inaugurated. The crisis caused by the new party had also paralyzed the board of aldermen, preventing the election of a quorum until 20 January.

As it turned out, Davis's election did not end the government crisis. Long a victim of tuberculosis, Davis suffered a major lung hemorrhage in May; his health rapidly declined, and on 7 October he resigned. The problem was that the city charter made no provision for the election or appointment of a new mayor in such circumstances. Because the mayor presided over the board of aldermen, the board could neither legally function nor put a new mayor in his place. The board and the common council grappled with this legal conundrum until a crisis provoked by the city treasurer's refusal to pay the bills finally forced it to take action. It then appointed the chairman of the board, Benson Leavitt, acting mayor.

Because of all these problems, the Davis administration accomplished very little. It succeeded in obtaining authorization from the state for the introduction of water from Long Pond on the condition that a majority of the voters accept it. In the 19 May referendum, however, the voters rejected it by a small vote. The city council also finally passed an appropriation to build the South Boston county jail. The protests of the people there, however, again forced this plan's abandonment. Mayor Davis died on 22 November 1845.

SOURCES: *Boston City Documents* (Boston, 1845); James M. Bugbee, "Boston Under the Mayors," in Justin Winsor, ed., *The Memorial History of Boston* (Boston, 1881); *Inaugural Addresses of the Mayors of Boston 1822–1851* (Boston, 1844); John Pierce, *An Address at the Funeral of the Honorable Thomas A. Davis* (Boston, 1845).

Christine M. Rosen

DAYTON, LEWIS P. (1824–1900), Mayor of Buffalo (1874–75). A physician better remembered for his activities in promoting Buffalo's public health than serving as its mayor, Dayton was born in 1824 in Eden, Erie County, New York, of a modest farm family of New England origin. Dayton was educated locally in private schools and graduated from the Geneva Medical College, Geneva, New York, in 1846. Returning to Buffalo, he began an immensely popular practice. As a physician, Dayton was noted for his great concern for the poor. His first wife was Grace Webster Holley of Canandaigua, New York, daughter of a wealthy businessman, whose family was originally from Salisbury, Connecticut. The Daytons had four children, two of whom died when very young. Widowed in youth, Dayton married Mrs. Alice M. Vogt Hayes later in life, and after her death, married Margaret Vogt in 1892, when he was sixty-eight. His children, John Guernsey Dayton and Jennie Louise Dayton Vogt, became prominent in Buffalo society. Dayton served as alderman, assemblyman, county clerk, and county treasurer before his election as mayor. He was also the official city physician of Buffalo, 1871–74.

When Dr. Dayton took office in 1874, Buffalo had approximately 135,000 people and a mayor-council form of government. Apparently, Dayton's short term was rather uneventful. He is noted, however, for his organization of a fine city health department and for his continued concern for the poor. Elected on the Democratic ticket with a small plurality of 3,112 votes, Dayton was reportedly ineffective as a mayor. Although a devoted party member, he could not muster sufficient forces to counterbalance the influence of the local Republican party.

Choosing not to run for reelection, Dayton resumed his medical career, though he did also serve as alderman. He was the commissioner of public health in Erie County until shortly before his death on 13 May 1900.

SOURCES: J. F. Barry, ed., *The Buffalo Text Book* (Buffalo, 1924); Buffalo *Express*, 15 May 1920; Buffalo *Times*, 2 December 1919.   *W. Andrew Achenbaum*

DEMING, HENRY C. (1815–72), Mayor of New Orleans (1862–63). One of a line of New Englanders who ruled New Orleans in the Civil War, Deming was born on 23 May 1815 in Colchester, Connecticut, and came from a Yankee family that traced its origin in Connecticut to 1641. His father, David Deming, was a prominent merchant; his mother came from an equally prominent family, the daughter of General Henry Champion who served in the Revolutionary War. Deming received a privileged education, graduating from Yale in 1836 and Harvard Law School in 1839. After admission to the Massachusetts bar, he opened a law office in New York City where he also served on the editorial staff of *New World*, a literary monthly.

In 1847, Deming returned to Connecticut to practice law in Hartford and three years later married Sarah Clerc, the daughter of Laurent Clerc of France, who had initiated the education of deaf mutes with Thomas Gallaudet

in 1816. Deming and his first wife had three sons and one daughter. While in Hartford, Deming also began a prominent career as a Democratic politician, serving in the following positions: state representative (1849, 1850, 1859–61); state senator (1851); and mayor of Hartford (1854–58, 1860–62), the latter term as mayor overlapping with his position in the state legislature. The Civil War dramatically reshaped his career. Although he had attended the Charleston convention in 1860 as an outspoken Democrat and threatened not to allow Union troops to pass through Hartford on their way to the South, Deming quickly changed his views as the crisis developed. After the Republican majority made him speaker *pro tempore* of the state legislature in 1861, he began aggressively to recruit Union troops for the invasion of New Orleans which was to be led by his former Democratic compatriot, Benjamin Butler. As the lieutenant colonel of the Twelfth ("Charter Oak") Connecticut Regiment, he led the first body of troops into New Orleans.

Butler appointed Deming as the occupied city's first military-mayor in October 1862, but Deming served only a short time, resigning in February 1863 in order to run for Congress as a Republican. His role in New Orleans was purely clerical and too brief to establish policy. The problems of administering an occupied city of 168,675 (1860) people were immense, but the commanding general, Benjamin Butler, clearly remained in charge of running the city. Deming's fame in New Orleans stems from his connection with Butler's famous "Woman's Order." Because Deming and Admiral David Farragut were drenched with dirty water by an unknown woman, Butler scorned Southern convention by threatening to arrest such offenders as prostitutes.

Deming was elected to the Thirty-eighth and Thirty-ninth Congresses (4 March 1863–3 March 1867), losing a race in 1866 to the Fortieth Congress. In 1869, he was appointed collector of internal revenue and served until his death. In his last years, he completed a biography of Ulysses S. Grant (1868) and married Annie Putnam Jittson (1871); he died on 8 October 1872 and is buried in Spring Grove Cemetery, Hartford.

SOURCES: Benjamin F. Butler, *Butler's Book* (Boston, 1892); Gerald Capers, *Occupied City, New Orleans Under the Federals 1862–1865* (Lexington, Ky., 1965); John S. Kendall, *History of New Orleans* (Chicago, 1922), vol. 1.   *Joseph Logsdon*

DEMPSEY, EDWARD J. (1858–1930), Mayor of Cincinnati (1906–1907). Cincinnati's only Democratic mayor in the first decade of the twentieth century, and an Irish Catholic, Dempsey was born on 26 September 1858 in Cincinnati. His parents, John Shiel Dempsey and Anna

(Brereton) Dempsey—"famine Irish"—left Ireland in 1848 and moved to Cincinnati, where they established a family grocery. The third son of their five children, Edward Dempsey attended Catholic primary school, Hughes High School, and earned his LL.B. from the Cincinnati Law College in 1879. Dempsey practiced law in Cincinnati and Chicago, and was associated with Clarence Darrow, 1886–89, but in 1892 he returned permanently to his home city. In 1898, he was elected judge of the Cincinnati Superior Court. Dempsey married a Catholic Cincinnatian of Irish parentage, Mary A. O'Leary, on 5 September 1894, and they had four children (John C., Margaret, Edward J., and Virginia).

Cincinnati in 1905 was a mayor-council city with a population of some 380,000 and a dominant Republican party, run by a political machine. Judge Dempsey, a Democrat, accepted his mayoral nomination from a reform coalition calling itself the Citizen's party, and he defeated the Republican candidate, Vice-Mayor Harry L. Gordon, by a vote of 40,865 to 34,335. As mayor, Dempsey's program for reform was very similar to that of his Republican predecessor, Julius Fleischmann (q.v.). Like Fleischmann, Dempsey promoted park acquisition and the commissioning of a comprehensive municipal park plan, improvement of city health and educational services, and efficient municipal administration. Unlike Fleischmann, whose tenure saw the city tax rate fall, Dempsey did not believe that a low valuation rate was a mark of municipal effectiveness, and during his two-year term, Cincinnati's rate rose from $22.38 per $1,000 valuation to $29.17. Dempsey attempted to manage his city by calling on an expanded, higher paid staff, and consultants. He increased the size and the budget of the health department to deal with school medical inspection, and he established a tuberculosis detection and treatment dispensary. Dempsey's political position, however, weakened during his two years of battling a Republican majority city council and raising taxes, and at the same time the coalition that had backed his candidacy in 1905 disintegrated. Dempsey faced the election of 1907 with only Democratic support; a coalition "City Party" challenger, Frank Pfaff, as well as the very popular Republican, Colonel Leopold Markbreit (q.v.), contended for his office. Markbreit won handily with 43,841 votes to Dempsey's 23,566 and Pfaff's 10,508.

After losing his bid for a second term in 1907, Dempsey returned to the practice of law and to a professorship at the Cincinnati College of Law, with a specialty in contracts. Dempsey also served on the Cincinnati Charter Commission in 1917. Dempsey's other associations were principally Democratic, Catholic, or ethnic, including Holy Family Church, the Friendly Sons of St. Patrick, and the Duckworth Democratic Club. Dempsey died in Cincinnati on 14 March 1930.

SOURCES: Annual Reports of the City of Cincinnati for 1906 and 1907; Cincinnati Bar Association, *The Bench and Bar of Cincinnati* (Cincinnati, 1921); *Cincinnati Enquirer*; Charles Theodore Greve, *Centennial History of Cincinnati and Representative Citizens* (Chicago, 1904); Zane L. Miller, *Boss Cox's Cincinnati: Urban Politics in the Progressive Era* (New York, 1968).
                                                      Judith Spraul-Schmidt

DENNY, EBENEZER (1761–1822), Mayor of Pittsburgh (1816–17). First mayor of Pittsburgh, and a Revolutionary War veteran, Denny was born at Carlisle, Pennsylvania, on 11 March 1761, the eldest son of William Denny (a merchant and first coroner of Cumberland County) and Agnes (Parker) Denny, a Presbyterian family of British descent. At thirteen, "a slender, fair, blue-eyed, red-haired boy," he was sent as a messenger to Fort Pitt during the Indian wars. Crossing the mountains on horseback, he was twice chased into Fort Loudon by Indians. While still a youth, he worked at his father's store. After moving to Philadelphia, at the age of sixteen, he was put in command of the quarter-deck on board a ship going to the West Indies.

Before he turned twenty-one, Denny was commissioned an ensign in the First Pennsylvania Regiment and saw his first action near Williamsburg, Virginia, on 18 June 1781. Although he became sick upon seeing the wounded, he took command of the company when both his captain and lieutenant were disabled. As youngest ensign at Yorktown, he had the honor of planting the first American flag in the captured British fortification. He would have received the sword from Cornwallis, but Baron Von Steuben pushed him aside and took it himself. Denny later served in the Carolinas and was adjutant of the First Regiment under Harmar and an aide-de-camp under Arthur St. Clair in expeditions against the western Indians. Denny was with St. Clair at his defeat in 1791 and relayed the news to General Washington. In 1794, Denny, commissioned as captain, tried to lay out a town at Presque Isle but was opposed by the Indians of the Six Nations. He served in the first Pennsylvania Constitutional Convention of 1789.

On 1 July 1793, Major Denny married Nancy Wilkins (d. 1806), daughter of Captain John Wilkins, Sr., of Carlisle and later founder of Wilkinsburg, Pennsylvania. They had five children: a daughter who died in infancy, another daughter, Nancy, and three sons, William, Harmar (who later married the daughter of Pittsburgh industrialist James O'Hara), and St. Clair.

In 1795, Denny moved from Bedford to the Streets Run area south of Pittsburgh to farm and to operate a mill. One year later, he was elected Allegheny County commissioner. At this time he moved into the city and opened a store. He also had a commissary in Philadelphia. A Federalist, he was named county treasurer in 1803 and again in 1808. In 1804, he was appointed a director of the Pittsburgh branch of the Bank of Pennsylvania, the first west of the Alleghenies. During the War of 1812, he supplied William Henry Harrison's troops as commissary of purchases for the Erie and Niagara frontier. Denny was a trustee of the First Presbyterian Church and was a Mason. He served as first president of the "Moral Society," founded in 1809, and helped establish Western Theological Seminary in Allegheny City. He was a charter member of the Society of Cincinnati.

In 1816, Pittsburgh's population was about 6,400, and on 19 July Denny was elected by councils from among twelve aldermen, receiving fifteen votes. Robert Graham got six votes, and John M. Snowden two. Denny established an excellent record as mayor. He encouraged the "night watch" to combat noise and rowdiness (a police force later discontinued by councils), put the city's operations on a business basis, and improved streets and wharves. Ahead of his time, he ordered a survey of Pittsburgh's business and sent a representative to Harrisburg and then to Washington, D.C., to promote the city. The councils unanimously voted to reelect him on 14 January 1817, but he declined because of ill health. He continued in office until his successor, John Darragh (q.v.), was elected on 31 July. In 1822, just after a trip with his daughter to Niagara Falls, Denny died suddenly and was buried with his wife in the Presbyterian churchyard in Pittsburgh. Later, both bodies were removed to Allegheny Cemetery.

SOURCES: *History of Allegheny County, Pa.* (Chicago, 1889), vol. 2; Allen H. Kerr, *"The Mayors and Recorders of Pittsburgh, 1816–1951"* (typescript, Carnegie Library of Pittsburgh, 1952); "The Mayors' Notebook, No. 1," *by George Swetnam," The Pittsburgh Press,* 16 September 1973.   *Helene Smith*

DEVER, WILLIAM EMMETT (1862–1929), Mayor of Chicago (1923–27). Reform mayor, born on 13 March 1862 at Woburn, Massachusetts, Dever was one of six children of Patrick James and Mary A. (Lynch) Dever, a Roman Catholic couple. His father was a successful leather manufacturer. Dever attended public schools in Woburn, graduating from high school in 1870; he worked in his father's leather business, 1881–84, and then for White and Company Tannery in Olean, New York. In 1886, he moved to Chicago and worked for Grey, Clark and Engle Leather Company. He attended night school at the Chicago College of Law and received his LL.B.

in 1890. Dever began practicing law in 1890 and became an active Democrat. On 5 January 1885, he married Katherine E. Conway (1865–1939) from Olean, New York. They had no natural children but adopted two boys, Daniel M. and George A. Dever was a member of the Iroquois Club, Knights of Columbus, and the Press Club.

In 1902, Dever, urged by reformers like Graham Taylor (Chicago Commons founder), ran as a Democrat and was elected alderman of the Seventeenth Ward. He served for eight years and chaired the Judiciary Committee. He resigned to run for judge of the superior court of Cook County in 1910. He was reelected in 1916 and 1922. In 1916 and 1918, he was selected to serve on the Illinois Appellate Court, First District.

In 1923, Chicago had a population of almost 3 million and was governed by a weak mayor-strong council structure. Since 1921, the council had consisted of fifty wards, with one alderman each, elected on a nonpartisan basis. Dever was selected to run for mayor because of his reputation and his long years of party service. On 3 April 1923, he defeated two opponents with 390,413 votes—54.5 percent to Arthur C. Lueder, Republican, 285,094—39.8 percent; and William A. Cunnea, Socialist, 41,186—5.7 percent. Dever ran for reelection against former Mayor William Hale Thompson (q.v.) in 1927 on a campaign of "Dever and Decency." Despite a satisfactory record, he was defeated by Thompson, 515,716 (51.6 percent) to 432,678 (43.3 percent).

Dever's administration was characterized by high-quality appointments, plans, and programs for physical growth, and a vigorous campaign for law and order. Chicago's first zoning ordinance was passed while he was mayor, and the double-deck Wacker Drive was completed. In addition, the Chicago River was straightened, Union Station finished, traffic lights installed in the downtown Loop, and extensive paving of streets and alleys took place. Dever's zeal to enforce Prohibition antagonized many voters and contributed to his defeat by Thompson.

In 1927, Dever became vice-president and trust officer of the Bank of America. He retired a year later because of ill health, and he died from cancer on 3 September 1929. He was buried in Calvary Cemetery.

SOURCES: Donald S. Bradley, "The Historical Trends of the Political Elites in a Metropolitan Central City: The Chicago Mayor," Center for Social Organization Studies Working Paper no. 10 University of Chicago, Department of Sociology, May 1963; Douglas Bukowski, "William Dever and Prohibition: The Mayoral Elections of 1923 and 1927," *Chicago History* (Summer 1974); William E. Dever Papers, 7 vols. (5 feet, 12,000 items), Chicago Historical Society; Lloyd Wendt and Herman

Kogan, *Big Bill of Chicago* (Indianapolis, 1953).

Andrew K. Prinz

DICKMANN, BERNARD F. (1888–1971), Mayor of St. Louis (1933–41). New Deal mayor of St. Louis, Dickmann was a German-American, born in St. Louis on 7 September 1888, the son of a merchant, Joseph F. Dickmann, and Maria (Eilers) Dickmann, both born in Germany. The third of six children, Dickmann attended St. Louis public schools until 1904 when he worked for a lumber company. In 1906, he began a successful career in real estate, establishing the firm of B. F. Dickmann and Company (1906–33). During World War I, he served in the Marine Corps, along with his younger brother Otto. He was three times an exalted leader of the Elks Lodge in St. Louis and president of the city's Real Estate Exchange in 1931.

Dickmann held no political office until 1933 when he was the Democratic nominee for mayor, defeating Walter J. Neun 156,567 to 140,976. In 1937, he defeated Oliver Remmes, by a vote of 159,494 to 111,324. St. Louis had 821,960 people in 1930 and 816,048 by 1940, with a mayor-council form of government.

Dickmann, the first unmarried mayor of St. Louis in half a century, was a popular politician, known simply as "Barney." During his two terms in office, he balanced the city's budget, reorganized several departments, improved the sewer system, and secured passage of the nation's first successful anti-smoke ordinance. He was criticized for the speed with which he organized a strong personal machine to control the city's Democrats. Dissatisfaction with this political power may have been responsible for his defeat by Judge William Becker (*q.v.*) in 1941 by a vote of 183,112 to 147,428.

Although defeated, Dickmann did not abandon politics. He was a delegate to the 1943 constitutional convention and served as the city's postmaster, 1943–58. While attending a national postal officials convention in New York City in 1948, he met Beula Pat Herrington, the widowed postmistress of Mount Olive, Mississippi, and they were married the following February 1949. He served as director of the Department of Welfare, 1958–61, and then resumed his career in real estate. Later, in the 1960s, he retired to Mount Olive, Mississippi, where he died on 9 December 1971, after a severe fall outside his home.

SOURCES: Charles H. Cornwell, *St. Louis Mayors: Brief Biographies* (St. Louis, 1965); St. Louis *Post-Dispatch*, 5 April 1933, and 10 December 1971; Floyd C. Shoemaker, *Missouri and Missourians*, 5 vols. (Chicago, 1943).

Thomas R. Bullard

DIEHL, CONRAD (1843–1918), Mayor of Buffalo (1898–1901). The first mayor of Buffalo born in the city, on 17 July 1843, was Dr. Conrad Diehl, a German-American physician. Diehl was the son of a German-born immigrant stone mason; and his mother came from Alsace. One of four children, Diehl attended public and private schools and graduated from the Medical Department of the University of Buffalo in 1866. He spent the next year in Europe, studying medicine; there he met his wife, Caroline Trautman of Weissemburg. They were married on 5 May 1869 and had three children. Diehl began practicing medicine in Buffalo in 1867 and was elected Erie County coroner that same year, serving until 1870. He was on the staff of Buffalo General Hospital (1867–1907) and was surgeon for the Sixty-fifth Regiment of the New York National Guard (1870–78). Diehl was also a member of the Buffalo Board of School Examiners (1892–97). His German wife died in 1888, and on 28 May 1892, he married Lois Masten (d. 1915) of Somerset, Massachusetts.

Dr. Diehl was elected mayor of Buffalo as a Democrat in 1897, becoming the first Buffalo mayor to serve a four-year term, as well as the first native-son mayor. He defeated Republican John N. Scatcherd, 29,131 to 21,593. Buffalo had 352,387 people by 1900 and a mayor-council form of government. Diehl had been nominated because of his reputation as a nonpolitical, honest professional man, but he had been expected to lose the election. Only one newspaper backed his campaign (the Buffalo *Times*), and there was some surprise when he won. Dr. Diehl was a strong supporter of civil service reform and thus did not necessarily follow the advice of more traditional party leaders. He was also responsible for the Pan-American Exposition, which he hoped would be a symbol and memorial to the soldiers of the Spanish-American War. Unfortunately, the assassination of President McKinley destroyed this dream. Diehl did not seek another term and returned to his medical practice. He died on 20 February 1918.

SOURCES: Buffalo *Sunday Times*, 22 June 1924; *The Men of New York*, 2 vols. (Buffalo, 1898); *Who's Who in New York, City and State* (New York, 1907 ed.).

Thomas R. Bullard

DIEHL, WILLIAM J. (1845–1929), Mayor of Pittsburgh (1899–1901). The son of William V. (1821–76), and Jane Elliott Diehl (1821–1905), and scion of a prominent Pittsburgh family, of German and Scotch-Irish descent, settled in the city since 1750, Diehl was born on 22 January 1845. After receiving his education in the public elementary and secondary schools, he attended Western Academy, also in Pittsburgh. When his father experienced business reverses, young William dropped out for a period to work in a brush store but later returned to complete his education. For six years, Diehl worked in a shoe and jewelry store until he obtained a clerical position in the sheriff's office; he was soon elevated to deputy sheriff. After four years in that position, he was called to the office of city treasurer to head the new department of city bond clerk. Along with this job, Diehl was business manager of the *Sunday Critic* and later secretary of the Western Telegraph and Telephone Company.

In 1885, Diehl was appointed personal property tax record examiner for Allegheny County, the county in which Pittsburgh is located. At this same time, he also held positions with local natural gas and oil companies. In addition, Diehl was the treasurer of the Central Masonic Hall Association and a member of the school board.

In 1898, Diehl won a position on the select council, perhaps as prefatory to a nomination for mayor which he later received on the Republican ticket. The Democrats nominated John C. O'Donnell, whom Diehl defeated by more than a 2 to 1 margin. During his administration, the city was planning a technical school when Andrew Carnegie offered to donate the entire school now called Carnegie-Mellon University.

Throughout his political career, Diehl had been allied with the Magee-Flinn Republican machine which was at odds with the Republican political boss of the state, Matthew Stanley Quay of Beaver, Pennsylvania. When in 1901 the Magee faction introduced a bill in the state legislature to annex the city of Allegheny, which was Quay territory, the Quay forces amended the bill to leave out the annexation provision but to replace the office of mayor of Pittsburgh with a city recorder appointed by the governor. On 6 April 1901, the governor appointed Adam M. Brown (*q.v.*) as recorder, and Mayor Diehl's term thus suddenly ended.

Diehl continued in the oil and gas interests after his term. He was a member of the Episcopal Church, the Royal Arcanum, the Masons, the Keystone Bicycle Club, and the Pittsburgh Athletic Association. He died on 22 September 1929 leaving two daughters. He was buried in Allegheny Cemetery, Pittsburgh.

SOURCES: Pittsburgh *Post-Gazette*, 24 September 1929; Pittsburgh *Press*, 23 September 1929; Frank W. Powelson, *Founding Families of Allegheny County* (Pittsburgh, unpublished manuscript, 1963), vol. 1.

Joseph F. Rishel

DILWORTH, RICHARDSON (1898–1974), Mayor of Philadelphia (1957–61). Reform mayor, born on 29 August 1898, in Pittsburgh, Pennsylvania, Dilworth was the son of Joseph R. (1860–1928) and Annie Hunter (Wood) Dilworth (1866–1941). Both parents came from old blue-blood families involved in the Pennsylvania iron and steel industry. Dilworth's father, Joseph, headed a Pittsburgh-based firm that manufactured railroad equipment. Richardson received a "proper" education at St. Marks

School, Massachusetts, and at Yale University undergraduate and law school.

In 1918, Dilworth joined the Marines and served with distinction in France. He served in World War II as a Marine intelligence officer in the Pacific theater. He married Elizabeth Brockie in 1921. Dilworth took his law degree at Yale in 1926 and established a reputable law practice in Philadelphia specializing in libel law. The Philadelphia *Inquirer* was a major client. Dilworth's marriage to Brockie ended in 1935. In August of that year, he married the recently divorced Anne E. Kaufman Hill. With Brockie, Dilworth had four children: Patricia (b. 1923), Anne (b. 1926), Brockie (b. 1928), and Warden (b. 1932). Anne Kaufman Hill bore Dilworth two children, Deborah (b. 1936) and Richardson (b. 1938).

Dilworth dabbled in Philadelphia Democratic politics in the 1930s, and after World War II, buttressed by the Americans for Democratic Action, he sought and won a voice in the then demoralized city Democratic party. In 1947, Dilworth lost his bid for mayor against Bernard Samuel (*q.v.*), but his vigorous streetcorner campaign laid bare the canker of political corruption. Dilworth ran for city treasurer in 1949 and was elected district attorney in 1951 when Joseph Clark (*q.v.*) won the mayoralty. The next year he ran unsuccessfully for governor, losing to John S. Fine. In 1955, Dilworth ran for mayor when Clark chose to run for the Senate.

In 1955, Philadelphia had a population of approximately 2,050,000 and a strong mayor-council form of government. In 1955, Dilworth defeated his opponent, W. Thatcher Longstreth (423,035 to Longstreth's 293,329). In 1959, he was reelected over his opponent Harold Stassen (438,278 to Stassen's 229,818). However, the handy margin of victory convinced the party leaders that the Democrats could win in Philadelphia without the reform label.

Dilworth was described by Clark as a "D'Artagnan in a double breasted suit." Dilworth's demeanor often appeared flippant, and his rhetoric occasionally outrageous. He was a political realist who recognized the need to balance efficient party organization with good government. Like Clark, Dilworth as mayor emphasized the physical development of the city and undertook urban renewal on a grand scale. Under his administration, in addition to the food distribution center and the Society Hill restoration, thousands of units of public housing were built and a mass transit program was launched.

Toward the end of his first term, Dilworth acknowledged the weakness of the city's tax base. His proposal to raise some money by installing parking meters in South Philadelphia proved politically damaging, and disclosures of a "payola" scheme in his administration marred his image. In 1961, Dilworth resigned, to make an unsuccessful bid for governor. In 1965, his successor,

James Tate (*q.v.*), appointed Dilworth to the school board, inaugurating a brief but controversial era of educational reform in the city. He resigned from the school board in 1971 and died three years later (1974) of a malignant brain tumor.

SOURCES: John Guinther, "The Last of the Fitzgerald Heroes," *Philadelphia Magazine* (April 1974); John G. McCullough, "A Man and His City," Philadelphia *Evening Bulletin*, 3 January 1960; Kirk R. Petshek, *The Challenge of Urban Reform: Politics and Progress in Philadelphia* (Philadelphia, 1973); Anthony Roth, ed., "Mayors of Philadelphia, 1691–1977: Collection of the Genealogical Society of Pennsylvania," (unpublished collection found in the Historical Society of Pennsylvania, Philadelphia).   *John F. Bauman*

DOCKSTADTER, NICHOLAS (1802–71), Mayor of Cleveland (1840). Third mayor of Cleveland, Dockstadter was born on 4 January 1802 in Albany, New York, of Dutch ancestry. He was the son of Jacob and Angelica Hanson Dockstadter (1771–1840), whose family numbered four sons and four daughters. When Nicholas Dockstadter came to Cleveland in 1826 at age twenty-four, he was accompanied by his two brothers, Richard and Butler. Nicholas married Harriett Judd (1805–37), and they had five children (William, Richard, Charles, Julia, and Elizabeth). Nicholas Dockstadter was the leading hat, cap, and fur dealer in Cleveland with his store on Superior Street (the first hat firm in Ohio), dealing in furs brought by local Indians.

Cleveland was in a period of rapid growth as the Lake Erie terminus of the Ohio and Erie Canal, its population increasing from 5,080 in 1835 to 6,071 in 1840. Ohio City, on the west side of the Cuyahoga River, had a population of 1,577. In 1835, Dockstadter was treasurer of the village of Cleveland, and in 1836, when Cleveland was incorporated as a city with a board of aldermen, he was elected alderman. An active businessman, he was treasurer of the Cleveland and Newburg Railroad incorporated in 1834 and helped to organize the Cleveland, Warren and Pittsburgh Railroad. He was a director of the Bank of Cleveland. A Whig in politics, he was a delegate to the Whig county and state conventions of 1837–38. In 1838, he was again elected alderman. Dockstadter was elected mayor of Cleveland in 1840, defeating H. B. Payne (Locofoco Democrat) 463 to 362. He served a single one-year term. He died on 9 November 1871 and was buried in Cleveland.

SOURCES: Elroy McKendree Avery, *A History of Cleveland and Its Environs: The Heart of New Connecticut* (Chicago, 1918); Gertrude Van Rensselaer Wickham, *The Pioneer Families of Cleveland 1796–1840* (Cleveland, 1914); Works Progress Administration, *Annals of Cleveland: Bibliographical Series* (typescript, 1939).   *Ronald E. Shaw*

DOLBEY, MRS. DOROTHY N. (1908–   ), Acting Mayor of Cincinnati (1954). First woman mayor of Cincinnati and first woman to head any large U.S. city, and an active reformer, born in Cincinnati, on 28 April 1908, Mrs. Dolbey was the daughter of Herbert Wood Nichols (d. 1958), owner of the city's first carbon-coated paper supply company, and Harriet (Short) Nichols (d. 1973), both old-stock Americans. The first of three children, she attended public schools, the University of Cincinnati (B.S., 1930), and Columbia University (M.S., 1934). In 1935, she married James M. Dolbey (b. 1910), an executive with the Edison Corporation of Cincinnati (and later of the 3M Corporation). They had two children, and Mrs. Dolbey spent the next few years as a housewife and mother. She and her husband are Methodists.

In 1950, Dolbey became director of the Better Housing Bureau, director and chairwoman of the World Fellowship Council, YWCA, and a member of Church Women United, beginning a long career in social and reform organizations. She was the first woman elected to the city council of Cincinnati, serving four terms (1953–61). In her first term, she was selected vice-mayor, and when Mayor Edward Waldvogel (*q.v.*) died of a heart attack in May 1954, she became acting mayor. She served in this post for six months, until the council selected a new mayor in December. She was the first woman chief executive of a large American city. Cincinnati had by then 503,998 people. A member of the Charterite faction, she supported the city manager and proportional representation systems which governed Cincinnati politics, and made numerous public appearances.

Mrs. Dolbey retired from active politics in 1961, declining to seek a fifth term on the council. She continued with her reform and social organization work, such as Goodwill Industries, League of Women Voters, Conference of Christians and Jews, and American Association of University Women (since 1953), and as a member of the board of directors of the Hospital Care Corporation.

SOURCES: Cincinnati *Enquirer*, May to December 1954; Personal Interview, 17 July 1979; Ralph A. Straetz, *PR: Politics in Cincinnati* (New York, 1958); *Who's Who of American Women, 1977–1978* (Chicago, 1978).   *Thomas R. Bullard*

DOREMUS, FRANK E. (1865–1947), Mayor of Detroit (1923–24). Born on 13 August 1865 in Venango County, Pennsylvania, to Sylvester and Sarah Peake Doremus, Frank moved with his family to Portland, Michigan, and was educated in the public schools. At age seventeen, Doremus worked for a small local newspaper, the Pewamo (Michigan) *Plain Dealer*, and in 1885, he established his own paper, the Portland *Review*. He was appointed Portland postmaster, 1895–99 and then went to Detroit where he studied law at the Detroit College of Law. Doremus began his long-term political career as a Democrat in the Michigan legislature, 1890–92, assistant corporation counsel of Detroit, 1903–1907 and city controller in 1907–10; and was elected to the U.S. Congress, 1910–20. In 1920, he decided against seeking reelection and returned to Detroit to practice law. He married Elizabeth Hartley on 26 June 1890.

Detroit in 1923 had a population of more than 1 million and a mayor-council form of government. One of the leaders of the Democratic party, Doremus ran for the mayoralty on 2 April 1923 to replace an incumbent who had accepted appointment to the U.S. Senate. In this special election, he won a landslide victory, with 83,391 votes to 34,649 for Dr. James W. Inches. The short term lasted only a matter of months and in November 1923, Doremus ran for reelection and polled one of the largest majorities ever recorded, crushing his opponent, Thomas C. O'Brien, by 84,468 votes to only 8,610. His administration accomplished very little because Doremus was in ill health; he resigned in June 1924. At that time, he was still a powerful figure in the Democratic party—in local parlance a "wheelhorse." Detroit newsmen, who liked to hang labels on the city's mayors, dubbed him the "bare-footed country boy that came to town." Despite his poor health Doremus lingered on until the ripe age of eighty-three, dying on 4 September 1947, at Howell, Michigan.

SOURCES: Clarence M. Burton. *The City of Detroit, Michigan 1701–1922* (Detroit-Chicago, 1922), vol. 3; Detroit *News*, 4 September 1947, Biographical file, Detroit Public Library; John C. Lodge, *I Remember Detroit* (Detroit, 1949); Albert N. Marquis. *The Book of Detroiters* (Chicago, 1914); New York *Times* Obituaries Index 1958–68 (New York, 1970).

Ben C. Wilson and *Finny Ike Mlemchukwu*

DORGENOIS, LE BRETON, Acting Mayor of New Orleans (6 November–4 December 1812).

DOWD, BERNARD J. (1891–1971), Mayor of Buffalo (1946–49). Pharmacist and mayor, born in Buffalo on 5 December 1891, Dowd was the son of a city fireman. He attended P.S. 51 and Technical High School, graduating in 1907, and worked for the Erie and New York Central Railroads as a car checker until 1916 when he began studies at the University of Buffalo School of Pharmacy. In 1917, he enlisted in the Army and saw combat at the battles of St. Mihiel and the Meuse-Argonne, where he was gassed and was initially listed as

killed in action. Dowd returned to the University of Buffalo in 1919 and graduated in 1920. He opened Dowd's Pharmacy that same year and remained in business for twenty-five years. On 22 October 1922, he married Grace Nolan (d. 1975); they had no children. The Dowds belonged to St. Margaret's (Catholic) Church, and Dowd was a member of most pharmacists' professional organizations.

A Republican, Dowd served on the board of supervisors, 1935–45, and was elected mayor in 1945, defeating Democrat Thomas Holling (*q.v.*) 80,383 to 60,461 (35,256 votes went to Frank Schwab, the People's party candidate). He reportedly spent only about $1,500 on his mayoral campaign, one of the most inexpensive on record. Buffalo had 575,901 people in 1940 and a mayor-council form of government.

The first Republican mayor in Buffalo in sixteen years, Dowd stressed strict economies and supported efforts to reduce city salaries. He actively backed efforts to modernize the city's major hospitals, securing a complete rehabilitation of the Adam Hospital. Dowd also sponsored a major rebuilding of the street-lighting system. He supported measures to provide better care for city trees and to build additional playgrounds. Mayor Dowd never became a professional at politics: he told an interviewer that the job of mayor was hard work, but he found it interesting and enjoyable. After leaving city hall, he worked as a pharmacist for various drugstores until he retired in the late 1960s. He died on 1 November 1971.

SOURCES: Buffalo *Courier-Express*, 2 November 1971; Buffalo *Evening News*, 1 November 1971; Sister Mary Jane and Sister Mercedes, "Mayors of Buffalo, 1832–1961," (B.A. thesis, Rosary Hill College, 1961).

Thomas R. Bullard

DRAKE, MARCUS M. (1835–1907), Mayor of Buffalo (1882). Great Lakes steamship captain and a reluctant, appointed mayor for only one month, Drake was born in Homer, New York, on 7 September 1835, of mixed English-German ancestry, and moved with his family to Fredonia in 1837. He attended local schools and the Fredonia Academy until 1851 when he left home to become a sailor on the Great Lakes. By 1855, he was a steamer mate, and by 1860, he had achieved the position of captain for the Erie Railroad's fleet of ferries. In 1862, he joined the Army, serving with the Seventy-second New York Volunteers through three years of Civil War combat. Drake returned to the Erie ferries in 1865, remaining with that company until 1889, when he formed his own company, the Lackawanna Transportation Company. In 1867, he married Mary A. Ludlow (d. 1880), and they had six children. Drake was a Mason and member of the Grand Army of the Republic. He also served as vice-president of the Niagara Bank.

A staunch Republican, Drake began his political career as a Buffalo alderman in 1878, serving until 1890. When Grover Cleveland (q.v.) resigned as mayor to become governor on 20 November 1882, the Council selected Drake as his successor. He did not enjoy this new responsibility and resigned a month later, on 22 December 1882. Drake's public career ended with a four-year term as commissioner of public works, 1896–99. In 1900, he took a second wife, Lillian Quest, and continued operating his steamship company, winning a reputation as a leading transportation executive on the Great Lakes. He died on 28 September 1907.

SOURCES: Buffalo *Evening News*, 29 September 1907; William H. Dolan and Mark S. Hubbell, *Our Police and Our City* (Buffalo, 1893); New York *Times*, 29 September 1907; Sister Mary Jane and Sister Mercedes, "Mayors of Buffalo, 1832–1961," (B.A. thesis, Rosary Hill College, 1961).   *Thomas R. Bullard*

DUNCAN, WILLIAM CHAMBERLAIN (1820–77), Mayor of Detroit (1862, 1863). Democratic mayor during the Civil War, Duncan was born in Lyons, Wayne County, New York, on 18 May 1820. At age five, he moved with his parents to Rochester, New York, where he attended public schools. From 1841 until 1849, he was employed as a steward on various passenger steamers on the Great Lakes. He assisted in moving the steamer *Julia Palmer* on rollers through the streets of Sault Ste. Marie around the falls to Lake Superior. The ship became the first sidewheel steamer to ply the waters of that lake. In 1849, he moved to Detroit and entered the malt and brewing business. Duncan Brewery became one of the leading producers of ale in Detroit.

Duncan was elected mayor in 1861 by a vote of 3,329 to 2,650 over H. P. Baldwin. Before 1861, Duncan had served as an alderman for five years. During his term as mayor, he was elected to the state Senate. He served as both mayor and senator during 1863. Duncan as one of Detroit's Civil War mayors was in office when the battle of Gettysburg took place. At his request, the council appointed a relief committee to travel to the Pennsylvania battlefield to offer aid to the Michigan soldiers.

While Duncan was in Lansing attending a session of the State Senate, a race riot erupted on 6 March 1863. Francis B. Phelps, the council president who was serving as acting mayor, called in troops who restored order in the city. A life-long Democrat, Duncan served on the board of estimates following his term as mayor. Efforts were made in 1871 to persuade him to stand for election to the office of mayor, but poor health forced him to decline. He died in Detroit on 19 December 1877, leaving a wife, one son, and one daughter.

SOURCES: Detroit *Free Press*, 19 December 1877; Silas Farmer, *The History of Detroit and Michigan* (Detroit, 1889); *Journal of the Proceedings of the Common Council of the City of Detroit*, 1862, 1863; Scrapbooks, Burton Historical Collection, Detroit Public Library.   *John Cumming*

DUNNE, EDWARD FITZSIMMONS (1853–1937), Mayor of Chicago (1905–1907). Progressive mayor and late governor of Illinois, born on 12 October 1853 at Waterville, Connecticut, Dunne was the son of P. W. and Delia M. (Lawler) Dunne, Irish Catholic immigrants. His parents moved to Peoria, Illinois, when he was two, and he attended grammar and high school there, graduating in 1870. Dunne enrolled in a three-year program at Trinity College, Dublin University, but left before completing because of his father's business failure. He received an LL.B. from Union College of Law in 1877 and began practicing law in 1878. He was selected for a vacancy on the circuit court of Cook County in 1892 and won election in 1897 and reelection in 1903. Dunne married Elizabeth J. Kelly (?–1928) on 16 August 1881, and they had ten children and twenty-nine grandchildren. Dunne was active in the Iroquois Club, served as vice-president of the National Civic Federation, and was president of the League of American Municipalities, 1906–1907.

Chicago in 1905 had a population of almost two million with a weak mayor-strong council form of government. There were thirty-five wards, each represented by two aldermen. Dunne received the Democratic nomination for mayor in recognition of his brilliant judicial career and because Mayor Harrison (q.v.) hesitated opposing the Republican nominee. Dunne won on 4 April 1905 by 163,189—49.3 percent, to his Republican opponent John M. Harlan, 138,548—42.2 percent, John Collins, Socialist, 23,034—7 percent, and Oliver W. Stewart, Prohibition party, 3,294. On 2 April 1907, Dunne lost a close reelection bid to Republican Fred A. Busse (q.v.), 164,702—48.6 percent, to 151,779—45.7 percent. He practiced law, 1907–11, and sought the Democratic nomination for mayor in 1911, losing to former Mayor Harrison by 1,500 votes. This defeat turned out to be a blessing, as he subsequently secured the Democratic gubernatorial nomination in 1912. Because Theodore Roosevelt's Progressive party caused a split in the Republican party, Dunne won an upset victory (a plurality of almost 125,000) and became the first Democratic governor in twenty years. In his final bid for reelection as governor, Dunne lost to Frank O. Lowden—696,535 to 556,654 in 1916.

Dunne began his administration with a strong focus on municipal ownership of public utilities and was the first mayor to go to Springfield to push for legislation to allow cities the power to regulate gas and electric light utilities. He accomplished little during his tenure, however, and he was the last mayor to have a two-year term. His term as governor was much more successful and saw accomplishments in labor and welfare. Dunne was the only Chicago mayor ever elected governor or to any other higher office.

From 1917 on, Dunne practiced law and continued his activity in the Democratic party. He was appointed attorney for the Cook County Board of Election Commissioners in 1930 and served until his death. In his eightieth year, he published a five-volume *History of Illinois* (1933). President Franklin D. Roosevelt designated Dunne the official federal government representative to Chicago's "Century of Progress" Fair. Dunne died on 24 May 1937 in Chicago.

SOURCES: Donald S. Bradley, "The Historical Trends of the Political Elites in a Metropolitan Central City: The Chicago Mayor," Center for Social Organization Studies Working Paper No. 10, University of Chicago, Department of Sociology, May 1963; John D. Buenker, "Edward F. Dunne: The Urban New Stock Democrat As Progressive," *Mid-America* 50, No. 1 (January 1968); Paul Michael Green, "The Chicago Democratic Party 1840–1920: From Factionalism to Political Organization" (Ph.D. dissertation, University of Chicago, 1975); William L. Sullivan, comp. and ed., *Dunne: Judge, Mayor, Governor* (Chicago, 1916); Ralph R. Tingley, "From Carter Harrison II to Fred Busse: A Study of Chicago Political Parties and Personages from 1896–1907" (Ph.D. dissertation, University of Chicago, 1950).

Andrew K. Prinz

DYER, THOMAS (1805–62), Mayor of Chicago (1856–57). Proslavery Democratic mayor, born on 13 January 1805 in Canton, Connecticut, the son of a Revolutionary War officer, Dyer grew up on a farm in rural New England and was raised as a Catholic. After a grade school education and a career as a clerk in a Canton general merchandise store, he made his way west to Chicago in 1835. Shortly thereafter, Dyer joined the warehousing firm of Wadsworth and Chapin, and he and Chapin subsequently formed a new business as meat-packers. In 1847, Dyer was elected a member of the board of directors of the Galena and Chicago Union Railroad, and in 1850, he became one of the first directors of the Chicago Gas Light and Coke Company. He was elected the first president of the Chicago Board of Trade and served as president of the city's Chamber of Commerce. Dyer represented Chicago in the Illinois General Assembly of 1851–52.

In 1856, Chicago had over 84,000 people and a mayor-council form of government. Dyer was Stephen A. Douglas's candidate for mayor that year, campaigning on the merits of the Kansas-Nebraska Act of 1854. He was opposed by Francis C. Sherman, a Democrat who opposed the extension of slavery. Violence, bribery, intimidation, and rowdyism marred the campaign; almost 9,000 votes were cast, approximately 1,500 more than could be legally polled. Dyer edged Sherman by a total of 4,712 to 4,113.

Dyer's administration was marked by the beginning of a nation-wide economic depression during which there was a general curtailment of business and a series of financial disasters. During the winter of 1856–57, the streets were thronged with idle men, and crime increased alarmingly. Both Dyer and his police force were denounced for their ineffectiveness. During his term, work was begun on raising the grade-level of the city's business district. In the process, which took twenty years to complete, some streets were raised as much as ten feet above the swamp, and buildings were jacked up to higher foundations or moved. It was also during Dyer's mayoralty that Fort Dearborn was razed, and the ground on which it stood was leveled to form Randolph Street.

Saddled with his inability to boost the sagging economy and faced with an increasingly antislavery feeling among Chicagoans, Dyer chose not to seek reelection after his term in city hall. Instead, he resumed his business career and eventually retired to New England. He died on 6 June 1862 and was buried in Middleton, Connecticut.

SOURCES: A. T. Andreas, *History of Chicago* (Chicago, 1884), vol. 1; *Chicago City Manual: 1911*; Bessie Louise Pierce, *A History of Chicago* (New York, 1940), vol. 2; Frederick Rex, *The Mayors of the City of Chicago* (Chicago, 1947).

W. Roger Biles

EARHART, FRED A. Acting Mayor of New Orleans (15 July 1936).

EATON, FREDERICK (1855–1934), Mayor of Los Angeles (1898–1900). ''Father of the Los Angeles Aqueduct,'' Eaton was born in Los Angeles on 23 September 1855 of a leading settler family. His father, Judge Benjamin S. Eaton, from Connecticut, was district attorney, justice of the peace, and a businessman, including viticulture. His mother, Mary Hays Eaton, was from Maryland. Eaton was educated in the Los Angeles public schools and at Santa Clara University. His first wife, Helen B. Burdick, whom he married in 1874 and divorced in 1906, came from a Los Angeles settler family and brought property to the union. They had six children. On 18 June 1906, Eaton married Alice Slosson in Los Angeles.

Eaton combined business and public service throughout his career. He was city surveyor and engineer, 1885–86, and city engineer, 1889–90, during which time he mapped the city and designed its water system. As chief engineer of the Los Angeles Railway Company, he built one of the first electric railroads in the United States. From these activities as well as his role as rancher and landowner, he became interested in the problem of water supply, and as early as 1890 was talking about the need and possibility of bringing Owens Valley water to the Los Angeles basin.

As Republican opponent of incumbent Mayor Meredith Snyder (q.v.) in 1898, Eaton made inadequate water supplies part of his campaign. He also supported more schools and public ownership of electric power. Eaton defeated Snyder 8,273 to 7,698.

During Eaton's mayoralty, Los Angeles was a rapidly expanding city which went over the 100,000 mark. It had a mayor-council form of government and was the county seat of Los Angeles County. Its major issues were associated with growth, particularly in terms of adequate resources, such as water. Business groups were increasingly asserting themselves, primarily behind the Republican party, to promote and direct economic development. As such, Eaton was very much a mayor for that community, reflecting business interests and principles; public power and public control of water supplies were interests that he shared not only with most businessmen, but also with most residents of the city as a whole.

Eaton served only one term and was not a candidate in 1900. He continued to be very involved in problems of water supply, and in his own land and ranching interests—the two never being entirely separate—until his death in Los Angeles on 11 March 1934. His own land options were sold to the city, guaranteeing it sufficient land in the Owens River Valley to implement the aqueduct project.

SOURCES: California Biography File, Los Angeles Public Library; Harris Newmark, *60 Years in Southern California*, 4th ed. (Los Angeles, 1970); Vincent Ostrom, *Water and Politics: A Study of Water Policies and Administration in the Development of Los Angeles* (Los Angeles, 1953); Leonard A. Sanders, ''Los Angeles and Its Mayors, 1850–1925'' (Master's thesis, University of Southern California, 1968).   *John M. Allswang*

EDSON, FRANKLIN (1832–1904), Mayor of New York (1883–84). An anti-Tammany, Democratic mayor of New York City, Edson was born in Chester, Vermont, in 1832. His mother, Soviah Williams, was a descendant of Roger Williams. His father, Ophir Edson, was a descendant of a prominent deacon and one of the founders of the Massachusetts Bay Colony. Franklin helped out on his father's farm while attending the local school until the age of fourteen. Then, for five years he taught school and farmed while a student at the Chester Academy. At the age of twenty, he moved to Albany, New York, where he worked in his brother's distillery. By 1855, he had become a full partner in this prosperous business. The next year he married Fanny C. Wood, the granddaughter of Jethro Wood, the inventor of the cast-iron plow. They had seven children. He soon became a director in the New York State Bank, a vestryman of St. Paul's Protestant Episcopal Church, a member of the board of trade, and president of the Young Men's Association. By 1866, he had embarked upon a career in the produce business in New York City. This resulted in his presidency of the New York produce exchange in 1873, 1874, and 1878. He also became a major figure in the trading and transportation of grain. His political experience and reputation grew in part from his work to abolish tolls on the state's canals. He also rationalized the system of rail delivery of grains to storage elevators. Edson was the driving force behind the construction of the Produce Exchange Building in New York.

In 1882, New York was a mayor-aldermanic city of well over a million people. Always known as an anti-Tammany Democrat, Edson was nominated for mayor in arrangements whereby his county Democrats allotted other offices to Irving Hall and Tammany Democrats. He defeated the Citizens' movement candidate, Allen Campbell, by 97,802 votes to 76,385. During his term, contracts were let out for the new Croton Aqueduct, new park land was acquired, the Brooklyn Bridge was completed, and monies for new armories were appropriated. Edson attempted to battle the corrupt rival bribes to alderman for surface railway contracts. He was active in the civil service reform movements of the time. In 1890, he became president of the Genesee Fruit Company. He maintained an active interest in banking and in St. James Church at Fordham until his death in New York in 1904.

SOURCES: Gordon Atkins, *Health, Housing and Poverty in New York City 1865–1898*, (Ann Arbor, Mich., 1947); William Herman, *Factbook: Mayors and Burgomasters* (New York, n.d.); Mark D. Hirsch, *William C. Whitney* (New York, 1948); Charles Morris, *Makers of New York* (New York, 1895).   *Howard R. Weiner*

ELIOT, SAMUEL ATKINS (1789–1862), Mayor of Boston (1837–39). The seventh mayor of Boston, Eliot was born there on 5 March 1789, the sixth of seven children of Samuel Eliot, a rich merchant, and Catherine (Atkins) Eliot, his father's second wife. They were an old New England family of British descent. Eliot was a divinity student at Harvard, graduating in 1817. He then followed his father into business, becoming a successful merchant in the East India trade. His interests were wide, and he distinguished himself as an educator, music lover, reformer, and writer, and as president of the Boston Academy of Music, president of the Prison Discipline Society, school commissioner, and treasurer of Harvard. He married Mary Lyman of Newburyport (d. 1869), and they had four daughters and a son, Charles, who later became president of Harvard.

A Whig, Eliot became mayor of Boston in 1837. He served three consecutive one-year terms, the maximum term of office a mayor could then serve in the city's mayor/bicameral council government. In 1837, Boston had about 85,000 people and was growing. This growth produced the most pressing social and political problems that Eliot faced. The Panic of 1837 complicated the task, forcing city officials to look for ways to cut expenditures, even as demand increased for public services. Nevertheless, Eliot made impressive strides toward alleviating some of the difficulties, by Whig standards of the day, at least.

Eliot's greatest achievements were his reforms of the city's fire and police departments, both of which were prompted by the Broad Street riot, which occurred in June 1837 after a fire engine company collided with an Irish funeral. Both forces were professionalized, with paid firemen replacing the volunteer companies and regular day police officers replacing the constabulary force. Eliot built several schools, the Hospital for Lunatics and Idiots, and an addition to the House of Corrections. He appointed a superintendent of alien passengers to turn away destitute immigrants who could neither give bond that they would not become wards of the city or state within ten years, nor pay $2 to commute the bond. Like his predecessors, however, Eliot made no progress on the problems of establishing a public water supply and replacing the inadequate Leverett Street jail. He could not make a start on the construction of a greatly needed new city hall and, despite some budget-slashing in 1837 and 1838, failed to reduce the city debt.

Eliot was elected to the state Senate in 1850 and from there was appointed to the U.S. Congress in 1851 to fill the unexpired term of Robert C. Winthrop. Near the end of his life, he lost all his money, when a firm in which he was a silent partner failed. He died on 29 January 1862.

SOURCES: *Boston City Documents* (Boston, 1837, 1838, 1839); James M. Bugbee, "Boston Under the Mayors," in Justin Winsor, ed., *The Memorial History of Boston* (Boston, 1881), vol. 3; Charles Philips Huse, *The Financial History of Boston from May 1, 1822 to January 31, 1909* (Cambridge, Mass., 1916); *Inaugural Addresses of the Mayors of Boston 1822–1851* (Boston, 1894); *Our First Men: A Calendar of Wealth, Fashion, and Gentlemen Containing a List of Those Persons Taxed in the City of Boston Credibly Reported to Be Worth 100 Thousand Dollars* (Boston, 1846).

Christine M. Rosen

ELLERT, LEVI RICHARD (1857–1901), Mayor of San Francisco (1893–95). First native-born San Franciscan to be elected mayor, Ellert was born on 20 October 1857. Ellert was a druggist, opening the L. R. Ellert and Company drugstore in 1883 at the corner of California and Kearny streets. After trying without success to be elected school director, Ellert won a place on the board of supervisors in 1888 and was reelected in 1890. A humorous political story in *The Wave* (November 1890) suggests that voters who opposed Ellert scratched his name incorrectly and inadvertently gave him their support. He seems to have been an able administrator, honest and "unimpeachable" as a supervisor, and in 1892, abandoning his Republican identity to run as a nonpartisan, he was elected mayor.

Ellert apparently had problems with the Republican party leadership; he was independent-minded, perhaps headstrong, having little patience with political bosses. His close friend was the local engineering genius, Adolph Sutro. During his term, Ellert studied law and was admitted to the bar. He presided over the Midwinter Exposition of 1894 held in Golden Gate Park, 27 January to 1 September, which attracted 2,225,000 visitors. Very successful in business, he was a director of the California Title Insurance and Trust Company, and the Continental Salt and Chemical Company, and president of the Sanitary Reduction Works until October 1899. In later life, he became involved in spiritualism and published a book on *séances* in San Francisco. He died in his native city on 21 July 1901.

SOURCES: L. R. Ellert, *Do The Dead Return? A True Story of Startling Séances in San Francisco* (San Francisco, 1900); B. Millard, *History of the San Francisco Bay Region* (Chicago, 1924); *Official History of the California Midwinter International Exposition* (San Francisco, 1894); *The Olympic*, 3 November 1894; *San Francisco News Letter*, 7 January and 28 October 1893; *The Wave*, 22 November 1890, 30 June 1894.

Peter d'A. Jones

ELY, SMITH, JR. (1825–1911), Mayor of New York (1877–78). The second post-Tweed mayor, Ely was born on 17 April 1825 at the residence of his maternal grandfather, Ambrose Kitchell, at Hanover, New Jersey. Judge Aaron Kitchell, his maternal great-grandfather, was a Revolutionary soldier, U.S. representative, and senator. Two remote paternal ancestors, William and Richard Ely, were colonial captains in the French and Indian War. His father, Epaphras C. Ely, a leather merchant, served in the War of 1812, and his paternal grandfather in the Revolutionary War. Thus, Ely had considerable social standing as a member of the Society of the Colonial Wars, Sons of the American Revolution, and the Society of the War of 1812. He studied law in the office of Frederic DePeyster and graduated from New York University Law School.

After pursuing the leather business while maintaining active interest in Democratic politics, Ely was elected a school trustee of the Seventeenth Ward (1856–59). In 1857, he was elected to the state Senate, the first Democrat from his district. He was the only Democrat on both the Committee on Cities and the Subcommittee of the Whole through which urban legislation passed. As a man of military ancestry, he was elected to the board of county supervisors in 1860 in order to raise men and money for the Civil War. He held this post for eight

years and developed into a vigorous opponent of public expenditures and corruption. He was reelected to the board in 1867 and in the same year was made commissioner of public instruction. His election to Congress in 1870 and 1874 and his nomination for mayor in 1876 were based upon his personal distinction and his acceptability to the various Democratic factions of the post-Tweed era. Ely never married, devoting his time to public life and to various elite clubs. On the board of supervisors, he became noted for his exposure of Tweed's corruption, particularly with his procedures against the infamous "Tweed Courthouse." (Ely and Tweed sat beside each other at board meetings for four years without exchanging a word.) In Congress his fiscal reputation grew as a member of the Railroad, Public Buildings and Treasury Expenditures committees.

In 1876, New York was a city of over one million people with a mayor-aldermanic system of government. The Tweed Ring had been overthrown, and unblemished candidates were now required. The Republicans nominated General John A. Dix, a distinguished soldier and former governor, whom Ely defeated by a majority of over 55,000. In each year of his term, the city debt and taxes were reduced despite increases in population. In 1877, a year of national labor violence, Ely skillfully criticized but permitted rallies of the unemployed. He preached economy, limitations on public construction and distribution of coal, in the face of calls for strong government action. Mayor Ely made an abortive effort to remove the police commissioner, charging that street cleaning (a police function) was a disgrace. A new decentralized sweeping plan was adopted. This issue, like others of his term, had overtones of private-public, state-city, and machine-reform political infighting. "Honest John" Kelly, the party leader and comptroller, continued to handle everyday finances and politics, while Ely took the high road. Ely refused a congressional nomination; instead, he retired to private life and membership in the Century, Drawing Room and Presbyterian Union clubs. He died at Livingston, New Jersey, on 1 July 1911.

SOURCES: Gordon Atkins, *Health, Housing and Poverty in New York City, 1865–1898* (Ann Arbor, Mich., 1947); Edwin A. Ely, *Personal Memoirs* (New York, 1929); William Herman, *Fact-book: Mayors and Burgomasters* (New York, n.d.); Charles Morris, *Men of Affairs in New York* (New York, 1906); Gustave Myers, *The History of Tammany Hall* (New York, 1901); New York *Times*, 2 July 1911; Paul T. Ringenback, *Tramps and Reformers* (Westport, Conn., 1973).

Howard R. Weiner

EWING, WILLIAM L. (1843–1905), Mayor of St. Louis (1881–85). Businessman and politician, Ewing was born in St. Louis on 16 March 1843, the second son of William L. Ewing (1809–73), a wholesale grocer, and Clara (Berthold) Ewing (1819–99), both Roman Catholics. One of eleven children, young William graduated from the Christian Brothers Academy (equivalent to college) and almost immediately began working as a clerk in his father's successful firm. He worked for the W. L. Ewing Company until 1873 when he left for a career as a banker (specializing in investments) and farmer. In 1880, he married Mary Flemming of Indianapolis, and they had one child, William, Jr.

Ewing, a Republican, entered politics in 1877, the first election after the new charter of 1876, which had split the city from the county. He served four years in the city's House of Delegates, acting as presiding officer of that body for the entire period. In 1881, he was elected mayor, defeating incumbent Henry Overstolz (q.v.), then running on the Democratic ticket, 24,608 to 11,353. Four years later, Ewing was defeated by Democrat David R.

Francis (q.v.) 20,861 to 19,349. (A third candidate, veteran Chauncey Filley (q.v.), running as an Independent candidate, got only 809 votes.) St. Louis had 350,518 people by 1880 and a mayor-council form of government.

As might be expected, Ewing ran a businesslike administration, supporting various civic improvements. He reorganized the police department in response to complaints that it had become too political. He supported a large-scale street-paving plan and the building of the city's first cable railway, replacing some of the old horsecars. He also supported measures to improve the fire department. After leaving office, he resumed his career as a banker, until his death on 4 June 1905.

SOURCES: Charles H. Cornwell, *St. Louis Mayors: Brief Biographies* (St. Louis, 1965); William Hyde and Howard L. Conrad, eds., *Encyclopedia of the History of St. Louis*, 4 vols. (New York, 1899); J. T. Scharf, *History of Saint Louis City and County*, 2 vols. (Philadelphia, 1883).

Thomas R. Bullard

F

FARAN, JAMES J. (1808–92), Mayor of Cincinnati (1855–57). Newspaperman and Democratic mayor, Faran was born in Cincinnati on 29 December 1808 and attended local schools and Miami University, graduating in 1832. He studied law with Judge Oliver M. Spencer, 1832–33, beginning practice in 1833. In 1834, he became editor of the *Democratic Reporter*, and ten years later he assumed the same post with the Cincinnati *Enquirer*. In 1840, he married Angelina Russell (d. 1898) of Columbus, and they had five children.

A Democrat, Faran was a member of the state general assembly in 1835–36 and 1837–39 (speaker during 1838–39) and then of the Ohio Senate, 1839–41. He was a member of the commission to plan a new statehouse in 1845. He was elected to Congress in 1844 and was reelected in 1846, serving two terms in all (1845–49). As a Democrat, Faran supported the Polk administration, but he also backed efforts to limit the expansion of slavery. In 1855, Faran was the Democratic candidate for mayor, defeating James Taylor (Know-Nothing) 9,558 to 8,225. Cincinnati had 115,435 people in 1850 and a mayor-council form of government.

The bitterness of the mayoral campaign showed the continuing strength of the nativist and anti-Catholic movement in local politics, and this issue dominated Faran's mayoral term. He was personally popular and was considered a man of absolute integrity, but political conditions limited his opportunities as mayor. In 1857, Faran was appointed postmaster of Cincinnati but was removed in 1859, since he had supported Stephen A. Douglas in the Illinois senator's intraparty feud with President James Buchanan. He resumed working for the *Enquirer* and continued in this newspaper career until his death on 12 December 1892.

SOURCES: *The Biographical Encyclopedia of Ohio of the Nineteenth Century* (Cincinnati, 1876); Lewis A. Conrad, ed., *Greater Cincinnati and Its People*, 4 vols. (New York, 1929); Charles T. Greve, *Centennial History of Cincinnati and Representative Citizens*, 2 vols. (Chicago, 1904); *History of Cincinnati and Hamilton County, Ohio* (Cincinnati, 1894). *Thomas R. Bullard*

FARGO, WILLIAM G. (1818–81), Mayor of Buffalo (1862–65). Internationally famous through the Wells, Fargo express company, and mayor of Buffalo in the Civil War, though a Democrat, Fargo was born on 20 May 1818 at Pompey, New York, the oldest of twelve children of William C. Fargo (1791–1878), farmer and distiller of English descent, and Tacy (Strong) Fargo (1799–1869). Fargo was obliged by poverty to leave school at age thirteen. He subsequently carried mail on horseback and worked in taverns and groceries, and as a railroad freight agent. At twenty-one (in 1840), he married Anna H. Williams of Pompey, New York. They had eight children, but only two outlived them.

When in 1842 Fargo became a messenger with an express line operating between Albany and Buffalo, he associated himself with the type of undertaking that would one day make his name a household word. Thereafter, wrote an admirer, Fargo proved that in America "fortune and fame do not depend upon birth or inheritance." Working with associates, such as Henry Wells and William Livingston, he took the infant express enterprise and, by destroying or consolidating with his competitors, organized it into successively larger units, until, as the American Express Company (1850) and Wells, Fargo and Company (1852), the express business carried from coast to coast. Perhaps naturally, his reputation brought him into politics.

A life-long Democrat but a political neophyte, Fargo was nominated mayoral candidate by the Democrats of Buffalo (population 81,129) in 1861. In the city election, swept by his party generally, he defeated Republican James Adams (*q.v.*) by 5,658 votes to 4,479. Two years later, he was reelected, though with a smaller majority (6,431 to Chandler J. Wells' *q.v.* 5,968). Those were trying times, the mayor told the common council in his first inaugural. A "rebellion . . . threatens the life of the nation"; yet, local government had to continue; and the schools, police force and harbor facilities had to be maintained. Fargo nevertheless urged economies: by virtually discarding the "remarkably efficient" voluntary fire department for a professional organization, his predecessor, he implied, had spent excessively. Himself Buffalo's most successful businessman, the mayor encouraged new business to locate in the city.

Fargo also took care as a Democrat, to support the Union war effort. He fostered enlistments and cooperated with federal conscription. In November 1863, when the secretary of war warned that "rebel" sympathizers were preparing to cross the border from Canada, the mayor dispatched plain-clothed policemen to Canadian ports. They reported no unusual activity, and Fargo regarded "the rumor . . . as groundless." Still, he asked the council to add fifteen men to the city police force.

Once leaving office, apart from being a presidential elector in 1868, Fargo concentrated on business interests, further expanding the express lines and acting as officer and director of various national railroads and local insurance and publishing enterprises. Locally, too, he found time for religious and civic matters. An Episcopalian, he was long a member of St. John's Church and in 1879 a founder and vestryman of Christ Church. Fargo served on the first board of the Buffalo State Hospital which opened in 1880. When, after a long illness, William Fargo died, on 3 August 1881, his name, it was noted, "was far more widely known than that of any citizen of Buffalo who survives him."

SOURCES: Buffalo *Commercial Advertiser*, 4 August 1881; Buffalo *Daily Courier*, 4 August 1881; Buffalo *Morning Express*, 4 August 1881; J. J. Gibbin, *Record of the Fargo Family* (Buffalo, 1907); Grace C. Sheldon, "William G. Fargo," Buffalo *Times*, 7, 14, and 21 September 1919; "William George Fargo," *Magazine of Western History* (April 1886); H. Perry Smith, *History of the City of Buffalo and Erie County* 2 vols., (Syracuse, N.Y., 1884).   *John D. Milligan*

FARLEY, JOHN HARRINGTON (1846–1922), Mayor of Cleveland (1883–84, 1899–1900). Commonly called "Honest John," Cleveland's Democratic mayor at the turn of the century Farley was born there on 5 February 1846. Both parents, Patrick Farley and Anna (Schwarz) Farley, were immigrants who met and settled in Cleveland during the first half of the nineteenth century. His father, coming from Northern Ireland, was an avowed Mason of unknown occupation. His mother, a Roman Catholic from Rhenish Bavaria (Rhineland, Germany), was a housewife. They had four children. The future mayor attended Cleveland public schools, William Wakefield's Private School, and the local business college. His chief interest, however, lay in mechanics, which led to his securing a number of patents. By profession a businessman, Farley gained his first practical experience managing his late brother's mercantile firm as executor of the estate. Later, he assumed management of the financially plagued Farman Brassworks which he returned to solvency, despite depressed economic conditions.

A life-long Democrat, Farley was elected city councilman from a predominantly Republican ward in 1871.

Declining renomination, he was reelected to two more terms (1873, 1875) by even larger majorities. During this third term, the Democratic majority on the council voted him council president from which position he presided over legislation adding $60,000 to the city treasury. In 1877, he left the council, but both parties subsequently elected him decennial appraiser, that is, real estate valuator, for the affluent First District (1879)—a high compliment. Two years later, Cuyahoga County Democrats drafted him to run against incumbent Mayor R. R. Herrick (*q.v.*) for the mayoralty. Although ahead of his ticket by a thousand votes, he nevertheless, lost by over 3,000 votes.

"Honest John" Farley campaigned a total of five times for the city's chief executive post, winning it twice. In 1883, he defeated George W. Gardner (*q.v.*) 14,768 to 10,776, and repeated this performance sixteen years later over incumbent Robert E. McKisson (*q.v.*) 33,198 to 30,343. These two terms came at a time when Cleveland was governed by a mayor and council under the federal system. Its population was 227,760 in 1883 and 409,617 in 1900. Farley's leadership, if unspectacular, was marked by close attention to fiscal affairs and a real concern for public improvements. He was also remembered as a strict party man who filled even the most minor public positions from Democratic patronage lists. Interestingly, he openly attributed his 1899 victory to a $20,000 contribution from Republican Senator Marcus A. Hanna, the "uncrowned boss" of Cleveland, who held a grudge against Farley's rival Robert McKisson, also a Republican. Near the end of his first term, on 23 September 1884, the mayor married Margaret (Kenney) Farley, the daughter of an early Cleveland pioneer family. There were no children.

When not sitting in the mayor's office, Farley was never far from politics. President Grover Cleveland (*q.v.*) appointed him collector of internal revenue for the Eighteenth Ohio District in 1884, and he also served as Cleveland director of public works (1893–94). He held high corporate positions as vice-president of the Guardian Trust Company and president of the Mutual Building and Investment Company.

An unpretentious, charitable man, fond of sports, animals, and long country walks, who valued his privacy and avoided notoriety, Farley died in Cleveland on 10 February 1922.

SOURCES: The Cleveland City Directory, 1870–1900; Cleveland *Plain Dealer*, April 1883 to April 1885, April 1899 to April 1901, and February 1922; "John H. Farley," *Biographical Cyclopedia and Portrait Gallery of Representative Men of the State of Ohio* (1887), vol. 4; *Memorial Record of the County of Cuyahoga and City of Cleveland, Ohio* (Chicago, 1894); Robert I. Vexler, ed., *Cleveland: A Chronological and Documentary History, 1760–1976* (Dobbs-Ferry, N.Y., 1977); James Beaumont Whipple, "Cleveland in Conflict: A Study in Urban Adolescence, 1876–1900," (Ph.D. dissertation, Western Reserve University, 1951).

Eric C. Lewandowski

FEINSTEIN, DIANNE (1933–   ), Mayor of San Francisco (1978–   ). First woman mayor of San Francisco, Feinstein was born in San Francisco on 22 June 1933 as Dianne Goldman, daughter of a Jewish physician and teacher, Dr. Leon Goldman, and a Roman Catholic, Russian-American mother, who modeled clothes in exclusive boutiques, Betty (Rosenburg) Goldman. She went to a convent school, Sacred Heart (graduating in 1951), while at the same time attending temple—a very American situation. From the age of sixteen, she knew her career would be in public service. An uncle in the garment business would take her to meetings of the city council and the board of supervisors. She went on to Stanford University, majoring in politics and history and graduating in 1955.

Firmly believing that women deserve careers but must develop real expertise and specialties first, Dianne Goldman turned to criminal justice as a field, working for a year as an intern in public affairs on a foundation grant, 1955–56, and later as administrative assistant to the California Industrial Welfare Commission, 1956–57. The responsibilities of child-rearing and divorce from her first husband, Jack Berman, an attorney, delayed her career temporarily, but in 1962 Governor Edmund Brown appointed her to the state women's parole board and for four years she learned the prison system at close hand. She worked on the city and county adult detention committee, 1967–69, and the mayor's crime committee. In 1962, she was remarried, to a prominent neurosurgeon, Dr. Bertram Feinstein (who died in June 1978).

A moderately liberal Democrat, Mrs. Feinstein was elected to the board of supervisors in 1969, serving three terms and acting as its president three times, 1970–71, 1974–75, and 1978. She was the first woman president in the city's history. Supervisor Feinstein threw herself into the job, abandoning housecares to paid help. "I've always felt that the important thing was the kind of time you spend with your family, not the amount. I like to spend Class A time with them. . . ," she explained, with characteristic honesty and directness to a reporter. Ambitious for the job, Mrs. Feinstein tried twice to be elected mayor—in 1971 (encouraged by Democrats more liberal than Alioto [*q.v.*] to try to unseat that incumbent mayor), and in 1975 when George Moscone (*q.v.*) won.

With the tragic assassination of Mayor Moscone in November 1978, Board President Feinstein assumed control of the city without hesitation. On 4 December 1978, her board colleagues selected her as mayor *pro tem*, and a city election a year later, first in November, then a runoff, on 11 December 1979, returned her to office for a full term. Mrs. Feinstein defeated Supervisor Quentin Kopp in a hard-fought election by 102,233 to 87,226. Voter turnout was low—fewer than half the total of 372,000 registered. At age forty-six, Dianne Feinstein was now legally elected the city's first woman mayor. She had held the city together in the dark days of 1978, which had seen not only the assassinations in city hall and the tensions that followed, but also the mass murders/suicides in Guyana of the San Francisco temple led by Reverend Jim Jones. Mayor Feinstein was careful to choose another homosexual, Harvey Milk, to replace Kopp (who was murdered along with Moscone), while at the same time avoiding the appointment of a radical lesbian activist, Anne Kronenberg, who had been Milk's assistant. While sympathetic to minority rights, the mayor understood that she also had obligations to the more conservative majority. She saw her task as one of bringing the city together and of reducing friction among ethnic, sexual, and political groups.

SOURCES: Dianne Feinstein, *Women in Government* (draft article for *Daily Commercial News*, 8 August 1979); election campaign material, November–December 1979; Office of the Mayor, *Biography of Mayor Dianne Feinstein* (San Francisco, n.d.); personal interviews, San Francisco City Hall, November 1979; press reports, New York *Times*, San Francisco *Chronicle; State of the City Address* (San Francisco, Office of the Mayor, 15 October 1979).

Peter d'A. Jones

FILLEY, CHAUNCEY IVES (1829–1923), Mayor of St. Louis (1863–64). Prominent Republican leader, born in Lansingburg, New York, on 17 October 1829, Filley was the son of Augustus and Amelia (Filley) Filley, and the cousin of a previous mayor, Oliver D. Filley (*q.v.*). He attended public schools and a local academy, followed by two years at a law school in Saratoga. He was offered an appointment to West Point but declined. On 16 September 1850, he married Anna Adams (d. 1896), also from Lansingsburg, and the young couple moved to St. Louis that same year. Filley joined his cousin's pottery company as a clerk and became a full partner in 1855. Although the Filley family was originally Democratic, Chauncey Filley joined the Republicans during the late 1850s.

In 1863, Filley was nominated by the anti-Blair faction of that party, and when the political leaders rejected his efforts to refuse this nomination, he went on to win the election with 5,908 votes to 3,202 for his cousin O. D. Filley (a pro-Blair Republican) and 4,071 for Democrat

Joseph O'Neill. St. Louis had a population of 160,773 in 1860 and a mayor-council form of government. As wartime mayor, Filley actively supported plans for a new water and sewer system and measures to preserve the city's trade. He also hoped to secure city ownership of the St. Louis Gas Company. His health gave way under the strain of office, and he resigned in April 1864, desiring to tend to his pottery company.

In fact, Filley's political career was just beginning. In 1865, he was chairman of the state's constitutional convention, which ratified the antislavery amendments to the Constitution. He was also a delegate to every Republican national convention from 1876 through 1892. He refused offers to become ambassador to Great Britain in 1881 and postmaster general in 1897. In 1885, he came in third in the mayoralty campaign. Running as an Independent, he received only 809 votes to 20,861 for Democrat David Francis (q.v.) and 19,349 for Republican W. L. Ewing. In 1894, he organized a Republican sweep of the Missouri congressional elections. He served on the city's board of trade (1871–79) and as a director of the Missouri Historical Society. As late as 1901, he again attempted to become mayor but fell well behind. He died at his home in Overland, Missouri, on 14 September 1923.

SOURCES: Charles H. Cornwell, *St. Louis Mayors: Brief Biographies* (St. Louis, 1965); William Hyde and Howard L. Conrad, eds., *Encyclopedia of the History of St. Louis* 4 vols. (New York, 1899). There are a few items in the Filley Family Papers (a total of 150 items) in the Missouri Historical Society Library in St. Louis.

Thomas R. Bullard

FILLEY, OLIVER DWIGHT (1806–81), Mayor of St. Louis (1858–61). First Republican mayor of St. Louis, Filley was a New Englander, born 23 May 1806 in Bloomfield, Connecticut the son of Oliver Filley, a tinsmith and Annis (Humphrey) Filley. One of six children, Filley attended public schools and business school, planning to follow his father's trade. He worked in sheet-metal shops in Pittsburgh and Philadelphia until 1833 when he moved west to St. Louis. He established a stove manufacturing firm with his younger brother Giles F. Filley (b. 1815), and it soon became the largest in the city. In 1835, he married Chloe Velina Brown, and they had seven children, all of whom reached adulthood. During the 1850s, Filley became a director of the Bank of the State of Missouri and a promoter of the Kansas and Pacific Railroad Company.

Filley was a personal friend of Senator Thomas Hart Benton and thus a Jacksonian Democrat in his earlier years. During the 1850s, he abandoned that party and joined the new Republican party, motivated at least in part by a belief in the doctrine of free soil. In 1858, he was elected mayor, defeating George R. Taylor (Democrat) 7,024 to 6,600. In 1859, he became the first mayor in St. Louis to be elected to a two-year term, with 8,277 votes to 4,682 for E. Wyman (American party) and 2,911 for L. V. Bogy (Democrat). At that time, St. Louis had 160,773 people and a mayor-council form of government.

During Filley's tenure in office, St. Louis got its first paid fire department and first street railway. A strong believer in the Sabbath, Filley insisted that saloons be closed on Sundays. He became chairman of the Committee of Public Safety upon the outbreak of the Civil War at the end of his second term. In 1863, he unsuccessfully sought another term, winning 3,202 votes as the candidate of the pro-Blair faction of the Republican party. He came in third, behind Democrat Joseph O'Neill (4,071 votes) and his cousin, C. Filley (q.v.) (anti-Blair Republican, with 5,908 votes). He continued his work with the Safety Committee until 1865, when he resumed his manufacturing pursuits. He moved back east to Hampton, New Hampshire, where he died on 21 August 1881.

SOURCES: Charles H. Cornwell, *St. Louis Mayors: Brief Biographies* (St. Louis, 1965); William Hyde and Howard L. Conrad, eds., *Encyclopedia of the History of St. Louis*, 4 vols. (New York, 1899); J. T. Scharf, *History of Saint Louis City and County*, 2 vols. (Philadelphia, 1883); There are a few Filley items within the Filley Family Papers in the Missouri Historical Society (St. Louis), which total only 150 items.

Thomas R. Bullard

FITLER, EDWIN HENRY (1825–96), Mayor of Philadelphia (1887–91). Philadelphia's first mayor under the reform Bullitt Charter of 1887, Fitler was the tenth of eleven children born in 1825 to William Fitler, a prominent tanner and leather dealer whose Protestant family came to America from Germany in 1750, and Elizabeth (Wonderly) Fitler. After receiving what his biographers call an "academic" education, Fitler read law in the office of Charles E. Lex of Philadelphia for four years. He did not enjoy his studies, however, and at the age of twenty-one he went to work in his brother-in-law's cordage manufacturing firm, George J. Weaver and Company, becoming a partner at age twenty-three. In 1859, he bought out Weaver, and the business became Edwin H. Fitler and Company. Fitler was well known as an innovator with labor-saving machinery. His sons joined the company, and by 1890 it was producing 10,000 tons of rope, cables, and binder twine for sale throughout the United States and abroad. In 1850, Fitler married Josephine Baker, by whom he had two sons and two daughters. Fitler was a director of the National Bank of the Northern Liberties, the Northern Pennsylvania Railroad Company, and the Northern Liberties Gas Company. He served as president of the American Manufacturers Association and the Union League.

Philadelphia's population increased from 847,170 in 1880 to 1,046,964 in 1890. Fitler had never held office prior to 1887, but in that year he accepted the Republican nomination for mayor, and he received 90,211 votes to his opponent, Democrat George deB. Keim's 62,263. Under the Bullitt Charter, Fitler was ineligible for re-election. The charter reduced the powers of the councils, strengthened the mayor's powers, and was widely heralded as a reform measure. However, J. Donald Cameron's state Republican organization had also supported the bill, theorizing that a strong mayor would be easier to deal with than the factionalized councils, many members of which supported Philadelphia Gas Works trustee and Cameron opponent, James McManes. Fitler's administration indicated that the changes had been primarily structural. His director of public safety, former Mayor William S. Stokley (q.v.), began firing police officers immediately, thus inaugurating a return to a partisan police force. Fitler's director of public works retained several McManes supporters in the Gas Works. His administration was also marred by the embezzlement of public funds by the city treasurer, an elected official. But Fitler's reputation upheld him, and he left office receiving widespread praise for a smoothly run administration.

In the second year of his administration, Fitler received a flurry of votes for the Republican presidential nomination from Pennsylvania delegates to the Republican national convention of 1888. He returned to his business following his mayoralty, and he never again held public office. Fitler was a member of the Centennial Exposition and was on its board of finance. He was a director of the Arch Street Theater Company and the Edwin Forrest Home as well as a trustee of the Jefferson Medical College. He was a founder of the Philadelphia Art Club and a member of several private clubs. Fitler died after a long illness on 31 May 1896, and was buried in Philadelphia.

SOURCES: W. W. Fitler, *Genealogy of the Fitler and Allied Families* (Philadelphia, 1922); Howard F. Gillette, Jr., "Corrupt and Contented: Philadelphia's Political Machine, 1865–1887" (Ph.D. dissertation, Yale University, 1970); Ellis Paxon Oberholtzer, *Philadelphia: A History of the City and Its People* (Philadelphia, 1911); obituaries in *Public Ledger, Inquirer, Evening Bulletin, North American*, 1 June 1896; *Philadelphia North American, Philadelphia and Popular Philadelphians* (Philadelphia, 1891); J. Thomas Schart and Thompson Westcott, *History of Philadelphia, 1609–1884*, 3 vols. (Philadelphia, 1884).

John F. Sutherland

FITZGERALD, JOHN FRANCIS (1863–1950), Mayor of Boston (1906–1907, 1910–13). Powerful Irish ward boss and twice mayor of Boston, John Francis Fitzgerald was also maternal grandfather of future President John Fitzgerald Kennedy and Senator Robert F. Kennedy of New York and Senator Edward M. Kennedy of Massachusetts. He was born on 11 February 1863 in a four-story, eight-family slum tenement on the Irish North End of Boston, the third of eleven children of poor "Famine Irish" immigrant parents who left County Wexford in the 1840s: Thomas Fitzgerald, a grocery and liquor store owner, and his wife, Rose Mary (Murray). The first Irish boy and first Roman Catholic to attend the Boston Latin School, he survived hostilities and became captain of both the baseball and football teams (though he was small) and editor of the school paper. After one year at Harvard Medical School, his father died and he had to drop out to father the large family, vowing: "We'll never break up!". His ethnic sense of family was very deep—when he married Mary Josephine ("Josie") Hannon on 18 September 1889, he soon allowed some of his brothers to move in. The handsome Josie bore him six children: Rose, Thomas, Agnes, John F., Jr., Eunice, and Frederick. The eldest, Rose, married into the formerly rival political family of the Kennedys in 1914, wedding Joseph P. Kennedy.

For three years, Fitzgerald worked at the customhouse and then began a profitable North End fire insurance business. But politics absorbed him. He was elected to the Boston Common Council in 1892 and set out to build his own ward machine. He joined every association and club; supported the Church; and kept a card index of all men in the district who needed work. He was on speaking terms with most residents. Short, dapper, bouncy, handsome, and very athletic, he was known in younger days as "Johnny Fitz" to his political gang, later as "Honey Fitz" for his eloquence and his singing voice. A journalist wrote: "Honey Fitz can talk you blind, On any subject you can find." It was in the 1910 mayoral election that Fitz first sang "Sweet Adeline" in public; the treacly song became his trademark.

Boston, a city of 750,000, had no single Tammany-type machine; the ward bosses ruled like feudal barons. Fitz consolidated his power on the North End; the West End was the satrapy of the "Mahatma," Martin Lomasney, the East End of Patrick Joseph Kennedy, and the South End (later) of Michael James Curley (q.v.). Fitzgerald left the insurance business to brother Henry and was no sooner on the council than he announced for the state Senate race, with Lomasney's support. It was a shoo-in, and he served, 1893–94, chairing the liquor and election committees and defending Irish and immigrant rights. Again with Lomasney behind him, Fitzgerald fought a rough election for the U.S. House in 1894 (Eleventh District) and served three terms, 1895–1901, in Washington. In 1895, he entered Congress as the only Democrat and only Catholic from New England. His tenure was not distinguished, although he defended black civil rights in the South, joined in the general Progressive attack on the meatpacking industry, and supported President Cleveland's (q.v.) veto of the literacy test for immigrants.

In 1901, Fitzgerald left Congress and bought a moribund weekly, *The Republic*, which, with politically inspired revenues from advertisers, he built up into a little moneymaker ($25,000 a year). A single issue once carried fourteen pages of lucrative ads by Boston banks. "The Napoleon of Ward 6" was a powerhouse. In December 1905, he was elected mayor for the first time, with the ward chiefs, including Lomasney, now opposing and fearing him. They allied with their arch-enemy, the Good Government Association, to run the innocent city clerk, Edward Donovan, against Fitzgerald. Promising "Bigger, Better, Busier Boston," Fitzgerald gave the city its first political motorcade, barnstorming to victory with ten speeches a night, thirty on pre-primary night. He took twenty out of twenty-five wards. On the election itself he spent $120,000, twice as much as his chief Republican opponent, Louis Frothingham, a Harvard blue-blood of inherited wealth and an easy target of Fitzgerald's scorn. Fitzgerald won by a plurality of 8,143. The opposition vote was split by a second Republican candidate, Judge Henry Dewey, smeared by Fitzgerald as being anti-Irish and anti-Catholic.

As mayor, Fitzgerald was a city booster, pushing seaport and harbor facilities and industrial development, building the High School of Commerce for boys and the School of Practical Arts for girls, and many playgrounds, public baths, and other facilities. He tolerated vice and manipulated graft in public contracts, creating hosts of sinecure jobs, ranging from city dermatologist to the new job category, tea-warmer. A tavern-keeper became superintendent of public buildings, a bartender superintendent of streets. Brother Henry ran the patronage department, while Fitzgerald attended, in his first term, an estimated 1,200 dinners, 1,000 meetings, and 1,500 dances—partnering 5,000 women. His energy was boundless; he was seen everywhere.

In 1907, the enraged anti-Fitzgerald Democratic bosses ran Representative John Coulthurst, while the Republicans picked postmaster George A. Hibbard (q.v.), a thrifty Yankee. Lomasney switched back to Fitzgerald, but Hibbard was elected. By 1909, the wheel had turned again, back to a spending policy, and Fitzgerald beat the Republican and reform candidate James Jackson Storrow in a vitriolic campaign. Fitzgerald vilified his rival's personal wealth, and Storrow coined the word "Fitzgeraldism" to mean graft. Fitzgerald addressed thirty-five rallies on the final night. The results were Fitzgerald, 47,177; Storrow, 45,775, and Hibbard (dying of TB of the throat), 1,614. Hibbard's vote made the difference for Fitzgerald, who had encouraged him to run. A fourth candidate, Nathan Taylor, received 613 votes.

Ironically, Fitz now served the first four-year term under the new reform charter which had arisen partly out of dissatisfaction with his own graft. His second regime was an extension of the first, with more public works and patronage jobs, and infighting among ward bosses to prevent him from building a city-wide machine. In 1914, he withdrew from the election under strong attack from J. M. Curley, who threatened, among other things, to expose Honey Fitz's sex life, an alleged affair with a lady known as "Toodles." Hating Curley, Fitz allied with Lomasney and the Good Government Association, but Curley was victorious. The 1914 election failure marked the real end of Fitzgerald's official political career, though he remained a force in Boston, out of office, for years to come. He ran unsuccessfully for the U.S. Senate (1916) and House (1918) and twice for governor (1922, 1930), withdrawing from the primary in 1930. In the 1916 Senate race, he ran against Henry Cabot Lodge; thirty-six years later, his favorite grandson, John F. Kennedy, ran against Lodge's grandson, Henry Cabot Lodge, Jr., and won. "Honey Fitz," however, had already died, aged eighty-seven, on 2 October 1950. His last campaign had been at age eighty-three, singing "Sweet Adeline" when JFK was first elected to Congress in 1946.

SOURCES: L. Ainley, *Boston Mahatma: Public Career of Martin Lomasney* (Boston, 1949); J. H. Cutler, *"Honey Fitz": Three Steps to the White House* (Indianapolis, 1962); J. F. Dinneen, *The Purple Shamrock* (New York, 1949); J. J. Huthmacher, *Massachusetts People and Politics, 1919–39* (New York, 1969); Francis Russell, *The Great Interlude* (New York, 1964), especially Chapter 11: "John The Bold."

Peter d'A. Jones

FITZGERALD, WILLIAM SINTON (1880–1937), Mayor of Cleveland (1920–21). English-American mayor of Cleveland, Fitzgerald was born in Washington, D.C., on 6 October 1880, the son of David Fitzgerald (1844–97), a London-born librarian of the War Department, and Esther (Sinton) Fitzgerald, born in Scotland. He attended local schools in Washington and then volunteered for duty during the Spanish-American War. He entered George Washington University, graduating with an LL.B. in 1903. After two years of legal practice, Fitzgerald moved to Cleveland in 1905. He eventually became an assistant to the Ohio attorney general. He married Margaret Chilton Tucker of Chicago, but they were divorced; he then married Carolyn Granger of Cleveland. Fitzgerald was a Mason, a Phi Sigma Kappa, and a member of the Chamber of Commerce.

Fitzgerald's political career began in 1911 when he was elected to the Cleveland City Council as a Republican. He became the recognized Republican floor leader, serving until 1915. The Welshman Harry Davis (q.v.) was elected mayor in 1915, and he promptly made Fitzgerald the city's law director. Thus when Davis resigned to run for governor, Fitzgerald assumed the mayoral post, serving from 1 March 1920 to 31 December 1921. He accomplished little of mark, and critics claimed he was no more than a figurehead, lacking any real political flair or imagination. In November 1921, he was defeated in the regular mayoral election, with 58,158 votes to 62,348 for Fred Kohler (Independent Democrat), 39,496 for Edward Haserodt (regular Democrat), 30,613 for James R. Hirchcliff (regular Republican), and 22,904 votes scattered among three other candidates. Kohler, the ex-police chief, was a colorful candidate who outperformed Fitzgerald in the election. Fitzgerald returned to legal practice and took no further part in Cleveland's political life. He died on 30 October 1937.

SOURCES: W. R. Coates, *A History of Cuyahoga County and the City of Cleveland*, 3 vols. (Chicago, 1924); William G. Rose, *Cleveland: The Making of a City* (Cleveland, 1950).   *Thomas R. Bullard*

FITZPATRICK, JOHN (1844–1919), Mayor of New Orleans (1892–96). Political boss mayor against whom impeachment proceedings were begun, Fitzpatrick was born of a New Orleans family on 1 May 1844 in Fairfield, Vermont where his mother was visiting. Orphaned at an early age, he grew up in the New Orlean's St. Mary's Orphan Asylum, began work as a newsboy, and as an adult became a carpenter. Fitzpatrick became a professional politician, known to his cronies as the "Big Boss of the Third Ward," and held a series of low-level patronage jobs including clerking in the courts beginning in 1872 and finally to what New Orleans called Criminal Sheriff, 1878–80. By 1884 he was commissioner of public works and expanded the city's payrolls with what the New Orleans *Mascot* called "Irish spade-and-shovel voters."

Immensely popular with working-class voters, Fitzpatrick accepted the Ring-dominated Democratic-Conservative party's nomination for mayor in 1892 and beat Joseph A. Shakspeare by 20,547 to 17,298 votes. New Orleans in 1890 had a population of 242,039 and a mayor-council form of government. The first half of Mayor Fitzpatrick's term (prior to 1894) was generally successful because Fitzpatrick carried out public improvements begun by his predecessor, including paving, sewage, and drainage projects, a new courthouse, a jail, and several firehalls. The second half of his term proved disastrous. The administration let out a private garbage contract which was expensive, unsatisfactory, and ultimately a failure. Garbage rotted in the streets, the incinerator failed to function at first, and when it did begin working, it filled some neighborhoods with noxious fumes and smoke. Fitzpatrick not only defended his new contractor but threatened to arrest householders who did not comply with the new rules that required the sorting of garbage and the use of specially prescribed trash containers. In addition, the city council assigned a 99-year franchise to the Illinois Central for a belt-line railroad that would encircle the city and would close several streets. The fact no bond was required, no restrictions were attached, or franchise payment made to the city, aroused vigorous protest meetings by reformist groups that suspected boodle, bribery, and the mayor's connivance in securing this windfall for the line. At the same time a chain of other minor and major scandals broke out with twelve councilmen and city officials indicted for bribery or other favors extended for payoffs. An investigation of the new courthouse under construction revealed that the plumbing contracting company was owned partly by Mayor Fitzpatrick's wife, suggesting graft. On 14 September 1894 the district attorney asked for the impeachment of Mayor Fitzpatrick on the charges of favoritism, corruption, and gross misconduct, but was unable to produce sufficiently strong evidence to convict the mayor in a civil suit or to remove him from office. The "Big Boss" limped through the remainder of his administration leaving office in 1896 when the reformers came back into power.

With the demise of Mayor Fitzpatrick's administration in 1896 (Joy Jackson wrote) an "entire era of Crescent City politics came to an end. It had been a raucous, corrupt, and debt-ridden age. . . . It was alright to cheat the other side, since they were all scoundrels and Republicans anyway."

Fitzpatrick continued to be active in Democratic party politics until his death 8 April 1919 in New Orleans.

SOURCES: Joy J. Jackson, *New Orleans in the Gilded Age: Politics and Urban Progress, 1880–1896* (Baton Rouge, 1969); John S. Kendall, *History of New Orleans* (Chicago, 1922), vol. 2; "Biographies of the Mayors of New Orleans, 1803–1936," (typescript, New Orleans, 1936).   *Melvin G. Holli*

FLAHERTY, PETE F. (1924–   ), Mayor of Pittsburgh (1970–77). Flaherty was born in Pittsburgh on 25 June 1924, the son of Peter F. Flaherty and Anne (O'Toole)

Flaherty, both Irish Catholic immigrants. His father operated a small grocery store, where Pete worked during off-hours. Pete was also timekeeper at an industrial plant and graduated from high school with high honors.

At seventeen, Flaherty enlisted in the Air Corps in World War II and became a navigator. He served in the Pacific area, winning two battle stars and the Air Medal, and was discharged with the rank of captain. He entered the University of Pittsburgh, transferred to Notre Dame, and graduated in law in 1951 with honors. Later, he earned a Master's degree in business administration from the University of Pittsburgh.

Flaherty began practice as a trial lawyer and ran for the school board as a Republican, but he missed nomination. Beginning in 1957, he was assistant district attorney for eight years. On 29 August 1958, he married Nancy Houlihan, a public relations specialist of Irish-German, Catholic background. They have five children, four boys and a girl.

As assistant district attorney, Flaherty prosecuted an important "no work" investigation in 1960. In private practice, he was attorney for the Brotherhood of Locomotive Trainmen and the United Steelworkers. In 1965 Flaherty was slated by the Democratic organization for city council and led the ticket. Later, he was offered endorsement for county commissioner but refused. Near the end of his term he broke with the party machine, ran for mayor, and was elected in 1969: 118,936 to Tabor's 62,586. His reelection bid in 1973 was uncontested. His first term was hectic, but at its end he won both Democratic and Republican nominations. Pittsburgh at this time had about 520,000 people and a strong mayor–small council form of government.

Flaherty ran for the U.S. Senate in 1974 and was defeated. He resigned as mayor in 1977 to become assistant U.S. attorney general. In 1978, he ran for governor of Pennsylvania but was defeated. He retired to private practice.

SOURCES: New York *Times*, 26 February 1977; Bill Rodd, "Goodbye Pete, Hello Who?" *Pittsburgh* (magazine), May 1977.

George Swetnam

FLANDERS, BENJAMIN FRANKLIN (1816–96), Mayor of New Orleans (1870–72). Reconstruction mayor, Flanders was born in Bristol, New Hampshire, on 16 January 1816, the son of Joseph and Relief Flanders. He studied at New Hampton Academy in New Hampshire and graduated from Dartmouth College in 1843. Flanders relocated in New Orleans, and although he had studied for the bar, he progressed through jobs in teaching, journalism, and then politics. He taught in the city's public schools, attained the rank of superintendent by 1850, and had earlier taken up the editorship of a local newspaper,

the New Orleans *Tropic*, of which he was part-owner. He was elected and reelected alderman in 1849 and 1852, respectively; in 1852, he also became secretary-treasurer of the Opelousas and Great Western Railroad (1852–61). When the city was occupied by federal troops in 1862, Union General Benjamin F. Butler appointed Flanders city treasurer. He was elected to Congress in 1862 as a Unionist and the following year was appointed supervising agent of the U.S. Treasury in Louisiana (a post he held until 1867). In 1864, he was already president of the First National Bank of New Orleans. In the same year, Flanders had been an unsuccessful candidate for governor of Louisiana, and in June 1867 General Philip H. Sheridan appointed him military governor of Louisiana, a position he held for seven months and then resigned. Flanders married Susan H. Sawyer on 20 September 1847.

New Orleans in 1870 had a population of 191,000 and a weak-mayor administrator government appointed by a Radical Reconstruction governor. Benjamin Flanders, a Republican, was appointed mayor under a new 1870 charter and held his office until 7 November 1870 when an election was to be held. Renominated by the Republicans, Flanders beat Democrat L. A. Wiltz by a vote of 18,216 to 11,826.

Flanders' first act as mayor—selling a city-owned railroad, the Jackson and Great Northern Railroad to a syndicate of private capitalists—met with general approval, even though the sale was snarled by litigation. The other major event of Flanders' first term was the slaughterhouse case by which the city nullified in court a monopoly over the cattle business granted by the state legislature to a single firm. Flanders' second term, beginning in November 1870, resulted in a new drainage system being planned and a land purchase for a city park, while New Orleans' debt climbed to a "colossal figure." Flanders was not a candidate for reelection and was replaced by a Democrat—although not gracefully. He refused to recognize as valid the election of a new mayor, delayed the inauguration for more than a week, but finally bowed to public pressure and surrendered the mayoralty.

After leaving office, Flanders was appointed assistant U.S. treasurer in New Orleans (1873–82). He made an unsuccessful race as a Republican for state treasurer in 1888 and died some years later in 1896 in New Orleans.

SOURCES: "Biographies of the Mayors of New Orleans" (New Orleans, 1939); John S. Kendall, *History of New Orleans* (Chicago, 1922) vol. 1.

Melvin G. Holli

FLEISCHMANN, JULIUS (1872–1925), Mayor of Cincinnati (1900–1905). Prosperous distiller and businessman-mayor of Cincinnati, and the first man of Jewish extraction to hold the post, Fleischmann was born in the Cincinnati suburb of Riverside on 8 June 1872 to Charles Fleischmann and Henrietta (Robertson) Fleischmann. German-Jewish but Hungarian-born Charles Fleischmann (1835–97) had already established a very successful distilling and yeast production enterprise. He, his New York born wife (who was of Scots descent), and their children Julius, Max, and Bettie, ranked with the city's wealthiest, most socially prominent families. After attending city schools, Fleischmann studied at the Franklin School of Business; then in 1889, he joined Fleischmann and Company. He quickly became a prominent figure in the city's commercial life, serving as president of the Market National Bank, founded by his father, and on the boards of several manufacturing companies, and was a part-owner of the Cincinnati baseball club. In 1894, Julius succeeded Charles Fleischmann as aide-de-camp to Governor William McKinley and retained that position through the next two administrations. Fleischmann married Cincinnatian Lillie Ackerland (1873–1947), a Presbyterian, on 3 April 1893, and they had three children, Louise, Charles, and Julius, Jr., before divorcing in 1919. He then married Laura Hyland Hemingway on 23 January 1920 and lived in New York, but that marriage soon ended in divorce. Fleischmann remained in New York to oversee his large, national corporation's finances.

At the turn of the twentieth century, Cincinnati had a mayor-council form of government with a population of 326,000, which would grow to some 380,000, in part through annexations, by the end of Fleischmann's term in 1905. Always active in Republican politics and Cincinnati affairs, Fleischmann was elected mayor in 1900 as a prominent business and civic leader pledged to giving the city a business-like administration, defeating by 34,357 to 28,839 votes a Citizen's party ticket headed by state Senator Alfred Cohen. In 1903, Fleischmann won reelection by a vote of 42,871 to 27,275 over reform-coalition candidate Melville E. Ingalls. Backed by the Cincinnati Republican party and its "Boss" George B. Cox, Fleischmann presented himself as an active reform mayor and a successful businessman supported by an effective, lasting political organization. Fleischmann argued that a well-administered city would be attractive to business and would draw new investment if it kept city tax rates low. The same well-managed city, in his plan, would raise the additional revenues needed for a full, progressive range of municipal services. Fleischmann set the tone for the succeeding Republican administrations: annexations, street resurfacing, and the beginnings of a park plan were all part of his program. Fleischmann strongly supported the construction of a new municipal hospital, establishment of free kindergartens, the up-

grading of the city's primary and secondary schools, and the opening of the city's first public bath.

Although he was out of public office after 1905, Fleischmann remained active in Republican politics and community affairs. Active in the Republican Blaine and Lincoln clubs, Fleischmann also belonged to the Commercial, Queen City and Optimists clubs, and to the Masons, Elks, Nights of Pythias, and North Cincinnati German ethnic *Turnverein*, among many other organizations. Fleischmann continued his father's practice of philanthropy, giving widely as the already prosperous Fleischmann Company grew larger. Fleischmann maintained Cincinnati ties, and after his death during a polo game in Miami, Florida, on 5 February 1925, his body was returned to Cincinnati for burial.

SOURCES: Annual Reports for the City of Cincinnati for the years 1900, 1901, 1902, 1903, 1904, 1905, especially the Mayor's Annual Messages; Charles Frederic Goss, *Cincinnati: The Queen City, 1788–1912* (Chicago and Cincinnati, 1912); Charles Theodore Greve, *Centennial History of Cincinnati and Representative Citizens* (Chicago, 1904); Zane L. Miller, *Boss Cox's Cincinnati: Urban Politics in the Progressive Era* (New York, 1968).   *Judith Spraul-Schmidt*

FLINT, EDWARD SHERRILL (1819–1902), Mayor of Cleveland (1861–63). A railroad executive, born in Warren, Ohio, on 3 January 1819, Flint moved to Portland, Ohio, during the 1840s, where he worked as a bookkeeper. He also married a New Yorker, Caroline E. Lemen, and they had two children. The family was Protestant. In 1851, they moved to Cleveland, where Flint went into real estate but soon discovered railroad promotion to be of greater interest. He was superintendent of the Cleveland, Columbus and Cincinnati Railroad, 1859–78. He served on the school board, 1860–61.

A War Democrat, Flint was elected mayor in 1861, defeating incumbent Mayor George B. Senter (*q.v.*) 3,890 to 3,172. Cleveland had 43,417 people in 1860 and a mayor-council form of government. Flint backed the Civil War effort and supported measures to aid families of local soldiers. He favored street improvements and measures to protect the city's business interests. In 1863, he was defeated by Irvine Masters (*q.v.*) 3,899 to 3,558 and returned to his railroad work. He lived in retirement after 1879, until his death on 29 January 1902.

SOURCES: Cleveland *Plain Dealer*, 30 January 1902; Contemporary business directories; William Rose, *Cleveland: The Making of a City* (Cleveland, 1950).   *Thomas R. Bullard*

FLOWER, WALTER C. (1850–1900), Mayor of New Orleans (1896–1900). Reform mayor, born in 1850 in

East Feliciana, Louisiana, Walter was the son of Richard Flower, a well-known planter who also had cotton business interests in New Orleans and Minerva A. Scott, a plantation owner's daughter. Flower was educated at Pass Christian College and studied law at Tulane University. After graduation, he was a reporter for the New Orleans *Picayune*, practiced law for a short time, and in 1888 entered the cotton business with a partner, Branch M. King. He was president of the Cotton Exchange, 1891–92, and his business met with such success that he was able to retire by 1896. He married Adele McCall in 1885 and was the father of four children.

New Orleans in 1896 had a population of 285,000 and a mayor-council form of government. Although a life-long Democrat, Flower accepted nomination by the Citizens' League to lead a reform ticket against the corruption-ridden regular Democrats in city hall. He was charged by the regulars with being a "sugar republican" because of his brief association with a national Republican administration in seeking a protective tariff for sugar and for allegedly being unsympathetic with the "laboring classes" because of his wealth. Expecting the worst, the Citizens' League scattered a force of 1,500 men armed with revolvers to guard against ballot-box mayhem on election day. A surprisingly quiet election day, 21 April 1896, saw Charles Flower overwhelm his regular opponent, Charles F. Buck, 23,345 to 17,295.

The Flower administration nullified the charter of an inadequate private water contractor and brought in a municipally owned and operated water, sewer, and drainage system which would eventually provide for better drainage and sewage and purified drinking water. Flower also sought to improve the city's commerce by bringing the port and dock facilities under a publicly controlled board. Fear of the spread of bawdy houses throughout the city resulted in the passage of the famous "Story ordinance" which created the restricted vice district called "Storyville" in 1897. One of the Crescent City's leading historians considered the Flower mayoralty to be a "turning point" in New Orleans history whereby Reconstruction Era politics ended, elections became less violent, and general prosperity began. Despite Flower's achievements, he was turned out of office by the regulars in 1900.

Mayor Flower had reorganized the city government under a new 1896 charter which halved the city council to seventeen members, expanded the mayor's appointive powers, and brought in a civil service commission (which the regulars would throw out when they returned to power in 1900). Opposition to the civil service was so vehement that Flower was unable to appoint a board of examiners until his second year in office. Other reforms included closer control over financial disbursements and the re-

capture for the city of overpayments to contractors by previous administrations. The single most important achievement of the Flower reforms was in the police department which was put on a more professional, civil service footing and closer supervision. The administration took measures to combat epidemic disease, such as the yellow fever of 1897 that took 298 lives. Flower died of tuberculosis in his country home at Covington, Louisiana, on 11 October 1900.

SOURCES: Joy J. Jackson, *New Orleans in the Gilded Age* (Baton Rouge, La., 1969); John S. Kendall, *History of New Orleans* (Chicago, 1922), vol. 2.

Betsy B. Holli and *Melvin G. Holli*

FORD, HENRY PARKER (1837–1905), Mayor of Pittsburgh (1896–99). Ford was born in Hudson, New York, on 15 October 1837. His father soon moved to Clarion County, Pennsylvania, to engage in the lumber business, and in about 1840 to Pittsburgh. Both parents, John and Susan (Carpenter) Ford, died soon after 1850, and at the age of fourteen Henry was apprenticed to a lithographer. He had inherited enough money to take a business course, and he specialized in accounting. At nineteen, he became secretary of one of Pittsburgh's school boards. Later, he was a member of that board for many years. In 1861, Young Ford became bookkeeper for an insurance firm and then chief accountant for one of Pittsburgh's largest iron firms, a position he held for nine years.

In June 1870, Ford married Rebecca Gillespie of Philadelphia, who bore him three daughters. He was a Protestant, and he became a Mason, later rising to a high position in that order. Ill and out of work, Ford moved to Philadelphia in 1871, but upon inheriting a large lumber business in 1876, he sold it and returned to Pittsburgh. He was a partner in a sawmill from 1876 to 1881, and then secretary-treasurer of a firm of pipe manufacturers.

Entering politics actively, Ford was elected to the select council in 1881, serving for fifteen years, and as council president for six. He was active in many Republican organizations in the city, county, and state, and was a trustee of Western University, now the University of Pittsburgh.

The city's population was about 300,000 with a mayor and two councils. In the 1895 election, his opponent was George W. Guthrie (*q.v.*), nominated by the Democrats and backed by the Citizens League for Reform. Ford won 20,552 to 19,234 and immediately named his predecessor, Democrat Bernard McKenna (*q.v.*), police magistrate.

As mayor, Ford was largely a figurehead, but the city made some progress toward water filtration, set up a bureau of bridges, and began putting wires under ground.

Ford died on 21 April 1905 and was buried in Homewood Cemetery.

SOURCES: *Allegheny County Pennsylvania Illustrated* (Pittsburgh, 1896); Pittsburgh *Dispatch, Post*, and *Gazette*, all 22 April 1905; *Prominent Pennsylvanians of the 19th Century* (Philadelphia, 1898); George O. Seilhamer, *Leslie's History of the Republican Party* (New York, n.d.).

George Swetnam

FOSTER, STEPHEN C. (1820–98), Mayor of Los Angeles (1854–55, 1856).

Foster was born on 17 December 1820 in Machias, Maine, the oldest of eight children of Alfred and Rebecca Foster, both of long-time Maine families. After graduating from Yale in 1840, Foster taught school in the South, but by 1846 he engaged in trade in Santa Fe. When the Mormon Battalion passed through on its way to war in California, it hired Foster as interpreter. When he arrived in Los Angeles in March 1847, the fighting had ended, but he stayed on in the city. At the end of the year, the military governor appointed him *alcalde* until May 1849. In 1848, Foster converted to Roman Catholicism and married a widow, Maria de la Merced Lugo de Perez (1815–1913), daughter of a prominent *Californio*. Of the Fosters' four or five children, only two sons, Alfred and Stephen, Jr., survived past infancy.

In 1849, Foster became a delegate to the state constitutional convention and then returned to Los Angeles to participate in local government. A Democrat, in December 1850 he was elected to fill a vacancy on the common council and then won a full year's term in May 1851. Concurrently, he also filled a vacancy in the state Senate, qualifying in February 1851. He did not attempt reelection to the common council in 1852, but he did win two more Senate terms. In July 1853, the council appointed Foster a member of the first board of education. The following May, when Los Angeles had approximately 2,700 residents, he ran for mayor and received 158 of the 281 ballots cast. His annual message emphasized education, and the council approved construction of a schoolhouse and appointed Mayor Foster superintendent of schools.

In January 1855, Foster resigned to appease a mob of the city's Hispanic population, angry because a Mexican had been executed legally, while a similarly convicted Anglo had obtained a stay of execution. As he had previously promised, Foster led the mob in lynching the Anglo; two weeks later, in the election to name a new mayor, he received 296 votes, apparently the only candidate. When his term expired at the regular time in May 1855, Foster did not run for reelection, but a year later he did run, defeating fellow Democrat Columbus Sims 283 to 183. He called for improvement of the schools

and water system, but again resigned, on 22 September 1856, to serve as executor of the estate of a wealthy relative. Later in the 1850s, he served as a county supervisor and as a common councilman, but after 1859 he no longer held public office.

Foster lived until 28 January 1898 as a farmer, expert on Spanish archives, and frequent witness in legal disputes over property.

SOURCES: Hubert Howe Bancroft, *The Works of Hubert Howe Bancroft*, 39 vols., *History of California* (San Francisco, 1884–90), vols. 18–24; H. D. Barrows, "Stephen C. Foster," *Historical Society of Southern California* 4 (1898); Stephen C. Foster, "I Was Los Angeles' First American Alcalde," *Historical Society of Southern California Quarterly* 31 (December 1949).

R. David Weber

FOSTER, THOMAS (1814–62), Mayor of Los Angeles (1855–56).

Physician-mayor of Los Angeles, Foster was born about 1814 in Pennsylvania and migrated westward in stages. His wife Catherine (of Scottish extraction) was born in Ohio, in 1818. Their oldest daughter Martha was born in Indiana in 1839, and two younger daughters, Laura and Janette were born in Kentucky in 1842 and 1846 respectively. Somewhere along the way Foster acquired a medical education so when he arrived in Los Angeles in 1851 he quickly became one of the town's leading physicians. Other Angelenos considered him the epitome of a Southern gentleman, as he always appeared in public in a Prince Albert coat and a silk hat, and his home, presided over by his well-educated wife, was one of the cultural centers of town. He participated in the formation of the city's first Masonic lodge, served as its third worshipful master, and helped raise funds to construct the first Protestant church in Los Angeles.

Although he had not participated in politics during the early 1850s, in May 1855 he defeated fellow Democrat William G. Dryden 192 to 179. In becoming mayor of the mayor-council city, which had grown to an approximate population of 3,000, Foster urged the common council to hire a professional engineer to design a comprehensive system of water distribution to portions of the city that were then unserved. Although water was consistently the most pressing problem for mid-nineteenth century Los Angeles, the council reported that Foster's ambitious scheme would require either higher taxes, which only the state legislature could authorize, or a loan, which depended on a vote of the people. As neither was likely, the council shelved his suggestion. Foster also attempted to halt the "unrighteous traffic" in liquor between small dealers and Indians and the resulting "disgusting scenes" in the streets, but with little success. For the most part, Foster played a very passive and inconspicuous role as mayor.

Foster did not attempt reelection in May 1856, but when his successor resigned on 22 September 1856, he was one of three Democratic ex-mayors who ran to replace him. Foster, however, received only 12 votes to 163 for John G. Nichols (q.v.) and 144 for Antonio Coronel (q.v.). Foster still retained his prestige as a physician, and in April 1860 he won appointment to the board of education, where he served until he resigned on 23 January 1862. Five days later, while en route to San Francisco, he fell overboard from a steamer off the coast of Monterey County. Although his friends in Los Angeles denied it, rumors persisted that he had committed suicide.

SOURCES: J. Gregg Layne, "Annals of Los Angeles," *California Historical Society Quarterly* 13 (December 1934); Maurice H. Newmark and Marco R. Newmark, eds., *Sixty Years in Southern California, 1853–1913; Containing the Reminiscences of Harris Newmark*, 4th ed. (Los Angeles, 1970); Leonard Ross Sanders, "Los Angeles and Its Mayors, 1850–1925" (M.A. thesis, University of Southern California, 1968).   *R. David Weber*

FOX, DANIEL, Mayor of Philadelphia (1869–71). Unlike his predecessors as mayor of the consolidated city, Fox attracted only the scantest amount of public attention. Although he received the Democratic nomination for mayor three consecutive terms and won the office in 1868, none of the many biographical directories published in Philadelphia at the turn of the century lists his name, and city histories say virtually nothing about his background or his term in office.

Various sources do confirm he was a conveyancer from the Northern Liberties section of the city. He ran for mayor unsuccessfully against Alexander Henry (q.v.) in 1862 and against Morton McMichael (q.v.) in 1865. In 1868, he edged his Republican opponent, Civil War veteran Hector Tynsdale, 61,517 to 59,679. Republican newspapers charged that Fox owed his election to wholesale naturalization frauds, a claim that appeared substantiated by a striking 29-percent increase in the vote over the previous mayoralty campaign. Such an increase could be attributed, however, to the close association of the election with a heated national campaign and a general growth in the electorate which had increased 23 percent in the previous three years.

As a candidate for mayor, Fox had drawn criticism from Republican newspapers for opposing public improvements to develop the outer reaches of the city, and clearly he ran behind in most of those outer wards. But as mayor, he himself called for increased expenditures, particularly for street lighting and water mains. While he was often criticized for failing to maintain security, appeals to expand the police department and to insure public safety were central items in his annual reports. He was not renominated for office in 1871 and presumably retired quietly from public life.

SOURCES: Ellis Paxon Oberholtzer, *Philadelphia: A History of Its People* (Philadelphia, 1912); J. Thomas Scharf and Thompson Westcott, *History of Philadelphia, 1609–1884* (Philadelphia, 1884).
Howard Gillette, Jr.

FRANCIS, DAVID ROWLAND (1850–1927), Mayor of St. Louis (1885–89). Mayor of St. Louis and later state governor, cabinet officer, and ambassador to Russia, Francis was born on 1 October 1850 in Richmond, Kentucky, the son of John B. Francis, a county sheriff, and Eliza Caldwell (Rowland) Francis, both of Anglo-Scottish and Welsh ancestry. He attended Reverend Robert Brook's Richmond Academy and Washington University in St. Louis, the family having moved there in 1866. He was a shipping clerk for Shyrock and Rowland (merchants) in 1870, becoming a partner by 1877. Francis and his brother Sidney then formed D. R. Francis and Brother, grain merchants, which remained his main occupation for the next half century. He married Jane Perry on 20 January 1876, and they had six children. Francis was president of the St. Louis Merchants' Exchange in 1884–85 and belonged to numerous business organizations.

Francis was elected mayor in 1885, as a Democrat, with 20,861 votes to 19,349 for Republican William Ewing (q.v.) and 809 for Independent Chauncey Filley (q.v.). St. Louis had 451,770 people by 1890 and a mayor-council form of government. As mayor, Francis supported efforts to improve the water supply, street sprinkling and paving, and milk inspection in the city. He also opposed higher gas rates and collected a $1 million judgment against the Missouri Pacific Railroad. He did not seek a second term as mayor.

Francis' political career continued, however, for he served as governor of Missouri, 1889–93, supporting lower taxes, better schools, and the Australian ballot system. In 1896, his friend Grover Cleveland (q.v.) appointed him secretary of the interior. Later, Francis became director of various banks and was president of the Louisiana Purchase Exposition in 1904. For a number of years, he owned the St. Louis *Republic* (a prominent Democratic newspaper). In 1916, Woodrow Wilson appointed Francis U.S. ambassador to Russia, and he remained at his post until the end of 1918. He always supported the anti-Bolshevik leaders and spent the remainder of his life urging U.S. military action to prevent the spread of international communism. Francis continued his business interests until his death on 15 January 1927.

SOURCES: Charles H. Cornwell, *St. Louis Mayors: Brief Biographies* (St. Louis, 1965); James Cox, *Old and*

New St. Louis (St. Louis, 1894); David R. Francis, *Russia from the American Embassy* (New York, 1921); John W. Leonard, ed., *The Book of St. Louis* (St. Louis, 1906). The David R. Francis Papers (some 50,000 letters, etc.) are in the Missouri Historical Society.   *Thomas R. Bullard*

FRENCH, JONAS HERROD (1829–1903), Military

Mayor of New Orleans (1862). During his Civil War service as the federal provost marshal of occupied New Orleans, French briefly discharged mayoral duties. He was born in Boston on 4 November 1829 to Massachusetts natives Jonas and Sarah (Baldwin) French. Upon graduation from the English High School, he worked first in the grocery business and then in distilling. As a young man, French enrolled in the City Guard and joined the Democratic party. By age thirty-two, he had served on a governor's staff, been three times elected to the Boston Common Council, and became commander of the Ancient and Honorable Artillery. Meanwhile, in 1856, French married Fanny Elizabeth Thompson, also of Boston, who bore him a son and a daughter.

When the Civil War erupted, French helped raise and temporarily commanded the Eastern Bay State (later Thirteenth Massachusetts) Regiment. This unit joined General Benjamin F. Butler's expedition to the Gulf Coast, and Captain French, though never commissioned by the governor of Massachusetts, became Butler's aide-de-camp and assistant inspector general with the rank of acting lieutenant colonel. Upon occupying New Orleans in early May 1862, General Butler named this able associate the federal provost marshal of New Orleans. French's first task was to reorganize the police force, dismissing officers who refused to take the oath of allegiance to the United States and appointing unionists and federal soldiers in their stead. He then proceeded to enforce sanitary regulations, collect intelligence, issue permits to travel from Union to Confederate lines, and maintain order in this unruly city of 140,000. During August, Godfrey Weitzel (*q.v.*), the assistant military commandant and acting mayor, was called to Baton Rouge, so French functioned as the city's chief executive, 6–20 August 1862. The administrative personnel and aldermen did not change during his brief tenure, and many letters from the mayor's office were still issued over Weitzel's name. Two of French's chief tasks as acting mayor were overseeing responsibilities he already performed: administering loyalty oaths and licensing businesses. On 1 October 1862, Butler promoted Colonel French to provost marshal of all of occupied Louisiana, a position he held until dismissed on 2 May 1863 by Butler's successor, General Nathan P. Banks. During his year's service in Louisiana, the rebel citizenry found

French to be courteous and fair—which was quite a compliment for an official so closely associated with the man they called "Beast" Butler.

After the war, French settled in Gloucester, Massachusetts. In 1869, he organized the Cape Ann Granite Company, which prospered, supplying stone for public buildings. As a director of the Maverick Bank of Boston, he and others were charged with making illegal loans. All were acquitted. French also served as a director on the boards of several railroads. Remaining active in politics, he sat in the Massachusetts Senate in 1879 and 1880, was a delegate to the Democratic national conventions of 1880 and 1888, chaired the Democratic State Central Committee for three years, and lost an 1890 bid to become a congressman from the Essex district.

French's first wife died, and in 1883 he married Nella J. Foss, a widow. Following a brief illness, French died on 22 February 1903 of apoplexy in Boston, where he is buried. He was survived by his second wife and his daughter.

SOURCES: Boston *Evening Transcript*, 24 February 1903; "Jonas H. French Documents," New England Genealogical Society, Boston; New Orleans *Daily Picayune* and *Daily Delta*, May 1862–May 1863; John Smith Kendall, *History of New Orleans*, 2 vols. (Chicago, 1922), vol. 1; "Letterbooks of New Orleans Mayors" (1862), New Orleans Public Library; Works Progress Administration, "Mayors of New Orleans, 1803–1936" (Typescript in the New Orleans Public Library, New Orleans, 1940).   *D. Blake Touchstone*

FRERET, WILLIAM (1799–1864), Mayor of New

Orleans (1840–42, 1843–44). Born in New Orleans in 1799, the son of an English emigré merchant, Jeanne Baptiste Freret, who married a French Creole woman, Eugenie Rillieux, William was the second oldest in a large family. His father sent the mechanically adept William to England to be trained in engineering and the mechanical arts at a time in New Orleans when such skills were more often frowned upon than respected in the South. William joined his father in the cotton-pressing business working for the Freret Cotton Press, which was considered to be one of the industrial pioneers in the American quarter of the city. Freret married Fanny Sakeld of Liverpool, England, and they had four children.

New Orleans in 1840 had a population of 102,000 and a mayor-multicouncil form of government (three municipal councils drawn from three city districts and one general council). The antagonism between the Creoles and Americans had become so intense that the legislature in 1836 decided that separation was the best solution. Accordingly, it divided the city, until 1852, into three separate governing bodies called municipalities: the

French Quarter containing the Creoles, the American sector, and the immigrant Irish and German sector. Each municipality had its own council, governed its own affairs, and sent representatives to a city-wide general council.

Nominated for mayor in 1840 by a new party, the Native Americans, who opposed the "Creole and foreign element," Freret beat Whig incumbent Charles Genois (q.v.) by a vote of 1,051 to 942, with a scattering of votes to several other candidates. Freret was renominated by the Native Americans in 1842 but lost the election, hotly contested over the foreign-born franchise, to Democrat Denis Prieur (q.v.) by a vote of 1,069 to 1,334. The winner, Prieur, remained in office only eight months, accepted a state job, and another election had to be held on 20 February 1843 to fill out his term. Freret accepted the Whig party nomination and defeated Joseph Genois, a Democrat, by a vote of 1,289 to 974. The election day turnout was low because a bank collapse caused a run on other banks by anxious depositors, who otherwise might have been at the polls.

A disastrous flood in 1840, the suspension of specie payment, and the perilous state of city finances restrained the Freret administration from undertaking needed public improvements. Three separate city councils representing three different city districts wrangled unproductively over riparian and wharf rights. Despite these inauspicious conditions, Freret was given high marks by the city's chroniclers for carefully supervising public works and public institutions and for his vigorous support of free public education, which New Orleans got in 1841. Although not the most popular mayor, Freret was regarded as one of the most efficient mayors New Orleans had up to 1850. He died in 1864 and was buried in New Orleans.

SOURCES: "Biographies of the Mayors of New Orleans" (New Orleans, Typescript, Works Progress Administration, 1940); L. V. Howard and R. S. Friedman, *Government in Metropolitan New Orleans* (New Orleans, 1959); John S. Kendall, *History of New Orleans* (Chicago, 1922), vol. 1; Leon C. Soule, *The Know Nothing Party in New Orleans* (Baton Rouge, La., 1961).
Melvin G. Holli

FUHRMANN, LOUIS P. (1868–1931), Mayor of Buffalo (1910–17). German-American businessman and Progressive reform mayor, born in Buffalo on 7 November 1868, Fuhrmann was the son of Philip and Alicia (Steiss) Fuhrmann, immigrants born in Germany. He attended public schools and Central High School. After leaving school, he went to work for Christian Klinck, a prominent Buffalo meatpacker. In 1886, he was sent to Kansas City, where he was superintendent of the wholesale dressed beef department of Jacob Dold Packing Company. He returned to Buffalo in 1892 and started his own meatpacking firm. He married Alice S. Meald on 13 July 1900, and they had two children.

A Democrat, Fuhrmann was elected to the board of aldermen in 1905 and served two terms (1906–1909). The council selected him as acting mayor, and he virtually ran the city during Mayor James Adam's (q.v.) absence. Local party leaders considered him to be a good candidate for the mayoralty and in 1909 nominated him rather than James Adam. His Progressive reform career as alderman had attracted public interest, and he was elected, defeating Republican Jacob Siegrist 35,484 to 34,156. In 1913, Mayor Fuhrmann won a second term, defeating Thomas Stoddard (Republican) and John L. O'Brien (Progressive) by 30,219 votes to 13,447 and 23,757, respectively. In 1917 however, Fuhrmann was defeated in his bid for a third term, losing to Republican George S. Buck (q.v.) 38,144 to 27,391. Buffalo had 423,715 people in 1910 and a mayor-council form of government. In 1916, the city adopted a new charter, which produced a mayor-city commission system.

Well known throughout the city simply as "Louis," Fuhrmann was one of the most popular men to hold the post of mayor of Buffalo. He strongly supported the Progressive measures then popular in national and local politics, and was a backer of the city commission plan adopted by Buffalo in 1916. With the outbreak of World War I, Fuhrmann supported the initial war measures but was defeated before the full impact of the war was felt in Buffalo. He returned to his packing business and served a short period in the 1920s as a member of the board of education and as chairman of the Erie County Democrats, 1928–29. He died on 23 February 1931.

SOURCES: Buffalo *Sunday Times*, 13 July 1924; Henry W. Hill, ed., *Municipality of Buffalo, New York, A History, 1720–1923*, 2 vols. (New York, 1923); *Who's Who in New York, City and State* (New York, 1911).
Thomas R. Bullard

FULTON, ANDREW (1850–1925), Mayor of Pittsburgh (1884–87). Fulton, whose family had been brass founders in Pittsburgh for three generations, was born in the city on 21 December 1850, a cousin of political ringmaster Chris Magee, and the son of Samuel M. and Agnes Fulton. He was a Protestant and a Mason, tall, friendly and well liked even by political enemies. His wife was the former Mary Hammond.

Fulton held a number of minor political posts, served on both select and common councils, and was city assessor. In the 1884 election, he faced former mayor Robert Liddell (q.v.), a formidable Democratic opponent. Pittsburgh, then a city of about 185,000, was controlled by the Republican Flinn-Magee ring, which had suffered two successive defeats for mayors, but had lost little ground, keeping majorities in the city's two councils. Magee cracked the whip, and Fulton won easily, 15,036 to 7,179.

Even among his friends, Fulton was known as a "do nothing" mayor, except for giving traction franchises to friends and relatives and handing out street contracts to Boss William Flinn's construction firm at outrageously high prices. Unable to succeed himself, Fulton went to Colorado as a rancher after leaving office. He spent a year in New York and then returned to Pittsburgh in 1892 as promoter for an ice company.

By 1897, he began holding minor offices again—chief city assessor, director of public safety, and delinquent-tax collector. Following the ring's defeat by a fusion reform ticket, Fulton retired in 1906, moving to Cambridge Springs. But when a friend returned to power in 1915 he came back as a clerk in the county treasurer's office. He continued in minor political posts until shortly before he died on 7 February 1925.

SOURCES: Allen H. Kerr, "The Mayors and Recorders of Pittsburgh, 1816–1951" (typescript, 1952, Carnegie Library of Pittsburgh); Pittsburgh *Press* and *Post*, both 7 February 1925.   *George Swetnam*

G

GALLAGHER, THOMAS JOSEPH (1883–1967), Mayor of Pittsburgh (1959). Gallagher was born in Pittsburgh, on 20 November 1883, the oldest of eleven children of a second-generation Irish Catholic toolmaker, and attended St. John's School, dropping out at twelve to sell papers. He worked briefly in a steel plant, and at thirteen he became a carrier in a glass plant. He became a glassblower at nineteen, helped organize the workers at the plant, where he worked for thirty-seven years, and became a national union officer. In about 1904, he married Florence Cleis, who died in 1921, leaving seven children, ranging in age from eighteen months to sixteen years. He kept the family together until all were grown.

In 1932, Gallagher ran for the state House of Representatives as a Republican and got both nominations, with 4,500 more Democratic write-in votes than Republican. He switched to the Democratic side and headed a commission investigating sweatshops and child labor. In 1933, he was elected to the city council as a Democrat, serving a recordbreaking thirty-two years. He was council president for fourteen years except for the eleven months spent as mayor. In 1937, he married a widow, Mrs. Ann Wilson, who died before 1952.

As council president, Gallagher became mayor when David Lawrence (*q.v.*) became governor in 1959. At seventy-five, he was the oldest man to become mayor of the city, which then had a declining population of 610,000 and a strong mayor-small council system. He did not run for election. He resigned on 2 December following the election of Joseph M. Barr (*q.v.*), having served the shortest term on record. He resumed his council post and was reelected in 1961. Gallagher retired in 1966 and entered a nursing home, where he died on 14 March 1967. He was buried in Calvary Cemetery.

SOURCES: Clipping file, Carnegie Library of Pittsburgh; Pittsburgh *Press*, 15 January 1959, 15 March 1967; *Sun-Telegraph*, 5 November 1958.

George Swetnam

GALVIN, JOHN (1862–1922), Mayor of Cincinnati (1909, 1918–21). Mayor of Cincinnati in 1909 by succession and wartime mayor by election after 1917, Galvin was an Irish Catholic born in Cincinnati on 13 June 1862. His blacksmith father Maurice Galvin emigrated from Ireland in 1851 to Cincinnati where in 1857 he married a local woman, Ellen Cronin (b. 1836). One of their ten children, John Galvin graduated from St. Xavier College and, in 1883, from the Cincinnati Law School. Galvin was assistant city solicitor (1887–94) and on 28 February 1889 married Julie Edair Cusson (1862–1915) at Covington, Kentucky, in a Protestant (Christian) church, though he was Catholic. Their daughter Julia Elizabeth was born in 1900, the only one of three children to survive into adulthood. In addition to his affiliation with city Republican clubs, including the Blaine Club and the Stamina League, Galvin held membership in the Businessman's Club, and in 1898 and 1899 he became grand exalted ruler of the USA of the Benevolent Paternal Order of Elks.

Galvin was elected vice-mayor of Cincinnati, a mayor-council city with a population of 380,000, in 1907, and became mayor at the death of the incumbent Leopold Markbreit (*q.v.*) on 27 July 1909. As acting mayor from the onset of Markbreit's illness in February 1909, Galvin carried on his predecessor's program, standard since Fleischmann's (*q.v.*) administration. A May 1909 referendum on nine bond issues saw all nine issues supported by majorities, but four got the two-thirds majorities required for passage: new hospital construction, equipment for the hospital, street improvements, and sewer work. Galvin chose not to run for the mayor's office in 1909, but he became vice-mayor once more, this time under Republican physician Dr. Louis Schwab (*q.v.*). After serving this term, Galvin continued in his legal practice and institutional affiliations.

In 1917, Galvin was the Republican machine's candidate for mayor against former Congressman Alfred G. Allen, Democrat. Galvin won, 43,418 to 38,887; the socialist candidate got 11,073 votes. Galvin's latter term as mayor was marked, in addition to wartime demands, by a police strike for higher wages and for the right to unionize. Galvin replaced striking police with the Home Guard, used Boy Scouts to aid in traffic direction, and came to a compromise situation with the strikers, allowing them to form a neutral protest organization. In 1920, Galvin emerged as a strong supporter of Warren G. Harding. During his tenure, Galvin became ill, but managed to finish his term before he died on 1 March 1922. He was buried in Cincinnati.

SOURCES: Annual Reports of the City of Cincinnati; Cincinnati Bar Association, *The Bench and Bar of Cincinnati* (Cincinnati, 1921); Cincinnati *Post,* 2 March 1922; Charles Frederic Goss, *Cincinnati: The Queen City, 1788 to 1912* (Chicago and Cincinnati, 1912); Louis Alexander Leonard, ed., *Greater Cincinnati and Its People: A History* (New York, 1927); Zane L. Miller, *Boss Cox's Cincinnati: Urban Politics in the Progressive Era* (New York, 1968).

Judith Spraul-Schmidt and George B. Engberg

GARDNER, GEORGE WARREN (1834–1911), Mayor of Cleveland (1885–86, 1889-90). Businessman-mayor of Cleveland and a transplanted old-stock Yankee, Gardner was born on 7 February 1834 in Pittsfield, Massachusetts. His father, Colonel James Gardner (d. July 1861), was a local businessman and past commander of the Massachusetts state militia. His mother, Griselda (Porter) Gardner (d. January 1861), was a housewife of old Yankee stock descended from Elihu Yale of Connecticut, founder of the college. Both were Presbyterians. The Gardners had seven children between 1829 and 1847, one of whom died in infancy; George W. was their third child. In 1837, the family moved to Cleveland, and at age fourteen the future mayor left home and the city's common schools to sail the Great Lakes. In 1853–57, he began a business career as a clerk in the banking house of Wicks, Otis and Brownell, subsequently becoming a junior partner in Otis, Brownell and Company, grain merchants. In 1859, he joined M. B. Clark and John D. Rockefeller to found Clark, Gardner and Company, also grain merchants and dealers. In 1861, he built the Union Elevator, largest grain elevator in the region. His firm purchased the National Flourmills in 1878. Meanwhile, his business interests branched into furnace and stove manufacturing and banking, and, in 1869, he was an incorporator, and later president, of the Cleveland Board of Trade (Chamber of Commerce). Before his election as mayor, Gardner was a Cleveland city councilman for eight years and council president for the last three. In 1857, he married Rosaline (or Rosilda) L. Oviatt (1839–99), a housewife and descendant of early Cleveland settlers. They had seven children, of whom George Henry and Burt M. became widely known in local business circles. Gardner was a life-long member of the First Presbyterian Church, enjoyed travel, and was regularly engaged in philanthropic activities.

Located in Cuyahoga County, Cleveland in 1885–86 had 238,953 residents. Five years later, this figure stood at 299,475 (1891). At this time, too, the city was governed by a mayor-council form of government under the federal system. Gardner's Republican ties led him to seek the mayor's office three times (1883, 1885, and 1889), winning the last two over Waldemar Otis (15,945 to 12,439) and John H. Farley (*q.v.*) (15,878 to 14,970), respectively.

In his first term as mayor, 1885–86, Gardner took a strong stance against labor violence, refusing to allow any "anarchist" to hold meetings or to speak within the city. He also advised Polish strikers at the Cleveland Rolling Mill Company that he would open artillery on them if any more violence occurred. In 1886, he convinced the board of police commissioners to establish civil service for police appointments, an accomplishment that alienated the regular Republican politicians and led to his defeat in the party convention, which chose William M. Bayne instead as its mayoral candidate in March 1887. Bayne lost the ensuing election to a Democrat, and in the following election of 1889, apparent public pressure for fewer politically determined appointments led the Republicans to hold their first direct vote primary. Gardner was nominated again and defeated Democrat and ex-Mayor John H. Farley in the election.

Although Gardner was noted for appointments regardless of party, his terms also provided some minor scandals regarding politically influenced contracts and conflict-of-interest sales of goods to the city. His introduction of civil service standards and his personal generosity (he often gave away his weekly salary) did much to mitigate this bad impression. Gardner left office in April 1891, later serving as fire department director under Mayor William G. Rose (*q.v.*), to whom he had lost his party's nomination in 1891. Gardner died at his daughter's home in Dayton, Ohio, on 8 December 1911 but was buried at Woodland Cemetery in Cleveland.

SOURCES: Elroy M. Avery, *A History of Cleveland and Its Environs; Biographical* (Chicago, 1918), vol. 2; *The Cleveland City Directory,* 1870–1911; Cleveland *Plain Dealer,* April 1885–April 1887, April 1889–April 1891, and December 1911; "George W. Gardner," *Biographical Cyclopedia and Portrait Gallery of Representative Men of the State of Ohio,* vol. 2, 1887; Charles Kennedy, *Fifty Years of Cleveland, 1875–1925* (Cleveland, 1925).

Eric C. Landowski and William D. Jenkins

GARRETT, AUGUSTUS (1801–48), Mayor of Chicago (1843–44, 1845–46). Two-term Democratic and "Locofoco" mayor of Chicago, Garrett was born in New York City in 1801 and lived in Cincinnati and New Orleans, working as an auctioneer before arriving in Chicago in 1836. He came to Chicago penniless and had to leave his wife in New York until he had accumulated sufficient funds to send for her. He prospered as an auctioneer, handling $1.8 million in one year alone (1836).

He also entered the real estate business and soon acquired a considerable fortune. Garrett was very active in the Methodist Church and in the temperance movement.

Chicago in 1843 had 7,580 citizens and a mayor-council form of government, with a one-year term for mayor. Garrett, a Democrat, served as alderman for one term in 1840 before running for mayor in 1842. That year he was defeated by Benjamin Raymond (*q.v.*), the Whig candidate, 490 to 432; Liberty party (abolitionist) candidate Henry Smith received 53 votes. On 7 March 1843, Garrett defeated his Whig opponent, Thomas Church, 771 to 381, with Henry Smith getting 45 votes. In this election, Garrett had the active support of the "Locofocos." In 1844, Garrett ran for mayor for the third time and defeated George Dole, his Whig opponent, 805 to 798. The election was nullified, however, after it was discovered that a Democratic election judge in a ward that had gone decisively for Garrett was not yet a citizen of the United States. The city council ordered a new election and this time Garrett was defeated by A. S. Sherman (*q.v.*), who ran as an Independent Democrat 837 to 694; Smith, of the Liberty party, received 126 votes. Garrett ran again in 1845, and this time was elected for a second term, as he defeated John Kinzie 1,072 to 913.

Throughout his career, Garrett was a staunch foe of abolitionism and government spending. During his first term, he ended the teaching of music in the public schools in order to save money. Another major act, apparently, was to get the city council to pass an ordinance that forbade citizens to allow their hogs to run freely in the streets. Newspapers had soundly condemned the practice because it only added to the filthiness of the neighborhoods. During his second term, Garrett led an unsuccessful campaign to sell the city's first permanent school building to a private organization that wanted to turn it into an insane asylum. Garrett argued that this plan would make better use of the building and raise money at the same time, but a majority of the city council did not agree with him. Chicago "firsts" in Garrett's time (with which he had little to do) included the first meat to be packed and shipped from the city to a foreign market and the first book to be compiled, printed bound, and published in Chicago (*Norris's Directory of 1844*). Garrett himself was a do-nothing, negative, unimaginative mayor.

After his second term, Garrett returned to the real estate business. He died suddenly, on 30 November 1848. His widow (d. November 1855), left his fortune to Northwestern University for the construction of the Garrett Biblical Institute.

SOURCES: A. T. Andreas, *History of Chicago* (Chicago, 1884); Don Fehrenbacher, *Chicago Giant: A Bi-*ography of *"Long John" Wentworth* (Madison, Wis., 1957); Bessie L. Pierce, *History of Chicago* (New York, 1937–57).   *Leslie V. Tischauser*

GARRISON, CORNELIUS KINGSLAND (1809–85), Mayor of San Francisco (1853–54). Reform mayor of San Francisco, Garrison was also a leading American entrepreneur and millionaire. Born on 1 March 1809 at Fort Montgomery, near West Point, New York, he had a distinguished Huguenot colonial background. His father, Oliver G., was descended from one Isaac G., a Huguenot immigrant from Montauban, France, who was naturalized in 1705 at New Rochelle, New York. Other family members settled in Putnam County and for several generations owned a large estate there called "Garrison's." His mother, Catherine Schuyler Kingsland, was seventeenth-century Dutch on one side and British on the other. Cornelius, however, the second of five brothers, suffered when his father lost his estates and wealth. At age thirteen, he became a cabin-boy on a Hudson River sloop, attending school only in the winter months. At age sixteen (1825), he moved to New York City to study architecture and engineering, pressed by his mother. Three years later, he went to Canada, designing buildings, lake steamboats, and other projects, such as the bridge at Goderich, Ontario. He was local manager for the Upper Canada Company until 1833 when a war scare with England caused him to move to St. Louis (a city where three of his brothers prospered). He married Mary Noye Re Tallack, a Cornish girl, in Buffalo, New York, on 1 August 1831 and they had seven children. His surviving son, William Re Tallack, also became a successful business leader. Mary died on 28 September 1876, and Cornelius married Letitia Willet Randall on 10 October 1878.

Garrison built and operated Mississippi River steamboats from St. Louis, serving river ports down to New Orleans; he built the largest such boat, the *Convoy*, to carry cotton. It was a hazardous business, and though he profited, such incidents as a steamboat fire in February 1849 made Garrison keep his options open. With the California Gold Rush, he moved to Panama and established a successful banking and trading firm. Visiting New York in 1852 to create a branch bank, he was offered $60,000 a year to run the San Francisco office of the Nicaragua Steamship Company. The firm's affairs were in poor condition, but within six months he had restored it to prosperity. By then, he was also asked to run for the mayoralty of San Francisco.

Garrison had arrived in San Francisco on 23 March 1853; he was elected mayor in September, and his term ran from 3 October 1853 to 1 October 1854. Elected mainly for his financial genius and honesty, Mayor Garrison began with many misgivings. He was by nature a reformer and an activist. He immediately gave an inaugural address to the council, and one month later announced a detailed agenda of reform. He denounced public gambling and Sunday theatricals; he demanded industrial schools for juvenile delinquents, to avoid throwing them in the almshouses and jails with common adult criminals; he called for an "African" school to educate Negroes and was convinced (as early as 1853) that they should be given the vote; and because his reforms involved big spending, he demanded taxes on nonresident and foreign capital and on carriage cab fares. Local cabs were overcharging; he imposed city regulation of fares. His biggest impact was on city education—he encouraged the building of new schools (to replace existing shanties) and at one point used his own money to pay for them. Mayor Garrison increased the fire department budget and built more water cisterns, extending Geary's (q.v.) projects. He even began a city beautification scheme, planting trees and shrubs on main squares like Portsmouth Plaza. Most important, he introduced the first street lighting to the city on 11 February 1854, by gas. He was an early advocate of the transcontinental railroad (and had an engine named after him) and of telegraph lines. A true philanthropist, he sent his own money to aid yellow fever victims in New Orleans (September 1853) and once gave his year's salary as mayor to Protestant and Catholic orphanages in San Francisco.

Returning east in 1859, Garrison became a well-known New York financier, investing in gas companies, railroads (he was president of the Missouri Pacific from 1876), steamship companies, and other industries. He even was a part owner of New York City's first elevated railroad ("El") with A. M. Billings. Although he suffered losses at one time, he recovered before the end of his life.

Despite his great vision and his contributions to the city, Garrison failed to be reelected in September 1854. He was defeated by a bigoted, Know-Nothing, anti-Chinese candidate, S. P. Webb (q.v.). The city gave Mayor Garrison a $10,000 gold dinner service at retirement in recognition of his service. He died in New York City on 1 May 1885.

SOURCES: Julia C. Altrocchi, The Spectacular San Franciscans (New York, 1949); W. F. Heintz, San Francisco's Mayors (Woodside, Calif., 1975); New York Genealogical and Biographical Record, "Cornelius Garrison," January 1906; New York Tribune, 2 May 1885; O. T. Shuck, Representative and Leading Men of the Pacific (San Francisco, 1870); F. Soule, J. H. Gihon, and J. Nisbet, Annals of San Francisco (New York, 1855); W. W. Spooner, ed., Historic Families of America (New York, 1907), vol. 2.   Peter d'A. Jones

GASTON, WILLIAM (1820–94), Mayor of Boston (1871–72). Mayor of Boston during the great fire (1872) and later governor of Massachusetts (1875), Gaston was born in Killingley, Connecticut, on 2 October 1820, the son of Alexander Gaston (1772–1856) of French Huguenot descent and Kesia (Arnold) Gaston (c. 1780–1856), of Baptist, old-stock Yankee descent. The Gastons had been merchants and lawyers in Connecticut for a century, and he was educated at private academies and at Brown College (A.B., 1840). In 1838, the family migrated to Roxbury, Massachusetts, a thriving small city of 25,000 on the outskirts of Boston. Here Gaston studied law and was admitted to the Massachusetts bar in 1844. Here, too, he married Laura Beecher in 1852, with whom he had three children.

Gaston quickly established a political-legal role for himself in Roxbury, serving on the common council, representing the city in the state House of Representatives, and acting as city solicitor in the years between 1849 and 1860. He climaxed these years of activity by becoming mayor of Roxbury, 1861–62. Political allegiances were reshaped in these years, and Gaston's were no exception. Initially a Whig, he was swept into the Democratic party when the Whig party dissolved over the slavery issue. He endeared himself to Irish constituents by refusing to accept nativist demands, and their support became an important part of his political strength. He ran for mayor of Boston as a Democrat, but his fiscal conservatism allowed him to receive considerable nominally Republican support in his municipal campaigns.

Boston was experiencing considerable growth and prestige. It was now a city of over 250,000, and the advantages of annexation appeared persuasive to neighboring towns. Gaston's political activism, his flourishing law practice, and his real estate interests made it logical that he should be a leader in the move to annex Roxbury. The union was accepted by both cities in 1867, and in December 1870 Gaston ran for mayor of Boston as a Democrat but with considerable "nonpartisan" (that is, Republican) support. He defeated the Republican, George Carpenter (10,836 to 7,836). He was successful again in December 1871, defeating Republican Newton Talbot handily (9,838 to 6,231). In December 1872, however, he was narrowly defeated by the Republican/Citizens coalition candidate, Henry L. Pierce (q.v.) (8,798 to 8,878).

By 1870, neither the population growth of the past two decades nor the growth of municipal expenses showed any signs of abating. Gaston's policy was to proceed very cautiously on the matter of further municipal initiatives in city improvements. His other policy, a tacit one, seems to have been to integrate the Irish into the city through the Democratic party. Gaston was defeated not because of these strategies, however, but because of apparent lack of administrative decisiveness and vigor. In the fall of 1872, the city experienced the devastating fire and an outbreak of smallpox. The mayor was faulted for his indecision during and after the fire, as well as for his failure to transform the health department into a more effective body. He was narrowly defeated in December 1872.

Gaston's political career continued, however, as he ran as a Democrat for governor in 1873, 1874, and 1875. In staunchly Republican Massachusetts, he was elected only in 1874, as a protest against national Republican corruption and local Republican temperance. In contrast to his political career, his law career flourished: his firm of Gaston and Whitney, later Gaston, Snow, Saltonstall, and Hunt, became one of the most prestigious in Boston. He was prominent professionally, becoming president of the Boston and Massachusetts bars, and was awarded honorary LL.D. degrees from Harvard and Brown universities. He died of natural causes on 19 January 1894 and was buried in Forest Hills Cemetery, Boston.

SOURCES: Boston *Transcript*, 19 January 1894 (obituary); J. M. Bugbee, "Boston Under the Mayors," in Justin Winsor, ed., *The Memorial History of Boston*, 4 vols. (Boston, 1881), vol. 3; City of Boston, Massachusetts, *Documents, 1871, 1872, 1873*; William Gaston Papers, Brown University Archives, Providence, R.I.; The great fire of 1872 is treated in Diane T. Rudnick, "Boston Fire of 1872: The Stillborn Phoenix" (Ph.D. dissertation, Boston University, 1971, Ann Arbor, Mich., University Microfilms, 1971). However, Gaston is scarcely mentioned in the work; Edward F. McSweeney, *Colonel William A. Gaston, a Biographical Study* (Boston, 1912—this pamphlet is about Gaston's son); *A Memorial of William Gaston from the City of Boston*, Boston, 1895; *New England Historic Genealogical Society Register* 48 (July 1894).   *Constance Burns*

GAYNOR, WILLIAM J. (1848–1913), Mayor of New York (1910–13). Born on 2 February 1848 in Whitesboro, New York, Gaynor was the son of Keiron K. Gaynor, a blacksmith and farmer born in Dublin, Ireland, and Elizabeth (Handwright) Gaynor. Both parents were Roman Catholic. After attending Assumption Academy, Gaynor enrolled at De La Salle Institute in 1863 and was subsequently admitted to the lay brotherhood of the Christian Brothers order. Following four years of teaching at parochial schools in St. Louis and Baltimore, Gaynor left the order and renounced Catholicism in 1868, eventually joining the Episcopal Church. He taught in Boston public schools and then studied law in Utica, New York.

Admitted to the bar in 1871, Gaynor settled in Brook-

lyn where he worked as a reporter for the Brooklyn *Argus* and New York *Sun*. As a young lawyer in Brooklyn, he became known as a crusader, defending the public interest against unscrupulous businesses. In 1893, he parlayed his reformist image into election as a state supreme court judge. In 1905, Gaynor was designated a member of the Appellate Division of the state's second department and was reelected to the bench two years later. His 1874 marriage to Emma Vesta Hyde ended in divorce in 1881; in 1886, he wed Augusta Cole Mayer, and they had seven children.

In 1910, New York City had 4,766,883 people and a mayor-board of aldermen form of government. Tammany Boss Charles F. Murphy chose the celebrated reformer-judge Gaynor to run for mayor in 1909 against the fusion candidate Otto T. Bannard, a well-known banker and philanthropist, and William Randolph Hearst of the Civic Alliance. Gaynor polled 250,678 votes to Bannard's 177,662 and Hearst's 153,843, but apart from the mayor's office, virtually the entire fusion slate was elected. To compound the Democratic machine's trepidation, Gaynor himself not only hired businessmen and experts as commissioners instead of the party faithful, but also actually fired many Tammany appointees. In the stormy first year of his mayoralty, Gaynor firmly established his independence from the political organization that had so recently helped to elect him.

In the summer of 1910, Gaynor was shot in the throat at close range by a discharged city worker. While his convalescence resulted in only a two-month absence from city hall, the long-term effects of the shooting were profound. The bullet remained in his throat, leaving him with a chronic cough and rasping voice. But most significant was the apparent change in personality, as Gaynor became increasingly vindictive and irascible. Once the darling of the reformers, Gaynor's obstinance and inflexibility earned him the enmity of the city's progressive community. (As a staunch defender of personal liberty, Gaynor resisted reformers' efforts to curb Sunday drinking, gambling, and prostitution.) Police scandals further sullied Gaynor's reputation.

In August 1913, Tammany Hall announced that Gaynor would not be renominated in the upcoming election. On 4 September the mayor accepted the nomination of an independent citizen's committee and subsequently left on a transoceanic steamship voyage to restore his failing health. On 10 September, his son Rufus found him dead on the ship's deck, a casualty of the shooting and the rigors of office. His body was brought back to New York and buried in Greenwood Cemetery, Brooklyn.

SOURCES: August Cerillo, Jr., "The Reform of Municipal Government in New York City: From Seth Low to John Purroy Mitchel," *New York Historical Society*

Quarterly 57:1 (January 1973); New York *Times*, 12 September 1913; Louis H. Pink, *Gaynor, The Tammany Mayor Who Swallowed the Tiger* (Freeport, N.Y., 1931); Mortimer Smith, *William Jay Gaynor: Mayor of New York* (Chicago, 1951); Lately Thomas, *The Mayor Who Mastered New York* (New York, 1969).

W. Roger Biles

GEARY, JOHN WHITE (1819–73), *Alcalde*/Mayor of San Francisco (1849–50; 1850–51). First mayor of San Francisco when that office was created upon statehood, Geary was a Mexican War hero, and subsequently governor of Kansas Territory, Civil War general, and governor of Pennsylvania. Reputedly born in a log cabin near Mount Pleasant, Westmoreland County, Pennsylvania, on 30 December 1819, Geary was the son of a failed ironmaster, Richard Geary, who was for a time principal of his own academy. Some sources claim Scottish-Irish descent for his father, but others suggest he came from an old Shropshire family, original English pioneers in Franklin County, Pennsylvania. Geary's mother, Margaret (White), was widowed while John attended Jefferson College at Canonsburg, Pennsylvania. John had to leave college without graduating in order to support the family. He had various jobs, briefly teaching school and clerking in a store, and then studying civil engineering and law. Admitted to the Pennsylvania bar, he never practiced law. He took a surveying expedition to the Green River, Kentucky, and made enough money in land speculation there to pay off his father's debts. For a few years he worked as assistant superintendent of the Allegheny Portage Railroad. In 1843, he married Margaret Ann Logan of Westmoreland County, a local girl. They had two sons. She died in 1853, and in 1858 he married Mrs. Mary Church Henderson of Cumberland County, Pennsylvania.

A longstanding interest in the Army (he was a militia lieutenant at the age of sixteen) paid off in 1846 with the outbreak of the Mexican War. Geary raised a company of mountain volunteers, the "American Highlanders," and joined up with the Second Pennsylvania Regiment and General Scott at Vera Cruz. Wounded at Chapultepec, the hero was made a full colonel and commander of the captured Mexican capital. After the war, he moved to California, apparently with great reluctance. On 22 January 1849, President Polk appointed him the first postmaster of San Francisco, with power to give out mail contracts and to create routes. The job was shortlived, since Tyler soon replaced Polk. Geary and his family had arrived on the Pacific steamship *Oregon* on 31 March 1849, bringing with him 5,000 letters from the East—the first regular mail service in California history.

After dabbling in business, Geary was elected *alcalde* (an executive-judicial office that preceded the mayoralty) in August 1849, replacing Thaddeus Leavenworth (*q.v.*). He wielded wide powers and took a large political role in framing the new state constitution and getting California admitted as a nonslave state. Elected mayor on 1 May 1850, under the new U.S. rules, Geary—a tall, 6′5½″ figure of military bearing with a hero's reputation—commanded respect. The city, with perhaps 25,000 people, was growing fast, with tents and shacks spreading out in all directions. Dismayed at his new job, Geary complained in August 1849:

> At this time we are without a dollar in the public treasury, the city is greatly in debt. You are without an office for your mayorship nor any public edifice. You are without a single police officer or watchman, and have not the means of confining a prisoner for an hour; [nor] a place to shelter while living, sick and infant strangers . . . , or to bury them when dead. Public improvements are unknown in San Francisco.

Although he seemingly ached to return home to Pennsylvania, Geary dutifully tackled the city's problems. As *alcalde*, he introduced the first local tax law (27 August 1849), realistically legalized gambling and taxed the tables, bought the brig *Euphemia* to use as a jail, created a police force, began orderly recording of land titles, and appointed the first fire chief, F. D. Kohler. He had underground cisterns installed to help combat the city's many fires. Geary tackled the problem of mob violence, especially urban gangs such as the "Hounds" and the "Sydney Ducks" (some were Australians).

The new city charter of 1850 removed many of the duties carried out by the former *alcalde*, defining the mayor's job more narrowly. Besides its mayor, the city was to have a recorder, treasurer, comptroller, street commissioner, tax assessors, city marshal, city attorney, and a board of aldermen—all elective offices. Geary was elected mayor against a weak Whig rival, Charles Brenham (*q.v.*). The election may have been illegal, since statehood had not yet been granted. Although Geary amassed $200,000 in under three years and engaged in land speculation with city lots, he contributed enormously to San Francisco as *alcalde* and mayor. Like those before and after, he failed to control the growing crime of the "Barbary Coast" area. What is now the famous Union Square is land given to the city by Geary in 1850.

Geary refused to run for reelection in April 1851. He left California in February 1852 to retire to a farm in western Pennsylvania. Declining the offer of the governorship of Utah, he finally accepted President Franklin Pierce's appointment as governor of "Bleeding Kansas" in 1856, during that territory's most violent period. An antislavery man, he resigned upon Buchanan's accession (1857) to the presidency. In April 1861, one hour after hearing about the attack on Fort Sumter and the outbreak of Civil War, Geary began recruiting volunteers to fight on the Union side. Wounded several times, he became a general and fought at Chancellorsville, Gettysburg, and Lookout Mountain, where his eldest son, Edward Ratchford (born on 14 September 1845) was killed on 28 October 1863. A second son graduated from West Point after the war (1874). Geary served as military governor of Savannah after its capture, having marched with Sherman to the sea. He was elected governor of Pennsylvania for two terms (1867–73) as a Republican, reducing state debts, and demanding state regulation of railroads, insurance, utilities, and public health. A labor reform candidate, he had short-lived presidential ambitions in 1872. Geary was tough, opinionated, shrewd, sometimes erratic and headstrong, and of violent temper. He made some enemies but was loved by his troops. He died suddenly, on 8 February 1873, and was buried in Harrisburg Cemetery, under a state monument in his honor.

SOURCES: W. C. Armor, *Lives of the Governors of Pennsylvania* (Philadelphia, 1872); W. J. Davis, *History of Political Conventions in California, 1849–92* (Sacramento, 1893); C. M. Drury, "J. W. Geary and His Brother Edward," *California Historical Society Quarterly* 20 (March 1941); J. H. Gihon, *Geary and Kansas* (Philadelphia, 1857); W. F. Heintz, *San Francisco's Mayors* (Woodside, Calif., 1975); Bernard Moses, *Establishment of Municipal Government in San Francisco* (Baltimore, 1889); *Sketch of the Early Life of the Civil and Military Service of Major General John W. Geary, Candidate of the National Union Party for Governor of Pennsylvania* (Philadelphia, 1866); Mary F. Williams, *History of the San Francisco Committee of Vigilance, 1851* (Berkeley, Calif., 1921).   *Peter d'A. Jones*

GENOIS, CHARLES (1793–1866), Mayor of New Orleans (1838–40). Born in New Orleans in 1793, the Creole mayor, Genois, labored long and effectively in two principal political causes: Jacksonian Democracy and division of the city of New Orleans into semi-autonomous municipalities shaped by ethnic identification. His latter crusade began in the mid-1820s, when he resided in the suburbs above Faubourg St. Mary, upriver from the heart of the metropolis. This crusade was largely responsible for his election to the city council in 1824.

Typical of Louisiana Jacksonians, Genois was active in the business community, serving on various bank and improvement corporation boards throughout the 1820s and 1830s. When his predecessor, Denis Prieur (*q.v.*), retired from the mayor's office in 1838 to seek the governorship, two years after the realization of Genois's long-held dream of a divided city, Genois received Jacksonian party support and won the New Orleans mayoralty

with a vote of 1,838 to 1,048 over the Whig L. U. Gainnie.

By then, the effects of the Panic of 1837 were paralyzing the city's economy, and Genois was forced to preside over an administration largely committed to retrenchment and curtailment of municipal expenditures. By August 1838, the city had defaulted on a $1 million debt to New Orleans banks and was unable to meet its payroll. Planned extension of street paving and canal connections to Lake Ponchartrain were necessarily canceled. Despite heroic efforts by Genois and Prieur, who managed to shore up the city's finances by arranging a New York loan of $100,000 in December 1838, the economic slide continued and by October 1839 the "American" second municipality of New Orleans was over $3 million in debt. Even sorely needed reform of the police of the city was insufficient to save Genois from the political effects of this debacle, and in April 1840 the Whig William Freret (*q.v.*), with massive support in the second municipality, ousted him from office. By 1840, New Orleans had a population of about 100,000.

Genois's later life was largely nonpolitical. Never married, he preferred the not uncommon Creole arrangement of maintaining a *ménage* with a free woman of color. He died in New Orleans on 30 August 1866.

SOURCES: New Orleans *Argus*, 27 May 1833; New Orleans *Louisiana Advertiser*, 22 December 1826; New Orleans *Louisiana Courier*, 8 October 1832, 7 April 1840; Orleans Parish Succession Records, Second District Court, 1846–80.   *Joseph G. Tregle, Jr.*

GILPIN, CHARLES (1809–91), Mayor of Philadelphia (1850–53). Born in Wilmington, Delaware, on 17 November 1809, Charles was the son of Edward and Lydia Grubb Gilpin. Educated at the Germantown Academy in Philadelphia, he then read law with a local attorney and was admitted to the bar in 1834. He practiced law in Philadelphia for a half century.

Gilpin was U.S. district attorney during Lincoln's presidency. He was elected to the common council in 1839 and then in 1840 to the select council where he served for nine years until elected mayor in 1850. He married Sarah Hamilton on 5 April 1843 and was the father of six children.

Philadelphia had a mayor-council form of government in 1850; the city proper had a population of 121,000, but the area population was much larger: 389,000. (In 1854, the city size jumped dramatically, on paper, when the consolidation with the county took place.) Accepting the Whig nomination, Gilpin was elected mayor in 1850 by a vote of 7,373 over his opponent, Joel Jones' 5,081. Mayor Gilpin was reelected in 1851, 1852, and 1853.

He was appointed solicitor to the sheriff in 1858 and filled that position, with the exception of two terms, until 1883. He also served as the U.S. attorney for the Eastern District of Pennsylvania from 1864 to 1868. He made his home in Philadelphia and died there in 1891.

SOURCES: *City of Firsts: Complete History of Philadelphia* (Philadelphia, 1926); J. W. Jordan, ed., "Gilpin Family," in *Colonial and Revolutionary Families of Pennsylvania* (New York, 1911), vol. 1.

Melvin G. Holli

GILROY, THOMAS F. (1839–1911), Mayor of New York (1893–94). A quintessential Tammany leader of his time, born in Sligo, Ireland, and brought to New York City seven years later by his newly widowed mother, Gilroy rose to the mayoralty through astute and devoted service to the great Democratic organization. He attended the city's public schools and graduated, according to an 1892 *World* campaign profile, from the Free Academy. His mother had settled in New York to be near relatives, and their help may have permitted him to remain long in school, but he apparently could not afford college or professional training. Following a brief stint as errand boy for G. P. Putnam's publishing house, in about 1859 he apprenticed himself to a politically well-connected printer, who placed him in increasingly responsible positions.

In 1864, Gilroy's experience and political connections secured him a $1,250 clerkship on the Croton Aqueduct Board. In that year he also married Mary Sheridan, a relative of General Phil Sheridan, in a ceremony conducted by the diocesan vicar-general at old St. Patrick's Roman Catholic Church. During the next few years, Gilroy prospered as messenger for Boss William Marcy Tweed and as confidential clerk to "Prince Hal" Genet, one of Tweed's closest associates. Both Tweed and Genet were subsequently convicted and imprisoned, but Gilroy, setting a pattern for his own career, avoided legal entanglement in the Tweed Ring's fall.

The 1870s and early 1880s were a time of troubles for Tammany, but Gilroy had nothing to do with bolters or reformers and remained loyal both to the organization and to John Kelly, its new boss. He became leader of the heterogeneous, rapidly growing Twenty-third Assembly District on the Upper East Side, and served as secretary of Tammany's General Committee through most of the 1880s. Meanwhile, he held a series of county and court clerkships in which he distinguished himself by reducing title-search delays and by displaying unexpected ability and honesty as the dubiously qualified receiver for a bankrupt firm. According to the *World*, his Algeresque qualities of "clockwork regularity," perseverance, and willingness to perform "unpleasant" duties made

him a "safe man for his superiors to lean upon" and accounted for his rise. He also earned a reputation for "invariably sound" judgment on matters of party policies, alliances, and personnel. And he was unusually literate: as mayor he published in the *North American Review* three cogent articles defending Tammany's financial management of the city. Although E. L. Godkin's *Evening Post* featured Gilroy in its critical "Tammany Biographies" of 1890 and 1894, it found no serious blemishes on his record except for the questionable drafting of some paving contracts.

Gilroy emerged as one of Tammany's three top leaders during the organization's resurgence after 1886. Although closely associated with Boss Richard Croker, he was, according to George B. McClellan, Jr.'s memoirs, "too much of a personage to take orders from anyone." As public works commissioner (1889–92) and then as mayor (elected, with Cleveland Democratic support, with 173,510 votes to Republican Edwin Einstein's 97,923 and Socialist Alex Jonas's 6,295), Gilroy successfully sought to reduce the tax rate while improving the streets, building an uptown trotting-horse speedway, looking after Tammany's patronage needs, and "harmonizing" potential Irish-German conflicts. (He does not seem to have made a point of membership in Irish or Catholic organizations himself.)

Gilroy did not play a leading public role in major policy decisions. Repeated state investigations failed to damage him personally, but the Lexow Committee's investigation of the police in 1894, his appointment of men who came under fire, and his vulnerability to the charge of neglecting the newest immigrants forced him to step aside after one term. He continued as a top Tammany leader and high public official until 1897, and then retired to small-time banking and real estate activities in uptown Manhattan and Far Rockaway, Queens. He died in Far Rockaway on 1 December 1911.

SOURCES: *Harper's Weekly*, 13 July 1889; Letters to Mayor Gilroy, Mayors' Papers, New York City Municipal Archives and Records Center; Samuel T. McSeveney, *The Politics of Depression: Political Behavior in the Northeast 1893–1896* (New York, 1972); Mary Gilroy Mulqueen, "Thomas F. Gilroy," *Journal of the American Irish Historical Society* 11 (1912); *New York Times*, 2 December 1911; Martin Shefter, "The Electoral Foundations of the Political Machine: New York City, 1884–1897," in Joel Silbey et al., eds., *American Electoral History: Quantitative Studies in Popular Voting Behavior* (Princeton, N.J., 1978); Martin Shefter, "The Emergence of the Political Machine: An Alternative View," in Willis D. Hawley, et al., eds., *Theoretical Perspectives on Urban Politics* (Englewood Cliffs, N.J., 1976).

David C. Hammack

GIROD, NICHOLAS (1747–1840), Mayor of New Orleans (1812–15). The fifth mayor of New Orleans, and the first to be popularly elected, Girod was born in 1747 in French Savoy, from which he migrated to Spanish New Orleans in the late 1770s. With his brothers Claude Francois and Jean Francois he prospered there as a commission merchant, eventually owning extensive property throughout the city, especially in the new "American" section upstream from the original settlement.

Creation of the state of Louisiana allowed for the first popular election of a mayor of New Orleans, which Girod won by defeating James Pitot on 12 September 1812 by a vote of 859 to 461. The town then had about 33,000 people. The exigencies of the War of 1812 prevented any expansive programs under Girod's leadership; his administration centered largely on attempts to ameliorate the city's war-torn economy. However, he was able to improve drainage by expanding the Girod Canal behind Congo Square and by laying the first brick sidewalks in the city.

Reelected on 5 September 1815 over Augustin Macarty by 309 to 286 votes, Girod assisted Andrew Jackson in opposing the 1814–15 British campaign against New Orleans, largely by collection of military supplies for the commander and by vigilance against internal subversion, for which he won Jackson's particular thanks after victory at Chalmette.

Girod resigned the mayoralty on 4 September 1815 to attend to his depleted personal fortunes. His later years were unburdened by public service except for brief tenure as city alderman in 1824–25 and as a "church warden" for the Roman Catholic St. Louis Cathedral. Girod was linked to the alleged New Orleans plot to rescue Napoleon from St. Helena in the early 1820s, reportedly offering the emperor refuge in a house adjoining his own home at the corner of Chartres and St. Louis streets, a building complex still famous as "The Napoleon House." Memories of the glorious days of 1815 made him an ardent Jacksonian in national politics.

At his death on 1 September 1840, he left bequests of several hundred thousand dollars to close friends and to various New Orleans charities, particularly to a planned asylum for French orphans, but legal attacks against the validity of title in many of his properties severely reduced the estate's value. Girod never married.

SOURCES: Henry Castellanos, *New Orleans as It Was* (New Orleans, 1895, new edition, Baton Rouge, La., 1979); John S. Kendall, *History of New Orleans*, 3 vols. (Chicago, 1922), vol. 1; New Orleans *Bee*, 2 September 1840.   *Joseph G. Tregle, Jr.*

GOODMAN, PHILIP H. (1915–76), Acting Mayor of Baltimore (1962–63). Acting Mayor, Goodman was born in Poland in 1915, but soon after was taken by his parents to Hamburg, Germany, where he lived until he was six, when the family emigrated to the United States.

Goodman was elected as a Democrat to the Baltimore City Council in 1951 and to the state Senate in 1953. Shortly after reelection to the Senate post in 1957, he resigned to run for president of the city council on the Grady (*q.v.*) ticket. He became acting mayor on 6 December 1962, finishing the remaining five months of his predecessor's term. Goodman ran for the office of mayor in 1963 but was defeated by the former Republican mayor and governor, Theodore R. McKeldin (*q.v.*). He died in 1976.

SOURCES: Biographical information from Mrs. Fay T. Albert, 1 March 1980; *U.S. Congressional Record*, 94th Congress, 2d S. 6., 6 May 1976.   *W. T. Durr*

GOURLEY, HENRY L. (1838–99), Mayor of Pittsburgh (1890–93). Gourley was born in Juniata County, Pennsylvania, on 3 October 1838, the second in a family of three. His father, a farmer, died in 1843, and his mother brought him to Pittsburgh, where he was bound out to work on a farm until he became eighteen. He worked overtime as a woodcutter and at harvesting, saved his money, and enrolled for four months at Witherspoon Institute, in Butler, Pennsylvania. He then transferred to Duff's Business College in Pittsburgh, where he graduated in 1857. He was a Presbyterian.

Young Gourley went to Iowa, but returned to Pennsylvania, where he taught in country schools in winter and worked on farms in summer. In 1861, he became principal of the Troy Hill school, and in 1867 he married Virginia Lenonia Brenneman, daughter of a German foundryman. They had no children. Later, he taught at various schools, was a schoolbook representative for Charles Scribner's Sons, and became a partner with A. H. English in printing school books in Pittsburgh. The company failed, and after a brief time in New York, he returned to teaching in Pittsburgh. Soon, he entered politics and was elected to the select council in 1876. Three years later, he became its president, holding the post for ten years. Pittsburgh at this time had a population of 240,000 and a government by mayor and two councils.

Gourley's Democratic opponent for mayor was J. H. Bailey, a highly respected former judge, whom he defeated 15,267 to 12,332, largely through a last minute slander campaign. Surprisingly, he turned reformer, built new waterworks, paved streets, and tried to give the city an honest government.

Gourley ordered Public Safety Director J. O. Brown to close the city's brothels, and when Brown refused, he sought to impeach him but was refused by the councils. Then Brown closed the houses of prostitution for a day and had all the women march on city hall, demanding food and shelter.

During Gourley's term, Pittsburgh was enriched by Schenley Park, Phipps Conservatory, and Carnegie Library, and downtown streets were widened.

Out of favor with the Flinn-Magee political ring, Gourley was still nominated for city controller but refused to accept. He was nominated for the same post as a Democrat, ran, and was elected. In this post, he discovered irregularities in the city's Law Department which sent the city attorney and city clerk to jail. At the end of his term, he accepted renomination as a Republican and was again elected.

Within a short time, Gourley became ill with tuberculosis and sought a cure in Colorado and Florida, but in vain. He died on 27 May 1899 and was buried in Homewood Cemetery.

SOURCES: *Encyclopedia of Contemporary Biography of Pennsylvania* (New York, 1898); *History of Allegheny County, Pa.* (Chicago, 1889); Pittsburgh *Post* and *Dispatch*, both 28 May 1899.   *George Swetnam*

GRACE, WILLIAM R. (1832–1904), Mayor of New York (1881–82, 1885–86). The first Roman Catholic mayor of New York and a millionaire shipowner, Grace was an immigrant, born in Queenstown, Ireland, on 10 May 1832. His father, James Grace, was a wealthy estate owner of Irish-Norman ancestry, and his mother was Ellen Mary (Russell) Grace; both were Catholics. William, the first-born of the four Grace children, ran away from home at age fourteen after his father blocked his plan to join the Royal Navy. He obtained a clerkship in a New York shipping house. After returning to Ireland, he moved to Liverpool, England, and established the firm of William R. Grace and Company. In 1851, he moved his operations to Peru, from whence he soon controlled much of the shipping of Central and South America. He traveled to and from the United States, Europe, and South America, building up a business that involved many kinds of vessels and import-export items. Grace's interest in New York developed after he opened a permanent business there in 1865. He sat on the boards of four New York banks and was influential in the insurance and lumber communities in addition to shipping.

As early as 1868, Grace was mentioned as a possible mayoral candidate. His philanthropic and political reputation rose in 1880 with his major contribution to a plan to relieve poverty in Ireland. Throughout the 1870s, his firm's influence in Peruvian affairs grew by supplying most of Peru's army and navy equipment. After Peru's failure in a war with Chile, Grace and Company took over most of the country's debt in return for silver mines, guano deposits, oil and mineral lands, and railroad prop-

erties. Grace married Lillius Gilchrist, the daughter of a prominent Maine shipbuilder in 1859. They had eleven children, two of whom died in infancy.

In 1880, New York had 1,164,673 people and had a weak mayor-aldermanic system of government. The Democratic party had split into three factions in the wake of the battle against the Tweed Ring. Candidates were chosen by truces and battles among the factions. The Irving Hall group, thinking that Grace, as an unusual selection, would be unacceptable to Boss "Honest John" Kelly, placed his name on a list in order to ensure another choice. It later turned out that Grace was Kelly's choice. A fierce campaign ensued with many Irving Hall Democrats opposing Grace on religious grounds. They joined with Republicans to support William Dowd, who received 98,715 votes to 101,760 for Grace. Grace's official power was limited by state legislation which had made the tenure of department executives longer than his own. He often spoke of the evils of legislative interference and soon broke with Kelly. As New York's first Irish Catholic mayor, Grace exemplified the strivings of that group. He resisted the efforts of the Manhattan Elevated Railway Company to be relieved of back taxes. Various street railway firms were also compelled to pay their taxes. Grace returned temporarily to his business interests in 1883 when a combination of three Democratic conventions chose Franklin Edson (*q.v.*) as the Democratic candidate. But at the Chicago convention of 1884, when Tammany interests opposed the nomination of Cleveland (*q.v.*), the coalition broke up. Grace, who was nominated by the County and Irving reform factions, was elected by a vote of 95,288 against 86,361 for Tammany's Hugh J. Grant and 45,386 for the Republican candidate, W. Wales. His second term was marked by the fall of "Honest John" Kelly and the emergence of Richard Crocker of County Cork as the new Democratic leader. Grace, although asked, refused to run again for mayor or for governor.

After leaving office, Grace established the pioneer direct steamship service between New York and the west coast of South America. In 1897, he and his brother founded the Grace Institute in New York for the education of young women in domestic science. Grace maintained homes in New York City and Great Neck, New York. He died in New York City on 21 March 1904.

SOURCES: Gordon Atkins, *Health, Housing and Poverty in New York City 1865–1898* (Ann Arbor, Mich., 1947); William T. Bonner, *New York, The World's Metropolis* (New York, 1924); Florence E. Gibson, *The Attitudes of the New York Irish Toward State and National Affairs 1848–1892* (New York, 1951); Henry Hall, *America's Successful Men of Affairs I* (1895); William Herman, *Factbook: Mayors and Burgomasters* (New

York, n.d.); *New York Genealogical and Biological Record* (July 1904); New York *Herald*, 22 March 1904; New York *Times*, 22 March 1904; New York *Tribune*, 5 October 1880; John Thompson, ''A Career of Romantic Achievement,'' *World's Work* (May 1904).

Howard R. Weiner

GRADISON, WILLIS DAVID, JR. (1928–   ), Mayor of Cincinnati (1971). Cabinet-level administrator, mayor and U.S. Representative, Gradison was born 28 December 1928, the only child of Willis D. Gradison (1899–   ), stock-broker, and Dorothy (Benas) Gradison, both members of old Cincinnati Jewish families. Gradison attended local schools, Yale (B.A. in 1948), and Harvard's Graduate School of Business Administration (D.C.S., 1954). In 1949, he joined his father's stock brokerage firm, Gradison and Company, Inc., becoming a full partner in 1958. Gradison was a research assistant at Harvard's Business School, 1951–53, an assistant to the undersecretary of the Treasury Department, 1953–55, and then assistant to the secretary of Housing and Urban Development, 1955–57. On 25 June 1950, Gradison married Helen Ann Martin (b. 1929; J.D., University of Cincinnati, 1971), and they had five daughters; the marriage ended in divorce in 1975. Gradison served as chairman of the board, Federal Home Loan Bank of Cincinnati, 1970–74, and was a member of the National Advisory Council on Economic Opportunities, 1971–74.

A Republican, Gradison was elected to the city council in 1961, soon becoming one of his party's major aldermanic spokesmen. He was vice-mayor, 1967–71, and thus automatically became mayor when Eugene Ruehlmann (*q.v.*) resigned in April 1971. In 1970, Cincinnati had 451,455 people and a council-city manager-mayor form of government.

Gradison later claimed that his only disappointment was the short length of his sole mayoral term (April-December 1971). He followed his predecessor's program of attempting to rebuild the city by attracting more business capital. Considered a strong mayor, Gradison actively urged cooperation between the city and surrounding county political organizations, especially the local Republican leadership. He hoped to bridge the gap between the public and government by touring the different neighborhoods. In October, he was part of a delegation of American mayors that traveled to Poland and West Germany, seeking ideas on municipal problems and their solution from a European viewpoint. After his short mayoral term ended, Gradison continued as an alderman until the spring of 1974 when he resigned to run for Congress. Although defeated in the special election in the First District, Gradison ran again in the regular elec-

tion for Congress that November and was elected. He was reelected in 1976 and 1978.

SOURCES: Congressional Directory, 95th Congress, 1st Session (Washington, D.C., 1977); *Who's Who in American Law* (Chicago, 1977); *Who's Who in American Politics* (New York, 1979); *Who's Who in the Midwest* (Chicago, 1978).

Thomas R. Bullard

GRADY, J. HAROLD (1917–   ), Mayor of Baltimore (1959–62). Grady was born in Williamsport, Pennsylvania, on 27 February 1917, the son of Thomas Leo Grady (1888–1937) an Irish-American Catholic railroad worker, and Edythe Augusta Grange (1888–1978), Lutheran of English descent. Grady, one of four children, married Patricia Grogan, a graduate of Mount de Sales High School on 2 May 1942. They had four children: Maureen (b. 1943), Joseph (b. 1947), Kathleen (b. 1953), and Thomas (b. 1955). Mayor Grady received the A.B., cum laude, in 1938 from Loyola College (Baltimore), and the LL.B. from the University of Maryland in 1942. Prior to becoming mayor, he served as a Federal Bureau of Investigation Special Agent (1942–47) and then as state's attorney of Baltimore (1956–59). When Grady became mayor, Baltimore's population totaled approximately 850,000 and the city had a mayor-city council form of government.

Grady was elected to office, on 5 May 1959, on a Democratic reform ticket, defeating former Governor and Mayor Theodore McKeldin (*q.v.*) by a vote of 155,001 to 72,745. With Grady were Philip Goodman (*q.v.*) who became president of the city council and R. Walter Graham, Jr., candidate for comptroller. Known as the ''3-G'' ticket, the men resisted the power held by some of the city's ethnic machines, especially the one led by James A. (Jack) Pollack who still controlled some votes in the city council.

Grady incorporated many recommendations of the Commission on Governmental Efficiency and Economy (now merged with the Chamber of Commerce) into his plans. This included the search for a new tax base, greater cooperation with surrounding subdivisions in the Baltimore SMSA, streamlined government, elimination of welfare abuse, capital planning, expansion of urban renewal projects in the center of the city, and improved mass transit and roadways. The ''3-G team'' was more concept than reality; it lacked a political base, and each of the reformers was independent of mind and will. During his term, Grady consulted the others less and less, and they reciprocated.

On 16 November 1962, Maryland Governor Millard Tawes announced the appointment of Harold Grady as associate judge of the supreme bench of Baltimore City. This appointment, sought by the increasingly frustrated mayor, opened the way for Philip Goodman, city council president, to become mayor. The Grady administration could list as accomplishments the improvement of housing inspection, establishment of a metropolitan transit authority, merger of park police with the Baltimore City Police Department, and improved governmental management and fiscal accountability. Mayor Grady, however, failed to find new revenues for the city and to unite the independently minded Democrats with whom he aspired to eliminate ward and precinct corruption common to old Eastern cities.

SOURCES: Biographical files of the Maryland Historical Society, the Enoch Pratt Free Library, and the Baltimore *Sun*.   *W. T. Durr*

GRANT, HUGH J. (1852–1910), Mayor of New York (1889–92). The most effective wheelhorse among Tammany's top-of-the-ticket candidates during the 1880s, Grant was a born insider. His father was a well-off Democratic politician, saloon-keeper, and real estate speculator. Although Hugh was left an orphan at an early age, he inherited both wealth and political connections. His guardian, a successful pawnbroker, saw to it that he had a good education. After passing through the city's common schools and Manhattan College, a private Catholic academy, he went at age sixteen to study in Berlin; on his return he spent three years at St. Francis Xavier College and two years at Columbia Law School. In the late 1870s, he worked in the office of D. M. Porter, then prominent at the bar, and in the office of a leading Tammany politico. He then set up his own law firm as well as a separate real estate office to manage both his own upper West Side properties and the estates formerly under his father's care.

Taking advantage of his inherited wealth and connections, Grant entered politics in a serious way in 1879, as leader of the upper West Side Kelly Campaign Club, a Tammany organization that persisted, as the Jefferson, then as the Narragansett Club, well into the 1890s. In 1881, Grant became Tammany's leader of the very large Nineteenth Assembly District. By the mid-1880s he was also a prominent member of the Friendly Sons of St. Patrick. His effective leadership, winning personality, shrewd distribution of patronage, and ability to provide opportunities for real estate and traction investments quickly made him the leader of a new group of ambitious young uptown politicians. It was largely through this group that by 1886 Tammany was drawing more votes from second-generation Irish-Americans than from immigrants.

First elected to the board of aldermen in 1882, Grant made his reputation when, as a member of the notorious "Boodle Board" of 1884, he was one of two aldermen not accused of taking a bribe and the only one to vote against the assignment of the immensely valuable lower Broadway streetcar franchise to Jacob Sharp, the bribe-giver. Several of the boodlers belonged to anti-Tammany factions or were closely associated with boss John Kelly, making Grant's action particularly valuable to a Tammany Hall struggling to overcome the Tweed Ring stigma and to Richard Croker, who was already ambitious to displace Kelly.

As Tammany's mayoral nominee in 1884, Grant ran well, though unsuccessfully, against anti-Tammany Democrat William R. Grace (*q.v.*) and Republican Frederick S. Gibbs. In 1885, he was elected sheriff in Tammany's sweep of county offices, and in 1888 he won the mayoralty with 114,111 votes to County Democrat Abram S. Hewitt's (*q.v.*) 71,979, Republican Joel B. Erhardt's 73,037, United Labor's James J. Coogan's 9,809, and Socialist Alex Jonas's 2,645. With this election, Tammany resumed its place as the dominant Democratic faction in the city. It consolidated its position two years later when Grant, despite his admission to a state investigating committee that while sheriff he had given $10,000 to Croker's baby daughter, won reelection with 116,581 votes to 93,382 for Francis M. Scott, who had Republican, Independent, and what remained of anti-Tammany Democratic support, and 4,604 votes for the Socialist August Delabar. Grant did not run in 1892, but in the wake of the Lexow Committee's revelations of police corruption, he reluctantly accepted the 1894 mayoral nomination, to be defeated by Republican-Independent William L. Strong (*q.v.*).

As mayor, Grant stressed real estate interests: low property taxes, high franchise fees, and alternatives to the tax on real property; the importance of placing overhead wires, which interfered with firefighting operations, underground; and the development of uptown districts. A Catholic himself, he increased the number of Catholics and Jews in city offices, thus rebuking nativists among Hewitt's and Scott's supporters while serving his organization's need for patronage. Both as mayor and afterwards, he frequently acted to impose discipline and restraint on the organization's least scrupulous district leaders.

Grant married an Irish-American Catholic, Julia M. Murphy, daughter of U.S. Senator Edward Murphy of Troy, New York, in 1895. Out of active politics after 1897, he devoted his time to his real estate interests, a series of lucrative receiverships, his famous trotting horses, and his family. He died of a heart attack at his New York home on 3 November 1910.

SOURCES: *Harper's Weekly*, 13 July 1889; Mark D. Hirsch, *William C. Whitney: Modern Warwick* (New York, 1948); Letters to Mayor Grant, Mayors' Papers,

New York City Municipal Archives and Records Center; Samuel T. McSeveney, *The Politics of Depression: Political Behavior in the Northeast, 1893–1896* (New York, 1972); New York *Evening Post*, "Tammany Biographies," October 1894; New York *Times*, 14 August 1893, 4 November 1894, and 4 November 1910; Martin Shefter, "The Electoral Foundations of the Political Machine: New York City, 1884–1897," in Joel Silbey et al., eds. *American Electoral History: Quantitative Studies in Popular Voting Behavior* (Princeton, N.J., 1978); Martin Shefter, "The Emergence of the Political Machine: An Alternative View," in Willis D. Hawley, et al., eds., *Theoretical Perspectives on Urban Politics* (Englewood Cliffs, N.J., 1976); Daniel Greenleaf Thompson, *Politics in a Democracy* (New York, 1893); M. R. Werner, *Tammany Hall* (New York, 1928).

David C. Hammack

GRAY, CHARLES McNEILL (1807–85), Mayor of Chicago (1853). An early city planner and industrialist, in whose factory the first McCormick reaper was made, Gray was born on 7 March 1807 in Chenango County, New York, to a family of Scottish Presbyterian immigrants. Gray had little formal education, working with his father as a carpenter's apprentice. At age twenty-five in November 1832, he married Mary Ann Haines of Pennsylvania, and two years later in 1834, the couple moved to Chicago, where their only son, Reuben, was born. In the young city, Gray worked as a carpenter and manufactured wheat cradles. He also tried his hand at the wholesale grocery business for a time. Gray soon met Cyrus McCormick, and in 1844 they became business partners. Three years later, in 1847, the first reaper factory in Chicago was built near the mouth of the North Bank of the Chicago River under the firm name of McCormick and Gray. In 1848, the restless Gray left Chicago for the Gold Rush to California and returned in 1852 with a small fortune. He promptly invested in a Chicago-Buffalo steamship line.

On 1 March 1853, Gray was elected mayor of Chicago on the Democratic ticket, defeating J. L. James, despite the fact that he had held no previous political offices. Although his term of office was lackluster, the city continued its rapid development and had increased to over 59,000, a growth of nearly 75 percent since the year before. Under Gray's direction, Union Park was first planned on eighteen acres of land donated to the city by S. S. Hayes, and with its "lake . . . rustic bridge and gliding swans" was perceived as one of the man-made wonders of the West and, perhaps more important, set the stage for Chicago's later primacy in the field of urban planning. The first substantial bridge across the river was built at Randolph Street, and in early May 1853, under

the direction of Frank Parmelee, the first regular omnibus line in Chicago and the West was begun. Gray was also interested in the development of public education, serving as a school trustee prior to his election. During his term, he continued this commitment and in November of that year, primarily through his urging, the city council created the office of the superintendent of schools.

In 1861, Gray was again a mayoral candidate, opposing Thomas B. Bryan of the People's Union party and the Republican candidate, Julian S. Rumsey (*q.v.*). The attack on Fort Sumter made a Republican vote an obligation, and the Democratic Gray was easily defeated.

Gray, then fifty-seven, began another career as assistant general freight agent for the Lake Shore and Michigan Southern Railroad. Gray and his family were able to purchase a comfortable $10,000 home located on Edina Street between VanBuren and Harrison, where they lived with Gray's younger brother George, a boat captain, and his wife Maria. The family employed one young female servant. Gray was an early friend of George M. Pullman and was associated with the Pullman Palace Car Company from 1867. Gray died on 17 October 1885 at the age of seventy-eight.

SOURCES: A. F. Andreas, *History of Chicago* (Chicago, 1884), vol. 1; Chicago *Daily Tribune*, 17 October 1885, 18 October 1885; *City of Chicago Census, 1850*; Bessie Louise Pierce, *A History of Chicago* (New York, 1940), vol. 1.

D. H. Parkerson

GREEN, SAMUEL A. (1830–1918), Mayor of Boston (1882). Civil War surgeon, local historian, and Republican mayor of Boston, Green probably possessed a wider range of nonpolitical experiences than nearly any other mayor in the city's history. Member of a Boston family dating back to 1636, he was born in Groton, Massachusetts, on 16 March 1830, one of five children of Dr. Joshua Green and Eliza Lawrence.

Green attended Lawrence Academy and graduated from Harvard in 1851 and from Harvard Medical School in 1854. He studied abroad and in 1858 was appointed surgeon to the Second Massachusetts Military Regiment, serving during the Civil War, planning one of the first war cemeteries, and for a time commanding a hospital ship.

A member of the Boston School Board from 1860 to 1862, after the war he returned to this duty between 1865 and 1872. At the same time, he was superintendent of the Boston Dispensary and, from 1868 to 1878, a trustee of the Boston Public Library. From 1871 until his election to the mayoralty in 1882 over Albert Palmer (*q.v.*), he held the post of city physician.

As mayor, Green favored allocating city funds for the improvement of the public school system. He was also a strong supporter of the continuing effort to design and build an extensive public park system for the city. However, the tax revenues collected during his administration were not sufficient to pay for park construction. Green was a prime mover in an effort to have one of the parks in the system named after Benjamin Franklin, which came to fruition when the "jewel" of the "emerald necklace" of parks designed by Frederick Law Olmsted, Franklin Park, was dedicated in 1884.

In later years, Green wrote a variety of topical histories of his birthplace, Groton. He also remained active in the Massachusetts Historical Society from 1860 until his death on 5 December 1918.

SOURCES: John Koren, *Boston, 1822–1922* (Boston, 1923); Albert P. Langtry, ed., *Metropolitan Boston: A Modern History* (New York, 1929), vol. 2; State Street Trust Company, *Mayors of Boston* (Boston, 1914).

Donald M. Jacobs

GREEN, WILLIAM JOSEPH (1938–   ), Mayor of Philadelphia (1979–   ). Born on 24 June 1938 to William Joseph Green, Jr., an insurance broker, and Mary Elizabeth Kelly, in the Kensington section of Philadelphia, Green's first ambition was the priesthood, but his interests seem to have been deflected when his father was elected to Congress in 1944 (and, with one exception, reelected until his death in 1963). William attended St. Joseph's College (B.S., 1960) where he was voted the "best campus politician." He matriculated at Villanova Law School but before graduating entered Congress as a Democrat in a special election held in 1964 to fill a vacancy caused by his father's death. He served twelve years in Congress and completed his law degree through night courses. Described as "brash, combative and handsome," Green, a Roman Catholic, married Patricia Anne Kirk on 13 June 1964 and is the father of three children.

An unsuccessful candidate in the Democratic mayoral primary against Frank Rizzo (*q.v.*) in 1971, Green finished his last term in Congress in 1976 and ran as a Democrat for the U.S. Senate and lost. Then, at the age of thirty-eight, Green was unemployed, and, since he had not taken his bar examination, not very employable. Green took a "cram course," passed the bar exam, and joined a Philadelphia law firm, which by 1978 was paying him an income far beyond that generally earned by second-year lawyers. He entered the race for mayor as a Democrat in 1979, winning with 313,345 votes to Republican David W. Marston's 174,083 and Consumer party Lucien E. Blackwell's 108,447.

SOURCES: *Biographical Directory of the American Congress, 1774–1971* (Washington, D.C., 1971); New York *Times* Biographical Service, 10 (November 1979).

Melvin G. Holli

GRIBBS, ROMAN S. (1925–   ), Mayor of Detroit (1970-74). First Polish Catholic mayor of Detroit born on 29 December 1925 in Detroit, Michigan, Gribbs was the son of Roman Grzyb (1890-1967), an automobile factory worker, and Magdalena (Widziszewski) Grzyb (1894–1976) a farmworker. The elder Roman and Magdalena emigrated separately from Poland, married in Detroit, and had four sons, only two of whom survived infancy; Roman Stanley was the elder. After living for a while in Detroit, the Grzyb family purchased a 100-acre farm near rural Capac, Michigan, where Roman attended public schools and worked on the farm. In his early adulthood, Roman anglicized the spelling of his name from Grzyb to Gribbs. During World War II, Gribbs served two years in the Army and was discharged as a sergeant. He entered the University of Detroit in 1948, earning a B.S. degree in 1952. While a student in the University of Detroit Law School, Gribbs worked as a store salesman and also taught accounting and law to undergraduates in 1952. He received an LL.B. in 1954, graduating third in his law school class.

In 1952, Gribbs married Detroit-born Katherine Stratis (1933–   ), a former college student of Greek descent, working as an airline hostess. They had five children: Paula, Carla, Christopher, Rebecca, and Elizabeth.

From 1956 to 1964, Gribbs worked as an assistant Wayne County prosecuting attorney. He practiced law privately, 1964–66, until he was appointed to serve as a presiding referee in Detroit's traffic court, 1966–68. He was twice an unsuccessful candidate for judge of Detroit's recorder's court. On 1 June 1968, he was appointed Wayne County sheriff, serving the seven months remaining of his predecessor's unexpired term. He was elected, as a Democrat, for a full term as Wayne County sheriff in November 1968 and served until December 1969, making several significant reforms in the administration of the sheriff's office.

Detroit in 1970 had 1,511,482 people, a strong mayor-council form of government, and nonpartisan elections. Because blacks accounted for more than 40 percent of Detroit's population by 1969, newspapers and white civic leaders were seeking a respectable white moderate to run for the Detroit mayoralty as a viable alternative to the well-qualified black who had already announced his candidacy. Gribbs agreed to seek the mayor's post and filed as a Democrat only twenty-four hours before the deadline.

Gribbs stressed "crime in the streets" as the number 1 issue and proposed strong but reasonable methods to achieve "order and justice under law." In November

1969, he narrowly defeated Richard H. Austin (258,010 to 251,816), a black man who was elected secretary of state in Michigan in 1970.

As mayor, Gribbs eliminated a $20 million deficit, cut jobs, trimmed services, and achieved a budget surplus. Neighborhood city halls were established, crime was reduced, and a billion dollars of new construction was started, including the outstanding riverfront complex containing office buildings, retail stores, and a major hotel known as the "Renaissance Center." Gribbs also helped develop federal revenue-sharing for cities and started riverfront ethnic festivals. Gribbs was president of the National League of Cities in 1973 and also served as president of the Michigan Conference of Mayors and trustee of the U.S. Conference of Mayors. Gribbs declined to run for reelection in 1973, becoming a partner in a law firm in 1974. He was also appointed a director of the Bank of the Commonwealth and a trustee of the University of Detroit in 1974. Gribbs was elected judge of the Wayne County Circuit Court in 1975. He was nominated and defeated as a Democratic candidate for the Michigan Supreme Court in 1976.

SOURCES: Detroit Archives, Mayor's Papers, Roman S. Gribbs, Burton Historical Collection, Detroit Public Library; Marvin Diamond and William T. Noble, "The Making of the Mayor," *Detroit News Magazine*, 4 January 1970; Roman S. Gribbs, biography file and miscellaneous material, Burton Historical Collection, Detroit Public Library; L. H. Whittemore, *Together: A Reporter's Journey into the New Black Politics* (New York, 1971).

De Witt S. Dykes, Jr.

GRIFFIN, JAMES D. (1929–   ), Mayor of Buffalo (1978–   ). Born in Buffalo on 29 June 1929, Griffin was the son of Thomas J. Griffin (1904–   ), salesman for a tool and die company, and Helen Margaret (O'Brien) Griffin (1907–72), both Buffalo-born Irish-American Catholics. Thomas Griffin's parents were born in Ireland. The second of four children, Griffin attended St. Brigid's Elementary School and South Park High School until he was sixteen, when he started working in a grain elevator. After a short period, he completed his secondary education at Our Lady of Victory High School. Griffin worked at a feed mill until the Korean War when he volunteered for the U.S. Army, serving from February 1951 to November 1953 and rising from private to lieutenant. He attended Erie County Technical Institute, graduating in 1958. Griffin worked as a railroad engineer and unsuccessfully ran for the city council in 1959. He subsequently served in that body 1961–65, followed by six terms in the state Senate (1961–77). On 4 May 1968, Griffin married Margaret McMahon of Buffalo, a fellow

ethnic, and they had three children. Griffin is a member of the St. Brigid Holy Name Society and the Knights of Columbus.

In 1977, Griffin sought the Democratic nomination for mayor but was defeated by Arthur D. Eve. Griffin then won the backing of the Conservative party and was elected, with 57,642 votes to 43,240 for Eve (Democrat), 34,171 for John J. Phelan (Republican), 1,856 for Donald L. Turchiarelli (Liberal), 260 for Khushra Ghandhi (Labor), and 167 for Reverend Bob Lily (Sunshine party). Buffalo had a declining population of 462,768 in 1970 and a mayor-council form of government.

Griffin had been aware of Buffalo's financial problems while a member of the city council and had supported measures to increase state aid to New York's cities while in the legislature. As mayor, he supported a reduction in the city budget, including a decrease in the level of spending for city schools. He also pushed efforts to rebuild the downtown region and to make the city streets safer. Griffin helped secure a minor league baseball franchise for Buffalo. Critics have charged that his political independence has led him to be inconsistent in his policies.

SOURCES: Buffalo *Courier-Express*, 31 December 1977; Buffalo *Evening News*, 12 November 1977; Data provided by Mayor's Office, Buffalo; Interviews of 8 August 1979 (with Griffin's brother, Parks Commissioner Thomas Griffin), and 9 August 1979 (with Mrs. Griffin); *Who's Who in American Politics* (New York, 1977).

Thomas R. Bullard

GRUMMOND, STEPHEN B. (1834–94), Mayor of Detroit (1884–85). Republican mayor of Detroit and Great Lakes shipping owner, Grummond was born near Marine City, Michigan, on 18 September 1834. He was the son of Stephen Benedict (d. 1856), and Mary (Harrow) Grummond, who migrated from New York State to Michigan, where they operated a farm and general store on the St. Clair River. In 1861, Stephen married Louisa B. Prouty, daughter of Colonel Nathaniel Prouty, a prominent pre-Civil War tavern-owner in Detroit. From that city, Grummond became a sailor on the Great Lakes and over the years built up for himself a fleet of tugboats and wrecking outfits that were reputed to be the largest and best on the lakes. Known as "Captain" Grummond, he also owned and operated sailing vessels and steamers, maintaining extensive warehouses and docks on the Detroit waterfront. In 1881, he was elected to the upper house of the common council.

Detroit in 1880 had 116,340 people and a mayor-council form of government. Grummond, highly regarded by the business community, won in November 1883 as the Republican candidate for mayor over the Democrat,

Marvin H. Chamberlain (q.v.), a prominent liquor dealer: Grummond 9,770, Chamberlain 9,304. The earliest post-Civil War reform group, known as the Civic Federation of Detroit, threw its support behind Grummond, who was the dry candidate, but reform with dry overtones was not to prove popular in wet Detroit. The Democratic press generally respected Mayor Grummond while excoriating alleged Republican corruption among the councilmen. The *Free Press*, however, accused the mayor of pushing the Eagen Bill, which was designed to disfranchise foreign-born voters (mostly Democrats). The unsuccessful bill had the full support of the Michigan Club, the insiders who ran the party, as well as Grummond's enthusiastic backing. In November 1885, Grummond reluctantly agreed to run for reelection. Once more Marvin H. Chamberlain, president of the council, was his Democratic opponent. In a short caucus of only a week, Chamberlain and the Democrats reversed the 1883 results. This time, it was 11,992 for Chamberlain and 10,104 for Grummond and the Republicans, with 129 votes for Carleton H. Mills and the Prohibition party.

Grummond, returned to private life, told reporters he was pleased not to have to run back and forth between Detroit and Mackinac, his shipping headquarters. He purchased a Detroit hotel, which he renamed ''The Benedict,'' operating it a few years after his term as mayor. He died on 2 January 1894 and was buried in Detroit. His reputation as mayor was largely that of a conservative chief executive who escaped censure despite well-publicized corruption in Detroit's city government.

SOURCES: Silas Farmer, *The History of Detroit and Wayne County and Early Michigan* (Detroit, 1890), vol. 2; Phoenix Publishing Company, *Detroit of Today: The City of the Strait* (Detroit, 1893); Robert B. Ross and George B. Catlin, *Landmarks of Detroit: A History of the City* (Detroit, 1898).   *Donald W. Disbrow*

GUILLOTTE, J. VALSIN (1850–1917), Mayor of New Orleans (1884–88). Democratic ''Ring'' mayor and lifetime professional politician, Guillotte was born on 29 June 1850 in Jefferson Parish (County) Louisiana to parents of Creole and Franco-Germany ancestry who were Roman Catholics. When Guillotte was five, his family moved to New Orleans' Ninth Ward, a perennial incubator of prominent New Orleans and Louisiana politicians.

Early in his career, Guillotte acquired the skills of expert penmanship required to become a clerk, a profession much more highly esteemed in the pre-typewriter and computer era than it is today. After performing as a ''White League'' company commander in the ''battle of Liberty Place'' (a riot against carpetbag rule) on 14 September 1874, Guillotte was rewarded with two successive court clerkships. He next served as administrator

of police and public buildings in the first administration of Mayor Joseph Shakspeare (q.v.) (1880–82), and followed that with two years as city comptroller under Mayor William J. Behan (q.v.) (1882–84). Irritated by Behan's independence and integrity, Democratic ''Ring'' leaders in 1884 gave their support instead to Guillotte, a more reliable, if personally honest, politician. Behan sought reelection anyway as an Independent but received only 6,512 votes to Guillotte's 18,278, many of which were bogus.

Although he was a man of experience and ability, Guillotte let his administration become an impressive disaster by always catering to the patronage wishes of his ''Ring'' mentors and by failing to demonstrate any leadership. To increase the number of patrolmen in crime-infested New Orleans, Guillotte appointed a number of ''special'' policemen, most of them drunken and rowdy minions of the ''Ring.'' They rarely wore their uniforms and spent their time brawling. The result of their employment was an increase rather than a decrease in crime. Many people were murdered in New Orleans while Guillotte was mayor. Among the victims were two city officials who were gunned down in personal vendettas.

City government became slack on other levels as well: paving, drainage, and garbage collection deteriorated while municipal deficits grew larger; meetings of the council (when a rare quorum was present) were boisterous and indecisive; and an extensively promoted cotton centennial exposition held in New Orleans from 1884 to 1886 was a financial fiasco. After four years of these and other calamities, even Guillotte was disgusted. He declined to seek a second term and was succeeded by a reform administration under the able former mayor, Joseph Shakspeare.

For the remainder of his life, Guillotte sporadically practiced law but essentially remained in politics. After several years in the state Senate, he was appointed a federal marshal. When he died on 24 July 1917, Guillotte was still on the public payroll as assistant secretary of the New Orleans Police Department. Guillotte's wife predeceased him by six months; they were survived by seven children.

SOURCES: Joy J. Jackson, *New Orleans in the Gilded Age: Politics and Urban Progress, 1880–1896* (Baton Rouge, La., 1969); John S. Kendall, *History of New Orleans* (Chicago, 1922), vol. 1; Works Progress Administration typescripts, ''Administrations of the Mayors of New Orleans, 1803–1936,'' and ''Biographies of the Mayors of New Orleans, 1803–1936'' (New Orleans, 1940).   *Mark T. Carleton*

GUNTHER, CHARLES GODFREY (1822–85), Mayor of New York (1864–66). Gunther, a Civil War mayor, was born in New York on 7 February 1822; his parents were immigrants from Germany, who had arrived in 1820. His father, Christian G. Gunther, prospered as the proprietor of the largest fur business in the country. His first-born son, Charles, attended the Moravian Institute in Nazareth, Pennsylvania, and then Columbia College Grammar School. In youth, he joined Eagle Hose Company No. 1 and was an active efficient fireman.

In 1844, the future mayor voted for Polk and Dallas on the Democratic ticket and became known as one of the hardest workers in the party. After a brief trip to Europe, possibly on a honeymoon (he later had four children), Gunther returned to politics to push the election of Franklin Pierce. In 1854, Gunther received the nomination of Tammany to the board of governors of the New York Almshouse and was elected by a 5,000 vote majority. In 1857, he was named president of the board. His popularity was not unnoticed. In 1856, he was elected a sachem of Tammany Hall, and in 1861 he ran for the mayoralty but was defeated by Republican George Opdyke (q.v.): Gunther, 24,746; Opdyke, 25,380; Fernando Wood (q.v.) 24,167. In the fall of 1863, he ran as a non-Tammany Peace or Copperhead Democrat and in another three-cornered campaign was handily elected. Gunther had a vote of 28,938, out of 70,770 votes cast, 4,000 more than his nearest rival.

The city's population was 815,254 in 1860, and it had a complex mayor-council form of government, with weak executive power. Gunther's reputation was a consideration, but the usual fratricidal wars among the Democrats were a major contribution to victory. As mayor, he sought to remove slaughterhouses from the city. He refused a Washington's Birthday celebration as a "reckless extravagance." He emphasized a frugal administration, relieving congestion in city traffic and expanding the executive power of the mayor, especially in the right to dismiss heads of departments. Toward the end of his second term, Gunther and other city officials were accused of improper handling of street-cleaning contracts. The affair did not go beyond the press, and Gunther was cleared. After retirement, Gunther promoted "Gunther's Road," a railroad to Coney Island from Brooklyn, and a large hotel at Locust Grove, Gravesend, Long Island. In 1868, he was named president of the German Hospital—evidence of his sense of community involvement, as well as the regard of his German constituency. In 1878, he attempted to return to politics but was defeated in a bid for state senator. He died at his residence in New York City on 22 January 1885, and he was interred at Greenwood Cemetery, Brooklyn.

SOURCES: Walter Barrett. *Old Merchants of New York City*, 5 vols. (New York, 1885); Augustine E. Costello. *Our Firemen. A History of the New York Fire Department* (New York, 1887); Allan Nevins and Milton H. Thomas eds., *The Diary of George Templeton Strong, 1835–1872* 4 vols. (New York, 1952); David T. Valentine. *Manual of the Corporation of the City of New York* (Albany, 1860–70); James G. Wilson. *The Memorial History of the City of New York*, 4 vols. (New York, 1893).

Leo Hershkowitz

GURNEE, WALTER S. (1813–1903), Mayor of Chicago (1851–52). Gurnee, founder of the village of Winnetka, and Democratic mayor of neighboring Chicago, was born on 9 March 1813 in Haverstraw, New York. His father, J. S. Gurnee, was among the first Haverstraw settlers and owned one of the principal stores, making a fortune in the tanning and saddlery business. J. S. died when Walter was eight, and the young boy was sent to live with his uncle, Judge John D. Coe, in Romulus, New York.

When Gurnee reached maturity, he went west and opened a saddlery business in Detroit in 1835 at the age of twenty-two. Sensing greater opportunities in Chicago, Gurnee moved the following year and opened a saddlery and tanning shop which later became one of the largest and most successful in the Midwest, known as the Chicago Hide and Leather Company (1843). Gurnee also invested in real estate and founded the suburban village of Winnetka. Gurnee's fortunes rose quickly, and soon he purchased a beautiful home near the corner of Michigan Avenue and Monroe Street where he lived with his wife and four children. In 1840, 1843, and 1844 he was elected city treasurer.

When Gurnee ran for mayor of Chicago as a Democrat on 4 March 1851, the population of the city had grown to 34,000. That year there were three leading campaign issues: temperance (which he did not favor); the question of a city-owned water company (which he favored); and a proposed land grant to the Illinois Central Railroad (which he did not favor). Gurnee was opposed by the incumbent mayor, James Curtiss (q.v.) (also a Democrat) and by Eli B. Williams and John Rogers. Gurnee violently opposed the railroad land-grant issue because his home was on Michigan Avenue, and he was afraid that the railroad's presence would decrease property values. John Wentworth (q.v.), another prominent Chicagoan and later Gurnee's arch-critic and political rival, fought hard for the railroad, claiming it would create new jobs and benefit the city as a whole. Later, Wentworth was partly discredited when it was discovered that he was a prominent stockholder in the Illinois Central.

Gurnee was reelected on 2 March 1852 over former mayor Curtiss, Peter Page, and the perennial temperance candidate, Amos G. Throop. During both terms he concentrated on city finances. By issuing bonds at a lower rate of interest and for longer periods of maturity, he was able to relieve the financial pressures on the young city and in so doing further solidified the executive powers of the mayor. Eight years later, when Gurnee was again nominated by the Democrats as their mayoral candidate in 1860, his Republican opponent John Wentworth accused him of having mishandled municipal funds. The entire campaign was clouded by accusations, and Gurnee was dubbed "Count Gurnee" by his opponents. Although Gurnee was supported by both the Isaac Cook machine and the powerful Stephen A. Douglas forces, the rising political fortunes of the Republican party were enough to push Wentworth into office, 9,998 to 8,739 for Gurnee.

Gurnee held no subsequent public offices, but remained a Chicago booster, investing in real estate in the region. Shortly after his second term, he became president of the Chicago and Milwaukee Railroad and a trustee of Bell's Commercial College in Chicago. Gurnee was also one of the first directors of the board of trade and one of the charter members of the Young Men's Association which established the city's first (subscription) library. In 1865, Gurnee returned to his native New York, where he died at the age of ninety on 18 April 1903.

SOURCES: A. F. Andreas, *History of Cook County* (Chicago, 1884), vol. 1; Chicago *Daily Tribune*, 18 and 19 April 1903; Frank B. Green, *History of Rockland County* (New York, 1886); Bessie Louise Pierce, *A History of Chicago* (New York, 1940), vol. 2; Frederick Rex, comp., *The Mayors of the City of Chicago* (Chicago, 1947).   *D. H. Parkerson*

GUTHRIE, GEORGE WILKINS (1848–1917), Mayor of Pittsburgh (1906–1909). Guthrie was born into an upper class Pittsburgh family on 5 September 1848. Both his father, John Brandon Guthrie (*q.v.*), and his grandfather, Magnus M. Murray (*q.v.*), had been mayors of Pittsburgh. Through much of his life, his father held various positions in the federal government, including that of customs collector for the port of Pittsburgh; he dealt in oil and owned a barrel factory. Guthrie's mother was Catherine Stevenson Murray (1814–91); the family was Episcopalian.

Guthrie graduated from Western University of Pennsylvania (now the University of Pittsburgh) in 1866. Following a brief period in business, he studied law in Washington, D.C., graduating in 1869. That same year he was admitted to the Pennsylvania bar.

In the early 1880s, Guthrie became interested in politics when he associated himself with the municipal reform group of Reverend George Hodges of Calvary Episcopal Church. In 1884, he was the secretary of the Democratic national convention. Reacting to the corruption in city government, Guthrie was active in organizing the Citizens League for Reform in 1895. The following

year he was the league's candidate for mayor, but he lost, possibly through fraud, for in some wards the number of votes cast exceeded the number registered. That same year Guthrie joined the Civil Service Reform Association and worked not only for civil service reform but also for ballot reform and uniform primary laws.

In 1906, a new direct primary law went into effect, and Guthrie ran for mayor as a Democrat, although he also had the endorsement of the Independent City party as well as other reform groups. He defeated the Republican candidate, A. M. Jenkinson, by almost 3,000 votes. However, the Republican organization maintained control of the city councils; consequently, most efforts at reform were effectively blocked.

Under Mayor Guthrie, the city purchased the Monongahela Water Company and by 1914 was able to provide pure water for the South Side. Pittsburgh also adopted a reformed civil service. After many court delays, the city of Allegheny was finally annexed on 7 December 1907. The municipalities of Montooth, Sheraden, West Liberty, Beechview, and parts of Union and Scott were also added during Guthrie's term. Many of the annexations had occurred with the provision that the municipality enter as a separate ward, but by 1908 so many had entered that the city had forty-four wards. In 1908, the wards were completely redistricted, and the number was reduced to twenty-seven. The practice of admitting a municipality as a separate ward did not stop, however.

After his term expired, Guthrie's interests shifted to the national level. As early as 1911, he had planned to have the reform governor of New Jersey, Woodrow Wilson, nominated for president in 1912. As head of the Pennsylvania delegation, Guthrie kept the delegates solid for Wilson and, after his nomination, conducted the campaign in the state. In 1913, President Wilson appointed him American ambassador to Japan. On 8 March 1917, Guthrie died suddenly of a stroke. His body was returned home to Pittsburgh where he was hailed with speeches and newspaper editorials.

Guthrie was survived by his wife, Florence Howe Guthrie (1849–1929), of an equally prominent Pittsburgh family, whom he married in 1886. They had no children. Guthrie was a member of Calvary Episcopal Church, and was also a Mason. He was buried in Allegheny Cemetery, Pittsburgh.

SOURCES: Frank M. Eastman, *Courts and Lawyers of Pennsylvania* (New York, 1922); vol. 4; John W. Jordan, *Encyclopedia of Pennsylvania Biography* (New York, 1914), vol. 2; Frank W. Powelson, *Founding Families of Allegheny County* (Pittsburgh, unpublished manuscript, 1963), vol. 2.

Joseph F. Rishel

GUTHRIE, JOHN BRANDON (1807–85), Mayor of Pittsburgh (1851–52). Guthrie was born on 28 July 1807, in Kittanning, Armstrong County, Pennsylvania. One of many Scots-Irish Presbyterian mayors of Pittsburgh, he was the son of James V. Guthrie (?–1827), a boat-builder born in Carlisle, Pennsylvania, and Martha Brandon, daughter of John Brandon, a captain in the Revolutionary War and later sheriff of Westmoreland County, Pennsylvania. On 8 December 1834, John B. Guthrie married Catherine Stevenson Murray, a descendant of Scottish immigrants who first came to America in 1715 and a daughter of Magnus M. Murray (q.v.), a lawyer, progressive businessman, and mayor of Pittsburgh (1828–30, 1831–32). The Guthries had eight children, five of whom lived to adulthood. One son, George W. (q.v.) (1848–1917) later served as reform mayor of Pittsburgh (1906–1909). During the Mexican-American War, John B. Guthrie served as an officer in the Duquesne Greys, a volunteer company from the Pittsburgh area.

A life-long Democrat, Guthrie held several public offices which made him a prominent member of his party and an influential resident of Pittsburgh. He served as commissioner of emigration of the Indians from the South under President Andrew Jackson. In 1845, President James K. Polk appointed Guthrie collector of customs at the port of Pittsburgh. Later, he accompanied mails to and from California as a special agent for the U.S. government—a post he acquired in 1847. Guthrie also held the position of pensions agent for the Western District of Pennsylvania.

Located in Allegheny County, Pittsburgh in 1850 had a population of 46,601 and was operated by a mayor-council form of government. Exercising both executive and legislative powers, the councils (select and common) held most municipal authority. The mayor was primarily a police chief and magistrate. Guthrie was a steamboat captain and surveyor of customs for Pittsburgh when the Democratic party sponsored him as an independent Citizens' candidate for mayor. He barely lost the election in January 1850, with 1,584 votes to 1,787 for Joseph Barker (q.v.) (People's and Anti-Catholic candidate), and 1,034 for Robert McCutcheon (Whig and Anti-Mason). In December 1850, Guthrie received the Democratic nomination and easily won the election of 11 January 1851 with 1,911 votes, defeating John J. Roggen (Whig) with 1,206 votes, and incumbent Mayor Barker with 924 votes. Guthrie was reelected on 13 January 1852 by a vote of 1,429 to 1,382 for B. C. Sawyer (Whig and Anti-Mason) and 785 for Joseph Barker (Independent). In January 1853, Guthrie lost his bid for a third one-year term, receiving 1,568 votes to 1,887 for winner Robert M. Riddle (q.v.) (Whig) and 251 for J. Heron Foster (Free-Soil).

As mayor, Guthrie restored order to a municipal administration previously disrupted by labor riots and the stormy term of Mayor Barker. Guthrie expanded the police force by an additional nineteen watchmen and five city constables. He strengthened the mayor's police powers by restoring old ordinances and by weakening the authority of the police committee of the councils. With augmented authority, Guthrie vigorously suppressed disorder—crime, ethnic and religious conflict, and labor unrest—with over 500 persons sentenced to jail in one year alone.

Guthrie's election victories symbolized a break in the traditional Whig party domination of Pittsburgh and the mayor's office. The Democratic triumphs primarily resulted from the third-party candidacy of Joseph Barker, who, with his anti-Catholic, anti-immigrant, and anti-business rhetoric, fused nativist and reform sentiments and thereby drew the votes of working-class Protestants who usually voted Whig. In January 1853, with Barker no longer a candidate and Guthrie accused of enriching himself through the collection of fines, the Whigs regained the mayor's office. Guthrie received another blow when he lost his party's nomination for mayor in December 1853.

Knocked out of municipal government, Guthrie moved into national public office. President Franklin Pierce appointed him special agent of the Treasury Department in 1854. In this capacity, he also served as U.S. collector of customs until he resigned in 1861. At the request of President Abraham Lincoln four years later, he returned to his Treasury post; he served under President Andrew Johnson.

In 1869, Guthrie retired and returned to Pittsburgh. Still a prominent member of his party, he served as a delegate to the Pennsylvania Constitutional Convention of 1872–73. A Presbyterian and a member of the Duquesne Club, he died quietly on 17 August 1885 at Cresson, Pennsylvania.

SOURCES: Christine Altenburger, "The Pittsburgh Bureau of Police: Some Historical Highlights," *Western Pennsylvania Historical Magazine* 49 (January 1966); Michael Fitzgibbon Holt, *Forging a Majority: The Formation of the Republican Party in Pittsburgh, 1848–1860* (New Haven, Conn., 1969); Allen Humphreys Kerr, "The Mayors and Recorders of Pittsburgh, 1816–1951" (unpublished manuscript, Historical Society of Western Pennsylvania, Pittsburgh, 1962); Pittsburgh *Gazette*, 18 August 1885; Pittsburgh *Post*, 18 August 1885; Erasmus Wilson, ed., *Standard History of Pittsburgh* (Chicago, 1898).

Matthew S. Magda

H

HAINES, JOHN C. (1818–96), Mayor of Chicago (1858–60). Second Republican mayor of Chicago, Haines was born on 26 May 1818 near Deerfield, New York. After rudimentary schooling in rural New York, he moved to Chicago in 1835 where he worked as a miller. In 1848, Haines and Jared Gage bought the Chicago Flour Mills which they quickly turned into a profitable business. Haines married a woman from Watertown, New York, and they had four children. From 1848 to 1854, Haines served on the Chicago City Council as alderman from the Fifth Ward and, from 1853 to 1858, was one of three members of the City Water Commission. In keeping with his growing reputation as a leading man of the city, Haines was elected a member of the Chicago Historical Society in 1857.

Chicago, a thriving community of 90,000 in 1858, was just recovering from the tempestuous mayoralty of "Long John" Wentworth (*q.v.*). When Wentworth declined to run for reelection, his handpicked successor was Haines, who subsequently defeated his Democratic opponent, Daniel Brainard, 8,642 votes to 7,481. Haines was reelected in 1859, defeating Marcus G. Gilman by a vote of 8,587 to 7,728.

As mayor, Haines organized Chicago's first salaried fire department. In 1859, the first horse-drawn streetcars appeared on State Street, and Haines presided over the construction of the city's principal street railway lines. It was over the traction issue that the major controversy of Haines' administration revolved, for he vetoed a street railway ordinance which gave traction companies a perpetual franchise if the city failed to buy the lines after twenty-five years. Like Wentworth before him, Haines refused to replace the short-term city debt with long-term bonds; the result was a floating debt of over $230,000 in 1859. When he declined to run for reelection in 1860, his successor, previous friend, and mentor, John Wentworth, blamed Haines' administration for the city's financial difficulties.

After two terms in city hall, Haines temporarily abandoned politics for the life of banker and businessman. In 1861, he became the first president of the State Savings Institution of Chicago and in 1863 a member of the syndicate which bought controlling interest in the Chicago West Division Railroad. In 1869, he was chosen a member of the Illinois State Constitutional Convention, and in 1874 he was elected to the state Senate. In the 1877 session, Haines received sixty-nine votes for a seat in the U.S. Senate but lost to Judge David Davis. In 1879, Haines retired to his farm near Waukegan, Illinois, where he died of peritonitis on 4 July 1896. He was a Universalist.

SOURCES: Chicago City Manual: 1911; Chicago *Tribune*, 5 July 1896; Bessie Louise Pierce, *A History of Chicago* (New York, 1940), vol. 2; Frederick Rex, comp., *The Mayors of the City of Chicago* (Chicago, 1947). *W. Roger Biles*

HALL, ABRAHAM OAKEY (1826–1898), Mayor of New York (1868–72). "Boss Tweed's mayor" was born on 26 July 1826 in Albany, New York, the son of Morgan James Hall, an English immigrant who settled in New York City. His mother was Elsie Lansing Oakey, a daughter of Abraham Oakey, a deputy treasurer of the state. At the death of her husband in 1830, widow Hall took her two children, one a younger daughter, Marcia, to New York City. Abraham Hall entered New York University, wrote essays in the local press, and graduated in 1844. After one year at Harvard Law School, followed by private study in New Orleans, he was admitted to the bar in Louisiana in 1846. Returning to New York in 1848, he opened a law partnership with Aaron J. Vanderpool and prospered. On 14 February 1850, Hall married Katherine Louise Barnes, daughter of Joseph Nye Barnes, owner of several Vermont marble quarries; the couple had seven children. The family was Episcopalian.

First appointed assistant district attorney in 1849, Hall won the election for district attorney in 1852, an office he held until 1860. During the Civil War, Hall, a Republican, became disgruntled with the failure of his party to insure civil liberties and switched to the Democrats. He joined the Tammany machine in 1864. In 1868, he was elected mayor, defeating Colonel F. A. Conkling, with 75,054 out of 96,054 votes cast. The city had almost one million people and a weak mayor-council form of government. With Hall as mayor, William Tweed as state senator, John Thompson Hoffman as governor, and Peter Barr Sweeney as president of the Parks Department, a "Tweed Ring" was formed and was in the process of robbing the city and state treasury of millions of dollars. Under a reform charter granted to the city in 1870, Hall, Tweed, and Sweeney, corrupt anti-reformers, became part of a board of audit meant to check all city expenditures; this, together with rising taxes and a mounting public debt, loosed a storm of protest stirred by Republican opponents, such as the New York *Times*. Hall always maintained his innocence but the disclosures led to indictments and a trial (February 1872). Hall's chief defense was that his auditing of warrants was merely ministerial. A declaration of a mistrial led to a second trial in October 1892 at which Hall was found innocent.

Hall, who had written children's books and short plays, tried the theater and spent a number of years in London persuading Lord Bryce to modify the Tweed chapter in his exposé of urban politics in his *American Commonwealth*. Hall's first wife died on 9 March 1897, and the ex-mayor married Mrs. John Clifton. The couple was baptized into the Roman Catholic Church in March 1898. A few months later, on 7 October 1898, Hall was dead of heart failure. He was buried in the family vault at Trinity Cemetery in New York City.

SOURCES: Croswell Bowen, *The Elegant Oakey* (New York, 1956); *Evidence Before the Grand Jury in the Case of A. Oakey Hall* (New York, 1871), a pamphlet; Leo Hershkowitz, *Tweeds' New York, Another Look* (New York, 1978); Allan Nevins and Milton H. Thomas *The Diary of George Templeton Strong, 1835–1875*, 4 vols. (New York, 1952); David T. Valentine, *Manual of the Corporation of the City of New York* (New York, 1960–70).   *Leo Hershkowitz*

HARMON, JOHN H. (1819–88), Mayor of Detroit (1852–54).

Mayor of Detroit and Democratic politician, Harmon was born on 21 June 1819 in Portage County, Ohio. His father, John Harmon, had moved from Connecticut to Ohio in 1800 and ran a newspaper at Ravenna. John H. Harmon had at least one sister and two half-brothers, Seth Harmon and W. E. Harmon. John H. learned the printing trade from his father and while a teenager founded the *Cuyahoga Journal* at Ohio City (later West Cleveland). Harmon sold his paper and arrived in Detroit in about 1838 where he found employment with the Detroit *Free Press*. Within a few years, he rose from printer to part-owner. Harmon also became active in Democratic politics in the city and was elected to the city council from the Second Ward in 1847. Harmon, a Presbyterian, married Sarah S. Rood in 1841 and had three children.

In 1852, Detroit (in Wayne County, Michigan) had 26,648 people and a mayor-council form of government. Mayors were elected annually by popular vote and served without pay, presiding over a city council of sixteen members (two from each of eight wards). In the election of 1 March 1852, Harmon won in every ward and defeated his Whig opponent, John Owen, 2,564 to 2,007. The Democrats won all city-wide offices and swept most of the ward positions. At first, the main issues Harmon dealt with—paving streets and sidewalks and constructing sewers—were similar to those his predecessors had faced. In the final months of Harmon's first term, however, divisive ethnic conflicts became obvious. The legislature endorsed a state-wide ban on the manufacture and sale of liquor (February 1853), which stirred tensions between prohibitionists and their adversaries in Detroit. Catholic-Protestant antagonism intensified when the city council proposed a city waterworks, a public almshouse, and street-paving projects. Catholic officials fought them, since they meant taxation of church property and the creation of a rival welfare agency (January 1853). The Catholic hierarchy also launched a campaign for public funds for parochial education and demanded an end to the exclusion of Catholic teachers from the public schools. These controversies divided the Democrats between regulars and independents. The independents, unhappy with Catholic political activism, allied with the Whigs in the city election of 7 March 1853. Both regulars and independents chose Harmon for reelection, and he ran unopposed, receiving 4,659 votes. In the contests for lesser offices, the independents succeeded, reversing earlier Democratic majorities.

Although he did not stand for a third term as mayor, Harmon remained active in politics. From 1853 to 1857, he was collector of the port of Detroit, a federal patronage job. Thereafter, he lived in Washington, D.C., taking part in national Democratic party business. He served on the Democratic National Committee and attended national party nominating conventions. He died on 6 August 1888 while staying at a Detroit hotel, possibly from the effects of pneumonia. Harmon was buried in Elmwood Cemetery, Detroit.

SOURCES: Detroit *Free Press*, 7 August 1888; *The Evening News* (Detroit), 7 August 1888; Silas Farmer, *History of Detroit and Wayne County and Early Michigan* (Detroit, 1890); Ronald P. Formisano, *The Birth of Mass Political Parties: Michigan, 1827–1861* (Princeton, N.J., 1971).   *Michael W. Homel*

HARPER, ARTHUR C. (1866–1948), Mayor of Los Angeles (1906–1909).

Born on 13 March 1866 in Columbus, Mississippi, Harper was the son of Charles F. Harper (1832–1915), a veteran of the Confederate Army and hardware merchant, and Martha W. (Mullen) Harper (1838–1922) of Southern lineage. The Harper family moved to San Francisco in 1867 and the following year came to Los Angeles. Arthur C. Harper attended Los

Angeles public schools and graduated from the University of Southern California in 1885. He managed the sales Department of his father's large hardware firm for a number of years. He left the hardware business to become cashier of the State Bank and Trust Company and later organized a packing firm. Harper married Minnie Hamilton (1867–1938) in 1887, and they had five children, three sons and two daughters. Harper was an active member of the local Democratic Club, a Mason, and a member of the socially prominent Jonathan Club. He was a Christian Scientist.

Los Angeles in 1906 had 214,500 people. The city's Democratic party nominated Harper for the mayoralty. Running against him were Dr. Walter F. Lindley, candidate of the Republican organization, Lee C. Gates, nominee of the Non-Partisan Committee of 100, and Stanley B. Wilson, candidate of the Public Ownership party. Harper won the election with 10,604 votes to Gates' 8,465. Lindley trailed Gates by 1,539, and Wilson was fourth with 3,877 votes.

The population of Los Angeles reached 280,000 in 1908. Harper's administration came under fire from a deputy district attorney, Thomas L. Woolwine, who uncovered evidence of graft that appeared to involve the mayor and prominent local businessmen. Several Los Angeles newspapers later revealed that Harper and his business associates, along with top police officials, were selling worthless stock to illegal bars and brothels in return for protection from police raids and prosecution. Harper appointed Police Chief Edward Kern, who had refused to close prostitution houses, to the city's board of public works. The board was responsible for building the $23 million Owens Valley aqueduct. Leading civic organizations collected enough signatures for a recall election in March 1909. Harper resigned from office shortly before the election. George Alexander (q.v.), candidate of the Good Government Organization, won the recall contest by a narrow margin.

Three years after his resignation from the mayoralty, Harper experienced bankruptcy. He then went to Bakersfield, California, and established a pipe company of which he became vice-president. He also served as president of an oil firm and owned a 400-acre farm in Kern County.

Harper died at his daughter's home in Palmdale, California, on 25 December 1948 and was buried in Los Angeles.

SOURCES: "Arthur C. Harper," *California Biography File*, Los Angeles Public Library; Albert H. Clodius, "The Quest for Good Government in Los Angeles, 1890–1910" (Ph.D. dissertation, Claremont Graduate School, 1953); J. M. Quinn, *A History of California and an Extended History of Its Southern Coast Counties* (Los Angeles, 1907), vol. 2; Los Angeles *Times*, 26 December 1948; William A. Spalding, *History of Los Angeles City and County, California. Biographical* (Los Angeles, 1931), vol. 3.

Martin J. Schiesl

HARPER, JAMES (1795–1869), Mayor of New York (1844–45). Founder of the famous New York publishing house of Harper Brothers and creator of the first U.S. police force, Harper was born at Newtown, Long Island, on 13 April 1795. He was the eldest of four brothers and the son of a prosperous Long Island farmer and fervent Methodist, who made the family home a center for visiting circuit preachers and Methodist worthies. Harper Senior was of British descent, and his wife of Dutch background.

James left his father's firm at age sixteen (1811) to become apprenticed in the printing trade in New York City. A strict craftsman and a perfectionist, James saved enough money during the apprenticeship to set up his own firm. Joined by his younger brother John (b. 1797), he established the house of J. & J. Harper. They prospered and later took in their two remaining younger brothers, becoming "Harper and Brothers"—one of America's most distinguished publishing houses from the 1820s down to the present day.

The tall, erect, dominating figure of James Harper became well known in the printing and publishing trades. He was genial, humorous, and a good public speaker, and set the highest professional standards. Thus, he was a natural choice as candidate for mayor of New York in 1844, as a Whig with much support from conservative reformers and Good Government dissenters. Elected on 9 May 1844 with what was claimed to be the largest vote known in New York City, Harper demanded from the outset as across-the-board, cost-cutting regime, threatening even to reduce public school expenditures, what he called "wilful pauperism," street-cleaning costs, and other city "improvements." As to the streets, he argued that other cities paid their contractors nothing, since they made enough profit selling the garbage. New York spent $100,000 a year on cleaning contracts. On schools, Harper wanted the state to impose upper tax limits. On paupers, he complained that the United States in general and New York in particular were a "paradise" for those who would not work, and suggested they be put to farm labor. The city also needed a workhouse for children, he argued. Harper firmly advocated Sabbatarian laws and the closing down of saloons.

Yet, Harper's administration is best known for the creation of the first organized metropolitan police force in the United States—the ordinance of 29 November 1844 which established "a Municipal Police or Night Watch."

After his brief foray into urban government, Harper devoted the rest of his life to his publishing business and led a quiet, serene existence, rarely leaving the city. He kept a strict regimen, beginning with players at breakfast, a few hours at the office, and a return home in the early afternoon. He was killed in a carriage accident caused by a runaway horse in Central Park, dying at St. Luke's Hospital in a coma on 27 March 1869.

SOURCES: *Annual Message of His Honor, Mayor James Harper*, 14 May 1844, Document No. 1, Board of Aldermen (New York, 1844), New York Public Library; James Richardson, *The New York Police* (New York, 1970); *Trade Circular Annual for 1871* (New York, 1871).   *Peter d'A. Jones*

HARRINGTON, ISAAC R. (1789–1851), Mayor of Buffalo (1841–42). Harrington was the proprietor of the well-known Buffalo inn and the Eagle Tavern; he also owned much of the surrounding real estate. He was married and the father of five children. Both Harrington and his mayoral opponent of 1841, Ira Brown, were substantial men of the community and both were Whigs, but the election could not thereby be said to be free of political overtones. Harrington found his constituency principally among the radical Locofoco Jacksonian Democrats, and he won the office by a margin of only 126 votes. As mayor, he viewed his own executive power as "merely nominal" and ceremonial, but he thought that Buffalo would play an important role in what he foresaw as the "inevitable expansion" of the United States to the Pacific Ocean.

In the decade before Harrington took office, Buffalo had grown from a village of fewer than 6,000 persons to a city of over 18,000. In 1830, Buffalo could boast of only four steamboats and twenty other vessels. In his inaugural address of 1841, Harrington reminded his constituents that business had increased by a factor of ten; fifty steamboats at a tonnage of 30,000 operated from Buffalo; canal tolls amounted to nearly $500,000. To encourage Buffalo's further growth, Harrington advocated improved harbor and water facilities, and the dredging and reinforcement of the Erie Canal. As sanguine as Harrington was about the progress that Buffalo had registered, he was also mindful of the high taxes necessary to finance the city's $60,000 debt. He also thought that the inflation of paper currency had "threatened the extermination of commercial prosperity." Harrington remained hopeful, however, that because the city's credit was still good, Buffalo provided adequate city services, and the outmoded "workhouse system" had been abolished. Buffalo therefore had a bright future.

At the time of his death on 20 August 1851, Harrington was serving as postmaster of Buffalo. He was buried in Forest Lawn Cemetery, Buffalo.

SOURCES: T. Horton, *Old Erie: The Growth of an American Community*, vol. 1, *History of North-Western New York* (New York, 1947); Crisfield Johnson, *Centennial History of Erie County* (Buffalo, 1876); Scrapbooks, Buffalo and Erie County Historical Society.   *Scott Eberle*

HARRIS, JOSIAH A. (1808–76), Mayor of Cleveland (1847–48). Yankee-born mayor of Cleveland and leading newspaper editor, Harris was born in Becket, Massachusetts on 15 January 1808, the son of Josiah Harris (1782–1867), a farmer and judge, and Charity (Messenger) Harris (d. 1837), both New England Protestants. One of four children, Harris moved to Amherst, Ohio, with his parents in 1818. He worked on his father's farm until 1828, attending night school for a few years. In 1828–29, he studied law and served as deputy sheriff of Lorain County, 1830–34. He bought the Lorain *Gazette* in 1832, edited it for two years, sold it in 1834, and moved to Columbus. He then spent some time in Mississippi and seriously considered buying a plantation there. In 1837, he moved to Cleveland, buying two newspapers (the *Gazette* and the *Herald*) and forming the successful *Daily Herald* which he edited and owned until 1865. In 1830, he married Esther Race (1809–1903), and they had five children.

Harris became a major figure in Cleveland as editor, noted for his humor and ability to collect information rapidly by telegraph and print it for the next day's paper. His paper's importance was shown by his frequent service as the city printer (1839–42, 1843–45, 1846–48, and later). He also was reporting clerk of the state legislature, 1856–57. He served as an alderman in 1840–41 and 1846–47. A Whig, Harris was elected mayor in 1847, defeating Democrat W. T. Goodwin 725 to 660. Cleveland had grown to about 13,000 and had a mayor-council form of government.

As mayor, Harris supported the plans for a city high school, plus other civic improvements. He strongly urged completion of a telegraph system to link Cleveland to the rest of the nation. He also raised city salaries and cut the city debt. After leaving office, he showed little interest in politics, preferring to edit his newspaper. After retirement in 1865, he moved to Lake Cliff, Ohio, where he raised prize-winning grapes. He died on 21 August 1876.

SOURCES: *The Biographical Dictionary of Ohio in the Nineteenth Century* (Cincinnati, 1876); J. F. Brennan, ed., *A Biographical Cyclopedia and Portrait Gallery of Distinguished Men, with an Historical Sketch of the State of Ohio* (Cincinnati, 1879); Harriet U. Taylor, *History of the Western Reserve*, 3 vols. (Chicago, 1910);

Gertrude Wickham, *The Pioneer Families of Cleveland, 1796–1840*, 2 vols. (Chicago, 1914).

Thomas R. Bullard

HARRIS, LEONARD A. (1824–90), Mayor of Cincinnati (1863–66). Reform-minded, popular Civil War mayor, born on 11 October 1824 in Cincinnati, Harris was educated in the common schools and attended higher institutions of learning. On 18 April 1854, he married Catherine Griffith. Upset by the fall of Fort Sumter in April 1861, he raised an infantry company and distinguished himself in the first battle of Bull Run. With presidential authorization, Harris raised the Second Ohio Volunteer Infantry. As its colonel, he continued his brilliant military career until bad health forced his resignation and return to Cincinnati.

Cincinnati in 1860 had 161,044 people and a mayor-council form of government. Harris accepted the nomination on a Union ticket for city mayor in 1863, which election he won by 13,102 votes to his opponent Joseph D. Torrence's 11,958. He was reelected mayor in 1865 and won by 11,252 votes to Torrence's 4,683. Harris became the first Cincinnati mayor not to complete a term of office, when he resigned in August 1866 to accept a presidential appointment as collector of internal revenue for the First Ohio District. He declined the Democratic nomination for state senator and a gubernatorial appointment to the state board of police commissioners, but he did accept another presidential appointment and served for several years as a member of the National Board of Soldiers' Homes.

Harris was one of Cincinnati's most popular mayors. During his first term, a gift of $8,000 was raised by popular subscription and a house was donated by a local businessman to encourage him to stand for reelection. He squelched anti-Union riots in the city, reorganized the police department to remove it from politics, and paved the way for construction of a municipal workhouse and hospital. By invitation of the governor, Mayor Harris drafted the law to create the Ohio National Guard providing for the "one hundred day men." He commanded one of the state regiments for its term of enlistment.

Harris was the principal founder and a long-time president of the Cuvier Club, noted for the advancement of ornithology and other natural sciences. He served two terms as a trustee of the city hospital. After an illness, of several months, Harris died of cancer of the liver, on 5 July 1890, in Cincinnati.

SOURCES: Cincinnati *Evening Post*, 5 July 1890; Charles Theodore Greve, *Centennial History of Cincinnati and Representative Citizens*, 2 vols. (Chicago, 1904); [Robert Herron], *Cincinnati's Mayors* (Cincinnati, 1957); Henry Howe, *Historical Collections of Ohio*, 2 vols. (Cincinnati, 1908); James Lundy, *Cincinnati Past and Present* (Cincinnati, 1872).

Dwight L. Smith

HARRIS, STEPHEN RANDALL (1802–79), Mayor of San Francisco (1852). Third mayor of San Francisco, Harris was born in Poughkeepsie, New York, in 1802, the son of Isaac Harris, a merchant who was killed in the War of 1812. Stephen was brought up by relatives and was apprenticed out to a surgeon, later entering the College of Physicians and Surgeons at Columbia University and graduating in 1826. Dr. Harris went immediately into local practice in New York City, staying there twenty-three years, until 1849. He was well known in New York, serving for six years as health commissioner and also as surgeon of the local Ninth Military Regiment and the city almshouses. He worked nobly and freely in the tragic cholera epidemic of 1832–34, but the lure of gold took him out to California (on a difficult route, via Panama, where he again worked against disease, freely) in June 1849.

Harris went straight out to the High Sierra goldfields of the American River, scraped together enough gold to open a drugstore, and settled in San Francisco to practice medicine. The drugstore was not, as is sometimes claimed, the first in San Francisco. (That honor goes to an earlier *alcalde*, Dr. Thaddeus M. Leavenworth [*q.v.*].) But Harris and his partner Panton kept it going with determination: they were burnt out three times in the city fires of May 1850, June 1850, and May 1851. After the last fire, Harris returned to the Sierras and found more gold to reopen the store yet again. Dr. Harris may have been the first *mayor* of San Francisco (as one authority claims) actually to work the goldfields. Yet, an earlier doctor, John Townsend (*q.v.*), the city's fourth American *alcalde* (1848), also tried to mine.

Politics interested Harris. He was a stalwart Democrat and was elected alderman and common council member in August 1849. He sat on the nominating committee of the Democratic party at the October convention, 1849 (called "the first political mass meeting in California history") and was vice-president of the Democratic state convention at Sacramento in February 1852. When the new city charter advanced the date of elections to September 1851 and Mayor Brenham's (*q.v.*) Whigs offered no ticket, Harris was elected unopposed as mayor of San Francisco. He could not take office until the state supreme court confirmed the legality of the process, on 27 December 1851. Harris was mayor from 1 January to 9 November 1852.

Dr. Harris faced two major political issues: city financing, in which he opposed the spending policies of the common council; and the growing opposition to Chinese immigration. With popular support, Mayor Harris vetoed various spending proposals of the council, though they passed over his veto a measure to buy the Jenny Lind Theater for $200,000 (and to spend a further $200,000 on it) to turn into a new city hall. The former hall had been burned down, and the city was spending $40,000 a year to rent space for offices. As for the Chinese, Harris probably favored Governor Bigler's proposed state law to limit their immigration. The act was too strong, and it failed.

Although he demanded economy, like Brenham (*q.v.*), Harris was easily replaced by that former Whig mayor, in November 1852. A year later Harris was elected comptroller, and he remained in public service for some years, serving as city coroner from 19 September 1864 to 2 December 1867, for example. He died at Napa, California, on 27 April 1879.

SOURCES: W. J. Davis, *History of Political Conventions in California, 1849–92* (Sacramento, 1893); W. F. Heintz, *San Francisco's Mayors* (Woodside, Calif., 1975); J. S. Hittell, *History of the City of San Francisco* (San Francisco, 1878); J. M. Read and M. E. Mathers, *History of the San Francisco Medical Society* (San Francisco, 1958); *San Jose Pioneer*, "Dr. Stephen R. Harris," 10 May 1879; F. Soule, J. H. Gihon and J. Nisbet. *Annals of San Francisco* (New York, 1855).

Peter d'A. Jones

HARRISON, CARTER H. (1825–93), Mayor of Chicago (1879–87, 1893). Machine politician and the first American mayor to be assassinated in office, Carter Harrison was born on 25 February 1825 near Lexington, Kentucky, the son of Carter Henry Harrison (d. 1825), a Southern plantation owner and descendant of a prominent Virginia family (which included President Benjamin Harrison and President William Henry Harrison), and Caroline (Russell) Harrison, of Kentucky ancestry. The family was Episcopalian. His father died eight months after his son's birth, leaving Harrison the only child of a widowed mother who taught him reading and writing. At the age of fifteen, he studied with Lewis Marshall, brother of Chief Justice John Marshall. He entered Yale University in 1842, and received his A.B. in 1845. After travel in Europe, Harrison studied law at Transylvania University Law School and graduated in 1855. In April 1855, he married his first wife, Sophonisba Preston (1835–76), sold his plantation, and moved to Chicago where he practiced law and speculated in real estate. The Harrisons had ten children, only four of whom, Caroline, Carter H. Harrison II (*q.v.*) (later mayor of Chicago), William Preston, and Sophy, survived to adulthood. After Sophonisba died in 1876, Harrison remained a widower until 1882 when he married Mar-

guerite Stearns, a Catholic. This marriage lasted until her death in 1887. Shortly before he was assassinated in 1893, Harrison had become engaged to Annie Howard of New Orleans.

Chicago in 1879 was a city of half a million, with a mayor-council form of government. Harrison, who had previously served as a county commissioner and U.S. congressman, was elected the first Democratic mayor of Chicago since 1865, by 25,685 to his Republican opponent Abner Wright's 20,496 and Socialist Ernest Schmidt's 11,829. Mayor Harrison served four terms in a row: he was reelected in 1881 (35,668 to John Clark's 27,925, Timothy O'Mara's 764, and George Schilling's 240); in 1883 (41,225 to Eugene Cary's 30,963); and in 1885 (43,352 to Sidney Smith's 42,977). Harrison declined to run for reelection in both 1887 and 1889. In 1891, Harrison's independent Democratic candidacy divided the Democratic vote and allowed a Republican, Hempstead Washburne (*q.v.*), to be elected, 46,957 votes to Democrat DeWitt Cregier's (*q.v.*) 46,558 and Harrison's 42,931. In 1893, however, Harrison was elected to a fifth term, as "the World's Fair Mayor," by 114,237 to Republican Samuel W. Allerton's 93,148. By then, Chicago's population, aided by annexation, had passed 1,250,000—a 25 percent growth since his first term as mayor.

Harrison's electoral triumphs transformed Chicago from normal Republican majorities to Democratic leads in municipal contests. Harrison forged a coalition of foreign-born and ethnic voters, workingmen, and moderate socialists who were attracted to his liberal stance on personal liberty; businessmen who admired his businesslike approach to the operations of government; and gamblers and saloon-keepers who appreciated his "live and let live" attitudes towards vice and gambling. Harrison was Chicago's first professional politician to build a personal organization that remained loyal even when he was out of office. As mayor, he improved the city's financial posture, restored competitive bidding for public works contracts, and increased the revenues the city received from the street railway companies.

On 28 October 1893, Harrison was assassinated in his home by Patrick Eugene Prendergast after he refused to appoint Prendergast corporation counsel. He was buried in Graceland Cemetery, Chicago.

SOURCES: Willis J. Abbot, *Carter Henry Harrison: A Memoir* (New York, 1895); Carter H. Harrison II, *Stormy Years* (Indianapolis, 1935); Claudius O. Johnson, *Carter Henry Harrison I: Political Leader* (Chicago, 1928); Frederick Rex, *The Mayors of the City of Chicago from March 4, 1837 to April 13, 1933* (Chicago, 1947).

Edward H. Mazur

HARRISON, CARTER HENRY, II (1860–1953), Mayor of Chicago (1897–1905, 1911–15). Harrison, a popular five-time, Democratic mayor, was born in Chicago, on 23 April 1860, the son of a five-time mayor, Carter Henry Harrison (1825–93) of Lexington, Kentucky, and Sophonisba (Preston) Harrison (1835–76) of Henderson, Kentucky. Only six of the ten Harrison children survived to adulthood. Harrison's ancestors included a signer of the Declaration of Independence and two U.S. presidents. The Harrisons came to Chicago in 1855 where the elder Harrison practiced law, became involved in Democratic politics, and became a famous mayor. The younger Harrison attended schools in Chicago and Germany. He received an A.B. from St. Ignatius College in 1881 and an LL.B. from Yale in 1883. On 14 December 1887, he married Edith Ogden (1861–1955), daughter of a distinguished Catholic family from New Orleans. Harrison practiced law and worked in the family real estate office, 1883–89. He became editor/publisher of the Chicago *Times*, 1891–95. Harrison was active in fraternal, veterans, and socially prominent organizations.

Chicago in the late 1890s was approaching a population of 1.7 million (1900 Census) and had a weak mayor-strong council form of government. The council consisted of thirty-five wards, each represented by two partisan aldermen. Harrison began his political career as the Democratic nominee for mayor in 1897. In the first of his five elections, he defeated a field of eight candidates on 6 April: Harrison, 148,880; John M. Harlan, Independent Republican 69,730; Nathaniel C. Sears, Republican 59,542; and others 18,238. Harrison was reelected on 4 April 1899, 148,496; Zina R. Carter, Republican, 107,437; John P. Altgeld, Municipal Ownership 47,169; and three others 2,565. On 2 April 1901, Harrison defeated six challengers: 156,756; Elbridge Hanecy, Republican 128,413; and five others, 12,462. His fourth consecutive election, on 7 April 1903, was his closest: 146,208; Graeme Stewart, Republican 138,548; and four others 24,849. Harrison did not seek renomination in 1905 but remained a party leader. He won a 1,500 vote primary fight over former mayor Edward F. Dunne (*q.v.*) in 1911 and was reelected mayor on 4 April 1911: 177,997; Charles E. Merriam, Republican 160,672; and three others 28,122. In 1915, Harrison, physically tired and mentally strained, lost a bitter primary battle to Robert M. Sweitzer.

Harrison, the first mayor to be born in the city, was a highly successful politician who appealed to upper class Republicans and to immigrant Democrats alike. He was flexible and willing to compromise; though considered honest, his two strongest allies were the notorious ward bosses, Michael "Hinky Dink" Kenna and "Bathhouse" John Coughlin. He gained initial respect in a battle against traction magnate Charles Yerkes. A mildly reformist patrician, he skillfully utilized patronage while supporting civil service reform.

In 1915, Harrison, though fifty-five years of age and no longer running for office, remained active in community concerns. He served as collector of the Internal Revenue Service, 1933–45, and published two autobiographical volumes. He died on 25 December 1953 and is buried with his wife in Chicago's historic Graceland Cemetery.

SOURCES: Donald S. Bradley, "The Historical Trends of the Political Elites in a Metropolitan Central City: The Chicago Mayor," Center for Social Organization Studies Working Paper No. 10, University of Chicago, Department of Sociology, May 1963; Paul Michael Green, "The Chicago Democratic Party 1840–1920: From Factionalism to Political Organization" (Ph.D. dissertation, University of Chicago, 1975); Carter H. Harrison, *Growing up with Chicago* (Chicago, 1944); Carter H. Harrison, *Stormy Years: The Autobiography of Carter H. Harrison, Five Times Mayor of Chicago* (Indianapolis, 1935); Carter H. Harrison IV (1860–1953), Papers, about 4,000 items, Newberry Library, Chicago; Ralph R. Tingley, "From Carter Harrison II to Fred Busse: A Study of Chicago Political Parties and Personages from 1896–1907" (Ph.D. dissertation, University of Chicago, 1950).

Andrew K. Prinz

HART, THOMAS N. (1829–1927), Mayor of Boston (1889–90, 1900–1902). Conservative Republican Mayor Hart, son of Daniel and Margaret (Norton) Hart, was descended from old-stock Yankee farmer Isaac Hart, a founder of Lynnfield, Massachusetts. Born in North Reading on 20 January 1829, he attended local schools until the age of thirteen, when he entered a Boston dry goods store as a clerk. In 1844, he joined a hat, cap, and fur store, moved in 1850 to Philip A. Locke's wholesale and retail hat and fur shop, where he became a partner, and in 1860 established the firm of Hart, Taylor and Company, which became one of the largest hat and fur dealers in New England. On 30 April 1850, he married Elizabeth Snow, daughter of John and Elizabeth (Ridley) Snow of Bowdoin, Maine. They had one daughter. Hart was treasurer of the American Unitarian Association, a member of the Algonquin Club, the Boston Art Club, Hull Yacht Club, and the Unitarian Club.

Retiring from business in 1879, Hart accepted the presidency of the Mount Vernon National Bank and turned his attention to Boston city politics. He was elected a member of the common council for three terms, 1879–81; alderman, three terms, 1882, 1885, 1886; and in addition was the Republican candidate for mayor in 1886 and

1887, both times opposing incumbent Democratic Mayor Hugh O'Brien (*q.v.*) and both times losing—23,426 to 18,685 in 1886 and 26,636 to 25,179 in 1887. In 1888, in his third campaign against O'Brien, Hart was elected 32,712 to 30,836.

Boston in 1889 had a population of approximately 390,000 with a mayor-bicameral, alderman-common council city government. Elected as the "citizens' " mayor, a reaction to the supposed excesses of the O'Brien machine, Hart initiated a policy of retrenchment and reform, proposing consolidation of overlapping city boards and agencies, trimming of all nonessential expenditures and services, extension of the civil service idea, longer terms for mayor and council members, and individual, paid department heads rather than government by commissions. After serving two rather undistinguished terms—he defeated Owen A. Galvin in 1889 by a vote of 31,133 to 25,673—he declined renomination in 1890. Instead he accepted a commission as postmaster of Boston, which he held until 1893 when he was once again the Republican candidate for mayor. He lost to Democratic incumbent Nathan Matthews (*q.v.*) 36,354 to 31,255. In 1899, Hart was again a candidate for mayor, and, as in 1888, he ran as a financial conservative against the alleged extravagance of the city Democratic machine. Once again he faced an Irishman, Patrick A. Collins. Campaigning on a platform of honesty, lower taxes, the eight-hour day, home rule for Boston, and sound business practices, Hart was elected with help from the Democratic faction of John R. Murphy, which refused to endorse Collins. The vote was 40,678 to 38,594. During his two-year terms, Hart brought an end to what he considered reckless spending of city revenues on recreational facilities. Declining renomination in 1902, Hart, occupied his post-mayoral years with participation in various social and charitable organizations. He died on 2 October 1927.

SOURCES: Boston *Evening Transcript*, 4 October 1927; Boston *Post*, 5 October 1927; Carl W. Ernst Collection of Scrapbooks, 18 vols., 1886–1901, Boston Public Library; "Famous Persons at Home: Thomas N. Hart," *Time and the Hour* (4 October 1899); Thomas N. Hart, *Inaugural Address of Thomas N. Hart* (Boston, 1889).   *Robert V. Sparks*

HATCH, GEORGE (   ), Mayor of Cincinnati (1861–63). Hatch, an unpopular Democratic mayor during the Civil War, was a Cincinnati businessman who maintained a tenuous connection with a soap and candle factory, was a cashier in the Bank of Cincinnati, and promoted real estate. In 1849, he offered to donate to the city as a park, a strip of land that adjoined a subdivision he was planning. For its part, he wanted the city

to fence and grade the streets on both sides of the park. The council did not take his offer seriously and rejected it.

Cincinnati in 1860 had 161,044 people and a mayor-council form of government. Hatch was nominated for city mayor in that year by a combination of otherwise uncooperative political groups, including the Democratic and Know-Nothing organizations, which appealed to the Crittenden Compromise in the national crisis. He won the 1 April 1861 election by 12,587 votes to his Republican opponent and future Mayor Charles F. Wilstach's (*q.v.*) 10,404, and to a minor candidate, Crusel F. Robinson's 589.

Hatch was a strongly partisan Democrat who represented the extreme sentiment of concessions to the South. With the outbreak of the Civil War, he managed to alienate most of the people of Cincinnati by his persistent continuation of this position. His popularity declined rapidly, and the leaders of the community refused to consult with him on matters of the city's involvement in the war. During his tenure he dealt with otherwise noncontroversial matters in a routine fashion. When his term as mayor ended, he left Cincinnati and disappeared into oblivion. He was succeeded by Leonard A. Harris (*q.v.*), a popular local war hero.

SOURCES: Charles Frederic Goss, *Cincinnati the Queen City, 1788–1912*, 4 vols. (Chicago, 1912); Charles Theodore Greve, *Centennial History of Cincinnati and Representative Citizens*, 2 vols. (Chicago, 1904); [Robert Herron], *Cincinnati's Mayors* (Cincinnati, 1957).   *Dwight L. Smith*

HAVEMEYER, WILLIAM F. (1804–74), Mayor of New York (1845–46, 1848–49, 1873–74). Millionaire sugar king and three times mayor of New York, Havemeyer was born in that city on 12 February 1804, the son of the rich sugar refiner William Havemeyer. The family was of German descent, originating in Bueckenburg, the capital of Schaumburg-Lippe. The family name, dating back to at least 1600, was originally spelled "Hoevemeyer." The mayor's father emigrated to London at the age of fifteen and rose in the English sugar business. He came to New York on behalf of Edmund Seaman and Company in 1799 and ran their sugar house on Pine Street until 1807. Thereafter, he became an independent and prospered. His son William F. was educated at private schools and at Columbia College (1819–23) where he excelled in mathematics. He then entered his father's business as a clerk. On 5 March 1828, Havemeyer set up his own firm with a cousin, W. F. and Frederick Christian Havemeyer and Company. He married Sarah Agnes, daughter of the Honorable Hector Craig, at Craigville, New York, on 15 April 1828 and continued in the sugar business until 1 January 1842 when he sold the company to his brother Albert.

Havemeyer's first connections with local politics came in the summer of 1844 when he was elected one of three delegates from the Eighth Ward to the New York City Democratic Committee. He later attended the state convention in Syracuse (4 September 1844) where he served as presidential elector. On 3 December, he voted for Polk. Havemeyer was elected mayor of New York City on 8 April 1845; he served a one-year term and declined renomination, despite requests from both parties.

Havemeyer's administration faced the problems that typified the era: urban poverty and costs of almshouses, street cleaning, police, water supplies, property assessments, and relations with the state government. He proved sensitive to immigrant housing conditions and to the need for New York to improve its port and dock facilities rapidly. "I . . . feel a profound sense of the arduous responsibilities of the trust," he declared in his inaugural message to the council. But he proceeded to the task with vigor.

Havemeyer was unusually enlightened and modern in his view of the positive contributions of immigrants—at that time heavily Irish—of whom 160,000 entered the city in 1844. "The immigration from the over-populated countries of Europe, which our free institutions and our fertile and unoccupied soils had invited, has received a new impulse from the (potato) famine which has recently added to the evils of (British) misgovernment," he commented. He saw migration as "one of the most remarkable characteristics of the age in which we live"—and a benefit:

> Aside from the vast increase of the productive power of the country thus created and the considerable additions to its capital from those who bring with them the accumulations of their former industry, the effects upon our foreign commerce . . . is by no means unimportant. The passage money received from immigrants during the past year has contributed more to the prosperity of our navigation than the freight from all our commerce with Europe.

He pushed for the creation of a board of emigration and then served as its president in 1847.

In 1848, Havemeyer again ran for mayor and was elected to a second term on 11 April, again serving for one year. In that administration, he proposed the unification of Brooklyn with New York (28 January 1849). During the 1850s and 1860s, he moved into banking, serving as president of the Bank of North America and of the New York Savings Bank, and he was vice-president of the Pennsylvania Coal Company for some years. During the Civil War, he was solidly pro-Union and was by then a Republican.

In the spring of 1870, Havemeyer helped to organize the good-government New York City Council of Reform and served as president of the Committee of 70 (1871–72), an anti-Tweed group. He played a large role in the defeat of the corrupt Tweed Ring and was swept into office for the third time, becoming mayor a quarter of century after his last term of office began. Havemeyer declared in January 1873: "In a great degree we have to rebuild the entire governmental edifice" (to recover from the Tweed years). He thought that county and city governments had to be consolidated "at the outset" and many offices abolished. Department heads, previously independent of the mayor, would have to be brought into line and the common council exert its authority more. In particular, he said, "that sink of political corruption, the New County Court House, should be finished."

Mayor Havemeyer had almost completed an energetic two-year term when he collapsed from overwork, after a long, hurried walk in the cold, and died of a heart attack in city hall on 30 November 1874.

SOURCES: Annual Message of Mayor W. F. Havemeyer, 9 May 1848, Board of Aldermen (New York, 1848); *Communication from the Mayor*, Document No. 7, Board of Aldermen, 14 April 1873 (New York, 1873); Howard B. Furer. *The Public Career of W. F. Havemeyer* (microfilm thesis, New York University, 1963); *Inaugural Message of Hon. W. F. Havemeyer, Mayor of the City of New York, 6 January 1873* (New York, 1873); *In Memoriam: W. F. Havemeyer, Mayor of the City of New York* (New York, 1881). (All documents are in the New York Public Library). *Peter d'A. Jones*

HAVEN, SOLOMON G. (1810–61), Mayor of Buffalo (1846). Early mayor of Buffalo and U.S. congressman, Haven was born on 27 November 1810 in Easton, New York, the second of four children of two old-stock Protestant Yankees, Asa Haven, Jr., a farmer and wheelwright, and Asenath (Eastwood) Haven, the daughter of a Methodist minister, Reverend Daniel Eastwood. Haven, who studied classics and medicine in Easton, remained in his hometown until 1828 when he moved to Geneseo, New York. He studied law there under a future governor of New York, John Young, and taught school, 1828–30. He was deputy clerk of Livingston County, New York (1830–34) and then county commissioner of deeds. In 1835, Haven settled in Buffalo and joined the prestigious law firm of Fillmore and Hall, not long afterwards becoming a full partner. He was the district attorney of Erie County, 1843–45. On 2 May 1838, Haven married Harriet N. Scott (1817–99) of Greenfield, New York, the daughter of Dr. William K. Scott. Harriet was an Episcopalian, a charity worker, and a socialite, who authored a study of Haven's friend, Millard Fillmore. The Havens had four daughters.

In 1845, Buffalo had 29,773 people and a mayor-council form of government. In the March 1846 election, the Whig Haven defeated his Democratic opponent, Issac Sherman, 2,025 to 1,704 votes. A single-term mayor, Haven actively sought funds to build a post office, a customshouse, and other public buildings.

After his term expired, Haven returned to practicing law. In 1850, he was elected to the U.S. House of Representatives, where he strongly supported President Fillmore. He was reelected to Congress in 1852 and 1854, but lost reelection bids in 1856 and 1860. Haven returned once more to his distinguished law practice in 1856. After his death on 24 December 1861, a funeral service was held at the Central Presbyterian Church. He was buried in Buffalo's Forest Lawn Cemetery.

SOURCES: Buffalo *Daily Courier; Commercial Advertiser and Journal*; Buffalo *Evening Post*; Cristfield Johnson, *Centennial History of Erie County, New York* (Buffalo, 1876); Grace Carew Sheldon, "Buffalo Mayors, 1832 to 1901" (Scrapbook in Buffalo Historical Society); Sister Mary Jane and Sister Mercedes, "The Mayors of Buffalo, 1832 to 1961" (B.A. thesis, Rosary Hill College, 1961); H. Perry Smith, *History of the City of Buffalo and Erie County, New York* (Syracuse, N.Y., 1884).

Daniel B. Karin

HAY, ALEXANDER (1806–82), Mayor of Pittsburgh (1842–45). Hay was born in Pittsburgh of Scottish parents and went to work in a glasshouse at the age of eleven. His father died soon afterward, and in 1816 he was apprenticed to a cabinetmaker, practicing that trade most of his life. In 1832, he married Jane Hubley, who bore him eleven children. She died on 17 August 1884.

Hay was captain of the Jackson Independent Blues and fought in the Mexican War, but he came home sick after a year of service. In the Civil War he was captain of Company E, Sixty-first Pennsylvania Volunteer Infantry, and saw action in the Peninsular campaign, but again he became ill and returned home.

A newcomer to politics, Hay was nominated by the Whig and Anti-Mason parties, and nosed out William M. Shinn, a prominent druggist (Jacksonian Democrat and Citizens' party) and Patrick McKenna, an auctioneer (anti-Jackson Democrat). Shinn's backers carried eighteen of the thirty common council posts. (Pittsburgh, then a town of 27,000, had select and common councils.) Hay began his term with a squabble over police promotion, which he won in the courts. In March 1842, Charles Dickens visited the city.

In his reelection bid in 1843, he squeaked out an 89-vote plurality as a Volunteer candidate (858 votes) over Thomas Dickson, Democrat, 769, and former Mayor James Thomson (*q.v.*) Whig and Anti-Mason, 755. A year later, on the Independent and Volunteer tickets, Hay

got 974 votes, defeating John Birmingham, Democrat, with 709, and M. Earle, Whig, 531. Always a minority mayor, Hay ran third on a try for a fourth term in 1845.

Following the end of his third term, Hay returned to his furniture business. He died on 5 November 1882 and was buried in Allegheny Cemetery.

SOURCES: Biographical Encyclopedia of Pennsylvania (Philadelphia, 1874); Allen Humphreys Kerr, "The Mayors and Recorders of Pittsburgh, 1816–1951" (typescript, 1952, Carnegie Library of Pittsburgh); Pittsburgh *Gazette*, 6 November 1882.   *George Swetnam*

HAYES, THOMAS G. (1844–1915), Mayor of Baltimore (1899–1903). Reform mayor, born on 5 January 1844 in Anne Arundel County, Maryland, Hayes was the son of Juliana (Gordon) Hayes and Reverend Thomas C. Hayes, a Methodist minister. He attended private schools, graduated from Virginia Military Institute (VMI), and fought for the Confederacy during the Civil War. Afterwards, he taught briefly at VMI and at Kentucky Military Institute in Frankfort where he also read law and was admitted to the bar. Hayes moved to Baltimore in 1872, became active in Democratic politics, was elected to the state House of Delegates in 1879, and to the state Senate in 1883, 1885, and 1891. President Cleveland (*q.v.*) appointed him a federal prosecuting attorney in 1886. Popular with organized labor as well as with farmers, Hayes was a leading gubernatorial candidate in 1895 when his nomination was blocked by the party bosses. An angry Hayes turned against the Rasin-Gorman machine, served as city counselor under Republican mayors from 1895 to 1899, and became the reform candidate in the 1899 mayoral election.

Baltimore in 1899 had 508,937 people and a mayor-council form of government under a new city charter. As city counselor, Hayes had played a significant role in drafting the charter, the first since 1796. He ran for mayor as a Democrat, independent of the bosses, won the primary, and defeated the reform Republican incumbent, William T. Malster (*q.v.*), 57,660 to 49,948. Hayes failed at reelection in 1903 when he was beaten in the Democratic primary by Robert M. McLane (*q.v.*).

As mayor, Hayes implemented Baltimore's new charter of 1899 by generally appointing qualified people to run governmental agencies, on a nonpartisan basis. His school board appointments began a major upgrading of the city's schools. Contemporaries believed his administration to be honest, efficient, and economical. Hayes gradually lost reform support, however, by his attempt to build his own political organization at city hall. While H. L. Mencken remembered Hayes as "a very shrewd lawyer, an unreconstructed Confederate veteran, a pious Methodist, and a somewhat bawdy bachelor," contemporaries increasingly saw Hayes as a stubborn, quarrelsome man who developed an alcohol problem in office, and they returned him to private life.

After 1903, Hayes retired from politics and practiced law. He died on 27 August 1915.

SOURCES: Baltimore *News*, 1899–1903; Wilbur F. Coyle, *The Mayors of Baltimore* (Baltimore, 1919); James B. Crooks, *Politics and Progress: The Rise of Urban Progressivism in Baltimore, 1895–1911* (Baton Rouge, La., 1968); H. L. Mencken, *Newspaper Days, 1899–1906* (New York, 1941); *Sun Almanac for 1900* (Baltimore, 1900).   *James B. Crooks*

HAYS, WILLIAM BRATTON (1844–1912), Mayor of Pittsburgh (1903-1906). Hays was born in Pittsburgh on 19 October 1844, the son of William Bratton Hays, Sr., and Mary Byerly. William, Sr., was a lime and coal merchant who supplied local iron mills. Young William attended local public schools, Norwich Military Academy, and Western University of Pennsylvania (now the University of Pittsburgh).

After graduation, Hays engaged in the coal business in Indiana, but within three years returned to Pittsburgh and joined the family firm. Soon the firm was sold, and Hays and his father entered the porkpacking business together. After his father's death, William, now head of the firm, endorsed the paper of a friend who subsequently failed, bringing Hays down too. After two years as a deputy sheriff of Allegheny County, he began speculating in oil and opened a poultry and commodities supply business in 1868.

In 1868, Hays was appointed to the Pittsburgh Board of Health, serving until 1874. Then, for eleven years, he held an influential position as a member of the board of fire commissioners. In 1882, he was appointed to the position of chief city assessor, during which time he became associated with Thomas S. and Edward M. Bigelow, cousins of Republican political boss Christopher Magee. In a fight with William Flinn, developing over the removal of Edward Bigelow as director of public works for the city, the Bigelows and Hays broke with the Magee-Flinn faction and joined the Matthew Quay faction. At this time, the office of city recorder (which had replaced the mayoralty) was changed from an appointed to an elected position. In the raucous politics of the day, William B. Hays, backed by a reform Citizens' party and the Democrats, ended up opposing the Quay-backed Republican candidate, John C. Haymaker, whom he defeated by 7,300 votes.

Hays' term was to have begun on 6 April 1903, but after the resignation of Joseph O. Brown (*q.v.*), Hays was appointed to the office of recorder on 16 March. The state legislature then changed his title from recorder to mayor, effective 23 April 1903.

Under Hays, the long-awaited water filtration plant was finally begun. The Wabash Railroad, long excluded from the city through the influence of the Pennsylvania Railroad, at last was able to obtain a franchise. In addition, the Pennsylvania Railroad agreed to remove its tracks from Liberty Avenue in the city's downtown area, in return for permission to construct an elevated line along the Allegheny River.

In 1905, the adjacent municipalities of Elliott, Esplen and Strett were annexed to the city, and the legislature passed enabling legislation for the consolidation of the cities of Pittsburgh and Allegheny. After numerous court delays, a joint referendum was held in 1906 with Allegheny voting 2 to 1 against. However, Pittsburgh voted 5 to 1 in favor, thus annexing Allegheny City against its will, as only the combined total was used to compute the outcome.

After the expiration of his term on 2 April 1906, Hays retired to his "model" farm on Thompson's Run in Allegheny County. He also had interests in North Carolina lumbering, an Ohio tool company, and the Liberty Electric Company. From 1870 to 1880, he had been a director of Allegheny National Bank.

Hays died in Pittsburgh of pneumonia on 16 September 1912. He was survived by three daughters.

SOURCES: Pittsburgh *Dispatch*, 17 September 1912; Pittsburgh *Post*, 17 September 1912.

Joseph F. Rishel

HAYWARD, NELSON (–1857), Mayor of Cleveland (1843). Fifth mayor of Cleveland, Hayward moved to Cleveland in 1825 from Lebanon, Connecticut. He was the son of William and Marjory Thayer Hayward of Braintree, Massachusetts, the third-born after his brothers Joseph and John. Nelson never married. All three brothers arrived in Cleveland together, at a time when the city was in a period of rapid growth as the Lake Erie terminus of the Ohio and Erie Canal. Cleveland was chartered as a city in 1836 with a board of aldermen; its population passed the 6,000 mark in 1840, while the neighboring Ohio City on the west side of the Cuyahoga River numbered more than 1,500.

Hayward was a radical Jacksonian Democrat in politics, known as a "Locofoco." He was elected alderman in 1841 and 1842, and then mayor of Cleveland in 1843, 482 votes to 437 for J. L. Weatherly (Whig) and 30 for John Stoddard (Independent). His "Locofoco" politics were illustrated in his inaugural address pledging to "avoid all extraordinary and new sources of expenditure not absolutely necessary for the general prosperity of the city, and observe a judicious economy in all necessary expenditures." He was vice-president of the city temperance society in 1842 and a member of the Cleveland Lodge of the Odd Fellows when it was organized in

1843. Hayward died in April 1857 and was buried in Cleveland.

SOURCES: Crisfield Johnson, *History of Cuyahoga County, Ohio* (Philadelphia, 1879); Gertrude Van Rensselaer Wickham, *The Pioneer Families of Cleveland 1796–1840* (Cleveland, 1914); Works Progress Administration, *Annals of Cleveland: Bibliographical Series* (typescript, 1939). *Ronald E. Shaw*

HAZARD, HENRY THOMAS (1844–1921), Mayor of Los Angeles (1889–92). Los Angeles' first home rule mayor, Hazard was born on 31 July 1844 in Evanston, Illinois, to Captain Americk M. Hazard (?–1873) of Vermont Yankee ancestry and to Eleanor (Alexander) Hazard, born in Scotland. One of eight children, Henry and his parents came to Los Angeles in 1854. Henry finished the public schools and went on to graduate from the University of Michigan Law School in 1868. Upon graduation, he plunged into politics by becoming a delegate to the Republican convention that nominated U. S. Grant for the presidency. Hazard remained a life-long Republican, extremely active in California politics.

On 1 October 1873, Hazard married Carrie B. Geller (1856–1918) in San Gabriel, California. The couple had no children. Within a year after her death, he married an Arizona woman. The marriage was annulled at his request because she allegedly refused "to perform wifely duties." Hazard was an Episcopalian, a member of the Pioneer Society of Los Angeles, and a charter member of the Los Angeles Bar Association.

Hazard's legal practice and real estate speculation provided him with a fortune of $500,000 by 1880. Hazard's political career also blossomed. During the 1870s, he worked to bring the Southern Pacific Railroad to Los Angeles. He was elected city attorney from 1880 to 1882, and in 1884 he became one of the city's representatives to the state assembly. Hazard was also elected to the Los Angeles Board of Freeholders (1887–88), a fifteen-member body which drew up the first charter giving Los Angeles home rule. An enthusiastic booster, Hazard had been one of the leading organizers of an 1881 effort to call a constitutional convention to divide California into two separate states.

In 1889, Los Angeles had approximately 50,000 people and a mayor-council form of government. Because of the new charter, Los Angeles was faced with another election just two months after John Bryson (*q.v.*) had won the mayoralty. Hazard won the nomination and with 5,322 defeated the Democrat Bryson (2,991) and a Prohibitionist (1,268) on 22 February 1889. Hazard was reelected on 1 December 1890 for a full term by defeating his Democratic and Municipal Reform opponents—4,665 to 2,698 and 1,766 votes, respectively. He declined to run for another term. Except for seeking and winning a

term (1896–98) on the board of freeholders, Hazard was not an active politician after 1892.

Hazard was not a reformer, but he was respected as an efficient and honest politician interested in stimulating Los Angeles' growth, as his efforts in enticing railroads and ocean-going vessels to Los Angeles testified. Hazard had refused to run for state assembly in 1886 because he strenuously opposed the Southern Pacific's domination of Republican state politics. As mayor, he reclaimed public lands which the railroads had illegally taken. In all other respects, Hazard followed the Republican party line during his term as mayor.

Hazard died of arterial sclerosis on 7 August 1921 in Los Angeles.

SOURCES: James E. Condon, *Southern California Blue Book of Money* (Los Angeles, 1913); Great Register of Voters for Los Angeles County, California, 1877, 1879, 1884, 1886, 1888, and 1890; Los Angeles City Directory 1872 to 1910, UCLA and Los Angeles Public Libraries; Special Collections, UCLA Library; U.S. Bureau of the Census, Manuscript Rolls of the 1880 Census for Los Angeles. *Christopher Cocoltchos*

HEATH, EDWARD (1819–92), Mayor of New Orleans (1867–68). Born in Lisbon, Maine, in 1819, Heath settled in New Orleans in 1842. He had worked in the customshouse, was a member of the board of Straight University, a Mason, and an active member of the Unitarian Church. He married a cousin named Heath in 1855. He was appointed Radical Reconstruction mayor on 27 March 1867 by General Philip H. Sheridan.

Heath served a troubled term under Reconstruction and military rule. Having replaced Mayor-elect John T. Monroe (*q.v.*), he identified himself fully with the radical cause. He engaged in acrimonious conflict with the citizens and city council over the forced admission of black children into white schools, the removal of Confederate sympathizers from the city government, the reconstitution of the police force, and the issuance of depreciated municipal paper money which contributed to the ever-mounting city debt. When the election of a Democratic mayor in 1868 challenged his appointment, Heath resisted and had to be forcibly ejected from city hall. He died on 1 January 1892 in Malden, Massachusetts, having long since returned to his native New England.

SOURCES: "Biographies of the Mayors of New Orleans" (New Orleans, typescript, Works Progress Administration, 1940); John S. Kendall, *History of New Orleans* (Chicago, 1922). *C. David Tompkins*

HEATH, MONROE (1828–94), Mayor of Chicago (1876–79). Mayor of Chicago during the labor turmoil of 1877, Heath was born at Grafton, New Hampshire, on 27 March 1828, the eldest of three children of Johnstone Heath and Nancy (Sanborn) Heath. Johnstone Heath, a Baptist of remote English ancestry, operated a farm near Grafton and served in several local offices, including that of justice of the peace. The younger Heath attended local farm district schools; orphaned at the age of twelve, he took up work as a farmhand and then as a millhand at Concord, New Hampshire.

While still in his teens Heath rose to the post of manager of a Vermont woolen mill, owned by the state's governor. Very mobile, he subsequently worked in Boston as a salesman for a dry goods firm and in New Orleans as a clerk for a paint manufacturer. In 1849, Heath journeyed to California to seek his fortune in the Gold Rush, but he soon began a paint business there instead. This business he quickly sold and, in late 1850 he moved to Chicago, where he began the paint manufacturing and retailing firm of Heath and Milligan in February 1851.

In 1853, Heath married Julia Dickerman of Jefferson, Illinois, and they had four children. A Republican, Heath served as a Chicago alderman between 1871 and 1875. Chicago in 1876 had a population of 407,661 and a mayor-council form of government. In 1877, when Heath was reelected, the population had already increased to 430,000.

A special mayoral election was held on 12 July 1876 to resolve a dispute over the proper length of the term of the incumbent mayor, Harvey Colvin (q.v.). Heath was nominated for the mayoralty by the Republican party, with the support of those who wished to see city expenses cut and corruption reduced. Heath received 19,248 votes against 7,509 for Democrat Mark Kimball and 3,363 for Independent J. J. McGrath. Heath retained office in a regular election on 3 April 1877, gaining 30,881 votes against 19,449 for Democrat Perry H. Smith.

Chicago's finances were in disarray at the outset of Heath's term because of a default by the city treasurer under the previous administration. They were further disrupted by an 1878 suit challenging the city's tax base. Heath therefore consolidated city departments and reduced some public services, although the council blocked cuts in the police and fire departments. Efforts were made to collect taxes in arrears, and the city's floating debt was nearly eliminated. In 1878, the city began issuing tax anticipation warrants.

The labor disturbances of July 1877 caught Heath unprepared. Once aroused, however, he called in the state militia and advised citizens to arm themselves. Heath approved the use of federal troops and afterward added 100 men to the police force.

At the conclusion of his second term in 1879, Heath retired from political life and moved to the suburb of Arlington Heights. He died on 21 October 1894 in Ashe-

ville, North Carolina, and was buried in Chicago. Heath was a 32d degree Mason and a member of the Knights Templar.

SOURCES: Fremont O. Bennett, *Politics and Politicians of Chicago, Cook County, and Illinois* (Chicago, 1886); Chicago *Daily News*, 22 October 1894; Chicago *Tribune*, 22 October 1894; *Notable Men of Chicago and Their City* (Chicago, 1910); Frederick Rex, *The Mayors of the City of Chicago from March 4, 1837 to April 13, 1933* (typescript dated 1933 held by the Municipal Reference Library of Chicago). A few official documents from Heath's mayoralty are in the Chicago Historical Society; a smaller number, mostly proclamations, are in the Newberry Library, Chicago.   *Paul Barrett*

HENRY, ALEXANDER (1823–83), Mayor of Philadelphia (1858–65). Born in Philadelphia on 11 April 1823, Henry was the grandson of prominent Philadelphia merchants on both sides of his family, Alexander Henry and Silas E. Weir. Although his father, John Henry, a Presbyterian, died at an early age, Henry received an excellent education, graduating from Princeton and receiving admission to the Philadelphia bar in 1844. He married the daughter of Comegys Paul the same year, and they had one child, John Snowden Henry. During his career, Henry was prominent in civic affairs, serving as a trustee of the University of Pennsylvania, inspector of the Eastern State Penitentiary, and president of the state board of Centennial Supervisors.

Entering local politics during a period of transition, Henry won election to the select council from the Seventh Ward in 1856 as an Independent over the opposition of the city's Know-Nothing faction. Two years later, he was named the first mayoralty candidate of the People's party, which was formed locally to solidify opposition to the Democrats. Identified as an old-line Whig, Henry broadened his ticket with the inclusion of several former nativists. Campaigning on a platform that favored high tariffs, free soil, and restrained opposition to "foreign paupers," he defeated Richard Vaux 33,159 to 29,120. Philadelphia then had over 500,000 people.

Henry's term of office was beset by the difficulties of protest and war. During his first term, he maintained a conservative position, seeking conciliation with non-slaveholding Southerners and supporting the Constitutional Unionist candidate over Lincoln. His active defense of the principle of free speech cost him support, however, when he marshaled his police force in December 1859 to protect New York abolitionist George W. Curtis from possible mob action. While Henry managed to quell anti-seccessionist mobs as well, he faced stiff opposition to his reelection in 1860, barely edging his opponent, John Robbins, 36,658 to 35,776.

Although national issues dominated the headlines during his tenure, Henry also took an active interest in urban development, calling for better services for outlying areas of the consolidated city, rationalization of the city's legal and tax systems, and expansion of the police force equal to the growth of the city. Such positions helped enhance his political position, as he beat his Democratic opponent Daniel Fox (*q.v.*) in 1862, 34,613 to 30,049, drawing new strength from the city's developing outer suburban wards.

With his retirement from office in 1865, Henry took up legal practice and played a major role in planning the 1876 Centennial Exposition. Apparently saddened by the death of his only son in 1880, Henry's health faltered. A trip to Europe in 1883 helped revive him, but shortly after his return to Philadelphia he fell ill again and died on 6 December 1883.

SOURCES: William Dusinberre, *Civil War Issues in Philadelphia 1856–1865* (Philadelphia, 1965); J. Thomas Scharf and Thompson Westcott, *History of Philadelphia*, 3 vols. (Philadelphia, 1884).   *Howard Gillette, Jr.*

HERRICK, RENSSELAER RUSSELL (1826–99), Mayor of Cleveland (1879–82). Two-term Republican mayor of Cleveland, Herrick was born on 29 January 1826 in Utica, New York. His father, Sylvester Pierce Herrick, a successful merchant in Vernon, New York, whose forebears were English Puritan immigrants (1629), died when the boy was two. Maria Marcia (Smith) Herrick (1798–1886), his mother, grew up on the New York estate of the Van Rensselaer family, hence her son's name. A remarkable woman, she raised four children (of whom the future mayor was the youngest), kept house, and edited the fairly successful *Mother's Magazine* after her husband's death. Young Rensselaer received intermittent formal schooling and was largely self-taught. At age ten he traveled west to Cleveland where he worked first as an apprentice printer and later learned carpentry. This latter skill served as a springboard for his ultimate success as owner of a Cleveland building and contracting firm. Herrick's diverse interests also led him to become president of the Dover Bay Grape and Wine Company. At twenty, on 10 May 1846, he married his first wife, Adelaide (Cushman) Herrick; little is known about her or his second wife, a Norwalk, Ohio, widow, Mrs. Laura (White) Hunt. He had no children. Before retiring from active business in 1870, Herrick also served five terms in the Cleveland City Council (1855–58 and 1869) and was subsequently elected member of the city board of improvements (1873–76 and 1877).

A leading Republican, Herrick received the Cuyahoga County Republican nomination for the Cleveland mayoralty in late March 1879. Opposed by Waldemar Otis, a perennial Democratic contender, he was elected in April of that year by a total of 11,766 to 9,528 votes. Two years later, he was reelected over another future mayor, John H. Farley (*q.v.*) (11,918 to 8,660 votes). During his two terms, Cleveland was governed by a mayor and council under the federal system and witnessed its population swell from 180,684 (1879–80) to 214,634 (1881–82).

Herrick's tenure in office established his reputation as a successful administrator of public funds. Between 1879 and 1881, primarily through his efforts, the tax valuation jumped from $71 million to $79 million, while the levy rate for the entire expense fell from $17.85 to $14.05. Cleveland's indebtedness (1879–81) also dropped by $2.1 million from $61.89 per capita (1879) to $38.00 per capita (1 January 1882). Among his other achievements, the mayor instituted an annual census by the police department, a reform thought unique to Cleveland at the time. As Cleveland's leading citizen, Herrick presided over the funeral services of assassinated President James A. Garfield (September 1882), a native Clevelander whose body was brought to rest there, largely through the mayor's intercession.

After leaving city hall, Herrick remained in the public eye as a vice-president of the prominent Society for Savings Bank and as director of public works under Mayor William G. Rose (*q.v.*) (1891–92). He died in Cleveland one day after his seventy-third birthday, on 30 January 1899, and was buried in Lake View Cemetery.

SOURCES: *The Cleveland City Directory*, 1879–80, 1881–82, and 1899–1900; Cleveland *Plain Dealer*, March 1879 to March 1882 and January 1899; Jedediah and Lucius C. Herrick, *A Genealogical Register of the Name and Family Herrick, etc.* (Columbus, Ohio, 1885); "R. R. Herrick," *Biographical Cyclopedia and Portrait Gallery of Representative Men of the State of Ohio* (1883), vol. 1; Gertrude Van Rensselaer Wickham, *The Pioneer Families of Cleveland, 1796–1840* (Cleveland, 1914), vol. 2.   *Eric C. Lewandowski*

HERRON, JOHN (1815?–?), Mayor of Pittsburgh (1849). Whig Mayor Herron was born around 1815 in Pittsburgh. He was a descendant of Scotch-Irish Presbyterians who first came to America from Ireland in 1734. His father, Reverend Francis Herron (1774–1860), was born in Shippensburg, Cumberland County, Pennsylvania. His mother, Elizabeth Herron (1777–?), was also a native-born Pennsylvanian. In 1811, Reverend Herron moved to Pittsburgh where he became pastor of the First Presbyterian Church and an influential clergyman. Nothing is known of John Herron's early life, education, work, or marriage. Herron was a captain in the

Duquesne Greys, a volunteer company from the Pittsburgh area, during the Mexican-American War. He participated in the siege of Vera Cruz and was mustered out of service in July 1848.

Located in Allegheny County, Pittsburgh in 1850 had a population of 46,601 and a mayor-council form of government. The councils (select and common) held most municipal authority, exercising both legislative and executive powers. The mayor served mainly as a police chief and a magistrate. Although he was a war veteran and a member of a prominent Pittsburgh family, Captain Herron barely defeated Charles B. Scully for the Whig mayoral nomination in December 1884. On 9 January 1849, he won the election with 1,868 votes to 1,514 for Calvin Adams (Democratic, Citizens' and Workingmen's Candidate), 251 for Neville B. Craig (Free-Soil), 213 for John S. Moorehead (Independent), and 13 for Isaac Harris (Independent Whig). Herron did not run for reelection.

Captain Herron's electoral victory continued the traditional Whig control of Pittsburgh's mayoralty. Herron's mediocre one-year term was characterized by strict enforcement of city ordinances and particularly stern judgments in the mayor's court. The main achievement of his administration was the breakup of a gang of arsonists who had for some time terrorized the city and destroyed several thousands of dollars worth of property. Herron angered some elements of his party and the *Gazette*, a Whig daily, by appointing the *Chronicle*, a Free-Soil newspaper, city printer. The highlight of Herron's term in office was the visit of President Zachary Taylor and Governor William F. Johnston to Pittsburgh on 18 August 1849.

Nothing is known of Herron following his mayoralty.

SOURCES: *History of Allegheny County* (author unknown) (Chicago, 1889), Part 2; Allen Humphreys Kerr, "The Mayors and Recorders of Pittsburgh, 1816–1951" (unpublished manuscript, Historical Society of Western Pennsylvania, Pittsburgh, 1952); Pittsburgh *Gazette*, 28 December 1848, 9 and 20 March 1849; Erasmus Wilson, ed., *Standard History of Pittsburgh* (Chicago, 1898).

Matthew S. Magda

HERRON, JOHN S.* **(1872-1947)**, Mayor of Pittsburgh (1933-34). Herron, president of the city council during the second term of Mayor Charles H. Kline (*q.v.*), served out the last nine months of the term after Kline's resignation. Herron was born in Oswego, New York, in 1872, and his father, Hugh H. Herron, was an Irish-born printer and composing-room foreman. The senior Herron

and his wife, Margaret Skinner Herron, had at least five children, of whom John was the fourth-born. The other four were Anne (b. 1867), Josie (b. 1869), George (b. 1871), and Alice (b. 1878). Herron attended Oswego public schools and was apprenticed as a bricklayer. He moved to Pittsburgh in 1901, and two years later, while working for a Pittsburgh contractor in Canton, Ohio, eloped with Cora W. Wagner, the daughter of a Canton saloon-keeper (October 1903). They had one daughter, Margaret.

By 1905, Herron was president of the Pittsburgh bricklayers' union local and remained a union member throughout his political career. After an unsuccessful candidacy for clerk of courts in 1911 on the Keystone ticket, Herron was appointed to the public health department in 1913 by Mayor William A. Magee (*q.v.*). The following year he won a seat on the city council and served five consecutive terms, being elected president of the council, 1918–21 and 1930–33. During Kline's mayoralty, Herron allied himself firmly with the mayor and attempted to deflect the scandal that enveloped that administration. After Kline's resignation in March 1933, Herron served two weeks as acting mayor, and then eight-and-a-half months as mayor *pro tempore*.

In 1933, Herron received the Republican nomination for a full term as mayor, but he lost the election to Democrat William N. McNair (*q.v.*) by a vote of 75,786 to 103,119. In May 1934, the judges of the court of common pleas named him to a life position on the board of viewers and then, in December 1935, to the county commission to serve the term of James F. Malone who had died shortly after his election. Herron was elected county commissioner in his own right in 1938 and reelected in 1941 and 1944. He was renominated in 1947, but before the election, he died of a kidney ailment in Magee Hospital on 13 September 1947, and was buried in Homewood Cemetery.

SOURCES: Allen Humphreys Kerr. "The Mayors and Recorders of Pittsburgh, 1816–1951: Their Lives and Somewhat of Their Times" (Typescript, 1952, Carnegie Public Library, Pittsburgh); Pittsburgh *Post-Gazette*, 14 September 1947; Pittsburgh *Press*, 13 September 1947; Bruce M. Stave, *The New Deal and the Last Hurrah: Pittsburgh Machine Politics* (Pittsburgh, 1970).

Douglas V. Shaw

HEWITT, ABRAM S. (1822–1903), Mayor of New York (1887–88). A professional Democratic politician of the reform variety and a famous iron manufacturer, Hewitt was born on a farm near Haverstraw, New York, to John Hewitt (1777–1857), an immigrant cabinetmaker, machinist, and farmer who had been born in Staffordshire, England, and Ann (Gurnee) Hewitt, a

*Not to be confused with the earlier John Herron (1815–?), also mayor of Pittsburgh.

Haverstraw native of Huguenot and English (like her husband, Protestant) stock. The fifth of seven children, Hewitt was raised in New York City, where his father established a moderately successful furniture-making and wholesaling business. Hewitt attended the public common school and obtained scholarships to the distinguished Columbia College Grammar School and to Columbia College, from which he graduated as salutatorian in 1842. He read law and taught school, and in 1844 he made a tour of Europe with Edward Cooper (*q.v.*), a Columbia classmate. In 1845 Edward's father, the famous New York industrialist and philanthropist Peter Cooper, provided the two friends with enough capital to establish an iron mill in Trenton, New Jersey. By the 1850s, Cooper and Hewitt was one of the largest establishments in the industry, and Hewitt had begun to establish himself as an unusually shrewd entrepreneur. Diversifying his business into a variety of iron and steel products, keeping up with new techniques, and adding facilities and ore lands in Pennsylvania and the South, Hewitt rose as far in the industry as his eastern location would permit. But after the late 1860s further expansion would have required a move to western Pennsylvania which Peter Cooper, who had become Hewitt's father-in-law as well as his principal creditor refused to approve.

His career as an industrialist blocked, Hewitt devoted an increasing portion of his energies to politics. Drawn during the 1860s into New York City affairs through the Citizens' Association (of which Peter Cooper was president) and through his developing friendship with Samuel J. Tilden, Hewitt and Edward Cooper were active in Tilden's anti-Tweed Committee of 70 in 1871 and in the subsequent effort to "purify" Tammany under the leadership of "Honest John" Kelly. Campaigning as a master artisan who treated his men well and as an advocate of honesty, hard currency, and a low tariff, he won election to Congress from the lower East Side, gashouse district in 1874. Two years later he was reelected, while serving as Tilden's chairman of the Democratic National Committee. Left out of Congress during a split with Kelly in 1879–80, Hewitt, Edward Cooper, William C. Whitney, and others set up the County Democracy as a rival to Tammany; Hewitt returned to Congress under its banner.

In 1886, Hewitt accepted the joint Tammany-County Democracy mayoral nomination after it had become clear that the radical tax reformer Henry George would run very well as the nominee of the United Labor party. Insisting on the fundamental unity of interests between employers and workers, and campaigning against Marx more than against George, Hewitt won with 90,552 votes to 68,110 for George and 60,435 for the Republican, young Theodore Roosevelt. The city was then over 1.4 million in size, with a weak mayor-council system. As

mayor, Hewitt sought, so far as his limited powers over city departments permitted, to reduce corruption and to increase efficiency while remembering his political debts, to enforce the Sunday closing laws, and to improve the city's basic services. He also tried to exert leadership over long-term policies in such areas as rapid transit, port development, and the construction of small parks in poor neighborhoods. As a result of accumulating patronage conflicts with Tammany, his refusal to review the 1888 St. Patrick's Day Parade, his increasingly vocal opposition to organized labor, as well as his bitter feud with Cleveland, Mayor Hewitt undertook an independent reelection campaign with a remnant of the County Democracy. Even though he polled nearly 28 percent of the vote, he lost to Tammany's Hugh J. Grant (*q.v.*).

Following this defeat, Hewitt continued active in business and local affairs, and in building up Cooper Union Institute. He consistently sought to reconcile the interests of taxpayers with those of manufacturers, merchants, and common carriers. His most lasting contribution to New York was a rapid transit plan that combined public financing with private ownership and management, all under Chamber of Commerce supervision. Hewitt died of jaundice at his New York home on 18 January 1903, aged eighty-one.

SOURCES: Thomas J. Condon, "Politics, Reform, and the New York City Election of 1886," *New-York Historical Society Quarterly* 44 (July 1960); Matthew T. Downey, "Grover Cleveland and Abram S. Hewitt: The Limits of Factional Consensus," *New-York Historical Society Quarterly* 53 (1970); A. S. Hewitt Mayoral Letterpress Copybooks, and Cooper-Hewitt Letterpress Copybooks, *New York Historical Society*; Letters to Mayor Hewitt, Mayors' Papers, New York City Municipal Archives and Records Center; Allan Nevins, *Abram S. Hewitt, With Some Account of Peter Cooper* (New York, 1935); Allan Nevins, *Selected Writings of Abram S. Hewitt* (New York, 1937); Louis F. Post and Fred C. Leubscher, *Henry George's 1886 Campaign* (Westport, Conn., 1976 reprint edition).   *David C. Hammack*

HEWSTON, GEORGE (1826–91), Mayor of San Francisco (1875). Very little is known about Hewston, who served as mayor of San Francisco for thirty-two days in 1875. Born in Philadelphia on 11 September 1826, the son of a businessman, Hewston was of English, Irish, and Scottish ancestry. He was trained in medicine at the University of Pennsylvania and the Philadelphia College of Medicine. With his wife Emily, two sons, and a daughter, he moved to San Francisco in 1860. There he practiced as a physician and spent most of his time teaching medicine. Hewston was also a leading light in the San Francisco Medical Society.

In 1873, Hewston was elected to the board of supervisors on the People's party ticket, an offshoot of the Republicans. When Mayor James Otis (*q.v.*) died in office on 30 October 1875, city leaders had to decide how to replace him. Elections had already determined a new mayor who would be inaugurated in December, and all but one of the supervisors had been turned out of office. Nevertheless, the board of supervisors decided to elect one of themselves as interim mayor for the month that remained in Otis's term. On the twenty-second ballot the supervisors chose Hewston as a compromise candidate, giving him seven of the eleven votes cast. He became mayor in a city of more than 200,000 people.

Hewston did virtually nothing as a lame-duck, interim mayor, but his rhetoric reflected the transition from one type of San Francisco executive to another. Like his predecessors, Hewston stood for fiscal conservatism and more police, but like his successor he spoke out against the Chinese. Characteristically for a doctor, perhaps, he also urged better public health programs.

After his brief stint as mayor, Hewston returned to teaching and medical practice. He became a member of the state centennial commission in 1876 and later joined the California Academy of the Sciences. In 1884, he became chairman of the National Anti-Monopoly party, an organization devoted to reducing the length of the working day, repaying the public debt, and legalizing greenbacks as public and private tender. Hewston died of Bright's disease on 4 September 1891.

SOURCE: William J. Heintz, *San Francisco's Mayors 1850–1880* (Woodside, Calif., 1975).

John M. Findlay

HIBBARD, GEORGE ALBEE (1864–1910), Mayor of Boston (1908–10). Postmaster of Boston who became Republican mayor for a single term during the John F. ("Honey Fitz") Fitzgerald (*q.v.*) years, Hibbard was born in Boston on 27 October 1864, the son of a strong abolitionist, Alonzo D. Hibbard, and Janette (Turner) Hibbard. He attended Roxbury High School (class of 1880) and went to work as a clerk in Quincy Market in his father's wholesale produce business. Later he was in insurance, stock dealings, and Hibbard and Mason tailors (as treasurer). Hibbard was not a business success. On 27 October 1886, he married M. Adelaide Ford.

A staunch Republican, Hibbard entered local politics, being elected to the Massachusetts House in 1894. He was made postmaster of Boston (1900–1908) until elected mayor in a close race in 1908. A parsimonious Yankee who believed in efficient, cheap government, Hibbard was brought in, ostensibly as a reformer, to defeat the incumbent mayor, "Honey Fitz." At first, Hibbard told Fitzgerald: "I decline to be your under-

taker''—to which the quick-witted Fitz replied: "Well, I prefer to have a respectable undertaker!" But Hibbard won with 38,000 votes, a plurality of 2,177 over Fitzgerald. Anti-Fitzgerald Democratic ward bosses had run John A. Coulthurst as a quasi-Independent; he made a respectable showing of 15,811 votes.

Although Hibbard promised to "clean up the mess," he was no genuine reformer or independent, and it was said that he had won "by the grace of God and the blunders of Fitzgerald." The victory was mainly a temporary anti-Democratic, anti-spending vote. Mayor Hibbard immediately made cuts: he sacked a thousand city workers, cut street maintenance costs in half, and reduced the city debt. His parrot-like nose, the delight of political cartoonists, seemed to fit the economy image. Hibbard favored the new city charter, pushed through the Massachusetts legislature in 1909, which gave more power to the mayor, as opposed to the council, and established a permanent Finance Committee, selected by the governor. The new charter was adopted by the city itself on 2 November 1909 by a majority vote of 3,894. A common problem with U.S. cities at this time was too strong a fear of executive power and overly ambitious city councils, which were the seat of corruption and patronage.

Hibbard made many enemies, and in 1910 the reformers would not back him for reelection, choosing instead James J. Storrow. With little support and no money, the ailing Hibbard ran, encouraged, it is said, by "Honey Fitz," who wanted to split the vote. Fitzgerald triumphed and returned to power on 11 January 1910. Out of 95,000 votes, Fitzgerald won 47,177, Storrow 45,775, and Hibbard 1,614. An obscure fourth candidate, Nathan Taylor, got 613 votes. Hibbard had made the difference for Fitzgerald, who could easily have lost such a close count. He offered Hibbard the post of city collector, which was refused. Soon after, on 29 May 1910, Hibbard died of tuberculosis of the throat, a disappointed man who felt that his reforms had never been appreciated.

SOURCES: L. Ainley, *Boston Mahatma: The Public Career of Martin Lomasney* (Boston, 1949); J. H. Cutler, *"Honey Fitz": Three Steps to the White House* (Indianapolis, 1962); John Koren, *Boston, 1822–1922* (Boston, 1923); Francis Russell, *The Great Interlude* (New York, 1964).

Peter d'A. Jones

HILLEN, SOLOMON (1810–73), Mayor of Baltimore (1842–43). Hillen, a member of an old and prominent Maryland Catholic family, was born in 1810 on the family estate near Baltimore. He was the fifth child of Thomas and Robina Kennedy (McHaffle) Hillen. Originally, the Hillens were Quakers, but on the death of the first Solomon Hillen and the remarriage of his widow, Elizabeth Raven Hillen, to Thomas Wheeler, a Catholic,

Hillen's grandfather was brought up in the Catholic faith. At the age of ten, in September 1820, Hillen was enrolled in Georgetown College, the Jesuit school in Washington, D.C. He received his A.B. degree in 1827 and continued to do additional work there until July of the following year. He probably was entitled to an M.A. degree. In his youth, Hillen also studied law and was admitted to the bar. He practiced law until ill health forced him to retire.

Hillen was a popular figure in Baltimore. He married Emily O'Donnell, daughter of General Columbus O'Donnell of Baltimore, and they had two children, Thomas and Emily. Hillen became involved in local military affairs and was a member and captain of the Independent Blues. Later, he became a colonel in the old Fifth Regiment. Politically, Hillen became a Democrat, and he held several political offices after his entry into politics. He served in the Maryland House of Delegates from 1834 to 1838 and was subsequently elected to the U.S. House of Representatives to represent Maryland in the Twenty-sixth Congress (March 1839–March 1841) for one term. Upon returning to Baltimore, he resumed his law practice. However, one year later, with the sudden resignation of Mayor Samuel Brady (*q.v.*), Hillen at the age of thirty-two was elected the city's youngest mayor in a special election over two other candidates: Hillen, 5,156 General S. C. Leakin (*q.v.*) 1,846, and Colonel Jacob Small (*q.v.*), 3,190. Hillen's majority over the combined vote of his two rivals was 120.

Baltimore, then a part of Baltimore County, had a population of 102,313 in 1840 and a mayor-council form of government, although the mayor's office possessed little power. In the early 1840s, no party dominated Baltimore, and victories were won by small margins. However, when Hillen ran for reelection in 1842, he was overwhelmingly elected by nearly a 3 to 1 margin—7,296 to 2,853—over his Whig opponent, Jacob Small.

Hillen's term of office was fairly uneventful. The city council created a special commission, with Hillen serving as a member, to investigate the possibility of reorganizing municipal departments. A number of civic improvements were made and approved. In the 1840s, Baltimore merchants and entrepreneurs continued to seek to expand the city's commercial base, and during Hillen's administration, the Baltimore and Ohio Railroad completed its line to Cumberland in its push for western markets. However, in the fall of 1843 Hillen resigned.

Hillen, having been in poor health for some time, died in the Fifth Avenue Hotel in New York City on 26 June 1873.

SOURCES: Wilbur F. Coyle, *The Mayors of Baltimore* (Baltimore, 1919); Dielman File and Filing case A, Maryland Historical Society; J. Thomas Scharf, *Chron-* *icles of Baltimore* (Baltimore, 1874); J. Thomas Scharf, *History of Maryland* (Hatboro, Pa., reprint, 1967).
                                              Richard R. Duncan

HINKS, SAMUEL (1815–87), Mayor of Baltimore (1854–56). Baltimore's first Know-Nothing mayor, Hinks was born on 1 May 1815 in Ellicott City, Maryland. His parents, William Hinks of Ellicott City and Mary Dent Hinks from an area near Washington, D.C., were quite poor and unable to provide Samuel with a formal education. Although often referred to as "a courtly and refined gentleman of the old school," Hinks was not a member of Maryland's traditional elite. His humble background, however, allowed him to be extolled by American party literature as "self-made, sound, unobtrusive, honorable, amiable, and upright." Hinks was at first a steam engineer, but on moving to Baltimore, he and his brother, Charles Dent Hinks, entered the grain and flour commission business. As a mill merchant, Samuel Hinks made a sizable fortune and with his wife produced seven children—four sons and three daughters. His eldest son, William, became a lawyer and also served as a Republican member of the state legislature.

Hinks' own political credentials were as inconspicuous as his origins. Although he had Democratic antecedents before his stint as mayor from 1854 to 1856, Hinks did not consider himself a politician. Indeed, he only accepted the Know-Nothing mayoral nomination after having been assured that he would not be required to campaign for his own election. The city's press registered surprise at the American party's selection of such a political unknown, the secrecy associated with his nomination, and the lateness of the Know-Nothings' announcement of Hinks' candidacy: only two weeks prior to the 11 October 1854 municipal elections. The Know-Nothings hoped that Hinks could rely on his business associates and the numerous connections he had secretly cultivated as a nativist lodge member. But as a precautionary measure, the Know-Nothings carefully printed their ballots with the same blue stripes on the back as had the Democrats, in hopes of benefiting from the voters' confusion. On election day, Hinks defeated his Democratic opponent William G. Thomas by a vote of 13,845 to 11,104. Moreover, the Know-Nothings scored significant triumphs in the city council, displacing earlier Democratic majorities in both branches.

Baltimore's population was rapidly increasing from the 1850 Census figure of 169,054, and, as mayor, Hinks responded by authorizing construction of a new city jail and taking important first steps in the establishment of a municipally operated water plant. As a political novice in Baltimore's mayor-council form of government, Hinks attempted to fill his 500 patronage positions with "the best men,'' thereby alienating Know-Nothing council members, who adamantly refused to approve the appointments of non-nativist Whigs and Democrats. This move helped to split the American party. After his term ended on 10 November 1856, Hinks continued in his profitable career as commission merchant and later served as Baltimore's water registrar (1860–63). He died on 30 November 1887.

SOURCES: Jean H. Baker, *Ambivalent Americans: The Know-Nothing Party in Maryland* (Baltimore, 1977); Wilbur F. Coyle, *The Mayors of Baltimore* (Baltimore, 1919); Enoch Pratt Free Library, Baltimore: Vertical File (newspaper clippings), Maryland Room; J. Thomas Scharf, *History of Baltimore City and County: From the Earliest Period to the Present Day* (Philadelphia, 1891); Richard Walsh and William Lloyd Fox, ed., *Maryland: A History, 1632–1974* (Baltimore, 1974).

Jo Ann Eady Argersinger

HOADLEY, GEORGE (1781–1857), Mayor of Cleveland (1846–47). Hoadley was born in Branford, Connecticut, on 15 December 1781, the son of Timothy Hoadley (1739–1816), a Revolutionary War officer, and Rebecca (Linley) Hoadley, both old-stock New England Protestants. Hoadley attended local schools and Yale, graduating in 1801. He was a Yale tutor, 1803–1806, while pursuing legal studies with Charles Chauncey. Hoadley was in Washington, D.C., as correspondent for the *U.S. Gazette*, 1806–1808. He then moved to New Haven, Connecticut, became a successful lawyer, and served as that city's mayor, 1822–26. On 8 November 1819, he married Mary Anne Woolsey Scarborough (1793–1871) of New York, and they had four children. Hoadley was president of the Eagle Bank, and, following its failure in 1830, the family moved west to Cleveland.

Arriving in Cleveland, Hoadley took out an ad in the *Herald*, seeking clients, and soon developed a flourishing practice, earning enough in fees to gain the nickname ''Squire Hoadley.'' He was a justice of the peace in Cleveland, 1835–47, hearing some 20,000 cases during that period. In 1846, Hoadley was elected mayor as a Whig, although he apparently had been a Democrat in Connecticut. He won 579 votes to 564 for William T. Goodwin (Democrat) and 85 for William Adair (Abolitionist). At that time, Cleveland had over 10,000 people and a mayor-council form of government.

As mayor, Hoadley supported a new high school over the opposition of some local politicians who claimed it would be too expensive and too elitist. He showed no desire to continue in politics after his single term and retired. He spent his time raising flowers, winning several prizes. He died on 20 February 1857, following an attack of pleurisy.

SOURCES: Benjamin W. Dwight, *The History of the Descendants of John Dwight of Dedham, Mass.*, 2 vols. (New York, 1874); *The New England Historical and Genealogical Register and Antiquarian Journal*, N.S.1:2 (April 1857); Gertrude Wickham, *The Pioneer Families of Cleveland, 1796 to 1840*, 2 vols. (Chicago, 1914).

Thomas R. Bullard

HOAN, DANIEL WEBSTER (1881–1961), Mayor of Milwaukee (1916–40). Socialist mayor of Milwaukee a record twenty-four years, Hoan was born on 31 March 1881 at Waukesha, Wisconsin, the youngest of five children of Irish-Canadian Socialist Daniel Webster Hoan (1841–95)—formerly Horan—a blacksmith and boarding-house owner, and Margaret A. (Hood) Hoan (d. 1927), a Waukesha native of English-German ancestry. Hoan and his three surviving siblings lived with their father following their parents' divorce in 1889. After his father's death, Hoan left school in the sixth grade but later worked as a cook to finance his education at the University of Wisconsin (B.A., 1905). Even though he was an active Socialist in 1898, he was chosen senior class president and associate editor of the newspaper. In Chicago after graduation, Hoan operated his own restaurant from 1906 to 1907, earned a Kent College of Law degree in 1908, and, in 1909, married his former cashier, an Irish Catholic, Agnes Bernice Magner (1883–1941) of Morris, Illinois; their two children were Daniel Webster, Jr. (b. 1910) and Agnes (b. 1916). In 1944, three years after his first wife's death, Hoan married Gladys Arthur Townsend, a Muncie, Indiana, schoolteacher who served as Wisconsin's Democratic national committeewoman before her death in 1952.

Recruited to Milwaukee in 1908 by local Socialists, Hoan assured his success as a labor lawyer by drafting the nation's first workmen's compensation law (1911). Milwaukee voters, weary of Democratic and Republican corruption, chose Hoan as city attorney in the 1910 Socialist sweep and, despite the defeat of the Socialist mayor in 1912, reelected Hoan in 1914. In 1916, Hoan toppled incumbent Mayor Gerhard A. Bading (*q.v.*) (33,863 to 32,206). Reelected six times, Hoan defeated Percy Braman in 1918 (37,504 to 35,394); Clifton Williams in 1920 (40,530 to 37,205); former Mayor David S. Rose (*q.v.*) in 1924 (74,418 to 57,495); Charles Schallitz in 1928 (64,874 to 46,657); Joseph P. Carney in 1932 (108,279 to 62,511); and Joseph J. Shinners in 1936 (111,561 to 98,897). In 1940, Carl F. Zeidler (*q.v.*) ended Hoan's tenure with a 111,957 to 99,798 win. During Hoan's administrations, Milwaukee's population rose from an estimated 436,535 in 1916 to 587,472 in 1940.

Although Milwaukee's elections had been officially

nonpartisan since 1912, Hoan consistently emphasized his Socialist party allegiance. Yet, he proved more interested in improved services and government ("sewer socialism") than in political theory, and in 1917, he refused to support the Socialists' St. Louis Proclamation opposing the war. Handicapped by nonpartisan majorities in the common council and unsuccessful in securing municipal ownership of street railways and electric power, Hoan nonetheless forged an enviable record, eliminating graft, bettering the city's health and safety, supporting harbor improvement, and reducing debt by financing improvements on a pay-as-you-go basis. Always the workingman's champion, Hoan backed governmentally subscribed housing in the 1920s, municipal marketing of surplus foodstuffs to combat profiteering during the Depression, a minimum wage for city employees, and the right to strike.

Following his 1940 defeat, Hoan left the Socialist party, joined the Progressives, and, in 1944, became a Democrat, running unsuccessfully for governor in 1944 and 1946 and for Congress in 1948. He also finished fourth of fifteen in the 1948 Milwaukee mayoral primary. After several strokes, Hoan died on 11 June 1961 at the age of eighty.

SOURCES: Daniel W. Hoan, *City Government: The Record of the Milwaukee Experiment* (New York, 1936); Daniel Webster Hoan Papers, 45 boxes, Milwaukee County Historical Society; Daniel Webster Hoan Mayor's Papers, 7 boxes, Milwaukee Public Library; Edward S. Kerstein, *Milwaukee's All-American Mayor: Portrait of Daniel Webster Hoan* (Englewood Cliffs, N.J., 1966); Bayrd Still, *Milwaukee: The History of a City* (Madison, Wis., 1966).

Barbara M. Posadas

HODGES, ALPHEUS P. (1822–n.a.), Mayor of Los Angeles (1850–51). First mayor of Los Angeles under its American charter of 1850, Hodges is also one of its most obscure. It is known that he was born in Virginia, was unmarried, and became a physician. According to the 1850 Census, he was not involved in municipal affairs prior to that year. He did not sign a fee schedule established by four other city physicians in 1850, and no evidence exists of his ever practicing medicine. Yet, he managed to come to the attention of the power elite in Los Angeles when the candidate for coroner, secretly selected by the group of insiders organizing city and county government, declined to serve. At its first meeting on 24 June 1850, the county court of sessions, the prime agency of county government, appointed Hodges as replacement. Hodges then became the only candidate for mayor in the first city election on 1 July 1850, establishing a council-mayor form of government for the city of 1,610 persons.

As mayor, Hodges' activities consisted primarily of performing those tasks assigned to him by the common council, which were mainly supervising the cleaning of the streets and collecting the monthly business licenses. He did recommend the establishment of a city police force, a suggestion not followed in favor of continued reliance on volunteer police forces, in which Hodges also served. When his term expired at what became the regular date, the first week in May 1851, he did not seek further city office, although he continued to serve as county coroner.

In October 1851, Hodges became the manager of the city's leading hotel, the Bella Union. According to recollections of Angelenos, he tended bar "with a perpetual smile," serving "the most bandit, cut-throat looking set" of men. Another resident recalled that Hodges could manufacture a potent cactus brandy. He operated the Bella Union in partnership with gambler Alexander Gibson until 28 July 1852, but shortly thereafter he reopened in partnership with James B. Winston, a physician and son-in-law of one of the area's leading *rancheros*. The firm of Winston and Hodges operated the hotel for only a few months. Hodges attended the first meeting of Los Angeles' Masons on 17 December 1853, after which there is no record of his presence in the city.

SOURCES: Maymie R. Krythe, "First Hotel of Old Los Angeles: The Romantic Bella Union," *Historical Society of Southern California Quarterly* 33 (March 1951); William W. Robinson, *Lawyers of Los Angeles: A History of the Los Angeles Bar Association and of the Bar of Los Angeles County* (Los Angeles, 1959); Leonard Ross Sanders, "Los Angeles and Its Mayors, 1850–1925" (M.A. thesis, University of Southern California, 1968).

R. David Weber

HODGES, JAMES (1822–95), Mayor of Baltimore (1885–87). Hodges was born at Liberty Hall, Kent County, Maryland, on 11 August 1822. Both his father, James, Sr., and his mother, Mary Hanson Ringgold, were English and Episcopalian. James was the eldest of five children. Educated in private schools, James subsequently moved to Baltimore and established a dry goods importing firm. On 30 November 1847, he married Josephine A. Bash, and they had four children: Mary Ella, Ida Virginia, Lily Hanson, and William Ringgold. Although a life-long Democrat, Hodges was never a professional politician, and he returned to his business after being mayor.

In 1890, Baltimore had a population of 434,439 and a mayor-council form of government. Hodges ran on the regular Democratic party ticket in 1885 against Judge George William Brown (*q.v.*) who represented the fusion of Republicans and Independent Democrats. On 28 October, Hodges polled 30,897 votes and Brown 28,667; there were 79,514 registered voters in the city at the time. Hodges' administrative achievements related chiefly to the expansion of the city during a period of prosperity. The city established a new observatory on Federal Hill. Five new schoolhouses and several new firehouses were built, new bridges were constructed across Jones Falls, the Patapsco River channel was deepened and widened, several city markets were rebuilt and enlarged, and the decimal system for numbering houses was established. Hodges died on 15 February 1895.

SOURCES: Wilbur F. Coyle, *The Mayors of Baltimore* (Baltimore, 1919); "James Hodges," the Dielman File, Maryland Historical Society, Baltimore; The *Sun Almanac* for 1886.   *Gary L. Browne*

HOFFMAN, JOHN THOMPSON (1828–88), Mayor of New York (1866–68). Mayor of New York and later governor, Hoffman was born in Sing Sing, later Ossining, New York, on 10 January 1828. His father, Dr. Adrian Kissan Hoffman, was an Episcopalian of Dutch-English extraction and was related to Philip Livingston, a signer of the Declaration of Independence. His mother, Jane Ann Thompson, also an Episcopalian, was allied with several prominent upstate families. Hoffman first attended Mount Pleasant Academy and at the age of fifteen entered Union College. He graduated with honors in 1846 and studied law with Judge Albert Richmond and Congressman Aaron Ward, being admitted to the bar in 1849. He immediately began a New York City practice. During those years, Hoffman took an active part in politics and joined the "Hunkers," conservative Democrats who opposed the radical Van Buren "Barnburners." In 1854, he married Ella Starkweather, daughter of Henry Starkweather, a merchant in the city. The couple had one child, Ella.

In 1860, Hoffman received the Democratic nomination for recorder and was elected by a good majority. He was the youngest person to hold that office, which dealt with criminal prosecutions. After the Draft Riots of 1863, he earned public approval for the severity of sentences he handed out to convicted rioters. In the fall of 1863, he was renominated by the Republicans as well as the Democrats and won 60,000 votes out of 64,000 cast—an unheard of occurrence. Nominated by the Democrats for mayor in 1865, he accepted, reluctantly, what he knew to be a "thankless" job. Opposed by Republican Marshall O. Roberts, the reform Citizens' Union candidate, John Hecker of the famed flour company, and the anti-Tammany faction candidate, C. Godfrey Gunther, Hoffman won a considerable personal victory, having 1,200 votes over Roberts, the next highest candidate. In 1866, Hoffman was nominated to run for governor.

Tall, dignified, with a distinguished appearance and an excellent reputation for independence, honesty, and sincerity, Hoffman "stumped" the state but could not overcome charges of being a war Democrat of the Stephen A. Douglas type. The support of Andrew Johnson proved a final straw. He lost the election to Reuben Fenton by a little over 13,000 votes out of 718,000 cast. However, he was reelected mayor at the end of the year. In 1868, he was again nominated for governor and defeated John A. Griswold of Troy by more than 27,000 votes. At that time, New York had a population of over 800,000 and a mayor-council form of government, with a weak executive.

In November 1870, Hoffman was reelected governor over Stewart L. Woodford by a 33,000-vote majority. Hoffman's rising star as a presidential candidate was destroyed by the press exposé of William A. Tweed and his corrupt "Ring." Hoffman's career was seemingly unjustifiably destroyed without a trial and with little, if any, evidence. His relationship with Tweed was official and casual, and his appointment of "Tweed judges" was in keeping with their legal reputation. Although he attended the national Democratic convention in Baltimore in July 1872, he had no hope for the nomination. He did not run again for public office, despite an apparent offer from President Cleveland (*q.v.*). He died suddenly on 24 March 1888 in Wiesbaden, Germany, and was interred at Dale Cemetery, Ossining, New York.

SOURCES: John T. Hoffman, *Public Papers of John T. Hoffman* (Albany, N.Y., 1872); Adrian H. Joline "John Thompson Hoffman" *New York and Genealogical and Biographical Record* 42 (April, 1911); Allan Nevins and Milton H. Thomas, eds., *The Diary of George Templeton Strong, 1835–1870*, 4 vols. (New York, 1952); David T. Valentine *Manual of the Corporation of the City of New York* (New York, 1860–70).

Leo Hershkowitz

HOLLING, THOMAS LESLIE (1889–1966), Mayor of Buffalo (1938–41). Printer and reform mayor, born in Bad Axe, Michigan, on 23 April 1889, Holling was the son of Thomas Holling (d. 1889) and Louisa (Knight) Holling, both of Anglo-Scottish descent. The last of three children, Holling spent his early childhood in Wyoming, Ontario, where his widowed mother had brought the family in 1890. He attended local Canadian schools until 1900 when he entered the printing business. In 1906, he moved to Buffalo, joining the McLoughlin Press. In 1911, he established the Holling Printing Company and soon earned a substantial fortune. On 14 June 1910, he married Mary F. Lenhard (1887–1955), and they had one daughter. The Hollings belonged to St. Vincent De Paul (Catholic) Church and were active in church-backed social work. Holling belonged to the Chamber of Commerce and Knights of Columbus, and in 1942 became a director of the Industrial Bank.

An Independent Democrat, Holling unsuccessfully campaigned for the state legislature in 1932 and 1934. In 1937, he was elected mayor, with 94,037 votes to 92,610 for Republican, Edwin F. Jaeckle, 11,392 for Joseph Kaszubowski (Ecpole party), 6,794 for Frank Schawb (*q.v.*) (People's party), and 966 for Herman Hahn (Socialist). Buffalo had 575,901 people in 1940 and a mayor-council form of government.

As mayor, Holling was considered the first real reformer in Buffalo since 1909. Following a pay-as-you-go plan, he took a 20 percent reduction in his own salary and also cut the city budget. He supported the construction of new housing and was fond of reminding his public that Thomas Jefferson was the greatest American of all time. He insisted that city workers had to be punctual, courteous, and neatly dressed. Under the city charter, he did not seek another term in 1941 but ran again in 1945, losing to Republican Bernard Dowd (*q.v.*), 80,383 to 60,461. Former Mayor Frank Schwab, on the People's ticket, got 35,256 votes.

Holling served briefly on the board of safety, 1958–59, resigning after an argument over the city's highway program. His wife died in 1955 and Holling married Mrs. Helen Busch Steele in November 1956. He retired and began spending winters in Florida, but as late as 1965 he was approached by local reform Democrats who urged him to seek the mayoral nomination. He died in Florida on 25 November 1966.

SOURCES: Buffalo *Evening News*, 15 June 1955, and 26 November 1966; Sister Mary Jane and Sister Mercedes, "Mayors of Buffalo, 1832–1961" (B.A. thesis, Rosary Hill College, 1961). *Thomas R. Bullard*

HOLLINS, JOHN SMITH (1786–1856), Mayor of Baltimore (1852–54). Hollins was born in 1786 in Baltimore. He was the son of John Hollins, a successful Liverpool banker who had emigrated to Maryland in 1783 and had married Jane Smith, a sister of General Samuel Smith (*q.v.*), a powerful Republican politician. The family was Presbyterian and Scots-Irish. Hollins' father became involved in local politics and served as a member of the powerful Second Branch of the city council between 1813 and 1820.

During the War of 1812, Hollins joined the Army and helped to defend Baltimore as an officer in the First Baltimore Hussars, part of the Fifth Maryland Cavalry led by his uncle, General Smith. With powerful political connections, Hollins entered politics and in October 1852 became the Democratic party's candidate for mayor. In the election, he scored an impressive victory over his Whig opponent, Richard France, 12,687 votes to 9,081. The Democratic party also carried both branches of the city council over a crumbling Whig party. Baltimore had a population of about 170,000 by this time.

During Hollins' administration, Baltimore's public water system was laid. The city council authorized a study of Baltimore's water supply in comparison with practices in other cities. The commission, which included the mayor, recommended that the city buy the private water corporation, and the general assembly granted the city the necessary bond authority to purchase the old Baltimore Water Company in 1853. Hollins also supervised additional municipal improvements such as eight school buildings, three bridges over Jones Falls, sewers, and the construction of Hanover Market House.

Two significant events occurred during Hollins' mayoralty. The Baltimore and Ohio Railroad completed its road to Wheeling on the Ohio River and thereby opened greater markets for Baltimore merchants. Meanwhile, in politics, a renewed and more virulent burst of nativism erupted in the form of the Know-Nothing movement which was to dominate Maryland for the remainder of the decade.

At the end of his term Hollins retired, and he died two years later at the age of seventy on 28 November 1856.

SOURCES: Wilbur F. Coyle, *The Mayors of Baltimore* (Baltimore, 1919); Dielman File, Maryland Historical Society; Clayton Colman Hall, ed., *Baltimore: Its History and Its People* (New York, 1912); J. Thomas Scharf, *History of Maryland* (Hatboro, Pa., reprint 1967). *Richard R. Duncan*

HOOKER, DAVID G. (1830–88), Mayor of Milwaukee (1872–73). Born in Poultney, Vermont, on 4 September 1830 of old-stock Anglo-American parents, Hooker graduated from Middlebury College in 1853. He studied law and was admitted to the bar in 1856, beginning the practice of law in Milwaukee. He married Sarah P. Harris of Middlebury, Vermont, in 1869. In 1872, he married Julia Ashley, an Episcopalian, and they had four children—Edward, Alice (McCutcheon), Edith (Greenwood), and Julia. In 1864, Hooker joined with H. L. Palmer in the law firm of Palmer and Hooker. A lifelong Democrat, Hooker served as city attorney (1867–1870). At that time, Milwaukee had a population of about 75,000 and a mayor-bicameral council form of government.

Hooker was elected mayor of Milwaukee in 1872, serving a one-year term. During his term, the problems of water and sewage dominated city government. Thirteen miles of water pipe were laid, pumping engines were installed, and a reservoir built.

Upon leaving office, Hooker returned to the practice

of law. The firm of Palmer and Hooker had often represented the Northwestern Mutual Life Insurance Company, and in 1878, he was appointed general counsel to that company, until his sudden death on 7 March 1888.

SOURCES: Frank A. Flower, *History of Milwaukee, Wisconsin* (Chicago, 1881); John S. Gregory, *History of Milwaukee, Wisconsin* (Chicago, 1931); Bayrd Still, *Milwaukee: The History of a City* (Madison, Wis., 1965); Jerome A. Watrous, *Memoirs of Milwaukee County*, 2 vols. (Madison, Wis., 1909).   *Donald F. Tingley*

HOOPER, ALCAEUS (1859–1938), Mayor of Baltimore (1895–97). Hooper was born in the suburbs of Baltimore in 1859 and was named for a Greek poet who was a favorite of his father, William E. Hooper (1812–85), a wealthy Scots-Irish manufacturer of cotton duck for sails. Alcaeus was the eighth of eleven children who were brought up in an imposing mansion overlooking Jones Falls and the family textile mills. His mother was Catherine (Bell) Hooper (1812–81). The Hoopers were active members of the Methodist Episcopal Church, and Alcaeus was an important figure in the church throughout his life. He took life very seriously, was quick to anger, and "scathing of tongue" against those who fell short of his own high standards. He attended a Quaker school in Baltimore and then entered his father's business. Young Alcaeus took an interest in the education of the workers employed at the Hooper mills, and in 1888, the year in which the locality was annexed to the city, he was appointed to the Baltimore City School Board. In 1893, he agreed to run for the city council on the Republican ticket and was elected. Two years later, he was asked to run on a fusion ticket of Republicans and reform Democrats, and he felt it his duty to accept the call. The election was a bitterly fought contest because the ruling Democratic machine, under the control of I. Freeman Rasin, was fighting for its life. After a tumultuous and violent election, Hooper was declared the winner, and the victory was cheered by municipal reformers throughout the nation. He was then thirty-six years old.

Unfortunately, the alliance between the Republicans and reform Democrats was fragile, born more of political necessity than of any deep mutual commitment to the principles of nonpartisan or honest municipal administration. Hooper, while adhering to the Republican party throughout his life, took the principle of local nonpartisanship very seriously. After entering office, he proceeded to appoint many worthy Democrats and Independents to office along with a generous portion of Republicans, which outraged those regular Republicans who had hoped to gain the full spoils. The Republican-dominated city council refused to confirm his appointees, and he, in turn, refused to confirm the council's appoin-

tees. Hooper next chose an entire new school board consisting of nonpartisan reformers headed by Daniel Coit Gilman, president of Johns Hopkins University. The council backed the old "political" board. Both cases were finally settled in the Maryland Court of Appeals, where the mayor won the appointment battle but lost the school board battle.

At the close of his term, Hooper was utterly anathema to the regular Republicans and was not even considered for a second term in spite of strong backing from many of the city's most prominent reformers. Reformer pressure forced Hooper's appointment to the city school board in 1900, and for the next eleven years he used this position to lash out against any intrusion of politics or, in his opinion, inefficiency in the school system. In 1911, his attacks on the president of the school board became so outspoken that he was taken to court by the embattled president. The issue was finally resolved when both Hooper and the president agreed to resign from the board. This finally ended Hooper's political activities. He was urged a number of times to run for office thereafter but always refused. He spent the remainder of his life managing the family's financial affairs. He died on 1 July 1938.

SOURCES: Wilbur Coyle, *The Mayors of Baltimore* (Baltimore, 1919); James B. Crooks, *Politics and Progress: The Rise of Urban Progressivism in Baltimore, 1895–1911* (Baton Rouge, La., 1968); Bernard Steiner, *Men of Mark in Maryland* (Washington, D.C., 1907).   *Joseph L. Arnold*

HOPKINS, JOHN PATRICK (1858–1918), Mayor of Chicago (1893–95). Chicago's first Irish Catholic mayor, born on 29 October 1858 in Buffalo, New York, Hopkins was the only son of seven children born to John and Mary (Flynn) Hopkins, Irish-born, immigrant parents. Educated at St. Joseph's College in Buffalo, he served as an apprentice machinist with the David Bell Company in Buffalo, 1871–74. For the next six years, he was the weighmaster for the Evans Elevator Company. In 1880, Hopkins moved to Chicago and was employed by the Pullman Palace Car Company, eventually becoming the firm's paymaster. By 1885, Hopkins, an enterprising suburban businessman, had established two general merchandise department stores, the Arcade Trading Company in Pullman and the Secord and Hopkins Company in Kensington. He was a leader in the pro-annexation movement that was successfully consummated on 29 June 1889 in which 120 square miles and more than 220,000 people were added to Chicago, making it the second largest American city. Hopkins, a bachelor, was a member of the Knights of Columbus, Chicago Athletic Club, South Shore Country Club, Catholic Order of Foresters, Washington Park, Columbus, and Sheridan Clubs.

Hopkins became active in Democratic politics upon his arrival in Chicago. He was chairman of the Democratic campaign committee, 1890–92; a delegate to the Democratic national conventions in 1892, 1900, and 1904; a vice-chairman of the National (Gold) Democratic Committee in 1896; and chairman of the Democratic State Committee (1901–1904).

On 19 December 1893, Hopkins was elected to fill the term of assassinated Mayor Carter H. Harrison I (*q.v.*). He received 112,959 votes to his Republican opponent and mayor *pro tem*, Alderman George B. Swift's (*q.v.*) 111,660 votes, while the Socialist and Peoples' party candidates polled only 2,599 combined.

Chicago in 1893 had 1,250,000 people and a mayor-council form of government. As mayor, Hopkins was a "political businessman" who realized great personal profits in franchise manipulation, building construction, and other politically related activities. Positive achievements under his direction included three further annexations of territory which increased Chicago's total acreage to over 186 square miles, the establishment of free public bath-houses, and the development of a non-partisan civil service board to select candidates for the police department.

Mayor Hopkins conspired with political boss Roger Sullivan and a group of aldermen known as the "Gray Wolves" to pass legislation granting virtually unlimited franchise rights and favorable lease arrangements in exchange for payoffs. Of course, the leases were detrimental to the public welfare. In several instances, dummy corporations such as the Ogden Gas Company, whose most prominent shareholder was Mayor Hopkins, were established and used to blackmail legitimate utility companies with the threat of actually operating as a competitor. The ploy proved successful, and in 1906 the Ogden Gas Company was purchased for more than $6 million, making Hopkins and his cohorts rich men. The franchise grabs led an aroused electorate, under the leadership of the newly formed Municipal Voters League, to a reform of Chicago government. The Ogden Gas Affair ended Hopkins' elective career.

Hopkins returned to private business but remained active in Democratic party affairs. In 1917, he was appointed secretary of the Illinois State Council of Defense. He died in Chicago on 13 October 1918, a victim of the great influenza epidemic, and was buried in Calvary Cemetery, Evanston, Illinois.

SOURCES: Paul M. Green, *The Chicago Democratic Party 1840–1920: From Factionalism to Political Organization* (Ph.D. dissertation, University of Chicago, 1975); Carter H. Harrison, II, *Stormy Years* (Indianapolis, 1935); Claudius O. Johnson, *Carter Henry Harrison I: Political Leader* (Chicago, 1928); Edward R. Kantowicz, *Polish-American Politics in Chicago* (Chicago, 1975); Frederick Rex, *The Mayors of the City of Chicago from March 4, 1837 to April 13, 1933* (Chicago, 1947).   *Edward H. Mazur*

HOPKINS, WILLIAM R. (1869–1961), City Manager of Cleveland (1924–30). The second Welsh-American to govern Cleveland, born on 26 July 1869, in Johnstown, Pennsylvania, Hopkins was the son of David J. Hopkins, coalminer and ironworker, and Mary Jeffreys Hopkins, both immigrants from Wales. The family moved to Cleveland when Hopkins was a small boy. Third of ten children, Hopkins worked in the rolling mills before he was able to return to school and finish his education. He nevertheless earned his A.B. in 1896 and his LL.B. in 1899, both from Western Reserve University. He practiced law in Cleveland and engaged in a number of business enterprises, including the building of the successful Cleveland Short Line Railroad, also known as the Belt Line. His principal associate in this venture was his brother Ben. He married Ellen Louize Cozad in 1903, from whom he was divorced in 1926. The couple had no children, and he never remarried. Hopkins was a Republican, a Presbyterian, and a Mason.

In 1920, Cleveland was the fifth largest city in the country, with 795,841 people. The following year the voters approved a new charter providing for a city manager appointed by a twenty-five-member council elected from five districts, in place of an elected mayor and a larger council elected by wards. Hopkins, who had served one term on the council from 1897 to 1899 but who had not held public office since, was chosen manager by an arrangement between Republican organization leader Maurice Maschke and Democratic leader Burr Gongwer. Included in the agreement was a proposal to divide patronage on the basis of two-thirds to the majority Republicans and one-third to the Democrats. Hopkins served as manager from the initiation of the new charter in January 1924, until his ouster by the council by a 14 to 11 vote in January 1930. He claimed that he was removed because of his opposition to a new franchise, supported by Maschke, giving the East Ohio Gas Company higher rates. In general, Hopkins had acted independently of the party organization during his later years as manager. His removal was one of the most sensational and heavily reported events in Cleveland's political history.

A promoter and builder in private life, Hopkins approached the office of manager in the same spirit. Therefore, he concentrated on such projects as the airport (known today as Cleveland Hopkins), new wings for the public auditorium, street openings and widenings, the

Municipal Stadium, and major bridges. His supporters praised his energy and vision, while his opponents attacked his neglect of administrative detail and his autocratic manner. In theory, the city manager was supposed to let the council set policy while he administered the city's affairs. Hopkins took a more expansive and political view. He initiated policy and served as the city's spokesman in ceremonial matters, a function the charter envisioned for the leader of council, who served as mayor. True to his Welsh background, Hopkins was a good speaker (sometimes known as Chautauqua Bill), and his assertive style led opponents of the manager system to argue that no one not directly responsible to the voters should exercise so much power. Hopkins and his followers defeated several attempts to overthrow the manager charter in the 1920s, but in 1931 the city did return to the mayor-council system. Hopkins was a member of the council from 1932 to 1934 and practiced law in Cleveland. He died on 8 February 1961 at the age of ninety-one.

SOURCES: Biographical clipping file, Cleveland Public Library; Thomas F. Campbell, *Daniel E. Morgan, 1877–1949: The Good Citizen in Politics* (Cleveland, 1966); R. O. Huus, "Cleveland Removes City Manager Hopkins," *National Civic Review* 18 (May 1929). The publication of the Citizens League, *Greater Cleveland*, had a number of favorable articles about Hopkins during his time in office.   *James F. Richardson*

HOTCHKISS, ELISHA (1778–1858), Mayor of Cincinnati (1831–33). Hotchkiss was the second elected mayor of the city of Cincinnati. His origins and family ancestry are uncertain, with some sources placing his birthplace in England and others in New Haven, Connecticut. Little is known of his early adult years, but he did move to Cincinnati around 1815 to practice law. No record exists of any outstanding or newsworthy civic contribution by Hotchkiss during the next twelve years of his residence in the Queen City.

Hotchkiss first ran for mayor of Cincinnati in 1827 but lost to Isaac G. Burnet (*q.v.*) by a vote of 1,004 to 984. He did not run in the 1829 mayoral contest but did defeat Samuel W. Davies (*q.v.*) in 1831 by 1,637 to 931. As Hotchkiss began his term, Cincinnati had a population of 26,071. His political appeal was based at least in part upon his genial personality and distinguished appearance. Hotchkiss's political preference was probably Whig. He got along well with the Cincinnati City Council, and during his two years in office the municipal regulation of burials was begun, public waste collection service was initiated, and the basis for an orphans home was laid. Hotchkiss lost his bid for reelection in 1833 to Samuel W. Davies by a vote of 1,882 to 1,479 and went on to become a perennial losing candidate in the next three mayoral campaigns, coming in third in 1835 with 364 votes to Samuel W. Davies' 1,560 votes and John C. Avery's 1,168 votes, finishing second in 1837 with 1,521 votes to Samuel W. Davies' 1,754 votes; and ending up third again in 1839 with 1,084 votes to Samuel W. Davies' 2,048 votes and John A. Wiseman's 1,173.

Hotchkiss returned to a private law practice after leaving the political arena. He eventually retired to the southeastern Indiana community of Aurora, about thirty miles down the Ohio River from Cincinnati, and died there in 1858.

SOURCES: Cincinnati Municipal Reference Bureau, *Origins of Municipal Activities in The City of Cincinnati* (Cincinnati, 1935); Charles Cist, *Cincinnati in 1841: Its Early Annals and Future Prospects* (Cincinnati, 1841); Charles T. Greve, *Centennial History of Cincinnati and Representative Citizens*, 2 vols. (Chicago, 1904).

Gary Kocolowski

HOUGHTON, DOUGLASS (1809–45), Mayor of Detroit (1842). To ardent Democrats in the 1840s, "their" Mayor Houghton was the one redeeming city executive in a decade otherwise dominated by Whigs. Like many prominent leaders in his own and the opposition party, Houghton was a transplanted New Englander. He was the fourth-born child to Jacob (1777–1861), and Mary Lydia (Douglass) Houghton of Troy, New York. His father, a lawyer and jurist, was of aristocratic English lineage. The Houghtons had first come in 1658 from Bolton, Lancashire, and had settled in Boston, Massachusetts. His mother, also of English ancestry, came from New London, Connecticut.

Houghton attended Fredonia Academy and Rensselaer Institute from which he received his medical degree in 1829. One year later, he became assistant professor of chemistry and natural history at the institute. In 1831, he was appointed surgeon and botanist on a government-sponsored expedition to explore the sources of the Mississippi River. This assignment coincided with an invitation to visit Detroit and to give a series of lectures on scientific subjects. He spoke in Detroit, went west, returned to Detroit, and settled permanently. In 1833, he married Harriet Stevens from Fredonia, New York; together they had three children: Hattie, Mary, and Douglass, Jr. The family was Protestant, probably Episcopalian.

Houghton was briefly associated in practice with Dr. Zina Pitcher (*q.v.*) three-time mayor of Detroit, but he soon became involved in geology and, in 1837, he was appointed state geologist. He held this position until his death, and he did much to attract the attention of capitalists to the mineral wealth in northern Michigan. Houghton also founded and served as professor in the

Department of Geology at the University of Michigan.

According to local practice, Houghton was nominated for the mayor's office by a party convention; it was customarily held about two weeks before the March election. In the 1842 Democratic nominating convention, a total of thirty votes were cast. The Whig opposition charged that Houghton's post as state geologist would prevent him from attending to the duties of mayor, but Houghton defeated his Whig opponent, John R. Williams, by a vote of 624 to 474.

Houghton was a temperance advocate, although the Democratic party was divided on that issue. He was a founder of the Detroit Young Men's Society, which many immigrant voters in the Democratic party would soon come to view as an elitist, Protestant organization. Yet, he was a popular mayor whose views of municipal government were described later in the century as "enlightened and liberal."

Dr. Houghton declined to be renominated and devoted his full attention to geology. On an expedition in 1845, on 13 October, he drowned in Lake Superior. His body was not found until spring, and he was buried in Detroit in May 1846.

Houghton was typical of many Detroit mayors throughout the nineteenth century; his importance derived from his professional rather than his political role. He was a scholar and a scientist of national reputation. Locally, he was remembered as a man who only 5'4" in his boots had an indomitable will and energy and a "remarkable imagination" which could clearly picture the future of Michigan.

SOURCES: Alvah Bradish, "Doctor Douglass Houghton," *Michigan Pioneer Collections* 4 (1906); C. B. Burr, ed., *Medical History of Michigan* (Minneapolis and St. Paul, 1930), vol. 1; George B. Catlin, *The Story of Detroit* (Detroit, 1923); Silas Farmer, *The History of Detroit and Michigan* (Detroit, 1889), vol. 2; Edsel K. Rintala, *Douglass Houghton: Michigan's Pioneer Geologist* (Detroit, 1954); Palmer Scrapbook and Douglass Houghton Papers, Burton Historical Collection, Detroit Public Library.   *JoEllen Vinyard*

HOW, JOHN (1813–85), Mayor of St. Louis (1853–55, 1856–57). Born in Philadelphia in 1813, How remains one of the lesser known St. Louis mayors. He moved to St. Louis in the 1830s and began a business career. Some time in the 1840s, he married. He and his wife had two sons, one of whom later married the daughter of the legendary James B. Eads, a major American business leader.

How held no political office prior to his decision to run for mayor in 1850. Running as the pro-Thomas H. Benton Democratic candidate, he won 2,018 votes to

3,329 for the victorious Whig, Luther Kennett (*q.v.*), 644 for D. A. Magehan (anti-Benton Democrat) and 73 for George Morton (Independent). In 1853, How was elected as a regular Democrat, defeating Whig Charles P. Choteau 4,194 to 3,228. In 1854, he defeated Whig John B. Carson 4,293 to 3,465. He did not run in 1855, but in 1856 he was elected to a third term, again defeating Carson 6,974 to 4,404. In this election, Carson had abandoned the Whigs for the nativists, the American, or Know-Nothing party. St. Louis had 77,860 people in 1850 and a mayor-council form of government.

As mayor, How supported construction of a new workhouse and jail, more city parks, and city investment in local railroads. He created the office of inspector of buildings, mainly to prevent fires. He once said that the mayor should serve a three-year term, since that would allow more freedom of action. A single year was simply too short for any major accomplishments.

After leaving office, How resumed his mercantile career. He ran once more for mayor, as the Democratic candidate in 1861. He was defeated by Republican Daniel G. Taylor (*q.v.*) 12,992 to 9,434. In 1869, he left St. Louis and went to Elko, Nevada, as the local Indian agent, serving in that capacity for four years. He subsequently moved west to San Francisco, where he died on 3 January 1885.

SOURCES: Howard L. Conrad, ed., *Encyclopedia of the History of Missouri*, 6 vols. (New York, 1901); Charles H. Cornwell, *St. Louis Mayors: Brief Biographies* (St. Louis, 1965); J. T. Scharf, *History of Saint Louis City and County*, 2 vols. (Philadelphia, 1883).   *Thomas R. Bullard*

HOWARD, CHARLES (1804–83), Mayor of Detroit (1849–50). Democratic mayor of Detroit, Howard was born on 7 August 1804 in Chenango County, New York. He had two brothers, Sebre and William, and their father, Sebre Howard, was a farmer of English and Scottish ancestry. Charles Howard received his schooling at Port Jervis, New York, where his family had moved. In about 1830, they settled in the Lake Ontario port of Sackett's Harbor, where Charles and his father became ship captains on Lakes Ontario and Erie. Charles Howard later worked for Bronson and Crocker, a large mercantile firm, and rose from clerk to branch manager. In 1840, Howard moved to Detroit and became a successful businessman. He founded Charles Howard and Company, Forwarding and Commission Merchants (1840), and a similar firm with Nelson P. Stewart (1848–54). In addition, Howard served as president of the Farmers' and Mechanics' Bank (1846–51), was a founder and first president of the Peninsular Bank (1849–57), and helped organize the Detroit Fire and Marine Insurance Company (1849). While in

New York, he married Jane Maria Strowger (1802–33). On 10 December 1834, he married Margaret Elizabeth Vosburgh (d. May 17, 1859), who traced her Dutch family lines to seventeenth-century colonial Manhattan. Charles and Margaret Howard had three sons and a daughter: Oren S., Bronson (1842–1908), Charles Scott (October 1848–July 1849), and Ella (Waterman) (d. 1892).

In 1849, Detroit (in Wayne County, Michigan) had about 20,000 people and a mayor-council form of government. Mayors were elected annually by popular vote and served without pay, presiding over a city council of sixteen members (two from each of eight wards). Howard, who had not been politically active prior to accepting the Democratic mayoral nomination, defeated Whig candidate Buckminster Wight on 5 March 1849, 1,362 to 1,226, winning five of the city's eight wards. Howard's victory was part of a Democratic sweep, typical of Detroit elections of his time. During Howard's year in office, he obtained public support for an additional school building, hired a city physician, and dealt with a cholera epidemic (June–September 1849) that took some 300 lives. As mayor, Howard was host to vice-president Millard Fillmore and historian George Bancroft during their visits to Detroit.

Howard did not stand for reelection, and when his term expired he resumed full-time attention to his business interests. During the 1850s, he headed a railroad construction firm (S. and C. Howard Company, 1854) and served on the board of directors of the Detroit and Pontiac Railroad. His construction company suffered financial reverses, and the depression of 1857 weakened the Peninsular Bank, which forced Howard to relinquish its presidency. He soon left for New York City, where he maintained a gun business (c. 1863–74). In about 1879, he moved back to Detroit and lived with his daughter and son-in-law, a real estate agent. Howard died of "lung congestion" at their home on 6 November 1883.

SOURCES: Frederick Carlisle, *Chronography of Notable Events in the History of the Northwest Territory and Wayne County* (Detroit, 1890); Silas Farmer, *History of Detroit and Wayne County and Early Michigan* (Detroit, 1895); Pat M. Ryan, "Charles Howard, Detroit Mayor and Merchant Adventurer" (unpublished paper submitted to *Detroit in Perspective*).   *Michael W. Homel*

HOWARD, HENRY (1801–78), Mayor of Detroit (1837). Howard, one of a line of New England-born mayors of early Detroit, was born in Hinsdale, Massachusetts, on 15 September 1801, the son of Colonel Joshua Howard. He later moved to Geneva, New York. He had a very limited education. In 1827, he moved to Detroit where he began a lumber business with Ralph

Wadhams and established a dry goods store. He was elected an alderman for Detroit in 1833 and 1834. In this position, he worked with Charles C. Trowbridge (*q.v.*), another alderman and mayor in 1834, in preparing the plans for a new city hall. He also served on a committee with Stevens T. Mason that urged a reduction in the number of places licensed to sell alcohol. While in Detroit, he belonged to the Democratic party but later became a Republican.

Detroit had a mayor-council form of government and a population of about 7,000 when Howard, a Democrat, won the mayoralty election on 3 April 1837, defeating the Whig Marshall Chapin (*q.v.*) by 682 to 411. Shortly thereafter, a smallpox epidemic broke out, and the common council agreed to pay for the vaccination of the poor. Howard encouraged the council to build a tower for the city's new water plant. Because of financial problems that year, the council passed an ordinance, hoping to prevent paupers from landing in Detroit. At a meeting in July 1837, the city officials discussed with Canadian authorities the possibility of increasing the number of ferries crossing the Detroit River. In August, the council approved the issuance of $25,000 worth of bonds to pay for the new Hydraulic Works in the city.

The Panic of 1837 and the refusal of banks to redeem their paper money in specie had caused a shortage of money in Detroit. Howard and the council authorized the issuance of $5,000 in paper to take care of the debts of the city. In February 1838, a shortage of small coins caused the council to issue a further $10,000 worth of paper in small units.

The rebellion in Canada in 1837–38 caused great unrest in Detroit. An increase in false fire alarms, the shooting of weapons in the city, and the difficulties in enforcing the laws caused Mayor Howard and Governor Stevens T. Mason to set up a city watch of 200 armed men on 13 January 1838. The city adopted a policy of strict neutrality towards the Canadian affair.

In June 1837, the mayor and council approved the route of the Detroit and St. Joseph Railroad (later the Michigan Central) through the city. In March 1838, they approved the route of the Detroit and Pontiac Railroad. Continued financial difficulties caused the mayor to call a meeting of the freemen of the city on 5 February 1838, to authorize the city to borrow an additional $50,000 to pay its debts.

Howard served as the first state treasurer, 1836–39. He then became auditor general, 1839–40. In 1840, he moved back to Buffalo, where he served as treasurer of the Buffalo Savings Bank for nearly thirty years. He died in Buffalo on 15 July 1878.

SOURCES: Clarence M. Burton, *History of Detroit, 1780–1850* (Detroit, 1917); Frederick Carlisle, comp.,

Chronology of Notable Events in the History of the Northwest Territory and Wayne County (Detroit, 1895); Detroit Common Council, *Journal of the Proceedings of the Common Council of the City of Detroit, 1824–1843* (n.p., n.d.); Silas Farmer, *History of Detroit and Wayne County and Early Michigan*, 3d ed., (1890, reprint, Detroit, 1969); legal and business papers, 1805–1834, in the Thomas Allen Papers, Burton Historical Collection, Detroit Public Library.   *William T. Bulger*

HOWARD, WILLIAM JORDAN (1799–1862), Mayor of Pittsburgh (1845–46). Howard was born in Delaware on the last day of the eighteenth century. His father, William Howard, was an English immigrant papermaker, who moved to eastern Ohio soon after 1800 and to Pittsburgh in 1815, following the death of his wife Elizabeth. The senior Howard soon became one of the principal merchants of the city. Later he was a federal pensions agent. Both he and his wife had been born in England; they had one other son. William Howard, Jr., became an important local businessman. On 14 May 1824, he married Lydia Updegraff, who bore him at least nine children. The family was Episcopalian.

The election of 1845 was hectic. Howard, running as a Whig and Anti-Mason, received 1,366 votes to defeat Henry McGraw, Democrat, with 1,337. Two minor candidates got a total of 451 votes. On the following day, Howard held open house for all friends and supporters, serving turkey, roast beef, hot coffee, and cakes. Pittsburgh, a city of 30,000, had a mayor and select and common councils.

Howard's election brought him little but grief. The main event during his term was the great fire of 10 April 1845, which destroyed almost three-fifths of the city. Other cities sent huge sums for relief, and Mayor Howard was accused of giving "the rich too much, the poor too little." An investigation disclosed his partner received a large sum.

In 1846, Howard ran again as a Whig and Anti-Mason, and lost by a narrow margin. He later served on the Poor Board and continued in the mercantile business until his death on 2 October 1862. He was buried in Allegheny Cemetery.

SOURCES: John W. Jordan *Encyclopedia of Pennsylvania Biography* (New York, 1914); Allen H. Kerr "The Mayors and Recorders of Pittsburgh, 1816–1951" (typescript, 1952, Carnegie Library of Pittsburgh); Pittsburgh *Post*, 16 January 1845.   *George Swetnam*

HOYT, STEPHEN A. (   ), Mayor of New Orleans (1864-65). An appointed military mayor, Hoyt was a commissary captain in the Union Army, appointed by General Nathanial Banks in February 1864. In 1860, the city had a population of 168,675. Hoyt was reported to be from the West when he entered the Army and supposedly returned there after his dismissal in March 1865. He worked actively in the political process which led to a new state government reconstructed under Abraham Lincoln, urging greater cooperation with the local radical elements than the commanding generals who supervised the process, Nathanial Banks and Stephen Hurlbut. He was particularly helpful to black citizens in arranging a mass meeting on 11 May 1864 to celebrate the abolition of slavery by the new state government in Louisiana.

Hoyt was dismissed from his post by Governor James Madison Wells. To conciliate returning Confederates, Wells replaced Hoyt with a local businessman and prosecessionist, Hugh Kennedy (*q.v.*).

SOURCES: Gerald Capers, *Occupied City: New Orleans Under the Federals, 1862–1865* (Lexington, Ky., 1965); John S. Kendall, *History of New Orleans* (Chicago, 1922); Peyton McCrary, *Abraham Lincoln and Reconstruction, the Louisiana Experiment* (Princeton, N.J., 1978).   *Joseph Logsdon*

HUNT, HENRY JACKSON (1788–1826), Mayor of Detroit (1826). Little is known of Hunt, the second elected mayor of Detroit. His father Thomas was descended from an old Massachusetts family and reputedly was wounded at the battle of Bunker Hill. Henry was born in Watertown, Massachusetts, in 1788; his father, a soldier, moved to Michigan with Wayne's Army in 1796, the family joining him there in 1800. His mother, Eunice Wellington, had eleven children, Henry being the oldest. When Thomas died, on 18 August 1809, Henry became the head of the family. Hunt joined the local militia at a fairly young age and worked as a merchant. After the War of 1812, he began practicing law with his brother-in-law Abraham Edwards. He married a Canadian, Ann Mackintosh (1789–1856) in 1811. They had no children. In 1815, he was appointed one of the judges of the county court, and two years later he served as city assessor. In 1819, he ran as a delegate to Congress. Two years later, he served as trustee of the University of Michigan and helped to organize the Protestant Society. He was an Episcopalian himself. He became trustee of the Corporation of Detroit and associate justice of the county court in 1823. Through most of his Detroit years, Hunt had been a friend of Governor Lewis Cass and apparently went into partnership with him to purchase real estate at one point.

Hunt was elected mayor in 1826 by a vote of 105 to William Woodbridge's 92 and D. McKinstry's 1. Detroit had a population of 2,000. Hunt died on 15 September of that year having served less than one year in office.

SOURCES: Clarence Burton, *History of Wayne County*

and the City of Detroit (Detroit, 1930); Silas Farmer, *History of Detroit and Michigan* (Detroit, 1889).   *Francis X. Blouin, Jr.*

HUNT, HENRY T. (1878–1956), Mayor of Cincinnati (1912–13). Reform mayor, who fought the Boss Cox machine, born on 29 April 1878 in Cincinnati, Ohio, Hunt was the son of Samuel T. Hunt (1850–1905), railroad president, and Martha (Trotter) Hunt. The first of two sons born into a conservative Democratic family, Hunt, a Methodist, graduated from Yale in 1900 and returned home to attend the Cincinnati Law School from which he graduated in 1903. He went on to pass the bar. He married Tomassa Haydock of Cincinnati.

In 1905, Hunt was elected to the Ohio House of Representatives in a Democratic sweep of Cincinnati which defeated the machine of George B. Cox, the notorious Republican boss. Hunt fought the machine by securing a committee to investigate political affairs in Cincinnati; it found that Cox's henchmen had been receiving interest paid on deposits of public funds. The receivers soon returned over $200,000 to the public treasury.

In 1908, Hunt was elected to the first of two terms as Hamilton County prosecuting attorney, an experience that gave him an opportunity to continue his fight against Cox. Hunt secured an indictment against Cox for taking interest on public funds which, although later ruled out, was an important move in the eventual defeat of the Republican machine. Cincinnati at that time had about 370,000 inhabitants living under a boss-ridden mayor-council form of government.

Although Hunt did not seek the Democratic nomination for the mayoral race of 1911, he conducted an aggressive campaign based on his record as prosecutor. With the strong support of the Cincinnati *Post*, Hunt declared war on Cox and announced that he would insist on competitive bidding for public contracts and would attack prostitution, bookmaking, and cocaine selling. Hunt defeated Louis Schwab (*q.v.*), the Republican candidate, 43,673 to 39,771. In pursuing efficient municipal operation as a chief goal, Hunt made appointments in a nonpartisan search for excellence. He brought in scientific budgeting and obtained public participation by extended hearings on proposed expenditures. Hunt improved social services and fought vice, but his attempt to improve traction service had little positive result.

Developments during the second year of Hunt's term undermined his electoral support. Textile, shoe, and traction strikes drew away the support of both capital and labor; patronage and public ownership quarrels split reform groups. The Republicans under adroit Cox leadership accused the mayor of failing to live up to his campaign promises and to uncover dishonesty in the administration. On 4 November 1913, Judge Frederick S. Spiegel defeated Hunt's bid for reelection 45,363 to 42,251. Hunt said the public had failed to understand his position on the traction question and his emphasis on civil service reform.

After serving as a major in the Army during World War I, Hunt moved to New York where he gained prominence as a labor lawyer. During the New Deal, he was general counsel of the Federal Emergency Administration of Public Works. Following a prolonged illness, he died in 1956 at the Veterans Hospital at Martinsburg, West Virginia.

SOURCES: Cincinnati *Post*, 13 October 1913; Zane L. Miller, *Boss Cox's Cincinnati: Urban Politics in the Progressive Era* (New York, 1968); New York *Times*, 24 September 1913; Landon Warner, "Henry T. Hunt and Civic Reform in Cincinnati, 1903–13," *Ohio State Archaeological and Historical Quarterly* 62 (April 1953).   *George B. Engberg*

HUNT, JESSE (1793–1872), Mayor of Baltimore (1832–35). First popularly elected mayor of Baltimore and chief executive during the Baltimore Bank riots, Hunt was born on 3 July 1793, into an old Maryland family in what is now the Greenspring Valley section of Baltimore County. His father, Job Hunt Jr., a prosperous farmer, moved from Calvert County and married Margaret Hopkins. She died shortly after Jesse, her sixth child and third son, was born (in February 1794). Hunt was orphaned at fifteen when his father died in 1809. Like many Baltimoreans, Jesse Hunt volunteered in the War of 1812 and helped raise a company. Wounded at the battle of North Point, he rose to a captaincy. After the war, he was apprenticed to a saddler and soon headed his own saddlery and harness-making business on Baltimore Street. At the same time he pursued a political career, identified with the Jacksonians, and served three terms in the Maryland House of Delegates.

At the time of his first term in 1832, Baltimore, despite its population of 80,000, still used the indirect elector system with each ward selecting an elector who then voted, in the same manner as presidential electors, for a mayor. But Hunt was popularly elected to his second term in 1834 by a vote of 5,468 votes to his opponent's 4,415 when the Maryland legislature changed elective procedures and instituted direct elections. During his first term, 1832–34, routine city business was forgotten as a result of a cholera epidemic and flood. During his second term, Hunt was identified with the Bank of Maryland default and was unable to deal with riots and destruction of property (including an attack on his own house). Hunt resigned his office in August 1835 after a procession of citizens demanded his removal. Later, he was appointed city registrar, served as volunteer president of the Association for the Improvement of Condition of the Poor, and was president of the Eutaw Savings Bank until his death on 8 December 1872.

SOURCES: Wilbur Coyle, *Mayors of Baltimore* (Baltimore, 1919); Dielman-Hayward File; Hunt Papers, Maryland Historical Society.   *Jean H. Baker*

HYDE, GEORGE (1819–90), *Alcalde* of San Francisco (1847–48). Third American *alcalde* (a Mexican executive and judicial office that preceded the mayoralty) of San Francisco in the prestatehood years, Hyde was born in Philadelphia on 22 August 1819 of Scottish-English stock on his father's side and pretensions of links with English nobility. He was related to the Revolutionary hero, Commodore John Barry, and on his mother's side (the Butchers) to a New Jersey family of New England, colonial descent. However, Hyde's father died at age twenty-eight, his mother remarried, and his Philadelphia education was cut short. Hyde was sent with his brother to Mount St. Mary's College in Emmitsburg. Forced to take up an early career because of straitened circumstances, he did brilliantly at his law exams and entered a Philadelphia firm, working there until 1845.

With the coming of the Mexican War, Hyde became secretary to Commodore Robert F. Stockton on the frigate *Congress* to Monterey. He reached Yerba Buena overland, on 10 August 1846 shortly after California had been declared American territory. Hyde opened the first law office in San Francisco and prospered. When the first American *alcalde*, Lieutenant Washington Bartlett (*q.v.*), was captured by rebels, Hyde served as second *alcalde*, effectively being in charge for a month or so. Then, on 1 June 1847, General Stephen W. Kearny appointed him *alcalde* to replace Edwin Bryant (*q.v.*). Hyde served 11 months, until 1 April 1848.

On 20 July 1847, Hyde began a huge sale of beach and water property rights. He also appointed (subject to later election) the town council, "six gentlemen to assist him in disposing of the great and daily accumulation of municipal business." The real estate operations apparently involved him in great controversy and enmities. Serious complaints of official misconduct were brought against him, "nine or ten charges of a criminal nature" of which few held up. He "resigned his trust," amid popular clamor.

In 1848–49, Hyde lived in a historic house, later known as the "Sazerac." He later built a more pretentious mansion, with lawns surrounding it—something new for the San Francisco of that day. He married Ellen McCoy in Philadelphia and had a daughter, Frances (d. 1931), who married the Spanish consul in San Francisco. A second daughter of Hyde's, Mrs. Alexander Garceau,

married a prominent city physician in 1891. After establishing himself and his family in the higher echelons of San Francisco social life, Hyde died on 16 August 1890, the charges against him of 1848 long-forgotten.

SOURCES: L. F. Byington, ed., *History of San Francisco* (Chicago, 1931), vol. 3; Z. S. Eldredge, *The Beginnings of San Francisco*, 2 vols. (San Francisco, 1912); W. H. Murray, *Builders of a Great City* (San Francisco, 1891), vol. 1; F. Soule, J. H. Gihon and J. Nisbet. *Annals of San Francisco* (New York, 1855).

Peter d'A. Jones

HYDE, OLIVER MOULTON (1804–70), Mayor of Detroit (1854–55, 1856–57). Old-stock Yankee and Whig mayor of Detroit, Hyde was born at Sudbury, Vermont, on 10 March 1804, the son of Pitt William Hyde, who traced his family to William Hyde (who had settled in New England in 1633). Oliver Hyde attended a local school and a seminary at nearby Castleton, where he later opened a dry goods store. In about 1834, he sold his business and moved to Mount Hope, New York, where he owned a pair of blast furnaces. Four years later, he moved to Detroit and became a successful businessman and politician. He first operated a hardware store on Woodward Avenue where, according to an early Detroit historian, "he would furnish for a price anything from a mousetrap to a meeting-house." Hyde also ran a foundry and machine shop where he made steamboat equipment, owned a sawmill in East Saginaw (1852–54), and built a floating drydock on the Detroit riverfront (1852). Hyde, a Whig, was also active in politics. He represented the Fifth Ward on the city council in 1844–45 and again in 1847–48, and was collector of the port of Detroit, a federal patronage job, 1849–53. Meanwhile, Hyde had married Julia Ann Sprague of Poultney, Vermont, in 1827. The couple had four children: Henry S., Julia Ann (1839–41), Hattie S. (Dickinson) (b. 1842), and Louis C.

Detroit in 1854 had a population of 41,375, and the Wayne County (Michigan) city had a mayor-council form of government. Mayors were elected annually by popular vote and served without pay, presiding over a city council of sixteen members (two from each of eight wards). In the 1854 city election campaign, the religious and ethnic issues of public education and temperance dominated debate. Hyde favored both and benefited from persisting divisions among Democrats. In the 6 March election, the Whig candidate Hyde won seven of eight wards and buried his Democratic opponent John Patton (*q.v.*) 2,791 to 1,595. During Hyde's first term, disputes over liquor sales as well as clashes between the Roman Catholic bishop and the city over downtown property showed that campaign issues remained unsettled. A cholera epidemic

(May 1854) added to the city's problems. Hyde did not run for reelection when his term expired, but in 1856 he ran as a Republican against Democratic hopeful Alexander W. Buel. Hyde, with Know-Nothing support, campaigned against the expansion of slavery, an issue previously absent from mayoral campaigns in Detroit. The verdict in the 5 February election was mixed: Hyde defeated Buel by a vote of 2,523 to 2,257, but the Democrats won seven of eight council seats. During Hyde's second term, enforcement of anti-liquor laws and encroachment by private fences and buildings on public streets attracted the attention of the city council. Hyde also proposed the creation of a house of correction, which was eventually established.

In November 1857, Hyde ran for a third term as mayor. However, John Patton, whom Hyde had decisively beaten in 1854, won the mayoralty by a wide margin, 3,512 to 2,714. In addition, the Democrats seized every city-wide post and filled nine of twelve available council seats. During the Civil War, Hyde helped to recruit for the Union Army. His active career ended suddenly as a result of two disabling strokes (1863, 1867). He was an invalid when he died in his home on 28 June 1870.

SOURCES: [Clarence Monroe Burton], *The Hyde House and the Garrick Theatre on Griswold Street Detroit* (Detroit, [1929]); Silas Farmer, *History of Detroit and Wayne County and Early Michigan* (Detroit, 1890); Ronald P. Formisano, *The Birth of Mass Political Parties: Michigan, 1827–61* (Princeton, N.J., 1971); Friend Palmer, *Early Days in Detroit* (Detroit, 1906).

Michael W. Homel

HYLAN, JOHN F. (1868–1936), Mayor of New York (1918–25). Tammany mayor, born on 20 April 1868 near Hunter, New York, Hylan was the son of Thomas H. Hylan, an Irish Catholic immigrant farmer, and Juliette (Jones) Hylan of New York. The third-born of five children, John F. Hylan attended New York rural schools. While working for the railroad, first as a tracklayer and later as an engineer, he attended Long Island Business College at night. After graduating from New York Law School in 1897, Hylan was admitted to the bar and opened a law firm in Brooklyn. In 1905, he ran unsuccessfully for a municipal judgeship but was appointed city magistrate the following year. His election as judge of Kings County Court in 1915 followed his appointment to that position the preceding year. On 24 September 1889, Hylan married Marian O'Hara (1886–1942) of Irish Catholic ancestry, and they had one daughter, Virginia.

New York City in 1918 had a population of 5,488,222 and a mayor-board of aldermen form of government. The obscure Hylan's selection as mayoral candidate of the Democrats in 1917 by Tammany chief Charles F. Murphy was a means of placating William Randolph Hearst, who opposed incumbent John Purroy Mitchel (q.v.). Hylan received 313,956 votes that year to Mitchel's 155,490, Socialist Morris Hillquit's 145,328, and Republican William S. Bennett's 56,438. In 1921, Hylan was reelected; he received 755,234 votes, while the Coalition party's Henry H. Curran got 336,398 and Socialist Jacob Panken, 82,019.

As mayor, Hylan's patronage policy proved him a faithful Tammanyite and subjected him to charges of cronyism. His most noteworthy achievement was securing the municipal operation of the third major division (Eighth Avenue) of the city subway system with a 5-cent fare. Hylan championed municipal ownership of all transit lines and home rule for New York City, but he was most noted for his pro-German sentiments, particularly his investigation of allegedly "pro-British" American history textbooks in the city's public school system.

When Tammany chiefs Al Smith and George W. Olvany boosted Jimmy Walker (q.v.) for mayor in 1925, Hylan failed to reverse that decision, losing the party primary and control of city hall. After Walker's election, the new mayor appointed Hylan as justice of the children's court in Jamaica, Long Island, a position he held until his death. In 1929, Hylan was nominated for mayor by the Better City Government League but withdrew to the advantage of Walker. In 1932, he ran for mayor as an independent but again withdrew for the regular Democratic candidate, John P. O'Brien (q.v.). His last foray into electoral politics was in 1934 with his losing campaign for the governorship on the Recovery party ticket. He died at his home in Forest Hills, Long Island, of a coronary thrombosis on 12 January 1936 and was buried in St. John's Cemetery, Long Island.

SOURCES: William Bullock, "Hylan," *American Mercury* 1 (April 1924); John F. Hylan, *Autobiography of John Francis Hylan* (New York, 1922); New York *Times*, 9 May 1942, 12 January 1936 (obituary).

W. Roger Biles

HYNES, JOHN B. (1897-1970), Mayor of Boston (1950-60). Three-term mayor, born on 22 September 1897 in Boston, Hynes was the son of Bernard J. Hynes, an Irish Catholic immigrant, railroad-car inspector for the Boston and Albany Railroad, and Anna (Healy) Hynes, also an Irish immigrant. Economic necessity forced Hynes to leave school at age fourteen and to work for the American Bell Telephone Company as an office-boy. By the time he entered the U.S. Army Air Corps during World War I, Hynes had become a skilled stenographer-clerk. In 1920, following his discharge, he began a long career in city government by passing a civil service examination and taking a clerk's job in the Boston Health Department. Two years later, he was moved to the Auditing Department and then was named chief clerk in the office of Mayor James Michael Curley (*q.v.*). When Curley's term expired in 1926, Hynes was shifted to the city's Budget Department. In 1929, he was made chief assistant to City Clerk Wilfred J. Doyle. When Doyle retired in 1945, Hynes, back from another stint in the Army, became city clerk by a vote of the Boston City Council. Hynes attended evening high school classes to obtain his diploma and went nights to Suffolk University Law School in the 1920s. He received his LL.B. in 1927 and passed the bar in 1928. Hynes married Marion H. Barry, an Irish-American secretary born in South Boston, on 25 April 1928, and they had six children, five of whom survived to adulthood.

In 1947, the Massachusetts legislature made City Clerk Hynes acting mayor to replace James Michael Curley, who had been convicted of mail fraud and sentenced to federal prison. Hynes served for five months until President Harry Truman pardoned Curley. Upon his return to Boston, the controversial Curley went out of his way to belittle Hynes' performance, causing a serious rift between the two former allies. As a result, Hynes, who had worked in many campaigns but had never run for office himself, became the candidate of a bipartisan coalition of middle and upper class Democrats and Republicans against Curley in the municipal election of 1949. Running on a simple platform of honesty and dignity, the quiet city clerk was elected with 137,930 votes to Curley's 126,000, Patrick J. "Sonny" McDonough's 22,230, George F. Oakes's 7,171, and Walter A. O'Brien, Jr.'s 3,659. After serving an experimental charter-mandated, two-year term, Hynes finished first in a September preliminary election and won a four-year term in November 1951, defeating Curley 154,206 to 76,354. He was reelected in 1955 with 124,301 to John E. Powers' 111,775.

Boston had a population of 801,444 in 1950. After Curley's troubled reign, Hynes saw his mission as one of restoring Boston's good name. The mayor reduced the number of city departments, attempted to lessen political influence in matters of pay increases and promotions for city employees, and installed the first computer in the Auditing Department. In 1955, Hynes won a measure of respect nationally by being elected president of the U.S. Conference of Mayors. He also took the city's first steps in the new program of urban renewal. A major effort, the West End project, demolished one of Boston's oldest neighborhoods and received community criticism. However, the Hynes administration did draw up a plan for a government center in the rundown Scollay Square area and helped to convince the Prudential Insurance Company to develop the railroad yards where the mayor's father had toiled. Both projects were brought to fruition by the administration of Hynes' successor, John F. Collins (*q.v.*).

Hynes retired from the mayoralty in 1960. He tended to his duties as Democratic national committeeman, wrote columns and verse for the local newspapers, and practiced law. In 1963, Massachusetts Governor Endicott Peabody appointed Hynes state commissioner of banks and banking. He served in that post until 1967. In 1969, Hynes, a member of the American Legion and the Catholic Order of Foresters, was made treasurer of Suffolk University. He died of a heart attack on 6 January 1970 and was buried in Boston's West Roxbury section. Later in 1970, the city's war memorial auditorium was named for Hynes.

SOURCES: Edward C. Banfield and Martha Derthick, eds., *A Report on the Politics of Boston* (Cambridge, Mass., 1960); Boston *Globe*, 7 January 1970 (obituary); *City Record, 1950–1960*, Government Documents Department, Boston Public Library; Documents of the City of Boston, 1950–60, Microtext Department, Boston Public Library; John B. Hynes, *From Boston to Beirut* (Boston, 1953); John B. Hynes, *Boston, a Poem* (Boston, 1956); John B. Hynes, *The European Odyssey of Mayor John B. Hynes* (Boston, 1954); John B. Hynes, "On Shifting Federal-State-Local Responsibilities," *American City* (November 1957); John B. Hynes clippings, Newspaper Morgue, School of Public Communication, Boston University; John B. Hynes Papers, Boston Public Library; Lorin Peterson, *Day of the Mugwump* (New York, 1961); *Proceedings of the City Council of Boston, 1950–1960*, Government Documents Department, Boston Public Library; John J. Sexton, Jr., "The Hynes Campaign: A Study in Coalition Politics" (senior honors thesis, Harvard University, 1950).

Richard H. Gentile

IMPELLITTERI, VINCENT RICHARD (1900–), Mayor of New York (1950–53). First Italian mayor of New York, Impellitteri was born on 4 February 1900, in Isnello, Palermo, Sicily, to Salvatore and Maria Antonia (Cannici) Impellitteri, both Roman Catholics. Vincent's father, a shoemaker and son of a shoemaker, brought his family to America in 1901, settling in Ansonia, Connecticut. Graduating from the local high school in 1917, Impellitteri joined the Navy and served overseas on the destroyer *Stockholm* as a radioman third class before being discharged in 1919. On 25 April 1922, Impellitteri became a naturalized citizen of the United States. He married Elizabeth Agnes McLaughlin, a legal secretary, on 21 August 1926.

Working his way through Fordham University, Impellitteri received his law degree in 1924 and joined Griggs, Baldwin and Baldwin. He was admitted to the New York bar in 1925. A member of the New York Democratic organization since the early 1920s, Impellitteri became assistant district attorney of New York County in 1929, a position he held until 1938 when he returned to private practice. In 1941, he became secretary to Peter Schmuck, the state supreme court justice, and from 1943 to 1945 he served Justice Joseph A. Gavagan in the same capacity.

Although Impellitteri was then a politically obscure figure, Mayor William O'Dwyer (*q.v.*) in 1945 chose him as a running mate, at least in part so that the Democratic ticket which included (Irish) O'Dwyer from the borough of Queens and (Jewish) Lazarus Joseph from the Bronx would be balanced with (Italian) Impellitteri from Manhattan. The slate was elected, and for the next five years Impellitteri served as president of the city council.

On 2 September 1950, O'Dwyer filed his resignation papers (effective 22 October) to accept the ambassadorship to Mexico. As president of the council, Impellitteri then became mayor. In the required special election that November, Impellitteri ran as an anti-boss, anti-corruption candidate. Running as an Independent and calling his following the "Experience" party, Impellitteri received 1,156,587 votes to 937,060 for Ferdinand Pecora, the Democratic-Liberal candidate and 382,795 for Edward Corsi, the Republican candidate. Although he was

the first person to be elected mayor of New York City running as an Independent, the term is misleading, and Impellitteri acted quickly to reestablish ties with the Democratic party.

During his forty months as mayor, Impellitteri gave Robert Moses, then at the height of his fame and power, a free hand, and while little was done for school or hospital construction, twenty-four huge public housing projects and many miles of highway were completed. At the same time, the city sales tax was increased from 2½ percent to 3 percent, and the subway and bus fare rose from 10 cents to 15 cents.

In 1953, Impellitteri was defeated in the Democratic primary by Tammany candidate Robert Wagner (*q.v.*), who was subsequently elected and who later appointed Impellitteri to the position of justice of the court of special sessions in New York City. Most observers agree that, while personally honest, Impellitteri made little effort to wrestle with the city's major problems and that the quality of life in the city deteriorated during his administration.

SOURCES: Robert Caro, *Robert Moses and the Fall of New York* (New York, 1974); Citizens Union, "An Appraisal of the Impellitteri Record," *The Searchlight* (May 1952); Vincent Impellitteri, *Scrapbooks*, 2 vols., Municipal Archives, New York City; Warren Moscow, *The Last of the Big-Time Bosses* (New York, 1971); Wallace S. Sayre and Herbert Kaufman, *Governing New York City* (New York, 1960).

Lurton W. Blassingame

IRWIN, WILLIAM W. (1803–56), Mayor of Pittsburgh (1840–41). Pittsburgh's ninth mayor, Irwin was born in that city in 1803, a son of John and Agnes Irwin. They were well-to-do, and he was nicknamed "Pony" for a pony he rode, a name that clung to him all his life. He attended private schools and Allegheny College, then studied law and was admitted to the bar in 1828. The following year he married Frances Smith, who died on 24 February 1836, apparently childless.

Irwin achieved the mayoralty on his fourth attempt, a year after being named district attorney by Joseph Ritner, Pennsylvania's only Anti-Mason governor. Nominated by the Whigs and Anti-Masons in 1840, Irwin was opposed by John Birmingham, the Democrat and Anti-

Bank candidate. He won a resounding victory, with a majority of 700 votes out of some 2,500 cast (Irwin, 1,562 to Birmingham's 854). His supporters also carried nearly all seats in the select council and all twenty-five in the common council. Pittsburgh at the time was a growing city of about 21,000.

Irwin, quiet and businesslike, proved a good mayor, and in his first term was elected (as a Whig) to the national House of Representatives. He was defeated for reelection to Congress in 1842 but was named chargé d'affaires to Denmark, serving through 1845. He then returned to Pittsburgh and was elected to the common council. Irwin, a wealthy man, was very popular but lost almost his entire fortune through endorsing the notes of his friends. He came of a short-lived family; he died on 10 September 1856, aged fifty-three.

SOURCES: Allen H. Kerr, ''The Mayors and Recorders of Pittsburgh 1816–1951'' (typescript, 1952, Carnegie Library of Pittsburgh); Pittsburgh *Dispatch*, 15 September 1856; Pittsburgh *Post*, 16 September 1856.

George Swetnam

JACKSON, HOWARD WILKINSON (1877–1960), Mayor of Baltimore (1923–27, 1931–43). A strong and popular mayor, Jackson was born on 4 August 1877 in Stemmers Run, Baltimore County, the first of three children born to Andrew Columbus Jackson (d. 1930), a railroad section hand, and Temperance Wilkinson Jackson (1857–1944), of an old Baltimore County family. Both were Methodists. Jackson spent his childhood in Magnolia, Harford County, Maryland, and attended the Baltimore public schools, Burnett's Business College in Baltimore, and the Baltimore Law School. Before becoming a partner in the Riall-Jackson Insurance Company, Jackson worked in a can factory, as a baker, and as a printer. On 14 September 1898, he married Ella May Galloway (1878–1964) of Havre de Grace, Maryland, a descendant of an old Maryland family and a graduate of Havre de Grace High School. They had five children: Carle A., H. Riall, Ella M. (Sheehan), E. Virginia (Mattingly), and William who died at age nine. Jackson was a member of the Wilson Memorial Methodist Church, the Elks, Moose, and several Masonic orders, including the Shrine and Commandry.

Jackson began his political career doing Democratic party precinct work, was elected to a term on the Baltimore City Council in 1907, and served as register of wills in Baltimore (1909–23).

Baltimore, with a mayor-council form of government, was expanding during Jackson's years as mayor (804,874 in 1930; 859,100 in 1940). He won nomination for mayor in 1923 as the candidate of the Sonny Mahon machine of the Democratic party. With 74,124 votes in the general election, he defeated both Republican incumbent William Broening (*q.v.*), who had 49,919 votes, and former Democratic Mayor James Preston (*q.v.*), who got 39,042 votes running on the Citizens' party ticket. Jackson's personal popularity made victory possible despite the Democratic split. But he failed to win the Democratic primary in 1927. When he did win the primary in 1931, he went on to defeat Republican mayoral candidate William Albrecht by a vote of 120,355 to 57,191. Jackson continued to win primary elections and in 1935 was reelected mayor over Republican Blanchard Randall, Jr., by a vote of 114,321 to 75,368 and in 1939 over Republican Theodore R. McKeldin (*q.v.*), by a vote of

109,368 to 84,832. Although renominated in 1943, Jackson lost to McKeldin 77,402 to 57,291. The defeat came in part because Democratic boss Jack Pollack gave his support to McKeldin, in part because of the low voter turnout, and in part, because of Jackson's well-known alcoholism.

Jackson was a strong mayor, a doer rather than a reformer or housekeeper. His administration saw the construction of the Baltimore Art Museum, the Enoch Pratt Free Library, and an airport, as well as numerous schools and streets. It was generally considered that he spent New Deal monies on valuable and lasting projects. He modernized the city government by reducing the number of independent boards and commissions and by establishing more centralized control.

Jackson held no further public offices and returned to the insurance business. He died on 31 August 1960.

SOURCES: Biographical files at the Maryland Historical Society, the Enoch Pratt Free Library, and the Baltimore *Sun*.   *Suzanne Ellery Greene*

JACOB, CHARLES, JR. (1835–1913), Mayor of Cincinnati (1879–81). First German-born mayor of Cincinnati and a prosperous meatpacker, Jacob emigrated to the United States at age sixteen from Rhenish Bavaria, where he was born on 24 November 1835. Having attended school in Germany until age thirteen, Jacob learned the trade of butchering from his father, Charles Jacob, Sr., and joined his uncle's Cincinnati butchering concern soon after arriving in the United States in 1852. In October 1857, Jacob, a member of St. John's Evangelical Protestant Church, married a fellow ethnic, Katherine Wust; they had three children, only one surviving to adulthood. With his father-in-law, Jacob established the porkpacking business of Charles Jacob, Jr., and Company. Later, he helped create the German Banking Company and dabbled in street railroad promotion. He joined a gymnast club, the Masons, and the Hanselmann Lodge.

After serving several terms on the city council, Jacob received an appointment to the Police Commission in 1876 and later became commission president. His role there won him plaudits in 1877 when he quelled a potential railroad strike riot without any bloodshed.

Cincinnati's population of 253,139 in 1880 was governed through a mayor-council structure. Jacob received the Republican nomination for mayor in 1879 because of his close association with the city's German community. In a fierce campaign in which the Democrats challenged Jacob's citizenship while the Republicans waved the "bloody shirt," Jacob defeated his Democratic opponent L. A. Harris by a vote of 21,391 to 21,030. Two other opponents, L. H. Sawyer and H. T. Orden, received 360 and 180 votes, respectively. Despite his pledge to the city's Moral Reform Committee to enforce all the city's laws, Jacob did not root out vice, Cincinnati remained wide open during his administration. This may have helped defeat him two years later when he ran for reelection and lost against Democrat William F. Means (*q.v.*) 23,804 votes to 21,384.

After his mayoralty, Jacob remained active in city affairs. He is given credit for forming the "Order of Cincinnatus" in 1883, an association for the promotion of business. In 1886, the governor appointed him a member of the Board of Municipal Affairs. His business fortunes sank to low tide at the turn of the century, and he needed a city job as packinghouse inspector to make ends meet. He quit that job in 1909 after three years and died of pneumonia on 27 February 1913 in Cincinnati, where he was buried at Spring Grove Cemetery.

SOURCES: Max Burgheim, *Cincinnati in Wort und Bild* (Cincinnati, 1888); Cincinnati *Daily Gazette*, 26 March 1879; Cincinnati *Enquirer*, 9 April 1879, 31 March 1879; Cincinnati *Commercial Tribune*, 28 February 1913; Cincinnati *Post*, 28 February 1913.

Robert B. Fairbanks

JEFFRIES, EDWARD J., JR. (1900–50), Mayor of Detroit (1940–48). A mayor who restored integrity to Detroit city government after a preceding corrupt administration, Jeffries, born on 3 April 1900 in Detroit, was the son of Edward J. Jeffries, a Detroit recorder's court judge for thirty-five years, and Minnie (Stott) Jeffries. One of three children, Edward, Jr., attended the Detroit public schools, graduating from Northwestern High School in 1917. He then went to the University of Michigan (A.B. 1920, LL.B. 1923). Jeffries did postgraduate work in Roman and British constitutional law at Lincoln's Inn in London. He was admitted to the Michigan bar in 1923 and began a Detroit law practice in partnership with Paul E. Krause the following year. On 24 January 1930, he married Florence Bell, whose father had been director of the Detroit Conservatory of Music. In 1940, they adopted a three-year-old boy, Gary Edward, their only child. Jeffries held memberships in the Delta Theta Phi and Alpha Sigma Phi fraternities, the Michigan Bar Association, the Maccabees, Odd Fellows,

Moose, Eagles, the Detroit Golf Club, and the Detroit Athletic Club.

In 1931, Jeffries successfully ran for a seat on Detroit's common council and served from 1932 to 1940. He was president from 1938 to 1940. In 1939, he ran for mayor and defeated incumbent Richard Reading (*q.v.*) by a 226,181 to 108,993 count. Subsequently, he defeated Joseph Gillis in 1941 (219,338 to Gillis's 72,041); Frank Fitzgerald in 1943 (207,821 to Fitzgerald's 175,360); and Richard Frankenstein in 1945 (275,159 to 217,425). By so doing, he gained the distinction of being a Detroit mayor for a longer period than any previous incumbent. He retired from the office in January 1948, after losing to Eugene Van Antwerp (*q.v.*) 224,310 to 205,543.

In 1940, Detroit, a city with a population of 1,618,549 and a mayor-council form of government, had been shaken by scandals that eventually sent Jeffries' predecessor, R. W. Reading, to prison. During his eight years as mayor, Jeffries did much to restore dignity and integrity to Detroit's government. Although a friend of labor, he resisted attempts by the CIO to exert undue influence, maintaining that government should not be beholden "to a single group in the community." He launched an extensive slum clearance program on Detroit's East Side. During his administration, Detroit adopted its first city-wide zoning ordinance. An ordinance was passed setting up a city insurance reserve; this measure saved Detroit taxpayers a significant sum that would have gone to defray outside insurance company overhead charges. The city's expressway system was begun during Jeffries' term, after a contract financing the project had been concluded with Wayne County and the state of Michigan. Jeffries helped organize the Michigan conference of mayors. As its president, he successfully lobbied for an amendment that gave cities and schools a portion of the state sales tax revenue.

In 1949, Detroiters again elected "Jeff," as he was popularly known, to the common council. On 2 April 1950, while vacationing in Miami Beach, Florida, he died of a heart attack. He was buried in Detroit's Woodlawn Cemetery.

SOURCES: Detroit *Free Press*, 3 April 1950; Detroit *News*, 3 April 1950; Edward J. Jeffries, Jr., Papers, 7 boxes of miscellanea, Burton Historical Collection, Detroit Public Library; New York *Times*, 3 April 1950; Robert I. Vexler, *Detroit: A Chronological and Documentary History, 1701–1976* (Dobbs Ferry, N.Y., 1977).

Robert Bolt

JEROME, JOHN H. T. (1814–63), Mayor of Baltimore (1850–52). John H. T. Jerome, a native Marylander, was born in 1814. Quite early, he entered the grocery business and became very successful in that occupation. On 12

November 1837, he married Henrietta Dyer of Pennsylvania, and they had four children. Jerome joined the Whig party, and in 1850 he became his party's candidate for mayor. Fortunately for him, the Democratic party in the city was badly divided over the mayoralty contest, and a seceding wing of the party nominated its own candidate. With division in the Democratic ranks and with some of the dissidents willing to support the Whigs, Jerome defeated the regular Democratic nominee, J. M. Turner, 9,952 to 9,183. However, all of the Whig city candidates for the legislature lost to their Democratic opponents.

As mayor, Jerome proposed an ambitious municipal program, although the office possessed little power. He advocated the acquisition of Federal Hill as a city park, the purchase of the city water company, which was still under private control, and the possibility that the city should build its own gas plant to illuminate the streets. More important, the move for constitutional reform in the state produced a new constitution which provided for the separation of Baltimore City from Baltimore County and increased the representation in the legislature for the city. Prior to the new constitution, Baltimore, a rapidly growing city of 169,054 in 1850, had approximately 25 percent of the state's population, but its proportionate share of representation in the House of Delegates was only one-sixteenth. With the separation, Baltimore doubled its representation. The city gained five delegates and was entitled to one senator.

Following his retirement from office, Jerome was elected by the city council to represent Baltimore on the board of directors of the Baltimore and Ohio Railroad. He also served on the school board. Later, Jerome moved to Baltimore County and in the fall of 1861 was elected to the House of Delegates as a unionist. He was a member of that body when he died suddenly of a hemorrhage of the lungs at his home near Govanstown on 28 January, 1863.

SOURCES: Baltimore *Sun* and Baltimore *Daily Gazette*, 28 January 1863; Wilbur F. Coyle, *The Mayors of Baltimore* (Baltimore, 1919); Dielman File, Maryland Historical Society; Clayton Colman Hall, ed., *Baltimore: Its History and Its People* (New York, 1912); J. Thomas Scharf, *History of Maryland* (Hatboro, Pa., reprint 1967).

Richard R. Duncan

JEWETT, EDGAR B. (1843–1924), Mayor of Buffalo (1895–97). Military officer and mayor, Jewett was born in Ann Arbor, Michigan, on 14 December 1843, the son of John Cotton Jewett (1820–1904), manufacturer, and Priscilla (Boardman) Jewett, both old-stock New Yorkers. The first of six children, Jewett attended public schools until age sixteen. He then joined his father in the

John C. Jewett Manufacturing Company (established following the family's arrival in Buffalo around 1850). Upon the outbreak of the Civil War, he joined Company C of the Seventy-sixth Regiment of the New York National Guard and saw action at Gettysburg. A first sergeant by 1865, he was promoted to captain in 1866, major in 1877, lieutenant colonel in 1880, and brigadier general in 1884, meanwhile being transferred through three different regiments. In 1885, he resigned to become president of his father's company, but he retained a military outlook throughout his life. On 3 October 1865, Jewett married Elizabeth Foster Danforth (1845–1905), an old-stock New Yorker, and they had four children. General Jewett was a Mason and a member of seven prominent clubs in Buffalo. The Jewetts attended the Episcopal Church of the Good Shepherd.

Early in 1894, Jewett was appointed Buffalo's commissioner of police and swiftly organized the police department along military lines, instilling a strong sense of discipline. He was elected mayor that November, as a Republican, defeating Jacob Stern (Democrat) 30,770 to 21,191. Buffalo had 255,664 people in 1890 and a mayor-council form of government. Jewett believed that a city's municipal powers, as exercised through the mayor's office, should be increased and protected. He vetoed all contracts awarded to "favored bidders." Jewett pushed new franchises for the Buffalo Traction Company and the Niagara Power Company. He also supported new schools and municipal ownership for the city's waterfront. To ease the impact of the economic depression, he adopted the so-called Detroit Plan whereby vacant land was used by unemployed workers and their families, thus providing money through sales of crops grown and reducing welfare costs. Jewett did not seek reelection and returned to business in 1898. His wife died in 1905, and he married Augusta Elizabeth Fiske on 6 January 1909. In 1910, he became president of the Jewett Association and spent his later years supporting it. He retired to Clifton Springs, where he died on 28 March 1924.

SOURCES: Buffalo *Sunday Times*, 15 June 1924; Frederick C. Jewett, *History and Genealogy of the Jewetts of America*, 2 vols. (New York, 1908); *The Men of New York*, 2 vols. (Buffalo, 1898).

Thomas R. Bullard

JOHNSON, EBENEZER (1786–1849), Mayor of Buffalo (1832–33, 1834–35). First mayor of Buffalo, Johnson was a transplanted Yankee physician, born on 7 November 1786 in Wells, Vermont, son of Captain Ebenezer Johnson (1760–1841), who was originally from Maine or eastern Massachusetts, and Deborah (Lathrop) Johnson (1767–1834), originally from Norwich, Connecticut. The family was Episcopalian, and Ebenezer was the second of thirteen children. He studied medicine with a Dr. White in Cherry Valley, New York, before moving to Buffalo in 1809 to rejoin his parents who had settled there earlier. On 11 January 1811, he married Sally M. Johnson of Cherry Valley, the daughter of Jesse Johnson (b. 1745), formerly a ship's carpenter from Middletown, Connecticut, and Abigail Johnson. Dr. Johnson had three children by his first wife: Mary, William, and Sally. His daughter Mary married Dr. John C. Lord, a prominent Presbyterian clergyman of Buffalo. On 7 December 1835, eighteen months after the death of his first wife, he married Lucy E. Lord (c. 1814–50), the sister of Dr. John C. Lord, and had three additional children: Cecilia, Sarah Louise, and Herbert.

Dr. Johnson practiced medicine for a short time and was a surgeon's mate in the militia during the War of 1812, but he soon left medicine to engage in more profitable banking and mercantile pursuits. During the 1820s and 1830s, he formed business partnerships with Samuel Wilkeson, H. H. Sizer, and Philander Hodge. As one of the original members of the Buffalo Harbor Company in 1819, Johnson played an important role in the construction of Buffalo's first harbor. He was surrogate judge of Niagara County, which at that time included Buffalo (1815–21), and surrogate judge of Erie County (1821–25).

Between 1832, the year Buffalo received its city charter, and 1835, the city grew in population from 10,119 to 15,661. It was governed by a common council, consisting of two aldermen elected from each of the five wards, which appointed the mayor and other city officials. Dr. Johnson was unanimously chosen to be Buffalo's first mayor in April 1832. During the summer following his selection, an epidemic of Asiatic cholera hit Buffalo; Johnson acted as the presiding officer of the board of health established by the common council to meet the emergency. In March 1833, the new common council unanimously reappointed him mayor, but he declined to serve. However, he did accept a second term in 1834–35.

Like many others in Buffalo, Dr. Johnson suffered financial reverses in 1836 and 1837. He returned briefly to the practice of medicine, then went to Tellico Plains, Tennessee, to look after his interests in an iron mine, which he owned with his elder brother Elisha Johnson (1784–1866), a former mayor of Rochester, Dr. Johnson died in Tellico Plains on 23 September 1849.

SOURCES: F. M. Inglehart, "Buffalo's First Mayor, Dr. Ebenezer Johnson," *Publications of the Buffalo Historical Society* 4 (1896); George W. Johnson, "William Johnson and His Descendants," *New England Historical and Genealogical Register* 33 (1879); Grace Carew Shel-

don, "Ebenezer Johnson, First Mayor, Came Here in 1809 to Get Granger's Advice," Buffalo *Times* 19 January 1919.
                                                    Christopher Densmore

JOHNSON, EDWARD (c. 1767–1829), Mayor of Baltimore (1808–16, 1819–1820, 1822–24). Johnson's origins are obscure. He was a relatively prosperous brewer who married Elizabeth Mackubin in 1798. They had at least one child, a son who died before reaching maturity at age fifteen.

Baltimore was undergoing significant change during the first two decades of the nineteenth century. It grew from 26,114 people in 1800 to 62,738 inhabitants in 1820. The dislocations of the War of 1812 and the Panic of 1819 retarded its transformation from a commercial to an industrial economy. Baltimore had a mayor-city council form of government in which the mayor was elected indirectly to a two-year term. The city was the arena for furious competition between minority Federalists and majority Democratic Republicans. Johnson, a Democratic Republican, served in the upper house of the city council (1797–1801) and as a Jeffersonian presidential elector, before becoming mayor in 1808. His electoral ticket won in 1808, 1810, 1812 (when he was unopposed), and in 1814. After his retirement in 1816, he replaced the ailing Mayor George Stiles (q.v.) in February 1819 but lost an indirect election to a full term in 1820 to John Montgomery (q.v.) polling 3,319 votes to 2,917 for his electors. In an 1822 rematch, his ticket won by 18 votes (3,518 to 3,500) but lost in 1824 (Montgomery, 3,333; Johnson, 2,994; Jacob Small (q.v.), 950) in the city's indirect election for mayor. Johnson retired a second time from office.

Mayor Johnson presided at a volatile period in Baltimore's history. Popular violence against an ultra-federalist newspaper in 1812 enhanced the city's reputation as a mob-town. Although the editor precipitated this disturbance, inaction by the civil government condoned the mob's actions, with unfortunate results. Civil government evaporated during the invasion crisis of 1814, and Mayor Johnson assumed the position of chairman of the *ad hoc* Committee of Vigilance and Safety. Prior to the war, urban government was concerned primarily with facilitating trade, regulating municipal services, and controlling an increasingly heterogeneous population—all at a minimum public expenditure. After the war, efforts to continue these policies were undermined by the Panic of 1819, the appearance of yellow fever in 1819, and the enormous financial burden incurred in Baltimore's defense. Mayor Johnson was a popular politician, but at the same time enjoyed the support of the elite who controlled the economic and political resources of the community. He died on 18 April 1829 and was buried in a Presbyterian cemetery.

SOURCES: Baltimore *American and Commercial Advertiser,* 2 October 1810, 6 November, 1810, 6 October 1812, 3 November 1812, 30 September 1814, 9 November 1814, 8 October 1816, 6 November 1816, 5, 6 October 1818, 18 September 1820, 3 October 1820, 7 November 1820, 7 October 1822, 5 November 1822, 5 October 1824, Donald R. Hickey, "The Darker Side of Democracy: The Baltimore Riots of 1812," *Maryland Historian* 7:2 (Fall 1976); William D. Hoyt, Jr. ed., "Civilian Defense in Baltimore, 1814–1815," *Maryland Historical Magazine* 39:3 (September 1944); Mayor's Messages (Baltimore, 1809–24); Whitman H. Ridgeway, *Community Leadership in Maryland, 1790–1840* (Chapel Hill, N.C., 1979); Dielman-Hayward File, Maryland Historical Society.   *Whitman H. Ridgway*

JOHNSON, JOHN W. (1775–1854), Mayor of St. Louis (1833–34). Third mayor of St. Louis, and a Southerner, Johnson was born in about 1775 in Howard County, Maryland, the son of Thomas Johnson, a gunsmith and a native Marylander of English ancestry, and Ann (Risteau) Johnson. John was the sixth son and last born of his parents' ten children. In 1808, the brother-in-law of John's eldest brother became superintendent of Indian trade, and that same year John received a commission as government factor to the Indians in the upper Mississippi Valley. He first traded at Fort Madison in present-day southeastern Iowa and then at a post in Prairie du Chien, Wisconsin. While at Prairie du Chien, he served as justice of the peace and as chief justice of the Crawford County court. He also acquired a share in the lead mines in the Dubuque region. During his years as Indian factor, he fathered three daughters (Eliza, Mary, and Rosella) by a Sauk Indian woman, Tapassio, who supposedly was the daughter of Chief Keokuk.

In 1822, Johnson moved to St. Louis and in 1831, married Mrs. Lucy Gooding, widow of his friend, Captain George Gooding. Johnson was regarded as one of St. Louis's leading citizens, and in 1833 he was chosen by the "downtown" interests as Whig candidate for mayor in their battle against the North Ward candidate, Hugh O'Neil, Sr. The son of Johnson's opponent, Hugh O'Neil, Jr., was leader of the North Ward and had originally supported the mayoral candidacy of Dr. Samuel Merry, a partner in medical practice with former Mayor William Carr Lane (*q.v.*). Merry had won the mayoral contest in April 1833, but the board of aldermen ruled that Merry was ineligible because he was already serving as U.S. receiver of public monies, and under the Missouri constitution no one could hold two public offices simultaneously. The Missouri Supreme Court upheld the

position of the board of aldermen, and in November 1833, in a second election, Johnson assumed leadership of the anti-Merry-O'Neil-North Ward faction. Johnson won in a close contest, garnering 286 votes to O'Neil's 252. O'Neil won 73 percent of the votes cast in the North Ward, while Johnson won 87 percent of the downtown Middle Ward. The Johnson-O'Neil battle represents the beginning of partisan politics in St. Louis mayoral elections, anticipating the Whig-Democrat split of the late 1830s.

Johnson's year-and-a-half term as mayor of the frontier city of about 8,000 residents was relatively uneventful. Moreover, it seems to have marked the conclusion of his public service. There is no record of his further activities. He died on 1 June 1854 and is buried in Calvary Cemetery in St. Louis.

SOURCES: Kate L. Gregg, "A Man Named Johnson," *Missouri Historical Review* 37 (January 1943); Maxmilian Reichard, "Urban Politics in Jacksonian St. Louis: Traditional Values in Change and Conflict," *Missouri Historical Review* 70 (April 1976); James H. Lockwood, "Early Times and Events in Wisconsin," *Second Annual Report and Collections of the State Historical Society of Wisconsin for the Year 1855* (Madison, Wis., 1856); J. D. Warfield, *The Founders of Ann Arundel and Howard Counties, Maryland* (Baltimore, 1905).   *Jon C. Teaford*

JOHNSON, TOM LOFTIN (1854–1911), Mayor of Cleveland (1901–1909). Famous reform mayor, Johnson was born in the South, in Blue Springs, Kentucky, on 18 July 1854, the son of Albert W. Johnson (a slave-holding cotton planter and police chief) and Helen Loftin of Jackson, Tennessee, both old-stock Protestants. Tom, the eldest of three children, had to begin work at eleven, after completing less than two years of grade school in Evansville, Indiana. In 1869, he became an office-boy with a streetcar company in Louisville, Kentucky, beginning a thirty-year career in that industry. He subsequently invented the glass-sided farebox that bears his name and became a superintendent. By 1876, he owned a streetcar company in Indianapolis, and by 1880, he had moved to Cleveland and bought additional companies in Cleveland, St. Louis, Brooklyn, and Detroit. He sold his local streetcar interests in the early 1890s and concentrated on his steel mills in Johnstown, Pennsylvania and Lorain, Ohio. On 8 October 1874, he married Maggie J. Johnson, and they had three children, two of whom survived: Loftin and Bessie. During his Cleveland years, the Johnsons attended the Disciple of Christ Church on Cedar Avenue.

Cleveland had a population of 381,768 in 1900, rising swiftly to 560,663 by 1910, and a mayor-council form of government. Johnson entered politics as a Democrat and a reformer after reading Henry George's *Progress and Poverty* (1879). He became a friend and follower of George, although he was also deeply influenced by reform Mayor Hazen Pingree (*q.v.*) of Detroit. After an unsuccessful campaign for Congress as a Democrat in 1888, Johnson won the seat in 1890 and 1892. He was defeated again in 1894. In 1897, he managed Henry George's campaign for the mayoralty of New York, during which the great Single Tax leader died. In 1901, Johnson narrowly won the Democratic primary for the mayoralty of Cleveland (6,123 to 5,118) and went on to defeat W. J. Akers (Republican) in the election: 35,811 to 29,764. His Progressive platform consisted of opposition to any franchise that would charge more than 3 cents for streetcar fares, and the advocacy of a property tax reappraisal.

In the next six years, Johnson defeated three Republican contenders for the mayoralty: 1903 (Johnson 36,060 to Harvey D. Goulder's 30,275); 1905 (Johnson 41,591 to W. H. Boyd's 29,466); and 1907 (Johnson 48,342 to Congressman T. E. Burton's 39,016). But in 1909, Johnson was finally defeated by a popular German-American, Herman C. Baehr (*q.v.*) (41,405 to 37,711), amidst a backlash of voter discontent over a prolonged streetcar strike.

In his four terms as mayor, Johnson commanded national attention, not only for his opposition ''to the forces of Privilege'' that he felt were corrupting urban America, but also for his ability as a progressive and humane administrator. While much was said of his Single Tax ideology, as mayor he never put the concept in practice. Rather, his Progressivism was based on his struggle to secure a lower streetcar fare, municipal ownership of utilities, just taxation, home rule for cities, women's suffrage, and a progressive and a graft-free administration. The tent that he pitched in Cleveland's multitongued neighborhoods to draw the immigrants into the political process was an exciting example of his ability to execute social reform. His challenge to the economic and social values of the business community aroused their anger and suspicion, but in the long run he provided a yardstick of municipal leadership.

After his defeat, Johnson was broken in health but not in spirit. He made a triumphant tour in Europe and the British Isles, and returned to Cleveland where he dictated his memoirs. He died on 4 May 1911. Johnson's final journey, on his way to be buried beside Henry George in Brooklyn, New York, demonstrated the affection that his adopted city had for Mayor Tom. Over 200,000 people lined the streets in a final tribute to the man who ''forsook the few to serve the mass,'' in his struggle to make Cleveland a ''city on a hill.''

SOURCES: R. H. Bremner, ''The Civic Revival in Ohio: The Fight Against Privilege in Cleveland and Toledo, 1899–1912'' (Ph.D. dissertation, Ohio State University, 1943); Frederick C. Howe, *Confessions of a Reformer* (New York, 1925); Tom L. Johnson, *My Story* (Seattle, 1970; special introduction by Melvin G. Holli, with analysis of Johnson as a social reformer and evaluation of his business career); Johnson Papers, Municipal Archives, Cleveland City Hall; Hoyt L. Warner, *Progressivism in Ohio* (Columbus, 1964).

Thomas F. Campbell

JOHNSTON, GEORGE W. C. (1829–79), Mayor of Cincinnati (1873–77). The first Democratic mayor of Cincinnati since the Civil War and a corrupt machine politician, Johnston was born in that city to parents of Northern Irish descent in 1829. Trained in the city's common schools, he became a house and sign painter at an early age, turning to mercantile pursuits in 1850. Six years later, he became a firewood and coal dealer. Johnston, who was married and had three daughters, also ran a line of omnibuses in Cincinnati.

As an active Democrat throughout his life, Johnston served on the local executive committee of the party and eventually chaired it. In 1872, he headed the Hamilton County delegation which attended the state Democratic convention whose task that year included choosing the delegates for the national Democratic convention. Johnston held numerous public offices, being elected to the city council in 1859, to the school board in 1861, and to the trusteeship of the waterworks in 1872. The Republican-dominated city council also appointed him in 1861 to the board of health. Johnston lost in his race for city auditor in the 1860s.

In 1873, Cincinnati had over 216,000 people and was governed by a mayor and city council, with twenty-one auxiliary boards. With the support of the Liberal Republicans, Johnston defeated the incumbent mayor, S. S. Davis (*q.v.*), 16,509 votes to 14,872. After his unanimous renomination two years later, he defeated Republican opponent John Robinson 21,595 votes to 15,198, the largest majority ever registered thus far in a contest for mayor. Two years later still, in 1877, he attracted only 16,606 votes and lost to Republican Robert M. Moore (*q.v.*) who won 18,240 votes. A third-party candidate that year, Charles H. Thompson, received 3,594 votes and may have cut into the mayor's strength.

Johnston's four-year mayoralty was marked by charges of lawlessness, graft, and machine politics. In 1874, he abolished the board of police commissioners, assuming personal responsibility for the police force. He later blamed intraparty squabbling for his failure to win reelection. Soon after his defeat, he refused a nomination for state senator and later lost in a bid for county sheriff. After leaving the mayoralty, Johnston remained active in his fuel business and also helped build a street railroad in Portsmouth, Ohio.

The former mayor died of rheumatic gout on 30 March 1879 in Cincinnati and was buried in the city's Spring Grove Cemetery.

SOURCES: *The Biographical Encyclopedia of Ohio of the Nineteenth Century* (Cincinnati and Philadelphia, 1876); Cincinnati *Enquirer*, 2 April 1879; Alvin F. Harlow. *The Serene Cincinnatians* (New York, 1950); *In Memorium. Containing Proceedings of the Memorial Association, Eulogies at Music Hall, and Biographical Sketches of Many Distinguished Citizens of Cincinnati* (Cincinnati, 1881).   *Robert B. Fairbanks*

JONES, DeGARMO (1787–1846), Mayor of Detroit (1839–40). Jones, a wealthy businessman, served as mayor for one year in a pattern common to Detroit during this era. He was born on 11 November 1787, most probably in Albany, New York, though some accounts give his birthplace as Erie, Pennsylvania. The family's records were lost in a fire, and little is known about his parents, early life, or schooling. Contemporaries did describe him as "well educated." One favorite tale told by friends, years after Jones' death, was that he had served as a drummer boy in the War of 1812. But it is more likely, as local newspaper biographers reminisced, that he was a sutler in the Army and first came through Detroit with General William Henry Harrison during the war.

Jones took up permanent residence in the city in 1818 after arriving on *Walk-in-the-Water*, the first steamship on the Great Lakes; the boat had made its maiden voyage to Detroit that same year. With him came his new bride (married on 28 March 1818) Catherine H. Annin (1799–1865) from Cayuga, New York. She, like Jones, was of old-line Yankee Protestant stock. Her father was a judge, and her mother, the daughter of Colonel Seth Reed, a Revolutionary soldier from Erie, Pennsylvania. Between 1823 and 1838 the couple had seven children. The first four children died while young, but Matilda, DeGarmo, Jr., and Alice survived to adulthood. The family was among the congregation of the prestigious First Protestant Society.

Profitably involved in numerous business ventures, Jones was one of the first stockholders of the Bank of Michigan, a contractor for the capitol building in Detroit, one of the first directors of the Detroit and St. Joseph Railroad, and operated a forwarding business from his large warehouse. Ever an innovator, he also erected the first plaster mill in the state.

A Whig, Jones served as alderman three times before becoming mayor and, during 1829, was adjutant general

of Michigan. In 1833, he was a trustee of the Detroit High School. In April 1839, Jones was elected mayor by an "unprecedented" majority of 514 votes in a contest against Democrat and former mayor Jonathan Kearsley (*q.v.*). Beginning with this election, city offices were filled in the spring, thus separating them from state and national races.

The census of 1840 revealed that Detroit had reached a population of 9,102, compared to only 2,222 a decade earlier. The city had a mayor-council form of government, and as mayor, Jones sat with the twelve-member common council. The mayor also presided over sessions of the mayor's court which dealt with all violations of city ordinances.

After leaving the mayor's office, Jones continued his business activities and also served as state senator in 1840 and 1841. He died on 14 November 1846 and was buried in Detroit. His able wife managed his considerable estate for the next nineteen years and doubled its value, capitalizing on the land boom and continued city growth.

SOURCES: Clarence M. Burton, *The City of Detroit, Michigan, 1701–1922* (Detroit, 1922), vol. 2; *Burton Scrapbook*, vol. 5; Silas Farmer, *The History of Detroit and Michigan* (Detroit, 1889), vol. 2; Letters included in the Burton, Woodbridge, Taylor, Sheldon, and Cass manuscript collections in the Burton Historical Collection, Detroit Public Library; *Michigan Biographies* (Lansing, Mich., 1924), vol. 1.   *JoEllen Vinyard*

JONES, JOEL (1795–1860), Mayor of Philadelphia (1849). Born in Coventry, Connecticut, on 25 October 1795, Jones was the son of Amasa and Elizabeth (Huntington) Jones. Joel Jones graduated from Yale in 1817 and studied law at Litchfield and New Haven, Connecticut, and then settled in Easton, Pennsylvania, where he practiced law for several years. He was appointed to a legal commission in Pennsylvania in 1830 and authored "Reports of a Commission to Revise the Civil Code of Pennsylvania." He became an associate judge of the district court of Philadelphia in 1835 and in 1845 its presiding judge. He wrote and edited several books including *A Manual of Pennsylvania Land Law: Notes on Scriptures, Or Jesus and the Coming Glory; Knowledge of One Another in the Future State*; and *Outline of a History of the Court of Rome . . . .* He also edited several English works of prophecy and took an active interest in theological inquiry and speculation about the "second coming of Christ." A founder of Lafayette College in Easton, Pennsylvania, Jones also became the first president of Philadelphia's Girard College, 1847–49. A Presbyterian, he married Eliza Sparhawk on 14 June 1831 and was the father of six children.

Philadelphia in 1850 had a population of 121,000 and a mayor-council form of government. Jones was elected to a one-year term for mayor in 1849. He died in Philadelphia on 3 February 1860.

SOURCES: Appleton's Cyclopedia of American Biography (New York, 1892), vol. 3; *City of Firsts: Complete History of Philadelphia* (Philadelphia, 1926).   *Melvin G. Holli*

JUNEAU, LAURENT SOLOMON (1793–1856), Mayor of Milwaukee (1846–47). Famous French Canadian Catholic pioneer and Milwaukee's first mayor, Juneau was born on 9 August 1793, at L'Assumption, near Montreal, Canada, the son of François Juneau (1758–1832), an immigrant farmer, and Thérèse (Galerneau) Juneau (d. 1809), both French-born. The family name had been LaTulipe but was changed after Francois and Thérèse left France. Solomon, the sixth of fourteen children in a devout Catholic family, had a brief education in village schools, and became a fur-trapper in his teens. He worked for the Hudson Bay Company in 1817, switching to Astor's American Fur Company the following year. He moved to Wisconsin in that year and worked for some time with Jacques Vieau, whose daughter Josette (1803–55) married Juneau on 14 September 1820. Josette, a *Canadienne* with some Menominee Indian blood, had seventeen children, several of whom died in infancy. The Juneaus settled in a cabin in 1822 which was considered the first permanent house on the site in Milwaukee, and Solomon is usually considered the founder of the city. Juneau, who became an American citizen in 1831, was a successful Indian trader, winning popularity among the local tribes, and a wealthy real estate promotor. The Juneaus devoted much of their time to charity work and to aiding local Catholic churches.

Juneau was Milwaukee's first postmaster (1835–43) and a village trustee (1837–39). He began the Milwaukee *Sentinel* in 1837, although his newspaper activity was limited to about one year. A staunch Democrat, Juneau was elected Milwaukee's first mayor in 1846, defeating John Tweedy (Whig) 749 to 404. Milwaukee had 9,655 people in 1846 and a mayor-council form of government. Juneau did little as mayor. He did not really want the job, although he did make an effort to support schools and suppress local gambling. He appears to have felt a desire to move on to greener pastures, for in 1849 he moved to Therese, Wisconsin, where he opened a new trading post and general store. While returning to his home after voting in the election of 1856, he became ill and died on 14 November 1856.

SOURCES: H. Russell Austin, *The Milwaukee Story* (Milwaukee, 1946); Eugene J. Connerton and L. Paul Landry, *Genealogy of the Juneau Family, 1600–1965* (1971); Isabella Fox, *Solomon Juneau* (Milwaukee, 1911); *History of Milwaukee* (Chicago, 1881).

Thomas R. Bullard

K

KALLOCH, ISAAC SMITH (1831–87), Mayor of San Francisco (1879–81). Workingman's party Mayor Kalloch was born on 10 July 1831 in Thomaston (today Rockland), Maine, to Mercy (Hathorn) Kalloch (1812–33) and Amariah Kalloch (1808–50), a Baptist minister whose Scots-Irish family had lived in the area since the early eighteenth century. His mother's only child, Kalloch had four half-brothers and half-sisters through his father's two subsequent marriages. Growing up in Maine, Kalloch attended private schools in Camden and graduated from an academy in Rockland. In 1848, he entered Colby College but after two-thirds of a year was expelled for a prank, and he quit only a few weeks after reentering in 1849. Despite his expulsion, he was ordained to preach in 1850 and became pastor of the Rockland Baptist Church, having previously taught and worked on the Rockland *Lime Rock Gazette*. In 1850, Kalloch married Caroline E. Philbrook (1829–1908 or 1909), and they had five children: Isaac Milton (b. 1851), Anne (b. 1858), Randolph (b. 1862), Carrie (b. 1869), and Halsey Knapp (b. 1871).

Kalloch rapidly developed a reputation as a public speaker, for he preached with a fervid style, and his large size and bright red hair gave him an impressive appearance. An abolitionist sympathizer, in 1855 he was asked to become minister of Boston's Tremont Temple, an antislavery Baptist church established in 1839 by merchant Timothy Gilbert, and he rapidly transformed the previously debt-ridden church into one of the city's largest congregations. In early 1857, Kalloch's career met a serious obstacle when he was accused of adultery. Although defended in court by Richard Henry Dana, Jr., and others, his reputation was damaged because the sensational trial, which ended in a hung jury, gave rise to news stories, printed ballads, and lurid pamphlets enjoying large sales. Kalloch resigned from the Temple in 1858 to pursue various activities in Kansas, including assisting the free state movement but returned later that year. In 1860, after his church acquitted him of new charges of adultery, Kalloch resigned again and moved to Kansas. In 1861, However, after returning east to raise funds for settlers, he accepted the pastorate of New York City's Laight Street Baptist Church. In 1864, apparently out of boredom, he quit that ministry and moved back to Kansas.

In Kansas, Kalloch engaged in a wide range of activities. He was a founder of Ottawa, on the Marias des Cygnes River, helped begin Ottawa College and served on the board of trustees, published the *Western Home Journal*, and became involved with the projected Leavenworth, Lawrence, and Galveston Railroad. In 1869, after moving from Ottawa to Lawrence, he published the *Daily Republican Journal* and, later, the *Spirit of Kansas*. He also farmed and participated in politics, allying himself with U.S. Senator Samuel C. Pomeroy. In 1874, after Pomeroy's political career ended in scandal and after Kalloch lost substantial amounts of money, he returned to the ministry, becoming pastor of Leavenworth's First Baptist Church. The next year, claiming he felt a duty to reform San Francisco's multitudes of sinners, Kalloch abandoned Kansas and moved to the West Coast.

In San Francisco, Kalloch quickly persuaded the city's Baptists to offer him a ministry and to build Metropolitan Temple, the largest church in the city when finished. Through his pulpit talks on city affairs, Kalloch rapidly became involved in San Francisco politics and, despite his initial opposition, joined the Workingmen's party, led by Denis Kearney. Along with the party, which drew its strength largely from disaffected Democrats, he called for expulsion of the Chinese and attacked the city's rich for their monopolistic practices. In 1879, he received the party's nomination for mayor of the city, which numbered 233,959 in 1880. Marked by personal attacks, the bitter and sensational campaign climaxed on 23 August when San Francisco *Chronicle* publisher Charles de Young shot Kalloch who had attacked de Young's mother in response to a Chronicle-financed pamphlet detailing his alleged adulteries.

Kalloch won the election on 3 September 1879 with 20,964 votes to his Republican opponent Briswold P. Flint's 19,550 and to Democrat Walcott N. Griswold's 862. Because Republicans dominated the board of supervisors, Kalloch's years as mayor were marked by constant conflict, during which he called for restraint by Workingmen's party members. Although defeating an 1880 charter revision favored by Republicans, he achieved relatively little, his attempts to secure unemployment relief and to close Chinatown as a nuisance being unsuccessful. He also was handicapped by a city charter which dispersed power through the municipal government. Twice during 1880, the board of supervisors unsuccessfully attempted to impeach him—the first time for corruption and incitement of civil disorder and the second for misadministration of city hiring. On 28 April 1880, shortly before the *Chronicle* was scheduled to publicize Kalloch's past anew, his son Milton went to the newspaper's office and killed Charles de Young, who had not yet been tried for shooting Kalloch. That killing and the gradual disintegration of the Workingman's party because of internal splits and improving economic conditions ended Kalloch's political career, and he did not run for reelection. After unsuccessful attempts to enter Democratic party politics, Kalloch resigned his pastorate and left San Francisco in 1883. He moved to Whatcom (now Bellingham), Washington Territory, where he practiced law, involved himself with railroad ventures, and farmed. He died on 9 December 1887 of a stroke and was buried in the territory.

SOURCES: Cyrus Eaton, *History of Thomaston, Rockland, and South Thomaston, Maine* (Hallowell, Me., 1865); Jerome A. Hart, *In Our Second Century: From an Editor's Note-Book* (San Francisco, 1931); Irving McKee, "The Shooting of Charles de Young," *Pacific Historical Review* 16 (August 1947); M. Marion Marberry, *The Golden Voice: A Biography of Isaac Kalloch* (New York, 1947); San Francisco *Examiner Election Supplement*, 29 October 1879; Alexander Saxton, *The Indispensable Enemy: Labor and the Anti-Chinese Movement in California* (Berkeley, 1971).   *Michael Griffith*

KANE, GEORGE PROCTOR (1817–78), Mayor of Baltimore (1877–78). Kane was born on 17 August 1817 in Baltimore of Irish ancestry. He learned the grocery business, served as an officer in various units of the state militia, and later acted as an agent for the Imperial Insurance Company. He married Anna Griffith, daughter of Captain John Griffith of Dorchester County, Maryland. They did not have any children.

In 1880, Baltimore had a population of 332,190 and a mayor-council form of government. Kane had served in various political offices—including sheriff of Baltimore County—as a Whig during the antebellum period. He typified the drift of many Maryland Whigs into the Democratic party following the Civil War. Kane became identified with Isaac Rasin's Democratic machine which controlled Baltimore during the 1870s. On 24 October 1877, he polled 33,188 votes for mayor. His Whig rival, Joseph Thompson, received 17,367, and Henry M. Warfield, running as an Independent, 536 votes. The achievements of Kane's brief tenure in office were minimal, for he fell ill and died on 23 June 1878, cutting his term short by seventeen months.

SOURCES: Wilbur F. Coyle, *The Mayors of Baltimore* (Baltimore, 1919); "George Proctor Kane," Dielman

File, Maryland Historical Society, Baltimore.

Gary L. Browne

KAUFMANN, ALOYS P. (1902–), Mayor of St. Louis (1943–49). One of a series of German-American mayors of St. Louis, Kaufmann was born on 23 December 1902 in St. Louis, the son of John Kaufmann, an insurance agent, and Sophia (Woehr) Kaufmann (1864–1965), both Roman Catholics of German descent. The youngest of four children, Kaufmann attended local schools and Brewster Law School, receiving an LL.B. in 1928 and an L.C.M. in 1929. In 1943, he married Margaret C. Uding (1911–?), belonging to the Disciples of Christ Church. They had one son, born during Kaufmann's mayoral term.

A Republican, Kaufmann was a leader of the Republican Central Committee from 1936 to 1943. In 1943, he was elected president of the board of aldermen, and when Mayor Becker (*q.v.*) was killed in a glider crash later that year, Kaufmann became mayor. In November 1944, he won the election to complete Becker's term, defeating P. J. Burke (Democrat) 182,787 to 154,540. In 1945, he was elected to a full four-year term, defeating H. F. Chadeayne (Democrat) 108,675 to 54,083. St. Louis had 816,048 people in 1940, 856,796 by 1950, and a mayor-council form of government.

Kaufmann was an active reform mayor, supporting the city's master plan, the large-scale postwar public improvements program financed by a $43 million bond issue. He backed the city's first earnings tax, first race relations commission, and a comprehensive restaurant code. He supported a new city building code and efforts to enlarge the city's boundaries. Rat control and modernized garbage collection programs were also key features of his term in office. Looking ahead, Kaufmann strongly urged construction of a new municipal airport across the Mississippi River in Illinois.

After leaving office in 1949, Kaufmann resumed his legal career. After 1953, he served for several years as president of the St. Louis Chamber of Commerce. A lifelong aviation "buff," he continued to support plans for a new airport and helped Mayor Cervantes (*q.v.*) in his unsuccessful efforts to win federal funding for such a project.

SOURCES: Charles H. Cornwell, *St. Louis Mayors* (St. Louis, 1965); Letter from A. P. Kaufmann to author, 24 March 1980; *Who's Who in American Politics* (New York, 1966).   *Thomas R. Bullard*

KEARSLEY, JONATHAN (1786–1859), Mayor of Detroit (1826, 1829). Sources disagree on the birthplace of Detroit's third mayor, Kearsley—either Virginia or Dauphin County, Pennsylvania, on 20 August 1786. His father, Samuel, served in the Revolutionary Army. In

1811, Jonathan Kearsley graduated from Washington College, intending a military career, and on 6 July 1812 was commissioned a first lieutenant in the Second Regiment of Artillery and soon became assistant deputy quartermaster-general in Philadelphia. One year later, he was appointed adjutant to general Winfield Scott's regiment and brevetted captain for conduct at the battle of Stony Creek. He was then promoted to garrison major and brigadier major. In 1814, Kearsley was commissioned assistant adjutant general with the rank of major and was placed in charge of the state arsenal at Harrisburg. There he was also made collector of internal revenue.

In 1819, Major Kearsley moved to Detroit as receiver of public money, an office he held until 1850. In 1826, he became recorder of the city, and the following year was named justice of the peace. From 1836 to 1850, he served as a regent of the University of Michigan. In September 1826, he replaced the incumbent Mayor Henry Hunt (q.v.) who died and served out the remaining months of his term. In 1829, Kearsley was elected mayor with 123 votes to John R. Williams' (q.v.) 45 and Shubael Conant's 89. Kearsley, known as a "staunch Jacksonian Democrat," presided over a city of 2,000. In 1839, he made another run at the office but lost to Whig businessman DeGarmo Jones (q.v.) by 514 votes, a heavy defeat.

Kearsley married twice, first to Margaret Hetich of Chambersburg, Pennsylvania. They had three children; one, Edward R., died as an infant. After his first wife's death, he married Rachel Valentine, another Pennsylvanian, from Chester County. She died on 6 January 1859. Kearsley died six months later, on 31 August 1859, at age seventy-three. He had been an active Episcopalian.

SOURCES: Stephen Bingham, *Early History of Michigan* (Lansing, 1888); Silas Farmer, *The History of Detroit and Michigan* (Detroit, 1889); *Representative Men of Michigan* (Cincinnati, 1878).

Francis X. Blouin, Jr.

KELLY, EDWARD J. (1876–1950), Mayor of Chicago (1933–47). Mayor of Chicago and co-leader of the city's Democratic machine, Kelly was born on 1 May 1876 in Chicago, the son of an Irish Catholic immigrant, Stephen Kelly, and Helen (Lang) Kelly, who was of German descent. The oldest of nine children, Kelly grew up in poverty, leaving school early to help his policeman father provide for the family. Attracted to civil engineering while observing construction of Chicago's 1893 Columbian Exposition, Kelly supplemented his lack of formal training through night school classes at the Chicago Athenaeum. First joining the Metropolitan Sanitary District, he eventually became its chief engineer by 1920. Appointed president of Chicago's South Park Board in 1924,

Kelly supervised a considerable expansion of its facilities. On 20 March 1910, he married Mary Edmunda Roche, a Roman Catholic from Chicago who died in 1918; their only child, Edward Joseph, died in 1926. Kelly married his second wife, Margaret Ellen Kirk (d. 1955) of Kansas City, Missouri, on 25 January 1922, they adopted three children, Patricia Ann, Joseph Michael and Stephen Edward.

Although he never held elective office before becoming mayor, Kelly enjoyed the close friendship of Patrick A. Nash, a wealthy contractor and powerful leader of Chicago's Democratic party. When Mayor Anton J. Cermak (q.v.) died in 1933, Nash used his influence as Democratic county chairman to arrange Kelly's election as mayor by the Chicago City Council. The Midwest metropolis of 3.3 million was nearly bankrupt, unemployment brought on by the Depression was high, and control over federal relief funds soon became a source of contention between Kelly and Governor Henry Horner. By rolling up impressive majorities in the 1936 election, the Kelly-Nash machine became the Roosevelt administration's agent for dispensing patronage and federal grants in Illinois. In turn, Mayor Kelly closely identified himself with the New Deal and used the WPA work-relief program to strengthen his machine's control over Chicago politics.

Building on the ethnic coalition perfected by Cermak, Mayor Kelly was successful in turning the city's black population from its traditional Republican allegiance to the Democratic party. As a result of the dependable majorities his machine could deliver, Kelly became a key political adviser to Franklin D. Roosevelt and a kingmaker within the national party. As mayor of Chicago, he stabilized the city's finances, using federal funds to aid the unemployed and to begin public works projects. However, he could not stop the spread of urban blight, while crime syndicate-controlled gambling was widespread. Nevertheless, Kelly's powerful Democratic machine assured his election in 1935 over Emil C. Wetten, 799,060 to 167,106; in 1939, against Dwight H. Green, 822,469 to 638,068; and in 1943 over George B. McKibbin, 685,567 to 571,547.

In 1946, Kelly bowed to pressure from his ward committeemen to retire rather than risk defeat in the following year's election. Returning to private life as an engineering consultant, he continued to serve as the Illinois Democratic national committeeman. He died of a heart attack on 20 October 1950 and was buried in Chicago.

SOURCES: Lyle W. Dorsett, *Franklin D. Roosevelt and the City Bosses* (Port Washington, N.Y., 1977); Harold F. Gosnell. *Machine Politics: Chicago Model* (Chicago, 1937); Gene Delon Jones, "The Origin of the Alliance Between the New Deal and the Chicago Machine," *Journal of the Illinois State Historical Society* 67 (June 1974); "The Kelly-Nash Political Machine," *Fortune* (August 1936); Thomas B. Littlewood, *Horner of Illinois* (Evanston, Ill., 1970).   *Peter J. O'Malley*

KELLY, JOSEPH JAMES (1897–1965), Mayor of Buffalo (1942–45). Mayor of Buffalo during World War II, Kelly was born in Buffalo, on 5 July 1897, the son of James W. Kelly (d. 1929), a tavern-owner and local Democratic politician, and Mary (Brodie) Kelly, both Catholic Irish-Americans. He attended parochial schools, Annunciation High School, and St. Joseph's Collegiate Institute. After serving with a training unit in World War I, Kelly attended the University of Buffalo Law School, graduating in 1920. He joined Locke, Babcock, Spratt and Hollister that same year. In 1924, he formed a new partnership with Robert E. Miller, which lasted until 1931.

Kelly was elected assistant county district attorney in 1931 and a city court judge in 1933, serving on the bench until 1941. As judge, Kelly earned a reputation for fairness and efficiency. In 1941, he was the Democratic candidate for mayor, defeating Republican William P. Fisher 101,135 to 96,955. Buffalo had 575,901 people in 1940 and a mayor-council form of government. At this time, Kelly was Buffalo's first unmarried mayor since Jonathan Scoville (1884).

Most of Kelly's mayoralty was devoted to the war effort, and he actively backed all measures to strengthen war industries in the city. He made trips to Washington seeking federal funds. He also cut the city debt by over $30 million. Kelly gained much publicity by backing a special reduced fare for schoolchildren riding the city's transit system. Perhaps Buffalo's youngest mayor, Kelly was one of the most popular, noted for his keen sense of humor.

On 7 March 1949, he married Laura Stephenson; they had no children. Kelly served with the Office of Price Stabilization, 1950–53, and was deputy state comptroller, 1955–63. He resigned early 1963, citing poor health, and died on 7 July 1965.

SOURCES: Buffalo *Evening News*, 7 July 1963; John T. Horton, *History of Northwestern New York*, 3 vols., (New York, 1947); Sister Mary Jane and Sister Mercedes, "Mayors of Buffalo, 1832–1961" (B.A. thesis, Rosary Hill College, 1961).   *Thomas R. Bullard*

KELSEY, LORENZO ALSON (1803–90), Mayor of Cleveland (1848–49). Steamboat captain and mayor of Cleveland, born in Port Leyden, New York, on 22 February 1803, Kelsey was the son of Eber Kelsey (1763–1837-38), a shipowner and land agent, and Lucy Ann (Leete) Kelsey (d. 1824), both New Yorkers. The

last of eleven children, Kelsey attended public school for a few years. In 1825, he married Sophia Smith (1806–93) of Windsor, Connecticut, and they had seven children, all of whom apparently reached adulthood. They were a Protestant family. The Kelseys moved to Cape Vincent, New York, and then to Youngstown, New York, where Kelsey was a lumber merchant. Located at the mouth of the Niagara River, his firm owned the first schooner to sail through the Welland Canal. In 1837, the Kelseys settled in Cleveland, where Lorenzo became manager of the Cleveland House, a prosperous hotel. After a couple of years, Kelsey became captain of the steamship *Chesapeake*, on the Buffalo to Chicago route. He later was captain of the *General Harrison*, largest on the lakes at that time. In the middle of the 1840s, he bought the New England Hotel.

Kelsey was elected mayor in 1848, with no previous political experience. Nominated by the Democrats, he defeated Charles Bradburn (Whig) and M. Hickox, 794 votes to 751 and 59, respectively. Cleveland had 17,034 people by 1850 and a mayor-council form of government. Kelsey did little as mayor, except for the traditional duty of supporting civic improvements. He once remarked that the mayor's salary was not enough to tempt him into a full-time political career. He returned to his hotel business in 1849, retiring in the late 1850s. He died on 13 February 1890.

SOURCES: Edward A. Claypool and Azalea Clizbee, *A Genealogy of the Descendants of William Kelsey*, 3 vols. (New Haven, Conn., 1928–47); Cleveland *Plain Dealer*, 14 February 1890; Gertrude Wickham, *Pioneer Families of Cleveland, 1796–1840*, 2 vols. (Chicago, 1914).   *Thomas R. Bullard*

KENDRICK, W. FREELAND (1874–1953), Mayor of Philadelphia (1924–28). Republican regular, born on 24 June 1874 in Philadelphia's Tenth Ward, Kendrick attended public schools through grammar school. His early occupation was in a steam laundry. Not much is known about his business activities in the intervening years, but by 1910 he headed his own company as a distributor of mineral waters. Far more evident was Kendrick's involvement in Masonic orders, in which he became a national figure as past imperial potentate. He was credited with originating the idea of the Shriners hospitals for crippled children. His critics frequently accused Kendrick of exploiting Shriner popularity for his business interests, a charge dismissed by the Shriner body. He was married to Mabel Benard, and they had two children.

In 1924, Philadelphia had a population of nearly two million and a mayor-council form of government. Kendrick, who as early as 1911 spoke of his interest in the mayoralty, rode the crest of his popularity as a Shriner and as receiver of taxes (1914–24). He reformed the latter office by establishing sound business practices, stressing efficiency and follow-up. Characterized by Republican boss Edwin H. Vare as the "biggest vote-puller in the state," Kendrick confirmed Vare's assessment by defeating Democrat opponent A. Raymond Raff 286,398 to 37,239 (on 6 November 1923).

Kendrick's mayoralty was marred by two fiascos. First, in his attempt to reform the city's notoriously corrupt police department during the Prohibition era, Kendrick appointed Marine General Smedley D. Butler as public safety director. Butler's prohibitionist zealotry in conspicuously wet Philadelphia brought the city national attention but discomfited Mayor Kendrick as well as numerous other Philadelphians, bootleggers and elite alike, and the embarrassed mayor removed Butler from office. A second episode involved the Sesquicentennial Exposition of 1926. Designed to boost the city, the exposition was both an artistic and financial failure, enabling Kendrick's critics to charge waste and extravagance in the election of 1927.

Kendrick's administration was not entirely negative. The vital Broad Street subway was initiated, and work on it speedily performed; the urban landscape was also refashioned with new architecture. But essentially Kendrick was a polished and ingratiating public figure who owed his career to his shrewdness rather than to his vision, and to the support of the contractor-combine of William S. Vare. Kendrick introduced the big city budget to Philadelphia without the means of sustaining it.

Kendrick resumed his business career after the 1928 election and died on 29 March 1953. He was buried in Philadelphia.

SOURCES: Fred D. Baldwin, "Smedley D. Butler and Prohibition Enforcement in Philadelphia 1924–25," *Pennsylvania Magazine of History and Biography* 84 (July 1960); Herman A. Collins and Wilfred Jordan, *Philadelphia: A Story of Progress* (Philadelphia, 1941); *The Mayors of Philadelphia*, Collections of the Genealogical Society of Pennsylvania; *Philadelphia*, Federal Writers Project, Pennsylvania Historical Commission, 1937; Adrienne Segal, *Philadelphia: A Chronological Documentary History* (New York, 1975); Edwin Wolf II, *Philadelphia: A Portrait of an American City* (Harrisburg, Pa., 1975).   *Richard A. Varbero*

KENNEDY, HUGH (1810–88), Mayor of New Orleans (1865). An appointed mayor of New Orleans, Kennedy was born on 1 July 1810 in Belfast, Ireland. His parents were born in Glasgow, Scotland, but moved to Ireland when his father opened a cotton mill and calico printing plant in Dublin. After Kennedy's three older brothers became professionals or civil servants, Kennedy started out on a similar path: he graduated from the Belfast Academical and Collegiate Institution, a Presbyterian school, and went to London to practice law. His life took a different turn when he left for America in 1833, moving to New Orleans via New York.

He kept the title of Dr. Kennedy throughout his life after working for more than a decade as a druggist in New Orleans, but he eventually turned to journalism and served as the editor of the New Orleans *True Delta*, working closely with several other Irish immigrants in the leadership of the Democratic party. He married Annie White, the daughter of the city's most prominent Irish immigrant, Maunsel White; Kennedy and his wife had three daughters.

Just before the Civil War ended, Kennedy was appointed mayor of the city by James Madison Wells, a governor in the provisional state administration established under the Reconstruction program of Abraham Lincoln in 1864. In 1860, the city had a population of 168,675. Kennedy, a former secessionist sympathizer, proceeded to fire most of the civilian employees appointed by the city's former military government. When Nathanial Banks returned to the city in May, he challenged Well's authority by removing Kennedy and replacing him with Captain Samuel M. Quincy (*q.v.*), a commander of black troops and the grandson of Boston's former popular mayor, Josiah Quincy (*q.v.*). Wells and Kennedy quickly left for Washington, D.C., for a meeting with President Andrew Johnson, who honored their demand to reverse Banks' order and to restore Kennedy to his former office. Under his renewed administration, Kennedy leased city-owned wharves to private parties in return for the lessees' renovating of those facilities. He also established a new school board and successfully lobbied with federal officials to have quasi-public railroad corporations (seized earlier by military authorities) returned to stockholders. He left office when the first mayor elected since military occupation took office on 12 May 1865. Kennedy did not run for the position; indeed, he never held an elective post in his life.

After his brief term in office, Kennedy entered the streetcar business and became president of the Crescent City Railroad Company in 1875. He later moved to Louisville in order to invest in coal mining operations. He died there on 19 May 1888.

SOURCES: Gerald Capers, *Occupied City: New Orleans Under the Federals, 1862–1865* (Lexington, Ky., 1965); John S. Kendall, *History of New Orleans* (Chicago, 1922); Peyton McCrary, *Abraham Lincoln and Reconstruction, the New Orleans Experiment* (Princeton, N.J., 1978).   *Joseph Logsdon*

KENNELLY, MARTIN H. (1887–1961), Mayor of Chicago (1947–55). Moderate Irish Catholic reform mayor of a city firmly controlled by a Democratic machine, Kennelly was born on 11 August 1887 in the Bridgeport neighborhood of Chicago. His Irish-American father, Jeremiah, a packinghouse worker, died when he was two, leaving the mother, Margaret (Carroll) Kennelly, to raise five children in poverty. After completing primary school, Kennelly spent a year working as a stockboy for Marshall Field Department Store before returning to De La Salle High School and graduating in 1905. Finding employment in the Becklenberg warehouse, he began a life-long career in the moving and storage business. During World War I, Kennelly served with the Army Quartermaster Corps and was discharged a captain in 1919. He soon began his own moving company, became a founder of Allied Van Lines, and in 1931 president of the National Furniture Warehousemen's Association. A bachelor, he devoted much of his time to civic activities, especially the Chicago Red Cross during World War II.

Kennelly allied himself with the "good government" wing of Chicago's Democratic party in opposition to the Kelly-Nash machine. Nevertheless, when Mayor Edward J. Kelly (*q.v.*) was compelled to retire in 1946, party leaders turned to Kennelly as their blue-ribbon candidate to face the resurgent local Republicans. The businessman-civic leader, who had never before held political office, defeated his opponent, Russell W. Root, 919,593 to 646,239 in the April 1947 mayoral election. Kennelly considered himself a municipal administrator rather than a politician and declined to take an active role in Democratic party affairs.

Turning his attention instead to solving the severe postwar housing shortage in a city of 3,620,962, Kennelly launched Chicago's first comprehensive housing program. The worst slums were cleared, and public housing projects were constructed with federal funds. The long-awaited transfer of Chicago's mass transit system to public ownership was accomplished, and subway lines were extended. Airport development and expressway construction became items of high priority with Kennelly's administration, reflecting the growth of Chicago's postwar airline and auto traffic. The police and fire departments were upgraded, and civil service expanded to include most of the city's municipal employees.

In 1951, Kennelly won a second term over Republican Robert L. Hunter, 697,871 to 545,326, but his difficulties in office began to increase. Chicago's reform groups were disappointed because he had not initiated the sweeping reform of city government they desired. Evidence uncovered by a U.S. Senate crime investigating committee revealed organized crime's continued power in Chicago, contradicting Kennelly's claim of improved law enforcement. Expansion of the city's black ghetto into white neighborhoods created racial friction for which both sides held the mayor responsible.

In 1955, the Democratic machine, exasperated by the mayor's indifference to party interests, denied his bid for a third term, and in a sharply contested primary election, Kennelly was defeated by Richard J. Daley (*q.v.*). Returning to the direction of his warehouse firm, Kennelly, a devout Catholic, also involved himself with fund-raising efforts for church institutions. He died in his sleep on 29 November 1961 and was buried in Chicago.

SOURCES: Perry R. Duis and Glen E. Holt, "The Real Legacy of 'Poor Martin' Kennelly," *Chicago* 27 (July 1978); Martin H. Kennelly Papers, 90 vols., scrapbooks, 16 drawers of correspondence, speeches, documents, UICC Library; Martin Meyerson and Edward C. Banfield, *Politics, Planning and the Public Interest: The Case of Public Housing in Chicago* (Glencoe, Ill., 1955).

Peter J. O'Malley

KENNETT, LUTHER M. (1807–73), Mayor of St. Louis (1850–53). Merchant and politician, born in Falmouth, Kentucky, on 15 March 1807, Kennett was the son of Press Graves Kennett (banker and local court clerk) and his wife. Young Kennett attended local schools and spent two years in Georgetown, Kentucky, studying under noted Baptist scholar Reverend Burton Stone. In 1822, Kennett's father suffered financial problems, and young Kennett quit school and worked in a nearby country store. Kennett served a short while as deputy clerk of Pendleton County, moving to St. Louis in 1825. He became a clerk in a local store, soon opening his own store in Farmington, Missouri. He moved back to St. Louis and opened a large store in partnership with Hugh White, gaining enough money to retire temporarily from business activity by 1840. He married Martha Ann Boyce in 1832, and they had one daughter, before Martha died in 1835. In 1842, he married Agnes M. Kennett, a distant relative, and they had seven sons.

Kennett served as an alderman, 1843–46, followed by a tour of Europe. In 1848, he was an unsuccessful candidate for mayor: running on the Whig ticket, he was defeated by Democrat John Krum (*q.v.*) 3,201 to 2,630. He subsequently served on a special committee in 1849, created to help the city recover from the serious cholera epidemic. In 1850, he was elected mayor, defeating Democrats John How (*q.v.*) and D. A. Magehan and Independent George Morton 3,329 to 2,018, 644, and 73, respectively. He was reelected in 1851, again defeating How, 4,015 to 3,335. In 1852, Kennett won a third term, defeating Democrat F. R. Conway 3,998 to 3,432. St. Louis had a population of 77,860 (1850) and a mayor-council form of government.

In his three years in office, Kennett supported a wide range of civic improvements: schools, a new harbor, and a better fire department. He was considered a popular mayor and a successful vote-winner for the Whigs. After leaving office, he became president of the Iron Mountain Railroad Company. He continued this interest in railroads during a single term in Congress, 1855–57. With the Whig party disintegrated, Kennett had switched to the nativist American or Know-Nothing party. After being defeated for reelection in 1856, Kennett retired from politics and returned to railroad promotion. In 1867, he went to Europe and died while in Paris, on 12 April 1873.

SOURCES: Charles H. Cornwell, *St. Louis Mayors: Brief Biographies* (St. Louis, 1965); William Hyde and Howard L. Conrad, eds., *Encyclopedia of the History of St. Louis*, 4 vols. (New York, 1899); J. T. Scharf, *History of Saint Louis City and County*, 2 vols. (Philadelphia, 1883); Walter B. Stevens, *St. Louis, The Fourth City 1764–1909* (Chicago, 1909).   *Thomas R. Bullard*

KERR, WILLIAM (1809–53), Mayor of Pittsburgh (1846). Democratic mayor and physician, Kerr was born on 15 September 1809 in St. Clair Township, Allegheny County, Pennsylvania. One of eleven children, he was the second son born to Reverend Joseph Kerr, a Scots-Irish Presbyterian minister, and Agnes Reynolds Kerr. Reverend Kerr, who came to America from Ballygoney, County Tyrone, Ireland, in 1801, was pastor of the St. Clair and Mifflin churches in Allegheny County, and later pastor of the Second United Presbyterian Church in Pittsburgh, editor of the *United Presbyterian* for forty years, and vice-president of the Pittsburgh Colonization Society. William Kerr married Mary Warden, daughter of John and Anna Leeds Warden of Pittsburgh, on 26 March 1840 and had four children. A graduate of the University of Pennsylvania Medical Department, Kerr began a medical practice at Pittsburgh in 1833 and later opened a drug store. He became a well-known and admired physician in the city.

Located in Allegheny County, Pittsburgh in 1840 had a population of 21,115 (which more than doubled by the end of the decade) and a mayor-council form of government. The councils (select and common) held most municipal authority, exercising both executive and legislative powers. The mayor was primarily a magistrate and police chief. Dr. Kerr retired from medical practice and accepted the Democratic nomination for mayor on 16 December 1845. On 13 January 1846, he won the election with 1,532 votes to 1,425 for William J. Howard (Whig

and Anti-Mason) and 22 for B.T.C. Morgan (Native American). Although urged by his party to continue as mayor, Dr. Kerr refused to run for reelection in January 1847. A year later, however, he was again Democratic mayoral candidate. He barely lost the election of 11 January 1848, with 1,556 votes to 1,642 for incumbent mayor Gabriel Adams (*q.v.*) (Whig and Anti-Mason), and 312 for Samuel Stackhouse (Native American).

Dr. Kerr's election victory in 1846 was the only time the Pittsburgh Democrats defeated the Whigs for the mayoralty during the 1840s. The Democratic triumph was the result of several factors: questions concerning the distribution of relief money for victims of the great fire of 10 April 1845, resentment over the political purges of the police force by the Whig mayor, William J. Howard (*q.v.*), and the extraordinary personal reputation of Dr. Kerr and his following among workingmen's groups. During his one-year term, Mayor Kerr helped reorganize the fire relief program, assisted the rebuilding of sections of the city destroyed by the fire, resolved tensions between the mayor's office and the police, conducted a liberal policy of patronage (appointing a Democratic and a Whig newspaper as city printers), and maintained municipal order when Pittsburgh became an important embarkation point for troops and a transshipment center for war materials during the Mexican-American War. A man of high esteem, Dr. Kerr was praised for his competent handling of municipal affairs, his wise legal judgment at mayor's court, and his sympathy for the poor.

After his mayoralty and his unsuccessful second campaign for mayor, Dr. Kerr moved to Chartiers Township where he lived quietly in retirement. A life-long Presbyterian, he died on 11 August 1853.

SOURCES: Leland D. Baldwin, *Pittsburgh: The Story of a City* (Pittsburgh, 1937); *History of Allegheny County* (Chicago, 1889); Michael Fitzgibbon Holt, *Forging a Majority: The Formation of the Republican Party in Pittsburgh, 1848–1860* (New Haven, Conn., 1969); Allen Humphreys Kerr, ''The Mayors and Recorders of Pittsburgh, 1816–1951'' (unpublished manuscript, Historical Society of Western Pennsylvania, Pittsburgh, 1952); Pittsburgh *Post*, 17 and 27 December 1845, 13 and 20 January 1846, 9 and 12 February 1846, 30 April 1846; Pittsburgh *Gazette*, 3 December 1847; Erasmus Wilson, ed., *Standard History of Pittsburgh* (Chicago, 1898).   *Matthew S. Magda*

KERRIGAN, JOHN E. (1907–   ), Mayor of Boston (1945–46). Interim mayor, born on 1 October 1907 in South Boston, Kerrigan was the son of Michael Kerrigan, an Irish immigrant fireman at Boston City Hospital, and Annie (Laffey) Kerrigan, also a Catholic from Ireland. His father died when John, the third-born of four boys, was five. His mother hired out to do housework, and young Kerrigan eventually helped the family by doing odd jobs after school. After graduation from South Boston High School in 1926, Kerrigan became a salesman for a soft drink concern. He also interested himself in local politics and participated in the Democratic campaigns of John W. McCormack for Congress and William J. Foley for Suffolk County district attorney.

In 1933, Kerrigan was elected from his ward to the twenty-two-member Boston City Council and was reelected in 1935 and 1937. He was chosen city council president in 1938. That same year, Kerrigan, as acting mayor, directed the relief effort in the city after a severe hurricane and won election to a term in the Massachusetts Senate. In 1940, he left the Senate and lost a bid to become county sheriff. Two years later, he forsook a campaign for the governor's council and joined the U.S. Army. Kerrigan held the rank of sergeant upon discharge in 1943.

The soft-spoken bachelor was elected to the city council again in November 1943 and was reelected in 1945. The other councillors again chose him to be the body's president in 1944 and 1945. In 1944, Kerrigan lost a second race for sheriff. In 1945, however, he was made acting mayor for a year when the incumbent, Maurice J. Tobin (q.v.), became governor of Massachusetts. The Bay State legislature subsequently voted to confer upon Acting Mayor Kerrigan the full powers and salary of an elected chief executive.

In 1940, Boston had a population of 770,816. As World War II wound down and the city moved into the postwar era, there were the familiar population shifts and shortages of necessities, and economic disarray. Attempting to gain the confidence of the business community, Kerrigan saw to it that city land was sold to the New England Telephone Company and that unused streets were made available for the expansion of industrial firms. He also fought successfully for the refinancing of the bonds of the East Boston Sumner Tunnel, so that the city could take advantage of low interest rates. In addition, Kerrigan reopened the East Boston Relief Station, closed since the Depression, and he proposed an ambitious long-range revitalization plan for the whole city which included a massive input of public housing.

Kerrigan's administration was nonetheless short-lived. In the municipal election of 1945, the thirty-eight-year-old Kerrigan, who had never been elected city-wide, was opposed by Congressman James Michael Curley (q.v.), a former governor and three-term mayor, the premier political figure in Boston. Four other candidates complicated matters by dividing the anti-Curley forces. Curley won the election with 111,824 votes to Kerrigan's 60,413, William Arthur Reilly's 46,135, John J. Saw-

telle's 12,743, Joseph Lee's 10,042, and Michael Paul Feeney's 3,298.

In 1951, after a change in the city charter, Kerrigan won a city-wide election for a seat on a nine-member city council. He was returned to the council in the elections of 1953, 1955, 1957, 1959, 1961, 1963, 1965, 1967, 1969, and 1971. As a city councillor, Kerrigan generally supported the housing and urban renewal programs of Mayors John B. Hynes (q.v.), John F. Collins (q.v.), and Kevin H. White (q.v.). Kerrigan, a member of the American Legion and the Knights of Columbus, retired from public office in 1974 to become a real estate consultant.

SOURCES: *City Record*, 1945–46, Government Documents Department, Boston Public Library; Documents of the City of Boston, 1945–46, Microtext Department, Boston Public Library; John E. Kerrigan clippings, Newspaper Morgue, School of Public Communication, Boston University; *Proceedings of the City Council of Boston*, 1934–38, 1944–46, 1952–74, Government Documents Department, Boston Public Library.

Richard H. Gentile

KETCHUM, WILLIAM (1798–1876), Mayor of Buffalo (1844). A Whig mayor and local business leader, active in reforming city fiscal operations, Ketchum was born on 2 March 1798 in Bloomfield, New York, the son of Joshua Ketchum, a small farmer, and Lucy (Parsons) Ketchum, both of Yankee Protestant stock. Ketchum moved to Buffalo in 1819 and began to work for Stocking and Bull, a merchant house handling furs and hats; he soon became a partner. Before being elected mayor, Ketchum was a Buffalo village trustee in the 1820s and a common school trustee in the early 1830s. On 18 March 1823, he married Lamira Callendar (1803–66), a native of Vermont, educated in Buffalo's common schools, and the daughter of Amos Callendar, who was a deacon of the First Presbyterian Church of Buffalo. Ketchum and Lamira had two daughters and a son. On 7 September 1871, Ketchum married a Canadian, Elizabeth Palmer (d. 1911), of Brantford, Ontario. He was an active Presbyterian.

Buffalo's population of 1840 was 18,213, rising to 26,503 by 1844. The city had a mayor-council form of government. Ketchum accepted the Whig nomination for mayor and defeated the Democratic candidate, Oliver G. Steele, in the March 1844 election, 1,602 to 1,389.

As mayor, Ketchum was primarily concerned with reordering the way the city handled work contracts and tax assessments. As a result of his efforts, taxes were levied and collected before work orders were issued. Not only did this reversal of previous procedure save tax revenue, it also meant that city government would not be encumbered with large debts each year, growing out of advances, since local projects were now financed on the basis of local assessments. During his one-year term, Ketchum strongly urged broader support for the public school system. He did not run for reelection in March 1845.

After leaving the mayoralty, Ketchum continued his partnership in the fur and hat business until his retirement in 1857. His friendship with President Millard Fillmore led to his appointment as customs collector for the port of Buffalo. He was also a county supervisor, 1847–50. Ketchum devoted much of his later attention to local history and was active in the Buffalo Historical Society. He suffered a heart attack while attending services at the First Presbyterian Church and died soon afterwards on 30 September 1876.

SOURCES: Buffalo *Daily Courier*; Buffalo *Morning Express; Commercial Advertiser and Journal*; John T. Horton, Edward T. Williams, and Harry S. Douglass, *History of Northwestern New York* (New York, 1947); Cristfield Johnson, *Centennial History of Erie County, New York* (Buffalo, 1876); J. N. Larned, *A History of Buffalo* (New York, 1911); Sister Mary Jane and Sister Mercedes, "Mayors of Buffalo, 1832–1961" (B.A. thesis, Rosary Hill College, 1961); Grace Carew Sheldon, "Buffalo Mayors, 1832–1901" (Scrapbook in Buffalo Historical Society).   *Daniel B. Karin*

KIEL, HENRY W. (1871–1942), Mayor of St. Louis (1913–25). German-American businessman-mayor, Kiel was born in St. Louis on 21 February 1871, the son of a successful building contractor, Henry F. Kiel (1843–1908), and Minnie C. (Daues) Kiel (d. 1879), both of German, probably Lutheran, descent. One of five children, Kiel attended public schools and graduated from Smith Academy before starting work for his father's firm, the Kiel-Daues Company. He eventually became president and reorganized the company into the Boaz-Kiel Construction Company, which built many hotels, theaters, and stores in St. Louis during the first quarter of the twentieth century. On 1 September 1892, he married Irene H. Moonan, and they had four children. The Kiels were members of St. Mark's English Lutheran Church and were active supporters of the St. Louis Municipal Opera. Kiel was also a Mason and an Odd Fellow.

Kiel entered politics in 1907, when elected chairman of the Republican City Central Committee. In 1913, he was elected mayor, with 54,811 votes to 51,526 for Democrat John Simon and 4,635 for Socialist Frank Gerhart. Kiel thought he had been defeated and was on a train for an Arkansas vacation when he learned he had been elected. In 1917, he was reelected, defeating W. C. Connett (Democrat) 70,193 to 46,792. He won a third

four-year term in 1921, with 104,320 votes to 94,748 for James W. Byrnes (Democrat) and 4,330 for William Brandt (Socialist). St. Louis had 687,029 people in 1910 and 772,897 by 1920, with a mayor-council form of government.

As mayor, Kiel actively supported the fund-raising drives of World War I, winning several awards for his efforts. He also backed an $87 million bond issue for major construction projects. He supported a new city charter and construction of the city's new zoo. Kiel served longer in office than any St. Louis mayor to date. After his third term ended, he returned to his construction firm. In 1931–32, he served as president of the city's board of police commissioners. He was an unsuccessful Republican nominee for the U.S. Senate in 1932. He retired later and died on 26 November 1942.

SOURCES: Charles H. Cornwell, *St. Louis Mayors: Brief Biographies* (St. Louis, 1965); Floyd C. Shoemaker, *Missouri and Missourians*, 5 vols. (Chicago, 1943).   *Thomas R. Bullard*

KILBOURN, BYRON (1801–70), Mayor of Milwaukee (1848–49, 1854–55). Promoter and politician, Milwaukee's third mayor was an old-stock New Englander and an Episcopalian. He was born on 8 September 1801 in Granby, Connecticut, the son of James Kilbourne (1770–1850), land agent and politician, and Lucy (Fitch) Kilbourne (d. 1805), daughter of John Fitch, the pioneer steamboat builder. The sixth of seven children, he dropped the final letter of his name and moved to Worthington, Ohio, with his parents in 1803. After a few years of local school, he became a surveyor and was selected to superintend the construction of several canals in Ohio during the early 1830s. In 1834, he became surveyor of public lands, migrated further west to Wisconsin, and led several surveying teams during 1834–37. In 1835, he stopped off at the home of Solomon Juneau (*q.v.*), Milwaukee's founder and first mayor, and was made aware of the possibilities of the region. Many authorities feel Kilbourn should share the title of "founder of Milwaukee" with Juneau. Kilbourn married Mary Cowles (d. 1837) in the later 1820s, and they had two children, both of whom died in their teens. On 16 June 1838, he married Henrietta Kerrick (c. 1807–1887) of Baltimore, and they also had two children, only one of whom survived childhood. The Kilbourns belonged to the Episcopal church, and Henrietta was active in church activities.

A prominent Democrat, Kilbourn was West Side president (1837–39). In 1840, he ran for Congress and was defeated. Kilbourn served in the state legislature in 1845 and on the board of aldermen, 1846–47. He was elected mayor in 1848, defeating Rufus King (Whig) 1,198 to

998. He was again elected in 1854, defeating incumbent Mayor George Walker (*q.v.*), 2,340 to 1,760 (Both men were Democrats.) Milwaukee had 20,061 people by 1850 and a mayor-council form of government. As mayor, Kilbourn adopted what may be called the pay-as-you-go plan of limiting city expenses. He also supported improved schools and projects to enlarge the harbor.

Kilbourn's later years were devoted to railroad work. He served as president of the Milwaukee and Mississippi Railroad and the LaCrosse and Milwaukee Railroad (1847–57). In 1858, he was called before a legislative committee and was charged with using bribery to influence a Wisconsin land grant to his railroad companies. He resigned his railroad directorships and almost dropped out of public life. In 1868, he moved to Florida where he died on 16 December 1870 of a stroke.

SOURCES: H. Russell Austin, *The Milwaukee Story* (Milwaukee, 1946); Godwin F. Berquist, Jr., "Byron Kilbourn's Ohio Heritage," *Historical Messenger* 27:1 (April 1971); *History of Milwaukee* (Chicago, 1881); Payne K. Kilbourn, *The Family Memorial* (Hartford, Conn., 1845 + later appendix).   *Thomas R. Bullard*

KING, SAMUEL GEORGE (1816–99), Mayor of Philadelphia (1881–84). Reform mayor, King was born in Philadelphia on 2 May 1816, the only son of George M. King, a coppersmith of old-stock English ancestry, and Mary Gougler King, whose German ancestors settled in Bucks County, Pennsylvania, in 1700. One of five children, King was born into the Lutheran Church; however, he was educated at a Friends School, and he attended Orthodox Friends meetings for most of his life. Nevertheless, in his old age he joined St. Clement's Protestant Episcopal Church. King briefly studied law, but he learned the brushmaking trade as a young man, started his own business at the age of twenty-one, and retired at thirty-five. A life-long Democrat, he entered politics as an election inspector and later became a ward committeeman. In 1854, he received an appointment as a customs inspector, a position he held until 1860. In 1860, King was elected to the select council from the Eleventh Ward, a post he held for over twenty years until his election as mayor. While on the council, he established a reputation as a reformer devoted to economy in government. In 1864, he was a delegate to the Democratic national convention.

Philadelphia in 1880 had 847,170 people and a mayor-bicameral council form of government. In 1881, King received the support not only of his party, but also of many reform-minded Republicans who belonged to the recently formed Committee of 100, a Good Government organization composed primarily of merchants and manufacturers. In addition, many followers of Republican state boss J. Donald Cameron supported King in an effort to weaken an opposing faction led by James McManes, a powerful trustee of the Philadelphia Gas Works. King defeated the Republican incumbent William S. Stokley (*q.v.*) 78,215 to 72,428. King ran for reelection in 1884 and was defeated by Republican William B. Smith (*q.v.*) 70,440 to 79,552.

Serving in an office that possessed few powers other than the appointment of police officers, it is not surprising that King, like his predecessor, made his reputation with Philadelphia's police force. In this instance, however, the mayor made nonpartisan appointments, even to the point of retaining the Republican chief of police. His major innovation, however, was the appointment of black police officers. King also spoke out frequently against corruption in government. By such measures, he failed to build a broad base of support during his administration, and, like many Good Government mayors, he failed to win reelection in 1884.

King's defeat marked the end of his political career. He refused the Democratic mayoralty nomination in 1891. A life-long bachelor, King was a Mason, and a student of the Bible, Shakespeare, and English poetry. He occasionally wrote poetry himself. He died on 21 March 1899 and was buried in Philadelphia.

SOURCES: Donald W. Disbrow, "The Progressive Movement in Philadelphia, 1910–1916" (Ph.D dissertation, University of Rochester, 1956); Howard F. Gillette, Jr., "Corrupt and Contented: Philadelphia's Political Machine, 1865–1887" (Ph.D dissertation, Yale University, 1970); Ellis Paxon Oberholtzer, *Philadelphia: A History of the City and Its People*, 4 vols. (Philadelphia, 1911); *Public Ledger, Inquirer, Evening Bulletin, North American*, 22 March 1899 (obituaries).

John F. Sutherland

KING, WASHINGTON (1815–61), Mayor of St. Louis (1855–56). Know-Nothing mayor and railroad promoter, born on 5 October 1815 in New York City, King was the son of English immigrants. After attending public schools, he became a teacher in New York City and eventually a school principal. On 2 December 1836, he married Cynthia M. Kelsey of Connecticut, and they had two children. In 1844, the Kings moved to St. Louis, where he entered the manufacturing and mercantile business. In 1849, he was virtually wiped out by the great fire which swept the business district of St. Louis. He then spent two and a half years touring Europe, observing the conditions within the various countries. By the time he returned, the Democrats had become the dominant party in the city, with the Whigs gradually losing strength. As a result, King joined the American or Know-Nothing party, the organization of the nativists.

In 1855, King won the mayoralty on that party's ticket, defeating Democrat John H. Lightner and Independent Democrat John Hogan by 3,781 to 3,050 and 2,595, respectively. St. Louis had 77,860 people and a mayor-council form of government. As mayor, King spent most of his energies supporting the various railroads that were linking St. Louis to the rest of the state. He also backed the 1856 annexation which enlarged the city. Among other civic improvements that won his support were a comprehensive program of street paving (by wooden blocks) and the construction of a new reservoir. Both improvements resulted from the earlier annexation. After leaving office, King was president of the Adams Express Company and remained in that position until his death on 27 August 1861.

SOURCES: Howard L. Conrad, ed., *Encyclopedia of History of Missouri*, 6 vols. (New York, 1901); Charles H. Cornwell, *St. Louis Mayors: Brief Biographies* (St. Louis, 1965); J. T. Scharf, *History of Saint Louis City and County*, 2 vols. (Philadelphia, 1883).

Thomas R. Bullard

KINGSLAND, AMBROSE C. (1804–78), Mayor of New York City (1851–53). The last Whig mayor of New York City, Kingsland was a native New Yorker born on 24 May 1804 of old British stock, first settled in New Jersey in 1665. Educated at Friends' Seminary, he and his brother in 1820 opened a dry goods store which they soon expanded into overseas trade. D. and A. Kingsland and Sutton specialized in the importation of sperm oil, quickly prospered, and eventually equipped its own ships for hunting whales. Kingsland, an Episcopalian, married Mary Lovett in 1833, and they had ten children.

In 1850, New York City had a population of 515,547 and was beginning a decade of spectacular growth. Under a new city charter imposed by a Whig-controlled legislature in 1849, the government was a mixed municipal federalist system with authority divided among a weak mayor, a bicameral common council of aldermen and assistant aldermen, and nine municipal departments. Fortunately for Kingsland, his Democratic opponents in Tammany Hall were split into feuding factions, and he defeated Fernando Wood (*q.v.*) 22,546 to 17,993.

As mayor, Kingsland proposed a far-reaching program to curb crime, improve sanitation, alleviate traffic problems, improve sanitation, pave avenues, create a central city park and light the streets. His ideas largely died stillborn. The police, appointed by the aldermen, ignored him; disease, filth, and congestion increased with population; the question of improving city services bogged down in bribery and differences over means of improvement; and Kingsland could not control the common council which was soon nicknamed "The Forty Thieves" for its purported corruption. Kingsland's only positive achievement lay in his sponsorship of Central Park.

Not renominated, he returned to his company, renamed A. C. Kingsland and Sons, and built a flourishing export trade with markets in Great Britain, China, and the East Indies. Kingsland, although no longer interested in elective office, fought a futile battle to preserve the Whig party in the late 1850s. For the remainder of his life, he served as a commissioner of the Croton Aqueduct, busied himself with civic improvements, and was an active member of the Chamber of Commerce. He died on 13 October 1878.

SOURCES: Gustavus Myers, *The History of Tammany Hall* (New York, 1917); Laura Roper: *FLO: A Biography of Frederick Law Olmsted* (Baltimore, 1973); George Wilson, *Portrait Gallery of the Chamber of Commerce of the State of New-York* (New York, 1890).

Jerome Mushkat

KIRBY, ABNER (1818–93), Mayor of Milwaukee (1864–65). The last Civil War, Democratic mayor of Milwaukee was born in New England on a farm in Somerset County, Maine, near the town of Starks on 11 April 1818. After working on the farm and serving an apprenticeship in the jewelry trade, Kirby migrated to Milwaukee in 1844. He was successively a jeweler, lumber dealer, manufacturer of threshing machines, shipowner, and, finally, a hotel owner, with the well-known "Kirby House."

Kirby's first wife, Rebecca Chase of Hartland, Maine, died in 1849. He then married her sister, Mary Jane, but she also died, in 1852. On 8 October 1854, he married Letitia Chase (according to one account, no relation to the departed sisters) of Amsterdam, New York. His wives bore him three sons and three daughters.

A life-long Democrat, Kirby was also an ardent unionist. In 1864, he was elected mayor without Republican opposition. Milwaukee was a growing community of about 50,000, with a mayor-council form of government.

Although the city and visitors considered the Kirby House to be the finest hotel in Milwaukee, Kirby suffered a number of financial reverses. Prior to his death, on 21 September 1893, he was active in various real estate development schemes and charitable activities.

SOURCES: Frank Flower, *History of Milwaukee, Wisconsin* (Chicago, 1881); John G. Gregory, *History of Milwaukee, Wisconsin* (Chicago, 1931); James A. Watrous, ed., *Memoirs of Milwaukee County* (Madison, Wis., 1909).

David J. Maurer

KLINE, ARDOLPH L. (1858–1930), Acting Mayor of New York (1913). Acting mayor for under four months in 1913, Kline was born on 21 February 1858 in Sussex

County, New Jersey, the son of Anthony Kline and Margaret (Busby) Kline. He was educated in public schools in Newton, New Jersey, and at Phillips Andover Academy, and was Episcopalian. Kline moved to Brooklyn in 1875 and enlisted in Company D of the Fourteenth U.S. Infantry National Guard the following year. Colonel Kline served in the Spanish-American War and remained in the National Guard until 1906 when he retired as a brevet brigadier general. He worked at W. C. Peet and Company in Brooklyn, a manufacturer of neckwear, from 1877 to 1886. In 1902, he ran unsuccessfully for sheriff of Kings County, and in 1904 he was elected a member of the board of aldermen, a position he held in 1904–1905, 1906–1907, 1912–13, and 1914–15. President Theodore Roosevelt named Kline assistant appraiser of the port of New York in 1908. Kline married Frances A. Phalon on 25 November 1886.

In 1913, New York City had 5,048,827 people and a mayor-board of aldermen form of government. When John Purroy Mitchel (q.v.) resigned as president of the board of aldermen, Kline replaced him. In that capacity, Kline was named acting mayor upon the death of Mayor William J. Gaynor (q.v.). Kline's brief mayoralty lasted from 10 September to 31 December 1913. During these months, John Purroy Mitchel was elected mayor, and Kline was reelected to the board of aldermen.

From 1914 to 1918, Kline served as tax commissioner of New York City, and from 1921 to 1923 he was a member of the Sixty-seventh Congress representing New York's Fifth Congressional District. In 1923, he was appointed the New York agent of the Sea Service Bureau of the U.S. Shipping Board. Kline died on 13 October 1930 at Methodist Episcopal Hospital and was buried in Newton, New Jersey.

SOURCES: *The Greater City: New York, 1898–1948* (New York, 1948); New York *Times* 12 September 1913, 14 October 1930.   *W. Roger Biles*

KLINE, CHARLES HOWARD (1870–1933), Mayor of Pittsburgh (1926–33). Kline was the son of an Indiana, Pennsylvania, dry goods merchant of Huguenot and German descent, Wellington B. Kline, and his wife, Maria Margaret (Custer) Kline. The couple, both of whose parents were also Pennsylvania-born, had four children: Laura E. (b. 1862), George K. (b. 1864), Horace M. (b. 1867), and Charles H. (b. 1870). The youngest, Kline attended Kiskiminetas Springs preparatory school, Indiana Normal School, and the University of Michigan Law School, from which he graduated in 1897. He arrived in Pittsburgh in 1899. On 24 October 1900, he married Katherine Whitsell Johnson of Pittsburgh, also a graduate of Indiana Normal School, and a Presbyterian, like Kerr. They had no children.

Kline began his political involvement early in his career. He was elected to a term in the state House of Representatives in 1904, and in 1906, he began three successive terms in the state Senate, becoming chairman of the appropriations committee in 1915. In that capacity, he was instrumental in increasing state funding for education. Appointed to the county court of common pleas in 1919 by Governor William C. Sproul, Kline retired from elective office to the judicial bench.

In 1925, when Andrew W. Mellon, the local Republican leader, opposed William A. Magee's (q.v.) bid for a second term, Kline became a compromise Republican candidate. In return for the nomination he agreed to reappoint twenty-five Magee men to their city positions. Handily defeating token primary opposition, Kline won an overwhelming victory in the general election, with 66,422 votes. Carman C. Johnson, Democrat, received 5,436 votes, and William L. Smith, an Independent Republican, received 15,935. In 1920, Pittsburgh had a mayor-council form of government and a population of 588,343.

Working in the shadow of the Mellons, Kline began soon after his inauguration to construct a personal patronage-based organization. As mayor, he supported a $19 million bond issue for road and bridge improvements and worked to enlarge the playground system. The city grew both physically and bureaucratically with the annexation of several peripheral townships and the creation of a department of city planning and a bureau of recreation.

Although the Mellon interests opposed him, Kline sought and was elected to a second term in 1929, defeating Thomas A. Dunn with slightly more than 80,000 votes to Dunn's 37,000. His program for his second term included securing rapid transit, widening and improving streets, allowing Sunday night cinema, and establishing metropolitan government for the Pittsburgh region. Through his organization, he controlled the city council, the county commission, and the county's delegation to the state legislature.

Early in his second term, however, a scandal broke in the department of supplies, and despite his strenuous attempt to avoid investigation and prosecution, in May 1931, a grand jury charged Kline and department head Bertram L. Succop with forty-three counts of misfeasance and malfeasance in office. Convicted in March 1932, Kline had exhausted all appeals by March 1933. With his health and reputation declining concurrently, he traded resignation from office for cancellation of a six-month jail term. He died four months later, on 22 July 1933.

SOURCES: Clipping file, Pennsylvania Division, Carnegie Public Library, Pittsburgh; Allen Humphreys Kerr,

"The Mayors and Recorders of Pittsburgh, 1816–1951: Their Lives and Somewhat of Their Times" (typescript, 1952, Carnegie Public Library, Pittsburgh); Bruce M. Stave, *The New Deal and the Last Hurrah: Pittsburgh Machine Politics* (Pittsburgh, 1970).

Douglas V. Shaw

KNIGHT, ERASTUS COLE (1857–1923), Mayor of Buffalo (1902–1905). Businessman-mayor, born in Buffalo, on 1 March 1857, Knight was the son of Theodore Columbus Knight, a businessman, and Sarah Minerva (Cole) Knight, both old-stock New Englanders. One of at least four children, Knight attended public schools and the Bryant and Stratton Business College. In 1877, he served with the Seventy-fourth Regiment of the New York National Guard seeing action against railroad strikers. In 1880, he became a traveling salesman for Bell Brothers wholesale produce merchants, and then worked as a member of the firm of Knight, Lennox and Company, 1880–87. He sold real estate from 1887 until 1892, when he formed the construction company of Jenkins and Knight. He was also involved with the grain elevator firm, Sloan, Cowles and Company. Knight married Mary Elizabeth Cowles on 14 May 1881, and they had six children, one of whom died in infancy. The Knights were Presbyterians, and Knight himself was also a Mason and a Knight Templar.

Knight was a Republican whose political career began with his election as one of Buffalo's city supervisors (1890–94). He was the city comptroller, 1895–1900, and the New York State comptroller, 1901. That November he was elected mayor, defeating Democrat H. P. Bissell 32,188 to 21,593. Buffalo had 352,387 people in 1900 and a mayor-council form of government. Mayor Knight won the election on the political theme that the city needed a businessman-mayor. He strongly backed public improvements and limited reforms. A believer in city economy, Knight won support for a new charter giving the mayor more control over the city budget. He retired from politics in 1906, devoting his time to the E. C. and G. L. Knight Company (coal dealers), organized in 1903, and the Isle of Pines (fruit exporting) Company, organized in 1905. Knight continued as president of both companies until his death on 3 September 1923.

SOURCES: Buffalo *Sunday Times*, 29 June 1924; *The Men of New York*, 2 vols. (Buffalo, 1898); *Who's Who in New York City and State* (New York, 1907 ed.).

Thomas R. Bullard

KOCH, EDWARD I. (1924–   ), Mayor of New York (1978–   ). Koch was born on 12 December 1924 in New York City, the second of three children born to Louis (1894–   ), and Joyce (Silpe) Koch (1900–60), both of Polish Jewish ancestry. When Edward was six, the family moved to Newark, New Jersey, and ten years later to Ocean Parkway in Brooklyn.

Koch worked at various jobs while attending high school and earning honor grades. From 1941 to 1943, he attended the City College of New York. In 1943, he entered the Army, served in Europe as a combat infantryman, earned two battle stars, and was discharged in 1946 with the rank of sergeant. In 1946, Koch entered New York University Law School, in 1948 obtained his LL.B. degree, the following year was admitted to the bar, and for the next twenty years was a practicing attorney. He was a senior partner of the law firm of Koch, Lankenau, Schwartz and Kovener.

Beginning active participation in politics during Adlai E. Stevenson's 1952 presidential campaign, Koch in 1956 became a charter member of a group of Greenwich Village Independent Democrats. In 1963, he defeated the Tammany Hall candidate and leader Carmine De Sapio for the post of Democratic district leader, a feat he repeated in 1965. In 1966, he was elected to the city council.

In 1968, Koch was elected to the U.S. House of Representatives from Manhattan's Seventeenth Congressional District, the first Democratic representative of that district since 1934. The voters returned him to office four times. While in Congress, he was a member of the Banking and Currency Committee, the Committee on House Administration, and the Appropriations Committee. He was also one of four congressional observers on the Emergency Financial Control Board set up to cope with New York City's fiscal crisis. He was allied with the opponents of Vietnam policy; worked for federal subsidies for mass transit, aid to Israel, health care for the aged, and family assistance; and worked against supersonic transport landing rights and federal park logging. His liberal voting record earned him a 100 percent rating from the Americans for Democratic Action and high marks from the League of Women Voters.

After an abortive run for the mayoralty in 1973, Koch in 1977 entered and won the seven-person Democratic primary. He was elected, receiving 712,976 votes to 597,257 for the Liberal party candidate, Mario Cuomo; 60,599 for the Republican party candidate, Roy Goodman; and 58,498 for the Conservative party candidate, Barry Goldin.

The most important of the myriad problems that faced Koch upon assuming office was New York City's disastrous financial condition. His first fiscal program was accepted by the city. The U.S. Congress, at President Jimmy Carter's initiation, voted the city well over $1 billion in federal loan guarantees. By mid-term, Mayor Koch could report with pride the first increase in available jobs in a decade, the general positive spirit of New Yorkers, and the new merit-selection process for criminal and family court judges. The threat of bankruptcy remained.

SOURCES: Ken Auletta, "The Mayor," *The New Yorker* (10 September, 17 September, 1979); John Corry, "The Koch Story," New York *Times Magazine* (30 October 1977); Dennis Duggan, "Mayor Ed Koch," *Newsday* (1 January 1979); Edward Koch, Collected Papers, Municipal Archives, New York City; *The Reminiscences of Edward I. Koch* in the Oral History Collection of Columbia University (closed until 1996).   *Lurton W. Blassingame*

KOCH, JOHN C. (1841–1907), Mayor of Milwaukee (1893–96). German immigrant, businessman, and mayor, Koch was born in Hamburg on 18 October 1841, the first of four children for John and Helena Koch, a Lutheran family. They emigrated to Milwaukee in 1854, and John attended the public elementary schools before learning the tinsmith's trade from his father. He took a job with the wholesale hardware firm of John Pritzlaff in 1866; by 1886, Koch had advanced to a vice-presidency of the company. He also established his own woodenware supply company. In 1864, he married Elizabeth Pritzlaff, and together they raised a family of nine children. A devout Lutheran, Koch was a member of the board of vestrymen of Trinity Lutheran Church in Milwaukee and a trustee of Concordia College, a Lutheran seminary.

Koch had little practical political experience other than an unsuccessful bid on the Republican ticket in 1892 for lieutenant governor. What he lacked in experience Koch compensated for with ethnicity. His extraction made him a popular candidate for mayor among Republicans eager to rebuild the party after defeats in 1890 and 1892. Germans made up about one-third of the population of Milwaukee, but the GOP had lost traditional German support because of its endorsement of a state measure—the Bennett law—in 1889 that required all school instruction be in English. Seeking to mend fences, the party ran Koch as its mayoral candidate in a special election in 1893 in light of Mayor Peter J. Somers' (*q.v.*) resignation. The Democrats had problems of their own, especially with the Polish community, which felt it had been ignored by Somers. Popular in both business and German circles, Koch captured the election, defeating Democrat Garrett Dunck by a vote of 11,689 to 8,420. He repeated his success in the regular election of 1894, polling 24,053 votes to 18,815 for Democrat Herman Fehr. By the end of Koch's second term, Milwaukee was a city of 250,000 and was still growing.

Koch sought to bring efficient administration to city government (which had a mayor-bicameral council form), and to meet the needs of a rapidly expanding metropolis. He increased the city's regulatory powers, police and fire protection, and the construction of streets, bridges, and sewers. He met the Depression of 1893 in the orthodox fashion of the day by moving to cut municipal expenditures and forego any tax increases. Declining to seek a third term in 1896, Koch returned to his business ventures. He died of pneumonia in Milwaukee on 8 November 1907.

SOURCES: Andrew Aikens and Lewis Proctor, eds., *Men of Progress of Wisconsin* (Milwaukee, 1897); Clay McShane, *Technology and Reform: Street Railways and the Growth of Milwaukee* (Madison, 1974); Bayrd Still, *Milwaukee: History of a City* (Madison, 1948); *Wisconsin Necrology* (compilation by State Historical Society of obituaries of prominent Milwaukeeans, on microfilm).   *Douglas Bukowski*

KOHLER, FRED (1864–1934), Mayor of Cleveland (1922–23). German-American mayor of Cleveland and former police chief, born on 2 May 1864 in Cleveland Kohler was the elder of two sons of Christian Kohler, a grocer and stonecutter who had emigrated from Germany, and Fredericka Kohler of Bohemian background. Fred Kohler left school after the sixth grade to work at a variety of manual jobs. In 1889, at age twenty-five, he joined the Cleveland Police Department and rose rapidly through the ranks. In 1903, Mayor Tom L. Johnson (*q.v.*) appointed him chief of police, a post he held until 1913, when he was removed on charges of neglect of duty and gross immorality because of his involvement with the wife of a traveling salesman. Kohler had married Josephine Modroch on 16 August 1888, and the couple had no children. Kohler was an imperious, autocratic police chief who gained a national reputation for his golden rule policy and the discipline of the Cleveland department. He also made many enemies within and without the police who resented his domineering and sometimes erratic behavior. After two unsuccessful tries for public office, Kohler was elected commissioner of Cuyahoga County in 1916.

Cleveland in 1920 had 796,841 people and a mayor-council form of government. In 1921, Kohler won the mayoralty over six other opponents with a total of 62,246 votes. His closest opponent, Republican incumbent William Fitzgerald (*q.v.*), had 57,442 votes. At this same election, the voters abolished the elected mayor system in favor of an appointed city manager system, in a charter to go into effect in January 1924.

Kohler met the city's financial crisis by ruthlessly slashing payrolls and cutting services. He left his successor a surplus of $500,000 at the cost of unperformed services and neglected city property. He did not neglect paint, however: he had city facilities all over town painted orange and black, his favorite colors. After appointing an excellent cabinet, he fought continually with almost all its members. He respected only one or two members of the city council. His few friends cheered and his more numerous enemies jeered at his valedictory statement on his administration: "Good or bad, right or wrong, I alone have been your mayor."

Kohler was elected sheriff of Cuyahoga County in 1924 but was defeated for reelection in 1926. During his term as sheriff, he was accused of allowing gambling to go unchecked and of underfeeding prisoners and pocketing the difference. Hungry prisoners could buy additional food from a commissary controlled by Kohler and run by one Louie the Pieman. When he died on 31 January 1934, he left a safety deposit box with more than $450,000 worth of cash and negotiable instruments.

SOURCES: George Condon, *Cleveland: The Best Kept Secret* (Garden City, N.Y., 1967); N. R. Howard, "I, Fred Kohler: Forty Years of Cleveland Politics" (Photocopied articles from the Cleveland *Plain Dealer* located in the Cleveland Public Library); Philip W. Porter, *Cleveland: Confused City on a Seesaw* (Columbus, 1976).

James F. Richardson

KOWAL, CHESTER W. (1904–66), Mayor of Buffalo (1962–65). Republican politician and mayor, born in Buffalo on 17 August 1904, Kowal was the son of John Kowalczewski, a blacksmith, and Katherine (Kotas) Kowalczewski, both Polish-American Catholics. The oldest of eight children, Kowal attended public schools until the age of thirteen when illness forced his father to abandon his job as a blacksmith and open a grocery store. Kowal enlisted in the Army during World War I but was discharged when his true age was discovered. While working at the family's grocery, and, later, beverage business, Kowal attended night school to earn enough credits to enter the University of Buffalo's School of Business Administration. He earned additional money by playing professional basketball with the German Orioles and the Buffalo Lincolns. He also played semipro baseball and was a boxer. In World War II, Kowal again enlisted and spent five months in the Pacific with the U.S. Army Air Corps. He married Stephanie Adamski, and they had two children. Kowal belonged to the Polish Union of America, the Polish Alliance, and the American Legion.

A strong Republican, Kowal served in local party posts during the 1930s. He was city comptroller, 1956–57 and 1960–61, earning publicity by saving money through new tax methods. In 1957, he narrowly lost the mayoralty election to Frank Sedita (*q.v.*), by 72,246 to 72,306. (Independent Frank Lux had 45,759 votes and Liberal

James Peak had 1,835.) Kowal became Buffalo's third Polish-American mayor in 1961, with 74,995 votes to 51,889 for Victor Manz (Democrat), 62,196 for Frank Sedita (Independent), and 8,016 for Peter Carr (Peoples'). At that time, Buffalo had 532,759 people and a mayor-council form of government.

Kowal reorganized the police department to depoliticize its members. He unsuccessfully sought to hire Robert Moses as head of the planning board and supported all efforts to rebuild the city and its financial structure. In state politics, he was an active backer of liberal Republican Governor Nelson Rockefeller. An ex-serviceman, Kowal actively supported civil defense measures for Buffalo. His health deteriorated while in office, and he was hospitalized nine times, 1957–65. Mayor Kowal was indicted in 1965 as part of a growing garbage collection scandal. While awaiting trial, he suffered a fatal heart attack on 28 September 1966.

SOURCES: Buffalo *Evening News*, 23 October 1957, and 28 September 1966, and other newspaper sources; New York *Times*, 29 September 1966.

Thomas R. Bullard

KREISMANN, FREDERICK H. (1869–1944), Mayor of St. Louis (1909–13). German-American businessman-Mayor Kreismann was born in Quincy, Illinois on 7 August 1869, the son of Frederick Kreismann (1827–1893) and Frances (Bruner) Kreismann. One of four children, he attended public schools in Quincy and Central High School in St. Louis, after the family moved to that city in the 1870s. He was a civil engineer and surveyor, 1888–90, then turned to the insurance business. Kreismann was the Aetna Insurance Company's special adjustment agent for Nebraska, 1891–93, when he formed the Kreismann-Theegarten Insurance Company. On 25 June 1902, he married Mrs. Pauline Whitman, a widow with two sons by a previous marriage. They had two daughters. The Kreismanns were Episcopalians, and he apparently belonged to a number of German social organizations in St. Louis.

Kreismann was a circuit court clerk, 1907–1909, resigning to campaign as the Republican candidate for mayor. He won the election, defeating Democrat G. Woerner 61,947 to 50,204. St. Louis had 687,029 people in 1910 and a mayor-council form of government. As mayor, Kreismann supported such civic improvements as a new bridge and a large public library building. He also showed a strong interest in medical matters and worked to improve the city's public health department. Kreismann also helped establish the city's first municipal testing laboratory. After leaving office, Kreismann continued working for his successful insurance company until he finally retired in 1939. He then moved to Webster

Groves, Missouri, where he died on 1 November 1944.

SOURCES: Charles H. Cornwell, *St. Louis Mayors: Brief Biographies* (St. Louis, 1965); Walter B. Stevens, *Centennial History of Missouri*, 4 vols. (Chicago, 1921).   *Thomas R. Bullard*

KRUM, JOHN MARSHALL (1810–83), Mayor of St. Louis (1848–49). German-American mayor of St. Louis, born in Hillsdale, New York, on 10 March 1810, Krum was the son of Peter Krum (d. 1854), a farmer, and Jane (Trowbridge) Krum, both New Yorkers. The Krum family was German and first arrived in the United States in the eighteenth century. Krum attended Smith Academy, Fairfield Academy (where he taught for about a year), and Union College in New York. Poor eyesight forced him to leave college in 1830, and he began the study of law. In 1832, he moved to Alton, Illinois, and began practicing law the following year. He was probate judge for Madison County (1836–37) and the first mayor of Alton (1837–38). During his short tenure, the Lovejoy riots occurred, and Krum was held responsible for the abolitionist's murder. He moved to St. Louis in 1839, where, in October, he married Ophelia Harding. They had five children.

Krum soon gained prominence in St. Louis and served as circuit court judge, 1843–48, when he resigned to campaign for mayor. He was elected as a Democrat, defeating Whig Luther M. Kennett (*q.v.*) 3,201 to 2,630. St. Louis had a population of 77,860 and a mayor-council form of government. As mayor, Krum strongly supported more schools and a broadened tax base to finance them. He also backed an enlarged sewer system in order to improve the city's health.

After leaving office, Krum continued to practice law and was also appointed a professor at St. Louis Law School. He helped revise the city ordinances and wrote several articles urging changes in the city code. In 1860, he was chairman of the credentials committee at the Democratic national convention, and his report helped secure the nomination of Stephen A. Douglas, a close personal friend. Krum died at his home on 13 September 1883.

SOURCES: Charles A. Cornwell, *St. Louis Mayors: Brief Biographies* (St. Louis, 1965); William Hyde and Howard L. Conrad, eds., *Encyclopedia of the History of St. Louis*, 4 vols. (New York, 1899), vol. 2; J. T. Scharf, *History of Saint Louis City and County*, 2 vols. (Philadelphia, 1883).   *Thomas R. Bullard*

KUCINICH, DENNIS J. (1946–   ), Mayor of Cleveland (1977–79). Independent Democrat and maverick mayor, Kucinich was born on 8 October 1946 in Cleveland, Ohio, the son of Frank Kucinich (1922–   ), a truck driver of Croatian background, and Virginia (Norris) (1924–   ) of Irish ancestry, both Catholics. The oldest of seven children, Kucinich grew up in poverty and attended parochial schools. After graduation at seventeen from St. John Cantius High School, he resided in an old mixed ethnic area on the city's near West Side. While working at a variety of menial jobs, Kucinich took courses at Cleveland State University. As a copy-boy for the *Plain Dealer*, he worked so hard he developed ulcers. In 1967, he lost a race for city council, but in 1969, aged twenty-three, he won that seat and was reelected again in 1971 and 1973 in a new ward. As councilman, he survived three recall attempts and earned a reputation as a feisty champion of the "Little People" with a confrontational style of politics. He was clearly ambitious. Kucinich lost two races for Congress in 1973 and 1974. Meanwhile, he secured a B.A. and M.A. in communications at Case Western Reserve in 1973. In 1969, Kucinich married Helen Lentz, and after his divorce in 1976 he married Sandra Lee McCarthy, a high school teacher of Irish American descent.

In 1975, Kucinich was elected clerk of Cleveland's municipal court and two years later ran for mayor as an Independent Democrat. He beat the Democratic party's nominee, Edward F. Feighan, by 93,476 to 90,074 votes. (The incumbent Republican mayor, Ralph J. Perk (*q.v.*), 1971–77 had been defeated in the nonpartisan primary.)

As Cleveland's youngest mayor, Kucinich attracted national attention by his boyish appearance, his populist speeches and proposals, his attacks upon the business community, and his vigorous opposition to tax abatement proposals. The mayor's attack upon the city council, the firing of his own appointee police chief, Richard Hongisto, on prime TV time, and the combative attitude of his administration brought charges of arrogance and led to a recall movement. Although the recall was very narrowly defeated, the overall impact was a legislative-executive deadlock.

Meanwhile, the city was facing a financial crisis that had been brewing for about ten years. As a result of the legislative-executive deadlock and the lack of confidence the bankers had in the total Kucinich administration, the city went into default in December 1978. In early 1979, the mayor, the city council leadership, and the business community successfully supported an income tax increase. However, on a vote to sell or keep the municipal light plant the mayor fought a vigorous and successful populist battle against business and council leadership. Despite the victory, and the mayor's ability to articulate the frustrations of poor citizens, the reputation of the administration continued to deteriorate among Clevelanders who resented its cynical and abrasive style. The press called him "Dennis the Menace."

Kucinich ran second in the 1979 nonpartisan primary and lost in the runoff election in November to a Republican, Lieutenant Governor George V. Voinovich (*q.v.*), by a 94,541 to 73,755 margin. After his defeat, Kucinich became a lecturer and engaged in writing about urban politics. He moved to Los Angeles to write an autobiographical novel.

SOURCES: David M. Alhern, with Tony Fuller, "Oh Cleveland," *Newsweek*, 1 January 1979; Thomas F. Campbell and Roberta Steinbacher, "Reflections on the Seventies," *Cleveland Magazine*, January 1980; Dennis J. Kucinich, "Speech on Urban Populism," before the National Press Club, Washington, D.C., September, reprinted in *Cleveland Press*, 3 October 1978; Dennis J. Kucinich, "Remarks Before Reclaiming the Future Conference," Columbus, Ohio, 28 April 1979; Frank Kuznik, "The Prime and the Power," *Cleveland Magazine*, April 1978; Brent Larkin, "Kucinich's Final Days," *Cleveland Magazine*, January 1980; Dan Marshal, *The Battle for Cleveland* (Cleveland, 1980); Jonathan Evan Maslow, "Cleveland's Woes," *Saturday Review*, 17 February 1979; Philip W. Porter, *Cleveland: Confused City on a Seesaw* (Columbus, 1976); Robert Scheer, "Dennis Kucinich: A Candid Conversation with the Controversial Young Mayor of Cleveland about Civic Greed and Corruption and His Feisty New Brand of Politics," *Playboy* Magazine, May 1979; Terrence Sheridan, "Denny the Kid and the Contest of Confrontation Politics," *Cleveland Magazine*, April 1972; E. P. Whelan, "Dennis Kucinich: The Punking of Cleveland," *Esquire* 90:12 (15 December 1978); Estelle Zannes, *Checkmate in Cleveland* (Cleveland, 1972).   *Thomas F. Campbell*

LADUE, JOHN (1803–54), Mayor of Detroit (1850–51). Ladue was born on 18 November 1803 at Lansingburgh, New York. His parents were Peter and Mary Tallman Ladue. In 1827, John married Mary Angel; four children survived him: John, Charlotte, George, and Austin. The family was Presbyterian. Ladue operated a business with his brother Andrew in New York, but in 1847, he arrived in Detroit and opened a large tannery on Rivard Street.

In 1850, Detroit (in Wayne County, Michigan) contained 21,019 residents and had a mayor-council form of government. Mayors were popularly elected each year and served without pay, presiding over a city council of sixteen (two members from each of eight wards). In the mayoral election of 4 March 1850, Ladue, a Democrat, defeated Whig candidate David Smith 1,420 to 1,352, carrying five of the city's eight wards. Democratic strength had declined since the 1849 election, however, as Whigs captures four of nine city-wide offices and took five of eight council seats. The fugitive slave issue was the most dramatic question in Ladue's year in office. When a mob formed, following the seizure of an alleged runaway slave, Ladue, according to Detroit historian Silas Farmer, ''was compelled to request the military to preserve the peace.''

Ladue did not run for reelection. He died at home on 4 December 1854 and was buried in Elmwood Cemetery, Detroit.

SOURCES: Detroit Daily *Advertiser*, 6 December 1854; Silas Farmer, *History of Detroit and Wayne County and Early Michigan* (Detroit, 1890).

Michael W. Homel

LAGUARDIA, FIORELLO (1882–1947), Mayor of New York (1934–45). Reformer and perhaps the most outstanding mayor in U.S. history, LaGuardia was born on 11 December 1882 in the Italian section of New York City's Greenwich Village. Fiorello was the second of three children of Achille Luigi Carlo LaGuardia (1849–1915), middle-class, lapsed Catholic from Foggia, Italy, and Irene Coen (1859–1915), daughter of a Jewish merchant from Trieste, Austria. Achille and Irene had emigrated to New York City in 1880, raising their children as Episcopalians. Achille enlisted in the U.S. Army as a bandmaster (1885–98), living at Western posts, including Prescott, Arizona, where Fiorello was educated through the eighth grade. Upon Achille's discharge the family emigrated to Trieste. Fiorello served in the U.S. consular service from age seventeen to twenty-three, in South Central Europe but returned, multilingual, to New York City in 1906. He graduated in 1910 from the New York University School of Law, evening division. While enrolled there, he supported himself primarily as an interpreter at Ellis Island. In the process, he became deeply concerned about the inequities endured by immigrants. As a young lawyer on Manhattan's lower East Side, he served a heavily ethnic clientele. In 1919, he married Thea Almerigiotti (1894–1921), a native of Trieste; she and their infant daughter died in 1921. He was married again in 1929 to Marie Fischer (1894–   ), a New York City native of German stock, his long-time secretary; childless, the couple adopted a son and daughter.

Fiorello LaGuardia sought elective office fourteen times, 1916–41, winning eleven contests. He joined a Republican club in 1910, apparently believing the party offered greater mobility than the Irish-dominated Tammany Democrats, to whom he became anathema. LaGuardia rose quickly, being named district captain in 1912 and a deputy attorney general in 1915, and was elected to Congress in 1916, the first Republican from the lower East Side since the Civil War. Reelected in 1918, he had previously taken leave to serve as a much-decorated Army flyer on the Austrian-Italian front, returning as a major. In 1919, he was elected president of the New York City Board of Aldermen. He returned to Congress in 1923 from the East Harlem district, serving until defeated in 1932. In his second congressional tenure, LaGuardia moved perceptibly to the left, espousing Progressive stands on a multitude of issues. As a result, his Republican affiliation became increasingly tenuous. He co-sponsored, with Senator George W. Norris, the Anti-Injunction Act, passed in 1933. As a lame duck, he worked closely with the new Democratic administration of Franklin Roosevelt.

Long interested in the mayoralty, LaGuardia had sought the Republican nomination unsuccessfully in 1921 and refused to run as a Progressive in 1925. As the Republican nominee in 1929, he lost to incumbent Democratic ''Jimmy'' Walker (*q.v.*) (865,549 to 368,384). He was mentioned in the 1920s as a potential candidate for other offices but refused appointment as an assistant secretary of labor in the Roosevelt administration after his 1932 congressional defeat.

New York City's 1930 population as 6,930,446; by 1950, it was 7,891,957. Under the 1898 charter, the city had a mayor-council form of government; a new 1937 charter ended the bicameral council structure. LaGuardia ran for mayor in 1933 on the fusion ticket that included the Republican endorsement. In the aftermath of the Walker ouster, he defeated insurgent Democrat Joseph V. McKee, regular Democrat John P. O'Brien and Socialist Charles Solomon (868,552 to 609,053, 586,672, and 59,828 respectively). Once more the fusion candidate (Republican, American Labor, and Communist, the last unsought and repudiated) in 1937, he became the first reformer in the city to win reelection, defeating Democrat Jeremiah F. Mahoney (1,344,630 to 889,756). In 1941, again running on a fusion ticket (Republican and American Labor), LaGuardia beat Democrat William O'Dwyer (*q.v.*) (1,186,518 to 1,054,235) in the closest of his three successful mayoral contests. When he declined to seek reelection in 1945, his protégé, Newbold Morris, ran unsuccessfully as a third-party candidate, with Democrat O'Dwyer winning the mayoralty.

LaGuardia's twelve years as chief executive of the nation's greatest city were characterized by especially high public visibility; intense, often rabid, involvement in every facet of the city's affairs; strong antipathy for traditional politicians, Republicans no less than Democrats; and New Deal reform and spending policies. He attracted notables to public service like A. A. Berle, Robert Moses, and Rexford Guy Tugwell; he instilled a sense of honesty and demanded excellence from civil servants. Ardently devoted to improving urban life, he closely cooperated with the New Deal for funds to underwrite advances in transportation, recreation, education, health, housing, and general public welfare. On the negative side, he was egocentric as an executive and unable to fashion a permanent political organization to perpetuate his concerns. In his final term, LaGuardia revealed obvious signs of lethargy, but he never received a hoped-for federal appointment offering him new opportunities beyond city government.

After the mayoralty, LaGuardia held a series of appointive posts, some honorific, the most important being director general of the United Nations Relief and Rehabilitation Commission in 1946. None of the jobs genuinely satisfied him. Except for his devotion to music, he had few outside interests. The ex-mayor died of cancer of the pancreas at home in Riverdale, Bronx, on 21 September 1947. A funeral was held at an Episcopal cathedral, with burial at Woodlawn Cemetery.

SOURCES: Leonard Chalmers, ''Fiorello LaGuardia, Paterfamilias at City Hall: An Appraisal,'' *New York History* 56 (April 1975); Charles Garrett, *The LaGuardia Years, Machine and Reform Politics in New York City* (New Brunswick, N.J., 1961); August Hecksher with Phyllis Robinson, *When LaGuardia Was Mayor, New York's Legendary Years* (New York, 1978); Arthur Mann, *LaGuardia, A Fighter Against His Times, 1882–1933* (Philadelphia and New York, 1959); Arthur Mann, *LaGuardia Comes to Power, 1933* (Philadelphia and New York, 1965); Fiorello LaGuardia Papers, Municipal Archives and Record Center, New York City.

Michael H. Ebner

LAMBERTON, ROBERT E. (1886–1941), Mayor of Philadelphia (1940–41). Lawyer, judge, and politician, born on 14 September 1886 in South Bethlehem, Pennsylvania, Lamberton was the only son of William A. Lamberton (1847–1910), a college professor, and Mary (McCurdy) Lamberton (1856–1913), both born in Ireland. One of three children, Robert attended public schools, the Episcopal Academy, and the University of Pennsylvania, where he was a successful college football player. He then went to that university's Law School, graduating in 1910. The following year he married Helen Wright Henderson, and they had five children. The Lambertons were prominent members of the First Presbyterian Church in Germantown, and Lamberton was one of its trustees.

Lamberton began his legal practice in 1910, coaching at the Germantown Academy in his spare time. He served as a member of the city council during 1915–19, emerging as a promising Republican leader. In 1919, he formed a partnership with Francis S. McIlhenny. His political career grew parallel with his legal work, and he served as county sheriff during 1920–24. He was appointed judge of the court of common pleas in early 1931 and was elected to a full term later that year, remaining at his post until 1939. Lamberton's growing reputation led to offers to run for various city and state offices, but he did not really decide until 1939 when he was persuaded to be the Republican candidate for mayor. In the November election, he defeated Democrat Robert C. White 398,384 to 361,143. At that time, Philadelphia had a population of 1,935,086 and a mayor-council form of government.

As mayor, Lamberton supported a balanced city budget, the use of Works Progress Administration funds to create new city construction projects, and an $18 million loan for additional work. He worked to settle disputes with the sewer and street railway companies, winning additional popularity. A modest man who shunned the ceremonies of the office, Lamberton seemed destined for a lengthy career. Unfortunately, he suffered from a severe case of peripheral neuritis and died quite suddenly at his home on 22 August 1941.

SOURCES: Philadelphia *Evening Bulletin*, 23 August 1941; Philadelphia *Record*, 23 August 1941; New York *Times*, 23 August 1941.   *Thomas R. Bullard*

LANDRIEU, MOON (Maurice Edwin) (1930–   ), Mayor of New Orleans (1970–78). Born on 23 July 1930 in New Orleans, Landrieu was the son of Joseph Landrieu, a small neighborhood grocer, and Loretta (Bechtell) Landrieu, who lived in their modest flat connected to the store. His family had only limited means. Maurice, or "Moon" as his boyhood friends called him, set records as a championship baseball player and won a four-year scholarship to Loyola University in New Orleans (B.A., Business 1952; LLB.B. 1954). He legally changed his given name, Maurice, to his boyhood nickname, Moon. After three years in the judge advocate's office, U.S. Army, he was discharged in 1957 and opened a modest law office in New Orleans which soon became the firm Landrieu, Calogero, and Kronlage. As a member of the Young Crescent City Democratic Association, Landrieu was elected in 1959 and later reelected (1960–66), from a working-class biracial district, to the Louisiana legislature. In 1966, he was elected councilman-at-large in New Orleans, subsequently reelected (1966–70), and became a vigorous spokesman for racial justice. In 1967 a civic watchdog group charged him with conflict of interest in his elected office and alleged connections to organized crime, but he was cleared by Crime Commission hearings in New Orleans and a federal investigation. He married Vera Satterlee in 1954 and fathered nine children. The Landrieus are Roman Catholic. They make their home near the center of New Orleans.

New Orleans in 1969 had a population of 600,000 and a mayor-council form of government. In December 1969, Landrieu won a Democratic party primary and a runoff, and emerged as the candidate the following April to beat Republican Ben C. Toledano by vote of 94,055 to 65,323. Building upon a coalition of white middle-class and black voters, he won a second four-year term, the maximum permitted by law.

Mayor Landrieu worked hard to rebuild the tourist industry. He opened up the city to private real estate development, and the resulting demolition of some historic buildings brought him into conflict with the preservationists. The historic French Market was refurbished with a riverside promenade, nicknamed the "Moon Walk." Even more daring and controversial was Landrieu's vigorous support of the construction of a $163 million Superdome, one of the largest enclosed sports stadiums in the nation. To critics who charged that the mammoth project was an exercise in madness, Landrieu pointed to the thousands of additional motel rooms and other facilities that had been built to accommodate the new business from the Superdome, and that critics had also charged Bavarian castle builder King Ludwig with madness, "But now thousands of tourists come to see the castles. So Bavaria's rich, and old Ludwig's a hero again." Landrieu established a record as an effective financial administrator working closely with the state legislature for additional funds and garnering from the federal government far more than a proportional share of federal aid. His reputation for having a "Midas" touch with Washington made him a spokesman for America's ailing cities, helped to win him the presidency of the U.S. Conference of Mayors, 1975–76, and put him in a position to assist in formulating a federal revenue-sharing program for cities. A liberal on racial issues, he appointed many blacks to high-level jobs and encouraged the city's business community to be responsive to black needs.

When his second term ended in May 1978, Landrieu returned to private life to become president of a major New Orleans land development company, Joseph C. Canizaro Interests, Inc. President Jimmy Carter appointed Landrieu secretary of housing and urban development in September 1979.

SOURCES: *Current Biography*, January 1980: Mayor's Office press releases, 1971; *Time* Magazine, 6 August 1979.   *Melvin G. Holli*

LANE, WILLIAM CARR (1789–1863), Mayor of St. Louis (1823–28), 1838–39). First mayor of the city of St. Louis, and an Army doctor of Southern extraction, Lane was born on 1 December 1789 in Fayette County, Pennsylvania, the son of Presley Carr Lane, a well-to-do Virginia-born farmer of English ancestry, and Sarah (Stephenson) Lane. The third son in a family of eleven children, William attended a country school in Fayette County. At age thirteen, he began two years of study at Jefferson College, in Pennsylvania, followed by two years of apprenticeship with his eldest brother, the prothonotary of Fayette County; two more years at Dickinson College; a medical apprenticeship with a physician in Louisville, Kentucky; and medical studies at the University of Pennsylvania. In 1813, he joined the Army to fight in the Indian wars of the Old Northwest, serving first as surgeon's mate at Fort Harrison and then as post surgeon. In 1818, while an Army physician, he married Mary Ewing of Vincennes, Indiana, the daughter of Nathaniel Ewing, receiver of the Vincennes land office. The Lanes had three children.

The following year, Dr. Lane left the Army and began a medical practice in St. Louis. In 1821, he was named aide-de-camp to Governor McNair of Missouri; the next year he was appointed state quartermaster-general.

In 1823, Lane was elected mayor of St. Louis, receiving 122 votes to 70 for Auguste Chouteau and 28 for M. P. Leduc. During the 1820s, St. Louis was a frontier settlement of about 5,000, and Mayor Lane dedicated his administration to providing such amenities of civilization as graded and paved streets. He easily won reelection throughout the 1820s, and the board of aldermen rarely opposed his wishes. At this time, Lane was a Democratic supporter of Andrew Jackson, but in the 1830s he broke with the Jackson forces and became a Whig.

After six one-year terms, Lane voluntarily stepped down as mayor, only to be reelected to two consecutive terms in 1838 and 1839. In 1838 he was elected with 769 votes against 566 for Charles Collins; in 1839, he was reelected with 452 votes against 283 for Collins, 98 for Samuel Daniels, and 4 for John Heller. By this time, the population of St. Louis had risen to 15,000, and in 1839, the city received a new charter that extended the city boundaries and created a bicameral legislative council.

Following his terms as mayor, Lane continued his medical practice in St. Louis and also served as professor of medicine at a local college. In 1852, President Millard Fillmore appointed Lane governor of the New Mexico Territory, and he occupied that post until Franklin Pierce became president. Lane then returned to St. Louis and in his last years campaigned for creation of a municipal waterworks. On 6 January 1863, he died, survived by his wife and two daughters. Lane was an Episcopalian. He was buried in Bellefontaine Cemetery in St. Louis.

SOURCES: John Fletcher Darby, *Personal Recollections of Many Prominent People Whom I Have Known, and of Events* . . . (St. Louis, 1880); Richard Edwards and M. Hopewell, *Edwards' Great West and Her Commercial Metropolis, Embracing a General View of the West, and a Complete History of St. Louis* (St. Louis, 1860); William Hyde and Howard L. Conrad, eds., *Encyclopedia of the History of St. Louis*, 4 vols. (New York, 1899); Missouri *Republican* 2 April 1838, 3 April 1839; J. T. Scharf, *History of Saint Louis City and County* (Philadelphia, 1883); Walter B. Stevens, *St. Louis, The Fourth City 1764–1909* (St. Louis, 1909).

Jon C. Teaford

LANGDON, GEORGE C. (1833–1909), Mayor of Detroit (1878–79). Langdon was a well-to-do Yankee, born in Geneva, New York, in 1833. He attended boarding school at Batavia, New York, and an academy in Farmington, Connecticut. In the 1850s, he came to Detroit and studied accounting at Gregory's Commercial College, graduating in 1858. The next year he married Fannie Vallee of Detroit; they had three daughters. Langdon entered the brewing business and accumulated a sizable fortune, most of which he lost during the depression of 1877.

In 1878, Langdon was the Democratic candidate for mayor, winning 6,905 votes to his opponent Republican John Greusel's 5,480. Detroit in 1874 had a population of 101,225 and a mayor-council type of government. Langdon's term was notable only for his successful efforts to have the city purchase for $200,000 a swampy, snake-infested island in the Detroit River for use as a city park. Belle Isle became one of the several city parks throughout the country landscaped in the 1880s by Frederick L. Olmsted. In 1879, Langdon was soundly defeated for reelection by William G. Thompson (*q.v.*), a popular Republican lawyer. Langdon never again ran for elective office but was later appointed a custodian of records, a position that entitled him to a pension. Known for his pleasant, easy-going manner and his benevolence, in his later life he was affectionately called "Uncle George." Langdon returned to New York and died at the home of one of his daughters in Geneva, on 5 June 1909, after a long, debilitating illness.

SOURCES: Detroit *Free Press*, 7 June 1909; Detroit *Graphic*, 4 October 1879; Detroit *News*, 6 June 1909; Silas Farmer, *History of Detroit and Wayne County and Early Michigan*, 3d ed., (Detroit, 1890, reprint 1969); Robert B. Ross and George B. Catlin, *Landmarks of Detroit*, revised by Clarence W. Burton (Detroit, 1898).

W. Patrick Strauss

LAPHAM, ROGER DEARBORN (1883–1966), Mayor of San Francisco (1944–48). One of San Francisco's more flamboyant mayors, Lapham was born in New York City on 6 December 1883. His father, Lewis Henry Lapham, was a founder of the Texas Company, and his mother, Antoinette (Dearborn) Lapham, came from a long line of New England sea captains. The family was Protestant. Lapham himself grew up in New York City, and, in 1901, he entered Harvard from which he graduated four years later. After completing college, he began a successful business career with the American-Hawaiian Steamship Company which had been organized by one of his maternal uncles. Lapham successively worked his way up through the company until, in 1925, he became president and then, in 1938, chairman of the board. His first official act as chief administrative officer was to relocate the company headquarters in San Francisco rather than New York. Lapham himself had moved west permanently in 1915 and had taken his wife Helen with him. Although Mrs. Lapham was born in Brooklyn, she came from an old New England family. The Laphams were married on 30 October 1907, just about two years after he graduated from Harvard and she from Smith.

They had four children, two sons, Lewis and Roger, and two daughters, Carol and Edna.

Between 1905 and 1943, Lapham devoted himself to the American-Hawaiian Steamship Company except for the years between September 1917 and April 1919 when he served as an infantry captain in France. As a shipping executive in San Francisco, Lapham's most demanding role was during the violent waterfront strikes of 1934 to 1936. During 1936, Lapham earned respect and a national reputation by publicly debating Harry Bridges at a longshoremen's meeting. Lapham's frankness and sense of fair play earned him the applause of the men in attendance, as did his conviction, soon accepted reluctantly by other shipping men, that collective bargaining was inevitable. Lapham's activities on the San Francisco waterfront soon brought him to the attention of President Franklin Roosevelt who, in 1941, appointed him to the National Defense Mediation Board. He served for two years on the board and on its successor, the National War Labor Board (NWLB), as the leading industry representative.

In 1943, Lapham resigned from the NWLB in order to run for mayor of San Francisco. At that time, the city had a population of over 650,000 and had been governed for twelve years by Mayor Angelo Rossi (q.v.) and the city's board of supervisors. A group of independent citizens who felt that San Francisco needed a change of leadership approached Lapham (a life-long Republican) and asked him to make the race against Rossi. A third major candidate was George Reilly, head of the State Liquor Control Board. On election day, Lapham won a sweeping victory, receiving 90,646 votes to Rossi's 47,626 and Reilly's 57,741. As mayor, Lapham tried to govern San Francisco according to sound business and financial principles. He personally campaigned to rationalize the city's transportation system and successfully fought to purchase the privately owned Market Street Railway Line. He also raised fares on the system and won approval of the highest tax rate in the city's history. He placed a substantial number of city officials under bond for the first time and generally conducted city affairs in a more satisfactory fashion than had previously been done.

Perhaps the two most dramatic events of Lapham's administration were the first meeting of the United Nations which took place in San Francisco in the spring of 1945 and the attempt to recall Lapham in May 1946. The recall election grew out of dissatisfaction with the mayor's transit policies and resulted in a sweeping vote of confidence as nearly three-fourth of the voters supported Lapham's retention in office.

Lapham's term expired in January 1948, and, true to a campaign promise made in 1943, he did not run for reelection. However, his political career was not over. In May 1948, President Truman selected him to head the Economic Cooperation Administration's mission to China. Starting in June, the former mayor guided all American outlays to China other than direct military assistance. He remained in China until 1949 when the American mission was withdrawn. Then, in September 1950, Lapham accepted a two-year position as head of the economic mission to Greece. After returning from this assignment, he retired and spent the remainder of his life traveling, playing golf and participating in social and civic activities. He died on 16 April 1966 following a severe fall in which he fractured his skull. At the time of his death, he was eighty-two years old.

SOURCES: "California, 'City I Love,' " *Time* 48 (15 July 1946); Helen Abbott Lapham, *Roving with Roger* (San Francisco, 1971); "Lapham, Roger D.," *Current Biography* (New York, 1948).   *Neil L. Shumsky*

LATROBE, FERDINAND C. (1833–1911), Mayor of Baltimore (1875–77, 1878–81, 1883–84, 1887–89, 1891–95). A political boss, and also a Baltimore worthy, born into one of Maryland's most prominent families, on 14 October 1833, and married in 1860 to the daughter of Governor Thomas Swann (q.v.), Latrobe was likely to succeed in almost any career he might choose. He chose politics. Having passed the Maryland bar, he was elected to the state legislature in 1867 and was appointed by Governor Swann to be judge advocate general. He was reelected to the state House of Delegates in 1869 and served that term as speaker of the House. He ran for mayor of Baltimore in 1873 but was defeated in the primary election. In 1875, he gained the nomination with the backing of the regular Democratic boss, I. Freeman Rasin, and, in a campaign of extraordinary excitement, violence and fury defeated a "fusion" ticket of Republicans and anti-Rasin Democrats. This was the first of seven electoral victories for Latrobe and Rasin, and it inaugurated a quarter century of "boss rule" in the city.

Latrobe was not simply a tool of the political machine. He was given a free hand in the management of the city, and under his seven administrations very substantial progress was made in the expansion of city services and the general efficiency of city government. The job of dispensing patronage and contracts, however, he left to Rasin and other Democratic bosses. Under Latrobe's leadership, street-paving, storm-sewer construction, school building, and harbors were dramatically improved. His most personal success in office was the ten-year campaign to convince Baltimore's suburban residents to annex themselves to the city—a step they took in 1888. During these years, Latrobe was often criticized as a "spendthrift mayor," but he was convinced that expensive public improvements could safely be financed by municipal loans. The improvements, he argued, would attract suburbanites into the municipality by annexation, and the increased tax base would pay the cost of the original changes. The annexation of 1888 and the subsequent financial history of the city verified Latrobe's assumptions. Considering the very slow growth in the city's economy and tax base, and the general unwillingness of most middle- and upper class taxpayers to increase rates, Mayor Latrobe was able to make remarkable progress. In many ways, he anticipated the reforms and accomplishments of Progressive era mayors. In spite of continual charges of graft and corruption during these years, there appears to have been very little misuse of public funds.

As a campaigner, Latrobe was a formidable opponent. He was, as one writer said, "an institution in the city." His aristocratic background always made him an acceptable candidate to large sectors of the middle and upper classes in the city. Yet his constant appearances at Irish balls, German beer-fests, Italian festivals, Polish picnics, and labor union outings (all of which he appears to have genuinely enjoyed) made him very popular with ethnic and working-class voters. However, as the most visible member of the Rasin machine, Latrobe was the target of reformers bent on ending "machine" rule and Latrobe's program of municipal deficit financing. This is why his terms in office were continually interrupted by so-called businessmen mayors who ran on a low-taxation, low-spending platform. As opposition to the Rasin machine grew stronger in the 1890s, Latrobe's position became more tenuous. At the completion of his seventh term in 1895, he was willing to run again, but by this time even many loyal Rasin men had come to believe that Latrobe was too tall a lightning rod for the reformers. He was never again given the chance to run. He died on 13 January 1911.

SOURCES: Biographical Cyclopedia of Representative Men of Maryland (Baltimore, 1879); Wilbur Coyle, *The Mayors of Baltimore* (Baltimore, 1919); "The Reminiscences of F. C. Latrobe" (typed copy of mss., copy on deposit at the Maryland Historical Society).

Joseph L. Arnold

LAUSCHE, FRANK J. (1895-   ), Mayor of Cleveland (1941-44). A Slovenian Catholic, mayor of Cleveland and governor of Ohio, Lausche was born in Cleveland on 14 November 1895, the second son of Louis and Frances (Milavec) Lausche, Slovenian immigrants. One of ten children of a steelworker's family, Lausche attended city schools until his father's illness forced him to start working at the family store. He played profes-

sional baseball, earning enough money to pay for a college education and graduating from John Marshall Law School in 1920. Lausche had also spent 1918–19 in the U.S. Army, reaching the rank of second lieutenant. He joined the law firm of Locker, Green and Woods in 1920, quickly gaining a reputation as a successful trial lawyer. He also sought political office, unsuccessfully campaigning for Congress (1922) and the state Senate (1924). He served as a judge on the Cleveland Municipal Court, 1932–37, and Cuyahoga County Court of Common Pleas, 1937–41, earning an anti-organized labor reputation. On 17 May 1928, he married Jane O. Sheal, an interior decorator.

Although considered independent by many party leaders, he was chosen as the Democratic candidate for mayor in 1941, defeating Edward Blythin (*q.v.*) 145,324 to 94,534. In 1943, he was reelected, overwhelming Edward Stanton 113,032 to 45,954. Cleveland had 878,336 people in 1940 and a mayor-council form of government. Lausche was personally popular and actively worked to improve the city, supporting beautification projects, the City Plan Commission, and a new transit organization. He cut city taxes and stressed the need for "clean government." Lausche also pushed for better health measures and actively supported wartime fund-raising efforts. Initially conservative on social issues, his 1943 campaign stressed the needs of blacks and labor (the CIO) as well as business.

Lausche's ability to win votes led to his selection as Democratic gubernatorial candidate in 1944, and he served as governor of Ohio for many years, 1945–47 and 1949–57, having lost the 1946 election. The first Roman Catholic Ohio governor, Lausche emphasized right-to-work laws, law and order, as well as the need to conserve natural resources. He was a U.S. senator for two terms, 1957–69, gradually becoming more conservative, supporting the Vietnam War, and backing national Republicans more than his own Democrats. These positions cost him the 1968 nomination, and he retired from politics, moving to Bethesda, Maryland, where he still resides.

SOURCES: Current Biography (New York, 1946); Nelson Lichtenstein, ed., *The Johnson Years* (New York, 1976); Nelson Lichtenstein, ed., *Political Profiles: The Kennedy Years* (New York, 1976).

Thomas R. Bullard

LAW, JAMES O. (1809–47), Mayor of Baltimore (1843–44). Law, the eighth child of Presbyterian Irish immigrants, was born in Baltimore to James (1768–1830) and Elizabeth (Davies) Law (1774–1838) on 14 March 1809. His father came from Bally Shannon, Donegal. After receiving a rudimentary classical education, Law went to work in a counting house owned by his cousin, Jacob G. Davies (*q.v.*), who was later to succeed him in the mayor's office in 1844. On coming of age, Law entered business on his own and soon became a prominent Baltimore merchant. At the age of twenty-six, he married Louisa Douglass of Alexandria, Virginia, on 21 January 1836. The married produced four children.

Law was very active in the affairs of Baltimore. He was a member of several societies, such as the Young Men's Temperance Society, the Odd Fellows' Association, and the Hibernian Society, and was president of the Independent Fire Company. His activities also included military affairs, and he was a member of the Independent Greys. In 1837, he was elected captain of the company. Later in 1842, he was elected a major in the Fifty-third Regiment, Maryland Volunteers Infantry, a position he held until his death.

On the resignation of Mayor Solomon Hillen (*q.v.*) in the fall of 1843, Law, the Whig candidate, was elected in a special election to serve the remainder of Hillen's term by a 332 majority, out of a total vote of 14,928, over his Democratic opponent, William H. Marriott. In the election, the Whigs also carried the First Branch of the city council. During Law's short term in office, Baltimore, containing a population of 102,313 in 1840, was connected with Washington by telegraph. Also during his administration, Baltimore in 1844 added two female high schools to its rudimentary public school system and thereby became a national leader in this movement. School enrollments increased from 675 pupils in 1839 to 3,366 in 1844.

In the mid-1840s, Law and the Whig party were threatened in Baltimore by an upsurge of nativism which spilled over into political activity. The Democrats attempted to link the Whigs with the nativists. The upsurge died down temporarily, but it foreshadowed a much more powerful movement which was to erupt in the 1850s. Law's attempt to secure a second term in October 1844 was unsuccessful. His own cousin, Jacob Davies, the Democratic candidate, defeated him by a margin of 498 votes. However, Law was rewarded for his party services with an appointment as a state flour inspector, a position he held until his untimely death on 6 June 1847. Law, at the age of thirty-eight, succumbed to ship-fever after having ministered to sick Irish immigrants at Canton, Maryland.

SOURCES: Wilbur G. Coyle, *The Mayors of Baltimore* (Baltimore, 1919); Dielman File and Filing Case A, Maryland Historical Society; Clayton Colman Hall, ed., *Baltimore: Its History and Its People* (New York, 1912); Reverend G. W. Musgrave, *Biographical Sketch of Major James O. Law* (Baltimore, 1847).

Richard R. Duncan

LAWRENCE, CORNELIUS VAN WYCK (1791–1861), Mayor of New York (1834–37). First mayor to be popularly elected in New York since the late seventeenth century, Lawrence was a descendant of eighteenth-century English settlers in Flushing, New York. He was the fifth child born to Henry Lawrence, a wealthy landowner of Flushing, New York, and Harriet Van Wyck, a descendant of an influential New Netherland Dutch family. Raised on his family estate, Lawrence apparently attended common schools. He moved to New York City in 1812 and was employed in the auction house of Shotwell, Hicks and Company. He prospered and became a partner in the firm of Hicks, Lawrence and Company, continuing in business until politics called.

A Jacksonian Democrat, Lawrence was elected to the Twenty-third Congress but served only until May 1834 when he resigned to become New York's popularly elected mayor. Lawrence supported Andrew Jackson's bank policy, a move which alienated many of his business associates. According to the Whig diarist and former New York Mayor Philip Hone, Lawrence was "compelled by his party to accept the nomination of mayor." In an extremely close contest, Lawrence received 17,575 votes to his Whig rival Gulian C. Verplanck's 17,372. The riots that ensued during the three days of voting in April 1834 were quelled by state militia. While the Democrats won the mayoral seat, the Whigs controlled the common council. Political power in the city of some 280,000 remained with the council, the office of mayor being a figurehead. Lawrence easily won reelection in 1835 when the Whigs offered no opposing candidate. Lawrence received 17,696 votes, with opposition votes split among John Y. Cebra, Hubert Van Wagenen, Philip W. Engs, Job Haskell, and Andrew L. Ireland.

It was during Lawrence's second term that the notorious anti-Catholic *Six Months in a Convent* made its appearance. Such literature found a receptive market in a city where recent Irish immigrants numbered in the thousands. A riot ensued in June 1835 which led to many bloody heads among the so-called Native Americans and the newly arrived immigrants. The local alliance of Whigs and Native Americans desperately sought to locate an acceptable mayoral candidate and finally settled on Samuel F.B. Morse. Although an ardent Jacksonian, Morse was a rabid nativist. Lawrence handily won reelection over three opponents, gaining 15,954 votes. Seth Geer, Whig, got 6,136; A. Ming, Jr., Equal Rights party, 2,712; and Samuel F.B. Morse, Native American, only 1,496. The city continued to be plagued by various riots during Mayor Lawrence's third term.

After the mayoralty, Lawrence became associated with several banks, serving as president of the Bank of the State of New York, a director in both the Branch Bank of the United States and the Bank of America, and a trustee of the New York Life and Trust Company. President James K. Polk appointed him collector of the port of New York (1845–49). Lawrence retired to his Flushing estate in 1856 and died there in 1861.

SOURCES: Leo Hershkowitz, ''The Native American Democratic Association in New York City, 1835–1836,'' *The New-York Historical Society Quarterly* 46: 1 (January 1962); New-York *Herald*, 21 February 1861; Bayard Tuckerman, ed., *The Diary of Philip Hone 1828–1851* (New York, 1889), vol. 1; David T. Valentine, ed., *Manual of the Common Council of New-York 1854* (New York, 1854).   *Jacob Judd*

LAWRENCE, DAVID LEO (1889–1966), Mayor of Pittsburgh (1946–59). Lawrence, mayor during the ''Pittsburgh Renaissance,'' was born of second-generation Irish Catholic parents on 18 June 1889 in the teeming Point area of Pittsburgh, a zone of freight yards, slums, and squalor. His father, Charles B. Lawrence, was a road worker; his mother was Catherine (Conwell) Lawrence. A few years after David's birth, the family moved to Herron Hill, another crowded and decaying district.

Young Lawrence attended public elementary schools and a brief high school business course, and at fourteen became stenographer in the law office of the city Democratic chairman. He quickly entered politics and was a page at the 1912 national Democratic convention. He was a delegate or official at every succeeding convention until his death. In 1914, he became registration commissioner, holding the post for ten years except for service in World War I, in which he rose from private to second lieutenant.

Returning from war, Lawrence went into the insurance business, in which he continued for life. In 1920, he became his party's county chairman. On 8 June of the next year, he married Alyce Golden (c. 1896–1968), an Irish Catholic, and they had three sons, two of whom were killed in an auto accident, and two daughters. In 1931, he ran for county commissioner but lost.

An early backer of Roosevelt's New Deal, Lawrence became collector of internal revenue in 1933. In 1934, he became state Democratic chairman, an office he held most of the time until he became mayor. During Governor George H. Earle's administration, he was secretary of the commonwealth and was made whipping-boy in the graft scandal of 1938. He was acquitted by an all-Republican jury when the charges fizzled out, but the scars remained for years.

In 1945, Lawrence was elected Democratic mayor of Pittsburgh by a narrow margin, defeating Republican Robert N. Waddell, 111,878 to 99,088. At this time, the city had a strong mayor, small council form of government, and a population of 635,000, near its peak in size; but Pittsburgh was dirty and in a state of decay. As mayor, Lawrence formed an unimaginable alliance with his old political enemies, the Mellon interests, and began the ''Pittsburgh Renaissance,'' which attracted international attention. During his unprecedented four terms as mayor, the city reduced smoke and other pollution, cleared slums, provided housing, rebuilt the decayed downtown area, attracted capital and corporation headquarters, and made other gains. In 1949, he was reelected 152,081 to Ryan's 95,498; in 1953 he got 137,338 to L. P. Kane's 82,016; and in 1957, he got 128,532 to J. Drew's 68,708.

Lawrence ran for governor in 1958, winning by 60,000 votes. He proved an able and progressive administrator, promoting education, highway construction, and conservation. He was considered principally responsible for the nomination of John F. Kennedy for president in 1960.

Following the end of his term, Lawrence became head of the Commission on Equal Housing and Opportunity. He suffered a heart attack while making a campaign speech on 4 November 1966 and lay in a coma for seventeen days until his death. He was buried in Calvary Cemetery.

SOURCES: Frank Hawkins, ''Lawrence of Pittsburgh,'' *Harpers*, August 1956; Gerald Lawrence ''Profile of David Leo Lawrence,'' Pittsburgh *Quote*, Summer 1959; Lawrence files and scrapbooks, Carnegie Library of Pittsburgh.   *George Swetnam*

LEAKIN, SHEPPARD C. (1790–1867), Mayor of Baltimore (1838–40). A member of the Whig party, Leakin served as mayor from 1838 to 1840. He was born in Baltimore County in 1790 to an old, wealthy, English-stock landowning Maryland family. His father, John Leakin, was a merchant in the Baltimore firm of Leakin and Davey, and Sheppard was apprenticed in a printer's shop. Married sometime before the War of 1812 to Margaret Dobbin, Leakin was the father of nine children. The family was Episcopalian. During the War of 1812, he was a captain in the infantry and became a colonel, and later, general in the state militia. Meanwhile, his career as a journalist prospered, and he was the owner and editor of a newspaper—the Baltimore *Chronicle and Daily Advertiser*—as well as proprietor of a bookstore. In 1824, he became the sheriff of Baltimore County.

By 1840, Baltimore's population (including the adjacent county) was 102,313. The city was governed by a two-branch council, but the Maryland legislature still had significant power over its affairs. In 1840, Leakin defeated his Democratic opponent 6,012 votes to 5,545. As mayor, he prevented a nativist mob from burning the Catholic Carmelite Convent; he also organized a city militia, which after the failure of the Bank of Maryland protected the houses of its directors. In 1840, Leakin was defeated for a second term by Democrat Samuel Brady (*q.v.*) by 7,119 to 6,887 votes, but he remained active in politics—as a Henry Clay supporter and as collector of the port—and in business—as director of the Baltimore and Susquehanna Railroad and president of the Fells Point Savings Bank.

SOURCES: Wilbur Coyle, *The Mayors of Baltimore* (Baltimore, 1919); Dielman-Hayward File, Maryland Historical Society; Leakin Papers, Maryland Historical Society; Mayor's Papers (1838–40), Baltimore City Archives.   *Jean H. Baker*

LEAVENWORTH, THADDEUS M. (1820?–93), *Alcalde* of San Francisco (1848–49). Leavenworth, an Episcopalian minister, physician, and druggist, was American *alcalde* of San Francisco just before California attained statehood, in a time of intense political confusion. He was born in Connecticut perhaps around 1820. Trained in medicine and theology, he moved to California as chaplain to Colonel Stevenson's regiment, the Seventh New York Volunteers, in March 1847.

Leavenworth opened the first drug store in San Francisco in a small frame house on Washington Street. He served as second *alcalde* (a Mexican executive and judicial office that preceded the American mayoralty) under George Hyde (*q.v.*) and Dr. John Townsend (*q.v.*) before being made *alcalde* himself (elected 29 August 1848; second election, 3 October 1848, at which a total of only 158 votes were cast). He served as *alcalde* from September 1848 to August 1849, during months of great confusion, violence among ethnic groups, and rival claims for political control.

In 1849, the population of San Francisco grew by the day, gold poured in from the mines, the bay filled with shipping (about 200 square-rigged vessels at anchor in late July), and the saloons and gambling dens overflowed. Tension between Americans and Hispanics produced bar fights and gang violence, the newer immigrants rejecting Mexican customs and laws, and the older "aristocratic" American settlers seeking to uphold the old ways. The rougher, anti-Hispanic leaders, known as "regulators" or the "Hounds," resorted to physical intimidation of so-called foreigners, culminating in a savage attack on a Chileno tent ghetto at the foot of Telegraph Hill on 15 July 1849. This anti-Hispanic riot produced a sharp, shocked response from the older, more settled American community: a confrontation with *alcalde* Leavenworth that he prosecute the mob leaders (he was suspected of sympathy for the Hounds), and a special tribunal to put them on trial.

Meanwhile, as *alcalde*, Leavenworth had other, re-lated problems. Because he was elected under the old, semi-Mexican system, his authority was rejected by newer settlers, who pressed for fresh elections, American-style and the abolition of the *alcalde* system. At one time in 1849, three rival town councils existed, each claiming power to run San Francisco. An armed group seized some of Leavenworth's official papers in May 1849, threatening him at gunpoint. He appealed to the military governor of the Pacific, General P. F. Smith, who told him to stand firm. But the civil governor suspended Leavenworth. A new governor reinstated him in June, but the racist excesses of the Hounds the next month, together with other complaints against Leavenworth—that he favored land speculators and was a weak leader—brought him down in August.

The following year, Leavenworth moved to Sonoma County, where he fought a land grant case, claiming part of the Agua Caliente *rancho*. He lived in San Rafael until 1874 and at Sonoma until 1891; he died at Santa Rosa on 30 January 1893. He was the last of the old-style American *alcaldes* of San Francisco, for his successor, John Geary (*q.v.*), soon changed his title to mayor.

SOURCES: Z. S. Eldredge, *Beginnings of San Francisco*, 2 vols. (San Francisco, 1912); Guy J. Giffen, *California Expedition: Stevenson's Regiment of New York Volunteers* (Oakland, Calif., 1951); W. R. Ryan, *Personal Adventures in Upper and Lower California in 1848–49* (London, 1881), vol. 2; F. Soule, J. H. Gihon, and J. Nisbet, *Annals of San Francisco* (New York, 1855).   *Peter d'A. Jones*

LEAVITT, BENSON (1797–1869), Acting Mayor of Boston (1845). Merchant, and Boston's first acting mayor, born in Hampton Falls, New Hampshire, 21 June 1797, son of Thomas Leavitt (1774–1852), a surveyor, and Hannah (Melcher) Leavitt. Both parents were old-stock descendants of New Hampshire pioneers, and Thomas Leavitt surveyed many towns in New Hampshire and was considered the first Democratic politician in that part of the state. Oldest of seven children, Benson Leavitt married Abigail Ward (1801–51), also an old-line Yankee, in 1826, and they had three children. Benson Leavitt and his brother Joseph took their families to Boston in the late 1820s to improve their lot. They formed a partnership, initially importing and handling West Indian goods, until 1843 when they formed the successful B. & J. M. Leavitt Co., a leading supplier of salted fish. Benson Leavitt was a director of the Granite Bank from 1837 to 1843. The Leavitts were Protestants.

He entered politics as a member of the Massachusetts House of Representatives in 1840, serving two more years in 1842 and 1843. Leavitt was also an Alderman in 1841 and 1845. At this time the Aldermen were elected in the city at-large, and they shared executive power with the mayor. During Leavitt's second term he was chosen as president of the Board of Aldermen. When Mayor Thomas Davis became ill, he offered to resign on 6 October 1845, but the City Council rejected his resignation and Davis was forced to remain in office until his death, on 22 November 1845. By virtue of his post as aldermanic leader, Leavitt was named acting mayor and served in that capacity until 11 December when Josiah Quincy, Jr. was sworn in as mayor. Boston had a mayor-council government and a population of 93,383. Leavitt had little opportunity to develop any programs and merely served as a caretaker-leader.

After 1845 he held no political office and returned to his fish business. His brother Joseph died in 1849 and Leavitt operated the firm alone for two years. In 1851 his son Charles joined the company and gradually assumed control. Benson Leavitt remained active with the firm until his death in 1869 at the age of 72.

SOURCES: Warren Brown, *History of the Town of Hampton Falls, New Hampshire* (Manchester, N.H., 1900); Joseph Dow, *History of the Town of Hampton, New Hampshire* 2 vols. (Salem 1893); Leavitt Family Association, *The Leavitts of America* (Salt Lake City, 1924); Justin Winsor, *The Memorial History of Boston* 4 vols. (Boston, 1881); *U.S. Census Records, 1850, Suffolk County* vol. 1. (1950).

Thomas R. Bullard and Richard Gentile

LEDYARD, HENRY (1812–80), Mayor of Detroit (1855–56). Diplomat and Democratic mayor of Detroit, Ledyard was born on 5 March 1812 in New York City, the son of attorney Benjamin Ledyard and Susan French Livingston Ledyard. Of Henry's grandfathers, one (Benjamin Ledyard) was a major in a New York regiment during the Revolution, and the other (Brockholst Livingston) was a justice of the New York Supreme Court and U.S. Supreme Court. Henry Ledyard graduated from Columbia (1830) and became an attorney in New York. From 1836 to 1844, he worked in the American legation in Paris as an attaché (1836–39), secretary of the legation (1839–42), and chargé d'affaires (1842–44). On 19 September 1839, Ledyard, a Presbyterian, married Matilda Frances Cass (d. 1898), daughter of General Lewis Cass, at the time U.S. ambassador to France. The five Ledyard children were Elizabeth Cass (b. 1840), Henry B. (b. 1844), Susan Livingston (1844–73), Lewis Cass (b. 1850), and Matilda Spencer (b. 1860).

When Cass left his diplomatic post in Paris, Ledyard also moved, to Detroit, where for fourteen years he was active in the city's business and civic affairs. Ledyard helped establish the State Bank (1845), Elmwood Cemetery (1846), and Michigan's first plank road company (1848). In addition, he served on the school board (1846–47), represented the Fourth Ward on the city council (1849–50), and was an early member of the board of water commissioners (1853–59). In 1855, Detroit (in Wayne County, Michigan) had about 42,000 people and a mayor-council form of government. Mayors were chosen by popular vote for one-year terms; they served without pay, presiding over a sixteen-member city council (two from each of eight wards).

Ledyard, described by a contemporary as an old Jacksonian democrat [who seemed] to represent the aristocracy of the town, was elected mayor on 5 March 1855. Winning four of eight wards, he defeated Independent Know-Nothing Henry P. Baldwin 3,975 to 2,313. Democrats won all city-wide offices, but Independents and Democrats evenly divided eight council seats. Liquor was the major issue during Ledyard's year in office. The council rejected the mayor's attempts to obtain local enforcement of the 1853 state prohibition law.

Ledyard did not run for reelection at the end of his term. He was sent to the state Senate in 1857 but resigned the next year and went to Washington, D.C., to work once more for the State Department under Lewis Cass. In 1861, Ledyard left the federal government and settled in Newport, Rhode Island, where he resided for the rest of his life. There he served on a city charter commission and was president of the city's hospital and library. Ledyard died on 7 June 1880 while visiting London.

SOURCES: *Compendium of History and Biography of the City and Detroit and Wayne County, Michigan* (Chicago, 1909); Detroit *News-Tribune*, 31 October 1897; Silas Farmer, *History of Detroit and Wayne County and Early Michigan* (Detroit, 1890) reprint, 1969.

Michael W. Homel

LEE, GIDEON (1778–1841), Mayor of New York (1833–34). Last of the mayors to be chosen by the New York City Common Council before the advent of popular elections, Lee was born in Amherst, Massachusetts, a child of Gideon Lee and Lucy (Ward) Lee, both of Yankee stock. Left fatherless at the age of fourteen, Lee was apprenticed in the tanning and shoemaker's trade and at age twenty-one started his own business in Worthington, Massachusetts. During these early years, he attended Westfield Academy at his own expanse. Lee had moved to New York by 1807, as a sales agent for a New England leather firm. He continued as agent for several firms until 1817 when he helped establish a major New York tannery under the name of Lee and Shepherd Knapp Company. He introduced the practice of accepting time payments from his customers. By the 1820s, he was regarded as one of the wealthiest men in the city, worth $25,000 to $50,000.

Twice married, Lee left offspring by both wives. He first married, on 23 September 1806, Laura Buffington (1790–1818) of Worthington, Massachusetts, by whom he had Lucy Ward Melvin, Samuel Buffington, and Laura Theresa. They lost one child in infancy. On 28 April 1823, Lee married Isabella Williamson (1800–?), daughter of a Scottish minister. Their children were Gideon, David Williamson, Charles Henry, who died at the age of three, and William Creighton. Lee left an estate valued between $50,000 to $100,000.

Lee was a Jacksonian Democrat. His political career began as a state assemblyman (1822), and he served as an alderman (1828–29, 1830). His fellow councilmen chose him as mayor in April 1833. At that time, rapidly expanding New York contained a population of some 250,000 with an ever-increasing number of Irish immigrants. By state law the city was to be given the opportunity of popularly electing its mayor in 1834, but Lee declined the Democratic mayoral nomination.

While mayor of New York for one year, Lee was confronted with two major issues: the request to the state legislature by the neighboring village of Brooklyn for incorporation as a city, and a major riot attributed to the coming first popular election of mayor. While not unalterably opposed to Brooklyn's incorporation as a city, Lee was not overly enthusiastic. He warned that New York must seek adequate protection for its maritime and replevin rights over the waterways of New York Harbor and the East River.

The mayoral election of April 1834 was accompanied by drunken brawls and street fighting. Attempting to intervene in one altercation, Lee was knocked unconscious. Order was eventually restored through the use of the state militia. Not surprisingly, he declined to run in 1835. He returned to his business until elected to fill a vacancy in the U.S. Congress (November 1835–March 1837). He was later elected to a full term in the following session. His last political act was to serve as a presidential elector on the Van Buren Democratic ticket in 1840. He retired to Geneva, New York, in 1836 and resided there until his death on 21 August 1841.

SOURCES: Freeman Hunt, ed., *Lives of American Merchants* (New York, 1858), vol. 1; Benson J. Lossing, *History of New York City Embracing an Outline Sketch of Events from 1609 to 1803* . . . (New York, 1884), vol. 1; Edward Pessen, "The Wealthiest New Yorkers of the Jacksonian Era: A New List," *The New-York Historical Society Quarterly* 54:2 (April 1970); David T. Valentine, ed., *Manual of the Corporation of the City of New York* (New York, 1853).

Jacob Judd

LEEDS, CHARLES J. (1823–98), Mayor of New Orleans (1874–76). A conservative (Democratic) Yankee mayor, born in 1823 in Stonington, Connecticut, Leeds was the son of Jedediah Leeds, an ironmaker, and Mary Stanton Leeds, both of English ancestry. The Leeds family moved to New Orleans while Charles was an infant, and in 1824 his father established Leeds Foundry at the corner of Delord and Constance streets. After Jedediah died in 1844, Charles became a partner in the foundry. Nothing is known of his life during the next thirty years, except that on 21 May 1856, he was married to Mary Josephine Rawle (by whom he fathered eight children) and that by 1874 he was regarded as a man of "means and position" in the community.

New Orleans, about 200,000 in size, was the state capital during the corrupt and violent period of Radical Reconstruction in Louisiana (1868–77). In 1872, however, the city's voters terminated Radicalism on the local level by electing a Conservative (Democratic) administration headed by Louis A. Wiltz (q.v.), a banker and former Confederate officer. Opposition to Radicalism increased tremendously while Wiltz was mayor. Near the end of his term, a bloody climax occurred in the "battle of Liberty Place" between heavily armed members of the "White League" (composed mostly of ex-Confederate officers and soldiers), Governor W. P. Kellogg's Metropolitan Police, and about 3,000 Radical black militia. After a brief engagement in which thirty-two men were killed and seventy-nine wounded, Kellogg's Radical government was sustained and order restored in the city by a reinforced garrison of federal troops.

The "battle" firmly established Conservative prestige in New Orleans, and less than two months later, Charles Leeds—in whose foundry many of the White Leaguers' weapons had been stored—was easily elected mayor to succeed Wiltz by a vote of 25,921 to 14,227 for the Republican candidate, Felix Labatut.

For two years, Leeds presided over a debt-ridden and virtually bankrupt city, laid low by the Panic of 1873, an onerous system of occupational license fees, burdensome property taxes, and Radical legislative interference in the operation and funding of several municipal departments. Leeds administration was not, on the whole, a success. The city's oppressive bonded indebtedness was only partially reduced by a bizarre funding scheme resulting in costly litigation. (This so-called premium bond plan was conceived and implemented in 1875 by Leeds' commissioner of finance and successor Edward Pillsbury—q.v.). Fees and taxes remained high. Drainage and other public works were delayed or aborted as a result of lack of funds, and Radical meddling in municipal affairs continued into the next administration.

But Leeds himself remained popular owing to a widespread belief that the city's many problems resulted from causes over which he had no control. Returning to private life and relative obscurity, when his term expired, Leeds disassociated himself from the foundry and became secretary of the Carondelet Canal and Navigation Company at an unknown date between 1876 and his death on 6 July 1898.

SOURCES: John S. Kendall, *History of New Orleans* (Chicago, 1922), vol. 1; Joe Gray Taylor, *Louisiana Reconstructed: 1863–1877* (Baton Rouge, La., 1974); Works Progress Administration typescripts, "Administrations of the Mayors of New Orleans, 1803–1936," and "Biographies of the Mayors of New Orleans, 1803–1936" (New Orleans, 1940).   *Mark T. Carleton*

LEWIS, ALEXANDER (1822–1908), Mayor of Detroit (1876–77). Lewis was born in Sandwich, Ontario, on 24 October 1822, the son of Thomas Lewis, a prosperous farmer of Welsh Catholic extraction and Jeanette (Velaire) Lewis of Windsor, Ontario, who was of French descent, also a Catholic. One of eight children (four boys and four girls), Alexander attended a private school near his home until 1837, when he moved across the border to Detroit and began his career as a clerk. By 1842, he had formed his own freight forwarding and commission company; in 1862, he also opened a flour and grain business from which he built a comfortable fortune, retiring in 1884. Lewis owned a substantial amount of downtown Detroit property and served as a director of several important financial institutions in the city. On 10 June 1850, he married Elizabeth J. Ingersoll (d. 1894), daughter of one of Detroit's most influential and successful businessmen. They had thirteen children, eight of whom survived to adulthood; several were later associated with their father in his various business enterprises.

Detroit in 1874 had a population of 101,225 and a mayor-council type of government. Lewis, who had served as police commissioner from 1865 to 1875, was a staunch Democrat who was elected mayor following a two-term Republican in 1875, winning 7,367 votes to his Republican opponent William G. Thompson's (*q.v.*) 5,691. Lewis served one term. His administration was not notable; his chief contribution was planning and executing a mammoth celebration for America's centennial on 4 July 1876.

After he retired from office, Lewis retained his interest and influence in local Democratic politics and served from 1881 to 1887 as a member of the board of commissioners for the Detroit Public Library. He died in Detroit on 18 April 1908.

SOURCES: Detroit *Free Press*, 18 April 1908; Detroit *News*, 18 April 1908; Detroit *News Tribune*, 28 July 1895; Silas Farmer, *History of Detroit and Wayne County and Early Michigan*, 3d ed., (Detroit, 1890, reprint 1969); Robert B. Ross and George B. Catlin, *Landmarks of Detroit*, revised by Clarence W. Burton (Detroit, 1898).   *W. Patrick Strauss*

LEWIS, JOHN L. (1800–86), Mayor of New Orleans (1854–56). Born in Lexington, Kentucky, on 26 March 1800, of pioneer stock, Lewis moved with his parents to New Orleans in 1803, where Lewis's father was appointed judge of the supreme court of the Louisiana Territory. Young John was educated at the academy of the Reverend James F. Hull, an Episcopalian rector. Leaving school at the age of eighteen, Lewis studied law in his father's office and made law his profession. His first political job was an assistant to the clerk of the Louisiana First Judicial District Court, of which he became clerk in 1846. Showing an aptitude for military affairs, Lewis joined a local militia unit, rose rapidly in rank to inspector general of the First Division of the Louisiana Militia and then commander in 1842. In 1852, he was elected to the state Senate and in 1854 won election as sheriff of the parish of New Orleans. Having married in 1837, Lewis fathered three children, all of whom died of scarlet fever, along with his wife.

New Orleans at the time of Lewis's election in 1854 had a population of about 140,000 and a mayor-council form of government. Although defeated in his bid for mayor in 1852, Lewis accepted the Democratic nomination in 1854 and with strong Creole support beat James Breedlove, the Independent Reform candidate, by a vote of 6,899 to 4,382. The election was a disorderly affair in which rowdy gangs attacked their opponents. In one precinct, this resulted in the death of two men and one police officer.

Lewis's term as mayor was undistinguished, except for the city's subsidization of two private railroads with a $3.5 million stock purchase to be paid for by the taxpayers. The council also leased out public wharves to private interests and engaged in a brouhaha over whether firemen should be paid, with the result that firefighters returned to their voluntary status. At the end of Lewis's term, an 1856 charter revision enlarged the mayor's control over the police department, a measure necessitated by increasing disorder between Know-Nothings, Creoles, and the foreign-born. Lewis died on 15 May 1886.

SOURCES: John S. Kendall, *History of New Orleans* (Chicago, 1922) vol. 1; Leon C. Soule, *The Know Nothing Party in New Orleans* (Baton Rouge, La., 1961).   *C. David Tompkins*

LIDDELL, ROBERT (1837–93), Mayor of Pittsburgh (1878–81). Liddell was born in England, attended private schools to the age of thirteen, and came to America in 1852. In about 1861, he married Maria Spencer and became a coal merchant. Later he was a brewer. He and Maria were the parents of six children. Liddell became interested in politics soon after reaching his majority, and was elected to the common council and later to the select council. He was a Mason, an Episcopalian, and a popular man-about-town.

Liddell's Democratic nomination for mayor in 1877 came at an opportune time. The Flinn-Magee political ring held the city of 150,000 in a tight grip, but its debt had become enormous and caused a revolt. Just at the climax of the election fight, Liddell was taken sick, and on election day he was at the point of death from peritonitis. Nevertheless, he defeated Republican Miles Humphreys 9,394-8,309; he recovered and was able to take the oath of office when his term began.

Both councils—Pittsburgh then had two—retained solid Republican majorities, but Mayor Liddell was a good politician, and though a Democrat, achieved an effective administration. The city annexed large areas to the south and west. A law was also passed to have mayors take office in April, extending his term by three months. Liddell was so popular that when his term ended he was able to name and elect his successor. But when he ran again in 1884, he lost badly. After leaving office, Liddell went into glass manufacturing and later wholesale liquor. He was an avid sports fan and an early mainstay of the Pittsburgh baseball club. He died on 2 December 1893.

SOURCES: History of Allegheny County Pennsylvania (Chicago, 1889); Allen H. Kerr. ''The Mayors and Recorders of Pittsburgh, 1816–1951'' (typescript, *Carnegie Library of Pittsburgh*, 1952); *The Manufactories and Manufacturers of Pennsylvania etc.* (Philadelphia, 1875).   *George Swetnam*

LINCOLN, FREDERIC WALKER, JR. (1817–98), Mayor of Boston (1857–59, 1863–66). Civil War mayor of Boston, Lincoln was born in Boston on 27 February 1817, the son of Louis Lincoln (1787–1827), a sailmaker, and Mary (Knight) Lincoln (c. 1896–1825), both of whom were descended from old Yankee stock. Orphaned at age ten, he was apprenticed to an instrument-maker at age thirteen and prospered in this career. He eagerly attended the lectures and mechanics organizations of the time for self-improvement and began his lifelong dedication to the Second Unitarian Church in Boston. He was married twice: first, in 1848, to Emeline (Hall) Lincoln, who died after the birth of their daughter in 1849; second, in 1854, to Emma (Lincoln) Lincoln. They had three children. Lincoln's financial success, serious demeanor, and administrative skills made him well known in the city, but he was always proud of his

identity as a mechanic. He became president of the Massachusetts Charitable Mechanics Association (1854–56). His brief career in politics before the mayoralty included two terms in the Massachusetts House of Representatives (1847–48) and service at the Massachusetts Constitutional Convention of 1853.

A heavy influx of Irish immigrants, antislavery agitation, and the Prohibition question had shattered traditional political allegiances in Boston. In an effort to keep the mayor's office above this turmoil, a nonpartisan ''Citizens'' convention had nominated and elected Alexander H. Rice in 1856–57. They nominated Lincoln in the same way in December 1857; he was victorious over Republican Charles B. Hall (8,110 to 4,193). In December 1858, he defeated Moses Kimball, an antislavery Republican, Julius Palmer, a Temperance candidate, and Jerome V. C. Smith (*q.v.*), the former nativist mayor (Lincoln, 6,298; Kimball, 4,449; Palmer, 1,007; Smith, 183). Running with both a Republican and Citizens endorsement in 1859, he defeated Democrat Joseph Wightman (*q.v.*), (5,932 to 4,208). He chose to retire, with the high esteem of the city, at the end of that term, but was called out of retirement in December 1862 because of wartime emergency to oppose Joseph Wightman, the Democratic incumbent. Lincoln was successful (6,352 to 5,287). In succeeding years, he easily won reelection three times: over Thomas Rich in 1863 (6,206 to 2,142) over Thomas Amory in 1864 (6,877 to 2,732), and over Nathaniel Shurtleff (*q.v.*) in 1865 (4,520 to 3,690). He retired once again at the end of 1866, to the appreciation and applause of his fellow Bostonians: he had had their confidence through troubled and expansive times alike.

Despite the upheavals of immigration, ideology, and war, Boston was experiencing urban growth in the midnineteenth century, its population rising from 136,880 in 1850 to 250,526 in 1870. Mayors had differing views of the municipal government's role in this expansion. During Lincoln's first administration, he took few initiatives on behalf of the city, preferring instead to carry through the various landfill and street extension activities of his predecessors and engaging the federal government in projects to improve the harbor. In his second administration, however, he was caught in the dynamism of the war and postwar years, and was more aggressive in espousing city initiatives. Always acting with decorum, he saw the new city hall and city hospital projects through to their completion in wartime, began the enlargement of the water system, the leveling of Fort Hill, and expansion of the waterfront in the old city, encouraged negotiations to annex neighboring communities, and developed a rational plan for dealing with the street extensions that were a never-ending task.

Lincoln was best remembered by Bostonians of the

time for his role as mayor during the Civil War. His most noted service was his prompt action in putting down the Draft Riot of 14–15 July 1863. Aware of what had happened in New York, he was ready to call out the troops at the first sign of trouble, and the event was quickly put down. He also carried on wartime activities that involved such projects as bounties, the coordination of relief efforts, and the maintenance of mustering stations.

After his retirement from the mayoralty, Lincoln served two further terms in the legislature (1872 and 1874). He also served on the Overseers of the Poor and on the Board of Harbor Commissioners, as well as boards of religious and charitable institutions. He died of natural causes on 13 September 1898 and was buried at Mount Auburn Cemetery.

SOURCES: Boston *Transcript*, 14 September 1898 (obituary); J. M. Bugbee, "Boston Under the Mayors," in Justin Winsor, ed., *The Memorial History of Boston*, 4 vols. (Boston, 1881), vol. 3; City of Boston, Massachusetts, *Documents, 1858, 1859, 1860, 1864, 1865, 1866*; Mary Knight Lincoln, ed., *In Memoriam, Frederic Walker Lincoln* (Boston, 1899).   Constance Burns

LINDSAY, JOHN VLIET (1921–), Mayor of New York (1966–73). Controversial liberal Republican mayor of New York, Lindsay was born on 24 November 1921 in that city, one of five children of George Nelson Lindsay (1888–1962), an investment banker of Scots-English descent, and Flore Eleanor (Vliet) Lindsay (1890–1947) of Dutch-Irish stock. The upper class family was Episcopal.

Lindsay attended private schools in New York and New Hampshire before entering Yale. He graduated in 1944 and then served as a U.S. naval officer in both the Mediterranean and South Pacific before being discharged in 1945, as a full lieutenant with several battle stars. He entered Yale Law School, received his LL.B. in 1948, and the following year was admitted to the New York State bar and joined Webster, Sheffield, Fliesmann, Hitchcock, and Chrystier. That year he married Mary Anne Harrison of Richmond, Virginia, a Vassar College graduate and businesswoman. They had four children: Katharine, Margaret, Anne, and John, Jr.

Invited to Washington to serve as executive assistant to U.S. Attorney General Brownell, Lindsay in 1955 and 1956 was the Justice Department's liaison with Congress and the White House, participated in drafting legislation, and argued cases before the U.S. Supreme Court.

Returning to New York in 1957, Lindsay ran successfully for Congress from Manhattan's Seventeenth District in 1958 and was reelected in 1960, 1962, and 1964, each time with an increasingly large margin. This record was remarkable in a city where registered Democrats outnumbered registered Republicans about three to one.

As a congressman, Lindsay worked for civil and individual rights, medical care for the elderly, anti-pollution safeguards, advancement of the arts, improved immigration procedures, and fair employment practices. In 1964, he declared his independence from the national Republican ticket and beat his Liberal-Democratic opponent 135,807 to 44,533.

In 1965, when Lindsay ran for mayor of New York as a liberal Republican, he received 1,156,915 votes to 1,030,771 votes for the Democratic candidate, Abraham Beame (*q.v.*), and 339,137 votes for the Conservatives' William Buckley. Lindsay was the first Republican to win the mayoralty since Fiorello La Guardia (*q.v.*). In 1969, he ran for reelection as a Liberal-Independent (having lost the Republican primary), and received 981,810 votes to Democrat Mario Procaccino's 821,824 votes and Republican John Marchi's 544,758.

As mayor, Lindsay had notable successes and failures. On the positive side, New York was the only major Northern city whose ghettos did not burn during the urban riots of the late 1960s, he reorganized city government by establishing ten administrations that consolidated some fifty separate departments and agencies, and he instituted changes that resulted in better utilization of police manpower. His administration, however, was also beset with crippling and bitterly divisive strikes, and the city's budget deficit increased dramatically, a fact for which he was blamed, if not with complete justification. Lindsay himself stated that excellence of management was one of his most substantial contributions. Others will remember him as the man who did most to call national attention to the plight and importance of America's cities, and who took walking tours of the ghettos.

In the summer of 1971, Lindsay joined the Democratic party, and the following spring he entered the Florida and Wisconsin presidential primaries, both of which he lost. Declining to run for reelection in 1973, Lindsay returned to his law practice. He has since been a novelist, a TV commentator and lost the Republican primary election for the U.S. Senate in 1980.

SOURCES: Robert Caro, *The Power Broker* (New York, 1974); August Heckscher, *Alive in the City* (New York, 1974); Nat Hentoff, "The Mayor," *The New Yorker* (3 May and 10 May 1969); Woody Klein, *Lindsay's Promise: The Dream That Failed* (New York, 1970); John V. Lindsay, *The City* (New York, 1969); John V. Lindsay, *Journey into Politics* (New York, 1966); Oliver R. Pilat, *Lindsay's Campaign* (Boston, 1968); Roger Starr, "John V. Lindsay: A Political Portrait," *Commentary* (February 1970).

Lurton W. Blassingame

LITTLE, WILLIAM (1809–87), Mayor of Pittsburgh (1839–40). Little, the eighth mayor of Pittsburgh, was born in Pittsburgh in 1809, but details of his early life, parentage, and education are unknown. He must have come of good family, for he was the original third lieutenant of the Duquesne Greys, a prestigious militia company, and an original member of the Washington Fire Company, organized in 1832. (His sister was the wife of a popular hotel proprietor.) He was a Protestant.

Pittsburgh, located in Allegheny County in southwestern Pennsylvania, was a city of about 20,000 in the 1830s, politically divided among Whigs, Anti-Masons, and two factions of Democrats. A month before the mayoral election of 1839, the city's volunteer firemen, mostly young, held a convention and nominated Little for mayor. He received the backing of the conservative Whigs and radical Democrats, while his opponent, William W. Irwin (q.v.), was nominated by conventions of regular Democrats, dissident Whigs, and Anti-Masons.

Little defeated Irwin by a vote of 1,294 to 1,050, but his hands were tied. Anti-Masons won majorities in both of the two councils, the common and select. He proved a popular mayor in an uneventful term and was urged to seek reelection, but he declined, in order to go into business. Following the end of his term, Little became forwarding agent for a canal freight transportation firm. Soon afterward, he moved to a farm he owned in Ohio. He sold it and opened a successful furniture business in Muscatine, Iowa.

Around 1855, Little returned to Pittsburgh to work for the Monongahela Navigation Company until the beginning of the Civil War. He became deputy U.S. assessor and then was appointed assessor by President Abraham Lincoln, serving until 1866. In that year, he became secretary and treasurer of the city's first trust company. After he retired from this post because of age, the firm continued his salary for life. He died on 25 August 1887. Little was interested in all public movements and was a member of the city's first historical society and vice-president of the second.

SOURCES: *History of Allegheny County, Pa.* (Chicago, 1889); *The Mercury*, 9 January 1839; Pittsburgh *Gazette*, 27 August 1887.   *George Swetnam*

LOCHER, RALPH SIDNEY (1915–   ), Mayor of Cleveland (1962–67). Democratic mayor of Cleveland during the turbulent 1960s, Locher was a classic example of American ethnic pluralism: he was born 24 July 1915 in Moreni, Romania, the second of two children of Ephraim Locher (1871–1933), a Swiss-American Mennonite and Natalie Voig (1881–1973), a Roman Catholic Austrian born in Romania. His father was an itinerant oil-field worker and had gone to Ploesti, Romania to work, returning with his new family during World War I. Locher graduated from Bluffton High School and earned a B.A. (1936) and LlD from Western Reserve in 1939. He married Eleanor Worthington, a school teacher and a Presbyterian of English-German ancestry on 18 June 1939, and they had one child, Virginia (b. 1940).

Locher practiced law and then served as secretary of the Ohio Industrial Commission (1945) before becoming secretary to Governor Frank J. Lausche (q.v.) (1945–49, 1949–53). From 1953 to 1962, Locher served as law director of Cleveland under Mayor Anthony J. Celebrezze (q.v.) (1953–62), whom he succeeded as mayor when Celebrezze became secretary of HEW. Locher was elected to complete the term, with 179,376 votes to 61,910 for W. Brown (Republican). In 1963, running unopposed, Locher secured 156,000 votes, and he won again—narrowly—in 1965 with 87,858 votes against Republican Ralph J. Perk (q.v.) (41,045) and two independent Democrats, Ralph A. McAllister (22,650) and Carl B. Stokes (q.v.), a black state legislator, the closest to winning (87,716).

Locher became mayor of a city experiencing major social, economic, and demographic changes. Migrating from the South, the number of blacks had increased from 73,464 in 1930 to 250,818 by 1960, while thousands more Appalachians and Hispanics also arrived during this period. Yet, the total population decreased from 914,000 to 810,857 (1965 estimate) as freeways, federal home loans, and the economic boom supported the exodus of the white middle class from the city.

Locher's administration, characterized by his personal honesty, presided over extensive but incomplete neighborhood urban renewal programs and the first extensive downtown development since the 1920s. He implemented efficiency recommendations of the Little Hoover Commission, secured passage of the city's first income tax, and used the revenue for shoring up the city's declining tax base and for expanding services and facilities.

But overcrowded slums, rising social tensions, and heavy unemployment among blacks aggravated racial conflict. While Locher sought to ameliorate the situation by appointing two blacks to his cabinet and by promoting interracial understanding through the city's community relations board, national trends and local events over which he had no control thwarted his good intentions. The accidental death of a white activist clergyman protesting racial segregation in the schools, the increased militancy among blacks, and the intransigence of the predominantly white police, contributed to a tension-filled atmosphere. In the summer of 1966, a minor incident erupted into a major race riot that shocked a complacent community and caused the business and civic leadership to look to Carl B. Stokes to replace Locher and in this way pacify the black community.

After Locher left office, he practiced law until 1968 when he was elected a Cuyahoga County Common Pleas judge (1969–72). In 1972, he was elected a probate court judge (1973–77), and in 1977 he won a seat on the Ohio Supreme Court (1978–   ).

SOURCES: Cleveland Urban League, Research Development, *The Negro in Cleveland 1950–1963: An Analysis of the Social, and Economic Characteristics of the Negro Population between 1950–1963* (Cleveland, 1964); William E. Nelson, Jr., and Philip J. Maranto, *Electing Black Mayors* (Columbus, 1977); Philip W. Porter, *Cleveland: Confused City on a Seesaw* (Columbus, 1976); Carl B. Stokes, *Promise of Power: A Political Biography* (New York, 1973); Kenneth G. Weinberg, *Black Victory and the Winning of Cleveland* (Chicago, 1968); Walter William, "Cleveland's Crisis Ghetto," *Transition* (September 1967); Derward C. Witzke, *Project 29 Wrap-up Report* (Cleveland, 1967); Estelle Zannes, *Checkmate in Cleveland* (Cleveland, 1972).   *Thomas F. Campbell*

LOCKWOOD, TIMOTHY T. (1812–70), Mayor of Buffalo (1858–59). Physician and conservative mayor of old-stock Yankee origins, Lockwood was born at North East, New York, in 1812. The son of pioneer farmers Ebenezer and Betsy (Seymour) Lockwood, he was the fourth of ten children. In 1816, the Lockwoods took their family to Hamburg, New York, where they purchased the farm on which Timothy spent his youth. In 1834, Timothy moved to Buffalo to enter the office of Dr. James P. White as a medical student. Continuing his studies at Philadelphia (Pennsylvania) Medical College, Lockwood received his M.D. and for some years practiced medicine in White's Corners. Returning to Buffalo, he joined the Erie County Medical Society in 1842 and served as its "censor" in 1845. In 1852, he was appointed city physician of Buffalo.

Lockwood married twice: a Hamburg woman, Charlotte (maiden name unknown), who bore him two daughters before she died, and Louise C. Francher (1815–69), of Buffalo, who also bore him two daughters.

Without previous political experience, Lockwood was the Democratic mayoral nominee in 1857. He defeated Republican Frederick P. Stevens (*q.v.*) by 1,274 votes and became the third physician-turned-mayor of the city, then a community of 74,214 people. Inasmuch as the effects of the Panic of 1857 were being sorely felt, Lockwood in his inaugural address to the common council emphasized "economy in the public expenditure." The county board of supervisors should, he said, reduce the "oppression" property taxes were imposing on city folk. Indeed, since the citizens were underrepresented on the

board, they were being forced to pay "nearly seventy-five *per centum* of the tax levied," when they constituted only 56 percent of the county's population. Lockwood admitted that the revenue had been used to finance a remarkable program of municipal improvements in new streets, sidewalks, and gaslights, but wondered "whether the city has not, of late, pressed forward too rapidly in its improvements." The wealthy, he claimed, were having difficulty meeting their "liabilities," and many mechanics and laborers were having to sell their property for taxes.

Whether Lockwood's economies were observed or helped slow down decline is unclear. What is clear is that in the election of 1858 the Republicans virtually swept the Democrats out of state, county, and city offices. Serving a two-year term, Lockwood, in his address to the new council, supported the project dear to his predecessor—construction of an international bridge to Canada, for which engineers had submitted specifications. Otherwise, he still urged economic stringency. By January 1860, when he left office, Buffalo was on its way to fiscal recovery.

Resuming his medical practice, in which he reputedly attended rich and poor alike . . . without regard to their ability to pay, Dr. Lockwood also continued to serve the Medical Society, as secretary in 1862, treasurer in 1866, and vice-president in 1868. The last-named office was honorary; two winters earlier, while alighting from a sleigh, Lockwood had fallen, and the resulting spinal injury had left him an invalid and totally blind. He died on 23 December 1870 and was buried between his two wives in Forest Lawn Cemetery.

SOURCES: Buffalo *Commercial Advertiser*, 27 December 1870; Buffalo *Daily Courier*, 26 December 1870; "Mayor's Inaugural," Buffalo *Daily Courier*, 5 January 1858; *Proceedings of the Common Council* (Buffalo, 1859); Grace C. Sheldon, "Dr. Timothy Lockwood," Buffalo *Times*, 24 August 1919; H. Perry Smith, *History of the City of Buffalo and Erie County*, 2 vols. (Syracuse, N.Y., 1884).   *John D. Milligen*

LODGE, JOHN C. (1862–1950), Mayor of Detroit (1922–23, 1924, 1927–29). Lodge was born on 12 August 1862 in Detroit, Michigan, the son of Edwin Albert Lodge (1822–87), a homeopathic physician who was born in England. His father was a Republican and an earnest antislavery man, who contributed heavily to the Underground Railroad fund in Detroit headed by Seymour Finney. The sixth of eleven children, John C. Lodge attended Philo M. Patterson's private school for boys and then Detroit public high school. He later went to Michigan Military Academy at Orchard Lake. His mother, Christina Hanson, was of Scots, Norwegian, and

Irish descent. The family was Presbyterian. Lodge loved sports and was a member of the Resolute Baseball Club of 1875. He was also a member of the Detroit Athletic Club and was elected captain of the Cinder Track Club in 1889.

Lodge started his career in 1886 as a copy boy with the Detroit *Free Press* and became city editor in 1893, later resigning to go into public service as chief clerk to the board of county auditors (1897).

Lodge's political career started in 1907 when he was elected to the legislature. He was a supporter of the brewers' slate introduced by Judge Guy A. Miller. In 1912, Lodge was appointed chairman of a committee that was to go to Pittsburgh to interview the officials of the Pennsylvania Railroad on the possibility of extending its service to Detroit. It failed. From 1909 Lodge served on the board of aldermen and in 1918 was elected president of the new council, a post he held for thirteen years. He was ten times a member of the common council and was generally regarded as the elder statesman of Detroit. Lodge strongly opposed radical changes in the government; he was a conservative Republican.

Lodge served as acting mayor from 5 December 1922 to 9 April 1923 and from 2 August to 21 November 1924, and in 1927 was elected mayor. In 1928 Detroit had a population of well over 1 million. At first Lodge was hesitant to run, even though he had experience as acting mayor, but was persuaded by friends. He resigned his post as president of the council, rendering his papers to a man who was to be his opponent—Mayor John Smith (*q.v.*). Smith was defeated. Lodge's campaign established a precedent, being devoid of speeches, interviews, and the usual trappings of a political contest. In 1929, he offered a plan to the city's ways and means committee for an $8 million bond issue to erect a new administrative building at Woodward and Jefferson avenues. Lodge served as mayor only one term, being defeated in 1929 by Charles Bowles (*q.v.*). Lodge's defeat did not mean an end to his public life; he continued as a councilman until 1947 when ill health forced him to quit. Regaining his health in 1948, he was appointed to the board of supervisors. By that time, he had served a half century as a Republican public office holder and was a living link connecting horse-and-buggy Detroit to the modern automobile capital of the world. He died on 6 February 1950 and was buried in Detroit.

SOURCES: Clarence M. Burton, *The City of Detroit, Michigan 1701–1922*, vol. 3 (Detroit-Chicago, 1922); John C. Lodge, *I Remember Detroit* (Detroit, 1949); Albert N. Marquis, *The Book of Detroiters* (Chicago, 1914); New York *Times Obituaries Index 1958–1968* (New York, 1970).

Ben C. Wilson and *Finny Ike Memchukwa*

LOW, SETH (1850–1916), Mayor of New York (1902–1903). A leading reform mayor, born on 18 January 1850 in Brooklyn, New York, Low was the son of Abiel Abbot Low (1811–93), an old-stock Yankee merchant, and Ellen (Dow) Low of Boston. The youngest of four children, Seth Low attended Brooklyn Polytechnic Institute and Columbia College, from which he was graduated as valedictorian in 1870. Low went to work for his father's company, A. A. Low and Brothers, which imported silk from China. In 1881, he became first president of the Young Republican Club of Brooklyn and the same year was elected Brooklyn's mayor. In 1886, after serving two terms, Low returned to the family business. In 1889, he was named president of Columbia College and subsequently engineered the move of the campus from its Forty-ninth Street site in Manhattan to Morningside Heights. In 1897, Low was nominated by the Citizen's Union for the mayoralty of the newly created "Greater New York," but Robert Van Wyck (*q.v.*), the Tammany candidate, was elected. In 1880, Low married Annie Wroe Scollay Curtis of Boston; they had no children.

New York City in 1902 had 3,437,202 people and was governed by a mayor and board of aldermen. Low ran for mayor in 1901 on a fusion ticket; both the Republican party and the Citizen's Union backed him in an effort to supplant the corrupt Van Wyck administration. Endeavoring to defuse the charges of corruption, Tammany Boss Richard Croker chose Edward Morse Shepard, a long-time Tammany critic and reformer, as the Democrats' candidate. Low won, however, beating Shepard 296,813 to 265,177. When Low ran for reelection as the fusion candidate in 1903, the new Tammany boss, Charles F. Murphy, chose George B. McClellan, Jr. (*q.v.*), the son of the famous Civil War general, to oppose him. McClellan beat Low 314,782 to 252,086.

As mayor, Low sought to apply sound business principles to municipal government; his watchwords were economy and efficiency. Despite lowering taxes and trimming the city budget, Low's health, charities, and tenement house departments scored notable improvements. One of his primary aims was reform of the city's much-maligned police department, and, under his direction, the bribery system was largely abolished. To the chagrin of many of the city's reformers, Low encouraged the police not to enforce the Sunday ban on liquor sales. Late in his term, when a new police commissioner insisted on strict compliance of the law, Low was roundly assailed by ethnic groups, notably the German-Americans. While he put the awarding of franchises on an honest basis, Low's opposition to municipal ownership caused many former supporters to question his legitimacy as a reformer. His brand of reform was too mild for some and yet vital enough to threaten others accustomed to Tammany rule, and Low was repudiated by the voters after a single term.

In 1904, Low retired to a farm in Westchester County but remained active in several Progressive causes. In 1907, he was elected chairman of the board of Tuskegee Institute and president of the National Civic Federation. In 1914, he was elected president of the New York Chamber of Commerce. Low died in his home on 17 September 1916.

SOURCES: Gerald Kurland, *Seth Low: The Reformer in an Urban and Industrial Age* (New York, 1971); Benjamin R.C. Low, *Seth Low* (New York, 1925); New York *Times*, 18 September 1916; Steven C. Swett, "The Test of a Reformer: A Study of Seth Low," *New York Historical Society Quarterly* 44 (January 1960).

W. Roger Biles

LOWRIE, MATTHEW B. (1773–1850), Mayor of Pittsburgh (1830–31). Scottish-born fifth mayor of Pittsburgh, Lowrie was born on 12 May 1773 in Edinburgh. He emigrated to America in 1792 with his Presbyterian family, settling in central Pennsylvania and five years later, in Butler County, north of Pittsburgh. There he and a younger brother opened what became a prosperous grocery business. Some time later, between 1800 and 1810, Matthew moved to Pittsburgh and operated another grocery in partnership with one Carter Curtis.

Lowrie and his wife, the former Sarah Anderson, had five daughters and three sons. His oldest son, Walter H. Lowrie, became a judge in Pittsburgh, going on to become a justice of the Pennsylvania Supreme Court from 1851 to 1863, serving as chief justice the last six years. Following Sarah's death, Lowrie married Mary Gilchrist. He was a Mason and one of the twelve original aldermen named by Governor Simon Snyder when Pittsburgh became a city. He received three out of the twenty-four votes cast when John M. Snowden (*q.v.*) was elected mayor in 1825. Lowrie was a religious leader in the First Presbyterian Church.

On 12 January 1830, Lowrie was elected mayor by joint action of the councils, defeating incumbent Magnus M. Murray (*q.v.*). Although a former member of the Masons, Lowrie ran as an Anti-Mason, swept into office during a panic of sentiment against secret societies, which forced the disbanding of all but two of southwestern Pennsylvania's Masonic lodges. This is the first mention of partisanship in Pittsburgh's mayoralty contests, and from that time candidates were designated by party.

After one year in office, Lowrie was defeated by Murray in an upsurge of Jacksonian Democracy. He ran for the office in 1832 and 1833 before the councils, and

again in 1834 when the office was made elective by popular vote, but he was defeated by Samuel Pettigrew (*q.v.*) in these campaigns and by Jonas McClintock (*q.v.*) in his final race in 1836. At the time Lowrie was mayor, Pittsburgh had a population of 12,568.

During Lowrie's administration, the Workingmen's party was organized, and plans were started for a second market house. At this time, the city was first divided into wards—North, South, East, and West. Not wanting to usurp authority, Lowrie inquired of the councils as to whether or not to charge for a license during the exhibition of a religious painting, and for showing a miniature steam locomotive and railroad car. (Folklore attributes the city's first steam fire-engine to Lowrie, but this type of engine was not used until around the time of his death, and until after 1870 individual fire companies bought their own engines.)

Lowrie died on 28 July 1850 of what was then called "cholera morbus" but was more likely a coronary attack. In his obituary, he was called "the oldest and most respected citizen" of Pittsburgh.

SOURCES: Allen H. Kerr. "The Mayors and Recorders of Pittsburgh, 1816–1951" (typescript, 1952, Carnegie Library of Pittsburgh); Pittsburgh *Gazette*, 29 July 1850; Pittsburgh *Press*, "The Mayors' Notebook, No. 5" by George Swetnam, 20 September 1973; Erasmus Wilson. *Standard History of Pittsburgh* (SIC), (Chicago, 1898).

Helene Smith

LOWRY, JAMES (1820–76), Mayor of Pittsburgh (1864–66). Lowry was born in Scotland in 1820 and came to Pittsburgh as a small child with his parents. His father was a linen weaver but soon opened a foundry business. After a common school education James went into business with his father and married Eliza Shore, who bore him eleven children.

Young Lowry was a Whig and an early backer of the Republican party, taking part in its first national convention in 1856. Beginning with 1863, his party decided to elect delegates to its nominating conventions, but only a few wards adopted the plan. It proved an utter fiasco, with many irregularities. As a result, the Republican party offered no candidate for mayor in the election of January 1864. Lowry, who would have been its logical nominee, ran with the backing of the Union City party, defeating Democrat Joseph R. Hunter 2,509 to 1,830. Pittsburgh at that time had a population of about 70,000, with a mayor and select and common councils. Lowry's administration was uneventful.

By December 1865, Lowry's party had a firm primary system, and he appeared to have won the nomination by 158 votes, but there was a contest, and William C. McCarthy (*q.v.*) was named the winner. Lowry continued in politics and later was elected coroner. He ran his foundry for several years, went into the coal trade, and was collector of customs for the port of Pittsburgh. Later, he moved to St. Louis as agent for a group of coal producers. He died there on 20 July 1876.

SOURCES: Allen H. Kerr, "The Mayors and Recorders of Pittsburgh, 1816–1951" (typescript, 1952, Carnegie Library of Pittsburgh); Pittsburgh *Gazette*, 23 July 1876; Pittsburgh *Post*, 22 July 1876.

George Swetnam

LOYD, ALEXANDER (1805–72), Mayor of Chicago (1840–41). Fourth Chicago mayor, born on 19 August 1805 in Orange County, New York, Loyd (sometimes spelled incorrectly as Lloyd), was the son of British immigrants. After attending public school, he began work as a carpenter. Seeking better opportunities, he moved west to Chicago in 1834 and quickly became a successful carpenter and contractor. During 1841–44, he was a partner of Benjamin W. Thomas; otherwise, Loyd operated by himself. During the 1850s, he branched out into other fields, buying a combination grocery and dry goods store and selling lumber.

Loyd's political activities began soon after his arrival in Chicago. In 1835, he was elected a town trustee. By 1836, he was identified as one of a group of local politicians forming the town's first Democratic machine. Loyd was chief engineer of the city's second fire company (the "Metamora" Engine Company) 1837–38. In 1840, he was elected mayor, defeating Whig incumbent Benjamin W. Raymond (*q.v.*) 582 votes to 423. Chicago then had a population of 4,479 and a mayor-council form of government. Mayor Loyd built the city's First Unitarian Church. His mayoralty was politically uneventful.

Loyd did not seek reelection, and his subsequent political career was brief. He served as a trustee of the school board and as a member of the city's board of health during the 1840s. In 1850–51, he served as alderman from the Second Ward. He then traveled to Pike's Peak, Colorado, where he invented a crusher for separating gold from quartz. The Panic of 1857 seriously depleted his financial resources, and he lost possession of a valuable lot in Chicago and a new building being constructed. His last major public appearance came at the Springfield, Illinois, memorial services for the slain President Lincoln in 1865. Following the death of his wife in 1871, Loyd moved to Lyons, Illinois, where he died on 7 May 1872.

SOURCES: A. T. Andreas, *History of Chicago*, 3 vols. (Chicago, 1884–86); *Chicago's Semi-Centennial Memorial with Engraved Portraits of the 24 Mayors of Chicago* (Chicago, 1887); Francis A. Eastman, comp., *Chicago City Manual, 1911* (Chicago, 1911); Bessie L.

Pierce, *A History of Chicago,* 3 vols. (New York, 1937–57).

Thomas R. Bullard

LUDINGTON, HARRISON (1812–91), Mayor of Milwaukee (1871–72, 1873–74, 1875). Ludington was born on 31 July 1812 in Ludingtonville, New York, the son of Frederick Ludington and Susannah (Griffith) Ludington of old-stock Anglo-American ancestry. One of fifteen children, Harrison Ludington received his education in the grammar school of the local village. After working as a store clerk, he moved to Milwaukee in 1838. In 1842, he joined with his brothers, James and Nelson, in the lumber business. In 1851, he formed the company of Ludington, Wells, and Von Schaick, buying several sawmills in the Greenbay area. The company became one of the largest manufacturers of lumber, controlling extensive forest tracts in Michigan, Louisiana, and Texas. Ludington also had an interest in the Ludington Mine at Iron Mountain, Michigan, as well as extensive real estate holdings in Milwaukee, including a parcel leased to the Pabst Brewery for $10,000 per year. He maintained a farm at Wauwatosa, Wisconsin, where he raised pure-bred stock and promoted scientific agriculture. He was a leader in St. Paul's Episcopal Church; he was a member of the city's volunteer fire department in the 1850s.

Originally a Whig, Ludington became a Republican with the organization of that party in 1856. He was elected to Milwaukee's common council in 1861 and 1862. The people elected Ludington mayor of Milwaukee in 1871, 1873, and 1875. He served only part of the third term, resigning to assume the governorship of Wisconsin to which he was elected in 1875, defeating Democrat William R. Taylor by a vote of 85,164 to 84,374. He ran for mayor again in 1882 but was defeated by a substantial margin by John M. Stowell (*q.v.*).

Milwaukee in the time of Ludington's mayoralty had a population of approximately 75,000. The city government consisted of a mayor and a bicameral body called the common council. One house consisted of one alderman from each ward and the other of two councillors from each ward. From 1857 to 1872, there were nine wards; a tenth was added in 1872, two more in 1873, and the thirteenth in 1874.

Known as "Bluff Old Hal," Ludington in 1871 defeated incumbent Joseph Phillips (*q.v.*). In 1872, Ludington was defeated by David G. Hooker (*q.v.*). In 1873, Ludington contended with Democrat Levi H. Kellogg, a member of the common council. Ludington lost the election by 217 votes, but Kellogg's election was declared void because the city charter prohibited a member of the common council from running for any other city office. By the time of the special election, Kellogg's term on the council had expired so he again stood against Ludington. This time Ludington won by 1,263 votes.

As mayor, Ludington advocated lower taxes as a measure to bring industry and population to Milwaukee. Yet, in his administration the fire department was changed from a volunteer unit to full-time paid firemen. A survey was made of Milwaukee streets and of the best kinds of street-building materials. Ludington warned against false economy in street building. Also during this time, there was great improvement of the waterworks. The great Chicago fire occurred during Ludington's administration, and he reacted promptly by sending firefighting equipment and, later, successive car-loads of clothing and food to the destitute of this neighboring city.

During Ludington's mayoralty, the Wisconsin legislature passed the Graham law which required a $2,000 bond for a license to sell liquor, civil penalties for miscreant saloon-keepers, and heavy penalties for drunkenness. Ludington defied state authorities and refused to enforce the law. This action won him wide acclaim with the brewers, distillers, and the German population. It was on this wave of popularity that he was nominated to and won election as governor of Wisconsin. He assumed the governor's chair on the heels of the radical Granger Movement which had caused the legislature to pass the Potter law. This law provided for a three-man railway commission with power to fix rates, regulate the railways, and forbid free passes on the railroads for public officials.

Ludington was conservative and business-oriented and had been an advocate of the railroads since the 1840s. Under his leadership, the Potter law was repealed and the Railway Commission was replaced by a single commissioner with no regulatory powers.

Ludington refused to run for reelection as governor. He returned to his business interests. In 1885, he suffered a bad fall and his health deteriorated. On 17 June 1891, he had a stroke and died.

SOURCES: *Dictionary of Wisconsin Biography* (Madison, Wis., 1960); John G. Gregory, *History of Milwaukee, Wisconsin* (Chicago, 1931); Robert C. Nesbit, *Wisconsin: A History* (Madison, Wis., 1973); William Francis Raney, *Wisconsin: A Story of Progress* (New York, 1940); Bayrd Still, *Milwaukee: The History of a City* (Madison, Wis., 1965); Jerome A. Watrous, ed., *Memoirs of Milwaukee County*, 2 vols. (Madison, Wis., 1909).   *Donald F. Tingley*

LUKEN, JAMES T. (1921–79), Mayor of Cincinnati (1976–77). The only labor union leader ever chosen mayor of Cincinnati, and a liberal Democrat, Luken was born in Cincinnati on 31 December 1921, the son of Walter J. Luken (1887–1969), an employee of a local printing company, and Philomenia (Kispert) Luken. He was the sixth of nine children, and his parents were both Roman Catholics of Irish-German ancestry. Luken's formal education ended when he graduated in 1938 from Norwood High School in Norwood, Ohio. He married Ida Mae Smith, also of Cincinnati, and they had four children, James Thomas, Diane, Stephen Phillip, and William Phillip. The Lukens were divorced in 1975 but remarried each other in 1979. They attended St. Peter-in-Chains (Catholic) Church.

Following his discharge from the Navy as an enlisted man in World War II, Luken took a job as a milk route driver and later as a milk salesman. At the age of twenty-seven, in 1948, Luken became president and business manager of Local 98, Dairy Worker's union, an organization that represents more than 1,800 workers in southeastern Indiana, southwestern Ohio, and northern Kentucky. After eight years as regional head of the Teamster's Union in southwestern Ohio, he successfully led a revolt in 1961 against the Teamster's national president, James Hoffa. After disaffiliating from the Teamsters, Luken continued to lead the Dairy Worker's Union, presently affiliated with the AFL–CIO.

Long active in Democratic party affairs, and a friend of both John F. and Robert Kennedy, Luken served as local aide and manager for John Gilligan's successful councilmanic, congressional, and gubernatorial campaigns, as well as heading the regional presidential campaigns for John Kennedy in 1960, Lyndon Johnson in 1964, and Robert Kennedy in 1968. Following John Kennedy's election, Luken turned down several offers to serve in the national administration, including the posts of assistant secretary of labor, assistant secretary of commerce, and ambassadorships to the then Belgian Congo and Argentina. In his first campaign for public office, Luken was elected in 1972 to the lower house of the Ohio General Assembly and was reelected in 1974, but he resigned to become a city councilman and the mayor-designate of Cincinnati after winning a seat on the city council in November 1975.

Cincinnati in 1976 had 410,000 people when Luken was selected mayor. The city, since adopting a charter form of government in 1925, maintained a small council-city manager system. The mayor, chosen by the council from among its nine members, all of whom are elected at large, exercises no statutory functions as such. The traditional role the mayor fulfills is to develop support for the majority's program within the council and to act as its spokesperson. Since 1971, when the Democrats joined with the Charterite party to form a coalition majority on the council, the mayoralty has alternated between the two parties, each party claiming the mayoralty for one year during each two-year councilmanic term.

Luken, running as a Democrat, finished seventh and garnered 46,532 votes in 1975, but in November 1977, while serving as mayor, he was reelected to the council and finished third with 66,318 votes.

During his three years on the city council, including his one year as mayor, Luken repeatedly emphasized that Cincinnati was becoming a city of old buildings and old people—losing population and losing an income tax base. "It cannot," he insisted, "support services it acquired at a time when it was 75% to 80% of the population of Hamilton County." In 1978, the city had 40 percent of the population of Hamilton County.

Among his successes in shifting costs to other governmental entities were the transfers to the state of Ohio of the operation of Cincinnati General Hospital and to the county of the financial obligation for the Hamilton County Municipal Court. While he served as mayor, his favorite project came to fruition when the University of Cincinnati became a state institution. He was less successful in terminating city support for an area-wide transit system that receives no support from surrounding municipalities.

As mayor, Luken was characterized as blunt but open-minded, realistic but gutsy, with a toughness reminiscent of Mayor Daley (*q.v.*) of Chicago. Some critics, however, complained that he ran the city council like a union meeting and failed to delegate powers. Luken stayed on the council after his mayoralty, but he died of cancer on 12 July 1979.

SOURCES: *The City Bulletin* (Official publication of the City of Cincinnati), 1975–78; newspaper clippings, Municipal Library, Cincinnati City Hall, 1974–78. Much of the above biography derives from communication, both oral and written from Mr. Luken.

Gene D. Lewis and *Thomas R. Bullard*

LUKEN, THOMAS A. (1925–   ), Mayor of Cincinnati (1971–72). Luken was born on 9 July 1925 in Cincinnati, one of eight children, of a Roman Catholic family of German descent. He attended local schools and Bowling Green State University (1943–44) and saw action in World War II with the Marines (1944–45). Returning to Cincinnati, he attended Xavier University, graduating in 1947 (A.B.) and then S. P. Chase Law School, receiving an LL.B. in 1950. Luken began his legal practice that same year. In 1947, he married Shirley Ast, and they had ten children. A Catholic himself, Luken is a member of the Knights of Columbus, American Legion, and the Jaycees. He is also a member of city, state, and national bar associations.

A Democrat, Luken was city solicitor in Deer Park, Ohio, during 1955–61. He was then appointed federal district attorney for the Southern District of Ohio,

1961–64, and served on the Cincinnati City Council, 1964–67 and 1969–74. After his reelection to the council in 1971, he was chosen mayor for a single year—the first such term of office under the charter system. Theodore M. Berry (*q.v.*) took the office for the second year of what was normally a two-year term. Cincinnati had 451,455 people in 1970 and a city manager-mayor-council form of government.

Although serving only one year, Luken was determined to be a strong mayor, and some critics (notably within the Charterite party) considered him too strong and too likely to interfere in areas usually left to the city council. He believed in an "open door" policy to allow the public easier access to his office. Luken tried to visit all neighborhoods in the city on foot in an effort to make the public realize the need to work with the political leadership. He attempted to win greater financial aid from state, county, and federal sources in order to provide better health, police, and recreational services for the city. At one point, he admitted that Cincinnati faced huge financial problems, but he was convinced they could be overcome. At the 1972 U.S. Conference of Mayors, Luken led an unsuccessful effort to have that organization attack the U.S. role in the Vietnam War.

After leaving the mayor's office, Luken continued as a member of the city council until 1974 when he resigned to run for Congress. In the special election held in the First District that spring, he was elected, but in the regular election in November, Luken was defeated by W. D. Gradison (*q.v.*), his predecessor as Cincinnati mayor. However, Luken was elected from the Second District in 1976 and reelected in 1978.

SOURCES: Cincinnati *Enquirer*, 2 December 1971; *Congressional Directory, 95th Cong., 1st Sess.* (Washington, D.C., 1977).

Thomas R. Bullard

LYMAN, THEODORE, JR. (1792–1849), Mayor of Boston (1834–35). Born in Boston on 20 February 1792, Lyman was the second son of Theodore Lyman, a wealthy Yankee merchant, and Lydia Williams, niece of Timothy Pickering of Salem, a prominent Federalist and secretary of state under President John Adams. Lyman attended Phillips Exeter Academy, graduated from Harvard in 1810, and planned to pursue a literary career. After nearly ten years of extensive travel and study, he returned to Boston and eventually published several works dealing with European and American history. He married Mary Elizabeth Hendersen of New York in 1821.

Almost inevitably, as a result of his family's social and political relationships, Lyman was drawn into local politics. From 1820 to 1825, he served in the state legislature where he was outspoken in his opposition to John Quincy Adams, Daniel Webster, and the platform of the

National Republican party. Indeed, during the campaign of 1828, Lyman wrote such a scathing newspaper editorial that Webster brought suit against him for criminal libel. Gradually, Lyman came to be the leader of a group of die-hard Federalists who decided to stop the Adams faction by throwing their support to the new Democratic party of Andrew Jackson and came to be known as "silk-stocking Democrats." Although Lyman slowly became disenchanted with Jackson and his bank policies, especially when he did not get the patronage he expected, he was still on good enough terms with local Democratic groups to get their support when he ran for mayor of Boston in 1833 and again in 1834.

Mayor Lyman was the first to confront violence rising out of new racial and ethnic tensions in the city created by the slavery controversy and by the influx of foreign immigrants. Boston was then about 70,000 in size. On 11 August 1834, an angry mob attacked and set fire to a convent of Ursuline nuns who operated a school for girls in Charlestown. Fearing a city-wide conflict between Catholic immigrants and native inhabitants of Boston, Lyman organized special police forces and called up units of the state militia to prevent any further disturbances. The following year Lyman had to confront another major riot—this time organized by elements in the city opposed to the movement begun in 1831 by William Lloyd Garrison and his followers calling for the total and immediate emancipation of slaves. On 21 October 1835, a mob broke into an abolitionist meeting, caught hold of Garrison, pummeled him severely, threw a rope around him, and dragged him through the streets of Boston. Although Lyman was unable to disperse the rioters with personal appeals, he saved the abolitionist leader from more serious harm by spiriting him off to the local jail and booking him as a "rioter." The next day the mayor dismissed the charges, released Garrison, and advised him to leave town.

When his two terms as mayor were over, Lyman spent his remaining years in a number of charitable and philanthropic enterprises, concerning himself especially with the education and rehabilitation of juvenile offenders. He helped establish the State Reform School for boys at Westboro, which he generously provided with funds out of his own income, and he recommended a similar school for girls at Lancaster. He died on 18 July 1849, shortly after returning from a visit to Europe with his son.

SOURCES: J. H. Benton, Jr., *A Notable Libel Case: The Criminal Prosecution of Theodore Lyman Jr. by Daniel Webster* (Boston, 1904); *Inaugural Addresses of the Mayors of Boston, 1822–1852* (Boston, 1894); Robert H. Lord, et al., *History of the Archdiocese of Boston*, 3 vols. (Boston, 1945), vol. 2; Theodore Lyman III, *Papers Relating to the Garrison Mob* (Cambridge, Mass., 1870); *Records of the City of Boston: Mayor and Aldermen* (microfilm, Boston Public Library); Leonard L. Richards, *"Gentlemen of Property and Standing": Anti-Abolition Mobs in Jacksonian America* (New York, 1970); Justin Winsor, ed., *Memorial History of Boston . . . 1630–1880*, 4 vols. (Boston, 1880), vol. 3.

Thomas H. O'Connor

LYNDE, WILLIAM PITT (1817–85), Mayor of Milwaukee (1860–61). Born in Sherburne, New York, on 16 December 1817, Lynde was the second of four children born to Telly (d. 1857) and Elizabeth (Warner) Lynde. His parents were Congregationalists, emigrants from Massachusetts, and of British descent, and his father established himself as a successful merchant and served in the New York legislature. William Lynde attended Hamilton College for two years and then transferred to Yale College, graduating in 1838. He entered Harvard Law School and graduated in 1841. On 24 May of the same year, he married Mary E. Blanchard of Truxton, New York; she was a graduate of the Albany (New York) Female Academy and a Presbyterian. They had seven children, six of whom survived.

By 1842, Lynde had established his first law offices in Milwaukee and became active in the Democratic party. His antislavery views pleased the growing German population of the city. In 1844, he was elected attorney general of Wisconsin and the following year was appointed U.S. district attorney for Wisconsin. Lynde served his only pre-Civil War term in Congress in 1846. In 1857, he helped establish one of the city's most prestigious law firms, Finches, Lynde, and Miller. The Milwaukee Democrats overwhelmed the Republicans in 1860 and elected Lynde as mayor. Milwaukee then had 46,396 people and a mayor-council form of government. Lynde remained a Democratic wheelhorse, and in 1874 and again in 1876 was elected to Congress from Wisconsin's Fourth District. During the 1874 term, he served as one of the House of Representatives' managers for the Senate impeachment trial of Secretary of War W. W. Belknap.

Lynde had rather extensive and lucrative real estate holdings in Milwaukee. He died in Milwaukee on 18 December 1885.

SOURCES: James S. Buck, *Milwaukee Under the Charter* (Milwaukee, 1886), vol. 4; Bayrd Still, *Milwaukee: The History of a City* (Madison, Wis., 1965); *Wisconsin Magazine of History* (1972).

David J. Maurer

LYON, ROBERT W. (1842–1904), Mayor of Pittsburgh (1881–84). Lyon was born on 22 May 1842 in

Butler County, Pennsylvania, the son of John Lyon, a farmer, and Mary Lyon. He lived on a farm until he was nineteen, when he enlisted as a blacksmith with the 102d Pennsylvania Volunteer Infantry, a famous fighting outfit. When fighting time came, he laid down his hammer for a gun.

Lyon quickly rose from private to orderly sergeant, and in 1862 he was commissioned a second lieutenant for conspicuous gallantry. The following year he became a captain and staff officer, and in 1864 he was first brevetted and then commissioned a major. When mustered out, he was made lieutenant colonel, but he never used the title, and only a few friends knew of his promotion. Although he was wounded in the face at Fair Oaks and in the thigh at Cold Harbor, he returned to duty each time.

Lyon was a fine physical specimen, standing ''six foot two in his socks'' and weighing 260 pounds. After the war, he worked in the oilfields around Oil City, and then came to Pittsburgh and took a business course. He became successively a bookkeeper, a cashier in a steel mill, and the mill's superintendent.

On furlough in 1864 Lyon had married Harriet Barclay (1841–99). They had eleven children, six girls and five boys, only six of whom survived him. He was a Protestant, a Mason, and a leader in the Grand Army of the Republic.

Nominated for mayor in 1880, Lyon was opposed by Republican Miles Humphreys, and there was a record turnout despite zero temperatures. Lyon won by 11,865 to 10,358, but he was hampered by the fact that both councils were against him. Pittsburgh, with a population of 160,000, had a mayor and council form of government. The one outstanding event of his term was a blunder: Andrew Carnegie's offer to the city of $250,000 to build a library was refused.

Unable to succeed himself, Lyon became superintendent of a steel mill at nearby McKees Rocks until 1902. After retiring there, he worked as clerk in the coroner's office until he became ill. He died on 9 October 1904. He and his wife, who had died five years previously, were buried in Mount Calvary Cemetery, McKees Rocks.

SOURCES: *History of Allegheny County Pennsylvania* (Chicago, 1889); Allen H. Kerr. ''The Mayors and Recorders of Pittsburgh, 1816–1951 (typescript, 1952, Carnegie Library of Pittsburgh); Pittsburgh *Post* and *Dispatch*, 9 October 1904.   *George Swetnam*

M

McALEER, OWEN (1858–1944), Mayor of Los Angeles (1904–1906). Born on 3 February 1858 in Liscard, Canada, McAleer was the son of Owen McAleer (1830–65), an Irishman, and Mary (Miller) McAleer (1830–1908) of Scottish ancestry. The McAleer family moved to Youngstown, Ohio, in 1863. One of eight children, Owen McAleer attended the Youngstown public schools. When poverty forced him to leave school at nine years of age, he went to work in a boiler factory. He remained in this job, eventually becoming proprietor of his own shop. Moving to Los Angeles in 1888, he became superintendent of an iron factory's boiler department and made the first boiler ever manufactured in the city. McAleer married Gertrude E. Mullally in 1898.

Los Angeles in 1901 had 108,800 people (but had doubled by 1906) and a mayor-council form of government. McAleer served on the city's examining board of engineers. Elected to the common council in 1902, he helped establish the city's first municipal playground, pushed through a law making it illegal to gamble on horse races, and sponsored an ordinance for the regulation of utility rates. McAleer accepted the Republican nomination for the mayoralty in 1904 which he won by 14,293 votes to Democratic incumbent Meredith P. Snyder's (*q.v.*) 10,949. It was the largest majority given any Los Angeles mayor up to that time. The Republican party did not renominate McAleer for another term.

Los Angeles's population rose to 176,600 in 1905. McAleer's administration launched the massive Owens River project. A delegation of city officials, which included Mayor McAleer, toured the proposed aqueduct route and examined the Owens River water supply. They approved a plan for a 225-mile aqueduct and made the arrangements to acquire the necessary land and water rights. McAleer also advocated the municipal ownership of public utilities which required the use of city streets. He vetoed several council measures designed to benefit gas and traction companies.

After his term of office, McAleer formed a partnership with Nat Wilshire and established an iron and steel firm. McAleer also headed two local water companies. In 1915, he managed the mayoral campaign of Police Chief Charles E. Sebastian (*q.v.*) who won the election. Sebastian appointed McAleer to the Los Angeles Board of Public Works, and he retained that position until 1920 when he retired. McAleer was a member of the local Union League and Elks and Sierra Madre clubs. He was a Baptist.

McAleer died after a long illness on 7 March 1944 and was cremated in Los Angeles.

SOURCES: Albert H. Clodius, "The Quest for Good Government in Los Angeles, 1890–1910" (Ph.D. dissertation, Claremont Graduate School, 1953); Los Angeles *Times*, 10 March 1944; "Owen McAleer," *California Biography File*, Los Angeles Public Library; Press Reference Library, *Notables of the Southwest* (Los Angeles, 1912); Leonard R. Sanders, "Los Angeles and Its Mayors, 1850–1925" (M.A. thesis, University of Southern California, 1968).

Martin J. Schiesl

McCALL, PETER (1809–80), Mayor of Philadelphia (1844–45). Born on 30 October 1809 in Philadelphia, the future mayor was the son of Peter McCall, scion of one of the oldest families of Pennsylvania, and Sarah (Gibson) McCall. Peter, the youngest of five children, attended schools in Philadelphia and graduated with distinction from Princeton in 1826. He read law in a local attorney's office, was admitted to the bar in 1830, and practiced for nearly a half century. McCall traveled frequently, spending the years 1837, 1853, and 1870 in Europe. In 1846, he married Jane Byrd Mercer of West River, Maryland, and was the father of eight children. McCall, an Episcopalian, was a member of the vestry and church warden of Christ Church, Philadelphia.

Philadelphia in 1844 had a population of about 105,000 and a mayor-council form of government. McCall's political experience included several terms on the city council before he accepted the nomination for mayor. McCall won by a vote of 5,506 to Democrat Samuel Badger's 5,065 and Native American party E. W. Keyer's 4,032.

Mayor McCall was a frequent public speaker and held a professorial chair at the University of Pennsylvania Law School. He died on 4 November 1880 in Philadelphia and was interred at Christ Church burial ground.

SOURCES: Biographical file at the Historical Society of Pennsylvania, Philadelphia; Information file, Department of Records, City of Philadelphia.

Melvin G. Holli

McCALLIN, WILLIAM (1842–1904), Mayor of Pittsburgh (1887–90). McCallin was born in Mercer, Pennsylvania, on 8 August 1842. His parents, James and Sophia McCallin, Scots-Irish Presbyterians, moved to Pittsburgh in 1845, the father operating a livery stable, aided later by the son. The place became a hangout for politicians and was jokingly referred to as "The Senate." McCallin married Marian Marshall, daughter of an elevator manufacturer. They had one child, a daughter, and Mrs. McCallin died in 1893.

Always interested in politics, McCallin was elected sheriff in 1881. A year after his term ended, he was nominated as mayor on the Republican ticket, facing Democrat Bernard McKenna (q.v.), a surprisingly strong opponent. He won narrowly by 13,908 to 12,428. One of his first acts was to appoint McKenna police magistrate.

McCallin's term of office saw extensive construction, through which he acquired a considerable fortune. Soon after the term ended, however, he lost the money through the default of a friend whose bond he had signed. During his incumbency, laws were passed which increased the power of the city's two councils, weakening the mayor. Pittsburgh at this time had a population of about 225,000.

When Bernard McKenna became mayor in 1893, he returned an old favor by appointing McCallin police magistrate. In 1901, McCallin was made city assessor and later worked in other political offices. He was an invalid the final year of his life, dying on 4 September 1904.

SOURCES: Allen Humphreys Kerr, "The Mayors and Recorders of Pittsburgh, 1816–1951" (typescript, 1952, Carnegie Library of Pittsburgh); Pittsburgh *Bulletin*, 10 September 1904; Pittsburgh *Post* and *Dispatch*, both 5 September 1904.   George Swetnam

McCARTHY, PATRICK HENRY (1863–1933), Mayor of San Francisco (1910–12). One of San Francisco's least known mayors, McCarthy was born in County Limerick, Ireland, on 17 March 1863. He was raised in a Roman Catholic household in Ireland and emigrated to the United States in 1880, spending six years in Chicago and St. Louis before moving to San Francisco in 1886. His occupation was carpentering, and, from an early date, he took an active interest in labor affairs. In San Francisco, he affiliated with the Carpenters' Union and later became its president. Eight years after his arrival in the city, he was already a powerful figure in the labor movement and was elected president of the Building Trades Council, a local affiliation of unions. As a leading figure in the economic life of San Francisco, McCarthy soon became an important political figure as well. He served on the committee that framed the city charter of 1900 as well as on the Civil Service Commission. Unlike most San

Francisco labor leaders of the day, McCarthy did not join the Union Labor party of Abe Ruef and Eugene Schmitz (q.v.), and he remained a loyal Democrat in the elections of 1901 and 1903. He swung his support to Union Labor in 1905, however, a move that would ultimately bring him the mayoralty.

In 1907, Schmitz, the mayor, and Ruef, the city's boss, were both convicted of taking bribes, and Schmitz was replaced in office by Edward R. Taylor (q.v.). A few months later, a regular election was held, and McCarthy was able to control his party's convention and receive its nomination for mayor of the city. Although he lost the 1907 election to Taylor, he immediately began preparing for the 1909 campaign. Once again, he received his party's nomination. In the general election, he defeated the Republican candidate, William Crocker, and the Democrat, Thomas Leland, by a vote of 29,455 to 13,766 and 19,564, respectively.

When McCarthy was elected, San Francisco had a population of nearly 417,000, and the city was governed by a mayor and a board of supervisors. During his administration, several of the major issues were similar to those faced by his predecessors and successors—public transit and municipal control of water supplies. Even before his election, McCarthy campaigned for the passage of bond issues favoring municipal ownership of street railways. He also supported public, rather than private, ownership of the city's water supply. However, neither of these goals was attained during his administration. The other crucial issue during his two years in office was dismissal of the graft prosecutions. McCarthy had campaigned on a platform advocating the end of prosecution, and all remaining indictments were, in fact, dropped on 15 August 1911. Other than this, McCarthy, as mayor, seems to have had no permanent, long-term effect on the life of the city.

In 1911, McCarthy ran for reelection against James "Sunny Jim" Rolph (q.v.) and was soundly defeated. His defeat as a political leader, however, did not end his position as a labor leader. He remained active in the Building Trades Council until 1923. After retiring from the council, he became an investment banker with particular interest in stocks. On 30 June 1933, he suffered a cerebral hemorrhage and died the next morning at the age of seventy.

SOURCE: Millard Robert Morgen, "The Administration of P. H. McCarthy, Mayor of San Francisco, 1910–1912" (M.A. thesis, Department of History, University of California, 1949).   Neil L. Shumsky

McCARTHY, WILLIAM C. (1820–1900), Mayor of Pittsburgh (1866–68, 1875–78). McCarthy, popularly nicknamed "Roaring Bill," was born in Pittsburgh on 14 October 1820. Little is recalled of his family, though they were probably Scots-Irish and Presbyterian. He took up printing and then became a newspaper pressman. He was a member of the Duquesne Engine Company, a volunteer firemen's group, and early became prominent in city ward politics. Little is known of his marriage, but he had one daughter and an adopted son.

In the Republican primary of December 1865, McCarthy appeared to have lost to Mayor James Lowry (*q.v.*) by 158 votes but filed a challenge and became the nominee. Former Mayor George Wilson (*q.v.*) supported his opponent, James Blackmore of the People's party, but McCarthy won 2,936 to 2,883. During his second year in office, the city annexed what is now its East End and changed the date for electing municipal officers.

McCarthy was extremely partisan and refused to meet President Andrew Johnson when he visited the city. McCarthy dropped out of a primary fight in 1867, was defeated for city treasurer in 1868, but was elected to the select council the following year. At the time of his first term, Pittsburgh had a population of about 75,000 (120,000 at the time of his second term) with a mayor and two councils.

Nominated for mayor as an Independent in 1874, McCarthy used a faked charge of treason on the morning of election day to defeat John B. Guthrie (*q.v.*), Democrat, 7,515 to 6,445, for a three-year term. By this time, he was high in the Flinn-Magee political ring. During this administration, the city installed an equalization board to prevent inequities in assessment between wards. But Mayor McCarthy failed to keep the city in order at the time of the 1877 railroad riots.

In 1878, McCarthy was elected city controller and later was superintendent of the city poor farm, director of property, councilman, and alderman until he became senile. He died in Dixmont Hospital on 27 January 1900.

SOURCES: Allen Humphreys Kerr, "The Mayors and Recorders of Pittsburgh, 1816–1951" (typescript, 1952, Carnegie Library of Pittsburgh); Pittsburgh *Dispatch*, 26 January 1900; Pittsburgh *Post*, 28 January 1900.   *George Swetnam*

MACARTY, AUGUSTIN (1774–1844), Mayor of New Orleans (1815–20). Born in New Orleans on 10 January 1774, Macarty was descended from a family that had had great prominence during the Spanish period of control in Louisiana. Son of Augustin Guillaume de Macarty and Jeanne Chauvin, both Roman Catholics of French and Spanish ancestry, he was thus related to Don Esteban Miro, governor of the colony from 1785 to 1792.

By the early 1800s, the Macartys were among the prominent landholders in the new American territory of Orleans. Below New Orleans in St. Bernard Parish was Augustin's own plantation, bordered by the Rodriguez

Canal along which Jackson strung his earthworks defense against the British in 1814–15, and site of the Macarty mansion which served as the commander's field headquarters.

Macarty was elected to succeed the resigned Nicholas Girod (*q.v.*) as mayor of New Orleans in September 1815, without opposition. In the regular election of 1816, he defeated Ferdinand Percy by a vote of 813 to 87 and was successful again in 1818 with 354 votes to Nathan Morse's 222 and Joseph Roffignac's (*q.v.*) 69. Macarty's term was highlighted by the creation of the city's first board of health in 1817 and by the beginning of cobblestone-paving of the streets in that same year. Appointment of an inspector general of police brought some improvement to the community's safety, while public convenience was advanced by granting a contract for the city's first waterworks to the famous architect, Benjamin Latrobe, in March 1819. Cultural life was nurtured by a public loan of $15,000 to John Davis for completion of the Théâtre d'Orléans, center of much of the musical life of the community in the years ahead. New Orleans had 41,000 people at that time.

Macarty retired from office in May 1820 without seeking reelection. His attempt to win a place on the city council in 1824 failed badly. In national politics, he was a firm supporter of John Quincy Adams and Henry Clay against the Jacksonian Democrats.

Like many of his French-speaking compatriots, Macarty chose a domestic life with a free woman of color rather than one centered in the more conventional marriage relationship. His connection to Celeste Perrault lasted for a half century and was, of course, a matter of common knowledge. He died in New Orleans on 16 October 1844.

SOURCES: Marie L. Badillo et al., v. Francesco Teo, 6 La. Ann. 130 (1854); New Orleans *Daily Delta*, 31 December 1854; New Orleans *Louisiana Gazette*, 22 August, 7 and 23 September 1815; Succession Records, Orleans Parish (Louisiana), Second District Court, 1844.   *Joseph G. Tregle, Jr.*

McCLELLAN, GEORGE B., JR. (1865–1940), Mayor of New York (1904–1909). McClellan, born on 23 November 1865 in Dresden, Saxony, was the son of Civil War General George B. McClellan (1826–85) and Ellen (Marcy) McClellan, an Episcopalian family of Scots, Philadelphia descent on his father's side. The elder of two children, McClellan was educated at St. John's Boarding School and the College of New Jersey. He served as a newspaper reporter (New York *Morning Journal*, New York *World*, and New York *Herald*, in succession) while attending New York Law School; in 1892, he was admitted to the bar. In 1889, McClellan joined

Tammany Hall and eventually rose to the position of sachem. That same year he was appointed treasurer of the New York and Brooklyn Bridge, and in 1892 he was elected president of the city's board of aldermen. In 1895, McClellan began serving the first of five consecutive terms in the U.S. House of Representatives where he was a member of the Ways and Means Committee. McClellan married fellow New Yorker Georgiana L. Heckscher on 30 October 1889; they had no children.

In 1904, New York City had more than 3.5 million people and a mayor-board of aldermen form of government. In 1903, McClellan was recalled from Washington by Tammany chief Charles F. Murphy to run against incumbent reform Mayor Seth Low (*q.v.*), and he won by a total of 314,782 to 252,086. Two years later, McClellan was reelected, this time to a four-year term, by defeating William Randolph Hearst of the Municipal Ownership party and Republican William M. Ivins. When Hearst demanded a recount in the extremely close contest, McClellan's victory was upheld. The final vote totals were McClellan 228,397; Hearst 224,929; and Ivins 137,198.

During his first term, McClellan remained loyal to Tammany Hall, but after the 1905 election he broke with Murphy over a patronage dispute. His second term, therefore, was characterized by political independence and moderate attempts at reform. McClellan's achievements as mayor included the building of new bridges across the East River, the establishment of municipal ferries, the creation of a new system of docks, and construction of the city's Municipal Building. In 1904, the city's first subway was opened, and plans for its second were adopted during McClellan's second term. The mayor also received praise for authorizing a young lawyer, John Purroy Mitchel (*q.v.*), to investigate the presidents of Manhattan, Bronx, and Queens boroughs. As a result, two presidents were removed from office, and one resigned.

In 1909, McClellan decided not to run for reelection and opened a law practice in New York. The following year he accepted a professorship of economic history at Princeton University. McClellan also served in World War I, rising to the rank of lieutenant colonel in the Army. After the armistice, he returned to Princeton, where he remained until his retirement in 1931. An authority on Italian history, he wrote *The Oligarchy of Venice, Venice and Bonaparte*, and *Modern Italy*. He died in Washington, D.C., on 30 November 1940 and was buried in Arlington National Cemetery.

SOURCES: August Cerillo, Jr., "The Reform of Municipal Government in New York City: From Seth Low to John Purroy Mitchel," *New York Historical Society Quarterly* 57:1 (January 1973); New York *Times*, 27 December 1905, 14 February 1915, 1 December 1940; Harold C. Syrett, ed., *The Gentleman and the Tiger: The Auto-Biography of George B. McClellan, Jr.* (New York, 1956).

W. Roger Biles

McCLINTOCK, JONAS R. (1808–79), Mayor of Pittsburgh (1836–39). The "boy mayor" of Pittsburgh, and an exponent of strong mayoral power, McClintock was born on 8 January 1808 in Pittsburgh of an Irish Presbyterian family. His father, John McClintock, came from Ireland to Philadelphia and eventually moved to Pittsburgh where he bought property in 1812. He was first a farmer and later a hotel-keeper and became prosperous as owner of the Iron City Hotel. Young McClintock enrolled in Western University (now the University of Pittsburgh) and graduated in 1830 in medicine at the University of Maryland. He married Elizabeth Aubuthnot and, following her death, Rachel Graham in 1837. He and Rachel Graham had three sons and one daughter. McClintock was one of the organizers of the Duquesne Greys (15 July 1831), serving first as lieutenant and later as captain. He also was the founder of the Vigilant Fire Company. McClintock refused a commission as assistant surgeon in the regular army. He served as the almshouse and prison physician and worked heroically during the 1832 cholera epidemic, which earned him local popularity.

As a strong supporter of Andrew Jackson, McClintock was elected to the common council on 14 January 1834. He played an important mediating role during the "Vashon" interracial riots of 1834. He became president of the common council the following year but was never a member of the board of aldermen. Running against Matthew B. Lowrie (*q.v.*), McClintock won his first election as mayor on 12 January 1836, receiving 849 votes to 598. A Democrat, he was at twenty-seven the youngest man to be elected mayor of the city. During his service as mayor, the city had a population of about 18,500, with 1,826 houses assessed for water at that time. McClintock organized a police force with a captain, two lieutenants, and sixteen watchmen. The mayor went to Philadelphia to negotiate a $60,000 loan, at which time the councils voted to issue $100,000 in unsecured small notes ("shinplasters"). Upon his return, McClintock refused to sign the bills since they were unauthorized; the councils threatened his impeachment. McClintock stood firm, and the threat was not carried out.

McClintock ran again for office on 10 January 1837 on a nonpartisan "city" ticket and defeated William W. Irwin (*q.v.*) (1,061 to 204), the Anti-Mason and anti-Van Buren candidate. Pittsburgh enlarged its boundaries at this time (which resulted in a fifth ward), and the

Monongahela Navigation Service was improved with the erection of dams and locks, and the pavement and grading of the wharf. This established Pittsburgh as the future center of the United States for heavy industry. In 1838, McClintock ran on a city improvement ticket and again defeated Irwin (1,242 to 1,156), the Anti-Mason and Whig. McClintock did not run for a fourth term because of his father's death.

During his terms in office, McClintock was one of the more publicly active mayors in the country. He promoted the waterworks and gasworks, but did not fulfill his promise to plant shade trees on Duquesne Way. Following his service as mayor, he took a job as chemist of the Philadelphia mint (1840–47). He served as a member of the state legislature (1850–52) and during this time protested the repeal of the Ten Hour Law which prohibited children under twelve years of age from working in factories. McClintock was elected to the state Senate in 1853 and introduced legislation that resulted in Pittsburgh's first public high school.

During the Civil War, McClintock served as adjutant general to General William Wilkins, organizing a force of 3,500 men. In 1864, McClintock refused a nomination to run for Congress. He spent the latter part of his life compiling a history of Pittsburgh, writing it from 1876 until the time of his death. Unfortunately, this history was lost. McClintock died on 25 November 1879.

SOURCES: History of Allegheny County Pennsylvania (Philadelphia, 1876); Allen Humphrey Kerr, "The Mayors and Recorders of Pittsburgh, 1816–1951," (unpublished manuscript, Historical Society of Western Pennsylvania, Pittsburgh, 1952); Pittsburgh Press; Mayors' Notebook, No. 7, by George Swetnam, 22 September 1973.   Helene Smith

McCOPPIN, FRANK (1834–97), Mayor of San Francisco (1867–69). Second foreign-born mayor of San Francisco, McCoppin was an Irish Catholic, born in Longford, Ireland, on 4 July 1834. Little is known of his early life. An anti-Irish diatribe in a San Francisco political paper, Thistleton's Jolly Giant (15 November 1873), later claimed that he had been trained as a Dublin policeman, serving in Westmeath. Since he was only eighteen when his parents came to the United States in 1852, this claim seems doubtful. However poor in origin, he did manage to marry the daughter of a former blue-blood mayor, James Van Ness (q.v.). The McCoppin family lived in New York for six years, where Frank acquired engineering training, for in 1858, when they moved to San Francisco, he was made superintendent of construction of the city's first transit system, the Market Street Railroad. The railroad was formally dedicated by Mayor Henry Teschemaker (q.v.) on 4 July 1860.

McCoppin planted ground cover along the lines to prevent drifting sand—a major problem in those early days. He was elected to the board of supervisors in 1860 and served for four terms.

The street railroad engaged McCoppin's attention on the board; he opposed municipal ownership, though he favored regulation. (Street railroads became the classic issue in the history of many U.S. cities at this time, as a source of graft and political leverage.) McCoppin sided with Mayor Henry Coon (q.v.) in opposing the transfer of bonds to the Central Pacific Railroad, and he endorsed the federal government's action in finally ceding its pueblo land title claims to the city in 1866, an action attacked by the Evening Bulletin and those citizens who had hopes to land claims. In 1867, however, McCoppin was brought to power as mayor when the Democrats swept the state.

McCoppin's first months were promising, witnessing such events as the opening of a new drydock, the largest on the Pacific Coast, at Hunter's Point, financed by W. C. Ralston's local Bank of California. The mayor was involved in such issues as regulation of house-moving, which he claimed tore up the wooden-block streets and caused congestion. The city rejoiced when the transcontinental railroad was completed at Promontory Point, Utah, in May 1869, but the end of work there released thousands of "Crocker's Pets"—Chinese laborers imported for the work, who added to the growing numbers of unemployed in San Francisco. The city was going into a serious slump. Mining foundries and other factories closed, and the Chinese were often blamed for the depression and unemployment. Dennis Kearney, a drayman, led American workmen toward anti-Chinese agitation. The long boom was temporarily over.

In July, the Republican platform urged denial of citizenship to "Mongolians." McCoppin himself was attacked in the press, which claimed that he did not become a naturalized citizen until 12 December 1864, and had therefore been illegally elected to the board of supervisors in 1860. He was accused of rigging the Democratic convention when he was nominated for mayor. A new independent group selected Thomas H. Selby (q.v.), a native-born American from New York and a prominent local business leader. McCoppin lost his reelection bid on 1 September 1869 by a narrow margin—10,789 to 10,673. He relinquished the office of mayor on 6 December 1869.

McCoppin, being an Irish politician and a Democratic party stalwart, remained in public life to the very end. In 1871, he sought the party nomination for governor and served on the state central committee at the Sacramento convention. He was vice-president of the convention in 1872 and attended the national convention (along with the radical, Henry George) that summer. He was the Democratic nominee for state senator in September 1873 and lost, but was finally elected in 1875. In the state Senate, he sponsored fare-fixing (at 5 cents) for California street railroads and authored the McCoppin Act to impose upper limits on city spending. He was reelected for a second term. As late as 1886, he was still active in the party; he was nominated for the federal House of Representatives, losing only narrowly. In 1890, at least one paper, *The Wave*, suggested McCoppin as a likely candidate for mayor of San Francisco. The idea came to nothing, however. He died in San Francisco on 26 May 1897.

SOURCES: W. J. Davis, *History of Political Conventions in California* (Sacramento, 1893); W. F. Heintz, *San Francisco's Mayors* (Woodside, Calif., 1975); J. S. Hittell, *History of the City of San Francisco* (San Francisco, 1878); *Overland Monthly*, March 1910; R. R. Parkinson, *Pen Portraits* (San Francisco, 1878); *Thistleton's Jolly Giant* 1:10 (15 November 1873); *The Wave*, 11 October 1890.   *Peter d'A. Jones*

MacDOUGALL, FREDERICK ALEXANDER (1814–78), Mayor of Los Angeles (1876–78).

A relatively noncontroversial mayor, born in Scotland on 2 November 1814, and with an M.D. from Edinburgh University, MacDougall joined the Gold Rush and was naturalized in Monterey County on 22 August 1859. He settled at San Juan Bautista in the early 1850s and practiced his profession, becoming a local hero during a severe smallpox epidemic. Bishop Francis Mora, who knew him there, said he gave medical services to all who required them, regardless of whether they were able to remunerate him or not. Another townsman described MacDougall as "ready to go at any time of the day or night to treat a patient . . . it is doubtful if he ever got a quarter of the money due him for his services. He was never known to send any patient a bill."

At San Juan Bautista, in about 1859, MacDougall married a wealthy, landed Mexican Californian widow, María Antonia Castro de Anzar, who was also noted for many kindnesses. She died, in about 1867, leaving him with their stepchildren and two children of their own. MacDougall managed his late wife's estates well and through land developments became very prosperous. As a Democrat, he was elected to the Monterey Board of Supervisors (1860–61 and 1863–64); and from 1867 to 1871, he was a California state senator representing Monterey and Santa Cruz counties.

In the early 1870s, MacDougall moved to Los Angeles, where he was involved in land management and politics more than medicine. On 24 October 1868 he remarried another Mexican Californian, the widow of

Robert S. Carlisle by whom she had three children. She was Francisca Williams Carlisle, and she and MacDougall had three more children.

Like almost all nineteenth-century Los Angeles mayors, MacDougall was a self-made man. He was worth $47,000 in 1876 when the Democrats nominated him for mayor. Popular with all groups, MacDougall won an easy victory in December 1876; 921 votes against 621 (Esaac W. Lord) and 455 (Prudent Beaudry—*q.v.*). The new mayor promised to lower the general tax levy; city growth had brought more taxable wealth. He requested the appointment of a city auditor and, like other mayors, vainly sought a full-scale sewer system, primarily for health and convenience. As his city of nearly 15,000 was growing rapidly, the mayor advocated opening new streets and funds for increasing public school enrollments. In 1877, he admitted that city expenses had mounted, despite his efforts to hold them down, as a result of a smallpox outbreak. Happily, he could report improvements in street gas lighting and efficiency of the small fire department. During his term, the office of police chief was created, and he named its first holder in 1877. As mayor, MacDougall functioned as police commissioner. In spite of a disastrous drought, a national depression, limited powers, and, soon, reduced funds, he accomplished a great deal. In 1877, MacDougall recommended radical city charter changes, despite public opposition to such "tinkering." Ironically, he wanted a provision for clear succession in case of the deaths of mayor or councilmen.

On 13 November 1878, MacDougall, aged sixty-four, suffered a stroke of apoplexy while attending a political meeting, and he died on 16 November. His funeral took place the next day at the Roman Catholic plaza church. His remains were interred in the local Catholic cemetery. Even critics agreed that his large income had not conflicted with his public duties.

SOURCES: Fred W. Atkinson, *100 Years in the Pajaro Valley* (Watsonville, 1934); Esther Boulton Black, *Rancho Cucamonga and Dona Merced* (Redlands, Calif., 1975); *California Blue Book; Or, State Roster* (Sacramento, 1903); Council proceedings in files of 1876–78 Los Angeles *Star, Herald*, and *Express; History of San Benito County, California* (San Francisco, 1881); *Los Angeles County Great Register* (Los Angeles, 1872); Los Angeles Public Library pamphlet, "City Officials: Frederick A. MacDougall"; Marriage and death records, Los Angeles County Hall of Records; Isaac L. Mylar, *Early Days at the Mission San Juan Bautista* (Watsonville, 1929); Harris Newmark, *Sixty Years in Southern California, 1853–1913* (New York, 1916); *U.S. 8th Census, 1860*, "California: Population Schedules, Monterey County."   *John E. Baur*

MACK, ANDREW (1780–1854), Mayor of Detroit (1834–35). Mack was born in New London, Connecticut, on 19 November 1780. He had a limited education. As a youth, he became a sailor and eventually a ship's captain, sailing around the world three times. In 1808, he drove a herd of sheep from the East to Cincinnati where he settled. He was a captain and, later, a colonel of an Ohio company during the War of 1812, and served as a member of the Ohio legislature while he ran a hotel in Cincinnati. In 1829, Mack moved to Detroit where he was appointed collector of customs at the port, a position he held until 1839. He purchased the Mansion House Hotel in 1830 and ran it for three years. He became one of the proprietors of the *Democratic Free Press* in 1831. He married and had a son and an adopted daughter. He had no religious affiliation.

Mack, a Democrat, was elected mayor of Detroit on 24 September 1834, without opposition and received 91 votes to fill out the term of Charles C. Trowbridge (*q.v.*) who had resigned. Detroit had a population of 4,973 people in 1834 and a mayor-council form of government. Under Mack's leadership, the council decided to move to better quarters until a new city hall could be built. Early in 1835, the city government agreed to hire an accountant who could prepare a proper bookkeeping system for the city. The city watch was disbanded after a number of its members were found either drunk or neglecting their duties. In March 1835, Mayor Mack presided over a public meeting that protested Ohio's efforts to take the area around Toledo from Michigan—an action that failed and which has been known by the deceptive name "Toledo War." Mack's term as mayor ended 11 April 1835.

Mack was the Democratic-Republican candidate for appointment as governor of the Michigan Territory in 1836 but lost to Stevens T. Mason. He served in the state legislature in 1839. In the 1840s, he moved to his farm on the St. Clair River where he died on 12 July 1854.

SOURCES: Frederick Carlisle, comp., *Chronology of Notable Events in the History of the Northwest Territory and Wayne County* (Detroit, 1894); George B. Catlin, *The Story of Detroit* (Detroit, 1923); Detroit Common Council, *Journal of the Proceedings of the Common Council of the City of Detroit, 1824–1843* (n.p., n.d.); Silas Farmer, *History of Detroit and Wayne County and Early Michigan*, 3d ed. (1890; reprint, Detroit, 1969); *The Sunday News-Tribune*, 17 October 1894.

William T. Bulger

McKEE, JOSEPH V. (1889–1956), Acting Mayor of New York (1932). Acting mayor for four months in 1932, McKee was born on 8 August 1889 in Newark, New Jersey, the son of John B. McKee, an engraver from Glasgow, Scotland, and Margaret (Cotterson) McKee, also of Scottish ancestry. The family was Roman Catholic. McKee was educated in the Bronx public schools and Fordham University (B.A. and LL.B.). While studying law, he was a Greek and Latin instructor at Fordham and later taught the classics for three years at DeWitt Clinton High School in New York. He served for six years as a Tammany Democrat in the New York State Assembly and in 1924 was appointed to the city court by Governor Al Smith. The following year, McKee was elected president of the city's board of aldermen and was reelected four years later. On 27 November 1918, he married Cornelia Kraft, and they had two children (Joseph V., Jr., and Richard Phillip).

New York City in 1932 had a population of 7,218,223 and a mayor-board of aldermen form of government. McKee was serving as the president of the board of aldermen when embattled Mayor Jimmy Walker (*q.v.*) resigned on 1 September 1932. By provision of the city charter, McKee became acting mayor the next day and served in that capacity until a special election was held. Tammany Hall Democratic slate makers bypassed McKee in favor of John P. O'Brien (*q.v.*) as their mayoral candidate. While O'Brien was triumphant in the 8 November 1932 special election, McKee received 232,501 write-in votes. On 1 January 1933, McKee stepped down to resume the presidency of the board of aldermen.

McKee resigned on 15 May 1933 to become president of the Title Guarantee and Trust Company. In the 1933 election, Bronx Democratic leader Ed Flynn organized the Recovery party with McKee as its mayoral candidate, but the fusion candidate, Fiorello H. LaGuardia (*q.v.*), outpolled both McKee and the Tammany Democratic candidate, incumbent John P. O'Brien. The electoral results were LaGuardia 868,522, McKee 609,053, and O'Brien 586,672.

Following this last political defeat, McKee returned to the banking business. In 1949, he was named commissioner of commerce for New York City. McKee died of a heart attack in his home on 28 January 1956 and was buried in Gate of Heaven Cemetery in Valhalla, New York.

SOURCES: Paul Blanshard, "LaGuardia Versus McKee," *The Nation* 137 (25 October 1933); Arthur Mann, *LaGuardia Comes to Power, 1933* (Chicago, 1965); Allan Nevins and John A. Krout, eds., *The Greater City: New York, 1898–1948* (New York, 1948); New York *Times,* 29 January 1956 (obituary).

W. Roger Biles

McKELDIN, THEODORE ROOSEVELT (1900–1974), Mayor of Baltimore (1943–47, 1963–67). McKeldin was the tenth of eleven children born to James

A. McKeldin, a Scots-Irish, Methodist stonemason and later policeman who had emigrated from Belfast, and Dora Grief McKeldin, daughter of a German-American immigrant Baltimore family. Theodore attended Baltimore City public schools, Milton College, Baltimore College of Commerce, and Johns Hopkins University Graduate School (in economics), and graduated from the University of Maryland Law School in 1925. On 7 October 1924, McKeldin married Honolulu Clair Manzer (1900–), descended from an old New York family and a graduate of the Maryland Institute of Art. She worked at the First National Bank of Maryland and was an active painter. The McKeldins had two children, Theodore, Jr., and Clara Whitney (Mrs. Peter Ziegler).

Before becoming mayor, McKeldin served as secretary to Republican Mayor William Broening (q.v.) (1927–1931) and was a partner in the law firm of McKeldin and Moylan. McKeldin and his wife were members of the Episcopal Church of the Redeemer. He was a member of the Masons, Shrine, Moose, Knights of Pythias, Kiwanis, and the German Society of Maryland, and helped organize the Baltimore Junior Chamber of Commerce.

Baltimore in 1940 had 859,100 people and a mayor-council form of government. McKeldin was defeated in the 1939 mayoralty election by the popular Democrat Howard Jackson (q.v.), whom he then defeated in 1943, with the help of Democratic boss Jack Pollack, by a vote of 77,402 to 57,291. After two terms as governor of Maryland (1951–59), McKeldin was reelected mayor of Baltimore in 1963 over Philip Goodman (q.v.) by 108,365 votes to 103,741.

McKeldin, known as a liberal, was always popular with the city's black voters as well as ethnic groups, whose support he actively cultivated. His personality, manner, and liberal programs drew the support of many Democrats. While mayor, he sponsored the building of Friendship Airport and the Baltimore Civic Center. He was an active leader in a revision of the city charter.

After his second term as mayor, McKeldin was appointed to the Indian Claims Commission by President Lyndon Johnson. He continued to live in Baltimore until his death on 10 August 1974.

SOURCES: Biographical files at the Maryland Historical Society, the Enoch Pratt Free Library, and the Baltimore *Sun*; McKeldin Papers, University of Baltimore, Baltimore Region Institutional Studies Center.   *Suzanne Ellery Greene*

McKENNA, BERNARD (1842–1903), Mayor of Pittsburgh (1893–96). Irish Catholic Mayor McKenna was born in Pittsburgh on 16 February 1842, the son of James McKenna, an Irish immigrant who had been elected county commissioner as a Whig. He was apprenticed as

moulder in an iron foundry, and about the time this training ended, the Civil War began. He enlisted in the Gunboat Squadron which patrolled the Ohio and Mississippi valleys.

After the war, McKenna became treasurer of the Moulders' Union. He was captain of the Allegheny Volunteer Fire Company and became a paid fireman when the city adopted the plan in 1870. Two years later, he married Mary McShane, an Irish girl, who bore him a daughter and two sons. In 1875, McKenna was elected an alderman and was reelected three times, serving twenty years in all.

McKenna was helped by the tide that swept Grover Cleveland (q.v.) into office for a second term in 1892, but he was also a popular Civil War hero and fireman, and, though a Democrat, had been on good terms with the Republican machine for some years. He narrowly defeated Republican John S. Lambie (15,497 to 14,117). Pittsburgh was then a city of about 275,000 people, governed by a mayor and two councils.

When William McCallin (q.v.) defeated McKenna for mayor six years earlier, he named the loser police magistrate. McKenna's first action was to return the favor, naming McCallin magistrate. Despite the fact that Republicans controlled both councils, McKenna managed to work with them, for a generally successful term. The city got its first board of health, some bridges were freed of toll, and the Highland Park Zoo was built. When the Grand Army of the Republic held its national meeting in Pittsburgh in 1894, Mayor McKenna was elected national commander.

At the end of his term as mayor, Henry P. Ford (q.v.) named McKenna police magistrate, as did the following three city heads. He held the post until shortly before his death on 18 June 1903. He was buried in St. Mary's Cemetery, in the Lawrenceville section.

SOURCES: Allen Humphreys Kerr, "The Mayors and Recorders of Pittsburgh, 1816–1951" (typescript, 1952, Carnegie Library of Pittsburgh); Pittsburgh *Dispatch*, *Post* and *Press*, all 19 May 1903.   *George Swetnam*

MACKEY, HARRY (1873–1938), Mayor of Philadelphia (1928–32). Republican regular, born on 26 June 1873 in Susquehanna, Pennsylvania, Mackey was the son of George Mackey, a small-town, Baptist lawyer, and Isadora (MacCollum) Mackey. Young Mackey's early schooling was rural; he was a capable student and an athlete, and his football exploits gave him instant recognition. He was handsome and also vain, going out of his way to be photographed in public throughout his career. After obtaining his LL.B. from the University of Pennsylvania, he practiced law with the Honorable W. W. Porter and with the firm of J. W. Gordon (1898–1902);

from 1902 on he practiced alone. On February 1900 Mackey married Ida Boner; they had one daughter, Lorna. Mackey was an Episcopalian, Mason, Elk, Eagle, Red Man, and Forester; he was recognized as a "joiner" with rare oratorical skills.

Philadelphia in 1928 was a city of two million people. Mackey had been active in city politics since the reform movement of 1905. He was acting director of the Department of Health and Charities (1905–1907), a member of the common council (1908–10), director of the Department of Public Works (1911), chairman of the Pennsylvania Workmen's Compensation Board (1915–23), and city treasurer (1925–27). On 8 November 1927, running as a Republican regular, he defeated former Mayor J. Hampton Moore (q.v.) (Citizens' party, 296,959 to 128,611), Thomas A. Logue (Democrat, 9,902), and Joseph S. MacLaughlin (Charterite party, 3,605). Like his predecessor in Philadelphia's turbulent machine-oriented politics of the 1920s, Mackey experienced executive difficulties and was acutely embarrassed in August 1928 by a grand jury investigation of the connection among bootleggers, racketeers, and the police. Mackey broke with his sponsor, boss William S. Vare, over the issue of police appointments, but the mayor had suffered a great loss in public esteem. He later allied himself with Albert M. Greenfield, the Lithuanian-born real estate speculator and future Democratic financier, a relationship that brought Mackey considerable criticism.

Despite his apparent skills, Mackey's mayoralty was routine and workmanlike. Mackey was an ambassador of good will who left no discernible impression on the city or its politics. In 1932 he was unsuccessful in a bid for the state legislature. He returned to private practice and died on 17 October 1938.

SOURCES: *Annual Messages of the Mayor*, City of Philadelphia, Reports of the various departments; Herman L. Collins and Wilfred Jordan, *Philadelphia: A Story of Progress* (Philadelphia, 1941), vol. 1; *The Mayors of Philadelphia*, Collections of the Genealogical Society of Pennsylvania; J. T. Salter, *The People's Choice: Philadelphia's William S. Vare* (New York, 1971).

Richard A. Varbero

McKISSON, ROBERT E. (1863–1915), Mayor of Cleveland (1895–98). Cleveland's youngest mayor elected to that time and a reformer, McKisson was born on 30 January 1863 on a farm in Northfield, Ohio, the third of four children born to Martin Van Buren McKisson (1827–91), a Scots-Irish farmer, and Finette Adeline Eldridge, both old-stock Protestants. After moving to Lagrange, Ohio, where he attended high school, McKisson paid his own way through Oberlin College and taught before finally moving to Cleveland in 1887 as an

assistant in the law office of Webster and Angell. In 1889, he was admitted to the bar and became a partner in Webster, Angell and McKisson in 1891. After political defeat in 1899, he returned to private practice, forming the firm of McKisson and Minshall in 1905.

McKisson was married three times (1891, to Celia Watring, 1901 to Mamie Langenau, 1915 to Pauline E. Reed), the first two marriages ending in divorce (1900, 1912) and without any children. His third marriage, to Pauline Reed, also divorced and formerly from Buffalo, was performed while he was ill in bed, just prior to his death in October.

In 1894, McKisson entered Cleveland politics by winning a seat on the city council. Backed by Senator Theodore Burton, his law teacher, by Senator Joseph Faraker, and by a youthful faction of the Republican party, McKisson defeated the candidate of Mark Hanna in the Republican primary of 1895 and vigorously attacked and defeated Robert Blee (q.v.), the incumbent Democratic mayor, 25,058 to 17,850 in the regular election. At that time, the city's population was 352,600.

Like an earlier mayor, W. G. Rose (q.v.), McKisson believed that city government was a business corporation in which the citizens were stockholders. As mayor, he appointed a number of commissions composed of prominent citizens to study the needs of the city and called for increased bonded indebtedness at a time when most mayoral candidates spoke of retrenchment. Major projects started during his administration included widening and straightening of the Cuyahoga River, construction of a new water tunnel and an east-west sewer intercept, a program to purify the Cuyahoga, and the building of a garbage reduction plant, eventually taken over by the city. In 1897, McKisson was reelected over the Democratic nominee, John H. Farley (q.v.), 26,969 to 24,500, at a time when Cleveland's population totaled 385,500.

McKisson was not simply a pro-business mayor. In an action presaging that of reformer Tom Johnson (q.v.), he refused to grant fifty-year franchises to the street railways and called for a reduced fare, universal transfers, and contribution of a portion of gross receipts to the city. He also instituted a suit against the railroads, which were claiming some of the lakefront land owned by the city.

In early 1898, McKisson made a major political blunder by feuding with Mark Hanna and opposing his nomination for senator. Combining with the Democrats, McKisson came very close to defeating Hanna and taking the Senate seat for himself, but that ploy cost him the local support of many Republicans and of the *Leader*, the Republican newspaper. Running again in 1899, McKisson was accused of building a personal political machine and of having a "flower fund." He was opposed by a coalition of Hanna Republicans, Democrats, and middle-class reformers, and lost to John H. Farley, former Democratic mayor 30,329 to 33,234, while other Republicans were winning. In 1910, McKisson lost again in a primary bid against the Republican nominee, Herman Baehr (*q.v.*). He died on 14 October 1915 after an extended illness described as resulting from overwork.

SOURCES: William and Miriam Alburn, *This Cleveland of Ours* (Cleveland, 1933); Thomas F. Campbell, ''Background for Progressivism: Machine Politics in the Administration of Robert E. McKisson, Mayor of Cleveland, 1895–99'' (M.A. thesis, Western Reserve University, 1960); William R. Coates, *A History of Cuyahoga County and the City of Cleveland* (New York, 1924); Cleveland *Plain Dealer* and the *Leader; First, Third and Fourth Messages of R. E. McKisson as Mayor of the City of Cleveland* (Western Reserve Historical Society); W. R. Hopkins, ''The Street-Railroad Problem in Cleveland,'' *Economic Studies* (December 1896), vol. 1; Charles Kennedy, *Fifty Years of Cleveland, 1875–1925* (Cleveland, 1925); Samuel P. Orth, *A History of Cleveland, Ohio* (Cleveland, 1910); Joseph C. Smith, ed., *History of the Republican Party in Ohio*, 2 vols. (Chicago, 1898).

William D. Jenkins and *Thomas F. Campbell*

McLANE, ROBERT M. (1867–1904), Mayor of Baltimore (1903–1904). Democratic mayor during the 1904 fire, McLane was born on 20 November 1867 in Baltimore, the son of a wealthy capitalist, James F. McLane, and nephew of Robert M. McLane, ex-governor of Maryland (1883–85) and ambassador to France for President Cleveland (*q.v.*). The McLanes were an old established, Episcopal Maryland family. The future mayor attended private schools and was graduated from Johns Hopkins University and the University of Maryland Law School. He practiced law, was appointed assistant to the state's attorney in 1891, and deputy state's attorney in 1895. In 1899, he was elected state's attorney on the Democratic gubernatorial ticket and kept that position until his mayoral election in 1903.

Baltimore in 1903 had more than half a million people (508,937 by the 1900 Census), with a mayor-council form of government. McLane successfully challenged the incumbent mayor, Thomas G. Hayes (*q.v.*), in the Democratic primary, supported both by reformers and by the party organization. He narrowly defeated his Republican opponent, Congressman Frank Wachter, 46,852 to 46,288 in the mayoral election. He died in office a year later from a self-inflicted gunshot wound.

In his brief tenure, McLane continued the honest, efficient administration begun by his predecessor under the new charter of 1899. He supported a substantial program of planned public improvements for Baltimore, including construction of a sanitary sewage system, a park system, schools, firehouses, and paved roads. Following the great Baltimore fire of 7 February 1904, which destroyed much of the central business district, McLane appointed a citizens' emergency committee of business and professional leaders to plan the reconstruction of the burned district. Contemporaries praised McLane's first mayoral year as enlightened and progressive. He committed suicide on 30 May 1904.

SOURCES: Baltimore *News*, 1903 to 1904; Wilbur F. Coyle, *The Mayors of Baltimore* (Baltimore, 1919); James B. Crooks, *Politics and Progress: The Rise of Urban Progressivism in Baltimore, 1895–1911* (Baton Rouge, La., 1968); Clayton Colman Hall, *Baltimore, Its History and Its People* (New York, 1912); *Sun Almanac for 1904* (Baltimore, 1904); *Sun Almanac for 1905* (Baltimore, 1905).

James B. Crooks

McMICHAEL, MORTON (1807–79), Mayor of Philadelphia (1866–68). Born in Bordentown, New Jersey, on 2 October 1807, McMichael was the son of John McMichael (1777–1846), a Protestant Irishman who worked as a groundskeeper, and Hannah (Masters) McMichael. He was educated in local schools before his family moved to Philadelphia where he read law with a local lawyer, gaining admission to the bar in 1827. In 1831, he married Mary Estell of Philadelphia. They had eight children.

McMichael began an active career in journalism in 1826 when he became editor of the *Saturday Evening Post*. He resigned in 1831 to become editor of the newly established *Saturday Courier*. In 1836, he started the *Saturday News and Literary Gazette* with Louis A. Godey, serving as an editor of *Godey's Lady's Book* from 1842 to 1846. In 1847, he became joint owner with George Graham of the city's leading Whig paper, the *North American*, which merged later that year with the *U.S. Gazette*. He acquired sole ownership in 1854.

McMichael mixed his journalism with politics, serving as an alderman and police magistrate in the 1830s. In 1843, Whigs who hoped to pry loose traditionally loyal Irish voters from their Democratic allegiance, nominated McMichael for the county office of sheriff, claiming he was ''like General Jackson, the son of Irish parents, and, like him, every inch an Irishman.'' He won the sheriff's election, only to be faced with the responsibility in 1844 for quelling the worst riots in the city's history, which stemmed from conflicts between Irish and native-born workers. McMichael never adopted the strong law and order stand promoted by the nativist American Republicans. Instead, on his retirement from office in 1846, he turned to promoting the city's economic growth through the expansion of railroads and public improvements. Like Alexander Henry (*q.v.*), he helped form and lead the People's party in Philadelphia and sought reconciliation with the South before the Civil War, only reluctantly adopting an antislavery position.

When Henry declined to seek reelection in 1865, McMichael received the Republican nomination. Campaigning on a promise to extend Henry's commitment to develop the outer reaches of the city, McMichael swept the city's newer suburban wards, beating his Democratic opponent, Daniel Fox (*q.v.*), 44,617 to 39,511.

McMichael dedicated much of his administration to extending vital urban services to the suburbs. He also helped guide the acquisition of properties which were to form the city's first major park. Instead of seeking reelection in 1868, he joined the newly formed Fairmount Park Commission, serving as its president until his death in 1879. He remained active in politics, serving as temporary chairman of the national Republican convention in 1872, as a delegate to the Pennsylvania's fourth constitutional convention in 1873, and as a member of the board of overseers for the Centennial Exposition. He was a founder of the Union League Club during the Civil War and served as its president from 1870 to 1874. He died of heart disease on 6 January 1879.

SOURCES: Robert L. Bloom, "Morton McMichael's *North American*," *Pennsylvania Magazine of History and Biography* 77 (April 1953); William Dusinberre, *Civil War Issues in Philadelphia, 1856–1865* (Philadelphia, 1965); Michael Feldberg, *The Philadelphia Riots of 1844: A Study of Ethnic Conflict* (Westport, Conn., 1975); Howard Gillette, Jr., "Corrupt and Contented: Philadelphia's Political Machine, 1865–1887" (Ph.D. dissertation, Yale University, 1970); Charles Morris, ed., *Makers of Philadelphia* (Philadelphia, 1894). *Howard Gillette, Jr.*

McNAIR, WILLIAM NISSLEY (1880–1948), Mayor of Pittsburgh (1934–36). McNair's mayoralty was one of Pittsburgh's more tumultuous. He was born on 5 October 1880 in Middletown, Pennsylvania, to Alvin McNair, a building contractor, and Maria (Schwartz) McNair. They had at least one other son. McNair graduated from Harrisburg Academy in 1896, Gettysburg College in 1900, and the University of Michigan Law School in 1903. In 1904, he was admitted to the bar in Pittsburgh and on 14 April 1914 married Helen E. Seip, a daughter of Dr. C. P. Seip, a member of one of Pennsylvania's oldest families. The McNairs had two children: Helen (b. 1918), and Elizabeth (b. 1923).

McNair entered politics as a Democrat who opposed the common practice of the local party of trading Democratic votes to the Republican offering the most patronage. Several times an unsuccessful candidate before his mayoral race in 1933, McNair ran for district attorney in 1911; state secretary of internal affairs in 1914; mayor, opposing William A. Magee (*q.v.*), in 1923; and the U.S. Senate in 1928. In his 1933 mayoral bid, McNair had the backing of David Lawrence's (*q.v.*) Democratic organization and, benefiting from a reaction to Republican machine excesses, received substantial support from middle-class Independents and Republicans. These shifts, added to the Democratic gains of 1932, gave McNair a substantial victory of 103,119 to Republican John S. Herron's (*q.v.*) 75,786. McNair thus became Pittsburgh's first Democratic mayor in more than a quarter of a century. In 1930, the city had a mayor-council form of government and a population of 699,817.

Ideologically, McNair was closer to the Progressives of 1900 than to the New Dealers of 1932; he was an admirer of the late radical Henry George (1839–97), and a regular lecturer for the Henry George Lecture Association. As mayor, McNair devoted much of his attention to battling utilities and high transit fares. Breaking with the Democratic organization and pursuing his own course, McNair made questionable appointments, interfered in the health department, and fired four successive safety directors in his first year in office. McNair opposed New Deal relief measures and battled his own city council, as well as state and federal officials, to prevent installation of the programs in Pittsburgh. Overridden by his city council on participation and funding, McNair fought a rear-guard battle to limit the New Deal's effect on Pittsburgh. His efforts outraged local Democrats, and the party sought unsuccessfully to have him removed by the legislature. In April 1936, McNair spent two hours in jail for contempt of court; in the fall, the city experienced financial chaos when McNair fired his city treasurer and could not get a replacement confirmed by the council. On 6 October 1936, beaten and bitter, McNair resigned.

McNair resumed his practice of law and his propaganda for the Single Tax. In 1944, he served a term in the state legislature, and in 1948 he declared as a Democratic presidential candidate on a platform of unrestricted immigration, a return to the gold standard, an end to all tariffs, and the implementation of the Single Tax. He was not successful. McNair died soon after, on 9 September 1948, in the St. Louis union depot, while on his way to make a dinner speech. He was buried from Calvary Protestant Episcopal Church.

SOURCES: Allen Humphreys Kerr, "The Mayors and Recorders of Pittsburgh, 1816–1951: Their Lives and Somewhat of Their Times," (typescript, 1952, Carnegie Public Library, Pittsburgh); McNair papers, Archives of Industrial Society, Hillman Library, University of Pittsburgh; Bruce M. Stave, *The New Deal and the Last*

Hurrah: Pittsburgh Machine Politics (Pittsburgh, 1970).   *Douglas V. Shaw*

McSHANE, ANDREW JAMES (1865–1936), Mayor of New Orleans (1920–25). McShane was born in New Orleans on 2 January 1865, the son of Bernard and Rose (Fitzpatrick) McShane, both Irish-American Catholics. His early education in parochial schools was curtailed upon the death of his father. At the age of nine, he entered the hide business of Fitzpatrick and Hall (later H. F. Hall and Company). Five years later, he was promoted to the post of traveling salesman. He became a full partner when he was nineteen, and at the age of twenty-one he became sole owner of the firm, with offices in New York and New Orleans. Under his management the business was very successful. On 4 April 1918, he married Agnes Burns of New Orleans.

Throughout his adulthood, McShane was associated with the anti-machine faction in municipal politics. During the administrations of Walter Flower (*q.v.*) and Paul Capdeville (*q.v.*), he served on the board of fire commissioners. In 1912, McShane ran for the commission council on the Good Government League ticket and lost despite an impressive showing.

In July 1920, the Orleans Democratic Association nominated McShane for mayor. With the backing of Governor John M. Parker, he narrowly defeated Martin Behrman (*q.v.*), the incumbent, by a vote of 22,986 to 21,536. On 2 December 1920, McShane became mayor. The population of New Orleans was then 387,000. Attempts to reorganize city government, however, created political friction that persisted throughout his administration. Inexperience and diverging goals among his supporters also caused disruption. Nonetheless, his administration did improve the garbage collection system, revitalize the Department of Public Works, reform the municipal financial structure and institute a system of one-way streets to alleviate traffic problems.

In 1925, McShane made a last-minute attempt to win reelection, but he finished third behind Martin Behrman and Paul Maloney. On 4 May 1925, McShane left office and entered retirement. He died on 17 April 1936 in New Orleans.

SOURCES: Richard Dixon, ''New Orleans Mayors . . . Pilsbury to Behrman,'' *Roosevelt Review* 27 (May 1964); John Smith Kendall, *History of New Orleans* (Chicago, 1922), vol. 3; Andrew J. McShane, ''Administrations of the Mayors of New Orleans, 1803–1936'', (typescript compiled and edited by Works Progress Administration, New Orleans, 1940, New Orleans Public Library); New Orleans *Times-Picayune*, 18 April 1936.

Edward F. Haas

MAESTRI, ROBERT SIDNEY (1889–1974), Mayor of New Orleans (1936–46). Maestri was born in New Orleans on 11 December 1889, the son of Francis and Angele (Lacabe) Maestri, Italian-American Catholics. He attended public and parochial schools and the Soule College of Commerce, but his formal education was limited. At an early age, he worked in the family furniture store, ultimately becoming its manager, and developed substantial holdings in real estate and financial securities. During World War I, he served in the U.S. Army.

After the war, Maestri used his wealth to enter politics. In 1928, he contributed heavily to the successful gubernatorial candidacy of Huey P. Long and directed Long's campaign in New Orleans. The next year, he financed the defense when the state legislature launched impeachment proceedings against the new governor. In November 1929, Maestri became commissioner of conservation, a post he administered with businesslike efficiency while he sat on the Kingfish's inner council and headed the Louisiana Democratic Association, Long's organization.

After the death of Huey Long in September 1935, Maestri allied closely with Seymour Weiss and guided the Long machine in Louisiana. In 1936, he endorsed Richard W. Leche for governor and presided over the surrender of the New Orleans old regulars to the Longites. When Mayor T. Semmes Walmsley (*q.v.*) resigned on 30 June 1936, Maestri became the Democratic nominee to fill the unexpired term and ran without opposition. On 18 August 1936, he became mayor. At that time, New Orleans was 460,000 in size, with a mayor/commission-council form of government. New powers that the Leche-controlled state legislature had recently bestowed upon the urban chief executive permitted Maestri to dominate city government and politics in New Orleans. A constitutional amendment postponed the forthcoming mayoralty election of 1938 for an additional four years.

Maestri ran an active administration that renovated the city's fiscal structure in order to correct the financial shambles that the state legislature had created during the Long-Walmsley controversy. The new mayor improved municipal tax collection and embarked upon an economy program that featured the conservation of city funds and the renegotiation of municipal loans. By 4 March 1938 this new system had freed the city from its massive debts. An additional aid was the use of federal funds to finance public works projects. During these early years, Maestri showed special concern for the people and their needs.

The mayor, however, allowed vice and gambling to go unchecked in New Orleans and continued his political manipulations. In 1939, he became implicated in the Louisiana ''hot oil'' scandals, but he escaped conviction.

In 1940, Maestri backed the gubernatorial candidacy of Earl K. Long, Huey's brother. When Sam Houston Jones, the anti-Long candidate, won the election, Maestri negotiated a temporary alliance that helped to moderate the anti-Long reforms and lasted until 1942.

In that year, Maestri ran for reelection and won decisively over Shirley Wimberly by a vote of 75,713 to 10,919 and Herve Racivitch's 49,479. In the following years, negligence and the shortages of World War II undermined the virtues of Maestri's administration and highlighted its flaws. In 1945, complacency and factional conflict between the old regulars and the Louisiana Democratic Association further weakened the Maestri forces. On 22 January 1946, DeLesseps Story Morrison (*q.v.*), a war veteran and state representative, narrowly defeated Maestri in the mayoralty election.

A subsequent reorganization of the old regulars drove Maestri from power. In 1950, he again announced his candidacy for mayor, but he soon withdrew when Governor Earl Long favored another candidate. For the remainder of his life, Maestri tended his business affairs, lived quietly in the Roosevelt Hotel that Seymour Weiss owned, and worked periodically behind the scenes. He died in New Orleans on 6 May 1974.

SOURCES: Edward F. Haas, "New Orleans on the Half-Shell: The Maestri Era, 1936–1946," *Louisiana History* 13 (Summer 1972); "Robert S. Maestri," Administrations of the Mayors of New Orleans, 1803–1936 (typescript compiled and edited by Works Progress Administration, New Orleans, 1940, New Orleans Public Library).
Edward F. Haas

MAGEE, WILLIAM ADDISON (1873–1938), Mayor of Pittsburgh (1909–14, 1922–26). Magee was born in Pittsburgh on 4 May 1873, a son of Edward S. and Elizabeth Steel Magee. His father was a builder's supply dealer and a half-brother of Chris Magee, the city's Republican political boss. The Magees were Roman Catholic. After high school, Magee worked as a law clerk, studied law, and was admitted to the bar in 1893. From 1897 to 1899, he was an assistant district attorney, and from 1898 to 1901, a member of the city's select council. On the death of Christopher Magee, he was named to finish his uncle's term in the state Senate, and in 1901 he was elected to another term.

Magee left politics briefly, and then in 1906 was chosen Republican county chairman to lead a youth revolt against William Flinn, the surviving member of the Flinn-Magee ring. Three years later, he was elected mayor with 48,060 votes to a total of 19,549 for two reform rivals. At this time, Pittsburgh had a population of about 500,000 and a weak mayor-two-council system. An act of 1911 extended his term to almost five years

and changed the city to a strong mayor-small council system.

Magee's first term achieved a great deal, cutting a "hump" downtown and raising low streets, building bridges, removing grade crossings, motorizing police and firemen, reducing smoke by half, and making other improvements. In 1914, he returned to law practice, and two years later, he became a member of the state's first public service commission. Later he was elected to the council.

By 1922, the city had grown to about 620,000, and Magee defeated William N. McNair (*q.v.*), a Democratic fellow councilman, for mayor, 72,186 to 32,448. The city's borrowing power had been depleted by intervening regimes, but he achieved some improvements. Although eligible under a 1921 act to succeed himself, Magee was not nominated in 1925. He left politics until 1933, when he was elected to the council as an Independent Republican, also nominated as a Democrat. He doublecrossed his Democratic and Independent supporters in his council voting and tried for mayor again in 1937, but he failed to be nominated. He died of pneumonia on 25 March 1938.

SOURCES: Book of Prominent Pennsylvanians (Pittsburgh, 1913); *Greater Pittsburgh* (June 1941); Pittsburgh *Bulletin*, 24 August 1933; Pittsburgh *Press* and *Post-Gazette*, both 26 March 1938; *Western Pennsylvanians* (Pittsburgh, 1912).
George Swetnam

MAGUIRE, GEORGE (1796–1882); Mayor of St. Louis (1842). St. Louis's first Democrat, first Irish, and first foreign-born mayor, Maguire was born at Omagh, Ireland, in 1796. When he was a small child, his family emigrated to the United States and settled in Virginia. Little is known of Maguire's youth except that he served as a clerk in the federal Office of Indian Affairs. Around 1820, he moved from Virginia to St. Louis where he established a prosperous business in real estate. A Democrat, he was also active in the political affairs of the community and held a number of municipal offices. He worked in the City Land Office, served on the city council, and was a member of the House of Delegates, 1839–40. In 1833, he married Mary Amelia Provenchere; they had one child, a daughter, named Eulilie.

St. Louis had a population of 27,000 and a mayor-council form of government in 1842 when Maguire was elected to a one-year term as mayor of St. Louis, winning with 1,212 votes against 1,170 for Edward Chapless, 458 for Wilson Primm, and 38 for B. Cleland. Not surprisingly, since this was a time of rapid growth for St. Louis, the decisions of Maguire's administration reflected the city's growing complexity. Voting by secret ballot was introduced and, in order to accommodate the increasing population, another ward was added to the five already in existence. The comptroller was required to supply the council with semiannual budget reports to aid them in their deliberations. Street inspectors were also ordered to furnish the mayor with information concerning the number and type of violations of city ordinances. Finally, systems of inspection were instituted for wood and lumber as well as for pork and beef coming into the city.

After his term as mayor, Maguire again served on the city council and was a member of the board of aldermen, 1848–49. He remained a resident of St. Louis until his death on 11 October 1882.

SOURCES: Charles H. Cornwell, *St. Louis Mayors: Brief Biographies* (St. Louis, 1965); Richard Edwards and M. Hopewell, *Edwards' Great West* (St. Louis, 1860); Walter B. Stevens, *St. Louis: History of the Fourth City, 1764–1909* (St. Louis, 1909).

Jeanette C. Lauer

MAHOOL, J. BARRY (1870–1935), Mayor of Baltimore (1907–11). Progressive Democratic mayor, born on 14 September 1870 in Baltimore County, Maryland, the son of a textile manufacturer and Confederate veteran, Colonel James M. Mahool, and Fannie (Hammond), of Scots-Irish descent, Mahool attended Baltimore public schools and then entered the grain commission business with a prominent local firm eventually becoming a partner. He married the boss's daughter (Mary Frame, 19 October 1893) and had two sons. He was ordained a Presbyterian elder and was listed in the Baltimore *Social Register* for 1909. Mahool entered politics in 1903 as an elected city councilman and spoke in support of urban reform.

Baltimore's population in 1907 was approaching 558,485 (1910 Census), and the city had a strong mayor-council form of government. Mahool's nomination for mayor in 1907 unified party supporters in this predominantly Democratic city, and he defeated his popular opponent, the incumbent E. Clay Timanus (*q.v.*) 48,254 to 43,584. Mahool entered office with reform well underway. The power of the political bosses had been curtailed; honest elections had become the norm; a new charter of 1899 had modernized city government; the passage of bond referenda had authorized a planned program of public improvements, including the construction of a sewage system, parks, schools, firehouse, roads, and docks; and child labor and public health laws had been passed. Mahool identified himself as a Progressive. He supported woman's suffrage, home rule, reapportionment, charter revision, civil service reform, governmental regulation of public utilities, recreation programs, tenement reform, clean air and water, hygienic standards

for dairies, bakeries, restaurants and slaughterhouses, and improved services for the poorer neighborhoods of Baltimore. He was an energetic administrator; the Baltimore *News* called him "the greatest human dynamo it has known in office." Mahool supported the formation of the first city-wide congress in Baltimore to discuss a wide range of urban issues, including public health, administration, city planning, taxation, and social justice.

Mahool was defeated by James H. Preston (*q.v.*) in the 1911 Democratic primary 30,000 to 20,715, when a revitalized political machine under John J. "Sonny" Mahon once again directed the future of the Democratic party. Mahool subsequently served as a member of the state tax commission in 1913, was appointed president of the Second Branch of the city council in 1918, was defeated for election as a city councilman in 1919, and was appointed to the Public Improvement Commission of Baltimore under Mayor William Broening (*q.v.*). Mahool died on 29 July 1935.

SOURCES: Baltimore *News* and Baltimore *Sun*, 1907–11; Wilbur F. Coyle, *The Mayors of Baltimore* (Baltimore, 1919); James B. Crooks, *Politics and Progress: The Rise of Urban Progressivism in Baltimore, 1895–1911* (Baton Rouge, La., 1968); The Mayors' Papers (Mahool), Baltimore City Hall; *Sun Almanac for 1908* (Baltimore, 1908); *Sun Almanac for 1912* (Baltimore, 1912).

James B. Crooks

MAIER, HENRY WALTER (1918–), Mayor of Milwaukee (1960–). Maier was born Henry Walter Nelke at Dayton, Ohio on 7 February 1918, the son of Marie L. (Kniseley) Nelke (1898–1977), an Ohio-born Lutheran of Pennsylvania Dutch heritage, and Henry Nelke (1898–1919), a photographer. Widowed at nineteen, Marie Nelke left her son with her parents in Springfield, Ohio, and moved to Milwaukee where she married a Wisconsin contractor, Charles P. Maier (1898–1974). Following high school graduation, Henry Nelke came to Milwaukee and changed his name to Maier. After graduating from the University of Wisconsin in 1940, Maier served as a Navy lieutenant during World War II. In 1941, he married an Irish Catholic, Mary Ann Monaghan, a Springfield, Ohio, nurse. Two daughters, Melinda and Melanie, were born during a thirty-two year marriage which ended in divorce in 1973. In 1976, Maier married Atlanta-born Karen Lamb, a nursing professor formerly active in Arizona feminist and Democratic politics.

Maier entered politics in the late 1940s, finishing sixth of fifteen in the 1948 Milwaukee mayoral primary. Elected to the state Senate in 1950, he became Democratic floor leader in 1953. In 1960, Maier topped Henry

S. Reuss 132,332 to 96,642, to become mayor of Milwaukee, a city of 741,324 residents. Maier was reelected four times: he defeated Arthur W. Else in 1964 (122,476 to 90,346); David L. Walther in 1968 (172,156 to 27,936); Bernard Novak in 1972 (140,390 to 66,395); and Jan Olson in 1976 (126,692 to 36,925). In 1964, Maier earned an M.A. in political science in night school at the University of Wisconsin-Milwaukee, while working as mayor. His *Challenge to the Cities: An Approach to a Theory of Urban Leadership* was published in 1966.

In twenty years as mayor, Maier has secured tremendous power in Milwaukee's mayor-council government through his ability to "enroll" support for his programs and through appointment power enhanced by his longevity in office. Effective opposition is infrequent, and Maier's control of the budget is rarely challenged.

But Milwaukee's problems during the Maier years have presented a continuing challenge. Civil rights advocates criticized Maier's employment of the National Guard during rioting by blacks in 1967, his opposition to "city only" open housing legislation, and his failure to encourage low-income public housing while supporting it for the elderly. Economically, the city retains a triple-A credit rating, but attracting industry and keeping established businesses have been difficult. Seeking to stem suburban flight, Maier has attempted a downtown "renaissance" with property tax incentives and has opposed most additional expressway construction. "Summerfest," an annual festival introduced in 1968, has successfully promoted tourism and recreation.

Maier has sought an image as a national urban spokesman. He was among the first in the mid-1960s to urge a reordering of national priorities to channel more money into cities. He lobbied effectively in the early 1970s for Wisconsin's tax-sharing reform and for federal revenue-sharing legislation. Past president of the U.S. Conference of Mayors, the National League of Cities, and the National Coalition of Democratic Mayors, Maier was mentioned as a possible Democratic vice-presidential candidate in 1972 and 1976.

SOURCES: Henry W. Maier, *Challenge to the Cities: An Approach to a Theory of Urban Leadership* (New York, 1966); "Henry W. Maier," City Government Clipping File, Milwaukee County Historical Society; "Henry W. Maier," Mayor's File, Municipal Reference Library, Milwaukee; "The Maier Years," Milwaukee *Journal*, 19–24 October 1975; Milwaukee *Sentinel*, 25 September 1971, 20–31 March 1972; *Newsweek*, 23 August 1971.   *Barbara M. Posadas*

MAKOWSKI, STANLEY M. (1923–   ), Mayor of Buffalo (1974–77). Born in Buffalo on 22 April 1923, Makowski was the son of Stanislaw Makowski

(1889–1965), a laborer, and Rosalia (Orzel) Makowski, both Polish Catholic immigrants. The youngest of two children, Makowski attended local schools and Millard Fillmore High School. He served with the U.S. Army, 1943–46, after which he returned to school, graduating from the State University of New York and Cornell University. He worked for several years as a machine press operator and as a grain mill worker. On 7 August 1954 he married Florence Ziolo, also a Catholic (1930–   ) of Buffalo, and they had eight children. Makowski belonged to the American Legion, Veterans of Foreign Wars, and other veterans' organizations.

A Democrat, Makowski entered public life as a member of the Erie County Board of Supervisors in 1956–59. He served as alderman (1960–69), becoming Democratic floor leader in the city council in his last term. In 1970–71, Makowski was confidential aide to Mayor Sedita (*q.v.*) and was considered Sedita's protégé. He was deputy mayor in 1972–73, and when Sedita resigned in 1973, Makowski became the city's fourth Polish mayor. Buffalo had 462,768 people in 1970, a declining population, and a mayor-council form of government. In November 1970, Makowski was elected to a full term, defeating Republican Stewart M. Levy 77,569 to 24,423.

As mayor, Makowski faced serious financial problems, including a 15-percent unemployment rate. He supported all efforts to win additional federal and state aid, and by the time his term ended Buffalo had overcome a $16 million deficit. Makowski backed plans to rebuild the downtown area, using city bond sales to finance construction. He supported a new theater district, new parks, better public transit, and an improved urban environment. At the beginning of his term, he laid off 800 city workers, saving the city $7.5 million but alienating the workers. Critics charged that Makowski was indecisive and lacked Sedita's flair for politics. The mayor himself felt he was too sensitive and too concerned about human problems. He thought his major success was getting the public more involved in political affairs. His declining standing in public opinion polls, and continuing problems (including his handling of the recordbreaking snowfall of 1976–77) caused Makowski to abandon plans to seek a second term in 1977. He was appointed to the State Industries Board of Appeals in 1978 for a five-year term.

SOURCES: Buffalo *Courier-Express*, 14 November 1977; Buffalo *Evening News*, 17 September 1977; Letter from Mayor Stanley M. Makowski to author, 24 September 1979.   *Thomas R. Bullard*

MALSTER, WILLIAM T. (1843–1907), Mayor of Baltimore (1897–99). Republican mayor in a predominantly Democratic city, and born on 4 April 1843 in Chesapeake City, Cecil County, Maryland, of obscure origins, Malster moved to Baltimore as a young man. He first worked as a watchman on the wharves and then became a fireman on the Bay Steamship line. Later an engineer and machinist, he opened his own machine shop in 1871 and built his first ship in 1878. By 1884, Malster was president of the Columbian Iron Works and was constructing ships for the U.S. Navy. Although circumstances subsequently forced him into bankruptcy, he later returned to head the Columbian Iron Works and Dry Dock Company.

Malster enjoyed participating in local Republican politics. He ran for mayor in 1893, losing to eight-time Mayor Ferdinand C. Latrobe (*q.v.*) 38,423 to 31,627 votes. He tried again in 1895 and failed to secure the Republican nomination when reformers defeated the incumbent Democratic machine for the first time since the Civil War. On his third try, after his party had repudiated the reform incumbent, Alcaeus Hooper (*q.v.*), Malster defeated machine-backed Democrat Henry Williams in the mayoral election of 1897 by 54,588 to 47,929.

Baltimore in 1897 was a city of about 500,000 people with a weak mayor-council form of government. It was also the largest unsewered city in the nation, with many unpaved streets, a backward school system, a large and segregated black population, and a strong Democratic boss. Since the long reign of Democratic mayors had ended two years previously, Malster rode the crest of a reform surge. He appointed a commission of leading citizens to draft a new charter to modernize city government, replacing the original document of 1796. The commission proposed professionalizing the school administration, limiting utility franchises, and shifting political power away from the boss- and ward-controlled council to the mayor. The document was similar to charters passed earlier in New York, Detroit, and Toledo, although it failed to introduce full civil service reform or a unicameral council. A Republican state legislature enacted the new charter in 1899.

While applauding the charter, reformers became increasingly critical of Malster's appointments to city jobs and of the increasing cost of local government. They believed the big, good-natured, well-intentioned mayor was being manipulated by party spoilsmen, and they organized to defeat him in 1899. Malster ran for reelection but was beaten by his Democratic opponent, Thomas G. Hayes (*q.v.*), 49,948 to 57,660.

After 1899, Malster returned to his shipbuilding business and served as naval officer for the port of Baltimore. He died on 2 March 1907.

SOURCES: Baltimore *News*, 1897–1899, *passim*; Wilbur F. Coyle, *The Mayors of Baltimore* (Baltimore, 1919); James B. Crooks, *Politics and Progress: The Rise of Urban Progressivism in Baltimore, 1895–1911* (Baton Rouge, La., 1968); *Sun Almanac for 1894* (Baltimore, 1894); *Sun Almanac for 1898* (Baltimore, 1898); *Sun Almanac for 1900* (Baltimore, 1900).

James B. Crooks

MANNING, JOHN BAKER (1833–1908), Mayor of Buffalo (1883). Businessman and Democratic politician, born on 13 July 1833 in Albany, New York, Manning was the son of John Manning (d. 1837), an Irish Catholic immigrant, and Eleanor (Oley) Manning, of Dutch ancestry. He attended local Albany schools until 1845 when he was appointed a page to the General Assembly. In 1847 he became a page in the state Senate, serving for two years. Manning moved to Buffalo in 1856 and entered the malting business, becoming successful and opening a branch in Canada in 1859. He was the Albany correspondent for the Brooklyn *Eagle*, 1860–61, beginning his association with Democratic politicians in New York State. He served as a member of the board of trade in Buffalo (president in 1881). In 1856, he married Elizabeth House of Cambridge, New York; they had seven children. The Mannings were Roman Catholics, and John Manning was also a Mason and a member of the Knights Templar.

Manning was elected First Ward supervisor in 1871 and held the same position in the Eighth Ward in 1873. Manning and his more famous older brother, Daniel (1831–87), gained some prominence by helping Grover Cleveland (*q.v.*) win the 1882 gubernatorial nomination. Manning was chosen by the local Democratic machine to run in the special election, 9 January 1883, to complete the remainder of Cleveland's mayoral term. He defeated Republican Robert Hefford 11,036 to 7,321. Buffalo had almost 200,000 people in 1883 and a mayor-council form of government.

Although a Democrat, Manning was not a strong partisan, claiming that the mayor should represent all elements in society. He vetoed measures for street lighting and a special land grant to local railroads, insisting that he would not support ''grabs'' by private business. Accused of trying to build a personal machine, Manning was denied his party's renomination in November 1883. He returned to his malting business and died on 28 April 1908.

SOURCES: William H. Dolan and Mark S. Hubbell, *Our Police and Our City* (Buffalo, 1893); Sister Mary Jane and Sister Mercedes, ''Mayors of Buffalo, 1832–1961,'' (B.A. thesis, Rosary Hill College, 1961); H. Perry Smith, ed., *History of the City of Buffalo & Erie County*, 2 vols. (Syracuse, N.Y., 1884).

Thomas R. Bullard

MANSFIELD, FREDERICK W. (1877–1958), Mayor of Boston (1934–38). New Deal era Mayor, born on 26

March 1877 in East Boston, Mansfield was the fourth-born of five children of Michael Read Mansfield (1843–1913), an Irish immigrant carpenter, and Catherine (McDonough) Mansfield (1845–1916), also a native of Ireland. He attended local schools and worked as an errand boy and apprentice in an East Boston drugstore. Mansfield became a registered pharmacist and served as an apothecary on the U.S.S. *Vulcan* during the Spanish-American War. Upon discharge from the Navy in 1899, Mansfield managed a pharmacy and studied law at Boston University Law School. He received his LL.B. and was admitted to the bar in 1902. Mansfield married Helena Elizabeth Roe, an Irish-American bookkeeper from East Boston, in 1904. They had one son, Walter R.

As a young attorney, Mansfield took on the job of counsel for a number of labor organizations, including the Massachusetts branch of the American Federation of Labor. He argued labor's cases before the courts and drafted the eight-hour bill and most of the other major labor legislation considered by the state legislature. A devout Roman Catholic, Mansfield founded the Catholic Lawyers League, which was dedicated to convincing Catholic attorneys not to take divorce cases, and was a Knight of the Equestrian Order of the Holy Sepulchre and a member of the Catholic Alumni Sodality, the Catholic Order of Foresters, and the Knights of Columbus.

Also active in Democratic party politics, Mansfield was nominated for state treasurer in 1913. When the majority Republicans split into opposing regular and Theodore Roosevelt Progressive camps, he was elected in a Democratic sweep. At the head of his ticket, David I. Walsh became the Bay State's first Catholic governor. In 1914, the Progressive vote diminished and, although Walsh survived, Mansfield and most of the other Democrats were defeated for reelection. Mansfield nonetheless remained a strong party figure and was the unsuccessful Democratic candidate for governor in 1916 and 1917 against Republican Samuel W. McCall.

In the 1920s, as president of the Massachusetts Bar Association, Mansfield prosecuted the disbarment of former state Attorney General Arthur Reading, who had been accused of improper conduct in public office. In 1929, the Good Government Association (GGA) of Boston, a Progressive Era relic on its last legs, chose Mansfield as its candidate for mayor. He lost, with 96,626 votes to James Michael Curley's (*q.v.*) 117,084. In 1933, with Curley forbidden by law to succeed himself, Mansfield ran again as the GGA's last endorsed candidate. This time he won with 70,035 to Malcolm E. Nichols' 68,312, William J. Foley's 60,776, Henry Parkman, Jr.'s 29,012, Joseph F. O'Connell's 9,961, and Michael H. Sullivan's 9,127.

Boston in the Great Depression was a city of some 781,000. By 1934, over 40,000 families were on relief, and the city had a cash deficit of $15 million. Thus, Mansfield, who had run on a platform of fiscal conservatism, had to adjust his views to the crisis situation. Although he was unable to reduce taxes, the mayor did manage to cut costs some by modernizing the accounting system and reorganizing the city welfare department. At the same time, he resisted business demands for wholesale layoffs of city employees and saw to it that more families were made eligible for relief. In addition, although he was a member of the conservative Ely-Walsh wing of his party and often disagreed with the philosophy and methods of the New Deal, Mansfield dutifully traveled to Washington and successfully obtained Works Progress Administration funds for projects and thousands of jobs for Boston. When he left office in 1938, Mansfield had reduced the city debt and had a modest record of achievement in putting people to work and easing suffering in a Boston wracked by depression. Perhaps as a result, voters chose Maurice J. Tobin (*q.v.*), a like-minded Democrat, to succeed him.

After his mayoralty, Mansfield practiced law, lectured on labor relations at Boston University Law School (1940–45), and was legal adviser for his friend William Cardinal O'Connell and the Catholic Archdiocese of Boston. In the last-named role, he led the fight against changes in the birth control laws of Massachusetts in the 1940s. Mansfield died of a heart ailment on 6 November 1958 and was buried in Brookline, Massachusetts.

SOURCES: City Record, 1934–1938, Government Documents Department, Boston Public Library; Documents of the City of Boston, 1934–38, Microtext Department, Boston Public Library; *Proceedings of the City Council of Boston*, 1934–1938, Government Documents Department, Boston Public Library; Good Government Association of Boston Papers, Massachusetts Historical Society; Frederick W. Mansfield, *Keeping Faith* (Haverhill, Mass., 1920); Frederick W. Mansfield, "The Relations of Labor Unions to Church and State," in *Addresses at Patriotic and Civic Occasions by Catholic Orators, 1915*, vol. 1; Frederick W. Mansfield clippings, Newspaper Morgue, School of Public Communication, Boston University; Frederick W. Mansfield Papers, Boston Public Library; Boston *Globe*, 7 November 1958 (obituary); Charles H. Trout, *Boston, The Great Depression and the New Deal* (New York, 1977).

Richard H. Gentile

MARCHESSAULT, DAMIEN (1821–68), Mayor of Los Angeles (1859–60, 1861–65, 1867). Multiterm, and first French-Canadian mayor of Los Angeles, Marchessault was born in Montreal in about 1821. According to some accounts, he went to New Orleans where he worked as a gambler, a profession he may also have followed when he first arrived in Los Angeles. The city's sizable French-speaking community from Canada, Switzerland, and France included several relatives. In partnership with them, Marchessault opened a restaurant in 1857, which was later expanded to an ice cream saloon and ice house. The ice was imported from the San Bernardino Mountains by 30-mule teams. The following year, he also organized a company to mine for gold in the Santa Anita district, about twenty miles east of Los Angeles. Neither business seems to have been particularly successful.

In May 1858 Marchessault ran unsuccessfully for the common council. The next year he ran for mayor as a proslavery Democrat against antislavery Democrat "Juan" Warner and won 400 to 258. After his one-year term, he did not run for reelection as mayor but received the largest number of votes for the council. When his successor as mayor died in office in late 1860, Marchessault ran to replace him in January 1861 and received 249 votes to 116 for William Potter and 114 for John Nichols (*q.v.*). He then won four more consecutive terms, winning without opposition in 1861 and 1862, defeating W. H. Peterson of a "Peoples' Ticket" 347 to 223 in 1863 and outpolling Union candidate Nichols 295 to 287 in 1864. The following year the Union party swept city offices, but in 1866 Marchessault ran again as an Independent Democrat and received 206 votes but lost to regular Democrat Christopher Aguilar's (*q.v.*) 213. Regular Republican Moore received 121 votes, and Independent Republican Mascarel (*q.v.*) got 71. The political situation was less fragmented in 1867, and Marchessault defeated Mascarel 388 to 296. The state, however, invalidated that election and Marchessault served only from May to August 1867.

During Marchessault's interrupted tenure as mayor, from May 1859 to August 1867, Los Angeles grew from about 4,000 to 5,300 residents. For the growing city, a major concern was to replace its crude water system of open ditches with regular pipes. Marchessault attempted to arrange the lease of the city's water rights to a private concern, several of which failed financially and technically. He himself participated in some of the water companies and reportedly was severely embarrassed when pipes leaked and turned the streets into quagmires. On 20 January 1868, he shot and killed himself in the deserted council chambers, with subsequent accounts attributing his suicide to his humiliation over the water issue. The day after his death, however, his widow Mary, for whom no previous records existed, released a note in which he blamed his drinking, gambling, indebtedness, and rejection of her advice to earn an honest living.

SOURCES: Los Angeles *Semi-Weekly News*, 24 January 1868; Maurice H. Newmark and Marco R. New-mark, eds., *Sixty Years in Southern California, 1853–1913; Containing the Reminiscences of Harris Newmark*, 4th ed. (Los Angeles, 1970); Leonard Ross Sanders, "Los Angeles and its Mayors, 1850–1925" (M.A. thesis, University of Southern California, 1968).

R. David Weber

MARKBREIT, LEOPOLD (1842–1909), Mayor of Cincinnati (1908–1909). Austrian-born mayor and ethnic newspaper publisher, Markbreit was born in Vienna on 13 March 1842. With his parents, Leopold (d. 1849) and Jane (Abiele) Markbreit (d. 1890), and two sisters, Markbreit emigrated to Cincinnati in 1848, the year of revolutionary upheavals in Central Europe. Markbreit attended schools in Cincinnati, Sandusky, and Philadelphia, and concluded his education by reading law with the Cincinnati *Volksblatt* editor, Frederick Hassaurek. A venture into law practice with future U.S. President Rutherford B. Hayes ended with the outbreak of Civil War when both men enlisted. Markbreit served with the Twenty-eighth Ohio Valley Infantry as a sergeant until his capture and imprisonment at Libby Prison, Richmond, in late 1863. After release, Markbreit returned to Cincinnati a major and earned the rank of colonel on the staffs of Governors James M. Cox and Rutherford B. Hayes. Markbreit was sent to Bolivia in 1869 as a special U.S. ambassador, and to Bolivia and Brazil in 1872 as the representative of American steamship and railway lines. In February 1882, Markbreit became the U.S. assistant treasurer at Cincinnati, and in 1886, he gave up that appointment to assume editorial and corporate responsibility for the German language newspaper, the *Volksblatt*. On 19 July 1887, he married a German actress born in Breslau, Bertha Fiebach (d. 1937), who had made successful stage tours of Europe and America; they had no children.

Markbreit was an active Republican and served as a commissioner of waterworks, 1896–1907. He was selected in 1907 as the mayoral candidate of the Cincinnati Republican party, which had split during and after the municipal elections of 1905. The election of 1907 saw Markbreit pitted against the incumbent Democratic mayor, Edward J. Dempsey (*q.v.*), who had lost the support of a 1905 coalition, and a "City party" candidate, Frank Pfaff. Markbreit's 43,841 votes gave him a large plurality over Dempsey, with 23,566, and Pfaff, with 10,508.

Markbreit came to office in a city of some 380,000 people, with a mayor-council form of government. His term of office was especially short, for he became ill in the winter of 1908–1909 and died in July 1909. While in office, Markbreit followed the kind of policies introduced by Julius Fleischmann (*q.v.*) in 1900 and followed by all succeeding Republican mayors of the first decade of the twentieth century. These included improvement of municipal services, with emphasis on health, parks, and street resurfacing, and the maintenance of a low city tax rate. Markbreit's successor, John Galvin (*q.v.*), stood behind a bond issue presented at the 1909 elections to determine citizen priorities and to obtain their funding.

Markbreit died in office on 27 July 1909; the city prepared public tributes in German and in English, at an Episcopal and a German Lutheran church. Active in civic affairs, Markbreit was closely associated with the Republican party and, through his newspaper, with the city's German population and its journalists. He was buried in his home city of Cincinnati, where his wife remained in their home in fashionable Walnut Hills until her death in 1937.

SOURCES: Annual Reports of the City of Cincinnati for the years 1908 and 1909; Cincinnati *Enquirer*; Cincinnati *Volksblatt*; Charles Theodore Greve, *Centennial History of Cincinnati and Representative Citizens* (Chicago, 1904); Zane L. Miller, *Boss Cox's Cincinnati: Urban Politics in the Progressive Era* (New York, 1968).

Judith Spraul-Schmidt

MARTIN, AUGUSTUS PEARL (1835–1902), Mayor of Boston (1884). Martin was born on 23 November 1835 at Abbott, Maine, the son of Pearl Martin (a storekeeper) and Betsey Verrill (Rollings) Martin of New Gloucester, Maine. He was descended from Robert Martin of Dover, New Hampshire, a farmer and veteran of the French and Indian War, and, on his mother's side, from Nicholas Rollings, a veteran of King Philip's War. At age seven, he accompanied his parents to Boston, where he attended the public schools, a private school in Melrose, and the Wesleyan Academy in Wilbraham. He began professional life as a salesman in the boot and shoe firm of Fay and Stone, but following the outbreak of war in April 1861, he joined the Third Massachusetts Battery (Twenty-Second Regiment) and two years later assumed command of the artillery brigade for the Fifth Corps, Army of the Potomac, distinguishing himself at Gettysburg with a courageous defense of a strategic position.

Following the war, Martin returned to Fay and Stone for two years, joined the firm of Francis Dane and Company as partner, and in 1871 founded A. P. Martin and Company, producers of boots and shoes. Meanwhile, he was director of the John Hancock Life Insurance Company and the Howard National Bank; president of the New England Shoe and Leather Association, the Tapley Machine Company, and the New England Mutual Aid Society; and member of the Athletic and Algonquin clubs of Boston and the Norfolk Unitarian Church in Dorchester. On 3 February 1859, he married Abbie Farmer Peirce, daughter of Jonathan and Elizabeth Barry (Leavitt) Peirce. They had four children—Flora E., Franklin Pearl, Charles Augustus, and Everett Fay.

As early as 1880, Martin was spoken of as a mayoral candidate, but he declined to run, citing the excessive demands of private business. When, however, in 1883 Democratic Mayor Albert Palmer (*q.v.*) declined a second term and the name of Hugh O'Brien (*q.v.*), the common council president, was put forward by the Democrats, a group of prominent citizens headed by ex-Mayor Samuel C. Cobb (*q.v.*) prevailed upon Martin to accept the independent citizens' nomination.

A Democrat in national politics, Martin campaigned on a nonpartisan ticket and picked up the Republican nomination as well. The short campaign pitted Martin—successful Yankee entrepreneur and Civil War hero—against O'Brien, Irish Catholic, and the alleged corruption and partisan spirit of the city Democratic machine. Elected over O'Brien in a record turnout, 27,494 to 25,950, Martin followed a policy of retrenchment, hoping to eradicate waste and extravagance while continuing necessary city programs. To accomplish this, he raised the tax rate, attempted to reform the board of aldermen by having them elected by district rather than at large, actively supported the passage of the 1884 state Civil Service Act, and labored to implement a policy of municipal autonomy, believing the city and not the state should regulate Boston's financial affairs.

The renewed business depression in 1884, together with opposition toward his nonpartisan handling of city affairs, resulted in Martin's defeat in the mayoral campaign of December 1884; he lost to O'Brien 27,494 to 24,168. During his postmayoral years, Martin served as Boston water commissioner under Mayor Patrick A. Collins (*q.v.*). He died on 13 March 1902.

SOURCES: "Ex-Mayors of Boston," Boston *Sunday Globe*, 16 November 1890; Augustus P. Martin, *Inaugural Address of Augustus P. Martin* (Boston, 1884); "Men Who Ruled the Hub," Boston *Sunday Herald*, 16 August 1891; John L. Parker, *History of the Twenty-Second Massachusetts Infantry* (Boston, 1887).

Robert V. Sparks

MARTIN, JOSEPH A. (1888–1928), Mayor of Detroit (1924). Born in Detroit on 26 June 1888, Martin was educated in the public schools and graduated from the University of Detroit in 1905. Beginning as an office-boy in the Union Trust Company, he became a bookkeeper and rose to head the real estate department. In 1915, he worked out a cost-accounting system for an Ontario automobile factory, then became chief auditor of a Detroit firm, the People's Outfitting Company, and three years later took a job with the central accounting division of Studebaker in Chicago. Mayor James Couzens (*q.v.*) appointed him commissioner of public works in Detroit in 1920. Martin held the job until 1923, after which he returned to private business.

Elected to the city council, Martin became acting mayor on 10 June 1924, when the ailing Mayor Frank E. Doremus (*q.v.*) resigned. Martin held that position only until 2 August 1924. He ran unsuccessfully against John W. Smith (*q.v.*) for mayor. He died in October 1928.

SOURCES: C. M. Burton, *History of Wayne County and Detroit* (Detroit-Chicago, 1922); Burton Historical Collection clipping file, Detroit Public Library; Detroit *Free Press*, 4 September 1924.

Ben C. Wilson and *Finney Ike Mlemchkwu*

MARX, OSCAR B. (1866–1923), Mayor of Detroit (1913–18). Marx was born in Detroit on 14 July 1866 of German-born parents, local farmer Stephen Marx (d. 1900), an immigrant from Baden, and Eleanore (Busch) Marx from Saxony. He attended a Detroit grammar school and at the age of fourteen entered Goldsmith's Business College. As a young man, he worked on his father's farm in Hamtramck township outside of Detroit. He invested a small sum in the U.S. Optical Company in 1891, eventually becoming president of that firm. Marx was also active in real estate, serving as vice-president of the Robert Oakman Land Company for many years. On 4 February 1897, he married Lydia Darmstaetter, a local Detroit German girl, and they had two children, Emma and Oscar, Jr. Marx was a popular social figure, belonging to the Harmonie, the Turners, the Detroit Yacht Club, the Detroit Athletic Club, and the Essex County Club of Canada.

Marx was mayor of Detroit during a time when the population of that city doubled from 450,000 to over 990,000. He was the last mayor to serve under the old city charter which provided for a large city council elected by wards. In 1918, a new charter was adopted which streamlined the city government by reducing the size of the city council and strengthening the powers of the mayor.

Marx entered Detroit politics in 1894 as an estimator-at-large, and in 1895 he was elected alderman of the Fifteenth Ward, a position he held for eight years. In 1910, he was elected city assessor, and in 1912 he won a three-way mayoral race over the Democratic incumbent William B. Thompson (*q.v.*) 36,067 to 25,268 and the Progressive candidate's 7,985. A popular mayor, Marx was reelected in 1914 with 36,845 votes over Frederick F. Ingram's 21,677 and in 1916 with 63,305 votes over William F. Connolly's 49,702. Like his predecessors,

Marx grappled with the streetcar franchise and municipal ownership issue. However, he came up with a solution that included a plan to provide for a 3-cent fare immediately and the formation of a street-railway commission that would work out the steps toward eventual municipal ownership. After some initial resistance, the Detroit United Railway relented and accepted Marx's plan.

Marx's three terms were also notable for an aggressive building program which included the construction of the Receiving Hospital, the Municipal Courts building, and a new public library. Marx appointed a woman to the city's recreation commission. Marx served as mayor during a time of extreme population growth, which placed severe pressure on urban services; his administration was generally successful. A new charter, a municipal ownership plan, and new public buildings marked his success.

Retiring from politics after 1918 except for an unsuccessful attempt to become a Republican national committeeman in 1920, he continued to busy himself with his optical and real estate businesses until the time of his death on 23 November 1923 in Detroit.

SOURCES: Clarence M. Burton, *The City of Detroit, Michigan, 1701–1922* (Detroit-Chicago, 1922); Burton Historical Collection Biographical Index, Drawer No. 138; Jack D. Elenbaas, "Detroit and the Progressive Era: A Study of Urban Reform, 1900–1914" (Ph.D. dissertation, Wayne State University, 1968); Oscar B. Marx Papers, annual messages to the common council, reading room file, scrapbooks, Burton Historical Collection, Detroit Public Library.

Jack D. Elenbaas

MASCAREL, JOSÉ (?–?), Mayor of Los Angeles (1865–66). Mayor of Los Angeles at the end of the Civil War, José Mascarel (*q.v.*) was a Frenchman who arrived in the settlement as early as 1844. He served on the common council several times and was elected mayor, serving from 5 May 1865 to 10 March 1866. A determined unionist and Republican, Mayor Mascarel opposed secessionist and pro-Confederate sentiments in the town. On Lincoln's assassination, open-air memorials were held and all shops were closed. During Mascarel's term, oil companies were established; the town's population was under 6,000. He ran for reelection but lost to Damien Marchessault by a vote of 388 to 296.

Very little is known of Mascarel, although he was still in Los Angeles as late as 1889 and had built several fine buildings in the city.

SOURCES: Illustrated History of Los Angeles County, California (Chicago, 1889); *Mayors of Los Angeles* (Los Angeles, 1968); William A. Spalding. *History of Los Angeles City and County, California. Biographical* (Los

Angeles, 1931 on p. 634—contains only a picture of Mascarel).
Peter d'A. Jones

MASON, ROSWELL B. (1805–92), Mayor of Chicago (1869–71). Canal and railroad engineer and Republican mayor of Chicago at the time of the great fire of 1871, civil engineer, and co-founder of the Western Society of Engineers, Mason was born at New Hartford, New York, on 19 September 1805. He was one of thirteen children of Arnold Mason, a farmer and public works contractor, and Mercy (Coman) Mason, both old-stock Yankees of New England origin and Presbyterian faith.

Despite frequent illnesses which took the younger Mason out of academies at Newfield, New Hampshire, and Utica, New York, Roswell assisted his father, beginning in 1821, in his business as a stone contractor for the Erie Canal. Between 1822 and 1826, young Mason worked on several canal projects in upper New York State. In 1826, he was named assistant engineer on the Mauch Chunk Canal in Pennsylvania, and in 1831 he became the canal's superintendent. Canal projects occupied him through 1837; thereafter, Mason was concerned chiefly with railroad construction. He was chief engineer for the New York, New Haven, and Hartford from 1846 and, beginning in 1851, surveyed and supervised construction for the Illinois Central Railroad. During the 1850s and 1860s, Mason supervised construction on railroads, canals, and bridges in New York, Illinois, and Iowa.

On 6 September 1831, Mason married Harriet L. Hopkins, daughter of Royal Hopkins, a contractor for the Morris canal, and they had eight children, seven of whom survived to adulthood.

Mason established his home in Chicago in 1851 and came to public notice when he represented the Illinois Central Railroad in negotiations for trackage rights in 1855. He also participated in an unsuccessful project to build the city's first street railway in 1856 and, in 1865, worked on a city commission for the improvement of local sanitation. A long-time Republican, Mason reluctantly accepted the mayoral nomination of an anti-corruption coalition in 1869.

In 1869, Chicago had a mayor-council form of government and a population of approximately 280,000. On 2 November 1869, Mason defeated his Republican opponent, George W. Gage, by a vote of 19,878 to 11,381. A temperance advocate, as mayor Mason proposed a limitation on the number of saloons. Aside from the beginning of construction of a new house of correction, however, Mason's actions left little mark on the city.

In response to the fire of 8–10 October 1871, Mason issued proclamations banning the sale of liquor and limiting personal liberties. He placed the city under the authority of federal troops and appealed to the rest of the nation for material aid which he subsequently channeled through the Chicago Relief and Aid Society, of which he had been director. Relief and reconstruction were accomplished in consultation with the city's business leaders.

Mason declined to run for reelection in 1871 and thereafter returned to engineering. During his remaining twenty-one years, he was at various times a founder and president of the Western Society of Engineers, an elder of the Fourth Presbyterian Church of Chicago, director of the Chicago Relief and Aid Society, board member of McCormick Theological Seminary, trustee of the Illinois Industrial University, and an active Republican. Mason died at Chicago after a brief illness on 11 January 1892. He was buried in his adopted city.

SOURCES: Fremont O. Bennett, *Politics and Politicians of Chicago, Cook County, and Illinois* (Chicago, 1886); Letters in "Engineering Papers" held by Illinois Central Gulf Railroad; Trowbridge Mason, *Family Annals* (typescript dated 1958, held by the Chicago Historical Society); Minor papers in "Mayoral Papers" file, Chicago Historical Society; C. H. Muttier, *Biography of Roswell B. Mason* (typescript dated 3 January 1938, commissioned by the Western Society of Engineers, held by the Chicago Historical Society); Fredrick Rex, *The Mayors of the City of Chicago from March 4, 1837 to April 13, 1933* (typescript dated 1947, Municipal Reference Library of Chicago).
Paul Barrett

MASTEN, JOSEPH G. (1809–71), Mayor of Buffalo (1843, 1845). Democratic mayor concerned with city improvements, Masten was born at Red Hook, New York, on 24 June 1809, of a well-to-do Episcopal family. First-born of three brothers, he attended a college preparatory program in Granby, Connecticut, graduated from Union College in 1828, and studied law in Kingston, New York. Masten practiced law for several years in Bath, New York, and then settled in Buffalo in 1836, becoming a member of several law firms. He married Christina Cameron, a Scots-Presbyterian from Bath, New York, and they had two sons and a daughter. Masten was a founding member of Christ Church (Episcopalian).

In 1844, Buffalo had 26,503 people, growing to 29,773 by 1845. The city had a mayor-council form of government. In the March 1843 city election, Democrat Masten defeated Whig candidate Walter Joy 1,639 to 1,197 votes. Although Masten did not run for reelection in 1844, he did so in March 1845 and defeated the Whig Hiram Barton (*q.v.*) 1,837 to 1,538.

During both of his one-year terms as mayor, Masten promoted various urban services. Largely through his efforts, new streets were laid out and old ones enlarged.

He actively enforced city ordinances requiring all residents to keep sidewalks and gutters clear of snow, dirt, and other obstructions. Mayor Masten helped improve the efficiency of municipal departments and encouraged the development of lake and canal commercial facilities. Finally, a new city charter was adopted during his 1843 term. He did not seek a third term.

Masten returned to his law practice and occupied several public offices. He was a city recorder's court judge (1848–52) and then a city superior court judge (1856–71). He was also a trustee of the Grosvenor Library of Buffalo. He served as a delegate in the 1867 state constitutional convention and sat on the Judiciary Committee. He was a member of the Buffalo Board of Trade. Masten died on 14 April 1871 and was buried in his family plot in Buffalo's Forest Lawn Cemetery.

SOURCES: Buffalo *Daily Courier*; Buffalo *Daily Gazette*; Buffalo *Morning Express; Commercial Advertiser and Journal*; J. N. Larned, *A History of Buffalo* (New York, 1911); Sister Mary Jane and Sister Mercedes, "Mayors of Buffalo, 1832–1961" (B.A. thesis, Rosary Hill College, 1961); *Publications of the Buffalo Historical Society*; H. Perry Smith, *History of the City of Buffalo and Erie County, New York* (Syracuse, N.Y., 1884).   *Daniel B. Karin*

MASTERS, IRVINE U. (1823–65), Mayor of Cleveland (1863–64). Shipbuilder and politician born in New York in 1823, Masters moved west to Ohio around 1851, along with his wife Naomi, also a native New Yorker. They were Protestants and had three children, all born in Ohio City, a community next to Cleveland. Masters served as a trustee of Ohio City in 1853 and 1854, helping Mayor William B. Castle (*q.v.*) arrange for the merger of the two cities in 1854. He was elected a member of the Cleveland City Council, serving from 1854 to 1863, and president of the council, 1859–61, and 1862–63. This activity paralleled a successful career as a shipbuilder, mostly during 1855–65, as a member of Peck and Masters.

A Republican, Masters was elected mayor in 1863, defeating incumbent Edward S. Flint (*q.v.*) 3,899 to 3,558. Cleveland had over 50,000 people and a mayor-council form of government. Masters was generally well liked as mayor and supported measures to improve the city's business. He also actively supported the war effort and hosted various war meetings and special public ceremonies for returning and departing soldiers. This excessive patriotism weakened his already poor health (he suffered from tuberculosis) and forced him to resign as mayor in May 1864. He went to New England for the summer, in an effort to regain his health. This was unsuccessful, and the following year he was also forced to

retire from business. Masters' wife had died in 1863, and he had immediately remarried. The family went to Pine Island, Minnesota, where he died, on 13 November 1865.

SOURCES: Cleveland *Herald*, 14 November 1865; Cleveland *Plain Dealer*, 15 November 1865; scattered references in earlier editions of newspapers and in the 1850 U.S. Census records.   *Thomas R. Bullard*

MATTHEWS, NATHAN (1858–1927), Mayor of Boston (1891–94). Reform Mayor Matthews, born on 28 March 1858, first of six children of Nathan Matthews, an old-stock Yankee merchant, real estate developer, and philanthropist, and Albertine (Bunker) Matthews of New York, inherited a family tradition of public service and Democratic party loyalty. A graduate of Dixwell's private school, Harvard University, and Harvard Law School, he opened a law office in 1880 specializing in tax and realty cases. He married Ellen Bacon Sargent, daughter of Lucius Manlius and Letitia Sullivan (Amory) Sargent, and had two children, Ellen Nathalie and Sullivan Amory. Matthews was an Episcopalian and a member of the Massachusetts Historical Society, American Law Institute, American Academy of Arts and Sciences, Free Trade League, the Union, Algonquin, and Somerset Clubs, and an editor of the *American Architect and Building News*.

Following the nomination of James G. Blaine by the Republicans in 1884, Matthews worked closely with dissatisfied "Mugwumps" and local Democratic leaders in gathering support for Grover Cleveland (*q.v.*). In 1888, Matthews joined with Josiah Quincy (*q.v.*) and others to found the Young Men's Democratic Club of Massachusetts, where he proved instrumental in forging a Yankee-Irish alliance in state politics. As a member of the Democratic State Committee, he directed fund-raising and registration campaigns, revealing an instinctive grasp of politics, if not for politicking. In 1890, he managed the gubernatorial campaign of William E. Russell with such precision that he was offered the nomination for mayor of Boston in the December 1890 contest. Trusted by the Irish community for his outspoken defense of their interests and equally so by economy-minded Republicans, Matthews carried twenty of Boston's twenty-five wards defeating Moody Merrill 32,210 to 19,957.

At the age of thirty-six, Matthews brought little legislative or executive experience to public office. Yet, he cut an impressive figure—tall, handsome, with *pince-nez* and bushy mustache—and, unlike Mayors O'Brien (*q.v.*) and Hart (*q.v.*), he fully exercised the executive powers granted under the Charter Ammendments of 1885. He required municipal departments to furnish monthly itemized budgets, consolidated unruly agencies, eliminated overlapping jobs, secured the enactment of legislation prohibiting city employees from lobbying for private interests, and conducted a successful court fight against the Boston gas monopoly. As a result, he was reelected in 1891 with 34,716 votes to H. G. Allen's 1,891, and in 1892 he beat Homer Rogers by 38,851 to 26,648. The depression of 1893, during which he maintained an uncompromising attitude toward relief, split the Yankee-Irish alliance, and only the crossover votes of hundreds of conservative Republicans won him a fourth term in 1894 with 36,345 votes to T. F. Hart's 31,239. A year later he was defeated by Edwin U. Curtis (q.v.).

In his postmayoral years, Matthews engineered the bolt of the Massachusetts Gold Democrats from Bryanism and Free Silver in 1896, chaired the 1907–1909 Finance Commission which resulted in the charter reforms of 1909, lectured on municipal government at Harvard (1909–12), sat on the Commission on a Segregated Budget (1915) and the Commission on New Sources of Revenue (1920–21), and following U.S. entry in World War I, acted as special counsel to the U.S. Railroad Commission. He died on 11 December 1927 while recovering from surgery.

SOURCES: Nathan Matthews, Jr., *The City Government of Boston* (Boston, 1895); Nathan Matthews Papers, Littauer Library, Harvard University; George R. Nutter, "Nathan Matthews," *Harvard Graduates Magazine* 36 (March 1928); Robert A. Silverman, "Nathan Matthews: Politics of Reform in Boston, 1890–1910," *New England Quarterly* 50 (December 1977).

Robert V. Sparks

MAYBURY, WILLIAM C. (1848–1909), Mayor of Detroit (1897–1904). Democratic mayor, born in Detroit on 20 November 1848, Maybury was the son of Protestant Irish-born immigrants, Thomas Maybury (1809–80), a wealthy Republican self-made contractor, and Margaret (Cotter) Maybury (d. 1851). William was a product of the Detroit public schools and the University of Michigan (B.A., 1870, M.A., 1880). Never marrying, he was both a prominent Mason (33rd degree) and a Protestant Episcopal layman.

Practicing law in Detroit after 1871, Maybury served as city attorney, 1875–80, and was elected to the First Congressional District of Michigan in 1882 and 1884. After his second term in Congress was over, he resumed law practice until 1897, when the Democrats chose him to run for the unexpired term of the reform mayor, Hazen Pingree (q.v.) (now governor of Michigan). In March, Maybury carried the Democrats to victory over Captain Albert E. Stewart, a Republican Great Lakes shipper, by a close vote of 17,978 to 17,451. Maybury won reelection over Clarence A. Black, Republican business leader,

by a 20,611 to 18,490 vote in the regular November mayoralty contest of the same year.

Detroit in 1900 had 285,704 people and a mayor-council form of government. As mayor, Maybury restored tranquility to Detroit politics following the turbulent Pingree era. According to his critics, he stood for, but did not fight hard enough for, most of the Pingree policies, including advocacy of municipal ownership of street railways. Liberals denounced him for what they regarded as timidity, yet, many Detroiters liked the conservative Maybury style. This was especially true for the downtown business and professional men who appreciated his espousal of industry, success in attracting conventions to the city, and business-in-government philosophy.

In 1899, Maybury won again over the Republican, Stewart—this time by a 20,081 to 16,664 vote. The Republican state legislature proceeded to pass "ripper" bills in 1901, bills that removed from the mayor the power to appoint cabinet heads, giving the councils (Republican) that power temporarily (eventually passed on to the governor). The three anti-Maybury men were appointed by the councils to head the departments of public works, police, and parks and recreation but proved corrupt and heavyhanded and later had to be removed by the Republican councils. Made even more popular by the actions of the independent department heads, Mayor Maybury in 1901 won over Dr. J. Henry Carstens, an eminent German-American physician, by a 23,391 to 21,748 vote. The Republican state legislators of 1901 had also changed the odd-years mayoralty elections to even-years, beginning with 1904, and as they had anticipated, the popular President Theodore Roosevelt, sweeping the city by about 70 percent of the vote in 1904, carried the Republicans to total victory in both city and state. This time, George P. Codd (q.v.), Republican lawyer, defeated Maybury—34,865 to 28,915. Republican dominance, attained by Pingree in the 1890s, resumed its course until the 1930s. Maybury's five Democratic victories had been a reflection both of the esteem voters held for Maybury and of the Republican split in Detroit between the McMillan state machine and the local Pingree reformers.

In 1904, the defeated mayor once again returned to his law practice. In 1900, he had run for governor, losing overwhelmingly to Aaron Bliss, the Republican, whose winning slogan had been "McKinley, Roosevelt and Bliss." Maybury died on 5 May 1909, and by popular subscription a bronze statue of him, facing a similar one already there of Pingree, was placed in Grand Circus Park—two statues symbolizing two popular but quite different mayors.

SOURCES: Ashod R. Aprahamian, "The Mayoral Politics of Detroit, 1897 through 1912," (Ph.D. dissertation, New York University, 1968); David E. Heineman Scrapbooks for 1899–1909 (they end in 1912), Michigan Historical Collections, Ann Arbor; Melvin G. Holli, *Reform in Detroit: Hazen S. Pingree and Urban Politics* (New York, 1969); William C. Maybury Papers (mostly scrapbooks), Burton Historical Collections, Detroit.   *Donald W. Disbrow*

MEANS, WILLIAM F. (1831–?), Mayor of Cincinnati (1881–83). Iron manufacturer and mayor, born at Union Furnace in Lawrence County, Ohio, in 1831, Means was the second of eight children born to Thomas W. Means (1803–90), a successful iron producer of Scots-Irish descent from South Carolina, and Sarah (Ellison) Means (1810–71), a daughter of early settlers in Adams County, Ohio. After a public education in Lawrence County, Means attended both Marietta College and Farmer's College, the latter after moving to Cincinnati to represent his father's iron business. Marietta awarded him an M.A. degree in 1880.

Means began his iron career at the Ohio Furnace, Scioto County, in 1852 and two years later, with his father, built a blast furnace in Vinton County, Ohio. He also pursued banking in Portsmouth, Ohio, and Ashland, Kentucky, and assumed the management of the iron and coal interests of Means, Kyle and Company.

On moving to Cincinnati in 1868, Means became an energetic participant in community life, acting as a commissioner of the Cincinnati Industrial Exposition, vice-president for the Chamber of Commerce, as well as an incorporator of the Music Hall and a guiding force behind the completion of the Exposition buildings, with his wife, Martha (Campbell), Means had four children, three of whom (Gertrude, Pearl, and Patty) survived to adulthood.

Cincinnati, with a population of 253,139 and a mayor-council form of government, acquired a reputation of wide-openness in the late 1870s. The Democrats' decision to nominate Means, a political novice, in 1881 was an attempt to appeal to the middle-class citizen and to wrestle the mayoralty from the Republicans. His victory over incumbent Charles Jacob (*q.v.*) (23,804 to 21,384) and W. D. Wilson (280) justified such a strategy. Means probably conducted one of the most effective administrations since the Civil War: he reduced city expenditures, increased receipts, and ran an honest government. Hailed even by his political opponents, Means declined renomination to assume the presidency of the Metropolitan Bank, a position he had been offered before the expiration of his term.

Means retired to his summer home at Yellow Springs in 1894 and died there after a long life.

SOURCES: The Biographical Cyclopedia and Portrait Gallery with an Historical Sketch of the State of Ohio (Cincinnati, 1884). Cincinnati *Enquirer*, 8 April 1881, 24 March 1881; *Cincinnati Graphic* 3 (2 May 1885).   *Robert B. Fairbanks*

MEDILL, JOSEPH E. (1823–99), Mayor of Chicago (1871–73). Mayor of Chicago, newspaperman, and founding member of the Republican party, Medill was born in rural Nova Scotia (now Canada) on 6 April 1823, the son of Presbyterian parents of Irish birth and Scots-Irish and French ancestry, who had migrated there in 1819. Medill's father, a farmer, moved to Stark County, Ohio, shortly after the boy's birth and settled at Massillon, Ohio, in 1832. Young Medill attended public schools to the age of sixteen, received tutoring from a clergyman at Canton, Ohio, and studied law under a practicing attorney, Hiram Griswald. Medill was admitted to the Ohio bar in 1856; for four years thereafter, he practiced law at New Philadelphia, Ohio.

In 1849, Medill abandoned law and bought the *Coshocton* (Ohio) *Whig*; two years later, he sold his paper and purchased the *Daily Forest City* (Cleveland, Ohio). In 1853, he began the Cleveland *True Democrat* (a Free-Soil organ) and soon consolidated it with his other paper to form the Cleveland *Leader*. In 1854, Medill, Horace Greeley, and four others formed the nucleus of the National Republican party at a meeting in Medill's Cleveland office.

In January 1855, Medill moved to Chicago and, with two others, bought the Chicago *Tribune*. A friend of Abraham Lincoln from 1858, Medill helped to convince the 1860 Republican convention of Lincoln's desirability as a presidential candidate. Medill was a delegate to the Illinois Constitutional Convention of 1869 but sought no political office before 1871. Married on 9 September 1852 to Katherine Patrick (daughter of James Patrick, a New Philadelphia newspaper publisher, county judge, and former Indian agent), Medill had three daughters, Elinor (Mrs. Robert W. Patterson), Katherine (Mrs. Robert McCormick), and Josephine.

Chicago in 1871 had a mayor-council type of government and a population of 334,270. Following the great fire of October 1871, business and political leaders sought out Medill as a person of national reputation who would restore confidence in the city's future and reorder its finances. Medill, running on the "Union-Fireproof" ticket, defeated Democrat C.C.P. Holden by a vote of 16,125 to 5,988 on 7 November 1871.

At the time of his nomination, Medill insisted that the mayor be given full control of all city boards and of all appointments, subject to council approval. State legislation made these changes possible during his administration and also permitted establishment of the city's first public library. Medill failed, however, in his attempt to extend to the city limits a ban on construction with flammable materials, and he aroused major opposition among the ethnic working-class and foreign-born by trying to close saloons on Sundays. Mass meetings against Medill and his policies ensued through the summer of 1873. He resigned on 18 August 1873, largely in frustration over the Sunday closing measure and a struggle between his police superintendent and the city police board. The remaining ten weeks of his term were filled by an interim mayor elected by the council.

Medill bought full control of the *Tribune* in 1874 and devoted most of the remainder of his life to writing and publishing. He died following a heart attack in San Antonio, Texas, on 16 March 1899, while doing a story there for the *Tribune*. He was buried in Chicago.

SOURCES: Fremont O. Bennett, *Politics and Politicians of Chicago, Cook County, and Illinois* (Chicago, 1886); Francis A. Eastman, *Chicago City Manual* (Chicago, 1911); Joseph Medill, ''Letters'' (not mayoral correspondence) in various files, Chicago Historical Society; *Joseph Medill: A Brief Biography and an Appreciation* (Chicago, 1947).   *Paul Barrett*

MELLUS, HENRY (1816–60), Mayor of Los Angeles (1860). Longtime Californian, Mellus, born on 4 August 1816 in Dorchester, Massachusetts, the sixth of eleven children of old-stock Yankees William Mellus and Amelia (Lyon) Mellus, followed his father and older brothers to sea. In 1834, he sailed aboard the *Pilgrim*, in a voyage later made famous by shipmate Richard Henry Dana in *Two Years Before the Mast*, for the California hide trade, and then stayed in California as a company agent for the next ten years. He lived at Los Angeles and other ports, disposing of the cargoes of the company's ships, in exchange for hides from local *ranchos*. In 1845, he formed a partnership with William D.M. Howard originally in Monterey but soon in San Francisco. Howard was also a Massachusetts man who had been in California for many years as a consignee.

Despite his long involvement with Mexican officials, Mellus assisted the United States in its conquest of California. He worked with Marine officer Archibald Gillespie and, at a decisive point in the battle for Los Angeles, provided powder and lead to American forces.

The eventual American victory, and especially the subsequent Gold Rush, proved a windfall for Mellus and Howard, who became the leading merchants in San Francisco. They also invested heavily in real estate, becoming the largest owners of waterfront lots in town, with annual rental income near $500,000. One estimate placed Mellus among the six wealthiest individuals in San Francisco, until he sold his interest in the firm to his partner in 1850 and returned to Salem, Massachusetts.

While amassing a fortune in San Francisco, Mellus retained ties to Los Angeles. In 1847, he married Roman Catholic Anita Johnson, daughter of an English merchant and a Mexican mother, in Los Angeles, where the couple's first son was born. Four daughters and another son were born in Salem during the 1850s.

After a series of bad investments in the East cost him his fortune, Mellus and his family returned to Los Angeles in 1859. With his brother's assistance, he acquired the Pacific Salt Works near the city. In May 1860, when the city's population had reached 4,300, he ran for mayor under its mayor-council form and defeated Henry R. Myles, a local druggist, 277 to 226. Although party politics had not played a part in the local election in the solidly Democratic city, during the summer and fall Mellus supported the Douglas Democrats. Mellus' partial term as mayor was generally undistinguished. Like other mayors of that period, he emphasized the need to improve the city's waterworks and to economize on expenses, but he actually accomplished little. He died on 26 December 1860 before he had completed his one-year term.

SOURCES: Doris Muscatine, *Old San Francisco; The Biography of a City from Early Days to the Earthquake* (New York, 1975); Adele Ogden, ''Alfred Robinson, New England Merchant in Mexican California,'' *California Historical Society Quarterly* 23 (September 1944); John W. Robinson, *Los Angeles in Civil War Days, 1860–65* (Los Angeles, 1977).   *R. David Weber*

MICKLE, ANDREW H. (1805–63), Mayor of New York (1846–47). ''The leading tobacconist in New York,'' Mickle at the age of forty-one was elected mayor of New York on the Democratic ticket, 14 April 1846. He served one year. At that time, the city had a population of 380,000 and was growing rapidly. Most of New York City proper still lay below Fourteenth Street; Washington Square, a former potters' field, was emerging as a fashionable residential district.

Mickle married the boss's daughter and eventually inherited the rich tobacco business. He had little or no political background when elected mayor, being advanced to the station without experience, or previous official connection with the city government. His first annual message betrayed a certain diffidence about the job, but as mayor he was not short of reform ideas. Although Mickle demanded cost reductions (the city indebtedness stood at over $14 million in 1846), he was not rigidly conservative in spending matters. He advocated a new workhouse, technical improvements in fire engines, and a new lunatic asylum.

Mickle asked why as many as 1 in 800 New Yorkers were in the city's overcrowded asylum, compared with a rate of only 1 in 2,000 for other great cities in the

United States and abroad. His answer was that other communities were presuming upon New York's generosity. His argument is reminiscent of New York City's financial problems of the 1970s and 1980s: "Such discrepancies can only arise from a systematized practice of fraud upon the benevolent feelings of our citizens, by casting upon them the insane of other communities." Mickle asked the council for measures to restrict this practice.

SOURCES: *Annual Message of His Honor the Mayor*, Andrew H. Mickle, 12 May 1846, Document No. 1, Board of Aldermen (New York, 1846); *The Renascence of City Hall: Mayors of New York* (New York, 1956).   *Peter d'A. Jones*

MILLER, JAMES F. (1831–73), Military Mayor of New Orleans (1863–64). One of a line of New Englanders to serve as temporary mayor, Miller was born on 13 October 1831 in Hollis, Maine. After graduation from Bowdoin College in 1856, he studied law with Fessenden V. Butler. A young enthusiastic Republican, he was appointed as an aide to Governor Israel Washburne in 1861 and was quickly given the rank of lieutenant colonel to oversee military recruitment for the Civil War. He resigned on 31 March 1862 to become captain and serve General George F. Shepley, military governor of Louisiana.

Before his appointment by General Nathaniel Banks as military mayor of New Orleans on 1 February 1863, Miller served as secretary of state of the military state government. His major accomplishment as mayor was to consolidate the small public school libraries into the public library for the city of New Orleans. In 1860, New Orleans had a population of 168,675. He served as mayor one year, until 3 February 1864 when he was transferred out of the city.

Miller left New Orleans for Norfolk to become assistant adjutant general of the Department of Virginia and North Carolina under Benjamin Butler, retiring on 16 July 1864. He returned to Portland, Maine and worked as a lawyer except for a term in the state legislature from Portland (1865–66). He died on 12 December 1873.

SOURCES: Gerald Capers, *Occupied City, New Orleans Under the Federals, 1862–1865* (Lexington, Ky., 1965); John S. Kendall, *History of New Orleans* (Chicago, 1922); William E. Morris, comp., (MS., Biographical Catalogue, Maine Historical Society, Portland Maine).   *Joseph Logsdon*

MILLER, RAY T. (1893–1966), Mayor of Cleveland (1932–33). Democratic mayor, born on 10 January 1893 in Defiance, Ohio, Miller was the son of Martin E. Miller (1865–1930), of German extraction and a superintendent of the Defiance Machine Works, and Anne (Riley) Miller (1864–1949), an Irish-American. The third of eight children in a Roman Catholic family, Miller graduated from the University of Notre Dame in 1914. His four brothers also attended Notre Dame, and all played football. Miller moved to Cleveland to practice law and served in the Army on the Mexican border in France during World War I, attaining the rank of captain. After the war, he returned to his Cleveland law practice. After two unsuccessful attempts, he won the office of prosecuting attorney of Cuyahoga County, holding that office from 1928 until elected mayor in 1932. Miller was a vigorous prosecutor who secured convictions against public officials for corrupt acts. In 1926, Miller married a Cleveland social worker, Ruth Hamilton (1896–1969), and the couple had six children. Miller was very active in the Knights of Columbus and Notre Dame alumni affairs.

Cleveland in 1930 had 900,429 people, and the following year its voters abolished the city manager form of government in favor of a return to a mayor-council type. In February 1932, Miller won the first election under the new charter by 102,730 votes to Republican and former City Manager Daniel E. Morgan's (*q.v.*) 95,039. Miller was the first Democrat to preside at city hall since Newton D. Baker (*q.v.*) in 1915. The long Democratic drought combined with the impact of the Depression put the Miller administration under intense patronage pressure. Opponents attacked the partisanship of Miller and his aides while there were far too few jobs available to satisfy unemployed Democrats. As mayor, Miller had to deal with severe drops in revenue and mounting relief needs. He was an enthusiastic supporter of the National Recovery Administration. Overall, he was considered to be less successful as mayor than he had been as prosecutor. In 1933, he lost his bid for reelection to former mayor and governor of Ohio Harry L. Davis (*q.v.*) by 147,515 to 133,163 votes. A major cause of his defeat was the continued opposition of fellow Democrat, Congressman Martin Sweeney.

After his mayoralty, Miller again practiced law and engaged in a number of business ventures. He became a wealthy man and was a major power in Cleveland business and political affairs. In 1938, after a bruising battle, he ousted Burr Gongwer as chairman of the Cuyahoga County Democratic party and held that position until 1964. He died at his home in Shaker Heights, Ohio, on 13 July 1966 after a heart attack.

SOURCES: Richard L. Maher, "Cleveland: Study in Political Paradoxes," in Robert S. Allen, ed., *Our Fair City* (New York, 1947); "Ray T. Miller," Biographical clipping file, Cleveland Public Library; Philip W. Porter, *Cleveland: Confused City on a Seesaw* (Columbus, 1976).   *James F. Richardson*

MILLER, VICTOR J. (1888–1955), Mayor of St. Louis (1925–33). Lawyer and politician, Miller was born in Joplin, Missouri, on 6 December 1888. He attended local schools in that community, graduated from Washington University Law School, and began practicing law in St. Louis in 1911. In 1918, he married Mabel Catherine Cooney. Miller served as president of the St. Louis Police Board, 1921–23. He earned considerable publicity by his habit of speaking freely with reporters. Miller caused some controversy by stating that numerous teenage prostitution rings (male and female) were active throughout the city's high schools. As disagreements among board members became obvious, the governor removed Miller in 1923. The following year, he was the unsuccessful Republican candidate for governor.

In 1925, Miller was elected mayor, defeating Democrat William L. Igoe 120,232 to 117,223. In 1929, he defeated Laurence McDermott 108,639 to 101,648. St. Louis had 772,897 people in 1920 and 821,960 by 1930. As mayor, Miller supported a widespread reconstruction of the city's lighting system. Subsequently, there were charges that the contractor for this new construction had been overpaid with the connivance of city officials. A series of indictments resulted, although the contractor's death in 1930 halted court proceedings. Miller also helped reach an agreement with the Wabash Railroad to remove a dangerous grade crossing. A new city hall was begun, and the fire department was fully motorized.

Most of this work was accomplished during Miller's first term in office. Apparently, he suffered a stroke shortly before winning reelection in 1929, and as a result, his staff did much of the work during his second term. After leaving office in 1933, he traveled to New York, hoping to find medical treatment. His wife divorced him in 1934, and he moved in with his brother in Kentucky. They finally settled in Kansas City, where Miller died on 6 January 1955.

SOURCES: Charles H. Cornwell, *St. Louis Mayors: Brief Biographies* (St. Louis, 1965); New York *Times*, 7 January 1955; St. Louis *Post-Dispatch*, 6 January 1955.   *Thomas R. Bullard*

MILLIKEN, ISAAC LAWRENCE (1815–89), Mayor of Chicago (1854–55). Promoter of the first permanent brick schoolhouse in Chicago (later known as the Dearborn School, School Number 1), Milliken was born on 29 August 1815 in Saco, Maine. His family was of Scottish origin, and Isaac was a member of the Christian Church. Milliken spent his early years in rural Saco and became apprentice to his blacksmith father. Following his marriage in 1837 to Almira Dene, a native New Yorker, the two went west to seek their fortune, settling in Chicago on 17 June 1837, where Isaac became a mod-

erately successful blacksmith on Randolph Street (site of the later Sherman House). For several years, Milliken independently read the law and was eventually admitted to the Illinois bar. He was twice elected alderman for the Second Ward and was once an assistant county judge.

Although the Millikens were childless, Isaac continued to be interested in education at all levels, and in 1844 and 1845 he supported the construction of a schoolhouse at the corner of Madison and Dearborn streets. Originally dubbed "Miltimore's Folly" (after Milliken's partner in the effort) by Augustus Garrett (q.v.), then mayor of Chicago, the school was later renamed the Dearborn School, admitting 543 pupils the first year. This building was the first permanent brick school structure in Chicago and became the foundation of the Chicago school system.

On 7 March 1854, Milliken successfully ran for mayor, defeating the temperance candidate Amos G. Throop, a rich lumber merchant. The population of the city at this time had grown to over 65,000. During his short term, he continued his support of education and appointed John C. Dore as Chicago's first superintendent of public education. But the liberal Milliken's career was in danger during the turbulent years 1854–55. The massive immigration of Irish and Germans into Chicago during the previous decade had spawned the bigoted Native American or Know-Nothing party. Just two months after Milliken's election, Stephen Douglas, with 500 Irish bodyguards, gave a speech in Chicago which became a mob scene. Mayor Milliken, Douglas, and his small Irish army barely escaped with their lives over the Clark Street bridge, drawn up behind them to the chagrin of the mob on the other side. This same political climate defeated Milliken in his second bid for mayor in 1855 against the American party candidate, Dr. Levi Boone (q.v.).

A major achievement during Milliken's term was the new state law creating a city board of sewage commissioners, empowered to tax and borrow funds to build an adequate sewage and drainage system for the growing city. The locally well-known expert E. S. Chesebrough, was appointed engineer and became the main architect of Chicago's sewage system. The plan was encouraged by the repeated cholera outbreaks in Chicago, 1849–1855. There were 1,424 deaths from cholera in 1854 alone.

Following his term, Milliken remained active in Chicago politics and for a number of years served the city as chief of police, justice of the peace, and, in 1856, chief magistrate of the police. He later retired from public office to Monee, in Will County, to pursue a career as a gentleman farmer. Milliken died on 2 December 1889 at the age of seventy-four.

SOURCES: A. F. Andreas, *History of Chicago* (Chicago, 1884), vol. 1; Chicago *Tribune*, 3 and 4 December 1889; *City of Chicago Census 1850*; Bessie Louise

Pierce, *A History of Chicago* (New York, 1940), vol. 2; Frederick Rex, comp., *Mayors of the City of Chicago* (Chicago, 1947).   *D. H. Parkerson*

MILLS, JOSHUA (1797–1843), Mayor of Cleveland (1838–39, 1842). Second mayor of Cleveland and brother-in-law of the first, Mills was born in 1797. Little is known of his origins before he came to Cleveland as a physician in 1827, though he was most likely a New Englander. He was married to a Protestant Yankee, Phoebe Stafford Higby in 1826. She was the daughter of Dexter and Rosanna Ellsworth Higby of Castleton, Vermont, and moved with them to Chillicothe, Ohio. She was first married (1820) to Sylvester Norton with whom she lived in Granville, New York; they had two children. She had two more children with Dr. Mills, Harriett and John Willey Mills, both of whom died of scarlet fever within a few days of each other in 1835. Mrs. Mills' sister was the wife of John Willey (*q.v.*), first mayor of Cleveland. She was Episcopalian, attending Cleveland's "Old Stone Church."

Dr. Mills was elected alderman in the first election after the incorporation of the city in 1836 and was apparently a Whig at that time. As the Lake Erie terminus of the Ohio and Erie Canal, Cleveland was in the midst of rapid growth, from 5,080 in 1835 to 6,071 in 1840. On the west side of the Cuyahoga River, the smaller settlement of Ohio City reached 1,577 by 1840. Dr. Mills opened a drug store on Superior Street and rendered great service in the cholera epidemic of 1832. He was one of three physicians on the first board of health, caring for the sick at a hospital established on Whiskey Island. The disease came to Cleveland on a troop boat bound for the Blackhawk War and resulted in about fifty deaths. Mills later shared a medical partnership with Dr. J. M. Ackley.

Mills was elected mayor on 5 March 1838 apparently unopposed and then was reelected, 507 to 379, over J. M. Wolsey on 5 March 1839. Mills ran for mayor again in 1841, this time as a "Locofoco" (Jacksonian Democrat), but was defeated by John W. Allen (*q.v.*) (Whig) by fifteen votes, 421 to 407. In 1842, he was successfully reelected to a third term as Locofoco mayor, but supported by both Whigs and Democrats, defeating John W. Allen by a vote of 458 to 338 (with a scattering of four votes elsewhere) in a city of more than 6,000. When Charles Dickens visited Cleveland by boat on 25 April 1842, he took such offense at a "Whip England" article copied in the Cleveland *Plain Dealer* that he refused to receive Mayor Mills. Mills died of tuberculosis on 29 April 1843 and was buried in Cleveland.

SOURCES: Elroy McKendree Avery, *A History of Cleveland and Its Environs: The Heart of New Connecticut* (Chicago, 1918); William Gransome Rose, *Cleveland, The Making of a City* (Cleveland, 1950); Gertrude Van Rensselaer Wickham, *The Pioneer Families of Cleveland 1797–1840* (Cleveland, 1914).   *Ronald E. Shaw*

MILLS, MERRILL I. (1819–82), Mayor of Detroit (1866, 1867). Transplanted New Englander and mayor of Detroit, born in Canton, Connecticut, on 4 November 1819, Mills attended common school, then went on to study at the Connecticut Literary Institute in preparation for entry to Yale University. However, he decided to join his father in the manufacture of gunpowder rather than continue his education. In 1838, he went to Alabama to represent family business interests. Called home in 1840 by his father's illness, he remained in Canton, Connecticut, for the next five years. At this point in his career, Mills decided to establish his own business in the West. Purchasing an extensive stock of dry goods, he headed for Fort Wayne but was delayed in Detroit by the close of the lake shipping. He altered his plans and established his business in Detroit.

Mills employed a number of teams and wagons to travel throughout the West, trading goods for raw furs and becoming one of the leading fur merchants in Detroit. In 1850, he started the manufacture of cigars, and in 1861, he entered into partnership with Frank Nevin in the manufacture of tobacco. This company eventually became the Banner Tobacco Company. He was one of the principal investors in the Detroit and Michigan stove companies, the Detroit Iron and Brass Works, and the Detroit Transit Railway Company. He also invested in banking and insurance and owned a large amount of Detroit real estate.

As a Democrat, Mills was elected mayor of Detroit in November 1865 by a vote of 3,851 to Henry P. Bridge's 2,958 and served for two years in that post. In 1868, he ran for Congress but finished second to his Republican opponent. He remained active in Democratic politics, serving as chairman of the State Central Committee of the Democratic party and as delegate-at-large to the national Democratic convention at St. Louis in 1876.

Mills died on 14 September 1882 and was survived by his wife, a son, Merrill B. Mills, and a daughter, Mrs. William B. Smith. His estate was valued at more than $1 million.

SOURCES: Detroit *Free Press*, 15 September 1882; Silas Farmer, *The History of Detroit and Michigan . . .* (Detroit, 1889); *Journal of the Proceedings of the Common Council of Detroit* (1866, 1867); Scrapbooks, Burton Historical Collection, Detroit Public Library.   *John Cumming*

MIRIANI, LOUIS CHARLES (1897–   ), Mayor of
Detroit (1957–62). Born on 1 January 1897 in Detroit,
Michigan, Miriani was the son of Roman Catholic Italians who emigrated to the United States in the 1890s:
Charles (Carlo) Miriani (1869–1918), a laborer, and
Caroline (Venegoni) Miriani (1875–1948). The eldest of
three sons, Louis attended public schools and graduated
from Eastern High School before serving one year in the
U.S. Navy, 1918–19. To help support his family, Miriani
did odd jobs, post office and bank clerk work. He enrolled in the University of Detroit Law School and received an LL.B. in 1923. He also took courses at Wayne
University in Detroit. He first practiced law and then in
the late 1920s joined the staff of the Legal Aid Bureau,
funded by the Detroit Bar Association. Miriani served
as chief counsel of the Legal Aid Bureau from 1930 to
1954.

On 11 April 1929, Miriani married Verona M. Vachon
(1908–   ), a Roman Catholic native of Calumet, Michigan, and they had two daughters, Dolores and Carol.
In the 1930s and 1940s, Miriani was active in civic affairs: president of the Detroit Welfare Commission,
member of the Detroit Street Railway Commission
(1934–44), member of the State Welfare Commission
(1940–47), vice-chairman and chairman of the Regional
War Labor Board (1943–45), and a lecturer on social
legislation at Wayne University.

Detroit in 1950 had 1,849,568 people, a strong mayor-
council form of government, and nonpartisan elections.
Miriani remained independent of political parties during
his public career. Elected to the Detroit Common Council
in 1947, he served as council president, 1950–57. He
was acting mayor during Mayor Albert Cobo's (*q.v.*)
convalescence from a severe heart attack in 1952–53,
and again upon Cobo's death in September 1957. Miriani
won the 1957 election by 290,947 to his opponent John
J. Beck's 48,074. As mayor, he sought to continue the
building and redevelopment programs started by previous
mayors. He was able to complete a major facility, the
$70 million Cobo Hall and Convention Arena, and to
continue slum clearance, freeway construction, and efforts to regenerate downtown Detroit. Yet, an inherited
budget deficit, a thirty-month economic recession na-
tionwide, inflation, loss of state aid as a result of declining population (1960 Census), and a rural-dominated
state legislature prompted Miriani to reduce the city
budget by a cumulative $27 million and city employees
by 2,000 during his four-year term. In 1961, Miriani was
considered a favorite for reelection, but a midcampaign
Time Magazine article (October 1961) critical of Detroit,
combined with his rival Jerome C. Cavanagh's (*q.v.*)
criticism of the city's continuing budget deficits, high
unemployment, flight of population and industry from

the city, and harsh police relations with the black community, resulted in Miriani's upset defeat (158,679 votes
to Cavanagh's 200,773).

From 1962 into the 1970s, Miriani was executive vice-
president of the Aronsson Printing Company in Detroit.
A prominent Roman Catholic, Miriani was appointed to
the lay board of trustees of Mercy College in Detroit in
1962. Reelected to the Detroit Common Council in 1965,
Miriani served from 1966 to 1970, voting as part of a
liberal bloc. In 1966, Miriani was indicted on charges
of evading federal taxes on $259,495 of income from
1959 to 1962. He was convicted in 1968 and, after losing
appeals, served almost a year in federal prison (1970–71)
and paid a $40,000 fine. After his release in 1971, Mir-
iani continued to live quietly in Detroit.

SOURCES: Robert Conot, *American Odyssey* (New
York, 1974); Detroit Archives, Mayor's Papers, Louis
C. Miriani, Burton Historical Collection, Detroit Public
Library; Louis C. Miriani, biography file, Burton His-
torical Collection, Detroit Public Library; Robert J.
Mowitz and Deil S. Wright, *Profile of a Metropolis*
(Detroit, 1962); *Time* Magazine, 27 October 1961.

De Witt S. Dykes, Jr.

MITCHEL, JOHN PURROY (1879–1918), Mayor of
New York (1914–17). ''Boy-mayor'' and reformer
Mitchel was born on 19 July 1879 in Fordham, New
York, the son of James Mitchel, a fire marshall, and
Mary (Purroy) Mitchel. His father was of Irish, and his
mother of Spanish, descent; both were Roman Catholic.
He attended St. John's Prep School, Columbia College,
and New York Law School from which he was graduated
with honors in 1902. After first working in the law office
of Eugene A. Philbin, Mitchel and two other young lawyers formed the partnership of Mullan, Cobb, and
Mitchel. Mitchel was hired by New York's corporation
counsel to investigate corruption in various city departments and soon established a reputation as a fearless
muckraker. Serving as Mayor McClellan's commissioner
of accounts, he ferreted out illegal practices by administrators in each of the city's boroughs. In 1909, Mitchel
was elected president of the board of aldermen with the
backing of the Republicans, Citizen's Union, and the
nonpartisan Committee of 100. When Mayor Gaynor
(*q.v.*) was shot in an assassination attempt, Mitchel
served as acting mayor for two months. In 1909, Mitchel
married Alice Olivia Child of Boston.

New York City in 1914 had 5,333,537 people and a
mayor-board of aldermen form of government. In 1913,
Mitchel was the anti-Tammany candidate of the fusion
movement and defeated Democrat Edward E. McCall by
the largest plurality since the formation of the Greater
City in 1897: Mitchel won 355,888 votes to McCall's

234,679. As mayor, Mitchel sought to improve the machinery of government and appointed as department heads men with professional and managerial backgrounds. New York City became the first in the nation to adopt a comprehensive zoning plan, and the police department functioned more honestly and efficiently. Yet, Mitchel's preoccupation with economy and balancing the budget led many to argue that he ignored the needs of the growing city. (Robert Moses, an ardent critic of Mitchel's brand of reform, described the mayor's efforts as "saving rubber bands" and "using both ends of the pencil.") Mitchel's support of the Gary Plan in the city's school system highlighted the criticism that he was more interested in saving money than in the welfare of the school children.

Mitchel's uncompromising preparedness advocacy after the outbreak of World War I and his indifference to politics cost him much of his support by 1917. That year he ran for reelection as a fusion candidate but without the support of the Republicans. In a four-sided race, Mitchel finished a distant second. Tammany Democrat John F. Hylan (q.v.) got 297,282 votes, Mitchel 147,975, Socialist Morris Hillquit 142,178, and Republican William S. Bennett 53,678.

After leaving the mayoralty, Mitchel received a commission in the Air Force. While undergoing advanced flight training at Gerstner Field, Lake Charles, Louisiana, Mitchel died in a plane crash on 6 July 1918. After lying in state in New York's city hall, he was buried in the city's Woodlawn Cemetery.

SOURCES: August Cerillo, Jr., "The Reform of Municipal Government in New York City: From Seth Low to John Purroy Mitchel," *New York Historical Society Quarterly* 57:1 (January 1973); Edwin R. Lewinson, *John Purroy Mitchel: Boy Mayor of New York* (New York, 1965); New York *Times*, 8 November 1913, and 7 July 1918 (obituary). W. Roger Biles

MOFFAT, HUGH (1810–84), Mayor of Detroit (1872–75). Immigrant mayor of Detroit, Moffat was born in Coldstream, Scotland, in 1810 of a Presbyterian family. His schooling is not known, but at the time of his arrival in Detroit in 1837 after a brief stay in Albany, New York, he was already a master carpenter. Moffat soon became Detroit's best known builder, constructing such landmarks as St. Paul's Church, the Marriner's Church, and the old Moffat Building (razed in 1922). By 1852, he had shifted to the lumber business, owning a large mill and several tracts of timber in northern Michigan, all of which added considerably to his fortune. Moffat married twice and had five children: Isabella, Margaret, Alice, William, and Addison. The last-named became a partner with him in the lumber business. Moffat

was a life-long Scots Presbyterian until he broke with the local church during the Civil War because the minister refused to tell him whether slavery was morally right or wrong. Moffat, always quick tempered, grew more curt and blunt with age, and his dislike of sham and anything he considered weakness made him a public, but not always, popular figure. From his business dealings rather than from politics came the sobriquet "honest Hugh." He was a penny-pinching, conservative Republican.

Detroit in 1870 had a population of 79,619, which rose to 101,225 by 1874, and a mayor-council form of government. In 1871, Moffat became the Republican candidate for mayor. The Democratic party nominally controlled the mayor's office and the city council (called the common council), but Moffat was elected on his pledge to curtail city spending. He won in 1871 by 5,522 votes to his Democratic opponent William Foxen's 4,695. He was reelected mayor in 1873 with 5,560 votes to his Democratic opponent Charles M. Garrison's 4,178.

Moffat's terms in office were characterized by his frugality, evidenced by his veto in one year of 28 of the 120 measures passed by the common council. Much of his ability to uphold his veto resulted from the economic depression that engulfed the nation and Detroit at the end of his first term. Few of his strictures were permanent, and he was succeeded in office by a Democrat.

Moffat continued as spokesman for the conservative Republican business community but never again held public office, devoting himself to his lumber interests. He died after a long illness at his home in Detroit on 6 August 1884 and was buried in Elmwood Cemetery in Detroit.

SOURCES: Detroit *Evening News*, 7 August 1884; Detroit *Free Press*, 2 August 1939; Detroit *News*, 10 April 1938; Silas Farmer, *History of Detroit and Wayne County and Early Michigan* (Detroit, 1890, reprint 1969); *Michigan Pioneer Society Collections* (1884), vol. 7; Robert B. Ross and George B. Catlin, *Landmarks of Detroit*, revised by Clarence W. Burton (Detroit, 1898). W. Patrick Strauss

MONROE, JOHN T. (1823–71), Mayor of New Orleans (1860–62, 1866–67). Born in 1823 in Dinwiddie County, Virginia, while his kinsman James Monroe was president, Monroe soon moved with his family to Missouri. By 1837, young Monroe was on his own, working as a laborer on the New Orleans levee. He rose to leadership in the stevedore's union and eventually organized his own company of longshoremen. Considered a champion of the workingmen, he entered politics on the Native American ticket and in 1858 was elected an assistant alderman. Monroe proved to be the leader in this lower chamber of the common council and so was made his party's mayoral candidate. When the municipal elections were held on 5 June 1860, New Orleans was a thriving port of 168,675 inhabitants.

In a large voter turnout, the incumbent Know-Nothings won handily: Monroe received 3,727 votes; Lucius W. Place of the Citizens' ticket 1,993; and the Independent, Alexander Grailhe, 1,873. During Monroe's first year as mayor, secession ripped the nation apart; however, few changes occurred in Crescent City government. Monroe continued Mayor Gerard Stith's (*q.v.*) public works projects with emphasis on building and improving streets. By the fall of 1861 the blockaded city was beset by inflation, food shortages, a crime wave, and Yankee spies. City hall fixed the price of bread, augmented the police force, and helped organize a "Free Market" to feed the families of Confederate soldiers. Nevertheless, the situation continued to deteriorate. By early 1862, the poverty, filth, and malaise of New Orleans dramatically contrasted with the exuberant prosperity that had accompanied secession one year before.

In mid-March, with federal forces preparing to attack from the Gulf, Mayor Monroe and the common council readily accepted martial law. When the federals fought past the forts guarding river access to New Orleans, chaos spread through the city and distraught Confederates wreaked havoc on the wharves. By April 25, a fleet of warships capable of leveling the city anchored in the Mississippi River at New Orleans, and rebel troops departed. Refusing to lower the Confederate flag and peacefully surrender his city, Monroe offered passive resistance. He even made a dramatic speech while standing in front of the enemy's howitzers. Much of the population (now only 140,000) rallied behind him. Monroe did not resign, believing he could mitigate the harshness of military rule. He grudgingly cooperated with General Benjamin Butler who hoped to use this popular magistrate to maintain order and develop unionist support. However, by 16 May 1862, Butler had to remove Mayor Monroe, who refused to swear allegiance to the United States and was held in custody in Louisiana and Florida until 1865.

In early 1866, Monroe reappeared in New Orleans to campaign in the first postwar municipal elections, held on March 12. Running as a Democrat, he defeated the Republican, Joseph H. Moore, by a margin of some 300 of the 6,600 votes cast. Having received the tacit approval of President Andrew Johnson, Monroe took office on 11 May amid the turmoil of Reconstruction. Monroe's complicity in the Mechanics Institute riot of 30 July 1866, his police department's many shortcomings, and his old animosity toward Union officers caused General Philip Sheridan to dismiss him from office once again (19 March 1867).

Monroe moved to Savannah, Georgia, in 1868 and established a stevedoring business. He died there on 23 February 1871. One year later, he was reinterred with Masonic rites in New Orleans.

SOURCES: Edwin L. Jewell, ed., *Jewell's Crescent City Illustrated* (New Orleans, 1873); Howard P. Johnson, "New Orleans under General Butler," *Louisiana Historical Quarterly* 24 (1941); John Smith Kendall, *History of New Orleans*, 2 vols. (Chicago, 1922), vol. 1; J. Peyton McCrary, *Abraham Lincoln and Reconstruction: The Louisiana Experiment* (Princeton, N.J., 1978); John T. Monroe, "Broadside," 25 April 1862; New Orleans *Daily Picayune*, 25 February 1871 and 14 February 1889; Works Progress Administration, "Mayors of New Orleans, 1803 to 1936" (typescript in New Orleans Public Library, New Orleans, 1940).

D. Blake Touchstone

MONTEGÚT, EDGAR (1806–80), Mayor of New Orleans (1844–46). Born in 1806 in Louisiana, Montegút was referred to as a "true representative of the old Creole race." Very little is known of Montegút's personal life or of his administration.

New Orleans in 1844 had a population in excess of 105,000 and a complex mayor-multicouncil form of government (three municipal councils drawn from three city districts and one general council). In the election for mayor in 1844, Montegút who had Democratic support, defeated the Whig incumbent, William Freret (*q.v.*), by a vote of 557 to 465. Election day was marred by charges of fraudulent voting, the throwing out of many ballots, and other election disturbances.

Five days after Montegút took office, a fire on 18 May destroyed a large section of the city. The mayor was preoccupied with relief measures for the disaster victims, and with a lawsuit by the Orleans Theater Company in which the theater sued for money past due from the city on its stock subscription. Meanwhile, the city's private economy was on a sharp upswing toward prosperity. Montegút died on 3 April 1880.

SOURCES: John S. Kendall, *History of New Orleans*, 2 vols. (Chicago, 1922), vol. 1; Works Progress Administration, "Mayors of New Orleans, 1803–1936" (typescript in New Orleans Public Library, New Orleans, 1940).

C. David Tompkins

MONTGOMERY, JOHN (c. 1764–1828), Mayor of Baltimore (1820–22, 1824–26). Before becoming mayor, Montgomery had a long public career. His father, John Montgomery, Sr. (1722–?), emigrated from Ireland and settled in Carlisle, Pennsylvania, in 1745. John Montgomery, Jr., was born there in 1764, eventually studied law, and established a practice in Harford County, Maryland, in 1791. He became a prominent Harford County

Democratic-Republican politician. Between 1793 and 1811, he served six times in the state House of Delegates (1793–98), three times as states' attorney (1793–96), and twice in the U.S. Congress (1807–11) before resigning to move to Baltimore and become the states' attorney (1811–18) again. During the War of 1812, he fought with distinction as captain of the Union Artillery Company at the battle of North Point. He was elected to the House of Delegates from Baltimore City in 1819. He was twice married: first to Mary Harris, and on 3 April 1809 to Maria Nicholson, by whom he had two sons. The Nicholsons were an active Democratic-Republican family.

Baltimore grew in several important ways during the 1820s. Its population increased from 62,738 (1820) to 80,620 (1830). Community boosters, trying to cope with the large War of 1812 debt and the stagnation following the Panic of 1819, sought to assure its future growth through economic expansion. Baltimore had a mayor-city council form of government in which the mayor was elected indirectly to a two-year term.

Mayor Montgomery placed an important role in the city's early development. His rivalry with Mayor Edward Johnson (q.v.) represented a competition within the urban mercantile elite. In 1818, Montgomery's ticket lost to George Stiles' (q.v.) ticket (2,576 to 4,298 votes), but in 1820 it was victorious against incumbent Mayor Edward Johnson's, attracting 3,319 votes to 2,917 for electors pledged to pick the mayor. Johnson unseated Montgomery in 1822 (3,518 to 3,500), and Montgomery won the rematch in 1824 (Montgomery, 3,333; Johnson, 2,994; Jacob Small [q.v.], 950). In 1826, Small defeated Montgomery (4,841 to 2,646).

During his administrations, Montgomery tried to deal with the city's crushing debt structure, to rationalize its administration and operations, and to cut municipal costs. He advocated an ambitious harbor improvement program, partially to reduce the threat of yellow fever, and city investment in improving navigation on the Susquehanna River. Montgomery's attitude and his program to develop efficient, economical, and responsible government were unique for the period. Montgomery died within two years of retirement as mayor, on 17 July 1828, and was buried in a Methodist Episcopal cemetery in Harford County.

SOURCES: Baltimore *American and Commercial Advertiser*, 5, 6 October 1818, 18 September, 3 October, 7 November 1820, 7 October, 5 November 1822, 27 September, 5 October, 2 November 1824, 3 October 1826; Gary L. Browne, "Baltimore in the Nation, 1789–1861" (Ph.D. dissertation, Wayne State University, 1973); Wilbur F. Coyle, *The Mayors of Baltimore* (Baltimore, 1919); Dielman-Hayward File, Maryland Historical Society; *Mayor's Messages* (Baltimore, 1821–26).   *Whitman H. Ridgway*

MOORE, JOSEPH HAMPTON (1864–1950), Mayor of Philadelphia (1920–24, 1932–36). Old Guard, conservative Republican, born on 8 March 1864 in a farmhouse in Woodbury, New Jersey (adjacent to Philadelphia), Moore was the son of Joseph B. Moore, a produce farmer and grocer who claimed descent from New Jersey's earliest settlers, and Mary J. (Dorf) Moore. Young Moore attended a country school and then a grammar school in Camden, New Jersey, leaving at the age of thirteen to enter a law office. He subsequently earned a reputation as a superior student of the law, although he was never admitted to the bar. He worked both as a legal reporter and a labor journalist for the Philadelphia *Public Ledger*. Moore also published a history entitled *Roosevelt and the Old Guard* (1925), and light verse. In 1889, he married Adelaide Stone, who bore him nine children, six of whom survived. He was a member of the Five O'Clock Club, the Union League, the National Press Club, and president of the Atlantic Deeper Waterways Association, a life-long interest.

In 1920, Philadelphia's population was 1,823,779, and the city was operating under a new charter (1919) that revised its mayor-council system (unicameral replacing bicameral and reducing executive power). Moore entered the race in 1919 with considerable political experience both locally and nationally. He was chief clerk to the city treasurer (1895–97), secretary to the mayor (1898–99), city treasurer (1901–1903), a Theodore Roosevelt appointee to the Bureau of Manufacturing of the Department of Commerce (1905), and a U.S. congressman for seven terms, representing the Third Congressional District (1907–20), where he gained his reputation as a conservative Republican. Moore won the mayoralty on 4 November 1919 by claiming independence from the notorious Vare machine, 227,739 to 30,408 (Harry Wescott, Democrat), 17,900 (Joseph S. MacLaughlin, Charterite party), and 6,320 (Charles Bauer, Socialist).

Moore's first term revealed his political limitations. Incorruptible, he was unalterably conservative, an "old fashioned Republican" whose principles rested upon Victorian verities. He made few effective alliances; reformers deserted him; the Vare-dominated council thwarted him. Although Moore was effective in advocating public transportation (Frankford El, Broad Street Subway), street and sewer improvements, and other civic amenities, his first term ended with little except voter affection, which was insufficient to reelect him in 1927. In 1931, public sentiment for "Hampy" again found expression in a victory over Democrat Michael Donahue by 362,329 to 31,330 (3 November 1931).

Moore's Depression era tenure in a city of two million was even less effective than his first. The mayor rejected relief funds for a city facing bankruptcy and instead pushed for a balanced budget. He even drew the barbs of conservative New Dealer Harold Ickes for his refusal to aid the city's jobless and poor. Moore and his otherwise competent cabinet reflected the values of an age long past. His chief accomplishments were the promotion of the Atlantic intercoastal system, earning him the title "Father of the Waterways," and the securing of public respect for the integrity of the mayoralty. He died in 1950.

SOURCES: *Annual Messages of the Mayor*, City of Philadelphia, reports of the various departments; Robert E. Drayer, *J. Hampton Moore: An Old Fashioned Republican* (Ph.D. dissertation, University of Pennsylvania, 1961); *The Mayors of Philadelphia*, Collections of the Genealogical Society of Pennsylvania; Edwin Wolf II, *Philadelphia: Portrait of an American City* (Harrisburg, Pa., 1975).   *Richard A. Varbero*

MOORE, ROBERT M. (1816–80), Mayor of Cincinnati (1877–79). Civil War hero of Scottish descent, Moore was born in Cookstown, Ireland, on 29 October 1816 to Robert and Jane (Knox) Moore. After obtaining a common school education there, he was apprenticed to Edward Patterson, a cabinetmaker, and emigrated to Canada with him in 1832. They moved to Cincinnati the next year, and Moore soon bought his remaining apprenticed time from his employer, entering into the furniture business for himself. With Robert Mitchell, he established the Mitchell, Rammelsberg Furniture Company. In 1847, Moore left the partnership and helped build an omnibus line from Sedanville to Cincinnati. Moore married a wealthy local resident, Anna E. Price (1825–?), on 1 May 1843, and she had four children.

At the outbreak of the Mexican War, Moore became captain of Company A, First Ohio Volunteers, and accompanied them to Mexico. Following that conflict, he served as a staff officer for Governor Salmon P. Chase (1856–60). In the Civil War, Moore joined Company D of the Tenth Regiment Ohio Volunteers as a captain. By 1863, he was promoted to lieutenant colonel.

After the war, Moore returned to Cincinnati, participating in a variety of organizations and groups, such as the Horticultural and Wine-Growers' Association. In 1871, he helped form the News Boy's Union, an organization to aid city paperboys. He also served several terms in the city council representing the Twenty-first Ward.

Cincinnati's population in 1877, approaching its 1880 total of 253,139, was directed by a mayor-council form of government. Moore secured the Republican nomination for mayor in 1877 and defeated the popular Democratic incumbent, George W.C. Johnston (*q.v.*), and Workingman's party candidate Charles A. Thompson (18,240 to 15,198 to 3,594). Although he had campaigned on a reform platform, the city under Moore remained wide open, while his own administration was marked by corruption and graft, including a swindle by one of his clerks for several thousand dollars. Moore, who appears to have been honest himself, paid back the missing funds shortly after leaving office in 1879, when he failed to gain his party's renomination for the mayor's post.

Soon after vacating the mayoralty, Moore became ill with a kidney ailment and died in the city on 23 February 1880. He was buried at Spring Grove Cemetery.

SOURCES: *The Biographical Cyclopedia and Portrait Gallery with an Historical Sketch of the State of Ohio* (Cincinnati, 1884); Cincinnati *Enquirer*, 27 February 1880; Charles Theodore Greve, *Centennial History of Cincinnati and Its Representative Citizens* (Chicago, 1904); *In Memoriam. Containing Proceedings of the Memorial Association, Eulogies at Music Hall, and Biographical Sketches of Many Distinguished Citizens of Cincinnati* (Cincinnati, 1881).   *Robert B. Fairbanks*

MORGAN, DANIEL EDGAR (1877–1949), City Manager of Cleveland (1930–31). Reform city manager and third Welsh-American to govern Cleveland, Morgan was born on 7 August 1877 in Oak Hill, Jackson County, Ohio, the eldest son of Elias Morgan (1846–93), a brickmaker who became a banker, and Elizabeth (Jones) Morgan, both Welsh and Calvinistic Methodists. Morgan was a church member in his youth. He attended grade school in Oak Hill, Marietta College, and Oberlin College, where he graduated (B.A.) in 1897. He earned a law degree from Harvard in 1901 and began to practice law in Cleveland. On 22 April 1915, Morgan married Ella A. Mathews (1881–1923) of Chester, Illinois, a high school teacher and an organizer for the suffrage movement in Chicago and Cleveland. She died in 1923 after the birth of a child, Nancy Olwen, and on 16 June 1926, Morgan married Wilma Irene Ball, a teacher and consumer activist.

In 1909 Morgan ran successfully for city council as a Republican but in 1911 lost a bid for city solicitor. For the next seventeen years, he was heavily involved in civic activities in Cleveland (its City Club, the Municipal League, the Home Rule Campaign, the Municipal Research Bureau) but avoided direct politics.

In 1928 Morgan was elected state senator and earned a reputation as an excellent legislator. He resigned in 1930 when appointed city manager (the incumbent, W. R. Hopkins, had run afoul of the Republican leadership).

Thus, Morgan initially faced considerable opposition from reformers and city editors, but his prudent management and progressive policies overcame much criticism. As city manager, Morgan faced the problem of over 50 percent unemployment as the Depression hit Cleveland. He got the Cleveland School Board and county officials to work together to put a $31 million bond issue on the ballot, and the money was used to build hospitals, sewage facilities, and exhibition hall facilities. These and other projects, such as city parks and the municipal stadium, provided jobs, while Morgan's skills as a negotiator ended disputes with the suburbs over water rates, and with the gas company over their rates. Morgan ended the long-entrenched policy of not allowing black doctors and nurses to train at the municipal-owned city hospital.

In 1931, Clevelanders restored the mayor-council form of government, and, in the ensuing primary election for mayor in January 1931, Morgan and Ray T. Miller (*q.v.*) the Democratic county prosecutor, emerged as winners. But in the runoff election in February 1931 Miller beat Morgan by 7,707 votes out of the 198,824 cast. Morgan had been city manager from 28 January 1930 to 13 November 1931.

Morgan lost the gubernatorial Republican primary of 1934 and served briefly as Republican county chairman in 1936–37. In 1939, Governor John W. Bricker appointed him to the Eighth District Appellate Court of Ohio—a position he held until his death in 1949. As judge, Morgan continued to display his commitment to social justice. During the war he served as chairman of the Cleveland Metropolitan Council on Fair Employment. Later, he sat on the city's Post-War Planning Council. After a long illness, Morgan died on 1 May 1949 and was buried in Cleveland.

SOURCES: Thomas F. Campbell, *Daniel E. Morgan: The Good Citizen in Politics: 1877–1949* (Cleveland, 1966); Frederic C. Howe, *The Confessions of a Reformer* (New York, 1925); Daniel E. Morgan Papers, Western Reserve Historical Society, Cleveland, Ohio; Hoyt Landon Warner, *Progressivism in Ohio 1897–1917* (Columbus, 1964).   *Thomas F. Campbell*

MORIAL, ERNEST NATHAN (1929–   ), Mayor of New Orleans (1978–   ). This first black mayor of the Crescent City was born on 9 October 1929 in New Orleans, the youngest of six children of a French-speaking, middle-class family. His father, Walter Etienne Morial, a "black Creole" cigarmaker, was descended from a group called in the South "free men of color." His mother, Leonie V. (Moore), was a seamstress. Nicknamed "Dutch," Morial attended public and private schools and was graduated from Xavier University in

1951 and from Louisiana State University Law School in 1954. Having served two years in the Army, he returned to New Orleans to his law partnership, 1956–60. He represented the Standard Life Insurance Company of Louisiana as general counsel, 1960–67, and was appointed assistant U.S. attorney in New Orleans, 1965–67. Morial was elected, 1968–70, to the Louisiana legislature as the first black state representative since Reconstruction, and, according to a New Orleans newspaper, left a record that was unexceptional and a style described as "one of the boys."

Morial lost an at-large election for the city council in 1969 and was appointed the following year by the governor as juvenile court judge (1970–74). Undeterred by his council loss, Morial won a seat on the Louisiana Court of Appeals, New Orleans, where he served as judge, 1974–77. He also lectured at Tulane University, was active in civil rights cases, and served as president of the New Orleans chapter of the National Association for the Advancement of Colored People, 1962–65. On 17 February 1955, Morial married Sybil Gayle Haydel, a member of a prominent New Orleans family; they have three daughters and two sons. In addition to serving on the governing boards of several local-area universities, Morial is a member of several fraternal organizations, including the Elks and the Knights of Columbus. He is a Roman Catholic. *Ebony* magazine named him one of the 100 most influential blacks in 1971, 1972, 1973, and 1978.

New Orleans in 1978 had a population of under 600,000 and a mayor-council form of government. Morial, who had been the city's first black councilman, entered the mayoral primary in 1977 and was the top votegetter. In the election, Morial beat his old council opponent, Joseph V. DiRosa, by a vote of 89,800 to 84,300. Carrying 51 percent of the total vote cast, Morial won with 95 percent of the black vote and 20 percent of the white vote—the latter mostly "uptown liberals," according to his critics.

A controversial and sometimes abrasive figure since he entered the mayoral scene (he sued for $1 million a former candidate who criticized his ability to get along with people), the stocky 5 foot 8 inch former youth boxer arouses sharply differing assessments. When his critics call him "vindictive and ruthless" and "pompous and arrogant," Morial retorts that he is "decisive" and that his arrogance is the "arrogance of excellence." As mayor, he has faced strikes of sanitation workers and teachers, and a Mardi Gras-time police strike that made national headlines and lost the city possibly $10 million in tourist income. Against the police, Morial took a "hard line," brought in National Guardsmen, and won: demoralized strikers returned to police duty without a contract. Meanwhile, New Orleans continued to suffer from an inadequate tax base, general decay, and a heavy dependency upon federal funds to operate the city. Sensitive to federal overdependency, Morial has sought to reinvigorate the economy by inducing expansion in the private sector. He has also committed New Orleans to a policy of affirmative action and hiring quotas on private contractors with the city.

SOURCES: Chicago *Tribune*, 20 May 1979; New Orleans Times-Picayune, 14 November 1977; New York *Times Biographical Service*, 9 November 1977; A. Poinsett, ''Mayor Ernest N. Morial Finds Running New Orleans Is No Mardi Gras,'' *Ebony* 34 (December 1978).   *Melvin G. Holli*

MORRIS, BUCKNER STITH (1800–79), Mayor of Chicago (1838–39). Lawyer, politician, and Chicago's second mayor, Morris was born in Augusta, Kentucky, on 19 August 1800 the son of Dickinson Morris (1762–1849), a Delaware-born surveyor and farmer, and Frances (Buckner) Morris (b. 1782, Virginia). The family was Protestant, probably Episcopalian. The oldest of six children, Morris attended local schools until aged ten, and then worked on the farm. He studied law, 1824–27, starting practice in 1827. Morris served two terms in the Kentucky legislature (1830–34), where he supported bills attempting to abolish slavery. A conservative Whig, he opposed Jacksonian fiscal policies. In 1832, he married Evelina Barker of Mason County, Kentucky, and they had two daughters, only one of whom survived to adulthood.

Morris visited Chicago briefly in early 1834, returning with his wife in the autumn. Chicago's third lawyer, Morris soon developed a flourishing practice, investing his earnings in real estate. He served on the town's board of health (1835–36) and helped draft the first city charter (1836–37). In 1838, Morris was elected Chicago's second mayor, defeating Democrat William Jones 377 to 318. Chicago then had approximately 4,000 people and a mayor-council form of government. As mayor, Morris responded to the depression of 1837 by urging fiscal retrenchment and by donating his salary to the relief of unemployed canal workers.

Morris subsequently served as Sixth Ward alderman (1839–40, and briefly in 1844) and as a Whig presidential elector in 1840. In 1842, he spent six months as adjutant of the Sixtieth Regiment (Illinois Militia). He was defeated in both the 1839 state Senate election and the 1844 congressional campaign. Morris also ran unsuccessfully for governor in 1852 (as a Whig), 1856 (as the Know-Nothing candidate) and 1860 (supporting the Bell-Everett Constitutional-Union ticket). During 1853–55, Morris was judge of the Seventh Circuit Court, refusing a second term for fear of having to impose the death penalty, which he considered immoral.

During 1842, Morris owned the Chicago *Daily American*, supporting the presidential hopes of Henry Clay. He was on the board of directors of both the Chicago Hydraulic Company and the Chicago Marine and Fire Insurance Company, and was a prominent Mason.

Morris's first wife, Evelena, was murdered in March 1848 and two years later, on 1 August 1850, he married Eliza Stephenson (1815–55), the English-born daughter of a wealthy businessman. Their two children died in infancy, and Eliza herself died of heart disease. A year after her death (1856), Morris married Mrs. M. E. Parrish, a Southerner like himself, and the widowed sister of two of his law partners, from a prominent Kentucky family. They had no children. In 1864, Morris and his third wife, who were naturally pro-Southern, were arrested and charged with complicity in the Northwest Conspiracy, a strange Confederate plot to free prisoners by an attack on Chicago. The Morrises did know some of the conspirators, but the couple was eventually acquitted in 1865, Morris resuming his law practice and his wife opening a boarding house. Impressed by the relief work of the nuns, both had converted to Catholicism in prison. Dwindling resources forced Mrs. Morris to return home to the South, and the now elderly Buckner was forced to live with his widowed daughter in Chicago. He died there on 16 December 1879 after a lengthy illness.

SOURCES: A. T. Andreas, *History of Chicago*, 3 vols. (Chicago, 1884–86); Chicago *Daily Tribune*, 16 December 1879 (an exceptionally fine obituary); Henry E. Hamilton, ''Buckner S. Morris,'' 5-typed MS. in the Chicago Historical Society: information on family background obtained from Mrs. Louise Poage of Brookville, Kentucky; Bessie L. Pierce, *A History of Chicago*, 3 vols. (New York, 1937–57); *The United States Biographical Dictionary and Portrait Gallery of Eminent and Self-Made Men, Illinois Volume* (Chicago, 1878).

Thomas R. Bullard

MORRIS, ROBERT HUNTER (1802–55), Mayor of New York (1841–44). Democratic reform mayor of New York City, Morris was the ninth child of Robert and Frances (Ludlum) Morris. The father was the son of Richard Morris, the second chief justice of the state of New York. Although born in New York City, Morris grew up in Hudson, Columbia County, New York, where the family moved soon after his birth. While there, his sister Mary met and married James A. Hamilton, son of Alexander Hamilton. Morris was privately tutored, read law, and then opened a law practice in Johnston, Columbia County. He moved to New York in 1827 to serve as assistant district attorney (1827–33) under his brother-in-law, James A. Hamilton.

Morris was elected as a Democrat to a state assembly seat (1833–34). He became recorder of the city of New York in 1838 and remained in that capacity until removed by Governor William H. Seward in 1841 in the midst of an election scandal.

Morris uncovered a scheme in 1840, by which Philadelphia workmen were to be brought into New York for the ostensible purpose of laying water mains for the Croton Water Works. They were, however, expected to cast their ballots for the Whig presidential candidate, William Henry Harrison. For uncovering this so-called Glentworth Papers scheme, Morris was catapulted to Democratic prominence and in April 1841 was narrowly elected to the first of three terms as mayor by a vote of 18,602 to 18,206 cast for the Whig J. Phillips Phoenix and 77 votes for the Native American Samuel F.B. Morse.

Morris soon realized that real political power lay with the common council. While he was a Democrat, the council was Whig-dominated. This struggle came to a head after Morris was reelected in 1842. His opponents in the 1842 election were the Clay Whig candidate J. Phillips Phoenix, 18,755; the Abolitionist T. F. Field, 136; and the Tyler Whig James Monroe, 22. Against this disorganized opposition, Morris polled 20,633 votes.

Soon after the election, the council moved to create committees whose main purpose was to take all executive powers over the police, the Croton water system, and sanitation into their own hands. Morris fought this by suggesting a revision in the city charter to strengthen the mayor's executive powers. Recognizing that reform had become a dominant issue, the Democrats pledged to clean up city government if elected in 1843. Morris was swept into a third term by a vote of 25,398 to the Whig Robert Smith's 19,507.

The city of some 320,000 desperately needed improved municipal services, and Morris sought to move the government in a proper course. Politics intruded as usual, with the Democrats proving themselves as incapable as the Whigs at instituting reforms. Morris recommended a reorganized police system, an executive planning board to supervise municipal contracts, and a tighter control over the recently created Croton Water Works. He was all but ignored by his own party, while the Whig newspaper editor, William Cullen Bryant, dubbed him "The Standard of Reform." In a last-ditch effort to salvage their positions prior to the municipal elections of April 1844, the council adopted Morris's proposals concerning the police and passed a reform measure along lines he had originally proposed on 7 August 1843.

After completing his third term, Morris was appointed postmaster of New York City by President James K. Polk. In 1853, he was elected to an eight-year term as justice of the state supreme court of the first judicial district, but he died on 24 October 1855. Mayor Morris was characterized by contemporaries as having been "forcible, eloquent, sarcastic and jocose."

SOURCES: Ira M. Leonard, "The Rise and Fall of the American Republican Party in New York City, 1843–1845," *New-York Historical Society Quarterly* 50:2 (April 1966); New-York *Herald*, 26 and 28 October 1855; James G. Wilson, ed., *The Memorial History of the City of New York* (New York, 1893), vol. 3.

Jacob Judd

MORRISON, DE LESSEPS STORY (1912–64), Mayor of New Orleans (1946–61). Morrison was born in New Roads, Louisiana, on 18 January 1912, the son of Jacob Haight and Anita (Olivier) Morrison, Roman Catholics of Scottish and French ancestry. De Lesseps attended Poydras Academy in New Roads. In 1932, he graduated from Louisiana State University in Baton Rouge, and in 1934 he received his law degree from Louisiana State University. After graduation, Morrison became a trial attorney with the National Recovery Administration in New Orleans. In 1935, he began a partnership with his half-brother Jacob and with T. Hale Boggs.

In 1936, Morrison entered politics as a precinct captain in the gubernatorial election, and in 1939, he helped organize the People's League of Independent Voters. The next year he was a successful candidate for the state House of Representatives from the Twelfth Ward, on the Sam Houston Jones ticket. In Baton Rouge he became a Jones floor leader.

In late 1941, Morrison entered active duty with the Army. In 1942, he married Corinne Waterman of New Orleans, a Newcomb College graduate; they had three children. After a brief assignment in New Orleans, the next year he went overseas to Europe. He received the bronze star for his work in the Normandy invasion, fought in the Battle of the Bulge, and rose to the rank of colonel. In 1944, he won reelection to the Louisiana house in absentia, while becoming chief of staff of the Bremen Port Command the following year.

After the war, Morrison returned to New Orleans and became the last-minute mayoral candidate of the Independent Citizens' Committee. On 22 January 1946, he won a surprisingly narrow victory over Robert S. Maestri (*q.v.*) by a vote of 67,160 to 63,273 and Shirley Wimberly 1,888. After this election, Morrison established the Crescent City Democratic Association, his personal political organization. At the time, New Orleans had 500,000 people, reaching its peak population of about

630,000 by 1960 and like many U.S. cities, declining thereafter.

Morrison officially took office on 4 April 1946, quickly launching a municipal improvement program that included street construction, better drainage, creation of a city recreation department, a union passenger terminal-grade separation program (completed in 1954), and a modern civic center project (completed in 1957). The mayor also began to promote new industry and trade in the city. A municipal department of international relations fostered commerce with Latin America and Europe. Morrison extended his programs to the black community, although he publicly and personally professed a strong belief in racial segregation. Through his many municipal projects, he won favorable support in the city and established an admirable national reputation.

Morrison practiced spoils politics with a consummate skill that defied his reform image. He also permitted inadequate planning and waste in several municipal improvement projects, notably the municipal courts building and Lyons Center. In 1949, his loose attitude toward local vice and toward police and political contacts with the criminal underworld precipitated the resignation of Police Superintendent A. Adair Watters.

In 1948, Morrison endorsed Sam Houston Jones in the gubernatorial campaign and thus alienated Earl K. Long, the victor. Long and the state legislature soon retaliated with several laws and constitutional amendments that undermined New Orleans' financial and administrative structure, and they sought to force Morrison from office. This action won increased popular backing for the mayor. In 1950, he handily won reelection over Charles Zatarain, the Long nominee, 120,582 to 58,620; with Alvin Cobb's 4,751 and a scattered vote of 1,214 for two others. After the election, Governor Long restored financial and administrative control to the city and backed a home rule plan for New Orleans.

The victory over the Long forces raised Morrison's status in Louisiana politics. He took an increasingly active role in several state-wide campaigns. In 1951, he led a movement against a Long-dominated constitutional convention, and in 1951–52, he backed the unsuccessful gubernatorial bid of T. Hale Boggs.

Morrison supported the committee of 1952 which drafted a new charter for New Orleans in order to establish home rule and create a mayor-council form of government to replace the commission council. In 1953, he backed a comprehensive new zoning ordinance. The mayor won reelection in 1954 under the new charter polling 94,313 votes to Thomas Brahney's 49,849 and John T. Grosch's 11,193. The findings of a citizens' investigating committee that uncovered evidence of widespread graft in the police department seriously dam-

aged Morrison's reform reputation but did not defeat him. This investigation led to several reorganizations of the police department during the following years.

In 1956, Morrison lost to Earl Long in the gubernatorial primary. Although he handily won reelection to the office of mayor in 1958, polling 90,802 to his opponents' C. W. Duke's 43,213 and F. C. Donaldson's 18,999. Morrison's growing involvement in state politics and other outside activities precipitated several administrative setbacks. Many of his political supporters defected to the opposition. On 26 February 1959, his wife, Corinne Morrison, died suddenly. In January 1960, Morrison lost the governor's election to Jimmie H. Davis in a hotly contested second primary that featured segregationist diatribes. In September 1960, the mayor's decision to pursue a politically neutral path during the school desegregation crisis deprived the city of necessary leadership and contributed to racial unrest.

Morrison endorsed an unsuccessful charter amendment in April 1961 that would have permitted him another term in office. On 17 July 1961, he resigned to become ambassador to the Organization of American States. In 1964, he ran for governor for the third time and lost to John McKeithen in another second primary. Morrison died in a plane crash in Mexico on 22 May 1964.

SOURCES: Edward F. Haas, "DeLesseps S. Morrison and the Governorship: A Reassessment," *Louisiana Studies* 15 (Summer 1972); Edward F. Haas, *DeLesseps, S. Morrison and the Image of Reform: New Orleans Politics, 1946–1961* (Baton Rouge, La., 1974); DeLesseps S. Morrison, *Latin American Mission: An Adventure in Hemisphere Diplomacy*, edited by Gerald Frank (New York, 1965).   *Edward F. Haas*

MOSBY, JOHN BORDEN (1845–1928), Mayor of Cincinnati (1889–94). Wholesale grocer and first three-year term mayor, Mosby was born on 4 December 1845 in Cincinnati, Ohio, the son of Napoleon Bonaparte Mosby of Petersburg, Virginia, and Ann (Borden) Mosby of Pennsylvania. The youngest of five children, he attended the public schools and then followed his father into the wholesale grocery business. He worked for the grocery house of A. Ludington for eleven years. During the Civil War, Mosby served as a member of the Ohio Volunteer Infantry. In 1872, he began a partnership with A. J. Hodson which lasted until Hodson's death in 1889. Mosby then joined two other men and established the wholesale grocery firm of Mosby, Raum and Gogreve, which became one of the largest grocers in Cincinnati. On 19 October 1879, Mosby married Mary F. Ludington, a Virginian and the daughter of his former employer. The Mosbys had five children—Stella M., John F., Gertrude, Genevieve, and Grace. He was a Scottish Rite

Mason and a member of the Knights of Pythias, the Blaine and Lincoln clubs, Cincinnati Lodge No. 2, the Independent Order of Oddfellows, and the Grand Army of the Republic.

Cincinnati in 1889 had almost 300,000 people and a mayor-council form of government. An active Republican, Mosby won his first term as mayor in 1889. He was narrowly reelected in 1891, securing only 25,582 votes to Democrat Gustav Tafel's (*q.v.*) 24,444. With the 1891 election Mosby was the first mayor to serve under the new city charter of 1890 which raised the mayor's term from two to three years. Under the provisions of this charter, he governed with the assistance of a newly created board of administration consisting of four members with no more than two members from the same political party, appointed by the mayor. The board was designed to abolish governmental inefficiency and to ''purify'' Cincinnati's politics. During his two terms as mayor, Mosby enthusiastically promoted the Queen City, worked to abate the smoke nuisance, strove to improve and to expand the park system, and grappled with the traction franchise issue.

Mosby did not run for a third term. He retired from public life and returned to the grocery business. He died in Cincinnati on 21 November 1928.

SOURCES: Biographical Cyclopedia and Portrait Gallery (Cincinnati, 1895); *Cincinnati's Mayors* (Cincinnati, 1957); Charles T. Greve, *Centennial History of Cincinnati and Representative Citizens* (Chicago, 1904); Zane L. Miller, *Boss Cox's Cincinnati: Urban Politics in the Progressive Era* (New York, 1968); G. M. Roe, *Our Police* (Cincinnati, 1890). *Patricia Mooney Melvin*

MOSCONE, GEORGE RICHARD (1929–78), Mayor of San Francisco (1976–78). Liberal Democratic mayor of San Francisco whose career was cut short by assassination, Moscone was born in the city on 24 November 1929, the son of George J. Moscone and Lee (Monge) Moscone. He married Gina Bondanza (19 June 1954), and they had four children: Jennifer, Rebecca, Christopher, and Jonathan. Moscone attended local schools, took a B.A. in sociology at the University of the Pacific (1952), and a J.D. at the University of California, Hastings Law School, 1956. A strong liberal Democrat and a Roman Catholic, Moscone worked as playground director for the city's department of recreation and parks while taking his law degree (1952–56). He was admitted to the California bar in 1957; taught law at Lincoln University in San Francisco during 1960–64; and was an associate of the law firm of Hanson, Bridgett, Marcus and Jenkins, 1968–76. Moscone served in the U.S. Navy.

A member of the San Francisco Democratic Central Committee from 1960, Moscone was elected to the city board of supervisors (1963–66) at age thirty-three. He was one of the two youngest councillors in city history. In his first attempt at state-wide elective office, he won a seat in the state Senate in 1966 with the second largest plurality in California for a nonincumbent. During the first year in Sacramento, he was made caucus chairman and Democratic floor leader; he was reelected floor leader every year until he resigned to become mayor in 1976. Moscone, a very popular figure, was reelected to the state Senate in 1970 and again in 1974, with large votes.

Moscone's public career was consistently associated with liberal ideas and causes, ranging from the legal rights of indigents, mental health, autistic children, general medical care, tax reform, open government, civil rights, consumer protection, environmentalism, housing, and workers' rights, to education. He published articles on noise pollution and on the need for group legal services. Moscone was elected mayor of San Francisco in December 1975, defeating the conservative Republican John Barbagelata. He took office on 8 January 1976. He and Supervisor Harvey Milk were murdered by a disappointed ex-member of the board of supervisors, Dan White, on 28 November 1978 in Moscone's city hall office.

SOURCES: Mayor's Office, *Biographical Sketch, George R. Moscone* (San Francisco, n.d.); New York *Times*, 28 November 1978.   *Peter d'A. Jones*

MRUK, JOSEPH (1903–   ), Mayor of Buffalo (1950–53). A jeweler by trade and Buffalo's first Polish-American mayor, Mruk was born in Buffalo on 6 November 1903. A Roman Catholic, he attended P.S. 44, St. John Kanty School, and the South Side High School. Mruk opened his own jewelry store in 1926. In 1933, he first sought political office with an unsuccessful campaign to become one of the city's board of supervisors. Mruk was a Republican member of the city council, 1936–39, and councilman-at-large, 1941–42. He was elected to Congress in 1942, being assigned to the Rivers and Harbors Committee. Conservative and cautious, Mruk opposed plans for what would become the St. Lawrence Seaway, thus going against the wishes of many Republican party leaders. It was charged that this clash cost Mruk a chance for a second term in 1944. He ran as an Independent and was defeated in the general election.

In 1945, several city independents urged Mruk to run for mayor, but he refused, stating that he would run only as a Republican candidate. In 1949, he secured that party's nomination and was elected with 123,500 votes to 100,631 for John Hillery (Democrat), 1,254 for Robert Hoffman (Liberal), and 1,411 for James Annaccone

(American Labor party). Buffalo had 580,132 people in 1950 and a mayor-council form of government.

Mruk modernized the city's business methods in an effort to streamline operations, reduce waste, and cut costs. He supported an improved system for trimming the city's trees and urged drastic changes in the system of awarding bids for city projects. His refusal to support a new franchise for the International Railway Company caused an end to the city's streetcar system in 1950. He was accused of using the mayor's office to punish members of his party who had blocked his congressional nomination in 1944.

Mruk was a member of the comptroller's office (1954–58) and served for several years as the state commissioner of pensions. He retired from politics in the 1960s.

SOURCES: Contemporary newspaper references in the card file at the Buffalo and Erie County Public Library; *Official Congressional Directory, 78th Cong., 1st Session* (Washington, D.C., 1943); Sister Mary Jane and Sister Mercedes, "Mayors of Buffalo, 1832–1961" (B.A. thesis, Rosary Hill College, 1961).

Thomas R. Bullard

MULLANPHY, BRYAN (1809–51), Mayor of St. Louis (1847–48). Irish Catholic mayor of St. Louis, born in Baltimore in 1809, Mullanphy was the son of John Mullanphy (1758–1833), wealthy philanthropist and merchant, and Elizabeth (Browne) Mullanphy (1773–1843), both immigrants from Ireland. One of fifteen children, young Bryan received his education in France and England, starting in 1818. The family moved to St. Louis in 1819, and Mullanphy began the practice of law after his return from Europe. He never married and would be St. Louis's first bachelor mayor. Like his father, he was prominent in local Catholic charity work.

Mullanphy served as an alderman, 1835–36, and then as a St. Louis Circuit Court judge, 1840–45. A popular Democrat, he was elected mayor in 1847, winning 2,453 votes to 1,829 for William M. Campbell (Nativist) and 962 for James H. Lucas (Whig). St. Louis had a population of 16,469 in 1840 and a mayor-council form of government. As mayor, Mullanphy actively supported civic improvements, notably a new waterworks. He also sought to improve the city's telegraph and railroad links with the rest of the state. He was perhaps best remembered for his desire to help the poor. He leased dairy cows to elderly widows, paying them to care for the animals and for the privilege of selling the milk. This kind of activity earned Mullanphy a reputation for being rather eccentric. After leaving office, he spent several years handling the finances of the Mullanphy Emigrant Aid Society, which had been established by his father.

Mullanphy died at his home in St. Louis on 15 June 1851, sincerely mourned by the city.

SOURCES: Charles H. Cornwell, *St. Louis Mayors: Brief Biographies* (St. Louis, 1965); William Hyde and Howard L. Conrad, eds., *Encyclopedia of the History of St. Louis*, 4 vols. (New York, 1899), vol. 3; The Mullanphy Family Papers (five linear feet of material, at the Missouri Historical Society in St. Louis, relating mainly to John Mullanphy's charities and the battles resulting from his will, which left the bulk of his estate to them); Walter B. Stevens, *St. Louis: History of the Fourth City, 1764–1909* (Chicago, 1909).

Thomas R. Bullard

MURPHY, FRANK (1890–1949), Mayor of Detroit (1930–33). Reform mayor of Detroit and later New Deal governor of Michigan, born on 13 April 1890 in Sand Beach (now Harbor Beach), Michigan, Murphy was the son of John F. Murphy, who had been born in Canada in 1849 and was of Irish extraction, and Mary (Brennan) Murphy, born in Whitehall, New York, in 1850, of Catholic parents who had migrated from Ireland. Frank, who never married, was the third of four children: Harold (1886–) Margaret Mary (Marguerite) (1888–) and George (1894–). Frank was educated in the public schools of Harbor Beach and attended the University of Michigan from 1908 to 1914, receiving an LL.B. He practiced law from 1914 to 1917 and served in the Army during World War I, rising to the rank of captain.

Murphy became first assistant U.S. attorney for the Eastern District of Michigan in August 1919, a position he held until March 1922, when he returned to private law practice. He served as a judge on Detroit's Recorder's Court from January 1924 until August 1930, when he resigned to become a candidate for mayor of Detroit following the recall of Mayor Charles Bowles (*q.v.*). He received 106,637 votes in the September election, defeating Bowles (93,985), George Engel (85,650), John Smith (21,735), and Phil Raymond (3,508). Winning reelection in 1931, he defeated Harold H. Emmons by a vote of 166,748 to 91,657. Detroit's population in 1930 was 1,548,662, and the city had a nonpartisan, mayor-council type of government, the nine aldermen being elected at large.

The Murphy mayoralty was dominated by the Great Depression. Insisting that no one go hungry, Murphy supplemented the relief efforts of the Department of Public Welfare by creating the Mayor's Unemployment Committee, which registered the unemployed, maintained emergency lodges for homeless men, and sponsored a thrift-garden program. Since Detroit was unable to cope successfully with the problem of relief, Murphy convened a conference of mayors in June 1932 to secure

MURRAY, MAGNUS M.   267

federal aid. The mayors met again in February 1933 and established the U.S. Conference of Mayors, with Murphy as president. Despite Murphy's budget cutting, the Michigan banking holiday declared on 14 February 1933, forced Detroit into default on its debt.

A Democrat and supporter of Franklin D. Roosevelt for president, Murphy was selected by the president in 1933 to serve as governor-general of the Philippines. When the Philippine Commonwealth was inaugurated in November 1935, Murphy became high commissioner. Elected Michigan's governor in 1936, he was responsible for one of the few "little New Deals" at the state level. During the recession of 1937–38, he sought, as during his mayoralty, to provide government assistance for the unemployed. Following his defeat in 1938, he was appointed attorney general of the United States, and after serving in that capacity for one eventful year, he was elevated to the U.S. Supreme Court, where he served until his death as an ardent defender of civil liberties. He died of a coronary thrombosis on 19 July 1949 and was buried in Harbor Beach.

SOURCES: Sidney Fine, *Frank Murphy: The Detroit Years* (Ann Arbor, Mich., 1975); and *The Political Career of Frank Murphy* (Chicago, 1979); J. Woodford Howard, *Mr. Justice Murphy: A Political Biography* (Princeton, N.J., 1968); Richard D. Lunt, *The High Ministry of Government:* (Detroit, 1965); *Frank Murphy: The New Deal Years*; For manuscripts, Frank Murphy Papers, Michigan Historical Collections, University of Michigan, Ann Arbor, Michigan; and Mayor's Office Records, Burton Historical Collection, Detroit Public Library, Detroit, Michigan.   *Sidney Fine*

MURRAY, MAGNUS M. (1787–1838), Mayor of Pittsburgh (1829–30, 1831–32). Murray, fourth mayor of Pittsburgh and a Jacksonian Democrat, was born in Philadelphia on 22 February 1787. His father was a distinguished Navy commander from a well-to-do family. Young Murray enrolled in the University of Pennsylvania at the age of twelve, graduated at fifteen, and received a Master's degree three years later.

Coming to Pittsburgh soon afterwards, he studied law under William Wilkins, dean of the county's bar, who moved his admission in 1809. The following year, Murray married Mary Wilkins, a niece of his preceptor. They had three daughters and four sons. A number of mayors came from this family. John Darragh (q.v.) (Pittsburgh's

second mayor) married a Wilkins granddaughter, and Murray was father-in-law of John B. Guthrie (q.v.), mayor in 1851–52, and grandfather of George W. Guthrie (q.v.), who held the office from 1906 to 1909. Murray's greatgrandson, Francis S. Guthrie, was nominated for mayor in 1913 but was defeated.

Murray headed a troop of light dragoons which escorted Lafayette on his visit to Pittsburgh in 1825 and for about forty miles on his way to Erie. Murray, like Lafayette, was a Mason.

When John M. Snowden (q.v.) declined to run for reelection as mayor on 8 January 1828, Murray was an almost unanimous choice, his popularity aided by his being a Jacksonian. He was reelected on 13 January 1829 without opposition, but he was defeated in 1830 by an Anti-Mason, Matthew B. Lowrie (q.v.), whom he in turn defeated a year later, on 11 January 1831.

As mayor, Murray supported public improvements and humane causes. Shortly after he took office, Pittsburgh began work on its first waterworks and reservoir. At this time, the city had a population of about 12,000 (increasing to about 14,000 during his last term). Following the completion of the western end of the Pennsylvania Main Line Canal, he promoted wharf improvements and better trade relations with Philadelphia. Previously, much of Pittsburgh's business had been going to Baltimore, over the National Pike.

During Murray's second term, the councils defeated a proposal to light Pittsburgh streets with produced gas. In his third term, the councils voted $20,000 for public improvements, but they strongly opposed efforts to construct underground sewers for fear they would freeze in cold weather. Under Murray's leadership, Pittsburgh provided free smallpox vaccinations for the indigent. He also suggested taxing dog owners to reduce the number of dogs roaming the streets, rather than (under a recently passed ordinance) shooting any that were without collars. Late in his third term, plans were approved for constructing a new market house, with the novelty of dividing it into squares rented to farmers. Murray died on 4 March 1838.

SOURCES: Allen Humphreys Kerr, "The Mayors and Recorders of Pittsburgh, 1816–1951" (typescript, 1952, Carnegie Library of Pittsburgh); Pittsburgh *Press*, "The Mayors' Notebook," No. 4, by George Swetnam, 19 September 1973; *Western Pennsylvania Historical Magazine* 8 (1925).   *Helene Smith*

NICHOLS, JOHN GREGG (1812–98), Mayor of Los Angeles (1852–53, 1856–59). Nichols was born in Canandaigua, New York, on 29 December 1812 of a Scottish father and a Connecticut Yankee mother. In the winter of 1827–28, the family moved to Fulton county, Illinois, where young Nichols served in the 1832 Black Hawk War and then worked in the Galena lead mines. Following his 1838 marriage to Florida Cox (1819–77), of Illinois, he moved in 1842 to Jackson county, Iowa, where he served two terms as sheriff.

In May 1849, the Nichols, with their three children, left for the California goldfields. Bad weather forced their party south to Los Angeles, where Nichols opened a general store and helped "in establishing the American regime." He contributed several firsts in the Anglicization of the Mexican town: he held its first Protestant services in his home, helped organize the first English private school and import a Congregational minister to teach it, fathered the first American child born in Los Angeles (April 1851; three more children followed), and built, in 1854, the first brick building in the city.

In the first election held after issuance of the city's American charter (July 1850), Nichols ran successfully for recorder (police judge). Then in 1852, when the city contained approximately 2,150 residents, he was elected mayor. His main concern was disposing of communal land to private owners. An ordinance of 13 August 1852, allowed individuals to obtain thirty-five acres of free city-owned land, if they lived there for one year and made improvements of $200. Although Nichols personally boosted disposal of land, the council repealed the ordinance in May 1854.

By then, Nichols' one-year term had expired, and he had retired to business. Efforts at a grocery store and a livery stable evidently failed, so in May 1855 he ran for common council. A Democrat in a heavily Democratic town, he received the highest number of votes cast and also won appointment to the school board, only to resign both positions inexplicably in November. In May 1856, he lost the Democratic nomination for mayor, but the resignation of the winner gave him another chance, and in October he received 163 votes to 144 for Antonio Coronel (*q.v.*) and 12 for Thomas Foster (*q.v.*). Nichols served two more terms, defeating Nelson Williamson

257 to 63 in 1857 and Benjamin Eaton 295 to 278 in 1858. At his urging, the city constructed additional schoolhouses and irrigation ditches. He ran for mayor again in January 1861, following the death of the incumbent, but received only 114 votes to 249 for Damien Marchessault (*q.v.*) and 116 for William Potter. In May 1863, he·ran for the common council but trailed badly, and the following year, as a Union candidate, he lost the mayoralty to Democrat Marchesseault 295 to 287. The council appointed him pound keeper in 1865, but thereafter he had no involvement in public life. He remained rather obscure, listing himself as a farmer and miner until he died on 22 January 1898.

SOURCES: H. D. Barrows, "Pioneers of Los Angeles," *Publications of the Historical Society of Southern California* 4 (1898–99); J. Gregg Layne, "Annals of Los Angeles," *California Historical Society Quarterly* 13 (December 1934); Maurice H. Newmark and Marco R. Newmark, eds., *Sixty Years in Southern California, 1853–1913; Containing the Reminiscences of Harris Newmark,* 4th ed. (Los Angeles, 1970).

R. David Weber

NICHOLS, MALCOLM E. (1876–1951), Mayor of Boston (1926–29). One of the rare Yankee Republican mayors of Boston, Nichols was born in Portland, Maine, on 8 May 1876, the son of Edwin T. Nichols and Helen J.G. Pingree. He took a B.A. at Harvard in 1899 and worked as a newspaper reporter and political editor until 1908, when admitted to the Massachusetts bar. He then became a tax lawyer. He married Edith M. Williams on 16 December 1916 (she died on 9 May 1925), and they had two sons and a daughter. On 26 November 1926, he married Carrie M. Williams. Nichols was a Swedenborgian (Church of New Jerusalem).

Elected to the Boston Common Council (1905–1906) as a Republican and then to the Massachusetts House (1907–1909) and Senate (1914, 1917–19), Nichols was a faithful servant of the Republican party machine. He sat on the Boston school commission, the transit board, and the housing commission, and was appointed federal fuel administrator in Boston, 1920–21, and U.S. collector of internal revenue, 1921–25—which is, no doubt, why Mayor Curley's (*q.v.*) biographer, J. F. Dinneen, called Nichols "a well-born, innocuous accountant."

In 1924–25, the Democrats were badly divided in Boston, and J. M. Curley feuded with J. F. Fitzgerald (q.v.); party boss Martin Lomasney warned them to bury the hatchet, or the Republicans would gain office. Indeed, in 1925, nine Irish Democratic candidates filed and split the vote, shooing in the Republican, Nichols, a puppet of the Republican chiefs. Reporters said that Charles Innes, the real Republican powerhouse, was the day mayor and Nichols the nightmare.

As mayor, Nichols lacked all control. He made no decisions without checking with Innes. Even former Mayor Curley's influence was not totally gone: about half the city hall appointees were Democratic hangovers from the previous Curley administration. Curley's farewell banquet made Nichols' inaugural look pallid. Nevertheless, under Nichols was fathered the "Greater Boston" idea: persuading the U.S. Census to group forty-one communities under this head as a metropolitan area. Nichols presided over a building boom in the city, pushed still further by the pyramidal building law of 1929, which permitted more flexibility in skyscraper construction, a zoning relaxation that produced tapering buildings like the United Shoe Machinery Company. Mayor Nichols' four-year term rounded out the 1920s. He could not succeed himself by law in 1929, and failed to be reelected in 1933, losing to Democrat F. W. Mansfield.

In 1948, Mayor Curley defended Nichols, who was now in charge of the city project to extend the rapid transit subway under Boston harbor to the airport, against charges of payroll padding. It was a strange circumstance for two former political enemies. Not long after, Nichols died, aged seventy-three, on 7 February 1951.

SOURCES: J. H. Cutler, *"Honey Fitz": Three Steps to the White House* (Indianapolis, 1962); J. F. Dineen, *The Purple Shamrock* (New York, 1949).

Peter d'A. Jones

NOONAN, EDWARD ALOYSIUS (1849–1927), Mayor of St. Louis (1889–93). Irish Catholic mayor of St. Louis, Noonan was born in Reading, Pennsylvania, on 20 December 1849, the son of Martin and Johanna (Nagle) Noonan, both Irish-born Catholics. Noonan attended local schools and Albany Law College, graduating in 1870. He had studied law in Reading and moved to St. Louis soon after graduation. He married Margaret Brennan, an Irish Catholic woman, and they had three children. Noonan was a member of the Mercantile Club and the St. Louis Businessmen's Association. He served as assistant district attorney (1877–83) and judge of the court of common pleas (1883–89).

Noonan sought the Democratic mayoral nomination in 1885 but was defeated by David R. Francis (q.v.). In 1889, he was successful and defeated John Butler (Republican) 28,637 to 27,031—the only successful Democratic candidate in that election. To some degree, his victory resulted from the support of an organization called the Young Democrats, which Noonan had helped to organize several years before. St. Louis had 451,770 people by 1890 and a mayor-council form of government.

As mayor, Noonan backed conversion of the city's street railways to electric operation and supported bills that would result in a new central railroad station and a new city hall. Under his administration, St. Louis was the first city in the United States to light its alleys electrically. Noonan succeeded in floating some bond issues in London to pay for improvements in the city's schools and further construction of a sewage treatment plant. After leaving office, Noonan practiced law but apparently not too successfully. He spent his last years living in a hotel near the public library until his death on 23 September 1927.

SOURCES: Charles H. Cornwell, *St. Louis Mayors: Brief Biographies* (St. Louis, 1965); James Cox, *Old and New St. Louis* (St. Louis, 1894); John W. Leonard, ed., *The Book of St. Louisians* (St. Louis, 1906); Walter B. Stevens, *St. Louis: History of the Fourth City, 1764–1909* (Chicago, 1909).

Thomas R. Bullard

NORCROSS, OTIS (1811–82), Mayor of Boston (1867). Single-term mayor of Boston, Norcross was born in Boston on 2 November 1811, the son of Otis Norcross (1785–1827), a dealer in crockery, and Mary (Homer) Norcross (1790–1869). He studied in the public schools of Boston until age fourteen, at which time he entered his father's business as an apprentice. His father, an old-stock Yankee Congregationalist, died when young Otis was sixteen, but the business was continued by his father's associates, and young Norcross was able to take over its direction when he came of age. He showed considerable astuteness and was able to expand it into one of the largest importers and dealers of china and crockery in the nation. He established branches in the West. In 1835, he married Laura Ann Lane of Boston; they had eight children, only four of whom survived infancy.

Norcross's business success gave him a place of importance in Boston, and he developed many civic concerns. He was a founder of the Boston Board of Trade and of the Union Club; he was a trustee of the Museum of Fine Arts, the Massachusetts Institute of Technology, the Homes for Aged Men and Aged Women, and the Young Men's Christian Union, to name but a few. He also became active in municipal politics.

Originally a Whig, Norcross made the transition to the Republican party and stood for office from his elite Back Bay ward. in 1861, he was defeated for state representative but was elected as city alderman. He served on the board of aldermen (1862–64). Retiring at the end of his third term, he shortly again turned to politics, running for mayor against Democrat Nathaniel Shurtleff (*q.v.*) in December 1866, and was victorious (5,662 to 4,755). Shurtleff defeated him, however, in the next annual contest (8,383 to 7,867). Norcross served for a year in 1869 as a governor's councillor, but after that his political career was in an advisory capacity.

Boston's growth, 136,880 in 1850, 177,840 in 1860, and 250,526 in 1870, had been accompanied by considerable governmental initiative and expense, and the debts incurred during the Civil War added to municipal indebtedness. Norcross strongly opposed this growth of city debt as well as the private profit and public inefficiency he believed to be part of contemporary municipal politics. While alderman, he had led a successful attempt to have the Overseers of the Poor be appointive rather than elective offices and to have their accounts regularly audited. Now, as mayor, he looked for a lessening of city initiative in the further development of Boston. He vetoed plans for a new city Insane Hospital and for city initiatives in developing new land and wharfage. In each instance, he maintained that the initiative rightly belonged to the state and/or private interests. This policy of retrenchment, coupled with his aloof manner, led to his defeat, after only a single year in office, by the genial Nathaniel Shurtleff in December 1867.

Norcross was elected to the governor's council in 1869, but that was the extent of his further elective office. He continued his service to the city as a trustee of the city hospital, and the Overseers of the Poor, and as a member of the water board and the board of state charities, in addition to earlier concerns. He died of natural causes on 5 September 1882 and was buried in Mount Auburn Cemetery, Cambridge, Massachusetts.

SOURCES: *Boston Transcript*, 6 September 1882 (obituary); J. M. Bugbee, "Boston Under the Mayors," in Justin Winsor, ed., *Memorial History of Boston*, 4 vols. (Boston, 1881), vol. 3; City of Boston, *Documents, 1867* (Boston, 1867); *In Memoriam: Otis Norcross* (Boston, 1883); Otis Norcross, Diary, 1859–82 (at the Massachusetts Historical Society: laconic, as was its author); *Register of the New England Historic Genealogical Society* 37 (April 1883).

Constance Burns

O

O'BRIEN, HUGH (1827–95), Mayor of Boston (1885–88). O'Brien, the first Irish Catholic mayor of Boston, was born in Ireland on 13 August 1827. He arrived in Boston at the age of five and attended the Fort Hill Grammar School; at twelve he left school to learn the printer's trade in the offices of the Boston *Courier*. For a time, he worked as foreman in the book and job office of Tuttle, Dennett, and Chisholm, leaving in 1843 to establish the *Shipping and Commercial List*, for which he served as both editor and publisher. Over the next twenty years, he became a principal figure in Boston's Irish community. He was elected president of the Union Institution for Savings and of the Charitable Irish Society, treasurer of the Franklin Typographical Society, and a trustee of the St. Vincent's Orphan Asylum.

As a result of his newspaper work, O'Brien's influence and reputation broadened, and in 1875 he served as alderman, the first of six years in that office. He was suggested as a mayoral candidate in 1881 and 1882, but he refused to have his name brought forward. In 1883, however, he accepted the Democratic nomination to oppose Augustus P. Martin (*q.v.*), in a campaign focusing on O'Brien's Irish, Catholic extraction and his alleged connection with the city Democratic machine of Patrick J. McGuire. For many, his defeat, 27,494 to 25,950, represented deliverance from "Irish domination." In 1884, O'Brien again faced Martin, and this time carried the polls by more than 3,000 votes, 27,494 to 24,168, despite a Republican press which billed the contest as a choice between honest government and the spoils system.

Boston in 1885 had a population of 390,393 and a mayor bicameral-council form of city government. As mayor, O'Brien pleaded the cause of city laborers, favored statutory limitation of municipal borrowing, a tax cap, and executive control of the budget. To lure manufacturing interests to the city, he proposed favorable tax incentives; to promote public access, he had a complaint book placed in the mayor's office. In part a transitional figure between old Yankee Democrats and the newer Irish politicians, O'Brien represented continuation of the successful businessman-amateur politician type prevalent in Boston city politics. By December 1885, he had gone far toward quieting Yankee mistrust of an Irish Catholic mayor. Not surprisingly, then, more than one hundred prominent citizens supported him for reelection, pointing to his moderation, his independence, and his spirit of cooperation. In the mayoral campaign that year, he scored a brilliant victory, defeating ex-Sheriff John M. Clark by a vote of 26,690 to 17,992.

During 1886, O'Brien continued his reforms by instituting routine investigations and firing entire city boards when necessary. Although reelected in 1886 (23,426 to 18,686) and 1887 (26,636 to 25,179) over Republican candidate Thomas N. Hart (*q.v.*), he faced mounting opposition from a bitter Republican press, the recently founded anti-Catholic, anti-immigrant American Protective Association, and the badly divided city Democratic party. Thus, despite renewed prosperity, a lowering of the tax rate, general employment, and expansion of business, O'Brien lost his third campaign against Hart 32,712 to 30,836. Between 1889 and his death on 1 August 1895, he was vice-president of the Boston Electric Light Company.

SOURCES: Boston *Daily Advertiser*, 2 August 1895; Hugh O'Brien, Boston *Shipping and Commercial List* (Boston, 1843 +); Hugh O'Brien Papers, Boston Public Library, scrapbooks, letters and transcripts; Charles H. Taylor "Two Reform Mayors of Boston," *Bay State Monthly* 3 (September 1885).   *Robert V. Sparks*

O'BRIEN, JOHN P. (1873–1951), Mayor of New York (1933). O'Brien, born on 1 February 1873 in Worcester, Massachusetts, was the son of property manager Patrick O'Brien, born in Tipperary, Ireland, and Mary Elizabeth (Gibbons) O'Brien, a Roman Catholic couple. After attending parochial school in Massachusetts, O'Brien received a B.A. degree from Holy Cross College in 1894, an M.A. from Georgetown University in 1895, and an LL.B. from Georgetown in 1897. Following law school, he clerked for the New York firm of Delany, Farley and Murphy, and after admission to the bar in 1898, joined the firm of Whalen and Dunn. In 1901, O'Brien was named assistant corporation counsel for New York City. He subsequently served in the city's bureaus of Condemnation and Collection of Personal Taxes as well as the Franchise Division. After heading the city's Tenement House Bureau, O'Brien was appointed corporation counsel in 1920. Two years later, he left that office to run successfully for the office of surrogate of New York County, a position he held for the next decade. On 6 October 1908, he married Helen Elizabeth Callanan, a Roman Catholic, Irish-American girl from New York City, and they had five children.

In 1932, New York City had a population of 7,346,007 and a mayor-board of aldermen form of government. In that year, a special election was held to fill the unexpired portion of former Mayor Jimmy Walker's (q.v.) term. O'Brien, though little known, was chosen to represent the Tammany Democrats in the mayoral contest. He won by the greatest plurality yet amassed in U.S. mayoral history, totaling 1,014,505 votes to Republican Lewis H. Pounds' 419,386 and the Socialist Morris Hillquit's 241,885.

O'Brien took office on 1 January 1933 with the city on the verge of bankruptcy. He asked the governor to call a special session of the state legislature at which the city received broader powers to levy taxes. He negotiated a fiscal agreement with the city's banks to help stabilize the local economy and cut the municipal budget dramatically. O'Brien was also instrumental in the enactment of the executive budget law which, for the first time, charged the mayor with proposing a realistic budget. Despite these and other notable achievements in the battle for fiscal responsibility in the Depression, O'Brien was not reelected in 1933. He finished third behind Fiorello LaGuardia (q.v.) (868,522) and Joseph V. McKee (q.v.) (609,053) with 586,672 votes.

In 1934, O'Brien returned to the practice of law in partnership with two of his sons, Gerard J. and James A. He also held the positions of president of Western Hemisphere Corporation and director of Starrett Corporation. The former mayor kept in touch with politics by serving as a delegate to the Democratic national conventions in 1936, 1940, and 1944. For several years after his retirement, he acted as official referee of the state supreme court. O'Brien died at his home on 22 September 1951 and was buried in Gate of Heaven Cemetery, Westchester County.

SOURCES: Alva Johnston, "The Scholar in Politics: Profile of Mayor John P. O'Brien", *The New Yorker* 9 (1 and 8 July 1933); Arthur Mann, *LaGuardia Comes to Power, 1933* (Chicago, 1965); New York *Times*, 23 September 1951 (obituary).   *W. Roger Biles*

O'DWYER, WILLIAM (1890–1964), Mayor of New York (1946–50). Irish-born mayor and nationally known crimebuster, O'Dwyer was born on 11 July 1890 in Bohola, Ireland, the son of Patrick O'Dwyer and Bridget (McNicholas) O'Dwyer, both schoolteachers. O'Dwyer was one of eleven children. He attended Bohola National

School and St. Nathays College in Ireland before studying for the priesthood at the University of Salamanca in Spain. In 1910, he left the Catholic order and emigrated to America, becoming a naturalized citizen in 1916. He married Catherine Lenihan on 3 August 1916. After working as a laborer, he became a patrolman for the New York City Police Department in 1917. Concurrently, he attended night classes at Fordham University Law School, graduating in 1923. Two years later, he resigned from the police force and began a law practice with alderman George Joyce. In 1932, O'Dwyer was appointed a magistrate in Brooklyn and later became the first judge of that city's adolescent court. He was appointed judge of Kings County Court in 1937 and the next year was elected to that office for a fourteen-year term.

In 1939, O'Dwyer resigned to run successfully for the office of district attorney of Kings County. He subsequently won national acclaim as the crimebuster who prosecuted the Mafia leaders of organized crime's Murder, Incorporated. In 1941, O'Dwyer lost in his attempt to unseat mayoral incumbent Fiorello LaGuardia (q.v.). With the outbreak of World War II, O'Dwyer was commissioned in the Army and rose to the rank of brigadier general. President Franklin Roosevelt appointed him U.S. representative of the Foreign Economic Administration in Italy in 1944 and director of the War Refugee Board the following year. In 1949, three years after his first wife's death, he married Sloan Simpson; they had two children.

In 1946, New York City had 7,864,000 people and a mayor-board of aldermen form of government. O'Dwyer accepted the mayoral nomination of the Tammany Democrats and American Labor party in 1945 and won 1,125,323 votes to Republican Jonah J. Goldstein's 431,606 and the No Deal party's Newbold Morris's 408,278. He was reelected in 1949, amassing 1,264,600 votes to Newbold Morris's 956,170 and the American Labor party's Vito Marcantonio's 356,423.

Notable achievements during O'Dwyer's first term included the location of the permanent headquarters of the United Nations in New York City, the creation of a traffic department, establishment of a smoke control bureau, and the funding of a division of labor relations. Shortly after his reelection in 1949, O'Dwyer's administration was rocked by a police scandal uncovered by Brooklyn district of attorney Miles F. McDonald. O'Dwyer resigned on 2 September 1950 to accept President Truman's nomination as ambassador to Mexico.

In March 1951, O'Dwyer returned to New York City to appear before the Kefauver Committee, and, while no indictments were returned against the former mayor, covert associations between O'Dwyer and Mafia leaders had been revealed. In 1952, O'Dwyer resigned his ambassadorship and opened a law practice in Mexico. He returned to New York City in 1960 and worked in the law office of O'Dwyer, Bernstein, and Correa. On 24 November 1964, O'Dwyer died of coronary thrombosis at Beth Israel Hospital and was buried in Arlington National Cemetery.

SOURCES: Edward Robb Ellis, *The Epic of New York City* (New York, 1966); Norton Mackridge and Robert H. Prall, *The Big Fix* (New York, 1954); Allan Nevins and John A. Krout, eds., *The Greater City: New York, 1898-1948* (New York, 1948); *New York Times,* 13 October 1946, 25 November 1964 (obituary).

W. Roger Biles

OGDEN, WILLIAM BUTLER (1805–77), Mayor of Chicago (1837–38). The first Chicago mayor and a leading railroad promoter, Ogden was a Protestant Yankee, born on 15 July 1805 in Walton, New York, the son of Abraham Ogden (1778–1825), a lumber and real estate dealer, merchant, and lawyer, born in Norristown, New Jersey, of English descent, and Abigail (Weed) Ogden, of New Canaan, Connecticut. The oldest of five children, Ogden attended public school until age fifteen, when his father had a paralytic stroke and the son had to assume control of the family business interests. During the 1820s, Ogden was in the militia and was local postmaster. He served a single term in New York's state legislature (1835), where he urged state aid for railroads—his pet project. Politically, the young Ogden was a self-styled "Madisonian Democrat."

Moving west to Chicago in 1835 to sell land owned by his brother-in-law, Ogden saw the town's potential and settled permanently in 1836. For over thirty years, he was a leading real estate dealer (after 1844 a senior partner in Ogden and Jones). In 1836, he was elected a town trustee and a year later, helped draft the city's first charter.

Ogden became Chicago's first mayor in 1837, defeating the Whig pioneer, John Kinzie, 489 to 217. Chicago had 4,180 people and a mayor-council form of government. Ogden's mayoralty was politically uneventful, marked only by his support for civic improvements and payment of state debts.

The 1837 depression caused Ogden personal losses, not recovered until 1844, but by 1850 he was worth $1 million. He used this fortune to support the Chicago Historical Society, the board of trade, Cyrus McCormick's reaper works, the Lill and Diversey Brewery, and other ventures. He was president of Rush Medical College (1843–63) and the second president of the first University of Chicago (1861–77). Ogden was a leading member of St. James Episcopal Church.

A long-time railroad enthusiast, who wished to link Chicago to the Pacific, Ogden was president of the Gal

ena and Chicago Union Railroad (1846–51) and other Chicago-based lines, which he combined into the Chicago and Northwestern system in 1859, serving as its first president (until 1868). Ogden was also first president of the Union Pacific Railroad (1862–63) and a director of the Northern Pacific (1867–74). To secure railroad materials, Ogden established his own iron and steel mill at Brady's Bend, Pennsylvania (1856) and lumber mills at Peshtigo, Wisconsin (1860).

Ogden served two terms as Sixth Ward alderman (1840–41 and 1847–48). He lost the 1840 congressional campaign and refused to run again in 1850. Opposed to the Southern wing of the Democratic party, he became a Republican in 1856, representing that party in the Illinois Senate for two terms (1861–64). Business activities caused frequent absences from these posts, and his break with Lincoln's war policies caused him to retire from all political activity in 1864.

After 1868, Ogden spent most of his time in New York, buying the estate named "Boscobel" near Highland. He survived the financial losses of two fires in 1871—one destroying his Chicago landholdings and the other burning his Wisconsin lumber mills. In 1875, he married Mary Anne Arnot, daughter of a wealthy New York judge. He died at his estate on 3 August 1877.

SOURCES: A. T. Andreas, *History of Chicago,* 3 vols., (Chicago, 1884–86); Isaac N. Arnold, *William B. Ogden and Early Days in Chicago* (Chicago, 1882); *Biographical Sketches of the Leading Men of Chicago* (Chicago, 1876); Francis A. Eastman, *Chicago City Manual, 1911* (Chicago, 1911); The William B. Ogden Papers, Chicago Historical Society (3 letterbooks and 12 folders); Bessie L. Pierce, *A History of Chicago,* 3 vols. (New York, 1937–57).

Thomas R. Bullard

O'KEEFE, ARTHUR JOSEPH (1876–1943), Mayor of New Orleans (1926–30). O'Keefe was born in New Orleans on 8 November 1876, the son of Arthur and Sarah (Hanley) O'Keefe both Irish-American Catholics. In 1892, he graduated from St. Alphonsus High School. On 14 November 1901, he married Mamie McDonald of New Orleans.

An active businessman, O'Keefe headed Arthur J. O'Keefe Teas and Coffees, an importing firm. He was also vice-president of the American Bank and Trust Company and director of the Lafayette Fire Insurance Company and the Mutual Building and Loan Association.

O'Keefe was a member of the Choctaw Club of Louisiana (the Democratic party machine's headquarters) and a steady participant in Tenth Ward Democratic politics. In 1925, he became commissioner of finance in the administration of Mayor Martin Behrman (*q.v.*). When Behrman died on 12 January 1926, O'Keefe became acting mayor. The city was then 387,000 in size. In February 1926, he received the nomination of the Orleans Parish Democratic Committee and ran without opposition in a special election to fill Behrman's unexpired term.

On 15 March 1926, O'Keefe officially became mayor and president of the Choctaw Club. He and the Choctaws soon advocated the privately financed Watson-Williams Bridge over Lake Pontchartrain and opposed the free bridges at the Rigolets and Chef Menteur that Public Service Commissioner (and later Governor) Huey P. Long favored. In 1928, O'Keefe, the Choctaws, and New Orleans Public Service Incorporated allied against Long in an unsuccessful effort to prevent the piping of cheap natural gas into New Orleans. The O'Keefe administration also witnessed a police controversy, the completion of plans for the Criminal District Court Building and Parish Prison, and the driving of the first piling for the Municipal Auditorium.

On 15 July 1929, O'Keefe took a leave of absence from his office after a series of lengthy illnesses. On 14 February 1930, he formally resigned and began retirement. He died in New Orleans on 14 November 1943.

SOURCES: Works Progress Administrations typescript, "Administrations of the Mayors of New Orleans, 1803–1936" (New Orleans, 1940).

Edward F. Haas

O'NEILL, EDWARD (1820–70), Mayor of Milwaukee (1863–64, 1867–69). O'Neill was the first Irish-born Catholic mayor of Milwaukee (and its second Irish-born mayor), following the string of Yankees who governed the city in its early years. He was born in Kilkenny, Ireland, on 11 March 1820, the son of Laurence and Margaret (Swift) O'Neill, and after education in the local Kilkenny parish schools emigrated to New York in 1837. Becoming an apprentice tailor, he moved north to Manchester, Vermont, after two years and opened his own tailorshop. After another eleven years, he migrated west to Milwaukee, along with his wife of three years, Clarissa A. McLaughlin of Bennington, Vermont, who was also Roman Catholic.

In turn, O'Neill opened a clothing store, coal store, and wholesale grocery in Milwaukee. A local community booster, he served nine years on the Milwaukee Board of Education, was president of the board of the State Reform School at Waukesha, president of the Water Commission, and an officer in the local militia. He and his wife gave generously to Catholic charities.

O'Neill took control politically of the local Irish. As a Democrat he was elected twice to the General Assembly, 1853 and 1855, and with the support of the German vote won a seat on the state Senate in 1857. Milwaukee was a small but growing city of about 50,000 with a

mayor-council form of government when O'Neill first became mayor, 1863–64. The Democrats were so overwhelming in strength that the Republicans did not contest O'Neill. The Milwaukee *Sentinel* commented that the election was "a jug-handle affair—all on one side." After a period out of office, Mayor O'Neill was reelected in 1867 and 1869. As mayor, he installed an automatic fire alarm system and completed surveys for a waterworks and a new sewage system, built after his term was over. He created a board of assessors for more equitable taxing of property.

By 1870, O'Neill was the largest stockholder in the Milwaukee Bank of Commerce and served as its president until 1879 when it merged into the Merchants Exchange Bank. He was also president of the Merchants Bank up to his death, in the spring of 1870, at the young age of fifty.

SOURCES: James S. Buck, *Milwaukee Under The Charter*, 4 vols. (Milwaukee, 1886); Frank Flower, *History of Milwaukee, Wisconsin* (Chicago, 1881); Bayrd Still, *Milwaukee: The History of a City* (Madison, Wis., 1965); J. A. Watrous, ed., *Memoirs of Milwaukee County*, 2 vols. (Madison, Wis., 1909).

David J. Maurer and *Donald F. Tingley*

OPDYKE, GEORGE C. (1805–80), Mayor of New York (1862–64). New York City's first Republican mayor, Opdyke, born on 7 December 1805, the sixth of nine children of George and Mary (Stout) Opdyke, was of Dutch Reformed stock who emigrated to America in 1663. Educated in district schools, Opdyke became a teacher at age sixteen. He soon borrowed capital to establish mercantile houses in Cleveland and New Orleans before moving to New York in 1832 where he specialized in importing and manufacturing woolens. By the 1850s, he was one of the city's richest men and turned toward politics. A Barnburner Democrat, Free Soiler, and Republican, Opdyke became a state assemblyman in 1858 but lost the mayoralty the following year: Fernando Wood (*q.v.*) 30,125, William Havemeyer (*q.v.*) 26,843, and Opdyke 21,773. In 1862, he capitalized on Democratic factionalism and won by 25,380 votes to C. Godfrey Gunther's (*q.v.*) 24,746 and Wood's 24,167.

By 1860, New York had a population of 820,000. Its government was a jumble of crisscrossing jurisdictions split among a mayor, a series of municipal and county boards either popularly elected or chosen by the governor, and a legislature that often disrupted orderly home rule. Opdyke took office under difficult conditions. In addition to governmental fragmentation, his executive powers were limited; a Democratic governor tried to erode his authority; and New York was torn over support for the Union's war efforts. To resolve these problems, he recommended increasing the mayor's powers, decreasing state interference, forming a greater "Manhattan" consisting of New York County and its environs, and giving support to President Abraham Lincoln. Political friction with the Democratic common council, however, hindered Opdyke's efforts. The 1863 Draft Riot highlighted his tenure. A firm unionist, he resisted the rioters' demands, labored to restore authority, and vetoed a $2.5 million bill to pay commutation fees for poor men drafted. Not wishing a second term, he left office under a cloud when his party nemesis, Thurlow Weed, accused him of war profiteering. A subsequent libel trial ended in a hung jury.

Long interested in money management and the author of two books on the subject, Opdyke retired from business in 1869 and formed a bank. Even so, he retained enough interest in public affairs to serve in the state constitutional convention (1867–68) and on a special commission to revise the state's legal code (1872–73). He was a member of the Union Club, Chamber of Commerce, and various civic groups. Opdyke died on 12 June 1880, survived by his wife Elizabeth Hall (Stryker) Opdyke, whom he had married on 26 September 1829, and six children.

SOURCES: Adrian Cooke, *Armies in the Street* (Lexington, Ky., 1974); Jerome Mushkat, *Tammany: The Evolution of a Political Machine* (Syracuse, 1971); Charles Opdyke, *The Op Dyke Genealogy* (Albany, N.Y., 1889). *Jerome Mushkat*

OTIS, CHARLES A. (1827–1905), Mayor of Cleveland (1873–75). Iron and steelmaker and mayor of Cleveland, born in Bloomfield, Ohio on 30 January 1827, Otis was the son of William A. Otis (1794–1868), banker and railroad promoter, and Eliza (Proctor) Otis. One of five children, Otis attended local schools until 1837 when the family moved to Cleveland. He worked in his father's new ironworks until 1848, when he spent some time as a steamboat purser. In 1853, he organized Ford and Otis, a major iron foundry. He spent a few months in Prussia in 1866, observing the new iron and steel mills, and upon his return he organized the Otis Iron and Steel Company, later renamed the Otis Steel Company, remaining as president until 1899. Otis married Mary Shepard in 1853, and they had two daughters. She died in 1860, and he married Anna Elizabeth Shepard (his former sister-in-law) on 15 October 1863; they had two sons. Otis was a major backer of the city's library and was a Protestant.

Otis had little interest in politics prior to 1873 when he was the Democratic candidate for mayor. He defeated Republican John Huntington 7,498 to 2,340. Cleveland was growing rapidly, with well over 100,000 people and a mayor-council form of government. Business interests

required so much of his time that Otis refused to seek a second term. He established the city's first board of fire commissioners, and supported other civic and business measures. He subsequently served on the board of improvements (1878–79) and the board of the city's House of Correction (1882–84). Most of Otis's later years were spent in business pursuits. In addition to his steel company, he organized the American Wire Company, the American Steel Screw Company, and the Cleveland Electric Street Railway. In 1894, he became president of the new Commercial National Bank, retiring from this and other business pursuits in 1904. He died on 28 June 1905 while visiting his son.

SOURCES: Elroy M. Avery, *A History of Cleveland and Its Environs*, 3 vols. (Chicago, 1918); William G. Rose, *Cleveland: The Making of a City* (Cleveland, 1950); Gertrude Wickham, *The Pioneer Families of Cleveland, 1796–1840*, 2 vols. (Chicago, 1914). *Thomas R. Bullard*

OTIS, HARRISON GRAY (1765–1848), Mayor of Boston (1829–31). Boston's third mayor, born in the city on 8 October 1765, Otis was the eldest son of Samuel Allyne Otis, a Yankee merchant, and Elizabeth Gray, and the nephew of the Revolutionary pamphleteer James Otis and of the patriot poet and historian Mercy Otis Warren. His mother, however, was the daughter of Harrison Gray, a prominent loyalist. Otis was educated at the Boston Latin School, graduated first in his class from Harvard College in 1783, and became a prosperous figure in law and real estate after being admitted to the Boston bar in 1786. He married another Yankee, Sally Foster (1770–1836), on 31 May 1790, and they had eleven children. An ardent Federalist who never lost his disdain for democratic influences and republican politics, Otis served in Congress from 1797 to 1801 and then returned to Boston where his various homes became celebrated centers of gracious hospitality and convivial social gatherings. He also resumed his political interests, serving in the state legislature (1802–1805, 1813–14) and the state Senate (1805–1806, 1814–1817), consistently opposing the policies of Thomas Jefferson, denouncing the War of 1812, and participating in the Hartford Convention. After the war, in 1817, he was elected to the U.S. Senate, but he found the social atmosphere in the nation's capital so uncongenial that he resigned his seat in 1822 and became a candidate in Boston's first mayoral election. Not only did Otis fail in his first attempt to become mayor, but also, when he received the Federalist nomination for governor of Massachusetts the following year, 1823, he was badly defeated again.

In 1829, when the Boston Federalists withdrew their support from Mayor Josiah Quincy (*q.v.*), they turned to Harrison Gray Otis who defeated E. Eddy by a vote of 2,978 to 1,283. During his three years as mayor, Otis showed little interest in the details of purely political affairs, and was more concerned with the physical growth and development of the city itself (now about 60,000 in size) than with the health and welfare of its less prosperous inhabitants. While he continued to authorize expenditures for such capital projects as a new courthouse, a water supply, and a railroad line to the Hudson River, he cut back sharply on expenses for street cleaning and for expanding the sewers, reduced the salary of the city marshal, and refused to increase the number of constables on patrol. In 1831, Mayor Otis received angry letters from prominent Southerners demanding he take action against an "incendiary" abolitionist newspaper called the *Liberator*. Ordering an investigation of the offending publication, Otis was informed that it was being published by a man named William Lloyd Garrison, whose office was an "obscure hole" and whose supporters were a handful of "insignificant persons of all colors." He promptly assured his friends in the South that this new "fanaticism" had no influence among the "respectable classes" and therefore was of no consequence. "In this, however," wrote Otis some years later, "I was mistaken."

After he left the mayor's office and until his death seventeen years later, Otis continued his active concern with political affairs at both the state and national levels. He died on 28 October 1848, at the age of eighty-three, just before the election of the Whig candidate for the presidency, General Zachary Taylor, to whom Otis had given his political allegiance and support.

SOURCES: *Inaugural Addresses of the Mayors of Boston, 1822–1852* (Boston, 1894); Samuel Eliot Morison, *Harrison Gray Otis, Federalist, 1765–1848*, 2 vols. (Boston, 1913); Thomas H. O'Connor, *Lords of the Loom* (New York, 1968); W. A. Otis, *A Genealogical and Historical Memoir of the Otis Family in America* (Boston, 1924); *Records of the City of Boston: Mayor and Aldermen*, microfilm, Boston Public Library; Justin Winsor, ed., *Memorial History of Boston . . . 1630–1880*, 4 vols. (Boston, 1880), vol. 3.   *Thomas H. O'Connor*

OTIS, JAMES (1826–75), Mayor of San Francisco (1873–75). Otis was born in Boston on 11 August 1826. He was a direct descendant of Revolutionary agitator and Boston lawyer, James Otis. The future mayor's father, George W. Otis, was a physician. He sent his son to the Boston public schools, where young Otis graduated at the head of his class at age fifteen. James turned down an opportunity to attend Harvard, choosing instead a career in business. He first traveled to San Francisco in 1849 representing a Boston firm that traded with China.

After a respite in Boston from 1852 to 1858, he returned permanently to San Francisco. There Otis became head of an importing business and soon invested successfully in mining. He married Lucy Macondray in 1858, a union that produced four sons and two daughters. Throughout his life, Otis retained the Unitarian faith of his New England upbringing.

Otis, a staunch Republican, enjoyed immediate success in local and state politics. In the early 1860s, he served as city supervisor and state legislator. He became chairman of the state Republican Central Committee in 1864 and helped to nominate Abraham Lincoln for re-election at the national party convention. He similarly supported Ulysses S. Grant's candidacies in 1868 and 1872. Moreover, he served as president of the local Chamber of Commerce in 1869–70.

In 1873, rapid growth characterized San Francisco, a city of around 195,000 residents, and factionalization characterized its politics. Otis received the mayoral nomination of the People's Independent party that year and was endorsed by the Citizen's Union, the People's Union, and the People's party, support that amounted to a Republican coalition. On 3 September 1873, Otis outpolled his Democratic rival, James M. McDonald, by a margin of 13,699 to 11,545. Otis was inaugurated on 1 December; his term was cut short by his death from diphtheria on 30 October 1875. He was already doomed to one term since he had been supplanted in the elections of September 1875 by the Democratic and Workingman's party candidate. The fact that Otis was hardly considered for a second term demonstrated his lack of popularity and the shifting political climate.

A fiscal conservative like his immediate predecessors, Otis seemed ill prepared to meet the growing social unrest in San Francisco, and he achieved little as mayor. A sharp economic downturn in 1874–75 plagued the city, particularly workingmen. The spendthrift Republican businessmen, who had dominated San Francisco's executive since 1869 and whose typical response to hard times was to call for more police, lost favor as new political organizations sprang up around anti-Chinese sentiments. Otis's reputation was further tarnished by scandal when $1.5 million of city funds were found in the bank of the mayor's friend. While never indicted for wrongdoing, Otis was criticized for negligence. This scandal, combined with the changing tone of politics, assured that Otis would be the last in a line of fiscally conservative businessmen to be elected mayor of San Francisco.

SOURCES: Gunther Barth, *Instant Cities: Urbanization and the Rise of San Francisco and Denver* (New York, 1975); William J. Heintz, *San Francisco's Mayors, 1850–1880* (Woodside, Calif., 1975); Alonzo Phelps,

Contemporary Biography of California's Famous Men (San Francisco, 1881), vol. 1. *John M. Findlay*

OVERSTOLZ, HENRY C. (1822–87), Mayor of St. Louis (1876–81). German-born mayor of St. Louis, Overstolz was born in Munster on 4 July 1822, the son of William Overstolz (1780–1853) and Therese (Buse) Overstolz (1790–1862), both from the province of Westphalia. Young Henry attended a *gymnasium* in Germany and then public schools in Illinois after the family emigrated to the United States. He went on to St. Louis in 1846, starting work as a store clerk. He soon established his own mercantile business and felt he had made enough money to retire in 1853. Even so, he operated a successful lumber mill during 1855–67. He married Philippine Espenscheid on 7 May 1874.

Overstolz was an alderman, 1850–52, 1856–57, and 1870–74 (serving as president of the city council, 1873–74). In 1853, he was elected city comptroller, the first German elected to a city-wide office in St. Louis history. He first ran unsuccessfully for the mayoralty in 1875 as an independent Republican, gaining 12,175 votes to 12,949 for Democrat Arthur Barret (*q.v.*) and 4,445 for regular Republican Maguire. Overstolz ran again in the special election, being defeated by Democrat James Britton (*q.v.*), whom the election judges declared the winner. Overstolz contested this decision and was finally declared the real winner in February 1876 by 14,725 to 14,648. In 1877, he became the city's first four-year term mayor, defeating Democrat N. C. Hudson 21,293 to 11,815. In 1881, he ran as a Democrat, losing to W. L. Ewing (*q.v.*) 24,608 to 11,353. St. Louis had 310,864 people in 1870 and 350,518 in 1880 and a mayor-council form of government.

As mayor, Overstolz reorganized the city departments and supported the political separation of St. Louis City from St. Louis County. He spent much time feuding with local party leaders who considered him too independent, while local reformers felt he was too interested in creating a personal machine. He did not seek political office after 1881 and spent his time as president of the Fifth National Bank (1882–87). He was an active banker until his death on 29 November 1887.

SOURCES: Charles H. Cornwell, *St. Louis Mayors: Brief Biographies* (St. Louis, 1965); William Hyde and Howard L. Conrad, eds., *Encyclpedia of the History of St. Louis*, 4 vols. (New York, 1899); J. T. Scharf, *History of Saint Louis City and County*, 2 vols. (Philadelphia, 1883).

Thomas R. Bullard

P

PAGE, DANIEL D. (1790–1869), Mayor of St. Louis (1829–33). Second mayor of St. Louis and a transplanted Yankee, Page was born on 5 March 1790 in Parsonsfield, York County, Maine, the son of a farmer of English ancestry who had served in the Continental Army during the American Revolution. He attended country schools and at age fourteen left the farm for the city of Portland, Maine. There he took a job in a general store and learned the baker's trade. Lane then established a bakery in Boston and married Deborah Young. Very mobile, he moved southwest to New Orleans and was in the tobacco business until his wife's failing health and aversion to the Southern climate forced him to head northward. In 1818, he settled in St. Louis and established a grocery to which he later added a bakery.

In 1829, the people of St. Louis by an almost unanimous vote elected Page as their second mayor, and three times he won reelection. St. Louis had a population of approximately 6,000 at this time, but the city was growing and needed extensive public improvements. During Page's administration, work continued on the grading and paving of streets, and the mayor was especially active in advocating construction of a waterworks. In fact, he advanced money from his own pocket to the contractor of the waterworks in order to ensure the completion of this vital improvement. Moreover, during Page's mayoralty, the city of St. Louis purchased its first fire engine and in 1832 suffered its first cholera epidemic.

After retiring as mayor, Page devoted himself to business, establishing the first steam flour mill in St. Louis in 1833. He was also a leading landowner in the city and an incorporator of both the Boatmen's Savings Institution and the Pacific Railroad. In 1848, he joined with his son-in-law in establishing the banking house of Page and Bacon which proved for a time to be very successful. By 1854, it had the largest volume of transactions of any banking firm in the Mississippi Valley. However, the firm advanced excessively large sums for the construction of the Ohio and Mississippi Railroad, and in 1855, it was forced to suspend payment and close its doors. This failure ended Page's business career. He died in Washington, D.C., on 29 April 1869.

SOURCES: William Hyde and Howard L. Conrad, eds., *Encyclopedia of the History of St. Louis* (New York, 1899); L. U. Reavis, *Saint Louis: The Future Great City of the World* (Biographical Edition) (St. Louis, 1875); J. T. Scharf, *History of Saint Louis City and County* (Philadelphia, 1883). *Jon C. Teaford*

PAGE, HERMAN L. (1818–73), Mayor of Milwaukee (1859–60). Police official and Milwaukee mayor, born on 27 May 1818 in Oneida County, New York, Page was the son of Eli V. Page (1772–1858), a farmer, and his wife Jane, both Connecticut-born old-stock American Protestants. Fifth of eight children, Page attended public schools before moving to Nunda, New York, where he opened a general store in partnership with his brother-in-law John Sergeant. In Nunda, in about 1843, he married Maria Camp (1824–46), daughter of a local pipe-organ builder. They moved to Milwaukee in 1844, two years before Mrs. Page's sudden death; the couple was childless. Page operated a dry goods store, earning enough money to retire from business pursuits in 1850. In 1848, he married Cynthia Barber, daughter of a wealthy Horicon (Wisconsin) judge, and they had four children. Page was a Baptist and also a prominent member of the International Order of Odd Fellows, becoming Wisconsin's first grand patriarch.

Page entered politics in 1846 with an unsuccessful campaign for county treasurer on the Liberty party ticket. He then became a Democrat and was elected deputy sheriff of the county in 1850. During his term (1851–53), Page gained publicity for arresting a number of burglars and corrupt public officials. He then served as sheriff of Milwaukee County (1853–54 and 1857–59). Page sought the Democratic nomination for congress in 1856 but was not chosen by the party.

Page was elected mayor, however, in 1859, defeating People's party candidate Increase A. Bapham 5,634 to 2,178. Milwaukee had 46,396 people in 1860 and a mayor-council form of government. Mayor Page advocated fiscal caution, since the city had not fully recovered from the financial difficulties of 1857–58. He demanded increased expenditures in only two areas: public schools and the police department.

After leaving office, Page was an agent for the Connecticut Mutual Life Insurance Company (1860–70). He was also Milwaukee's chief of police, 1862-63. In 1862, he was lieutenant colonel of the Twenty-fourth Regiment for a few months. He again failed to win the Democratic congressional nomination in 1863. After 1870, he sold real estate, earning enough money to take annual vacations in Europe with his family. While on one of these trips, he became ill; he died in Dresden, Germany, on 15 October 1873, and was buried there.

SOURCES: John G. Gregory, *History of Milwaukee, Wisconsin*, 4 vols. (Chicago, 1931), vol. 2; H. Wells Hand, *Centennial History of the Town of Nunda, 1808–1909* (Rochester, N.Y., 1908); *History of Milwaukee, Wisconsin* (Chicago, 1881); Jerome A. Watrous, ed., *Memoirs of Milwaukee County*, 2 vols. (Madison, Wis., 1909).   *Thomas R. Bullard*

PALMER, ALBERT (1831–87), Mayor of Boston (1883). Palmer, the seventh child of Joseph and Abby (Wilson) Palmer of Candia, New Hampshire, was born on 17 January 1831. Of old Yankee stock, he was descended from Joseph Palmer, one of the earliest settlers of Rowley, Massachusetts, and from Stephen Palmer, grandson of Joseph, one of the founders of Candia. Palmer attended Kimball Union Academy in Meriden, New Hampshire, followed by three years at the Phillips Academy in Andover, Massachusetts, and four at Dartmouth College, graduating in 1858. He taught for two years in West Arlington, Massachusetts leaving in 1860 for a position in the Boston Latin School. Five years later, he left teaching to found the Jamaica Pond Ice Company, which he managed as president until his death. On 25 November 1863, he married Martha Ann Newell, daughter of Artemas and Martha (McIntosh) Newell of Needham, Massachusetts, and had two sons, Joseph N., Harvard graduate and Boston attorney, and Wilson N., also a Harvard graduate and a clerk for the Boston Ice Company. Palmer was also a member of the New England Historic Genealogical Society.

A boyhood admirer of Rufus Choate and Daniel Webster, Palmer ran in 1872 as a Republican candidate for state representative and was successful for three terms. By 1875, he had gained a reputation as a powerful speaker and also considerable experience as chairman of the joint committees on railroads and federal elections. In 1881, however, he changed parties, choosing to follow the popular and controversial Democrat, Benjamin Butler. When Frederick O. Prince (*q.v.*), four-time Democratic mayor of Boston, refused another term that year, Palmer unsuccessfully opposed Samuel A. Green (*q.v.*), losing 20,284 to 19,936. A year later, he again opposed Green and, because of his continued association with Butler and the city Democratic machine of Patrick J. McGuire, was vilified in the press as an agent of "Tweedism." He won nonetheless by a vote of 21,727 to 19,540.

Boston at that time had a population of approximately 380,000 with a mayor-alderman-common council form of government. In his inaugural address, Mayor Palmer opposed proposals for a limitation of the franchise, called for abolition of the poll tax, reform of the voter registration laws, and separation of city elections from state campaigns, and assured a worried Boston audience that his victory meant neither Irish domination nor the advent of Tweedism. His one-year term passed relatively peacefully. Palmer was, therefore, able to concentrate his efforts on implementing a policy of retrenchment and strict supervision of all municipal expenditures. He ordered major city improvements postponed and appropriations cut, and he moved cautiously in furthering the water, street, and sewer systems. Finding that the mayor ran a poor second to the city council in controlling patronage and purse strings, he called for municipal reorganization and consolidation of agencies and functions, but he left office before any reforms could be attempted. Reform-minded groups led by the Massachusetts Reform Club maintained a steady attack upon Palmer's alleged vassalage to Boss McGuire, and, not surprisingly, he declined a second term. He died of pneumonia on 21 May 1887 at his Roxbury home.

SOURCES: Boston *Daily Advertiser*, 23 May 1887; Samuel L. Gerould, *Biographical Sketches of the Class of 1858 Dartmouth College* (Nashua, N.H., 1905); Albert Palmer, *The Inaugural Address of Albert Palmer* (Boston, 1883); Wilson Palmer, Reminiscences of Candia (Cambridge, Mass., 1905).   *Robert V. Sparks*

PANKOW, STEVEN (1908–), Mayor of Buffalo (1954–57). Born in Buffalo on 29 March 1908, Pankow was the son of a worker for the Pennsylvania Railroad, and both his parents were Roman Catholics of Polish descent. He attended local schools and high school to the age of fifteen when he began working at a local junkyard. The following year, he became an employee of the U.S. Rubber Company and then worked as a crane operator at the local Bethlehem Steel plant. Pankow joined the Chrysler Company and was sent to Detroit where he attended its business school for automobile agents. Returning to Buffalo, Pankow sold cars for A. W. Julius and Company. In 1934, he left the company and began selling cars on his own; in 1938, Pankow obtained a Dodge-Plymouth franchise, which became Pankow Motors, a successful Buffalo automobile sales company. Pankow married Mary Conwell (born Konowalczak), a Buffalo Polish-American, in 1930, and they had three children. The Pankows belonged to St. Aloysius (Catholic) Church. Pankow was an Elk, a Moose, a member of the Chamber of Commerce, and director of the Buffalo Auto Club, 1947–50.

A Democrat like many Poles, Pankow was elected Erie County clerk in 1948. The following year he was an unsuccessful candidate for the Democratic mayoralty nomination. He was elected mayor in 1953, defeating Republican Harold J. Becker 93,206 to 90,490. Buffalo had 580,132 people in 1950 and a mayor-council form of government. As mayor, Pankow supported the reduction of city expenditures, especially after the voters rejected a proposed new sales tax. Pankow frequently urged the state legislature to pass bills allowing Buffalo and other cities to receive more state aid. He also supported new housing programs and a revitalized downtown, following suggestions of the Planning Commission. Pankow reorganized the police department, following charges of official misconduct by top officers. In 1959, however, he was indicted for failure to pay income tax and for accepting bribes. After several trials, both charges were dropped in 1962–63. Pankow had planned to run for mayor in 1961, but he soon quit the race. He was a member of the Municipal Housing Board, 1968–70 and an aide in the city's recreation department, 1970–75. In 1975, he was appointed to the board of assessors.

SOURCES: Buffalo *Evening News*, 15 October 1953 and other newspaper sources.   *Thomas R. Bullard*

PATTON, ISAAC W. (1828–90), Mayor of New Orleans (1878–80). Conservative (Democratic) mayor, Patton was born on 4 February 1828 in Fredericksburg, Virginia, the son of John W. Patton, a distinguished Richmond attorney and five-term U.S. congressman. After attending Fairfax Institute in Alexandria, young Isaac began the study of law in his father's office, only to be distracted by the Mexican War in which he served as a second lieutenant with the Tenth U.S. Cavalry. Transferred to the Third U.S. Artillery in 1849, Patton shortly thereafter married Frances Merritt of Richmond, resigned from the Army in 1855, and moved to Louisiana where he became a planter of cotton and sugar cane. He had three sons.

At the outbreak of the Civil War, Patton was elected captain of the Screwmen's Guards, a New Orleans infantry unit. After the fall of New Orleans in April 1862, he became colonel of the Twenty-third Louisiana Infantry serving at Vicksburg (where he suffered a severe hip wound) and later at Mobile. When the war ended, Patton returned to New Orleans and became a commission merchant. Elected criminal sheriff in 1872, he took part in the memorable "battle of Liberty Place" (a riot against Union carpetbagger government) on 14 September 1874 and in 1878 was elected mayor of New Orleans in a hotly contested campaign. He received a plurality of votes (13,932) against a combined total of 15,178 votes for his three opponents.

As mayor, Patton inherited from his immediate predecessors a nagging problem of heavy municipal indebtedness, payment of which continued to be a burden on city revenue. After suggested remedies failed, Patton persuaded the state legislature to create in 1880 a city board of liquidation, authorized and empowered to exercise "exclusive control" over the bonded indebtedness of New Orleans. (The board was strengthened by amendments to the original act in 1882 and 1884). Even so, all efforts to retire the debt were vitiated by the numerous state taxes collected in New Orleans which could not be devoted to local purposes.

Racially segregated public schools were legally sanctioned in New Orleans during Patton's administration, and considerable railroad construction connecting New Orleans with points north and west took place. Mayor Patton's attempts to reform the police force were not successful.

By 1880, the Conservative Democrats had controlled the city government for eight years and had assumed some of the corrupt and self-serving features of an entrenched machine. While Patton himself remained generally admired, the Conservatives were ejected from office by a group of "reform" Democrats led by Joseph Shakspeare (*q.v.*).

Between 1880 and 1884, Patton devoted himself to business pursuits. In 1884, he returned to public life as city treasurer in the "Ring" administration of Mayor J. Valsin Guillotte (*q.v.*), serving until 1888. On 9 February 1890 he died, allegedly from prolonged agony and complications caused by the hip wound he had received at Vicksburg almost thirty years before.

SOURCES: Joy J. Jackson, *New Orleans in the Gilded Age: Politics and Urban Progress, 1880–1896* (Baton Rouge, La., 1969); John S. Kendall, *History of New Orleans* (Chicago, 1922), vol. 1; Works Progress Administration typescripts, "Administrations of the Mayors of New Orleans, 1803–1936," and "Biographies of the Mayors of New Orleans, 1803–1936" (New Orleans, 1940).   *Mark T. Carleton*

PATTON, JOHN (1822–1900), Mayor of Detroit (1858–59). Scots-Irish Presbyterian mayor of Detroit, born in the County of Down, Ireland, on 1 March 1822, Patton emigrated to America at the age of eight with his parents, James and Eliza (Cathcart) Patton. One of six children, John attended public schools in Albany, New York, until the age of seventeen, when he was apprenticed to a carriage smith.

In 1843, Patton moved to Detroit, found employment at his trade, worked for two years, and then went into business for himself in 1845. In the same year, on 3 March, he married Eliza J. Anderson, also a Presbyterian. Three years later, he built his own factory and soon became one of the leading manufacturers of carriages in the city.

Patton began his civic career in 1848 with his election to the office of alderman for a two-year term. Although he was not reelected in 1850, he came back in 1852 to win another term. He took an active interest in the fire department, which at the time was volunteer. From 1852 through 1854, he served as chief engineer of the fire department and from 1855 to 1857, as president.

In a Democratic sweep in November 1857, Patton upset the incumbent Mayor Oliver M. Hyde (*q.v.*) by a vote of 3,512 to 2,714 to win the office of mayor of Detroit. When he first arrived in Detroit in 1843, Patton found a city that barely exceeded 10,000 residents; now as mayor, he headed a city more than four times that size (45,000). What had been farms upon Patton's arrival were now being transformed into subdivisions, and streets were being extended into every direction. With this expansion came problems of street improvement, sewage disposal, licensing, and crime. During his administration, the Sewer Commission was formed; the first paved streets were constructed; the first streetcar line was started; ordinances were adopted to control disposal of garbage, waste, and pollutants to streams; and laws were adopted in an effort to curb prostitution. A new fire ordinance established a paid fire department that would gradually replace the volunteer service.

Patton did not stand for reelection, but his public service career was not over. He served as county auditor (1864–69), as sheriff (1869–70), as justice (1880–91), and as U.S. consul at Amherstburg (1893–97).

When Patton died in Detroit on 15 November 1900, he was hailed as "the oldest living mayor of Detroit" and was buried with full Masonic honors in Elmwood Cemetery in Detroit. He was survived by five children.

SOURCES: Detroit *Free Press*, 16 November 1900; Silas Farmer, *The History of Detroit and Michigan . . .* (Detroit, 1889); Scrapbooks, Burton Historical Collection, Detroit Public Library.

John Cumming

PAYNE, NATHAN PERRY (1837–85), Mayor of Cleveland (1875–76). Payne was born on 13 August 1837 in Cleveland, Ohio. His father, the Honorable Henry B. Payne (1810–96), of old New England stock from Lebanon, Connecticut, was a well-known Cleveland attorney, business leader, and politician, being at one time a stockholder and director in eighteen business enterprises, including coal and iron mining, banking, and manufacturing, as well as U.S. congressman (1875–77) and U.S. senator from Ohio (1885–91). His mother, Mary (Perry) Payne (c. 1813–95), also claimed Yankee

English descent, her family being among the earliest settlers of Cleveland. The first of five children, Nathan attended Cleveland public schools and Pierce Academy, Middleborough, Massachusetts, in preparation for the scientific course at Brown University. Serious illness, however, caused his return to Cleveland where, after partial recovery, he assumed charge of the McIntosh nurseries (1855). Aided by this experience, Payne joined Perry, Cross and Company, a family-run Great Lakes coal mining and shipping concern, two years later. Over the better part of the next two decades, his involvement in the company grew as management changed hands. By 1875, he was senior partner of Payne, Newton and Company, successors to the original firm. Meanwhile, his political interest was growing under his father's influence, and Payne served two terms on the Cleveland Board of Education (1859–61) and, subsequently, six years on the city council.

Cleveland in 1875 had a population of 164,230 and a mayor-council form of government. The city's increasingly ethnic social character provided the ideal backdrop for Payne's mayoral campaign. His popularity stemmed from a lack of class consciousness and contributed to his unanimous nomination for mayor in spring 1875 by Cleveland Democrats and liberals. His election over Charles B. Pettengill (by a majority of 7,812 to 7,789 votes) is significant in that it broke a long period of traditionally Republican rule in the city.

Since his tenure as mayor was so brief, no major accomplishments mark the Payne administration, which was primarily caretaker in scope. Yet, always mindful of the public-spirited Payne family tradition of integrity and incorruptibility, the mayor in his inaugural address promised to "root out jobbery and corruption while favoring and aiding Cleveland's economic growth and prosperity." Preferring business to politics, however, Payne served only one term in the mayor's office, declining renomination in 1877.

A private, unassuming man and a perennial bachelor, Payne was a respected member of Cleveland's business community. Always of questionable health, he died in Cleveland at the early age of forty-eight on 11 May 1885 and was buried there, in Lake View Cemetery, two days later.

SOURCES: *The Cleveland City Directory, 1875–76, 1876–77*; Cleveland *Plain Dealer*, March 1875–April 1877 and May 1885; James Harrison Kennedy, *A History of the City of Cleveland* [Biographical Volume] (Cleveland, 1897); Carrington T. Marshall, ed., *A History of the Courts and Lawyers of Ohio* (New York, 1934), vol. 3; "Nathan P. Payne," *Biographical Cyclopedia and Portrait Gallery of Representative Men of the State of Ohio*, vol. 3 (1884).

Eric C. Lewandowski

PECK, GEORGE W. (1840–1915), Mayor of Milwaukee (1890). Popular humorist, mayor, and governor, Peck was the first of three children born to David B. and Alzina Peck of Hudson, New York. The elder Peck and his wife left their native New York in 1843 for Whitewater, Wisconsin, where their son received an eighth grade education in the public schools. Having little desire to become a tavern-keeper like his father, Peck chose instead to become a printer's devil in order to learn the trade at a number of area newspapers. In 1863, he enlisted in the Fourth Wisconsin Cavalry, attaining the rank of second lieutenant before his discharge in 1866. Peck returned to Wisconsin, founded a small paper, *The Ripon Representative*, and began writing humorous pieces. He then pursued fame and fortune in Manhattan as a columnist, only to return again to Wisconsin. In 1874, he established *La Crosse Sun*, which he in turn moved to Milwaukee four years later as *Peck's Sun*. The paper's weekly circulation ran as high as 80,000. This success was in great part attributable to Peck's literary creation, "Hennery," a lad who liked to sneak cod liver oil into the Sunday pancakes or a frog down the neighbor girl's back. Peck married Francena Rowley (1843–1906) of Delavan, Wisconsin, in 1860, and the couple raised two sons, George and Roy.

A war veteran and a writer compared favorably by some to Mark Twain, Peck proved a sound choice as the Democratic nominee for mayor in 1890. He was an astute campaigner and aggressively attacked the Republican Achilles' heel, their sponsorship of the Bennett Act in the state legislature in 1889. This law required that all school instruction be in English, and its passage infuriated immigrant voters throughout the state. Milwaukee's German community, comprising about 27 percent of the city's population, withheld its traditional support of the Republicans amidst Peck's charges that the new law infringed "on the natural liberty of conscience and on the natural right of parental control." The Democrat swept past Republican incumbent Thomas H. Brown and Citizens' party candidate N. S. Murphey by approximately 4,000 votes. Peck thus became mayor of a city of 204,468 with a mayor-council form of government.

Dubbed "the happy mayor" by pundits, Peck was deemed too valuable by state party figures to stay in Milwaukee. They tapped him to run for governor in the fall elections, and he again campaigned on the issue of the Bennett law. He handily defeated incumbent William Hoard by capturing 53.6 percent of the vote and a 28,000 vote plurality. He won a second term in 1892 by defeating Republican John C. Spooner but lost his bid for a third term in 1894 to William H. Upham. Peck attempted a comeback in 1904 but could not dislodge Robert La-Follette as governor.

In his two terms in Madison, Peck sought to increase Democratic popularity and strength state-wide. He repealed the Bennett law in 1891 and backed a reapportionment plan favoring the Democrats. After his defeat in 1904, Peck returned to private life as a writer and lecturer. He died on 16 April 1915.

SOURCES: Andrew Aikens and Lewis Proctor, eds., *Men of Progress of Wisconsin* (Milwaukee, 1897); Donald J. Berthrong, "Andrew Jackson Turner, 'Workhorse' of the Republican Party," in *Wisconsin Magazine of History* 38 (Winter 1954–55); Bayrd Still, *Milwaukee: History of a City* (Madison, Wis., 1948); *Wisconsin Necrology* (compilation by state historical society of obituaries of prominent Milwaukeeans, on microfilm).

Douglas Bukowski

PELTON, FREDERICK WILLIAM (1827–1902), Mayor of Cleveland (1871–73). Yankee businessman and mayor of Cleveland, born in Chester, Connecticut, 24 March 1827, Pelton was the son of Russell Pelton (1803–98), a quarry owner, and Pamelia (Abbey) Pelton, both Methodist-Episcopal New Englanders. The fourth of six children, Pelton attended public schools in Brooklyn, Ohio, where the family moved in 1835. He graduated from Brooklyn Academy in 1843 and moved to Akron, working for Wheeler and Chamberlain. He returned with them to Cleveland in 1848, but when their new store failed, he worked as a farmer and hotel owner in Richfield for ten years. In 1858, he moved back to Cleveland, opening a ships' chancellery, operated until 1867. On 26 August 1848, he married Susan Dennison of Massachusetts, and they had seven children, only three of whom outlived him. Pelton was a Mason and an Odd Fellow, and he and his wife attended St. Paul's Episcopal Church (later switching to St. Matthew's). In the early part of the Civil War, Pelton served with the First Ohio Artillery as a captain in Company E.

A Republican, Pelton entered public life in 1865–69 as a member of the city council. In 1871, he was elected mayor, defeating incumbent Democrat Stephen Buhrer (*q.v.*) 7,085 to 5,939. Cleveland had 92,829 people in 1870 and a mayor-council form of government. Pelton accomplished little that would be remembered while in office, mainly supporting civic and business measures. He also served on the board of directors of the city's infirmary in 1871. He did not seek reelection in 1873, temporarily retiring from politics. He became president of the Citizens' Savings and Loan Association, remaining at this post until 1907. He was also on the board of directors of the city's House of Corrections (1886–89) and the board of directors of the workhouse (1889–91). After this return to minor public office, Pelton completely retired from politics, confining himself to his banking interests until his death on 19 March 1902.

SOURCES: Cleveland *Plain Dealer*, 16 March, 1902; Crisfield Johnson, comp., *History of Cuyahoga County, Ohio* (Cleveland, 1879); J. N. Pelton, *Genealogy of the Pelton Family in America* (Albany, 1892).

Thomas R. Bullard

PERK, RALPH J. (1914–), Mayor of Cleveland (1971–77). Czech-American mayor of Cleveland during years of heightened white ethnic awareness, Perk was born on 19 January 1914 of first-generation Czech-American, Roman Catholic parents from Cleveland's industrial valley. He was the third of five children born to Joseph Charles Perk (1879–1964), a tailor and labor union organizer, and Mary (Smirt) Perk (1884–1964). Perk attended public and parochial schools, went into business with his brothers delivering ice and coal, finished high school by correspondence courses, and enrolled in evening college classes. In 1940, he married Lucille Gagliardi, a Clevelander of Italian background who had attended Catholic grammar school with him. They had six children.

During the 1950s, Perk became increasingly popular with white ethnic neighborhood groups who elected him to five successive terms on the Cleveland City Council beginning in 1953. His assiduous courting of the white ethnic vote made him a formidable candidate in Cuyahoga County and in 1962 helped him to unseat Democrat John J. Carney by a majority of 20,000 votes, to become the first Republican county auditor in fifty years. Perk was reelected in 1966 and again in 1970.

In 1971, after two unsuccessful tries, Perk became the first Republican in thirty years to be elected mayor of Cleveland. The race was a bitter three-way contest which split the Democratic vote between the party's official candidate, businessman James M. Carney, and black school board president and Independent Democrat, Arnold Pinkney (Perk 88,664, Pinkney 74,085, and Carney 65,725). Perk was reelected in 1973 with a majority (Perk 90,839 and Mercedes Cotner 57,488) and in 1975 by a 10 percent margin (Perk 98,341 and Pinkney 83,155). He ran unsuccessfully for U.S. Senate in 1974. In 1977, he was defeated by Democrats Edward F. Feighan and Dennis J. Kucinich (*q.v.*) in the nonpartisan primary.

As mayor, Perk's major problem—which his administration failed to confront—was the city's financial deficit: $13.5 million when he took office in 1971. Although Perk announced austerity measures, he was able to avoid facing the problem without imposing tax increases or service cutbacks because of a massive infusion of federal revenue-sharing which became available to the city under the Nixon administration. These monies, plus practices of "rolling over" short-term notes, "borrowing" from restricted city accounts, and selling sewer and transit systems, created a false sense of calm while only postponing the inevitable financial crisis.

Cleveland became the butt of national jokes when the mayor accidentally set his own hair on fire while cutting a ceremonial metal ribbon with an acetylene torch and when he required garbagemen to distribute a pornography poll. On the positive side, Perk also helped to ease the racial tensions that had marked the city in the 1960s by lowering the tone of rhetoric and working in close cooperation with the black city council president. During his administration, Cleveland saw the expansion of its major airport and several public buildings as well as the building of two new downtown hotels. Perk was the first Cleveland mayor to use CETA (Comprehensive Employment Training Act) funds for cultural purposes. His attempt to lure business back to the city with a plan for tax abatement became a major campaign issue in his primary campaign against Dennis Kucinich, the urban populist who went on to be elected his successor (Kucinich 36,498, Edward F. Feighan 39,742, and Perk 36,498). After leaving office in 1977, Perk became an urban consultant.

SOURCES: Thomas F. Campbell and Roberta Steinbacher, "Reflections on the Seventies," *Cleveland Magazine*, January 1980; Philip W. Porter, *Cleveland: Confused City on a Seesaw* (Columbus, 1976); Terrence Sheridan, "The Uncool Iceman," *Cleveland Magazine*, January 1973; Carl B. Stokes, *Promise of Power: A Political Biography* (New York, 1973); Edward P. Whelan, "Mayor Ralph J. Perk and the Politics of Decay," *Cleveland Magazine*, September 1975; Estelle Zannes, *Checkmate in Cleveland* (Cleveland, 1972).

Thomas F. Campbell

PETERS, ANDREW JAMES (1872–1938), Mayor of Boston (1918–22). One of the rare Yankee mayors of Boston, Peters was born on 3 April 1872 in West Roxbury, Massachusetts, the son of Andrew James Peters, a wealthy merchant of seventeenth-century English colonial stock, and Mary Richards Whitney. The family was Episcopal, and Andrew attended St. Paul's prep school (where he was a skipper and athlete), and Harvard (B.A., 1895, LL.B., 1898). He entered a law firm in Boston and became interested in Democratic party politics. (He was *not* a Republican, as reported in J. F. Dinneen's biography of Mayor Curley [*q.v.*].) Peters married Martha R. Phillips, a descendant of John Phillips (*q.v.*), the first mayor of Boston, on 23 June 1910, and they had six sons.

Peters was elected to the Massachusetts House (1902), to the state Senate (1904–1905), and then to the U.S. Congress (Eleventh District), where he served four consecutive terms, 1907–14, resigning to accept President Woodrow Wilson's appointment as assistant secretary of the U.S. Treasury (Customs), 1914–17. Peters served four years as mayor of Boston, 1918–22, and his administration was marked by the Boston police strike of 1919 and a very high level of graft. His election was close and bitter, mainly an anti-Curley movement led by Democratic boss Martin Lomasney ("the Mahatma"), who was determined to oust James Michael Curley, running Peters and two Irish Catholic candidates against him. The result was Peters 37,923; Curley 28,848; James A. Gallivan 19,400; and Peter Tague 1,700. Curley had dismissed Peters, in a typical phrase, as "a Brookline squire endowed with three apostolic names." Peters, an amiable, high-principled, utterly honest Yankee, was gullible, trusting, and perhaps lazy. Always tanned, a sailor and horseman, and used to the good life, Peters felt confined by deskwork and the everyday chores of the mayoralty, chores adored by professionals like Curley.

Mayor Peters hoped for a peaceful, happy administration. He gave patronage plums to the Boston Irish who had put him in power; he limited further city improvements but raised city employee salaries; he stood for fiscal responsibility and tax reductions; and he was loved by business. A disciple of metropolitan control, Peters pushed the "Greater Boston" concept later brought to fuller fruition under Curley in 1930 (creation of the Metropolitan District Commission). Yet, he was plagued by an unscrupulous, corrupt palace guard over whom he had little control (and of whom he had little knowledge). He presided over one of the most graft-ridden administrations in Boston history: a tragic irony for such a man.

The big issue in that growing city of 750,000 was the Boston police strike, which broke out on 8 September 1919. Supported by Police Commissioner (and ex-Mayor) E. U. Curtis (q.v.), Mayor Peters took a strong stand, refused all police demands, and used the militia to keep order. He broke the strike, although it was the governor, Calvin Coolidge, who gained most publicity and shot to the U.S. presidency as a result. Peters did not run for reelection in 1922; he was thoroughly disillusioned and never did understand what had happened to his administration. Curley said later that Peters was "an innocent dupe for a conscienceless corps of bandits." A story which typifies Peters (whether true or not) is that he would have been chosen to run for governor in 1929, but he was napping and refused to answer the telephone when the Democratic state chairman called. He died in Boston at the age of sixty-six, on 26 June 1938.

SOURCES: J. H. Cutler, *"Honey Fitz": Three Steps to the White House* (Indianapolis, 1962); J. F. Dinneen, *The Purple Shamrock: The Hon. James M. Curley of Boston* (New York, 1949); John Koren, *Boston, 1822–1922: The Story of Its Government* (Boston, 1923); Francis Russell, *The Great Interlude* (New York, 1964).   *Peter d'A. Jones*

PETTIGREW, SAMUEL (1790?–1860?), Mayor of Pittsburgh (1832–36). Little is known of Samuel Pettigrew, the first popularly elected mayor of Pittsburgh, not even his birth date or the year of his death. His first records appear in Masonic sources showing that on 13 April 1814 he was initiated into Ohio Lodge No. 113. He served the organization as worshipful master in 1821–22, was its secretary for three years, and a district official for two.

In 1814, Pettigrew married Martha Barclay, apparently the mother of his son James, who ran unsuccessfully for mayor in 1853 and 1854. Eighteen months after Martha died in 1823, Samuel married Charlotte Clayland. In 1815, he was listed in the city's first directory as a druggist, and seven years later, his name appears on a deed as a member of the firm of Trevor, Pettigrew and Troost. For a number of years, he served on the city's common council and became its president in 1828, resigning three years later when appointed an alderman.

A Democrat, Pettigrew was the last mayor of Pittsburgh to be chosen by councils and the first to be elected by popular vote, under provisions of an act of December 1833. On 10 January 1832 and 8 January 1833, he was chosen mayor with little opposition. On 14 January 1834, in the first popular election, running as the "Jackson and Clay" candidate, he received 844 votes to 485 for Cornelius Darragh (son of Pittsburgh's second mayor) and 96 for former Mayor Matthew B. Lowrie (q.v.), an Anti-Mason. With the adoption of the convention system of nomination in 1835, Pettigrew's opposition within his party nearly crumbled. While he was mayor, Pittsburgh had a population of about 16,000 to 17,500.

During Pettigrew's administration, much was accomplished. The city's waterworks (using the Allegheny River as a source instead of surface wells) commenced operation in 1832. In January of that year, Pittsburgh suffered a cholera epidemic, followed by another in 1833. Salt wells were struck in what is now Pittsburgh's South Side, resulting in a considerable development of a new industry for the city. Gasworks went into operation in 1834, and the Pittsburgh Board of Trade was organized in January 1835. There was a devastating flood in February 1832. The following year, Daniel Webster visited the city on 4 July with his daughter and was welcomed as "an apostle of righteousness" since he had surprised everyone by voting for a tariff act much desired by Pittsburgh industrialists. On 7 January 1834, the councils passed an ordinance that completed the division of the city into four wards (first initiated during Matthew B. Lowrie's term in office), for the convenience of voters. A new market house was completed during Pettigrew's administration.

SOURCES: Allen Humphreys Kerr, "The Mayors and Recorders of Pittsburgh, 1816–1951" (typescript, 1952, Carnegie Library of Pittsburgh); Pittsburgh *Gazette*, 29 July 1850; Pittsburgh *Press*, "The Mayors' Notebook, No. 6," by George Swetnam, 21 September 1973; Erasmus Wilson, *Standard History of Pittsburgh* (*sic*) (Chicago, 1898). *Helene Smith*

PHELAN, JAMES DUVAL (1861–1930), Mayor of San Francisco (1897–1902). Reform mayor of San Francisco and millionaire art patron, Phelan was born in the city on 20 April 1861, eight days after the outbreak of the Civil War. His father, James Phelan (1821–92), was a wealthy banker, a California pioneer from Ireland who had made various fortunes in commodities before going into real estate and banking. His mother, an Irish Catholic, was Alice Kelly, born in Brooklyn, New York, and married in San Francisco in June 1859 (d. 1902).

Phelan was educated at St. Ignatius College (B.A., 1881), a Jesuit institution which later became the University of San Francisco, and went on to take a law degree at the University of California, Berkeley. His real dream was to become a poet and writer; leaving Berkeley, he toured Europe for two years, studying the arts. James was a good-looking and wealthy young man-about-town, one of the first to own an automobile in San Francisco. After his father died in December 1892, James took over several of the family banking businesses, such as the First National Bank of San Francisco, the Mutual Savings Bank, and the United Bank and Trust Company. He became an art patron, encouraging sculptors, writers, and painters, and was president of the San Francisco Art Association, 1894–95 (to whom he bequeathed his famous Villa Montalvo on his death). Phelan was an unusual businessman—a close friend of Bohemian and artistic circles and a member of the *salon* led by Mary Edith Griswold (an editor of *Sunset Magazine*) at her Telegraph Hill mansion, which included such people as Jack London, David Belasco, Ambrose Bierce, Gertrude Atherton, Luther Burbank, and assorted poets and artists. Gertrude Atherton called him "California's most elegant gentleman." Phelan never married.

At this time San Francisco, a city of about 330,000, was one of the most boss-ridden and corrupt in the union, dominated by "Boss" Abraham Ruef (1864–1936) who ran the Republican (later Union Labor) machine. After Phelan gave a speech to the Mechanics' Institute in 1896 on "The New San Francisco," Fremont Older, crusading editor of the *Evening Bulletin*, asked him to run for mayor. With no political experience whatsoever, Phelan ran as a Democrat and won, being reelected twice, in 1898 and 1900. For three terms, Mayor Phelan managed the city well. He attacked graft, reduced inflated "jobs" (saving $300,000), and yet still managed to beautify the city, adding parks, fountains, and playgrounds. He was responsible for bringing the "Burnham Plan" (the ideas of the great Chicago city planner, Daniel H. Burnham) to San Francisco, one fruit of which was the future civic center. Phelan masterminded the Hetch Hetchy water supply system, which eventually fed water to the city from the Sierras, and during his second term, he helped to draft the new civic charter—over the opposition of both old party machines—which placed jobs on civil service and envisaged municipal ownership of utilities.

Despite such achievements, Phelan was brought down by a violent waterfront strike in which he used policemen to protect nonstriking workers—a fatal mistake. The Union Labor party emerged, directed by "Boss" Ruef, and swept its puppet, Eugene Schmitz (*q.v.*), into the mayor's office in January 1902.

Phelan's work was not over by any means. He struggled against the corrupt Schmitz-Ruef regime in 1906–1908, and, encouraged by President Theodore Roosevelt, he and Rudolph Spreckels financed the famous graft prosecutions which convicted the two criminals. Phelan showed great courage in the face of personal threats and much violence.

Meanwhile, the earthquake and the fire of 1906 had ravaged the city, and though Phelan himself had lost a great deal, including his mansion, he soon rebuilt the well-known Phelan Building downtown, gave at least a million dollars of his own money to aid, and was appointed by President Roosevelt as direct coordinator of the federal relief plan ($10 million was involved), circumventing the corrupt city government. In later years, Phelan undertook State Department missions abroad and was elected to the U.S. Senate for six years (1915–21), where he supported the exclusion of Oriental immigrants and was unsympathetic to the League of Nations idea. He was defeated for reelection in 1920 by a Republican. In 1924, Phelan gave the nominating speech for W. G. McAdoo at the Democratic national convention.

James Phelan died at his estate, Villa Montalvo, on 7 August 1930. Wrote Fremont Older, "He had a deep love for San Francisco and dreamed of making it a clean, beautiful city worthy of its magnificent natural advantages . . ." Phelan's role in rebuilding the city in 1906 was remarkable; he proclaimed: "Build! Build! Build! Here all are equal and the prizes will be to the ones who have courage and stamina to pass over the trying days of reconstruction." Phelan certainly lived up to his own words.

SOURCES: Gertrude Atherton, *Golden Gate Country* (New York, 1945); Walton Bean, *Boss Ruef's San Francisco* (Berkeley, Calif., 1952); *In Memoriam, James D. Phelan*, Meeting of Board of Supervisors of City and County of San Francisco, 11 August 1930; Dorothy Kaucher, *James Duval Phelan: A Portrait* (Saratoga, Calif., 1965); Fremont Older, *My Own Story*, 2d ed. (San Francisco, 1926); James D. Phelan, "The New San Francisco" (printed address, 1896).   *Peter d'A. Jones*

PHILLIPS, JOHN (1770–1823), Mayor of Boston (1822–23). Boston's first mayor, born there on 23 November 1770, Phillips was the son of William and Margaret Phillips, Anglo-Saxon Yankees who ran a dry goods store. After attending Phillips Academy, he was admitted to Harvard College and graduated in 1784 as salutatory orator of his class. He chose law and became prosecutor of the municipal court; in 1809 he became judge of the court of common pleas. He married a Yankee of British descent, Sarah Walley, and they had eight children, one of whom, Wendell Phillips (1811–84), became a leading abolitionist and radical reformer. In 1820, he served as delegate to the state constitutional convention and the following year was a member of a committee recommending the transformation of Boston from a town to a city.

For the first century and a half of its existence, Boston had been governed by town meetings, selectmen, and a variety of autonomous and semi-autonomous boards. After the Revolution, however, the population increased at such a rapid rate that Bostonians became aware of the inability of the town meeting system to deal effectively with the growing demands of a city of 45,000. In 1821, therefore, the town authorized several committees to explore new administrative structures, and eventually one committee recommended a system of city government. After a brief but highly emotional debate, on 7 January 1822, the voters of Boston adopted the proposal by a small margin, and on 23 February 1822, Governor John Brooks officially approved "an act establishing the city of Boston." Henceforth Boston would function under a charter providing for a mayor, an eight-person board of aldermen, and a representative body of forty-eight called the common council.

Boston now turned to the task of electing its first mayor. The older Federalists proposed Harrison Gray Otis (*q.v.*), former congressman and senator from Massachusetts; younger elements of the Federalist party nominated Josiah Quincy (*q.v.*), who had also served as congressman and state senator. When the National Republicans entered the name of Thomas L. Winthrop, the city-wide vote was further divided, and neither Federalist candidate was able to secure the required majority of votes. A second election was held on 16 April 1822, in which John Phillips, by now a well-known figure acceptable to both wings of the Federalist party, was selected as a compromise candidate, and almost unanimously elected as the first mayor of the city of Boston attracting 2,499 of the 2,650 votes cast.

On 1 May 1822, the new city government was organized in solemn ceremonies at Faneuil Hall where the chairman of the town's board of selectmen formally turned over to the new city authorities the town records and title deeds, as well as a copy of the city charter enclosed in a silver case. After acknowledging "the wisdom of our ancestors" whose traditions of town government had caused Boston to grow and prosper for nearly 200 years, Mayor Phillips displayed his spirit of conciliation by warning those who had agitated for the new city structure not to entertain "hopes which could not be realized." At the same time, he urged those who were saddened at the loss of the old town structure not to indulge in "unreasonable apprehension." For the most part, Phillips confined his activities to organizing the administrative machinery created by the new city charter and making the transition from town to city as painless and as acceptable as possible. Because his health was deteriorating badly, he entertained no thoughts of a second term as mayor. He died on 29 May 1823, less than a month after the close of his single term.

SOURCES: James M. Hubbard, *Boston's Last Town Meetings and First City Election* (Boston, 1884); *Inaugural Addresses of the Mayors of Boston, 1822–1852* (Boston, 1894); John Koren, *Boston, 1822–1922* (Boston, 1922); *Records of the City of Boston: Mayor and Aldermen*, microfilm, Boston Public Library; Henry H. Sprague, *City Government in Boston* (Boston, 1890); Justin Winsor, ed., *Memorial History of Boston . . . 1630–1880*, 4 vols. (Boston, 1880), vol. 3.   *Thomas H. O'Connor*

PHILLIPS, JOSEPH (1825–), Mayor of Milwaukee (1870–71). Born in Alsace, France, in 1825, Phillips came to the United States in 1834 and to Milwaukee in 1842. He started his career as a tanner, and subsequently, he was in the insurance business. In 1848, he married Mary End. After her death, he married a Miss Liginger, in 1871. He was the father of four sons and five daughters by his first wife. He served as alderman from the Sixth Ward (1859–62) and as city treasurer of Milwaukee (1866–69).

Phillips was elected mayor for a one-year term in 1870. He was defeated for reelection by Harrison Ludington (*q.v.*) in 1871. A life-long Democrat, Phillips vigorously enforced the Graham law and other laws for regulation of saloons and thus lost favor with many of his constituents, particularly the Germans. One of the critical issues of the times was the upgrading of the water and sewer systems. Mayor Phillips appointed a committee in 1870 to study the problem with former Mayor O'Neill (*q.v.*) as chairman, and in 1871 bonds were issued to establish a pumping station, a waterworks, and a reservoir.

Milwaukee was a city of about 72,000 persons at the time. The city government consisted of a bicameral common council and a mayor elected for a one-year term.

SOURCES: George William Bruce, *The Mayors of Milwaukee* (Milwaukee, 1942); Frank A. Flower, *History of Milwaukee, Wisconsin* (Chicago, 1881); John S. Gregory, *History of Milwaukee, Wisconsin* (Chicago, 1931); Bayrd Still, *Milwaukee: The History of a City* (Madison, Wis., 1965).   *Donald F. Tingley*

PIERCE, HENRY L. (1825–96), Mayor of Boston (1873, 1878). Republican mayor of Boston and a champion of reform in municipal services, Pierce was born in Stoughton, Massachusetts, on 23 August 1825, the son of Colonel Jesse Pierce and Elizabeth S. (Lillie), both of them strong-willed and outspoken Methodists. Pierce attended Milton Academy and the State Norman School in Bridgewater, and then worked for many years in his uncle's business, the Baker Chocolate Factory. He never married.

A staunch antislavery Free-Soiler, and a strong opponent of Know-Nothingism, Pierce became an early and active supporter of the Republican party and was made state party treasurer in 1857. He was elected to the state legislature in 1860 and served through 1862. He later turned to city politics, serving as a member of the Boston Board of Aldermen in 1869.

The city leadership's inability to cope with a severe smallpox epidemic, combined with the devastation caused by the great fire of 1872 that ravaged a large section of Boston's business district, led a group of independent businessmen to champion Pierce's nonpartisan candidacy for mayor. In one of the closest races in the history of the Boston mayoralty, Pierce won by a mere seventy-nine votes over incumbent William Gaston (*q.v.*). Responding to what he felt to be the city's immediate needs, Pierce helped establish a smallpox hospital and, in spite of strong opposition, forced the much needed reorganization of the health and fire departments. The efficiency of the fire department over the coming years led to a significant reduction in the city's fire insurance rates.

Many city streets were improved during his first term. However, his effort to revise the city charter and strengthen the central government was unsuccessful. Before his one-year term ran out, Charlestown, West Roxbury, and Brighton were officially annexed by the city, increasing Boston's population by over 42,000. The city's official size by 1875 was 341,919.

Elected to fill a vacancy in Congress, in November 1873, Pierce resigned from the mayoralty. After representing the Third District in Washington, D.C., he was again elected mayor in 1878, defeating Democrat Frederick Prince (*q.v.*) by 2,300 votes. Pierce's major efforts now included a reorganization of the municipal police and a reduction in the tax rate. He decided not to run for reelection in 1879. During the 1880s, he was involved in the Massachusetts Tariff Reform League, and in 1884 he became sole owner of the Baker Chocolate Factory. A skilled yachtsman, he became an ardent outdoorsman during his later years, in part to improve his health. Pierce became ill during a visit to Chicago and after being stricken with paralysis died in Boston on 17 September 1896 at the age of seventy-one.

SOURCES: Albert P. Langtry, ed., *Metropolitan Boston: A Modern History* (New York, 1929), vol. 2; State Street Trust Company, *Mayors of Boston* (Boston, 1914); Justin Winsor, ed., *The Memorial History of Boston* (Boston, 1880–83), vol. 3.   *Donald M. Jacobs*

PILLSBURY, EDWARD (1823–82), Mayor of New Orleans (1876–78). A conservative (Democratic) mayor of Yankee origin, Pillsbury was born in 1823 in Eastport, Maine, of old-line English parentage. His father, Timothy Pillsbury, was in the shipping business and at one time (c. 1841) was also a member of the Republic of Texas Congress. Edward and his father arrived in New Orleans in 1834. From then until his death, Pillsbury was engaged in business as a cotton factor and commission merchant. At some unspecified date, Pillsbury married Desiree Perret who bore him three children. Other events in Pillsbury's life are unknown until in 1874 he became commissioner of finance in the administration of Mayor Charles J. Leeds (*q.v.*).

Pillsbury's principal contribution to the welfare of New Orleans was a scheme known as the "premium bond plan" intended to reduce substantially $22 million of bonded indebtedness. One of the plan's essential requirements was the exchange of old bonds for new ones, and expensive litigation resulted from the unwillingness of many bondholders to accept the exchange. Put into effect in 1875, the "premium bond plan" was neither an immediate nor a total success. Nonetheless, as the creator of what was believed at the time to be the vehicle of the city's financial salvation, Pillsbury was nominated by acclamation as the Democratic candidate for mayor of New Orleans in 1876 and won easily over Republican C. B. White 25,031 votes to 15,022.

As mayor, Pillsbury was unable to pay off the city's *floating* debt, although his sale of the municipal waterworks for $2 million helped in that respect. Under Pillsbury's low-key administration, a number of streets and bridges were repaired, and construction of the impressive Robert E. Lee monument began. The most notable event of Pillsbury's mayoralty was the termination of Radical Reconstruction in Louisiana on 24 April 1877. Without the support of a nearby state administration, Republicanism in New Orleans soon became impotent and later virtually extinct. Consequently, for the past century, control of the city government has alternated only between various Democratic "rings" and reformers. As these developments began to formalize, Pillsbury died on 10 August 1882.

SOURCES: John S. Kendall, *History of New Orleans* (Chicago, 1922), vol. 1; Works Progress Administration, "Administrations of the Mayors of New Orleans, 1803–1936," and "Biographies of the Mayors of New Orleans, 1803–1936" (New Orleans, 1940).

Mark T. Carleton

PINGREE, HAZEN S. (1840–1901), Mayor of Detroit (1890–97). Reform mayor, born on 30 August 1840 near Denmark, Maine, Pingree was the son of Jasper Pingree (1806–71), an old-stock Yankee small farmer and itinerant cobbler, and Adeline (Bryant) Pingree of New England ancestry. The fourth-born of eight children, Hazen Pingree attended Maine rural schools in the winter months, not going beyond eighth grade. He went to work in a cotton factory in Saco, Maine, and in 1860 moved to a Hopkinton, Massachusetts, shoe factory to work as a leather cutter. In 1862, he enlisted in the First Massachusetts Heavy Artillery and was captured and imprisoned in the infamous Andersonville stockade. Upon discharge in 1865, Private Pingree went to Detroit, working again as a leather cutter and later becoming a salesman in a small boot and shoe factory purchased for a small sum ($1,360) in 1866 with his partner Charles H. Smith. By 1890, the sales of Pingree and Smith had reached $1 million annually, and the plant was judged one of the largest in the West. Pingree married a Mount Clemens, Michigan, schoolteacher, Frances A. Gilbert (1841–1908), in 1872, and they had three children; only two of the children, Hazel and Hazen, Jr., survived to adulthood. Pingree was a member of the socially prominent Woodward Avenue Baptist Church, a Maccabee, a Mason, and an active member of the Detroit Grand Army of the Republic, Post 384.

In 1890, Detroit had 205,876 people and a mayor-council form of government. Pingree, who had taken no active role in politics, accepted the Republican nomination for Detroit mayor in 1889. He won the election by 13,954 votes to his Democratic opponent, John Pridgeon, Jr.'s (q.v.) 11,616. He was reelected Republican mayor in 1891 (15,335 to his two opponents, William G. Thompson's (q.v.), 9,015, and John Miner's, 5,263); in 1893 (24,924 to Marshall H. Godfrey's 19,124); and in 1895 (21,024 to Samuel Goldwater's 10,432), winning four consecutive two-year terms. During his last term as mayor in 1896, he was elected Republican governor of Michigan, and he was reelected in 1898. He declined to run for reelection in 1900.

Pingree's mayoralty elections transformed Detroit from its normal Democratic majorities to Republican victories with the help of foreign-born and ethnic voters, whom he assiduously courted. As mayor, Pingree began a new depression relief program (urban farming in 1893) and engaged in heated controversies with Detroit's traction, gas, electric light, and telephone companies, forcing rate reductions. He won public approval for a citizen-owned electric light plant, and became an outstanding spokesman for both municipal ownership and state regulation of utilities, and achieved national acclaim as one of the preeminent social reformers of his time.

Although Pingree's achievements as governor were not as manifold as those as mayor, he corrected the most flagrant tax evasion by large corporations. He also forced through the state legislature the first significant statewide appraisal of railroad and corporate property which helped to establish a rational basis for regulation and taxation, emulated by later Progressive reformers in other states.

After a trip to South Africa to hunt elephants and to investigate the Boer War, Pingree took ill with dysentery, died in London on 18 June 1901, and was buried in Detroit.

SOURCES: Melvin G. Holli, *Reform in Detroit: Hazen S. Pingree and Urban Politics* (New York, 1969); Hazen S. Pingree, *Facts and Opinions* (Detroit, 1895); Hazen S. Pingree Papers, 285 vols., scrapbooks, Burton Historical Collection, Detroit Public Library; Charles R. Starring, "Hazen S. Pingree: Another Forgotten Eagle," *Michigan History* 32 (June 1948).   *Melvin G. Holli*

PITCHER, ZINA (1797–1872), Mayor of Detroit (1840, 1841, 1843). Known as the father of free education in Detroit, Pitcher considered this accomplishment as mayor to be the crowning achievement of his life. It was a milestone in a life marked by service. Pitcher was born on 12 April 1797 to Nathaniel and Margaret (Stevenson) Pitcher, a farm family in rural Fort Edwards, Washington County, New York. His mother, widowed in 1802, was left with five sons and an unproductive farm, but the Quaker woman managed to provide all her boys with fine educations. One of the brothers became lieutenant governor of New York in the mid-1830s; Zina Pitcher became a medical doctor, receiving his degree from Middlebury College in 1822.

From his graduation until 1836, Pitcher served in the Army as assistant surgeon and then as surgeon. During that time, he worked among the Indians at frontier outposts. A prolific medical writer throughout his life, he authored numerous articles about the value of certain Indian medicines based upon his early experiences.

In 1836, Pitcher moved to Detroit with his wife since 1824, Anne (Sheldon) Pitcher. She was from a prominent Kalamazoo, Michigan, family, and they had two children, Nathaniel and Rose. In 1867, three years after his wife's death, Pitcher married the widowed Emily L. (Montgomery) Backus from Rochester, New York. Their child, Sidney Rochester, died in infancy.

Dr. Pitcher had a life-long passion for justice and for the humane treatment of others, concerns that led him to diverse causes. He helped organize the State Insane Asylum at Kalamazoo, a progressive institution for its time. He also served as local president of the Irish Repeal Association which, according to the disgruntled Democratic Detroit *Free Press*, was a factor in his capturing the Irish vote and thereby the mayoralty.

In 1840, Pitcher, a Whig, was elected mayor by a ten-vote majority over M. Gillet, the Democrat. A year later, a split in the Whig party led to a three-way race in the 1841 election between Pitcher, Issac Rowland (a Whig running on the Young Men's Ticket) and B.F.H. Witherell (Democrat). Pitcher won this time by 103 votes. He did not run in 1842, but he returned to the race in 1843 and defeated Witherell 793 to 479 votes. Detroit was rapidly becoming a mixed community of Yankees, Irish, and Germans in the early 1840s; yet, the Whigs dominated local politics during most of the decade. The city had over 9,000 people and was growing.

During his second term, Pitcher prevailed upon the twelve members of the council to petition the state legislature for a law to authorize public schools in the city. He shamed citizens into taxing themselves to support primary education when money from the sale of school lands ran out.

After his terms as mayor, Pitcher continued his medical practice, serving also as county physician and city physician. He was tenth president of the American Medical Association, co-founder of the *Peninsular Journal of Medicine*, and associate editor of the *Richmond and Louisville Medical Journal*. He died on 5 April 1872 in Detroit and was buried from the Episcopal Church which he had attended but never joined.

SOURCES: Silas Farmer, *The History of Detroit and Michigan* (Detroit, 1889), vol. 2; Morris Fishbein, *A History of the American Medical Association, 1847–1947* (Philadelphia, 1947); *Medical History of Michigan* (Minneapolis and St. Paul, 1930), vol. 1; *Scrapbooks*, Burton,

Palmer, Walker, and Zug: in the Burton Historical Collection, Detroit Public Library. Miscellaneous Pitcher letters are to be found in the Sheldon, Woodbridge, Catlin, and Mason Papers, also located in the Burton Historical Collection. *JoEllen Vinyard*

POELKER, JOHN H. (1913–), Mayor of St. Louis (1973–77). Born on 14 April 1913 in St. Louis, son of John G. and Anna (Bongner) Poelker, the future mayor attended local schools and St. Louis University, graduating in 1934. Poelker was an assistant to the sales manager of the National Ammonia Division of E. I. Du Pont de Nemours Company, Inc., in St. Louis (1934–42). He then served as a special agent for the FBI (1942–53). On 19 October 1940, he married Ruth Cambron, and they had three children. Poelker belonged to the National Association of Accountants, the Municipal Finance Officers Association, and the International Association of Assessing Officers.

A Democrat, Poelker began his political career in 1953 when he was elected city assessor. In 1957, he was elected city comptroller, thus becoming an important aide to Mayor Raymond R. Tucker (*q.v.*). He was reelected in 1961, 1965, and 1969, serving a total of sixteen years at this post. During his last two terms, he provided support for Mayor A. J. Cervantes (*q.v.*). In 1973, Poelker decided to challenge Cervantes in the Democratic mayoral primary. Successfully winning the nomination, Poelker went on to defeat J. Badaracco (Republican) 76,601 to 57,962. St. Louis had 622,236 people in 1970, a heavy loss since 1960, and a mayor-council form of government.

As mayor, Poelker was able to win approval for federal grants to provide funds for a series of urban renewal programs. He backed construction of a new civic center as part of this rehabilitation plan. During his term, numerous older buildings were restored, instead of being razed, winning the approval of architects and local historians. Poelker also reached an agreement with the Missouri Pacific Railroad with regard to trackage rights along the city's waterfront. In 1977, he was defeated in the Democratic primary and retired from public life.

SOURCES: St. Louis newspapers, 1973, 1978; *Who's Who in America* (Chicago, 1978); *Who's Who in the Midwest* (Chicago, 1978). *Thomas R. Bullard*

POND, EDWARD B. (1833–1910), Mayor of San Francisco (1887–91). Pond was born on 7 September 1833 in Belleville, New York, to Congregational minister Charles Pond (d. 1876), an old-stock Yankee, and Abigail (Bates) Pond. The fifth of eight children, Pond received a college preparatory education but left the East in 1854 to seek his fortune in California. Arriving in

1855 after a trip overland, he settled in Butte County, part of the upper Sacramento River Valley, and began trading in livestock. In 1859, he opened a general store in Chico as one of the town's first settlers, but in 1866, after a two-year trip to the East Coast, he moved to San Francisco and entered the wholesale liquor business. In 1874, Pond associated with the San Francisco Savings Union and subsequently served as director, vice-president, and president until retiring in 1909. He also engaged in other enterprises, most notably grain trading. In 1861, Pond married Sarah McNeill, an Ohio native of Scottish and German ancestry; two of their three children, Charles Edward and Samuel Frank, lived to adulthood. In San Francisco, he was a long-time member of the First Unitarian Church.

In 1880, San Francisco had 233,959 people, a figure that increased to 298,997 by 1890, and the city, consolidated with the county of the same name, was run by a mayor-board of supervisors form of government. Pond began his political career with election to the board of supervisors in 1882 and was reelected in 1884. Because of his reputation as a watchdog of city funds, he received the 1886 Democratic nomination for mayor and won the 2 November election with 24,340 votes to Republican Abner Doble's 19,701 and William M. Hinton's 1,446. On 6 November 1888 he was reelected, with 21,002 votes to Republican Charles R. Story's 18,405 and Independent Charles C. O'Donnell's 15,491. Despite his two terms, Pond achieved relatively little, in part because the city charter limited his influence by dispersing power widely through city government. Like other San Francisco mayors of the 1880s, Pond conceived his responsibility to conduct a frugal administration of ongoing, limited city activities, not the introduction of new projects. His views coincided with the program of Democratic party boss Christopher Buckley who sought victory through a platform of low taxes and opposition to bond issues. During Pond's two terms, the Democrats controlled the board of supervisors, and Buckley ran the city to enrich and sustain his political organization. In 1890, during his second term, Pond accepted the Democratic nomination for governor, but he lost the election to Republican Henry H. Markham. This defeat ended his political career. During the 1890s, he worked with the Traffic Association, a group of San Francisco businessmen seeking to introduce railroad and shipping competitive with the Southern Pacific to California. He died of a heart attack in San Francisco on 22 April 1910 and was buried in Oakland.

SOURCES: [Anon.], *The Bay of San Francisco*, 2 vols. (Chicago, 1892), vol. 1; [anon.], *The Valley Road* (San Francisco, 1896); Alexander Callow, Jr., "San Francisco's Blind Boss," *Pacific Historical Review* 25 (August 1956); W. H. Murray, *Builders of a Great City* (San Francisco, 1891); [San Francisco Board of Supervisors], *San Francisco Municipal Reports, 1886/87* (San Francisco, 1887) and *1888/89* (San Francisco, 1889); San Francisco *Chronicle*, 23 April 1910; San Francisco *Examiner*, 23 April 1910; John Phillip Young, *San Francisco: A History of the Pacific Coast Metropolis*, 2 vols. (San Francisco, 1912), vol. 2.   *Michael Griffith*

PORTER, AUGUSTUS SEYMOUR (1798–1872), Mayor of Detroit (1838). Yankee mayor of early Detroit, Porter was born on 18 January 1798 in Canandaigua, New York, the son of Augustus and Lavinia (Steele) Porter, a well-to-do, established family. His grandfather, Joshua Porter, was a physician who served as a colonel in the state militia during the Revolutionary War and who was a long-time member of the state assembly in Connecticut. Augustus Porter attended Union College and graduated in 1818. He returned to Canandaigua to read law. He practiced law in Black Rock, New York, until 1827 when he moved to Detroit. He had a law office in Detroit for the next twenty years.

In 1830 and 1834, Porter served as recorder of the common council, and in 1832 he was elected superintendent of the poor. He was elected a commissioner of the district schools in 1833 but apparently never performed any service. In 1838, he became one of the owners of the *Daily Advertiser*.

Porter, a Whig, was elected on 2 April 1838 as mayor with 839 votes to Henry Howard's 508. Detroit, with a mayor-council form of government, had a population of about 8,000. On 1 May 1838, Porter presided over a meeting of the freemen of the city who authorized the mayor and council to borrow $50,000 to pay its growing debts and to help build new streets, walks, and sewers. Under Porter's leadership, the council made plans for revising the city charter, put up a town clock in the Presbyterian church steeple, and, in November 1838, authorized the increase of the Night Watch to 200 men because of anxiety over the rebellion that was still going on across the Detroit River in Canada. The first public schools were opened in 1838. On 8 March 1839, Porter announced that he was moving out of the city and was therefore resigning as mayor.

Porter was elected by the Michigan legislature to fill a seat in the U.S. Senate on 20 January 1840 and served until 3 March 1845. As senator, he helped to obtain federal aid for the construction of the St. Mary's ship canal at Sault Sainte Marie, Michigan. In 1848, he moved to Niagara Falls, New York, where his family owned Goat Island. He practiced law there until his death on 18 September 1872.

SOURCES: Clarence M. Burton, *History of Detroit*,

1780–1850 (Detroit, 1917); Frederick Carlisle, comp., *Chronology of Notable Events in the History of the Northwest Territory and Wayne County* (Detroit, 1895); Detroit Common Council, *Journal of the Proceedings of the Common Council of the City of Detroit, 1824–1843* (n.p., n.d.); Silas Farmer, *History of Detroit and Wayne County and Early Michigan*, 3d ed. (1890; reprint, Detroit, 1969); some items in the William Woodbridge Papers, Burton Historical Collection, Detroit Public Library.   *William T. Bulger*

PORTER, JOHN C. (1872–1959), Mayor of Los Angeles (1929–33). Born on 4 April 1872 in Leon, Iowa, Porter was the son of Josephus Clinton Porter, a farmer, and Matilda (Gardiner) Porter. As an only child, Porter moved to California with his family in 1885 when his father bought a farm in Artesia, and he attended Whittier Academy and a business college in Los Angeles. In 1892, Porter began working as a telegraph operator for the Southern Pacific Railroad, and one year later, on 10 January 1892, he married the former Mattie Lee, who provided him with two children, Lee Clinton and Helen Catherine. In 1906, he opened his own automobile sales agency in Los Angeles. He was a Mason, a Moose, and a Republican.

Porter's political career began in 1928 when he led the grand jury to indict the district attorney, Asa Keys, for bribery, and the gangster, Albert Marco, for murder. Their conviction catapulted Porter into the mayor's seat in the election of 6 June 1929: 151,905 to 106,515. During his only term, Porter completed final negotiations between the federal government and the Metropolitan Water District for vital Colorado River water, and settled a dispute between Los Angeles and Owens Valley, another water source. Porter also ended a longstanding dispute between Los Angeles and Long Beach for the unification of their harbor projects. Besides military parades, fiestas, aviation races, and conventions, Porter hosted the 1932 Olympic Games in Los Angeles.

Throughout his career, Porter was known as a Christian and an economizer. Like his mentor, the Reverend Robert P. "Bob" Shuler, Porter was a teetotaler, and during an official visit to Paris he refused to participate in a diplomatic toast. His economic measures had far greater significance than his religious scruples. By 1933, Porter had reduced the size of the city budget by 27 percent and the city tax rate by 14 percent. When he left office, the city was in sound financial health.

Porter nevertheless suffered the humiliation of being the first mayor of Los Angeles to face a recall election. The Municipal League claimed that he opposed the development of the municipally owned Department of Water and Power, that he dismissed Dr. George Parrish,

the finest health officer in the city's history, and that he discriminated against Catholics and Jews in the civil service. Porter successfully overcame this recall attempt in 1932, but the damage had been done and he was defeated for reelection in 1933.

Porter remained active in public life for nearly a decade after he left office. In 1936, he was appointed to the State Highway Commission, and in 1941, he again ran for mayor but was defeated in the primary. His first wife died in 1940, and he married the former Anna C. Webb in March 1945. For the remainder of his life, he was the director of Suburban Hospitals, Inc., in South Gate, California. He died on 27 May 1959.

SOURCES: Marshall Dimock, "Recall Movement Against Mayor Porter," *National Municipal Review* (December 1931); John Anson Ford, *John Anson Ford and Los Angeles County Government* (Oral History Project, UCLA, 1967); John R. Haynes Collection, Government Documents, UCLA Research Library; Los Angeles *Times*, 28 May 1959; Stanley Rogers, "The Attempted Recall of the Mayor of Los Angeles," *National Municipal Review* (July 1932).   *Fred W. Viehe*

POULSON, CHARLES NORRIS (1895–   ), Mayor of Los Angeles (1953–61). Poulson was born on 23 July 1895 in Baker County, Oregon, to Peter S. Poulson (1843–1928), a Danish-born Lutheran farmer, and Jenney E. (Rainey) (1867–1940) of Arkansas. Poulson grew up on his father's farm and attended local schools. In 1913, he entered the Oregon Agricultural College at Corvallis, and a year later he transferred to a business college in Baker, Oregon. The following February, the nineteen-year-old Poulson became an accountant for J. F. Bryant in nearby Haines but left and took up farming after he married the former Erna June Loenning on 25 December 1916. Their marriage produced three daughters, Erna Bea, Patricia, and Norrissa. In the spring of 1923, Poulson and his family moved to Los Angeles where he became a bookkeeper for the Square Oil Company. Two years later, he opened his own accounting business, and in 1933, he passed the California CPA examination.

Poulson's Republican political career began in 1938 when he was elected to the California State Assembly from the Fifty-sixth District. He was reelected two years later and was noted for his investigation of the California Athletic Commission. In 1943, Poulson was elected to the U.S. House of Representatives, but after he was defeated for reelection two years later, he worked as a state lobbyist for the California CPA Association. In 1947, Poulson again was elected to Congress and was reelected three consecutive times. While in Congress, as a member of the House Public Lands Committee, he began a life-long interest in southern California's water problem.

On 26 May 1953, at age fifty-eight, Poulson was elected mayor of Los Angeles, defeating a fourteen-year incumbent, Fletcher Bowron (*q.v.*), 287,619 to 252,721. Poulson was reelected with a far larger vote on 2 April 1957: 311,970 to 201,121. During his two terms, he racially integrated the fire department, settling a public housing dispute, and brought the Brooklyn Dodgers baseball team to Los Angeles. Poulson caught national attention in September 1959 when he challenged the visiting Soviet premier, Nikita Khrushchev, to explain his statement that the U.S.S.R. would "bury" the United States. In 1961, Poulson again sought reelection, but he was defeated in an upset by Samuel Yorty (*q.v.*).

After leaving office, Poulson maintained his interest in public affairs, and in 1965, he began serving a four-year term as a member of the California Water Commission. It was here that Poulson felt he made his greatest contribution to public welfare. As a member of the water commission, he led the fight to pass a state bond issue that brought water to southern California from the northern part of the state.

In 1969, Poulson retired from public life and moved to Tustin, California, to be closer to his family.

SOURCES: Interview by the author with Norris Poulson, 17 September 1979; Norris Poulson, *Who Would Ever Have Dreamed* (Oral History Project, UCLA, 1966); Norris Poulson Papers, Special Collections, UCLA Research Library.   *Fred W. Viehe*

PRATT, A. MILES (   ), Acting Mayor of New Orleans (30 June–15 July, 1936).

PRATT, HIRAM (1800–40), Mayor of Buffalo (1835–36, 1839–40). Pratt, the last mayor of Buffalo to be selected by the common council, was a Yankee Presbyterian, born on 28 June 1800 in Westminster, Vermont. He was a descendant of John Pratt, who had emigrated to Cambridge, Massachusetts, with the Reverend Thomas Hooker in 1632. In 1804, Hiram was taken to Buffalo on the Niagara frontier by his father, Captain Samuel Pratt (1764–1812), a fur trader and sea captain (born in East Hartford, Connecticut), whose dealings with the local Indians earned him the Seneca name *Hodanidoah* ("Man of Mercy"). In 1785, Captain Pratt had married Esther Wells (1766–1830), daughter of Samuel and Lucy (Evans) Wells, a native of Hatfield, Massachusetts. Hiram was the fifth of their eight children. His youngest sister, Marilla, married Orlando Allen (*q.v.*), who also became mayor of Buffalo in 1848.

Hiram's father opened the first general store in the Buffalo region, which placed him in the local center of business and community activities. Hiram's early grit was demonstrated when he shepherded young refugees to safety who fled the advancing British in the battle of Black Rock in December 1813. On 3 November 1825, he married Maria Fowler (1799–1868), daughter of Nathaniel and Rhoda Fowler, of Northampton, Massachusetts and they had three daughters. They were prominent members of the First Presbyterian Church of Buffalo.

Originally intending a career in medicine, Hiram worked in the drug store owned by Dr. Cyrenius Chapin, a family friend, managing it with Orlando Allen. Pratt eventually bought the drug store outright and abandoned the idea of a medical career. In 1824, he became a partner of Asa B. Meech in a warehouse and forwarding business; he acted as an exchange merchant in an agreement with the Canandaigua branch of the Utica Bank; and in 1831, he became cashier and director of the Bank of Buffalo. His freight firm, Pratt and Taylor, built and operated the steamboat *Daniel Webster*. He was also part owner of the burial ground criticized for its rundown condition, and subsequently closed, with removal of the bodies, in 1830.

In the year Buffalo was chartered as a city, 1832, its population was 10,119; it reached 15,661 in 1835 and 18,213 in 1840. Government was by a common council, consisting of two aldermen from each of five wards, elected for one-year terms. The mayor and other city officials were appointed by the council. Immediately after being appointed mayor in March 1835, Pratt became involved in a dispute over the powers of his office. When the council was divided on its choice for police constable, Pratt, as presiding officer, declared one of the candidates elected. The city attorney ruled the decision illegal, and the action was reconsidered by the council, which elected the other candidate by a substantial majority. Later that year, a committee of the council, reviewing the procedure for selecting a mayor, recommended the continuation of the existing system, but a minority report favored amending the city charter to make the office of mayor elective. Also of note during Pratt's first term was the purchase of land for a wholesale market, later known as the Elk Street Market.

Although Buffalo's city government in the 1830s was dominated by Whigs, elections were generally conducted without reference to the national parties. By the late 1830s, the picture had changed and seven of the ten aldermen elected in March 1839 had been nominated by the Whigs. Pratt himself was a Whig, and during his second and last term of office, 1839 to 1840 (to which he was elected by a vote of 6 to 4 of the council), he and the common council were attacked by the opposition party, particularly for the taxes levied to support city projects—education, parks, the militia, and fire protection. The office of mayor was made elective by state law in 1840.

Pratt suffered great financial losses in 1836–38, particularly through the failure of a local land speculator and builder, Benjamin Rathburn. In the Panic of 1837, his Bank of Buffalo had failed—a second financial loss in two years. This loss had wrecked his estate, and he never recovered financially before his death. Declining health brought a relatively early death to Pratt in Utica, where he had gone for treatment, on 1 May 1840. He was almost forty.

SOURCES: William C. Bryant, "Orlando Allen: Glimpses of Life in the Village of Buffalo," *Publications of the Buffalo and Erie County Historical Society* 1 (1879); William Pryor Letchworth, *Sketch of the Life of Samuel F. Pratt With Some Account of the Pratt Family* (Buffalo, 1874); Scrapbooks, Buffalo and Erie County County Historical Society; H. Perry Smith, *History of Buffalo and Erie County*, 2 vols. (Syracuse, N.Y., 1874); Truman C. White, *Our Country and Its People: A Descriptive Work on Erie County*, 2 vols. (Boston, 1898).   *Christopher Densmore* and *Scott Eberle*

PRATTE, BERNARD (1803–86), Mayor of St. Louis (1844–45). A French-American and the first native of St. Louis to serve as its mayor, Pratte was born on 17 December 1803 to one of the city's most respected and oldest French families. His father, General Bernard Pratte, Sr., a successful merchant and fur trader, had served as a territorial judge of Missouri and had distinguished himself in the War of 1812. The younger Pratte received his early education in St. Louis and, at age fifteen, was sent to Georgetown, Kentucky, to complete his schooling. In 1821, he returned to St. Louis and in 1824 married Louisa Chenie; they had seven children. After his education was finished, Pratte joined his father in the family merchandising business, Bernard Pratte and Company. Although over the years he changed partners several times, Pratte remained in this business until 1846. An enterprising man, he was a financial success. Indeed, in his determination to enlarge his business, he sent a steamboat expedition in 1832 up the Missouri River to its source at the mouth of the Yellowstone: a "first" in steamboat navigation. It marked a new era in the navigation of the Missouri River but also greatly extended the area of his trade.

Pratte was active in the political affairs of Missouri. In 1838, he was elected to the state legislature. In 1844 and again in 1845, he was elected mayor of St. Louis on the Whig ticket winning in 1844 with 2,258 votes, against a "Locofoco" candidate, Reily; winning in 1845 with 2,265 votes against 2,118 for Camden (Native American) and 326 for Watson (Locofoco). St. Louis had a population of 38,600 in 1844 and 44,600 in 1845, and was headed by a mayor-council form of government. Pratte secured improvements for the growing city during his administrations: gaslights were installed along many city streets; the levee was paved with stone blocks; there was continued work on the harbor and wharf; and construction was begun on a city hospital. In addition, the mayor helped direct relief for the many victims of the recordbreaking flood of the Mississippi River in June 1844.

Pratte continued to be active in local affairs until his death in Jonesburg, Missouri, on 10 August 1886. He was for many years a director of the Bank of the State of Missouri and also served as its president.

SOURCES: Charles H. Cornwell, *St. Louis Mayors: Brief Biographies* (St. Louis, 1965); Richard Edwards and M. Hopewell, *Edwards' Great West* (St. Louis, 1860); William Hyde and Howard L. Conrad, eds., *Encyclopedia of St. Louis* (New York, 1899); J. T. Scharf, *History of Saint Louis City and County* (Philadelphia, 1883); Walter B. Stevens, *St. Louis: History of the Fourth City 1764–1909* (St. Louis, 1909).

Jeanette C. Lauer

PRENTISS, WILLIAM AUGUSTUS (1800–92), Mayor of Milwaukee (1858–59). Prominent Milwaukee politician and mayor, Prentiss was born on 24 March 1800 in Northfield, Massachusetts, the son of Samuel Prentiss (1759–1818), a surgeon, and Lucretia (Holmes) Prentiss (1759–1841), both old-stock New England Protestants. The youngest of nine children, Prentiss attended public schools to age fifteen, but reduced family finances prevented his attending Hanover College. He moved to Cooperstown, New York, in 1815, working as a clerk. One year later, he went to Albany. He returned to Northfield in 1817, remaining as a clerk in a local store until 1822. He planned to move to North Carolina, but an older brother persuaded him to move to Montpelier, Vermont, where he operated a store (1822–31). Prentiss then lived in Chittenden, 1831–36, owning another store. He was a Vermont state legislator (1829–30) and local justice of the peace. In 1833, he married Eliza Sands (1812–57) of Saco, Maine, and they had six children.

Prentiss took his family to Milwaukee in 1836 where he opened yet another store, in partnership with Dr. Lemuel W. Weeks. The following year Prentiss began his local political career, soon becoming a leading Whig. He was an East Side trustee (1837–39 and 1845–46), a county justice of the peace (1837–45), chairman of the board of county commissioners (1837–40), president of the county board (1840), East Side clerk (1838–41), and city assessor (1850–51). Prentiss was especially renowned as an alderman (1852–54 and 1857–58). He unsuccessfully ran for the state legislature in 1854 and 1857. Around 1855 he joined the Republican party.

Prentiss was elected mayor in 1858, however, on the People's party ticket, defeating Democrat A.R.R. Butler (*q.v.*) 4,022 to 2,998. Milwaukee had 40,000 people in 1857 and a mayor-council form of government. Since his election was mainly a response to the financial scandals of the preceding administration, Prentiss followed a policy of strict economy. He fired some city employees and vetoed nearly all civic improvement bills. He traveled to New York where he arranged the sale of city bonds, restoring Milwaukee's credit.

After leaving office, Prentiss again was an alderman (1859–61 and 1869–71) as well as a member of the city's upper chamber, the council (1865–68). He rejected an offer of support for another mayoralty campaign in 1866. He was defeated in the 1861 legislative campaign but subsequently spent two terms in the state legislature (1867–68) as a Union party member. He was defeated in 1868 and 1869. After 1871, Prentiss was a notary public, and helped organize the Old Settlers' Club and the Pioneers' Association. He remained active in their behalf until his death on 10 November 1892.

SOURCES: History of Milwaukee, Wisconsin (Chicago, 1881); J. H. Temple and George Sheldon, *A History of the Town of Northfield, Massachusetts for 150 Years* (Albany, N.Y., 1875); *The United States Biographical Dictionary and Portrait Gallery of Eminent and Self-Made Men, Wisconsin Volume* (Chicago, 1871); Jerome A. Watrous, ed., *Memoirs of Milwaukee County*, 2 vols. (Madison, Wis., 1909).   *Thomas R. Bullard*

PRESTON, JAMES H. (1860–1938), Mayor of Baltimore (1911–19). "Handsome Harry" Preston was mayor of Baltimore for eight years and was one of the most important figures in the history of the modern city. The future mayor was born on 23 March 1860 at Preston's Hill in Harford County. His father, James Bond Preston, a Democrat, served several terms in the Maryland legislature. His mother, Mary Amelia Winks, was of British descent like her husband. The family was Episcopalian. Young Harry received his education in the public schools of Harford County, St. John's College in Annapolis, and the University of Maryland Law School in Baltimore. He graduated in 1881 and soon joined a prominent city law firm. In 1889, Preston was elected to the Maryland legislature from Baltimore and was reelected in 1893. He was speaker of the House of Delegates in 1894. During these years, he formed a close alliance with John J. (Sonny) Mahon, one of I. Freeman Rasin's chief lieutenants in the city Democratic machine. He served on the police board (1904–1908) and was an unsuccessful candidate for Congress from the Fourth District in 1910.

By 1911, old boss Rasin had died, and the city Democrats were split between Mahon and the followers of Frank Kelly. Mahon backed Preston for mayor, and together they defeated the incumbent Democratic mayor, J. Barry Mahool (*q.v.*), and went on to beat their Republican opponent in the general election. When Preston ran for a second term in 1915, he faced no internal opposition and soundly defeated the Republican opponent.

Mayor Preston was a politically ambitious man. He attempted to dominate all factions of the Democratic party in Baltimore and had a reputation for steamrolling anyone who stood in his way. Through his patronage chief, Daniel J. Loden, Preston rewarded his loyal supporters and cast into the outer darkness all those who disagreed with him—mainly the Kelly faction of the city Democratic machine. He ran the city government with an iron hand, using almost the entire staff from his private law firm to fill top posts in the city government.

With "czar" Preston presiding over an almost perfectly unified municipal administration, the city accomplished an amazing array of public improvements. These vast changes in the physical environment of the city were made possible in part because, for the first time in many years, the city tax base was increasing rapidly and the city treasury was larger than it had ever been. Even so, Preston's grand plans far exceeded immediate revenue, and he borrowed heavily to fund many of the larger projects. Chief among Preston's plans was a comprehensive harbor improvement program, including a municipal railroad linking all harbor areas, a series of park expansions, and several new parks, a civic center and a series of gardens in the central district, a modern sewage plant and sanitary connecting system, high-intensity lighting for downtown and all major highways, and many new boulevards and the widening and repaving of hundreds of miles of streets. But Preston's greatest political victory was the annexation in 1918 of a huge territory around the city, which brought almost 100,000 people along with all the prime suburban land for years to come.

By 1919, Preston's dictatorial rule in Baltimore and, more important, his split with the governor over the annexation issue, won him a large number of political enemies who all united in the mayoral primary and defeated him after a long, bitter campaign. Preston attempted to run once more for mayor in 1923 as an Independent, but was soundly defeated and retired from active politics. He married Helen Fiske Jackson (1874–1933) on 14 November 1893, and they had five children. He died on 14 July 1938, at the age of seventy-eight.

SOURCES: Joseph L. Arnold, "Suburban Growth and Municipal Annexation in Baltimore, 1745–1918,"

Maryland Historical Magazine 73 (June 1978); Wilbur F. Coyle, *The Mayors of Baltimore* (Baltimore, 1919); James B. Crooks, *Politics and Progress: The Rise of Urban Progressivism in Baltimore, 1895–1911* (Baton Rouge, La., 1968). *Joseph L. Arnold*

PRIDGEON, JOHN, JR. (1852–1929), Mayor of Detroit (1888–89). Democratic mayor of Detroit, John Pridgeon, Jr., was born in that city on 1 August 1852. He was the son of John (1829–94) and Emma (Nicholson) Pridgeon, English immigrants. The elder Pridgeon, becoming an American sailor in the Mexican War, later amassed a fleet of Great Lakes vessels, which evolved into the White Star Line. The younger Pridgeon was educated in public schools, the academy of Professor Bristow, and the Detroit Business University. In 1874, he married Cora Edgar of Pittsburgh. Going to work under his father in the marine business, he helped organize and thereafter manage the White Star Line, serving as treasurer and director. At one time, the Pridgeons owned the Detroit and Windsor Ferry Company. The family was Protestant. Unlike his Republican father, John, Jr., became a Democrat. He was appointed to the Detroit Park Board in 1883, was elected to the city council in 1885 for a two-year term, and during the second year he was designated president of the council.

Detroit in 1880 had 116,340 people and a mayor-council form of government. A popular spokesman for the business community, Pridgeon was nominated for mayor in 1887. Dr. Charles C. Yemans, the Republican candidate, unwisely endorsed temperance and was overwhelmed at the polls by a 12,300 to 7,363 vote and two minor candidates divided 2,829 votes. The Democrats also swept the council elections, giving the new mayor the support of twenty-two out of thirty-two seats. It was the most crushing defeat the GOP had ever suffered in Detroit, and Pridgeon was the youngest man elected mayor.

The victory turned out to be a Pyrrhic one because the triumphant Democratic council slate had been all Irish except for two Germans defeated by a crossover vote. The Germans, who then represented half the city's foreign-born population, resented Irish domination of the Democratic party, and they bided their time for revenge. Still, Pridgeon proved to be a fairly popular mayor. No scandals touched him, although certain Democratic aldermen were hurt by extortion charges in the sensational J. B. Lowder case.

In the 1889 election, Mayor Pridgeon was opposed by Hazen S. Pingree (*q.v.*) the Republican shoe manufacturer and reformer, who appealed to ethnic Democrats, especially Germans and Poles. In addition, labor harassed the mayor for not enforcing the eight-hour day on city contracts. Pingree's colorful campaign included surprise visits to saloons. Pridgeon, further handicapped by the all Irish council slate, lost to Pingree, who polled 13,954 votes to Pridgeon's 11,610. Critics felt Pridgeon should have heeded the clamor for more streetcar lines. Dr. Melvin G. Holli, Pingree's biographer, concludes that it was Pingree's opportunistic appeal to the ethnic blocs that won him the office.

Pridgeon returned full time to manage the White Star Line. In 1911, he was linked to a shadowy Boston lady; their affair was given thorough news coverage. His wife promptly sued for divorce; she died in 1914. Pridgeon's second marriage was to Mrs. Blanche Cota, widow of a relative and a New York City socialite. He retired to manage a small farm in Massachusetts and died in 1929.

SOURCES: Silas Farmer, *History of Detroit and Wayne County and Early Michigan* (Detroit, 1890), vol. 2; Melvin G. Holli, *Reform in Detroit: Hazen S. Pingree and Urban Politics* (New York, 1969); Paul Leake, *History of Detroit* (Chicago, 1912), vol. 2.

Donald W. Disbrow

PRIEUR, DENIS (1791–1857), Mayor of New Orleans (1828–38). Prieur, born in New Orleans in 1791 and thus a member of the creole and *ancienne population* segment of the community, served as mayor of his native city during what was probably its single most remarkable decade. Entering politics in 1824 with election as recorder of the municipal council, Prieur distinguished himself as an ardent Jacksonian in the violent party disputes of his day. This identification, plus exploitation of "American" and "Creole" antagonism to the "foreign French" element in New Orleans, gave him victory in the mayoralty campaign of 1828 by a vote of 888 to 531 over A. Peychaud, an Adams-Clay protagonist and French immigrant.

Prieur's administration was marked by unprecedented growth and expansion of New Orleans: bank funds and capital soared from $4.5 million to $55 million; the Pontchartrain Railroad began its run from the Mississippi to Lake Pontchartrain in 1831, the same year that construction began on the New Basin Canal linking the newer parts of the city to the lake; 1833–38 saw construction of the world-famous St. Charles, St. Louis, and Verandah hotels, the Merchants' Exchange, Banks' Arcade, the First Presbyterian, Methodist, and Christ churches, the St. Charles Theatre (for years the most imposing playhouse in the United States), and William Strickland's celebrated U.S. Branch Mint. New improvement banks also provided expanded city water service and illuminating gas outlets to light the city. By the mid-1830s, New Orleans had become the first port of the nation in volume of export trade. Its population was about 50,000.

Prieur was not the driving force in all this activity. His political strength apparently rested on his great personal charm and good looks, together with gregariousness that embodied the city's sense of its heady prosperity. On the darker side, his tenure saw the combined yellow fever-cholera plague of 1832–33, which in relative terms was the worst pestilence in the city's history. Ethnic rivalries forced division of the city into three semi-autonomous municipalities in 1836, and the economic depression of 1834 and the Panic of 1837 were probably nowhere as severe as in New Orleans.

Prieur flirted with a race for the governorship in 1834, in sympathy with John Slidell's break with the dominant Martin Gordon faction in the state Democratic party but soon withdrew to maintain his claim on the mayor's office. He had won reelection in 1830 over the Clay candidate, J. Bermudez, 1,045 to 452, and by defeating the Gordon Jacksonian, H. D. Peire, in 1832 by a vote of 1,255 to 412. A final victory came in 1836 against the Whig L. U. Gainnie. Prieur won the Democratic nomination for governor in 1838 but lost the election to the Whig A. B. Roman. His last political post was that of collector of the port of New Orleans by appointment of James K. Polk in late 1845.

Prieur never married, choosing instead to live with a free woman of color and their children in an openly acknowledged *ménage*. He died on 9 November 1857, in New Orleans, almost destitute.

SOURCES: New Orleans *Argus*, 5 March and 4, 7 April 1828; New Orleans *Bee*, 4 October 1833; New Orleans *Louisiana Courier*, 10 November 1857; Succession No. 13,392, Orleans Parish Succession Records, Second District Court, 1846–80.

Joseph G. Tregle, Jr.

PRINCE, FREDERICK OCTAVIUS (1818–99), Mayor of Boston (1877, 1879–81). Important force in national Democratic party politics and mayor of Boston, Prince came from one of Boston's oldest families dating back to 1633, and was born on 18 January 1818, the son of Thomas J. and Caroline Prince. He attended Boston Latin School and graduated from Harvard in 1836. He married Helen Henry in 1848 and was remarried in 1889 to a New Orleans widow, Mrs. Samuel P. Blane. He had five sons and a daughter.

A lawyer by training, Prince served in the Massachusetts House of Representatives from 1851 to 1853 and in 1854 was elected to the state Senate. A major power in Democratic politics, he served as secretary of the Democratic national convention continuously for twenty-eight years, from 1860 to 1888.

An excellent speaker, Prince built his popularity during his first term by reducing property taxes. However,

Prince's support for a questionable city council directive forcing the city to run the East Boston Ferry at its own expense negated his earlier image as a champion of economy in government. Although the city's sewage was improved and the major high schools were expanded, a "draft Pierce" movement convinced Henry Pierce (*q.v.*) to run again for mayor after a five-year absence, and he defeated Prince by 2,300 votes in 1878.

When Pierce decided not to run for reelection in 1879, Prince was again nominated by the Democrats and he defeated the Republican candidate, Charles Codman, by 700 votes. Sewage improvement was again emphasized, and a Department of Hospitals was established. Planning for a city-wide system of public parks continued, and during Prince's administration Frederick Law Olmsted was hired to design the city's park system. Boston celebrated its 250th anniversary during Prince's mayoralty with the unveiling of a statue of John Winthrop.

Prince later served as a trustee of the Boston Public Library and was instrumental in the movement to erect the library building that remains at Copley Square. He ran unsuccessfully as the Democratic candidate for governor of Massachusetts in 1885 and 1896. He died in Boston on 6 June 1899, at age eighty-one.

SOURCES: Albert P. Langtry, ed., *Metropolitan Boston: A Modern History* (New York, 1929), vol. 2; State Street Trust Company, *Mayors of Boston* (Boston, 1914); Justin Winsor, ed., *The Memorial History of Boston* (Boston, 1880–83), vol. 3.   *Donald M. Jacobs*

PUCHTA, GEORGE (1860–1937), Mayor of Cincinnati (1916–17). Puchta was born on 8 April 1860 in Cincinnati. He was the son of German-born parents, Lorenz Puchta (1833–81), a tavern/boarding house and shoe store operator, and Barbara (Schmidt) Puchta. George Puchta attended public schools and the Ohio Mechanics Institute, and graduated from Nelson's Business College in 1876. He also had private instruction in mathematics and mechanical drawing, and became proficient on the violin, which was his main hobby. Puchta started work at the age of fourteen and eventually rose to leadership in a company that dealt in machinists' supplies and machine tools. Later, he entered into partnership in a factory supply business of which he became president in 1911. Puchta served as president of the local Business Men's Club and of the National Supply and Machine Dealers Association. In 1911, he served on the board of park commissioners and was appointed by President William H. Taft as assistant U.S. treasurer for the subtreasury at Cincinnati. On 6 October 1886, Puchta married Anna M. Meinhardt a German American from Kentucky, with whom he had two children, Ella A. and Lawrence G.

When the Republican high command under Rudolph Hynicka, successor to George B. Cox as party boss, approached Puchta in 1915 to be its candidate for mayor, he told the party spokesmen that, if elected, he would consult them but that in case of conflict he would do what he thought best. In later years, he claimed that he had always acted independently of the machine. In the election he defeated Charles Sawyer (later to be secretary of commerce under President Truman) 57,243 to 35,105, the largest plurality that any mayoralty candidate in Cincinnati had received up to that time.

In spite of the Puchta victory, the power of the Cox machine was waning. Cox grew old and Hynicka lacked his touch, so that as World War I claimed public attention, the power of the machine declined. One precursor of reform came when Murray Seasongood (*q.v.*), eventually to be the first charter-reform mayor, broke with the local Republican party because Puchta did not support the merit system.

Puchta's mayoralty was dominated by concern with public utility service during his first year and by World War I during 1917. Bond issues to support water, fire, and street projects were passed by wide margins. After Congress declared war, Puchta organized a war council to take over war work on the municipal scene, but this did not prevent a serious shortage of gas and coal in the winter of 1917–18. A city home rule charter was overwhelmingly defeated by the electorate in November 1917. Puchta declined renomination and returned to his business interests until he retired in 1933. After leaving the mayoralty, he refused appointment as postmaster but was active in local affairs, especially as a leader of the Commercial Club. He was prominent in groups promoting transportation on the Ohio River. He belonged to the Cincinnati and Maketewah country clubs as well as the prestigious Queen City Club; he was both a Mason and an Elk. In his later years, he traveled widely; he died in Manila, the Philippine Islands in 1937. He was buried in Cincinnati.

SOURCES: C. F. Goss, *Cincinnati, the Queen City, 1788–1912* (Cincinnati, 1912); Leonard A. Lewis, ed., *Greater Cincinnati and Its People, a History* (Cincinnati, 1927); George Puchta, "Autobiography," typescript in Public Library of Cincinnati and Hamilton County; *Williams Cincinnati Director, 1916 to 1918*.

George B. Engberg

Q

QUINCY, JOSIAH (1859–1919), Mayor of Boston (1895–99). Quincy, Massachusetts blue-blood, the third and last Josiah Quincy to be mayor of Boston, was born at Quincy, Massachusetts, on 15 October 1859 of distinguished New England parentage. He was descended from an Edmund Quincy who left England in 1628; the first Josiah Quincy was a Revolutionary patriot, whose son was president of Harvard and whose grandson was the first Josiah to be mayor. The third mayor was the son of Helen F. Huntington and Josiah Phillips Quincy (1829–1910), a noted laywer, poet and dairy farmer. Josiah graduated from Harvard in 1880, having won the Bowdoin Prize (for oratory) and the Boylston Prize (for elocution). After a year of teaching, he entered Harvard Law School (LL.B., 1884) and opened a Boston law practice.

Quincy was interested in local politics and was elected to the Massachusetts House in 1887–88 and 1890–91. He chaired the Democratic state committee (1891–92 and 1906), for, despite his family background, he was a willing creature of the Boston Democratic machine. President Cleveland (q.v.) made him assistant secretary of state in return for political services, but he resigned after only six months (1893). In 1895, a candidate of political boss Martin Lomasney, Quincy was elected mayor of Boston, the first mayor to serve for two years under the new terms of office. He was reelected in 1897. Quincy was partly run by a Democratic caucus, the "Strategy Board," a small group of bosses who ran the city and selected mayors. The group was set up after the death of boss "Pea Jacket" Maguire, in 1896. Political patronage was rampant; under Quincy, the city's operating costs rose rapidly and its debt doubled to $80 million. He created jobs through contracts and public works, building playgrounds, gymnasia, bathing facilities, and summer camps. Streets, sewers, and subways all increased city taxes and expenditures. Quincy was determined to spend city money to enable the poor to enjoy some of the benefits known to Boston's rich. He was called "the embodiment of humanness and Democracy" by one admirer. But the "philanthropic mayor" left the city in debt and was replaced in 1899 by a more conservative candidate.

In later years, Quincy took an interest in street railways and served on the city transit commission. He was a director of the Quincy and Boston Street Railway Company. In retirement he followed his literary interests. He was twice married: first, in London, to Mrs. Ellen F. Tyler, daughter of Dr. Krebs of Boston (17 February 1900), who died in 1904; second, to Mary Honey, daughter of the Honorable Samual R. Honey of Newport, Rhode Island (1 November 1905). Quincy died in Boston on 8 September 1919.

SOURCES: J. H. Cutler, *"Honey Fitz": Three Steps to the White House* (Indianapolis, 1962); John Koren, *Boston, 1822–1922: The Story of Its Government* (Boston, 1923).   *Peter d'A. Jones*

QUINCY, JOSIAH, JR. (1802–1882), Mayor of Boston (1846–48). Whig Mayor, Quincy, born on 17 January 1802 in Boston, was the son of Josiah Quincy (q.v.) (1772–1864), a former mayor of Boston and president of Harvard, and Eliza Susan (Morton) Quincy (1774–1850). The second of eleven children and the eldest son, Josiah, Jr., attended Phillips Andover and graduated from Harvard in 1821. He married Mary Jane Miller (1806–74), the daughter of a wealthy Bostonian, and they had two sons and one daughter. Quincy was a Unitarian.

Before he became mayor of Boston, Quincy had a solid preparation for public service. A lawyer by profession, he served as a member of the common council from 1833 to 1837 and was president of it for at least three years. He broadened his experience in politics as a member of the Massachusetts General Court, first in the House and then in the Senate, rising to the presidency in each body.

Boston numbered about 120,000 people and had a mayor-aldermen-council form of government in 1845 when Quincy drew 5,333 votes to defeat Democrat John F. Heard, 1,354, and Native American William S. Damrell, 1,647. He was formally inaugurated on 5 January 1846. Having proposed to introduce water into Boston from Lake Cochituate near Framingham, he was assisted by his father, former Mayor Josiah Quincy, and former U.S. President John Quincy Adams, in turning over the first shovel that started the project, 20 August 1846. He was returned to office in 1846 with 3,846 votes to C. B.

Goodrich's 1,319 and N. C. Betton's 735. Thus, he had the joy of witnessing the project's completion as the roar of guns and the ringing of bells greeted the opening of the water supply on 25 October 1848. Quincy's third-term election saw the incumbent poll 4,756 votes to C. B. Goodrich's 1,657, W. Parker's 1,547, and N. C. Betton's 866.

Like his father, Mayor Quincy was a progressive and energetic public servant. Not only did his years as mayor of Boston see progress in the field of education with new facilities for primary and secondary students, but also he worked to prevent wealthy citizens from evading taxes on personal property. As chairman of the board of aldermen, he vetoed the issuance of liquor licenses and contributed to law and order by strengthening the police department by approving the construction of a county jail.

Quincy was also treasurer of the Boston Athenaeum, treasurer of the Western Railroad, and president of the Pioneer Cooperative Bank. A member of the Ancient and Honorable Artillery in Massachusetts, he was in the Union Club and the prestigious Wednesday Evening Club. He was buried from King's Chapel, Boston, after his death in Quincy on 2 November 1882. His grave is in Mount Wollaston Cemetery in Quincy.

SOURCES: Boston *Globe*, 3 November 1882 (obituary); H. Hebart Holly, comp., *Descendants of Edmund Quincy, 1602–1637* (Quincy, Mass., 1977); Josiah Quincy, Jr., *Figures of the Past from the Leaves of Old Journals* (Boston, 1883); Josiah Quincy, Jr., Papers, Massachusetts Historical Society; State Street Trust Company, *Mayors of Boston* (Boston, 1914); William H. Whitmore, ed., *The Inaugural Addresses of the Mayors of Boston*, 2 vols. (Boston, 1894–96).

Vincent A. Lapomarda

QUINCY, JOSIAH P. (1772–1864), Mayor of Boston (1823–28). Boston's second mayor, popularly known as the "Great Mayor," born in Boston, Massachusetts, on 4 February 1772, Quincy was the son of the lawyer Josiah Quincy, Jr. (*q.v.*) (1744–75) and Abigail Phillips, both Yankees of British descent. After attending Phillips Academy, he entered Harvard College and graduated first in the class of 1790. Although he was admitted to the Boston bar in 1793, his family income allowed him to pursue a career in politics instead of law. He married Eliza Susan Morton, of New York, on 6 June 1797, and they had five daughters and two sons, including Josiah, Jr. (*q.v.*) (1802–82), the eleventh mayor of Boston, and Edmund (1808–77) an abolitionist leader. He was elected to the state Senate in the spring of 1804 on the Federalist ticket, and that fall to the first of three successive terms in the U.S. House of Representatives, until he resigned

in protest against the War of 1812. Back in Boston, Quincy was again elected to the state Senate, until 1820 when Federalist leaders dropped him from their slate because of his outspoken views and unpredictable actions.

When Boston changed from a town to a city in 1822, Quincy was one of the first mayoral candidates. Although he lost his initial bid for city office, in 1823 he drew 2,504 votes to George Blake's 2,179 and was overwhelmingly elected second mayor of Boston. Quincy was subsequently reelected to six consecutive terms polling 3,867 of the 3,950 votes cast in 1824; taking 1,202 out of a total of 1,395 votes in 1825; defeating George Blake by a count of 3,163 to 1,750 in 1826; and winning with 2,139 over Amos Binney's 340 in 1827. He established an innovative program of city planning and urban renewal for the growing 200-year old city which was now about 55,000 in size. By appointing himself chairman *ex officio* of all executive committees, the mayor assumed a controlling voice in all major municipal decisions, including a much-needed modernization of the police and fire departments. He organized new methods of cleaning city streets, improved antiquated systems of sewerage and drainage, initiated a municipal water supply, and restricted burials in crowded locations. Vigorously enforcing the laws against drinking, gambling, and prostitution, he built a house of industry to segregate helpless paupers from lawbreakers, and constructed a house of reformation to separate juvenile offenders from hardened criminals. Perhaps his best known accomplishment was the improvement and expansion of the overcrowded market district behind Faneuil Hall. By draining the town dock, filling up the tidal flats, and renovating unused property in the waterfront area, he was able to create a new expanse of land in the heart of the city on which he constructed a large, two-story, granite market house which became the center of renewed commercial activity. Quincy's numerous plans and ambitious projects created such annoyance and apprehension among the members of his own party, however, that in November 1828, he lost the party's support, failed to get a majority of votes, and withdrew from the mayoral race, reflecting on the "fickleness of the popular will."

Almost as soon as he left public office, Quincy became president of Harvard College in January 1829, bringing with him obvious skills in business and management. He was president for sixteen years, selecting a prestigious faculty, expanding the law school, constructing a famous library, and launching the public fund drive that produced the Astronomical Observatory. Retiring in 1845 at the age of seventy-three, Quincy threw himself into a series of extensive literary projects dealing mostly with the history of Boston and took an active part in the violent political disputes of the late 1850s and early 1860s, speaking out against the institution of slavery and supporting President Lincoln in his struggle to preserve the Union. Quincy died on 1 July 1864 at the age of ninety-two.

SOURCES: A. W. Brayley, *Complete History of the Boston Fire Department* (Boston, 1889); *Inaugural Addresses of the Mayors of Boston, 1822–1852* (Boston, 1894); Roger Lane, *Policing the City: Boston 1822–1885* (New York, 1971); Edmund Quincy, *The Life of Josiah Quincy of Massachusetts* (Boston, 1868); Josiah Quincy, *Municipal History of the Town and City of Boston During Two Centuries* (Boston, 1852); *Records of the City of Boston: Mayor and Aldermen*, microfilm, Boston Public Library; E. H. Savage, *Police Records and Recollections* (Boston, 1873); Justin Winsor, ed., *Memorial History of Boston . . . 1630–1880*, 4 vols. (Boston, 1880), vol. 3.   *Thomas H. O'Connor*

QUINCY, SAMUEL MILLER (1833–87), Acting Mayor of New Orleans (5 May–8 June 1865). Acting military mayor of New Orleans in spring 1865, Quincy was born in Boston in 1833. His parents were Josiah Quincy (*q.v.*) (mayor of Boston, 1846–1848) and Mary Jane (Miller) Quincy. The Quincy family was noted in Massachusetts history for its distinguished merchants, lawyers, and writers. His elder brother, Josiah Phillips Quincy, was the author of several dramas. His grandfather, Josiah P. Quincy (*q.v.*), had been a congressman, mayor of Boston (1823–1828), and president of Harvard University.

Samuel Miller Quincy graduated from Harvard in 1852, was admitted to the bar in Boston, and edited the *Monthly Law Reporter*. When the Civil War began, Quincy was serving in the Massachusetts legislature. He accepted a commission as captain in the Second Massachusetts Infantry on 25 May 1861. At the battle of Cedar Mountain in August 1862, he was seriously wounded and captured. He spent eight weeks in the Confederate Libby Prison in Richmond, Virginia, where he kept a diary that was later published. After his parole in

October 1862, he was stationed in Washington until March 1863, recovering from wounds. On active duty in 1863, he commanded his regiment in the battle of Chancellorsville, but on 5 June 1863, exhausted by poor health, Quincy resigned from the Army. By November 1863, his health had improved enough for him to return as lieutenant colonel of the Seventy-third U.S. Colored Infantry. He served in the Port Hudson campaign and as president of the board of examiners set up in Louisiana to recruit black officers for the Union Army. On 13 March 1865, he was brevetted a brigadier general of U.S. Volunteers.

Quincy was appointed mayor of New Orleans by General Nathaniel P. Banks on 5 May 1865, replacing Hugh Kennedy (*q.v.*). He served as military mayor, 5 May–8 June 1865. During this period, acting under orders from Banks, he reinstated officials Kennedy had removed from office. The ousted mayor and the governor traveled to Washington to seek redress from President Johnson; they were successful. By the end of May, an expansion of the territory under the U.S. Army's Department of the Gulf put General Edward R.S. Canby in charge of the military in Louisiana. President Andrew Johnson instructed Canby to cooperate with Governor Wells. General Canby removed Quincy and restored Mayor Kennedy. In September 1865, Quincy was transferred to the Ninety-sixth U.S. Colored Infantry.

After returning to civilian life in 1865, Quincy edited the *Reports of Cases* of his great-grandfather, Josiah Quincy, returned to the practice of law, and served on the Boston Board of Aldermen, and in the Massachusetts legislature. He died at Keene, New Hampshire, on 24 March 1887.

SOURCES: "Administrations of the Mayors of New Orleans, 1803–1936" (typescript, Works Progress Administration, New Orleans, 1940) (located in the Main Branch of the New Orleans Public Library); Payton McCrary, *Abraham Lincoln and Reconstruction: The Louisiana Experiment* (Princeton, N.J., 1978); New York *Herald Tribune*, 25 March 1887; New York *Times*, 25 March 1887.   *Joy J. Jackson*

R

RADER, FRANK (1848–1897), Mayor of Los Angeles (1894–96). A businessman-politician, Rader was born in Easton, Pennsylvania, on 8 April 1848. He attended Heidelberg College in Tiffin, Ohio, and, although a journalist, he went into the hardware business in that state from 1874 to 1883, at which time he moved to California. He was the second husband of Clara Adelaide D. Bunnell (1854–1917), whom he married on 16 June 1880; she had one son by her previous marriage, Charles E. Bunnell, whom Rader helped to raise.

Rader a Protestant and a Mason, was active in real estate and banking in southern California, being one of the organizers of the Southern California National Bank. He was also very active in fraternal organizations, including the Masons, Knights Templar, Nobles of the Mystic Shrine, California Club, and Jonathan Club.

Los Angeles at the time of Rader's mayoralty was a city of 75,000 people. It had a mayor-council form of government and was the seat of Los Angeles County. The city was still in depression when Rader ran for office, which was perhaps the main reason for the change in party support of 1894.

A businessman rather than a politician, Rader was typical of many Republican activists of his day. He defeated former Mayor H. T. Hazard (*q.v.*) in the Republican primary and then the Democrat Ryan in the general election, where Rader's modest support for the very popular issue of public power helped him. The results were: Rader, 5,515; Ryan, 3,506; Hazard (Independent) 2,123; and Schnabel (Populist) 1,120. Nativism was also an issue, with the Roman Catholic Ryan being accused of having liquor dealer and church support, while Rader was endorsed by the American Protective Association.

Rader served only one term, dying the following year, on March 1897, in Los Angeles and was buried in a Masonic cemetery.

SOURCES: California Biography File, Los Angeles Public Library; Leonard A. Sanders, "Los Angeles and Its Mayors, 1850–1925" (Master's thesis, University of Southern California, 1968); John Waugh, "L. A. Mayors: The Great, Near-Great and Un-Great," *West Magazine* (25 May 1969). *John M. Allswang*

RAUSCHENBERGER, WILLIAM G. (1855–1918), Mayor of Milwaukee (1896–98). An immigrant businessman with close ties to the Milwaukee German community, Rauschenberger was born to John (1813–1906) and Amalia Rauschenberger on 6 December 1855 in Soldin, Prussia. The family emigrated to the United States in 1860, and the elder Rauschenberger in time established himself in Milwaukee as a woodenware dealer and cordage maker. William Rauschenberger, the third of four children, finished eight years at parochial (Lutheran) and public schools. He then joined his father as an apprentice and by 1880 had become the secretary and treasurer of a fairly prosperous business. Rauschenberger married Ida Anger of Milwaukee, also German, in 1883, and they raised two daughters, Ida and Reinhold. Rauschenberger served as a member of the Ancient Order of United Workmen, the National Union, and the North Side *Turnverein*.

Rauschenberger began his political career in 1880 when he successfully ran for alderman of the Tenth Ward on the Republican ticket. He was reelected and later served three years as the ward's school commissioner. After serving a term as ward school-board president, he was elected twice more as alderman from the Tenth Ward. Rauschenberger made an attractive candidate for mayor, with his dual appeal to city businessmen and the German community, itself comprising approximately 27 percent of Milwaukee's population. He beat back the challenge of Democrat Glenway Maxon and Populist Henry Smith, scoring a victory of 17,917 votes to 15,377 for Maxon and 9,121 for Smith. Rauschenberger presided over a city of 250,000 with a mayor-bicameral council form of government.

As mayor, Rauschenberger attempted to stay abreast of Milwaukee's growth by continuing a number of municipal construction projects and augmenting the city's inspection powers. During a lengthy traction strike in 1896, he kept the city from overt interference and, in fact, spoke in defense of the strikers. Although an adherent of municipal traction ownership, he was unable to pass any enabling legislation through the common council. Retiring from office in 1896, Rauschenberger returned to his business interests. He died on 6 April 1918.

SOURCES: Andrew Aikens and Lewis Proctor, eds., *Men of Progress of Wisconsin* (Milwaukee, 1897); William G. Bruce, *History of Milwaukee, City and County*

(1922); Clay McShane, *Technology and Reform: Street Railways and the Growth of Milwaukee* (Madison, Wis., 1974); Bayrd Still, *Milwaukee: History of a City* (Madison, Wis., 1948); *Wisconsin Necrology* (compilation by state historical society of obituaries of prominent Milwaukeeans, on microfilm).   *Douglas Bukowski*

RAYMOND, BENJAMIN WRIGHT (1801–83), Mayor of Chicago (1839–40, 1842–43). Businessman and third mayor of Chicago, Raymond was born on 15 June, 1801 in Rome, New York, the son of Benjamin Raymond (1774–1824), a surveyor and judge, and descendant of French Huguenots, and Hannah (Wright) Raymond of Weatherfield, Connecticut. The oldest of nine children, Raymond spent several years in public school and a few at an academy built by his father. He also attended school for one year in Montreal, having been sent there to sell lumber for his father. Raymond worked as his father's clerk until 1822 when he opened his own general store. William Wright became his partner in 1823, being replaced by Samuel Dexter in 1831. Raymond was then based in East Bloomfield, New York, where on 12 June 1835 he married Amelia Porter (1814–89) of Auburn, New York, a Protestant (and probably Presbyterian, like her bridegroom). They had three children, two of whom (George and Katherine) reached adulthood.

Raymond visited Chicago in 1834, to sell merchandise, returning as a permanent resident in 1835, with his new wife. From then until his death, the firm of B. W. Raymond and Company was a leading general merchandising business. In 1839, Raymond erected the city's first fireproof building. Dexter's financial aid enabled Raymond to survive the depression following the 1837 Panic, although he could not pay back the loans until 1842. Raymond helped establish the Second Presbyterian Church (1843), serving as an elder for forty years.

In 1839, Raymond accepted the Whig mayoralty nomination, expecting defeat in this Democratic city. He beat James Curtiss (*q.v.*) 353 to 212—much to his surprise. Chicago then had 4,200 people and a mayor-council form of government. As mayor, Raymond was the tie-breaker on an evenly divided city council. He supported civic improvements, the prosecution of canal scrip counterfeiters, and temperance. He donated his entire salary to the relief of unemployed canal workers and secured the site of the future Dearborn Park. Defeated in 1840, he was renominated in 1842 and won, with 490 votes to 432 for Augustus Garrett (*q.v.*) (Democrat) and 53 for Henry Smith (Liberty party). During his second term, Raymond backed fiscal retrenchment.

Business activity forced Raymond to decline the Whig legislative nomination in 1842 and the Temperance party's mayoralty nomination in 1852. He ran for the state House of Representatives in 1846 but lost. Raymond was Third Ward alderman, 1847–48.

As his political career waned, Raymond increased his business pursuits. By 1850, he was the Chicago agent for eastern insurance companies and a founder of the board of trade. He was a director of the Galena and Chicago Union Railroad and vice-president of the Elgin and State Line Railroad (1847–55). He helped establish both the Sacred Music Society and the Chicago Historical Society. He built a woolen mill in Elgin, Illinois, in 1846, and the world-famous Elgin Watch Company, which opened in 1864. He founded the town of Lake Forest, serving many years as a trustee for Lake Forest College.

After gradually retiring from business, Raymond died at his Chicago home on 6 April 1883.

SOURCES: A. T. Andreas, *History of Chicago*, 3 vols. (Chicago, 1884–86); Henry E. Hamilton, "Benjamin W. Raymond," typed two-page ms. in the Chicago Historical Society; Bessie L. Pierce, *A History of Chicago*, 3 vols. (New York, 1937–57); "Benjamin W. Raymond," *Chicago Magazine* 1 (April 1957); *The United States Biographical Dictionary and Portrait Gallery of Eminent and Self-Made Men, Illinois Volume* (Chicago, 1876); The Chicago Historical Society also has fourteen volumes of letterbooks for B. W. Raymond and Company, covering almost his entire career in Chicago.

Thomas R. Bullard

READING, RICHARD WILLIAM (1882–1952), Mayor of Detroit (1938–40). Reading was born on 7 February 1882, in Detroit, the son of Richard William Reading, an electrician, and Louise (Harrington) Reading. One of eight children, he attended the Detroit public schools and then took special night courses at Detroit College. As a boy, he worked for the Detroit *News* as a printer's devil for $3.00 per week. After he became an apprenticed printer, he left the *News* and in 1901 began working for Detroit *Today* (later the Detroit *Times*) where he eventually rose to be business manager. In 1918, he resigned his position in order to go into the real estate business. On 27 August 1901, he married his childhood sweetheart, Blanche White (d. 27 August 1952). Reading had four children, Richard, Clarence, Ralph, and Marion. Reading was a member of the Congregationalist Church, a Mason, an Eagle, an Elk, and an Odd Fellow. He also held memberships in the Detroit Athletic Club, the Detroit Golf Club, the Detroit Boat Club, and the Detroit Yacht Club.

Mayor James Couzens (*q.v.*) recognized Reading as someone active in civic affairs and a successful realtor and thus appointed him city assessor, 1921–24. In 1924, he became city controller. On 5 September 1925, Reading resigned to run for city clerk. Elected, he took office in January 1926 and held this office until he ran for mayor in 1937. On 2 November 1937, he decisively defeated Patrick H. O'Brien 261,048 to 154,048.

When Reading assumed the mayoralty, Detroit had a mayor-council form of government with a population of 1,650,000. In his victory message, the 5'3" mayor chortled, "The victory was one of all the people, the rank and file of our city, determined to preserve nonpartisan, clean progressive government here." In spite of this statement, Reading as mayor became involved in a serious scandal. After he lost the 1939 election to Edward J. Jeffries, Jr. (q.v.), by 226,181 to 108,993 and retired from the mayor's office in January 1940, he was accused, on 25 April 1940 of conspiring with eighty police officers to protect a $10 million a year numbers racket. Witnesses charged Reading had accepted $55,000 in monthly payoffs. When convicted, Reading charged: "This is the greatest injustice since the crucifixion of Christ." Sentenced, he went to prison on 20 January 1944 and was paroled on 13 February 1947. On another charge, he pleaded *nolo contendere* to income tax invasion and was fined $10,000.

After serving his prison term, Reading retired to White Lake. On 9 December 1952, he died in a Brighton, Michigan, hospital after suffering a heart attack. He was buried in Detroit.

SOURCES: Detroit *Free Press*, 10 December 1952; Detroit *News*, 10 December 1952; "Inside Story of How Handbook and Policy Racketeers of Detroit Corrupted Mayor Reading and Others in the Late 1930's," Detroit *News*, 14 January 1941; Richard W. Reading Papers, 2 vols., clippings, Burton Historical Collection, Detroit Public Library; Robert I. Vexler, *Detroit: A Chronological and Documentary History, 1701–1975* (Dobbs Ferry, N.Y., 1977).

Robert Bolt

REQUENA, MANUEL (1802–76), Acting Mayor of Los Angeles (1856). Acting mayor for eleven days, Requena, born around 1802 in Campieto, Yucatan, Mexico, engaged in trade which, in the 1830s, brought him to Mazatlán, where he was collector of customs, and to Guaymas, where he met and married Gertrudes Guirado. One of his sisters-in-law married an English merchant, James "Santiago" Johnson, who in 1834 persuaded many members of the large Guirado family to come to Los Angeles where Requena soon became an important merchant and landowner. He also figured prominently in local government, serving two terms (1836 and 1844) as *alcalde* (equivalent to mayor and justice of the peace) and playing an important military role in the bloodless civil wars of California's Mexican period. When the Americans invaded in 1846, however, he avoided any

involvement in the fighting.

Requena's prominence in the city under Mexican administration carried over to the American period, beginning in July 1850 when he served as a member of the first common council under the new American charter. He went on to four more consecutive terms on the council, serving most of that time as president. Concurrently, he was elected a member of the first board of supervisors of the county when that body was organized in 1852. He failed reelection to the council in May 1855, but he won again in 1856, thus serving as council president on 22 September 1856 when the mayor resigned. Requena was acting mayor until an election on 3 October produced a replacement. During his eleven-day term as acting mayor, Requena served strictly as a caretaker under the council-mayor form of government for the city of approximately 3,200. He did not run for the mayor's office to replace himself, although he continued to be a regular candidate for the common council and the board of supervisors. In the early 1850s, he had been a Democrat, but late in that decade he transferred to the new Republican party. As a Republican in a heavily Democratic city and a Mexican in an increasingly Anglicized city, Requena's campaigns through the late 1850s and early 1860s were mostly unsuccessful, although he did win a seventh council term in 1864 and an eighth in 1867.

Meanwhile, Requena had remained owner of substantial property within the city, and he concentrated on raising oranges and grapes. He had no children and was a widower after 1874. He died quietly on 27 June 1876.

SOURCES: Hubert Howe Bancroft, *The Works of Hubert Howe Bancroft*, 39 vols., *History of California* (San Francisco, 1884–90), vol. 18 to 24; Los Angeles *Evening Express*, 28 June 1876; Leonard Pitt, *The Decline of the Californios: A Social History of the Spanish-speaking Californians, 1846–1890* (Berkeley, Calif., 1966).

R. David Weber

REYBURN, JOHN EDGAR (1845–1914), Mayor of Philadelphia (1907–11). Born in New Carlisle, Ohio, on 7 February 1845, Reyburn was the son of William Stuart Reyburn. John was educated by private tutor and attended Saunders' Institute, West Philadelphia, studying law and beginning a law practice in Philadelphia in 1870. In 1871, he was elected to the state legislature as a Republican, serving in the House of Representatives (1871 and 1874–76) and in the state Senate (1876–92). He was elected and reelected to the U.S. Congress (1890–97) and served there again in 1905, resigning in 1907 when elected mayor. He married Margaret Crozier, and they had one son.

Philadelphia had a population of about 1.4 million and a mayor-council form of government in 1907. With Reyburn's mayoralty, the "contractors' gang" of the Vare brothers, Boies Penrose and "Sunny Jim" McNichol, and the political machine, were placed firmly in control of the city. Reyburn added another chapter to the history of graft in Philadelphia. Nonetheless, he was said to be only "next to" and "not on as low a level" as that of the incomparable boodler Mayor Samuel Ashridge (q.v.), whose corruption had been exposed by Progressive muckrakers like Lincoln Steffens. Reyburn died in Washington, D.C., on 4 January 1914 but was buried in Philadelphia.

SOURCES: *Biographical Directory of the American Congress, 1774–1971* (Washington, D.C., 1971); *City of Firsts: History of Philadelphia* (Philadelphia, 1926); Lincoln Steffens, *The Shame of the Cities* (New York, reprinted 1960).   *Melvin G. Holli*

RICE, ALEXANDER HAMILTON (1818–95), Mayor of Boston (1856–57). First Republican mayor of Boston and later state governor, born in Newton Lower Falls, Massachusetts, on 30 August 1818, Rice was the son of Thomas Rice (1781–1859), a papermill owner, and Lydia (Smith) Rice (1785–1873). The family was Episcopalian and came from old New England stock. Having received his early education in his native town and in neighboring towns, he went on to Union College in Schenectady, New York, where he graduated at the top of his class in 1844. On 19 August 1845, he married Augusta E. McKim (1817–68) of Lowell, and they had one son and two daughters. After her death he married Angie Erickson Powell of Rochester, New York, and they had one son.

Although Rice had been introduced to the papermaking business at an early age and continued in it during his adult life, he was very interested in politics. Originally a Whig, he was first elected to the Boston Common Council in 1853. Reelected in 1854, he became its president and that of the Boston School Committee. He was an organizer of the Republican party in Massachusetts, and an unaligned citizens' group in 1855 chose him to run against Dr. Nathaniel Shurtleff (q.v.), the Native American candidate for the mayoralty. Rice won 7,398 votes to 5,390. He was reelected in the following year 8,659 votes to J. Preston's 2,062.

Boston had a population of 160,490 in 1855 and a mayor-aldermen-council form of government when Rice came into office. His main objective as mayor of Boston was to reorganize the city's public institutions that cared for criminals, the mentally ill, and the poor. At the same time, he developed the Back Bay section of the city, improved the streets of Boston, launched Boston City Hospital, and strengthened the police force. These projects contributed to the rise in the city debt but were essential for the welfare of the city. Understandably partial to his own party, he was sufficiently independent in judgment and effective as a speaker to remain popular with Bostonians.

Rice was too valuable to the Republican party to remain long out of politics after he left city hall. Elected to the U.S. Congress in 1859, he served four terms, including one as chairman of the Committee on Naval Affairs, before he refused renomination in 1867. An experienced politician, he was three times elected governor of Massachusetts (1876–78) and manifested the same concern in supporting public institutions for the needy as he had when mayor of Boston.

Outside of public life, Rice not only was president of his own paper company, but also became the head of at least two other companies and held positions of trust in educational and cultural societies. He was active in the Protestant Episcopal church. He died of a stroke in Melrose, Massachusetts, on 22 July 1895 and was buried in Forest Hills Cemetery, Jamaica Plain.

SOURCES: Assorted Papers of Governor Alexander H. Rice, Massachusetts State Library; Boston City Council, *A Memorial of Alexander Hamilton Rice from the City of Boston* (Boston, 1896); Boston *Journal*, 23 July 1895 (obituary); Bradford M. Fullerton, "Hon. Alexander Hamilton Rice, LL.D.," *New England Historical and Genealogical Register* 50 (1896); Robert E. Moody, "Rice, Alexander H.," *Dictionary of American Biography* 15 (1935); Alexander H. Rice Congressional Speeches, U.S. Library of Congress; Alexander H. Rice Scrapbooks, 2 vols., Houghton Library, Harvard University; William H. Whitmore, ed., *The Inaugural Addresses of the Mayors of Boston*, 2 vols. (Boston, 1894–96); Clarence A. Wiswall, *One Hundred Years of Paper Making* (Reading, Mass., 1938).

Vincent A. Lapemarda

RICE, JOHN B. (1809–74), Mayor of Chicago (1865–69). Actor, theatrical manager, and two-term Republican mayor of Chicago, Rice was born in Easton, Maryland, on 28 May 1809. Nothing is known of Rice's family background except that his father, an Episcopalian possibly of Irish extraction, was a shoemaker by trade. Rice followed his father's profession to the age of twenty-seven; for twenty-one years thereafter (1836–57), he worked as an actor and theatrical manager and entrepreneur. This second career took Rice (who was "discovered" by a Baltimore theater manager who heard the future mayor singing at his cobbler's bench) to Philadelphia, New York City, Buffalo, Albany, Milwaukee, and, finally, Chicago. Rice married actress Mary Ann Warren (daughter of actor William Warren) in December

1837, and they had six children, including an only son, William Henry.

A theater manager from 1841, Rice came to Chicago in 1847 to open a playhouse, Rice's Theater. Both he and his wife acted, but, with the passing of time, Rice became more absorbed in the management of the theater and his stage appearances became less frequent. In 1857, both Rice and his wife retired from the stage, and in 1861, the theater was sold. Thereafter, Rice supported himself and his family through largely successful dealings in downtown real estate.

An ardent opponent of slavery and a Republican from 1856, Rice had no active political career before 1865. In that year, the Union (Republican) party nominated Rice for the mayoralty, apparently on the basis of his wide reputation as a "responsible" theater manager and businessman. Chicago in 1865 had a population of 178,492; in 1867, when Rice was reelected mayor, the population was approximately 225,000. Situated in northeastern Cook County, Illinois, Chicago during the 1860s had a mayor-council form of government, with the balance of power vested by the city's charter in the council.

Rice defeated his major opponent, Democrat Francis Sherman (q.v.), by a vote of 11,678 to 5,600 on 18 April 1865 and, again facing ex-Mayor Sherman, won the election of 16 April 1867 by a vote of 11,904 to 7,971. A man of practical rather than theoretical intelligence, Rice came to office with no clear program aside from his promise of low-cost, clean government. He steadfastly opposed the demands of the working-class faction in the council for an eight-hour day for city workers and labored to mitigate the effects of public support for a state eight-hour-day law. During his two terms, Rice attained a personal reputation for clean government, despite a police scandal and journalistic opposition to the rising cost of public education. Inevitably, however, the powers of the city grew during his time in office. For example, the city's public water system was expanded, and the council gained greater power over markets.

Rice declined renomination in 1869 but ran successfully for state representative in 1872. He was elected to the U.S. House from Chicago in 1873, running, as always, on the Republican ticket. Rice made no major contributions in his state or federal positions. In Washington, his health declined rapidly, and he died on 17 December 1874, at his winter home in Norfolk, Virginia.

SOURCES: W. T. Andreas, *History of Chicago* (Chicago, 1878); Chicago *Tribune*, 18 December 1874; "Mayoral Papers" file, Chicago Historical Society—two minor pieces of correspondence; *Memorial Addresses on the Life and Character of John B. Rice*, delivered in the U.S. Senate and House of Representatives, 2 February

1875 (Washington, D.C., 1875); Bessie L. Pierce, *History of Chicago* (Chicago, 1931), vol. 2; Frederick Rex, *The Mayors of Chicago from March 4, 1837 to April 13, 1933* (typescript dated 1933 held by the Municipal Reference Library of Chicago).   *Paul Barrett*

RICH, CARL WEST (1898–1972), Mayor of Cincinnati (1947, 1951–53, 1954–55). Teacher, lawyer, and mayor, born in Cincinnati on 12 September 1898, Rich was the son of David W. Rich and Rosa (West) Rich. After attending local schools and Walnut Hills High School, Rich graduated from the University of Cincinnati (A.B. in 1922 and LL.B. in 1924). He taught at the University of Cincinnati and Cincinnati Labor College. He was assistant city solicitor, 1925–28, assistant city prosecutor, 1928, judge on the court of common pleas, 1938, and Hamilton County prosecutor, 1939–47. He also served as vice-president of the Central Hyde Park Savings and Loan and as a trustee of the Cincinnati Zoological Association. He married Frances Ivins (d. 1965) on 8 September 1926; they had no children. Rich was a Mason, Shriner, Elk, and Moose, and a member of the Cincinnati Club. He served in both world wars (colonel in 1918, lieutenant colonel, Chemical Warfare Division, 1942–45).

A loyal Republican, Rich served on the city council, 1947–61. He was first chosen mayor in early 1947, when Mayor William Stewart (q.v.) resigned to go on the state supreme court. He then served one regular term in 1951–53, and in 1954, after Mayor Edward Waldvogel (q.v.) died in office, Rich was selected to complete his term (to 1955). In 1950, Cincinnati had 503,998 people and a city manager-mayor-council form of government.

Rich was one of the most popular mayors in Cincinnati history, largely because of his charm and remarkable ability to win elections. He did not take an active role as mayor, considering the job under the city manager charter mainly as a ceremonial post. After leaving the city council, he served one term in Congress (1965–67). He was also selected as chairman of the board of the Cincinnati Royals (a professional basketball team) and was a member of the boards of various city banks. He died on 26 June 1972.

SOURCES: Cincinnati *Enquirer*, 27 June 1972; Ralph A. Straetz, *PR: Politics in Cincinnati* (New York, 1958); *Who's Who in American Politics* (New York, 1967).   *Thomas R. Bullard*

RICHERT, WILLIAM (1859–1912). Acting Mayor of Detroit (1897). German-born, Republican mayor of Detroit, Richert was born in 1859 "somewhere along the Baltic." After coming to Detroit at the age of thirteen, he worked for years as a stove-molder at the Michigan

Stove Works. He married Bertha Berg of Detroit (1866–1940). They kept a grocery store at the corner of Joseph Campau and Chestnut streets, and he was also a tavern-keeper (presumably at the same place). They sold out in 1887 in order to buy a shingle mill in Bay City, Michigan. Richert was a prominent Mason and a Protestant.

Detroit in 1890 had 205,000 people and a mayor-council form of government. Tolerably well-off and active in ward politics, Richert was elected alderman from the Eleventh Ward in 1891 and served four successive two-year terms on the council. On 22 March 1897, as president *pro tem* of the council, he became temporary mayor of Detroit when Hazen S. Pingree (*q.v.*) reluctantly had to give up that office on the orders of the Michigan Supreme Court. Pingree had been elected governor the previous November and had been holding down both offices. In his fifteen days as acting mayor, Richert had little to do beyond making a few minor appointments. He had to step aside after William C. Maybury (*q.v.*), Democrat, won the special election to fill the rest of Pingree's unexpired term.

At that Republican city convention, on 22 March, the Pingree forces, in full command, were apparently behind Richert, whose supporters were pointing out that their candidate as an alderman had stood ''shoulder to shoulder'' with the then mayor, Pingree, in his fight against the street railway corporation. The *Abend-Post* endorsed Richert, the hope of the German community. But the Pingree blessing was not for Richert but rather for Captain Albert E. Stewart, the governor's handpicked choice. The final vote was Stewart 79 to Richert 52. The German voters were disappointed, and although Richert dutifully campaigned for Stewart against Maybury, the Democratic nominee and winner, there was considerable decline of the kind of support they had given Pingree in his four previous victories.

On 5 April 1897, Richert's fifteen-day term was over. He ran in Republican primaries for state senator a couple of years later but was defeated. He died on 16 June 1912 at age fifty-three and was buried in Elmwood Cemetery in Detroit.

SOURCES: Ashod R. Aprahamian, ''The Mayoral Politics of Detroit, 1897 through 1912'' (Ph.D. dissertation, New York University, 1968); Melvin G. Holli, *Reform in Detroit: Hazen S. Pingree and Urban Politics* (New York, 1969); Paul Leake, *History of Detroit* (Chicago and New York, 1912).   *Donald W. Disbrow*

RIDDLE, ROBERT M. (1812–58), Mayor of Pittsburgh (1853–54). Riddle was born in Pittsburgh on 17 August 1812, a son of Judge James Riddle and his wife, Jane. The Riddles were of an early family in the area,

Scottish or Scots-Irish, probably Presbyterians.

Young Riddle, one of eight children, was trained for business, working for a wholesale house. He quickly amassed a fortune, lost it, tried banking in Philadelphia, where he had inherited property, failed, and returned to Pittsburgh, where he became editor of the *Daily Advocate and Statesman* in 1837. He served as postmaster for almost four years under John Tyler and then bought the *Spirit of the Age*, changing its name to the *Commercial Journal*.

Riddle was elected mayor as a Whig, although he had met with other politicians the previous year to name and plan the formation of the Republican party. The city at that time had about 47,000 residents, and he received 1,887 votes to defeat incumbent John B. Guthrie (*q.v.*), with 1,568. Riddle was vice-president of the Allegheny (volunteer) Fire Company and a brother-in-law of Judge Charles L. Shaler. He married Mary Jane Johnston, seems to have divorced her around 1835, and married Mary J. Dickinson on 9 February 1839. He had five children.

At the end of his term, Riddle missed renomination and resumed the editor's chair at the *Commercial Journal* until the spring of 1858, when he retired to a farm in nearby Rochester because of arthritis. Visiting Pittsburgh on business, he suffered a sudden attack and died on 18 December 1858. He was buried in Allegheny Cemetery.

SOURCES: Allen Humphreys Kerr, ''The Mayors and Recorders of Pittsburgh, 1816–1951'' (typescript, 1952, Carnegie Library of Pittsburgh); Pittsburgh *Dispatch*, 20 December 1858; Pittsburgh *Gazette*, 20 December 1858; Frank W. Powelson, ''Founding Families of Allegheny County'' (typescript, 1963, Carnegie Library of Pittsburgh).   *George Swetnam*

RIZZO, FRANK L. (1920–   ), Mayor of Philadelphia (1972–79). The ''tough cop'' mayor of Philadelphia and the second Catholic to hold the office, Rizzo was born on 23 October 1920, the oldest of three children of Rafael (1894–1968) and Teresa Erminio (1900–39) Rizzo, Roman Catholic immigrants from Italy. Rafael first practiced tailoring in Philadelphia and then joined the police force. Frank Rizzo left high school in 1938 with a half-semester to complete, enlisted in the U.S. Navy, and was discharged a year later for medical reasons. In 1947, he signed on the city police force. By 1950, big (6'2" and 250 pound) Frank Rizzo had earned a reputation for toughness and immaculate grooming. Promoted to sergeant, he was assigned to a police district rife with pay-offs and promptly rooted out the corruption. In 1952, his strong-arm tactics against the bars and numbers rackets in black West Philadelphia drew protests from civil rights groups. After Mayor James Tate (*q.v.*) appointed Rizzo police commissioner in 1967, Rizzo enlarged the police force from 7,000 to 9,000 and with radio-equipped buses gave it strike-force capabilities. While white liberals and militant blacks condemned him, fearful working-class whites deemed him a savior.

In April 1942, Rizzo married Carmella Silvestri. The Rizzos had two children, Frank S. (b. 1943) and Joanna Ellis (b. 1948). Rizzo is active in organizations such as the Fraternal Order of Police.

Philadelphia in 1970 had 1,951,000 people (34 percent black) and a strong mayor-council form of government. Although Rizzo had abjured politics, in 1971 outgoing Mayor Tate saw him as the only candidate to preserve the shaky Democratic dominance. In 1971, Rizzo defeated his aristocratic opponent, W. Thatcher Longstreth (394,067 to 345,912). In 1975, this time without party organization support, Rizzo was reelected, defeating his opponents, Republican Thomas Foglietta and black independent Charles Bowser (311,879 to Foglietta's 101,001 and Bowser's 134,334).

Rizzo considered himself the champion of the little people, and his program reflected that support: hold the line on taxes, create a better business climate for jobs, control the school budget, and make the city safe. He never pretended to be liberal, and he antagonized Democrats by supporting Nixon. To hold the line of taxes, he sought increased federal revenue-sharing dollars and shut down the aging Philadelphia General Hospital. He opposed public housing and favored the reuse of old, existing housing.

The Rizzo administration was controversial. Investigatory reporters disclosed that the Rizzo "hold the line budget" included collecting close to $1.7 million from the bankrupt Penn Central Railroad, that the mayor had an opulent office in city hall, and was building a palatial home. Rizzo's campaign against his chief detractor, the Philadelphia *Inquirer*, culminated in the police condoning the blockade of the *Inquirer* offices. One futile attempt was made to recall Rizzo in 1977. In 1978, Rizzo lost a campaign to have the charter changed to allow him to run for a third term.

SOURCES: "Biography" of Frank Rizzo, Office of the Mayor News Release, 1 June 1978; Joseph R. Daughen and Peter Binzen, *The Cop Who Would Be King: Mayor Frank Rizzo* (Boston, 1977); Fred J. Hamilton, *Rizzo* (New York, 1973).   *John F. Bauman*

ROBINSON, ELMER E. (1894–   ), Mayor of San Francisco (1948–56). Mayor of San Francisco at the time of its peak population, Robinson was a native-born lawyer and judge. Born in San Francisco on 3 October 1894, Robinson was the son of Ralph Sydney and Edyth Alice (Rahlves) Robinson. He attended public schools and Kent Law School at night, being admitted to the California bar in 1915. He married Doris Gould in 1916 and after her death was remarried to Ora Norris Martin (1 April 1944). He had two daughters: Elizabeth Jane Bolton (b. 1919) and Rosemarie Kerr.

After graduation, Robinson began local law practice and also was intermittently employed in the district attorney's office, 1919–23. He was an able trial lawyer and was appointed to the municipal court in 1935 and then to the superior court, to which he was subsequently elected for two six-year terms (1938, 1942). He was presiding judge in 1936 and president of the California Conference of Judges, 1940–41. President Franklin Delano Roosevelt appointed Robinson director of adjusted compensation for World War I veterans in 1938.

In 1921, Robinson had been an unsuccessful Republican candidate for the California Senate. He retained party affiliation, and many years later in the spring of 1947, ran for the office of mayor. There were three candidates: Chester McPhee, a Republican with Scripps-Howard newspaper backing; State Representative F. R. Havenner, a CIO Democrat, and Robinson, who won the support of the Hearst press and the financial district of San Francisco. Robinson defeated Havenner 116,937 to 101,478; McPhee ran third.

Determined to boost the city's image, Mayor Robinson appointed a professional public relations expert, Francis V. Keesling, Jr., who served during 1948–55 and helped the mayor win federal aid (about $5 million) for the airport, extra cash (about $10 million) for the Hetch Hetchy water supply project, and contracts for the San Francisco naval shipyard. The mayor successfully opposed Senator William F. Knowland's plan to build a second bridge to Oakland because he thought its projected site was too close to the existing bridge.

By 1950, San Francisco had reached its peak historical population of 775,357 and occupied about forty-five square miles, with water on three sides. A major Pacific port with a growing international airport traffic, the city was also a naval and military center. The centenary of the San Francisco city charter was celebrated in 1950 along with that of California's admission to the Union, with pomp and pageantry. Mayor Robinson encouraged and joined the clamor over the need for urban civil defense in 1950–51. He was successfully reelected mayor for a second four-year term on 6 November 1951 and almost immediately began plans for a San Francisco subway system. He became president of the U.S. Conference of Mayors in 1953 and in 1954 pressed the federal government to declare the San Francisco airport a duty-free zone. A consistent city booster, Robinson demanded that harbor administration be handed over to the city. In June

1955, the board of supervisors let him appropriate $150,000 to invite the United Nations to return to San Francisco to celebrate its tenth anniversary, an elaborate six-day affair.

The mayor was a member of many fraternal organizations and an avid Americana collector. He was an Episcopalian. He retired from office on 7 January 1956, returning to his law practice and work as president and general manager of Woodlawn Memorial Park.

SOURCES: E. L. Barrett, Jr., *The Tenney Committee* (Ithaca, N.Y., 1951); L. Beebe and C. Clegg, *Cable Car Carnival* (Oakland, Calif., 1951); W. J. Davis, *Northern California and Its Builders* (San Francisco, 1954); *Time* Magazine 50: 24, 17 November 1947.

Peter d'A. Jones

ROCHE, JOHN A. (1844–1904), Mayor of Chicago (1887–1889). Engineer and manufacturer, reform mayor, and a transplanted Yankee, born on 12 August 1844 in Utica, New York, Roche was the son of William and Sarah Roche, a Protestant family. He attended primary and secondary school in Utica, and following his graduation from high school in 1858, he moved to New York City where he served as an apprentice pattern-maker and attended both the Cooper Institute and night school. He worked as a draftsman and designer in Boston, 1861–69 and joined the Corliss Steam Engine Company for two years.

Roche came to Chicago in 1869 and became a partner in the machinery firm of James, Roche, and Spencer until the Chicago fire of 1871. After the fire, Roche became the chief agent in the northwestern United States for the J. A. Fay and Company Woodworking Firm. He married Emma Howard in 1871, and they had four children, three of whom survived to adulthood. Roche became a member, and eventually president, of the board of trustees of the Lewis Institute, a vocational college, and was a member of the Union League and Illinois Club and the United Order of Deputies.

In 1887, Chicago had a population of 760,000 and a mayor-council form of government. Roche, who had served a term in the Illinois legislature in 1873, was elected the first Republican mayor since 1879 by 51,249 votes to his Labor party opponent Robert L. Nelson's 23,490 and Prohibitionist Joseph L. Whitlock's 372.

Chicago, the classic late nineteenth-century city, underwent rapid commercial, industrial, and heterogeneous population growth, accompanied by social disorganization and heightened criminal activities, including gambling and prostitution. The public exposure of frequent alliances between saloon-keepers, gamblers, and political figures aroused great concern by 1887. The Democratic party, split by the 1886 Haymarket Affair

and suffering from a series of defeats at the polls, did not enter a mayoral candidate in 1887. Many reform and business-oriented Democrats supported Roche's candidacy. Upon his election, Mayor Roche pledged to be "a reform and business mayor" and actively attempted to eliminate gambling and destroy the alliances between politicians, saloon-keepers, and gamblers. However, his success was limited because the majority of Chicago's residents supported a wide-open city.

During Roche's term in office, traction lines were expanded, construction of elevated systems was undertaken, and water supply and sewage-disposal systems were improved.

Roche sought reelection in 1889 but was defeated by Democrat DeWitt C. Cregier (*q.v.*) 57,340 to 45,328. Roche's candidacy was hampered by his membership in the United Order of Deputies, a secret anti-Catholic organization, his alleged pro-monopoly stance regarding the traction lines, and a relatively unified Democratic party opposition.

Following his defeat, Roche served as vice-president of the Crane Elevator Company, 1889–93, and as president of the Lake Street Elevated Company, 1893–1904. During a business meeting on 10 February 1904, he suffered an attack of uremic poisoning and died. He was buried in Rosehill Cemetery, Chicago.

SOURCES: A. T. Andreas, *The History of Chicago from the Earliest Period to the Present Time* (Chicago, 1886), vol. 3; Marshall Kravitz, *The Mayors of Chicago* (unpublished typescript, Chicago, 1976); Bessie L. Pierce, *A History of Chicago* (New York, 1957), vol. 3; Frederick Rex, *The Mayors of the City of Chicago from March 4, 1837 to April 13, 1933* (Chicago, 1947).

Edward H. Mazur

ROESCH, CHARLES EDWARD (1886–1936), Mayor of Buffalo (1930–33). Business-mayor born in Buffalo on 31 March 1886, Roesch was the son of Jacob M. Roesch (1858–1930), a leading meatpacker and dealer, and Julia (Fuellhart) Roesch, both of German descent. Roesch attended local grammar schools until 1901 when he joined his father in the meat business. In 1911, the firm was renamed Jacob M. Roesch and Son, and in 1916 it became Charles E. Roesch and Company. On 10 June 1914, Roesch married Mabel Carrie Klinck, and they had two sons. Roesch was a Mason, an Elk, and an Oriole. The Roesches were Universalists.

Roesch showed no apparent interest in politics until 1929 when he became the Republican nominee for mayor. He defeated incumbent Democratic Mayor Frank X. Schwab (*q.v.*) 77,175 to 69,593, with 9,031 votes going to Socialist-Independent Frank E. Perkins. At that time Buffalo had 573,076 people and a mayor-council form of government. Mayor Roesch took office as the Great Depression was underway, and he was forced to handle the city's economic problems. He pushed through a program of tax cuts, reducing the city's tax rate to the lowest level since 1909. Roesch intended to balance the loss of revenue with salary cuts and the sale of city bonds. He also supported charter amendments which would allow cities to win higher aid from the New York legislature. Property assessments were reduced, and Roesch went on record with a proposal that the (pre-New Deal) federal government should reimburse cities for amounts up to 50 percent of what they had spent on welfare and relief costs. The only major civic improvement which Roesch supported was a new courthouse. This planned construction followed revelations that the old building was in poor shape and crawling with cockroaches. Roesch retired from politics after leaving office in 1933. He continued running his meat business until his death on 15 January 1936.

SOURCES: Buffalo *Daily Courier*, 16 January 1936; various clippings in Local Biography Scrapbook in the Buffalo and Erie County Public Library.

Thomas R. Bullard

ROFFIGNAC, JOSEPH (1766–1846), Mayor of New Orleans (1820–28). Born in Angoulême, France, in 1766, Count Louis Philippe Joseph de Roffignac came to the United States in the first years of the nineteenth century as part of the French military personnel preparing for the eventual restoration of Louisiana to its ancient Gallic loyalties.

Adapting to American republican practice, the count henceforth called himself simply Joseph Roffignac. Extended terms in the Louisiana legislature and a stint in the New Orleans city council as alderman (1817) from the "American" suburb of St. Mary prepared his way to the mayoralty of New Orleans, which then had a population of about 45,000. His election over J. B. Gilly on 1 May 1820 by a vote of 537 to 388 ushered in one of the most tempestuous periods in the city's history. For the American section of the population, Roffignac became a symbol of the "aristocratic," "backward," and "corrupt" character of the French-speaking community. His administration was plagued by continuous allegations of inefficiency and dishonesty. Most serious was the common "American" charge that the city was in the grip of a "foreign faction" which was loyal to the restored Bourbons and was determined to hand over Louisiana to the Holy Alliance. The quarrel resulted in near civil war in New Orleans during 1823–25, with French attempts to deny certain "American" parishes representation in the legislature, clashes between Gallic and "American" militia units, and obscene Anglo-Saxon

ridicule of Roffignac's theatrical leadership in a supposed slave insurrection threat in 1823.

All this led to the beginning of demands for division of the metropolis along ethnic lines, a campaign that would not come to fruition until 1836. Accusations of blundering were heard again in 1828 when fire swept unchecked through the Louisiana Statehouse and other valuable property in the heart of the city. Nonetheless, Roffignac's administration prided itself on such civic improvements as the foundation of the New Orleans Physico-Medical Society and a free library in 1820, inauguration of the American Theatre in Camp Street in 1823, and creation of a Bank of Louisiana in 1824. Factional French support of Roffignac was sufficient to win him reelection without opposition in 1822, 1824, and 1826. The climax of his last term was the visit of Andrew Jackson in January 1828, in perhaps the first presidential campaign junket in American history.

Roffignac resigned in May 1828 to visit his homeland, where he remained until his death in 1846, caused when he accidentally shot himself in the head during an apoplectic seizure. He was married to Solidella Montegut, daughter of Dr. Joseph Montegut of New Orleans, royal surgeon of the colony during Spanish dominion.

SOURCES: Henry Castellanos, *New Orleans As It Was* (New Orleans, 1895; new edition, Baton Rouge, La., 1979); John S. Kendall, *History of New Orleans*, 3 vols. (Chicago, 1922), vol. 1; New Orleans *Argus*, 22 December 1826, 30 January 1827; New Orleans *Louisiana Advertiser*, 9 January 1828.   *Joseph G. Tregle, Jr.*

ROGERS, WILLIAM FINDLAY (1820–1899), Mayor of Buffalo (1868–1869). Newspaperman and politician, born March 1, 1820 in Forks Township, Pennsylvania, son of Thomas J. Rogers (1781–1832), Irish-born Congressman and newspaper editor and Protestant. The family moved to Philadelphia in 1824 and Rogers attended public schools in that city until his father's death in 1832. He then got a job in the print room of the *Whig* in Easton. In 1834 he joined the printing staff of the Philadelphia *Enquirer*. Rogers ran his own paper in Honesdale, Penn. during 1840–44. In 1846 he moved to Buffalo, working for both the *Courier* and the *Express* over the next fifteen years. During 1848-49 he owned the Buffalo *Republic*, established as a newspaper for the anti-slavery Democrats in New York. Rogers had joined Company D of the City Guards in 1846 and volunteered for action in 1861. He was elected Colonel of the 21st Regiment, New York Volunteers, and saw considerable combat in 1861–63. He was made Brigadier General in 1865, and later commanded the 8th Division of the New York National Guard. Rogers married Caroline Waldron of Honesdale (d. 1847), and they had one child. In 1849 he married

Phebe Demony of Buffalo, and they had three children. Rogers was Episcopalian, and a prominent Mason, as well as a member of the G.A.R.

A Democrat, Rogers began his political career immediately after his discharge from the Army, serving as Buffalo City Auditor in 1864–65 and City Comptroller during 1866–67. In 1867 he was elected Mayor, defeating incumbent Chandler J. Wells (Republican). Buffalo had 94,210 people in 1865 (State Census) and a mayor-council government.

As Mayor, Rogers is chiefly remembered for his strong support for a system of public parks. He was instrumental in establishing the Board of Park Commissioners. He also backed creation of a state hospital for veterans in Bath, N.Y. He did not seek reelection in 1869, but was soon appointed to the Board of Park Commissioners (serving as Secretary and Treasurer). In 1878 he was offered a state senatorial nomination, but declined to run. In 1882 he was elected to the 48th Congress, serving only one term (1883–85), and then retiring from political life. Rogers was Superintendent of the Soldiers and Sailors' Home at Bath, N.Y., from 1887–1897. He died at his home in Buffalo on Dec. 16, 1899.

SOURCES: *Who Was Who in America, Historical Volume* (Chicago: Marquis-Who's Who, Inc., rev. ed. of 1967), 523; *The Men of New York* (2 vols., Buffalo: George S. Matthews & Co., 1898), II:28–30C; Francis B. Heitman, *Historical Register and Dictionary of the United States Army* (2 vols., Washington: G.P.O., 1903), I:843; Sister Mary Jane, "Mayors of Buffalo (1832–1861)," B.A. Thesis, Rosary Hill College, 1961, 54–56.

Thomas R. Bullard

ROLPH, JAMES, JR. (1869–1934), Mayor of San Francisco (1912–30). The mayor who governed San Francisco for a longer period than any other individual, "Sunny Jim" Rolph was born in San Francisco on 23 August 1869. His father, James Rolph, Sr., was a native of London, England and his mother, Margaret (Nicol) Rolph, of Edinburgh, Scotland. They were Episcopalians. They met aboard an immigrant ship and were married in San Francisco shortly after their arrival in San Francisco in 1868. Rolph, Sr., a bank teller, established his family, which would ultimately include seven children, in the city's Mission District, and there his first-born, James, Jr., attended public schools and Trinity Academy. After graduating from Trinity in 1888, the younger Rolph took a job with a shipping and commission firm where he advanced to the position of head cashier. In 1900, he and a long-time friend, George Hind, established their own company, Hind, Rolph and Company, shipping and commission merchants, and Rolph was on his way to becoming one of San Francisco's

leading businessmen. During the next twenty years or so, he founded the Mission Bank (1903), the Mission Savings Bank (1906), and Rolph Navigation and Coal Company (1914), and the Rolph Shipbuilding Company (1917). He also took a leading role in business organizations such as the Merchants' Exchange, Merchants' Association, and Chamber of Commerce. Rolph's active business career did not preclude a full family life. On 26 June 1900, he married Annie Marshall Reid, and they had three children—Annette Reid, James III, and Georgina.

Rolph's rise to political, as opposed to commercial, prominence began in 1906 when he organized and administered relief efforts on behalf of victims of that year's fire and earthquake. Three years later, he was asked to run for mayor on the Republican ticket but declined the offer. When the municipal conference repeated the offer two years later, he accepted and received endorsements from the Republican and Democratic county committees, businessmen, conservative labor leaders, and the press. Rolph's opponent was the incumbent mayor, P. H. McCarthy (*q.v.*), and Rolph won handily by a vote of 47,427 to 27,067. This was the first of five large majorities over ineffective opposition. In 1915, Rolph defeated Eugene Schmitz (*q.v.*) (a former mayor) by a vote of 63,908 to 35,798. In 1919, he beat Schmitz once again, this time by a vote of 63,162 to 35,317. In 1923, he received 71,619 votes to James B. McSheehy's 43,640. And, in 1927, he overtook James E. Power by a vote of 90,359 to 59,335.

At the time of Rolph's first election, San Francisco was a city of about 417,000 people. Twenty years later, when he left office, it had grown to 634,000. Throughout the period, the city was governed by the mayor and board of supervisors. Rolph's two decades as mayor were a time of growth and expansion in the city. His years in office were marked by the construction of the Civic Center, the building of schools, and the development of parks. He advocated a public railway and power system, and fought for the acquisition of water rights for the city at Hetch Hetchy. In the always bitter labor struggle in San Francisco, Rolph supported collective bargaining. After two terms as mayor, Rolph set his political sights higher and decided to run for the governorship of California in 1918. Under California's unique system which allowed a candidate to enter the primary of both parties, Rolph, a registered Republican, captured the Democratic, but not the Republican, nomination and was declared ineligible to run. Twelve years later, he tried again for the governorship. This time around, he did capture his party's nomination and was elected by a large majority. Unhappily, his record as governor was much less satisfactory than that as mayor. His term was marked by massive unemployment, declining state revenues, and a general inability to solve the problems caused by the Depression. His refusal to pardon Tom Mooney and his public approval of a lynching in San Jose made him an extremely controversial figure. It gradually became clear that he did not have the ability to handle California's problems during the early 1930s. Nevertheless, he announced that he would run for reelection in 1934 and commenced a state-wide campaign tour. During that tour, he suffered a general collapse and died a few months later, on 2 June 1934.

SOURCES: Tom Bellew, "The Life of James Rolph, Jr.," serialized in the San Francisco *Chronicle*, 4–30 June 1934; Herman Gilbert Goldbeck, "The Political Career of James Rolph, Jr., A Preliminary Study" (M.A. thesis, Department of History, University of California, 1936); H. Brett Melendy and Benjamin F. Gilbert, *The Governors of California* (Georgetown, Calif., 1965); Moses Rischin, "Sunny Jim Rolph: The First 'Mayor of All the People,' " *California Historical Quarterly* 53 (Summer 1974); David Wooster Taylor, *The Life of James Rolph Jr.* (San Francisco, 1934).

Neil L. Shumsky

ROSE, DAVID S. (1856–1932), Mayor of Milwaukee (1898–1906, 1908–10). "All the time Rosy," the colorful five-time mayor of Milwaukee, was born in Darlington, Wisconsin, on 30 June 1856, the son of James S. Rose (d. 1890), an attorney of Scots descent, and Phebe A. Budlong (d. 1907), of German origin. Rose attended high school in Darlington, worked on a farm, and studied the printer's trade. After reading law in his father's office for two years, he became a member of the firm at the age of twenty. Seven years later, Rose was elected mayor of Darlington; he served for two terms and was elected county judge. In 1886, he moved to Milwaukee to practice law and immersed himself in Democratic politics. Although his parents were both Presbyterians, Rose married a Catholic on 10 November 1910, Rosemary Gilosz, a Hungarian-American singer and his third wife. In 1898, Rose ran for mayor on the combined tickets of the Democrats and Populists, and upset Republican William Geuder by a vote of 26,219 to 18,207. During the next decade, Rose was the perennial Democratic mayoral candidate, winning four of the next five elections held. During his tenure from 1898 to 1910, Milwaukee grew in population from 275,000 to 375,000. In 1900, Rose defeated Republican Henry Baumgaertner 25,166 to 22,772; in 1902, he overcame Republican Charles Anson 28,971 to 20,906; and in 1904, he beat Republican Guy Good 22,515 to 17,598. Significantly, Social Democrat Victor Berger polled about one-quarter of the vote cast, a percentage that the party's candidates steadily increased in each ensuing election. In 1906, Rose was upset by twenty-nine-year-old Republican Sherburn Becker (q.v.) 22,850 to 21,332. Two years later, Rose won his final term as mayor by a total of 23,106 to 20,887 for Socialist Emil Seidel (q.v.) and 18,411 for Republican Thomas Pringle.

Chameleon-like, Rose shifted his position on substantive issues as practical politics dictated, a habit that helped earn him the sobriquet "All the time Rosy." Despite a campaign stand in favor of municipal ownership, Rose engineered a controversial thirty-four-year streetcar franchise through the city council. Posing as an advocate of civil service in 1898, he later dismissed it as a "hypocritical pretense." Although generally friendly to utility companies, he persuaded the water company to equalize its rates to business and domestic consumers. Rose's most consistent stands were in favor of a wide-open city and in opposition to socialism, positions that usually guaranteed him the overwhelming support of many Irish, German, and Polish Catholics. By 1910, reaction against the alleged corruption and permissiveness of his administration prompted Rose to retire from public life.

Rose lived variously in New York, Chicago, and Los Angeles in the next decade, touring South America on behalf of a traction company. In 1924, he made one last race for mayor, on the nonpartisan ticket, promising to "bring back a little life to Milwaukee," but he lost to long-term Socialist Daniel Hoan (q.v.) by over 17,000 votes. Rose returned to law practice in his native Darlington in 1930 and made an unsuccessful race for county judge. He died in Milwaukee on 8 August 1932 and was buried there.

SOURCES: Milwaukee *Journal*, 8 August 1932; Bayrd Still, *Milwaukee: The History of a City* (Madison, Wis., 1965); E. B. Usher, *History of Wisconsin*, (Chicago, 1914), vol. 8, 1848–53; Robert W. Wells, *This Is Milwaukee* (Garden City, N.Y., 1970).   *John D. Buenker*

ROSE, HENRY H. (1856–1923), Mayor of Los Angeles (1913–15). A Midwestern Republican, born on 27 November 1856 in Taycheedah, Wisconsin, Rose was the son of Henry F. Rose, a lawyer, and Mary W. (Howard) Rose. Henry H. Rose attended the St. Paul's Parish schools (Episcopalian) and Fond du Lac High School in Wisconsin. He studied law in his father's office and was admitted to the Wisconsin bar in 1881. Preferring to acquire a practical knowledge of business life, Rose accepted positions as a traveling auditor in Illinois and Wisconsin, and later joined a company that sold farm machinery. He was a member of the Wisconsin National Guard from 1880 to 1888. Moving to Pasadena, California, in 1888, at age thirty-two, he resumed the practice of law. Rose married Gertrude C. Ruggles in 1884, and they had one child, Augustus. Rose's wife died in 1909, and he married Leonie E. Klein in 1910. He was a member of the prestigious California Club and a Mason, and he belonged to the Los Angeles and American Bar Associations.

Rose was justice of the peace for Pasadena in 1890, and in 1891 he was elected city recorder for a two-year term. He served as deputy district attorney of Los Angeles County from 1903 to 1905. In 1905, he was named Los Angeles city justice and police judge and retained these posts until the 1913 mayoral elections. Rose ran as an Independent (Republican) in the primary election. The other candidates were John W. Shenk, nominee of the Municipal Conference, and Job Harriman, a Socialist. Shenk received 35,395 votes, and Rose secured the second position with 22,042 to Harriman's 20,508. In the runoff, Rose won a surprising victory—46,045 votes to Shenk's 38,109. He retired at the end of his first term.

Los Angeles in 1913 had 430,000 residents. Mayor Rose presided over the opening of the 225-mile Owens Valley aqueduct. He persuaded the city council to adopt the policy that municipal surplus water be made available only to areas that would become part of Los Angeles and assume a share of the aqueduct expense. Rose helped win public approval of a $6.5 million bond issue in 1914 for the construction of a distributing system for aqueduct electricity. He also sponsored improvements in city administration and backed the efforts of department heads to furnish better services.

Rose remained active in the city's leading civic, social, and fraternal organizations. He died on 21 July 1923 and was buried in Los Angeles.

SOURCES: J. M. Guinn, *A History of California and Extended History of Los Angeles and Its Environs. Biographical* (Los Angeles, 1915), vol. 3; ''Henry H. Rose,'' *California Biography File*, Los Angeles Public Library; Press Reference Library, *Notables of the Southwest* (Los Angeles, 1912); Leonard R. Sanders, ''Los Angeles and Its Mayors, 1850–1925'' (M.A. thesis, University of Southern California, 1968); Martin J. Schiesl, ''Politicians in Disguise: The Changing Role of Public Administrators in Los Angeles, 1900–1920,'' in Michael H. Ebner and Eugene M. Tobin, eds., *The Age of Urban Reform: New Perspectives on the Progressive Era* (Port Washington, N.Y., 1977), chapter 7.

Martin J. Schiesl

ROSE, WILLIAM GREY (1829–99), Mayor of Cleveland (1877–78, 1891–92). First mayor of Cleveland under the new ''Federal plan'' in 1891 and one-time editor, attorney, and realtor, Rose was born on 23 September 1829 in Mercer County, Pennsylvania. His father, James

Rose, was a blacksmith and itinerant farmer of English descent from Doylestown. Through his mother, Martha (McKinley) Rose, a housewife of Scots-Irish ancestry, he was a first cousin of President William McKinley. The youngest of eleven children, William worked on a farm during the summers and attended local schools in the winter months until age seventeen. Afterward, he taught public school, pursued part-time studies at various academies (1847–52), and read law privately under the Honorable William Stewart of Mercer, Pennsylvania (1852–55), being admitted to the Pennsylvania bar on 17 April 1855.

Rose broke with his family's Democratic tradition over the slavery issue, founding first the weekly *Independent Democrat* and then serving two terms as a Republican in the Pennsylvania legislature (1857–58). In 1860, he was elected a delegate to the national Republican convention in Chicago which nominated Abraham Lincoln for president. An untimely illness, however, caused his place to be filled by an alternate. Twice nominated by the Mercer County Republican organization for U.S. Congress, Rose failed to receive district nomination because of Pennsylvania's county Republican system of rotating nominations. During the Civil War, he served a three-month enlistment as a private in a West Virginia volunteer regiment and, at war's end, in 1865, established himself as an attorney and real estate agent in Cleveland. Rose also helped found a meatpacking firm, the Cleveland Provision Company. Investments in the new and rising oil industry made him rich enough to retire by 1873. He made an extensive tour of California and the Far West before entering Cleveland politics. On 28 March 1858, Rose married Martha Emily (Parmelee) Rose (1834–1923), a Presbyterian whose family origins traced back to England via Guilford, Connecticut. Mrs. Rose, a graduate of Oberlin College and a local author, bore four children: Alice Evelyn, Hudson Parmelee, Frederick Holland, and Willie (or William) Kent Rose, all of whom survived to adulthood.

Run by a mayor and council, Cleveland in 1877 had 165,739 inhabitants. By 1891, under the federal system which Mayor Rose initiated during his first term, this total increased to 309,243. The Republican mayoral nominee in 1877 and again in 1891, Rose defeated Democrats Waldemar Otis and John H. Farley (*q.v.*) (10,492 to 9,520 and 18,378 to 15,493, respectively). In 1877, Rose, a Protestant, had the anti-Catholic support of Edwin Cowles, editor of the *Leader* and organizer of the nativist Order of American Union. After each term, he declined to run for reelection, although he campaigned unsuccessfully for lieutenant governor of Ohio with Governor Joseph B. Foraker (1883). He supported woman suffrage.

Generally considered an able administrator, Rose was known for his conservative policies of fiscal responsibility and retrenchment in the economically troubled 1870s and 1890s. He handled the railroad strike of 1877 with restraint and sympathy. He also introduced the new federal system of municipal government into Cleveland with its increased executive power. During his first term, too, owing to his persistence, the high-level Superior Avenue viaduct was completed on time. Mayor Rose also intervened to settle two major strikes in 1877, one by iron ore handlers and the other by streetcar drivers. In addition, he contracted for city street pavement in the amount of $1 million. Returned in 1891, he addressed the municipal gas issue by lowering rates and improved neighborhood playground facilities. He advocated the concept of the city as a corporation in which citizens held stock.

Rose retired after his second term. He died on 15 September 1899 and is buried in Cleveland.

SOURCES: Wilfred Henry Alburn, *This Cleveland of Ours* (Chicago, 1933), vol. 3; Elroy M. Avery, *A History of Cleveland and Its Environs: Biographical* (Chicago and New York, 1918), vol. 2; *The Cleveland City Directory*, 1877–78, and 1891–92; Cleveland *Plain Dealer*, March 1877–April 1879, April 1891–April 1893, and September 1899; S. P. Orth, *A History of Cleveland, Ohio* (Cleveland, 1910); Martha Emily (Parmelee) Rose, ed., *The Western Reserve of Ohio and Some of Its Pioneers, Places and Women's Clubs* (Cleveland, 1914), vol. 1; "William G. Rose," *Biographical Cyclopedia and Portrait Gallery of Representative Men of the State of Ohio* (1891), vol. 5.

Eric C. Lewandowski and *William D. Jenkins*

ROSSI, ANGELO J. (1878–1948), Mayor of San Francisco (1931–44). Rossi, who served longest as mayor of San Francisco except for James Rolph (*q.v.*), was born on 22 January 1878 in Volcano, California, a small mining town in the Mother Lode country. His parents, Angelo and Magdalena (Gueirolo) Rossi, were Italian immigrants who came to the United States during the 1860s. After settling in California's Amador County, the senior Rossi opened a grocery which he operated until his death in 1884. After that, Mrs. Rossi ran the business until it was destroyed by fire six years later, in 1890. She then moved her family to San Francisco where her son Angelo began working as a messenger boy for one of the city's leading florists. Within a dozen years, he had saved enough money to buy an interest in the company, and, over the course of time, he became sole proprietor of the Angelo Rossi Floral Company which he owned and operated until his death. In 1902, the same year that he bought his first share of the firm, Rossi

married Grace Allen of San Francisco; they ultimately had three children—Eleanor Grace, Clarence Angelo, and Rosamund.

As a prominent businessman, Rossi played an active role in San Francisco's commercial and civil life. He was a director of the San Francisco Advertising Club, president of Dante Hospital, and one of the founders of the Downtown Association, serving as president in 1920 and 1921. Rossi's involvement in community affairs brought him into close contact with the businessman-mayor of San Francisco, James Rolph, who appointed Rossi to the San Francisco Playground Commission in 1914. Rossi served as commissioner for seven years, until 1921, when he was elected to a four-year term on the city's board of supervisors. He was then reelected to a second term in 1929.

In 1931, Rolph, who had served as mayor for nineteen years, resigned to become governor of California. At that time, San Francisco's population was somewhat in excess of 634,000 people who were governed by a mayor and board of supervisors. Upon Rolph's resignation, the board of supervisors elected Rossi to fill out the unexpired term. Subsequently, Rossi won election on his own three times. Later, in 1931, he defeated Adolph Uhl by a vote of 76,550 to 69,743. In 1935, his opponent was Uhl once again, and the incumbent won 96,655 to 59,129. Then, in 1939, he defeated Franck Havenner 137,335 to 116,256. Rossi's thirteen-year tenure in office ended in 1944 when he was succeeded by Roger D. Lapham (*q.v.*) who had defeated him in the preceding fall's election.

During Rossi's term of office, a number of major additions were made to the city. The two great bridges—Golden Gate and San Francisco-Oakland Bay—were completed during the 1930s, as were the Veterans Building, War Memorial Opera House, and Aquatic Park. More than $11 million worth of new schools were built during his administration, and a new pipeline connected the city with its Hetch Hetchy Reservoir. However, even this massive construction program could not keep the Depression from hitting San Francisco severely. In fact, the conservative fiscal policies of Rossi's administration may have contributed to hard times. In 1930, San Francisco had a municipal deficit of $1 million. By 1939, after ten years of Depression and the great construction program, the city had a surplus of $3 million. Unemployment was, of course, the greatest problem Rossi faced as mayor, and, like other mayors of the day, he could do very little to help the situation despite his own personal feelings. His humanitarian concerns for the poor, sick, aged, and unemployed were well known in the city.

The mayor faced his greatest challenge between 1934

and 1936 when San Francisco experienced a large degree of labor unrest; during the two-year period, 561 strikes occurred. The most serious of these began on 9 May 1934 when 12,000 members of the International Longshoremen's Association, headed by Harry Bridges, walked off the job. When the Industrial Association attempted to break the strike with strikebreakers in early July, rioting broke out and the National Guard was mobilized. As a result, a general strike was called, and life in the city came to a halt on 16 July. The general strike lasted for four days, until 20 July, when federal mediation brought it to an end. Rossi himself was ineffective during the whole period. According to Louis Howe, the mayor was "badly frightened and his fear . . . infected the entire city and vicinity." Nonetheless, Rossi maintained his popularity for close to a decade, being reelected in 1935 and 1939, although he lost his bid for a fourth term in 1943. After losing the race in 1943, Rossi spent his remaining years running his floral business until he died of heart failure on 5 April 1948.

SOURCES: "Rossi, Angelo Joseph," *National Cyclopedia of American Biography* 37 (New York, 1951); Stanford Parlor No. 76, Native Sons of the Golden West, *Proceedings Attending the Funeral of Angelo J. Rossi* (San Francisco, 1948).   *Neil L. Shumsky*

ROWAN, THOMAS E. (c. 1842–1901), Mayor of Los Angeles (1892–94). An early Los Angeles professional politician, Rowan was born circa 1842 in New York, the son of James Rowan, who died in Los Angeles in about 1886. He and his father came to Los Angeles in 1856, where they started the predecessor of what became the American Baking Company. Rowan early left active involvement in the baking company to others and eventually sold it, working from then on only when he did not hold political office.

Rowan married Josephine Mayerhofer, the daughter of an Austrian military officer who emigrated as a political exile in 1854, in San Francisco in 1862. She was born in Austria on 26 November 1848 and died in Los Angeles on 31 December 1919. They had three children: Thomas E., Jr., Josephine Jane, and V. J. He was a pioneer member of the Los Angeles Social Club, one of the first such clubs in the city. He was also a founding member of the "38's"—the city's first volunteer fire department.

Los Angeles at the time of Rowan's mayoralty was a growing city of about 62,000 people; it had a mayor-council form of government, with a two-year mayoral term. Rowan, a Democrat, was a professional politician at a time when that was still rare in Los Angeles. He held numerous public positions, including under sheriff, county supervisor, county treasurer (1870–75), city treas-

urer (1869–70), and the mayoralty for one term (12 December 1892 to 12 December 1894).

Rowan was narrowly elected over Republican J. Q. Tufts in 1892 (4,901 to 4,209) in a highly charged campaign, where the influence of both the organized liquor dealers and the water company was important. He was mayor during the Depression starting in 1893, and he supported programs for public relief, including a public works program wherein the unemployed worked for $1 per day on roads, parks, and the like. He was also active in trying to promote business growth, playing a role in the establishment of the Fiesta de las Flores, a boosterish activity that continued for some years. The same year also saw the start of the Citizen's League, a business-led group seeking a new city charter, which was not successful during Rowan's mayoralty.

Rowan was not a candidate in the 1894 election, and while he held no further offices, he continued his active involvement in politics until his death in Los Angeles on 25 March 1901. He was buried in a Masonic cemetery.

SOURCES: *California Biography File*, Los Angeles Public Library; Historical Society of Southern California and the Pioneers of Los Angeles County Publications, vol. 5 (1900–1902); Harris Newmark, *60 Years in Southern California*, 4th ed. (Los Angeles, 1970); Leonard A. Sanders, "Los Angeles and Its Mayors, 1850–1925" (Master's thesis, University of Southern California, 1968).   *John M. Allswang*

ROZIER, JOSEPH ADOLPHUS (1817–96), Acting Mayor of New Orleans (19–20 March 1866). Eminent lawyer Rozier, acting mayor of New Orleans for two days in 1866, was born at St. Genevieve, Missouri, on 31 December 1817. His father, Ferdinand Rozier, was a native of Nantes, France, and his mother, Constance (Roy) Rozier, was a descendant of early French settlers in Missouri and like her husband a Roman Catholic. After graduating from St. Mary's College, Perry County, Missouri, Joseph studied law at Kaskaskia, Illinois, under Judge Nathaniel Pope and completed his law studies in Paris, France. In 1839, he came to New Orleans and was admitted to the bar in 1840. He quickly achieved an extensive practice. He was married in 1847 to Clothilde Vallee of St. Genevieve, Missouri. They had six children, only three of whom survived Rozier—Judge Thomas R., Kate, and Clothilde Rozier. In politics, he was a Whig before the Civil War, a conservative Unionist during Reconstruction, and a Democrat in his later years.

In 1861, Rozier was one of the New Orleans representatives to the Louisiana secession convention in Baton Rouge. He was opposed to secession without attempting first to reach a compromise over slavery, and he was one of seventeen members who voted against the secession ordinance.

During Reconstruction, Rozier was one of the chief spokesmen for the conservative Unionists, who had opposed secession, wished to see Louisiana back in the Union, but did not accept Lincoln's 10 percent plan as legal. Nonetheless, Rozier did have influence with military commanders assigned to Louisiana. He interceded successfully with General Benjamin Butler to have a death sentence commuted to imprisonment for three men convicted of spying. He was appointed to the board of administrators of the city's Charity Hospital in 1863 by General George F. Shepley. On 19 March 1866, following the election of Mayor John T. Monroe (q.v.) in New Orleans, General Edward R.S. Canby sent Rozier to inform Monroe that he was barred from the mayoral office under the amnesty terms issued by President Andrew Johnson. Rozier was named interim mayor by Canby until the next day when the president of the board of aldermen assumed the job. At this time New Orleans (which is contiguous with Orleans Parish) had a population of approximately 170,000. In 1867, when General Winfield Scott Hancock took command in Louisiana, Rozier served as his legal adviser.

After Reconstruction, Rozier continued to practice law and was president of the New Orleans Bar Association. He died on 14 December 1896 and was buried in New Orleans.

SOURCES: "Administrations of the Mayors of New Orleans, 1803–1936" (typescript compiled and edited by Works Progress Administration, New Orleans, 1940—manuscript located in the main branch of the New Orleans Public Library); Willie Malvin Caskey, *Secession and Restoration of Louisiana* (Baton Rouge, La., 1938); Edwin J. Jewell, ed. and comp., *Jewell's Crescent City Illustrated* (New Orleans, 1874); Peyton McCrary, *Abraham Lincoln and Reconstruction: The Louisiana Experiment* (Princeton, N.J., 1978); New Orleans *Daily States*, 15 December 1896.   *Joy J. Jackson*

RUEHLMANN, EUGENE PETER (1925–), Mayor of Cincinnati (1967–71). Lawyer and politician, born in Cincinnati on 23 February 1925, Ruehlmann was the son of John F. Ruehlmann, insurance company executive, and Hattie (Mehrckens) Ruehlmann, both Cincinnati-born Protestants of German origin. Ruehlmann and his twin sister were the last of nine children. He attended public schools and Western Hills High School. In 1942, he served as Boys' Week mayor in Cincinnati. He served in the U.S. Marines, 1943–44, and then attended the University of Cincinnati (B.A., 1948) and Harvard Law School (LL.B. in 1950). In 1947, he married Virginia Juergens (1924–), a University of Cincinnati graduate,

and they had eight children. Ruehlmann became a member of city, state, and national bar associations. He began practicing law in 1950 and joined the firm of Strauss, Troy and Ruehlmann in 1952.

A Republican, Ruehlmann sat on the city council, 1959–71. He was vice-mayor, 1963–67, and was chosen mayor by the council in 1967. Cincinnati had 452,524 people and a city manager-mayor-council form of government. Ruehlmann refused to accept the idea that the mayor should do little under this charter system, and he actively worked to improve the city's park system, housing, schools, and other needs. He supported renovation of the downtown area and completion of the new stadium and convention center. He also pledged to do what he could to ease social tensions and inequalities. Mayor Ruehlmann did not desire to serve another term and resigned the office on 6 April 1971, remaining in Cincinnati and continuing his legal practice.

SOURCES: Cincinnati *Enquirer*, 2 December 1963 and 2 December 1967; Personal Interview of 18 July 1979; *Who's Who in the Midwest* (Chicago, 1968).   *Thomas R. Bullard*

RUMSEY, JULIAN S. (1823–86), Mayor of Chicago (1861–62). Rumsey was born on 3 April 1823 in Batavia, New York. He was the son of Levi Rumsey (1776–1833), an attorney of Welsh descent, and Julia (Dole) Rumsey, both from a Congregationalist family. The younger of two children, Rumsey accompanied his brother George to Detroit and then to Chicago, arriving in 1835. He immediately began work as a clerk for his uncle, J.W.C. Coffin. With his brother and George W. Dole, he established the firm of Dole, Rumsey, and Company, originally a transfer freight company and later a grain purchaser. When Dole retired in 1852, the Rumsey brothers devoted their entire business to the buying and selling of grain. Julian Rumsey was a charter member of the Chicago Board of Trade and served as its president from 1858 to 1859. During his tenure, he was responsible for the adoption of a new charter and a new system of grain inspection. For these and other contributions, he was called the "father of grain inspection." In 1859, he was also elected president of the Chicago Chamber of Commerce.

Chicago in 1861 was a community of 120,000 people and had a mayor-council form of government. Elected mayor at the outbreak of the Civil War, Rumsey, a Republican and ardent unionist, defeated Democrat Thomas B. Bryan 8,274 votes to 6,601. In office but a few months, he raised a Committee of 100 which went to Washington to plead with President Buchanan for peace on a compromise basis. At a mass meeting in Chicago's Metropolitan Hall a few days after the firing on Fort

Sumter, Mayor Rumsey gave a stirring patriotic speech urging Chicagoans to enlist in the Union Army. During his mayoralty, over 30,000 soldiers were mustered into service in Chicago. When Union failures on the battlefield led to fears of defection in Northern cities, Rumsey required all citizens suspected of wavering loyalty to take an oath affirming their allegiance. During his year in office, the "war mayor" also served as an executive member of the First War Finance Committee. In a war economy, the city's manufacturers and trade boomed, and Rumsey's Chicago became known as the "granary and abattoir of the New World."

After deciding not to run for reelection in 1862, Rumsey devoted his time to fund-raising for the Union war effort. In 1870, he was elected president of the newly incorporated Corn Exchange National Bank in Chicago and served as the treasurer of Cook County, 1872–73. Rumsey was bedridden in his Chicago residence for three weeks prior to his death on 20 April 1886 of progressive general paresis. An Episcopalian, he was buried in Chicago's Graceland Cemetery.

SOURCES: *Chicago City Manual: 1911*; Chicago *Daily News*, 3 November 1939; Chicago *Tribune*, 21 April 1886; Frederick Rex, *The Mayors of the City of Chicago* (Chicago, 1947); Jean Rumsey, "Family History of Colonel William Rumsey," 1968 (Genealogical Collection, Newberry Library).

W. Roger Biles

S

SAMUEL, BERNARD (1880–1954), Mayor of Philadelphia (1941–52). Wartime mayor of Philadelphia and last of the Vare organization mayors, Samuel was born on 9 March 1880 in South Philadelphia, the only child of Samuel and Christina Samuel. Both were natives of the city. Samuel's father and grandfather had been active in South Philadelphia Vare organization politics. After graduating from prestigious Central High School at age sixteen (the youngest in his class), Samuel worked as an office-boy for a Philadelphia brokerage firm and advanced to become boardroom manager. At age twenty-one, bosses William and Edwin Vare made Samuel their protégé, and shortly he became boss of the Thirty-ninth Ward. In 1923, Samuel won election to the city council where in six months he chaired the finance committee. He headed that committee for twelve years.

Samuel married Eleanor Hamm in 1903. Their one son, Richard Russell, was later deputy secretary of the commonwealth of Pennsylvania. The Samuels were Episcopalian. Described as "jaunty," "good hearted," and "anxious to please everybody," "Barney" Samuel was active in the South Philadelphia Business Man's Association and enjoyed fishing and boating on the South Jersey coast.

Samuel presided over the city council in 1941 when Mayor Robert Lamberton (q.v.) died in office, and, as provided in the city charter, Samuel became acting mayor. The state Supreme Court upheld the wish of the Republican machine that Samuel serve out Lamberton's unexpired term. Philadelphia in 1940 had a population of 1,931,000 people and a mayor-council form of government. In 1943, Samuel ran for his own term and defeated his Democratic opponent, ex-Ambassador William C. Bullitt (346,297 to Bullitt's 282,832). Samuel attacked Bullitt with charges that he was pro-Nazi, anti-Catholic, and anti-Semitic. Running for reelection in 1947, Samuel handily overcame his young Democratic reform candidate opponent, Richardson Dilworth (q.v.) (413,091 to Dilworth's 321,469). Dilworth charged that the city during Samuel's term reeked with corruption.

During the war years, Samuel successfully managed the city's civilian defense establishment, created a city planning commission, and laid plans for the reemployment of returning veterans. However, he always operated with sorely inadequate funds. Despite campaign promises, he did little to improve Philadelphia's foul water supply; nor did the city address the problem of deteriorating streets, poor public transportation, and an undermanned police and fire department. Samuel requested $5 million in 1948 to meet the payroll demands of city workers. To get it he was forced to create the Committee of 15, which launched a thorough investigation of the whole structure of city government. The committee uncovered considerable scandal, which precipitated passage of a new city charter in 1951 and the overthrow of the Republican machine a year later.

After leaving office in 1952, Samuel returned to the brokerage business. He died suddenly on 1 January 1954 of a stroke.

SOURCES: Joseph R. Fink, "Reform in Philadelphia, 1946–1951" (Ph.D. dissertation, Rutgers University, 1971); Philadelphia *Record*, 1 October 1945; Anthony Roth, ed., "Mayors of Philadelphia, 1691–1977: Collection of the Genealogical Society of Pennsylvania," vol. 8 (unpublished collection found in the Historical Society of Pennsylvania, Philadelphia).

John F. Bauman

SANDERSON, GEORGE HENRY (1824–93), Mayor of San Francisco (1891–93). Republican Mayor Sanderson was born in July 1824 in Boston, one of at least five children who survived to maturity. Self-educated, he went to California when the Gold Rush began, arriving in 1850 after a voyage around Cape Horn. Mining proved unrewarding, and after a few months, Sanderson went into business as a wholesale grocer in Stockton. Immediately active in politics, he served as Stockton controller in 1853 and alderman in 1854, he helped form a volunteer fire company, and he was chief of the fire department for three years. During 1863, he also acted as secretary of the State Agricultural Society. While in Stockton, he married Sarah Dyer Rowe (d. 1911) of Maine, and they had four sons: Henry Ellis (b. 1858); George R., Edward H., and William W. In 1865, Sanderson moved to San Francisco where he continued his career as a wholesale grocer. Initially associated with Weaver, Wooster and Company, he became a partner of M. P. Jones in 1868 and then, in 1877, of Elliott M. Root, as Root and Sanderson. Sanderson was prominent in several business organizations, including a trustee of the Chamber of Commerce, a director and two-term president of the board of trade, and president of the Merchants' Club. He also was a member of the Territorial Pioneers of California.

In 1890, San Francisco had 298,997 residents, and the city, consolidated with the county of the same name, was governed by a mayor and board of supervisors. Sanderson received the Republican nomination for mayor that year, and he won the 4 November election, partly because the Democratic party was divided between reformers and boss Christopher Buckley's faction. Sanderson polled 20,957 votes to Democrat William F. Goad's 15,790, Independent Charles C. O'Donnell's 17,054, and Reform Democrat James M. McDonald's 1,408. Like earlier San Francisco mayors of the 1880s, Sanderson recorded few notable achievements during his term, in part because the city charter inhibited leadership by dispersing power, and in part because in San Francisco good administration typically was viewed as carefully limiting government expenditures. In 1892, Sanderson, along with ten Republican supervisors, failed to win renomination: factions led by party bosses Martin Kelley and Phil Crimmins controlled the convention and presumably preferred their own men. Sanderson also failed to win the mayoral nomination of the reform nonpartisan organization which ran Levi R. Ellert (*q.v.*) instead. On 1 February 1893, after having been ill for some time, Sanderson died in San Francisco of pneumonia and was buried in the city, after funeral services at the First Presbyterian Church.

SOURCES: Lincoln Grammar School records for Henry E. Sanderson (California Historical Society); San Francisco *Call*, 2 February 1893; San Francisco *Chronicle*, 30 November 1890 and 2 February 1893; San Francisco *Examiner*, September–October 1892 and 2 February 1893; George H. Tinkham, *A History of Stockton* . . . (San Francisco, 1880).

Michael Griffith

SAWYER, BENAIR C. (1822–1908), Mayor of Pittsburgh (1862–64). Sawyer was born in Pittsburgh on 18 October 1822, son of a wealthy soap manufacturer of the same name. With a good education he became a printer but returned to the family business. Politically minded, he was elected to both the common and select councils several times before he was twenty-seven. From 1849 he ran for mayor almost perennially as a Whig and Republican. The city, with about 55,000 population when he became mayor, had two councils.

In the election of 1862, Sawyer defeated former Mayor Henry A. Weaver (*q.v.*), Union party, by 2,701 to 2,167 votes. Little occurred during his administration until he

announced he would seek a second term. Then a storm broke out, with charges of scandalous misconduct. The charges were never proved, but in the primary he was low man in a three-man race, and his father was caught redhanded stuffing a ballot box.

Following this defeat, Sawyer returned to soapmaking to replace his father, who died in January 1865. The business failed during the Panic of 1873, sweeping away the whole fortune. In 1876, he went to Colorado and entered the mining business, quickly making another fortune. In 1880, he moved to Denver, became a major in the National Guard, and held a number of state political positions. Sawyer moved still further west to Los Angeles in 1895 and went into real estate, successfully.

At some time in his career, Sawyer married Catherine Aiken, who bore him a son and three daughters. Apparently he was married twice, for *two* sons and a daughter survived him. He died in Los Angeles on 13 March 1908.

SOURCES: Allen Humphreys Kerr, "The Mayors and Records of Pittsburgh, 1816–1951" (typescript, 1952, Carnegie Library of Pittsburgh); Los Angeles *Examiner*, 15 March 1908; Denver *Post*, 5 March 1908.

George Swetnam

SCHAEFER, WILLIAM DONALD (1921–   ), Democratic Mayor of Baltimore (1971–   ). Schaefer was born in Baltimore on 2 November 1921, the son of William Henry Schaefer and Tululu Irene Schaefer, both of German heritage and both Episcopalian.

His father was a lawyer, and the son followed in his footsteps, earning the LL.B. degree in 1942 and the Master of Laws in 1951 from the University of Baltimore. He served in the Army between 1942 and 1945, as a colonel.

The city of Baltimore, 850,000 in size, has a so-called strong mayor form of government. The city charter provides for a council of nineteen members, three elected from each of six districts, plus a president elected citywide. The council is empowered to set the property tax rate, cut the mayor's proposed budget, and confirm nominations. But the real power, particularly in an era of massive state and federal aid to cities, is given to the board of estimates, which makes all fiscal operational decisions. While the president of the city council is president of the board of estimates, the mayor is also a member and controls two more votes of the five-member board through appointment. A Democrat, Schaefer served on the city council, 1952–67 and was its president, 1967–71. In 1971, Schaefer won the mayoralty election, defeating R. Z. Pierpont by a vote of 120,725 to 17,680. The mayor, a bachelor, has devoted his life to his city. He also demands high levels of accomplishment from himself and others who work for him. This trait, together with the strength of his position and character, enables him to attract many able subordinates.

In 1975, Schaefer defeated the mayoral challenger, C. M. Chandler, by a 91,335 to 16,036 vote. A recent analysis of Schaefer's first eight years (two terms) gave him high marks for achievement but lower grades when compared with Thomas J. D'Alesandro (q.v.), on his image for humaneness and sense of identity with the less fortunate. Baltimore was at least 47 percent black by 1970. Mayor Schaefer encouraged economic development as an important source of jobs for lower class and middle-class people. More recently, the promotion of tourism, eight years in the planning, has taken a major priority. The mayor has cooperated with law enforcement officials only to see crime rates rise and fall and rise again. He has frequently become involved in fights over expressways. He sees them as an economic advantage but has often been forced to compromise with irate citizens of threatened local neighborhoods. In other ways, he encourages these same citizens to organize. Stadium improvements, an aquarium, and what some call the finest waterfront development program in the entire United States are among his achievements. He has also worked hard to improve the city's schools, which were victims of *de facto* segregation and ineffective leadership during the first half of the decade.

Schaefer cut his urban teeth as a member of Baltimore's prestigious Citizens' Planning and Housing Association. As mayor, he worked with Commissioner Robert Embry to bring many federal funds to the city and used them creatively. Schaefer is a fiscal conservative and has therefore been able to keep the city's bond rating high during a period of urban collapse elsewhere. Finally, Schaefer has claimed to push Baltimore's neighborhoods as major sources of civic strength. He continuously praises them and attends their events. He has decentralized city government by placing eleven mayor's stations throughout the city where citizens can receive help and can communicate with local representatives of city hall.

Schaefer has sought to blend fiscal accountability, public works improvements, political sensitivity, and civic pride to lift his city's hopes and aspirations. As a result, Baltimore is experiencing a claimed renaissance. In November 1974, he was reelected by a vote of 118,706 to 25,072 (S. A. Culotta) to his third four-year term. While some contemporaries speak derisively of his authoritarian style, history may well record him as one of Baltimore's greatest mayors.

SOURCES: Baltimore Mayor's office biography, New York *Times Biographical Service*.

W. T. Durr

SCHEU, SOLOMON (1822–88), Mayor of Buffalo (1878–79). German-born Democrat councilman, and briefly mayor, Scheu played a minor political role in Buffalo's past. Born on 6 January 1822 at Standenbuehl, Bavaria, he was the son of Henry Jacob Scheu, a prosperous farmer and landowner, and Catharina (Hepp) Scheu, neither of whom chose to leave Germany. One of several sons of a Lutheran family, he emigrated to the United States with one brother in 1839, at the age of seventeen, settling in Buffalo in 1844. Entering in business ventures which included lumber-dealing and bakery operations, the Scheu brothers became prominent in Buffalo's sizable German population. Scheu married German-born Catharina Rink (1824–99), a Bavarian Lutheran (as he was) in 1847, and they had seven sons and a daughter, all but two sons surviving into adulthood. After his marriage, Scheu and his wife began a small but prosperous grocery business, which the family maintained until his death in 1888. His political career began with election as an alderman from the predominantly German-ethnic Sixth Ward in 1853, a post he occupied consistently until his temporary election to city hall, twenty-five years later.

Buffalo in 1878 had approximately 150,000 inhabitants and a mayor-council form of government. A Democrat, Scheu actively pursued the nomination for mayor, beating the incumbent mayor, Republican Philip Becker (q.v.), a fellow Bavarian immigrant, by a small plurality. That he was defeated in a subsequent bid for the Democratic nomination suggests that Scheu was an unpopular mayor. His brief term of office appears to have been unsatisfying, for despite continued support from his ward constituency, he henceforth refrained from elected political office. Scheu was appointed to the Erie County Board of Trade, on which he served for several years.

Scheu continued to run his grocery business after his political retirement. All of his primary outside interests were associated with the Lutheran Church, from which he was buried with great honors upon his death on 23 November 1888.

SOURCES: J. F. Barry, ed., *The Buffalo Text Book* (Buffalo, 1924); Buffalo *Commercial Advertiser*, 24, 26, 28 November 1888; Buffalo *Times*, 16 November 1919.

W. Andrew Achenbaum

SCHIRO, VICTOR H. (1904–   ), Mayor of New Orleans (1961–70). Mayor of New Orleans when the South and the nation were experiencing great social and economic changes, Schiro provided calm, quiet leadership, and the result was peace and order in his city while other communities were torn by racial strife. Schiro was born in Chicago on 28 May 1904, second child of Andrew Edward Schiro and Mary (Pizzati) Schiro, both Roman

Catholics from Italy. His father's career was spent in banking.

Schiro was an insurance executive and civic leader. His political career began with his election as commissioner of public buildings and parks in 1950. With the advent of the home rule charter and strong mayor-council system, he was elected councilman-at-large in 1954 and reelected in 1958. When Mayor Morrison resigned (*q.v.*), the council unanimously elected Schiro interim mayor on 20 June 1961. Elected to a full term in 1962, he was reelected in the first primary four years later.

Always underestimated by opponents and opposed by the daily newspapers in both campaigns for mayor, Schiro was independent and unorthodox, abolishing courtesy parole powers for his own supporters and letting the Morrison political organization which he inherited become moribund. His administration built a police-courts complex and regional libraries, started the cultural center, initiated a code of ethics for city employees and a criminology degree program for police officers, and began the renowned jazzfests and foodfests.

Schiro secured local-option urban renewal in a state that had prohibited the program, got New Orleans included in the Model Cities Program, and started a regional planning commission, which made possible many federal programs that followed.

Committed to sound business operation of city government, Schiro adopted performance budgeting, invested idle funds, pushed development of New Orleans East, started the mosquito control program, and established the first pay program of planned raises for employees. His major achievements were the firm leadership he provided to insure the peaceful opening of integrated schools in 1961, in sharp contrast to the nationally publicized disturbances of 1960; the nonpolitical administration and cleanup of the police department after years of scandals; his successful campaign for professional sports and the Superdome; the widening of Poydras Street, which resulted in development of the Superdome-River Corridor; and the leadership he provided when Hurricane Betsy struck the city in 1965. He failed in efforts to spur "air rights" development of the downtown riverfront, but saw the concept accepted and the first projects built in his successors' administrations.

A life-long Democrat and party loyalist, Schiro was one of the few officials in Louisiana to support Hubert Humphrey for president in 1968 and was co-chairman of the national mayors for Humphrey committee.

Limited by the charter to two consecutive terms, Schiro left office in 1970. He has been active in business affairs as president of his insurance agency. His interests include boating and civic work, particularly promotion of trade through the port of New Orleans.

SOURCES: Morton Inger, *Politics and Reality in an American City: The New Orleans School Crisis of 1960* (New York, 1969); Mayor's Office, City of New Orleans, "Annual Report of the Mayor," issues for 1961 through 1970; Victor H. Schiro, interview, 18 September 1979; Victor H. Schiro, personal papers and memorabilia. (Mayor Schiro's reading file of outgoing letters is in the Special Collections Division of the Tulane University Library, New Orleans; other papers are in the city records in the main library of the public library, and various papers and memorabilia remain in his possession); Victor H. Schiro, with Allan Katz, "The Schiro Years," New Orleans *States Item*, 8 March–6 April 1971.

Jack B. McGuire

SCHMITZ, EUGENE E. (1864–1928), Mayor of San Francisco (1902–1907). Mayor of San Francisco at the height of "boss" rule and graft, Schmitz was born in the city on 22 August 1864, the son of pioneer parents. A musician and band leader, he began as a young drummer boy at the Standard Theater, ending up leading the Columbia Theater Orchestra by 1900. As president of the Musicians' Union, Schmitz was picked by political boss Abraham Ruef to run for mayor in 1901.

Beginning in 1900, a series of violent labor disputes had torn the city, despite the years of good government and the new charter instituted under the distinguished former Mayor James Phelan (*q.v.*). The City Front Federation of waterfront workers and the Employers' Association fought a relentless war, and Mayor Phelan fell back on police help. The unions were crushed and formed a new party, the Union Labor party. Abe Ruef, Republican political boss, changed parties and grasped control of the opportunity. Schmitz was elected and subsequently reelected twice, in 1903 and 1905, with increasing majorities, but the real power was Ruef.

"Handsome Gene" Schmitz was good-looking, genial, and well liked, and, although not "the smallest man mentally and the meanest man morally" ever to be mayor, as one opponent claimed, he was easily ruled by Ruef. With each passing day, the links between the city administration and the underworld ramified, especially after the large electoral victory of 1905, after which the city began taking "tributes" from respectable businesses. Three men counterattacked: the former mayor, Phelan; a local business leader, Rudolph Spreckels; and Fremont Older, crusading editor of the *Evening Bulletin*. Phelan and Spreckels financed a complex investigation by a rising U.S. Secret Service man, William J. Burns (recommended by President Theodore Roosevelt, who connived in the whole operation), with the help of an able prosecutor, Francis J. Heney.

The earthquake and fires of April 1906 intervened,

during which Mayor Schmitz displayed unusual initiative and leadership—only to regress to graft and shakedowns with Ruef once the crisis was over. Indeed, the rebuilding of the city invited still further graft. On 7 November 1906, a grand jury indicted Ruef and Schmitz for exacting ''legal fees'' from brothels. Many members of the board of supervisors confessed when offered state immunity. The investigation began to reach into the upper levels of San Francisco society—to the heads of large corporations, including the notorious United Railroads. At one stage, Fremont Older was kidnapped and taken to Santa Barbara, and prosecutor Heney was shot in open court by an ex-convict who later died mysteriously in jail. Ruef was finally convicted in 1908, receiving a fourteen-year sentence (paroled in 1915).

Mayor Schmitz was arrested on twenty-seven charges of graft and bribery, but his conviction was overturned by the appellate court and by the state supreme court, and he blithely returned to politics. He ran again, unsuccessfully, for mayor in 1915 and 1919, and he was even elected to the board of supervisors, 1917–25. He retired into private business in 1925 and died of heart disease in San Francisco on 20 November 1928, protesting his innocence until the end.

SOURCES: Walton Bean, *Boss Ruef's San Francisco* (Berkeley, Calif., 1952); Robert Glass Cleland, *From Wilderness to Empire: A History of California*, edited by Glen S. Dumke (New York, 1962); J. C. Kennedy, *The Great Earthquake and Its Fire* (New York, 1963); San Francisco Board of Supervisors, ''Report on the Municipal Corruption in San Francisco'' (1910); Lately Thomas, *A Debonair Scoundrel* (New York, 1962).

C. Peter d'A. Jones

SCHWAB, FRANK XAVIER (1874–1946), Mayor of Buffalo (1922–29). German-American brewer and a lively and controversial mayor, born in Buffalo on 14 August 1874, Schwab was the son of Frank and Anna (Bauer) Schwab, Roman Catholics of German descent. Schwab attended St. Ann's School but received a relatively limited formal education. He started working at the Wagner Palace Car Company shops, reaching the level of foreman, but left this firm around 1900 and eventually became a successful brewer. He was also president of Mohawk Products Company until 1922. On 24 September 1901, he married Theresa M. Lauser (1880–1943), a German Catholic like himself, and they had seven children. Schwab was an Elk, a Moose, an Eagle, and member of the Knights of St. John and of twenty-seven fraternal organizations.

Schwab was elected mayor in 1921 as a Democrat, defeating incumbent Republican Mayor George S. Buck (*q.v.*) 62,631 to 59,974, although Buffalo's elections

were technically nonpartisan at that time. He was re-elected in 1925, defeating Republican Ross Graves 77,587 to 55,354. In 1929, however, Schwab was defeated in his bid for a third term, with 69,593 votes to 77,175 for Republican Charles Roesch (*q.v.*) and 9,031 for Socialist-Independent Frank Perkins. Buffalo had 506,775 people in 1920 and a mayor-commission form of government. In the 1925 election, the voters had approved a return to a mayor-council form of government.

Schwab campaigned in 1921 on the theme of going to Washington and persuading Congress to repeal Prohibition. (He was, after all, an ethnic German and a brewer.) He backed city salary increases and civic improvements, supporting an $8 million bond issue. An active politician, Schwab liked to get in his car and ride to the scenes of fires. He was always in the news, especially with his opposition to the Ku Klux Klan (he was a Roman Catholic). Schwab sponsored the ''Hotel de Gink'' for transients, earning additional publicity. Newsmen called him the ''Peter Pan'' of local politics. Schwab dropped out of the 1933 and 1941 mayoral campaigns, but ran again on the People's party ticket in 1937 and 1945. In 1947, he polled only 6,974 votes to 94,037 for T. L. Holling (*q.v.*) (Democrat) and 92,610 for E. J. Jaeckle (Republican); in 1945 he ran stronger, with 35,246 votes to Republican Bernard Dowd's (*q.v.*) 80,383 and Holling's 60,461. The strain of this last race probably hastened his death, which occurred on 23 April 1946.

SOURCES: New York *Times*, 1 December 1929, 17 April 1943 and 24 April 1946; *Who's Who in New York* (New York, 1929).   *Thomas R. Bullard*

SCHWAB, LOUIS (1850–1926), Mayor of Cincinnati (1910–11). Schwab was born in Cincinnati on 26 November 1850 to Mathias Schwab (1808–65), a pipe-organ manufacturer from Freiburg, Baden, Germany, and Solomena Yeck of Basel, Switzerland. The third of six children, Louis Schwab attended Cincinnati public schools and served in the Fifth Ohio Valley Infantry during the Civil War. He trained in pharmacy and opened a pharmaceutical shop, and then returned to school at the Medical College of Ohio. After graduation in 1883, Dr. Schwab established a practice in the suburb of Cumminsville, and on 22 October 1885 married a local woman, Fannie Sheppard. The couple had three children, Mathias (b. 1886), Nelson (b. 1888), and Abigail (b. 1889), before their mother's early death in 1891.

Active in the medical profession, the Masons, and the Syrian Temple, Schwab played a role in Republican city politics, starting with membership in the Blaine Club and the Stamina League. He was a member of the board of medical directors for the new municipal hospital, and in

1898 and again in 1900 was elected coroner of Hamilton County. He won a seat on the board of education in 1904 and was reelected in 1906 for a four-year term of office, which ended with his election to Cincinnati's mayoralty in 1909.

Cincinnati had a mayor-council form of government and a population of some 380,000 when Schwab accepted the Republican party's mayoral nomination in 1909. Through his medical practice and school board activities, he had maintained a reputation for respectability and integrity that gained support for his candidacy even from some critics of the "Republican machine," and he defeated Democratic John Weld Peck by a vote of 41,903 to 34,118. In office, Schwab continued the policies of his Republican predecessors, including annexations, park planning and construction, tenement regulation, and improved health care delivery. Schwab expressed a disinclination to run for reelection in 1911 but ultimately agreed to accept his party's nomination. His Democratic opponent, Henry T. Hunt (*q.v.*), however, chose to run his campaign against Republican party "Boss" George B. Cox rather than against Schwab, and Hunt emerged the victor by a vote of 43,673 to Schwab's 39,771.

Schwab returned to his medical practice in 1912 but continued to be active in public life. From 1916 to his death, he served once more on the school board, and he held places on the city charter commission and the city planning commission. He died in Cincinnati on 4 June 1926 and was buried there in Spring Grove Cemetery.

SOURCES: Lewis Leonard Alexander, ed., *Greater Cincinnati and Its People* (New York, 1927); *Annual Reports of the City of Cincinnati* for 1909, 1910, 1911; Cincinnati *Enquirer*; Charles Frederick Goss, *Cincinnati: The Queen City, 1788–1912* (Chicago and Cincinnati, 1912); Charles Theodore Greve, *Centennial History of Cincinnati and Representative Citizens* (Chicago, 1904); Zane L. Miller, *Boss Cox's Cincinnati: Urban Politics in the Progressive Era* (New York, 1968).

Judith Spraul-Schmidt.

SCOTT, JOHN M. (?–?), Mayor of Philadelphia (1841–43). Scott, about whom very little is known, was mayor during the Native American turbulence which pitted the native-born against the foreign-born, mostly Irish. Philadelphia was in turmoil over these affairs, which saw mobs attacking each other's meetings and parades, churches and buildings. Earlier in 1842, the administration experienced a Negro riot, when a black temperance society paraded through the streets of south Philadelphia celebrating Jamaican Emancipation Day. Some bystanders misread the event as a celebration of the black massacre of whites on Santo Domingo, and attacked blacks in the parade, burned down a meeting hall, and assaulted blacks in the ghetto.

SOURCES: *City of Firsts: Complete History of Philadelphia* (Philadelphia, 1926); Michael Feldberg, *The Philadelphia Riots of 1844* (Westport, Conn., 1975); Sam Bass Warner, Jr., *The Private City: Philadelphia in Three Periods of Its Growth* (Philadelphia, 1968).

Melvin G. Holli

SCOVILLE, JONATHAN (1830–91), Mayor of Buffalo (1884–85). Iron manufacturer and mayor of Buffalo, born in Salisbury, Connecticut, on 14 July 1830, Scoville was the son of Samuel C. Scoville (1804–65), iron manufacturer, and Lois Dorcas (Church) Scoville (1805–90), both old-stock New Englanders. The oldest of seven children, Scoville attended local schools until 1846 when he began a two-year career as a clerk in a country store. He then took courses at Harvard in preparation for entering his father's iron business. He took charge of the mines at Canaan, Connecticut, and then moved to Buffalo in 1860, establishing a wheel foundry with his brother Nathaniel. In 1861, he opened a branch in Toronto, Canada, quickly amassing a fortune. He never married and apparently never joined any of the city's major clubs.

Scoville served in Congress, 1880–83, but did not enjoy political activity. Seeking a reform-minded candidate, the local Democratic leaders chose Scoville as their mayoral candidate in the 1883 election. He defeated Josiah Jewett, Republican, 13,823 to 13,668. Buffalo had almost 200,000 people in 1883 and a mayor-council form of government.

A strong believer in civil service reform, Scoville is usually described as the mayor who most strongly supported the concept in Buffalo. Following the lead of Mayor Grover Cleveland (*q.v.*), Scoville often found himself in opposition to his party's leaders. He had no desire for a lengthy political career and did not seek another term in 1885. He retired from business around 1886 and died on 4 March 1891. He left a $5,000 bequest to the Buffalo Academy of Fine Arts, the only major civic institution to earn his support.

SOURCES: Jennie M. Holley and Homer W. Brainerd, *Arthur Scovell and His Descendants in America* (Rutland, Vt., 1941); J. N. Larned, *A History of Buffalo*, 2 vols. (New York, 1911); Sister Mary Jane and Sister Mercedes, "Mayors of Buffalo, 1832–1961," (B.A. thesis, Rosary Hill College, 1961). *Thomas R. Bullard*

SCULLY, CORNELIUS DECATUR (1878–1952), Mayor of Pittsburgh (1936–46). A product of David Lawrence's (*q.v.*) Democratic organization, Scully set the stage for the Pittsburgh renaissance that followed his term. Scully was born in suburban Chartiers township, and he and his family moved into Pittsburgh when he was quite young. His father, John Sullivan Scully, a banker and businessman of Protestant Irish ancestry, and his mother, Mary Negley Scully, from a prominent Pittsburgh family, had three other children. Scully attended Pittsburgh public schools, graduated from the University of Pennsylvania in 1901, and from the University of Pittsburgh Law School in 1904. After admission to the bar, he joined the firm of Lee and Meeker where he practiced corporate law, specializing in oil and gas problems. In 1905, he married Rosalie Pendleton of Shephardstown, West Virginia; the Scullys had two sons and two daughters.

A progressive Republican, Scully ran for state treasurer on the Keystone ticket in 1910. For the next two decades, he remained a nominal Republican, but in 1932 he was drawn to the Democrats by Franklin D. Roosevelt. An adherent of Henry George's Single Tax philosophy, he worked as William N. McNair's (q.v.) campaign manager in Pittsburgh's 1933 mayoral contest and became McNair's first city solicitor. Quickly fired by the mercurial McNair, Scully was elected by the city council to a vacated council seat, and in 1936 he became council president. When, on 6 October 1936, McNair resigned, Scully became acting mayor for two weeks and then completed McNair's four-year term as mayor *pro tempore*.

In 1937, Scully, with the backing of the Lawrence organization, handily defeated P. J. McArdle in the primary and then secured 122,418 votes to 92,386 for Republican Robert N. Waddell. When Scully was reelected in 1941, he received 112,723 votes against 109,560 for Republican Harmar D. Denny. In 1940, Pittsburgh had a mayor-council form of government and a population of 671,659.

Scully restored order to the city's finances, cooperated with state and federal New Deal programs, and worked to strengthen the Lawrence Democratic organization. During Scully's term, interest in urban revitalization increased; in 1939, Robert Moses presented his downtown renewal plan to the Pittsburgh Regional Plan Association. In that same year, Richard K. Mellon began to direct the Chamber of Commerce and other groups toward expanding public powers to create a more hospitable economic environment. Scully appointed a point park commission and sponsored stronger smoke control and flood control measures. Much of the state legislation on which the post-World War II renaissance depended was passed in Harrisburg during Scully's second term.

In 1945, David L. Lawrence decided to run for mayor, and Scully was passed over for the nomination. Shortly after his term concluded, he was appointed to the Allegheny County Sewer Authority. In addition, Scully served on the board of directors of the Legal Aid Society,

a post he held from 1908 to 1947. He was a member of the Duquesne Club and a Mason. In 1949, his health failing, he retired from most of his activities. On 22 September 1952, he died in Winchester, Virginia, after a long illness.

SOURCES: Allen Humphreys Kerr, "The Mayor and Recorders of Pittsburgh, 1816–1851: Their Lives and Somewhat of Their Times" (typescript, 1952, Carnegie Public Library); Frank Hawkins, "David Lawrence: Boss of the Mellon Patch," *Harpers Magazine* 213 (August 1958), reprinted in Roy Lubove, ed., *Pittsburgh* (New York, 1976); Stefen Lorant, *Pittsburgh: The Story of an American City* (Garden City, N.Y., 1964); Roy Lubove, *Twentieth Century Pittsburgh: Government, Business, and Environmental Change* (New York, 1969); Bruce Stave, *The New Deal and the Last Hurrah: Pittsburgh Machine Politics* (Pittsburgh, 1970).

Douglas V. Shaw

SEASONGOOD, MURRAY (1878–   ), Mayor of Cincinnati (1926–29). Reformer, expert author on corporate law and Cincinnati's first mayor under the city manager system, Seasongood was born 27 October 1878 in Cincinnati the son of Alfred Seasongood (1844–1909), a wholesale clothing merchant and Emily (Fechheimer) Seasongood (1852–1941), both Jewish and both natives of Cincinnati. The youngest of four children, Seasongood attended public schools, Woodward High School Edgeborough School (in Guilford, England), and Harvard (B.A., 1900, M.A., 1901, and LL.B., 1903). He joined the law firm of Paxton and Seasongood in 1903, and was admitted to practice before the Supreme Court in 1907. During World War I, Seasongood was a legal adviser to the draft board. In 1912, he married Agnes Senior (1890–   ) of Cincinnati who was also Jewish, and they had one daughter. Seasongood was a Phi Beta Kappa and a member of various organizations.

Seasongood showed an early interest in political and social reform, and served on the Ohio Commission for the Blind, 1915–25. Initially a Republican, Seasongood grew dissatisfied with that party's support of boss rule in Cincinnati and was a leader in the reform movement that led to the city's new charter in 1925, resulting in adoption of the city manager system. He was elected alderman that same year and served two terms as Cincinnati's first charter mayor (and, indeed, as leader of the Charterite party). Cincinnati had 401,247 people in 1920 and a city manager-mayor-council form of government.

Throughout his four years in office, Seasongood defended the charter system and helped to defeat regular politicians' efforts to return to machine rule. He wrote articles and delivered many speeches, winning a national reputation as a reform leader. As mayor, Seasongood helped settle a longstanding dispute between the city and its major transit company. He also opposed the power company's efforts to increase its rates and saved money in nearly all departments of the municipal government.

Although Seasongood's elective political career ended on 31 December 1929, he continued his interest in reform, serving as a consultant to a presidential housing conference (1932), as a member of the Advisory Committee on Rules for Criminal Procedures for the U.S. Supreme Court (1941–44), and as president of the National Municipal League (1931–35). Seasongood served on the Loyalty Review Board of the U.S. Civil Service Commission (1947–53) and on the Personnel Security Board of the Atomic Energy Commission (1953–61). He taught at the University of Cincinnati Law School (1925–59) and lectured at Harvard, 1947–48. Seasongood wrote the standard *Casebook on Municipal Corporations*, which has gone through three editions. He has also continued his practice (still with Paxton and Seasongood) to the present—a legal career of more than seventy-five years.

SOURCES: Lewis A. Leonard, ed. in-chief, *Greater Cincinnati*, 4 vols. (New York, 1927); Letter of Mrs. Herbert Hoffheimer, Jr. (Seasongood's daughter) to author, 22 April 1980; Letter of Murray Seasongood to author, 11 April 1980; Agnes Seasongood, ed., *Selections from Speeches (1900–1959) of Murray Seasongood* (New York, 1960); Murray Seasongood, *Local Government in the United States* (Cambridge, Mass., 1934).

Thomas R. Bullard

SEAVER, BENJAMIN (1795–1856), Mayor of Boston (1852–53). Whig mayor, born in Roxbury, Massachusetts, on 12 April 1795, Seaver was the son of Benjamin Seaver (1766–1815) and Debby (Loud) Seaver, from a prominent local family. The eldest of five children, the younger Benjamin was educated at Roxbury Grammar School and entered business as an apprentice in 1812. He had become a successful auctioneer with Whitefield and Seaver by the time he ran for political office.

Previous to his election, Seaver held a number of offices. He won a seat on the Boston Common Council as a representative of the Fifth Ward in 1845, 1846, and 1847 before moving to the Fourth Ward, and he won election again to the council in 1848 and 1849. At the same time, he not only served as president of the common council (1847–49), but also held office in the Massachusetts General Court, first as a representative (1846–49) and then as a senator (1850–52).

Seaver won the mayority election of 1851 with 3,990 votes to J.V.C. Smith's (*q.v.*) 2,736, A. W. Thaxter Jr.'s 1,024, and H. B. Rogers' 188. In 1852, Seaver

squeaked in with only a one-vote margin over his four opponents. Seaver became mayor of a city of 140,000 people and with a mayor-aldermen-council form of government. Accused by the nativists of being elected with the help of Irish Catholics, he was a conscientious magistrate who fought against bigotry, ignorance, and poverty. He labored to place Boston on a sound fiscal foundation by advocating economy and efficiency in government. While his efforts resulted in the reduction of the city debt by some $250,000 because of taxes and the sale of property, his years are best remembered for the steps taken to provide a building for the Boston Public Library. Defeated in his third attempt for the mayoralty, he retired from public life but continued to fight against religious bigotry.

Benjamin Seaver married Sarah Johnson in August 1818, and they had four children. A Mayflower descendant, like his wife, he was active as a deacon in the Twelfth Congregational Church. He acquired a reputation for integrity and was known for his generosity to the poor. He died in Roxbury on 14 February 1856 and was buried in Forest Hills Cemetery in Jamaica Plain.

SOURCES: Boston *Bee*, 15 February 1856 (obituary); Benjamin Seaver, *Catalogue of the Entire and Select Library of the late Rev. Samuel Cooper Thacher* (Boston, 1818); Jesse Seaver, *The Seaver Genealogy* (Philadelphia, 1924); State Street Trust Company, *Mayors of Boston* (Boston, 1914); William Blake Trask, ''The Seaver Family,'' *New England Historical and Genealogical Register* 26 (1872); William H. Whitmore, ed., *The Inaugural Addresses of the Mayors of Boston*, 2 vols. (Boston, 1894–96).

Vincent A. Lapomarda

SEBASTIAN, CHARLES EDWARD (1873–1937), Mayor of Los Angeles (1915–16). Chief of police who became mayor of Los Angeles, Sebastian rose to power as a crime and vice crusader, but fell through exposure of personal scandals. Born in Farmington, St. Francois County, Missouri, on 30 March 1873, the son of Charles Layal and Selina Jane (Poston) Sebastian, representatives of old families of Missouri, Sebastian was taken to Ventura County, California, with his family in 1874 and subsequently to Los Angeles (1879). Law enforcement was in his family. A grandfather, Milton Sebastian, had been circuit judge and sheriff of St. Francois County.

For a while, Sebastian's father farmed in Ventura and also acted as deputy sheriff there and in Los Angeles. He died in 1886. Charles took various jobs: farming (1881–89, 1890–94), selling merchandise (1889–90, 1894–96), conductor on the Los Angeles Railway Company (1896), and city street inspector (1897) before becoming a special police officer in the Los Angeles Police Department, 24 April 1900, and a regular patrolman in

October. Then he worked his way up the bureaucracy: acting sergeant (1905), sergeant (1906), sergeant in charge of the "Oriental Squad"—a Chinatown vice squad—(1907–10), and lieutenant (August 1910). On the way he was awarded the Police Bronze Medal for fidelity (the only one awarded) in 1908. Sebastian was made chief of police, the youngest officer ever appointed (age thirty-seven) on 23 December 1910 and took over the department in the new year, 3 January 1911.

Already a well-known vice crusader and a darling of the progressive Good Government League, Chief Sebastian was encouraged by reform Mayor George Alexander (*q.v.*) to launch a war on crime. An able administrator and disciplinarian, and a courageous police officer, Sebastian proved successful as a crimebuster. In one dramatic episode, when threatened in his office by an angry man with a box of eighty sticks of dynamite, he kept talking to him until officers could maneuver to grab the man.

Encouraged by such a reputation, Sebastian ran for mayor in June 1915, but ironically he was indicted and put on trial during the campaign, for corruption of a minor. It was alleged that he carried on a torrid affair with one Lillian Pratt while her underage sister looked on (a jailable, criminal offense). A month of lurid evidence kept the local papers lively, but on the eve of the primary election a would-be assassin narrowly missed him with two bullets and the sympathy vote carried Sebastian through the primary and the final election with an overwhelming majority. Meanwhile, the jury acquitted him of the morals charges.

Sebastian's tenure as mayor was brief and ineffective. The press continued their attacks—regular front-page cartoons, for instance, in the Los Angeles *Record*, and Mayor Sebastian continued his love affair, dismissing his wife as a "haybag." An outraged delegation of civic leaders, no doubt remembering the glowing accounts they had given of Sebastian as police chief, placed a letter of resignation on his desk, which the mayor signed. His term had run from June 1915 to 2 September 1916: a meteoric career, from crusader to alleged corrupter. He died on 7 April 1937.

SOURCES: R. J. Burdette, *American Biography and Genealogy:* California Edition (Chicago, 1923), vol. 2; California Biography File, Los Angeles Public Library; B. Hentsell, *Los Angeles* Magazine, January 1978; Tom Moran, *Los Angeles* Magazine, March 1977; Los Angeles *Times*, 8 April 1937.   Peter d'A. Jones

SEDITA, FRANK ALBERT (1907–75), Mayor of Buffalo (1958–61, 1966–73). Mayor during years of turbulence and urban decline, Sedita was born in New Orleans on 20 June 1907, the son of Vincent (1879–1964)

and Crocifissa (Militello) Sedita, both Italian, Roman Catholic immigrants. One of eight children, Sedita moved to Buffalo with his family as a child. Attending local schools, he spent much of his childhood as a shoeshine boy. He worked his way through Canisius College as a busboy and graduated from the University of Buffalo in 1931 (LL.B.). Sedita began his legal practice in 1932, and his political career started the next year, with a stream of public offices. He served as deputy sheriff (1933–35), assistant corporation counsel (1935–38), secretary of the city's water division (1938–41), clerk of the city court (1941–47), first deputy of the surrogate court (1947–49), and associate judge of the city court (1949–57). On 11 July 1934, he married Sara R. Vacanti, a Buffalo Italian-American Catholic, and they had two children. The Seditas attended Holy Cross Church.

A life-long Democrat, Sedita was elected mayor in 1957, defeating Republican Chester Kowal (*q.v.*) in a close race, with 72,306 votes to 72,246 for Kowal, 45,759 for Elmer Lux (Independent Citizens), and 1,835 for James Peck (Liberal). In 1961, Sedita ran as an Independent and lost, with 62,196 votes to 74,995 for Kowal, 52,899 for Victor E. Manz (Democrat), and 8,016 for Peter Carr (Peoples). In 1965, Sedita was elected over Roland Benzow (Republican) 92,950 to 81,191. In 1969, he defeated Mrs. Alfreda Slominski (Republican-Conservative), and Ambrose I. Lane (Unity Independent), 87,319 to 67,880 and 7,430, respectively. Buffalo had 632,759 people in 1960 (a figure that declined to 462,768 in 1970), and a mayor-council form of government.

Personally popular, Sedita was a supporter of increased state and federal aid to big cities. He also backed tax cuts in his first term but supported a modest sales tax in his second term. He actively campaigned for civic improvements to halt the decline of downtown Buffalo. He backed housing improvements and civil rights, claiming he was a mayor for all ethnic groups. Although privately supporting the salary grievances of city workers, Sedita successfully prevented major strikes by the police and fire department. Sedita's political career continued in a minor way outside the mayor's office, for he was collector of customs for Buffalo, 1961–65 (between terms), and a member of the Crime Victims' Compensation Board. He was appointed to the latter post after resigning as mayor in 1973, because of ill health, and served until his death on 2 May 1975.

SOURCES: Buffalo *Evening News*, 2 May 1975; New York *Times*, 3 May 1975.   Thomas R. Bullard

SEIDEL, EMIL (1864–1947), Mayor of Milwaukee (1910–12). First Socialist mayor of Milwaukee, Seidel was born in Ashland, Pennsylvania, on 13 December

1864, the eldest of eleven children born to German-Lu-theran parents, Otto and Henrietta (Knoll) Seidel. His parents were Pomeranian immigrants; his father was a carpenter. The family moved first to Prairie du Chien, Wisconsin, then to Madison, and finally to Milwaukee, in the early 1870s. Emil attended public school until he was thirteen, when he became an apprentice woodcarver. His occupation and his German background involved Seidel in the activities of Milwaukee's growing Socialist movement; he became a party organizer at the age of nineteen. In 1886, he went to Germany where he lived for the next six years, refining both his woodcarving skills and his knowledge of socialism. Returning to Milwaukee in 1892, he married a German Lutheran, Lucy Geissel, on 8 May 1895, a union that ended in divorce in 1924 and produced two children, Lucius and Viola. Rising through Social Democratic circles, Seidel was elected alderman in 1904 and made an unsuccessful race for mayor in 1908, losing to perennial Democratic Mayor David Rose (*q.v.*) 23,106 to 20,887.

In 1910, Seidel was elected mayor of the city of 375,000 by a vote of 27,608 to 20,530 over Democrat Vincerz Schoenecker. Campaigning on a platform of municipal ownership and promising honest and efficient administration, the Social Democrats swept the city council and the entire range of city and county offices, gaining support from labor, Progressives, and structural reformers. As mayor, Seidel established a bureau of efficiency and economy, improved municipal services, and won a minimum wage at union scale for most city employees. He was unable to effect municipal ownership of any of Milwaukee's utilities, however, because of the existence of state franchises and the opposition of non-Socialists. Seidel also came under fire for appointing only Social Democrats to office, clashed with the Electric Company over trolley transfer policy, and fought with Police Chief John T. Janssen over endorsement of anti-vice ordinances. In a campaign marred by red-baiting, Seidel lost his bid for reelection in 1912 to Gerhard Bading (*q.v.*), a fusion candidate supported by both major parties, 43,176 to 30,272.

For the remainder of his life, "Unser Emil" (Our Emil) remained active in Social Democratic politics. In 1912, he was Eugene Debs' running mate in the U.S. presidential election, and in 1914, he lost his final mayoral race to Bading 37,673 to 29,122. In 1917, he openly opposed the city's loyalty ordinance and was arrested and fined for an antiwar speech in November that year. Reelected alderman in 1916, he served periodically in that post for the next twenty years, and in 1932, he was an unsuccessful candidate for the U.S. Senate. Seidel died in Milwaukee on 24 June 1947 and was buried there.

SOURCES: Edward S. Kerstein, *Milwaukee's All-*

American Mayor: Portrait of Daniel Webster Hoan (Englewood Cliffs, N.J., 1966); Milwaukee *Journal*, 25 June 1947; Frederick I. Olson, "The Milwaukee Socialists, 1897–1941" (Ph.D. dissertation, Harvard University, 1952); Emil Seidel, "Unpublished Autobiography," Area Research Center, University of Wisconsin-Milwaukee, n.d.   *John D. Buenker*

SELBY, THOMAS HENRY (1820–75), Mayor of San Francisco (1869–71). Selby, millionaire mayor of San Francisco, was born on 14 May 1820 in New York City. His parents, who had three sons and four daughters besides Thomas, were Captain John Selby, merchant and shipowner descended from old English colonist stock, and Sarah (Carmer) Selby, of Dutch and Scots extraction. Tutored privately until the age of sixteen or seventeen, Selby then joined a New York mercantile firm. When business failed in 1849, Selby entered the Gold Rush to California to repay the firm's debts and to build his fortune. He quickly prospered from trade, mineral investments, and a thriving San Francisco metalworks. His phenomenally rapid business success helped to launch his political career.

In April 1851, Selby was selected assistant alderman as a member of the Whig party. The following year he became a full alderman for one two-year term. Afterwards, he shunned public office until 1869 but remained active as president of the city's merchant exchange.

Selby married Jane Williams (d. 1848), and they had two children. In San Francisco, he met and married Henrietta I. Reese from Tuscaloosa, Alabama, who had a daughter by a previous marriage. Selby and his second wife added four more offspring, finally totaling three sons and four daughters. Selby was an active Presbyterian all his adult life.

Selby reluctantly accepted the independent Taxpayers party nomination for mayor in 1869 and was soon endorsed by the Republicans as well. In the close election of 1 September, Selby received 9,415 votes in the city of 160,000, while his opponent, Democratic incumbent mayor Frank McCoppin (*q.v.*), tallied 9,298. This victory helped to break the Democrats' control of state and local politics. Sworn in on 5 December, Selby served one two-year term as mayor, working with San Francisco's board of supervisors, the legislative arm of municipal government. Involved in an unsuccessful bid for the state gubernatorial nomination in 1871, Selby declined to seek reelection and ended his term in December. Throughout his time in office, this wealthy businessman refused to accept the mayor's salary.

A socially-conscious millionaire, Selby brought cultural sophistication to public office, a quality desperately sought in the young city of San Francisco. This trait probably encouraged Selby to begin construction of a new city hall. Perhaps his most noteworthy quality was the fiscal conservatism reflected in his maintenance of the status quo and his twenty-one vetoes of measures passed by the largely Democratic board of supervisors. One key veto canceled a far-fetched scheme to drain Lake Tahoe in order to supply San Franciscans with water. Selby's fiscal conservatism contributed to the city's inability to cope with a rapid influx of unemployed men from slumping western mines.

Selby returned to his business in 1872. He died of pneumonia three years later, on 9 June 1875.

SOURCES: Gunther Barth, *Instant Cities: Urbanization and the Rise of San Francisco and Denver* (New York, 1975); William J. Heintz, *San Francisco's Mayors 1850–1880* (Woodside, Calif., 1975); "Memoir of Thomas H. Selby, Together with the Funeral Discourse, by Rev. John Hemphill," 1875 (Bancroft Library, University of California, Berkeley); Alonzo Phelps, *Contemporary Biography of California's Representative Men* (San Francisco, 1881), vol. 1.

John M. Findlay

SENTER, GEORGE B. (1827–1870), Mayor of Cleveland (1859–61, 1864–65). Senter was born in Potsdam, New York, in 1827. He moved west to Cleveland in 1851, beginning a successful legal practice. He had been married before his arrival in Cleveland, and he and his wife Delia had at least one child; they were Protestants. Senter was a director of the Washington Union Insurance Company in 1853 and a member of the city council, 1858–59. A Republican, Senter was elected mayor in 1859, defeating Democrat James Coffinberry 3,491 to 2,871. He was defeated in 1861 by Edward S. Flint (q.v.) (Democrat) 3,890 to 3,172. Cleveland had 43,417 people in 1860 and a mayor-council form of government.

Personally popular, Senter supported civic improvements in his first term in office. Strenuously pro-Union, in 1863 he became commander of Camp Cleveland, with the rank of colonel. He became mayor again in May 1864, when Mayor Irvine U. Masters (q.v.) resigned, chosen by the city council to complete the unexpired term. Senter's efforts to support the Union cause in the Civil War weakened his health, and he retired in 1865. His health never recovered, and he died on 16 January 1870.

SOURCES: Cleveland *Leader*, 17 January 1870; Cleveland *Plain Dealer*, 17 January 1870; William C. Rose, *Cleveland: The Making of a City* (Cleveland, 1950). *Thomas R. Bullard*

SHAKSPEARE, JOSEPH A. (1837–1896), Mayor of New Orleans (1880–82, 1888–92). Reform mayor, born in New Orleans on 12 April 1837, Shakspeare was the son of Samuel Shakspeare, a Quaker, and Mariane Mathias, a native of Switzerland. The oldest of seven children, Joseph went to New York to study iron design and returned to New Orleans to become proprietor of a local ironworks. In 1863, he married Antoinette Kroos, who was born in Berlin, Germany, and they had five children.

New Orleans in 1880 had a population of 216,000 and a weak mayor-council form of government. The politically inexperienced Shakspeare accepted the nomination for mayor in 1880 on the reformers' ticket, to oust a scandal-ridden Democratic administration. Shakspeare won the election closely, 9,803 votes to the "Ring" candidate's (Jules Denis) 9,362. Being the only reformer elected, Shakspeare faced a hostile administrative board and an intractable city council. Even so, his accomplishments were considerable: he straightened out the city's chaotic budget and rescheduled its repayment plan, and also sold a city street railway franchise which produced sorely needed revenue. He worked out the famous "Shakspeare Plan," an extralegal technique by which gambling houses (all of which were illegal) paid a regular monthly tribute into the city treasury. Shakspeare's reform record was tarnished by a struggle against the council and police board to take patronage control of the police for the mayor's office. An anomalous situation developed which produced a three-way gun battle that killed one of the mayor's appointees in 1881 and led to a new charter for the city.

In 1888, Shakspeare was again a candidate for the reform ticket for mayor and beat the "Ring" favorite and regular Democrat, Judge Robert C. Davey, by a vote of 23,313 to 15,635. Shakspeare's second four-year term (as provided for in the new charter) saw additional street paving, the introduction of electrically operated street lights and street railways, and a new debt settlement scheme of 1890 that improved upon his first plan of 1880. He also created a professional fire department, and, by replacing the volunteer companies, he provoked some criticism. The mayor's efforts to exert patronage control over the police department turned some reformers against him. Shakspeare then appointed David C. Hennessy, described as one of the most brilliant and dedicated law enforcement officers the city had ever known, as chief. Hennessey's assassination in 1890, allegedly by the "mafia," and the lynching of several Italian immigrant suspects, led to a serious international incident. When Shakspeare's second term drew to a close in 1892, the controversial and somewhat tarnished reformer ran again but lost to the regular Democratic candidate for mayor. He died on 22 January 1896 in New Orleans.

SOURCES: "Biographies of the Mayors of New Orleans" (typescript, Works Progress Administration, New

Orleans, 1940); Joy J. Jackson, *New Orleans in the Gilded Age* (Baton Rouge, La., 1969).

Melvin G. Holli

SHAW, FRANK L. (1877–1958), Mayor of Los Angeles (1933–38). A big city mayor who was recalled, Shaw was born in Canada on 1 February 1877 near Warwick, Ontario. He was the son of John Shaw, a Scots-Irish farmer, rancher, and coal dealer, and Katherine S. (Roche) Shaw. The elder of two children, Frank Shaw attended a series of public and private schools, while his family moved first to Detroit in 1883, then to Joplin, Missouri, Hays City, Kansas, and finally to Denver, Colorado. While working on a ranch, Shaw was afflicted with polio which left him with a noticeable limp the rest of his life. Beginning in 1895, he began his business career as a clerk in a country store, and over the next thirty years, he worked in every facet of the wholesale and retail grocery trade representing such firms as the Cudahy Packing Company and the Haas-Baruch Company. In 1905, he married the former Cora H. Shires, a Texas schoolteacher, and in 1909, they moved to Los Angeles and settled in a home near the corner of Fifty-ninth and Main streets. Shaw was a member of the Chamber of Commerce, the United Commercial Travelers of America, and the Los Angeles Athletic and Jonathon clubs. He was a Presbyterian, Mason (32°), Shriner, Elk, Moose, Eagle, and Maccabee.

Shaw's Republican political career began in 1925 when he was elected to the city council, and he was reelected two years later. In 1928, elected to the county board of supervisors, he became popular for his ability to obtain federal funds; in 1932, he became chairman. On 6 June 1933, Shaw was elected mayor 187,053 to 155,513.

At the beginning of Shaw's term, Los Angeles was suffering from a 40 percent unemployment rate. Shaw traveled to Washington, D.C., and obtained $3 million of an eventual $100 million in federal funds for the Works Progress Administration and other New Deal projects. He was noted for his total commitment to public ownership, and during his administration, he made the Department of Water and Power the sole distributor of electricity within the city limits.

Shaw was the first mayor of Los Angeles to be recalled. After winning reelection on 4 May 1937, with 54 percent of the vote (169,848 to 144,079), his administration was riddled with scandal. The climax came on 14 January 1938, when Harry Raymond, an investigator for a reform group, was nearly killed by a bomb planted by Captain Earl Kynette of the police intelligence squad. Kynette's conviction, along with that of two city commissioners for vice and labor racketeering, led to Shaw's recall on 16 September 1938. The vote was 122,196 for Shaw and 232,686 for Fletcher Bowron (*q.v.*), a superior court judge.

Following the recall, Shaw's brother and personal secretary, Joseph Shaw, was convicted of civil service fraud, and *Liberty* magazine claimed that the Shaw administration had been in league with the underworld. But the former mayor was exonerated of all malfeasance when the state supreme court overturned his brother's conviction and when *Liberty*, faced with a libel suit, settled out of court for $50,000 and a public apology. Shaw ran again for mayor in 1941 but was defeated in the primary. He sought to fill a vacancy on the board of supervisors in 1944, to no avail.

On his return to private life, Shaw became the president of the NO Flame Chemical Corporation, and later, he led a successful career in real estate. Shaw died of cancer on 24 January 1958.

SOURCES: John R. Haynes Collection, Government Documents, UCLA Research Library; *Los Angeles Times*, 25 January 1958; Joseph E. Shaw Papers, and Clifford E. Clinton Papers, Special Collections, UCLA Research Library; Harold H. Story, *Memoirs of Harold H. Story* (Oral History Project, UCLA, 1967).

Fred W. Viehe

SHELLEY, JOHN FRANCIS (1905–74), Mayor of San Francisco (1964–68). Shelley was a Roman Catholic and a native son of the city, born there on 3 September 1905, the son of Denis Shelley and Mary (Casy) Shelley. Educated in local parochial and public schools, Shelley attended the University of San Francisco Law School, specializing in labor law and graduating in 1932 (LL.B.). He married Genevieve Giler, and they had a daughter, Joan Marie (born on 15 June 1933). After his first wife's death, Shelley married Thelma Smith in Washington, D.C. (6 June 1953). They had two children, Kathleen Patricia (b. 12 August 1954) and Kevin Francis (b. 6 November 1955).

Shelley served thirteen years as president of the San Francisco Labor Council, AFL, and four years as president of the California State Federation of Labor, AFL. A Democrat, he was elected to the state Senate, 1939–46, and was very popular in his Fifth District. He was always known familiarly as "Jack." In 1946, he was elected to the U.S. House of Representatives and served eight terms—no candidate had even filed against him.

On 5 November 1963, Shelley defeated Supervisor Harold Dobbs for mayor of San Francisco, 120,560 votes to 92,627, with the help of labor support from longshoreman Harry Bridges. Shelley refused a second term because of ill health. Despite his years in other elected office, he regarded the mayoralty of San Francisco with some distaste. He complained: "The job of Mayor is an endless, impossible and exhausting drain, trying not only to keep a city intact, but on the right track." Shelley nevertheless retained enough enthusiasm for his city to work as its lobbyist in Sacramento until his death on 1 September 1974.

SOURCES: R. E. Burke, *Olson's New Deal for California* (Berkeley, Calif., 1953); *San Francisco Business*, July 1967; San Francisco *Examiner*, 30 April 1967.   *Peter d'A. Jones*

SHEPLEY, GEORGE FOSTER (1819–78), Military Mayor of New Orleans (1862). Following the federal occupation of Confederate New Orleans, Shepley served briefly as the first military mayor. A native of Maine, Shepley was born on 1 January 1819 to Anna (Foster) Shepley and Ether Shepley, a Congregationalist, a lawyer, and later a U.S. senator and justice of the Supreme Court of Maine. Upon graduation from Dartmouth in 1837, Shepley studied law at Harvard and worked in his father's office. In 1839, he began practicing law in Bangor, Maine. During 1844, the young lawyer married Lucy A. Hayes, and they moved to Portland, Maine. Rising in Democratic political circles, Shepley secured the post of U.S. district attorney for Maine under Presidents Polk, Pierce, and Buchanan. As a delegate to the 1860 national Democratic conventions in Charleston and Baltimore, he met Benjamin Butler of Massachusetts (who would later appoint him mayor of New Orleans). Although Shepley lost his federal appointment when the Republicans won the presidency, the Civil War enabled him to continue in public service as the colonel of the Twelfth Regiment of Maine Volunteers. This unit accompanied General Benjamin Butler's New England division to the Gulf in early 1862.

Soon after the Union forces captured New Orleans, Butler appointed Shepley military commandant of the city. Butler eventually removed the intransigent Confederate Mayor John T. Monroe (*q.v.*) and on 20 May 1862 installed Shepley as acting mayor. Governing an occupied city of some 140,000, many of them rebels, was no easy task, nor was dealing with his imperious superior officer from Massachusetts. Shepley's relations with Butler were sometimes strained. Moreover, Shepley was eventually implicated in some of the scandals that resulted from Butler's service in Louisiana.

Mayor Shepley is best remembered as the firm, though dignified, administrator who tackled the problems of worthless currencies and terrible filth in New Orleans by issuing city notes and creating a public works program. He also fixed the price of bread, which was in very short supply, and began registering Confederates and aliens. Shepley dismissed the civilian aldermen in June because

they refused to take the oath of allegiance to the United States; a system of martial law modeled on the previous government of New Orleans began at this time and lasted four years. The effort to clean up the Crescent City was well underway when the acting mayor was replaced on 11 July 1862.

President Lincoln so thoroughly approved of Shepley's performance that he appointed this prominent Democrat the military governor of Louisiana and promoted him to brigadier general. Shepley held this position for two years, his primary task being to encourage a native unionist movement. After supervising elections in occupied Louisiana in 1864, he was placed in command of the District of Eastern Virginia. Shepley then served as the military governor of Richmond until resigning his commission on 1 July 1865 to return to his law office in Maine.

Shepley left the private practice of law in 1869 to become a judge on the federal circuit court. His first wife having died in 1859, Judge Shepley married Helen Merrill in 1872. He died in Portland, Maine, of Asiatic cholera on 20 July 1878, survived by his second wife and two daughters.

SOURCES: John Smith Kendall, *History of New Orleans*, 2 vols. (Chicago, 1922), vol. 1; "Letterbooks of New Orleans Mayors" (1862), New Orleans Public Library; "Mayors of New Orleans, 1803–1936," (Works Progress Administration, typescript in New Orleans Public Library, New Orleans, 1940); Peter Ripley, *Slaves and Freemen in Civil War Louisiana* (Baton Rouge, La., 1976).   *D. Blake Touchstone*

SHERMAN, ALSON SMITH (1811–1903), Mayor of Chicago (1844–45). Eighth mayor of Chicago, Sherman was a transplanted Yankee, born in Barre, Vermont, on 21 April 1811, the oldest child of Nathaniel and Deborah (Webster) Sherman. Trained by his father, a mason and builder, he moved to Chicago, arriving on 1 November 1836, and became a successful building contractor and building materials wholesaler. He founded the important Lemont Marble quarries, from which came the so-called Athens marble of which many of Chicago's fine buildings were constructed. The quarry was twenty-one miles to the southeast, convenient to the Illinois and Michigan Canal, between Lemont and Joliet. Sherman also opened Chicago's first sawmill and traded in lumber and ice. He had nine children and was an active Methodist.

Chicago in 1844 had over 10,000 people and a mayor-council form of government, with a one-year term for mayor. Sherman had been chief of the fire department, 1841–44, and was elected alderman (Third Ward in 1842, and again in 1849 and 1850 for the Fourth Ward). He ran successfully for mayor in 1844 as an Independent

Democrat in a special election called after the regular election, won by Augustus Garrett (*q.v.*), 805 to 798, over a Whig opponent, George Dole. This election was nullified because a Garrett election judge was discovered to be not yet a U.S. citizen. In the special election, Sherman had the support of the Whigs and defeated Garrett 837 to 694, with an abolitionist (Liberty party) candidate, Henry Smith, getting 126 votes.

At this time, Chicago's main business thoroughfare, Lake Street, was first planked. There was still no real police department, order being maintained by a city marshal and a few constables. Water was privately supplied by pipes from Lake Michigan and by water carts. Sherman's chief accomplishment was to help establish a municipal waterworks to secure a better water supply for the growing city. He also promoted public schools. He served as mayor from 7 April 1844 to 5 March 1845.

Sherman was one of the original trustees of Northwestern University, at that time still located in the city. (It moved to Evanston in 1854.) He died in Waukegan, Illinois, on 22 September 1903.

SOURCES: A. T. Andreas, *History of Chicago* (Chicago, 1884); Don Fehrenbacher, *Chicago Giant: Long John Wentworth* (Madison, Wis., 1957); Bessie L. Pierce, *History of Chicago* (New York, 1937–57); Frederick Rex, comp., *The Mayors of the City of Chicago* (Chicago, 1933). *Leslie V. Tischauser*

SHERMAN, FRANCIS CORNWALL (1805–70), Mayor of Chicago (1841–42, 1862–65). Businessman, politician, and fifth mayor of Chicago, Sherman was born 18 September 1805 in Newtown, Connecticut, the only child of Ezra and Mary Sherman, both Protestants of English descent. After public school, Sherman became a clerk, eventually moving to Danbury, where he married a local girl, Electa Trowbridge (1806–81), on 30 January 1825. They had six children, four of whom reached adulthood.

Seeking success, Sherman and his family arrived in Chicago in 1834, where he opened a tavern. By 1835, Sherman had added a line of wagons between Chicago and Galena, Illinois. He also opened the town's first brick kiln and the City Hotel in 1836. The hotel was renamed the Sherman House in 1844 and became a Chicago landmark. Sherman was vice-president of the Chicago Gas-Light and Coke Company, 1848–50. By 1850, at the age of forty-five, he had earned enough money to retire from most business activity.

In 1835, Sherman had been elected a town trustee. He was known as a Jacksonian Democrat. In 1837, he was elected Second Ward alderman. He lost the 1840 election for city treasurer but was elected a county commissioner, serving until 1845. In 1841, he was elected Chicago's

fifth mayor, defeating the Whig Issac Gwinn 460 to 419. At that time, Chicago had 5,500 people and a mayor-council form of government. Sherman also served as city treasurer (1842–43) and then was elected to three terms in the state assembly (1844–49) where Sherman supported all legislation favorable to Chicago's interests. In 1847, he was a delegate to the state's constitutional convention, supporting clauses restricting banks. Chairman of the board of county supervisors (1851–53), Sherman was an unsuccessful candidate for the mayoralty in 1852 and for the legislature in 1858.

In 1862, Sherman was again elected mayor, defeating Republican Charles Holden 7,437 to 6,254. Chicago had by then grown to 138,186 people. A "War Democrat," Sherman backed civic reform and the building of new water and sewer lines. He lost the 1862 congressional election but won reelection as mayor in 1863, defeating Unionist Thomas Bryan 10,252 to 10,095. Both the 1862 congressional and 1863 mayoral elections were characterized by bitter partisan attacks. Despite charges that he was a Copperhead, Sherman actively supported the Union war effort and opposed all corruption and profiteering. Wartime hysteria caused his defeat in 1865 and 1867.

Sherman was vice-president of the Merchants' Farmers' and Mechanics' Savings Bank (1861–70), his last major activity at the time of his fatal heart attack on 7 November 1870.

SOURCES: A. T. Andreas, *History of Chicago*, 3 vols. (Chicago, 1884–86); *The Biographical Encyclopedia of Illinois of the Nineteenth Century* (Philadelphia, 1875); Francis A. Eastman, comp., *Chicago City Manual, 1911* (Chicago, 1911); Bessie L. Pierce, *A History of Chicago*, 3 vols. (New York, 1937–57); Roy V. Sherman, *The New England Shermans* (Akron, Ohio, 1974). *Thomas R. Bullard*

SHURTLEFF, NATHANIEL BRADSTREET (1810–74), Mayor of Boston (1868–70). A noted antiquarian, Shurtleff was born in Boston on 29 June 1810, the son of Dr. Benjamin Shurtleff (c. 1774–1847) and Sally (Shaw) Shurtleff (d. 1865). He was educated at Boston Latin School, the Round Hill School in Northampton, Harvard College (A.B., 1831), and Harvard Medical School (M.D., 1834). In 1836, he married Eliza Susan Smith (d. 1887) of Boston. They had seven children.

Shurtleff joined his father in the practice of medicine, but his interests soon turned elsewhere. Descended from *Mayflower* families on both sides, Shurtleff was conscious of his heritage and developed a strong interest in antiquarian affairs, especially those pertaining to the early history of Massachusetts. His antiquarian concerns were matched by his concerns for the contemporary condition of Boston. He became a tireless worker for the cultural institutions, public and private, and were prominent in the rapidly growing city (250,000 by 1870). These included the School Committee, the Boston Public Library, Harvard University, the Massachusetts Historical Society, the Society for Natural History, and the Masons. He also became interested in Boston politics.

Boston municipal politics had traditionally been factional or single-issue in nature, but the growth of the population in size and diversity made such traditional forms less useful. Shurtleff's political career reflected the uncertain experimentation with political organizations of the time. He first ran for mayor of Boston in 1855 as a candidate of the Native American party, losing to Alexander H. Rice (q.v.), candidate of the nonpartisan Citizens Convention (5,390 to 7,401). A decade later, he ran as a Democrat against the incumbent, Citizen-Republican endorsed, Frederic W. Lincoln (q.v.) and was defeated again, (3,690 to 4,520). The following year, 1866, he ran against the Republican Otis Norcross (q.v.) and was defeated yet again (4,755 to 5,662). Finally, in December 1867 he triumphed against Norcross (8,383 to 7,867) and began the first of three terms. In 1868, the Republicans reverted to endorsing an old antislavery partisan, Moses Kimball, and Shurtleff won in a hotly contested race (11,005 to 9,156). Finally, in 1869, amid rumors of Shurtleff's nativism and anti-Democratic bias, the city's Democrats abandoned him and nominated George Baldwin as their candidate. Shurtleff, however, was endorsed by the Citizens and belatedly by the Republicans, and he won easily (13,054 to 4,790). Thoroughly vindicated, he retired at the end of his 1870 term.

Inspired by the dynamism of Boston in the post-Civil War years, Shurtleff supported the activist and expensive policies of a municipal government that was an initiator in civic improvements. This was a tradition espoused by Frederic W. Lincoln in his second administration (1863–66) but rejected by his one-term successor, Otis Norcross (1867). Shurtleff was not an initiator himself, but his enthusiasm for these improvements made his administration very supportive of them. Thus, by the end of his administration, Shurtleff could glory in the annexation of Dorchester and Roxbury, which enlarged the original small city fourfold; expansion of the waterfront and construction of Atlantic Avenue; aggressive policy of extending, paving, and even raising streets; and enlargement of water, police, fire departments.

After his mayoralty, Shurtleff continued his public service and wrote the *Topographical and Historical Development of Boston* (1871). His amiable, if somewhat diffuse, personality made him a popular figure. He died

unexpectedly of a stroke on 17 October 1874. Funeral services were held at his home in newly annexed Dorchester, and burial was in Mount Auburn Cemetery, Cambridge, Massachusetts.

SOURCES: Boston *Transcript*, 18 October 1874 (obituary); J. M. Bugbee, "Boston Under the Mayors," in Justin Winsor, ed., *The Memorial History of Boston*, 4 vols. (Boston, 1881), vol. 3; City of Boston, Massachusetts, *Documents, 1868, 1869, 1870*, (Boston, 1868–70); *Proceedings of Massachusetts Historical Society* 13 (December 1874); Shurtleff Family Papers, Massachusetts Historical Society, Boston (small, miscellaneous collection); Works by Shurtleff include his editing of *Records of the Governor and Company of Massachusetts Bay in New England 1630–1686*, 5 vols. (Boston, 1853–54) and of *The Records of the Colony of New Plymouth in New England*, 8 vols. (Boston, 1855–57); also *The Topographical and Historical Development of Boston* (Boston, 1871); and minor tracts such as *The Epitome of Phrenology* (Boston, 1837) and *Thunder and Lightning & Death in Marshfield*.

Constance Burns

SMALL, JACOB (c. 1772–1851), Mayor of Baltimore (1826–31). Small was Baltimore's first mayor to rise from its artisan class. His father, Jacob Small, Sr. (d. c. 1794), was a builder-architect who built the Otterbein Church in 1785. While both parents were buried in the Episcopal cemetery, little is known about his mother, Anne Barbara Small (d. 1791). Jacob Small, Jr., was probably born in Baltimore in 1772. He followed his father's profession, submitted plans for the federal capitol in 1792, and became a successful Baltimore builder. He married twice: in 1794, to Nancy Fleetwood (c. 1772–1824) with whom he had three children, all of whom died by 1824; and in 1827 to Catherine Young of Chambersburg, Pennsylvania, by whom he had at least two children. He joined the militia, fought in the defense of Baltimore in 1814, and rose to the rank of colonel in the Thirty-ninth Regiment.

Prior to becoming mayor, Small was elected to the lower house of the city council (1805–10) and to one term in the upper house (1823). He belonged to the Democratic-Republican party, but became a National Republican in the 1820s and a Whig in the 1830s. Following an unsuccessful bid for reelection in 1832, he returned to his profession until his death in 1851. Small was a member of St. Peter's Episcopal Church.

Baltimore underwent important political and economic changes during this era. Its population grew from 62,738 (1820) to 80,620 (1830), and ward boundaries were redrawn in 1831. It had a mayor-city council form of government in which the mayor was elected indirectly to a two-year term. The very title of the "Mechanics ticket" for Small in 1824, when he served as a spoiler in the traditional rivalry between Edward Johnson (*q.v.*) and John Montgomery (*q.v.*), illuminates an important change in local politics. Now men with resources other than ties to the merchant elite could compete successfully for the mayor's office. Jacob Small represented small businessmen. Although he lost in 1824 in the city's indirect elections (Montgomery, 3,333; Johnson, 2,994; Small, 950), his ticket beat the incumbent mayor's in 1826 (Small, 4,841; Montgomery, 2,646), and he won reelection in 1828 (Small, 4,551; James Mosher, 3,150) and again in 1830 (Small, 4,844; Colonel Barry, 3,821). He temporarily resigned for reasons of health in 1831 but ran for reelection in 1832 against the popular Jacksonian politician, Jesse Hunt (*q.v.*), and lost (Hunt, 5,369; Small, 3,532).

The emergence of a national two-party competition so heated municipal elections in this period that the poll was changed from early to late October in an unsuccessful effort at depoliticization. During Small's administration, there was a subtle shift in municipal priorities. City government continued to deal with its traditional problems, such as harbor improvements, sanitation, water, and lighting, and to work on new ones, such as the establishment of a public school system, but it recognized that Baltimore's growth could be guaranteed only by direct linkage to the Ohio Valley. From the mid-1820s on, the city government invested heavily in internal improvements, especially in railroads, in an effort to assure future prosperity.

SOURCES: Baltimore *American and Commercial Advertiser*, 27 September, 5 October 1824, 3 October, 7 November 1826, 20 and 21 October, 4 November 1828, 19 October, 2 November 1830; Baltimore *Patriot and Mercantile Advertiser*, 16 October 1832; Gary L. Browne, "Baltimore and the Nation, 1789–1861" (Ph.D. dissertation, Wayne State University, 1973); Jeanne F. Butler, "Competition 1792: Designing a Nation's Capitol," *Capitol Studies* 4: 1 (1976); *Mayor's Messages* (Baltimore, 1827–31); Dielman-Hayward File, Maryland Historical Society; Whitman H. Ridgway, *Community Leadership in Maryland, 1790–1840* (Chapel Hill, N.C., 1979).   *Whitman H. Ridgway*

SMITH, AMOR, JR. (1840–1915), Mayor of Cincinnati (1885–89). Smith, energetic reform mayor of Cincinnati and of English descent, was born in Dayton, Ohio, on 22 October 1840. He was the son of a Yorkshire woman, Sarah (Spencer) Smith, born in Hull, England, and Amor Smith of Newcastle County, Delaware. In 1847, the Smith family moved to Cincinnati. After attending Herons Private School and the Swedenborgian

University, Smith, in 1865, joined Amor Smith and Company, his father's and brother's fertilizer and candle manufacturing business. Shortly thereafter, his brother moved to Baltimore and established a branch there. On 27 May 1863, Smith married Mary Jane (Kessler) Smith of Cincinnati, a German from Saxony, and in 1872 moved with her to Baltimore to help his brother. Following the death of this wife in 1873, Smith and his three children, Kessler (b. 1865), Alvin (b. 1867), and Leonora (b. 1871), returned to the Cincinnati branch of the business.

In Cincinnati, Smith became an active Republican. In 1875, he was chairman of the Republican Executive Committee of Hamilton County and was appointed an internal revenue collector. He worked tirelessly for the election of Rutherford B. Hayes. He was the chairman of the campaign committee to raise the bond to finance the Cincinnati Southern Railway. He was nominated, although not elected, for Congress in 1882, and in 1884, he served as a delegate to the Republican national convention. In 1885, he received the Republican nomination for mayor and defeated George Gerke by a vote of 14,834 to 13,168.

Cincinnati in 1885 had over 225,000 people and a mayor-council form of government. Smith campaigned as the representative of the party dedicated to restoring law and order to Cincinnati, to eliminating corruption and extravagance in city affairs, and to reducing taxes. He won the election, carrying fourteen of the city's twenty-five wards. In 1887, Smith won a second term with 11,351 votes to W. H. Stevenson's 10,008 and Isaac B. Matson's 6,820. His challenge in this election did not come from the Democratic candidate Matson, but from the recently established Union Labor party's candidate W. H. Stevenson. Under Smith's management, Cincinnati became a "model" municipality. He reorganized the municipal police force and served as the head of Cincinnati's first professional police department. Smith handled the 1886 labor uprising skillfully. When the freight handlers of the Cincinnati, Hamilton, and Dayton Railroad struck for higher wages, Smith, unlike Mayor Thomas J. Stephens (*q.v.*) during the 1884 riots, dealt with the situation adeptly. Before the situation got out of hand, he called a meeting of representatives from all the labor organizations and companies involved in the strike and settled labor-management difficulties through peaceful arbitration.

At the conclusion of his second term, Smith was appointed surveyor of customs for the port of Cincinnati (1889–94, 1903–10). Smith and his second wife, Ida (Sennett) Smith (married on 3 August 1887), were familiar figures in Cincinnati society. Smith was a Scottish Rite Mason and an active member of the Syrian Temple,

Nobles of the Mystic Shrine, the Young Men's Blaine Club, the Protective Order of the Elks, and apparently a Swedenborgian by religion. He died in Cincinnati in 24 August 1915.

SOURCES: *Cincinnati's Mayors* (Cincinnati, 1957); Charles T. Greve, *Centennial History of Cincinnati and Representative Citizens* (Chicago, 1904); Zane L. Miller, *Boss Cox's Cincinnati: Urban Politics in the Progressive Era* (New York, 1968); G. M. Roe, *Our Police* (Cincinnati, 1890); G. F. Wright, *Representative Citizens of Ohio* (Cleveland, 1918).   *Patricia Mooney Melvin*

SMITH, HENRY K. (1811–54), Mayor of Buffalo (1850–51). English mayor of Buffalo, Smith was born on 2 April 1811 in St. Croix (Virgin Islands), the son of Jeremiah Smith, a local architect, and Jane (Cooper) Smith, both English-born and members of the Anglican Church. In 1815, the island became Danish, but his father's career continued with success until he was blinded in an accident. Mrs. Smith then took over the raising of their four children, instilling a desire for success in all of them. Young Henry had attended local schools but in 1819 was sent to Baltimore to be educated by a prominent Anglican teacher. Smith joined the church in 1824, winning praise for his remarkable intellectual gifts. In 1828, he went to New York City, working as a clerk in a dry goods store. Convinced that he could do better in law, he quit and moved to Johnstown, New York, where he studied with Judge Daniel Cody. In 1832, he began a successful legal practice. He married a Miss Vorhees of that town in 1834, but she died after only a year. In 1837, Smith moved to Buffalo and opened a law firm with George Clinton as his partner. Through the years his partners would include General Isaac Verplank and R. U. Stevens, perhaps an indication of his popularity. In 1848, he married a Miss Thompson of Buffalo, they had one son before her early death in 1850.

Smith was a Jacksonian Democrat, and his first political role was as a highly gifted orator. His friends included such powerful politicians as Martin Van Buren and William Marcy. He served as district attorney for Erie County in 1839 and as recorder for the city court of Buffalo, 1844–48. Smith unsuccessfully sought election to the New York House of Representatives, New York Senate, and U.S. Congress. In 1850, he was elected mayor, defeating Whig candidate Luman Plimpton 2,678 to 2,301. At that time, Buffalo had 42,261 people and a mayor-council form of government. As mayor, Smith supported various civic improvements but did not earn a reputation as an activist. After leaving office, he continued his legal practice until his death on 23 September 1854, at the early age of forty-three.

SOURCES: Alden Chester and F. M. Williams, *Courts and Lawyers of New York*, 3 vols. (New York, 1925); L. B. Proctor, *The Bench and Bar of New York*, 2 vols. (New York, 1870); U.S. Census for 1850—Buffalo volumes.   *Thomas R. Bullard*

SMITH, JEROME VAN CROWNINSHIELD (1800–79), Mayor of Boston (1854–55). Native American mayor and famous medical author, born in Conway, New Hampshire, on 20 July 1800, Smith was the son of Richard Ransom Smith (1773–1830), a physician and dentist, and Sally (Cumings) Smith, both of New England ancestry. Having received his early schooling in his native town, he did his undergraduate work at Brown University (1818) and received a medical degree from Williams College (1822). On 29 December 1825, he married Eliza Maria Brown, a descendant of Revolutionary War hero John Brown, and they had one son. They were Congregationalists.

Before Smith became mayor of Boston, he was very active in the field of medicine. He had lectured in anatomy and physiology at the Berkshire Medical Institution and at the New York Medical College before he was elected port physician of Boston (1826–29). A member of the Massachusetts Medical Society since 1824, he edited the *Boston Medical and Surgical Journal*, predecessor of the *New England Journal of Medicine*, for more than twenty years. A prolific author and editor, he was famous for his textbook on anatomy which underwent eleven editions in the nineteenth century.

Although he was trained in medicine, Smith had an interest in the politics of his adopted state. Not only did he serve in the Massachusetts General Court after his election to that body in 1837 and in 1848, but he was also a member of the Boston School Committee and a justice of the peace. In his first attempt at the mayoralty in 1852, he was defeated in a five-man contest in Boston when Benjamin Seaver (*q.v.*) emerged as the victor.

Smith won in 1854 polling 6,840 votes to J. H. Wilkin's 3,170, J. Whiting's 1,731, and A. Hobart's 282. He was reelected in 1855 drawing 6,427 votes to G. B. Upton's 4,435. Smith became mayor of a city that had about 140,000 people and a mayor-aldermen-council form of government. Even though he proposed a number of projects to improve Boston, he failed to carry out most of them because his powers were rather weak under the city charter. Consequently, apart from his reform of the police department, his administration failed to make significant improvements in municipal services.

Smith was a member of the Know-Nothing party, but there are later indications that he did not adhere fully to its principles. For he not only indulged his penchant for sculpturing by producing a bust of John Bernard Fitzpatrick, the Catholic bishop of Boston (1846–66), but he also helped to raise a regiment of Irish immigrants to fight for the Union in the Civil War. Smith himself served as acting inspector general in New Orleans with the rank of colonel in the same conflict.

Smith spent his last years in New York City where he lectured at the New York Medical College. He died of lung congestion on a visit to Richmond, Massachusetts, on 20 August 1879, and was buried in the Forest Mount area of Pittsfield Cemetery next to his wife who had died on 4 July 1876.

SOURCES: James Spear Loring, *The Hundred Boston Orators* (Boston, 1855); Pittsfield *Sun*, 24 August 1879 (obituary); State Street Trust Company, *Mayors of Boston* (Boston, 1914); Jerome Van Crowinshield Smith, *The Class-Book of Anatomy* (Boston, 1830); Jerome Van Crowninshield Smith Assorted Papers (an unpublished diary, covering 1848 to 1852, New England Historical and Genealogical Society, and some unpublished letters in both the Massachusetts Historical Society and the Francis A. Countway Library of Medicine); William H. Whitmore, ed., *The Inaugural Addresses of the Mayors of Boston* 2 vols. (Boston, 1894–96).

Vincent A. Lapomarda

SMITH, JOHN W. (1883–1942), Mayor of Detroit (1924–28, 1933–34). Born on 12 April 1883 to John W. and Gertrude Wax Smith, a poor German Catholic family on Detroit's East Side, young John, one of seven children, was left fatherless at age six. He was forced to sell newspapers and his formal education never went beyond the elementary grades. One of his later mentors called Smith a streetwise boy from Dutchtown who never read a book until he was seventeen. Smith enlisted in the Spanish-American War of 1898, remained on to fight the Filipino insurrection, and returned to Detroit in 1901. He earned his livelihood as a plumber's apprentice and steamfitter.

Smith made his political debut in 1906 as a Republican campaign worker and was taken under the wing of John C. Lodge (*q.v.*), the veteran Detroit politician. Smith then went on to other mentors and passed through a series of patronage jobs, including deputy U.S. marshall (1911), campaign worker for Governor Chase Osborn (1912), deputy state labor commissioner, deputy sheriff of Wayne County (1913), and deputy county clerk (1918–20). He also found time to serve in the state Senate but was rewarded with his most important appointment, postmaster of Detroit (1920–24), for helping to swing the Michigan presidential convention delegates to Warren Harding in 1920. Smith was married and the father of two children.

When Mayor Frank E. Doremus (*q.v.*) died in 1924, Smith was elected to fill his unexpired term and then went on in 1926 to win election to a full two-year term by a vote of 115,772 over Charles Bowles' (*q.v.*) 105,902 and J. Martin's 83,769. Detroit then had a mayor-council form of government and a population of well over a million. Smith later served as acting mayor (from 8 September 1933 to 2 January 1934). Although neither of his terms was marked by any great distinction, he was known as a fighting mayor who opposed the Ku Klux Klan's intervention into city politics, as a strong supporter of fiscal integrity, and as pro-labor in his sympathies. After he left the mayoralty, he served almost continuously on the city council until his death. Although he lived from the public payroll for a goodly portion of his life, the Detroit *Free Press* credited him with "none of the oily attributes of the common political type." Smith was stricken by tuberculosis and other ailments and died on 17 June 1942.

SOURCES: Biographical file, Detroit Public Library; Clarence M. Burton, *History of Wayne County and Detroit, Michigan* (Detroit-Chicago, 1922); Detroit *Free Press*, 18 June 1942; Detroit *News*, 18 June 1942.

Ben C. Wilson and Finney Ike Mlemchukwu

SMITH, SAMUEL (1752–1839), Mayor of Baltimore (1835–1838). Hero of the American Revolution and War of 1812 as well as a veteran of thirty years in Congress, Smith was chosen mayor by popular acclamation in 1835. Born in Carlisle, Pennsylvania, in 1752, he was the son of John Smith (1722–94), an Irish immigrant of Scots-Irish, Presbyterian descent, and Mary Buchanan, also of Lancaster County. The Smiths moved to Baltimore when Samuel, the eldest of their ten children, was six (1758). John Smith, who founded the importing firm of Smith and Buchanan, was soon considered one of the city's wealthiest merchants. Samuel was educated at private academies in Elkton, Maryland, and Newark, Delaware, and was apprenticed, and later worked in his father's firm, both in England and the United States. During the revolution, he enrolled as a captain and served in Colonel Smallwood's regiment at Fort Mifflin, Monmouth, White Plains, and Valley Forge. In the 1790s, he returned to military duty as a brigadier general commanding troops in the Whiskey Rebellion, and in 1812 he organized Baltimore's defenses against the British.

In 1778, Smith married Margaret Spear, who was also a Presbyterian, and eleven children were born to the couple, only six of whom survived childhood. In 1792, after a term in the Maryland House of Delegates, Smith was elected, as a Federalist, to the House of Representatives, where he served four more terms until in 1803 the legislature elected him to two terms in the U.S. Senate. It was during this period that Smith became an enthusiastic Jeffersonian and opposed the United States

Bank. From 1816 to 1822, Smith served as a congressman, and from 1822 to 1833 as a U.S. senator.

In 1835, after the failure of the Maryland Bank and attacks on the homes of bank officials, Mayor Jesse Hunt (*q.v.*) resigned. Smith was chosen mayor by popular acclamation and vote by the two branches of the city council, which, along with the mayor, governed Baltimore's nearly 100,000 citizens. The following year, although eighty-four, Smith was nearly unanimously reelected mayor, and this municipal service capped his long public career. Smith died within months of his retirement from office, on 22 April 1839.

SOURCES: Frank Cassell, *Merchant Congressman in the Young Republic, Samuel Smith of Maryland, 1752–1839* (Madison, Wis., 1971); John S. Pancake, *Samuel Smith and the Politics of Business 1752–1832* (University, Ala., 1972); Smith and Buchanan Letterbooks, Maryland Historical Society, Samuel Smith Papers, Library of Congress.   *Jean H. Baker*

SMITH, THOMAS B. (1869–1949), Mayor of Philadelphia (1916–20). Republican machine mayor, Smith was born on 2 November 1869, the son of Thomas B. and Isabella (Cairns) Smith of Philadelphia. Smith left the city's public schools at the age of twelve and held a number of clerical jobs before securing a position in what was to be his life-long profession, the bonding and surety business. Eventually, Smith became a vice-president of the National Surety Company, which bonded post office, municipal, and county employees. In 1896, he married Elisabeth Barrett; they had six children, of whom four—Davis P., Thomas B., Harvey, and Elisabeth—survived. Smith was an Episcopalian and was active as a Mason Shriner Artisan; he also belonged to the Union League, the Manufacturers Club, and the Penn Athletic Club.

Philadelphia in 1916 had a population in excess of 1.5 million and a mayor-council form of government. Smith's prior political experience as a member of Philadelphia's Common Council (1902–1903) and the Pennsylvania Statehouse (1905–1906) was followed by an appointment in 1911 as postmaster of Philadelphia by U.S. Senator Boies Penrose, the state Republican boss. Penrose and his ally, James ("Sunny Jim") McNichol, viewed Smith as a likely candidate to wrest power in Philadelphia from their bitter rivals, the brothers Edwin A. and William S. Vare, who commanded the local Republican machine. In a three-way mayoral race on 2 November 1915, Smith defeated his opponents 166,643 to 88,135 and 4,741 (George D. Porter, Franklin party, and D. Gordon Bromley, Democrat), but the new mayor later surprised Penrose by embracing the powerful Vare combine.

Smith's victory and his alliance with the local Republican organization signaled the end of Philadelphia's mild flirtation with Progressivism. The mayoralty rapidly degenerated as Philadelphia resumed its corruption and contentment under stalwart rule and the social dislocations of war. Vice and violence permeated the city and irreparably damaged the mayor. Twice mayor, Smith himself was indicted: once after a 1917 primary during which a police detective was killed by an imported thug in an election brawl; and again in 1919, when the mayor was compelled to answer charges of corrupting elections. He was acquitted on both counts, but his reputation was ruined, and he earned the sobriquet "bungler."

Although Smith was earnest in his efforts to promote civic improvements, such as the Delaware River Bridge, wartime budget constraints and unrelenting charges of corruption stifled whatever positive goals for urban development he may have entertained. He resumed his business career after 1920 and died on 17 April 1949.

SOURCES: Herman L. Collins and Wilfred Jordan, *Philadelphia: A Story of Progress* (Philadelphia, 1941); *The Mayors of Philadelphia*, Collections of the Genealogical Society of Pennsylvania, Historical Society of Pennsylvania; George Morgan, *Philadelphia: The City of Firsts; A History of Philadelphia* (Philadelphia, 1926); Harold P. Quicksall, "Government by Murder," *The Outlook*, 24 October 1917.   *Richard A. Varbero*

SMITH, WILLIAM BURNS (1844–1917), Mayor of Philadelphia (1884–87). Smith was born in Glasgow, Scotland, on 14 November 1844. When he was seven, his parents, William W. and Annie (Simpson) Smith, brought him to Philadelphia where the elder Smith ultimately became a senior member of Smith and Campion, a Philadelphia interior decorating firm. Smith attended local public schools until he was eleven and then was apprenticed to learn woodcarving and interior decorating. Ultimately, he joined his father's firm. As a young man, Smith belonged to a Republican marching club, and he met influential citizens while employed by his father. In 1881, he was appointed to a vacancy on the select council. Three months later, he won election in his own right. Smith spoke against the Gas Trust, earning the enmity of the local machine which was controlled by Gas Works trustee James McManes. However, supporters of Pennsylvania Republican boss J. Donald Cameron rallied behind him, as did the reform Committee of 100 and many Democrats. In 1882, Smith won election as president of the select council, and in 1884, he won the Republican mayoralty nomination. Smith served for twenty-five years in the National Guard, rising from the rank of corporal to major; he saw action in the railroad strikes of 1877. Smith was twice married, first to Ellen B. Cochrane by whom he had a son and a daughter, and in 1898 to Charlotte Isabel Wellington.

Philadelphia in 1880 had 847,170 people and a mayor-bicameral council form of government. In 1884, Smith spoiled Democratic Mayor Samuel G. King's (q.v.) bid for reelection, defeating him 79,552 to 70,440. He did not run for reelection in 1887.

Known as the "Dandy Mayor" because of his hail-fellow-well-met personality, Smith was Philadelphia's last mayor prior to the implementation of the reform Bullitt Charter in 1887. Many Republicans sought to have the charter take effect prior to the end of Smith's term, thus strengthening his powers. However, this effort failed; thus, Smith's achievements were limited primarily to the area of law enforcement. He introduced police matrons, police surgeons, and police wagons to the city's law enforcement programs. But the major event of Smith's administration was probably his near-impeachment. Colonel A. K. McClure of the Philadelphia *Times* accused the mayor of delaying deposits of public funds. A councils investigating committee actually recommended impeachment, but no action was taken. Although Smith later recovered damages from the *Times*, he was now a political liability and was not renominated.

In 1901, Smith was appointed assistant fire marshal, a position he held until two years before his death. A "joiner," Smith belonged to several civic and fraternal groups, including the Masons, the Odd Fellows, and the Union League. He died at his home in Laurel Springs, New Jersey, on 23 November 1917.

SOURCES: Howard F. Gillette, Jr., "Corrupt and Contented: Philadelphia's Political Machine, 1865–1887" (Ph.D. dissertation, Yale University, 1970); George Morgan, *The City of Firsts: A Complete History of the City of Philadelphia* (Philadelphia, 1926); Ellis Paxon Oberholtzer, *Philadelphia: A History of the City and Its People*, 4 vols. (Philadelphia, 1911); *Public Ledger, Inquirer, Evening Bulletin, North American*, 24 November 1917 obituaries.

John F. Sutherland

SNELBAKER, DAVID T. (1804–67), Mayor of Cincinnati (1853–55). Early Whig mayor, Snelbaker was born in Philadelphia on 29 August 1804, the son of Philip Snelbaker (1764–1807). Largely self-educated, Snelbaker worked for a few years as a cooper in Philadelphia. In 1827, he married Elizabeth Duey (d. 1837), and they had three children. In 1833, they moved to Kentucky, and shortly afterwards the family moved on to Cincinnati. Snelbaker began the practice of law as a partner of Abel Dalzell; the firm lasted until 1846. In Cincinnati, Snelbaker married for a second time in 1839, his wife being Mary Hooper (1817–67). They also had three children. Snelbaker and his wife were Methodists.

A Whig, Snelbaker was elected mayor in 1853, with 5,928 votes to 2,878 for J. S. Ross (Independent Whig), 5,195 for J. D. Taylor (Anti-Catholic), and 977 for F. T. Chambers (Independent). Cincinnati had 115,435 people in 1850 and a mayor-council form of government. Snelbaker spent most of his term attempting to reduce tensions caused by a growing anti-Catholic movement which produced at least one full-scale ethnic riot. After leaving office, Snelbaker resumed his legal practice, dying on 15 February 1867.

SOURCES: *Biographical Encyclopedia of Ohio of the Nineteenth Century* (Cincinnati, 1876); Cincinnati *Commercial*, 7 April 1867; *Cincinnati Mayors* (Cincinnati, c. 1957); U.S. Census Schedules for 1850.

Thomas R. Bullard

SNOWDEN, JOHN M. (1776–1845), Mayor of Pittsburgh (1825–28). Snowden, third mayor of Pittsburgh, was born in Philadelphia in 1776. During the American Revolution, his father was a ship captain, was captured by the British, and died in prison in New York. As a youth, Snowden was apprenticed to the famous Philadelphia printer, Matthew Carey. At the age of twenty-one, he moved to Chambersburg, Pennsylvania, and then to Greensburg, where in 1798 he founded the *Farmer's Register*, the second newspaper published in western Pennsylvania. While living there, he married Elizabeth Moor (daughter of Judge John Moor), who bore him six daughters and six sons; two dying as children.

In about 1808, Snowden sold his paper. He moved to Pittsburgh in 1811, where he opened a bookstore and printing shop, and published a number of books. Soon after coming to Pittsburgh, he bought the anti-Federalist newspaper, *The Commonwealth*, and changed its name to *The Mercury*. A Democratic-Republican, in 1813 he became a member of the Pittsburgh borough council and was one of the original aldermen when the city was incorporated in 1816. Snowden in 1814 was a member of the group which organized the firm that became the Bank of Pittsburgh. He was an elder in the First Presbyterian Church, and in 1825 he served as Allegheny County recorder of deeds.

On the resignation of John Darragh (q.v.) as mayor on 28 June 1825, Snowden was elected to the post by the councils, receiving eleven votes to four for Magnus M. Murray (q.v.) and three for Matthew B. Lowrie (q.v.), both aldermen who later became mayors. At this time, Pittsburgh had a population of about 10,000. During 1825, the election date was changed to January, and Snowden was unanimously reelected in 1826 and 1827. Although he favored a high tariff, Snowden supported Andrew Jackson for the presidency. Yet, when Henry Clay visited the city on 20 June 1827, the mayor and his supporters gave a banquet in his honor. Snowden and a group of his friends did sponsor another banquet, in support of Jackson, on 4 July of that year on the banks of the Allegheny River, with more than 1,600 in attendance.

While in office, Snowden led the city in extensive street improvements, and in draining and filling-in two large ponds. After retiring at the end of his third term, he moved to Allegheny, now Pittsburgh's North Side, and served as county treasurer. Snowden was one of the organizers of the Historical Society of Western Pennsylvania, 27 February 1834. From 1840 to 1845, he was an associate or lay judge. He died at his home on 2 April 1845. Snowden Township was named in his honor.

SOURCES: George D. Albert *History of Westmoreland County, Pa.*, (Philadelphia, 1882); *History of Allegheny County, Pa.* (Chicago, 1899), vol. 2; Allen H. Kerr "The Mayors and Recorders of Pittsburgh" (typescript, Pittsburgh, 1952); Pittsburgh *Mercury*, 10 July 1827; Pittsburgh *Press*, "The Mayors' Notebook, No. 3," by George Swetnam, 18 September 1973.

Helene Smith

SNYDER, MEREDITH PINXTON (1859–1937), Mayor of Los Angeles (1896–98, 1900–1904, 1919–21). A farmer, merchant, banker, pioneer subdivider, and the only four-time mayor of Los Angeles, Snyder was born in Winston-Salem, North Carolina, on 22 October 1859, the son of Kehlin D. and Elizabeth (Heiher) Snyder, both of whom died when Meredith was a boy. The boy was left poor, in the stricken post-Civil War South. His education was desultory and broken, though he managed to attend Yadkin College, never graduating. At the age of twenty-two, he migrated to Los Angeles (1880) with $5 in his pocket and began work at $25 a month as a store clerk, sleeping behind the store. Four years later, he had saved enough money to buy a shoe store (1884); he began buying real estate, building up a fortune, pioneering in this field over the next eight years. Snyder's specialty became the art of subdividing lots. He was a staunch Democratic party wheelhorse and the leader of the party in Los Angeles for twelve years. From the start—from the day he followed the tall silk-hatted, Prince-Albert-coated man out of the dry goods store and discovered this was the mayor of Los Angeles—his ambition was to become mayor. Sixteen years later, Snyder became mayor. Before that date, Snyder married May Ross in San Diego on 14 February 1888. Born in about 1860 in Washington, D.C., May was the daughter of William W. Ross, Lincoln's bodyguard and later mayor of Topeka, Kansas, and niece of the governor of New Mexico, Edmund G. Ross. The Snyders had a son, Captain Ross Snyder, killed at Château-Thierry during World War I. A playground was named after him in Los Angeles.

In 1890, now a prominent banker and realtor whose name was closely associated with the physical development of the city, Snyder was elected police commissioner; he was reelected in 1893. He won a seat on the city council (Second Ward), 1894–96, and served ably on the finance committee, leading a movement which became his hobbyhorse—the demand for total municipal ownership of the water company. On that issue Snyder was first elected mayor in 1896, winning with a large majority (9,070 to 7,440), aided by Republicans who switched to vote for him. They liked his abstemious, tax-saving, pro-business attitudes. Snyder served three more terms, 1900–1902, 1902–1904, and 1919–21, winning as follows: *1900*: 10,067 to 6,946; *1902*: 8,736 to 6,039 and 2,976; *1919*: 26,779 to 15,578. Among his achievements were the consolidation of San Pedro and Wilmington with Los Angeles (1909) which gave the city a harbor; the boring of the Third Street Tunnel through Bunker Hill in the middle of the city (1901); and, during his third term, the city's adoption of the initiative, referendum and recall. His last term, years later, came during the Prohibition era. Golf was brought to Los Angeles, and the first all-movie theater, but Mayor Snyder's pet project, municipal ownership of the water supply, had come in 1902. The city grew from about 5,000 (in 1859, when Snyder was born) to 576,000 (in 1920). It kept the mayor-council form of government, though the mayoralty became at least officially nonpartisan after 1906.

Between mayoralties, Snyder reverted to his subdividing business, the Snyder Shoe Company (established 1892), and the California Savings Bank (which he created in 1904). He served on many boards, including the Home Telephone Company, Gardenia Bank and Trust, and California Guaranty Corporation. After 1921, Snyder withdrew mainly to his large farm in the San Joaquin Valley, which he, of course, subdivided. He kept 700 acres for personal use. His wife died on 7 February 1937, and he died only two months later, on 7 April, at Jonathans Club in Los Angeles, where he was then living. All his life Mayor Snyder had been affectionately known as "Pinky," a short form of his unusual middle name and a reference to his flowing red sideburns.

SOURCES: California Biography File, Los Angeles Public Library; J. M. Guinn, *History of California*, vol. 3: *Historical and Biographical Record* (Los Angeles, 1915); Leonard A. Sanders, "Los Angeles and Its Mayors, 1850–1925" (M.A. thesis, University of Southern California, 1968); John Waugh, "L.A. Mayors. . . ," Los Angeles Times, *West* Magazine, 25 May 1969.

Peter d'A. Jones

SOMERS, PETER J. (1850–1924), Mayor of Milwaukee (1890–93). Lawyer and Irish-American professional politician, Somers was born on 12 April 1850 in Menominee, Wisconsin. His parents, Peter and Ann Somers, Roman Catholic immigrants, had established themselves in Wisconsin after fleeing Ireland in 1837. The third of four children, Somers grew up on his parents' farm and attended local public primary and secondary schools. He graduated from the Whitewater Normal School and taught for a time before deciding on law as a profession in 1872. After establishing his practice in Milwaukee, Somers turned to politics and successfully ran for city attorney in 1882. In 1890, he was elected alderman of the Ninth Ward as part of a city-wide Democratic landslide. He married Catharine F. Murphy of Milwaukee, also a first-generation, Irish-American Catholic, in 1878, and together they raised nine children.

The Democrats centered their campaign strategy in 1890 around the Bennett law, a Republican-sponsored measure in the state legislature that required all school instruction be in English. So successful was Democrat George W. Peck (q.v.) in capitalizing on ethnic discontent with the GOP that he resigned the mayoralty and ran for governor. The resignation necessitated a special election in Milwaukee, with Somers, the Democratic candidate, again exploiting the Bennett issue. He won easily and repeated his victory in the regular election of 1892 by outpolling Republican Paul Bechtner by a vote of approximately 20,000 to 17,000. Somers presided over a rapidly expanding city of over 200,000 with a mayor-council form of government. He resigned his office in 1893 to finish the term in Washington of Congressman John L. Mitchell, who in turn had been elected to the Senate. Declining to run for Congress on his own, Somers returned to his legal practice in 1894.

As mayor, Somers combined politics with an interest in expanding municipal services. His administration saw increased course offerings by the school system, various construction projects, and increased concern over traction. (The common council debated, but neither it nor Somers moved to regulate traction company growth.) In making his patronage selections, Somers may have erred in not allotting enough recognition to Polish voters, who had hoped for sizable rewards in return for their strong support of him in 1890 and 1892. A Polish boycott of the special election after Somers' resignation in 1893 made possible the victory of Republican John C. Koch (q.v.).

In 1905, Somers moved further west to Nevada, where he entered into Democratic state politics and served as a district judge from 1908 to 1914. He died in Los Angeles on 15 February 1924.

SOURCES: Andrew Aikens and Lewis Proctor, eds., *Men of Progress of Wisconsin* (Milwaukee, 1897); Bayrd Still, *Milwaukee: History of a City* (Madison, Wis.,

1948); *Wisconsin Necrology* (compilation of obituaries of prominent Milwaukeeans by state historical society, on microfilm).
Douglas Bukowski

SPAULDING, ELBRIDGE G. (1809–97), Mayor of Buffalo (1847). Whig mayor, prominent citizen, and U.S. congressman, Spaulding was born in Summer Hill, New York, on 24 February 1809 to Edward Spaulding (1764–1845), a farmer, and Mehitable (Goodrich) Spaulding (1770–1838), both of whom were of New England, Protestant descent. The youngest of nine children, Spaulding entered preparatory studies and then read law in Batavia, New York. In 1834, he settled in Buffalo and joined the law office of Potter and Babcock. He was city clerk, 1836–40, and in 1841 became an alderman and chaired the common council's finance committee. On 5 September 1837, Spaulding married Jane Rich, a New York-born Presbyterian and daughter of an Attica, New York, bank proprietor. She died in 1841, and on 5 August 1842, Spaulding married Nancy Strong (1824–1852), born to Yankee-stock parents in Connecticut. Spaulding's third wife was Nancy's sister, Delia Robinson (d. 1895), whom he married on 6 May 1854. Spaulding and Nancy had two sons and a daughter. He was a member of the First Presbyterian Church, a Whig, a unionist, and then a Republican.

Buffalo's population in 1845 was 29,773; by 1850, it had increased to 42,261. The city had a mayor-council form of government. In the March 1847 election, Spaulding, a Whig, defeated his Democratic opponent, Isaac Sherman, 2,192 to 2,013.

While mayor, Spaulding actively sought projects to augment Buffalo's commercial base and health facilities. Largely through his efforts, the city government began to build a general sewage system and undertook a program of street-paving. He promoted the Buffalo Gaslight Company and helped design plans to improve Buffalo's harbor and canal facilities. He did not run for reelection.

After his single term as mayor, Spaulding was active in many pursuits. In 1848, he was elected to the state assembly and served in the U.S. House of Representatives (1849–51), where he strongly supported President Taylor. In 1853, he became the New York State treasurer. In 1858 and 1860, he was again elected to Congress. While serving in Washington, Spaulding helped to write the Greenback Act. He was active in party matters, helping to establish the Republican party in New York State and serving on Abraham Lincoln's congressional campaign committee. After retiring as a lawyer in 1850, he became president of a Buffalo bank and a stockholder in others. Spaulding was the director of two railroad companies and president of the International Bridge Company. A society leader, he was a member of the

Buffalo Historical Society, the Society of Natural Science, and the Buffalo Club. He died on 7 May 1897 and was buried in Buffalo's Forest Lawn Cemetery.

SOURCES: Buffalo *Daily Courier*; Buffalo *Daily Gazette*; Buffalo *Morning Express*; Buffalo Public Library, "Scrap Book: Local Obituary Notices and Biographical Sketches, 1861–64"; *Commercial Advertiser and Journal*; William R. Cutter, *Genealogical and Family History of Western New York* (New York, 1912); Henry W. Hill, *The Municipality of Buffalo, New York: A History, 1720–1923* (New York, 1924); Crisfield Johnson, *Centennial History of Erie County, New York* (Buffalo, 1876); J. N. Larned, *A History of Buffalo* (New York, 1911); H. Perry Smith, *A History of Buffalo and Erie County, New York* (Syracuse, N.Y., 1884); Elbridge G. Spaulding manuscripts in Buffalo Historical Society, inventory in *Niagara Frontier*, (1966) vol. 13; Truman C. White, *Our County and Its People: A Descriptive Work on Erie County, New York* (Boston, 1898); Merton M. Wilner, *The Niagara Frontier: A Narrative and Documentary History* (Chicago, 1931).   *Daniel B. Karin*

SPENCE, EDWARD FALLES (1832–92), Mayor of Los Angeles (1884–86). One of the founders of the University of Southern California, Spence was born on 22 December 1832 in Enniskillen, Northern Ireland, to Gabriel Spence, a wealthy farmer and cattle rancher, and his wife who was also Scots-Irish. Educated by private tutors, Spence assisted his father in managing his extensive interests.

In 1852, Edward emigrated to the United States, landing in New York City and moving to Philadelphia. His stay was brief. He caught gold fever and set off for San Francisco via Nicaragua, arriving in December 1852. He headed for the goldfields and continued mining until an injury forced him to quit. He then studied pharmacy and developed a profitable business in Nevada City, California. In 1860, he was elected to the state legislature.

In 1869, Spence moved to San Jose, California, where he continued his pharmaceutical enterprises. In 1872, he relocated in San Diego where he established a bank. From this time on, Spence became involved in banking. He moved to Los Angeles in 1876 and soon organized one bank, and was an officer of several others. He became involved in local politics, winning election to the city council from 1879 to 1881.

Spence married his Scots-Irish wife, Anna (1851–?), in 1872. They had three sons and a daughter. He was one of the prominent Methodists who founded the University of Southern California. He was also a Mason, an Odd Fellow, a Knight of Pythias, vice-president of the California Bankers Association, an officer of the American Bankers Association, and president of the Los Angeles Philharmonic Society.

Possessing a mayor-council form of government, Los Angeles had not yet experienced its land boom. In 1884, its population numbered 15,000 to 20,000. The Santa Fe Railroad entered the city during Spence's administration in 1885. The rate war which ensued between the Santa Fe and the Southern Pacific stimulated the rush of settlers and land speculation in 1886.

Spence obtained the Republican party's nomination for the 1 December 1884 mayoral election, which he won by receiving 2,068 votes to 1,549, 108, and 86 votes for the Democratic (C. E. Thom), and the minor Greenback and Prohibitionist candidates, respectively. In 1886, Spence retired from politics.

Like other booster-oriented mayors of this period, Spence sought to attract more people and industry to his city. Investing heavily in streetcar franchises and town promotion, he perceived no barrier to combining the concerns of public office with those of private real estate speculation. Realizing that the economic growth of Los Angeles required adequate public services, he effected internal reorganizations within city government, including the creation of the city's first professional fire department.

In 1887, Spence contributed to the advancement of science by donating $50,000 toward the construction of the Mount Wilson Observatory. He moved to Monrovia in 1888 and lived there until 18 September 1892 when he returned to Los Angeles for medical care. He died on 20 September 1892 of heart disease and was buried in Los Angeles.

SOURCES: City of Los Angeles, *Chronological Record of Los Angeles City Officials 1850–1938* (Los Angeles, 1940), vols. 1–3; Glenn S. Dumke, "The Boom of the Eighties in Southern California" (Ph.D. Dissertation, UCLA, 1942); John L. Wiley, *History of Monrovia* (Pasadena, Calif., 1927); Los Angeles *Times* 1884–86, 1888, 1892.   *Christopher Cocoltchos*

SPENCER, HENRY EVANS (1808–82), Mayor of Cincinnati (1843–51). Cincinnati's first native-born mayor, born in that city (actually in the then-independent town of Columbia) on 13 June 1808, Spencer was the son of Oliver Spencer (1781–1838), a prominent judge. The elder Spencer was well remembered by Cincinnati old-timers as the boy held captive by Indians for over a year in the 1790s. Spencer, like his father, became a lawyer. He was editor of the Cincinnati *Whig* in 1838, president of the Fireman's Insurance Company, and a leader of the local branch of the American Colonization Society. He married Henrietta Halsted (1810–   ), member of an old-stock New Jersey family, in the 1830s, and they had ten children.

A Whig, Spencer was elected mayor in 1843, with 3,196 votes to 3,122 for Henry Morse (Democrat) and 797 for Marcus Smith. He was elected to a second term in 1845, again defeating Morse, 3,388 to 3,091 (with 401 votes for George Jones of the American Republican party). In 1847, he defeated Mark P. Taylor (*q.v.*) (Democrat) 4,213 to 3,599. In 1849, he defeated John G. Gerard (Democrat) 5,580 to 4,468. In 1851, Spencer lost his bid for a fifth term to Taylor (Democrat) 6,923 to 6,800. Cincinnati had 46,338 people in 1840 and 115,435 in 1850, and a mayor-council form of government.

Spencer was a popular mayor, noted for his honesty, ability, and continued support for all civic improvements. Newspaper accounts of the period stressed his desire to secure the "best things" for the city. After 1851, Spencer returned to his legal practice. By 1856, he had abandoned the Whigs for the Democratic party, but he was not elected to any public office under his new political affiliation. He died of pneumonia, on 2 February 1882.

SOURCES: *Cincinnati's Mayors* (Cincinnati, 1957); Charles Cist, *The Cincinnati Miscellany*, 2 vols. (Cincinnati, 1845–46); *History of Cincinnati and Hamilton County, Ohio* (Cincinnati, 1894); W. Ogden Wheeler, *Descendants of Rebecca Ogden, 1729–1806 and Caleb Halsted, 1721–1789* (Privately printed, 1912).

Thomas R. Bullard

SPIEGEL, FREDERICK S. (1855 or 1858–1925), Mayor of Cincinnati (1914–15). Republican machine mayor and a Jewish immigrant, Spiegel was born 20 November 1855 or 1858 at Hovestadt, Prussia, the son of Simon Spiegel and Rosalie (Hersberg) Spiegel. After Frederick attended the *gymnasium* at Paderborn in Westphalia, the family emigrated in 1867 to Alabama, where Frederick graduated from the Southern Institute, Gadsden, in 1873. Spiegel moved to Cincinnati, graduated from Nelson's Business College in 1875, joined the Typographical Union, and became editor of the ethnic, German-language paper, *Freie Press*. He graduated from the Cincinnati Law School in 1880 and began a long career of public service by becoming chief of the Ohio State Bureau of Statistics and by being elected to the Cincinnati School Board. The next year he served on the Night School Committee and by 1882 was chairman of the Public School Committee on the German language.

In 1883, Spiegel married Minna Steinberg (1861–1937), and they had three children. By that time, he was practicing law in Cincinnati and in 1889 went back into public office as a member of the city council. He was county solicitor (1890–96) and judge of the common pleas court (1896–1906). He was also judge of the superior court (1902–13). Spiegel found time to be president of a number of *vereins*; he was a Mason and an active Republican. He was noted for his Progressive stands, particularly on personal liberty.

In 1913, Spiegel was the Republican choice to challenge Henry T. Hunt (*q.v.*), the Democratic reform mayor whose labor and liberal support had fallen into disarray. The city's 380,000 people and mayor-council form of government were seriously split, and the George B. Cox machine was determined to regain control. Spiegel's long record of public service made him an attractive candidate, and he won (45,363 to 42,251), carrying with him most of the GOP slate and a safe majority on the council. Spiegel was mayor in name, but much of the power was wielded by Rudolph K. Hynicka, who had succeeded Cox as Republican boss, and by Michael Mullen who managed the city council with the help of an advisory committee of business and professional men. Spiegel straddled the issues, lacked backbone and tact, and generally had an unsatisfactory record. He did not run for reelection, but he returned to the practice of law, including service as chief counsel for the Rapid Transit Commission. He died in Chicago in 1925 and was buried in Cincinnati.

SOURCES: *The City of Cincinnati and Its Resources* (Cincinnati, 1891); [Isaac M. Martin], *History of the Schools of Cincinnati* (1900); [W. W. Morris and] E. Bokrieger, *Bench and Bar of Cincinnati* (1921).

George B. Engberg

SPRINGER, GERALD NORMAN (1944–   ), Mayor of Cincinnati (1977–78). English-born mayor of Cincinnati, Springer was the son of Richard and Margot (Kallman) Springer, and was born in wartime London 13 February 1944. His parents were Jewish refugees from Hitler's Germany. The family moved to the United States in 1949, settling in New York City where young Springer attended local schools. They became U.S. citizens in 1954. He attended Tulane University (B.A., 1965) and Northwestern University (J.D., 1968). In 1968, he moved to Cincinnati and began practicing law with Furst and Jacobs (1969–70). Springer was a member of the U.S. Army Reserve but was also a critic of the Vietnam War, immediately winning support among the city's younger voters. He married Margaret Joann Velten on 16 June 1973, and they have one daughter. Springer became a member of the Cincinnati Bar Association.

Springer's appeal to the younger voters led him into politics in 1970 when he ran unsuccessfully for Congress. In 1971, he was director of the Ohio Youth Corps. That same year he was elected to the city council as a liberal Democrat. Upon his reelection in 1973, Springer became vice-mayor and was to become mayor in 1974 when Mayor Theodore Berry (*q.v.*) retired. This would have made Springer the city's youngest mayor. However, he was a witness in a local vice trial, and the resulting publicity caused him to resign from the city council in the spring of 1974. In 1975, he was elected to another term as an Independent, but he soon rejoined the Democratic ranks. In 1977, he was selected as mayor. Cincinnati had 451,455 people in 1970 and a city manager-mayor-council form of government.

Springer was a popular mayor who seemed to make personality a key political issue. He had a great sense of humor and seemed to enjoy being quoted by the local media. He believed that Cincinnati could surmount its economic problems and become a model city. Springer insisted that the mayor's office should be "open" to the public, to allow the voters a chance to participate in the political process. He made special efforts to aid the young and the city's minorities to attract them to the political process. Mayor Springer strongly backed all efforts to cut the city's rate of unemployment. After leaving the mayoralty, Springer continued his political career on the city council.

SOURCES: *Biography News* 1:5 (May 1974); Cincinnati *Enquirer*, 10 November 1977, C-1 and period from 30 April through 18 May 1974; *Who's Who in America* (Chicago, 1979).   *Thomas R. Bullard*

STANSBURY, ELIJAH, JR. (1791–1883), Mayor of Baltimore (1848–50). Described as an inflexible and uncompromising Democrat of the old school, Stansbury was a leading political figure in Baltimore during the turbulent years when the city became widely known as "mobtown" because of its political violence. Stansbury was born in Baltimore County sometime in May 1791, but his father, Elijah, Sr. (1756–1837), soon moved to neighboring Harford County where Elijah, Jr., and his twelve brothers and sisters grew up. The Stansbury family was Episcopalian, fairly prosperous, and well known in Harford County. Elijah received a common school education while helping on the family farm. In 1808, he expressed "an aversion to farming" and was allowed to go to Baltimore and to apprentice himself to one of his older brothers as a bricklayer. In the War of 1812, he enlisted in the Baltimore Union Artillery and helped defend the city at the battle of North Point, September 1814. He continued to serve in the state militia where he rose to the rank of colonel. He also prospered as a bricklayer and soon developed a building trades business which he pursued the rest of his life. Nevertheless, he often listed himself merely as a bricklayer even though he was usually addressed by others as "Colonel Stansbury." He married Eliza Eckel (1801–1877) in 1817, and they remained childless. Stansbury was active in fraternal organizations, including the Odd Fellows,

Druids, Red Men, Sons of Freedom, Sons of Temperance, and the Masons; he became senior grand warden of the Masons.

Stansbury's political career began with the Baltimore Union Artillery, commanded by John Montgomery (*q.v.*) who was a leading Democrat and three-time mayor of the city during the 1820s. Stansbury was elected to the city council in 1826 and continued there until 1830 (after which his brother, John E. Stansbury, served for a number of terms in the 1830s). In 1844, Elijah was elected to the state legislature. In 1848, he was selected by the Democrats to run for mayor and on 11 October defeated James Griffin, the Whig candidate, by a vote of 9,950 to 9,064. He served from 13 November 1848 to 11 November 1850. During his administration, the first systematic efforts were made to pave the city's streets with cobblestones, to construct a series of major storm sewers, and to build more bridges across Jones Falls (a wide stream dividing east and west Baltimore). The most complex problem facing the city during Stansbury's term was the continuing disagreement between the city and surrounding Baltimore County over a number of jointly financed and operated public institutions. Agreements were finally worked out for the complete separation of all city and county institutions, which resulted in what has been called the "final divorce" of the two local governments. Baltimore at this time was 164,000 in size.

Mayor Stansbury took the leading role in the city's welfare activities. By 1850, he had become very concerned over the growth of poverty in the city and thought the wretched condition of many of the city's poor was a civic disgrace. However, rather than expand the public facilities for the poor through an enlargement of the city's almshouse, he led the movement for the establishment of an Association for the Improvement of the Condition of the Poor which began operations in the fall of 1849. He remained interested in this private charitable organization for the rest of his life.

After leaving office in 1850, Stansbury retired from active political life and concentrated on his building business. He occasionally served in the state legislature as a delegate from Baltimore, but he never again sought full-time political office. He retired from active business in 1862 and died on 19 December 1883 at his home at 431 North Central Avenue.

SOURCES: *Biographical Cyclopedia of Representative Men of Maryland* (Baltimore, 1879); Wilbur F. Coyle, *The Mayors of Baltimore* (Baltimore, 1919); Archibald Hawkins, *The Life and Times of Hon. Elijah Stansbury* (Baltimore, 1874).   *Joseph L. Arnold*

STARKWEATHER, SAMUEL (1799–1876), Mayor of Cleveland (1844–46, 1857–59). An old-stock Yankee,

Starkweather was born in Pawtucket, Massachusetts (later Rhode Island), on 27 December 1799, the son of Oliver Starkweather (1759–1834), merchant and politician, and Mariam (Clay) Starkweather (1764–1805), both New England Baptists. The fifth of six children, Starkweather attended local schools while working on his father's farm until 1818. He attended Brown University, graduating in 1822, and taught there, 1823–24. He then studied law with John Swift (in Litchfield) and Chancellor Kent (in New York City). Starkweather married Julia Judd (1810–94) on 25 June 1825, and they had four children. The young couple moved west to Columbus, Ohio, in 1826, and Starkweather began practicing law. They moved again to Cleveland in 1827, seeking a larger legal practice. The Starkweathers were Episcopalian, attended the "Old Stone Church," and supported local charities.

Starkweather, a Jacksonian Democrat, entered politics in 1831–32, serving as the collector of the port of Cleveland. He was president of the Village of Cleveland (1836–37), followed by a year on the board of health, and was a member of the city council, 1837–38 and 1843–44, before winning election as mayor in 1844, defeating Whig Samuel Wilkinson 561 to 532. In 1845, he was reelected, defeating Whig Melincton Barrett and Abolitionist Thomas Richmond, 587 to 482 and 68, respectively. Cleveland had 6,071 people in 1840 and a mayor-council form of government. As mayor, Starkweather supported better streets, city aid to railroads, and construction of a medical college.

After leaving office, Starkweather served on the school board, 1846–47, and another term as alderman, 1848–49. He was a judge of the court of common pleas, 1852–57. He resigned from the bench in 1857 and was reelected mayor for a two-year term, defeating Republican incumbent Mayor William Castle (q.v.) 1,728 to 1,305 (incomplete returns). Cleveland had 17,034 people by 1850. Starkweather continued to support civic improvements and an enlarged fire department. After leaving office in 1859, he retired from all political pursuits, practicing law until his death on 5 July 1876.

SOURCES: J. R. Brennan, ed., *A Biographical Cyclopedia and Portrait Gallery of Distinguished Men, With an Historical Sketch of the State of Ohio* (Cincinnati, 1879); *Cleveland: Past and Present* (Cleveland, 1869); Carlton L. Starkweather, *A Brief Genealogical History of Robert Starkweather . . . and of His Descendants in Various Lines, 1649–1893* (Occuquan, Va., 1904).   *Thomas R. Bullard*

STEPHENS, THOMAS J. (1823–92), Mayor of Cincinnati (1883–85). Glue manufacturer and Democratic mayor during the 1884 riot, Stephens was born in 1823

of Northern Irish parents. He moved from Lexington, Kentucky, his hometown, to Cincinnati, Ohio, in 1836. Soon after his arrival, he helped build the Old Buckeye Race Course, one of Cincinnati's oldest race tracks, and opened a restaurant called the Millcreek House. After the Civil War, he established a glue manufacturing plant and by 1880 had amassed a comfortable fortune. He married and had three sons.

Cincinnati in 1883 had 225,139 people and a mayor-council form of government. In 1883, Stephens, a Democrat, became mayor of Cincinnati, beating the Republican candidate L. L. Sadler 25,192 to 22,335. His term of office was marked by emergencies in which Stephens failed to exercise firm leadership. The worst of the emergencies, the Courthouse Riot of 1884, broke out after the sentencing of William Berner, a German immigrant, on trial for the robbery and murder of a white livery man. The jury's decision to find Berner guilty only of manslaughter touched off an explosion. After a number of public meetings, a mob stormed the jail and demanded the hanging of Berner. The actions of the militia, called in by Stephens to restore peace, led to a series of violent clashes lasting one day and two nights, during which the mob burned the courthouse to the ground.

Stephens did not run for reelection in 1885. After his term expired, he devoted himself to his glue manufacturing plant and became a familiar figure at the Merchant's Exchange. In 1889, the Democratic party again nominated Stephens for mayor but he lost to the Republican candidate John B. Mosby (q.v.). On 2 June 1892, Cincinnati newspapers reported the death of Stephens, the "official reminder of the 1884 riot."

SOURCES: Cincinnati's Mayors (Cincinnati, 1957); Charles T. Greve, *Centennial History of Cincinnati and Representative Citizens* (Chicago, 1904); Zane L. Miller, *Boss Cox's Cincinnati: Urban Politics in the Progressive Era* (New York, 1968).   *Patricia Mooney Melvin*

STEPHENS, WILLIAM D. (1859–1944), Acting Mayor of Los Angeles (1909). Mayor for only two weeks but later state governor, Stephens was born on 26 December 1859 in Eaton, Ohio, the son of Martin F. Stephens and Alvira (Leibee) Stephens. He attended the public schools of Eaton, graduating from high school in 1876. During the next four years, he taught school and studied law and civil engineering. He left home in 1880 to work on railroad construction in Ohio, Iowa, Indiana, and Louisiana. Stephens moved to Los Angeles with his parents in 1888 and entered the wholesale grocery business. In 1902, he formed a partnership with J. E. Carr, and under the name of Carr and Stephens remained in the grocery business until 1909. Stephens married Flora Rawson in 1891, and they had one child, Barbara. Stephens served as director of the Los Angeles Chamber of Commerce from 1902 to 1911. He was also an officer in the California National Guard.

Stephens served on the Los Angeles Board of Education in 1907. Two years later, Mayor Arthur C. Harper (*q.v.*) resigned over charges of protecting organized vice. The city council appointed Stephens interim mayor for two weeks until a new chief executive could be elected. Los Angeles in 1909 had 293,300 people. Stephens helped complete the consolidation of the harbor towns of San Pedro and Wilmington with Los Angeles. In 1910, he was president of the city water commission and served on the advisory committee for the building of the Owens Valley aqueduct. The same year he defeated the Democratic congressman from the Seventh California District and was reelected in 1912. Two years later, Stephens ran successfully on the Progressive ticket from the Twelfth District and served a third term in Congress.

California state politics took Stephens from Congress and put him in the lieutenant governor's office in 1916. Governor Hiram Johnson resigned in 1917, and Stephens became governor; he was reelected in 1918. Stephens reorganized the executive branch of the state government along the lines of economy and efficiency, forced through the legislature a tax bill which increased corporation taxes, and provided more funds for the expansion of social services. He lost the Republican nomination in 1922 to Friend W. Richardson who won the governorship.

Stephens returned to Los Angeles and entered private law practice. He was a member of numerous civic and fraternal organizations. He died on 24 April 1944 and was buried in Los Angeles.

SOURCES: Charles F. Lummis, *Out West. Los Angeles and Her Makers: A Record* (Los Angeles, 1909); John Steven McGroarty, *Los Angeles: From the Mountains to the Sea. With Selected Biography of Actors and Witnesses of the Period of Growth and Achievement* (Chicago, 1921), vol. 3; H. Brett Melendy and Benjamin F. Gilbert, *The Governors of California: Peter H. Burnett to Edmund G. Brown* (Georgetown, Calif., 1965); "William D. Stephens," *California Biography File*, Los Angeles Public Library.   *Martin J. Schiesl*

STERNE, BOBBI LYNN (1919–), Mayor of Cincinnati (1975–76 and 1978–79). The first lady mayor of Cincinnati was Acting Mayor Dorothy N. Dolbey (*q.v.*) but Cincinnati's first full-time woman mayor was Bobbie Lynn Sterne, born 27 November 1919 in Moran, Ohio, the younger of two children of Vernon C. Lynn (1864–1932), a storekeeper, telegrapher, and farmer, and Eva Douglas (Dodds) Lynn (1881–1954). Both parents were of mixed Scots-French stock. Sterne attended local

schools and then chose a nursing career, attending Akron City Hospital's school, 1940–41, and Akron University, 1941–42. She served with the U.S. Army's Nurse Corps in Europe (1942–45), reaching the rank of first lieutenant. In 1944, she married Dr. Eugene Sterne (1910–1977), a Harvard M.D. of German-Jewish descent, whom she met while stationed in England. They had two daughters, Lynn and Cynthia. Returning to the United States, Mrs. Sterne completed her education at the University of Cincinnati, 1946–47. She served on the board of directors of the Cincinnati Scholarship Fund in 1958 and was a member of the Cincinnati Charter Commission, 1955–71. She joined the League of Women Voters, Community Chest, Planned Parenthood, National Women's Political Caucus, and the Women's City Club. The Cincinnati *Enquirer* gave her a Special Award for Outstanding Community Service in 1967 and chose her as Woman of the Year in 1976.

Mrs. Sterne became interested in active politics in 1969 when she ran unsuccessfully for the city council. Joining the Charterite faction, she was elected to the council in 1971 and served on that body thereafter. Quickly recognized as an expert on health problems and public finances, she was chosen mayor in 1975, becoming the city's first full-time lady mayor. The city, after adopting a charter form of government in 1925, maintained a small council-city manager system. The mayor, chosen from among the nine-member council elected at large, exercises no statutory functions as such. The traditional role that the Mayor fulfills is to develop support for the majority's program within the council and to act as its spokesperson.

Prior to her first campaign for city council in 1969, Sterne served as the head of the Field Division of the Charter Committee for twelve years and as a member of the Cincinnati Charter Committee Board. Running as a Charterite against a slate of Republicans and Democrats, she finished fifteenth in 1969. In 1971, she was elected, finishing seventh and garnering 58,555 votes; in 1973, 53,226, running seventh again; in 1975, 49,353 finishing second; and in 1977, 67,260, also finishing second. Since 1971, when the Charter Committee joined with the Democrats to form a coalition majority on the council, the mayoralty has alternated between the two parties. Under this arrangement, Sterne became mayor for one year, on 1 December 1975, and for another year commencing 1 December 1978.

Cincinnati in 1975 had 427,000 people and only slightly less than that number in 1978 when Mrs. Sterne became mayor for the second time. In her two terms, she earned a reputation for leadership and strength. As befitting her background, she actively campaigned for improved health care, especially for small children and senior citizens. She supported efforts to attract more tourists to Cincinnati, seeing this as a way to bring money into the city. Sterne was described as a liberal with regard to social issues (notably women's rights) and a conservative with respect to spending. She supported those programs which could be carried out with a minimal expenditure. Although critics claimed she was too tough, her mayoralty (especially her second year in office) showed that she had a sense of humor and an ability to absorb political and fiscal information quickly. Ironically, her first term witnessed a sizable reduction in city services as a consequence of the failure of the voters to approve an increase in the city earnings tax shortly before she became mayor. She did succeed in gaining approval for an environmental quality district zoning ordinance, upgrading environmental controls in addition to regular zoning requirements. She also led in the efforts to control upstream pollution of the Ohio River.

Mayor Sterne's major resolution came when she proposed preventing the use of city funds for travel to conventions and seminars held in states that have not adopted the equal rights amendment (ERA). Despite the debate and controversy, her proposal carried, and the travel ban remains. Following her ERA resolution, Mayor Sterne has brought other proposals to the council, especially in the areas of human rights and health. She has been particularly identified with gaining additional funds for the city's health clinics. She has also become the major spokesperson for changes in a fair housing ordinance that would ban discriminating against renters with children or discriminating against renters on the basis of marital status or source of income. During Mayor Sterne's first term, the *Saturday Review* named Cincinnati as one of the five most livable American cities. After the end of her second year, she continued as a council member.

SOURCES: Cincinnati *Enquirer*, 1 December 1976, 1 and 2 December 1978, 12 November 1979; The *City Bulletin* (official publication, City of Cincinnati), 1971–78; Newspaper clipping file, Municipal Library, City Hall, Cincinnati, 1969–78; *Who's Who in American Politics* (New York, 1979).

Gene D. Lewis and *Thomas R. Bullard*

STEUART, WILLIAM (1782–1839), Mayor of Baltimore (1831–32). An interim mayor appointed by the city electors after his predecessor resigned, Steuart (whose name is spelled the traditional Scottish way and is often misspelled as Stewart in contemporary as well as later sources) served as mayor for eighteen months. Little is known of his ancestry or personal life, although he was born in 1782, the son of Robert Steuart who had come to Maryland from Falkirk, Scotland, as an indentured servant and later became a stonecutter. Married to Eliz-

abeth Hagerty of Alexandria, Virginia, William Steuart served as an apprentice to his father, and the Steuart family contributed the stone and marble work to two important Baltimore buildings, the Washington Monument, and the courthouse completed in 1805. During the War of 1812, Steuart was appointed lieutenant colonel of the U.S. Infantry defending Baltimore and gained prominence as a defender of the city. In 1826, he was appointed a receiver of subscriptions to the Baltimore and Ohio railroad stock. He served several terms on the city council and Maryland House of Delegates before becoming mayor. He was an active Mason.

In 1831, Baltimore did not popularly elect its mayor. Instead, each of the twelve wards voted for an elector, usually identified with a candidate, and, in the same manner as presidential politics, these electors met and selected a mayor. At the time of Steuart's election, Baltimore had a population of 80,625 (which included 14,900 free Negroes and 4,100 slaves) and was governed by the mayor and a two-branch city council. During his brief tenure, Steuart approved the sale of the old Alms House, presided over the construction of the city's second public school, and supported several ordinances permitting urban improvements such as the Chatsworth Run Bridge. After leaving office, Steuart served as president of the Maryland Institute of Arts and just before his death, on 12 February 1839, was appointed city collector.

SOURCES: Baltimore City Register; Wilbur Coyle, *Mayors of Baltimore* (Baltimore, 1919); Dielman-Hayward file, Maryland Historical Society.

Jean H. Baker

STEVENS, FREDERICK P. (1810–66), Mayor of Buffalo (1856–57). Lawyer, judge and active mayor, and a Welsh-American, Stevens was born on 26 October 1810 in Pierpont, New Hampshire, the eighth of twelve children born to Archelaus Stevens, an impecunious farmer of Welsh ancestry, and Hanna (Hastings) Stevens. After a youth spent laboring on the family farm and attending local schools, Stevens in 1831 began to study law with an older brother, Robert, who practiced in Lockport, New York. After two years of training, Frederick finished his studies in Rochester and was admitted to the bar.

Coming to Buffalo in 1835, Stevens gained professional prominence; in 1836, the governor appointed him a judge of the Erie County Court of Common Pleas on which he served first as puisne (associate) judge and, after 1845, as presiding judge. When the new constitution of 1846 mandated the popular election of county judges, Stevens, who had always acted with the Democratic Party, was in 1847 elected on that ticket as presiding judge. Although never a great judge, noted one newspaper, Buffalo *Morning Express*, "he was generally regarded as a fair and safe one."

His judicial term ending, Stevens was elected in 1854 to the Buffalo Common Council and in 1855 to a two-year term as mayor of Buffalo's 74,214 inhabitants. He received 4,080 votes for mayor to the combined 3,939 votes of his two opponents—William A. Bird and Lewis L. Hodges. Elected with him was the entire Democratic city ticket. As mayor, Stevens demonstrated "superior executive ability." Under him the council appropriated large sums ($300,000 a year) for a program to lay out new city streets, pave old ones, plank over sidewalks, and erect gas streetlights. Stevens is also credited with being one of the originators of a city streetcar system and one of the initiators of the idea of an international bridge from Buffalo to Canada.

Before he left office, Stevens fell out with the Democratic party. Deeming its actions "a departure from its original principles," he thenceforth identified with the Republican party. He became its mayoral candidate in 1857 but was defeated by the Democratic nominee, T. T. Lockwood (*q.v.*). In 1863, the second county district elected Stevens to the state assembly, in which he chaired the influential Ways and Means Committee. The following year, his defeat for reelection ended his political career. Commented one observer: "Like every public officer, his conduct was sometimes severely criticized, but no one ever . . . question[ed] his integrity."

His failing health permitting, Stevens continued his law practice. He suffered a lung hemorrhage in 1865 and a second attack while in court on 21 March 1866. He died two days later. More than a professional and political figure, "Judge" Stevens had been active in civic affairs. In 1836, he was a founder of the Buffalo Young Men's Association for "mutual improvement in literature and science" and became its first corresponding secretary. Incorporated by the legislature in 1837, the association in time became "the pride and glory of the city." When the new Episcopal Church was incorporated in 1855, Stevens was elected a vestryman.

SOURCES: Buffalo Morning Express, 26 March 1866 (obituary); J. N. Larned, *A History of Buffalo* 2 vols. (New York, 1911); Sister Mary Jane and Sister Mercedes, "Mayors of Buffalo, 1832–1961," (B.A. thesis, Rosary Hill College, 1961); Stevens Family Papers, Buffalo and Erie County Historical Society. *John D. Milligan*

STEWART, JAMES GARFIELD (1881–1959), Mayor of Cincinnati (1938–47). Lawyer and politician, born in Springfield, Ohio, on 17 November 1881, Stewart was the son of James Stewart, a bank teller, and Mary Emily (Durbin) Stewart, both old-stock Episcopalians. He attended local schools in Springfield, taking odd jobs after

hours, since his father had died while still a young man. He graduated from Kenyon College in 1902 and from the University of Cincinnati Law School in 1905 (with an LL.B.). Beginning his legal career in 1905, Stewart moved permanently to Cincinnati in 1908, practicing with a variety of partners over the next half century. For a few years, he served as attorney for the city's street railway system. On 7 September 1910, he married Harriet Loomis Potter of Jackson, Michigan, and they had three children, one of whom eventually was appointed to the U.S. Supreme Court (Justice Potter Stewart). The Stewarts were Episcopalians and were active in supporting social work. Stewart was a Phi Beta Kappa, Phi Delta Phi, a Mason, an Elk, a Moose, and a member of the Cincinnati Club.

A Republican, Stewart was first elected to the city council in 1933. In 1938, he was selected by the council as mayor and was to serve four two-year terms. Cincinnati had 455,610 people in 1940 and a city manager-mayor-council form of government. The first Republican mayor under the charter, Stewart was a strong leader and an equally strong partisan who frequently suggested that the charter system was not effective. He hinted that the old party system was better, and he often clashed with the Charterite faction in the council. Stewart was hostile to public housing and many other reform issues popular with the Charterites.

After leaving office, Stewart was appointed to the Ohio Supreme Court in 1947. He was subsequently reelected in 1952 and 1958. In addition, he maintained his private legal practice. While preparing to give a speech to a gathering of lawyers in Louisville, Stewart suffered a fatal heart attack on 3 April 1959.

SOURCES: Ralph A. Straetz, *PR: Politics in Cincinnati* (Washington Square, 1958). *Thomas R. Bullard*

STILES, GEORGE (c. 1760–1819), Mayor of Baltimore (1816–19). Merchant and sea captain, Stiles had a colorful background. He was probably born in Harford County, Maryland, to Phoebe and Joseph Stiles in 1760. He moved to Baltimore and became a sea captain. During the American Revolution, he operated a ship for Samuel (*q.v.*) and John Smith and thereafter sailed for the firm of Smith and Buchanan. On 6 June 1786, he married Anne Steele, and they had at least five children. By the War of 1812, he was a partner in the firm of Stiles and Williams, tea and grocery dealers, and a prosperous merchant. During that war, he successfully operated several privateers and formed the First Marine Artillery Company which he commanded on the waterfront during the bombardment of Fort McHenry in 1814. Captain Stiles, an ardent Democratic-Republican since 1798, aligned himself with his former mentor and urban party leader, Samuel Smith. He was an early proponent of steam-powered vessels and built a factory to manufacture maritime engines.

Baltimore was trying to recover from the War of 1812 during his term of office. Its population grew from 35,583 in 1810 to 62,738 in 1820. The annexation of the precincts in 1817 contributed to this growth, and the number of wards increased from eight to twelve. Baltimore had a mayor-city council form of government in which the mayor was elected indirectly to a two-year term. In 1816, the Stiles ticket for mayor defeated the Abner Neal ticket (3,024 votes to 1,239) and in 1818 beat John Montgomery's (q.v.) ticket (4,298 to 2,576 votes) in selecting electors who picked the mayor. Mayor Stiles was a popular but undynamic leader. During his administration, the city had to deal with its huge war debt and to replace bridges unexpectedly destroyed by the Jones Falls flood of 1817, while he advocated harbor improvements and the establishment of new town markets. The economic stagnation of 1819 further hampered his plans. Plagued by ill health during most of his term as mayor, Stiles resigned in February 1819 and died on 16 June 1819. He was buried in the Second Presbyterian Church graveyard.

SOURCES: Joseph L. Arnold, "Suburban Growth and Municipal Annexation," *Maryland Historical Magazine* 73:2 (Summer 1978); Baltimore *American and Commercial Advertiser*, 3, 8 October, 16 November 1816; 5, 6 October 1818; Dielman-Hayward File, Maryland Historical Society; Jerome R. Garitee, *The Republic's Private Navy* (Middletown, Conn., 1977); *Mayor's Messages* (Baltimore, 1817–19); Whitman H. Ridgway, *Community Leadership in Maryland, 1790–1840* (Chapel Hill, N.C., 1979).   *Whitman H. Ridgway*

STITH, GERARD (1821–80), Mayor of New Orleans (1858–60). An astute politician, Stith gained control of the Native American party in New Orleans and supported a major program of public improvements. Born in Fairfax County, Virginia, into the family of Griffin Stith and his fourth wife, Mary (Dent) Alexander, Gerard Stith left home at an early age to reside amid the excitement of the nation's capital. There he began his career as a printer, worked for the Washington *Globe*, and married Clara Morsell. The young couple migrated in 1845 to the prosperous port of New Orleans, which then was the fourth largest city in the United States. After brief employment at the New Orleans *Bulletin*, Stith began his long association with the *Picayune*. During most of his remaining years, he worked for this influential, conservative newspaper as the composing room foreman and an editor in all but name. Meanwhile, he became a leader in the New Orleans Typographical Union (or Printers'

Association). Stith's newspaper and union interests drew him into New Orleans politics. Running as a Whig, he was elected to the state legislature in 1847. He also won a minor judgeship, and in 1854 he began service as an assistant alderman in the lower chamber of the common council. In 1856, he was chosen recorder of the First District. When the Whig party died, this energetic politician joined the Know-Nothings, bringing organized labor into the party of Native American merchants and aristocrats. Although Stith's party literally fought the Creole-dominated Democrats for control of New Orleans, it did not become anti-Catholic and it appealed to German-American voters.

The vicious struggle to control the Crescent City culminated in the municipal elections of 1858. Stith was the mayoral candidate of the "Americans," who had long been economically dominant but politically subordinate. Avoiding the Democratic party label, the "Creoles" and "progressive" businessmen supported the independent candidacy of Major P.G.T. Beauregard. As election day approached, a heavily armed Vigilance Committee captured a state arsenal and occupied part of the French Quarter to prevent the Know-Nothings from intimidating voters. Rival forces gathered near the city hall in the American sector. Municipal government nearly collapsed, so the boards of aldermen removed Mayor Charles Waterman (q.v.) and had his replacement swear in a special police force designed to keep the two armies apart. A battle was miraculously prevented in this violent city of 160,000, and Gerard Stith's 3,581 votes narrowly bested the 3,450 of his rival, Beauregard.

Mayor Stith and most of his ticket assumed office on 21 June and immediately launched an ambitious program of much needed public improvements. Paving the streets with granite blocks and rebuilding the drainage system would combat the ever-present problems of mud, filth, and disease. Despite difficulties in getting support for such expensive projects, Stith persisted and succeeded. He also directed work on wharves, a new normal school, a pumping station, the Boys' House of Refuge, and telegraph service for the police and fire departments. Meanwhile, the mayor purged the police department, assiduously employed patronage, and cultivated the working man.

Although Stith and his machine remained controversial, serious political opposition nearly vanished. The mayor picked John T. Monroe (q.v.), a stevedore, as his successor in 1860. The American party, with Stith serving as president of the board of aldermen, dominated city government until mid-1862, when the Union occupation forces removed all Confederates from office. Federal troops briefly imprisoned Stith and several other New Orleans officials.

After a short stint with the *Daily Delta*, Stith returned

in 1863 to his position at the *Picayune*, where he remained until shortly before his death at Wytheville, Virginia, on 11 June 1880. He was survived by his wife and a daughter.

SOURCES: John Smith Kendall, "The Municipal Elections of 1858," *Louisiana Historical Society Publications* 5 (1923); New Orleans *Daily Picayune*, 13 June 1880; Leon Soulé, "The Creole-American Struggle in New Orleans Politics, 1850–62," *Louisiana Historical Quarterly* 40 (January 1957); Works Progress Administration, "Mayors of New Orleans, 1803–1936" (typescript in New Orleans Public Library, New Orleans, 1940).

D. Blake Touchstone

STOKES, CARL B. (1927–), Mayor of Cleveland (1967–71). The first black mayor of a major American city and a reform Democrat, Stokes was born on 21 June 1927 in Cleveland, one of three children born to Charles Stokes (1897–1928), a laundry worker from Alabama, and Louise (Stone) Stokes (1895–1978), a homemaker and domestic worker from Wrens, Georgia. Carl's brother Louis was elected a U.S. congressman in 1968.

Stokes grew up in poverty, shining shoes to supplement his mother's earnings as a domestic servant. He attended Cleveland public schools, dropped out of high school in 1944 to take a job, and then served with the Army of Occupation in Germany, 1945–46. After finishing high school, Stokes attended West Virginia State College and Cleveland College, then worked as an Ohio State liquor enforcement agent before taking a B.A. in law from the University of Minnesota (1954) and an LL.D. from Cleveland-Marshall Law School in 1956. He was married three times—to Edith Shirley Smith (1951, divorced 1955) to Shirley Edwards (1958, divorced 1975), and to Raija Salmoniv (1977), a Nordic beauty and former Miss Finland of 1969 (b. 1947). He has three children from his second marriage—Carl Jr., Cordi, and Cordell.

Stokes practiced law until elected state representative in 1962. He was the first black Democrat to serve in that body, to which he was reelected for two more terms. He entered the 1965 Cleveland mayoralty as an Independent Democrat and lost to Democratic incumbent Ralph Locher (*q.v.*) (87,858 to 85,716). Two years later, following the 1966 Hough Riots, Stokes won the mayoralty, narrowly defeating Republican Seth Taft, the grandson of President Taft, to become the first black mayor of Cleveland (129,396 to 127,717). He had appealed to both white and black Americans.

Mayor Stokes governed a city of 810,857 (1965 estimate) that was 36.6 percent black. Following the assassination of Martin Luther King on 4 April 1968, Stokes walked the Cleveland ghetto, restoring calm and averting an outburst of rage and frustration. Three months later, the Glenville shootout, an encounter between police and black militants, resulted in eleven deaths. Stokes avoided further violence, but he angered police and others by ordering all white police out of the area and allowing only blacks to act as a peacekeeping force.

On the political front, Stokes advocated scatter-site public housing, opened employment opportunities in public and private sectors for blacks, opposed the expansion of the freeway system through the central city, and pushed affirmative action legislation through the city council. With the backing of Cleveland business and community leaders, Stokes raised $4 million for "CLEVELAND Now," a multifaceted booster program aimed at securing matching federal dollars for urban programs. But even a charismatic figure like Stokes could do relatively little to alleviate the hardcore problems, while the energies of the federal government were increasingly mired in Southeast Asia.

Stokes won reelection over Republican County Auditor Ralph J. Perk (*q.v.*) in 1969, 120,464 to 117,013, but the revelation that militants had used "CLEVELAND Now" money to buy weapons used in the Glenville shootout, and the mayor's removal of white police during that period, developed into major stumbling blocks to further achievements as the city council, business, and civic leadership turned against him.

Stokes declined to run for a third term in 1971 and left Cleveland in 1973 to become a TV anchorman with the National Broadcasting Company in New York and to lecture and write his autobiography, *Promises of Power*.

SOURCES: Louis H. Massoti and Jerome R. Corsi, *Shootout in Cleveland* (New York, 1969); William E. Nelson and Philip J. Meranto, *Electing Black Mayors* (Columbus, 1977); Philip W. Porter, *Cleveland: Confused City on a Seesaw* (Columbus, 1976); Carl B. Stokes, *Promises of Power: A Political Autobiography* (New York, 1973); Carl B. Stokes Papers, Western Reserve Historical Society, Cleveland, Ohio; Kenneth G. Weinberg, *Black Victory: Carl Stokes and the Winning of Cleveland* (Chicago, 1968); Estelle Zannes, *Checkmate in Cleveland* (Cleveland, 1972).

Thomas F. Campbell

STOKLEY, WILLIAM STURMBURG (1823–1902), Mayor of Philadelphia (1872–81). Long-ruling political boss of Philadelphia, Stokley was born there on 25 April 1823, the son of a boot and shoe merchant who suffered severe economic losses and died in 1834. One of three children, young Stokley was forced to work, first in a bookbinder's shop and then in the employ of a boot and shoe merchant. At the age of seventeen, he became an apprentice in a confectioner's shop and ultimately owned his own establishment. In 1845, he married Mary A. Miller (1822–1900), and they had five children. Stokley was a Mason and a member of the Bethlehem Presbyterian Church. As a young man, he served in a volunteer fire department where he became acquainted with local politicians. He moved from the Whigs to the Republican party, and his antislavery views attracted the notice of the Quakers. In 1860, he won election to the common council from the normally Democratic Ninth Ward, and he became president of that body in 1865. In 1867, he was elected to the select council, becoming its president in 1868. Stokley built a wide base of support through his control of expenditures for public buildings, his attacks on the unpopular Gas Trust, and his surprising support for a paid fire department. Prior to his mayoralty, he was also assessor of internal revenue for the Second District of Pennsylvania.

Philadelphia's population rose from 674,022 in 1870 to 847,170 in 1880. The city had a mayor-bicameral councils form of government. In 1871, Stokley won election to his first term as mayor, defeating his Democratic-Reform opponent James S. Biddle 58,508 to 50,307. He was reelected in 1874 (60,128 to Democratic-Independent A. K. McClure's 49,133), and in 1877 (64,779 to Joseph Caven's 61,913). In 1881, he was defeated for reelection by Democrat Samuel G. King (q.v.) 72,428 to 78,215.

During Stokley's tenure, the councils exercised great power through control of most appointive offices. Stokley maximized the political potential of his greatest power—the appointment of police officers. The years prior to his election had been characterized by numerous disturbances and riots, especially during elections. Stokley promoted himself as a champion of law and order, and he acquired local fame by leading a posse of police to break a gas workers' strike in 1872 and by maintaining peace during the railroad strikes of 1877. Citing the need for public safety during the nation's centennial celebration, he persuaded the councils to add 200 permanent policemen to the force. Stokley effectively used the police as a source of patronage and campaign workers. In 1881, the reform Committee of 100 rejected his candidacy, as did many disgruntled suburban voters who feared the downtown area was receiving too large a share of the city's appropriations for public works. Thus, Samuel G. King defeated Stokley, ending if not bossism, the career of Philadelphia's longest ruling boss.

In 1887, Mayor Edwin H. Fitler (q.v.) appointed Stokley as director of public safety, a position he held until 1891. He also served on the Public Buildings Commission and on the Fairmount Park Commission until his death. On 21 February 1902, Stokley died of a paralytic stroke which resulted from an attack of Bright's disease. He was buried in Philadelphia.

SOURCES: Howard F. Gillette, Jr., "Corrupt and Contented: Philadelphia's Political Machine, 1865–1887" (Ph.D. dissertation, Yale University, 1970); Ellis Paxon Oberholtzer, *Philadelphia: A History of the City and Its People*, 4 vols. (Philadelphia, 1911); *Public Ledger, Inquirer, Evening Bulletin, North American*, 22 February 1902 (obituaries); J. Thomas Scharf and Thompson Westcott, *History of Philadelphia: 1609–1884*, 3 vols. (Philadelphia, 1884); John D. Stewart II, "Philadelphia Politics in the Gilded Age" (Ph.D. dissertation, St. John's University, 1973).   *John F. Sutherland*

STOWELL, JOHN M. (1827–1907), Mayor of Milwaukee (1882–84). Iron and steel manufacturer and single-term mayor, Stowell was born in Alexander, New York, on 9 March 1827, the son of Azel Stowell, a carpenter and farmer, and Abigail (Maxwell) Stowell, both old-stock Americans. The youngest of five children, Stowell attended public schools and the Alexander Classical Institute. The family moved west to Marietta, Ohio, and Stowell graduated from Marietta College. By 1849, Stowell had moved again to St. Louis, working for the Eagle Foundry and Machine Company. In 1855, he went to Moline, Illinois, and was employed by Orlando Child, an iron manufacturer. He started his own company the following year but was wiped out by the 1857 depression. Moving to Milwaukee, he worked for a local foundry and also edited the Milwaukee *News* in 1862. He joined forces with Jacob Filer in 1867 to establish the highly successful Cream City Iron Works, later renamed Filer and Stowell. In 1880, it became the Stowell Manufacturing and Foundry Company. He married Ellen E. Downey (1824–1909) in St. Louis on 10 July 1849, and they had at least three children. While Stowell was a Swedenborgian, his wife was Episcopalian.

A Democrat, Stowell had served a single term in the state legislature in 1862. In 1882, he was elected mayor, defeating Republican Harrison Ludington (q.v.) 9,635 to 7,321. Milwaukee had about 120,000 people and a mayor-council form of government. Stowell essentially supported various business measures and civic improvements while in office. He does not seem to have been interested in continuing his political career, and he held no other political offices after 1884. He returned to his foundry which soon became the city's largest iron and steel producing firm. He died on 30 August 1907.

SOURCES: *Biographical Dictionary and Portrait Gallery of Representative Men of Chicago, Wisconsin and the World's Columbian Exposition* (Chicago, 1895); *History of Milwaukee, Wisconsin* (Chicago, 1881).   *Thomas R. Bullard*

STRONG, WILLIAM L. (1827–1900), Mayor of New York (1895–97). A businessman, reform mayor, and a millionaire, born on 22 March 1827 near Loudenville, Richmond County, Ohio, Strong was the son of Abel Strong (1792–1840), a farmer born in Hartford, Connecticut, of old New England stock, and Hannah (Burdine) Strong (1798–?) of old-stock Pennsylvania ancestry. The first-born of five children, Strong had only a country school education before the death of his father forced him to seek employment. At age sixteen, he went to Wooster, Ohio, to work in a dry goods store; two years later, he moved on to a better job in the larger town of Mansfield. He moved to New York City in 1853 to take a position with L. O. Wilson and Company, a large wholesale dry goods firm that failed in the Panic of 1857. Strong then joined Farnham, Dale, and Company, staying with its successors through three reorganizations until it emerged in January 1870 as William L. Strong and Company. This firm prospered, opening branches in Philadelphia and Boston, and its owner became one of the leading merchants of New York. By the mid-1890's, Strong was president of the Central National Bank, director of several banking, trust, and insurance companies, and a vice-president of the Chamber of Commerce of the State of New York. At the time of his death, the *World* estimated his fortune to be $5 million. In 1866, Strong married Mary Aborn (1842–1921), of Orange, New Jersey; they had two children, Putnam Bradlee and Mary (later Mrs. Albert R. Shattuck). An active member of the Protestant Episcopal Church, Strong attended services at St. Thomas's, served as vestryman at the Church of the Incarnation, and was for several years treasurer of the charitable St. John's Guild.

Strong was active in politics as a business Republican from the early 1880s. An unsuccessful candidate for Congress in 1882 and a founder of the Ohio Society of New York in 1886, he worked through such organizations as the Union League Club, the Businessmen's Republican Club, and the Dry Goods Republican Club for the election of Republicans and for such causes as the gold standard. Neither a Mugwump nor a leader in the "respectable" Republican opposition to state boss Thomas C. Platt, Strong was suggested as a possible candidate for mayor in 1890. In 1894, he accepted the Committee of 70 nomination when other businessmen turned it down. He proved acceptable to Platt as well as to the Chamber of Commerce and the Independents, and won with 154,094 votes to 108,907 for Hugh J. Grant (*q.v.*), his Tammany opponent, and 7,255 for Socialist Lucien Sanial.

The contemporary press gave Mayor Strong most praise for his appointments, particularly those of Theodore Roosevelt as police commissioner and of noted san-

itary expert George E. Waring as sanitation commissioner, and for his support of school and civil service reform. The very fact that he provided a businesslike administration helped him to gain support for increased expenditures for schools and public health as well as for streets and bridges. Higher taxes, Roosevelt's policy of enforcing the state law against Sunday drinking, anti-Catholic overtones in the school reform program, his decision to give patronage to Union League Club opponents of Platt and of both reform Democrats and principled nonpartisans, made it politically impossible for Strong to seek a second term. Tammany celebrated its 1897 victory with the chant "Well, well, well, Reform has gone to Hell!"

Strong resumed his business and political career, but he continued to be troubled by chronic gout. He died at home from that ailment on 2 November 1900.

SOURCES: Harold F. Gosnell, *Boss Platt and His New York Machine* (New York, 1969 reprint of 1924 edition); David C. Hammack, "Participation in Major Decisions in New York City, 1890–1900: The Creation of Greater New York and the Centralization of the Public School System" (Ph.D. dissertation, Columbia University, 1973); George F. Knerr, "The Mayoral Administration of William L. Strong" (Ph.D. dissertation, New York University, 1957); Letters to and from Mayor Strong, Mayors' Papers, New York City Municipal Archives and Records Center; Samuel T. McSeveney, *The Politics of Depression: Political Behavior in the Northeast* (New York, 1972); New York *Times*, Evening *Post*, and *World*, 3 November 1900; Frand D. Pavey, "Mayor Strong's Experiment in New York City," *The Forum* 23 (1897); Martin Shefter, "The Electoral Foundations of the Political Machine: New York City, 1884–1897," in Joel Silbey, et al., eds., *American Electoral History: Political Behavior in the Northeast* (Princeton, N.J., 1978); Simon Sterne, "The Reconquest of New York by Tammany," *The Forum* (January 1898).

David C. Hammack

STUART, EDWIN SYDNEY (1853–1937), Mayor of Philadelphia (1891–95). The first son of Scots-Irish Protestant immigrants from Northern Ireland, Stuart was born in Philadelphia on 28 December 1853. His mother, Anna (Newman) Stuart, was the second wife of Hugh Stuart, a furniture manufacturer. Stuart had at least one brother and one sister. After completing grammar school, he began work as an errand boy at Leary's Book Store at the age of fourteen. Nine years later, he purchased the store from the estate of its former owner. By 1890, it enjoyed a reputation as the largest bookstore in the country. In 1880, Stuart helped organize the local Young Republican Club, later becoming its treasurer and president. In 1886, he successfully ran for the select council to which he was reelected in 1889. He was a presidential elector in 1884 and 1900 and a delegate to the Republican national conventions of 1888, 1896, and 1908. In 1891, Stuart became the youngest man to have been elected mayor of Philadelphia. He was a life-long bachelor.

Philadelphia in 1890 had 1,046,964 people and a mayor-bicameral councils form of government. Stuart won his mayoralty by the largest majority in the city's history, defeating Democrat Albert H. Ladner 108,978 to 69,913. He was ineligible for reelection.

Stuart became mayor during a scandal involving the embezzlement of city funds by the city treasurer, and he won high praise for restoring honesty in government. During his administration, the streetcar companies abandoned horses for trolleys, and Stuart successfully championed an ordinance requiring the companies to pay for the paving of roads after the new tracks were laid. Stuart's administration combatted the Depression with a combination of public works and cooperation with private charitable agencies. These efforts provided sewers, gas mains, and resurfaced streets and alleys in some of the city's crowded immigrant neighborhoods. Citizens were beginning to express concern over these issues, and a well-publicized abolish-the-slums movement helped provide Philadelphia with its first, albeit limited, tenement house law in 1895. Stuart's support for these measures appears to have been relatively passive compared to the active involvement of his health officer, Moses Veale.

In 1906, Stuart was elected governor, becoming the first person to serve both as mayor of Philadelphia and governor of Pennsylvania. Again he took office as a scandal broke, this time involving inflated billings during the construction of the state capitol. Stuart vigorously assisted the investigations which marked the highlight of his otherwise quiet administration. Following his term, Stuart abandoned active politics and returned to his bookstore. He was a deputy governor of the Federal Reserve Bank of Philadelphia, a director of both the Bell and Diamond States Telephone companies, and president of the board of city trusts, and served four terms as president of the Union League. Stuart was an ardent bibliophile and Philadelphia Athletics (baseball) fan. He received honorary degrees from Lafayette, the University of Pennsylvania, and the University of Pittsburgh. Edwin Stuart died on 21 March 1937 at the age of eighty-three.

SOURCES: Philadelphia *North American, Philadelphia and Popular Philadelphians* (Philadelphia, 1891); *Public Ledger, Inquirer, Evening Bulletin*, 4 March 1937 (obituaries); John F. Sutherland, ''A City of Homes: Philadelphia Slums and Reformers, 1880–1918'' (Ph.D. dissertation, Temple University, 1973); John Russell Young, *Memorial History of Philadelphia* (New York, 1898).   *John F. Sutherland*

SUTRO, ADOLPH HEINRICH JOSEPH (1830–98), Mayor of San Francisco (1895–97). Populist mayor of San Francisco towards the end of his life and a famous engineer, Sutro was born in Rhenish Prussia at Aachen on 29 April 1830 of Jewish descent. He was one of a family of seven sons and four daughters, born to Emmanual Sutro, a cloth manufacturer who died in 1847. Adolph ran the business, giving up polytechnic school to do so, but as a result of the revolutions of 1848 in Germany the family emigrated to New York in 1850. They finally settled in Baltimore while Adolph went further west, arriving at San Francisco on the steamship *California* on 21 November 1851. There and in Stockton he spent a decade in the tobacco trade and married Leah Harris (1856). They had six children, two boys and four girls. Adolph was separated from his wife for some years before her death in 1893.

News of the silver strike at Comstock, Nevada, came in 1859, and Sutro moved to East Dayton, Nevada, in 1860, starting the Sutro Metallurgical Works, a quartz-reducing mill, with John Randohr. They succeeded and by 1862 had grown to a ten-stamp mill. The silver mines were plagued by flooding, gas, and heat, and Sutro devised the idea of driving a great tunnel, ten feet high and four miles long, into the mountain to the Comstock Lode for ventilation, drainage, and transportation of timbers and ore. Financed initially on Ralston's Bank of California group, who turned against him, Sutro tried New York backers and then toured Europe, seeking supporters in 1867. He pieced together enough cash and began building the Sutro Tunnel on 19 October 1869. It was completed on 8 July 1878 at a cost of $6 million. Since Sutro took a royalty of $2 a ton on ores moved through his magnificent tunnel, he became an instant millionaire. He sold out in 1879 and used the profits to buy up land in San Francisco and its suburbs. Soon he came to hold about one-twelfth of San Francisco.

In the 1880s and 1890s, Sutro was a benefactor of the city, owning the Cliff House Ranch overlooking the ocean. A thousand acres there became known as Sutro Heights (eventually deeded to the city as a park). The Sutro Baths, opened in February 1896 as another public gift, were the finest then available and had cost $1 million. A Sutro Forest was planted. Sutro protected the seals in the area and gave land to the University of California. But he was authoritarian, used to giving orders and dispensing *largesse*, and when the radical third party, the Populists, asked him to be their nominee for mayor, they chose badly. He was a sure winner in 1894 but a poor mayor.

Sutro had long favored the working-class cause, opposed the large railroad companies, especially the Southern Pacific, and fought for classic goals, such as cheap mass transit—the 5-cent city fare. His own Sutro Street Railroad opened in San Francisco in March 1896, helping to ensure this victory. He won 31,254 of the 60,000 votes cast in the winter of 1894. At that time, San Francisco, with a mayor-council system, had a population of about 320,000. Sutro's single term ran from 7 January 1895 to 3 January 1897. At his inaugural, he promised better paved streets, improved fire controls (he warned, eleven years before the fire of 1906, that the city was open to "general fire"), better schools (emphasizing technical education, gymnastics, and kindergartens), and a rejection of machine politics. Sutro's Populist rhetoric accused the Southern Pacific (the "Octopus") of exerting a stranglehold on the city and the press. Only one paper supported him. However, he was his own worst enemy. Failing in physical and mental health (diabetes and exhaustion after such an amazing life) and unable to compromise with the twelve-member board of supervisors, Sutro also failed to grasp the ambiguities of some of the stubborn positions he took. For instance, demanding better pavements, when in fact he himself owned blocks and blocks of unimproved lots; or opposing street railroad contracts, after the board had approved one for his own firm. As the *Examiner* said: "He passed his term in a state of exasperation."

Sutro was glad to give up office in January 1897, asking plaintively, "What have I accomplished as Mayor? Very little. The Mayor is little more than a figurehead. . . . I have always had a number of men under my employ, and they did as I told them. I could not manage the politicians." He was pleased, however, when his old enemy, the Southern Pacific Railroad, did not get its refunding bill passed a few days after his farewell.

The end was tragic and pitiful for the dynamic and powerful Sutro: he lost his mind first, while his family fought over his will, worth at least $3 million. He died on 8 August 1898 in San Francisco, his "simple" funeral and cremation being celebrated by Rabbi Jacob Nieto at Sutro Heights, with a twelve-carriage procession to Odd Fellows' Cemetery. Sutro left his name and benefactions around the Bay area. Few single individuals have had such importance in California history.

SOURCES: Eugenia K. Holmes, *Adolph Sutro, A Study of a Brilliant Life* (San Francisco, 1895); San Francisco *Call*, 2 January 1897; San Francisco *Examiner*, 9 August and 14 August 1898; R. E. and M. F. Stewart, *Adolph Sutro: A Biography* (Berkeley, Calif., 1962).   *Peter d'A. Jones*

SWANN, THOMAS (1809–83), Mayor of Baltimore (1856–60). Controversial Know-Nothing mayor, Swann was born into a wealthy family in Alexandria, Virginia, on 3 February 1809. His father, Thomas Swann, prac-

ticed law and served as U.S. attorney for the District of Columbia. Swann's mother, Jane Byrd Page, belonged to one of the first families of Virginia. After graduating from the Columbian College preparatory school and the University of Virginia, Swann practiced law with his father until 1833 when he became secretary to the U.S. commission to Naples negotiating spoiliation claims. A year later, on 20 May 1834, he married Elizabeth Gilmor Sherlock of Maryland's prestigious Gilmor family.

Refusing a parental request to live at Morven, the family estate in Virginia, Swann moved to Baltimore to use his own resources. After profiting from lobbying and railroad investments, he served as president of the Baltimore and Ohio Railroad from 1848 until 1853 when he became president of the Northwestern Virginia Railroad Company. At home he enjoyed his four daughters and son, Thomas Jr. All four daughters married prominent Baltimoreans, including Mayor Ferdinand Latrobe (*q.v.*). His son died in 1867 and his wife on 26 April 1876. Swann then married Josephine Ward Thompson of New Jersey (20 June 1878), sister of Speaker of the House Samuel Randall, but that marriage soon ended in separation.

Although a former Whig, Swann entered politics as a Know-Nothing mayoral candidate. In the violent municipal election of 8 October 1856, he defeated Democrat Robert Clinton Wright 13,892 to 12,338. In the city council, the Know-Nothings held their majority in the First Branch but divided the Second Branch evenly with the Democrats. The 1856 election-day violence that left 17 dead, 67 wounded, and countless disfranchised recurred on Swann's 13 October 1858 reelection, characterized by fewer casualties but an increase in his victory margin—24,008 to 4,859 over Independent Augustus Shutt. The Know-Nothings took majorities in both council branches. The press lambasted Swann for not curbing election-day intimidation and charged that he did not represent "the legal voters of the city." But in 1865 Swann was elected governor on the Union party ticket and later went to Congress as a Democrat (1869–79).

As the mayor of 212,418 people, Swann proved an able administrator, bringing the city streetcar service and revenue from the street railroad company to provide city parks. He reorganized the fire department, replacing volunteers with paid firemen; introduced the police and fire alarm telegraph system; and improved the water facilities.

A businessman first, whether as 1850s' railroad executive or 1860s' bank president, Swann was less consistent politically. As Know-Nothing mayor, Swann embraced nativism and joined the American Protestant Association; as Union party governor, he urged improvement of habor facilities to attract more immigrants; and as Democratic congressman, he defended the rights of Catholic Irish-Americans. Upon his political retirement in 1879, Swann returned to Morven where he died on 24 July 1883. He was buried in Baltimore.

SOURCES: Jean H. Baker, *Ambivalent Americans: The Know-Nothing Party in Maryland* (Baltimore, 1977); Wilbur F. Coyle, *The Mayors of Baltimore* (Baltimore, 1919); Enoch Pratt Free Library, Baltimore: Vertical File (newspaper clippings), Maryland Room; J. Thomas Scharf, *History of Baltimore City and County: From the Earliest Period to the Present Day* (Philadelphia, 1891); Laurence F. Schmeckebier, *History of the Know Nothing Party in Maryland* (Baltimore, 1899); Joanna H. Spiro, ''Thomas Swann and Baltimore: The Mayor and the Municipality, 1856–1860'' (M.A. thesis, Loyola College, 1964); Frank F. White, Jr., *The Governors of Maryland* (Annapolis, Md., 1970).

Jo Ann Eady Argersinger

SWIFT, GEORGE BELL (1845–1912), Mayor of Chicago (1893, 1895–97). Republican mayor, born on 14 December 1845 in Cincinnati, Ohio, Swift was the son of Samuel W. Swift and Elizabeth (Bell) Swift, a Protestant couple. His parents moved to Galena, Illinois, while he was an infant. After primary education in Galena, Swift came to Chicago in 1862, graduated from the West Division High School, and began working as a cashier for the Lord and Smith wholesale drug firm. In 1867, Swift became the junior member of Frazer and Swift, manufacturers of axle-grease and lubricating oil. Swift married Lucy L. Brown (1848–1937), an old-stock Yankee from Chicago, in 1868 and they had seven children. Swift was a Mason, an active member of the Knights of Pythias and of the Union League, Illinois, Hamilton, and Hyde Park clubs.

Swift was elected alderman of the Eleventh Ward in 1879; was appointed special U.S. treasury agent of Chicago in 1884, deputy city clerk in 1885, and commissioner of public works in 1887; and was reelected alderman of the Eleventh Ward in 1892. He was elected mayor pro tem upon Mayor Carter H. Harrison's (*q.v.*) assassination in 1893, serving until John P. Hopkins (*q.v.*) was installed as mayor on 27 December. Swift was elected to a full term in his own right in 1895, receiving 143,884 to his two opponents, Democrat Frank Wenter's 103,125 and Peoples' party hopeful Bayard Holmes' 12,882. Swift declined to run for reelection in 1897.

Chicago in 1895 had 1,366,000 people and a mayor-council form of government. Mayor Swift appointed the first civil service commission, making Chicago the first metropolis west of the Atlantic seaboard to adopt a comprehensive civil service law. He emphasized the application of business methods to city government and appointed businessmen as commissioners of health and of police. He attempted to bring uniformity and regularity into the assessment and valuation of real estate, particularly in the central business district. Swift unsuccessfully sought significant changes in the powers of the mayor and the composition of the city council. He wanted the mayor's office to be vested with appointive power, subject to city council confirmation, for the offices of city clerk and city treasurer. He argued that the public would be better served if the number of aldermen were halved from sixty-eight to thirty-four and a certain number were elected at large, to discourage parochialism.

Upon leaving office, Swift returned to his businesses, the Frazer Lubricating Company and the Swift Fuel Company. In 1911, he was appointed a member of the Chicago Board of Education. He suffered a heart attack and died in Chicago on 2 July 1912 and was buried in Rosehill Cemetery, Chicago.

SOURCES: Paul M. Green, *The Chicago Democratic Party 1840–1920: From Factionalism to Political Organization* (Ph.D. Dissertation, University of Chicago, 1975); Marshall Kravitz, ''The Mayors of Chicago'' (typescript, University of Illinois, M.A. thesis, 1976); Bessie L. Pierce, *A History of Chicago* (New York, 1957), vol. 3; Frederick Rex, *The Mayors of the City of Chicago from March 4, 1837 to April 13, 1933* (Chicago, 1947).

Edward H. Mazur

SWIFT, JOHN M. (1790–1873), Mayor of Philadelphia (1832–38, 1839–40, 1845–48). Quaker city's first mayor to face a popular election, Swift was born on 27 June 1790 in Philadelphia, the son of John White Swift, a former councilman, merchant, and purser of the ship *Empress of China*. John was admitted to the bar in 1811 and practiced law in Philadelphia. He was a leader of the Whigs of Philadelphia but is best remembered as a mayor who had to face many riots in his city.

Philadelphia had a population of 93,600 and a mayor-council form of government in 1840. Swift, who had been already mayor from 1832 to 1838, before popular elections, was a candidate for mayor in October 1839 when Philadelphia for the first time tried to elect a mayor. Swift drew a plurality with 3,343 votes to John C. Montgomery's (*q.v.*) 2,670 and John K. Kane's 3,294, but since no candidate had a clear majority the election reverted to the bicameral city councils, who chose Swift as mayor.

During Swift's mayoralty, Philadelphia was torn apart by antislavery agitation and nativist riots. Pennsylvania Hall, a center of abolitionist activity (where John Greenleaf Whittier edited the antislavery *Pennsylvania Freeman*), became a target for a mob which in May 1838 ignored Mayor Swift's counsel to disperse and burned down the hall. Other mobs threatened the Friends' Shelter for Colored Orphans, but the firemen were able to save the structure.

Swift, who was elected again as mayor, 1845–48, is known to have died in 1873.

SOURCES: *Appleton's Cyclopedia of American Bi-* *ography* (New York, 1889), vol. 6; *City of Firsts: Complete History of Philadelphia* (Philadelphia, 1926); Sam Bass Warner, Jr., *The Private City: Philadelphia in Three Periods of Its Growth* (Philadelphia, 1968).

Melvin G. Holli

T

TAFEL, GUSTAV (1830–1908), Mayor of Cincinnati (1897–1900). German immigrant, newspaperman, and mayor, Tafel was born in Munich, Germany, on 13 October 1830. His parents, Dr. Leonard Tafel and Caroline (Vayhinger) Tafel, came from Würtemberg, Germany. Dr. Tafel, a noted philologist, taught at the *gymnasium* of Ulm, where Gustav, one of fourteen children, received much of his education. In 1847, Dr. Tafel emigrated to the United States and settled briefly in Urbana, Ohio, where he had accepted a position as professor of languages at the New Church (Swedenborgian) College. At the end of 1849, when the Tafel family left Urbana for New York City, Gustav remained in Ohio and joined his grandparents, who had emigrated earlier, in 1832, settling in Cincinnati.

Tafel worked as a printer with the Cincinnati *Gazette*. In 1855, he left the *Gazette* and joined the *Volksblatt* staff as city editor. He also read law with Judge Stallo and Robert L. Cook. After his admittance to the bar in 1858, Tafel resigned from the *Volksblatt* and practiced law until the outbreak of the Civil War, when he helped organize the Ninth Ohio Volunteer Infantry. By 1862, he had been promoted to the rank of colonel. In 1866, he served one term in the state legislature. He married a fellow Swedenborgian, Teresa Dorn of Louisville, Kentucky, on 19 January 1870, and they had ten children. Tafel helped organize numerous ethnic *Turner Gymnasium* societies and was an active member of the Grand Army of the Republic, the Loyal Legion, the German Literary Club, and the German Old Men's Home Society.

Cincinnati in 1897 had over 325,000 people and a mayor-council form of government. After losing to John B. Mosby (*q.v.*) in 1891, Tafel ran successfully for mayor in 1897. Although he had switched his political affiliation several times by 1884, he had joined the Democratic party and was a very active member. In 1897, Tafel also received the backing of influential Republicans dissatisfied with a number of annexations secured under the outgoing Republican mayor. This "fusionist" ticket swept almost all the municipal offices in 1897. Tafel, with 35,868 votes, soundly defeated the Republican candidate, Levi C. Goodale, who received only 28,433.

Tafel proved to be an inefficient administrator and was not chosen to represent the "fusion" ticket again in 1900.

He retired from public life and returned to his law practice. He died in 1908.

SOURCES: Biographical Cyclopedia and Portrait Gallery (Cincinnati, 1895); *Cincinnati's Mayors* (Cincinnati, 1957); Charles T. Greve, *Centennial History of Cincinnati and Representative Citizens* (Chicago, 1904); *History of Cincinnati and Hamilton County Ohio* (Cincinnati, 1894); Zane L. Miller, *Boss Cox's Cincinnati: Urban Politics in the Progressive Era* (New York, 1968). *Patricia Mooney Melvin*

TAFT, CHARLES PHELPS (1897–), Mayor of Cincinnati (1955–57). Lawyer and reformer, born in Cincinnati on 20 September 1897, Taft was the son of William Howard Taft (1857–1930), U.S. President and chief justice of the United States, and Helen (Herron) Taft (1861–1943), both Unitarians of old-stock Yankee ancestry. The last of three children, Taft attended the Taft School in Watertown, Connecticut, Yale (1914–17), and Yale Law School (1919–21), during which time he coached the university football team. He served with the Third Field Artillery in World War I, winning several medals for valor. In 1917, Taft married Eleanor K. Chase (1894–1961) a Bennett College graduate, and they had seven children. The Tafts were active members of Christ Episcopal Church in Cincinnati.

Taft began the practice of law in 1919, and was a partner with his brother Robert, 1922–24, followed by a partnership with T. Stettinius. He served as prosecuting attorney of Hamilton County, 1927–28, and chairman of the County Charities Commission, 1934–35. Taft was a member of the Cincinnati City Council, 1938–42, 1948–51, and 1955–77, initially a reform Republican and then as a Charterite. He actively supported the charter (city manager) and proportional representation system, and was president of the City Charter Committee, 1946–48. He was director of the Commission of War Services and president of the War Relief Control Board, 1941–43, and worked for the State Department as director of the Office of Wartime Economic Affairs, 1944–45.

Selected by the council as mayor for a two-year term in 1955, Taft supported urban renewal and mass transit programs, as well as a revival of downtown Cincinnati. The city had 503,998 people in 1950. Taft was essentially a nonpartisan mayor, although he belonged to the charter faction. After his term ended in 1957, he continued working for reform and social groups. He did not retire from active politics until the end of his council term in 1977, when he was eighty years of age.

SOURCES: Henry F. Pringle, *The Life and Times of William H. Taft*, 2 vols. (New York, 1939); *Current Biography* (New York, 1945); Ishbel Ross, *An American Family* (Cleveland, 1964); Charles P. Taft papers in William Howard Taft Memorial Library, Cincinnati; and Charles P. Taft collection in Library of Congress.

Thomas R. Bullard

TALLMADGE, JOHN J. (1818–73), Mayor of Milwaukee (1865–66). Born in Claverack, New York, on 10 June 1818 of old Scottish-American stock, Tallmadge was educated in the common schools of his neighborhood. At the age of sixteen, he began work in a store in Lyons, New York, and stayed until he was twenty-one. He was married in 1840, and from 1840 to 1848 he was in the transportation business in Albany and in the same business in Buffalo from 1848 to 1855. In 1855, he moved to Milwaukee as agent for the Western Transportation Company where he had charge of steamboats linking Milwaukee to the New York Central Railroad and access to New York via Buffalo. He held this post for fifteen years, and then entered the provision and meatpacking business in a highly successful way. He was a founder of the Milwaukee Chamber of Commerce, serving as vice-president in 1862 and as president in 1863 and 1864. Tallmadge was a promoter of the Soldiers' Home Fair, a relief agency for retiring veterans of the Civil War, and served as its treasurer.

Tallmadge was elected mayor of Milwaukee in 1865 and 1866 by a combination of Democrats and the Eight-Hour League. Always a unionist, Tallmadge was a War Democrat during the Civil War supporting the efforts of the Lincoln administration. Much of his mayoralty was caught up in the war effort. Milwaukee, a city of 50,000, was governed at the time by a mayor and a bicameral common council.

Tallmadge was the Democratic nominee for governor of Wisconsin in 1867, losing to Republican Lucius Fairchild by 4,764 votes. He continued his interest in the transportation and meatpacking business until failing health forced him to retire to his farm in Summit, Wisconsin, where he died on 16 October 1873.

SOURCES: Frank A. Flower, *History of Milwaukee, Wisconsin* (Chicago, 1881); John S. Gregory, *History of Milwaukee, Wisconsin* (Chicago, 1931); Bayrd Still, *Milwaukee: The History of a City* (Madison, Wis., 1965); Jerome A. Watrous, *Memoirs of Milwaukee County*, 2 vols. (Madison, Wis., 1909).   *Donald F. Tingley*

TATE, JAMES HUGH JOSEPH (1910–   ), Mayor of Philadelphia (1962–72). The first Roman Catholic mayor of Philadelphia, born on 10 April 1910 in a small row-house in north Philadelphia, Tate was the first of six children born to James Edward Tate (d. 1951), a machinist, whose father had emigrated in 1846 from County Derry, Ireland, and Anna R. (Shea) Tate, also of Irish descent. Young James left high school early to work with his father at the Budd metal fabricating works. He finished high school in the evening, went to Strayer's Business College, and worked as secretary to Dean John Hervey of Temple Law School. Tate entered Temple Evening Law School and graduated in 1938. While in law school, the political boss of Tate's Thirty-fourth Ward, John Haney selected him to run for committeeman, and Tate won the first of seventeen straight election victories.

Failing his bar exams, Tate worked as an insurance adjustor and did legal research in the court of common pleas, until in 1940 he ran successfully for the state legislature. After serving three terms, "Big" Jim Clark, a kingpin in the pre-World War II Democratic party, chose Tate as the executive secretary of the city committee. Tate was elected real estate assessor in 1946.

On 20 January 1942, Tate married Anne M. Daley; they had two children, Francis X. and Anne Marie. Tate and his family were Roman Catholic, and he was especially active in Irish organizations such as the Friendly Sons of Saint Patrick.

Tate entered the city council in 1951 and until 1962 served successively as majority floor leader, president *pro tem*, and president. When Mayor Richardson Dilworth (*q.v.*) resigned to run for governor in 1962, under the provisions of the city charter, Tate as council president became mayor. Philadelphia in 1960 had 2,002,512 people (26 percent black) and a strong mayor-council form of government. In 1962, Tate won the mayor's seat over his opponent, James T. McDermott (401,714 to McDermott's 333,446). Again in 1967, Tate was returned to office against Arlen Specter (353,326 to Specter's 342,398).

Tate inherited the reform goals of the Joseph Clark (*q.v.*)-Richardson Dilworth administrations. While continuing the urban renewal phase, Tate eschewed the Americans for Democratic Action liberalism of his predecessors and worked successfully to solidify the political power base of the mayor's office. However, he enjoyed little more success than other big-city mayors in dealing with the festering racial ghetto, the deteriorating schools, and an insufficient urban tax base. He did advocate a regional approach to urban problems and helped to establish the Southeastern Pennsylvania Transportation Authority (SEPTA). Calling for "human not urban renewal,'' he compiled a mixed record in dealing with the city's racial ferment. He signed an anti-discrimination bill, appointed a progressive school board with black representation, and at the end of his second full term counted 43 percent of the municipal employees black. Yet, the Congress of Racial Equality blasted the ineffectiveness of his Human Relations Committee, and Tate fought with black leaders over the use of anti-poverty monies. Tate also appointed Frank Rizzo (q.v.) police commissioner and began the enormous strengthening of the city police force.

Tate left office in 1972 and retired to lead a quiet private life.

SOURCES: "Biographical Sketch" of James H. J. Tate, Office of the Mayor News Release, June 1970; Anthony Roth, ed., "Mayors of Philadelphia, 1691 to 1977: Collection of the Genealogical Society of Pennsylvania" (unpublished collection found in Historical Society of Pennsylvania, Philadelphia); William J. Speers, "Did Anyone Really Know Mayor Tate?" Philadelphia Inquirer Magazine, 28 November 1971; James H. J. Tate, with Joseph P. McLaughlin, "Memoires of Mayor Tate," Evening Bulletin, 18–26 January 1974.

John F. Bauman

TAYLOR, DANIEL GILCHRIST (1819–78), Mayor of St. Louis (1861–63). Scottish-American steamboat captain and Republican mayor, born in Cincinnati on 15 November 1819, Taylor was the son of James Taylor and his wife, the former Miss McLean, both Scots Presbyterian immigrants. Young Daniel attended public schools for a few years, until his parents died. He started working aboard steamboats on both the Ohio and Mississippi rivers during the 1830s. In 1845, he was captain of the *Clermont* on her lengthy voyage up the Yellowstone River. In 1849, he moved to St. Louis where he opened a boat furnishings company which was destroyed in the big fire of that year. He subsequently formed the company of Taylor and Hopkinson, a steamboat agency. In 1850, this firm was reorganized as Taylor and Harrington, lasting until 1857 when Taylor opened a successful liquor store. Around 1853 he married Angelique Henri of Prairie du Rocher, Illinois. They had two daughters, one of whom drowned, along with Mrs. Taylor, on 4 February 1858 when the steamboat *Crossman* exploded and sank in the Mississippi. In 1860, Taylor married another French woman, Emilie Lebeau of St. Louis, and they had three children. Taylor was a Mason, but joined the Roman Catholic Church in later years.

An ''old-style'' Democrat, Taylor served on the city council, 1852–53 and 1854–56. He soon drifted away from the Democrats—at least enough to run for mayor on the unionist ticket in 1861 when he defeated Democrat John How (q.v.) 12,992 to 9,434. St. Louis had 160,773 people (1860) and a mayor-council form of government. Mayor Taylor's major accomplishments in office arose out of the needs of the Civil War. He arranged for relief measures to aid soldiers' families and helped raise funds to prevent a business depression—necessary to balance the loss of the prewar trade with the South.

After leaving office, Taylor became president of the Boatmen's Insurance Company and also head of the Real Estate Savings Institution. He served two terms (1871–75) as city treasurer but otherwise showed little interest in political activities. He continued his banking interests until his death on 8 October 1878.

SOURCES: Charles H. Cornwell, St. Louis Mayors: Brief Biographies (St. Louis, 1965); William Hyde and Howard L. Conrad, eds., Encyclopedia of the History of St. Louis, 4 vols. (New York, 1899); J. T. Scharf, History of Saint Louis City and County, 2 vols. (Philadelphia, 1883).

Thomas R. Bullard

TAYLOR, EDWARD ROBESON (1838–1923), Mayor of San Francisco (1907–10). A reform mayor of San Francisco, Taylor was born on 24 September 1838 in Springfield, Illinois. He was the son of Henry West Taylor, a fairly well-to-do merchant and farmer, and Mary (Thaw) Taylor, who moved their family from Springfield to Boonville, Missouri, in about 1844. Taylor grew up in Boonville where he attended the Kemper School, now the Kemper Military Academy. Upon graduation, he became a typesetter and soon acquired part-ownership of the local Boonville *Observer*. In 1861, the future looked very bleak in a wartorn Missouri, and Taylor decided to leave for California. That fall, he made his way to San Francisco via New Orleans and Panama, and he arrived in February of the following year. Once in California, he went to Sacramento where he worked first as a typesetter and then as a purser on steamers between that city and San Francisco. Taylor quickly decided to become a physician and entered the Medical Department of the University of the Pacific in 1863. The following year, that institution became part of the Toland Medical College from which Taylor received his degree on 5 December 1865. He practiced medicine for about two years and then became the private secretary to the new governor of California, Henry H. Haight. He kept this position throughout Haight's term of office (1867–71) and also studied for the bar. He was admitted to the California State bar in January 1872 and immediately began a partnership with Haight whose term had expired the previous month. Taylor soon became one of San Francisco's leading attorneys and later served as president of the San Francisco Bar Association in 1890, 1891, 1894, and 1895. His legal career culminated in 1919 with his selection as dean of the Hastings College of Law, a position which he held for twenty years. During these busy years, Taylor found time for an active social and family life. On 20 April 1870, he married Agnes Stanford, the niece of Leland Stanford. They had five children, of whom only two, Edward DeWitt and Henry Huntly, survived to adulthood. The first Mrs. Taylor died on 27 November 1906, and on 8 February 1908, Taylor remarried. His new wife was Eunice Jeffers, a woman forty-three years his junior.

In 1907, San Francisco's population was approaching 416,000, and the city was governed by a mayor and a board of supervisors. During that year, it was also experiencing the sensational graft prosecutions of Mayor Eugene Schmitz (*q.v.*) and boss Abe Ruef. On 13 June 1907, Schmitz was convicted of extortion, and, a month later, on 8 July, he was sentenced to five years in the state penitentiary. With his conviction and sentencing, the office of mayor fell vacant, and the prosecution decided that Taylor, a registered Democrat, should be appointed. The special prosecutor directed the board of supervisors (many of whom had already confessed to bribery) to select Taylor. Once he was safely in office, the disgraced supervisors were ordered to resign, and Taylor appointed an entirely new board. Taylor finished out Schmitz's unexpired term and was elected in his own right for a new two-year term in November 1907. In that election, Taylor running as a Democrat, was opposed by P. H. McCarthy (*q.v.*), the candidate of the Union-Labor party, and Daniel A. Ryan, the Republican. He beat both of them handily, receiving 28,766 votes, with McCarthy getting 17,583 and Ryan 9,255.

During Taylor's term of office, San Francisco began to move in several important directions. The city rapidly rebuilt the downtown which had been devastated by fire and earthquake in 1906, and, by 1910, practically every major firm in the city had reestablished itself. At the same time, plans began to be made for the great new civic center which was ultimately approved in 1912, although the bond issue of 1909 lacked 3,215 votes of having the necessary two-thirds majority. Finally, Taylor and the board of supervisors hired John R. Freeman, an internationally known hydraulic engineer, to prepare a report on the water needs of the city. This report, finally issued in 1912, was one of the first steps in San Francisco's acquisition of the Hetch Hetchy water supply.

In 1909, Taylor declined to run for reelection, and when his term expired, he returned to the position of dean at Hastings Law School. He held no other political position than trustee of the public library. In 1919, he retired as dean and spent the remaining years of his life continuing to write poetry (as life-long hobby) and reading the classics of English and French literature. He died

on 5 July 1923 at the age of eighty-one.

SOURCES: Walton Bean, *Boss Ruef's San Francisco, the Story of the Union Labor Party, Big Business, and the Graft Prosecution* (Berkeley and Los Angeles, 1967); Franklin Hichborn Papers, Mss., Public Affairs Service, Research Library, UCLA, Los Angeles; Kenneth M. Johnson, *The Life and Times of Edward Robeson Taylor, Physician, Lawyer, Poet, and Politician* (San Francisco, 1968).   *Neil L. Shumsky*

TAYLOR, MARK P. (1812–53?), Mayor of Cincinnati (1851–53). Cincinnati's first Democratic mayor, Taylor was a Yankee, born in Massachusetts in 1812. He moved to Ohio by 1842 when he was listed in local directories as a cooper. In 1843, he was chosen as a constable in Cincinnati and became a justice of the peace shortly afterwards. He was also president of Washington Fire Company Number 1. Taylor and his wife Margaret (1816–?), from New York, had three children.

Taylor first attempted to become mayor in 1847, losing to incumbent Henry Spencer (*q.v.*) (Whig) 4,213 to 3,599. He defeated Spencer in 1851 by 6,923 to 6,800. Unfortunately, Taylor was in poor health, and contemporary accounts claim he spent almost the entire two years of his term in bed, arising only once—to attempt (without success) to halt a strike by firemen. He died sometime in 1853, after his term had ended.

SOURCES: Cincinnati's Mayors (Cincinnati, c.1957); Charles F. Goss, *Cincinnati: The Queen City*, 4 vols. (Chicago, 1912).   *Thomas R. Bullard*

TESCHEMAKER, HENRY FREDRICK (1823–1904), Mayor of San Francisco (1859–63). First foreign-born mayor of San Francisco, Teschemaker (sometimes spelled Teschemacher) was born in England on 16 February 1823. He moved to California as early as 1842, trading hides, furs, tallow, and other goods on the Pacific Coast for a Boston firm, William Appleton and Company. Settled in San Francisco by 1849, he began buying many land lots, as the Gold Rush got under way. He is also known as the artist of an early drawing of the city, dated 1846 (*A View of Place of Anchorage of Yerba Buena*). Teschemaker saw much of early San Francisco history—the gold days, the vigilantes, and the rise of crime—and he led the city during the silver boom and the Civil War.

A quiet, conservative man, Teschemaker supported the first Vigilante Committee of 1851, as juryman on arson trials of the "Sidney Ducks"—the Australian gang. He joined the second vigilante movement of 1856, and three years later was chosen as the Vigilante-People's party candidate to replace Mayor Burr (*q.v.*). The Democrats were hopelessly divided over slavery, and on 7 September 1859, Teschemaker swept into office as president of the board of supervisors, with 5,034 votes (the opposition being divided between Cutter, 3,181, and Knox, 2,065). Teschemaker's first term was quiet, with rare public appearances: he agreed to further street improvements (a leveling of Broadway which involved cutting away still more of Telegraph Hill) and to the plan to move the main city center from Portsmouth Plaza to the Yerba Buena Cemetery (today's civic center). He formally opened the first street railway, down Market Street on 4 July 1860.

Reelected without difficulty on 6 November 1860 (the same day as Abraham Lincoln), Teschemaker could point to a previous record of good government, probity, and economy. In fact, the city was calm because local politics lost interest with the coming of the silver boom and the Civil War. California was virtually cut off from the rest of the nation by the war, and San Francisco was forced to develop its own manufacturing and to extend new patterns of trade with the Orient. Both of these healthy necessities brought war prosperity and city growth. A state census of 1860 put the city at 56,802; the population had almost tripled by 1870 (149,473). During his second term, Teschemaker doubled the size of the police force (to 200 men). In April 1861, his title, president of the board, reverted back to the more popular form "mayor," and after only six months into the term, yet another charter change advanced his reelection date to May. These changes, in the name of "clean government," aimed to separate the city from state party politics. On 23 May 1861, Teschemaker was returned to office by the People's party, 6,247 votes to his opponent's 5,029. The new Republican party had run its first candidate in the city, Charles T. Fay.

Teschemaker's third-term achievement was a massive codification and revision of all city ordinances and their reduction to one general order of fifteen chapters. Fire codes were expanded, the chain gang abolished, and sidewalk, street, and sanitation laws revised. War and silver prosperity brought increased city tax revenues and better paved streets.

The mayor refused a fourth term, was given a farewell banquet, and was escorted to the steamer *Constitution* by a public parade on 23 July 1863, leaving for Europe—virtually forever. Although he returned for a brief visit in 1892, Teschemaker spent the rest of his long life, forty-one years, in Europe. He died in Territet, Switzerland, on 29 November 1904, age eighty-one. Mayor Teschemaker represented the *best* side of the Vigilante-People's party movement in California—its constructive, "good government" aspect.

SOURCES: W. F. Heintz, *San Francisco's Mayors* (Woodside, Calif., 1975); *North Pacific Review* (March 1863), (portrait and biography); San Francisco *Chroni-*cle, 1892; W. F. Swasey, *Early Days and Men of California* (Oakland, Calif., 1891).   *Peter d'A. Jones*

THOM, CAMERON ERSKINE (1825–1915), Mayor of Los Angeles (1882–84). Mayor during the "Great Boom," Thom was born on his father's plantation, "Berry Hill," in Culpeper County, Virginia, on 20 June 1825. His father, John Thom, was a scholar, planter, sheriff, and state senator, and had served in the War of 1812. Cameron was Episcopalian, and his ancestors were Scottish Highlanders. He was educated in private schools and studied law at the University of Virginia. In 1849, he went overland to California, mined briefly on the American River and Mormon Island, and then opened a law office at Sacramento, but he soon turned to supervising properties of a mercantile firm. In 1853, he was appointed assistant law agent for the U.S. Land Commission at San Francisco, and the next year he was sent to Los Angeles to take testimony in land cases. When this task was completed, Thom resigned and was appointed city attorney, shortly thereafter being named to an unexpired term as Los Angeles district attorney. For a while he held both offices simultaneously. Altogether, Thom served three terms as district attorney. In 1857, he was elected as a Democrat to represent Los Angeles, San Bernardino, and San Diego counties in the California State Senate, for one term.

Thom left his Los Angeles law practice in 1863 to enlist in the Confederate Army as a volunteer officer with the rank of captain. He remained in uniform until the war's end and then returned to Los Angeles where the community with its Southern feelings soon welcomed him. President Andrew Johnson pardoned Thom, and his active political life resumed.

Thom married three times, first in 1852 to Miss E. L. Beach, whose precarious health probably was a factor in his moving to Los Angeles's mild climate; she died in about 1857. Next, in June 1858, he married Susan Henrietta Hathwell, and after her death, in about 1868, he married her younger sister, Belle Cameron Hathwell, on 9 November 1874. He had one child by his second wife and four children by his third wife. Thom joined the Masons at Sacramento and in 1871 became a volunteer fireman in Los Angeles. In the latter year, he displayed heroism by risking his life to implore fellow townsmen to stop the murders of Chinese during early Los Angeles's bloodiest race riot, the Chinese lynchings of 24 October.

Among Thom's political services were: city attorney, 1856–58, emergency sanitation committeeman, 1876–77, member of the board of freeholders, 1887–88, and mayor, police commissioner, and police judge coterminously, 1882–84. In 1888, he attended a convention seeking the creation of a state of South California.

In business affairs, Thom was very successful, serving as a director of the prestigious Farmers and Merchants Bank, 1873–1915, a chief stockholder and director of the Bank of Glendale. He became a millionaire through real estate dealings, particularly in Glendale. As one of Los Angeles's most eminent attorneys, Thom was associated with Judge Albert M. Stephens and U.S. Senator Stephen M. White.

When Thom became mayor in 1882, Los Angeles was feeling the beginnings of the tremendous real estate boom of the 1880s. It had grown to about 30,000 people. At the time, Elysian Park was created, and the board of trade was founded. Occupied with modernizing Los Angeles, Thom worked to get the clearing of the river's debris and riverside levies against nearly perennial floods. Political parties were in flux, and when Thom, a Democrat, ran for reelection against Republican E. F. Spence (*q.v.*) in 1884, he was defeated; Spence won 2,063 votes to his 1,549.

Temperate in habits, Thom continued in good health to nearly the end of his eighty-nine years. He died of apoplexy at Los Angeles on 2 February 1915.

SOURCES: *Chronological Record of Los Angeles City Officials, 1850 to 1938* (Los Angeles, 1966), vol. 3; Robert Glass Cleland and Frank B. Putna, *Isaias W. Hellman and the Farmers and Merchants Bank* (San Marino, Calif., 1965); Jackson A. Graves, *My Seventy Years in California, 1857 to 1927* (Los Angeles, 1928); *Historical and Biographical Record of California and an Extended History of Los Angeles* (Los Angeles, 1915), vol. 2; James Franklin Burns, Pioneer: An Autobiographical Sketch,'' Historical Society of Southern California *Quarterly* (Los Angeles), 32 no. 1 (March 1950); J. Kurts, ''Reminiscences of a Pioneer,'' Historical Society of Southern California *Quarterly*, 7 (1906); Los Angeles County Hall of Records, Certificates of Death; Los Angeles *Semi-Weekly News, Star,* and *Times* files, containing reports on city council meetings and mayoral functions, and reflections on Thom's career, 1858 to 1889, *passim*; ''Members of the California Senate,'' *Hutchings' California Magazine* (San Francisco) 2 (April 1858). *John E. Baur*

THOMAS, JAMES S. (1802–74), Mayor of St. Louis (1864–67). Banker and politician, born in Maryland on 25 May 1802, Thomas moved to St. Louis in 1825 and opened the city's first successful bank, which he operated until 1838 when he formed a partnership with L. A. Benoist (Thomas, Benoist and Co.). The partnership lasted until 1850, when he then resumed banking on his own. In the early 1830s, he had married a Miss Skinner of St. Louis, but she died shortly afterwards. On 27

November 1837, he married Susan Hackney (also of St. Louis), and they had one daughter, In 1861, Thomas became head of the city's board of assessment.

When Mayor Chauncey Filley (*q.v.*) resigned in 1864, the Republican party leaders selected Thomas to replace him, and he defeated Democrat J. Gabriel Woerner 6,477 to 3,873. He was subsequently reelected to two full terms, defeating Daniel T. Wright (6,829 to 3,764) n 1865 and John Finn (8,237 to 5,471) in 1867. In 1869, Nathan Cole (*q.v.*) won the Republican nomination, so Thomas ran against him as a Democrat, losing by a vote of 8,961 to 6,033. St. Louis had 160,773 people in 1860 and a mayor-council form of government.

Thomas was a pro-business mayor who worked to restore the city's commercial activity to prewar levels. He carried on his predecessor's efforts to buy the city's gas company but failed. He improved the city's sewer system and waterworks, and launched a new house-numbering scheme. A cholera epidemic during his second term led to a complete overhauling of the public health structure, with the creation of a modern board of health, virtually eliminating the once-dreaded tradition of summer diseases. After leaving office, Thomas served as a park board commissioner until his death on 26 September 1874.

SOURCES: Charles H. Cornwell, *St. Louis Mayors: Brief Biographies* (St. Louis, 1965); William Hyde and Howard L. Conrad, eds., *Encyclopedia of the History of St. Louis*, 4 vols. (New York, 1899); J. T. Scharf, *History of Saint Louis City and County*, 2 vols. (Philadelphia, 1883); Walter B. Stevens, *St. Louis; History of the Fourth City, 1764–1909* (Chicago, 1909).

Thomas R. Bullard

THOMAS, NICHOLAS W. (1810–64), Mayor of Cincinnati (1857–59). Meatpacker and mayor, born in Jenkintown, Pennsylvania, on 23 May 1810, Thomas moved to Cincinnati in the 1830s. He founded N. W. Thomas and Company, one of the city's major porkpacking establishments; Cincinnati, a meatpacking center, was sometimes called ''Porkopolis'' by critics. Thomas was president of the Miami Exporting Company and one of the founders of the Chamber of Commerce. He married Arminda Bernard of New York, and they had at least two children. The Thomases were noted for their charity work and were among the leading backers of various social welfare organizations in the city.

Originally a Whig, Thomas was a Republican by 1857 when he was elected mayor, defeating C.J.W. Smith (Democrat) 8,785 to 8,559. Cincinnati had 161,044 people in 1860 and a mayor-council form of government. As mayor, Thomas supported all types of civic improvement. Personally a popular man, he donated his entire mayoral salary to charities. After leaving office in 1859, he resumed his business career. He died on 27 March 1864.

SOURCES: Homer W. Brainerd, *A Survey of Ishams* (Rutland, Vt., 1938); Cincinnati *Enquirer*, 29 March 1864; *Cincinnati's Mayors* (Cincinnati, 1957); U.S. Census for 1850. *Thomas R. Bullard*

THOMPSON, SHELDON (1785–1851), Mayor of Buffalo (1840–41). In a real sense, Captain Sheldon Thompson was the *first* mayor of Buffalo—at least, the first directly and popularly elected mayor. Until 1840, Buffalo mayors had been selected by the city council (itself an elected body, to be sure). The New York State legislature enacted a bill in January 1840 stating that mayors should be directly elected, and Thompson was the first. The election campaign was tough, according to a contemporary account, "without doubt the most severe one ever known." Hotly contested as it was, the 1840 election was not the most exciting episode in Captain Thompson's adventurous life.

Thompson was born on 2 July 1785 in Derby, Connecticut, of a long line of old-stock Yankee adventurers, dating back to 1687 in New Haven. His grandfather, Jabez, was an officer in the French and Indian War, later killed while commanding troops at Long Island. His father was lost at sea in 1794. Sheldon was pressured to become a cabin-boy at age ten because of the needs of a large, bereaved family, dependent on a small farm. In 1798, Thompson was taken prisoner by the French at Guadeloupe, at age thirteen. Later, he became master of his own vessel based in New Haven, trading with the West Indies. Persuaded by business partners that inland trade was safer and more profitable, he moved to Lake Erie to supervise the building of a 100-ton vessel in 1810; the ship was used in the War of 1812. Thompson's firm transshipped goods west, ascending the Niagara River into Lake Erie under power of what he called, in a fine metaphor, the "horn breeze" (oxen-hauled ships).

Thompson married Catheryn Barton (1793–1832) of Lewiston, New York, the daughter of Benjamin Barton (1770–1842), a pioneer surveyor on the Niagara frontier. The family was Episcopalian. They had ten children, only four of whom survived to maturity.

Thompson was the Whig candidate for mayor of Buffalo in 1840. His opponents, seeking to insult him, called him a Federalist. His opponent was a popular young Democrat and graduate of Union College of 1827, George Barker. Of the 2,300 ballots cast in this very first mayoral election in Buffalo, Thompson was the victor by only 10.

At the time, Buffalo had a population of about 10,000 and was growing. Thompson was made wealthy by his shipping interests, and mining and lumber investments in Ohio. He was a warder and vestryman of St. Paul's Episcopal Church from its founding. He died on 13 March 1851 and was buried in Forest Lawn Cemetery.

SOURCES: Henry Wayland Hill, *Municipality of Buffalo: A History, 1720 to 1923* (Buffalo, 1923), vols. 1–3; John T. Horton, *Old Erie: The Growth of an American Community*, vol. 1; *History of Northwestern New York* (New York and Chicago, 1947); Scrapbooks, Buffalo and Erie County Historical Society. *Scott Eberle*

THOMPSON, WILLIAM BARLUM (1860–1941), Mayor of Detroit (1907–1908, 1911–12). Thompson was born on 10 March 1860 in Detroit to Irish-born, Roman Catholic immigrant parents, Thomas Thompson, a Detroit policeman, and Bridget (Barlum) Thompson. Young William attended the Detroit public schools, graduated from Detroit Central High School, and went on to the Detroit Business University. He then secured a position in his uncle's meat market and in 1882 opened his own meat market in Cadillac Square, known as Thompson and Brother's. He later founded Robinson's Beef Company and Cadillac Square Improvement Company, became the treasurer of the Detroit Furnace Repair Company and the secretary-treasurer of Michigan Salt Pickle and Supply Company of Saginaw, and invested in real estate developments in Detroit. Thompson was a well-known and popular downtown businessman and local politician prior to his mayoralty. In 1887, he married Nellie Hymes, also a Catholic, and they had nine children, two boys and seven girls. Thompson attended SS Peter and Paul's Jesuit Church of Detroit, was a member of the Knights of Columbus, the Benevolent Paternal Order of the Elks, and the Harmonie Club, and was knight commander of the Order of St. Gregory.

Detroit in 1906 had over 450,000 people and a mayor-council form of government. Thompson had been active as an alderman from the Eighth Ward during the Hazen Pingree (*q.v.*) reform years (1892–98), and in 1897 he was elected city treasurer, the only Democrat to survive the Pingree Republican victories of that year. A popular Irish Catholic Democrat, Thompson claimed the friendship of politicians such as Mayor Pingree and Mayor Tom Johnson (*q.v.*) of Cleveland, both nationally known urban reformers. Tom Johnson came to Detroit and campaigned for Thompson in the mayoralty campaign of 1912. Thompson served as Detroit's city treasurer for nine years, giving up that position when he was elected mayor in 1906, by a vote of 30,042 over George P. Codd's (*q.v.*) 27,241.

Thompson, like his Republican predecessor, came to the mayor's office promising to settle the streetcar franchise issue by bringing about municipal ownership. He managed to settle a difficult streetcar workers' strike, but municipal ownership eluded him. As a result, he was defeated in his bid for reelection in the 1910 campaign. The failure of Thompson's successor, Philip Breitmeyer (*q.v.*), to accomplish municipal ownership brought new life to Thompson's political career, and in 1910 Detroit Democrats nominated him for a third time. Campaigning vigorously for municipal ownership, a 3-cent fare, and civil service reform, Thompson was returned to city hall by his 1910 victory of 27,608 votes over Proctor K. Owens' 22,461.

In his second term, Thompson unveiled a solution to the streetcar franchise issue known as the Thompson-Hally Ordinance, which provided for a new twelve-year franchise and a 3-cent fare. The ordinance was roundly defeated at the polls by 10,000 votes. In an attempt to salvage his 1912 bid for reelection, Thompson ordered the arrest of several city councilmen on charges of corruption. Claiming to have uncovered widespread corruption in the council, Thompson campaigned in 1912 on an anti-graft platform. But his inability to solve the streetcar franchise issue, coupled with Teddy Roosevelt's Republican sweep of Detroit, brought about his second defeat.

After 1912, Thompson returned to his business interests and became a successful merchant and realtor. He died at his home in Detroit on 13 February 1941.

SOURCES: Jack D. Elenbaas, "Detroit and the Progressive Era: A Study of Urban Reform 1900 to 1914" (Ph.D. dissertation, Wayne State University, 1968); Jack D. Elenbaas, "The Excesses of Reform: The Day the Detroit Mayor Arrested the City Council," *Michigan History* 54 (Spring 1970); A. N. Marquis, *The Book of Detroiters*, 2d ed. (Chicago, 1914); William Barlum Thompson Papers, scrapbooks, Reading Room File and Biographical Index, Drawer No. 224, First and Second Annual Messages to Detroit Common Council, 1907, 1908, Burton Historical Collection, Detroit Public Library.   *Jack D. Elenbaas*

THOMPSON, WILLIAM G. (1842–1904), Mayor of Detroit (1880–83). Republican mayor of Detroit and a popular lawyer, Thompson was born in Lancaster, Pennsylvania, on 23 July 1842, the son of a lawyer who was a direct descendant of the Revolutionary War general, Alexander McDougall. Thompson attended Amherst College, leaving in his senior year when the Civil War began. He first enlisted in a Pennsylvania regiment and then served in both Michigan and New Jersey units. He achieved the rank of first lieutenant and saw action in several battles, being severely wounded at Chancellorsville. In 1864, after his regiment was disbanded, he entered Columbia College of Law in New York City but

did not graduate. He returned to Detroit and in 1867 was admitted to the Michigan bar. In November 1867, he married Lillie Brush, daughter of A. E. Brush, a wealthy pioneer landowner in the city. They had one daughter before Lillie Thompson's death in 1875. Three years later, Thompson married Adele Campau, sister of Daniel J. Campau, Jr., a prominent Democratic politician, of a pioneer French Detroit family line.

Thompson began his political career in city government in 1872; before his election as mayor in 1880, he had served on the board of estimates, as alderman, and as president of the common council. During the 1870s, he was twice nominated for the office of mayor, once losing to Alexander Lewis (*q.v.*) and once declining to run.

Thompson was elected mayor in 1879, easily defeating the incumbent Democrat George C. Langdon (*q.v.*) 8,587 to 6,480. In 1880, Detroit had a population of 116,342 and a mayor-council type of government. After his first term, Thompson was reelected by 8,060 to Democrat William Brodie's 6,649. During both of his terms, Thompson pursued conservative economic policies in line with those of the local Republican party.

After leaving office, Thompson disagreed with the national party platform; he became a Democrat and in 1891 split the local party into two factions—one led by himself and the regulars led by his brother-in-law, Daniel J. Campau, Jr. In that year, Thompson ran unsuccessfully for mayor but soon returned to the Republican party. He was elected state senator in 1894 and during his term was a spokesman for conservative Detroit business interests as well as a bitter foe of the reform mayor and later governor, Hazen S. Pingree (*q.v.*).

Thompson had a reputation for brilliant oratory and was one of the best known and most popular politicians of his time in Detroit. He was first president (1881–85) of the Detroit baseball club. He was struck by a bicyclist in downtown Detroit in April 1904, never recovered, and died in a sanitarium in Yonkers, New York, on 20 July 1904. A gregarious man of wealth, he belonged to the Masonic Order, the Sons of the American Revolution, the Society of the Cincinnati, and several Detroit societies. He was buried in the family plot in Princeton, New Jersey.

SOURCES: Detroit *Free Press*, 21 July 1904; Detroit *News*, 20 July 1904; Silas Farmer, *History of Detroit and Wayne County and Early Michigan*, 3d ed. (Detroit, 1890, reprint, Detroit, 1969); Melvin G. Holli, *Reform in Detroit: Hazen S. Pingree and Urban Politics* (New York, 1969); Robert B. Ross and George B. Catlin, *Landmarks of Detroit*, revised by Clarence W. Burton (Detroit, 1898).

W. Patrick Strauss

THOMPSON, WILLIAM HALE (1867–1944), Mayor of Chicago (1915–23, 1927–31). Colorful, controversial Republican mayor, born on 14 May 1867 in Boston, Massachusetts, Thompson was the first son of Commander William Hale (1838–91) and Medora (Gale) Thompson. The elder Thompson, a successful businessman in Boston, took his family to Chicago where his father-in-law had figured prominently in the city's incorporation. Young Bill was educated at Charles Fessenden Preparatory School. He exhibited little interest in school and at the age of fifteen journeyed west to work on ranches, eventually to manage a family ranch in Ewing, Nebraska. In 1891, after his father's death, Thompson returned to Chicago to administer the family business interests. He married Mary Walker Wyse of Louisville, Kentucky, on 7 December 1901; they had no children. They remained married, although alienated from each other. Thompson was active in many sporting clubs and social groups.

Thompson's outgoing nature attracted the notice of prominent Republican businessmen who urged him to run for alderman. He served the Second Ward, 1900–1902, and was Cook County commissioner, 1902–1904.

Chicago in 1915 had a population of almost 2.5 million and a weak mayor-strong council form of government. The council consisted of thirty-five wards, represented by two partisan aldermen. Thompson was elected mayor on 6 April 1915, 398,538, to Robert M. Sweitzer, Democrat 251,061 and two others, 28,426. His plurality was the largest in any Chicago municipal election to that time. Thompson was narrowly reelected on 1 April 1919 (259,828, to Robert M. Sweitzer, Democrat, 238,206, Maclay Hoyne, Independent, 110,851, and others 81,917. In 1921, a major restructuring of the city council occurred, and there were now fifty wards, with only one nonpartisan alderman elected.

Thompson wisely did not seek reelection in 1923 because of scandals and a vigorous Chicago *Tribune* attack against him. On 5 April 1927, he returned to power, decisively defeating incumbent William E. Dever (*q.v.*), Democrat 515,716 to 432,678; and J. D. Robertson, Independent 51,347. Thompson was finally rejected by Chicago voters on 7 April 1931, losing to Democrat Anton J. Cermak (*q.v.*) 671,189 to 476,932. Chicago then had a population of 3,378,000, and more than one million voters participated.

Thompson was one of the most colorful mayors in Chicago's history. With his charisma, he appealed to all classes of voters, but a great base of his strength was the black voter. His administrations were characterized by publicity-oriented pronouncements. His isolationist, pro-German, anti-British stance earned him the title "Kaiser Bill" during his first term. His second-term push for public works construction earned him the sobriquet "The Builder." His election in 1927 was aided by Al Capone and was sparked with "America First" and anti-King George V slogans.

After his terms as mayor, Thompson sought to keep active politically, but he ran a weak third in the 1936 governor's race and lost in the Republican gubernatorial primary in 1939. His last years were spent tragically in illness and melancholy. He suffered a heart attack and died on 18 March 1944 in Chicago. The urban demagogue caused controversy even after his demise, when it was discovered he had left assets of over $2 million.

SOURCES: Donald S. Bradley, "The Historical Trends of the Political Elites in a Metropolitan Central City: The Chicago Mayor" Center for Social Organization Studies Working Paper No. 10 University of Chicago, Department of Sociology, May 1963; Alex Gottfried, *Boss Cermak of Chicago: A Study of Political Leadership* (Seattle, 1962); George C. Hoffman, "Big Bill Thompson His Mayoral Campaigns and Voting Strength" (M.A. thesis, University of Chicago, 1956); Reinhard H. Luthin, *American Demagogues: Twentieth Century* (Boston, 1954); George Schottenhamel, "How Big Bill Won Control of Chicago," *Journal of the Illinois State Historical Society* (Spring 1952); Lloyd Wendt and Hermand Kogan, *Big Bill of Chicago* (Indianapolis, 1953).

Andrew K. Prinz

THOMSON, JAMES (1790–1876), Mayor of Pittsburgh (1841–42). Thomson, whose grandfather had come from Scotland in 1771, was born on 18 December 1790 in Franklin County, Pennsylvania. Little is known of his father, Archibald Thomson, but James was apprenticed to a Chambersburg, Pennsylvania, clockmaker—almost certainly Alexander Scott. Thomson moved to Pittsburgh in 1812 and set up his own clock shop, later adding jewelry and watchmaking.

Prospering in business, Thomson married Elizabeth, daughter of William Watson, a Pittsburgh merchant, in 1824. The following year he went into partnership with Samuel Stackhouse, one of the city's earliest and most successful steam-engine builders. Later, he joined a former Stackhouse partner, John Tomlinson, in the same field. His engines powered many of Pittsburgh's mills, as well as many of the early steamboats on the local rivers. His firm also built iron steamers, including the *Allegheny*, which was the first metal hull to run on the rivers, and the *Michigan* (renamed *Wolverine*) which was moved in sections and assembled on Lake Erie.

Thomson was a minority mayor, receiving 1,144 votes in a four-man, seven-party race. He was backed by a fragile fusion of Whigs, Anti-Masons, and revived Federalists; William Graham got 604 votes on the Firemen's and Citizens' party tickets. Hammond Marshall, Workingman's party, and William McKelvy, Democrat, divided another 1,144 votes almost equally. The city had a population of about 24,000, with a government that included a mayor and select and common councils.

After failing to be renominated by any party, Thomson returned to the engine and boat business. He ran again in 1843 as a Whig and Anti-Mason, missing election by 104 votes and running a close third in a five-man race.

On the arrival of the first railroads in about 1850, Thomson began manufacturing freight cars. In 1853, he changed fields again, becoming chief engineer of the Pittsburgh Gas Company, making it a successful operation for the first time. He continued in the post until 1871 and as a consultant until his health failed in the spring of 1875. Thomson died on 10 August 1876. His son, William W. Thomson, admitted to the bar in 1855, was a successful lawyer. The family was most likely Presbyterian.

SOURCES: *History of Allegheny County, Pennsylvania* (Philadelphia, 1876); *History of Allegheny County, Pennsylvania* (Chicago, 1889); William G. Johnston, *Life and Reminiscences of William G. Johnston* (Pittsburgh, 1901).   *George Swetnam*

TIEMANN, DANIEL FAWCETT (1805–99), Mayor of New York (1858–60). A frustrated municipal reformer, Tiemann was born in New York City on 9 January 1805 to Anthony and Mary (Newell) Tiemann, of German-American stock. Educated briefly in the city's free school system, Tiemann in 1818 became a clerk in a wholesale drug company before joining his father's firm which manufactured paints and oils. After becoming a partner, he took over the organization when his father retired and built it into one of the largest in the nation. Married on 30 August 1826 to Martha Clowes, a niece of Peter Cooper, the Tiemanns had ten children. Tiemann served his political apprenticeship as a Democratic assistant alderman, almshouse governor, and on the board of education before running for mayor.

By 1858, New York City had a population of over 700,000 and was in the midst of staggering problems largely created by massive growth. Its new government, imposed by the 1857 Republican legislature, consisted of a bicameral common council, weak mayor, and municipal and county boards that were either popularly elected or chosen by the governor. Tiemann, running with bipartisan support from Tammany Hall, the Know-Nothings, and Republicans, defeated controversial Fernando Wood (*q.v.*) 43,216 to 40,889 in an election marred by violence and fraud on both sides.

As mayor, Tiemann sought to serve his fractious constituency while making needed reforms, including re-

organizing the board of education, improving granting street cleaning contracts, investigating fraudulent bills and kickbacks, easing state control over the police, halting aldermen from raising their salaries, and creating a thoroughly efficient government based on honesty and economy. Tiemann failed. He could not satisfy the conflicting patronage claims which his backers made; the city was too fragmented and decentralized for executive leadership; and the continued bitterness between Tammany Hall and Fernando Wood disrupted the political process. Tiemann's only accomplishment was the creation of the custom of placing the names of streets on street lamps.

Denied renomination, Tiemann returned to his factory but did not lose interest in politics. For a time a close friend of William Tweed, Tiemann broke with him and in 1872 aided anti-corruptionists by becoming a state senator. After his term, Tiemann officially retired from politics, stayed active in business until over ninety, and died after a short illness on 29 June 1899.

SOURCES: Jerome Mushkat, *Tammany: The Evolution of a Political Machine* (Syracuse, N.Y., 1971); Samuel Pleasants, *Fernando Wood of New York* (New York, 1948); I. N. Phelps Stokes, *The Iconography of Manhattan Island, 1498–1909* (New York, 1926).

Jerome Mushkat

TIMANUS, E. CLAY (1863–1923), Mayor of Baltimore (1904–1907). Republican mayor, born on 2 September 1863 in Baltimore County, Maryland, Timanus left school at fifteen to work for his father, John T. Timanus, in the family flour mill. Later he ran a flour, feed, and grain store, became active in the local corn and flour exchange, and was elected to the board of the Baltimore Chamber of Commerce. The family was Methodist and old-line Maryland settlers, of Scandinavian-Swiss descent. Timanus married Grace Lowry Hutchins in 1886 (d. 1947), and they had three children. Timanus ran successfully for city council in 1897, sat out the 1899 race, ran successfully again in 1901, and was elected president of the Second Branch (upper house) of the council in 1903. When the Democratic incumbent, Robert M. McLane (*q.v.*), shot himself in office in 1904, Timanus by charter succeeded to the mayoralty.

Baltimore in 1904 was a city of more than half a million people (508,936 by the 1900 Census), with a mayor-council form of government. In succeeding to the mayor's office at McLane's death, Timanus worked with urban reformers appointed by his predecessor. He supported McLane's program for building sewers, schools, and firehouses, reserving parkland and paving streets in the recently annexed suburbs. In 1905, he called for a public improvements conference, rallying support from a wide range of Baltimore business, neighborhood, professional, and political associations. A conference-appointed committee subsequently undertook a public education program and secured voter support for a series of referenda to carry out the improvements. Timanus ran for election in 1907 but was defeated by Democrat J. Barry Mahool (*q.v.*) 43,584 to 48,254 votes. His defeat reflected the dominant position of a united Democratic party in Baltimore. Running again in 1911 as a reform candidate against James H. Preston (*q.v.*), Timanus narrowly lost 46,809 to 47,508 votes. Personally, Timanus was a genial, popular man.

Timanus died in 1923.

SOURCES: Baltimore *News*, 1904–1907; Wilbur F. Coyle, *The Mayors of Baltimore* (Baltimore, 1919); James B. Crooks, *Politics and Progress: The Rise of Urban Progressivism in Baltimore, 1895–1911* (Baton Rouge, La., 1968); Clayton Coleman Hall, *Baltimore, Its History and Its People* (New York, 1912); The Mayor's Papers (Timanus), Baltimore City Hall; *Sun Almanac for 1908* (Baltimore, 1908); *Sun Almanac for 1912* (Baltimore, 1912).   James B. Crooks

TOBERMAN, JAMES R. (1836–1911), Mayor of Los Angeles (1872–74, 1878–82). Three-time, economy-minded mayor, Toberman was a Southerner born on 22 June 1836 in Richmond, Virginia. His father, John Toberman, was German-born, but his mother, Elizabeth (Campbell) Toberman, was a native Virginian. In 1845, the family moved west to Missouri where young Toberman worked in a mercantile business before taking a B.A. at the University of Virginia. In 1859, he moved to California via the Isthmus and engaged in various businesses. After Toberman achieved the rank of major in the Civil War, Lincoln appointed him U.S. deputy revenue assessor at Los Angeles, a position he held for about six years. Toberman spent the rest of his life in the region. He was also agent for Wells, Fargo and Company locally. He joined Los Angeles's pioneer bank, Hellman, Temple and Company, and by 1873 was also an insurance agent for the North British and Mercantile Insurance Company.

Toberman's political career began in 1868 when he was elected to the Los Angeles City Council, serving until 1870. In a community strongly Democratic, he was a supporter of that party, and in 1872, he was chairman of the Los Angeles Greeley Club. In December, he won the mayoralty against the popular Cristóbal Aguilar (*q.v.*), three times mayor, by 715 to 378 votes.

As mayor, Toberman immediately called for improving the city's financial condition. He reduced Los Angeles's indebtedness by over $30,000. When his first term ended, there was $25,000 in the city treasury. Toberman was proud that the tax rate had been reduced from $1.60 to $1.00 per $100 property evaluation. Toberman Street was named for him. The mayor's official messages became models of clarity and planning, admired by the press. During his second term, 1882, electric lights were first turned on, making the city one of America's best-lit communities. In 1872–74, he had seen the Los Angeles population grow from 8,000 to 10,000, while the number of public schools increased from eight to eighteen.

In 1878, Toberman sought a second term and won against Acting Mayor Bernard Cohn (*q.v.*) 1,422 to 562. The Workingman's party, then noted for its anti-railroad and anti-Chinese stance, had nominated him, much to the disgust of his opponents who said that he hired Chinese labor himself and had not done manual labor in many years. The kind of clothing he favored—high silk hat and gold-headed cane—were criticized by his workingclass supporters. During this second term, Toberman was accused of excessive leniency in his judgments in the mayor's court.

By the early 1880s, Los Angeles was feeling the first surge of the land boom, as real estate soared, construction increased, thousands of Midwesterners flocked in as settlers, and the telephone, electricity, oil pipelines, four-story buildings, and a vibrant Chamber of Commerce began to symbolize the modern metropolis of 15,000 or more people. Toberman presided over this transition time which swept away frontier ways. He boasted about the additions of public parks and street beautification, while calling for additions to the public library and other municipal amenities.

After leaving office, Toberman continued in his insurance and realty businesses. His wife of forty-two years, the former Emma J. Dye, an old-stock Methodist, died on 17 September 1909 of endocarditis. One of his two sons, Homer J. Toberman, had predeceased her on 4 June 1901. Never well after these losses, Toberman himself succumbed to pneumonia on 26 January 1911 in Hollywood and was buried in Evergreen Cemetery.

SOURCES: *Chronological Record of Los Angeles City Officials, 1850–1938* (Los Angeles, 1966); Arthur M. Ellis, comp., *Historical Review: Seventy-Fifth Anniversary: Los Angeles Lodge No. 42, F. & A.M.* (Los Angeles, 1929); "James R. Toberman," by F. Goddard, Municipal Reference Library, Los Angeles City pamphlet, Los Angeles Public Library; Los Angeles County Hall of Records, Death and Marriage Records; Los Angeles *Express, Herald, Star,* and *Times* files, 1872–1911; "Major James R. Toberman," *Annual Report* of Los Angeles County Pioneers of Southern California, 1911–12 (Los Angeles, 1912); Harris Newmark, *Sixty Years in*

Southern California, 1853–1913 (New York, 1916); Benjamin D. Wilson Papers, Huntington Library.

John E. Baur

TOBIN, MAURICE JOSEPH (1901–53), Mayor of Boston (1938–44). New Deal mayor and later governor, born on 22 May 1901 in Roxbury, Massachusetts, Tobin was the son of James Tobin and Margaret (Daly) Tobin, Roman Catholic immigrants from Ireland. He received his early education at Our Lady of Perpetual Help Elementary School in Roxbury and at the High School of Commerce in Boston before he undertook prelegal studies at Boston College. On 19 November 1932, he married Helen Noonan of Brighton, and they had two daughters and one son. The young Democrat decided to run for mayor of Boston when he rose to traffic manager in the New England Telephone and Telegraph Company.

Tobin came into city hall with a solid background in politics. Not only had he won a seat in the Massachusetts House in 1926, but also he won election to the Boston School Committee in 1931 by topping a field of twelve candidates and in 1935 by topping a field of twenty-nine. Although James Michael Curley (*q.v.*) had been his political mentor during these years, disagreements between them resulted in a political rivalry. Despite Curley's efforts to sidetrack him, Tobin was sufficiently resourceful as a campaigner to defeat him in 1937 by 105,212 votes to 80,376 and in 1941 by 125,786 to 116,430 votes for mayor of Boston.

Boston had a population of about 818,000 people and a mayor-council form of government when Tobin became mayor of Boston. The young mayor restored confidence in Boston's ability to pay its debts and used the New Deal programs to try to end the Depression in Boston. Despite the decline in the city's population, he was able to cut into the entrenched support of Curley and to endear himself to progressive elements in both major parties, while maintaining a good relationship with the establishment. Just as he gave his loyal support to Franklin D. Roosevelt's domestic policies in the late 1930s, so he defended the president's foreign policies in the early 1940s.

Elected governor of Massachusetts in 1944, Tobin was effective in bringing about a fair employment practice law in the state. Failing to win a second term in 1946, he was engaged in a potentially dangerous primary fight with Paul A. Dever for the gubernatorial nomination when President Harry S Truman called him to be his secretary of labor on 7 August 1948. In this capacity, the former governor campaigned energetically for the national ticket and contributed significantly to Truman's stunning victory that same year.

During the next four years, Tobin became one of the

president's chief campaigners as he continued his work at the Department of Labor and fought to repeal the Taft-Hartley law. Not only was he a strong link between the administration and the Roman Catholic community of which he was a part, but he was also a major bond between the president and the American Jewish community whose ideal of a homeland for its people Tobin had supported throughout his own political career. Tobin was a member of a number of fraternal organizations, including the Knights of Columbus, and was honored by several universities with doctoral degrees. Within six months of leaving Washington, he died of a heart attack at Scituate, Massachusetts, on 19 July 1953 and was buried in Holyhood Cemetery in Brookline. A bronze statue of him stands on the Esplanade in Boston.

SOURCES: Gerald F. Coughlin, comp., *Addresses and Messages . . . of his Excellency Governor Maurice J. Tobin . . .* (Boston, 1947); Vincent A. Lapomarda, ''Maurice Joseph Tobin,'' *New England Quarterly* 43 (1970); Vincent A. Lapomarda ''Maurice Joseph Tobin, 1901–1953,'' (Ph.D. dissertation, Boston University, 1968); Vincent A. Lapomarda, ''A New Deal Democrat in Boston'' *Essex Institute Historical Collections* 108 (1972); Maurice J. Tobin, *Inaugural Address . . . to the City Council* (Boston, 1938); Maurice J. Tobin Papers, Boston Public Library; Secretary Maurice J. Tobin File, National Archives.   *Vincent A. Lapomarda*

TORRENCE, JOHN FINDLAY (1819–83), Mayor of Cincinnati (1869–71). Torrence was born on 24 May 1819, the son of a judge. He had six brothers and an undetermined number of sisters. He received his education at the Pleasant Hill Academy, better known as ''Cary's Academy,'' which later became Farmer's College. Having a substantial inheritance, Torrence did not go into a business or a vocation.

Torrence was elected to the city council in 1840 and for several terms thereafter. He became its president in 1860. In 1867, he was elected as a Republican to the state Senate for the 1868–69 term. Cincinnati, whose population was to increase to 216,239 by the 1870 Census, had a mayor-council form of government. Torrence received the nomination of the Republican party for mayor of the city in 1869. He won the election by 13,654 votes to his Citizens' Reform opponent Charles Thomas's 11,733. He resigned his unexpired seat in the state Senate to accept the office of mayor.

Torrence was one of Cincinnati's most retiring and self-effacing mayors, who nevertheless was capable, unruffled, and efficient. He returned to private life with five of his unmarried brothers. He died on 28 January 1883, after fifteen years of intense suffering from the gout.

SOURCES: Cincinnati *Commercial*, 1 April 1869; Cincinnati *Enquirer*, 29 January 1883; Charles Theodore Greve, *Centennial History of Cincinnati and Representative Citizens*, 2 vols. (Chicago, 1904); [Robert Herron], *Cincinnati's Mayors* (Cincinnati, 1957); *History of Cincinnati and Hamilton County, Ohio* (Cincinnati, 1894).   *Dwight L. Smith*

TOWNSEND, JOHN (c. 1805–50), *Alcalde* of San Francisco (1848). Fourth American *alcalde* (a Mexican executive-judicial office that preceded the American mayoralty) of San Francisco in the prestatehood period before the office of mayor was created, Dr. John Townsend was also the city's first resident graduate physician. Born in Fayette County, Pennsylvania, around 1805, the son of an English pioneer of the same name, Townsend earned his M.D. at Lexington Medical College. An insatiable pioneer from the outset, called a perpetual seeker after the foot of the rainbow, Townsend practiced medicine in Pennsylvania, Ohio, Indiana, and Missouri, moving further west all the time and ending up as obstetrician, surgeon, and general practitioner in Buchanan County, Missouri, by 1843. In 1832, he married Elizabeth Louise Schallenberger in Stark County, Ohio. They had a son, John H. M. Townsend, born in San Francisco on 26 November 1848.

Dr. Townsend helped organize the second overland trip, the Stevens party, to California, the first to cross the Sierras via the Truckee River (which his party named after their Indian guide) and the first to bring covered wagons into California. The party left Missouri in May 1844, reached the Sierras in late fall, with early snows, were probably the first white men to view Lake Tahoe, suffered no loss of life, and had babies born during the journey. At Donner Lake, Townsend's seventeen-year-old brother-in-law, Moses Schallenberger was left with the wagons (full of silks, satins, shawls, and combs to sell to the Spanish ladies of California); they had built a log cabin, used later by the tragic Donner party (1846). Schallenberger suffered terribly over the winter but survived. Townsend and his wife reached Sutter's Fort on 13 December 1844 on horseback.

They arrived during revolutionary times and joined American forces to oust the Mexican governor, Micheltorena. After a brief stay in Monterey, the footloose Townsend took his patient wife off to Yerba Buena, where he opened, in 1846, the first doctor's office in San Francisco history. A prominent public figure, he was elected to the school board (21 February 1847), which built the first public school in the city (April 1848); speculated in real estate with a Dutchman, Cornelius de Boom, planning a suburb, *Potrero Nuevo*, on Mission Bay which failed to attract lot buyers; and was made

alcalde on 1 April 1848 (serving until October). The town's population, under 500 in 1846, shrank during the gold craze and then grew rapidly from 1849 with waves of migrants. Townsend replaced the unpopular George Hyde (*q.v.*), after popular petitions in his favor. From December 1848, he served on the new town council, initially as its first president.

Never satisfied, Townsend slipped away from his post as *alcalde* in June-August 1848 in order to try his luck at the gold mines; ironically, his absence produced petitions for his replacement. He returned to San Francisco, disappointed from the mines and in 1849 retired to a 195-acre ranch two miles from San Jose in the Santa Clara Valley, having tried everything else. His only satisfaction was his son, born after sixteen years of marriage. When cholera swept through the valley and wiped out the doctor and his wife, on December 1850 or January 1851, the little boy was discovered playing by his mother's dead body. Dr. Townsend was a pioneer of pioneers.

SOURCES: R. H. Cross, *The Early Inns of California* (San Francisco, 1954); H. Harris, *California's Medical Story* (San Francisco, 1932); G. D. Lyman, "The Scalpel Under Three Flags in California," *California Historical Society Quarterly* 4:2 (June 1925); F. Tomlinson, "John Townsend—the Peripatetic Pioneer," *California and Western Medicine*, 51:3–5, (September-November 1939).   *Peter d'A. Jones*

TROWBRIDGE, CHARLES CHRISTOPHER (1800–83), Mayor of Detroit (1834). Mayor and prominent businessman, Trowbridge was born in Albany, New York, on 29 December 1800, the son of Luther and Elizabeth (Tillman) Trowbridge, old-stock Yankees. His father, a merchant, was from Massachusetts and had served as a captain during the Revolution. Charles was one of six children, and after the early death of his father, the family was broken up. Charles lived at home until age twelve when he was indentured to a merchant in Oswego, New York. He worked in a store until the business failed in 1815, and then he held various jobs. In 1819, at the urging of his missionary friend, the Reverend John Montieth, he moved to Detroit. He became a deputy to the U.S. marshal and clerk of the courts. He also met General Lewis Cass. In 1820, he accompanied Cass's expedition around the Great Lakes, searching for the source of the Mississippi River. Trowbridge was presumably a good linguist because Cass hired him as an interpreter and accountant for Indian affairs. Trowbridge worked for Cass for several years and, in 1821, successfully negotiated a treaty with the Indians in the Green Bay area. He married Catherine Whipple Sibley, a native-born Ohian, in 1826, and they had four daughters and one son. Trowbridge was a Republican and an active

Episcopalian.

Trowbridge was appointed commissioner of bail, 1821–26, and served as secretary to the regents of the University of Michigan, 1821–35. In 1825, he began a career in banking when he was appointed cashier of the newly formed Bank of Michigan. He held this post until 1836. He also began to speculate in land and, with some Boston investors, was one of the founders of Allegan, Michigan, in 1834. He was elected alderman for Detroit in 1833 and served on a committee that called for better kept financial records for the common council. He helped to recover $15,000, owed to the city by purchasers of lots, and proposed that this money be used for a new city hall and market.

Trowbridge, a National Republican, was elected mayor on 8 April 1834 without opposition and received 170 votes. The city had a population of 4,973 and a mayor-council form of government. Trowbridge led the council in passing an ordinance that reduced the number of ''groceries'' selling liquor in the city. He appointed a surveyor who, by 1835, established a permanent grade for the city. Plans for new sewers were approved. Detroit was struck by cholera in the summer of 1834 for the second time in two years. The disease raged through the city, killing Governor George B. Porter and several hundred others. The mayor led the fight against the disease, directing the physicians, setting up emergency hospitals, and visiting the sick. When the epidemic subsided, Trowbridge resigned as mayor on 13 September 1834.

Trowbridge served as financial officer for the city in 1835. He visited several eastern cities, trying to find a purchaser for $100,000 worth of city bonds, issued for the construction of sewers. He failed to find a buyer in the East and returned to Detroit where he eventually sold the bonds to Oliver Newberry, a member of the common council.

In 1837, Trowbridge was the Whig candidate for governor of the new state of Michigan. He lost to Stevens T. Mason by 237 votes. He never again ran for political office.

In 1839, Trowbridge was appointed president of the Bank of Michigan and held this position until the bank's failure in 1843. He was president of the Michigan State Bank from 1845 to 1853 and was appointed secretary and resident director of the Detroit and Milwaukee Railroad in 1843, serving as its president from 1863 to 1875. He was a director of the Detroit and St. Joseph Railroad and an investor in real estate and plank roads.

Trowbridge was active in civic and religious affairs. He was a founder of the Historical Society of Michigan; a regent of the University of Michigan, 1839–42; president of the Detroit Association of Charities, 1882; a delegate to the general convention of the Episcopal Church from 1835 on; a member of the standing committee of the Diocese of Michigan; and senior warden of Christ Episcopal Church, 1865. A public testimonial dinner was held for Trowbridge on the occasion of his eighty-second birthday. He died in Detroit on 3 April 1883 and was buried in Elmwood Cemetery.

SOURCES: Stephen Bingham, comp., *Early History of Michigan with Biographies of State Officers, Members of Congress, Judges, and Legislators* (Lansing, Mich., 1888); James V. Campbell, ''Biographical Sketch of Charles Christopher Trowbridge,'' *Collections of the Pioneer Society of the State of Michigan* (Lansing, Mich., 1907), vol. 6; Detroit Common Council, *Journal of the Proceedings of the Common Council of the City of Detroit, 1824–1843* (n.p., n.d.); Detroit *Free Press*, 4 April 1883; Charles C. Trowbridge Papers, Burton Historical Collection, Detroit Public Library.

William T. Bulger

TROWBRIDGE, JOSIAH (1785–1862), Mayor of Buffalo (1837). Trowbridge, pioneer physician, early Buffalo mayor, and one of a series of Yankee mayors, was born on 29 September 1785, the third of four children of Captain John Trowbridge (1752–1825) of Framingham, Massachusetts, a farmer, local officeholder, and veteran of the American Revolution, and his wife, Mary (Bent) Trowbridge (1755–1844). The family, old-stock Puritans, was Congregationalist. At age fifteen, Josiah became a clerk in his elder brother John's store in Cambridgeport, Massachusetts, but soon took up the study of medicine. He studied under Dr. Willard of Uxbridge, Massachusetts, and Dr. Kittredge of Framingham before being licensed to practice in 1808 or 1809. After practicing for a short time in Weathersfield, Vermont, Trowbridge moved to Buffalo and then across the Niagara River to Fort Erie, Canada. At the outbreak of the War of 1812, though not in sympathy with the war party, he returned to Buffalo and served in the local militia. He returned to Fort Erie in 1813 to bring back Margaret Wintermute (1797–1863), the daughter of John and Mary Jane (Smith) Wintermute, a Canadian (Episcopalian) woman, whom he married on 22 September 1813. They had eleven children.

Early in his medical practice, Trowbridge was associated with pioneer Buffalo physician Dr. Cyrenius Chapin. He later formed partnerships with Drs. John E. Marshall (1828–29, 1830–31), Alden B. Sprague (1831), Charles Winne (1835–36, 1838–42), Bela H. Colgrove, and Thomas B. Clarke. He was a charter member of the Erie County Medical Society in 1821 and the short-lived Buffalo Medical Society in 1831, and he became the first president of the Buffalo Medical Association in 1845.

Buffalo had 15,661 inhabitants in 1835 and 18,213 by

1840. The city was governed by a common council consisting of two aldermen from each of five wards, elected for one-year terms. The common council appointed the mayor and other city officials. Dr. Trowbridge, originally a Federalist and then a Whig, whose sole previous political office was as a treasurer of the Village of Buffalo, 1816–17, was appointed mayor by the council in March 1837, following a full day of balloting. During the early part of his term, Trowbridge succeeded in raising city taxes to support the newly established city schools. In December 1837, radical refugees from Canada, including William L. Mackenzie, came to Buffalo in the wake of the Upper Canada Rebellion and received support in money, arms, and volunteers for the ''Patriot'' army. Mayor Trowbridge, in contact with federal officials, attempted to halt actions that might lead to conflict between the United States and British authorities in Canada. Feeling unable to maintain law and order in the city, Trowbridge resigned on 22 December 1837; the council appointed Pierre A. Barker (q.v.), collector of customs and alderman from the Fifth Ward, as acting mayor.

In 1836, Trowbridge left his medical practice to devote himself to the management of his land and property holdings, particularly the United States Hotel. Suffering financial losses in 1837 and 1838, Trowbridge returned to medicine as an active practitioner and then as a consultant until he was forced to retire because of ill health in 1856. He died on 18 September 1862.

Although his parents were Congregationalists, Trowbridge became an Episcopalian early in life and was an active supporter of St. Paul's Church in Buffalo.

SOURCES: Orrin Edward Tiffany, ''Relations of the United States to the Canadian Rebellion of 1837–1838,'' *Publications of the Buffalo Historical Society* 7 (1905); ''A Tribute of Respect to Josiah Trowbridge, M.D.,'' *Buffalo Medical and Surgical Journal* 2 (October 1862); Frances Bacon Trowbridge, *The Trowbridge Genealogy: History of the Trowbridge Family in America* (New Haven, Conn., 1908); John S. Trowbridge, *Biographical Sketch of the Late Josiah Trowbridge, M.D. of Buffalo* (Buffalo, 1869).   *Christopher Densmore*

TUCKER, RAYMOND R. (1896–1970), Mayor of St. Louis (1953–65). Three-term Democratic mayor, born on 4 December 1896 in St. Louis, Tucker was the son of William J. and Mary Ellen (Roche) Tucker, both Roman Catholics. He attended local schools, St. Louis University (A.B., 1917) and Washington University (B.S., 1920). Tucker was an instructor in mechanical engineering at Washington University, 1921–23, assistant professor (1923–24), and, finally, associate professor (1927–34). On 28 May 1928, he married Mary Edyth Leiber, and they had two children. The Tuckers were

Catholics, and Tucker belonged to Sigma Xi, Tau Beta Pi, and the University Club.

A Democrat, Tucker was Mayor Bernard Dickmann's (q.v.) secretary, 1934–37. From 1937 to 1942, he served as commissioner of smoke regulation and director of public safety, being responsible for the city's first effective antismoke ordinance. He retired from politics for nine years in 1942, being appointed chairman of the Department of Mechanical Engineering at Washington University. In 1951, he returned to public life, being appointed director of civil defense. In 1953, he was elected mayor, defeating C. G. Stifel (Republican) 144,298 to 82,348. In 1957, he was reelected, defeating R. J. Mehan, Jr., 102,448 to 30,713. In 1961, he defeated Ben Lindenbusch 101,994 to 59,917. Mayor Tucker lost the 1965 primary to A. J. Cervantes (q.v.), ending his hopes of being elected to a fourth term. St. Louis had 856,746 people in 1950 and 750,026 by 1960, and a mayor-council form of government.

Tucker supported a wide range of civic ventures in his twelve years as mayor: expressways, a civic auditorium, a new planetarium, a city art museum, a riverfront floodwall, the Gateway Arch, and new voting machines for the entire city. He was able to win public approval of a $110 million bond issue to finance these projects. He helped change the face of St. Louis. Tucker was also concerned with social problems and secured passage of the city's first fair housing and public accommodation acts, as well as the first fair employment practices act of 1956. During 1963–65, Tucker was president of the U.S. Conference of Mayors. After leaving public office, he was professor of urban affairs at Washington University, from 1965 until his death on 23 November 1970.

SOURCES: Charles H. Cornwell, *St. Louis Mayors* (St. Louis, 1965); New York *Times*, 25 November 1970.   *Thomas R. Bullard*

TURNER, JOEL H. (1820s?–1888), Mayor of Los Angeles (1868–70). A saloon owner who became mayor of Los Angeles in the late 1860s, Turner was also an active Democrat, attending most party conventions. In the early 1860s, he served as justice of the peace for Soledad Township and became mayor of Los Angeles on 9 December 1868 (reelected in 1869 and serving two terms until 9 December 1870). Critics claimed that he won with the help of local politicos he treated at his El Monte distillery.

During Mayor Turner's administrations, the city board of education was reorganized (April 1869) and the first town high school opened; the fruit-growing industry was developed; and a major hotel, the Pico House, was built. A short, twenty-two-mile railroad was completed from Los Angeles to Wilmington, the locomotive being brought around Cape Horn by ship. Despite recurring economic depressions and a smallpox epidemic, mainly north of the Plaza (Sonoratown, 1869–70), Los Angeles continued to grow. Its official population count was still under 6,000: 5,614 persons were served by 110 saloons in 1870.

Mayor Turner held personal, public auctions of city lands on the street in front of city hall. In 1870, the mayor and the council were indicted for falsely issuing warrants or scrip for water improvements and selling the paper for their own profit. They were exposed by former Mayor José Mascarel (*q.v.*). Mayor Turner got a sentence of ten years in jail, but the decision was overturned on appeal and he finished his term of office undisturbed, saying "It was all a mistake."

Turner became an avid apiarist in later life, raising bees on a large scale in San Joaquin County, where he died on 5 May 1888.

SOURCES: California Biography File, Los Angeles Public Library; Tom Moran, "The Thief, The Gambler, The Swine and Other Mayors Past," in *Los Angeles Magazine* 22:3 (March 1977).   *Peter d'A. Jones*

U

UPHAM, DON A. J. (1809–77), Mayor of Milwaukee (1849–51). Lawyer, politician, and a transplanted Yankee, Upham was born on 31 May 1809 in Weathersfield, Vermont, the son of Joshua Upham (1771–1849), a clerk, and Phebe Graves (Chamberlain) Upham (1775–1862), both old-stock Baptists. The third of five children, Upham attended local schools in Chester, Vermont, and Meriden, Connecticut, graduating from Union College (Schenectady) in 1831. He studied law with General James Tallmadge in New York City, starting practice in 1835. He then moved to Wilmington, Delaware, becoming that community's city attorney. Upham edited the Delaware *Gazette* until 1837, making it a strongly Democratic paper. In 1836, he married Elizabeth Jaques (1815–83) of Wilmington, daughter of a prominent Quaker physician of French Huguenot ancestry. They had ten children, five dying in infancy. Upham was a Phi Beta Kappa.

The Uphams moved west to Milwaukee in 1837 and for twenty-five years Don Upham was one of the city's leading lawyers. He served in the Wisconsin legislature (1840–41) and was presiding officer of the 1846 constitutional convention. He was elected mayor in 1849, defeating B. H. Edgerton (Whig) 1,513 to 683. The following year, he was reelected, defeating Rufus King (Whig) 1,981 to 556, with 305 votes going to the Peoples' party candidate John B. Smith. Milwaukee had 20,061 people by 1850 and a mayor-council form of government.

As mayor, Upham supported a good school system, claiming that this institution, imported from New England, was the road to democracy. He also urged economy and strict controls on taxes. His second term was marked by a series of clashes between native-born temperance groups and largely immigrant pro-saloon forces. In 1851, Upham did not seek a third term but ran unsuccessfully for governor of Wisconsin. Except for a two-term period in the city council (1862–64) Upham's political career virtually ended after leaving the mayor's office. He helped organize the Old Settlers' Society in 1869. After his retirement from a successful legal career in 1863, Upham devoted his spare time to astronomy. He died on 19 July 1877.

SOURCES: John G. Gregory, *History of Milwaukee, Wisconsin*, 4 vols. (New York, 1931), vol. 3; F. K. Upham, *The Descendants of John Upham* (Albany, N.Y., 1892).

Thomas R. Bullard

VAN ANTWERP, EUGENE IGNATIUS (1889–1962), Mayor of Detroit (1948–50). An unpredictable mayor who fought everything from squirrels to communism in city government, Van Antwerp was born on 26 July 1889 in Detroit. He was one of eight children. His father was Eugene Charles Van Antwerp, whose Dutch colonial forebears had migrated to New York in the 1650s, and his mother was Cecilia (Renaud) Van Antwerp. A devout Roman Catholic, like his parents, Van Antwerp graduated from SS Peter and Paul Parochial School and the University of Detroit. Although a civil engineer, he taught English and mathematics at Gonzaga College in Spokane, Washington (1910–11). He then returned to Michigan where he worked for the Michigan Central Railroad (1912–13) and the Grand Trunk Railway until he entered the U.S. Army in 1917. He served with the American Expeditionary Force in France, rising to the rank of captain. After World War I, he returned to work for the Grand Trunk Railway until 1926 when he became chief engineer for the National Survey Service. After two years, he left this position to go into practice for himself. Van Antwerp married Mary Frances McDevitt on 21 June 1911, and had eleven children. Van Antwerp was national commander of the Veterans of Foreign Wars in 1938–39. He was a member of several organizations, including the Elks, the Knights of Columbus, the American Legion, and the American Society of Civil Engineers.

In 1931, Van Antwerp ran for a seat on Detroit's common council and won. He served eight terms and then ran successfully for mayor in 1947, defeating Edward J. Jeffries, Jr. (q.v.) 224,310 to 205,543. When he became mayor, Detroit had a population of 1,815,000 and a mayor-council form of government. The victory was especially sweet for Van Antwerp, for he had been frustrated in his bid to become auditor of Wayne County in 1935 and Democratic candidate for governor in 1940.

As mayor, Van Antwerp was bluff and outspoken. As one Detroit newspaper put it, he "never became a politician." Colorful and unpredictable, he fought for stiffer control of slum landlords; he opposed taxi-dance halls and police speedtraps. He banned the wearing of dark glasses at council meetings explaining "they're as effective as a mask."

Van Antwerp served one term and was then defeated in the primary when he sought reelection. In 1950, he returned to the common council and served there until he died of a heart attack in Detroit on 5 August 1962. He was buried in Detroit's Holy Sepulchre Cemetery.

SOURCES: Detroit *Free Press*, 6 August 1962; Detroit *News*, 6 August 1962; Van Antwerp Genealogy, Burton Historical Collection, Detroit Public Library; Robert I. Vexler, *Detroit: A Chronological and Documentary History, 1701–1976*, (Dobbs Ferry, N.Y., 1977).

Robert Bolt

VANCE, SAMUEL B. H. (1814–90), Mayor of New York (1874). One-month mayor of New York, Vance was born in Pennsylvania in 1814, and soon moved to New York City, married, and in 1854 became a member of the firm of Mitchell, Vance and Company, manufacturers of gas fixtures. In youth, Vance saw service in the Mexican War as a captain of volunteers, was elected several times as a member of the board of education of New York City, and was elected to the common council in 1872. He was chosen its president in January of the following year. At that time, the city had over a million people.

On 30 November 1874, immediately upon the sudden death of Mayor William Havemeyer (q.v.), Vance, as president of the common council, was mandated to fill the remaining month of the late mayor's term. His first order of business was to act on a request of Governor John A. Dix to see if "Boss" William M. Tweed, then languishing in prison, was being accorded the privileges of a visiting dignitary, as well as having any opportunity to escape, as was being rumored. Such charges proved unfounded, although Vance removed the two commissioners of the Bureau of Corrections and Charity, Myer Stern and James Bowen, in accordance with the wishes of the incoming Mayor, William Wickham (q.v.), and Governor Dix.

In another mild attempt at change, Vance reappointed two commissioners of accounts, Lindsay Howe and George Bowland, who had been replaced by former Mayor Havemeyer. Havemeyer's appointments, John Joy and Ezra Kingsley were threats to patronage dispensed by Tammany Hall. Vance also overturned another

Havemeyer decision when he signed warrants giving Cornelius Vanderbilt several million dollars to sink the tracks of his Fourth Avenue Railroad. The surface tracks, long known as "Death Alley," needed to be removed, but Vanderbilt refused to pay the entire cost and the city had agreed to payment, previously voided by Havemeyer. Vance died on 11 August 1890 in Douglaston, Long Island, and was buried at Greenwood Cemetery.

SOURCES: Newspapers of the period, especially the New York *Times*, December 1874 and 12 August 1890.

Leo Hershkowitz

VAN DYKE, JAMES (1813–55), Mayor of Detroit (1847). A Pennsylvania Dutchman credited with straightening out Detroit's finances, Van Dyke was another in the long list of prominent Detroiters who served a turn in the mayor's office during the antebellum years. Born on 10 December 1813 in Mercersburg, Franklin County, Pennsylvania, Van Dyke was the first in what would become a family of four more boys and one girl. His father, William, was a Pennsylvania Dutch farmer-businessman whose seventeenth-century colonial ancestors were among the first builders of New Amsterdam. His mother, Nancy (Duncan) Van Dyke, was a native of Pennsylvania; her ancestors had come from Scotland.

Van Dyke was educated at Madison College in Uniontown, Pennsylvania, and then began legal studies, first with a lawyer in Pennsylvania and then in Maryland. He planned to practice in Pittsburgh but found it "unattractive" and moved on to Detroit where he settled permanently in 1834. In 1835, he married a Roman Catholic, Elizabeth Desnoyers, daughter of an old and wealthy French Detroit family whose first members had come to the area with Cadillac. The couple had eleven children, seven surviving to adulthood. Van Dyke was a partner in various law firms. In the early years of his practice, from 1835 to 1839, he was city attorney; in 1840–42, he was prosecuting attorney of Wayne County.

Van Dyke ran for mayor on the Whig ticket in March 1847 and won over his Democratic opponent, Gurdon Williams, by a majority of thirty-two votes. The Detroit population was fast approaching 20,000 by the late 1840s, but in 1847, the city remained divided into the six wards originally established in the 1820s, with each ward represented by two aldermen. Like the mayor's office, the common council was almost consistently dominated by the Whig party throughout the decade.

Cost of government was a persistent citizen concern, and the city finances were also in chaos, probably in part because of the continuous turnover of untrained public officers serving short terms. As an alderman in 1843 and 1844, Van Dyke was chairman of the Committee of Ways and Means, and he tackled the financial tangle. He con-

tinued the effort when he became mayor and was credited with saving the city from bankruptcy and with restoring its credit.

Van Dyke was also instrumental in helping organize and building up the Detroit Fire Department, and he went out regularly on fire runs. He chose not to run for reelection but continued to serve as president of the department, a post he held from 1847 to 1851. He was a member of the first board of commissioners of the Detroit Water Works, 1853–55. Meanwhile, in 1852, he retired from general practice and became an attorney for the Michigan Central Railroad, which he highly praised in court for all the benefits it had brought to the state.

Van Dyke remained nominally Protestant throughout his life, although his wife and children were Roman Catholic. One son became a priest and one daughter, a member and Mother Superior of the Ladies of Sacred Heart religious order. In his final illness he converted to Catholicism, and upon his death, on 7 May 1855, he was buried in a Catholic service in Detroit.

SOURCES: Clarence M. Burton, *The City of Detroit, Michigan, 1701–1922* (Detroit, 1922), vol. 3; Frederick Carlisle, comp., *Wayne County Historical and Pioneer Society Chronography* (Detroit, 1890); Silas Farmer, *The History of Detroit and Michigan* (Detroit, 1889), vol. 2; Robert B. Ross, *The Early Bench and Bar of Detroit* (Detroit, 1907). Items pertaining to Van Dyke are among the Desnoyers, Woodbridge, and Emmons papers, all located in the Burton Historical Collection, Detroit Public Library.

JoEllen Vinyard

VAN NESS, JAMES (1808–72), Mayor of San Francisco (1855–56). Seventh mayor of San Francisco during the second Vigilante upheavals, Van Ness was a blueblood from Vermont, who replaced as mayor a previous New Englander, S. P. Webb (*q.v.*). Born in Burlington, Vermont, in 1808, Van Ness came from a distinguished family of judges, descended from seventeenth-century Dutch settlers in New York. His father was Cornelius Peter Van Ness, successively district attorney for Vermont, governor of that state, chief justice of its supreme court, and Andrew Jackson's ambassador to Spain. His mother was Rhoda (Savage) Van Ness. An uncle, William P., was U.S. district judge for New York. James Van Ness went to the University of Vermont (graduated 1825) and was admitted to the bar in Burlington. He practiced law in Georgia, the state of his wife (of the Georgia Leslies), and then in Louisiana, where his children were born: a son, Thomas Casey (15 February 1847), who became a San Francisco lawyer, and a daughter, who married another mayor of San Francisco, Frank McCoppin (*q.v.*).

James arrived in San Francisco, coming from New

Orleans via Mexico and the sea route in 1851. He was elected alderman almost immediately, serving four years before being elected mayor in May 1855, as a Democrat. It was a determined campaign; even the state's governor went to San Francisco to support Van Ness in a torchlight parade. Van Ness began his tenure badly. The city's previous, Know-Nothing officers would not leave without legal action; the election was attacked as fraudulent, a longshoreman's strike in August brought violence, crime had returned on a large scale, and a reduction of the police force by forty men caused public anger at the administration (8 November). All these conditions produced a violent revival of the vigilante movement, which had been quiet since 1851. Vigilantism and crime dominated the Van Ness mayoralty.

Two spectacular murders were the initial spark. Charles Cora, a jealous lover, shot a city marshal in cold blood on 17 November 1855 and was kept protected from a lynch mob by his friend the sheriff in the city jail. When a veteran San Franciscan and former vigilante of 1851, Sam Brannan, harangued the crowd, he was briefly arrested, much to the anger of the people. The Cora case dragged on and Mayor Van Ness did nothing, despite calls for his own dismissal. Those calls came chiefly from the *Bulletin*, edited by one James King (who affected the name "James King of William" because there were several James Kings). A libelous writer, King of William attacked a fellow journalist and city alderman, James P. Casey, accusing him of being a jailbird from Sing Sing, New York, and a ballot-box stuffer. On 14 May 1856, with the Cora case still hanging on, Casey shot down King in the street.

As bells tolled, the Vigilance Committee of 1851 was formally reconstituted, and on Sunday 18 May, twenty-four fully armed companies of vigilantes (about 100 men per company) marched to the jail, grabbed both Cora and Casey, and, when James King of William finally succumbed of his wounds two days later, strung up the two assassins. Mayor Van Ness watched the hanging from the roof of the International Hotel—unable to do anything about it. In truth, the Vigilantes now ran the city.

Once more, harsh repression seemed to work; criminals were said to have fled the city. The Vigilante Committee made dozens of arrests and meted out tough sentences, including two more hangings (29 July 1856). Then they disbanded, after a triumphant torchlight procession in August. Van Ness at first refused to relinquish his office on 1 July but was forced out legally. He moved to San Luis Obispo in 1861 to farm and practice law. He remained active in Democratic party politics, became a state senator in 1871, and as late as 14 October 1872 was placed on the party's state central committee.

Van Ness is remembered for two very positive achievements. First, the *Van Ness Ordinance* (27 September 1855) codified and rationalized confused land titles in the city; one new street laid out under the law was named after Van Ness. A genuine planning act, the Ordinance, looked ahead for years, providing sites reserved for public uses as the city grew, including Golden Gate Park. Second, a farsighted Consolidation Act of 1856 combined the city with the county in a structural reform of local government which served San Francisco well for half a century. Under the act, the mayor's title was changed to president of the board of supervisors. The title proved unpopular, was never generally used, and was therefore rescinded in 1861.

Van Ness died at San Luis Obispo on 28 December 1872. He is buried at Laurel Hill Cemetery, San Francisco.

SOURCES: W. F. Heintz, *San Francisco's Mayors* (Woodside, Calif., 1975); Pauline Jacobson, *City of the Golden Fifties* (Berkeley, Calif., 1941); *San Francisco, Its Builders, Past and Present*, (Chicago and San Francisco, 1913), vol. 2; Alan Valentine, *Vigilante Justice* (New York, 1956); S. P. Webb, "A Sketch of the Causes, Operations and Results of the San Francisco Vigilance Committee in 1856," *Essex Institute Historical Collection*, 84 (April 1948).   *Peter d'A. Jones*

VANSANT, JOSHUA (1803–84), Mayor of Baltimore (1871–75). Vansant was born on 31 December 1803 in Millington, Kent County, Maryland, of Dutch and Quaker ancestry. At an early age, he moved to Baltimore where he was apprenticed to the hatter and furrier trade. On 24 January 1824, he married Mary Ann Menzies (1805–77) whose family had moved from Boston. They had two children, James and Joseph. They were Dutch Reform in faith.

Baltimore in 1870 had 267,354 people and a mayor-council form of government. Vansant served two terms as the regular Democratic party nominee. He was first elected on 28 October 1871, defeating his Reform party opponent, Charles Dunlap, 18,097 to 10,943 votes. Vansant was reelected on 22 October 1873, defeating a second Reform party opponent, David Carson, 22,751 to 12,657 votes. After his second term in office, Vansant was appointed city comptroller (1875) and retained the office until his death. His son, Joseph, continued to operate their family business as hatters and furriers.

Vansant's mayoralties coincided with the emergence of the city-wide Democratic party machine controlled by Isaac Freeman Rasin and witnessed the financial Panic of 1873. He began the municipal registration of births and deaths, the construction and completion of city hall (25 October 1875), two new city markets, two new police stations, the city library and city college, nine new public school buildings, the first German-English school, and the first public school for the now freed blacks. Vansant died on 7 April 1884.

SOURCES: Baltimore *Sun*, 27, 28, 29, October 1871, 21, 22, 23 October 1873; Wilbur F. Coyle, *The Mayors of Baltimore Illustrated from Portraits in the City Hall* (Baltimore, 1919); "Joshua Vansant," Dielman File, Maryland Historical Society, Baltimore.

Gary L. Browne

VAN WYCK, ROBERT A. (1847–1918), Mayor of New York (1898–1901). The first mayor of "Greater New York" and a Tammany mayor of the "front-man" variety, Van Wyck was the son of William Van Wyck (1803–c. 1867), a New York City lawyer of colonial Dutch and British stock who was born in Huntington, Long Island, and Lydia Anderson (Maverick) Van Wyck, born in Pendleton, South Carolina, of colonial British stock. William Van Wyck's chief occupation was managing his wife's family estate. The fifth-born of at least five children, Robert attended an academy in Pendleton, worked for several years as a store clerk, and graduated from Columbia University Law School in 1872 as valedictorian of his class.

Following his father, Van Wyck became a lawyer and a member of Tammany Hall. Less notable as a lawyer than as a convivial man-about-town at ease in the Holland and St. Nicholas societies as well as in political club-houses, he quickly gained a place in the adaptable middle ranks of Democratic politics. As a member of the Tammany General Committee in 1880, he publically denounced boss "Honest John" Kelly for knifing the presidential ticket, and then joined in the effort of Abram S. Hewitt (*q.v.*) and others to replace Tammany with a new organization, the County Democracy. In 1887, at the moment when it became clear that the County Democracy would fail, Van Wyck returned to Tammany. In 1889, he was elected judge of the city court; elevated to chief judge of that court in 1895, he then won another six-year term. By 1893, he had gained a small reputation for wide political experience, but he had established no independent base of support. In 1897, Boss Richard Croker, who was temporarily able to dominate Tammany and who was apparently seeking a candidate who would be entirely his own creation, secured Van Wyck's nomination to the mayoralty. Van Wyck made no speeches during the campaign, but he was elected with 233,997 votes to 151,540 for Citizens' Union Independent Seth Low (*q.v.*), 101,863 for Republican Benjamin F. Tracy, and 21,693 for Henry George, Jr. (standing in for his father, who had died a few days before the election).

As the first mayor of "Greater New York," containing Brooklyn, Staten Island, and the present boroughs of Queens and the Bronx in addition to Manhattan, Van Wyck faced a series of major administrative and political challenges. These proved to be much too difficult for him to master. As the New York *Times* said in his obituary, "Van Wyck became involved in probably more scandals than any Mayor in the city's history." The passive voice was appropriate, for Van Wyck did not make many of the scandalous decisions for which he was officially responsible. He outraged the business community by supporting the corrupt and expensive Ramapo water deal and by acquiescing in delay of the first subway; he offended school reformers by his appointments to the board of education; and he gave vote-getting issues to Tammany's opponents by supporting the oppressive regime of Police Chief "Big Bill" Devery and by personally joining in an "Ice Trust" that pushed up the cost of ice—hence of fresh milk—in the slums. The explanation for these and other failings lies in part with Van Wyck's personal and political weakness, and in part with the desire of Croker and his associates for a big payoff after years of disciplined work. The Van Wyck scandals and Tammany's defeat in 1901 spelled the end of Croker's brief ascendancy in city hall.

Following his term in office, Van Wyck reputedly made a fortune of $5 million as a lawyer. In March 1906, he married a divorcée, Kate E. Hertle, and retired with her to Paris, where he died on 13 November 1918.

SOURCES: Albert Fein, "New York City Politics from 1897–1908: A Study in Political Party Leadership" (M.A. thesis, Columbia University, 1954); *Harper's Weekly*, 13 November 1897; George B. McClellan, Jr., *The Gentleman and the Tiger*, edited by Harold C. Syrett (Philadelphia and New York, 1956); Gustavus Myers, *The History of Tammany Hall* (New York, 1917); *The Nation*, 3 February 1898; New York *Journal*, 1 October 1897; New York *Times*, 16 November 1918; New York *Times Illustrated Weekly Magazine*, 7 November 1897; Martin Shefter, "The Electoral Foundations of the Political Machine: New York City, 1884–1897," in Joel Silbey, et al., eds., *American Electoral History: Quantitative Studies in Popular Voting Behavior* (Princeton, N.J., 1978); Van Wyck Mayoral Papers, New York City Municipal Archives and Records Center; M. R. Werner, *Tammany Hall* (Garden City, N.Y., 1928).

David C. Hammack

VARIAN, ISAAC LEGGETT (1793–1864), Mayor of New York (1839–40). Scion of a substantial Knickerbocker family, Varian was the first of nine children born to Isaac and Tamar (Leggett) Varian, who traced their New York ancestry to the days of Dutch New Amsterdam. Isaac Varian was born on 25 June 1793 to his Presbyterian parents at the family farmhouse on the

Bloomingdale Road on Manhattan Island.

Varian was raised on the farm which lay just north of the rapidly expanding city and was privately tutored. Provided with an ample fortune, he was able to devote his adult career to politics. An ardent Tammany Democrat, Varian served in multiple capacities on both state and municipal levels. He sat in the state assembly from 1831 to 1834 and then switched to city affairs. He served as an alderman from 1833 to 1836 and as the president of the board of aldermen (1835–36). He made his first bid for the mayoralty in 1838 but was defeated by Aaron Clark (*q.v.*). Varian was successful in his second effort by polling 21,050 votes to the Whig Aaron Clark's 20,027.

Varian married the former Catherine Hopper Dusenbury (1789–1870) on 25 July 1811. Their first child was born the following May, and she gave birth to a total of nine children. Six children lived into adulthood.

Prior to his serving as mayor, Varian was a tax collector, census taker, tax assessor, and election inspector. He also found time to be a volunteer fireman, an essential ingredient in a New York politician's dossier. Varian was able to make his mark in local Democratic politics in a city of 312,000 at a time of flux. Many opposed the upstate political machine under Martin Van Buren, and Tammany split into warring splinter factions. He successfully united them in his 1839 bid and handily won reelection the following year with a vote of 21,242 to 19,622 for J. Phillips Phoenix, the Whig candidate. Varian served as mayor at a time when the real political power rested in the hands of aldermen and assistant aldermen organized as a common council. Varian went on to serve several terms as a state senator (1842–45).

At the conclusion of his service as state senator, Varian and his wife retired to a country retreat in Peekskill, Westchester County, New York. He died there on 10 August 1864. The mayor of New York at the time, C. Godfrey Gunther (*q.v.*), declared that Varian "was one of the sterling representatives of the City of New-York at a time when integrity of character and honesty of purpose were the essential qualities to secure popularity." His widow survived him, living in Peekskill until her death on 13 April 1870.

SOURCES: Samuel Briggs, *The Book of the Varian Family* (Cleveland, 1881); William R. Cutler, *Genealogical and Family History of Southern New York and the Hudson River Valley* . . . (New York, 1913), vol. 2; The New-York *Times*, 23 August 1864; James G. Wilson, ed., *The Memorial History of the City of New York* (New York, 1893), vol. 3.   *Jacob Judd*

VAUX, RICHARD (1816–95), Mayor of Philadelphia (1856–58). Reform mayor, born in Philadelphia on 19

December 1816, Vaux was the son of a widely respected Quaker philanthropist, Roberts Vaux (1786–1836), and Margaret (Wistar) Vaux, also of Philadelphia. One of two sons, Vaux was educated by private tutors and at the Friends Select School. He was admitted to the bar at the age of twenty after reading law with William Meredith, who later became secretary of the treasury under Zachary Taylor. After serving a year as private secretary of the American ambassador to London, Vaux returned to Philadelphia to practice law and to enter a long career of politics and public service. A perennial candidate for office, Vaux gained election to the board of controllers for public schools in 1839 and as recorder of the city (1841–47). But Philadelphia's overwhelming Whig majority sent him to defeat as the Democratic candidate for state assembly in 1839 and in his campaigns for mayor against John Scott (*q.v.*) in 1842 and John Swift (*q.v.*) in 1846.

Named the first Democratic candidate for mayor of the consolidated city in 1854, Vaux lost to Robert Conrad (*q.v.*) 28,883 to 21,020 when he failed to sway the city's working-class districts away from a nativist allegiance. But capitalizing on the Whig refusal to endorse his opponent, Vaux defeated the American Republican candidate, Congressman Henry D. Moore, 29,534 to 25,445 in 1856, carrying all but five of the twenty-four wards in this city of over 500,000. Vaux solidified his support among naturalized immigrant voters by reinstituting appointment of foreign-born police and among native artisans hurt by the Panic of 1857 by expanding the city's welfare policies. Both actions repelled his former Whig supporters, who combined a moderate strain of piety with planks supporting reduced city expenditures and a higher national tariff, to elect an old-line Whig, Alexander Henry (*q.v.*), over Vaux in 1858, 33,868 to 28,934. Vaux also appeared to have suffered defections from his own party when he refused to endorse the proslavery LeCompton Constitution in Kansas.

Following his father's lead in philanthropy, Vaux served fifty-three years (forty as president) on the board of governors of the Eastern State Penitentiary, which his father had helped found. He published several works on prison reform, served as president of the board of directors of Girard College, and was president of the socially conservative Philadelphia Club from 1888 to 1894. He was defeated for the position of congressman-at-large in 1872. He did serve the unexpired term of Congressman Samuel J. Randall in 1890–91 but was defeated in a bid for reelection. In March 1895, he guided a visiting delegation from the state legislature through the Eastern Penitentiary, appearing as usual without a topcoat. In the process, he caught a cold which, with complications, led to rapid decline and death, on 22 March 1895 at his home at 1900 Chestnut Street.

SOURCES: Richard Wistar Davis, *The Wistar Family* (Philadelphia, 1894); William Dusinberre, *Civil War Issues in Philadelphia, 1856–1865* (Philadelphia, 1965); Sam Bass Warner, Jr., *The Private City: Philadelphia in Three Periods of Its Growth* (Philadelphia, 1968).   *Howard Gillette, Jr.*

VOINOVICH, GEORGE VUTOR (1936–   ), Mayor of Cleveland (1979–   ). Born on 15 July 1936 in Cleveland, Voinovich was the son of George S. Voinovich (d. 1974), an architect, and Josephine (Bornot) Voinovich, both Roman Catholics. He attended Collinwood High School, Ohio University (1958), and the Ohio State University Law School (president of his graduating class in 1961). In 1962, he began law practice with Calfee, Halten and Griswold. On 8 September 1962, he married Janet Allen of Lakewood, Ohio, and they had four children, one of whom was killed in a traffic accident during his 1979 mayoral campaign. Voinovich belongs to the city, county, and state bar associations, and the International Association of Assessing Officers, and was a lecturer at the Lincoln Institute (Cambridge, Massachusetts).

A Republican, Voinovich was assistant to the state attorney general, 1963–67. He then served two terms (1967–71) in the state legislature, sitting on the finance and environmental committees. He was Cuyahoga County auditor in 1971–76 and a county commissioner in 1976–78, gaining a reputation for supporting strict government economies. In 1978, he was elected lieutenant governor but served only a few months in 1979 before beginning his campaign for mayor. He defeated incumbent Mayor Dennis Kuchinich (*q.v.*) in a nonpartisan election by 94,541 to 73,755. Cleveland had 750,879 people in 1970 and a mayor-council form of government.

During his campaign, Voinovich had indicated a need to reverse the city's financial crisis, which he saw as the direct result of Mayor Kucinich's inability to work with bankers and the city council. Voinovich felt his widespread popularity in both white and black wards gave him a mandate to prevent the decline. He announced plans to put the city on a sound business footing and said he would run Cleveland like a corporation. When Voinovich organized a special commission to study the city's financial crisis, critics (especially within the city council) attacked his appointees as being suburbanites who cared mostly for big business interests. He urged all urban school districts in the state to consolidate to increase lobbying power in Washington. Voinovich also made special radio and television tapes to give instant news to the public, in addition to more traditional press confer-

ences. By March 1980, he was forced to announce that the city was on the brink of financial disaster, caused by years of financial neglect by previous administrations. It thus seemed that Cleveland's fiscal problems were by no means close to solution.

SOURCES: Cleveland *Plain Dealer*, 1 December 1979 through April 1980; Information from the Mayor's Office, 22 January 1980; *Who's Who in American Politics*, (New York, 1973).   *Thomas R. Bullard*

VOLZ, FERDINAND E. (1823–76), Mayor of Pittsburgh (1854–56). Volz, the last Whig mayor of Pittsburgh, was born in that city in 1823. His father, Charles Volz, of German, Protestant descent, had been water assessor for a number of years until he was killed by a falling wall on 3 January 1846, while superintending demolition following the city's great fire of 1845. Ferdinand succeeded to his father's post until 1851.

Volz' principal opponent in the 1854 election was James C. Pettigrew, Democrat, son of a former mayor, who had been clerk in the mayor's office and in the post office. Others running were Neville Craig, editor, Free Soiler, and author, and former mayor Joseph Barker (*q.v.*). Volz ran away from the field, getting 2,172 votes to Pettigrew's 1,132, and the other two getting a total of 415. Pittsburgh had over 47,000 people at the time, with a government by a mayor and select and common councils.

A problem of the city had been hogs running loose on the streets. Volz succeeded in abating this nuisance. Other problems were beyond his control. In September 1854, the city's worst epidemic of cholera took nearly 500 lives in less than a month. A day of fasting and prayer was held on 21 September. There was also a great drought, with hardly any rain from May to 28 December. Crops were ruined, food was expensive, and there was much suffering among the poor.

For a second term, Volz ran as an Independent, getting 2,405 votes to 1,839 for B.T.C. Morgan, the Native American (Know-Nothing) candidate. Volz ran third in a try for a third term.

After leaving office, Volz returned to his old post as water assessor for ten years and then was collector of internal revenue (1866–69). For five years, he was paymaster of the Allegheny Valley Railroad. In 1874, he became city treasurer, a post he held until his death on 14 May 1876. He was buried in Allegheny Cemetery.

SOURCES: Allen Humphreys Kerr, "The Mayors and Recorders of Pittsburgh, 1816 to 1951" (typescript, 1952, Carnegie Library of Pittsburgh); Pittsburgh *Commercial*, 15 May 1876; Pittsburgh *Gazette*, 15 May 1876; Pittsburgh *Post*, 15 May 1876.   *George Swetnam*

W

WADSWORTH, JAMES (1819–91), Mayor of Buffalo (1851–52). Yankee born mayor and railroad promoter, born in Durham, Connecticut, on 25 August 1819, Wadsworth was the son of Wedworth Wadsworth (1782–1860), local politician, and Content (Scranton) Wadsworth, both Methodist-Episcopal New Englanders. The youngest of five children, Wadsworth attended local schools in Madison, Connecticut, and graduated from Yale in 1845. He had studied law in the offices of B. D. Silliman, a prominent New Haven lawyer, and moved to Buffalo in 1845, beginning practice that same year. On 8 September 1845, he married Rosetta F. Robinson (1821–66) of Connecticut, and they had four children. The Wadsworths were Presbyterians, then Congregationalists, although they belonged to no specific church.

A Democrat, Wadsworth was Buffalo's city attorney, 1850–51, until his election as mayor in 1851, defeating Whig Sherman Jewett 2,880 to 2,336. Buffalo had 42,261 people and a mayor-council form of government. Wadsworth backed various measures for the city's well-being and business growth. He served in the state Senate, 1856–57 and 1858–59, strongly supporting state aid to railroads. He had visited Great Britain several times, 1851–54, learning about the growing English railway system. In 1854, he became president of the Buffalo, Brantford and Roderich Railroad. He also was a director of the Schenectady and Catskill Railroad.

In 1859, Wadsworth moved to New York City where he actively promoted various railroads for the next twenty-five years. He also spent several years working for the Wells Fargo Express Company. In addition, Wadsworth found time to continue his legal practice. During the Civil War, he was chairman of the Union League. In 1870, he was an unsuccessful candidate for Congress. After his first wife's death (8 September 1866), he married Virginia Conklin of Norfolk, Virginia, in 1875. They had one daughter. Wadsworth continued his career as a lawyer until his health suddenly declined in 1888. He died on 18 May 1891, apparently from influenza.

SOURCES: William C. Fowler, *History of Durham, Connecticut* (Hartford, Conn., 1866); *Semi-Centennial Historical and Biographical Record of the Class of 1841 in Yale University* (New Haven, Conn., 1892); H. Perry Smith, ed., *History of the City of Buffalo and Erie County*, 2 vols. (Syracuse, N.Y., 1884); Horace A. Wadsworth, *Two Hundred and Fifty Years of the Wadsworth Family in America* (Lawrence, Mass., 1883).

Thomas R. Bullard

WAGNER, ROBERT FERDINAND (1910–   ), Mayor of New York (1954–65). Robert F. Wagner, Jr. (he dropped the junior soon after becoming mayor and later transferred it to his son) was born in New York on 20 April 1910, the only child of Robert F. and Margaret McTeague Wagner. His mother died when he was nine, and as a consequence the boy spent more than an average amount of time with his father, the famous U.S. senator (1927–49) and New Deal leader, which meant listening to, and later joining in, political talk. Naturally, Robert Wagner, Sr. (1877–1953), himself an immigrant German, was a major and continuing influence on his son.

Wagner was raised a Roman Catholic (his mother's faith). He attended public school in New York, the Taft School in Watertown, Connecticut, and Yale University, from which he graduated in 1933. In 1937, he graduated from Yale Law School, having spent an interim year at the Harvard Business School.

In 1937, Wagner began his political career with his election to the New York State Assembly, a position to which he was twice reelected. He served in Europe during World War II, was attached for a time to Supreme Headquarters, Allied Expeditionary Forces, and was discharged in 1945 as a lieutenant colonel, U.S. Army, with six battle stars and the Croix de Guerre.

Wagner married Susan Edwards of Greenwich, Connecticut, on 14 February 1942, and the couple had two sons, Robert F. Wagner Jr. and Duncan Wagner. Widowered in 1964, Wagner married Barbara Joan Cavanagh in 1965, and after their divorce in 1971 married Phyllis Fraser Cerf in 1975.

Soon after World War II, Wagner returned to politics. Mayor O'Dwyer (*q.v.*) appointed him in 1946 to the position of city tax commissioner and subsequently to that of commissioner of housing and buildings, and then chairman of the city planning commission. In 1949, he was elected president of the borough of Manhattan, and in 1953 he defeated the incumbent mayor, Vincent Impellitteri (*q.v.*), in the Democratic primary by a nearly two to one margin. In the election itself, Wagner, backed by Carmine De Sapio, leader of Tammany Hall, received 1,021,448 votes; his Republican opponent, Harold Rigelman, 661,410 votes; and the Liberal-Independent Candidate, Robert Halley, 468,392 votes. Running for reelection in 1957, Wagner drew 1,507,342 votes to Republican R. K. Christenberry's 587,440.

Among Wagner's accomplishments as mayor were modernization of the civil service; gains in slum clearance, zoning, and housing; an increase in the number of policemen; and a more functional budget. As late as 1960, an article in *Fortune* expressed the view that "the city's credit is as good as most," and complimented the mayor on the creation of the office of city administrator. In 1961, he broke with Tammany Hall and defeated the machine candidate, winning a third term in city hall.

Declining to run for reelection in 1965, Wagner returned to practice law as a partner in the firm of Finley, Kumble, Wagner, Heine, and Underberg. He served as U.S. ambassador to Spain, 1968–69, chairman of the board of directors of the Library of Presidential Papers, member of the New York State Law Revision Commission, and vice-chairman of the Port Authority of New York and New Jersey. He resigned his ambassadorship to run again in the New York mayoral primary in 1969 but failed.

SOURCES: Robert Caro, *The Power Broker* (New York, 1974); Seymour Freedgood, "The Vacuum at City Hall," *Fortune* (February 1960); Philip Hamburger, "The Mayor," *The New Yorker* (26 January 1957); and (2 February 1957); Edward Kenworthy, "The Emergence of Mayor Wagner," New York *Times Magazine* (14 August 1955); Warren Moscow, *The Last of the Big-Time Bosses* (New York, 1971).

Lurton W. Blassingame

WALBRIDGE, CYRUS PACKARD (1849–1921), Mayor of St. Louis (1893–97). Businessman-mayor of St. Louis, Walbridge was born in Madrid, New York, on 20 July 1849, the son of Orlo Walbridge, a Methodist minister, and Maria Althea (Packard) Walbridge, born in England. The family moved around the Eastern and Midwestern United States, as a result of which Cyrus attended schools wherever possible. In the 1860s, they settled in Minnesota, and Walbridge attended Carleton College, 1868–71, and the law school at the University of Michigan (graduating in 1874). He practiced law in Minneapolis, 1874–76, then moved to St. Louis, becoming legal adviser of Jacob S. Merrill, a wealthy druggist. In 1885, he became president of the J. S. Merrill Drug Company. In 1879, he married Merrill's daughter Lizzie, and they had one son. The Walbridges attended the First

Trinitarian Congregational Church. Walbridge was a Mason and a member of the Missouri Athletic and Mercantile clubs. He was also president of the Wholesale Druggists Association.

A Republican, Walbridge served in the House of Delegates, 1881–83 and was president of the city council, 1889–93. He was elected mayor in 1893, with 34,461 votes to 31,246 for James Bannerman (Democrat), 1,668 for Albert Sanderson (Socialist-Labor), and 259 for John Field (Prohibitionist). St. Louis had 451,770 people in 1890 and a mayor-council form of government.

Walbridge supported efforts to streamline the city's business contracts. He also was the first St. Louis mayor to appoint women to city positions. He backed measures to place all telegraph and telephone wires underground, and to pave all the city's streets. Walbridge also secured new contracts to improve collection of the garbage in St. Louis.

After leaving office, Walbridge returned to business. He was president of the Bell Telephone Company of Missouri in 1904. In that same year, he was the unsuccessful Republican candidate for governor. In 1908, Walbridge was appointed to the Missouri Waterways Convention. He died on 1 May 1921.

SOURCES: Howard L. Conrad, ed., *Encyclopedia of the History of Missouri*, 6 vols. (New York, 1901); Charles H. Cornwell, *St. Louis Mayors* (St. Louis, 1965); James Cox, *Old and New St. Louis* (St. Louis, 1894); John W. Leonard, *The Book of St. Louisians* (St. Louis, 1906).

Thomas R. Bullard

WALDEN, EBENEZER (1777–1857), Mayor of Buffalo (1838–39). By the time Ebenezer Walden was elected mayor unanimously by fifteen aldermen sitting in council, he had already become the wealthiest citizen of Buffalo. He owed his wealth to success in law and real estate speculation, and his prominence to an ambitious public life. Born in 1777 in Massachusetts, Walden attended Williams College and read law in Oneida County, New York. For two years after his arrival in the Niagara frontier in 1806, he remained the only practicing attorney west of Batavia. His wife, Suzanna Marvin, born in Bloomfield, New York, was seventeen years his junior, of an old New England Protestant family, and was educated at Bethlehem, Pennsylvania, and Hartford, Connecticut. She bore four children.

Some insight into Walden's character is seen by his performance in the War of 1812. Along with Samuel Wilkeson (*q.v.*), he was the last to remain, in a general route of the Chautauqua County regiment at the battle of Black Rock, in which forty or fifty soldiers died. He was not blindly heroic however; shortly thereafter, he counselled a group of convalescents, armed only with a ceremonial cannon, against making a foolhardy confrontation with British regulars advancing upon Williamsville. He was captured later the same day and, according to one account, managed to escape by quietly walking away from his captors, as if nothing [was] the matter. In 1812, Walden was a Federalist (later a Whig) member of the state assembly, representing the area now comprising Erie, Niagara, Chautauqua, and Catteraugus counties. Walden directed the Bank of Niagara, the first bank chartered in the newly incorporated village of Buffalo in 1816. He was also a member of the Buffalo Harbor Company which hoped to improve Buffalo's waterfront so that the village might compete better with Black Rock, a village to the north. In 1823, Walden was chosen first judge of the Erie County court; five years later, he acted as a presidential elector casting his vote for John Quincy Adams. He was a member of the committee that drafted a city charter in 1832 and was elected in April of that year as one of Buffalo's first city officers. Walden was appointed mayor in this Whig stronghold in 1838. As mayor, he helped reorganize the school system, and he advocated an aggressive, though unsuccessful, program of compensated expropriation of Indian lands. After his mayoral term, Walden retired from public life to a farm where he died fifteen years later, on 10 November 1857.

SOURCES: Henry Wayland Hill, ed., *Municipality of Buffalo: A History, 1720–1923* (New York, 1923), vol. 1; Crisfield Johnson, *Centennial History of Erie County* (Buffalo, 1876); Truman C. White, *Our County and its People: A Descriptive Work on Erie County, New York* (Boston, 1898).   *Scott Eberle*

WALDVOGEL, EDWARD NICHOLAS (1895–1954),

Mayor of Cincinnati (1953–54). Businessman and politician, born in Cincinnati, on 28 October 1895, Waldvogel, a German-American, attended local Catholic schools and Xavier University. He began working for the Pettibone Company (a major producer of uniforms) as an accountant in 1916 and became vice-president in 1924 and president in 1940. In 1953, he retired from the company and joined Westheimer and Company (investment brokers). In 1918, he married Mrs. Helen Breen (d. 1953), and they had two children. The Waldvogels were both Roman Catholics.

Waldvogel was a member of the state Senate, 1933–37, as a Democrat. He was elected to the city council in 1937, serving until 1954. He changed party affiliation from Democrat to Charterite during this period, becoming a strong backer of the city manager system. He was vice-mayor, 1940–41 and 1948–52, and in 1953 was chosen mayor by the council. Cincinnati had 503,998 people in 1950 and a city manager-mayor-council form of government.

Known as "Eddie," Waldvogel was a popular politician, always open to new ideas and willing to hear different points of view. He was known as one of the few men who never lost an election during his career. He backed amateur sports and supported the city's civic development. A rather flashy dresser, Waldvogel was also noted for his sense of humor. At one party he laughed so hard at a joke that he broke a rib. When selected mayor, there were some who expressed concern at his age and health. These fears were well founded, for Waldvogel died from a sudden heart attack while in office, on 7 May 1954.

SOURCES: Cincinnati *Enquirer*, 7 May 1954; *Cincinnati Mayors* (Cincinnati, 1957); Ralph A. Straetz, *PR: Politics in Cincinnati* (Washington Square, 1958).   *Thomas R. Bullard*

WALKER, GEORGE H. (1811–66), Mayor of Milwaukee (1851–52 and 1853–54). Milwaukee pioneer and mayor, born on 22 October 1811 in Lynchburg, Virginia, Walker was the oldest son of George R. Walker (1783–1873), a physician, and Rebecca Walker (1780–1872), old-stock Protestant Southerners. He attended public school until the family moved west to Illinois in 1826. He subsequently moved north and settled on the site of Milwaukee's South Side in 1834. His property, Walker's Point, was the subject of court suits until 1849 when the government finally recognized his claim. Walker was an Indian trader and real estate agent, acquiring wealth and a reputation for total honesty. He was a canal commissioner in 1840 and also promoted plank roads. He was a prominent member of St. Paul's (Episcopal) Church and a leading Mason, attaining the rank of grand master.

Walker served in the territorial assembly (1842–45; as speaker, 1843–45), he strongly defended the interests of south Milwaukee. He was land office registrar in 1845–49, a South Side trustee (1845–49), and an alderman (1850–51). In early 1851, he served a final term in the state assembly. He was recognized as the most popular Democratic leader in Milwaukee.

Walker ran for mayor on a pro-constitution platform in 1847, losing to anti-constitutionalist Horatio N. Wells (q.v.) 974 to 621. In 1851, he switched his candidacy to the Peoples' party and defeated Democrat A. B. Smith 1,832 to 1,488. Milwaukee had 20,061 people in 1850 and a mayor-council form of government. Mayor Walker supported city aid to schools and railroads, as well as other civic improvements. He did not seek reelection in 1852 but won a second term in 1853, defeating Democrat James Kneeland 2,083 to 1,607. Walker continued supporting internal improvements and gained local notoriety for settling a railroad strike by physically and verbally attacking the strikers. He stood six feet tall and weighed over 350 pounds. In 1854, he was defeated for reelection by Democrat Byron Kilbourn (*q.v.* 2,340 to 1,760. The defeat ended his political career.

Walker subsequently was a railroad promoter, serving as a director of the Milwaukee and Mississippi Railroad (1852–60, its vice-president in 1855–58), and as a director of the McGregor and Milwaukee Railroad (1857). In 1859–65, he was a director of the city's first street railway. He married Mrs. Caroline P. Brown, a local Milwaukee widow, on 1 March 1858, and they had no children. Although originally a Democrat, Walker actively supported the Civil War effort in 1861–65 and joined the Volunteer Guards. His wife was a director of the Women's Soldiers Aid Society. After the war, Walker helped establish the Soldiers' Home, traveling to Washington to lobby for aid. After the fourth such trip, Walker suffered a fatal heart attack in his home, on 20 September 1866.

SOURCES: H. Russell Austin, *The Milwaukee Story* (Milwaukee, 1946); John G. Gregory, *History of Milwaukee, Wisconsin*, 4 vols. (Chicago, 1931); *History of Milwaukee, Wisconsin* (Chicago, 1881); *Reminiscences of George H. Walker* (Milwaukee, 1921).

Thomas R. Bullard

WALKER, JAMES JOHN (1881–1946), Mayor of New York (1926–32). Debonair songwriter and man-about-town, and an immensely popular mayor, Walker was born on 19 June 1881 in New York City's Greenwich Village, the son of Irish immigrant William Henry Walker (1850–1916), a lumberyard owner and Tammany politico, and Ellen (Roon) Walker, a native New Yorker of Irish ancestry. The second-born of nine children, Jimmy Walker attended New York city Catholic parochial schools and, before dropping out of both, St. Francis Xavier College and business school. After graduation from New York Law School in 1904, he embarked on a career as a songwriter in Tin Pan Alley. In 1909, after serving as a Tammany district chief under his father, Walker was elected to a state assembly seat representing Greenwich Village. He was elected to the state Senate five years later, as a Tammany protégé of Al Smith, serving from 1921 to 1925. As a state senator and minority leader, Walker established a reputation as a sponsor of liberal social-welfare legislation. He married a Chicago entertainer, Janet Frances Allen, on 11 April 1912; their childless marriage ended in divorce in 1933. On 18 April 1933, Walker married British actress Betty Compton; they adopted two children, Mary Ann and James John, and were divorced in 1941.

In 1926, New York City had 5,924,138 people and was governed by a mayor and board of aldermen. In 1925, Walker was summoned from Albany by the Tammany leadership to run for mayor. He defeated Republican Frank D. Waterman 748,687 votes to 346,564. Four years later, he was reelected, polling 865,546 votes to fusion candidate Fiorello H. LaGuardia's (*q.v.*) 368,384 and Socialist Norman Thomas's 174,931.

Although Walker was best known for his free-wheeling, theatrical life-style and love of ceremony as mayor, the years of his administration were eventful ones in the city's history: the Department of Sanitation was created; public hospitals were brought under a single head; and transit reforms included construction of the Queens-Midtown Tunnel, the Triborough Bridge, Manhattan's West Side Highway, and a new subway. Yet, all these activities were overshadowed by an investigation of the Walker administration ordered by the state legislature in 1931. The investigating committee's chief counsel, Judge Samuel Seabury, submitted charges and evidence of corrupt payoffs against the mayor to Governor Franklin D. Roosevelt who ordered a hearing. On 1 September 1932, in the midst of his testimony before the governor, Walker submitted his resignation and immediately left for Europe.

Walker returned to New York City in 1935 and two years later was appointed assistant counsel of the New York State Transit Commission. In 1940, he was appointed as municipal arbiter of the garment industry by Mayor LaGuardia. From 1945 until his death, the former mayor served as president of Majestic Records, Inc. He died of a blood clot on the brain on 18 November 1946 at Doctor's Hospital and was buried at Gate of Heaven Cemetery in Westchester County, New York.

SOURCES: Gene Fowler, *Beau James: The Life and Times of Jimmy Walker* (New York, 1949); Milton Mackaye, *The Tin Box Parade* (New York, 1934); Herbert Mitgang, *The Man Who Rode the Tiger: The Life and Times of Samuel Seabury* (Philadelphia, 1963); New York *Times*, 19 November 1946 (obituary).

W. Roger Biles

WALLBER, EMIL (1841–1923), Mayor of Milwaukee (1884–88). A German-born Lutheran immigrant who became mayor, Wallber was born in Berlin on 1 April 1841, the son of Julius Wallber (d. 1879), a merchant, and his wife Henrietta (Krohn) Wallber (d. 1886). The family emigrated to the United States in 1850, reaching Milwaukee in 1855. Emil attended local schools in New York and Milwaukee, moving on to study law with G. Salomon. He became Salomon's protégé, and his chief clerk in 1863–64, when Salomon was governor of Wisconsin. Wallber was assistant state's attorney in 1864–65, city alderman in 1871, and Milwaukee's city attorney (1873–78). His private practice also prospered, and he became a spokesman for Milwaukee's large German community. On 5 September 1868, he married Minna Seeger of Milwaukee, and they had three children. The Wallbers were Lutherans, and members of German clubs and organizations. Wallber was also a Mason.

Wallber was elected mayor in 1884 as a Republican, largely through the party's desire to attract the German vote. Wallber defeated Samuel H. Dixon (Democrat) 11,780 to 8,692. In 1886, he was reelected, defeating John A. Hinsey (Democrat) 13,996 to 12,582. Milwaukee had 206,000 people by 1890 and a mayor-council form of government. Wallber proved to be a popular mayor, supporting better schools, parks, public baths, and civic honesty. He was criticized both for being too pro-German and for restricting the sale of liquor on Sundays. He supported the labor unions' right to strike, but when labor disturbances hit Milwaukee in 1886, he felt obliged to call for the state militia to stop a series of strikes, thus earning the dislike of many local union leaders. He did not seek a third term in 1888 and returned to his law practice.

Wallber was elected a judge on the municipal court in 1890, serving until 1895, when that court was divided. Wallber then became a judge on the civil court until 1900. He was elected county court judge but was defeated for reelection in 1902. In 1906–17, he served as a consular agent for the German government in Milwaukee. Wallber also spent much time working for the Old Settlers' Club and the Milwaukee Bar Association. He was the latter organization's oldest member (having joined in 1867) when he died on 4 June 1923.

SOURCES: William G. Bruce, ed., *History of Milwaukee City and County*, 3 vols. (Chicago, 1922), vol. 3; *History of Milwaukee, Wisconsin* (Chicago, 1881); Scrapbooks of obituary notices compiled by the Old Settlers' Club in the Milwaukee County Historical Society, vol. 2; Bayrd Still, *Milwaukee, The Story of a City* (Milwaukee, 1948).   *Thomas R. Bullard*

WALMSLEY, T. SEMMES (1889–1942), Mayor of New Orleans (1929–36). Walmsley was born in New Orleans on 10 June 1889, the son of Sylvester Pierce and Myra E. (Semmes) Walmsley. His father was a prominent cotton factor, and his grandfather, Robert N. Walmsley, was president of Louisiana National Bank. T. Semmes was educated at Spring Hill College in Mobile, Alabama, and at Tulane University Law School. At Tulane he was an outstanding athlete who won fourteen varsity letters. After graduation, he practiced law in New Orleans. On 15 April 1914, he married Julia Havard of New Orleans. During World War I, he served as a captain, and after the war, he continued his law practice.

In 1919, Walmsley was named assistant attorney general of Louisiana and held that position until 5 May 1924. He also became active in the Democratic headquarters, the Choctaw Club. From 1925 to 1926, he served as city attorney during the administration of Martin Behrman (*q.v.*). When Arthur J. O'Keefe (*q.v.*) became mayor upon Behrman's death, Walmsley was made commissioner of finance. On 15 July 1929, he became mayor when O'Keefe took a leave of absence.

In August 1929, Walmsley and the commission council came under attack from an incensed mob in the council chambers, because the council had not acted immediately to resolve a streetcar strike. After the assault, Walmsley declared his candidacy for mayor on a platform of law and order. In 1930, he defeated Public Service Commissioner Francis Williams by a vote of 43,133 to 36,724, with 761 to Fred C. Huff. On 5 May 1930, Walmsley officially took office; at the time, New Orleans had about 460,000 people and had a mayor-commission-council form of government.

Walmsley's early administration featured construction of the municipal auditorium, completion of the criminal courts building and the parish prison, the addition of seven giant pumps to the municipal drainage system, the development of the lakefront airport, the renovation of twenty-three public markets, the lighting of Canal Street, the paving of more than one hundred miles of city streets, the improvement of the streetcar service, and the extension of City Park to the lakefront. On 23 January 1934, Walmsley won reelection over Francis Williams and John Klorer, Sr.

Political conflict with Huey P. Long disrupted Walmsley's administration. After a brief truce, Long sought to unseat Walmsley and to overturn the "old regular" organization. In January 1934, Long's Louisiana Democratic association had backed the candidacy of Klorer in the mayoralty campaign. In the summer of 1934, Governor O. K. Allen, a Long cohort, ordered National Guardsmen into New Orleans and declared martial law in a successful attempt to control the forthcoming election of important state and national officials. The state legislature then acted to strip administrative and financial power from the city government. By July 1935, old regular leaders believed that municipal survival depended upon the mayor's resignation. Walmsley, however, did not step down until 30 June 1936, after he had received assurance from Governor Richard W. Leche, Huey Long's successor, that the state legislature would restore home rule to New Orleans.

Walmsley died in San Antonio, Texas, on 17 June 1942.

SOURCES: "T. Semmes Walmsley," Administrations of the Mayors of New Orleans, 1803–1936 (typescript compiled and edited by Works Progress Administration, New Orleans, 1940, New Orleans Public Library); T. Harry Williams, *Huey Long* (New York, 1969).   *Edward F. Haas*

WARWICK, CHARLES F. (1852–1913), Mayor of Philadelphia (1895–99). Born on 14 February 1852, Warwick was educated in the Philadelphia public schools and the University of Pennsylvania Law School. Active in politics since 1875, Warwick served as solicitor for the Board of Guardians for the Poor, as assistant district attorney, 1881–84, and then, from 1884 to 1895, as city solicitor. Known as an orator as well as a mimic, he once convincingly "posed as an Irishman" before a New York City Catholic-Irish audience. He married in 1873 and was the father of five children. He joined the Union League and the Union Republican and Young Republican clubs.

Philadelphia had a population of about 1.1 million in 1895 and a mayor-council form of government. Nominated during a factional quarrel in his party, Warwick accepted the Republican nomination for mayor and opposed Democrat and ex-Governor Robert E. Pattison, whom he beat by a vote of 137,863 to 79,879. The election was bitterly contested and spelled an overwhelming defeat of the reform movement.

After leaving office, Warwick indulged his literary penchant and authored several books on the French Revolution. He died in Philadelphia on 4 April 1913.

SOURCES: *The City of Firsts: Complete History of Philadelphia* (Philadelphia, 1926); *Harper's Weekly* 29 (2 March 1895).   *Melvin G. Holli*

WASHBURNE, HEMPSTEAD (1852–1918), Mayor of Chicago (1891–93). Reform mayor, born on 11 November 1852 in Galena, Illinois, Washburne was the son of Elihu B. Washburne (1816–87), an old-stock Yankee statesman, constitutional lawyer, and diplomat, and Adele (Gratiot) Washburne (1826–87) of Missouri and of French ancestry. Hempstead's father Elihu represented the Galena district in Congress (1853–69), was appointed secretary of state by President Ulysses S. Grant in 1869, and subsequently became ambassador to France.

Washburne attended Kent's Hill School in Maine, studied metaphysics at the University of Bonn, Germany, and read law at the University of Wisconsin and the Union College of Law in Chicago. He moved to Chicago in May 1875, passed the bar examination, and opened a law practice with Henry S. Robbins. Later, former U.S. Senator Lyman S. Trumbull and Theodore Brentano joined his firm. Washburne married Annie M. Clarke in 1883, and they had four children: Hempstead Washburne, Jr., Clark, Adele, and Gratiot. Washburne was

a member of the Chicago, Marquette, and Saddle and Cycle clubs.

Chicago in 1891 had 1,150,000 people and a mayor-council form of government. Washburne was elected mayor by a majority of 369 in a turbulent, violent, and closely fought contest. He received 46,957 votes; Dewitt Cregier (Democrat) 46,558; Carter Harrison (Independent Democrat) 42,931; Elmer Washburn (Citizens) 24,027; and a Socialist candidate 2,376. Mayor Washburne declined to run for reelection in 1893.

During Washburne's tenure of office, the World's Columbian Exposition was completed, and an almost entirely new city was erected in the vicinity of the Jackson Park fairgrounds on Chicago's South Side. The mayor established the city's first juvenile police courts, secured legislation that prohibited the employment of children under fourteen years of age, and forced the street railway companies to elevate dangerous ground-level grade crossings at their own expense. He won a reduction in the price of gas and forced the gas companies to pay 3 percent of their gross receipts for the privileges they enjoyed. He won public support for a milk inspection ordinance and the establishment of public bathing beaches.

During the waning days of his administration, Washburne called for a civil service for city employees, for lengthening the mayoralty to a single four-year term, and for consolidating the city, town, and county governments.

After leaving elective office, Washburne became a banker, managed his father's estate, and practiced law. He was a member of the Chicago Civil Service Commission, 1897–98. A victim of a stroke, Washburne died in Chicago on 13 April 1918 and was buried in Graceland Cemetery, Chicago.

SOURCES: Claudius O. Johnson, *Carter Henry Harrison I: Political Leader* (Chicago, 1928); J. B. Kingsbury, "Municipal Personnel Policy in Chicago, 1895–1915" (Ph.D. dissertation, University of Chicago, 1923); Bessie L. Pierce, *A History of Chicago* (New York, 1957), vol. 3; Frederick Rex, *The Mayors of the City of Chicago from March 4, 1837 to April 13, 1933* (Chicago, 1947).   *Edward H. Mazur*

WATERMAN, CHARLES M. (1809–60), Mayor of New Orleans (1856–58). Waterman was born in New York City in 1809, the son of a sailing captain for the Black Ball Line. Charles, who was raised in New Orleans, had become a successful hardware merchant at the time of his nomination for mayor.

New Orleans in 1856 had a population of about 150,000 and a mayor-council form of government. Waterman accepted the American party or Know-Nothing nomination for mayor and beat his Democratic opponent, W. A. Elmore, by a vote of 4,726 to 2,762. The election was punctuated by violence among the Know-Nothings, foreign-born, and Creoles. A clash at one polling place between "American" partisans and "Sicilians" resulted in the death of Norbert Trepagnier, killed by the Sicilians, who also lost one of their number in the continuing fight. The regular police were considered so useless that they were disarmed two days before the election for fear they would simply contribute to the disorder. Before the polls closed, six more people were wounded. The turnout was low because large numbers of naturalized citizens had been intimidated by the Know-Nothings.

Waterman's mayoralty ranks as one of the most turbulent in the city's history. When his term was drawing to a close in 1858, New Orleans was besieged by three armed mobs or "militias" that occupied different sectors of the city—Know-Nothing partisans who held the city hall area; a Vigilance Committee in the foreign-born section; and a private army under Captain J. K. Duncan who had just returned from an unsuccessful "filibuster" invasion of Nicaragua. A municipal "civil war" threatened as armed groups patrolled their sectors and occasionally exchanged gunfire. The greatest loss of life occurred by accident when Vigilance Committee sentinels opened fire in the dark upon one of its own returning patrols, killing four men (three identified as Irish and one German) and wounding four. Meanwhile, Mayor Waterman refused to deputize the Nicaragua filibuster as special police and refused the city council's demands that the mayor call for an armed force of volunteers to fight the Vigilance Committee.

Confusion reigned for the next few days as Waterman swore the filibusters in as a special police force which apparently was illegal; signed a city requisition to arm citizens at public expense from a local hardware store; was impeached and removed from office; and finally, switching sides, fled to the Vigilance Committee sector for safety. After these astonishing events, somehow an election was held for mayor on 7 June. There was only a small turnout and the American party candidate, Gerard Stith (*q.v.*), beat P.T.G. Beauregard 3,851 to 3,450. Waterman disappeared on the night of 14 June 1860 and was believed to have drowned in the river.

SOURCES: John S. Kendall, *History of New Orleans* (Chicago, 1922), vol. 1; Leon C. Soulé, *The Know Nothing Party in New Orleans* (Baton Rouge, La., 1961).

C. David Tompkins

WEAVER, HENRY A. (1820–90), Mayor of Pittsburgh (1857–60). Weaver, the first Republican mayor of Pittsburgh, was born at Freeport, Pennsylvania, on 1 April 1820 and came to the city ten years later with his parents, Benjamin and Nancy Shaffer Weaver, both of German descent and Episcopalian. His father operated the city's best hotel for years and served as sheriff from 1840 to 1845. Henry was one of a family of ten children and went into business as a retail dry goods merchant at eighteen, soon afterward becoming a wholesaler. In 1841, he and his brother Jacob opened a river and canal-boat supply house, which Henry operated until 1852. On 9 February 1843, Weaver married Eliza Arthurs, daughter of a businessman and county commissioner. She bore him four children, only one of whom lived past early childhood.

In 1854, Weaver went into the coal trade and the following year was elected to Pittsburgh's select council. The city, with a population of 48,000, had a mayor and select and common councils. An early supporter of the new Republican party, Weaver was a delegate to its first nominating convention in Philadelphia in 1856. In the January election, he received 2,749 votes to 2,323 for Captain J. D. White, Democrat, clerk of the U.S. district court, and a coal merchant.

Weaver proved a strong and active city head. He reorganized the police department and launched a state fair in the city, which proved a success. An act of 1857 changed the Pittsburgh mayoral term from one to two years, and he was the only man to be elected to both one- and two-year terms.

In the 1858 election, Weaver faced Democrat Christopher L. Magee (a cousin of the later Republican political boss of the same name), defeating him 3,149 to 1,915.

Weaver declined to run for a third term, going into the oil refining business in 1860 but continuing in politics as a strong backer of Abraham Lincoln. During the Civil War, he was commissioned in the Pennsylvania Reserve, with the rank of major. His later career included banking and gas and oil production, and a term as assessor of revenue. He was a Mason and an Episcopalian, and a member of the Chamber of Commerce and of the Pittsburgh Exposition Society. Weaver died on 26 September 1890 and was buried with Masonic honors in Allegheny Cemetery.

SOURCES: Biographical Encyclopedia of Pennsylvania (Philadelphia, 1874); John W. Jordan, *Encyclopedia of Pennsylvania Biography* (New York, 1914); Allen Humphreys Kerr, "The Mayors and Recorders of Pittsburgh, 1816–1951" (typescript, 1952, Carnegie Library of Pittsburgh); Pittsburgh *Gazette*, 27 September 1890; Pittsburgh *Post*, 27 September 1890.

George Swetnam

WEAVER, JOHN (1862–1928), Mayor of Philadelphia (1903–1907). Born on 5 October 1961 in Worcestershire,

England, the son of Benjamin and Elizabeth (Wilke) Weaver, the future mayor came to the United States in 1879, aged eighteen, was admitted to the bar in 1891 and began to practice law in Philadelphia. He was district attorney for Philadelphia from 1901 to 1903 and an Independent Republican. He married Emily Jennings on 21 October 1885.

In 1903, Philadelphia had a population of more than 1.3 million and a mayor-council form of government. Weaver was elected mayor by the Republican city machine and cooperated with them in matters of patronage jobs. He broke with the machine, however, over the question of extending a gas franchise from thirty to seventy-five years, because he and reformers suspected widespread boodling and believed the extension was not in the interests of city consumers. He brought in an advisory committee of reformers, experienced a falling out with them, and the "good government" supporters resigned from his administration. Weaver then switched his loyalties to the political machine, saying that the reformers were as bad as the "Gang." He died on 18 March 1928.

SOURCES: *City of Firsts: Complete History of Philadelphia* (Philadelphia, 1926); *Who Was Who in America* (Chicago, 1942), vol. 1.   *Melvin G. Holli*

WEBB, STEPHEN PALFREY (1804–79), Mayor of San Francisco (1854–55). Sixth mayor of San Francisco and the first Know-Nothing candidate, Webb was a native New Englander, born in Salem, Massachusetts, on 20 March 1804, the son of a sea captain. Webb was a Harvard graduate (May 1824) and a member of the Essex bar, who practiced successfully in Salem, becoming mayor of Essex (1842–45), and subsequently representative and then senator in the Massachusetts legislature. He was treasurer of the Essex Railroad Company.

Arriving in San Francisco in 1853, Webb opened a law office, and in May 1854, he joined the newly created Know-Nothing party, a racist, reactionary group opposed to foreigners, especially the Chinese, and Roman Catholics. Webb was elected mayor of San Francisco on 13 September 1854, on the Know-Nothing ticket. At the time, the Democrats were divided, some being opposed to former mayor Garrison (*q.v.*), and the Whigs were mainly absorbed into the Know-Nothings. Ballot-box stuffing probably fixed the election for Webb.

From the start, Webb's administration seemed tainted by the Meiggs Affair, a major financial scandal he inherited from the previous regime. "Honest Harry" Meiggs, a lumber merchant and owner of Meiggs' Wharf at North Beach in the city, absconded with city funds worth $385,000, together with $233,000 obtained by forged checks on two local businesses. On 6 October

1854, Meiggs sailed away with his family to Chile, where he spend thirteen years building railroads before moving to Peru, where he did the same, at exorbitant costs under corrupt contracts. In addition, four aldermen and two assistant aldermen were indicted by a grand jury on 31 March 1855. Although Webb had little connection with these incidents, his inactivity, a city financial crisis (it was short of $842,344 in March 1855), his Know-Nothing sympathies (he refused to appoint five policemen because they were not "native-born Americans"), and continuing popular anger over corrupt lot sales brought him down.

Since a new charter advanced the election date from September to May, Webb had only eight months in office, being defeated in the May elections by the reform Democrat James Van Ness (*q.v.*).

Webb returned to Salem in 1860; he served again as his hometown mayor (1860–62) and as city clerk (1863–70). In 1874, he published an account of the revived vigilante movement of 1856 in San Francisco, which remains a useful source for historians. He died in Salem on 29 September 1879. Earlier he had lost his sight and had suffered financial reverses.

SOURCES: J. W. Dwinelle, *Colonial History of the City of San Francisco* (San Francisco, 1866); W. F. Heintz, *San Francisco's Mayors* (Woodside, Calif., 1975); Peter d'A. Jones, *Since Columbus: Pluralism and Poverty in the History of the Americas* (London, 1975); "Mayor Stephen P. Webb," *City-County Record* (San Francisco), April-May 1957; Watt Stewart, *Henry Meiggs: Yankee Pizarro* (Durham, N.C., 1946); S. P. Webb, "A Sketch of the Causes, Operations and Results of the San Francisco Vigilance Committee in 1856," *Essex Institute Historical Collection* 84 (April 1948).

Peter d'A. Jones

WEITZEL, GODFREY (1835–84), Military Mayor of New Orleans (1862). During the Civil War, Weitzel, a career U.S. Army officer, served briefly as mayor of occupied New Orleans. He was born on 1 November 1835 in Cincinnati, Ohio, to Louis and Susan Weitzel, recent immigrants from Bavaria. In 1855, he graduated second in his class at the U.S. Military Academy and was commissioned in the Corps of Engineers. Weitzel's first assignment was rebuilding fortifications near New Orleans; then he taught engineering at West Point. While on the faculty, Assistant Professor Weitzel was promoted to first lieutenant, and, as the result of an accident, his first wife died of severe burns. The Civil War brought short tours of duty in Pensacola, Cincinnati, and Washington, D.C. His intimate knowledge of the New Orleans region contributed to his being named the chief engineer of General Benjamin Butler's Department of the Gulf.

Being both able and popular, Weitzel was repeatedly promoted during the war. In May 1862, soon after the fall of New Orleans, Butler named him assistant commandant of the city. He became acting mayor on 14 July 1862 when the first military mayor, George F. Shepley (*q.v.*), assumed the duties of military governor of Louisiana. Weitzel's principal tasks were disarming citizens, maintaining order in this turbulent city of 140,000, and continuing a much needed cleanup campaign. From 5 to 21 August, while he was away from New Orleans on official business, the federal provost marshal, Jonas H. French (*q.v.*), temporarily assumed the mayor's duties. Weitzel was reasonably well liked by the public—especially in comparison to "Beast" Butler—but his talents were needed elsewhere, so he was transferred on 30 September 1862.

Having become a brigadier general of volunteers on 29 August, Weitzel was assigned to field operations. At first, Weitzel objected to commanding black troops. Later, Weitzel's mostly black XXV Army Corps took possession of Richmond in April 1865, and General U. S. Grant promoted this much-decorated soldier to major-general in the regular army.

Following the war, Weitzel briefly commanded volunteer units along the Rio Grande, but returned to the Corps of Engineers in 1866 as a major. Thereafter he devoted his talents to river and harbor improvements. One of Weitzel's most important tasks (1867–73) was supervising the construction of large locks at Sault Sainte Marie, Michigan. He became a lieutenant colonel in 1882 after completing a huge lighthouse at Stannards Rock in Lake Superior. Weitzel died in Philadelphia on 19 March 1884, leaving his second wife, Louisa Bogen Weitzel, with one daughter. He is buried in Cincinnati.

SOURCES: John Smith Kendall, *History of New Orleans*, 2 vols. (Chicago, 1922), vol. 1; "Letterbooks of New Orleans Mayors" (1862), New Orleans Public Library; *The United States Army and Navy Journal* 21 (22 March 1884); Works Progress Administration, "Mayors of New Orleans, 1803–1936" (typescript in the New Orleans Public Library, New Orleans, 1940).

D. Blake Touchstone

WELLS, CHANDLER JOSEPH (1814–87), Mayor of Buffalo (1866–67). Known in Buffalo history as "the father of waterworks," Wells belonged to that select company of "best men" who served their city competently in various capacities out of a sense of duty. His father, Joseph Wells (1768–1834), was born in England and emigrated to Rhode Island before arriving in Buffalo in 1800, permanently settling there in 1808. The senior Wells was the village's first tanner and brickmaker, served as a major in the War of 1812, and was instru-

mental in rebuilding Buffalo after the devastation of that war. His wife (*nee* Prudence Grannis) was a native of Providence, Rhode Island, and an old-stock Yankee. They were Episcopalians. Chandler Joseph Wells was born on 10 June 1814, while his mother was visiting friends in Utica, New York. He was the fifth son and seventh child of eleven.

Joseph Wells left a modest estate when he died of cholera in 1834, but he had ensured that his son learn a suitable trade and had nurtured in him a fine business sense. After serving as an apprentice to his older brother in the joiner's trade, Chandler became an independent contractor at age eighteen. He prospered, 1835–55, by building shops and homes in the burgeoning Buffalo community. By 1857, Wells began to diversify his financial interests, investing profitably in grain elevators, sawmills, and real estate in Buffalo and Ontario. Wells married Susan Jane Wheeler of Buffalo in 1837; their two children died before reaching the age of sixteen and so they adopted two grandnieces.

As his fortune grew, Wells became involved in politics, serving as an alderman from 1854 to 1861. Nominated against his wishes for mayor by the Republicans in 1864, he was narrowly defeated; two years later, however, he won his election bid. During his one-year term, the city, which then had a population of approximately 104,000, purchased the waterworks from a private group. In 1868, a board of water commissioners was established. Wells served intermittently as its chairman for the next fourteen years, until declining health forced him to resign. Local accounts note that Wells supervised the expansion and modernization of the waterworks, and credit him with improving hygiene in Buffalo.

Wells offered his reputation and funds on behalf of many fledgling Buffalo institutions. He was one of the founders of the Erie County Savings Bank. Wells served as a director of the YMCA and Buffalo Historical Society, and was active in the Episcopal Church and in social clubs. He died in 1887 and was buried with fullest honors.

SOURCES: H. Perry Smith, ed., *History of the City of Buffalo and Erie County* (Syracuse, N.Y., 1884).

W. Andrew Achenbaum

WELLS, CHARLES B. (1786–1866), Mayor of Boston (1832–33). Fourth mayor of Boston and the first non-Federalist, born on 30 December 1786, Wells was a master carpenter of middle-class background and Republican political beliefs, in sharp contrast to his three predecessors—John Phillips (*q.v.*), Josiah Quincy (*q.v.*), and Harrison Gray Otis (*q.v.*)—who all came from prominent Boston families, were upper class Federalists, and were all graduates of Harvard. Having been on the common council and board of aldermen, Wells was nominated by the National Republican caucus to run in the 1831 mayoral campaign against William Sullivan, the Federalist candidate, and Theodore Lyman (q.v.), who was being supported by the newly organized Jacksonian Democrats. In the election held on 12 December 1831, the vote was so evenly divided that none of the three candidates received the required majority; but in a second election of 22 December Wells emerged as the victor. The choice of a relatively obscure person like Wells by the Republicans was seen as a reaction of the middle classes of the city against the "magnificent," but often high-handed, policies of upper class aristocrats like Quincy and Otis, as well as an attempt by the poorer classes to cut back on appropriations and thereby force down the city debt.

Because his administration took over at a time of general prosperity for the growing city of about 65,000, Wells was not inclined to depart radically from the fiscal policies of his predecessor. He presided over the construction of the new courthouse in Court Square and authorized the widening of such central thoroughfares as Broad, Commercial, and Tremont streets. As a result, the city's expenses continued to rise during 1832 and 1833. Wells did, however, show much greater concern with the health and safety of those people who lived in the less prosperous parts of the city. He restored the city marshal's salary, previously reduced by Mayor Otis, appointed more constables to patrol the troublesome districts, increased the number of city watchmen to meet the needs of Boston's expanding population, and greatly augmented appropriations for the department of internal health in order to cope with a dangerous outbreak of Asiatic cholera in 1832.

After leaving the office of mayor, Wells did not again become involved in political affairs. He died at the age of eighty on 23 June 1866.

SOURCES: Arthur B. Darling, *Political Changes in Massachusetts, 1824 to 1848* (New Haven, Conn., 1925); *Inaugural Addresses of the Mayors of Boston, 1822–1852* (Boston, 1894); Roger Lane, *Policing the City: Boston 1822–1885* (New York, 1971); *Records of the City of Boston: Mayor and Aldermen*, microfilm, Boston Public Library; Justin Winsor, ed., *Memorial History of Boston . . . 1630–1880*, 4 vols. (Boston, 1880), vol. 3.   Thomas H. O'Connor

WELLS, HORATIO N. (1807–58), Mayor of Milwaukee (1847–48). Milwaukee's second mayor was a transplanted Yankee, born in Hinesburg, Vermont, on 4 November 1807. Wells studied law in Burlington, Vermont, becoming the partner of A. Smalley. Seeking better opportunities, he moved west to Milwaukee in 1836,

quickly establishing himself as one of the young community's best lawyers. From 1837 to 1841, he was the partner of Hans Crocker and Anashel Finch, and then with Finch until 1847. On 22 December 1842, he married Augusta E. Vail, and they had at least two children, only one of whom lived to adulthood.

Wells was West Side clerk (1837–39), territorial attorney (1839–41), and a member of the territorial legislature (1839–40). In 1847, he played a prominent role in opposing the state's new constitution. A Democrat, Wells was elected mayor in 1847, defeating G. H. Walker (q.v.) 974 to 621. Both candidates were members of the same party, but Walker campaigned for the new constitution, while Wells opposed its adoption. Milwaukee had a mayor-council form of government and 9,655 people in 1846 rising rapidly to over 20,000 by 1850.

Wells accomplished little as mayor, since he was not partisan and disliked the need to dispense patronage. After his single term ended, he showed little desire to pursue a political career. He did serve as Milwaukee County's first judge during 1849–53 and then retired to his legal practice. It was said that he was one of the city's best after-dinner speakers and party hosts. The combination of high living and hard work gradually destroyed his health, and friends noticed a physical deterioration after 1850. He died on 19 August 1858.

SOURCES: John R. Berryman, *History of the Bench and Bar of Wisconsin*, 2 vols. (Chicago, 1898), vol. 2; *History of Milwaukee* (Chicago, 1881); D. W. Norris and H. A. Feldmann, comps., *The Wells Family* (Milwaukee, 1942).   Thomas R. Bullard

WELLS, ROLLA (1856–1944), Mayor of St. Louis (1901–09). Progressive, businessman-mayor, born in St. Louis on 1 June 1856, Wells was the son of Erastus Wells (1823–93), businessman and politician, and Isabella Bowman (Henry) Wells (d. 1877), both old-stock Episcopalians. The elder of two children, Wells attended an Episcopal school in Burlington, Vermont, and then St. Louis University (until 1871) and Princeton. In 1878, he took control of his father's street railway company (the oldest in the city). In 1882, he and Robert Brown organized an oil company which became the American Linseed Oil Company. In 1883, Wells worked for a few months on an Oklahoma cattle ranch and then a New Mexico gold mine. He finally returned to St. Louis and organized the St. Louis Steel Foundry Company in 1891, and the American Steel Foundry Company in 1894, enterprises that made him wealthy in a few years. On 2 October 1878, he married Jennie Howard Parker, and they had five children. They were both Episcopalians. Wells belonged to the University Club, Commercial Club, and various business groups.

A conservative Democrat, Wells supported Cleveland (*q.v.*) and opposed Bryan in the 1896 presidential election. He was elected mayor in 1901, although he tried to refuse the nomination, having little desire for political office. He received 43,023 votes to 35,038 for G. W. Parker (Republican), 2,121 for C. I. Filley (Good Government party), and 28,565 for Lee Meriweather (Public Opinion party). In 1905, he was elected to a second term, with 44,367 votes to 42,942 for John Talty (Republican) and 3,236 for the unfortunate Meriweather. St. Louis had 575,238 people in 1900 and 687,029 by 1910, with a mayor-council form of government.

Wells was a strongly progressive mayor who supported a new city charter, better water and sewage treatment facilities, a public utilities commission, municipal ownership of the lighting company, new parks, playgrounds, and public baths. He suggested the need to build a rapid transit system. Convinced that partisan attacks were undermining his plans, Wells refused to seek a third term.

Wells was president of the Chamber of Commerce (1911–13), governor of the St. Louis Federal Reserve Bank (1914–19), receiver for the United Street Railways (1919–27), and director of the David Ranken School of Mechanical Trades. He continued his interest in Progressive reform by backing Woodrow Wilson's presidency. His wife having died in 1917, Wells married Mrs. Carlota Clark Church on 17 November 1923. He died on 30 November 1944, at the age of eighty-eight.

SOURCES: Charles H. Cornwell, *St. Louis Mayors* (St. Louis, 1965); Rolla Wells, *Episodes of My Life* (St. Louis, 1933).

Thomas R. Bullard

WENTWORTH, JOHN (1815–88), Mayor of Chicago (1857–58, 1860–61). First Republican mayor of Chicago, born on 5 March 1815 in Sandwich, New Hampshire, Wentworth was the son of Paul Wentworth, (1782–1855), a dairy farmer and politician, and Lydia (Cogswell) Wentworth (1793–1872), both old-stock Yankee Congregationalists. The eldest of nine children, Wentworth attended public and private schools in New England and graduated from Dartmouth College in 1836. Shortly thereafter, he headed west, settled in Chicago, and immediately assumed the editorship of the city's oldest newspaper, the *Democrat*. By the spring of 1837, Wentworth had become the sole owner of the paper, school inspector, and aide-de-camp to the governor. In 1841, he attended lectures at Harvard Law School and returned to be admitted to the Illinois bar. Wentworth married Roxana Marie Loomis (1817–70) of Troy, New York, a Presbyterian, and they had five children (Riley, Marie, John, Roxana, and John Paul).

In 1843, Wentworth, then a Democrat, was elected to the U.S. House of Representatives for the first of seven terms. He quickly established himself as an ardent expansionist and the chief agitator for harbor improvements on the Great Lakes. As the only Illinois Democrat in Congress to vote for the Wilmot Proviso and against the Compromise of 1850, Wentworth aligned himself with those Northern Democrats opposed to the extension of slavery. His opposition to the Kansas-Nebraska Act led him to abandon the Democrats for the fledgling Republican party in 1856–57.

Chicago in 1857 had a population of 93,000 and a mayor-council form of government. Wentworth ran for mayor that year on the "Republican-fusion" ticket and outpolled his opponent, Democrat Benjamin F. Carver, by a count of 5,933 to 4,842. He chose not to run for reelection the following year but was elected again in 1860, defeating Democrat Walter S. Gurnee (*q.v.*) (9,998 to 8,739).

Wentworth's administrations were highlighted by his attempts to combat the lawless elements of Chicago. Most noteworthy was his highly publicized raid on "The Sands," a den of gambling and prostitution on the northside lake shore area, in which he personally led a squad of thirty policemen in razing the shanties and dispatching the inhabitants. Wentworth's terms in office were largely characterized by parsimony; he fought the creation of a municipal water system and arbitrarily burned $96,000 worth of long-term bonds issued by the city council.

Wentworth was elected to the Illinois Constitutional Convention in 1862 and to the U.S. House of Representatives (1865–67). During this term, while chairman of the House Ways and Means Committee, he sided with the Radical Republicans and championed the Freedmen's Bureau bills and the Fourteenth Amendment. In 1870, he unsuccessfully sought the Republican nomination for U.S. senator.

His legislative career concluded, Wentworth continued to serve the Republican party in the role of elder statesman, acting as vice-president of their national convention in 1880. His later years were spent administering his widespread Chicago real estate holdings. After a short siege of paralysis, Wentworth died on 16 October 1888 and was buried in Chicago's Rosehill Cemetery.

SOURCES: Chicago *Tribune*, 17 October 1888; Don Fehrenbacher, *A Biography of "Long John" Wentworth* (Madison, Wis., 1957); Paul Gilbert and Charles Lee Bryson, *Chicago and Its Makers* (Chicago, 1929); John Wentworth, *Congressional Reminiscences* (Chicago, 1882); John Wentworth, *The Wentworth Genealogy: English and American* (Chicago, 1878); John Wentworth Scrapbooks, vols. 1–4, Chicago Historical Society.

W. Roger Biles

WESTERVELT, JACOB A. (1800–79), Mayor of New York (1853–55). A wealthy shipbuilder, typical of the New York 1850s' business elite who considered public service a duty, Westervelt was born on 20 January 1800 in Tenafly, New Jersey, of Dutch stock who had emigrated in 1662. When his family moved to the city in 1801, Westervelt received limited formal education in Dutch Reform Church Schools but was expected to follow his father's trade of dock contracting. In 1814, following his father's death, he became an apprentice shipbuilder to Christian Bergh. After a brief stay in Charleston, South Carolina, Westervelt entered into partnership with his former master. He married on 25 April 1825 and had eight children. When Bergh died in 1835, Westervelt toured Europe to study modern techniques and in 1841 joined William Mackey in a new firm. Subsequently, Westervelt dissolved that company, took his sons into partnership, and enlarged operations by managing ships they constructed.

New York City in 1853 had a population of 520,000 and was in the midst of massive growth that placed a great strain on a government consisting of a weak mayor, aldermanic boards, and municipal departments. Westervelt, who had served as a Democratic alderman, ran for mayor on Tammany Hall's ticket and won over his Whig opponent, Morgan Morgans, 33,251 to 23,719.

Mayor Westervelt faced mounting crises. He repeatedly vetoed bills passed by a bipartisan group of corruptionists and cooperated with a grand jury investigation that uncovered systematic frauds involving kickbacks to contractors, unethical awarding of transportation franchises, padded bills, and bribery. Westervelt helped reformers amend the city charter by weakening aldermanic prerogatives and introducing stiff penalties for bribery. In particular, he actively reorganized the police department and was instrumental in forcing the use of uniforms over heated objections. During his administration, he tried to instill clean government through honesty, efficiency, and economy. He failed largely because of burgeoning growth, the decentralized nature of power, and social and religious fragmentation that exploded into bloody nativist rioting during his term.

Never an organizational politician, Westervelt lacked a strong constituency and returned to his company. Considered the city's richest shipowner before 1861, he built gunboats for the Union Navy but suffered economic reversals because of Confederate raiders and in 1866 terminated his business. In 1870, he became commissioner of docks and served until his death on 21 February 1879. He was a member of the Dutch Reformed Church, and he was survived by four sons and three daughters.

SOURCES: Robert Albion, *The Rise of New York Port* (New York, 1939); Jerome Mushkat, *Tammany: The*

Evolution of a Political Machine (Syracuse, N.Y., 1971); Walter Westervelt, *Genealogy of the Westervelt Family* (New York, 1905).   *Jerome Mushkat*

WHEATON, WILLIAM W. (1833–91, Mayor of Detroit (1868–71). Democratic mayor of Detroit and a transplanted New Englander, Wheaton was born in New Haven, Connecticut, on 5 April 1833, the son of John Orit C. Wheaton, a direct descendant of William Wheaton, a Revolutionary War officer. He attended schools in New Haven and Hartford, Connecticut. At sixteen, he entered a wholesale firm in Hartford. In 1853, he moved to Detroit and joined a wholesale grocery company, becoming a junior partner in 1855 and in 1859 going into business for himself. He later acquired several partners, branched out into other types of enterprise, and in 1873 became treasurer and general manager of the Marquette and Pacific Rolling Mill Company. He was married and had two daughters who survived him.

Detroit in 1868 had a population of 68,827 and was governed by a mayor-council type of government. Wheaton, a long-time Democrat, was elected mayor in 1868, winning 4,271 votes to his Republican opponent George C. Codd's 3,909. He was reelected in 1870, receiving 4,813 votes to the Republican John D. Standish's 4,102. Wheaton's two terms in office were not notable; his one lasting achievement was in building the city hall which was in use for eight decades.

Wheaton was a major figure in the Democratic party in Detroit and Michigan for nearly twenty years. After being mayor, he served as chairman of the Democratic state committee and in 1889 as state representative, but he failed in his bid for the state Senate the next year. Wheaton was a member of the Elks and other social and civic clubs. He died in Detroit on 11 November 1891.

SOURCES: Detroit *Free Press*, 12 November 1891; Detroit *Journal*, 12 November 1891; Silas Farmer, *History of Detroit and Wayne County and Early Michigan*, 3d ed. (Detroit, 1890).   *W. Patrick Strauss*

WHELAN, GEORGE J., Mayor of San Francisco (1856). The "missing" mayor of San Francisco, Whelan remains a mystery figure. Nothing is known of his origins or his end.

With the Consolidation Act of 1856 combining city and county government, a temporary form of government was created for San Francisco to cover the months between the end of James Van Ness's (*q.v.*) mayoralty and the new winter election date (July to November 1856). A temporary board of supervisors made up of four justices of the peace was to nominate a president of the board who would act as chief magistrate until the new election. After November, the office of mayor would be held by the new president of the board, who would be elected. The title "mayor" was abolished. However, few citizens understood this arrangement, and none liked it (the title "mayor" returned in 1861). The city was still ruled intermittently by the Vigilance Committee into August; people resented having a nonelected mayor, and nobody knew the man selected, George J. Whelan. He had been Know-Nothing nominee for district attorney on 19 August 1855.

According to city directories, Whelan shared a law office with Jasper J. Papy, at least in the years 1857-60. Attorney Whelan could do little as acting mayor because the members of the board often failed to attend his meetings, and he had no quorum. Under the Consolidation Act, private property-owners had been made financially responsible for street repairs; the city did carry out such repairs at this time and bill its angry citizens. Whelan complained strongly that the act failed to provide for adequate funding of the fire department.

City treasury records, which miraculously escaped the fire of 1906, were discovered in the city hall basement in August 1974 and attest that Whelan was paid a monthly salary as temporary mayor, or, strictly speaking, temporary president of the board of supervisors. More than that we do not know.

A Resolution of Mayor Joseph Alioto's (q.v.) board of supervisors on 12 November 1974 affirmed that Whelan was the official eighth mayor in San Francisco history, having served from 8 July to 15 November, 1856. The resolution was the result of insistent research by local historian William F. Heintz, aided by the city archivist Gladys C. Hansen.

SOURCES: Gladys C. Hansen, *San Francisco: A Guide to the Bay and Its Cities* (revised Works Progress Administration edition, New York, 1973); Gladys C. Hansen, *San Francisco Almanac* (San Francisco, 1975); W. F. Heintz, *San Francisco's Mayors* (Woodside, Calif., 1975); Oscar T. Shuck, *Bench and Bar in California* (San Francisco, 1889).   *Peter d'A. Jones*

WHELTON, DANIEL A. (1872–?), Acting Mayor of Boston (1905). Acting mayor, to fill out the unexpired term of Patrick A. Collins (q.v.) who died in office, Whelton was born in the west end of Boston on 1 January 1872 and graduated from St. Mary's School in 1886. After a few months of night school training, he worked for Henry A. Young and Company, book publishers, and later as a salesman for DeWolfe and Fisk Company. By 1895, he was U.S. revenue gauger, holding the post until 1903.

Whelton became interested in politics and served as a warden in caucus and as an election officer before being elected to the common council in 1894, being reelected

in 1895, and working on the Finance Committee. In 1905, he was chairman of the board of aldermen and so became acting chief executive of Boston upon Collins' death on 15 September 1905. He was quickly replaced by John F. "Honey Fitz" Fitzgerald (q.v.), who was elected mayor in that year. Later, in 1909, Whelton served as one of the deputy sheriffs of Boston.

SOURCES: *Boston's 45 Mayors* (Boston City Record, 1975); J. Koren, *Boston, 1822–1922* (Boston, 1923).   *Peter d'A. Jones*

WHITE, KEVIN H. (1929–   ), Mayor of Boston (1968–   ). The first Boston mayor elected to four consecutive four-year terms, White was born on 25 September 1929 of Irish Catholic parents in the West Roxbury section of Boston. He was the first-born of four children of Joseph C. White (1898–1967), a teacher and onetime state legislator, Boston City Council president, and school committee member, and Patricia (Hagan) White (1902–   ), the daughter of Henry E. Hagan, a shoe merchant and former Boston City Council president. White attended Tabor Academy and graduated from Williams College in 1952. He received his LL.B. from Boston College Law School and was admitted to the bar in 1955. He served briefly as corporation counsel for Standard Oil of California and from 1956 to 1958 was an aide to the district attorney of Middlesex County, Massachusetts. In 1958, White became an assistant to Suffolk County District Attorney Garrett Byrne. The young assistant sought political office for the first time in 1960. He won the Democratic nomination for Massachusetts secretary of state and defeated Republican Edward W. Brooke in the general election. White was reelected in 1962, 1964, and 1966. In 1956, he married Kathryn H. Galvin, a graduate of Newton College of the Sacred Heart and the daughter of William J. "Mother" Galvin, another former city council president. The Whites had five children.

In 1967, White entered the race to succeed retiring John F. Collins (q.v.) as mayor of Boston. He finished second in a field of ten in the preliminary election, beating out Republican John W. Sears and nationally renowned Boston Redevelopment Authority director, Edward J. Logue, for the right to take on popular anti-busing leader, Louis Day Hicks, in the final contest. With black and liberal support, White defeated Hicks by a vote of 102,706 to 90,154. In 1970, while still in his first term, White won the Democratic nomination for governor over three other candidates but lost to Republican Francis W. Sargent in November. In both the party primary and the general election, the mayor was defeated in the city of Boston. Nonetheless, White won a second mayoral vote in 1971 with 113,137 votes to Hicks's 70,331. In 1972,

Democratic presidential nominee George McGovern seriously considered White as a possible running mate before finally choosing Senator Thomas F. Eagleton of Missouri. White was elected for the third time as mayor in 1975, defeating Joseph F. Timilty 81,058 to 73,622. He won a record fourth term in 1979, besting Timilty again 78,048 to 64,269.

Boston's population was 641,071 in 1970, down some 56,000 since 1960. In the same ten-year period, the percentage of nonwhites in the city rose from 7.3 percent to 16.3 percent. As mayor, White acknowledged the demographic changes in his city and successfully maintained an electoral coalition of liberals, blacks, Irish, Italians, and Hispanic Americans by using his power of appointment to accommodate these diverse groups. White's administration also reached out to all of Boston's neighborhoods with the establishment of "Little City Halls" providing links to the downtown seat of government, and with the creation of a community-oriented program of warm weather activities and entertainment called "Summerthing." At the same time, White advanced a number of redevelopment plans for Boston. The showpiece of his administration thus far has been Quincy Market, a large area of shops and restaurants near city hall.

In 1974, when Federal District Court Judge W. Arthur Garrity ordered the integration of some of Boston's neighborhood schools through busing, local white groups engaged in frenzied demonstrations. With state and federal assistance, White and his administration assumed the duty of protecting the city's school children from harm during the implementation of the busing order. Although one school was taken into federal receivership for a time and the threat of racial trouble has remained, the initial crisis passed with only scattered instances of real violence. In 1976, Boston like other cities, was in a severe financial bind. Desegregation costs and the decision not to raise property taxes put the city considerably in arrears at a time when credit was scarce. White was forced to economize and to raise taxes, and persuaded Morgan Guaranty Bank to underwrite the city bond issue, averting disaster.

Mayor White undertook significant campaigns for reform in 1976 and 1978. He proposed a change in the city charter, enlarging Boston's city council and school committee and reinstituting partisan elections for the first time since 1907. White's plan was narrowly defeated in a state legislative committee. In 1978, the mayor was the principal leader of a movement favoring property tax classification, and his political organization played a major role in the landslide victory for the proposition in a statewide referendum. In these campaigns, commentators thought they saw a bold push for more power by White and the emergence of a formidable "machine" of city workers. A White machine, if it did exist, would be the first of consequence in the modern history of a city known for feudal and uncentralized politics.

SOURCES: City Record, 1968– , Government Documents Department, Boston Public Library; *Documents of the City of Boston*, 1968– , Microtext Department, Boston Public Library; Philip B. Heymann and Martha Wagner Weinberg, "The Paradox of Power: Mayoral Leadership on Charter Reform in Boston," in Walter Dean Burnham and Martha Wagner Weinberg, eds., *American Politics and Public Policy* (Cambridge, Mass., 1978); Arnold M. Howitt, "Strategies of Governing: Electoral Constraints on Mayoral Behavior in Philadelphia and Boston" (Ph.D. dissertation, Harvard University, 1976); Alan Lupo, *Liberty's Chosen Home: The Politics of Violence in Boston* (Boston, 1977); Eric A. Nordlinger, *Decentralizing the City: A Study of Boston's Little City Halls* (Cambridge, Mass., 1972); Daniel S. Pool, "Politics in the New Boston, 1960–1970: A Study of Mayoral Policy-Making" (Ph.D. dissertation, Brandeis University, 1974); *Proceedings of the City Council of Boston*, 1968– , Government Documents Department, Boston Public Library; Michael Ryan, "Confessions of a Mayor," *Boston* (October 1978); Martha Wagner Weinberg, "Kevin White: A Mayor Who Survived" (paper delivered at the Annual Meeting of the American Political Science Association, 1979); Kevin H. White clippings, Newspaper Morgue, School of Public Communication, Boston University; Kevin H. White speeches and press releases, Mayor's Office of Communications, City Hall, Boston.   *Richard H. Gentile*

WHYTE, WILLIAM PINKNEY (1824–1908), Mayor of Baltimore (1881–83). Whyte was born on 9 August 1824 in Baltimore. He was the third and last child of Joseph White (1791–1867), of Irish descent and cashier of the Baltimore branch of the Second Bank of the United States (a political appointee), and Isabella Pinkney, the only child of William Pinkney, a prominent Maryland lawyer. Both parents were Episcopalian. Whyte was educated in private schools and after a brief stint as a clerk in the firm of Peabody and Riggs, leading Baltimore dry goods importers, he attended Harvard Law School. Returning to Baltimore to practice law, Whyte then allied himself with another old Baltimore family by marrying Louisa Dorsey Hollingsworth on 7 December 1847. They had three children: Joseph, Edward Clymer, and William Hollingsworth. Louisa died on 28 October 1885, and on 27 April 1892, Whyte married Mary McDonald Thomas, a widow and his ward, who died eight years later (1900).

In 1880, Baltimore had a population of 332,190 and a mayor-council form of government. Whyte, who had

had a long and successful career as a Democratic officeholder and appointee since the late 1840s, was elected mayor on 26 October 1881 with 29,244 votes and no opposition. The achievements of his administration included the city's acceptance of the Enoch Pratt Free Library, the creation of the office of fire marshal and the Department of Street Cleaning, a manual training school, and a quarantine hospital. Following his tenure as mayor, Whyte served as attorney general of Maryland (1887–91), on the New Charter Commission for Baltimore City (1897–98), as city solicitor (1900–1903), and as U.S. senator (1906–1908). He died on 17 March 1908.

SOURCES: Wilbur F. Coyle, *The Mayors of Baltimore* (Baltimore, 1919); Frank F. White, Jr., *The Governors of Maryland, 1777–1970* (Annapolis, Md., 1970); "William Pinkney Whyte," Dielman File, Maryland Historical Society, Baltimore.   *Gary L. Browne*

WICKHAM, WILLIAM H. (1832–93), Mayor of New York (1875–76). First mayor of the post-Tweed era, Wickham was born at Smithtown, Long Island, on 3 July 1832. His ancestors had been prominent in New York City affairs for over a century. He was the son of Daniel and Ruth Wickham, and was early identified with shipping interests as well as his father's jewelry business. Wickham's grandfather, who came to New York City from Long Island in 1790, was a dry goods merchant and one of the original founders of the New York Stock Exchange. Wickham attended the Mechanic's Society School and subsequently graduated from a classical academy in Vermont. In 1850, he joined the New York City Volunteer Fire Department, of which he was later president for two years. Wickham was an active member of the Mercantile Library Association. He married a Miss Floyd of Long Island and had one daughter. He also adopted the three grown children of his deceased sister. A Democrat, Wickham was one of the "citizens' committee of seventy" which ousted the Tweed Ring. The first election under an amended charter took place in November 1874 and resulted in the victory of William Havemeyer (*q.v.*) a prominent anti-Tweed figure and former mayor. Havemeyer died of a heart attack on 30 November 1874, leading to Wickham's election.

New York at that time, had over a million people, with a mayor-aldermanic council form of government. Wickham had never held public office but was a member of the Tammany Hall General Committee, a founder of the Apollo Hall division of the Democratic party, and a person whose independent character was held in high esteem. Wickham's 70,071 votes represented a majority over the 37,011 of Salem H. Wales (Republican) and the 24,182 of Oswald Ottendorfer (Independent Democrat).

In the wake of the Tweed era, Wickham sought to reduce expenditures, to assert control over city departments, and to support private investment. He engaged in acrimonious battles with the police board, particularly with respect to its street-cleaning functions. Uptown real estate interests lauded his calls for development and public works. However, spending cuts and bickering over details of administration, especially with Andrew Haskell Green, a real estate ally of Governor Tilden, slowed efforts at improvement. The most important physical change of the era was the growth of rapid transit for which Wickham appointed New York's first Rapid Transit Commission. He worked with Tammany boss "Honest John" Kelly, whom he appointed as comptroller, first to halt and then to reduce the municipal debt. The press praised the high quality of his appointments. As a conservative reformer, Wickham feared labor unrest and the influx of poorly trained immigrants. Without the public schools, he asserted in 1876, "it might be doubted whether free institutions could long be maintained for a city like this." Cuts in municipal wages and the partial continuance of the spoils system under Kelly added to the unease of the times. After his term, he lost interest in politics but served on a coroner's jury after a subway tunnel accident, as a member of the Columbian celebration committee, and on the board of education. After suffering from heart disease and Bright's disease, he died on 13 January 1893.

SOURCES: Gordon Atkins, *Health, Housing and Poverty in New York City 1865–1898* (Ann Arbor, Mich., 1947); William T. Bonner, *New York—The World's Metropolis* (New York, 1924); John Ford, *The Life and Public Service of Andrew Haskell Green* (Garden City, N.J., 1913); William Herman, *Factbook: Mayors and Burgomasters* (New York, n.d.); Mark D. Hirsch, *William C. Whitney* (New York, 1948); Seymour Mandelbaum, *Community Politics: New York City in the Eighteen Seventies* (Princeton, N.J., 1962); J. F. McLaughlin, *The Life and Times of John Kelly* (New York, 1885); Scrapbooks in Kilroe Collection, Columbia University Libraries; *Wilson's Memorial History of the City of New York* (1893), vol. 13.   *Howard R. Weiner*

WIGHTMAN, JOSEPH M. (1812–85), Mayor of Boston (1861–62). First modern Democratic mayor of Boston, Wightman was born in Boston on 19 October 1812, the son of James P. Wightman and Martha (Stokes) Wightman. James Wightman, an immigrant English tailor, died when his son was only ten; the boy left school and was apprenticed to a machinist. Wightman became active in the Mechanics Institutes that were being established for the dissemination of popular scientific knowledge. He lectured at lyceums and institutes in Massachusetts on scientific topics and edited the *Boston Mechanic*, a short-lived magazine (1832–36). He was elected president of the Massachusetts Charitable Mechanics Association (1857–60). During these antebellum years, he developed one of the first firms in Boston for the importing and manufacturing of "philosophical" (i.e., scientific) instruments. Eventually, he was able to develop the company into a rewarding and well-known business. During these years, he married Bethia Wightman and had several children.

Wightman's political career began with service on the Boston School Committee (1846–51), in the Massachusetts legislature (1850–51), and on the board of aldermen (1856–58). National politics intruded on the factional or single-issue politics that had been usual in Boston affairs, and Wightman, nominally a Whig, was swept by the slavery and union agitation into the Democratic party. In December 1859, the Democrats nominated him for mayor, the first time in more than a decade that the party had run a candidate. Defeated by the popular incumbent, Republican-Citizens Frederic W. Lincoln (q.v.) (4,208 to 5,932), he ran again in December 1860, as a Democratic-Union candidate against the antislavery Republican, Moses Kimball, and was victorious (9,974 to 5,674). He was relected for a second term in December 1861, defeating the nonideological Republican Edward Tobey (6,765 to 5,795). However, after charges of serious laxness in office, he was defeated in December 1862 by Lincoln, who had been called out of retirement (5,287 to 6,352). Wightman remained active in Democratic city politics but did not again hold public office.

Wightman was elected on a national issue, the desire to maintain the union and to conciliate the South if at all possible. Once conciliation had proved impossible and the war had begun, he led the city in unprecedented activities to reinforce the war effort. Under his leadership, Boston was generous in the offering of bounties to recruits, in the payment of relief to families of servicemen, in coordinating many private relief activities, and in maintaining the mustering depots and aid stations. Beyond this war activity, Wightman was eager to continue municipal activities in expanding the city. He pushed for a monumental city hall to symbolize "the American Athens" and was active in encouraging further landfill and street extensions. The council agreed with these policies, and both mayor and council fell into considerable disfavor for their seemingly lax and lavish style of government and their inept administrative abilities. The old coalition of Citizens of the 1850s reemerged to persuade the respected Frederic W. Lincoln to run again and to lead the city during wartime. Although Wightman protested that the allegations were false and that under his direction the city had responded well, he was defeated.

After leaving the mayor's office, Wightman continued in city politics and in his business. After retirement he was given a place on the board of voter registration which he held at the time of his death on 25 January 1885. He was buried at Mount Auburn Cemetery in Cambridge, Massachusetts.

SOURCES: *Annals of the Boston Primary School Committee, from Its First Establishment in 1818 to Its Dissolution in 1855* (Boston, 1860); *Boston Mechanic*, 4 vols. (Boston, 1832 to 36); Boston *Transcript*, 26 January 1885 (obituary); J. M. Bugbee, "Boston Under the Mayors," in Justin Winsor, ed., *The Memorial History of Boston*, 4 vols. (Boston, 1881), vol. 3; City of Boston, Massachusetts, *Documents, 1861, 1862; Companion to the Air Pump* . . . , (Boston, 1845); Wightman's writings include "Letter of the Mayor in Relation to the Contribution of the Citizens of Boston for the Relief of the Soldiers," Boston, 1862 (a pamphlet written against allegations of mismanagement and lavishness during the campaign of December 1862.)   *Constance Burns*

WILKESON, SAMUEL (1781–1848), Mayor of Buffalo (1836–37). Fourth man to become mayor of Buffalo and a Scots-Irish Presbyterian, Wilkeson, born in Carlisle, Pennsylvania, on 1 June 1781, was the son of John and Mary (Robinson) Wilkeson, a farm family and emigrants to Delaware from Londonderry, Northern Ireland, in about 1760. In 1784, the Wilkeson family moved to Washington County in western Pennsylvania to farm land granted to John for service in the Revolution. In about 1802, Samuel Wilkeson married Jane Oram (1784–1819), also of Scots-Irish parentage, the daughter of Captain William Oram. They had seven children. After his first wife's death, Samuel married Sarah St. John (1797–1836) of Buffalo, and following her death, Mary Peters (c. 1797–1847), the daughter of Absolom Peters of New Haven, Connecticut. Wilkeson had no offspring from his second or third marriages.

About the time of his marriage to Jane Oram, Wilkeson moved to Youngstown, Ohio, where he built a grist mill. Later, in about 1810, he moved to Chautauqua County, New York, where he built boats and shipped salt. During the War of 1812, he built boats for General Harrison's forces on Lake Erie, and as a member of the militia he helped defend the town of Black Rock, near Buffalo. In 1814, he moved to Buffalo where he became a merchant and shipper; he also constructed Lake vessels and built the first iron foundry in Buffalo.

In 1820, the Buffalo Harbor Company needed to secure a loan for the construction of Buffalo harbor. Although not a member of the company, Wilkeson, along with Oliver Forward and Charles Townsend, pledged a security of $12,000 for the project. The following year,

WILLEY, JOHN W.   393

Wilkeson took over as supervisor of harbor construction. He was also active in promoting Buffalo, rather than neighboring Black Rock, as the western terminus of the Erie Canal.

Wilkeson was elected justice of the peace in 1815, appointed judge of the court of common pleas in 1821, elected to the New York Assembly in 1822, and to the state Senate in 1824. Elijah Efner, an early associate of Wilkeson, described Wilkeson as a "War Democrat" in 1812, who later allied himself with DeWitt Clinton and finally became a supporter of Henry Clay and the Whigs.

The population of Buffalo grew from 15,661 in 1833 to 18,213 in 1840. Government was in the hands of a common council consisting of two alderman from each of the five wards. The mayor and other city officials were appointed by the common council. Wilkeson, appointed mayor in 1836, was particularly concerned with enforcing the laws and strengthening the city's police force.

Although a Presbyterian, Wilkeson had not become acquainted with Christianity until the early 1830s when Charles G. Finney preached in Buffalo. By the middle of the 1830s, Wilkeson withdrew from his various businesses in favor of his sons and became increasingly involved with the Colonization Society of New York and the American Colonization Society. He moved to Washington, D.C., to serve as president of the American Colonization Society and to edit its magazine, the *African Repository*. Wilkeson died on 7 June 1848, in Kingston, Tennessee, while on a visit to his daughter.

SOURCES: Albert Bigelow, "The Harbor Maker of Buffalo," *Publications of the Buffalo Historical Society* 4 (1896); Elijah D. Efner, "The Adventures and Enterprises of Elijah D. Efner," *Publications of the Buffalo Historical Society* 4 (1896); John C. Lord, "Samuel Wilkeson," *Publications of the Buffalo Historical Society* 4 (1896); John C. Lord, *"The Valiant Man": A Discourse on the Death of the Hon. Samuel Wilkeson of Buffalo* (Buffalo, 1848); Richard J. Perry, "Preliminary Inventory of the Wilkeson-Barringer Collection," *Niagara Frontier* 15 (Summer 1968); Richard J. Perry, "Preliminary Inventory of the Wilkeson Papers," *Niagara Frontier* 15 (Spring 1968); Samuel Wilkeson, "Recollections of the West and the Building of the Buffalo Harbor," *Publications of the Buffalo Historical Society* 5 (1902).   *Christopher Densmore*

WILLEY, JOHN W. (1794–1841), Mayor of Cleveland (1836–37). First mayor of Cleveland, Willey was a transplanted New Englander, born in 1794 in Goshen, New Hampshire, son of Allen Willey (b. 1760) and Chloe Frink Willey (b. 1760). The sixth-born of nine children, John W. Willey was named for president John Wheelock

of Dartmouth College, from where he later graduated. In 1829, he married Laura Maria Higby (1809–72), also of old-stock New England origins. They had no children. Willey studied law in New York and moved to Cleveland in 1822.

First elected village auditor in 1824, Willey entered the Ohio General Assembly in 1827, serving three years as representative and three as senator. A Jacksonian Democrat, he ran for Congress in 1838 but was defeated by a Whig, later Mayor John W. Allen (*q.v.*). At the mouth of the Cuyahoga River on the east side (with Ohio City on the west), Cleveland became a boom town as the Lake Erie terminus of the Ohio and Erie Canal was completed in 1834. The population grew from 1,075 in 1830 to 5,080 in 1835 and 6,071 in 1840. Ohio City then had 1,577 people. In 1836, the first Cleveland city directory recorded that 117 million pounds of goods valued at $2.5 million arrived by canal, while almost 2,000 lake vessels cleared the port. Willey participated in chartering the Cleveland, Columbus and Cincinnati Railroad, and was president of the Cleveland, Warren, and Pittsburgh Railroad in 1836, but neither railroad made progress for a decade.

Cleveland was incorporated as a city on 5 March 1836, with a mayor and a board of aldermen. A leader of the Cleveland bar, Willey wrote the city charter and ordinances, and was elected the first mayor on 13 April, defeating Leonard Case. In two of Cleveland's three wards, Nicholas Dockstadter (*q.v.*) and Joshua Mills (*q.v.*) were aldermen and later mayors. On 5 March 1837, Willey was reelected to a second term, apparently unopposed. The city charter called for common schools under a board of managers, one of whom was Willey, and on 7 July 1837, the Cleveland public school system was established. Willey was a central figure in the celebrated "Bridge War" of 1837. He speculated in lands called "Willeyville" south of Ohio City to which Cleveland built the Columbus Street Bridge, diverting trade from the south away from the Detroit Street Bridge connecting Cleveland to Ohio City. When Willey's administration removed the Cleveland side of the Detroit Street Bridge, an Ohio City mob set out to destroy the Columbus bridge. In the mêlée, three persons were seriously wounded, and many others were hurt. The issue helped to delay a union of the two cities until 1854.

In his law career, Willey was partner with Reuben Wood, later governor of Ohio. Willey became a judge in the court of common pleas in 1840. When he died of tuberculosis on 9 July 1841, he was chief judge of the Fourteenth Judicial Circuit for the counties of Geauga, Cuyahoga, and Lorain. He was buried in Cleveland.

SOURCES: Elroy McKendree Avery, *A History of Cleveland and Its Environs: the Heart of New Connect-*

icut (Chicago, 1918); E. Decker, *Cleveland Past and Present: Its Representative Men* (Cleveland, 1869); Gertrude Van Rensselaer Wickham, *The Pioneer Families of Cleveland 1796–1840* (Cleveland, 1914).

Ronald E. Shaw

WILLIAMS, JOHN R. (1782–1854), Mayor of Detroit (1824, 1825, 1829, 1830, 1844–46). First elected mayor of Detroit and the only son of Thomas Williams (c. 1750–85), and Mary Cecilia Campau (1764–1805), John (he later added the "R" to distinguish himself from another man in Detroit of the same name) was born in Detroit on 4 May 1782. He was baptized a Roman Catholic, following his French mother's faith, but left the church at age twenty-three. His father had arrived in the city in 1780, and was a storekeeper and justice of the peace. His mother's brother, Joseph Campau, was among the wealthiest pioneers of early Detroit. When his father died in 1785, Joseph Campau took charge of his nephew's upbringing, providing his education. Campau's store gave Williams his first job. In 1796, he received an appointment in the Army, serving primarily at Fort Marsac on the Cumberland River in Tennessee. Two years later, he returned to Detroit to form a trading partnership with his uncle. Williams thus traveled frequently. Many accounts mention a trip in those frontier days to Montreal during which he successfully challenged a Frenchman named La Salle to a duel, for which he was subsequently jailed for several months. In 1803, he dissolved the partnership with Campau and built his own store, which burned two years later but was rebuilt.

In 1802, when Detroit was incorporated as a township, Williams was chosen town clerk, the first of a series of public appointments. In 1804, he was chosen a trustee of Detroit, and shortly after, he was appointed to the local artillery and then as justice of the peace. He resigned both positions, it is said, because of personal differences with Governor William Hull and the judges. Apparently because of these differences, Williams chose to participate in the War of 1812 as a private in the militia. During the war, he ended up in Albany, where he briefly opened yet another store. After the war, Williams returned to Detroit, continued trading, and again immersed himself in public service. Long a supporter of the Woodward plan for Detroit, he was continually concerned about the appearance of the city. In 1818, he was appointed associate justice of the county court and county commissioner. From 1818 to 1829, he served as adjutant general of the territory. In 1818, he also became president of the Bank of Michigan. One year later Williams ran for Congress as a Democrat and lost. In 1820, he served as a trustee of the University of Michigan. In 1824, he helped write the charter for Detroit and was elected the first

mayor of the city under the new mayor recorder council form of government. He was reelected on 4 April 1825 for another one-year term, drawing 102 votes to a scattering for his opponents: Henry Hunt 6, Peter Desnoyers 1, James Abbott 1, M. Day 2, and Abner Wells 1. He ran unsuccessfully in the three subsequent elections but was elected again in 1829, 1830, and from 1844 to 1846.

During his various terms as mayor, the settlement grew from a village of 2,000 to a thriving town of 18,000. Meanwhile, Williams served a number of years on the board of education. In 1829, he was a major general in the Michigan militia. Two years later, he took a leading role, along with his uncle, in establishing the *Democratic Free Press*, the ancestor to the present-day Detroit *Free Press*. In 1832, he led the local militia to Chicago to defend the city against the reported danger of Indian attack. He went to Washington D.C. to present the resolutions of the state constitutional convention in 1835 to the U.S. Congress and in 1836, presided over the so-called Snap Convention which accepted the terms imposed by Congress for Michigan's admission into the Union. Williams died on 20 October 1854. His wife, Mary Mott, a cousin whom he had married on 24 October 1804, had died fourteen years before him. They had ten children.

SOURCES: Clarence Burton, ed., *History of Detroit* (Detroit and Chicago, 1922), vol. 1; Silas Farmer, *The History of Detroit and Michigan* (Detroit, 1885); Milo Quaife, ed., *The John Askin Papers* (Detroit, 1931), vol. 2; *Representative Men of Michigan* (Cincinnati, 1878); John R. Williams, "Sketch of the Life of General John R. Williams," *Michigan Pioneer and Historical Collections* 29. *Francis X. Blouin, Jr.*

WILSON, BENJAMIN DAVID (1811–78), Mayor of Los Angeles (1851–52). Wealthy landowner and town booster, Wilson was born in Nashville, Tennessee, on 1 December 1811 and was orphaned at the age of eight. At fifteen, he began trading in the Southwest, arriving in 1833 at Santa Fe. As a merchant there, he learned Spanish but in the fall of 1841, fearing Mexican retaliation against foreigners, joined a party across the desert to Los Angeles. In spring 1843, he purchased a *rancho* near present-day Riverside, where he engaged in several campaigns against hostile Indians and cooperated with the *Californios* in their February 1845 overthrow of an unpopular Mexican governor. The new governor appointed him a justice of the peace in February 1846. Hence, when war began between Mexico and the United States, Wilson, an American citizen but a Mexican official, tried to avoid military involvement and maintain peace in the area. When fighting broke out, he joined with other Americans in the minor battle of Chino Rancho, where he was captured and imprisoned for several months.

In 1844, Wilson married a *Californio* woman, Ramona Yorba (1828–49), by whom he had a daughter Mary and a son John. Before Ramona's death, he sold his rancho and moved into Los Angeles where he established a general store. In organizing local government for American Los Angeles's 1 April 1850 election, a secret meeting of the town's leading citizens selected him county clerk. He held that post until July 1853, although he assigned most of the actual work to a deputy in order to devote his attention to his business. He also became a member of the common council in September 1850, and in May 1851, when the city had around 1,800 residents, he won election as mayor by a large majority. The council disregarded his recommendations to improve water facilities and to discontinue the public school in favor of a college, although it followed his suggestions to determine city boundaries and to establish a volunteer police force.

After his one term as an inactive mayor, Wilson never again participated in city politics, although he held several county, state, and federal offices: Indian agent for southern California in late 1852 (as a Whig), four terms as state senator (1856 and 1857 as a Democrat, 1869 and 1871 as an Independent), and four terms in the early 1860s as a county supervisor.

Following his 1853 marriage to Margaret Hereford (1820–1893), a Virginia-born widow by whom he had two more daughters, Anne and Ruth, Wilson sold his store and moved to a *rancho* east of town. He acquired several other area *ranchos*, sometimes by foreclosing mortgages at 5-percent interest a month, and he developed areas such as Pasadena. Other investments included railroads and oil. He also lobbied in Congress to obtain appropriations for railroads and harbor improvements in Los Angeles. Until his death on 11 March 1878 at his home near the present city of San Marino, he remained one of the wealthiest men in Los Angeles county. Wilson was Episcopalian.

SOURCES: Hubert Howe Bancroft, *The Works of Hubert Howe Bancroft*, 39 vols., *History of California* (San Francisco, 1884–1900), vols. 18–24; "Benjamin David Wilson's Observations on Early Days in California and New Mexico," *Historical Society of Southern California, Annual Publications* 16 (1934); John C. Macfarland, "Don Benito Wilson," *Historical Society of Southern California Quarterly* 31 (December 1949).

R. David Weber

WILSON, GEORGE (1816–82), Mayor of Pittsburgh (1860–62). Wilson was born in Baltimore on 7 July 1816 and was brought to Pittsburgh at the age of two. His father, Robert Wilson, a millwright, probably of Scots descent, died in about 1820, and he was brought up by a sister, Mrs. Margaret Marshall. He apparently had little education, going to work in a tobacco factory when very young. Later, however, he became a banker, and was a school director and served on both the select and common council.

At the time of his election, Pittsburgh was a city of about 49,000, with a government by a mayor and two councils. Wilson received the Republican nomination after an apparent deal not to seek a second term and defeated Democrat Alexander McIllwaine 2,837 to 2,170. His party swept the elections for both councils. Except for visits by the prince of Wales "Baron Renfrew" in 1860 and Abraham Lincoln in February 1861, and a panic over the transfer of some outmoded guns in December 1860, Wilson's term was relatively colorless. The only important change was paying the mayor a salary of $1,000, instead of by fees as an alderman. (Immediately after the change, arrests in the city dropped by more than half.)

Wilson did not seek reelection. In 1867 and 1869, he was elected to the state House of Representatives. He was a family man, father of nine children—six by Mary Frances Howe Wilson, who died in 1854, and three by Emily Wilson who died in 1879. He was superintendent of the Presbyterian Sunday School and an organizer of Bellefield Presbyterian Church. He died at his East End home on 12 April 1882.

SOURCES: *Biographical Review of Pittsburgh and Vicinity* (Boston, 1897); Allen Humphreys Kerr "The Mayors and Recorders of Pittsburgh, 1816–1951" (typescript, Carnegie Library of Pittsburgh, 1952); Pittsburgh *Gazette*, 13 April 1882.   *George Swetnam*

WILSON, RUSSELL (1876–1946), Mayor of Cincinnati (1930–37). Newspaperman and mayor, Wilson was born in Cincinnati on 10 November 1876, the son of Moses F. Wilson and Lucy (Thorpe) Wilson, both old-stock Protestants. After attending local schools, Wilson spent one year in Princeton and then moved on to the University of Cincinnati, graduating with an LL.B. in 1900. He was drama editor for the Cincinnati *Post*, 1908–11, and associate editor of the Cincinnati *Times-Star*, 1913–30. Wilson also served as president of the Cincinnatus Association in 1924–25. He married Elizabeth Smith on 20 September 1923, and they had two children. The Wilsons were Presbyterians. Wilson was also a Mason and a member of Sigma Chi, Phi Delta Phi, Sigma Sigma, the Cincinnati Club, and other social organizations.

Wilson was elected to the city council in 1929 and was subsequently appointed mayor for four consecutive two-year terms. During his political career, Wilson was a Charterite, having originally been a Democrat. Cincinnati had 451,160 people in 1930 and a city manager-mayor-council form of government. As mayor, Wilson was an active defender of the charter form of government. He was a popular politician and always had solid press backing in his campaigns. He opposed municipal ownership of utilities, considering the existing companies adequate for the job. Wilson also once said that crime would be reduced only when the police department stayed out of politics. He was frequently asked to write articles and to give speeches to national groups, explaining and defending the charter and the city-manager system of government.

Wilson remained on the city council from 1938 to 1946. He also served during World War II as director or chairman of various organizations, including the Red Cross, the Committee to Defend America by Aiding the Allies, the Foreign Policy Association, and Bundles for Britain. His political career continued until his death on 27 November 1946.

SOURCES: *Cincinnati Mayors* (Cincinnati, 1957); New York *Times*, 14 November 1930; Ralph Straetz, *PR: Politics in Cincinnati* (Washington Square, 1958); The Russell Wilson Papers in the Cincinnati Historical Society comprise some four file drawers covering almost the entire 1929–46 era, mostly relating to Wilson's support for the charter.

Thomas R. Bullard

WILSON, SAMUEL D. (1881–1939), Mayor of Philadelphia (1936–39). Wilson was born in Cambridge, Massachusetts, on 31 August 1881. His father died when Samuel was a child, and he was raised by his mother who inspired him with a desire for success. He attended local schools and Phillips Exeter Academy. After his mother died in 1897, young Wilson began the study of law in John Long's office in Boston. He went to Vermont in 1901, gaining a job as vice-inspector for Windsor County. After killing a gambler in White River Junction in 1902, Wilson left and joined the U.S. Army Signal Corps for two years. In 1903, he went to Washington, D.C., and worked for Edward Hale, chaplain to the U.S. Senate. He also joined the International Reform Bureau, as a result of which he was invited to come to Philadelphia as a member of the Law and Order League in 1905. At this point, he began calling himself S. Davis Wilson (as there already was a Samuel D. Wilson). In 1908, he married a hometown girlfriend, Sarah, and they had four children.

During World War I, Wilson worked for the Justice Department and helped arrest a German agent. He lived for a time in Port Elizabeth, New Jersey, serving as a justice of the peace. He also operated an auto body shop. He returned to Philadelphia in 1925 and soon became a

protégé of William B. Hadley, the city comptroller. He became Hadley's deputy (1927–33) and succeeded him in 1933. Wilson collected delinquent taxes and sold city-owned land to raise funds, impressing the public. He also convinced the local Republican machine to support his ambitions of becoming mayor. Even though he was considered too independent, he secured the party's endorsement and won the 1935 election, defeating Democrat John Kelly 379,222 to 333,825. At that time, Philadelphia had a population of 1,950,961 and a mayor-council form of government.

As mayor, Wilson's name was constantly in the headlines, for he was a successful self-publicist. He settled labor disputes, used federal funds (through the Works Progress Administration) to finance building projects, and sponsored a new airport. He hoped to become either the next governor or a U.S. senator, and he actually sought support from the local Democrats. Two indictments for official misconduct halted these dreams in 1938. In early 1939, he suffered a stroke and spent only twelve minutes in his office during the rest of the year. Strong pressure finally forced him to resign on 11 August 1939; he was replaced by Acting Mayor George Connell (*q.v.*). Wilson died only eight days later.

SOURCES: Peter B. Bart and Milton C. Cummings, Jr., "Politics and Voting Behavior in Philadelphia" (undergraduate honors thesis, Swarthmore College, 1954); Herman L. Collins and Wilfred Jordan, *Philadelphia: A Story of Progress*, 4 vols. (New York, 1941), vol. 1; Philadelphia *Evening Bulletin*, 19 August 1939; Philadelphia *Record*, 20 August 1939.

Thomas R. Bullard

WILSTACH, CHARLES F. (1818–82), Mayor of Cincinnati (1866–67, 1867–69). Wilstach was born on 10 August 1818 in Philadelphia and moved to Cincinnati in 1839. He established a bookbinding firm which later expanded into book publishing and selling and related activities. He served as president of the First Cincinnati Industrial Exposition and for seventeen years as president of the Ohio Mechanics Institute in the city. During the Civil War, he became well known for his philanthropic activities.

When Mayor Leonard A. Harris (*q.v.*) resigned in August 1866, the city council appointed Wilstach to fill the remainder of the unexpired term to April 1867. Cincinnati, whose population was to increase to 216,239 by the 1870 Census, had a mayor-council form of government. In 1867, the Republican party nominated Wilstach to run for mayor in his own right, a race he won by 13,733 votes to his Democratic opponent James Saffin's 9,362.

Mayor Wilstach achieved notoriety of sorts when he

proclaimed that the greatness of a city is measured by its public indebtedness. In office, he persuaded the city to spend more than it ever had before, principally for civic improvements. Although the city debt nearly doubled during his administration, his integrity and judgment were never questioned by the business community.

Wilstach returned to his publishing business. He died of paralysis in Cincinnati on 17 April 1882.

SOURCES: Cincinnati *Enquirer*, 17, 19 April 1882; [Robert Herron], *Cincinnati's Mayors* (Cincinnati, 1957).   *Dwight L. Smith*

WILTZ, LOUIS ALFRED (1843–81), Mayor of New Orleans (1872–74). Born in New Orleans on 21 January 1843, the son of J. B. Wiltz of German ancestry and Louise I. Villanueva Wiltz, the daughter of a Spanish soldier, Louis Alfred was a Roman Catholic and attended the New Orleans public schools until about age fifteen. He then worked in a mercantile house and at the outbreak of the Civil War enlisted in the New Orleans Artillery. Wiltz rose to captain, but his career at Fort Jackson was cut short when he and his command were captured by Union forces in 1862. Exchanged as a prisoner of war, he returned to the South and served in the Confederate Army until 1865. After the war, he returned to New Orleans, where he went into business for himself, became active in the Orleans Democratic Parish Committee, and was elected to the state legislature in 1868. He served briefly on the conflict-ridden New Orleans City Council but was removed by the Radical Reconstruction party in power at the statehouse. He married M. Bienvenu in 1862 and was the father of seven children.

New Orleans in 1872 had a population of about 191,000 and a weak mayor administrator government. Having run unsuccessfully for mayor in 1870, Wiltz accepted the Democratic nomination in 1872 and beat his Republican opponent, W. R. Fish, by a vote of 23,896 to 12,984. Although elected in early November, Wiltz, because of state intervention in the recount, did not assume the mayoralty until 6 December when the Republican incumbent reluctantly vacated the office.

Wiltz's term as mayor was troubled. Finances were in perilous condition and to meet operating costs, the city turned to certificates (or scrip) which were heavily discounted when circulated. Wiltz, in desperation, turned to a pay-as-you-go policy, but that failed. The city cut back public improvements, tried to collect back-taxes by discounting delinquent bills, and as a last resort sold public land and a public building to meet expenses. In addition, the city was buffeted by shock waves from the open conflict between two rival Radical Republican governments fighting for control of the state, a conflict which included shootouts and cannonading by private militias

in the streets of New Orleans. On the positive side, the street railways were extended, and an area called Carrollton was annexed.

Wiltz lost his reelection campaign for mayor in 1874 but was returned to the state legislature the same year and was speaker of the House in 1875. In 1879, he was elected governor of Louisiana. He died of tuberculosis while still in office, on 16 October 1881, and was buried in New Orleans.

SOURCES: John S. Kendall, *History of New Orleans* (Chicago, 1922), vol. 1; Robert Sobel and John Raimo, eds., *Biographical Directory of the Governors of the United States, 1789–1978* (Westport, Conn., 1978), vol. 2.   *Melvin G. Holli*

WIMER, JOHN M. (1810–63), Mayor of St. Louis (1843, 1857). Wimer was elected mayor for two terms, fourteen years apart. He was a Southerner, born in Amherst County, Virginia on 8 May 1810. When he was eighteen, he moved to St. Louis and worked as a blacksmith. However, his business ventures eventually led him far beyond the blacksmith trade. He helped to establish several St. Louis enterprises and became president of both the Missouri Pacific Railroad Company and the Commercial Insurance Company. Furthermore, soon after his arrival in St. Louis, Wimer became active in city politics. For years he controlled the city's Fifth Ward from his frame blacksmith shop on the corner of Fourth and Chestnut streets. He held a variety of local offices, compiling a good record as constable, alderman, superintendent of the waterworks, postmaster, sheriff, and county judge. Since firefighting was a consuming interest for him, he was one of the founders of the Liberty Fire Company of the St. Louis Volunteer Fire Department.

St. Louis had a population of 32,800 and a mayor-council type of government in 1843 when Wimer was elected to his first term as mayor, defeating former mayor John Darby (*q.v.*) and A. Wetmore. Not surprisingly, given his interests, one of the city's first fire-control measures was put into effect under his leadership. Chimney and stove-pipe regulations were established, and a system of inspection was instituted. In addition, during his first administration, the duties and salaries of city officials were revised and more precisely described. The city engineer, who received $1,500 annually, was the city's highest paid official. The mayor's annual salary was set at $1,200. The city grew rapidly in the years between Wimer's two terms and by 1857 had a population of 133,000. In that year, Wimer was reelected, with 5,448 votes, against 3,753 for former Mayor Bernard Pratte (*q.v.*) (Whig) and 2,031 for former Mayor William Carr Lane (*q.v.*) (Know-Nothing). The most notable accomplishment of his second term was the organization of a regular, paid fire department which acquired the property of the volunteer companies.

When the Civil War began, Wimer supported the Confederate cause. In the spring of 1862, he was arrested and imprisoned by Union forces. However, in December 1863 he escaped and joined Confederate forces in southwestern Missouri. He served there under the command of General Emmett McDonald; Wimer was killed at Hartsville, Missouri, on 11 January 1863.

SOURCES: Charles H. Cornwell, *St. Louis Mayors: Brief Biographies* (St. Louis, 1965); William Hyde and Howard L. Conrad, *Encyclopedia of the History of St. Louis* (New York, 1899); Walter B. Stevens, *St. Louis: The Fourth City, 1764–1909* (St. Louis, 1909).   *Jeanette C. Lauer*

WOOD, FERNANDO (1812–81), Mayor of New York (1855–58, 1860–62). A prototype machine politician, Wood was born in Philadelphia on 14 June 1812, the middle son of Benjamin and Rebecca (Lehman) Wood, of Scottish Quaker ancestry. After five years of private schooling, Wood held various jobs before following his father into the dry goods business. Using shrewd, if unsavory, tactics in New York City, Wood made a fortune (quickly invested in real estate) by trade with California during the Gold Rush. He began politics as a Tammanyite and served one term in Congress (1841–43) before seeking the mayoralty. He was defeated in 1849 (receiving 17,793 votes to Ambrose Kingsland's (*q.v.*) 22,546) but won in 1854: Wood 19,993, James Barker 18,553, Wilson Hunt 15,386, John Herrick, 5,712.

In 1855, the city had a population of 629,904 and a mayor-bicameral system of government. Initially, Wood promised a people's-oriented administration, pledged to anti-corruption, home rule, civic improvement, and ending vice by closing brothels and gambling houses, plus enforcement of Sunday laws for saloons. A large part of this program rested on his control over the police. Before long, Wood's selective reformism, ties to criminal elements, and scarcely disguised graft disillusioned many well-wishers. Moreover, his long-term goal of dominating Tammany Hall, by building an independent power bloc through patronage and party discipline, alienated regular Democrats. Nonetheless, Wood's constituency, mainly poor immigrants, held firm in the 1856 election: Wood 34,860, Isaac Barker 25,209, Anthony Bleeker 9,654, James Libby 4,764, and James Whiting 3,646. Wood, by now the center of escalating controversy, faced a fresh challenge in 1857 when the Republican legislature created a new police force, which prompted a bloody riot when he denied its legitimacy, and passed a revised charter that cut his term by half. Forced to organize his own faction, Mozart Hall, and no longer considered a

reformer, Wood lost the 1858 election to Daniel Tiemann (*q.v.*) 43,216 to 40,889. In 1860, Wood regained the mayoralty by 29,940 votes to William Havemeyer's (*q.v.*) 26,913 and George Opdyke's (*q.v.*) 21,417. Usually adept at reading public opinion, Wood stumbled during the Civil War because of his pro-Southernism and Peace Democratic ideas. He lost the 1862 election: Opdyke 25,380, C. Godfrey Gunther (*q.v.*) 24,767, and Wood 24,167. A year later, he partly recovered by becoming a congressman (1863–65). In 1867, Wood again ran for mayor but lost badly: John Hoffman (*q.v.*) 63,061, Wood 22,837, and William Darling 18,483. Wood achieved little positive good as mayor. Nonetheless, he left the city with two indelible legacies—the desire for home rule and the "boss" model for William Tweed.

By 1866, Wood found his niche in Congress; he served fourteen years there and became chairman of the Committee on Ways and Means. He was married three times. He died on 14 February 1881, survived by his wife, Alice Fenner Mills, whom he had married on 2 December 1860.

SOURCES: Jerome Mushkat, *Tammany: The Evolution of a Political Machine* (Syracuse, N.Y., 1971); Samuel Pleasants, *Fernando Wood of New York* (New York, 1948); James Richardson, *The New York Police* (New York, 1970).   *Jerome Mushkat*

WOODHULL, CALEB S. (1792–1866), Mayor of New York (1849–51). Woodhull was elected mayor of New York City on 10 April 1849 on the Whig ticket, serving until 1851. Known for his attempts to beautify the city, he was an advocate of open squares and parks, arguing in his annual message of 7 January 1850 that such squares "not only greatly beautify a city, but are essential aids to the public health. They are the great *breathing-places* of the toiling masses, who have no other resort in the heat of the summer or in time of pestilence . . . ."

In 1850, New York had a population of 515,547; it already needed those "breathing-spaces" named by Mayor Woodhull (a phrase used ever since by urban reformers). Many of his original goals (outlined in his first message of 8 May 1849) remained tasks for the city's mayors for years thereafter. He demanded improvements in almshouses, the city jail, street-cleaning methods, "emigrant boarding-houses," property assessments and taxation, and the city's charter. He said New York needed a brand new market to handle an ever-growing trade.

An idea of the character of city life around 1850 is derived instantly in Woodhull's plaintive advice: "I would further suggest that manure should be put in all cases after being taken up, directly into cars or boats, and not again deposited in the streets in large masses, as is and has been the practice for many years."

SOURCES: *Annual Message of Mayor Caleb S. Woodhull*, Document No. 1, Board of Assistant Aldermen (New York, 1849); *Annual Message of Mayor Caleb S. Woodhull* (New York, 1850); *The Renascence of City Hall: Mayors of New York* (New York, 1956).

Peter d'A. Jones

WOODMAN, FREDERICK THOMAS (1872–1949), Mayor of Los Angeles (1916–19). Mayor of Los Angeles during World War I, Woodman, born on 25 June 1872 in Concord, New Hampshire, was the son of a New England sea captain, Alfred Woodman, and Maria T. (Gallap). Frederick attended White River Junction public high school until 1895 and then studied law in private practice with Honorable John L. Spring, being admitted to the New Hampshire bar in 1899. He went into practice for himself in Concord, New Hampshire, and married Etta M. Sanborn in that town on 6 February 1908. She died on 16 April 1916, whereupon Woodman married Katherine Potter Winter of Los Angeles on 2 February 1921. They had a son, Thomas, who died.

Woodman was elected to the New Hampshire House of Representatives as a Republican, 1901–1903. He moved to Los Angeles in 1908 and opened a new practice there. Four years later, he was made president of the Harbor Commission (1912–16) and was then appointed mayor of Los Angeles, 1916. He was subsequently elected mayor for a full term in his own right, 1917–19. During his term, Pershing Square was named after the World War I general; Westwood was annexed to the city; and the municipal Bureau of Power and Light was created, as was the Los Angeles Philharmonic. In Hollywood, already a movie capital, Mary Pickford signed the world's first million-dollar acting contract, and D. W. Griffith produced the epic, *Intolerance*, on the Sunset Boulevard movie lot.

After 1919, Mayor Woodman reverted to his law practice and private business. A member of many fraternal organizations and clubs, and of the California bar, he died on 25 March 1949 and is buried in Rosedale Cemetery, Los Angeles.

SOURCES: *Cyclopedia of American Biography; Mayors of Los Angeles* (Los Angeles, 1968).

Peter d'A. Jones

WOODWORTH, JAMES HUTCHINSON (1804–69), Mayor of Chicago (1848–49). Two-term mayor of Chicago, Woodworth was born in Greenwich, New York, on 4 December 1804, the son of Eleazar Woodworth, an old-stock Yankee farmer, and Catherine (Rock) Woodworth, also of New England ancestry. Woodworth

had eight siblings. He left school at age fourteen to work on his father's farm and moved to Chicago in 1833 where he eventually entered the milling and flour business. He also worked as a real estate salesman and speculated in land. In 1854, he was elected president of the Merchant's and Mechanics Bank, and a few years later he headed the Treasury Bank of Chicago. He was married in 1842.

Chicago in 1848 had a population of 20,000 and a mayor-council form of government with a one-year term. Woodworth, who had served in the state Senate (1838–40) and state House of Representatives (1842–44) and as a city alderman (1845 and 1847), ran for mayor on 7 March 1848 as an Independent Democrat, defeating the incumbent mayor, James Curtiss (*q.v.*), 1,971 to 1,361. On 6 March 1849, Woodworth was reelected, running now as a Whig Democrat on a fusion ticket, defeating Timothy Wait (Independent Democrat) 2,292 to 378, with 260 votes for Lewis C. Kerchival and 26 for S. D. Childs.

Under Woodworth, Chicago's first anti-gambling ordinance was passed in March 1848 to suppress keno; the Illinois and Michigan Canal was formally opened in April 1848—most important for the city's economic growth (and as a provider of jobs for immigrants); the first municipal market was opened (Randolph and Lake); and the first smallpox scare was met, with many free vaccinations given. In 1849, in Woodworth's second term, Chicago became a major outfitting post for would-be gold miners on their way west, and the city grew. But a bad flood caused by an ice-jam in the Chicago River caused thousands of dollars worth of damage to shipping and warehouse facilities on 12 March 1849. The following July, a bad fire destroyed twenty-one downtown buildings, including the famous Tremont House. Cholera followed—a bad year for Chicago. On the positive side, the dispute over railroad terminal facilities was resolved by allowing each separate railroad to build its own terminal in Chicago. Despite a money shortage at the time, the Chicago and Galena Railroad was completed to Elgin and opened on 22 January 1850.

After leaving city hall, Woodworth, who became a Free Soiler (Republican), was elected to Congress for two terms beginning in 1854. He opposed the Kansas-Nebraska Act, and he was Chicago's first Republican congressman. He had always opposed slavery and had led the movement against the Compromise of 1850 in Chicago. In later life, he was a banker. He died at home in Highland Park, Illinois, on 26 March 1869.

SOURCES: A. T. Andreas, *History of Chicago* (Chicago, 1884); Don Fehrenbacher, *Chicago Giant: A Biography of "Long John" Wentworth* (Madison, Wis., 1957); Bessie Pierce, *History of Chicago* (Chicago, 1937–57); Frederick Rex, *Mayors of the City of Chicago* (Chicago, 1947).

Leslie V. Tischauser

WOODWORTH, WALLACE (1832–82), Acting Mayor of Los Angeles (1860–61). Acting mayor of Los Angeles at the outbreak of the Civil War, Woodworth arrived in the settlement in 1853, becoming a prominent local merchant and lumber and furniture dealer, associated with William H. Perry. As acting mayor he remains obscure, but as a California pioneer and entrepreneur he is remembered for his adventures during the La Paz gold rush in 1862, when Perry and Woodworth took a party of about forty men, pack animals, and seven or eight wagons loaded with goods, including a small boat, to La Paz and the Colorado River on the little-used Morongo Trail, an ancient Indian pathway off the more famous Bradshaw route. Inexperienced with the High Desert country, the party vanished for weeks, presumed dead, but they eventually reached their destination, totally exhausted. By the Morongo, a bad choice, it took Woodworth and Perry forty days to reach the Colorado—and only nine days to return to Los Angeles on the more established main route. The party used the boat on the swollen Colorado River, giving rise to the legend of a ''Lost Ship'' in the High Desert, sometimes described as a Spanish galleon.

Today the Morongo Trail on which Woodworth nearly died is called the Baseline Highway, a chief boat-trailer-automobile route between Los Angeles and the Colorado River.

SOURCES: Harold O. Weight, ''A Desert Ship That Wasn't Lost,'' *Westways* 56:5 (May 1964). Woodworth is not included in the official city of Los Angeles handbook, *Mayors of Los Angeles* (1968).

Peter d'A. Jones

WORKMAN, WILLIAM HENRY (1839–1918), Mayor of Los Angeles (1886–88). A prime mover behind the adoption of the first charter for Los Angeles in 1889, Workman was born on 1 January 1839 in New Franklin, Missouri, to David Workman (1880–85), an English saddlemaker, and to Nancy (Hook) Workman (1807–?), an old-stock Yankee and German Pennsylvanian. William was the youngest of their three children. Completing eight years of public education, he then attended the Kemper Collegiate Institute in Missouri until age fourteen.

In 1854, Workman's family moved to Los Angeles. In the 1860s, he and his brother, Elijah, began manufacturing saddles. As the business prospered, Workman purchased what would later be known as Boyle Heights in 1867 (for $5 to $10 an acre) from his father-in-law, Andrew Boyle. He sold part of this tract for over $200 per acre during the 1880s.

On 17 October 1867, Workman married Marie Boyle (1847–?), a Roman Catholic native of New Orleans. Of Irish, British, and French ancestry, Mrs. Workman had four sons and four daughters. William was a Mason, a member of the Blue Lodge, the California Club, and the Jonathan Club, and an organizer of the Historical Society of Southern California.

During the 1870s, Workman became a banker and invested in streetcar franchises, which provided a comfortable livelihood for the rest of his life. An active booster, he was instrumental in getting three major railroads to enter the city. In 1875, he helped build a local railroad to combat the interests controlling freight hauling between Los Angeles and its port of San Pedro. Workman was politically active in the 1870s. A Democrat, he was elected to the city council from 1872 to 1874, 1874 to 1876, and 1878 to 1880.

In 1886, Los Angeles experienced a real estate and population boom. When Workman was elected mayor on 6 December 1886, the city had 30,000 inhabitants, but during the next two years its population grew to 50,000. Workman won (2,133) the mayoralty by defeating Republican L. W. French (1626), with a scattered vote to the Laborite (219), Prohibitionist (185), and American Protective Association candidate (119). In 1888, Workman did not stand for reelection. However, he later won seats on the boards of education and park commissioners, and served as city treasurer from 1901 to 1907 when he strongly supported the Owens Valley aqueduct by going to New York City to sell bonds for the project.

As mayor, Workman sought to extend public services such as street lights and paving and to acquire public parks. He began and completed the construction of a new city hall. Believing that the city's development depended upon a rapid system of streetcars, he supported the liberal granting of streetcar franchises. When the boom ended, he continued to believe in the city's growth, and he helped to organize the Chamber of Commerce in 1888. Perhaps Workman's best known achievement was his sponsorship of the home rule charter.

On 21 February 1918, Workman died of myocarditis at his home in Los Angeles.

SOURCES: Death records of Los Angeles City and County, Los Angeles County Recorder's Office; James Miller Gwinn, *A History of California and an Extended History of Its Southern Coast Counties* (Los Angeles); Los Angeles *Times*, 1886 to 88; Boyle Workman, *The City That Grew* (Los Angeles, 1936).

Christopher N. Cocoltchos

Y

YORTY, SAMUEL WILLIAM ("SAM") (1909–), Mayor of Los Angeles (1961–73). Three-term mayor of Los Angeles in the turbulent and radical 1960s, Yorty came from a Midwestern Populist tradition, but like some others of his generation, he turned conservative on major issues. Born in Lincoln, Nebraska, on 1 October 1909, he was the son of Johanna (Egan) and Frank Patrick Yorty; his father was a building contractor. Yorty moved to Los Angeles after completing high school in Nebraska and attended the University of Southern California and Southwestern University, studying law. He was admitted to the bar in 1939 and on 1 December 1931 married Elizabeth, the daughter of Peter Hensel, a local sales executive. They had one son, William Egan Yorty. The Yortys attended Christ Church, Los Angeles.

Yorty was already involved in politics in the early Depression years and seemed attracted to various idiosyncratic movements of that time, but his real public career began with his election to the state assembly as a Democrat in 1936. Being reelected in 1938, he served until 1940, at which time he hoped to enter the U.S. Senate but was defeated by the Republican isolationist, Senator Hiram Johnson. As a state legislator, Yorty was an active liberal Democrat, but he did sponsor the creation in California of the nation's first Un-American Activities Committee, chairing it until 1940. After a period in his private law practice, Yorty entered the Air Force in 1942 and rose to the rank of captain in intelligence. Returning to law after the war, he was reelected to the state legislature in 1948 and then to the U.S. House of Representatives, 1950 and 1952.

In Congress, Yorty protected the interests of the Air Force, supported California's water and oil claims, and secured places at the military academies for West Coast minorities. He failed to win a seat in the U.S. Senate in 1954 and 1956, and as his attitudes shifted to the right wing, he lost touch with state Democratic leaders. In 1960, he endorsed Republican Richard Nixon for the presidency rather than his party's nominee, John F. Kennedy.

His maverick personality helped to elect Yorty to the office of mayor of Los Angeles in 1961, in an upset victory, aided by an early use of television to reach out to the scattered Los Angeles electorate. The first mayor elected from a suburb (San Fernando Valley), Yorty made it a theme of his first term that he wished to integrate Los Angeles, transforming it from a collection of heterogeneous entities into a real "City of the Future." He brought department heads and commission members into regular contact with each other, in order to work on planned goals. He led the city during the huge boom years of the 1960s, boosting its share of the economic growth wherever possible. He began renewal of the decaying downtown, helped develop a master plan for the harbor, pushed the new international airport plans, consolidated county and city health facilities, averted a transit strike and a musicians' strike (which could have wiped out the Los Angeles Philharmonic—Yorty had a deep interest in music), and lowered property taxes. Above all, however, he kept the name of Yorty before the public eye through television talk shows, the press, and a series of worldwide tours. His vociferous support of U.S. involvement in the Vietnam War earned him the sobriquet "Saigon Sam."

With good media and business support, Yorty handily defeated Representative James Roosevelt and six other candidates in the May 1965 election, bringing a host of city and county officials into office with him on his coattails. Almost immediately, the first of the major city riots of the 1960s, Watts, broke out in August: thirty-four people died, and hundreds were injured as the city was held in the grip of violence for a week. Once it was over, the mayor, the state, and the federal authorities began apportioning blame. Yorty came out worst, officially condemned by the U.S. Civil Rights Commission in January 1966 for "gross negligence" and for poor attitudes which contributed to the bad racial atmosphere. Like other mayors at this time, Yorty was embroiled with the federal government over the distribution of poverty funds; he defended his police force against charges of brutality. But in U.S. Senate hearings in August 1966, Senator Abraham Ribicoff of Connecticut and Senator Robert F. Kennedy (New York) both blamed Yorty for failure to alleviate conditions in Watts. The mayor also found a running battle with the liberal Democratic governor of California, Edmund Brown.

Despite these problems, Yorty managed to squeeze by another mayoral election in 1969, after a bitter runoff against a rising star of black politics, Tom Bradley (*q.v.*). In 1973, Bradley defeated Yorty, and the maverick mayor retired from the arena.

SOURCES: E. Ainsworth, *Maverick Mayor: A Biography of Sam Yorty of Los Angeles* (Garden City, N.Y., 1966).   *Peter d'A. Jones*

YOUNG, COLEMAN ALEXANDER (1918–   ),
Mayor of Detroit (1974–   ). Detroit's first black mayor was born in Tuscaloosa, Alabama, on 24 May 1918, the oldest of five children born to Coleman and Ida Reese (Jones) Young. When Coleman was five years old, his father moved to Detroit's "Black Bottom" neighborhood where he set up a tailor shop and also worked for the post office. Young attended Roman Catholic elementary school and Eastern (public) High School, graduating with honors in 1934. He worked for the Ford Motor Company's Rouge plant, claimed participation in the sitdown strikes of 1937, and served in World War II as a second lieutenant and a bombardier-navigator. After the war, Young worked as a CIO union organizer but was fired because he claims to have clashed with Walter Reuther. In 1951, he was executive secretary of the National Negro Labor Council which the then U.S. attorney general labeled "subversive" and which was disbanded shortly thereafter. Young worked at various jobs in the 1950s, including spot cleaner in a laundry, took a hand at running his own cleaning service, was a taxi driver, butcher's assistant, insurance executive, and then plunged into politics in 1960, winning a delegate's seat to the Michigan Constitutional Convention. He was elected to the Michigan Senate in 1964–73 and became Democratic floor leader. Young has been twice divorced and has no children. He was formerly a Roman Catholic but became a Baptist as an adult.

Detroit's population in 1973 continued to decline from its 1970 figure of 1.5 million, and the city was governed by a mayor-council system. Coleman Young, who survived the nonpartisan mayoral primaries, opposed Detroit police chief John F. Nichols and beat him by a vote of 233,674 to 216,933 in a bitterly contested election. Detroit's 50-50 racial balance reflected itself in the vote in which an estimated 92 percent of the blacks voted for Young and 91 percent of the whites voted for Nichols. Although both candidates strove to keep the issue of race out of their rhetoric, they were not always successful. Nichols campaigned on the need to make Detroit a safe place to live. Young attacked the police force as a "white and racist" organization upholding an "unjust racist society," and promised to use a quota system to increase the number of black officers. Once the election results confirmed Young's victory, the mayor-elect took a harder line on crime, apparently hoping to end Detroit's 1973

reputation as "Murder City, USA." He told a prayer breakfast meeting in December: "I issue an open warning now to all dope pushers, to all rip-off artists, to all muggers. It's time to leave Detroit. I don't give a damn if you are black or white, or if you wear Super Fly or blue uniforms with silver badges: hit the road!"

Young's brave words were soothing to citizens who feared muggers and rapists, but it would take more than rhetoric to turn around Detroit's downward slide as an aging industrial city. Young promised to initiate a coherent public transit system, for, as he told *Ebony*, "Detroit is the only city among the nation's 10 largest which doesn't even have a plan for mass transit." This was perhaps a reflection of the power of the big three automakers who preferred to have their workers ride to the plant in Chevvies, Fords, and Plymouths. Young also wanted to revitalize the waterfront and had high hopes for the Renaissance Center which was under construction when he assumed office. The center, a $337 million phoenix of high-rise towers, rose out of the dilapidated and decaying downtown section, and when finished would stand in sharp contrast to its grubby and vacant-storefront downtown surroundings. Whether the center could usher in a "born again" Detroit, which had been torn by a firestorm of riot in 1967 and thereafter abrasive race relations, white flight, and an exodus of industry—was a serious question, with many experts placing the odds against it. Critics pointed out that at first the center simply emptied out more downtown buildings by attracting tenants to the new security-girdled, glass-encased towers. Yet, Young at one point was convinced that an urban "facelift" combined with high energy costs might force suburban expatriates back into the city and help revive it.

Reelected for another four-year term in 1977, Young also hoped to build more low-cost public housing, enlarge the city's tax base, attract more business and industry into the city, and transform the city of the straits into a convention center.

A rough-hewn, coarse, and blunt person, and occasionally as raw as the city he represented, Young blistered the police with profanities for living in the suburbs. He suspended police living outside the city limits, moved desk sergeants out into the streets, demoted others, promoted large numbers of blacks, and disbanded a special tactical crimefighting unit. Unable to ignore the serious economic problems of the city, Young finally asked his old foe the business community to help save Detroit: "I don't give a goddamn about them making money so long as it is not excessive and so long as they have the city's interests at heart," he told one reporter.

Despite the efforts of city hall and Young's brave and gritty macho rhetoric, economic decline, racial tensions, and exodus of business, and the white flight continued, and even accelerated, during the Young administrations. Some of the problems were beyond Young's control. The July 1974 U.S. Supreme Court decision mandating (forced) school busing in a system 70 percent black, triggered an exodus of whites to the suburbs. By 1977, fiscal deficits forced the layoff of 4,500 city workers, a job freeze, and the closing of two museums. Continued outbreaks of crime such as a rampage of young street toughs in August 1976 robbing and assaulting patrons at a Cobo Hall rock concert aggravated the city's problems and enraged the mayor. He threatened to crack down, called back laid-off policemen, ordered a 10:00 P.M. curfew, and ordered mass arrests of street youth who ignored it. Both street youth and civil rights groups protested the mayor's crime control measures.

With a new energy crisis in the making, an obsolescent auto industry, and a "boom and bust" employment and business cycle, Young, like his post-1967 riot predecessors had his hands full keeping the city from going under. The plucky chief executive seemed undaunted by the urban travail that rested upon his shoulders. He summed up his life with, "Just say I've had some peaks and valleys, baby."

SOURCES: Chicago *Tribune* 17 April 1977; *Current Biography* (New York, 1977); Detroit *Free Press*, 9 May 1974; *Detroit Magazine* 1 (December-January 1974); *Ebony* 29 (February 1974); Melvin G. Holli, *Detroit* (New York, 1977); Mayor's Office "Biography," Biographical file, Detroit Public Library; *Nation* 218 (19 January 1974); *Newsweek* 83 (14 January 1974).

Melvin G. Holli

ZEIDLER, CARL FREDERICK (1908–42), Mayor of Milwaukee (1940–42). The "singing mayor," killed in action in World War II, Zeidler was born on 4 January 1908 in Milwaukee to German-American Lutheran parents, Michael W. Zeidler, a barber, and Clara A.E. (Nitschke) Zeidler. Raised with his younger siblings, Clemens (b. 1910), Frank (q.v.) (b. 1912, mayor of Milwaukee, 1948–60), and Dorothy (b. 1915), Carl Zeidler attended Milwaukee public schools and worked his way through Marquette University where he was one of ten voted most likely to succeed. He received his undergraduate degree with honors in 1929 and his law degree in 1931. In 1936, Zeidler was appointed assistant city attorney. Reputedly eyeing a political career, he joined numerous civic and fraternal organizations and used his rich baritone voice in both speech and song at the many meetings he attended. By the time of his campaign for mayor in 1940, Zeidler maintained that he could call 50,000 Milwaukeeans by their first names.

Milwaukee, with a 1940 population of 587,472 and a mayor-council form of government, had enjoyed twenty-four years of good government under Socialist Daniel Webster Hoan (q.v.). Given little chance to unseat the veteran mayor, Zeidler won a spot on the April ballot and caused worry in the Hoan camp by polling an impressive 50,515 votes to Hoan's 75,313 in the eight-candidate primary. During his vigorous campaign, the tall, handsome, wavy, blond-haired, thirty-two-year old bachelor crooned "God Bless America," popular tunes, and old favorites, shook hands, and delivered 879 talks, most of them on the theme "Americanism and Good Government." Running as a nonpartisan, Zeidler took an anti-Socialist stand and pledged that he carried "no flag but the American flag." While he admitted that Milwaukee was well governed, he promised "A New Day for Milwaukee" and garnered enough support from Republicans and conservative Democrats to defeat Hoan 111,957 to 99,798. "I used nothing else than modern merchandising methods," he said: "See 'em, tell 'em, sell 'em."

In office for only two years, Zeidler claimed credit for small reductions in the city budget and property tax rate, worked to keep industry from leaving Milwaukee, made two minor departmental consolidations, and was the first American mayor to pledge his city's support of the national defense program.

Following U.S. entry into World War II, Zeidler volunteered for active service in the Navy in April 1942 and was granted leave from his Milwaukee post. Common council president John L. Bohn (q.v.) became acting mayor. In December 1942, Lieutenant (j.g.) Carl F. Zeidler, commander of a gun crew on a merchant vessel, and erstwhile mayor of Milwaukee, was declared missing in action when his ship disappeared in South Atlantic waters. He was officially presumed dead on 2 November 1944.

SOURCES: Milwaukee Journal, 20 April 1941; New York *Times*, 4 April 1940, 19 February 1942, 9 November 1944; *Time*, 15 April 1940; Carl F. Zeidler Papers, 63 boxes, Milwaukee Public Library; Carl F. and Frank P. Zeidler Papers, 1 box, Milwaukee County Historical Society.   *Barbara M. Posadas*

ZEIDLER, FRANK P. (1912–), Mayor of Milwaukee, 1948–60). Milwaukee's last Socialist mayor, Zeidler, the third of four children of German-American Lutheran parents, Michael W. Zeidler, a barber, and Clara A.E. (Nitschke) Zeidler, was born on 20 September 1912 in Milwaukee. With his siblings, Carl (q.v.) (b. 1908, mayor of Milwaukee, 1940–42), Clemens (b. 1910), and Dorothy (b. 1915), Frank attended Milwaukee public schools, becoming a Socialist during his high school years. Although he never graduated from college, the "gentle, bookish, bespectacled" Zeidler studied at Marquette University, the University of Chicago, and the University of Wisconsin. A land surveyor, Zeidler was elected county surveyor of Milwaukee County in 1938. He worked in the engineering department of the Milwaukee Road from 1943 to 1945 and operated his own land surveying business prior to his election as mayor. During the 1940s, Zeidler and his wife, Agnes, became the parents of six children.

In 1940, while his brother Carl campaigned successfully to unseat Milwaukee's veteran Socialist mayor, Daniel Hoan (q.v.) Frank Zeidler lost his bid to become county supervisor. From 1941 to 1948, he served as a member of the Milwaukee Board of School Directors. Following the death of Mayor Carl Zeidler during active duty in World War II, Frank Zeidler ran poorly in the 1944 mayoral primary. But in April 1948, supported by Socialists, liberals, and labor leaders allied in the Public Enterprise Committee, he defeated Henry S. Reuss 124,024 to 97,277 to head Milwaukee's mayor-council government at a time when the city's population was estimated at 627,000. Reelected twice, Zeidler topped Leonard C. Fons by 152,658 to 58,590 in the 1952 contest and in 1956, bested common council president Milton McGuire by 118,698 votes to 95,481, in a campaign which saw the mayor accused of advertising in the South for new black residents for Milwaukee. Zeidler did not seek reelection in 1960. He was, in his last term, America's sole surviving Socialist officeholder.

Hoping to secure new industrial sites and residential space, especially for low-income workers, Zeidler actively supported suburban annexation. During his twelve years as mayor, Milwaukee grew from 46 to 92 square miles, and the city's population rose from 637,392 in 1950 to 741,324 in 1960. Other interests of the Zeidler administration included urban redevelopment, preparation of a city master plan, construction of an expressway system, preservation of public transportation, promotion of the St. Lawrence Seaway, and expanded harbor facilities at Milwaukee. Although Zeidler originally campaigned for retention of the ''pay-as-you-go'' improvements policy initiated by Hoan, bonds began to be issued again in 1949. While Zeidler's critics charged that insufficient funding allowed further decay of downtown Milwaukee, the city maintained its triple-A credit rating.

After leaving office, Zeidler worked as a municipal consultant, publishing *Essays in More Effective Urban Renewal* (Madison, Wis., 1964) and numerous articles. Continuing as an active Socialist, Zeidler ran as the Socialist party's candidate for U.S. president in 1976. A member of the Evangelical Lutheran Church of the Redeemer, Zeidler continues to reside with his wife in Milwaukee.

SOURCES: Let's See, 25 January to 7 February 1957; New York *Times*, 6 April 1948, 2 September 1975; Dan Wakefield, ''The Socialist Survivors,'' *Nation*, 2 February 1957; Robert W. Wells, *This Is Milwaukee* (New York, 1970); ''Carl Zeidler'' and ''Frank Zeidler,'' Biographical Pamphlet File, Milwaukee County Historical Society; Carl F. and Frank P. Zeidler Papers, 1 box, Milwaukee County Historical Society; Frank P. Zeidler, *Essays in More Effective Urban Government* (Madison, Wis., 1964); Frank P. Zeidler Papers, 300 feet, restricted, Milwaukee Public Library; Frank P. Zeidler Collection, 3 boxes, Area Research Center, University of Wisconsin—Milwaukee.

Barbara M. Posadas

ZIEGENHEIN, HENRY (1845–1910), Mayor of St. Louis (1897–1901). Businessman and politician, Ziegenhein was born on 16 September 1845 in Bonhomme Township (near St. Louis), the son of Peter (who reputedly lived to be 106) and Mary Ziegenhein, both German immigrants. Henry attended local schools until the age of thirteen, working on a farm in the summers. He then became a carpenter's apprentice for four years. During the Civil War, Ziegenhein was a soldier. After 1865, he became a building contractor and soon grew wealthy. In 1869, he married Catherine Henkle, and they had nine children.

A Republican, Ziegenhein served in the House of Delegates (1879–81), city council (1881–85), state legislature (1885–89), and as city collector (1889–97). He was elected mayor in 1897 with 48,654 votes to 24,492 for J. Harrison (Democrat) and 18,285 for Lee Meriweather (Independent Democrat). St. Louis had 575,238 people by 1900 and a mayor-council form of government.

Ziegenhein's campaign for the mayoralty had stressed his desire for a businesslike and efficient administration, allowing progress for the entire city. In reality, Ziegenhein proved to be an inept chief executive. His major accomplishments included construction of the new city hall, rehabilitation of City Hospital, and securing a bond issue for the 1904 fair. Critics charged him with running a corrupt machine. One famous anecdote told about a citizens' group asking him to sponsor improved street lighting on their block: ''Uncle Henry'' simply smiled and said, ''What for? You have the moon, don't you?'' Ziegenhein did not seek another term and returned to his contracting business in 1901. He also served as a director of the Lafayette Bank for several years, until his death on 17 March 1910.

SOURCES: Howard L. Conrad, *Encyclopedia of the History of Missouri*, 6 vols. (New York, 1901); Charles H. Cornwell, *St. Louis Mayors* (St. Louis, 1965); John W. Leonard, ed., *The Book of St. Louisians* (St. Louis, 1906).

Thomas R. Bullard

ZIMMERMAN, GEORGE J. (1882–1938), Mayor of Buffalo (1934–37). Lumber merchant, one of a line of German-American mayors of Buffalo, and a New Dealer, Zimmerman was born on 19 June 1882 in Buffalo, the son of George M. Zimmerman (1854–1940), a lumber company owner, and Agnes (Steinmann) Zimmerman, both Roman Catholics of German descent. The fourth of fourteen children, Zimmerman attended local schools and spent two years at Canisius College in Buffalo. He then joined his father's lumber business and eventually became a partner. In 1923, he married Gertrude Cochrane (1891–1975), and they had three children.

In 1931, Zimmerman was selected chairman of the

Erie County Democratic party. He soon established a reputation for geniality, good humor, and popularity with the voters. These qualities helped him win the nomination and election in 1933 when he defeated Philip C. Schaefer, Republican, 99,292 to 83,678. To Zimmerman the election was an endorsement for President Franklin D. Roosevelt's New Deal policies, especially the National Recovery Administration. Buffalo had 573,076 people in 1930 and a mayor-council form of government.

As mayor, Zimmerman supported increased public works programs in an effort to combat the effects of the Depression in Buffalo. By 1934, there were complaints that some of his appointments were not of the highest caliber. By 1936, there were charges that he had used his office to win city contracts for his close friends. Continuing complaints led to his indictment on charges of accepting illegal fees from a $15 million sewer project. The indictment was dropped in 1937, but another was quickly drawn up and Zimmerman was convicted in 1938, after leaving office. While free on appeal, he suffered a heart attack and died, on 14 September 1938.

SOURCES: Buffalo *Evening News*, 15 September 1938; Henry W. Hill, ed., *Municipality of Buffalo, New York*, 4 vols. (New York, 1923); New York *Times*, 15 September 1938; Sister Mary Jane and Sister Mercedes, "Mayors of Buffalo, 1831–1961," (B.A. thesis, Rosary Hill College, 1961).

Thomas R. Bullard

APPENDIX I
CHRONOLOGICAL LIST OF MAYORS BY CITY

Baltimore

Edward Johnson (1808–16, 1819–20, 1822–24)
George Stiles (1816–19)
John Montgomery (1820–22, 1824–26)
Jacob Small (1826–31)
William Stewart (1831–32)
Jesse Hunt (1832–35)
Samuel Smith (1835–38)
Sheppard Leakin (1838–40)
Samuel Brady (1840–42)
Solomon Hillen, Jr. (1842–43)
James Law (1843–44)
Jacob Davies (1844–48)
Elijah Stansbury, Jr. (1848–50)
John Jerome (1850–52)
John Hollins (1852–54)
Samuel Hinks (1854–56)
Thomas Swann (1856–60)
George Brown (1860–61)
John Blackburn (1861)
Charles Baker (1862)
John Chapman (1862–67)
Robert Banks (1867–71)
Joshua Vansant (1871–75)
Ferdinand Latrobe (1875–77, 1878–81, 1883–84, 1887–89, 1891–95)
George Kane (1877–78)
William Whyte (1881–83)
James Hodges (1885–87)
Robert Davidson (1889–91)
Alcaeus Hooper (1895–97)
William Malster (1897–99)
Thomas Hayes (1899–1903)
Robert McLane (1903–1904)
E. Clay Timanus (1904–1907)
J. Barry Mahool (1907–11)
James Preston (1911–19)
William Broening (1919–23, 1927–31)
Howard Jackson (1923–27, 1931–43)
Theodore McKeldin (1943–47, 1963–67)
Thomas L.J. D'Alesandro, Jr. (1947–59)
J. Harold Grady (1959–62)
Philip Goodman (1962–63)
Thomas L. J. D'Alesandro, Jr. (1947–59)
Thomas L. J. D'Alesandro III (1967–71)
William Schaefer (1971–)

Boston

John Phillips (1822–23)
Josiah Quincy (1823–28)
Harrison Gray Otis (1829–31)
Charles Wells (1832–33)
Theodore Lyman, Jr. (1834–35)
Samuel Armstrong (1836)
Samuel Eliot (1837–39)
Jonathan Chapman (1840–42)
Martin Brimmer (1843–44)
Thomas Davis (1845)
Josiah Quincy, Jr. (1846–48)
John Bigelow (1849–51)
Benjamin Seaver (1852–53)
Jerome Smith (1854–55)
Alexander Rice (1856–57)
Frederick Lincoln, Jr. (1857–59)
Joseph Wightman (1861–62)
Otis Norcross (1867)
Nathaniel Shurtleff (1868–70)
William Gaston (1871–72)
Henry Pierce (1873, 1878)
Leonard Cutter (1873–74)
Samuel Cobb (1874–76)
Frederick Prince (1877, 1879–81)
Samuel Green (1882)
Albert Palmer (1883)
Augustus Martin (1884)
Hugh O'Brien (1885–88)
Thomas Hart (1889–90, 1900–1902)
Nathan Matthews, Jr. (1891–94)
Edwin Curtis (1895)
Josiah Quincy (1895–99)
Patrick Collins (1902–1905)
Daniel Whelton (1905)
John Fitzgerald (1906–1907, 1910–13)
George Hibbard (1908–10)
James Curley (1914–17, 1922–25, 1930–33, 1946–49)
Andrew Peters (1918–22)
Malcolm Nichols (1926–29)
Frederick Mansfield (1934–38)
Maurice Tobin (1938–44)
John Kerrigan (1945–46)
John Hynes (1950–60)
John Collins (1960–68)
Kevin White (1968–)

Buffalo

Ebenezer Johnson (1832–33, 1834–35)
Andre Andrews (1833)
Hiram Pratt (1835–36, 1839–40)
Samuel Wilkeson (1836–37)
Josiah Trowbridge (1837)
Pierre Barker (1837–38)
Ebenezer Walden (1838–39)
Sheldon Thompson (1840–41)
Isaac Harrington (1841–42)
George Clinton (1842–43)
Joseph Masten (1843, 1845)
William Ketchum (1844)
Solomon Haven (1846)
Elbridge Spaulding (1847)
Orlando Allen (1848)
Hiram Barton (1849–50, 1852–53)
Henry Smith (1850–51)
James Wadsworth (1851–52)
Eli Cook, Jr. (1853–55)
Frederick Stephens (1856–57)
Charles Pierce (1858)
Timothy Lockwood (1858–59)
Franklin Alberger (1860–61)
William Fargo (1862–65)
Chandler Wells (1866-67)
William Rogers (1868-69)
Alexander Brush (1870–73, 1879–81)
Lewis Dayton (1874–75)
Philip Becker (1876–77, 1886–90)
Solomon Scheu (1878–79)
Stephen Grover Cleveland (1882)
Marcus Drake (1882)
Harmon Cutting (1882–83)
John Manning (1883)
Jonathan Scoville (1884–85)
Charles Bishop (1890–94)
Edgar Jewett (1895–97)
Conrad Diehl (1898–1901)
Erastus Knight (1902–1905)
James Adam (1906–1909)
Louis Fuhrmann (1910–17)
George Buck (1918–21)
Frank Schwab (1922–29)
Charles Roesch (1930–33)
George Zimmerman (1934–37)
Thomas Holling (1938–41)
Joseph Kelly (1942–45)
Bernard Dowd (1946–49)
Joseph Mruk (1950–53)
Steven Pankow (1954–57)
Chester Kowal (1962–65)
Frank Sedita (1966–73)
Stanley Makowski (1974–77)
James Griffin (1978–)

Chicago

William Ogden (1837–38)
Buckner Morris (1838–39)
Benjamin Raymond (1839–40, 1842–43)
Alexander Loyd (1840–41)
Francis Sherman (1841–42, 1862–65)
Augustus Garrett (1843–44, 1845–46)
Alson Sherman (1844)
John Chapin (1846–47)
James Curtiss (1847, 1850)
James Woodworth (1848–49)
Walter Gurnee (1851–52)
Charles Gray (1853)
Isaac Milliken (1854–55)
Levi Boone (1855)
Thomas Dyer (1856–57)
John Wentworth (1857–58, 1860–61)
John Haines (1858–60)
Julian Rumsey (1861–62)
John Rice (1865–69)
Roswell Mason (1869–71)
Joseph Medill (1871–73)
Lester Legrant Bond (1873)
Harvey Colvin (1873–76)
Monroe Heath (1876–79)
Carter Harrison (1879–87, 1893)
John Roche (1887-89)
DeWitt Cregier (1889-91)
Hempstead Washburne (1891–93)
George Swift (1893, 1895–97)
John Hopkins (1893–95)
Carter Harrison, II (1897–1905, 1911–15)
Edward Dunne (1905–1907)
Fred Busse (1907–11)
William H. Thomspon (1915–23, 1927–31)
William Dever (1923–27)
Anton Cermak (1931–33)
Frank Corr (1933)
Edward Kelly (1933–47)
Martin Kennelly (1947–55)
Richard Daley (1955–76)
Michael Bilandic (1976–79)
Jane Byrne (1979–   )

Cincinnati

William Corry (1815–19)
Isaac Burnet (1819–31)
Elisha Hotchkiss (1831–33)
Samuel Davies (1833–43)
Henry Spencer (1843–51)
Mark Taylor (1851–53)
David Snelbaker (1853–55)
James Faran (1855–57)

Nicholas Thomas (1857–59)
Richard Bishop (1859–61)
George Hatch (1861–63)
Leonard Harris (1863–66)
Charles Wilstach (1866–69)
John Torrence (1869–71)
Simon Davis (1871–73)
George Johnston (1873–77)
Robert Moore (1877–79)
Charles Jacob (1879–81)
William Means (1881–83)
Thomas Stephens (1883–85)
Amor Smith, Jr. (1885–89)
John Mosby (1889–94)
John Caldwell (1894–97)
Gustav Tafel (1897–1900)
Julius Fleischmann (1900–1905)
Edward Dempsey (1906–1907)
Leopold Markbreit (1908–1909)
John Galvin (1909, 1918–21)
Louis Schwab (1910–11)
Henry T. Hunt (1912–13)
Frederick Spiegel (1914–15)
George Puchta (1916–17)
George Carrel (1922–25)
Murray Seasongood (1926–29)
Russell Wilson (1930–37)
James Stewart (1938–47)
Carl Rich (1947, 1951–53, December 1954–55)
Albert Cash (1948–51)
Edward Waldvogel (1953–May 1954)
Mrs. Dorothy Dolbey (May–December 1954)
Charles Taft (1955–57)
Donald Clancy (1957–60)
Walton Bachrach (1960–67)
Eugene Ruehlmann (1967–71)
Willis Gradison, Jr. (1971)
Thomas Luken (1971–72)
Theodore Berry (1972–75)
Bobbie Sterne (1975–76, 1978–79)
James Luken (1976–77)
Gerald Springer (1977–78)
John Blackwell (1979–   )

Cleveland

John Willey (1836–37)
Joshua Mills (1838–39, 1842)
Nicholas Dockstadter (1840)
John Allen (1841)
Nelson Hayward (1843)
Samuel Starkweather (1844–46, 1857–58)
George Hoadley (1846–47)
Josiah Harris (1847–48)
Lorenzo Kelsey (1848–49)

Flavel Bingham (1849–50)
William Case (1850–52)
Abner Brownell (1852–55)
William Castle (1855–57)
George Senter (1859–61)
Edward Flint (1861–63)
Irvine Masters (1863–64)
Herman Chapin (1865–67)
Stephen Buhrer (1867–71)
Frederick Pelton (1871–73)
Charles Otis (1873–75)
Nathan Payne (1875–76)
William Rose (1877–78, 1891–92)
R. R. Herrick (1879–82)
John Farley (1883–84, 1899–1900)
George Gardner (1885–86, 1889–90)
Brenton Babcock (1887–88)
Robert Blee (1893–94)
Robert McKisson (1895–98)
Tom Johnson (1901–1909)
Herman Baehr (1910–11)
Newton Baker (1912–15)
Harry Davis (1915–20, 1933–35)
William Fitzgerald (1920–21)
Fred Kohler (1922–23)
William Hopkins (1924–30)
Daniel Morgan (1930–31)
Harold Burton (1931–32, 1935–40)
Ray Miller (1932–33)
Edward Blythin (1940–41)
Frank Lausche (1941–44)
Thomas Burke (1945–53)
Anthony Celebrezze (1953–62)
Ralph Locher (1962–67)
Carl Stokes (1967–71)
Ralph Perk (1971–77)
Dennis Kucinich (1977–79)
George Voinovich (1979–   )

Detroit

John Williams (1824, 1825, 1829–30, 1844–46)
Henry J. Hunt (1826)
Jonathan Kearsley (1826, 1829)
John Biddle (1827–28)
Marshall Chapin (1831, 1833)
Charles Trowbridge (1834)
Andrew Mack (1834)
Levi Cook (1832, 1835, 1836)
Henry Howard (1837)
Augustus Porter (1838)
De Garmo Jones (1839–40)
Zina Pitcher (1840, 1841, 1843)
Douglas Houghton (1842)
James Van Dyke (1847)
Frederick Buhl (1848)
Charles Howard (1849–50)

John Ladue (1850–51)
Zachariah Chandler (1851–52)
John Harmon (1852–54)
Oliver Hyde (1854–55, 1856–57)
Henry Ledyard (1855–56)
John Patton (1858–59)
Christian Buhl (1860–61)
William Duncan (1862, 1863)
Kirkland Barker (1864, 1865)
Merrill Mills (1866, 1867)
William Wheaton (1868–71)
Hugh Moffat (1872–75)
Alexander Lewis (1876–77)
George Langdon (1878–79)
William Thompson (1880–83)
Stephen Grummond (1884–85)
Marvin Chamberlain (1886–87)
John Pridgeon, Jr. (1888, 1889)
Hazen Pingree (1890–97)
William Richert (1897)
William Maybury (1897–1904)
George Codd (1905–1906)
William B. Thompson (1907–1908,
    1911–12)
Philip Breitmeyer (1909, 1910)
Oscar Marx (1913–18)
James Couzens (1919–22)
John Lodge (1922–23, 1924,
    1927–29)
Frank Doremus (1923–24)
Joseph Martin (1924)
John Smith (1924–28, 1933–34)
Charles Bowles (1930)
Frank Murphy (1930–33)
Frank Couzens (1933–38)
Richard Reading (1938–40)
Edward Jeffries, Jr. (1940–48)
Eugene Van Antwerp (1948–50)
Albert Cobo (1950–57)
Louis Miriani (1957–62)
Jerome Cavanagh (1962–70)
Roman Gribbs (1970–74)
Coleman Young (1974–   )

Los Angeles

Alpheus Hodges (1850–51)
Benjamin Wilson (1851–52)
John Nichols (1852–53, 1856–59)
Antonio Coronel (1853–54)
Stephen Foster (1854–55, 1856)
Thomas Foster (1855–56)
Manuel Requena (1856)
Damien Marchessault (1859–60,
    1861–65, May–August, 1867)
Henry Mellus (1860)
Wallace Woodworth (1860–61)
Jose Mascarel (1865–66)

Cristobal Aguilar (September
    1867–68, 1871–72)
Joel Turner (1868–70)
James Toberman (1872–74, 1878–82)
Prudent Beaudry (1874–76)
Frederick MacDougal (1876–78)
Bernard Cohn (1878)
Cameron Thom (1882–84)
Edward Spence (1884–86)
William Workman (1886–88)
John Bryson, Jr. (1888–89)
Henry Hazard (1889–92)
William Bonsall (1892)
Thomas Rowan (1892–94)
Frank Rader (1894–96)
Meredith Snyder (1896–98,
    1900–1904, 1919–21)
Fred Eaton (1898–1900)
Owen McAleer (1904–1906)
Arthur Harper (1906–1909)
William Stephens (1909)
George Alexander (1909–13)
Henry Rose (1913–15)
Charles Sebastian (1915–16)
Frederick Woodman (1916–19)
George Cryer (1921–29)
John Porter (1929–33)
Frank Shaw (1933–38)
Fletcher Bowron (1938–53)
Charles Poulson (1953–61)
Sam Yorty (1961–73)
Tom Bradley (1973–   )

Milwaukee

Solomon Juneau (1846–47)
Horatio Wells (1847–48)
Byron Kilbourn (1848–49, 1854–55)
Don Upham (1849–50)
George Walker (1851–52, 1853–54)
Hans Crocker (1852–53)
James Cross (1855–58)
William Prentiss (1858–59)
Herman Page (1859–60)
William Lynde (1860–61)
James Brown (1861–62)
Horace Chase (1862–63)
Edward O'Neill (1863–64, 1867–69)
Abner Kirby (1864–65)
John Tallmadge (1865–66)
Joseph Phillips (1870–71)
Harrison Ludington (1871–72,
    1873–74, 1875)
David Hooker (1872–73)
A.A.R. Butler (1876–78)
John Black (1878–80)
Thomas Brown (1880–82, 1888–90)
John Stowell (1882–84)

Emil Wallber (1884–88)
George Peck (1890)
Peter Somers (1890–93)
John Koch (1893–96)
William Rauschenberger (1896–98)
David Rose (1898–1906, 1908–10)
Sherburn Becker (1906–1908)
Emil Seidel (1910–12)
Gerhard Bading (1912–16)
Daniel Hoan (1916–40)
Carl Zeidler (1940–42)
John Bohn (1942–44, 1944–48)
Frank Zeidler (1948–60)
Henry Maier (1960–   )

New Orleans

Le Breton Dorgenois (1812)
Nicholas Girod (1812–15)
Augustin McCarty (1815–20)
Joseph Roffignac (1820–28)
Denis Prieur (1828–38)
Paul Bertus (1838)
Charles Genois (1838–40)
William Freret (1840–42, 1843–44)
Edgar Montegút (1844–46)
Abdiel Crossman (1846–54)
John Lewis (1854–56)
Charles Waterman (1856–58)
Gerard Stith (1858–60)
John Monroe (1860–62, 1866–67)
George Shepley (1862)
Godfrey Weitzel (1862)
Jonas French (1862)
Henry Deming (1862–63)
James Miller (1863–64)
Stephen Hoyt (1864–65)
Hugh Kennedy (1865)
Samuel Quincy (1865)
Glendy Burke (1865)
Joseph Rozier (1866)
George Clark (1866)
John Monroe (1866–67)
Edward Heath (1867–68)
John Conway (1868–70)
Benjamin Flanders (1870–72)
Louis Wiltz (1872–74)
Charles Leeds (1874–76)
Edward Pillsbury (1876–78)
Isaac Patton (1878–80)
Joseph Shakspeare (1880–82,
    1888–92)
William Behan (1882–84)
J. Valsin Guillotte (1884–88)
John Fitzpatrick (1892–96)
Walter Flower (1896–1900)
Paul Capdeville (1900–1904)
Martin Behrman (1904–20, 1925–26)

Andrew McShane (1920–25)
Arthur O'Keefe (1926–29)
T. Semmes Walmsley (1929–36)
A. Miles Pratt (1936)
Jesse Cave (1936)
Fred Earhart (1936)
Robert Maestri (1936–46)
deLesseps Morrison (1946–61)
Victor Schiro (1961–70)
Moon Landrieu (1970–78)
Ernest Morial (1978–   )

New York

Gideon Lee (1833–34)
Cornelius Lawrence (1834–37)
Aaron Clark (1837–39)
Issac L. Varian (1839–40)
Robert Morris (1841–44)
James Harper (1844–45)
William Havemeyer (1845–46,
    1848–49, 1873–74)
Andrew Mickle (1846–47)
William Brady (1847–48)
Caleb Woodhull (1849–51)
Ambrose Kingsland (1851–53)
Jacob Westervelt (1853–55)
Fernando Wood (1855–58, 1860–62)
Daniel Tiemann (1858–60)
George Opdyke (1862–64)
Charles Gunther (1864–66)
John Hoffman (1866–68)
Thomas Coman (1868)
Abraham Hall (1868–72)
Samuel Vance (1874)
William Wickham (1875–76)
Smith Ely, Jr. (1877–78)
Edward Cooper (1879–80)
William Grace (1881–82, 1885–86)
Franklin Edson (1883–84)
Abram Hewitt (1887–88)
Hugh Grant (1889–92)
Thomas Gilroy (1893–94)
William Strong (1895–97)
Robert Van Wyck (1898–1901)
Seth Low (1902–1903)
George McClellan (1904–1909)
William Gaynor (1910–13)
Ardolph Kline (1913)
John Mitchel (1914–17)
John Hylan (1918–25)
James Walker (1926–32)
Joseph McKee (1932)
John O'Brien (1933)
Fiorello LaGuardia (1934–45)
William O'Dwyer (1946–50)
Vincent Impellitteri (1950–53)
Robert Wagner, Jr. (1954–65)

John Lindsay (1966–73)
Abraham Beame (1974–77)
Edward Koch (1978–   )

Philadelphia

John Swift (1832–38, 1839–40,
    1845–48)
John Scott (1841–42, 1843)
Peter McCall (1844–45)
Joel Jones (1849)
Charles Gilpin (1850–53)
Robert Conrad (1854–56)
Richard Vaux (1856–58)
Alexander Henry (1858–65)
Morton McMichael (1866–68)
Daniel Fox (1869–71)
William Stokley (1872–81)
Samuel King (1881–84)
William Smith (1884–87)
Edwin Fitler (1887–91)
Edwin Stuart (1891–95)
Charles Warwick (1895–99)
Samuel Ashbridge (1899–1903)
John Weaver (1903–1907)
John Reyburn (1907–11)
Rudolph Blankenburg (1912–16)
Thomas Smith (1916–20)
Joseph Moore (1920–24, 1933–36)
W. Freeland Kendrick (1924–28)
Harry Mackey (1928–32)
Samuel Wilson (1936–39)
George Connell (1939)
Robert Lamberton (1940–41)
Bernard Samuel (1941–52)
Joseph Clark, Jr. (1952–56)
Richardson Dilworth (1957–61)
James Tate (1962–72)
Frank Rizzo (1972–79)
William Green (1979–   )

Pittsburgh

Ebenezer Denny (1816–17)
John Darragh (1817–25)
John Snowden (1825–28)
Magnus Murray (1829–30, 1831–32)
Matthew Lowrie (1830–31)
Samuel Pettigrew (1832–36)
Jonas McClintock (1836–39)
William Little (1839–40)
William Irwin (1840–41)
James Thompson (1841–42)
Alexander Hay (1842–45)
William Howard (1845–46)
William Kerr (1846)
Gabriel Adams (1847–48)
John Herron (1849)

Joseph Barker (1850)
John Guthrie (1851–52)
Robert Riddle (1853–54)
Ferdinand Volz (1854–56)
William Bingham (1856–57)
Henry Weaver (1857–60)
George Wilson (1860–62)
Benair Sawyer (1862–64)
James Lowry (1864–66)
William McCarthy (1866–68,
    1875–78)
James Blackmore (1868–69, 1872–75)
Gerard Brush (1869–72)
Robert Liddell (1878–81)
Robert Lyon (1881–84)
Andrew Fulton (1884–87)
William McCallin (1887–90)
Henry Gourley (1890–93)
Bernard McKenna (1893–96)
Henry Ford (1896–99)
William Diehl (1899–1901)
Adam Brown (1901)
Joseph Owen Brown (1901–1903)
William Hays (1903–1906)
George Guthrie (1906–1909)
William Magee (1909–14, 1922–26)
Joseph Armstrong (1914–18)
Edward Babcock (1918–22)
Charles Kline (1926–33)
John Herron (1933–34)
William McNair (1934–36)
Cornelius Scully (1936–46)
David Lawrence (1946–59)
Thomas Gallagher (1959)
Joseph Barr (1959–70)
Peter Flaherty (1970–77)
Richard Caliguiri (1977–   )

San Francisco

Washington Allon Bartlett (1846–47)
Edwin Bryant (1847)
George Hyde (1847–48)
John Townsend (1848)
Thaddeus Leavenworth (1848–49)
John Geary (1849–50, 1850–51)
Steven Harris (December
    1851–September 1852)
Charles Brenham (May–December
    1851, 1852–53)
Cornelius Garrison (1853–54)
Stephen Webb (1854–55)
James Van Ness (1855–56)
George Whelan (1856)
Ephraim Burr (1856–59)
Henry Teschemaker (1859–63)
Henry Coon (1863–67)
Frank McCoppin (1867–69)

Thomas Selby (1869–71)
William Alvord (1871–73)
James Otis (1873–75)
George Hewston (1875)
Andrew Bryant (1875–79)
Maurice Blake (1881–83)
Washington Bartlett (1883–87)
Edward Pond (1887–91)
George Sanderson (1891–93)
Levi Ellert (1893–95)
Adolph Sutro (1895–97)
James Phelan (1897–1902)
Eugene Schmitz (1902–1907)
Charles Boxton (1907)
Edward Taylor (1907–10)
Patrick McCarthy (1910–12)
James Rolph, Jr. (1912–30)
Angelo Rossi (1931–44)
Roger Lapham (1944–48)
Elmer Robinson (1948–56)
George Christopher (1956–64)
John Shelley (1964–68)
Joseph Alioto (1968–76)

George Moscone (1976–78)
Dianne Feinstein (1978–   )

St. Louis

William Lane (1823–28, 1838–39)
Daniel Page (1829–33)
John Johnson (1833–34)
John Darby (1835–37, 1840)
John Daggett (1841)
George Maguire (1842)
John Wimer (1843, 1857)
Bernard Pratte (1844–45)
Peter Camden (1846)
Bryan Mullanphy (1847–48)
John Krum (1848–49)
James Barry (1849–50)
Luther Kennett (1850–53)
John How (1853–55, 1856–57)
Washington King (1855–56)
Oliver Filley (1858–61)
Daniel Taylor (1861–63)
Chauncey Filley (1863–64)

James Thomas (1864–67)
Nathan Cole (1869–71)
Joseph Brown (1871–74)
Arthur Barret (1875)
James Britton (1875–76)
Henry Overstolz (1876–81)
William Ewing (1881–85)
David Francis (1885–89)
Edward Noonan (1889–93)
Cyrus Walbridge (1893–97)
Henry Ziegenhein (1897–1901)
Rolla Wells (1901–1909)
Frederick Kreismann (1909–13)
Henry Kiel (1913–25)
Victor Miller (1925–33)
Bernard Dickmann (1933–41)
William Becker (1941–43)
Aloys Kaufmann (1943–49)
Joseph Darst (1949–53)
Raymond Tucker (1953–65)
Alfonso Cervantes (1965–73)
John Poelker (1973–77)
James Conway (1977–   )

APPENDIX II
MAYORS BY POLITICAL PARTY AFFILIATION

Not Known

Washington Allon Bartlett
William Brady
Edwin Bryant
George Clark
John Conway
William Corry
Alpheus Hodges
Stephen Hoyt
Henry J. Hunt
George Hyde
Edward Jeffries, Jr.
Ebenezer Johnson
Joel Jones
Thaddeus Leavenworth
Joseph Martin
Daniel Page
Joseph Roffignac
John Scott
George Shepley
William Stewart
Sheldon Thompson
John Townsend
Godfrey Weitzel
Daniel Whelton
Wallace Woodworth

Federalist

John Darragh
Ebenezer Denny
Harrison Otis
John Phillips
Josiah P. Quincy

Democratic-Republican (Jeffersonian)

Edward Johnson
Augustin McCarty
John Montgomery
Jacob Small
John Snowden
George Stiles
Charles Wells

Democrat

James Adam
Cristobal Aguilar
Joseph Alioto
Andre Andrews

Brenton Babcock
Charles Baker
Newton D. Baker
Robert Banks
Pierre Barker
Joseph Barr
Arthur Barret
James Barry
Washington Bartlett
Abraham Beame
Prudent Beaudry
William Behan
Martin Behrman
Michael Bilandic
Flavel Bingham
Charles Bishop
Richard Bishop
John Black
John Blackburn
James Blackmore
Robert Blee
Tom Bradley
Samuel Brady
James Britton
George Brown
James Brown
Joseph Brown
Abner Brownell
Andrew Bryant
John Bryson, Sr.
Stephen Buhrer
Thomas Burke
A.A.R. Butler
Jane Byrne
Richard Caliguiri
Paul Capdeville
Albert Cash
Jerome Cavanagh
Anthony Celebrezze
Anton Cermak
Alfonso Cervantes
Marvin Chamberlain
Horace Chase
Joseph Clark
Grover Cleveland
George Clinton
Bernard Cohn
John Collins
Patrick Collins
Harry Colvin
Thomas Coman
James Conway
Eli Cook

Edward Cooper
Antonio Coronel
Frank J. Corr
DeWitt Cregier
James Cross
James Curley
James Curtiss
Harmon Cutting
Richard Daley
Thomas D'Alesandro II
Thomas D'Alesandro III
Joseph Darst
Robert Davidson
Jacob Davies
Lewis Dayton
Henry Deming
Edward Dempsey
William Dever
Bernard Dickmann
Conrad Diehl
Richardson Dilworth
Frank Doremus
William Duncan
Edward Dunne
Thomas Dyer
Franklin Edson
Smith Ely, Jr.
James Faran
William Fargo
John Farley
Dianne Feinstein
John Fitzgerald
John Fitzpatrick
Peter Flaherty
Edward Flint
Stephen Foster
Thomas Foster
Daniel Fox
David Francis
Jonas French
Louis Fuhrmann
Thomas Gallagher
Augustus Garrett
Cornelius Garrison
William Gaston
William Gaynor
Charles Genois
Thomas Gilroy
Nicholas Girod
Philip Goodman
William Grace
Harold Grady
Hugh Grant

Charles Gray
William Green
Roman Gribbs
J. V. Guillotte
Charles Gunther
Walter Gurnee
George Guthrie
John Guthrie
Abraham O. Hall
John Harmon
Arthur Harper
Leonard Harris
Stephen Harris
Carter Harrison I
Carter Harrison II
George Hatch
Thomas Hayes
William Hays
Nelson Hayward
Abram Hewitt
Solomon Hillen, Jr.
James Hodges
John Hoffman
John Hollins
David Hooker
John Hopkins
Douglas Houghton
John How
Charles Howard
Henry Howard
Henry T. Hunt
Jesse Hunt
John Hylen
John Hynes
Vincent Impellitteri
Howard Jackson
Tom Johnson
George Johnston
Solomon Juneau
George Kane
Jonathan Kearsley
Edward Kelly
Joseph Kelly
Lorenzo Kelsey
Hugh Kennedy
Martin Kennelly
William Kerr
John Kerrigan
Byron Kilbourn
Samuel King
Abner Kirby
Edward Koch
John Krum
Dennis Kucinich
John Ladue
Moon Landrieu
William Lane

George Langdon
Ferdinand Latrobe
Frank Lausche
Cornelius Lawrence
David Lawrence
Henry Ledyard
Gideon Lee
Charles Leeds
Alexander Lewis
John Lewis
Robert Liddell
John Lindsay
Ralph Locher
Alexander Loyd
James Luken
Thomas Luken
William Lynde
Robert Lyon
George McClellan, Jr.
James McClintock
Frank McCoppin
Frederick MacDougal
Andrew Mack
Joseph McKee
Bernard McKenna
Robert McLane
William McNair
Andrew McShane
Robert Maestri
George Maguire
J. Barry Mahool
Henry Maier
Stanley Makowski
John Manning
Frederick Mansfield
Damien Marchessault
Augustus Martin
Joseph Masten
Nathan Matthews, Jr.
William Maybury
William Means
Henry Mellus
Andrew Mickle
Ray Miller
Isaac Milliken
Merrill Mills
Edgar Montegut
Ernest Morial
Robert Morris
DeLesseps Morrison
George Moscone
Bryan Mullanphy
Frank Murphy
Magnus Murray
John Nichols
Edward Noonan
Hugh O'Brien

John O'Brien
William O'Dwyer
William Ogden
Arthur O'Keefe
Edward O'Neill
Charles Otis
Henry Overstolz
Herman Page
Albert Palmer
Steven Pankow
Isaac Patton
John Patton
Nathan Payne
George Peck
Andrew Peters
Samuel Pettigrew
James Phelan
Joseph Phillips
Edward Pillsbury
John Poelker
Edward Pond
James Preston
John Pridgeon, Jr.
Denis Prieur
Frederick Prince
Josiah Quincy
Frank Rizzo
William Rogers
David Rose
Thomas Rowan
William Schaefer
Solomon Scheu
Victor Schiro
Frank Schwab
Jonathan Scoville
Cornelius Scully
Frank Sedita
Joseph Shakspeare
John Shelley
Alson Sherman
Francis Sherman
Nathaniel Shurtleff
Henry Smith
Samuel Smith
Meredith Snyder
Peter Somers
Gerald Springer
Elijah Stansbury, Jr.
Samuel Starkweather
Thomas Stephens
Carl Stokes
John Stowell
Gustav Tafel
John Tallmadge
James Tate
Edward Taylor
Mark Taylor

Cameron Thom
William B. Thompson
Daniel Tiemann
James Toberman
Maurice Tobin
Raymond Tucker
Joel Turner
Don Upham
Eugene Van Antwerp
Samuel Vance
James Van Ness
Joshua Vansant
Robert Van Wyck
Isaac Varian
Richard Vaux
James Wadsworth
Robert Wagner, Jr.
George Walker
James Walker
T. Semmes Walmsley
Horatio Wells
Rolla Wells
Jacob Westervelt
William Wheaton
Kevin White
William Whyte
William Wickham
Joseph Wightman
John Willey
John Williams
Louis Wiltz
John Wimer
Fernando Wood
James Woodworth
William Workman
Samuel Yorty
Coleman Young
George Zimmerman

Whig

Gabriel Adams
John Allen
Orlando Allen
Samuel Armstrong
Hiram Barton
John Biddle
John Bigelow
Charles Brenham
Frederick Buhl
Glendy Burke
Isaac Burnet
William Case
William Castle
Zachariah Chandler
John Chapin
Marshall Chapin
Jonathan Chapman

Aaron Clark
Samuel Cobb
Robert Conrad
Levi Cook
John Daggett
John Darby
Samuel Davies
Nicholas Dockstader
Samuel Eliot
Charles Gilpin
James Harper
Isaac Harrington
Josiah Harris
Solomon Haven
Alexander Hay
Alexander Henry
John Herron
George Hoadley
Elisha Hotchkiss
William Howard
Oliver Hyde
John Jerome
John Johnson
DeGarmo Jones
Luther Kennett
William Ketchum
Ambrose Kingsland
James Law
Sheppard Leakin
William Little
Theodore Lyman, Jr.
Peter McCall
Martin McMichael
Joshua Mills
Buckner Morris
Zina Pitcher
Augustus Porter
Hiram Pratt
Bernard Pratte
Josiah Quincy, Jr.
Benjamin Raymond
Robert Riddle
Joseph Rozier
Benjamin Seaver
David Snelbaker
Elbridge Spaulding
Henry Spencer
Gerard Stith
John Swift
James Thompson
Charles Trowbridge
Josiah Trowbridge
James Van Dyke
Ferdinand Volz
Ebenezer Walden
Samuel Wilkeson
Benjamin Wilson
Caleb Woodhull

Native American (Know Nothing)

William Bingham
Levi Boone
Ephraim Burr
Peter Camden
Thomas Davis
William Freret
Samuel Hinks
Washington King
John Monroe
Jerome Smith
Thomas Swann
Charles Waterman
Stephen Webb
George Whelan

Republican

Franklin Alberger
George Alexander
William Alvord
Joseph Armstrong
Samuel Ashbridge
Edward Babcock
Walton Bachrach
Gerhard Bading
Herman Baehr
Kirkland Barker
Philip Becker
Sherburn Becker
William Becker
Maurice Blake
Rudolph Blankenburg
Edward Blythin
Lester L. Bond
William Bonsall
Charles Bowles
Fletcher Bowron
Philip Breitmeyer
William Broening
Adam Brown
Joseph Owen Brown
Thomas Brown
Alexander Brush
Jared Brush
George Buck
Christian Buhl
Harold Burton
Fred Busse
John Caldwell
George Carrel
Herman Chapin
John Chapman
George Christopher
Donald Clancy
Albert Cobo

George Codd
Nathan Cole
George Connell
Frank Couzens
James Couzens
Hans Crocker
George Cryer
Edwin Curtis
Harry Davis
Simon Davis
William Diehl
Bernard Dowd
Marcus Drake
Frederick Eaton
Levi Ellert
William Ewing
Chauncey Filley
Oliver Filley
Edwin Fitler
William Fitzgerald
Benjamin Flanders
Julius Fleischmann
Henry Ford
Andrew Fulton
John Galvin
George Gardner
John Geary
Henry Gourley
Willis Gradison, Jr.
Samuel Green
Stephen Grummond
John Haines
Thomas Hart
William Havemeyer
Henry Hazard
Edward Heath
Monroe Heath
R. R. Herrick
John Herron
George Hibbard
Thomas Holling
Alcaeus Hooper
William Hopkins
Charles Jacob, Jr.
Edgar Jewett
Aloys Kaufmann
W. Freeland Kendrick
Henry Kiel
Ardolph Kline
Charles Kline
Erastus Knight
John Koch
Fred Kohler
Chester Kowal
Frederick Kreismann
Fiorello LaGuardia
Richard Lamberton
Roger Lapham

Frederic Lincoln, Jr.
John Lodge
Seth Low
James Lowry
Harrison Ludington
Owen McAleer
William McCallin
William McCarthy
Theodore McKeldin
Harry Mackey
Robert McKisson
William Magee
William Malster
Leopold Markbreit
Oscar Marx
Jose Mascarel
Roswell Mason
Irvine Masters
Joseph Medill
James Miller
Victor Miller
John Mitchell
Hugh Moffat
Joseph Moore
Robert Moore
Daniel Morgan
John Mosby
Joseph Mruk
Malcolm Nichols
Otis Norcross
George Opdyke
James Otis
Frederick Pelton
Ralph Perk
Henry Pierce
Hazen Pingree
John Porter
Norris Poulson
George Puchta
Samuel Quincy
Frank Rader
William Rauschenberger
Richard Reading
Manuel Requena
John Reyburn
Alexander Rice
John Rice
Carl Rich
William Richert
Elmer Robinson
John Roche
Charles Roesch
James Rolph, Jr.
Henry Rose
William Rose
Angelo Rossi
Eugene Ruehlmann
Julian Rumsey

Bernard Samuel
George Sanderson
Benoir Sawyer
Louis Schwab
Thomas Selby
George Senter
Frank Shaw
Amor Smith, Jr.
John Smith
Thomas Smith
William Smith
Edward Spence
Frederick Spiegel
William Stephens
Frederick Stevens
James Stewart
William Stokley
William Strong
Edwin Stuart
George Swift
Daniel Taylor
James Thomas
Nicholas Thomas
William G. Thompson
William H. Thompson
E. Clay Timanus
John Torrence
George Voinovich
Cyrus Walbridge
Emil Wallber
Charles Warwick
Hempstead Washburn
Henry Weaver
John Weaver
Chandler Wells
John Wentworth
George Wilson
Samuel Wilson
Charles Wilstach
Frederick Woodman
Henry Ziegenhein

Populist

Adolph Sutro

Socialist

Daniel Hoan
Emil Seidel
Frank Zeidler

Local Parties

Joseph Barker
Theodore Berry
John Blackwell
John Bohn

Charles Boxton
Henry Coon
Abdiel Crossman
Dorothy Dolbey
Walter Flower
James Griffin
George Hewston
William Irwin

Isaac Kalloch
Matthew Lowrie
Patrick McCarthy
Louis Miriani
William Prentiss
Eugene Schmitz
Murray Seasongood

Charles Sebastian
Bobbie Sterne
Charles Taft
Henry Teschemaker
Edward Waldvogel
Russell Wilson
Carl Zeidler

APPENDIX III
MAYORS BY ETHNIC BACKGROUND

Not Known

Samuel Ashbridge
Charles Baker
Charles Bishop
John Blackburn
James Blackmore
Lester L. Bond
Levi Boone
Charles Bowles
Charles Boxton
Samuel Brady
William Brady
Charles Brenham
Joseph O. Brown
Abner Brownell
Jared Brush
Edwin Bryant
John Bryson
George Buck
A.A.R. Butler
Peter Camden
Albert Cash
William Castle
John Chapin
Jonathan Chapman
Samuel Cobb
Robert Conrad
Eli Cook, Jr.
Levi Cook
Edward Cooper
Frank J. Corr
George Cryer
Leonard Cutter
John Daggett
Robert Davidson
Jacob Davies
Simon Davis
Ebenezer Denny
Frank Doremus
Bernard Dowd
William Duncan
Samuel Eliot
Levi Ellert
William Ewing
James Faran
Dianne Feinstein
Chauncey Filley
Oliver Filley
Benjamin Flanders
Edward Flint
Walter Flower
Henry Ford

Thomas Foster
Daniel Fox
George Gardner
Augustus Garrett
Henry Gourley
Willis Gradison, Jr
Hugh Grant
Samuel Green
Stephen Grummond
George Guthrie
John Haines
Isaac Harrington
Leonard Harris
Stephen Harris
George Hatch
Thomas Hayes
William Hays
Nelson Hayward
Edward Heath
George Hewston
Samuel Hinks
Alpheus Hodges
Elisha Hotchkiss
John How
Henry Howard
Stephen Hoyt
Henry Hunt
Jesse Hunt
William Irwin
Edward Jeffries
John Jerome
Edward Johnson
De Garmo Jones
Jonathan Kearsley
W. Freeland Kendrick
Luther Kennett
Abner Kirby
Erastus Knight
John Ladue
George Langdon
Thaddeus Leavenworth
John Lewis
William Little
Harrison Ludington
Theodore Lyman, Jr.
Robert Lyon
Peter McCall
Andrew Mack
Robert McKisson
William Magee
Henry Maier
William Malster
Joseph Martin

Joseph Masten
Irvine Masters
Andrew Mickle
Victor Miller
Joshua Mills
Merrill Mills
Robert Morris
John Mosby
Magnus Murray
Charles Otis
George Peck
Samuel Pettigrew
Joseph Phillips
Henry Pierce
John Poelker
Augustus Porter
John Porter
Frank Rader
Richard Reading
John Reyburn
Carl Rich
Elmer Robinson
John Roche
Thomas Rowan
Eugene Ruehlmann
Bernard Samuel
Benair Sawyer
John Scott
Murray Seasongood
George Senter
Alson Sherman
Jacob Small
Thomas Smith
David Snelbaker
John Snowden
Henry Spencer
Elijah Stansbury, Jr.
William Stephens
George Stiles
William Stokley
John Stowell
Thomas Swann
George Swift
Mark Taylor
James Thomas
Nicholas Thomas
John Torrence
Raymond Tucker
Joel Turner
Samuel Vance
George Voinovich
Charles Warwick
Charles Waterman

Charles Wells
George Whelan
Daniel Whelton
John Willey
Russell Wilson
Samuel Wilson
Charles Wilstach
John Wimer
Caleb Woodhull
Wallace Woodworth

Black

Theodore Berry
John Blackwell
Tom Bradley
Ernest Morial
Carl Stokes
Coleman Young

Canadian

Prudent Beaudry
Solomon Juneau
Damien Marchessault

Croat

Michael Bilandic
Dennis Kucinich

Czech

Anton Cermak
Ralph Perk

Dutch

Sherburn Becker
Henry Coon
Nicholas Dockstader
John Hoffman
George Opdyke
Eugene Van Antwerp
James Van Dyke
James Van Ness
Joshua Vansant
Robert Van Wyck
Isaac Varian
Henry Weaver
Jacob Westervelt

English

William Alvord
Newton Baker
James Brown

Andrew Bryant
George Carrel
John Chapman
Horace Chase
Frank Couzens
James Couzens
Harmon Cutting
Samuel Davies
Marcus Drake
William Fargo
William Fitzgerald
William Freret
John Geary
Abraham Hall
James Harper
Monroe Heath
Abram Hewitt
James Hodges
John Hollins
Douglas Houghton
Charles Howard
William Howard
John Johnson
Samuel King
Washington King
Ambrose Kingsland
Cornelius Lawrence
Charles Leeds
Robert Liddell
John Lodge
Alexander Loyd
William McNair
Daniel Page
Isaack Patton
Edward Pillsbury
James Preston
John Pridgeon, Jr.
James Rolph, Jr.
Thomas Selby
Joseph Shakspeare
Henry Smith
Henry Teschemaker
William H. Thompson
John Townsend
Richard Vaux
T. Semmes Walmsley
John Weaver
Stephen Webb
Chandler Wells
Joseph Wightman

French

John Black
Paul Capdeville
Albert Cobo
DeWitt Cregier
Cornelius Garrison

William Gaston
Charles Genois
Nicholas Girod
J. Valsin Guillotte
Moon Landrieu
Augustin McCarty
Jose Mascarel
Edgar Montegut
Bernard Pratte
Denis Prieur
Benjamin Raymond
Joseph Roffignac
Joseph Rozier

German

Franklin Alberger
Gerhard Bading
Herman Baehr
Philip Becker
William Becker
Martin Behrman
Richard Bishop
Rudolph Blankenburg
John Bohn
Philip Breitmeyer
Martin Brimmer
W. F. Broening
Christian Buhl
Frederick Buhl
Stephen Buhrer
Fred Busse
William Case
Joseph Darst
Bernard Dickmann
Conrad Diehl
William Diehl
Edwin Fitler
Julius Fleischmann
Louis Fuhrmann
Charles Gunther
William Havemeyer
Charles Jacob, Jr.
Aloys Kaufmann
Henry Kiel
Ardolph Kline
Charles Kline
John Koch
Fred Kohler
Frederick Kreismann
John Krum
James Luken
Thomas Luken
Leopold Markbreit
Oscar Marx
Ray Miller
Henry Overstolz
George Puchta

William Rauschenberger
William Richert
Charles Roesch
William Schaefer
Solomon Scheu
Frank Schwab
Louis Schwab
Emil Seidel
John Smith
Frederick Spiegel
Gerald Springer
Adolph Sutro
Gustav Tafel
Daniel Tiemann
Ferdinand Volz
Robert Wagner, Jr.
Edward Waldvogel
Emil Wallber
Godfrey Weitzel
Louis Wiltz
Carl Zeidler
Frank Zeidler
Henry Ziegenhein
George Zimmerman

Greek

George Christopher

Hispanic

Cristobal Aguilar
Alfonso Cervantes
Antonio Coronel
Manuel Requena

Irish

Gabriel Adams
Joseph Armstrong
Joseph Barr
James Barry
William Behan
Robert Blee
Thomas Burke
Jane Byrne
Jerome Cavanagh
Donald Clancy
George Codd
John Collins
Patrick Collins
Thomas Coman
James Conway
William Corry
Hans Crocker
James Curley
Richard Daley

John Darragh
Edward Dempsey
William Dever
Edward Dunne
Thomas Dyer
John Farley
John Fitzgerald
John Fitzpatrick
Peter Flaherty
Thomas Gallagher
John Galvin
William Gaynor
Thomas Gilroy
William Grace
Harold Grady
William Green
James Griffin
Alexander Henry
John Herron
Daniel Hoan
John Hopkins
John Hylen
John Hynes
George Kane
Edward Kelly
Joseph Kelly
Martin Kennelly
John Kerrigan
Richard Lamberton
James Law
David Lawrence
Patrick McCarthy
James McClintock
Frank McCoppin
Bernard McKenna
Martin McMichael
Andrew McShane
George Maguire
John Manning
Frederick Mansfield
John Mitchell
John Montgomery
Bryan Mullanphy
Frank Murphy
Edward Noonan
Hugh O'Brien
John O'Brien
William O'Dwyer
Arthur O'Keefe
Edward O'Neill
James Phelan
John Rice
William Rogers
Cornelius Scully
John Shelley
Peter Somers
James Tate
William B. Thompson

Maurice Tobin
James Walker
Kevin White
William Whyte

Italian

Joseph Alioto
Richard Caliguiri
Anthony Celebrezze
Thomas D'Alesandro II
Thomas D'Alesandro III
Vincent Impellitteri
Fiorello LaGuardia
Robert Maestri
Louis Miriani
George Moscone
Frank Rizzo
Angelo Rossi
Victor Schiro
Frank Sedita

Old-Stock American (Ancestors in the United States in the Eighteenth Century)

John Allen
Orlando Allen
Andre Andrews
Samuel Armstrong
Brenton Babcock
Edward Babcock
Robert Banks
Joseph Barker
Kirkland Barker
Pierre Barker
Arthur Barret
Washington Bartlett
Washington Allon Bartlett
Hiram Barton
John Biddle
John Bigelow
Flavel Bingham
William Bingham
Maurice Blake
William Bonsall
Fletcher Bowron
Adam Brown
Thomas Brown
Ephraim Burr
Harold Burton
Marvin Chamberlain
Zachariah Chandler
Herman Chapin
Marshall Chapin
Aaron Clark
Joseph Clark

Grover Cleveland
George Clinton
Nathan Cole
Henry Colvin
George Connell
James Cross
Abdiel Crossman
Edwin Curtis
James Curtiss
John Darby
Thomas Davis
Lewis Dayton
Henry Deming
Dorothy Dolbey
Frederick Eaton
Franklin Edson
Smith Ely, Jr.
Stephen Foster
Jonas French
Andrew Fulton
Charles Gilpin
Walter Gurnee
John Harmon
Arthur Harper
Josiah Harris
Carter Harrison I
Carter Harrison II
Thomas Hart
Solomon Haven
Henry Hazard
R. R. Herrick
George Hibbard
Solomon Hillen, Jr.
George Hoadley
David Hooker
Henry Hunt
Oliver Hyde
Howard Jackson
Edgar Jewett
Ebenezer Johnson
Tom Johnson
Joel Jones
Lorenzo Kelsey
William Ketchum
Byron Kilbourn
William Lane
Roger Lapham
Sheppard Leakin
Henry Ledyard
Gideon Lee
Frederic Lincoln, Jr.
Timothy Lockwood
Seth Low
William Lynde
Harry Mackey
Robert McLane
Augustus Martin
Roswell Mason

Nathan Matthews, Jr.
Henry Mellus
James Miller
John Monroe
Joseph Moore
Buckner Morris
Malcolm Nichols
Otis Norcross
William Ogden
Harrison Otis
James Otis
Herman Page
Albert Palmer
Nathan Payne
Andrew Peters
John Phillips
Hazen Pingree
Zina Pitcher
Edward Pond
Hiram Pratt
William Prentiss
Frederick Prince
Josiah Quincy
Josiah Quincy, Jr.
Josiah P. Quincy
Samuel Quincy
Alexander Rice
Henry Rose
William Rose
George Sanderson
Eugene Schmitz
Jonathan Scoville
Benjamin Seaver
Charles Sebastian
George Shepley
Francis Sherman
Nathaniel Shurtleff
Amor Smith, Jr.
Jerome Smith
Meredith Snyder
Elbridge Spaulding
Samuel Starkweather
James Stewart
Gerard Stith
William Strong
John Swift
Charles Taft
Edward Taylor
Cameron Thom
Sheldon Thompson
James Toberman
Charles Trowbridge
Josiah Trowbridge
Don Upham
James Wadsworth
Cyrus Walbridge
Ebenezer Walden
George Walker

Hempstead Washburne
Horatio Wells
Rolla Wells
John Wentworth
William Wheaton
William Wickham
John Williams
Benjamin Wilson
Frederick Woodman
James Woodworth
William Workman
Samuel Yorty

Polish

Walton Bachrach
Abraham Beame
Bernard Cohn
Philip Goodman
Roman Gribbs
Edward Koch
Chester Kowal
Stanley Makowski
Joseph Mruk
Steven Pankow

Scandinavian

Norris Poulson
E. Clay Timanus

Scottish

James Adam
George Alexander
Joseph Brown
Alexander Brush
Isaac Burnet
John Caldwell
Charles Gray
Alexander Hay
Thomas Holling
George Hyde
Hugh Kennedy
John Lindsay
Matthew Lowrie
James Lowry
Frederick MacDougal
George McClellan, Jr.
Joseph McKee
Isaac Milliken
Hugh Moffat
DeLesseps Morrison
John Nichols
David Rose
William Smith
Bobbie Sterne
William Stewart

John Tallmadge
Daniel Taylor
William G. Thompson
James Thomson
George Wilson
Fernando Wood

Scots-Irish (or Northern Irish)

George Brown
Glendy Burke
Richardson Dilworth
David Francis
John Guthrie
John Herron
Alceus Hooper
George Johnston

Isaac Kalloch
William Kerr
Owen McAleer
William McCallin
William McCarthy
Theodore McKeldin
J. Barry Mahool
William Maybury
William Means
Joseph Medill
Robert Moore
John Patton
Robert Riddle
Frank Shaw
Samuel Smith
Edward Spence
Thomas Stephens
Edwin Stuart
Samuel Wilkeson

Slovenian

Frank Lausche

Swiss

Ralph Locher

Welsh

Edward Blythin
James Britton
John Conway
Harry Davis
William Hopkins
Alexander Lewis
Daniel Morgan
Julian Rumsey
Frederick Stevens

APPENDIX IV
MAYORS BY RELIGIOUS AFFILIATION

Not Known

Samuel Armstrong
Samuel Ashbridge
Charles Baker
Kirkland Barker
Pierre Barker
Washington Allon Bartlett
Charles Bishop
John Blackburn
John Bohn
Lester Bond
Charles Bowles
Charles Boxton
William Brady
Charles Brenham
Martin Brimmer
Andrew Bryant
Edwin Bryant
Fred Busse
A.A.R. Butler
George Clark
Eli Cook
Frank J. Corr
William Corry
James Cross
Leonard Cutter
John Daggett
Robert Davidson
Bernard Dickmann
Conrad Diehl
Frank Doremus
William Duncan
Samuel Eliot
Levi Ellert
James Faran
Chauncey Filley
Oliver Filley
William Fitzgerald
Benjamin Flanders
Edward Flint
Walter Flower
Daniel Fox
Louis Fuhrmann
Samuel Green
Stephen Grummond
George Guthrie
Isaac Harrington
Leonard Harris
Stephen Harris
George Hatch
William Havemeyer
Alexander Hay

William Hays
Nelson Hayward
John Herron
George Hewston
Daniel Hoan
Elisha Hotchkiss
John How
Henry Howard
Stephen Hoyt
Jesse Hunt
John Jerome
George Kane
W. Freeland Kendrick
Abner Kirby
Fred Kohler
John Krum
George Langdon
Ralph Locher
Andrew Mack
Robert McKisson
George Maguire
William Malster
Joseph Martin
Oscar Marx
Irvine Masters
Andrew Mickle
Victor Miller
Merrill Mills
Edgar Montegut
John Mosby
Henry Overstolz
George Peck
Joseph Phillips
John Poelker
Augustus Porter
John Reyburn
John Rice
Carl Rich
William Richert
Benair Sawyer
Eugene Schmitz
John Scott
Joseph Shakspeare
John Smith
Henry Spencer
Bobbie Sterne
William Stokley
John Tallmadge
Edward Taylor
Mark Taylor
Henry Teschemaker
James Thomas
Nicholas Thomas

Daniel Tiemann
John Torrence
John Townsend
Joel Turner
Samuel Vance
Charles Warwick
Hempstead Washburne
John Weaver
Godfrey Weitzel
Charles Wells
Horatio Wells
John Willey
Samuel Wilson
Charles Wilstach
John Wimer
Fernando Wood
Caleb Woodhull
James Woodworth
Wallace Woodworth

Protestant

Unknown Denomination

Franklin Alberger
George Alexander
William Alvord
Andre Andrews
Brenton Babcock
Herman Baehr
Newton Baker
Joseph Barker
Arthur Barret
Hiram Barton
Sherburn Becker
James Blackmore
John Blackwell
Edward Blythin
Levi Boone
Fletcher Bowron
Tom Bradley
Samuel Brady
James Britton
James Brown
Joseph Brown
Thomas Brown
Abner Brownell
Jared Brush
John Bryson
Stephen Buhrer
Isaac Burnet
Ephraim Burr
Harold Burton
Peter Camden

William Case
William Castle
Marvin Chamberlain
John Chapin
Marshall Chapin
Jonathan Chapman
Aaron Clark
Samuel Cobb
George Connell
Robert Conrad
John Conway
Edward Cooper
DeWitt Cregier
Abdiel Crossman
Edwin Curtis
Harmon Cutting
John Darby
Samuel Davis
Lewis Dayton
Henry Deming
Nicholas Dockstadter
Marcus Drake
Frederick Eaton
Edward Fitler
Henry Ford
Stephen Foster
Thomas Foster
David Francis
Jonas French
William Freret
Andrew Fulton
Cornelius Garrison
William Gaston
John Geary
Charles Gilpin
Walter Gurnee
Josiah Harris
Carter Harrison II
Monroe Heath
R. R. Herrick
John Herron
George Hibbard
Samuel Hinks
George Hoadley
Alpheus Hodges
William Hopkins
Douglas Houghton
Charles Howard
George Hyde
Oliver Hyde
William Irwin
Charles Jacob, Jr.
Ebenezer Johnson
John Johnson
Tom Johnson
DeGarmo Jones
Joel Jones
Lorenzo Kelsey

Washington King
Roger Lapham
Cornelius Lawrence
Gideon Lee
Charles Leeds
William Little
Timothy Lockwood
Theodore Lyman
William Lynde
Robert Lyon
Frederick MacDougal
Robert McLane
Martin McMichael
William Means
Henry Mellus
James Miller
Isaac Milliken
Joshua Mills
Joshua Monroe
Joseph Moore
Robert Moore
Daniel Morgan
Buckner Morris
Robert Morris
Magnus Murray
John Nichols
Otis Norcross
Charles Otis
Harrison Otis
Daniel Page
Isaac Patton
John Patton
Nathan Payne
Samuel Pettigrew
John Phillips
Edward Pillsbury
Norris Poulson
William Prentiss
John Pridgeon
Frederick Prince
George Puchta
Josiah Quincy
Josiah P. Quincy
Frank Rader
John Roche
William Rogers
David Rose
William Rose
Thomas Rowan
Eugene Ruehlmann
Jonathan Scoville
Cornelius Scully
Charles Sebastian
George Senter
Frank Shaw
George Shepley
Francis Sherman
Nathaniel Shurtleff

William Smith
Meredith Snyder
Thomas Stephens
William Stephens
William Stewart
Gerard Stith
Carl Stokes
Edwin Stuart
Thomas Swann
George Swift
John Swift
William G. Thompson
E. Clay Timanus
James Toberman
James Van Dyke
James Van Ness
Robert Van Wyck
Ferdinand Volz
Robert Wagner, Jr.
Cyrus Walbridge
Ebenezer Walden
Charles Waterman
Stephen Webb
William Wheaton
George Whelan
William Whyte
William Wickham
Joseph Wightman
Frederick Woodman
William Workman
Carl Zeidler
Henry Ziegenhein

Baptist

Richard Bishop
Nathan Cole
Harry Davis
Isaac Kalloch
Luther Kennett
Owen McAleer
Herman Page
Albert Palmer
Hazen Pingree
Don Upham
Coleman Young

Christian Scientist

William Bonsall
Philip Breitmeyer
Arthur Harper

Congregationalist

Washington Bartlett
Maurice Blake
Albert Cobo
Thomas Davis
Edward Pond
Richard Reading

Benjamin Seaver
Jerome Smith
James Wadsworth

Dutch Reformed

George Updyke
Joshua Vansant
Jacob Westervelt

Episcopalian

John Allen
Robert Banks
John Biddle
George Carrel
John Chapman
George Clinton
Hans Crocker
Jacob Davies
Samuel Davies
William Diehl
Richardson Dilworth
Franklin Edson
William Fargo
William Gaynor
Carter Harrison I
Henry Hazard
Abram Hewitt
James Hodges
John Hoffman
David Hooker
William Howard
Henry J. Hunt
Edward Jeffries, Jr.
Edgar Jewett
Jonathan Kearsley
Byron Kilbourn
Ambrose Kingsland
Ardolph Kline
Frederick Kreismann
Fiorello LaGuardia
Richard Lamberton
William Lane
Ferdinand Latrobe
Sheppard Leakin
Thaddeus Leavenworth
John Lewis
Robert Liddell
John Lindsay
Harrison Ludington
Peter McCall
George McClellan, Jr.
Theodore McKeldin
Harry Mackey
William McNair
Joseph Masten
Nathan Matthews, Jr.
William Maybury
John Montgomery

William Ogden
Frederick Pelton
Andrew Peters
Zina Pitcher
James Preston
Alexander Rice
Elmer Robinson
James Rolph, Jr.
Henry Rose
Julian Rumsey
Bernard Samuel
William Schaefer
Jacob Small
Henry Smith
Thomas Smith
Elijah Stansbury, Jr.
Samuel Starkweather
Frederick Stevens
James Stewart
William Strong
Charles Taft
Cameron Thom
Sheldon Thompson
Charles Trowbridge
Josiah Trowbridge
George Walker
Henry Weaver
Chandler Wells
Rolla Wells
Benjamin Wilson
Samuel Yorty

German Reformed

Rudolph Blankenburg

Lutheran

Gerhard Bading
William Broening
Henry Kiel
John Koch
Henry Maier
Leopold Markbreit
William Rauschenberger
Solomon Scheu
Emil Seidel
Emil Wallber
Frank Zeidler

Methodist

Theodore Berry
William Bingham
Alexander Brush
Horace Chase
Dorothy Dolbey
Augustus Garrett
James Harper
Thomas Hayes

Henry T. Hunt
Howard Jackson
Henry Pierce
John Porter
Alson Sherman
David Snelbaker
Edward Spence
William H. Thompson

Methodist-Episcopal

Joseph Owen Brown
Alcaeus Hooper

Moravian

Charles Gunther

Presbyterian

Gabriel Adams
Orlando Allen
Joseph Armstrong
Edward Babcock
William Becker
Flavel Bingham
Adam Brown
George Brown
George Buck
Christian Buhl
Frederick Buhl
Glendy Burke
John Caldwell
Zachariah Chandler
Grover Cleveland
George Codd
Harvey Colvin
Levi Cook
Henry Coon
James Couzens
George Cryer
James Curtiss
John Darragh
Ebenezer Denny
Smith Ely, Jr.
George Gardner
Henry Gourley
Charles Gray
John Guthrie
John Harmon
Solomon Haven
Alexander Henry
John Hollins
Edward Johnson
George Johnston
Hugh Kennedy
William Kerr
William Ketchum
Charles Kline
Erastus Knight

John Ladue
James Law
Henry Ledyard
John Lodge
Matthew Lowrie
James Lowry
William McCallin
William McCarthy
James McClintock
J. Barry Mahool
Roswell Mason
Joseph Medill
Hugh Moffat
Hiram Pratt
Benjamin Raymond
Robert Riddle
George Sanderson
Louis Schwab
Thomas Selby
Samuel Smith
John Snowden
Elbridge Spaulding
George Stiles
James Thomson
Isaac Varian
T. Semmes Walmsley
John Wentworth
Samuel Wilkeson
George Wilson
Russell Wilson

Quaker

Samuel King
Richard Vaux

Swedenborgian

Malcolm Nichols
Amor Smith, Jr.
John Stowell
Gustav Tafel

Unitarian

John Bigelow
Herman Chapin
Joseph Clark
Thomas Hart
Edward Heath
Frederic Lincoln
Seth Low
Alexander Loyd
Augustus Martin
James Otis
Josiah Quincy, Jr.
Samuel Quincy

Universalist

John Haines
Charles Roesch

Roman Catholic

Cristobal Aguilar
Joseph Alioto
Joseph Barr
James Barry
Prudent Beaudry
Philip Becker
William Behan
Martin Behrman
Michael Bilandic
John Black
Robert Blee
Thomas Burke
Jane Byrne
Richard Caliguiri
Paul Capdeville
Albert Cash
Jerome Cavanagh
Anthony Celebrezze
Anton Cermak
Alfonso Cervantes
Donald Clancy
John Collins
Patrick Collins
Thomas Coman
James Conway
Antonio Coronel
Frank Couzens
James Curley
Richard Daley
Thomas D'Alesandro II
Thomas D'Alesandro III
Joseph Darst
Edward Dempsey
William Dever
Bernard Dowd
Edward Dunne
Thomas Dyer
William Ewing
John Farley
John Fitzgerald
John Fitzpatrick
Peter Flaherty
Thomas Gallagher
John Galvin
Charles Genois
Thomas Gilroy
Nicholas Girod
William Grace
Harold Grady
Hugh Grant
William Green
Roman Gribbs
James Griffin
J. Valsin Guillotte
Abraham Hall
Solomon Hillen, Jr.

Thomas Holling
John Hopkins
John Hylen
John Hynes
Vincent Impellitteri
Solomon Juneau
Aloys Kaufmann
Edward Kelly
Joseph Kelly
Martin Kennelly
John Kerrigan
Chester Kowal
Dennis Kucinich
Moon Landrieu
Frank Lausche
David Lawrence
Alexander Lewis
James Luken
Thomas Luken
Patrick McCarthy
Augustin McCarty
Frank McCoppin
Joseph McKee
Bernard McKenna
Andrew McShane
Robert Maestri
William Magee
Stanley Makowski
John Manning
Frederick Mansfield
Damien Marchessault
Jose Mascarel
Ray Miller
Louis Miriani
John Mitchel
Ernest Morial
DeLesseps Morrison
George Moscone
Joseph Mruk
Bryan Mullanphy
Frank Murphy
Edward Noonan
Hugh O'Brien
John O'Brien
William O'Dwyer
Arthur O'Keefe
Edward O'Neill
Steven Pankow
Ralph Perk
James Phelan
Bernard Pratte
Denis Prieur
Manuel Requena
Frank Rizzo
Joseph Roffignac
Angelo Rossi
Joseph Rozier
Victor Schiro

Frank Schwab
Frank Sedita
John Shelley
Peter Somers
James Tate
Daniel Taylor
William B. Thompson
Maurice Tobin
Raymond Tucker
Eugene Van Antwerp
George Voinovich
Edward Waldvogel
James Walker

Daniel Whelton
Kevin White
John Williams
Louis Wiltz
George Zimmerman

Greek Orthodox

George Christopher

Jewish

Walton Bachrach

Abraham Beame
Bernard Cohn
Dianne Feinstein
Julius Fleischmann
Philip Goodman
Willis Gradison, Jr.
Edward Koch
Murray Seasongood
Frederick Spiegel
Gerald Springer
Adolph Sutro

Not Known

Charles Baker (?)
William Bingham (1808)
John Blackburn (?)
William Brady (1801)
Daniel Fox (?)
Charles Genois (1793)
Charles Gilpin (1809)
Nicholas Girod (1774)
Isaac Harrington (1789)
Stephen Harris (1802)
George Hatch (?)
John Hollins (1786)
Elisha Hotchkiss (1778)
Stephen Hoyt (?)
Edward Johnson (1767)
Augustin McCarty (1774)
Andrew Mickle (1805)
Joshua Mills (1797)
Samuel Pettigrew (c. 1790)
John Scott (?)
Jacob Small (c. 1772)
William Stewart (1782)
William Stokley (1823)
James Thomas (1802)
John Torrence (1819)
Joel Turner (1820s)
Charles Waterman (1809)
Charles Wells (1786)
George Whelan (?)
Louis Wiltz (1843)
Caleb Woodhull (1792)
Wallace Woodworth (1832)

United States

Alabama

Coleman Young (1918)

California

Cristobal Aguilar (c.1825)
Joseph Alioto (1916)
Fletcher Bowron (1887)
Charles Boxton (1860)
Frederick Eaton (1855)
Levi Ellert (1857)
Dianne Feinstein (1933)
George Moscone (1929)
James Phelan (1861)
Elmer Robinson (1894)
James Rolph, Jr. (1934)

Angelo Rossi (1878)
Eugene Schmitz (1864)
John Shelley (1905)

Connecticut

John Allen (1802)
M. Andre Andrews (1792)
Henry Deming (1815)
Edward Dunne (1853)
Thomas Dyer (1805)
Oliver Filley (1806)
William Gaston (1820)
George Hoadley (1781)
Joel Jones (1795)
Byron Kilbourn (1801)
Thaddeus Leavenworth (c. 1820)
Charles Leeds (1823)
Andrew Mack (1780)
Merrill Mills (1819)
Frederick Pelton (1827)
Jonathan Scoville (1830)
Francis Sherman (1805)
Sheldon Thompson (1785)
James Wadsworth (1819)
William Wheaton (1833)

Delaware

Samuel Brady (1789)
William Howard (1799)

District of Columbia

William Fitzgerald (1880)

Georgia

Washington Bartlett (1824)

Illinois

Arthur Barret (1835)
William Becker (1876)
Michael Bilandic (1923)
George Buck (1875)
Fred Busse (1866)
Jane Byrne (1934)
Richard Daley (1902)
Carter Harrison II (1864)
Henry Hazard (1846)
Edward Kelly (1876)
Martin Kennelly (1887)
Frederick Kreismann (1869)
Victor Schiro (1904)
Edward Taylor (1838)
Hempstead Washburne (1852)

Iowa

Herman Baehr (1866)
John Porter (1872)

Kentucky

Theodore Berry (1905)
Richard Bishop (1812)
Levi Boone (1808)
Charles Brenham (1817)
Carter Harrison (1825)
Tom Johnson (1854)
Luther Kennett (1807)
John Lewis (1800)
Buckner Morris (1800)
Thomas Stephens (1892)

Louisiana

William Behan (1840)
Paul Capdeville (1845)
Walter Flower (1851)
William Freret (1799)
J. Valsin Guillotte (1859)
Moon Landrieu (1930)
Andrew McShane (1865)
Robert Maestri (1889)
Edgar Montegut (1806)
Ernest Morial (1929)
DeLesseps Morrison (1912)
Arthur O'Keefe (1872)
Denis Prieur (1791)
Frank Sedita (1907)
Joseph Shakspeare (1837)
T. Semmes Walmsley (1889)

Maine

Washington Allon Bartlett (c. 1820)
Maurice Blake (1815)
James Brown (1824)
Abdiel Crossman (1846)
Stephen Foster (1820)
Edward Heath (1819)
Isaac Kalloch (1831)
Abner Kirby (1818)
Augustus Martin (1835)
James Miller (1831)
Isaac Milliken (1815)
Malcolm Nichols (1876)
Daniel Page (1790)
Edward Pillsbury (1823)
Hazen Pingree (1840)
George Shepley (1819)

Maryland

Franklin Alberger (1825)
William Broening (1830)
George Brown (1812)
Glendy Burke (1805)
John Chapman (1812)
Thomas D'Alesandro II (1903)
Thomas D'Alesandro III (1929)
Jacob Davies (1796)
Thomas Hayes (1844)
Solomon Hillen, Jr. (1810)
Samuel Hinks (1815)
James Hodges (1822)
Alcaeus Hooper (1859)
Jesse Hunt (1793)
Howard Jackson (1877)
John Jerome (1814)
John Johnson (1854)
George Kane (1820)
Ferdinand Latrobe (1833)
James Law (1809)
Sheppard Leakin (1790)
Theodore McKeldin (1900)
Robert McLane (1867)
J. Barry Mahool (1870)
William Malster (1843)
Bryan Mullanphy (1809)
James Preston (1860)
John Rice (1805)
William Schaefer (1921)
Elijah Stansbury, Jr. (1791)
George Stiles (1760)
E. Clay Timanus (1863)
Joshua Vansant (1803)
William Whyte (1824)
George Wilson (1816)

Massachusetts

Samuel Armstrong (1784)
John Bigelow (1797)
Martin Brimmer (1793)
Abner Brownell (c. 1813)
Edwin Bryant (1805)
Harold Burton (1888)
Marshall Chapin (1798)
Jonathan Chapman (1807)
Aaron Clark (c. 1784)
Samuel Cobb (1826)
John Collins (1919)
Levi Cook (1792)
James Curley (1874)
Edwin Curtis (1861)
John Daggett (1793)
Thomas Davis (1798)
William Dever (1862)
Samuel Eliot (1798)
John Fitzgerald (1863)

Jonas French (1829)
George Gardner (1834)
Samuel Green (1830)
Josiah Harris (1808)
Thomas Hart (1829)
Nelson Hayward (1857)
George Hibbard (1864)
Henry Howard (1801)
Henry Hunt (1878)
John Hynes (1897)
John Kerrigan (1907)
Gideon Lee (1778)
Frederic Lincoln, Jr. (1817)
Theodore Lyman, Jr. (1792)
Frederick Mansfield (1877)
Nathan Matthews, Jr. (1858)
Henry Mellus (1816)
Otis Norcross (1811)
John O'Brien (1873)
Harrison Otis (1765)
James Otis (1826)
Andrew Peters (1872)
John Phillips (1778)
Henry Pierce (1825)
William Prentiss (1800)
Frederick Prince (1818)
Josiah Quincy (1859)
Josiah Quincy, Jr. (1802)
Josiah P. Quincy (1772)
Samuel Quincy (1833)
Alexander Rice (1818)
George Sanderson (1824)
Benjamin Seaver (1795)
Nathaniel Shurtleff (1810)
Samuel Starkweather (1799)
Mark Taylor (c. 1812)
William H. Thompson (1867)
Maurice Tobin (1901)
Josiah Trowbridge (1785)
Ebenezer Walden (1777)
Stephen Webb (1804)
Daniel Whelton (1872)
Kevin White (1929)
Joseph Wightman (1812)

Michigan

Charles Bowles (1884)
Philip Breitmeyer (1864)
Jerome Cavanagh (1928)
Marvin Chamberlain (1842)
Albert Cobo (1897)
George Codd (1869)
Frank Couzens (1902)
Roman Gribbs (1925)
Stephen Grummond (1834)
Thomas Holling (1889)
Edward Jeffries, Jr. (1900)
Edgar Jewett (1843)

John Lodge (1862)
Joseph Martin (1888)
Oscar Marx (1866)
William Maybury (1849)
Louis Miriani (1897)
Frank Murphy (1890)
John Pridgeon, Jr. (1852)
Richard Reading (1882)
John Smith (1883)
William B. Thompson (1860)
Eugene Van Antwerp (1889)
John Williams (1782)

Mississippi

Arthur Harper (1866)

Missouri

Alfonso Cervantes (1920)
Nathan Cole (1825)
James Conway (1933)
Joseph Darst (1885)
Bernard Dickmann (1888)
William Ewing (1843)
Aloys Kaufman (1902)
Henry Kiel (1871)
Victor Miller (1888)
John Poelker (1913)
Bernard Pratte (1803)
Joseph Rozier (1817)
Charles Sebastian (1873)
Raymond Tucker (1896)
Rolla Wells (1856)
William Workman (1839)
Henry Ziegenhein (1845)

Nebraska

George Cryer (1875)
Samuel Yorty (1909)

New Hampshire

Andrew Bryant (1832)
Zachariah Chandler (1813)
Herman Chapin (1823)
Leonard Cutter (1829)
Benjamin Flanders (1816)
Monroe Heath (1828)
Albert Palmer (1831)
Jerome Smith (1800)
Frederick Stevens (1810)
John Wentworth (1815)
John Willey (1794)
Frederick Woodman (1872)

New Jersey

Isaac Burnet (1784)
Grover Cleveland (1837)
Smith Ely, Jr. (1825)

Ardolph Kline (1858)
Joseph McKee (1889)
Martin McMichael (1807)
Joseph Moore (1864)
George Opdyke (1805)
Jacob Westervelt (1800)

New York

Orlando Allen (1803)
William Alvord (1833)
Brenton Babcock (1830)
Edward Babcock (1864)
Kirkland Barker (1819)
Pierre Barker (1790)
Hiram Barton (1810)
Martin Behrman (1864)
Flavel Bingham (1803)
Charles Bishop (1844)
Alexander Brush (1824)
George Clinton (1807)
Harry Colvin (1815)
Eli Cook (1814)
Henry Coon (1822)
Edward Cooper (1824)
Frank Carr (1877)
Dewitt Cregier (1829)
James Cross (1819)
Lewis Dayton (1824)
Conrad Diehl (1843)
Nicholas Dockstadter (1802)
Bernard Dowd (1891)
Marcus Drake (1839)
William Duncan (1820)
William Fargo (1818)
Henry Ford (1837)
David Francis (1850)
Louis Fuhrmann (1868)
Augustus Garrett (1801)
Cornelius Garrison (1809)
William Gaynor (1848)
Hugh Grant (1853–1858)
Charles Gray (1807)
James Griffin (1929)
Charles Gunther (1822)
Walter Gurnee (1813)
John Haines (1818)
Abraham Hall (1826)
James Harper (1795)
William Havemeyer (1884)
Solomon Haven (1810)
R. R. Herrick (1825)
John Herron (c. 1815)
Abram Hewitt (1822)
John Hoffman (1828)
John Hopkins (1858)
Douglas Houghton (1809)
Charles Howard (1804)
John Hylen (1868)

DeGarmo Jones (1787)
Joseph Kelly (1897)
Lorenzo Kelsey (1803)
William Ketchum (1798)
Washington King (1815)
Ambrose Kingsland (1804)
Erastus Knight (1857)
Edward Koch (1924)
Chester Kowal (1904)
John Krum (1810)
John Ladue (1803)
Fiorello LaGuardia (1882)
George Langdon (1833)
Roger Lapham (1883)
Cornelius Lawrence (1791)
Henry Ledyard (1812)
John Lindsay (1921)
Timothy Lockwood (1810)
Seth Low (1858)
Alexander Loyd (1805)
Harrison Ludington (1812)
William Lynde (1817)
Stanley Makowski (1923)
John Manning (1833)
Roswell Mason (1805)
Joseph Masten (1809)
Irvine Masters (1823)
John Mitchel (1879)
Robert Morris (1802)
Joseph Mruk (1903)
John Nichols (1875)
William Ogden (1805)
Herman Page (1818)
Steven Pankow (1908)
George Peck (1840)
Zina Pitcher (1797)
Edward Pond (1833)
Augustus Porter (1798)
Benjamin Raymond (1801)
John Roche (1844)
Charles Roesch (1886)
Thomas Rowan (c. 1843)
Julian Rumsey (1823)
Frank Schwab (1874)
Thomas Selby (1820)
George Senter (1827)
Elbridge Spaulding (1809)
John Stowell (1824)
John Tallmadge (1818)
Daniel Tiemann (1805)
Charles Trowbridge (1800)
Robert Van Wyck (1847)
Isaac Varian (1789)
Robert Wagner, Jr. (1910)
Cyrus Walbridge (1849)
James Walker (1881)
Chandler Wells (1814)
William Wickham (1832)

James Woodworth (1804)
George Zimmerman (1882)

North Carolina

John Darby (1803)
Meredith Snyder (1859)

Ohio

Walton Bachrach (1904)
John Blackwell (1948)
Robert Blee (1839)
William Bonsall (1846)
Stephen Buhrer (1825)
Thomas Burke (1898)
John Caldwell (1852)
George Carrel (1865)
William Case (1818)
Albert Cash (1897)
Donald Clancy (1921)
Harry Davis (1878)
Edward Dempsey (1858)
Dorothy Dolbey (1908)
James Faran (1808)
John Farley (1846)
Julius Fleischmann (1872)
Edward Flint (1819)
John Galvin (1862)
Willis Gradison, Jr. (1928)
John Harmon (1819)
Leonard Harris (1824)
Henry T. Hunt (1878)
George Johnston (1825)
Fred Kohler (1864)
Dennis Kucinich (1946)
Frank Lausche (1895)
James Luken (1921)
Thomas Luken (1925)
Robert McKisson (1863)
Henry Maier (1918)
William Means (1831)
Ray Miller (1893)
Daniel Morgan (1877)
John Mosby (1845)
Charles Otis (1827)
Nathan Payne (1837)
Ralph Perk (1914)
George Puchta (1860)
John Reyburn (1845)
Carl Rich (1898)
Eugene Ruehlmann (1925)
Louis Schwab (1850)
Murray Seasongood (1878)
Amor Smith, Jr. (1846)
Henry Spencer (1808)
William Stephens (1859)
Bobbie Sterne (1919)
James Stewart (1881)
Carl Stokes (1927)

William Strong (1827)
George Swift (1845)
Charles Taft (1897)
Daniel Taylor (1819)
George Voinovich (1936)
Edward Waldvogel (1895)
Godfrey Weitzel (1835)
Russell Wilson (1876)

Oregon

Norris Poulson (1895)

Pennsylvania

Joseph Armstrong (1867)
Samuel Ashbridge (1849)
Joseph Barker (1806)
Joseph Barr (1906)
John Biddle (1792)
James Blackmore (1822)
Adam Brown (1840)
Joseph Owen Brown (1846)
Jared Brush (1814)
John Bryson (1819)
Christian Buhl (1812)
Frederick Buhl (1806)
Richard Caliguiri (1931)
Joseph Clark (1901)
George Connell (1871)
Robert Conrad (1810)
Ebenezer Denny (1761)
William Diehl (1845)
Richardson Dilworth (1898)
Frank Doremus (1865)
Edwin Fitler (1825)
Peter Flaherty (1924)
Thomas Foster (1814)
Andrew Fulton (1850)
Thomas Gallagher (1883)
John Geary (1819)
Henry Gourley (1838)
Harold Grady (1917)
William Green (1938)
George Guthrie (1848)
John Guthrie (1807)
Alexander Hay (1806)
William Hays (1844)
Alexander Henry (1823)
John Herron (c. 1815)
George Hewston (1826)
William Hopkins (1869)
John How (1813)
George Hyde (1819)
William Irwin (1803)
Jonathan Kearsley (1786)
W. Freeland Kendrick (1874)
William Kerr (1809)
Samuel King (1816)
Charles Kline (1870)

Richard Lamberton (1886)
William Lane (1789)
David Lawrence (1899)
William Little (1809)
Robert Lyon (1842)
Peter McCall (1809)
William McCallin (1842)
William McCarthy (1820)
James McClintock (1808)
Bernard McKenna (1842)
Harry Mackey (1873)
William McNair (1880)
William Magee (1873)
John Montgomery (c. 1764)
Magnus Murray (1787)
Edward Noonan (1849)
Frank Rader (1848)
Robert Riddle (1882)
Frank Rizzo (1920)
William Rogers (1820)
William Rose (1829)
Bernard Samuel (1880)
Benair Sawyer (1822)
Cornelius Scully (1878)
Emil Seidel (1864)
Samuel Smith (1752)
Thomas Smith (1869)
David Snelbaker (1804)
John Snowden (1776)
Edwin Stuart (1853)
John Swift (1790)
James Tate (1910)
Nicholas Thomas (1810)
William G. Thompson (1842)
James Thomson (1790)
John Townsend (1805)
Samuel Vance (1814)
James Van Dyke (1813)
Richard Vaux (1816)
Ferdinand Volz (1823)
Charles Warwick (1852)
Henry Weaver (1820)
Samuel Wilkeson (1781)
Charles Wilstach (1818)
Fernando Wood (1812)

Rhode Island

Ephraim Burr (1809)

Tennessee

Benjamin Wilson (1811)

Texas

Tom Bradley (1917)

Vermont

A.A.R. Butler (1821)
William Castle (1814)

John Chapin (1810)
Horace Chase (1810)
James Curtiss (1803)
Simon Davis (1817)
Franklin Edson (1832)
John Fitzpatrick (1844)
David Hooker (1830)
Oliver Hyde (1804)
Ebenezer Johnson (1786)
Hiram Pratt (1808)
Alson Sherman (1811)
Don Upham (1809)
James Van Ness (1808)
Horatio Wells (1807)

Virginia

Robert Banks (1822)
James Britton (1817)
Peter Camden (1801)
John Conway (1825)
William Corry (1779)
Robert Davidson (1850)
Alpheus Hodges (1822)
John Monroe (1823)
Isaac Patton (1828)
Gerard Stith (1821)
Thomas Swann (1809)
Cameron Thom (1825)
James Toberman (1836)
George Walker (1811)
John Wimer (1810)

West Virginia

Newton Baker (1873)

Wisconsin

Gerhard Bading (1870)
Sherburn Becker (1876)
John Bohn (1867)
Thomas Brown (1839)
Daniel Hoan (1881)
David Rose (1856)
Henry Rose (1856)
Peter Somers (1850)
Carl Zeidler (1908)
Frank Zeidler (1912)

Foreign Countries

Austria

Leopold Markbreit (1842)

Canada

Prudent Beaudry (1819)
James Couzens (1872)
Solomon Juneau (1793)
Alexander Lewis (1822)

Owen McAleer (1858)
Damien Marchessault (1821)
Joseph Medill (1823)
Frank Shaw (1933)

Czechoslovakia

Anton Cermak (1873)

England

Abraham Beame (1900)
Harmon Cutting (1830)
Samuel Davies (1776)
Robert Liddell (1837)
Gerald Springer (1944)
Henry Teschemaker (1823)
John Weaver (1861)

France

John Black (1827)
Jose Mascarel (?)
Joseph Phillips (1825)
Joseph Roffignac (1766)

Germany

Philip Becker (1830)
Rudolph Blankenburg (1843)
Charles Jacob, Jr. (1835)
John Koch (1841)
George McClellan, Jr. (1865)
Henry Overstolz (1822)

William Rauschenberger (1855)
William Richert (1859)
Solomon Scheu (1822)
Frederick Spiegel (1855)
Adolph Sutro (1830)
Gustav Tafel (1830)
Emil Wallber (1848)

Greece

George Christopher (1907)

Ireland

Gabriel Adams (c. 1788)
James Barry (1800)
Patrick Collins (1844)
Thomas Coman (1836)
Hans Crocker (1815)
John Darragh (1772)
Thomas Gilroy (1829)
William Grace (1832)
Hugh Kennedy (1819)
Patrick McCarthy (1863)
Frank McCoppin (1834)
George Maguire (1796)
Robert Moore (1816)
Hugh O'Brien (1827)
William O'Dwyer (1890)
Edward O'Neill (1820)
John Patton (1822)
Edward Spence (1832)

Italy

Anthony Celebrezze (1910)
Vincent Impellitteri (1900)

Mexico

Antonio Coronel (1817)
Manuel Requena (1802)

Poland

Bernard Cohn (1835)
Philip Goodman (1915)

Romania

Ralph Locher (1915)

Scotland

James Adam (1842)
George Alexander (1839)
Joseph Brown (1823)
Matthew Lowrie (1773)
James Lowry (1820)
Frederick MacDougal (1814)
Hugh Moffat (1810)
William Smith (1844)

Virgin Islands

Henry Smith (1811)

Wales

Edward Blythin (1884)

APPENDIX VI
TOTAL AND URBAN POPULATION OF THE UNITED STATES:
1790-1970

Year	Total Population	Percent Increase over Preceding Census	Urban Population	Percent Increase over Preceding Census	Percent of Total Population Urban	Rural
1790	3,929,214		201,655		5.1	94.9
1800	5,308,483	35.1	322,371	59.9	6.1	93.9
1810	7,239,881	36.4	525,459	63.0	7.3	92.7
1820	9,638,453	33.1	693,255	31.9	7.2	92.8
1830	12,866,020	33.5	1,127,247	62.6	8.8	91.2
1840	17,069,453	32.7	1,845,055	63.7	10.8	89.2
1850	23,191,876	35.9	3,543,716	92.1	15.3	84.7
1860	31,443,321	35.6	6,216,518	75.4	19.8	80.2
1870	38,558,371	22.6	9,902,361	59.3	25.7	74.3
1880	50,189,209	30.2	14,129,735	42.7	28.2	71.8
1890	62,979,766	25.5	22,106,265	56.5	35.1	64.9
1900	76,212,168	21.0	30,214,832	36.7	39.6	60.4
1910	92,228,496	21.0	42,064,001	39.2	45.6	54.4
1920	106,021,537	15.0	54,253,282	29.0	51.2	48.8
1930	123,202,624	16.2	69,160,599	27.5	56.1	43.9
1940	132,164,569	7.3	74,705,338	8.0	56.5	43.5
1950*	151,325,798	14.5	96,846,817	29.6	59.6	40.4
1960*	179,323,175	18.5	125,268,750	29.3	69.9	30.1
1970*	203,211,926	13.3	149,324,930	19.2	73.5	26.5

Source: U.S. Bureau of the Census

*New urban definition includes those persons living in unincorporated parts of urbanized areas.

APPENDIX VII
THE FIFTEEN CITIES: POPULATION AND RANK,
BY DECADE, 1820-1960

Cities	1960 Rank	1960 Population	1950 Rank	1950 Population	1940 Rank	1940 Population	1930 Rank	1930 Population
New York	1	7,781,984	1	7,891,957	1	7,454,995	1	6,930,446
Chicago	2	3,550,404	2	3,620,962	2	3,396,808	2	3,376,438
Los Angeles	3	2,479,015	4	1,970,358	5	1,504,277	5	1,238,048
Philadelphia	4	2,002,512	3	2,071,605	3	1,931,334	3	1,950,961
Detroit	5	1,670,144	5	1,849,568	4	1,623,452	4	1,568,662
Baltimore	6	939,024	6	949,708	7	859,100	8	804,874
Cleveland	8	876,050	7	914,808	6	878,336	6	900,429
St. Louis	10	750,026	8	856,796	8	816,048	7	821,960
Milwaukee	11	741,324	13	637,392	13	587,472	12	578,249
San Francisco	12	740,316	11	775,357	12	634,536	11	634,394
Boston	13	697,197	10	801,444	9	770,816	9	781,188
New Orleans	15	627,525	16	570,445	15	494,537	16	458,762
Pittsburgh	16	604,332	12	676,806	10	671,659	10	669,817
Buffalo	20	532,759	15	508,132	14	575,901	13	573,076
Cincinnati	21	502,550	18	503,998	17	455,610	17	451,160

Cities	1920 Rank	1920 Population	1910 Rank	1910 Population	1900 Rank	1900 Population
New York	1	5,620,048	1	4,766,883	1	3,437,202
Chicago	2	2,701,705	2	2,185,283	2	1,698,575
Philadelphia	3	1,823,779	3	1,549,008	3	1,293,697
St. Louis	6	772,897	4	687,029	4	575,238
Boston	7	748,060	5	670,585	5	560,392
Baltimore	8	733,826	7	558,485	6	508,957
San Francisco	12	506,676	11	416,912	10	342,782
Cincinnati	16	401,247	13	363,591	11	325,902
Cleveland	5	796,841	6	560,663	8	381,768
Buffalo	11	506,775	10	423,715	9	352,387
New Orleans	17	387,219	15	339,075	12	287,104
Pittsburgh	9	588,343	8	533,905*	7	321,616
Detroit	4	993,678	9	465,766	13	285,704
Milwaukee	13	457,147	12	373,857	14	285,385
Los Angeles	10	576,673	17	319,198		102,479

Cities	1890		1880		1870	
	Rank	Population	Rank	Population	Rank	Population
New York	1	1,515,301	1	1,206,299	1	942,292
Chicago	2	1,099,850	4	503,185	5	298,977
Philadelphia	3	1,046,964	2	847,170	2	674,022
St. Louis	5	451,770	6	350,518	4	310,864
Boston	6	448,477	5	362,839	7	250,526
Baltimore	7	434,439	7	332,313	6	267,354
San Francisco	8	298,997	9	233,959	10	149,473
Cincinnati	9	296,908	8	255,139	8	216,239
Cleveland	10	261,353	12	160,146	15	92,829
Buffalo	11	255,664	14	155,134	11	117,714
New Orleans	12	242,039	10	216,090	9	191,418
Pittsburgh	13	238,617	13	156,389	16	86,076
Detroit	15	205,876	18	116,340	18	79,577
Milwaukee	16	204,468	19	115,587	19	71,440
Los Angeles	57	50,395	116	11,183	114	5,728

Cities	1860		1850		1840	
New York	1	805,651	1	515,547	1	312,710
Chicago	9	109,260	19	29,963	51	4,470
Philadelphia	2	565,529	4	121,376	4	93,665
St. Louis	8	160,773	8	77,860	20	16,469
Boston	5	177,840	3	136,881	5	93,383
Baltimore	4	212,418	2	169,054	2	102,313
San Francisco	15	56,802	**	**		
Cincinnati	7	161,044	6	115,435	6	46,338
Cleveland	21	43,417	34	17,034	45	6,071
Buffalo	10	81,129	13	42,261	18	18,213
New Orleans	6	168,675	5	116,375	3	102,193
Pittsburgh	17	49,217	10	46,601	13	21,115
Detroit	19	45,619	24	21,019	33	9,102
Milwaukee	20	45,246	29	20,061	71	1,712
Los Angeles	98	4,385	98	502		

Cities	1830		1820	
New York	1	197,112	1	123,706
Chicago				
Philadelphia	3	80,462	2	63,802
St. Louis	12	14,125	12	10,049
Boston	4	61,392	4	43,298
Baltimore	2	80,620	3	62,738
San Francisco				
Cincinnati	7	24,831	13	9,642
Cleveland	57	1,076	53	606
Buffalo	23	8,668	39	2,095
New Orleans	6	29,737	5	27,176
Pittsburgh	15	12,568	17	7,248
Detroit	52	2,222	46	1,422
Milwaukee				

*Pittsburgh annexed Allegheny City in 1907.

**The returns for 1850 for San Francisco were destroyed by fire; the state census for 1852 reports
a population of 34,766.

APPENDIX VIII
THE FIFTEEN CITIES: POPULATION INCREASE/DECREASE, BY DECADE, 1790-1970

	Population	Increase or Decrease over Preceding Census			Population	Increase or Decrease over Preceding Census	
		Number	Percent			Number	Percent

Baltimore / Buffalo

	Population	Number	Percent		Population	Number	Percent
Baltimore				**Buffalo**			
1970	905,787	− 33,237	− 3.5	1970	462,768	− 69,991	− 13.3
1960	939,024	− 10,684	− 1.1	1960	532,759	− 47,373	− 8.2
1950	949,708	90,608	10.5	1950	580,132	4,321	0.7
1940	859,100	54,226	6.7	1940	575,901	2,285	0.5
1930	804,874	71,048	9.7	1930	573,076	66,301	13.1
1920	733,826	175,341	31.4	1920	506,775	83,060	19.6
1910	558,485	49,528	9.7	1910	423,715	71,328	20.2
1900	508,957	74,518	17.2	1900	352,387	96,723	37.8
1890	434,439	102,126	30.7	1890	255,664	100,530	64.8
1880	332,313	64,959	24.3	1880	155,134	37,420	31.8
1870	267,354	54,936	25.9	1870	117,714	36,585	45.1
1860	212,418	43,364	25.7	1860	81,129	38,868	92.0
1850	169,054	66,741	65.2	1850	42,261	24,048	132.0
1840	102,313	21,693	26.9	1840	18,213	9,545	110.1
1830	80,620	17,882	28.5	1830	8,668	6,573	313.7
1820	62,738	16,183	34.8	1820	2,095	587	38.9
1810	46,555	20,041	75.6	1810	1,508		
1800	26,514	13,011	96.4				
1790	13,503						

Chicago

	Population	Number	Percent
1970	3,366,657	− 181,047	− 5.1
1960	3,550,404	− 70,558	− 1.9
1950	3,620,962	224,154	6.6
1940	3,396,808	20,340	0.6
1930	3,376,438	674,711	25.
1920	2,701,705	516,422	23.6
1910	2,185,283	486,708	28.7
1900	1,698,575	598,725	54.4
1890	1,099,850	596,665	118.6
1880	503,185	204,208	68.3
1870	298,977	186,805	166.5
1860	122,177	82,209	274.5
1850	29,963	25,493	570.3
1840	4,470		

Boston

	Population	Number	Percent
1970	641,070	− 56,127	− 8.1
1960	697,197	− 104,247	− 13.0
1950	801,444	30,628	4.0
1940	770,816	− 10,372	− 1.3
1930	781,188	33,128	4.4
1920	748,060	77,475	11.6
1910	670,585	109,693	19.6
1900	560,892	112,415	25.1
1890	448,477	85,638	23.6
1880	362,839	112,313	44.8
1870	250,526	72,686	40.9
1860	177,840	40,959	29.9
1850	136,881	43,498	46.6
1840	93,383	31,991	52.1
1830	61,392	18,094	41.8
1820	43,298	9,511	28.1
1810	33,787	8,850	35.5
1800	24,937	6,617	36.1
1790	18,320		

Cincinnati

	Population	Number	Percent
1970	451,455	− 51,095	− 10.2
1960	502,550	− 1,448	− 0.3
1950	503,998	48,388	10.6
1940	455,610	4,450	1.
1930	451,160	49,913	12.4
1920	401,247	37,656	10.4

	Population	Increase or Decrease over Preceding Census	
		Number	*Percent*
1910	363,591	37,689	11.6
1900	325,902	28,994	9.8
1890	296,908	41,769	16.4
1880	255,139	38,900	18.
1870	216,239	55,195	34.3
1860	161,044	45,609	39.5
1850	115,435	69,097	149.1
1840	46,338	21,507	86.6
1830	24,831	15,189	157.5
1820	9,642	7,102	279.6
1810	2,540		

Cleveland

	Population	Number	Percent
1970	750,879	−125,171	−15.3
1960	876,050	−38,758	−4.2
1950	914,808	36,472	4.2
1940	878,336	−22,093	−2.5
1930	900,429	103,588	13.
1920	796,841	236,178	42.1
1910	560,663	178,895	46.9
1900	381,768	120,415	46.1
1890	261,353	101,207	63.2
1880	160,146	67,317	72.5
1870	92,829	49,412	113.8
1860	43,417	26,383	154.9
1850	17,034	10,963	180.6
1840	6,071	4,995	464.2
1830	1,076	470	77.6
1820	606		

Detroit

	Population	Number	Percent
1970	1,511,482	−156,543	−9.4
1960	1,670,144	−179,424	−9.7
1950	1,849,568	226,116	13.9
1940	1,623,452	54,790	3.5
1930	1,568,662	574,984	57.9
1920	993,678	527,912	113.3
1910	465,766	180,062	63.
1900	285,704	79,828	38.8
1890	205,876	89,536	77.
1880	116,340	36,763	46.2
1870	79,577	33,958	74.4
1860	45,619	24,600	117.
1850	21,019	11,917	130.9
1840	9,102	6,880	309.6
1830	2,222	800	56.3
1820	1,422		

Los Angeles

	Population	Increase or Decrease over Preceding Census	
		Number	*Percent*
1970	2,816,061	337,046	13.3
1960	2,479,015	508,657	25.8
1950	1,970,358	466,081	31.
1940	1,504,277	262,229	21.0
1930	1,238,048	661,375	114.7
1920	576,673	257,475	80.7
1910	319,198	216,719	211.5
1900	102,479	52,084	103.4
1890	50,395	39,212	350.6
1880	11,183	5,455	95.2
1870	5,728	1,343	30.6
1860	4,385	2,775	172.4
1850	1,610		

Milwaukee

	Population	Number	Percent
1970	717,327	−23,997	−3.2
1960	741,324	103,932	16.3
1950	637,329	49,920	8.5
1940	587,472	9,223	1.5
1930	578,249	121,102	26.5
1920	457,147	83,290	22.3
1910	373,857	88,542	31.0
1900	285,315	80,847	39.5
1890	204,468	88,881	76.9
1880	115,587	44,147	61.8
1870	71,440	26,194	57.9
1860	45,246	25,185	125.5
1850	20,061	18,349	1,071.8
1840	1,712		

New York City

	Population	Number	Percent
1970	7,894,862	114,479	1.5
1960	7,781,984	−109,973	−1.4
1950	7,891,957	436,962	5.9
1940	7,454,995	524,549	7.6
1930	6,930,446	1,310,398	23.3
1920	5,620,048	853,165	17.9
1910	4,766,883	1,329,681	38.7
1900	3,437,202	1,921,901	126.8
1890	1,515,301	309,002	25.6
1880	1,206,299	264,077	28.0
1870	942,292	128,623	15.8
1860	813,669	298,122	57.8
1850	515,547	202,837	64.9
1840	312,710	110,121	54.4
1830	202,589	78,883	63.8

	Population	Increase or Decrease over Preceding Census	
		Number	Percent
1820	123,706	27,333	82.7
1800	60,515	27,384	82.7
1790	33,131		

New Orleans

	Population	Increase or Decrease over Preceding Census	
		Number	Percent
1970	593,471	− 34,054	− 5.4
1960	627,525	57,080	10.0
1950	570,445	75,908	15.3
1940	494,537	35,775	7.8
1930	458,762	71,543	18.5
1920	387,219	48,144	14.2
1910	339,075	51,971	18.1
1900	242,039	25,949	18.6
1890	242,039	25,949	12.0
1880	216,090	24,672	12.6
1870	191,418	22,743	13.5
1860	168,675	52,300	44.9
1850	116,375	14,182	13.9
1840	102,193	56,111	121.8
1830	46,082	18,906	69.6
1820	27,176	9,934	57.6
1810	17,242		

Philadelphia

	Population	Increase or Decrease over Preceding Census	
		Number	Percent
1970	1,948,609	− 53,903	− 2.6
1960	2,002,512	− 69,093	− 3.3
1950	2,071,605	140,271	7.3
1940	1,931,334	− 19,627	− 1.0
1930	1,950,961	127,182	7.0
1920	1,823,779	274,771	17.7
1910	1,549,008	255,311	19.7
1900	1,293,697	246,733	23.6
1890	1,046,964	199,794	23.6
1880	847,170	173,148	25.7
1870	674,022	108,493	19.2
1860	565,529	444,153	365.9
1850	121,376	27,711	29.6
1840	93,665	13,203	16.4
1830	80,462	16,660	26.1
1820	63,802	10,080	18.8
1810	53,722	12,502	30.3
1800	41,220	12,698	44.5
1790	28,552		

Pittsburgh

	Population	Increase or Decrease over Preceding Census	
		Number	Percent
1970	520,117	− 84,215	− 13.9
1960	604,332	− 72,474	− 10.7

	Population	Increase or Decrease over Preceding Census	
		Number	Percent
1950	676,806	5,147	0.8
1940	671,659	1,842	0.3
1930	669,817	81,474	13.8
1920	588,343	54,438	10.2
1910	533,905	82,393	18.2
1900	321,616	212,289	34.8
1890	238,617	82,999	52.6
1880	156,389	82,228	81.7
1870	86,076	70,313	74.9
1860	49,217	36,805	5.6
1850	46,601	2,616	120.7
1840	21,115	8,547	68.0
1830	12,568	5,020	69.0
1820	7,248	2,480	52.0
1810	4,768	3,203	204.7
1800	1,565		

St. Louis

	Population	Increase or Decrease over Preceding Census	
		Number	Percent
1970	622,236	− 127,790	− 17.0
1960	750,026	− 106,770	− 12.5
1950	856,796	40,748	5.0
1940	816,048	− 5,912	− 0.7
1930	821,960	49,063	6.3
1920	772,897	85,868	12.5
1910	687,029	111,791	19.4
1900	575,238	123,468	27.3
1890	451,770	101,252	28.9
1880	350,518	39,654	12.8
1870	310,864	150,091	93.4
1860	160,773	82,913	106.5
1850	77,860	61,391	372.8
1840	16,469	11,492	230.9
1830	4,977		

San Francisco

	Population	Increase or Decrease over Preceding Census	
		Number	Percent
1970	715,674	− 24,642	− 3.3
1960	740,316	− 35,041	− 4.5
1950	775,357	140,821	22.2
1940	634,536	142	
1930	634,394	127,718	25.2
1920	506,676	89,764	21.5
1910	416,912	74,130	21.6
1900	342,782	43,785	14.6
1890	298,997	65,038	27.8
1880	233,959	84,486	56.5
1870	149,473	92,671	163.1
1860	46,802		

APPENDIX IX
FOREIGN-BORN AND BLACKS IN SELECTED CITIES, 1860

City	Total Population	Foreign-Born	Percent	Blacks	Percent
New York	805,651	383,717	48	12,472	
Philadelphia	565,529	169,430	29	22,185	1.5
Brooklyn	266,661	104,589	39	4,313	3.9
Baltimore	212,418	52,497	25	27,898	1.6
Boston	177,840	63,791	36	2,261	13.0
New Orleans	168,675	64,621	38	24,074	1.3
Cincinnati	161,044	73,614	46	3,731	14.0
St. Louis	160,773	96,086	60	3,297	2.3
Chicago	109,260	54,624	50	955	2.0
Buffalo	81,129	37,684	46	809	0.9
San Francisco	56,802	28,454	50	1,176	1.0
Detroit	45,619	21,349	47	1,403	2.1
Milwaukee	45,246	22,848	50	106	3.1
Cleveland	43,417	19,437	45	799	0.2
					1.8

Source: U.S. Census.

APPENDIX X
FOREIGN-STOCK WHITES IN SELECTED CITIES, 1920

CITY	TOTAL POPULATION	FOREIGN-BORN WHITES		NATIVE WHITE FOREIGN OR MIXED PARENTAGE	
		Number	Percent	Number	Percent
New York	5,620,048	1,991,547	35.4	2,303,082	
Chicago	2,701,705	805,482	29.8	1,140,816	41.0
Philadelphia	1,823,779	397,927	21.8	591,471	42.2
Detroit	993,678	289,297	29.1	348,771	32.4
Cleveland	796,841	239,538	30.1	310,241	35.1
St. Louis	772,897	103,239	13.4	239,894	38.9
Boston	748,060	238,919	31.9	309,755	31.0
Baltimore	733,826	83,911	11.4	162,839	41.4
Pittsburgh	588,343	120,266	20.4	213,465	22.2
Los Angeles	576,673	112,057	19.4	140,349	36.3
Buffalo	506,775	121,530	24.0	215,377	24.3
San Francisco	506,676	140,200	27.7	182,643	42.5
Milwaukee	457,157	110,068	24.1	213,911	36.0
Cincinnati	401,247	42,827	10.7	121,665	46.8
New Orleans	387,219	25,992	6.7	69,283	30.3
					17.9

Source: Statistical Abstract of the U.S.: 1929 (Washington, D.C., 1929), pp. 46–49, and U.S. Bureau of the Census, Fourteenth Census of the U.S.: 1920.

APPENDIX XI
BLACKS IN CITIES, 1900, 1920, 1950, and 1970

	1900		1920		1950		1970	
	No.	*%*	*No.*	*%*	*No.*	*%*	*No.*	*%*
New York	60,666	1.8	152,467	2.7	747,610	9.5	1,688,115	21.1
Buffalo	1,698	9.5	4,511	9.9	36,645	6.3	94,329	20.4
Philadelphia	62,613	4.8	134,229	7.4	376,041	18.2	653,791	33.6
Pittsburgh	20,355	4.5	37,725	6.4	82,453	12.2	104,904	20.2
Baltimore	79,258	15.6	108,322	14.8	225,099	23.7	420,210	46.4
Cincinnati	14,482	4.4	30,079	7.5	78,196	15.5	125,000	27.6
Cleveland	5,988	1.6	34,451	4.3	147,847	16.1	287,841	38.3
Detroit	4,111	1.4	40,838	4.1	300,506	16.2	660,428	43.7
Milwaukee	862	0.3	2,229	0.5	21,772	3.4	105,088	14.7
Chicago	30,150	1.8	109,458	4.1	492,265	13.6	1,102,620	32.7
St. Louis	35,516	6.2	69,854	9.0	153,766	17.9	254,191	40.9
New Orleans	77,714	27.1	100,930	26.1	181,775	31.9	267,308	45.0
Los Angeles	2,131	2.1	15,579	2.7	171,209	8.7	503,606	17.9
San Francisco	1,654	0.5	2,414	0.5	43,502	5.6	96,078	13.4
Boston	11,591	2.1	16,350	2.2	40,057	5.0	104,707	16.3

Source: U.S. Census.

APPENDIX XII
THE FIFTEEN CITIES: FOREIGN-BORN / MIXED-PARENTAGE
AS PERCENTAGES OF POPULATION, 1970

	Total population		
	Number	*Percent foreign born*	*Percent native of foreign or mixed parentage*
Baltimore, Md.	905,757	3.2	7.9
Boston, Mass.	641,056	13.1	23.9
Buffalo, N.Y.	462,781	7.6	20.7
Chicago, Ill.	3,362,947	11.1	18.6
Cincinnati, Ohio	452,376	2.7	6.5
Cleveland, Ohio	750,932	7.5	14.4
Detroit, Mich.	1,511,322	7.9	14.7
Los Angeles, Calif.	2,815,998	14.6	19.2
Milwaukee, Wis.	717,110	5.5	17.3
New Orleans, La.	593,467	3.1	5.5
New York City, N.Y.	7,894,862	18.2	23.7
Philadelphia, Pa.	1,948,608	6.5	16.6
Pittsburgh, Pa.	520,146	6.0	19.9
San Francisco, Calif.	715,673	21.6	22.7
St. Louis, Mo.	622,234	2.4	7.8

INDEX

Note: Numbers in **boldface** indicate complete entries.

ABOUT THE EDITORS

MELVIN G. HOLLI is Professor of History and Director of the Urban Historical Collection at the University of Illinois, Chicago Circle. He is Co-Director of the Project for the Study of American Mayors. Among his earlier works are *Reform in Detroit, Detroit,* and, with Peter d'A. Jones, *The Ethnic Frontier.*

PETER d'A. JONES is Professor of History, University of Illinois, Chicago Circle. He is Co-Director of the Project for the Study of American Mayors. His earlier works include *The Consumer Society, The Christian Socialist Revival,* and *Economic History of the U.S. Since 1783.*